THE REVOLT

OF

MARTIN LUTHER

THE REVOLT

OF

MARTIN LUTHER

ROBERT HERNDON FIFE

COLUMBIA UNIVERSITY PRESS

NEW YORK 1957

© COLUMBIA UNIVERSITY PRESS 1957

PUBLISHED IN GREAT BRITAIN, CANADA, INDIA, AND PAKISTAN
BY OXFORD UNIVERSITY PRESS
LONDON, TORONTO, BOMBAY, AND KARACHI

LIBRARY OF CONGRESS CATALOG CARD NUMBER: 56-11910

MANUFACTURED IN THE UNITED STATES OF AMERICA

To the Memory of My Parents

ROBERT HERNDON FIFE

AND

SARAH STRICKLER FIFE

INTRODUCTION

THE appearance of a new life of Martin Luther needs no apology in spite of the number of previous efforts in this field—itself evidence of an enduring interest in one of the most remarkable figures in human history. Now, more than four hundred years after his death, Luther is still a problem for the theologian and an inviting theme for the student of profane history. Although many causes and personalities contributed their share to the development of the Reformation, it was Luther who set it in motion and gave it its peculiar character.

The present writer is no theologian. His interest in Luther dates from school-boy years and was planted in a home whose religious traditions had their roots in Scotland. In unwavering memory he recalls with gratitude the Virginia parents to whom he owes his early knowledge of Luther.

For the earliest suggestion that he put into print his ideas of Luther's character and development, the author was indebted to the late Archbishop Söderblom, former Primate of Sweden, at whose recommendation the Olaus Petri Foundation invited him to deliver at Uppsala University a course of lectures on Luther's early religious development. These lectures were published as *Young Luther* (New York: Macmillan Company, 1928).

The scope of the present work is limited to the development of Luther from his earliest years to the point where his stand before the Diet at Worms marked his final break with the Church of Rome. Much source material and many investigations by scholars have appeared to throw light on this development. Obviously no attempt could be made to take into account or evaluate all that has been published since older writers like Oergel, Böhmer, Müller, Grisar, and Scheel traversed various phases of the field of Luther research. The reader's attention is called particularly to the extensive bibliography in Roland Bainton's *Here I Stand* (New York: Abingdon Cokesbury Press, 1950) and to Josef Körner's *Bibliographisches Handbuch des deutschen Schrifttums* (Bern: A. Francke, 3d ed., 1949).

Although it is manifestly impossible to comment on the many titles listed by these scholars, the writer wishes to call attention to a work included in the Körner bibliography: *Die Reformation in Deutschland,* by Josef Lortz. Catholic scholars such as he and the Jesuit Hartmann Grisar, though necessarily viewing the life and character of Luther from the standpoint of their own sincere religious convictions, have provided an invaluable challenge to Protestant scholarship.

A perusal of Bainton's and Körner's listings, covering actually only a part of the vast body of Luther research that has come from the press or appeared in various periodicals, makes it clear that entirely new sources or a completely fresh viewpoint on Luther are hardly possible at this time. The present writer certainly lays no claim to novelty of background material or approach. His aim has been a careful reexamination of the sources and the opinions of competent critics, hostile or apologetic, in order to unfold before the reader more at home in English than in German the development of Luther from a viewpoint as free as possible of conscious confessional bias.[1]

Obviously a part of the detail in the following pages has been introduced not only because of its importance for a portrayal of Luther's character and growth, but also because it lends something of the dimensionality of life to the man himself and to the places, names, and events that left their impress upon him. The writer has not intended thereby to approximate Ranke's famous "How the things actually occurred." The combination of circumstance and individual genius which formed a man like the mature Luther does not yield all its secrets to so simple a formula, any more than to other ingenious patterns which the philosopher of history might deduce from the course of human events. Stimulating as such theories are to the insight and the imagination, they must always be tempered by the awareness that no portrayal of a great figure or an outstanding period can be definitive. Without eschewing necessary selection in the weighing of fact and theory, therefore, the writer has preferred to present in ample detail the background, actions, events, and traits of character as they appear in the sources in order to let the figure of Luther emerge, as it inevitably does from his writings, lectures, and letters, with the forcefulness, the weakness and strength, the contradictoriness—in short, with the mysterious alchemy of personality that will never cease to tantalize and attract the scholar and student.

For aid in gathering the material for the following work the writer wishes

[1] His bibliography on p. 695 will reveal at once the limits he has set himself.

to express his thanks to the libraries whose resources have been placed so generously at his disposal, particularly the libraries of Columbia University and Union Theological Seminary. Sincere thanks are due Miss Constance Winchell of the Interlibrary Loan Service of the Columbia University Libraries and her able staff, especially Miss Mary Cunningham, Kenneth Lohf, and Eugene Sheehy, for the patience and helpfulness with which they traced successfully many titles difficult of access.

Above all the writer wishes to express his profound gratitude to his wife, Hildegarde Wichert Fife, for the skill and devotion with which she verified the entire reference material as well as for her invaluable work in editing and preparing the manuscript for the press. Without her help, unstintingly given despite the demands of her own professional duties, publication of the present book, already delayed because of various contingencies, would not have been possible at this time nor in the present form.

CONTENTS

THE REVOLT
OF
MARTIN LUTHER

I

EARLY DAYS AT HOME
AND SCHOOL

THE family from which Martin Luther sprang was of Thuringian peasant stock. It belonged to the tough and vigorous race dwelling on the northwestern slope of the great ridge that cuts across central Germany from the southeast and forms a boundary line of historical importance. Many sources have contributed to the population of this rugged country. Archaeological finds in the valleys point back as far as an interglacial age. Since then waves of many migrant peoples have swept around and over the forested hills and left traces in the settlement and culture of the region. In prehistoric times the Frankish invasion halted at the western slopes, but many of this tribal group filtered through to mingle with the Thuringian stock. The racial character of the population is, as it was in the later Middle Ages and for many centuries before, of prevailingly Alpine type: stocky of figure, brown of eyes and hair and somewhat brownish in complexion, tough and elastic in body.

The village of Möhra, lying in the forest which overhangs Eisenach and its plain, was the focus of the clan of Luther, or Luder. This clan embraced a number of families. So numerous, indeed, were the Luthers that when Martin, on his return from Worms in 1521, made a visit to the home of his forefathers, he found that his relatives filled the whole neighborhood.[1] Like other small peasant proprietors of the region, the Luthers were not subject to the exactions that afflicted the rural classes in southern and southwestern Germany in the later fifteenth century. Under the mild rule of the Saxon electors the Thuringian villages enjoyed a considerable measure of local self-government. Nevertheless, families were large and their lives were a constant struggle for existence. Custom did not permit peasant farms to be divided, and the many sons were forced to fend for themselves.

One of these was Hans Luther, the father of Martin. As a young man he

[1] Letter from Luther to Spalatin, May 14, 1521, *WAB*, II, 338, ll. 55 f.

learned the trade of copper mining, an industry that seems to have just then awakened to life in the Möhra region. In the neighborhood he found a wife, Margarete Ziegler, the daughter, according to Philip Melanchthon, of an old and respected family of the vicinity of Eisenach.[2] Hans and Margarete live for us on the canvas of Lucas Cranach as they looked in later middle life. Their broad heads and earnest, careworn faces are those of the farming villagers of the Eisenach region at the present day. Not long after their marriage the young couple left their native district and moved to Eisleben, a hundred miles to the northeast. It is probable that the hope of better opportunities for his work drew Hans thither, as it did many others in those years. Eisleben was not a large city even in terms of the late Middle Ages, embracing perhaps 3,000 to 6,000 persons within its walls,[3] but the surrounding copper mines of the county of Mansfeld made it the home of a thriving industry.

Regarding the character of Hans Luther much has come down to us. A good deal of this information is derived from Martin himself, either directly or through friends and younger associates, while his enemies have contributed their share. Personal love and hate and polemical attitudes have colored the picture, but enough is known from reliable sources to attest the sturdy though temperamental character of the peasant-miner. He caught ground under his feet quickly in the new region and made steady progress up the economic and social ladder. His attitude when his son decided to enter the cloister gives evidence of practical sense and a resolute will. Hostile biographers of Martin passed down a tradition that the elder Luther killed a man in Möhra and for that reason was obliged to emigrate. The records furnish no evidence for this, although the judicial annals of the late fifteenth century show that the Thuringian peasantry was free enough in brawling and acts of violence with cudgel or knife. It is possible that Martin's father became a victim of the bad reputation of a younger brother, called "Little Hans" by neighbors in the county of Mansfeld to distinguish him from Martin's father, who went by the name of "Big Hans." [4] "Little Hans" also found his way from Möhra to the copper mining country beyond Eisleben,

---

[2] CR, VI, 157.

[3] See K. Gelbke, "Die Volkszahl der Stadt Eisleben von der Mitte des 15. Jahrhunderts bis zur Gegenwart," Mansfelder Blätter, IV (1890), 96 ff. Basing his figures on the number of houses, he estimates the population of the city at 4,240 for 1433 and 9,000 toward the end of the sixteenth century. Otto Scheel scales down these figures considerably. For his estimates see Martin Luther, I, 1 f. (all page references to Volume I are to the edition of 1916; all references to Volume II are to the edition of 1930 unless otherwise specified).

[4] See Julius Köstlin, "Rezensionen," ThStKr, LVII, II (1884), 373 ff., based on investigation of Mansfeld records.

where he gave much trouble to the magistrates and other guardians of the peace. As early as 1499 he begins to appear in the law records of Mansfeld for his ready use of a knife in quarrels, and during the next fourteen years he figures in encounters entailing wounds given and received in assaults, fist fights, beatings, and stabbings, within and without the local taverns.[5]

Such a record is not unusual for those years, but taken with other evidence it points to a strain of violence in the Luther family. "Big Hans" was also obstinate and stormy in his reactions, but a genial heart beat under his hard exterior. In later life Martin refers, half in jest to be sure, to his father's drinking, but he recalls also that when in his cups Hans was jovial of temper and inclined to jest and song.[6] The rigor with which he inflicted punishment on young Martin left resentment in its train, but through the years the son also remembered the generous impulse which led his father to seek a reconciliation afterward.[7] Over against evidence of an ardent and uncontrolled temper, the progress of Hans Luther in the world shows him to have been a man of industry and serious purpose. His neighbors entrusted him with an important office, that of representing his quarter as one of the four aids to the city council.[8] As time went by he followed his son's career with affection and evidently with understanding, and he made an effort to win the friendship of the clergy, who apparently respected him.[9] Martin carried through life a high regard for the older man's opinions, especially those concerning the cloister life. These he turned over and over in his mind through the crucial years, and after his break with Rome he dedicated his solemn renunciation of monasticism to Hans in a letter in which, with singular earnestness of tone, he recalls the doubts concerning his mission as friar that the practical miner had planted in his heart early in his career.[10] He carried through life also an affectionate memory of the self-sacrifice and loyalty with which his hard-working parent had supported his studies.[11]

Whereas the figure of Hans Luther stands forth in the sources in vigorous outline, that of his wife is pale in comparison. This is not altogether due to the spirit of the rugged age in which she lived, although north of the Alps

---

[5] W. Möllenberg, "Hans Luther, Dr. Martin Luthers Vater," *Zeitschrift des Harzvereins für Geschichte und Altertumskunde*, XXXIX (1906), 191 ff., cites the Mansfeld court records in detail regarding the misbehavior of "Hans Luder der junge" or "der kleine Hans Luder."

[6] *TR*, IV, No. 5050 (1540).   [7] *Ibid.*, II, No. 1559 (1532).

[8] The document substantiating this fact has evidently been lost, and the work in which it was published has not been available to the writer for checking. See Scheel, *Martin Luther*, I, 258, n. 38; see also n. 20 below.

[9] *CR*, VI, 156.

[10] *De votis monasticis* (1521), *WA*, VIII, 573 ff.

[11] *Eine Predigt, dass man Kinder zur Schule halten solle* (1530), *WA*, XXX, II, 576.

surprisingly few women interest the scribes of the Renaissance era. The clerical and scholarly writers who knew Luther's family would hardly have overlooked Margarete Ziegler if she had been marked by outstanding qualities. This does not necessarily imply that she was of a passive nature, for one of the two references which Martin makes to her notes the violence of a punishment that she inflicted on him for filching a single nut.[12] Apparently she was true to the German peasant type in her industry and self-abnegation, truc also to its world of mythology and the dread of the mysterious powers of earth and air which held it in its ban in those days. The two humanists of Martin's inner circle of friends, Georg Spalatin and Philip Melanchthon, note her domestic virtues and devout character, thus indicating, no doubt, that the little peasant woman possessed those qualities that were honored by her contemporaries.[13]

How long the young couple had been in Eisleben when Martin came into the world is uncertain. Uncertain it is also whether he was their first child.[14] Even the date of his birth cannot be fixed with absolute assurance, but the weight of evidence points to Monday, November 10, 1483, the day which Martin himself celebrated in later years and which has been generally accepted by succeeding generations.[15] He first saw the light in a small house which once stood in the present Doctor Luther Street near the Church of St. Peter's, not far inside the old south wall of Eisleben. The next day he was baptized in the chapel in the tower of St. Peter's and received his name, according to custom, from the calendar saint of that day, the gentle St. Martin of Tours, founder of Gallic monasticism and subject of many medieval stories of generosity and self-denial.

In the year following Martin's birth Hans Luther moved his little family out of Eisleben to the tiny city of Mansfeld. The new home lay several miles to the north in the center of the copper-mining region. Today the mines show little activity, but the landscape extends in weird vistas of innumerable mounds of refuse from earlier workings. Among these the town of Mansfeld lies in the gaunt valley in colorless repose, left aside by the pulsing traffic

[12] *TR*, III, No. 3566A (1537).

[13] Both knew her personally, Melanchthon evidently quite well. See *CR*, VI, 156. See also Krumhaar, *Die Grafschaft Mansfeld*, p. 83.

[14] In a very unreliable quotation in the *Table Talk* Martin is made to say that his parents brought a son with them from Möhra. *TR*, V, No. 5362 (1540).

[15] If we may trust poorly attested statements in the *Table Talk*, Martin himself was uncertain regarding the year of his birth. *TR*, V, No. 5573 (1543), and No. 5347. His mother shared this uncertainty. *CR*, VI, 156. Melanchthon makes it 1483 on the authority of Martin's brother Jakob. Oergel, *Vom jungen Luther*, pp. 15 f., made a valiant claim for December 7, 1482, but found little support. For opinions of authorities varying from 1482 to 1484 see Reu, *Thirty-Five Years of Luther Research*, pp. 36 f., and Scheel, *Martin Luther*, I, 256, n. 3.

of later days. In Luther's childhood it was undoubtedly more picturesque amid its forests and gardens. Its prosperity was then considerable, for it ruled the copper industry of northern Thuringia and had a strategic position on one of the chief commercial routes of late medieval Germany. Through its long street, the sole artery of traffic in the town, wagon trains, horsemen, and foot-travelers passed from Nuremberg and the South German cities toward the ports on the North Sea and the Baltic. Close at hand rises a steep ridge, where beside a modest chateau nestled among trees stand a tower and a few stone fragments, all that remains of the medieval castle to which Martin looked up as a boy. This was then the seat of two counts of Mansfeld, lords of the country round about. Here was the home of Martin's childhood. Here he ripened into adolescence amid surroundings which in great measure determined his attitude toward society.

The culture of Germany in the last decades of the fifteenth century and for nearly a century longer was solely an urban culture. Art and literature, scholarship and industry, liquid wealth and the comforts of existence were scarcely to be found elsewhere than within the walls of the cities, which from Augsburg and Strasbourg in the south to Danzig and Lübeck on the Baltic strung out across the land in a network of industrial centers whose activity and wealth had a generation earlier awakened the enthusiastic admiration of foreign observers. The walls and moat surrounding even a half-rural municipality like Mansfeld enclosed a life that in organization and sanctions differed radically from the life outside. Here patrician merchant, master-workman, journeyman, and apprentice moved in their narrow spheres, inter-locked with each other in a complex civic organization in which clergy and officials had also their well established part. The burghers viewed the world outside with feelings mingled of greed and suspicion. Toward the ruling nobility their attitude vibrated between servility and defiance; toward the peasantry they knew only the contempt so realistically shown in Albrecht Dürer's engravings of the brutish figures, men and women, as he caught them offering their eggs and geese on the market place in Nuremberg. This urban culture was to become Martin's; these prejudices were in a large measure to be his prejudices. Throughout life he was to meet the nobility, greater or less, with a mixture of humility and defiant independence. Not-withstanding his peasant ancestry and boyhood association with the rural world, he was to show little sympathy for the peasantry and scant under-standing for their problems. When the peasants tried to cure their economic ills by revolution in 1525 his reaction was to denounce the "murderous and thieving hordes."

It could only have been by degrees that the Luther family adapted itself to life in the new home. For a long time the struggle with poverty must have been a bitter one in mine and furnace, field and garden, even for the wiry limbs of peasant-bred Hans and Margarete. Half a century later, seated beside his comfortable professor's table in Wittenberg, surrounded by well-nourished children and students, Martin recalled the hard days of his youth, when his father was a poor laborer in the mines and his mother brought in all the wood on her back. "That is the way they brought us up." [16] This points to the early Mansfeld years when Hans still worked for others and Margarete followed the custom of poor families and fetched the firewood, peasantwise, from the communal forest. Many children came to add to the burden; how many we do not know, but several lived to maturity.[17] The terrible mortality of the later Middle Ages did not spare the Luther family. In 1505, by which time the father had become a man of some property,[18] the plague carried off two of his children. Brothers and sisters do not appear as individuals in the *Table Talk*, where Martin speaks freely on every aspect of his past. They played little part in his mature life; nevertheless their presence in early years must have been an important educational experience. Unlike some monastic and humanistic celibates of the period, Martin did not break the ties of affection that bound him to the home of his childhood.

Poor though the Luthers undoubtedly were in Martin's early years, it was a rising family, and the things essential to a child's development came in increasing measure. The archives of Mansfeld and the records of its court of mines show a constant improvement in the father's affairs.[19] By 1491, as we have seen, he had climbed to a position in the community that justified his election by his fellow-burghers as a representative on the "Commission of Four," associated with the city council in defending the rights of the citizens in contact with the administrative officers of the county of Mansfeld.[20] In 1501 Martin entered the university at Erfurt without other support

[16] *TR*, III, No. 2888a (1533).

[17] See the anecdote in Martin's sermon of 1538, *WA*, XLVII, 379, where Hans, ill abed, is said to have refused a priest importuning for a legacy on the ground that his many children needed the money more than did the Church. One son, Jakob, followed his father as mine owner in 1523. Möllenberg, "Hans Luther," pp. 174, 184, 186.

[18] *De votis monasticis*, *WA*, VIII, 573. See also Möllenberg, "Hans Luther."

[19] Möllenberg, "Hans Luther," pp. 169 ff., made a systematic study of the archives of the Mansfeld Grafschaft at Eisleben and the minutes of the Mansfeld city council (1495–1513), at Mansfeld, reproducing the original documents (pp. 175 ff.). This tireless digger into the records believed that he had identified the very slag pile where one of Hans Luther's furnaces stood! (p. 171).

[20] Krumhaar, *Versuch einer Geschichte von Stadt und Schloss Mansfeld*, p. 16. The city records used by this scholar seem now to be lost. Scheel, *Martin Luther*, I, 258, n. 38.

than that received from his father. In 1506 we find Hans in possession of a house, encumbered by only a small mortgage.[21] In the following year he appears as joint lessee of several mines and furnaces, one with three smelting hearths, and in the same year as one of a company engaged in dismantling shafts in abandoned mines. He seems to have been able to borrow money for his operations. Anyone could take up land for working copper mines if he was in a position to smelt the ore, and after 1506 Hans expanded his undertakings to include participation in several joint mining enterprises.[22] Even though a great part of Martin's youth after his fourteenth year was spent away from Mansfeld at school and in the university, and after 1505 in the cloister, it is evident that he belonged to one of the successful and respected households of Mansfeld. When at last on May 9, 1507, he celebrated his first Mass, Hans Luther marked the entry of his son into priestly office by riding over to Erfurt for the occasion with twenty companions and leaving behind a gift of twenty florins to Martin's cloister.[23]

It was, then, amid surroundings conducive to a sturdy development in body and in moral character that young Luther passed the formative years that led to adolescence. To this early background and to the stalwart heritage of peasant ancestry he owed the physical vigor that enabled him later to carry the burden of unremitting mental productivity and to stand without breaking the nervous strain of a succession of emotional upheavals.

With this physical preparation a moral steeling went hand in hand. Several times in later years Martin recalls the severity of the punishments that both parents visited on him. This was quite in accord with the custom of the times in home and school. It was against such brutal manhandling of children that the pedagogues of the Renaissance, including Martin himself, revolted and set in motion a reform. The severe punishments of his early years may well have built up in the boy a fear complex that played its part in psychological crises throughout life.[24] Many years later a reporter in the *Table Talk* has Martin say that this treatment made a coward of him.[25] If so, it was an experience that he shared with other sensitive boys of his generation. On the other hand, he voices gratitude that his parents brought him up in the knowledge and fear of God. Filial obedience was a scriptural command that Hans Luther took seriously. At the celebration of Martin's first

---

[21] Möllenberg, "Hans Luther," p. 185, cites the documents recording the payments.

[22] *Ibid.*, pp. 170 ff.   [23] *TR*, II, No. 1558.

[24] Preserved Smith, "Luther's Early Development in the Light of Psycho-Analysis," *American Journal of Psychology*, XXIV, 360 ff.

[25] "Usque ad pusillanimitatem coercuerent . . . ego pusillanimus tantum (factus sum)." *TR*, III, No. 3566A (1533).

Mass, his colleagues at the Erfurt cloister defended him for taking the cowl against his father's authority, but the uncompromising miner was prompt to answer: "Have you never read in the Scriptures that one is to honor father and mother?" The incident clung to Martin's memory and he repeats it again and again at widely separated periods.[26] Like every spirited youth he resented punishment, but its favorable effects on a naturally impulsive and violent nature cannot be overlooked in later years. He carried through life a respect for order and lay authority and on more than one occasion recorded regret for his outbreaks of violent temper and tried to curb them.

The cultural atmosphere that surrounded the growing child was not different from that in other small cities of north-central Germany in the later Middle Ages. Crude superstition and naïve religious beliefs were intertwined to make up the texture of the mind. Through his parents he absorbed relics of pagan mythology that the German peasantry had brought down from primitive days without essential modification by Christian patterns. The awakening imagination of the child sucked in with eagerness these animistic beliefs and wove them into fixations that reappear throughout later life in the sermons and in the *Table Talk*.[27] He learned that witches lurk on every side and cast their spell on man, beast, and food.[28] In early sermons he shows a certain grim pleasure in passing in review the manifestations of witches and evil spirits,[29] and he throws a vivid light on the atmosphere of his home when, many years later, in looking back on the way mothers were obliged to care for children under the attacks of these creatures, he adds, "that kind of witchery was especially general when I was a boy."[30] His poor mother, as he told his table companions, "was so tormented by one of her neighbors who was a witch that she was obliged to treat her with the highest respect and conciliate her, for she caused such agony to her children that they would scream like unto death."[31] When one of his brothers died, witchcraft was held to be responsible; and many victims of these malignant women were pointed out to the terrified boy.[32] When the crops failed, he learned that it was because evil spirits had poisoned the air;[33] and as a child he doubtless

[26] In 1521, *De votis monasticis*, *WA*, VIII, 574; in 1533, *TR*, I, Nos. 623 and 881; in 1539, *TR*, IV, No. 4574; and in 1545, *Enarrationes in Genesin*, *WA*, XLIV, 711 f.

[27] See Klingner, *Luther und Volksaberglaube*, for a detailed study of popular superstitions in Luther's works. The author's assembly of the sources is conscientious and methodical, but his interpretation is not devoid of an apologetic tone.

[28] *TR*, III, No. 2982b (1533); IV, No. 3979 (1538).

[29] E.g., in the series of sermons on the Ten Commandments, published in 1518, *Decem praecepta Wittenbergensi praedicata*, *WA*, I, 401 f. and 406 f.

[30] *In epistolam S. Pauli ad Galatos commentarius* (1531), *WA*, XL, II, 313.

[31] *TR*, III, No. 2982b.   [32] *WA*, XL, II, 314 f.

[33] *Ein Sermon von dem Gebet und Prozession in der Kreuzwoche* (1519), *WA*, II, 178.

took part in the Corpus Christi processions, when the clergy led the way to the fields and read the gospel to purify the air of such harmful beings. It was the latter, as he was told by his parents and neighbors, that caused the destructive storms, blasted the fruit, and brought the cattle plague. "We may not doubt," he declares in a well-accredited remark in the *Table Talk*, "that pestilences, fevers, and other grave diseases are the work of demons." Following Biblical authority he thought that insane persons were possessed of a devil, who took this way of tormenting them, and that the doctors attributed things of that kind to natural causes only because of their ignorance of the ways of demons.[34] Hidden in the house were little sprites who, like the fox-spirit in China, bring good luck; and his mother must often have whispered to him to avoid giving offense to these "little wights," for people feared to vex them "more than God and the whole world." [35] Satan, Martin learned, dwells in the woods and groves and is especially dangerous in the water. On the Pubelsberg, a mountain near Mansfeld, there was a lake which was thought to be a dwelling place of captive demons in his boyhood. "If a stone is thrown in, a great storm arises throughout the whole region." [36] The cases of drowning which occurred yearly at Wittenberg among bathers in the Elbe, a stream of shifting sandbanks and holes, Martin ascribed in a sermon of middle life to Satan, "who formerly worked through nixies"; and he warned his hearers to wash at home rather than go to the river alone.[37]

As he grew older, the simple animism that the boy had learned from his village-bred parents and neighbors was modified by theological influences. The literalism with which he came to interpret the Scriptures made him reject forms of magic commonly practiced in his day, such as communion with the spirits of the dead, foretelling the future by crystal-gazing, or finding treasure with a divining rod.[38] These and other hocus-pocus he found inconsistent with God's commands. He even mocked at astrology, which was accepted without hesitation by contemporary humanists of distinction: God has locked the future from us, Martin is convinced, and will reveal it at His own time. Nevertheless he joined his contemporaries in believing that comets and other exceptional celestial phenomena boded

---

[34] *TR*, II, No. 2267b (1531).   [35] *WA*, I, 406, ll. 30 ff.   [36] *TR*, III, 3841 (1538).

[37] *Predigt am 3. Sonntag nach Trinitatis* (June 13, 1529), *WA*, XXIX, 401. Open-air bathing was indeed very risky for pious Wittenbergers. A historian of the city, claiming to draw from archival sources, tells us that the Lutheran clergy sought to prevent their flock from bathing in the Elbe by threatening to withhold Christian burial from those who were drowned. It was believed that demons drew the bathers down by the feet and twisted their necks under water. Meyner, *Geschichte der Stadt Wittenberg*, p. 135.

[38] *WA*, I, 406, ll. 10 ff.; *TR*, III, No. 3618A (1537), and No. 3825 (1538). See Klingner, *Luther und Volksaberglaube*, pp. 69 f.

disaster, though not to the righteous man.[39] Likewise, the old Germanic superstition of the incubus and succubus, who beget children under the guise of dreams, and the demonic changeling that is substituted for the infant in the cradle appear repeatedly in Luther's *Table Talk* in richly decorated form.[40] From his father Martin learned also of resentful earth-spirits who appear to the workmen in the lonely corridors of the mine. The tricks which the devil plays on the miner stirred the imagination of the boy and like other mythology of Mansfeld days reappeared in colorful pictures in old age.[41] In Luther's years of restless self-examination many demons focus in the scriptural Satan, but this enemy, who figures repeatedly in Martin's physical and emotional crises, has his source above all in the animistic fixations of childhood that crowd each other in picturesque succession in a sermon on the Ten Commandments in 1518, one of the earliest publications of young Luther, and persist in the discourses of middle life and later.

In Martin's boyhood the primitive demonology of the Germans broke into hysterical expression in the pulpit and in literature. As soon as he was able to comprehend, he heard from parish priest and begging friar stories like those he tells afterward to his congregations and table companions. These religious sanctions extended to the picturesque figure of the medieval devil. This half-terrifying, half-humorous figure may well have caught his eye as it passed in the carnival procession of the city guilds or played hide-and-seek with other *dramatis personae* of a Shrovetide mask on the market place of Mansfeld or Eisleben. The imagination of the boy seized pictures of this sort and gave them reality. From these sources as from the folklore passed on by family and neighbors the character of the devil was built up for Martin: now full of malignant hatred, now touched with grim humor, always a resourceful and relentless enemy.

Over against this evil power the affrighted soul grasped eagerly the hand of divine protection. In the home and abroad demons were held in check by the triumphant figures of Christian mythology. What part thoughts of God the Father and Christ the Son and Savior played in the imagination of the growing boy cannot be disentangled in the sources from the soul experiences of maturer years. When Martin reviews his early religious impressions, it is

[39] *Vorrede zu Lichtenbergers Weissagung, WA*, XXIII, 10 (1527); see also letter from Luther to Wenceslaus Link, Jan. 14, 1521, *WAB*, II, 248, and n. 8.

[40] *TR*, II, No. 2528b (1532), and No. 2529b. See also *Predigten über das erste Buch Mose* (1523–24), *WA*, XIV, 185, ll. 10 f., where Luther declares that the belief that demons can beget children with women of the earth is no article of faith, but admits the possibility.

[41] See also the interesting story in the *Table Talk* of Hans's terror when he sees the deadly wound inflicted by the devil on a fellow miner. *TR*, II, No. 2370 (1532).

in the years following his conflict with the papacy, and the picture he draws shows polemical coloring. Here Father and Son appear as stern and frightful judges of mankind, an idea that becomes more definite as Martin's cloister life fades into the distance.[42] One picture, however, that of Christ seated on a rainbow judging the world, clearly goes back to a boyhood impression, for it appears repeatedly in the discourses of later days when Martin speaks of the fears that surrounded his early conception of the Savior.[43] As a boy this caught his eye on a painting behind the altar or on a church window and intensified his fears of Christ the Judge. In contrast with the terrors aroused by the thought of the Last Judgment, the Christmas festival must have awakened his imagination to the poetry of the Nativity, for on Holy Night he sang in the Mansfeld streets of the Christ Child born in Bethlehem. This too left a deep imprint, and in mature years bore fruit in the Christmas songs, such as "Vom Himmel hoch, da komm' ich her," in which he puts the old medieval Latin hymns into simple German.

The Virgin Mother and the saints greeted the eyes of the boy from altar and windows, and their glory became familiar in prayers and hymns. Here love and pity, protection and help came to him clothed in warm humanity. The Virgin, whose song, the *Magnificat*, Martin translated and interpreted while waiting for the summons to his hearing at Worms, was usually sung at vesper services. Her figure sank into his memory as she appears at the Last Judgment, showing to her Son the breasts that suckled Him and pleading for mercy on mankind.[44]

Singing the Litany and the Rogations in the choir he learned to know the saints, and these bright figures gave him protection against the severity of the Judge and the wiles of the demons. Beside the apostolic forms of John the Baptist, Peter, and Paul stood the titanic Archangel Michael with his sword, and the knightly St. George, the patron of the parish church of Mansfeld. Prominent in the galaxy of saints appeared St. Anne, the patron of the miners. Martin's boyhood saw a rapid increase in the brotherhoods of laymen devoted to the cult of an especial saint. Toward the end of the century St. Anne rose to great importance under an impulse given by the Franciscans, who had come forward as champions of the immaculate

[42] See Scheel, *Dokumente,* index, "Christus." Nearly all of the statements cited belong to the period of Luther's middle forties. Denifle, *Luthertum* (1904), I, 400 ff. One, however, appears in the sermons of 1522–23 and undoubtedly points back to ideas entertained during Martin's life in the cloister. *WA,* X, III, 357. See Scheel, *Dokumente,* Nos. 63 and 65 f., pp. 26 f.

[43] *Das 14. und 15. Kapitel St. Johannis gepredigt* (1537), *WA,* XLV, 482; see also *WA,* XLVI, 9; XLVII, 275; XXXIII, 90 and 677.

[44] He recalls this picture in sermons of 1531, implying that it was inspired by a description of the Last Judgment in the works of St. Bernard. *WA,* XXXIII, 83 and 539.

conception of the Virgin.[45] In one of his earliest sermons Martin recalls that the honor paid St. Anne rivaled, if it did not exceed, that shown to the Virgin herself.[46] The shining forms of the saints stamped themselves enduringly on the boy's imagination. Long afterward, in 1519, when he had launched his attacks on indulgences and broken with the scholastic theology, he continued to hold to the belief in miracles wrought through the saints: "Who can deny that openly to this very day God works miracles in His sacred name beside the bodies and graves of the saints?"[47] Slowly and with difficulty he turned away from the venerated company that had shielded his childhood from the powers of evil.[48]

Schooling in Martin's boyhood days began with the seventh year. The chronicle of his sixteenth-century biographer, Conrad Schlüsselberg,[49] states that he entered at a somewhat earlier age, and Martin's recollection confirms this. Two years before his death he recorded in the Bible of his brother-in-law Nikolaus Omeler that the latter, an old comrade, had carried him back and forth in school days more than once as a child.[50] In 1489 Hans Luther must still have been a poor man, for whom the cost of schooling would have been no slight burden. The evidence, therefore, seems to point to an early development of the boy's mind. The Mansfeld school lay across the square from the church of St. George, where its successor rests today on the same foundation. Nothing is known of its character during Martin's boyhood, though later on it became an important preparatory school for the Wittenberg university.[51] It cannot have been different from the other trivial schools of the type that had grown up in the German cities after the middle of the fourteenth century, supplanting in great part the old cathedral and parochial schools and sharing throughout the fifteenth century in the prosperity of the municipalities. It gave early instruction to those boys in the community who were to go on to the university as candidates for the legal or clerical calling.

Many years later, in 1524, Martin drew up a bitter indictment of the Latin

[45] See Schaumkell, *Der Kultus der heiligen Anna*, pp. 13 ff.

[46] *WA*, I, 415. See also Theodor Kolde, "Das religiöse Leben in Erfurt beim Ausgange des Mittelalters," *SVRG*, LXIII (1898), 17 f.

[47] *Unterricht auf etliche Artikel, WA*, II, 69 f.

[48] E.g., *Sendbrief vom Dolmetschen, WA*, XXX, II, 644: "Est ist mir selber aus der massen sauer worden, das ich mich von den Heiligen gerissen habe." In another work he asks patience for "weak" brethren who continue to address prayers to the saints. *Epistel oder Unterricht von den Heiligen, WA*, X, II, 166.

[49] *Oratio de vita et morte . . . Lutheri,* C 3. See Scheel, *Martin Luther*, I, 256, n. 3.

[50] De Wette, *Dr. Martin Luthers Briefe*, V, 709.

[51] See Förstemann, *Album der Studenten*, cited in Scheel, *Martin Luther*, I, 53.

schools of the cities for their stagnation in method and the lifeless character of the subjects they taught.[52] Standing as he did at the opening of a new social era after twenty years of humanistic reform, he conceived of education as training for life rather than merely for the priesthood or the law. Every age that is acutely conscious of its reforming mission finds in the narrowness of school traditions an explanation of the evils that afflict the culture of its day. Here the humanists were no exception. In their zeal for reform they overlooked the fact that the old trivial school had laid the foundation for the scholarship of educational leaders like Johann Reuchlin, and Latin poets like Eobanus Hessus and Ulrich von Hutten.

The archives of the late medieval cities in Germany show a constant effort on the part of the city fathers to maintain the standards of these schools. They were at pains to see that the principal carried out the program of instruction and disciplined his subordinates in order that they might hold the balance between too cruel treatment by brutal teachers and too great leniency due to the influence of indulgent parents. The principal, in turn, leaned for the maintenance of discipline on his monitors, or *locati,* whose office is symbolized in contemporary woodcuts by a bundle of switches; and for aid in teaching he depended on his older scholars, or *bacchanti.* In addition, each class was provided with a special monitor, or *lupus,* keeper of the dreaded "wolf list," a register of the demerits incurred for the two chief offenses against the school code: cursing and speaking German. Once a week the calendar was swept clean and the culprits duly punished, while day by day the poorest scholar was decorated with the wooden effigy of an ass.

Such was the organization of the German trivial school, and the one at Mansfeld cannot have deviated greatly from the pattern. Here as elsewhere the strenuous use of the rod was an accepted part of the mechanism of school life. The severity of the punishments is well attested in the acts and minutes of the councils of the German cities and by other school authorities at the period. One hundred years after Luther's birth the regulations of the Gymnasium of another Saxon city, Nordhausen, warned the teachers "not to behave like tyrants, not to beat the boys till the blood came or kick them or pluck them by the hair or ears, or strike them in the face with sticks or books, but to inflict moderate punishment." The instructors are urged also to refrain from "blasphemy, cursing, using insulting terms and violent abuse."[53] If warnings like this were necessary after half a century of

---

[52] *An die Ratsherren aller Städte deutsches Lands, WA,* XV, 27 ff.

[53] School directions for the Gymnasium, 1583, in *Mitteilungen der Gesellschaft für deutsche Erziehungs- und Schulgeschichte* (Berlin, 1892), II, 97.

humanistic reform, we may infer that brutal punishments were the order of the day at the Mansfeld trivial school during the eight years of Martin's attendance. In an educational pamphlet of 1524, *To the Councilors of All German Cities,* he denounces the cruelty of the teachers with an intensity that points to personal experience; and many years later he tells his table companions of teachers as cruel as executioners.[54] He feels that in school as in the home punishment may breed resentment and terror, and supports this in a lecture delivered late in life by a story from his own childhood.[55] With other boys he had sung at Shrovetide before a farmer's house in a lonely spot at the end of a village. At the cry of the householder, all fled incontinently and had to be enticed back to receive the food he was bringing them. Not so well attested is the story, repeated by nearly every biographer of Luther, that he was punished fifteen times in a single forenoon for failure to learn his Latin grammar lesson.[56] These incidents cannot be interpreted to mean that the teachers at Mansfeld were more cruel than elsewhere; for Martin certainly shared the experiences of other school boys of his day. They do give further indications, however, that his was a character that could not avoid punishment or bear it without resentment. Yet its effect on a boy of nervous and headstrong temperament in the years preceding adolescence was probably not altogether unfavorable, for his career in the school at Eisenach after his fifteenth year was a happy one.

"What have people learned in the upper schools and cloisters down to the present except to be asses, blocks, and stumps? One studies twenty to forty years and learns neither Latin nor German." [57] Thus Martin summarizes the achievements of the trivial schools of his time a generation after he left Mansfeld. The statement has, as is often the case at this period, a polemical background. He saw in the school the same tyranny of the law and lack of evangelical gentleness as in the Roman Church. It is, however, far from accurate as a characterization of the schools which he attended. The primary object of the trivial school was instruction in Latin. Martin began with a Latin reader, or *fibula,* which contained the Ten Commandments, the Apostles' Creed, the Lord's Prayer and prayers for morning and evening,

---

[54] *TR,* III, No. 3566B (1537).

[55] *Enarrationes in Genesin, WA,* XLIV, 548. The same incident is related in *TR,* I, 137 (1531–32). See Jürgens, *Luthers Leben,* I, 159 ff.

[56] *TR,* V, No. 5571 (1543). The tradition supporting the text (Caspar Heidenreich's notes) is somewhat unreliable. Many biographers, especially Adolf Hausrath, have dwelt on brutal treatment in school as a cause of Luther's nervousness and physical sufferings in later life. The contemporary sources give no support to this theory.

[57] *An die Ratsherren, WA,* XV, 31.

the Annunciation, the Confession, and other formulas.[58] From these he passed on to learn the forms as they were given in the grammar of Aelius Donatus, a work on which much of the Middle Ages built its knowledge of Latin. Like many generations before him, Martin conceived great respect for this father of language-teaching in the schools and refers to him in later years as the "best of grammarians." [59] It is not likely, however, that he or any of his fellow pupils possessed a copy of Donatus nor that there were any schoolbooks in Mansfeld except in the hands of teachers. A somewhat older Swiss boy, Konrad Kürsner, who later in humanistic fashion put his name into Latin as Pellicanus, attended school in the 1480s and had good instruction from Donatus's grammar and the popular Latin syntax of the Middle Ages, the *Doctrinale puerorum* by Alexander de Villa Dei. He tells us that during his entire school experience he never had a printed book but was obliged to write down everything with toil and pains. "In fact, there was not at that time a single printed copy of Donatus or Alexander in Basel." [60] After Martin had entered the university, another schoolboy, little Thomas Platter, set forth from Switzerland to find a school in Germany where he might acquire some of the "New Learning," the fame of which had penetrated into the high valley of the upper Rhone. On his wanderings, which led him to Silesia and back again, he came into many classes where the teacher alone had a book.[61] The scholars wrote down what was dictated, then repeated and memorized it. Under such discipline young Martin laid the foundation for the prodigious memory that enabled him later to take part successfully in the university disputations, where the participant must be ready to meet citation with citation, and to put his finger promptly on an authoritative passage in heavy volumes of William of Occam, Peter Lombard, or Augustine. The material on which the trivial scholar exercised his Latin had been burnished by three centuries of use in the German schools. It included the Distiches of Cato,[62] a storehouse of pithy wisdom; Aesop's

[58] See *Mitteilungen der Gesellschaft für deutsche Erziehungs- und Schulgeschichte*, I, 93, for a description of a Nuremberg *Teutsche Kinder-Tafel* of 1534, where these formulas appear for initiating the youngsters in "the beginning of Christian faith and the German language."

[59] *TR*, III, No. 3490 (1536).

[60] Pellicanus, *Die Hauschronik*, p. 8. A translation into English has been made by Frederick C. Ahrens, "The Chronicle of Conrad Pellican, 1478–1556, Translated from the Latin Manuscript . . . in 1950" (Ph.D. dissertation, Columbia University).

[61] See Gustav Freytag, "Bilder aus der deutschen Vergangenheit," II, in *Gesammelte Werke*, XIX (1911), 21.

[62] This well-worn collection of proverbial wisdom was retained by Luther's school visitors in the reformed program of the Saxon school. See "Unterricht der Visitatoren," in *The Visitation of the Saxon Reformed Church in the Years 1527 and 1528*, ed. by Richard Laurence (1839), p. 139. For the plan of instruction in the Wittenberg Latin school in 1533 see Scheel, *Martin Luther*, I, 56 f.

fables; the *Consolation of Philosophy* of Boethius; and possibly a Plautus or Terence, which found their way into some of the more advanced schools toward the end of the century.

Such an invasion by the spirit of humanism was, however, unusual. The subject matter of study, beside the medieval authors just mentioned, was likely to be religious. It is unlikely that the seven or eight years in the Mansfeld school took Martin beyond Donatus and the earliest part of the *Doctrinale* of Alexander, which taught the rules of Latin sentence structure in mnemonic hexameters. Though the procedure of instruction was slow and many boys learned nothing after years of schooling, as we know from Thomas Platter and from resentful criticism by Luther and his humanistic contemporaries, it nevertheless laid the foundation for a ready and fluent Latin. Practice in speaking Latin played an important rôle: for the older boys German was rigidly excluded in school and, so far as possible, on the playground as well.[63] At Mansfeld Martin must have begun to acquire the command of the language of scholarship which he afterward wielded with natural facility and an individual style.

The trivium, which embraced the first three of the liberal arts, that is, the "arts of the freeman," consisted of grammar, logic, and rhetoric. The last two were usually reserved for the university: only a larger school here and there brought them into its program, and it is unlikely that the school at Mansfeld could do so. However, one subject from the old quadrivium was found even in the smallest school, namely music. This was of high importance for Martin: he had unusual gifts for song and devoted himself to it with enthusiasm throughout life. As a schoolboy he sang on the streets of Mansfeld, earning a bit of bread or fish or sausage as one of a *currende* or troop of comrades who thus won the bounty of generous householders at Christmas or Carnival time.[64] To sing in the choir of the church was a communal duty expected of the schoolboys and their masters and called for their presence not only on Sunday, but at the regular daily offices as well. This was no simple art. The system of counterpoint was already finding its way across the Alps, and before the end of the fifteenth century the liturgical forms of worship in the German churches had become complex, foreshadowing the highly developed technique which the Italian choristers were to introduce by the end of the first quarter of the following century. The later Middle Ages had a passion for religious spectacles, and in the proces-

[63] Monitors (*lupi*) were secretly appointed in the Nordhausen school as late as 1583 to denounce boys from the three upper classes who lapsed into German. *Mitteilungen der Gesellschaft für deutsche Erziehungs- und Schulgeschichte*, II, 96.

[64] See n. 55 above.

sions and rituals that marked the great Church festivals or the passage through the city of an archbishop or a traveling Roman dignitary, music was an important feature. Here, too, young Martin and his school comrades played a rôle.

For an imaginative boy all this meant of course not merely an introduction to musical technique. The ancient formulas of Christianity: the Apostles' Creed, the Lord's Prayer, the Ten Commandments, the *Te Deum* and other Latin hymns, the Latin litany, the *Kyrie eleison, Magnificat,* and *Nunc dimittis* and all the rest, together with the solemn service of the Mass, were a part of Martin's daily life and entered into the very fiber of his being. It is not difficult to imagine that the sublime poetry of Christian faith as it rose on the wings of choral song must have lifted his impressionable young soul into a world of mystical emotion.

2

THE SCHOOLBOY ABROAD

IN his fourteenth year young Martin left the narrow scenes of childhood and went forth into a wider world of experience. Probably at Easter, 1496,[1] he set out from the valley of Mansfeld to carry on his schooling at Magdeburg, thirty miles to the north. The largest city of the region, Magdeburg lay strategically in the valley of the Elbe and dominated the country round about as the center of a lively trade and the seat of a bishop, as well as through the prestige of its churches and schools. The departure from home must have been a great adventure for the lad, but it was quite in accord with the spirit of the times. The wandering schoolboy, an heir of the vagrant scholars of the Middle Ages, was not an unusual sight on the highways of Saxony in a day when a great wave of school reform was spreading over Central Europe. Thomas Platter's autobiography pictures the troops of youths swarming along the German roads, many of them hundreds of miles from home, seeking food from charity and lodging wherever they could. Wandering was in the blood of the later Middle Ages. Schoolboys adapted themselves to it and fitted together into a social organization like that which had grown up among another class of wanderers, the artisans of the cities. The schools too had their apprentices, their journeymen, and their master-workmen. An older boy, the *bacchante,* was attended by a group of satellite fags, or *Schützen,* who begged and stole to keep their elders in food, receiving in return protection from other boys and perhaps a crust of bread or a bit of fish from such store as they collected. As the "New Learning" brought especial fame to certain schools, large numbers of scholars were often attracted from distant parts of Middle Europe and made serious trouble for school authorities and city fathers.

A system like this involved a cruel waste of life. Martin, however, escaped

[1] The date of Luther's removal to Magdeburg is a matter of some dispute. Barnikol, *Luther in Magdeburg,* p. 4, sets the date as Easter, 1496; the early biographers, Melanchthon, Ratzeberger, and Mathesius, make it 1497, which Scheel prefers.

the worst of its physical hardships and moral dangers. As the son of a respected and rising citizen of Mansfeld he enjoyed such protection as the social structure of the time permitted. He journeyed to Magdeburg in the care of an older lad, Hans Reinecke, son of a neighbor and business associate of Hans Luther.[2] In Magdeburg also he was not without protectors, for a native son of Mansfeld, Paul Mosshauer, who had attained some importance in the Elbe metropolis as an official of the archbishop, opened a friendly house and invited the boy repeatedly to his table.[3]

Thus the transfer to Magdeburg was no great hazard. Nevertheless it was a long step forward in Martin's education. From the narrow mining town of Mansfeld with its single street, which had been the world of his childhood, he came into the broad valley of Germany's greatest river and wandered on the crowded ways of a city that had at that time no commercial rival between the central mountains and the northern seas. Begirt with populous suburbs, Magdeburg enclosed perhaps 30,000 inhabitants [4] within far-extended walls and carried on a thriving trade in grain, wool, and textiles.[5] As the seat of an archbishop it had considerable political and cultural importance. To the southeast, somewhat aside from the busier centers of trade, lay the oldest quarter of the city, and here clustered a complex of religious buildings. Here was the great cathedral with its many richly decorated altars and its store of sacred relics; here the palace of the archbishop and its attendant structures. A half dozen churches raised their towers beside the cathedral square and in the streets leading from it, and cloister walls bordered the narrow ways.[6] This sacred precinct of Church hierarchy and religious orders was in all probability the scene of Martin's year of schooling at Magdeburg.

It can hardly be doubted that it was the high reputation of a school that drew him thither. Contemporary biographers attest this; the most competent of them, Melanchthon, vouches for the generally good repute of the grammar

[2] See n. 3 below; see also Enders, *Luthers Briefwechsel*, III, 402, n. 2. This companion developed into a life-long friend. When Reinecke died the Luther household kept the news of his passing from Martin for a long time. *TR*, V, No. 6030 (1538).

[3] Letter from Luther to Claus Storm, June 15, 1522, *WAB*, II, 563.

[4] Hoffmann, *Geschichte der Stadt Magdeburg*, I, 467, sets this figure for the last quarter of the fifteenth century. Population figures for German cities in the Renaissance era are largely a matter of guessing, as a single visit of the plague might destroy a large fraction of the inhabitants. Of Magdeburg, chronicles report that in 1450 one third of the population perished in this way (*ibid.*). During Luther's early school days the Hansa cities generally had passed the crest of their popularity.

[5] *Ibid.*, pp. 466 ff.

[6] Scheel, *Martin Luther*, I, 63 ff., has illustrated the location by a plan derived from a drawing made after the burning of the city by Tilly in 1632. Hoffmann, *Geschichte der Stadt Magdeburg*, Vol. I, Appendix, shows a map from 1551. See also *ibid.*, III, 181 ff., for a description of the churches in Magdeburg in 1513–1631.

schools of the city. It is not possible to say which school young Martin attended.[7] A quarter of a century later Luther mentions that he was at school "with the Null Brethren,"[8] a name usually applied to the Brethren of the Common Life. This was a semi-monastic brotherhood which had been founded in the later fourteenth century at Deventer in Holland by the famous mystics Geert Groot and Florentius Radewyn as an expression of the social tendency of late medieval monasticism.[9] In addition to cultivating the devotional life the Brethren had undertaken the care of schoolboys as an especial mission, and without giving themselves altogether to school instruction they had established homes for scholars so as to provide physical protection and moral training. These institutions extended into Westphalia, where a settlement of brothers flourished at Münster, and into lower Saxony. It was especially the poorer scholars who came under their care.[10] Erasmus lived with the Brethren of the Common Life during his early school days at Deventer. The house of the order at Hildesheim, from which that at Magdeburg stemmed, made definite efforts to draw poor scholars into its protection and had sheltered a considerable number of such boys during the decades that preceded Martin's year at Magdeburg.[11] At that time the foundation of the devout brotherhood in the Elbe metropolis was well established; indeed, it had just secured an extension of its privileges after a long struggle against local jealousies. Its house lay close to the cathedral beside the east wall of the city.[12]

It is probable that for at least a part of his stay at Magdeburg young Martin

[7] The question is discussed at length by Kawerau, "Welche Schule in Magdeburg hat Luther besucht?" *Geschichtsblätter für Stadt und Land Magdeburg,* XVI (1881), 309 ff., who thinks Martin attended a municipal school. See, however, n. 13 below.

[8] Letter from Luther to Claus Storm, *WAB,* II, 563. The name has been variously explained. Barnikol, *Luther in Magdeburg,* pp. 9 ff., derives it from *lollen* or *lullen* (to sing softly), and *Lollbrüder* seems, indeed, to have been more common. Lindener in his "Katzipori" (1558) applies the term *Nollbrüder* to monks in general, but especially to the Franciscans. *Bibliothek des Litterarischen Vereins in Stuttgart,* CLXIII (1883), 113, 150, 173 f. See also Kawerau, "Welche Schule," 309 ff.

[9] See Hyma, *The Christian Renaissance;* see also Mestwerdt, *Erasmus,* especially for the important rôle of the Brethren in early humanism.

[10] Mestwerdt, *Erasmus,* pp. 138 ff. One of the poor scholars who enjoyed happy relations with the brotherhood at Deventer was Johann Butzbach, a Rhenish contemporary of Luther (*ibid.,* p. 140, n. 1).

[11] "Annalen und Akten der Brüder des gemeinsamen Lebens in Lüchtenhofe und Hildesheim," ed. by R. Doebner, in *Quellen und Darstellungen zur Geschichte Niedersachsens,* IX (1903), 123 ff.

[12] The first brothers seem to have been sent to Magdeburg from Hildesheim in 1482. *Ibid.,* pp. 90 ff. The settlement was established in the following year in the so-called "Diebshorn," now the Fürstenwallstrasse in the "new city." When Luther came to Magdeburg, the community had grown to twenty brothers. See *Geschichtsquellen der Provinz Sachsen,* XXVIII, 407 f., 587.

found a home with this brotherhood. Some of its members were his teachers, either in a school attached to their house or, as seems more likely, in the cathedral school which lay on the New Market close at hand.[13] Wherever his abode, he tasted early of the hardships of the scholastic life. Like other schoolboys of the time, even those of families in easy circumstances, he was obliged to live, in part at least, from charity. This was in accord with the custom of the later Middle Ages. "He went after bread and sang before burgher houses," [14] relates the early biographer Mathesius, and Luther himself confirms it.[15]

It is clear that Martin's connection with the brothers, brief though it was, must have had a definite influence on the boy's religious character. He came into contact with a group of men of rich devotional spirit. Many years later he speaks of the members of the order as witnesses of Christian freedom and the apostolic way of life.[16] Their goal was not the traditional monastic ideal of prayer and contemplation, but the *devotio moderna,* an active mission in aid of the body and morals of youth. In the school and at their house young Martin must have listened to the devotional exercises and the pious conversation which were characteristic of the group here as at Deventer and elsewhere, for in spite of the modern trends within the order the brothers went the round of cloister observances. Among them he could follow the monastic succession of private prayer and liturgical exercise, and perhaps even his immature eyes noted how the religious zeal of these men was fired by their systematic devotion to spiritual growth and the reading of Holy Scripture. He must have watched them also at their deeds of practical mercy. In daily contact with these teachers and companions the adolescent boy could learn something of the magic appeal of self-sacrifice and the mystic attraction of the yoke of God.

The year amid the churches and cloisters of Magdeburg furnished the lad with vivid impressions of the pomp and majesty of religious life as well as its mystic charm. Many pictures of contemplative saint and ministrant monk must have remained in his mind. One of these rose to consciousness thirty-five years later, when he recalled having seen a gaunt figure stagger through

[13] Scheel, *Martin Luther,* I, 76 f., argues vigorously for the cathedral school, where the Null Brothers may have given instruction. There is no evidence that they ever had a school of their own in Magdeburg; but Luther's statement that he went to school to them is categorical.

[14] "Daselbst ist dieser Knabe wie manches ehrlichen und wohlhabenden Mannes Kind, nach Brot gegangen und hat vor den Bürgerhäusern gesungen." Mathesius, *Das Leben Luthers,* p. 2.

[15] *Eine Predigt, dass man Kinder zur Schule halten solle* (1530), *WA,* XXX, II, 576.

[16] Letter from Luther to the Council of Herford, Oct. 24, 1534, *WAB,* VII, 112 ff.

Broad Street of Magdeburg under a heavy sack of bread which he had begged
for his cloister, "like a death's head, nothing but skin and bone" from fasting
and self-castigation.[17] Some bystander must have told him then that under
the cowl of this humble Brother Ludwig of the Franciscans he saw a duke of
the reigning house of Anhalt-Zerbst, a priest and guardian of his cloister
who after many years of self-abnegation was now approaching the end of his
life. Among other religious impressions to which the soul of the young
student opened in those months, that of the musical services in church and
processional celebrations must here too have played a leading rôle, as they
did in Mansfeld. Beside the dreary exercises of Donat's grammar and
Alexander's rhetoric, the choral duties of the schoolboys were an aesthetic
counterbalance of lasting influence on one so musically gifted as young
Martin. The technical knowledge of music which he possessed in later years
was due to the training of his youth,[18] and for this Magdeburg gave rich
opportunity.

Just when the Magdeburg experience came to an end is not quite certain.
By Martin's own account and that of contemporary biographers it lasted a
year. Dr. Matthäus Ratzeberger, Luther's friend and physician at Wittenberg,
records that in the year 1498 Martin went to school at Eisenach, "sent by his
parents to his friends," [19] and Pastor Mathesius confirms this with the statement that his going was "at the bidding of his parents." [20] Here, therefore,
in the neighborhood from which his parents had migrated, the son of Hans
and Margarete Luther was to carry on his schooling. A quarter of a century
later Martin declared that the country round about still contained all his
relatives.[21]

To Eisenach, then, his "beloved Eisenach," as he calls it in mature years,
the young scholar did not come as a stranger. In childhood he must have
heard from his parents many fragments of history and legend that clung to
the peasant mind from livelier days in the annals of the city. It was a provin-

---

[17] *Verantwortung der aufgelegten Aufruhr* (1533), *WA*, XXXVIII, 105. See *TR*, VI, No.
6859. For an account of this striking example of the leveling power of the late medieval
Church see Leonhard Lemmens, "Aus ungedruckten Franziskanerbriefen des XVI. Jahrhunderts," *RgST*, XX (1911), 8 ff.

[18] See Preuss, *Luther der Künstler*, pp. 89 ff., for a detailed presentation of Luther's musical
training and ability.

[19] Ratzeberger, *Handschriftliche Geschichte*, p. 43. Melanchthon says that Luther was four
years in Eisenach, and this is supported by a passage in a somewhat unreliable part of the
Table Talk. *TR*, V, No. 5347. In that case, he must have gone to Eisenach in 1497. The
matriculation at the University of Erfurt in May, 1501, is the first date in Luther's life that
is authentically documented. See Biereye, *Die Erfurter Lutherstätten*, p. 5.

[20] Mathesius, *Das Leben Luthers*, p. 2.

[21] Letter from Luther to Spalatin, Jan. 14, 1520, *WAB*, I, 610.

cial place, possibly somewhat smaller than Eisleben, and it lacked the vigorous pulse of industry and commerce that the boy had known in the copper country and during his Magdeburg year. Nevertheless, it was one of the four chief cities of Thuringia, and it had, and still has, the charm that is the heritage of a romantic past. In the background of its towers and churches the Wartburg stood high on its forested ridge, in centuries past the home and fortress of the Thuringian landgraves. Three hundred years before Martin came with his light wallet to seek schooling in the town, Landgrave Hermann had dwelt at the castle, a Maecenas of epic poets and minnesingers. These came to beg hospitality from him and to be pushed about rudely enough by the crowds of knights and dependents in the halls and courts of the Wartburg. The greatest of German medieval lyric poets, Walther von der Vogelweide, was a guest there more than once, and warned away all who were sensitive of hearing and frail of limb. Even in the next generation, however, the prestige of the Eisenach princes had begun to fade; then in the course of the kaleidoscopic shifting that makes up the confusing story of central Germany in the later Middle Ages, city and land passed to other dynasties and finally came into the hands of the Wettin princes of Saxony. When these lords visited Eisenach they dwelt in a commodious residence on the market place, while the ancient Wartburg served only as a military post and potential refuge. Nevertheless, town and castle cultivated the legends of the colorful past, those of the minstrel contests of the minnesingers and more actively those of gentle Elizabeth of Hungary, who came as the wife of a rude landgrave in the early thirteenth century and lived in popular imagination as a typical representative of the Franciscan ideal of social godliness. As the Middle Ages drew to a close and the Eisenach princes turned their patronage from letters to religious foundations, the ecclesiastic burden lay heavy on the city, which at the time of Martin's coming offered a picture of economic stagnation and decay.[22] Only the churches and cloisters flourished. These lay close together within the walls, and many members of various orders crowded the mostly unpaved streets.[23]

In this "nest of priests," as he called it in a later, polemical mood, young Martin spent the three or four years necessary to complete his preparation for the university. Even in the next generation the fingers of romance began to weave colorful traditions about his stay in Eisenach. One of these con-

[22] See Helmbold, "Geschichte der Stadt Eisenach," *Bau- und Kunstdenkmäler Thüringens*, III, 1 (1915), 130, for repeated laments of citizens in the later fifteenth and early sixteenth century; also other abundant source material cited in Scheel, *Martin Luther*, I, 270 f.

[23] Rein, "Kurze Geschichte und mittelalterliche Physiognomie der Stadt Eisenach," *Zeitschrift des Vereins für thüringische Geschichte und Altertumskunde*, Vol. V.

nected the young scholar with a distinguished patrician house, that of the Cottas. A lady of this house, a Widow Cotta, is supposed to have been attracted by Martin's singing and to have become a second mother to the lad. This picture has been redecorated through three centuries; especially the nineteenth century made of the elderly patrician lady and the singing school-boy a genre-picture of true Biedermeyer style. Modern research has swept the romance away, but has established clearly that in the Eisenach years young Martin enjoyed a protection and kindness that saved him from the worst hardships of contemporary school life, as we shall see below. References by Luther to these days also attest that he was kindly received by his relatives, who were numerous. One of these, Margarete of Schmalkalden, a sister of his maternal grandfather, came into close contact with him. Her husband, Konrad Hutter, a sacristan of the ancient church of St. Nicholas, won the boy's affection, and a decade later received an invitation to come to Erfurt for the celebration of his first Mass.[24]

In spite of the affection and kindness of relatives, Martin was obliged to go the way of other schoolboys and beg his bread at the doors of the house-holders. "I also was a 'crumb-hunter' and fetched my bread at people's houses, especially in my beloved city of Eisenach." [25] This reminiscence, found in a sermon on school discipline, appears also in the early biographers. As at Mansfeld, so now in Eisenach, he doubtless sang his bread-song with other scholars before the doors of hospitable burghers.

One of these opened to a less precarious livelihood. Perhaps the gift for making friends, so marked a trait of Martin's mature years, began to show itself in the boy. An unknown scribe at Luther's table in Wittenberg forty years later noted down as a recollection from the Eisenach school days that after begging his bread from door to door, the boy finally came to "Henri-cianus" and was entrusted with the task of taking his son to school.[26] The reference points undoubtedly to a certain Heinrich Schalbe, a member of a distinguished Eisenach family and an official of the city during a part of Martin's stay. Luther refers to Schalbe elsewhere as his host [27] at Eisenach. The family biographer, Dr. Ratzeberger, tells us that Martin lodged with Cuntz (Conrad) Cotta, while Pastor Mathesius refers to a "devout matron" who took the schoolboy into her house and to her table because she conceived

---

[24] *WAB*, I, 11, and n. 10, p. 12. See also Clemen, *Beiträge zur Reformationsgeschichte*, II, 1 f.

[25] *Eine Predigt, dass man Kinder zur Schule halten solle* (1530), *WA*, XXX, II, p. 576.

[26] *TR*, V, No. 5362. The source, Georg Rörer's manuscript of the *Table Talk*, is undepend-able, but this particular passage has confirmation.

[27] Enders, *Luthers Briefwechsel*, V, 366; see *EA*, LIII, 398; LIV, 50.

a "longing affection" for him on account of his singing and his earnest prayers in church.[28] Perhaps it was this lady who coined or repeated a sentimental proverb which Luther caught up and which he quotes later with approval in a lecture, ascribing it to his Eisenach landlady: "Nothing on earth is dearer than woman's love if one can win it." [29] These sources, taken together, give a certain degree of reality to the story mentioned above, of the Widow Cotta and the singing schoolboy.[30] It is interesting to note, too, that Conrad Cotta, whose family had played an important rôle in the city for more than a century, was married to an Ursula Schalbe. Thus, while the more romantic features of the story as it developed from the accounts of early biographers fade on closer examination, there is evidence that at least in the later years of his Eisenach stay the young scholar found hospitality with two patrician families of the city, families that may well have been of influence on his studies and his character.

The Cottas and the Schalbes were not only among the wealthiest people in none too prosperous Eisenach; they were also noted for their piety. A little cloister that housed a handful of religious persons stood at the foot of the eminence from which the Wartburg looks down. Here it had been established in the fourteenth century by the margrave, Friedrich, beside the spot where St. Elizabeth had fed the poor and nursed the sick.[31] This little institution had been supported generously by the Schalbe family and was called the "Schalbe Collegium." The first group established there had been composed of six Franciscan friars, but at Luther's time it seems to have lost its cloister quality and the character of the inmates cannot be determined, except that they were pious men. Martin refers to Heinrich Schalbe many

[28] Mathesius, Das Leben Luthers, p. 3.

[29] TR, VI, 265: "Es ist kein lieber Ding auf Erden denn Frauenliebe, wem sie kann zuteil werden."

[30] The story of Frau Cotta is one of the most persistent of Luther legends and has kept the sentimentalists of three centuries occupied. It will probably continue to live so long as mankind demands romance. Apparently the kindhearted matron first appeared in 1593 in Matthias Dresser's De Festis Diebus Christianorum, p. 238; then in his Luther biography, Martini Lutheri Historia, unpaged. J. G. Walch, Luthers Schriften, XXIV (1750), 65, sentimentalizes still further. See J. Köstlin, "Geschichtliche Untersuchungen über Luthers Leben," ThStKr, XLIV, 35.

[31] For an account of the foundation of the so-called Schalbe Collegium, see the "Düringische Chronik" of Johann Rothe (d. 1434), reproduced in the Thüringische Geschichtsquellen, Vol. III. St. Elizabeth had a hospital built in 1225 below the Wartburg (ibid., pp. 352 f.), so that the poor and sick would not have to climb the hill to receive charity. In 1331 Margrave Friedrich built a chapel there and from timber that had stood on the spot a little cloister was erected, "unde satzte dor yn (sechs) barfussen brudir. . . . unde liess die tegelichen von Warpergk speisen" (ibid., p. 562). Paullini, Rerum et Antiquitatum Germanicarum Syntagma, p. 78, gives a somewhat different account. For theories of the character of the Collegium and its members see WAB, I, 13, n. 12.

years later as the "prisoner and servant of the barefoot monks," [32] and it is likely that the men of the Collegium had some connection with the Franciscan order. Quite probably through Schalbe the lad formed a friendly relationship with the little religious company. Since the Magdeburg year he had been no stranger to cloisters and their self-denying inmates. Six years later, in the first fully accredited letter from him that has come down to us, he praises the "best of men" as his benefactors, and shyly suggests that they be invited to the celebration of his first Mass.[33]

In Eisenach, then, the contact with godly men that had begun with the Null Brothers in Magdeburg continued and broadened. Lasting attachments began to emerge and to show themselves powerful in the life of the youth. Outstanding among these was the friendship of Johann Braun, one of the numerous vicars of the Cathedral Church of Our Lady, evidently a man with the charm to bind to himself the confidence of an ardent boy. With Vicar Braun, Martin maintained a correspondence when school years were over and he had gone on to the university and the cloister.[34] As the crucial moment of his first Mass approached, the young priest sends him an urgent invitation to come. "A pious man, my dearest friend," he calls him in another letter of that time.[35]

Beside these personal influences he can hardly have escaped the mystic attraction of Eisenach's patron saint, Elizabeth. This brilliant figure shone in the radiance of more than two centuries of adoration. The boy may have seen relics of her that were brought down each year from the Wartburg and exhibited in the city. He must surely have heard some of the beautiful stories about her which after four centuries of Protestantism have not entirely died out among the Thuringian and Hessian folk, stories of her care of the sick, of her pure joy in giving alms, and of the wonders of healing wrought by

[32] *WA*, XXX, III, 491, ll. 37 f. Many years later a certain Caspar Schalbe of Eisenach comes into Luther's Wittenberg circle. This man, who had relations with a number of humanists, was possibly the son of Luther's old benefactor, Heinrich Schalbe. In that case Martin had an opportunity to repay the elder man's kindness by exerting himself to help Caspar out of an affair involving a maid of Wittenberg, with what success we cannot tell. See letter from Luther to Spalatin, July 3, 1526, *WAB*, IV, 97; letters from Luther to Elector John Frederick, Nov. 15, 1526, *ibid.*, pp. 127 f., and March 1, 1527, *ibid.*, pp. 173 f.

[33] Letter from Luther to Johann Braun, April 22, 1507, *WAB*, I, 11.

[34] Two letters from Martin to Braun have been preserved: the first, April 22, 1507, is the earliest Luther letter that we know; the second, March 17, 1509, is from Wittenberg. The latter indicates that there had been other correspondence, now lost, between the two. Regarding two still earlier letters, supposed to have been written to Braun by Martin while he was still at the University, see H. Degering, "Aus Luthers Frühzeit," *Zentralblatt für Bibliothekswesen*, XXXII (1916), 69 ff., and Clemen, *WAB*, I, 1 ff. Clemen argues with some conclusiveness that neither content nor style justifies us in ascribing these letters to Luther.

[35] Letter from Luther to Wigand Guldenapf (?), April 28, 1507, *WAB*, I, 15.

her hands. In Luther's boyhood the life and death of the saintly woman shone through a web of miracles of grace. Beside bright apparitions like these, the Eisenach region was rich in wonder-stories of the primitive and mystic kind that had fed his childish imagination in Mansfeld. With the eagerness of youth he continued to absorb the grandiose and the bizarre and to bring them into the curious intimacy so characteristic of his mind in mature years. Four decades later he calls from memories of Eisenach one of these grotesque miracles and tells it to illustrate a serious theme in a lecture on Genesis: during his school days at Eisenach a wellborn and just matron of the city was delivered of a rat as the result of a shock she had suffered when a rat with a bell about its neck ran across her path! [36]

In the midst of these influences young Martin's schooling went on apace. Little is known of the Eisenach school. There is nothing to indicate that it was outstanding among the trivial schools of Thuringia nor in any way to be compared with institutions like those at Deventer in the Netherlands, Münster in Westphalia, or Schlettstadt in Alsatia, where under the influence of the Brethren of the Common Life a great series of headmasters had come to the fore and humanistic enthusiasm was developing. Had Martin been old enough to discriminate he might well have noted that his new surroundings were lacking in educational values as compared with those in Magdeburg. Nevertheless, conservative and pedestrian as the school seems to have been both in program and method, it was well adapted to give a sound preparation for a university which still moved in the old scholastic courses, as the Thuringian university at Erfurt did.

"Here he finished the study of grammar." [37] This remark of Melanchthon, based on Luther's recollections, is supported by a statement of Dr. Ratzeberger that at Eisenach he studied chiefly rhetoric and poetry.[38] This means that he continued to grind at the mill of Latin inflections with Donatus and to attack with all the fresh and undaunted energy of youth the rules of syntax and the categories of rhetoric. The book of instruction was here too the time-honored *Doctrinale* of Alexander de Villa Dei,[39] a truly appalling work which had probably first come to the awe-struck eyes of the young student in Magdeburg or even in Mansfeld, as we have seen. In three parts the rules for inflection, for syntax, and for accent, quantity, and figures are

---

[36] *WA*, XLIII, 692.   [37] *CR*, VI, 157.

[38] Ratzeberger, *Handschriftliche Geschichte*, p. 44.

[39] See "Das Doctrinale des Alexander de Villa-Dei," ed. Dietrich Reichling, *Monumenta Germaniae pedagogica*, Vol. XII, with a very informative introduction. In spite of the sneers of the humanists, the *Doctrinale* continued to flourish in the schools throughout the greater part of the sixteenth century. Reichling cites 267 editions in the hundred years after 1470 (*ibid.*, pp. clxxi ff.).

set forth in Latin in so-called "Leonine hexameters." The learning of grammar by means of verse was long established school practice, and Martin had doubtless chanted wooden hexameters and other Latin doggerel from an early age. Now he advanced to the rudiments of metrics and the basic definitions of Latin rhetoric. Sheer unending lists of Greco-Roman figures of speech were to be learned by heart, with their definitions and applications. On these "pleonasms," "acyrologias," "cacosynthetons," "amphibologias," and "macrologias" the memory of the youth exerted itself and acquired the astonishing vigor that marked the scholar in later years.[40]

This method of instruction contributed of course to his fluency in speaking Latin. He must have thrown himself into the task with persistent industry. Far more reliable than the statements of the early biographers regarding his diligence is the testimony of his capacity as a linguist in his cloister days. His fluent and highly personal style in writing medieval Latin and his wide and elastic vocabulary, the rapidity with which he acquired Greek and Hebrew in the midst of cloister and professional duties and the accuracy of his knowledge, all point to a scientific attitude in linguistic matters and to systematic and conscientious teaching. To his teachers, therefore, Martin owed much, and to at least one of them he seems to have clung with particular respect and affection. The identity of his Eisenach schoolmasters can not be established with certainty. According to Melanchthon, one was outstanding as an "exact and clever" teacher of grammar. Dr. Ratzeberger introduces as headmaster of the school Johann Trebonius,[41] who, he adds, was distinguished as scholar and poet; and he tells a charming story of his modesty. When the good rector entered the schoolroom, he would take off his scholar's beret and bow to his students and he instructed his assistants to do likewise; "for," he said, "God may intend many of them for burgomasters, chancellors, scholars, or rulers." Trebonius cannot be identified and

[40] The following selection describing a group of rhetorical figures is by no means an unusual illustration of the character of the *Doctrinale* (ll. 2361 ff., p. 157):

Pluribus est membris distincta figura loquelae.
Haec sunt schema, tropus, metaplasmus, rursus earum
Quamlibet in proprias species distinguere debes.
Sunt plures aliae scripto vel voce figurae.
Hinc sunt exempla: pleonasmos, acyrologia,
Et cacosyntheton et eclipsis, tautologia,
Amphibologia, tapinosis, macrologia,
Perissologia, cacenphaton, aleoteta.

[41] The existence of a "Rector Trebonius" is doubtful. Clemen, *WAB,* I, 14, thinks Ratzeberger may have confused him with the humanist Heinrich Trebellius, who taught with distinction at Eisenach after Luther left the school. It seems likely that the anecdote which Ratzeberger tells of "Trebonius," *ibid.,* p. 43, originally came from Luther and characterizes the type of scholar under whose influence he fell.

the anecdote is unconfirmed. Nevertheless, it has value as indicating that there was in the Eisenach school a kindly and modest spirit among the teachers. This is further attested by the loyal and affectionate tone of a letter which Martin wrote from Erfurt to one of his Eisenach teachers some years after he had left the school. In a tone that is mingled of affection and respect, he invites this "preceptor" to join Johann Braun in attending Martin's first Mass. Possibly the "preceptor" was a certain Wigand Guldenapf from Fritzlar in Hesse,[42] a former teacher with whom Martin kept in touch as the years went by. As priest at Walthershausen, Guldenapf received a copy of the first sermons with which Martin caused a stir in Thuringia.[43] A decade later Luther interceded with John Frederick, elector of Saxony, to get a pension for this aging friend.[44] One may conclude on the basis of such evidence that if the men who guided the boy's studies at Eisenach were faithful drillmasters of the older sort they certainly gave him something more, something of personal interest and affection that could attract and tame a youth of headstrong temperament.

[42] The letter to Guldenapf, April 28, 1507, *WAB*, I, 15, was one of those discovered by Degering and published in 1916. "Aus Luthers Frühzeit," p. 88. Degering thinks it was addressed to Trebonius; Clemen, *WAB*, I, 14 f., following Kawerau, prefers Guldenapf, which seems more likely.

[43] Letter from Luther to Johann Lang, Aug. 30, 1516, *WAB*, I, 52.

[44] Letter from Luther to Elector John Frederick, May 14, 1526, *WAB*, IV, 74 f.

3

EARLY YEARS AT THE UNIVERSITY

THE young scholar's choice of a university fell quite naturally on the great Thuringian seat of higher studies at Erfurt. He was now in his eighteenth year, in that day a somewhat advanced age to enter academic life. Many of his contemporaries began it at fifteen, and college doors were swung open freely to lads of thirteen and even younger.[1] Martin was evidently not a precocious youth, but his preparation had been solid and he had no need to avail himself of the pre-college training which the late medieval university provided for immature freshmen.[2]

At the opening of the summer semester in May, 1501, "Martinus Ludher ex Mansfeldt" was duly registered in the faculty of arts,[3] beginning a residence in Erfurt that was to last at university and convent for nearly ten years. Even as a wandering schoolboy, Martin may have explored the streets of Erfurt more than once, for the most convenient road from his home to Eisenach led through its gates. In later days he did not always speak respectfully of the city that witnessed so many crucial phases in his life. Nevertheless, the deep impression which its size and commerce and public life made on his youthful mind did not fade with the passing of the years, and it found expression repeatedly in the *Table Talk* and elsewhere.

When the Mansfeld boy came as a freshman, the ancient metropolis of Thuringia might well have impressed an observant and ambitious scholar. It passed for the most populous city in the German empire, although at least four others, Nuremberg, Strasbourg, Cologne, and Lübeck, disputed the claim.[4] The early biographers, confirmed by Luther's own statements, set

---

[1] Paulsen, "Organisation und Lebensordnung der deutschen Universitäten im Mittelalter," *Historische Zeitschrift*, XLV, N.F. IX (1881), 385 ff.

[2] Neubauer, *Frühzeit*, p. 50.

[3] For Luther's matriculation "class" see "Acten," VIII, II, 219.

[4] Neubauer, *Frühzeit*, p. 12.

the number of inhabitants as high as 50,000, but like most other population statistics of the later Middle Ages, these figures need revision downward.[5] Careful students of the period reduce this by more than half.[6]

Nature and rural industry had provided Erfurt with an idyllic setting. Even one accustomed to the smiling contrast of forest and rich, cultivated land which Thuringia offers must have been impressed by the surroundings of "Erfurt the towered," as Luther calls it, in its wreath of vineyards and its swelling background of hills covered with fruit and nut trees.[7] No destructive religious wars had as yet laid waste the villages and brought neglect to orchard and field; no factories marred the valleys with smoking chimneys. "If it burned down, a city would have to stand there." [8] Thus, long afterwards, from the sandy Wittenberg country Luther recalled the fertility of the neighborhood of Erfurt, which furnished the wine that had not yet given place to beer on the table of the German burgher, a wine so abundant that in productive years it had to be sold at the value of the casks alone.[9] He also recalled the wealth of the citizens.[10] This had been nourished by Erfurt's fortunate position on the great north-south road running through central Germany, and by the cultivation and marketing of woad, the popular dyestuff of that day, which was grown round about and stored in fine warehouses, some remains of which the curious traveler may still find in Old Erfurt.[11]

The walls were ringed with suburbs, where impoverished and wandering folk of all kinds dwelt in squalid poverty which sank in times of plague and civil disorder to a depth of misery now scarcely to be imagined.[12] In contrast to these unfortunates, called in the parlance of the day "those before the gates," not a few Erfurt burghers dwelt in houses that were, to be sure, much confined in space but equipped with many comforts.[13] One character-

[5] Even the most reliable reporters of the *Table Talk* have a liking for high figures. They quote Luther's estimate of Erfurt's population at 16,000 (*TR*, II, No. 2494b) to 18,000 (*TR*, II, No. 2494a; III, No. 3517) hearths.

[6] Neubauer, *Frühzeit*, p. 11, thinks 50,000 would include the whole area then under Erfurt's control, about 600 square kilometers. See also Scheel, *Martin Luther*, I, 125.

[7] For a description of the landscape of the Erfurt region in Luther's day, see Karl Herrmann, "Selbstbiographie," *Mitteilungen des Vereins zur Geschichte des alten Erfurt*, VII (1875), 85.

[8] *TR*, III, No. 2871b.

[9] *TR*, III, No. 3878. See Neubauer, *Frühzeit*, pp. 10 f.

[10] *TR*, III, No. 3878. See also II, Nos. 2494a and 2494b.

[11] Strangely enough, Luther thought woad (*isatis tinctoria*) destructive to the land. See *TR*, II, No. 2344b.

[12] Neubauer, *Frühzeit*, p. 13.

[13] Neubauer's description (*ibid.*, p. 15), on the basis of official documents of the sixteenth century, of the dwelling of Caspar Rindfleisch, a master weaver and council member, throws a cheerful light on the living conditions of a well-placed Erfurt burgher in the later Middle Ages. Indeed, many a German middle-class citizen of the later nineteenth century might well

istic, however, the Erfurt patrician and artisan of the later Middle Ages and the Renaissance seem to have lacked: the instinct for art. There is little remaining from that day to compare with the sculptures and paintings in the churches and burghers' houses of the South German and Rhenish cities.

Life in the city was marked by all the sharp contrasts of the later Middle Ages. Viewed through the haze of memory it seemed to Martin "a bawdy house and a beer house," and he adds that the "courses" given in these places were the ones most regularly attended by the students.[14] He declares in other passages in the *Table Talk* that the city had no proper Christian teaching or preaching, and that in political matters it had broken faith repeatedly.[15] Social conditions were those prevalent in other cities of this era. Erfurt had, to be sure, its official brothel, maintained by the council,[16] but so did other German cities of the time. On the other hand, religious zeal throbbed in all classes of the population. "Little Rome," as the city was called, maintained largely through the contributions of its citizens a vast number of religious institutions, including cloisters, parish churches, chapels, hospitals, and two great collegiate churches. Recent history had given evidence of the tremendous religious energy that could be awakened there.[17] A generation before Luther's coming, two great churches, those dedicated to the Virgin and to St. Severus, had burned. They were rebuilt in grander style in an incredibly short time. As in other parts of Germany, pilgrimages to foreign shrines had greatly increased in the preceding half century. Pious men and women set forth to Rome, to Jerusalem, and to distant Santiago of Campostella in western Spain in larger numbers than at any time since the crusades.[18]

A religious hysteria like that which marked the fourteenth-century flagellants still slumbered lightly in hard-working peasant and burgher, and it burst forth at times into frenzied orgies. In 1452 the fiery Franciscan, John of Capistrano, preached for three weeks to crowds that could find space nowhere save in the open, and though he spoke only in Latin, which had first

---

have envied the comfortable circumstances in which his predecessors lived in the heyday of the Renaissance.

[14] *TR*, II, No. 2719b.

[15] *TR*, II, Nos. 2800a and 2800b; cf. *EA*, LX, 280.

[16] The "Frauenhaus," picturesquely called "Muhmenhaus," was rebuilt by the council after the disastrous fire of 1472. See W. J. A. Freiherr von Tettau, "Beiträge zu einer vergleichenden Topographie und Statistik von Erfurt," *Mitteilungen des Vereins für die Geschichte und Altertumskunde von Erfurt*, Vol. XII (1885).

[17] Theodor Kolde, "Das religiöse Leben in Erfurt beim Ausgang des Mittelalters," *SVRG*, Vol. LXIII (1898).

[18] *Ibid.*, pp. 26 ff.

to be translated into German for the audience, he lashed his hearers into a violent religious emotion.[19] His sermons reached their conclusion with a bitter attack on the Jews, and his audiences turned to rid the city of these "enemies of God," not by deeds of blood, as a century earlier at the time of the Black Death, but by official decrees and economic pressure, so that in 1457, as a chronicle tells, not a Jew remained in the city.[20] The unfortunate victims may have derived a melancholy satisfaction later from the heavy economic losses that resulted to their persecutors, including severe financial penalties laid on the city by the emperor and its temporal lord, the archbishop of Mainz. In June, 1475, a chronicle records a sudden and unexplainable frenzy that seized the population and drove it to make pilgrimages to a miraculous bleeding Host at the neighboring town of Wilsnack. All classes streamed thither. Peasants left their oxen in the field, burghers their shops, and servants their tasks. Especially the young were seized by the hysterical desire to do reverence to the "holy blood." Tender maids defied decorum and maternal authority, even little children were affected by the contagion. When forcibly restrained, the victims frequently broke into a wild paroxysm. Only the coming of the plague at last stilled the madness.[21]

The years Martin spent in the city were an especially exciting period in its history. Erfurt had never won the rights of a free city. Since the days of St. Boniface it lay in the sphere of the Archbishopric of Mainz. "Faithful daughter of the See of Mainz" [22] ringed its seal, but the citizens and council carried on intermittently through centuries a struggle for political independence which continued until the beginning of the nineteenth century. Then Napoleon put a period to its claims by annexing the Mainz territories and making Erfurt a French enclave in the heart of Germany. Through the later Middle Ages the citizens sought support from the Saxon electors, but the archbishop had powerful clerical allies within the walls.

As the new century opened, economic difficulties came to swell the unrest. The hand of ecclesiasticism lay heavy on industry and trade. Fire and pestilence, floods and war contributions added burden to burden, so that at the time young Martin entered the university the interest on the city debt called for almost the entire income from taxes.[23] Finally, in 1509 came a

---

[19] "Die Chronik Hartung Cammermeisters," ed. R. Reiche, *Geschichtsquellen der Provinz Sachsen,* XXXV (1896), 131 ff.

[20] Kirchhoff, *Die ältesten Weistümer der Stadt Erfurt,* pp. 300 f.

[21] "Konrad Stolles Thüringische-Erfurtische Chronik," *Bibliothek des Litterarischen Vereins in Stuttgart,* XXXII (1854), 128 ff.

[22] Fidelis filia Moguntiae sedis. See Richard Thiele, "Erphurdianus Antiquitatum Variloquus incerti auctoris," *Geschichtsquellen der Provinz Sachsen,* XLII (1906), 1.

[23] For details regarding the hopeless economic situation in 1509, see the chronicle presumably by Johann Werlich, *ibid.,* pp. 142 ff.; see also Luther's recollections, *TR,* II, No. 2494a.

complete collapse, followed the next year by something like a reign of terror when the commons, led as it seems by the episcopal party, gained the ascendancy and took bloody revenge on the council.[24] Town and gown were in ever recurring conflict, which in the "terrible year" of 1510 gave rise to a first-class disaster for the university. A tavern brawl between students and artisans assisted by mercenary soldiers developed into a regular battle and resulted in the plundering of the "old college" with a part of its valuable library.[25]

Such was the city to which the young freshman from Mansfeld came to grasp the hand of Alma Mater. Through streets still for the most part unpaved and without illumination, past houses lying irregularly without building lines, one came to the university, wedged among a great complex of religious edifices in the heart of the city. The institution was already more than a century old. Like other universities north of the Alps, it had developed out of a group of clerical schools which pooled their courses into what was known as a *studium generale*.[26] This designation Erfurt received as early as 1362; [27] and a bull of Pope Clement VII on September 18, 1379, confirmed its right to teach grammar, logic, philosophy, canon and civil law, and medicine.[28] Due to the Great Schism, it lost to Heidelberg the honor of being the first university on German soil after Prague and Vienna. It finally elected a rector on April 28, 1392, and opened its doors to 523 students.[29] Gifts and endowments flowed in and freed the academic republic from dependence on the city council. After scarcely more than half a century it passed all German universities for a time in the number of its students.[30] Less than five years after the "old college" had been burned it was rebuilt from university resources. Of its faculties, that of arts, which was preparatory to the professional schools and included two thirds of all the students,

[24] The sources for the "terrible year" are treated in detail by C. A. H. Burkhardt, "Das tolle Jahr zu Erfurt," *Archiv für sächsische Geschichte*, XII (1874); see also Werlich's chronicle. A general account of the period is to be found in Benary, *Zur Geschichte der Stadt und Universität Erfurt*. Luther chronicles his recollections of the tragic events several times in the Table Talk. TR, I, No. 487; II, Nos. 2494a and 2494b, and No. 2709b.

[25] Neubauer, *Frühzeit*, p. 42.

[26] For the rise of the late medieval universities and their relation to the cloister schools, the most convenient general accounts are to be found in Rashdall, *Universities of Europe in the Middle Ages*, or Denifle, *Die Universitäten des Mittelalters*, Vol. I. For Erfurt, see W. Oergel, "Urkunden zur Geschichte des Collegium majus zu Erfurt," *Mitteilungen des Vereins für Geschichte und Altertumskunde von Erfurt*, Vol. XVI (1894), for a brief but well-documented survey.

[27] Denifle, *Universitäten*, p. 407.   [28] "Acten," VIII, 1, 1 ff.   [29] *Ibid.*, pp. 36 ff.

[30] Denifle, *Universitäten*, p. 412; Franz Eulenburg, "Die Frequenz der deutschen Universitäten von ihrer Gründung bis zur Gegenwart," *Abhandlung der sächsischen Gesellschaft der Wissenschaften*, XXIV, Part II (1904), 286.

enjoyed especial fame.[31] Shortly before the time Luther came an average of 324 freshmen entered each year.[32]

Into this great institution the Mansfeld scholar was now admitted, "Jodocus Trutvetter being rector," and was duly "entitled" as thirty-eighth of his group of freshmen.[33] The splendor of the festal rites of the university, such as the election and inauguration of the "rector magnificus," remained in his memory during later years. Solemn and awestruck must have been his mood when he took the long Latin oath which according to medieval custom was required of all matriculants. Here he swore by God and the Sacred Evangelists to obey the rector and statutes, to refrain from all strife within and without the university, to seek justice only in its courts, and to leave it if ever commanded to do so.[34] Such forms and ceremonies impressed on the entrant that he was no longer under the rule of parents and teachers, but was a member of an academic state whose powers and privileges were guaranteed by the highest authority in Christendom.

The son of the Mansfeld miner appears among those "possessing funds" (*in habendo*). Thanks to the thrift of his father his entire charges, twenty groschen, were paid in advance.[35] Probably young Martin was enrolled at once as a resident in a college, or *bursa,* for only in exceptional cases were students permitted to live in the houses of citizens. For a part of his study at Erfurt he was a member of the College of St. George; there is no evidence that he lived elsewhere.[36] Its home, now vanished, was a stone building among a group which made up the "Latin quarter" of the city. St. George's, or the "Beer-bag" as it was called in student parlance, seems to have been one of the less important colleges. From the statutes of the university, as well as those of another of the Erfurt colleges, founded in 1412 by the second rector of the university, Amplonius Ratingk, with the promising name of Porta Coeli (Gate of Heaven), we are able to construct a fairly detailed picture of life as it presented itself to the young student.[37] With its own lecture hall

---

[31] Neubauer, *Frühzeit,* p. 31.   [32] "Acten," VIII, ii, 170 ff.

[33] *Ibid.,* p. 219.   [34] The text may be found *ibid.,* VIII, i, 34.

[35] *Totum.* "Acten," VIII, ii, 219. See also *ibid.,* VIII, i, 12, Rubric IV, No. 3.

[36] Clemen, *Beiträge zur Reformationsgeschichte,* II, i. Biereye, *Die Erfurter Lutherstätten,* is a careful and well-documented study by the leading expert in this field. The *bursa* disappeared with the decay of the university in the sixteenth century and was eventually replaced by the present house, Nos. 27–29, on the Augustinerstrasse. *Ibid.,* pp. 6 ff.; see esp. p. 25.

[37] See "Acten," VIII, i, 19 f., Rubric VIII; VIII, ii, 145 f., Rubric XXV, for the regulations of the university. For those of the Amplonian college, see J. C. H. Weissenborn, "Die Urkunden für die Geschichte des Dr. Amplonius Ratingk de Fago auch genannt Amplonius de Berka," *Mitteilungen des Vereins für die Geschichte und Altertumskunde von Erfurt,* Vol. VIII (1877); and Weissenborn, "Die Urkunden zur Geschichte des M. Amplonius de Fago aus Rheinbergen," *ibid.,* Vol. IX (1880). These sources antedate Luther's student years by two

and chapel, the college formed a little state within the academic republic, and rules or traditions prescribed every step in the life of its inmates. Here the freshman, or *beanus,* underwent the painful process of initiation, the "deposition," a symbol, as the name indicates, of the laying aside of the old life and the entry into a higher form of existence. The victim of these rites was supposed to be shielded by university decrees from the worst forms of humiliation and brutality, but there is evidence that members of the faculty also joined in the crude and sometimes savage hazing.[38] Like many an alumnus who sees in perspective the disciplinary value of the early pains of college life, Luther in his maturity defended the "deposition," explaining to three Wittenberg freshmen that it was symbolical of a man's life, its misfortunes, hardships, and chastisement.[39]

The separation from the world and from individual freedom was emphasized in other ways. The university statutes demanded that the young student select a master of arts with whom he must be in constant contact.[40] They prescribed dignified dress both in the college and on the streets.[41] Hours of closing of the colleges were enforced by the university on pain of financial penalties. The students were sworn to obey the college head, "to listen to his instruction and direction with patience, to refrain from plots and cabals against him" and from anything that might damage the university.[42] Wandering about on the streets during the hours of college exercises was strictly forbidden.[43] Quarterly visits by the rector and the dean were to take note of the state of the *bursa* and to make inquisition into the behavior of its inmates.[44] In addition to this rigid discipline, constant devotional exercises gave to life in the college a monastic character, "in order that the religious life may keep step with the scholastic," as the statutes of Porta Coeli declare. In this *bursa* the inmates had to rise at four and retire at eight, unless specially exempted. They were required to pray through the entire psalter every two weeks; they heard the Bible and godly books read

---

and three generations respectively, but the second half of the fifteenth century seems to have been a static period in the Erfurt academic administration. It cannot be overlooked, however, that the picture of student life afforded by the statutes is very incomplete for any period.

[38] Neubauer, *Frühzeit,* pp. 46 ff. The university tried to hold down the cost of the deposition. "Acten," VIII, I, 18; VIII, II, 130. A contemporary account of the "depositio" is found in the *Manuale Scholarium,* reprinted in Zarncke, *Die deutschen Universitäten im Mittelalter.*

[39] *TR,* IV, No. 4714; see also No. 5024.

[40] The regulations covering the colleges and the faculty of philosophy emphasize in a number of places the relation of the student and his tutor. The master was expected to watch closely both his progress in studies and his moral conduct. See *inter alia,* "Acten," VIII, I, 18 ff., Rubrics VIII and IX; VIII, II, 145 f., Rubric XXV; also VIII, II, 7, ll. 18 ff.

[41] *Ibid.,* VIII, I, 18, ll. 15 ff.; cf. p. 21, ll. 28 ff.; VIII, II, 132, ll. 3 ff.

[42] *Ibid.,* VIII, I, 18, ll. 18 ff.   [43] *Ibid.,* p. 19, ll. 23 ff.   [44] *Ibid.,* p. 11, ll. 25 ff.

and interpreted at meals.[45] Before admission to the final examination for the baccalaureate degree the candidate's moral character had to be certified to before the examining commission by masters of arts in the college where he had studied.[46] We do not know whether Martin's college was equally strict, but there is no doubt that it held its students to stern religious requirements. In university and college statutes one feels the effort on the part of the institution to set bounds to the growing luxury of life.

Though life in the colleges was simple, it was not without its comforts. Porta Coeli, at least, brewed its own beer.[47] Both it and Collegium Magnus (Great College) had libraries, and it is probable that St. George's also had one. The students slept in dormitories and studied in a common room, where the supervising master saw to it that they were quiet and industrious and spoke only Latin.

The curriculum was exactly specified. The lecture courses which must be heard and the length of time assigned to each and the books to be used were all prescribed. It is not possible to say precisely what lectures young Martin heard, but the statutes in vogue at the university at the time of his residence there permit us to attempt a reconstruction of his course of study. These ancient ordinances, which had been in effect since 1449 and continued to govern the life of the student long after Martin had left academic walls, include the oath demanded of all candidates before they advanced to the first degree.[48] Here he swears by God and the sacred gospels that he has attended regularly the lectures and exercises in a list of prescribed subjects. In another chapter of the statutes the lecture courses appear in detail in what may be assumed to be the order that the undergraduate heard them.[49] Furthermore, a manuscript of an Erfurt master, Herbord of Lippe,[50] gives the requirements for the degree some eighty years earlier, and a work of Luther's professor of philosophy, Jodocus Trutvetter, interprets the courses in logic.[51] By means of the information thus available it is possible to deduce

[45] See the statutes in Weissenborn, "Amplonius aus Rheinbergen," IX, 147 ff., paras. I, II, and XL. In the *Collegium majus* a holder of a stipend was required to thank God once a week for having been born a man instead of a woman! See Scheel, *Martin Luther,* I, 139.

[46] Statutes of the philosophical faculty, "Acten," VIII, II, 145, ll. 33 ff. The statement regarding candidates for the master of arts is still more explicit. *Ibid.,* p. 137, ll. 18 ff.

[47] Neubauer, *Frühzeit,* pp. 38 ff.; also for the statements immediately following.

[48] "Acten," VIII, II, 143, para. 106. These were revisions of the ordinances of 1412.

[49] *Ibid.,* p. 134, para. 60: *Rubrica de libris legendum per quod tempus.*

[50] *Puncta materiarum librorum quasi omnium que pro baccalariatus gradu Effordiae leguntur et examinantur scilicet secundum colleccionem magistri Herbordi de Lippia Effordie promoti.* Quoted in Scheel, *Martin Luther,* I, 152 ff. (see also 282, n. 4) from a MS in the Erfurt Stadtbibliothek.

[51] See citations by Scheel (*Martin Luther,* I, 153 f.; also 282) from a MS in the Stuttgart Landesbibliothek. It is quite clear that the curriculum as reflected in the statutes and the

with some exactness the "points" required of the bachelor of arts, to outline
in a general way the plan of his course, to estimate the number of months
devoted to the series of lectures on each subject, and to identify, in part at
least, the books that were used. Inferences may even be made with some
possibility of correctness as to the daily schedule of lectures and exercises
prescribed for the undergraduate student.

For the baccalaureate the statutes set a minimum of one and one-half years
of study. Martin received his degree at the end of this period. His first
semester carried on the work in Latin grammar begun in his school years.
All progress in the university depended on the command of the language
of scholarship; indeed, the statutes required a preliminary examination to
show whether the young man was able to express himself in Latin,[52] and as
an annex to the Collegium Magnus Erfurt conducted a preparatory institute
for those who were found deficient. The course began, then, with a development of the trivium, grammar from the well-thumbed works of Donatus
and Priscian and the second part of the old *Doctrinale* of Alexander. Even
before he had disposed of these the young undergraduate may have been
introduced to the second of the liberal arts, rhetoric, and very soon to the
third and more difficult field of logic. Here he tried his teeth on one of
the toughest and to modern taste most unappetizing works of the whole
scholastic program, the *Summulae logicales* of Petrus Hispanus, usually
identified as Peter Giuliani, Pope John XXII (1276–77), a compendium of
logical formulas that burdened student memory with its mnemonic verses
throughout the later Middle Ages and well into the Renaissance.[53] The
logical training of the student began with the first and fourth books of this
work, the so-called "little logic," on which the Erfurt faculty laid especial

----

Puncta of the Herbord von Lippe MS cannot be accepted uncritically for the period of Luther's
study. In the sixty to eighty years intervening, the contents and particularly the emphasis in
the course required of the bachelor of arts probably underwent considerable change. In this
respect Trutvetter's five logical papers in the MS referred to give interpretations of contemporary
value. Also it cannot be overlooked that the university at Erfurt was of the conservative
scholastic character that adhered to tradition with a tenacity undreamed of by modern academic
institutions. This much should be said in defense of Scheel's rather dogmatic inference from
the early records. In Heidelberg, too, the plan of studies seems to have persisted with little change
throughout the entire fifteenth century. See Gerhard Ritter, "Studien zur Spätscholastik, II,"
Sitzungsberichte der Heidelberger Akademie der Wissenschaften, XIII (1922), 88 ff.

[52] "Acten," VIII, ii, 136, para. 71.

[53] See Prantl, *Geschichte der Logik im Abendlande*, III, 32 ff.; IV, 219. This authority, who
cites 48 versions of the work (pp. 35 ff., n. 143), calls the *Summulae* "[jene] sinnlose Ver-
quickung grammatischer und logischer Momente" (p. 73). For the rôle played by the work
in late medieval education, see Rashdall, *Universities of Europe in the Middle Ages*, I, 448,
n. 2, and 492; II, 242. See also Ritter, *Die Heidelberger Universität*, I, 166 ff., 417 ff.

emphasis.[54] Martin's professor, Trutvetter, regarded the series of propositions which make up the work as fundamental in preparing the young student's mind for the progressive order of logical concepts.[55]

This work, it seems quite certain, was Martin's introduction to the scholastic discipline. It was undoubtedly resistant material for the young mind, and to the modern student seems an utterly futile approach to the mechanics of thought. It was, however, a natural development out of the material and methods of grammatical analysis cultivated in earlier study. It led the way quite organically to the lectures Martin next heard on the so-called "old logic," the name given to the treatise which had developed out of Aristotle through Greco-Roman sources before the rediscovery of the works of Aristotle in the twelfth century. Here the basic text was the *Eisagoge* by the Neoplatonist Porphyrius, in the Latin translation of Boethius, another important fixture in the medieval program of studies. With a further deepening of his knowledge of Petrus Hispanus's compendium, Martin was then prepared for the "new logic" as set forth in the *Analytics* of Aristotle and possibly in his *Topics*.[56] With these he had now learned the laws of demonstration and proof, and was prepared to apply them in the disputational exercises which the practice of the university demanded of him. Of immediate value for the technique of the disputation was the course in Aristotle's *Sophisms* (*Elenci Sophistici*), which was specified on his program.[57]

[54] "Acten," VIII, II, 141, para. 99. The *parva logicalia*, with its intimate terminology, must have been an acid test of freshman intelligence. It is really an abstruse chapter of formal grammatical logical ideas: "suppositiones, ampliationes, restrictiones, appellationes . . . consequentie . . . obligatoria . . . insolubilia . . ." (*ibid.*, p. 134). The prescriptions of the faculty of philosophy assign to this subject lectures totaling two months and add, "Biligam per 1 mensem . . . logica Hertisbri per 4 menses" (*ibid.*, ll. 17 ff). Scheel, *Martin Luther*, I, 154, interprets this as meaning that Martin's course in "little logic" was not based on Hispanus's well-known seventh treatise, but on those of the Englishmen Thomas Maulfeldt and Richard Billingham. The latter was an Oxford scholastic at Merton College at the time of Edward III. See Bale, *Index Brittaniae Scriptorum*, Appendix VI, p. 518. About a dozen years earlier another boy, Konrad Kürsner (Pellicanus), was going through this material at the Rufach Gymnasium. In spite of the fact that he could not have been much more than twelve years of age, Konrad tells us in his autobiography that he made good progress, "sed cum multis laboribus, terroribus, plagis et virgis." Pellicanus, *Das Chronikon*, p. 7. I owe this reference to F. C. Ahrens. See above, p. 17, n. 60.

[55] Quoted in Scheel, *Martin Luther*, I, 282, n. 31.

[56] After the twelfth century the title "old logic" was given to those parts of the Aristotelian *Organon* that had come down through the Romans, i.e., the *Categories* and *On Interpretation*, including the *Eisagoge* of Porphyrius. Under "new logic" were included the works of Aristotle that had become available in the West through Persian-Arabian mediation: the *Prior* and *Posterior Analytics*, the *Topics*, and the *Sophisms*. Prantl, *Geschichte der Logik*, III, 3 f., 26, 206.

[57] "Acten," VIII, II, 143, ll. 17 ff.

Later courses widened the horizon of the young candidate and led beyond the trivium into the field of the other liberal arts, which from early medieval days tradition had grouped in the quadrivium. Here the subject of study was nature; not, to be sure, nature as an object of direct observation, still less of experiment, but nature described, classified, and categorized on the basis of its forms and processes. The guides to natural philosophy were Aristotle's *Physics*, to which an entire semester was devoted, and his work *On the Soul*.[58] To these a course in spherical astronomy was added.

This curriculum comprised perhaps two to three hours of lectures a day during the six undergraduate semesters.[59] For a gifted and diligent student it was a period of intense mental activity and rapid development. Dictation by the lecturer was frowned upon, if not forbidden. The youth must learn to select, digest the material, and reproduce it by his own mental processes. An aid to this were the so-called "resumptions," or quizzes, which were held by small groups in the college in the evening in preparation for the examination.

This was only a part of the training which the young student was obliged to undergo. The scholastic university of the later Middle Ages delivered to the learner a fixed body of knowledge, highly systematized and superbly rounded out. It laid tremendous burdens on the memory and was almost altogether lacking in visualization of the world around. Nevertheless, it did not limit its task to imparting information and insuring by examination that it was adequately understood and absorbed. It required that the materials and methods which it taught should be applied as tools for determining the truth. The goal of this effort was limited and the truth which was sought was restricted to the scholastic horizon; but within this range the young scholar was expected to make use of the weapons of scholarship as soon as his training permitted. The form of practice in this was the disputation, where the concepts contained in the treatise of Petrus Hispanus, the "little logic," and finally the categories of Aristotle were brought into play. It would be far from the truth to regard the disputation as merely an academic exercise. The age was convinced that the processes of logic led the way to certain truth, and it was accustomed to refer to the disputation of university scholars the weightiest problems of politics and morals. This explains the importance attached to memorizing the wearisome classifications in Petrus Hispanus and to the mastery of the systemization of pure thought in the

[58] In *philosophia naturali* phisicorum [et] de anima et speram materialem . . . Aristotelis . . . philosophie, scilicet in phisicorum et in de anima. *Ibid.,* ll. 18 ff.

[59] Scheel's reckoning. *Martin Luther,* I, 154.

Analytics of Aristotle. It explains also the zeal with which the student was trained in the technique of the disputation.

To these important exercises the freshman was introduced at the beginning of his course. Regular participation in them was a requirement for admission to the baccalaureate examination.[60] The training began in the college with exercises in finding questions for debate and casting them into the ethical form required.[61] Thus the young learner was prepared to take part in the disputation itself, first daily in the *bursa* and ultimately in the weekly public contests held in the hall of the faculty of the university, when all lectures were omitted.[62] Once a year, on August 24, rector, faculty, and students marched in solemn procession to the great *quodlibet,* a free-for-all affair which lasted the entire day under the eye of the dean.[63] Here any problem whatever from the field of the liberal arts might be proposed, attacked, and defended. The masters of arts seem to have been the chief contestants, though younger students also took part under their leadership.

This free-for-all disputation was evidently a tempting field for young masters and bachelors to display their cleverness, and the university authorities had to exert themselves to keep it on a serious plane. The urge to insinuate witty questions into the program was too strong to be resisted. One of these sophomoric jokes is recalled by Luther in his *Table Talk:*[64] "In a free-for-all disputation at Erfurt the question was proposed: Why is Dominic represented with threatening fingers, Francis, on the other hand, with outstretched hands? The solution was as follows: Dominic is reported to have raised the warning: 'O Francis, what naughty fellows you have in your order.' Francis answered in a lamenting voice with arms raised: 'What can I do about it?'" Little wonder that the university statutes devote attention to the matter of unbecoming conduct at the *quodlibet,* warning the contestants against improper questions and urging them to refrain from "rancors, contentions, vituperations, and useless babblings and abuse of one another"![65] On the other hand, there is no evidence that the weekly and monthly disputations were marked by other than a serious spirit.

The college day began at six in summer and at seven in winter. It opened with exercises or disputations followed by lectures. After dinner, which came in the late forenoon, the exercises and disputations began again at two

---

[60] "Acten," VIII, II, 144 f., paras. 109, 120.

[61] *Ibid.,* p. 140, para. 91; Weissenborn, "Amplonius aus Rheinbergen," IX, para. XV.

[62] "Acten," VIII, II, 128, para. 27. The importance of the disputations is emphasized throughout the statutes.

[63] *Ibid.,* pp. 139 f., para. 89.   [64] *TR,* III, No. 3656.

[65] "Acten," VIII, II, 140, para. 92.

o'clock. Vacations were short; that of the summer lasted only one month. The material to be covered in the brief eighteen months was for the most part new, and the student who wished to progress had to work diligently under the guidance of the master of arts who supervised his work in the college. Since the requirements of the graduation oath were formal and admitted of no abatement, they left little time for the so-called *allotria,* a small group of subjects lying outside the curriculum. Such were perhaps the ethical works of Seneca and of Boethius, and a course possibly based on Aristotle's *Poetics,* with collateral readings from classical authors. That Martin had some work of this kind seems very probable, but it must have come in the later years of study.

When, therefore, in the fall of 1502 young Martin Luther received his bachelor's degree, he had been introduced to the three liberal arts of the trivium, grammar, logic, and rhetoric, as well as to natural philosophy.[66] These had given him the implements of knowledge and showed him how to use them in the presentation of thought. The training in dialectics continued when he entered on studies for the master's degree; indeed, these seem to have begun with lectures on the *Topics* of Aristotle and to have included exercises covering the whole Aristotelian logic.[67] Now, however, his studies were also to take him into the realm of nature. The four arts of the quadrivium, music, astronomy, arithmetic, and geometry, formed the backbone of the curriculum, as may be seen from the oath required of the candidates. Mathematical studies, as the Middle Ages defined them, probably consumed fully half of his time and included arithmetic in the work of Joannes de Muris, Euclid's geometry, and also "the theory of the planets and metaphysics," as well as a subject that was perhaps the most congenial of all to a youth of Martin's gifts: music. Probably he had already made an excursion into the "mathematics" of nature in Aristotle's *Physics.*

Aristotle, who had in his *Organon* supplied him with the basic laws governing the mind and its operations, now furnished the material for his knowledge of the physical laws of the universe, of politics, social economy, and moral laws. The books on which his teachers fed and which Martin studied were those of this master rationalist of antiquity, by means of which the rationalists of the twelfth and thirteenth centuries had built the structure of medieval scholarship: his "little natural history," his works on the heavens, the universe, colors, generation and decay, animals; his *Politics, Economics,*

[66] *Ibid.,* p. 137, para. 74; see also p. 143, para. 106.
[67] See the lengthy graduation oath required of candidates for the master's degree, *ibid.,* p. 138, para. 78. What follows in the text is based on the subjects specified in the oath.

Nicomachean Ethics, and his *Metaphysics.* The sequence in which these subjects were presented cannot be derived from the statutes, but it would be
in tune with the mental practice of the later Middle Ages to assume that
the study of natural history and natural philosophy preceded and led up to
those dealing with the soul of man, ethics, and metaphysics. "Metaphysics,
that is the divine science, transcending nature." This remark, in the catalogue of the library of Amplonius, founder of Porta Coeli College, might
be called the motto of European scholarship in Luther's student days.[68]

How the young Mansfeld student comported himself at Erfurt is a question on which direct and contemporary information is slight. One of his
university associates, the Hessian Johann Jäger, does contribute favorable
evidence. This scholar and satirist, who in the fashion of the humanists
rebaptized himself in classic manner as Crotus Rubianus, will reappear in a
later crisis in Martin's career. Three years older than Luther, he had taken
his bachelor's degree at Erfurt in 1500 and remained for a time a junior
teacher in the faculty of philosophy. Many years later he recalled his close
student friendship for Martin and the latter's excellent qualities.[69] Like most
humanists, Crotus delighted in neat phrase-making, and the circumstances
under which he wrote do not encourage us to take his remark at full value.
Nevertheless, the university records show that Martin won his way at Erfurt
with increasing success. He received his bachelor's degree in the fall of 1502,
and his master's as the result of an application made at the beginning of
1505, both in the briefest time permitted by the statutes. In the list of bachelors he appears as thirtieth among fifty-seven candidates; in that of the
masters as second among seventeen.[70]

As we have seen, Erfurt, like other medieval universities, began early in
the student's course to set him tasks that required him to put his knowledge
to work. It carried this opportunity still further. When the young candidate
had been promoted to bachelor of arts, he was obliged to promise under
oath that he would lecture in the faculty of philosophy for two years unless
excused from the duty.[71] The subjects on which he might lecture were
grammar, rhetoric, and the "little logic." The books of Aristotle were withheld from his immature hands except by special authorization.[72] We do not
know whether Martin began his teaching at this time, but, energetic and
enthusiastic youth that he was, he may well have done so.

The investiture with the master's degree was a highly formal affair. In

---

[68] Schum, *Beschreibendes Verzeichnis der amplonianischen Handschriftensammlung zu Erfurt,*
p. 818.

[69] Hutten, *Opera,* I, 309.

[70] Neubauer, *Frühzeit,* pp. 60 ff.

[71] "Acten," VIII, II, 147, para. 128.

[72] *Ibid.,* p. 141, paras. 99, 100.

accordance with the medieval custom, an oath was required of the candidate by which he promised not to receive the degree at any other university and to observe faithfully the statutes of Erfurt.[73] He was then solemnly invested with ring and beret, and a feast followed for which the candidate had to pay the bill.[74] Safeguards were thrown around this ancient custom in an effort to cut down the expense, but the older masters were entitled to an invitation and the efforts of the university to spare the pocketbook of the novice seem to have been only half-hearted. When these formalities had been concluded, the young master entered on a new dignity, which implied much heavier responsibilities, for the faculty of philosophy was composed of the masters of arts. Theoretically, therefore, Martin now became a member of this body, authorized as eligible to preside at regular disputations, to stand at the head of a *bursa,* and to act as teacher and guide to younger students.

[73] *Ibid.,* p. 139, para. 81.
[74] *Statuta licenciam et licenciatos in artibus concernencia, ibid.,* p. 139, para. 82 ff.; see also p. 153, Rubric XXVIII.

4

THE SCHOLASTIC LEARNING

"THE university at Erfurt used to be of such standing and repute that all the others might be looked upon as junior colleges in comparison." [1] This remark of Martin's in the *Table Talk* belongs to a period more than a quarter of a century after his graduation. He could still recall his ecstasy when he was received into the rank of masters: "What majesty and splendor there was when one received his master's degree! They brought torches to him and presented them. I think that no earthly joy could be compared with it." These recollections and the regrets that he voiced at the decay of the university after the religious revolution give us some idea of the depth of the Erfurt experience. In later days he has, to be sure, many bitter things to say about university learning, particularly in the field of theology, and Erfurt does not escape: "It is no better than a stall full of sows," he declares in a well-attested remark in the *Table Talk;* [2] and six years later he speaks with sorrow of the decay of the university due to the attitude of the archbishop of Mainz. [3] These remarks stem from years of polemical bitterness and concern what he held to be an outworn theology. Occasionally also he recalls the pettiness and uselessness of the sophistry and word-splitting in his university training. The dialectic of his day was a "futile playing with words, with 'universals' and 'predicaments'" and a fighting of "horrible battles" about them without understanding their use. [4] On another occasion he is said to have remarked to his friend Justus Jonas: "If your son were twenty years old I could teach him all the sophistical expressions with their meanings in three hours." [5]

Nevertheless, intensive practice in the "little logic" and the Aristotelian *Organon* set an enduring stamp on young Martin's impressionable mind. The first subjects which a young teacher has to present to pupils are usually

[1] *TR*, II, No. 2788b.
[2] *TR*, III, Nos. 2871a and 2871b.
[3] *TR*, IV, No. 4033.
[4] *TR*, II, No. 2191.
[5] *TR*, IV, No. 5033.

those which cling to the memory longest, and this is perhaps a reason for believing that Martin taught the "little logic" and possibly fragments of the Aristotelian system before completing the master's degree. Throughout life he was fond of discussing "dialectics," as logical operations were called. He defines very adequately the "old logic" as the art of classification and the "new logic" as that of building up arguments to a syllogism; [6] he offers genuinely classical definitions of the difference between logic and rhetoric: [7] rhetoric moves us, logic teaches us; rhetoric decorates ideas while logic demonstrates them briefly and in their proper order. It is much better to be without rhetoric than logic. Rhetoric is color, logic is outline. Logic belongs to the intellect, rhetoric to the will. In later years he liked to set up arguments in syllogistic form for the benefit of his table companions.[8] He calls logical training a necessity, not only in the schools but especially in consistories and churches, and he dwells at length on the aid it gives in showing the hollowness of specious arguments. He acquired at the university and retained throughout life a belief in the importance of logical processes as a reliable basis for predicting future events. He also carried through life a deep respect for the training that logic gives in presenting knowledge; indeed, the art of logic as he sees it preserves the worship of God and the organization of human society.[9] Half seriously he considers in middle life the possibility of writing a work on logic.[10] In that case he would banish the Greek terms and substitute German words for them, and he gives examples of these. Logic is in his opinion as necessary a study as arithmetic. We shall have occasion again and again to refer to the results of this formal university training both for his use of technical terms and for the inner organization of his works, beginning with the *Marginalia,* written down in his years as an instructor, and continuing to the great treatises of the revolutionary year 1520. Upon his training in the disputation in the halls of the college and the university he built assiduously by further practice. What this meant in several great crises of his life we shall see in later chapters.

To a youth of ardent and dynamic temperament, teachers mean more than

[6] *TR,* IV, No. 4570.

[7] In several places in the *Table Talk:* very pungently in III, No. 3237. See also II, Nos. 2139, 2140. The subject seems to have been a frequent matter of discussion among the table companions.

[8] *TR,* IV, No. 4612 and No. 5082b.

[9] E.g., the illustration in *TR,* II, No. 2629b, p. 560, ll. 8 ff. See also V, No. 6244, where he shows the dialectical weakness of Demosthenes' argument concerning Philip of Macedon, "Whoever has a bad case will have no success; Philip has a bad case, therefore he will have no success." This syllogism led the Athenians astray because they did not examine the truth of the major premise; as a matter of fact, the greatest villains have the best luck. Such an error, he infers, would not be made by men trained in disputation.

[10] *TR,* III, Nos. 3237a and 3237b.

subject matter. We do not know all of Martin's instructors. Of several we know only that they touched his life in student days but we cannot determine whether they had any effect upon his growth. We do not even know the name of one who must have played an important rôle in his life, the master of arts at St. George's College who had charge of his work and watched carefully over his character as it developed. The fact that his name has not come down to us may be evidence that he made no lasting impression on young Martin. There were, however, two liberal-minded professors in the faculty of arts who perhaps expressed the spirit of the Erfurt institution at its best and who certainly set their stamp strongly on his development. The first of these was Jodocus Trutvetter of Eisenach.[11] He had been at Erfurt for a quarter of a century before Luther came, and had distinguished himself by persistent industry reflected in a series of works on scholastic philosophy. A genuine example of the late medieval scholar in Germany, this zealous and conscientious man produced six books on logic, traversing the whole field from the "ancient art" of Porphyrius to Peter of Spain and the *Organon* of Aristotle, all probably intended as manuals and class books for the Erfurt students. At the time when Luther came under his influence Trutvetter was putting together the greatest of these, his *Summary of all Logic, Commonly Called the Great Work, Laboriously Drawn in Recent Days from the Dogmas of All the Ancient and Modern Theologians, like the Juice from the Flowers.*[12] Perhaps Martin thumbed over more than once the 272 quarto pages of this massive work, assembled, as the author declares, from sixty-seven medieval writers through the whole alphabet from Aurelius Augustinus to Valerius Maximus.

Trutvetter was later to precede Martin to Wittenberg, where for a brief time he represented the "modernist" direction in philosophy. The young student was fortunate in coming under the hand of a thinker who was something more than a dry-as-dust exponent of logical distinctions, for Trutvetter was also a theologian, receiving his doctorate in that subject while Martin was still a student at Erfurt, and he had sufficient warmth of personality to win young Luther's liking. Later, at a critical point in his life, Martin turns to his revered teacher for a sympathetic understanding, and is deeply disappointed at the hostile attitude of Trutvetter and perhaps even more humiliated that the "chief of dialecticians"[13] should now denounce him as an ignoramus in the field of logic![14]

Even closer bonds drew Martin to another of his teachers, Bartholomäus

[11] Plitt, *Jodocus Trutfetter;* see also Prantl, *Geschichte der Logik*, IV, 241 ff.
[12] For contents see Prantl, *Geschichte der Logik*, IV, 241.
[13] Letter from Luther to Spalatin, Feb. 22, 1518, *WAB*, I, 150, ll. 20 ff.
[14] Letter from Luther to Trutvetter, May 9, 1518, *WAB*, I, 170, l. 38, and n. 1, p. 171.

Arnold von Usingen, a warm-hearted scholar still in his thirties when Martin came under his instruction. He was another of the interpreters of the older logic and the Aristotelian *Organon* and *Physics* who gave Erfurt its reputation as a center of scholastic learning.[15] Luther may have used Arnold's *Short Natural History,* which was well thought of in other universities besides Erfurt and highly praised for its brevity and simplicity.[16] Arnold as he appears to us in his writings lacks the industry of Trutvetter, but evidently he had a nature that endeared him to his students and made them his friends in after-life. In a later edition of his *Short Natural History,* after the author's death, an Erfurt fellow-professor gives what is perhaps the highest praise that can come to a devoted teacher: "His kindness in aiding and promoting the studies of his students was never withheld but was free and available to everyone." [17] In addition, he was of deeply religious temperament, and in 1512 he entered the Augustinian monastery at Erfurt. To a man like this Martin's ardent nature felt itself strongly drawn. "The best paraclete and consoler," he calls him many years later.[18] He continued to send greetings to his old teacher as late as 1520; then the wave of revolution whirled them apart.

Both Trutvetter and Arnold von Usingen belonged to the so-called "modernist" direction in philosophy. In the opinion of Christoph Scheurl, a juristic colleague at Wittenberg and a keen observer of times and men, Dr. Jodocus was "the prince of modernists." [19] If his works are anything like a faithful picture of the man, he must have emphasized constantly in his lectures the ideas of the nominalist school as propounded by the English Franciscan, William of Occam, and his latest German apostle, Gabriel Biel of Tübingen. In what seems to have been Trutvetter's first work, his *Breviary of Dialectics,* he formulates the nominalist declaration of faith in the trenchant phrase: "The universals are not entities but the names of entities." [20] Arnold, although more independent in his attitude, was also a confirmed Occamist, and his works set forth clearly and definitely the nominalist ideals of theology. When the religious revolt broke out both teachers parted company with Luther; and Arnold, whose works show his strongly conservative nature,[21]

---

[15] N. Paulus, "Der Augustiner Barth. Arnoldi von Usingen, Luthers Lehrer und Gegner," *Strassburger theologische Studien,* I, III (1893).

[16] *Parvulus philosophie naturalis* (Leipzig, 1499), reprinted in Erfurt, Basel, and Vienna.

[17] Johann Curio's dedication to Nikolaus Hoffner, abbot at Homburg, dated Feb. 27, 1543, quoted in Paulus, "Arnoldi von Usingen," p. 2, n. 4.

[18] Letter from Luther to Georg Leiffer, April 15, 1516, *WAB,* I, 37, ll. 8 f.

[19] Scheurl, *Briefbuch,* I, 123.

[20] *Breviarium dialecticum Jodoci Isennachcensis theologi studiosis logices apprime necessarium,* quoted in Plitt, *Jodocus Trutfetter,* p. 29, n. 5; *ibid.,* pp. 9 f.

[21] Note his remark to Luther on the interpretation of the Bible in the light of tradition: *TR,* II, No. 1240; also Paulus, "Arnoldi von Usingen," p. 26 and n. 1.

combatted vigorously Martin's ideas of faith and works. At the university, however, both set their stamp on young Luther's philosophy, and all the storms of mind and soul that came over him afterwards did not erase it. He accepted willingly the badge of "modernist" which the Erfurt university pinned on its graduates, and he wore it proudly in the years of his great collision with Rome. Proudly he declares: "I am of the faction of Occam." [22]

In addition to these two men, who took their philosophy, especially their logic, so seriously, there is no evidence that other personalities influenced Martin's development during early university years. Only one other instructor can be identified with certainty. This was Hieronymus Emser, a roving cleric with a slant toward humanism who came to Erfurt in the train of Cardinal Raymond Perault in 1504 and stopped for a semester to give a course on Reuchlin's comedy *Sergius, or the Head of the Head.* Emser was later to develop into one of Luther's most relentless enemies. In the midst of a furious polemic in the bitter years of the revolt Emser recalled that Martin had been among his hearers at Erfurt,[23] and he seized this opportunity to charge the heretic with immoral behavior at the university. Spoken in the midst of a fierce controversy, these charges remained unconfirmed.

Emser's statement regarding the lectures on this school comedy is interesting because the author of *Sergius,* the Swabian humanist Johann Reuchlin, was at that time preparing the first Hebrew grammar to be published in Germany. It provides a bit of evidence that Martin had some contact with the rising wave of humanistic interest in these critical years. So far as we are able to identify his teachers, they were otherwise all men of the older scholastic sort. Arnold von Usingen stood, to be sure, on terms of warm friendship with the humanistic group that was beginning to form in Erfurt when Martin graduated, and the most gifted poetic spirit of this coterie, Eobanus Hessus, sang his praise in a florid poem in honor of Erfurt (1507):

> Thee do grateful young men,
> Grateful old men revere, marvel at, admire, and love.[24]

A decade later Konrad Mudt, chief of the humanistic group of central Thuringia, spoke with respect of Arnold's learning. Nevertheless, nothing justifies us in thinking that the learned scholastic shared humanistic enthusiasms when he was Martin's teacher or at any time later. His friendship

[22] *WA,* VI, 600, l. 11; *ibid.,* p. 195.

[23] G. Kawerau, "Hieronymus Emser," *SVRG,* LXI (1898), 9 f.

[24] *De laudibus et praeconiis incliti Gymnasii litteratorii apud Erphordiam Carmen,* cited in Paulus, "Arnoldi von Usingen," p. 3. See also p. 14.

with the young men of Mudt's circle was probably due to his solid scholarship and his lovable, religious character. The good doctor fell at times into somewhat barbarous Latin and apparently knew no Greek. Nor is there evidence of any interest on his part in neo-Latin poetry, in the revolutionary expansion of the curriculum advocated by humanists like Celtes, or in any of the philological, pedagogical, or historical ideas which the humanists had brought back from Italy and were cultivating in Germany. A scholastic philosopher Arnold von Usingen was and remained, deeply devoted to medieval techniques of instruction, and occupied with a philosophy that acknowledged itself subservient to theology as maid to mistress. Trutvetter was a man of similar stamp. He was, however, not altogether blind to what had been going on in the world of scholarship in his lifetime. His references show that he knew many classical authors and, what is more significant, the work of the late medieval Voltaire, Laurentius Valla, the Italian rationalist of half a century earlier. Trutvetter's reading had indeed gone far beyond the writers of his own century. He had also personal relations with two younger humanists of the faculty, Nikolaus Marschalk and Maternus Pistorius. Nevertheless, his reigning interests lay in the scholastic field.[25]

Erfurt University was, indeed, never a focus for the activities of early humanists. Luther would have felt their influence more strongly had his studies taken him to one of the universities on the upper Rhine. At Erfurt the wandering scholars of humanism came and went, to be sure, bearing their enthusiasm for the new poetry, for the cultivation of the poetic personality, and for the extension of the program of university studies. A generation before Martin, Peter Luder, one of the most undisciplined of the wandering brood, stopped at Erfurt and lectured on Vergil, Terence, and Ovid. The great Celtes passed a semester there in 1486 and perhaps lectured also. Together with these scholars who had been in touch with Italy, new philological enthusiasm came to the fore at the end of the century. Marschalk, a master of arts of the university, published in the year of Luther's matriculation his *Orthography,* a list of Greek words with their Latin equivalents, and an *Exegetical Grammar,* the earliest attempt at a Greek grammar to be issued in Germany. He followed these the next year with his *Handbook of Celebrated Authors,* an anthology of Greek and Latin writers. If these beginnings of Greek scholarship aroused Martin's interest nothing came of it at this time, for the young student was absorbed in the traditional curriculum, and Marschalk, restless like most of the early humanistic scholars,

---

[25] Rommel, *Über Luthers Randbemerkungen,* pp. 5 f. See also Kaufmann, *Geschichte der deutschen Universitäten,* II, 529 ff.

soon journeyed on to Wittenberg.[26] For a decade no one appeared in Erfurt to imitate his efforts. Martin concentrated on scholastic studies and post-poned the learning of Greek to a later day.[27]

A new interest in classical Latin authors was in the air, however, and it can hardly be doubted that Martin felt the stimulus. Broad reading in the Latin classics was by no means lacking in the plan of the later medieval uni-versity. Boethius' *Discipline for Students,* five copies of which were in the library of the Amplonian College at Erfurt, had been prescribed as early as 1412 as the subject of a month's lectures at the university.[28] Here the students were called upon to read and memorize extracts from Vergil, Ovid, Plautus, and Horace.[29] In the century that followed, the program of lectures on classical works seems to have been considerably extended, even though Erfurt probably did not go so far in this respect as Heidelberg. There, in 1491, young Konrad Kürsner (Pellicanus), then a lad of thirteen or fourteen, later to become a leading scholar in Hebrew, heard lectures on the Heren-nian rhetoric of Cicero, the *Epistles* of Horace, the *Achilleid* of Statius, and Ovid's *Elegy on the Nut-tree,* all in addition to the regular program of studies for the baccalaureate.[30] At Erfurt the temptation to neglect the discipline of the old and the new logic for classical authors was probably less strong.

According to Melanchthon, Luther became acquainted with the classics at the university. There is no reason to doubt this, even though "select morsels," such as were offered in Boethius, may have been known to him beforehand. Many years later he told Veit Dietrich, his amanuensis, that the first poet he read was Baptist of Mantua.[31] In view of the serious atmosphere in the Erfurt colleges, this is very probable, for Baptist was above suspicion of worldliness or heathen inclinations. A general of the Carmelites in the generation just preceding Luther, his poems—epic, didactic, and lyrical—are a quaint mixture of the ancient spirit and Christianity. His *Eclogues,* first printed in 1498, had just come from the press in Germany when Martin matriculated at Erfurt. Their praise of monasticism was brightened for the youthful mind in search of beauty by a realistic touch and by the poetic charm of their descriptions of life among the peasantry.[32] After this poet,

[26] Paulsen, *Geschichte des gelehrten Unterrichts,* I, III, 72; Scheel, *Martin Luther,* I, 221.
[27] For the early history of humanism at Erfurt, see Bauch, *Die Universität Erfurt im Zeitalter des Frühhumanismus.* Later studies by Oergel, Benary, Neubauer, Kalkoff, and Burgdorf have modified somewhat the conclusions of this fundamental work.
[28] "Acten," VIII, II, 134, Rubric LX.   [29] Scheel, *Martin Luther,* I, 219 ff.
[30] Pellicanus, *Die Hauschronik,* p. 10.   [31] *TR,* I, No. 256.
[32] Ellinger, *Geschichte der neulateinischen Literatur Deutschlands,* I, 103 ff. See also Mustard, *The Eclogues of Baptista Mantuanus,* p. 35.

who disinfected the new poetry of all suspicions of heathendom, Martin declares that he read the *Heroides* of Ovid and also Vergil. He adds that scholastic theology forbade him to go further. He did go further, however, for it must have been during the university years that he made friends with Cicero and Livy. It was probably also at the university that he formed acquaintance, though less intimately, with the works of Juvenal, Horace, Plautus, and Terence. The amanuensis Dietrich, one of the most reliable of the Wittenberg Boswells, quotes a statement by Luther that when he entered the cloister he returned to the bookseller all his books except Plautus and Vergil, which he took with him into monastic life.[33] His reading was done with the intensity of concentration known only to an age in which access to books was a rare privilege. The results were clinched by a prodigious memory, for in later years Martin knew by heart whole sections of Baptist the Mantuan and was able to quote from memory with considerable accuracy from Ovid, Vergil, Cicero, and Livy. Only a few months before his death, when he came to draw up the account of his religious experiences, he illustrated it with numerous classical quotations, among them a hexameter from the second *Georgic* of Vergil:

> The blood about my heart congealed in ice.[34]

This experience with the ancients could not have been without its effect, even on a mind bound to the rationalistic curriculum by the sturdy cords of scholastic requirements. Melanchthon, thoroughgoing humanist that he was, probably goes too far in his statement that Luther learned at this time to honor the classical authors as guides of life, but it is quite possible that the young student found in the library of his own college or that of the Collegium Magnus other works than those of Aristotle that set forth the ethical ideals of the ancients. Perhaps he dipped into Seneca, in whom the Middle Ages discovered the maxims of a moral life founded on the natural law. Many years later, in his great controversy with Erasmus, Martin rails in polemical fury against the ancient philosophers as substitutes for the Scriptures, and mocks at their wisdom. In the Erfurt days this contrast almost certainly had no such vivid character for teachers or pupils.

Yet, although Martin's acquaintance with poets and prose writers of the Roman world was not superficial when he emerged from his master's examination, the humanizing influence of classical profane poetry did not mount very high in his mind. Certainly there were opportunities for contact with men in whom this enthusiasm burned, although we do not know

---

[33] *TR*, I, No. 116.   [34] *Georgicae*, II, 484. *WA*, LIV, 185.

enough of Martin's student friendships to be definite about such associations.[35] Some thirty miles away, at Gotha, Konrad Mudt, better known by his Latinized name, Mutianus, had established a sort of focus for young humanists before Luther left the university. Mutianus had come back to Germany after ten years in Italy and settled down in a comfortable living as canon. To Gotha he attracted a circle of friends, including young men from Erfurt, and carried on a correspondence with others. Georg Spalatin and Peter Eberbach, the former to become one of Luther's most intimate friends in later years at Wittenberg, were among the disciples of Mutianus. Crotus Rubianus, whom we know as a member of a student group with Luther at Erfurt, was also soon to become a correspondent of Mutianus. The latter was an earnest man, although a real epicurean. He was a foe of the old theologians, and in his letters has many sarcastic things to say about their scholastic narrowness and intolerance. Indeed, he goes further and does not spare the Mass or the confessional. Later on this group was to drift in various directions; one of them, Crotus, carried the satirical attack on scholastic theology and theologians to the point of caricature in the *Letters of Obscure Men*. But the so-called "Latin army" of Mutianus was a somewhat shadowy affair and seems not to have come into existence at all until after Martin had left the university. Young Luther's personal acquaintance with the satirical canon of Gotha did not begin until a decade later.[36]

There were, however, besides Crotus, two fellow-students at Erfurt whose acquaintance with Martin perhaps began in university years and who were to become important as humanistic influences upon him: Johann Lang [37]

[35] The subject of Luther's relations to humanism in the Erfurt period is a baffling one. Burgdorf, in *Einfluss der Erfurter Humanisten,* assembled an imposing array of possibilities that he was at this time under the influence of humanistic reformatory tendencies and of personalities related to humanism. It must be admitted that he could hardly have escaped some of these forces, but with our present information it seems quite impossible to define them or their effect upon him except in the most general way. For the university years some influence can hardly be denied, but it is striking that none of the current enthusiasms of humanism—philological, pedagogical, nationalistic, Neoplatonic, moral-rationalistic, and the like—can be discerned in his range of interest until long after he took his master's degree. When some of these ideas emerge in works of maturity and in the *Table Talk* they do not bear the stamp of early university experiences.

[36] Luther writes in a letter to Mutianus, May 29, 1516, of his friendship with the latter as being quite recent. *WAB,* I, 40. See also Lang's letter to Mutianus of May 2, 1515. K. Gillert, ed., "Der Briefwechsel des Conradius Mutianus," *Geschichtsquellen der Provinz Sachsen,* XVIII, II (1890), pp. 149 f., No. 490. The more one examines the sources regarding the "Latin army," the less real it seems. Burgdorf's assumption of an acquaintance of Martin's with Peter Eberbach in university years has no support in the sources. *Einfluss der Erfurter Humanisten,* p. 54.

[37] See Burgdorf, *Johann Lange* (Burgdorf insists on the spelling "Lange"; see p. 128, n. 18). Lang's early relations to humanism are fully attested. See letters of Peter Eberbach to Lang, 1506, 1507, and 1508, in Burgdorf, *Einfluss der Erfurter Humanisten,* pp. 122 ff.

and Georg Spalatin. Both were students in Luther's time at Erfurt, both were theologians, and both were to come into very close relations with Martin after his entry into monastic life. Lang followed him into the cloister, probably in 1506. He certainly preceded him in the study of Greek and may have been of help to him in this subject a few years later. It is possible that the three shared the interest in "good arts," the humanistic term for letters, to which, as Crotus says, Martin devoted himself at Erfurt.[38] Possibly also their common interests were not limited to enthusiasm for linguistic purism, but extended to embrace some knowledge of the critical and satirical attitude of the humanists toward the Church orders.[39] Perhaps with the iconoclasm of youth they discussed with each other certain questions of the day which enthusiastic students from the Rhine or from Vienna may have brought to Erfurt, such as the attack on the monks by the great Heidelberg critic and pedagogue, Jakob Wimpfeling.[40]

"Today the apes of theology occupy the whole university, teaching their students the figures of Donatus, a most unintelligible thing; the figures of Parvalus, pure nonsense; exercises in complexities, the silliest stuff. With such chatter they burden their students." Thus Mutianus writes to his friend Heinrich Urban in a neighboring cloister nearly a decade after Martin had graduated from the university.[41] The scholastic edifice at Erfurt was indeed so solidly built that no real breach was made in its walls until the religious revolt burst upon the city in 1520 and swept the university away from its old foundations.[42] "Letters make one stupid; only philosophy brings joy." This remark, attributed to John of Salisbury, might well have been the motto of those teachers to whom Martin owed his education at Erfurt. In this education classical authors, poetry—the humanities, in our terms—were an episode of little significance as compared with the system of knowledge for which Aristotle supplied both substance and framework. From this Martin drew the weapons which he was later to wield with such assurance in the face of his theological adversaries. In the fiery years after the promulgation of his Ninety-five Theses he upbraids his scholastic opponents for not knowing a single chapter of Aristotle.[43] To be sure, his professors did not

---

[38] Letter from Crotus to Luther, Oct. 16, 1519, *WAB*, I, 541, ll. 3 ff.

[39] Kalkoff, *Humanismus und Reformation in Erfurt*, pp. 6 ff.

[40] *De integritate*. Knepper, *Jakob Wimpfeling*, pp. 182 ff. See also Scheel's review of Burgdorf's work, *Der Einfluss der Erfurter Humanisten*, in *Theologische Literaturzeitung*, LIV, III (1929), 63 ff.

[41] 1514. Gillert, "Mutianus," p. 78, No. 418.

[42] The reform that took place under the leadership of Luther's younger friend Justus Jonas. Kalkoff, *Humanismus und Reformation in Erfurt, passim.*

[43] Letter from Luther to Egranus, March 24, 1518, *WAB*, I, 158, ll. 38 f.; also letter to

leave him in any doubt as to the unreliability of the Greek philosopher in treating the relation of God to man. Dr. Trutvetter makes this clear in his interpretations, and Martin took the distrust of Aristotelian philosophy into the cloister with him and gave full expression to it a few years later. Nevertheless, he believed in the value of the Aristotelian *Organon* and the *Poetics,* and in his revolutionary writings of 1520 he calls for the retention of these subjects in the educational system.[44]

In the field of nature it was Aristotle who continued to give him the foundation on which to build his ideas of the world about him. Both of the Erfurt professors whom we have learned to know wrote works on physics, and these give us a fairly accurate picture of the lectures that Martin heard from them on the laws of nature. For the scholastic period it was of course as natural that the professor of logic and moral philosophy should also lecture on nature as it had been in the Lyceum at Athens. Like their Greek master, the Erfurt philosophers presented to their students a rationalized universe in the form of classifications and sequences, for the art of defining and categorizing was cultivated as actively in natural philosophy as in the field of dialectics. In Arnold's *Compendium of Natural Philosophy,* from which Martin may well have drawn many of his ideas, the sharp logician is recognizable throughout. The entire work is based on Aristotle as he had been supplemented and adapted by Thomas Aquinas and Albertus Magnus. Arnold divides philosophy into physical, ethical, and logical. Physics, "the knowledge of divine things," breaks up into metaphysics, natural philosophy, and mathematics. Natural philosophy treats of things in nature which are in motion and subject to natural change. Nature's laws are resolved into premises, distinctions, and conclusions.[45]

Natural sciences were, then, decidedly on the program at Erfurt in Martin's university days. The works on this subject in the catalogue of Porta Coeli College were numerous, and an investigation of the curriculum of the university for this time shows that in the number of lectures and the time allotted to them natural philosophical subjects exceeded logical subjects.[46] To be sure the prevailing school of philosophy at Erfurt, the Occamist,

---

Spalatin, Jan. 14, 1519, *ibid.,* p. 301, ll. 19 f. The latter describes a fiery dispute with a Thomistic doctor in Dresden.

[44] *An den Christlichen Adel, WA,* VI, 458.

[45] *Compendium naturalis philosophie et studio singulari M. Bartholomei de Usingen. In Gymnasio Erphurdiensi publice litterarie perfectum* (1501). See also nn. 15 and 16, above.

[46] Neubauer, *Frühzeit,* p. 75, makes a minimum total of thirteen, covering forty-four months, in natural philosophy as against eight, covering thirty months, in logical subjects.

stressed the formal and logical character of all knowledge.[47] In later years Martin was inclined to make sport of the highly abstract and laborious classifications of simple natural objects and experiences by Aristotle and the medieval physicists. Yet the Aristotelian rationalism was stamped permanently upon him.[48]

Within these limitations his teachers gave him a surprising amount of factual material regarding astronomy, geography, biology, and psychology, based for the most part on accurate observation. Such material they exerted themselves to bring into line with Christian faith. Arnold in his *Compendium* is at pains throughout to show how the divine laws include the natural laws; and the pious author ends his disquisition on nature with a prayer that Christ may permit us to finish our lives with a happy conclusion in this vale of tears. The title of Trutvetter's *Summa* is significant—*A Summary of All Physics or Natural Philosophy Elucubrated and Set Forth with True Wisdom, i.e., with Theology.*[49]

What his professor thus "elucubrated and set forth" had its basis in Aristotle's nature lore. It jostled weirdly with the Christian mythology and the animism of Martin's childhood impressions, but wherever these do not interfere, his conception of the natural world retains the mark of Aristotle's rationalism. From Aristotle he knew that the earth is smaller than one of the stars and much smaller than the sun.[50] Founded on Aristotle and strengthened by his own religious ideas was Martin's scepticism in regard to astrology. Professor Trutvetter remained independent of the superstitions of the day with respect to this pseudo-science,[51] and he impressed his views on Martin, who later in life took a position contrasting sharply with that of the humanist Melanchthon, with whom he had many arguments on the subject. Luther declares repeatedly his disbelief in prophecy by means of the stars; [52] the most he is willing to concede to stellar influence is a certain disposition: "The stars give an inclination but no compulsion. There is no prophesying by means of them." [53] "To believe in the stars is idolatry,"

[47] As representatives of the so-called "sermocinal" disciplines the Occamists have been charged with neglecting the natural sciences. This has been definitely refuted. Scheel, *Martin Luther*, I, 194 ff. The very character of the epistemological approach to nature by these "modernists" necessitated an effort to define physical experiences with all possible sharpness.

[48] See the amazing illustrations he gives to Valentin Dietrich in TR, II, No. 2395.

[49] *Summa in totam physicem: hoc est philosophiam naturalem conformiter siquidem vere sophie: que est theologia . . . elucubrata et edita* (1514). Plitt, *Jodocus Trutfetter*, p. 44.

[50] TR, II, No. 2413b.

[51] See Scheel, *Martin Luther*, I, 194. Scheel's analysis of the ideas on natural philosophy held by Luther's teachers has been very helpful.

[52] See the long discussion in TR, I, No. 855; also No. 678; and II, Nos. 2413a and 2413b.

[53] TR, III, Nos. 3606A and 3606B.

because it violates the first commandment.[54] "Astrology is no art," he declared, according to one of his table companions, "for it has no proof or demonstration on which one can establish a solid foundation." [55] Between the miracle, whether God's or the devil's doing, and the phenomenon which can be classified logically there was for him no middle ground.

His Erfurt teachers could not, of course, admit a self-operating universe in the Aristotelian sense, and in later years Martin ridicules repeatedly the idea of a "sleeping" God.[56] Our earth is the center of the universe, his professors taught, surrounded by movable, revolving heavens.[57] Three decades later Luther recalled with some accuracy the Aristotelian differentiation between the universal movement of the different heavens and that of the planets, and ascribes the motive power to angels.[58] A comet, however, for which no laws of motion could be prescribed, is a "bastard" among the planets. Like other unclassified signs and wonders in the skies it may prophesy evil things to come.[59] For that there was scriptural authority.[60] He entertained the same doubts regarding the powers of alchemy as he found implied in Aristotle, doubts which had agitated his professor Trutvetter as well,[61] although Luther delighted in the laboratory procedure of the alchemists as a symbol of the purification of mankind.[62]

From Aristotle, then, Martin's teachers gave him the foundation for his knowledge of the world without. They showed him how to square this knowledge with the mythology of Christianity. A few years later he was ready to turn and rend the Greek philosopher as a heathen; nevertheless, the latter had given Martin a technique for seeking truth and presenting his findings, as well as much factual information that was to remain his equipment. In the social field too he had respect for the Greek. More than once he praises ideas drawn from Aristotle's *Economics* and admits the value of his authority as a political philosopher.[63]

"Dear friend, I know well what I am talking about. I know Aristotle just as well as you and your sort do. I have read him and heard lectures on him

---

[54] *Ibid.*, I, No. 1026.

[55] *Ibid.*, No. 855, p. 419, ll. 40 ff. The remarks on astrology in the *Table Talk* come from the most reliable reporters and are documented at unusual length.

[56] *EA*, LXII, 351; II, 297 ff.; XXXVIII, 251. See Nitzsch, *Luther und Aristoteles*, pp. 39 f.

[57] See Scheel, *Martin Luther*, I, 192, with an interesting reproduction of charts from Trutvetter's *Physics*.

[58] *TR*, II, Nos. 2730a and 2730b.

[59] *TR*, II, Nos. 2756a and 2756c; III, No. 3507, p. 366, ll. 31 ff.

[60] *TR*, V, No. 5621.

[61] "Gaudet genera et species! sagt Aristoteles wider die Alchemisten." *TR*, V. No. 5671.

[62] *TR*, I, No. 1149.   [63] *TR*, III, No. 3608d.

with a better understanding than St. Thomas or Scotus did. I can say that of myself without boasting and I can prove it if need be." [64] This statement of Luther in his *Address to the Christian Nobility* lacks something in modesty but it is a sincere declaration. In the perspective of fifteen years Aristotle must indeed have seemed to him the great source for the substance of his university training. A decade of association with humanists and a revolutionary theological experience now fired him with resentment against the worldly philosophy of the Greek: "the damned, arrogant, sarcastic heathen" who had deceived so many of the best Christians with his false words. Young Martin's professors at Erfurt were not among those Christians who had been fooled, nor did they permit their hearers to overlook the non-Christian elements in Aristotle: his failure to find the absolute transcendental reason in God, his belief in the eternity of matter, his idea of creation as the realization of a potentiality within the universe itself and not the fiat that called something out of nothing, his denial of the immortality of the soul. To accommodate this resistant material to Christian tradition and faith had been the great task of four centuries of theologians. The moral philosophy which Martin heard in his later years at the Erfurt university was the current attempt to apply the formulas of logic to metaphysics, physics, psychology, and ethics so as to serve the ideas of Christianity.

The system of philosophy accepted by Luther's teachers was the so-called "modernistic." This was of great significance for his future, a significance that will be apparent when we examine the development of his theological studies. More than once in the years of his final break with the Church, as mentioned above, he proclaims himself one of the party of Occam. This party, that of the nominalists, was an outgrowth of the development of scholastic thought in the fourteenth century.[65] In the history of European ideas it was a phase in the continual struggle of the mind to adjust itself to the world without. As a chapter in scholastic philosophy it represents a further spiraling from the abstract in the direction of the concrete, a tendency toward a psychological approach to knowledge. In theology it marks a wider opening of the cleft between reason and faith. Considered from the standpoint of mass psychology, Occam's theories reflect the same trend toward the development of individualism among intellectuals and burghers that was manifest at this time in politics, society, and in the observation of nature. Later generations have made merry over the medieval struggle about the

[64] *WA*, VI, 458.

[65] For a good recent account of William of Occam and the development of his theory, see Abbagnano, *Guglielmo di Ockham.*

so-called "universals," or general ideas, and their relation to the object of knowledge, although it may be doubted whether these generations with their vastly increased information regarding nature and human psychology have come any nearer to the fundamental problem of the essence of reality. Certainly none have attacked it with the powerful logical equipment of the fourteenth and fifteenth centuries. To the modern man, the struggle between realism and nominalism has the mustiness of a room without light and air. To the late medieval Schoolmen and their students the questions involved were burning with vital interest.

In accordance with the rhythm of medieval speculation, with its general movement from the simplicity of a rationally organized universe toward the recognition of non-rational forces, realism was the earlier theory. The twelfth century seems to have found no difficulty in accepting the statement of Abelard that the general idea is a predicate which is arrived at by comparing individual objects. It was but a further step to assume that general ideas have a real existence as archetypes in the mind of God. This was the conception of Thomas Aquinas and the basis of his great theological system. Such an assumption simplified greatly the problem of theology, for it supported the theory that all human individuals are one "universal" with merely accidental differentiations. Also, for St. Thomas and his generation the conception that humanity dwells as an archetype in God's mind opened the door wider for predetermination. The balancing of this against the concept of freedom of the human will was a triumphant achievement of the great theologians of the thirteenth century. From a rational standpoint the system which they evolved was a perfect one, so perfect, indeed, that nothing could be done with it by the next generation except to attack its foundation. Duns Scotus, an Englishman and a Franciscan, found himself unable to accept the subordination of the individual will altogether under a generic form. For Scotus, whose keenness of analysis was the marvel of his day, the individual was of an essentially primal character, a substantialization, as it were, of the generic idea. The soul of man was, however, a self-contained reality. The Scotists thus moved in the direction of giving reality to the individual. Another Englishman, William of Occam, took a further step. The universals are deduced, he declares, from a knowledge of the objects which we have acquired by sensation and by an intuitive knowledge of ourselves.[66] At long last he was not willing to concede the absolute certainty that the

---

[66] Occam thus took a direction which led past the English empiricists of the eighteenth century, with whom he has much in common, toward the path later followed by Kant. For an illuminating study of Occam's epistemology and its relation to Kant's transcendentalism, see

sensation came from an object: the mental picture might come from God's own action on the mind. But whether derived from a physical sensation or from divine intervention, the universal exists only in the mind of man. Knowledge is thus an experience within ourselves. In consequence the universal loses its reality and becomes only a name.

There is no doubt that the nominalist ideas dealt a staggering blow to the rationalistic system of theology with its fine adjustment of checks and balances. If one accepts Occam's theory, the bases for substantiating even the existence of God and the Trinity by arguments built on reason alone would be seriously undermined, for knowledge rests on an inner experience and it is beyond human power to experience God.[67] However, medieval thinker that he was, Occam had no idea of extending his scepticism beyond the domain of the human mind: the structure of faith remained untouched. The result of his theory was to complete the rift between the realm of the intellect and that of the soul. Reason dominates the one; the other is left to the irrational workings of faith. Philosophy continued to build its structures by logical techniques and these the followers of Occam now developed with stern consistency; but theology was freed from all subtle compromises with the reason. The truths of revelation are accepted; what is true in theology must also be true in philosophy, but in the domain of the spirit the laws of cause and effect do not apply. Philosophically only the object of knowledge may have a real existence, the universal is simply a name; but God's province is the supernatural world, and there the acts of His will are impenetrable to human reason.[68] As Luther phrases it a few years later, reason does not decide, but because the Holy Ghost says it is true,[69] it is true.

Occam was of a combative nature and his followers girded themselves for a struggle with the older school. Much of his productive life had been spent in southern Germany, where he had close relations with the emperor, Louis the Bavarian, and his ideas found many adherents, particularly among the German Franciscans. They seem to have avoided carrying the more radical implications of his theories into the theological field, but they did press the fight for his philosophy. The scene of the conflict between realists and nominalists in Germany was at first the "general studies," the groups of

---

H. Siebeck, "Occams Erkenntnislehre in ihrer historischen Stellung," *Archiv für Geschichte der Philosophie*, X, N. F. III (1897), 317 ff. A more extended investigation is found in Hochstetter, *Studien zur Metaphysik und Erkenntnislehre Wilhelms von Ockham*.

[67] Siebeck, "Occams Erkenntnislehre," p. 327.

[68] For the ethical-social tradition which appears in Occam, see *ibid.*, esp. p. 321. The influence of this on Luther's teachers at Erfurt cannot be overlooked.

[69] *WA*, IX, 35, ll. 3 f.

cloister schools. With the rise of the universities the battle was transferred to them. The intolerance of the age impelled one school of thought to exclude the other, and the universities swore their professors and graduates to the banners of the realist or nominalist cause.[70] With the early fifteenth century the acute stage of the conflict passed and compromises followed which allowed both doctrines to be taught side by side in the same institution. After the middle of the century a reaction in the realistic direction showed itself and bitter conflicts broke out between the defenders of the *via antiqua,* as the realist philosophers came to be called, and the *via moderna* of the nominalists. Such a strife blazed up in Paris after 1471. In Germany, Cologne and Heidelberg became arenas for the conflict as a result of outside interference. In Heidelberg in 1452 the "ancient way" was introduced by direct action of the Elector Palatine, the pro-rector of the university; and elsewhere in Germany political authorities took the field to support the older theory. The prejudice of these conservative officials was possibly aroused by the fear that heresy lurked somewhere in the nominalist system, with its ardent cultivation of logic.[71]

In Erfurt, the Occamist tradition established itself early and persisted. The reputation of the university as a citadel of nominalism is reflected in the dialogues found in a student's handbook of the day,[72] but bitter strife against the *via antiqua* seems to have been lacking. The statutes of Porta Coeli College admitted both directions, at least in the first half of the fifteenth century; indeed the Thomistic theology and the "modern" school of logic seem to have dwelt together in a sort of amity. When Luther came to the university, however, the adherents of the *via moderna* were in full possession.[73] The professors who introduced him to the thorny field of scholastic philosophy were thoroughgoing modernists. The intricate path on which they led him can be followed in the works of both Trutvetter and Arnold. The importance of the doctrine for his whole subsequent experience makes it worth while to follow its windings in some detail.

The world without penetrates to the soul of man through the senses,

---

[70] For the various phases of the conflict in the university, see the intensive studies by Gerhard Ritter, "Studien zur Spätscholastik," Parts I and II, *Sitzungsberichte der Heidelberger Akademie der Wissenschaften,* Vols. XII, XIII (1921, 1922).

[71] For an account of this revival of the "ancient way," see *ibid.,* Part II, esp. pp. 64 ff.

[72] *Manuale Scholarium qui studentium universitates aggredi . . . ,* reprinted in Zarncke, *Die deutschen Universitäten im Mittelalter,* p. 12.

[73] This seems to be generally admitted except by Benary, *Zur Geschichte der Stadt und Universität Erfurt,* Part III. See pp. 57 f. for a summary of Benary's conclusions. Ritter, "Studien zur Spätscholastik," II, 15 ff. and 44 ff., disposes of Benary's arguments quite effectively, at least for the period of Luther's studies.

whence the spirit conducts impressions to the brain, the seat of the general mind. Here repetition gives rise to an inclination (*habitus*) to recall the impressions to memory and to bind them together into pictures (*phantasma*). The intellect then classifies the concepts and derives the general ideas from them. All our knowledge of the outer world is thus a form of experience, not a reality. "The exterior sense does not perceive its object as a reality, but through its own effort." [74] This maxim from Arnold's brief interpretation of natural philosophy Martin must have heard many times. The universal is present in the soul only as a symbol (*terminus*) for a number of individuals: man is the *genus,* the universal for all human beings, that is, creatures having common characteristics. The knowledge of nature is therefore built up by deduction. Such, in brief, was the epistemology of the school which Martin observed. It can be seen easily why Occamist students enjoyed a reputation for logical mastery in the disputation.

No teacher of philosophy in a scholastic age could separate this discussion from theology, and Luther's teachers would have been the last to do so. The implications of the nominalists' theory of cognition have already been mentioned. Knowledge is derived from phenomena. This basic principle Martin absorbed and reflected a decade later in the earliest of his theological courses of lectures. The process by which knowledge is derived is inner experience. It is not possible for us to have an experience of God; consequently, we can have no knowledge of Him. Here a great gulf yawns before the investigator. Reason halts, for it can go no further. Beyond lies a world of revelation, not demonstrable by rational processes, a supernatural realm where the word of God is omnipotent and works in its own way to save or to destroy.

It is not difficult to imagine that these theories as set forth in the measured dialogues of a Trutvetter or the warm accents of an Arnold thrilled their hearer. Martin, by nature of a religious character, was deeply impressed, as succeeding events will show. He had no gift for philosophic theorizing but he was well trained in logic, and he was most certainly before the close of his study for the master's degree profoundly concerned about the relation of God to man. In these formative years it is probable that he accepted the ideas presented to him passively and blindly and that certain implications of the nominalist philosophy thus took lasting hold upon him. Occam's conception of the will as the essence of the soul dominated his thought through the succeeding years. The differentiation between reason and revelation, knowledge and faith, became a lasting impression.

[74] Arnold von Usingen, *Parvulus philosophie naturalis figuralis interpretatio.* Quoted by Neubauer, *Frühzeit,* p. 141, n. 21.

His Erfurt professors also inoculated him with a prejudice against the philosophy of the Thomistic school, with its subtle balancing of the rights of the divine will and human will. As a reaction to these studies and strengthened, perhaps, by a natural lack in this direction, he developed a violent repugnance for philosophical speculation, both within the university and without. Ten years later, when he begins to stretch his limbs in the lectures on Paul's Epistle to the Romans, he is already raging against the philosophy of the schools and declaring that one must know it only in order to refute it.[75] It is the scholastics, headed by Thomas Aquinas, who have smuggled it into the world, although the Apostle Paul expressly forbade it.[76] In 1518 he wrote to his teacher Trutvetter that he prayed to God every day that in place of perverse studies in philosophy a wholesome study of the Bible and the Fathers might be introduced.[77] The significance of these philosophical studies will become apparent when we follow him into his cell and examine his early lectures and theological studies.

[75] Denifle, *Luthertum* (1906), I, 609 f.   [76] *WA*, VIII, 127.
[77] *WAB*, I, 170, ll. 36 ff.

5

ENTRANCE INTO THE CLOISTER

WHEN young Martin Luther presented himself for the master of arts examination early in 1505 he had carried on studies for a minimum period of two years.[1] He had attended thirty regular disputations and taken part in fifteen of them, and his moral character had been approved.[2] In accord with the statutes his examination must have taken place before four masters of arts and the dean or his representative.[3] His preparatory career closed amid the solemn festivities with which Alma Mater blesses her well-behaved children. On this occasion the rector of the university bestowed on Martin the coveted master's beret, and as we noted, he swore not to accept the award from any other university. The ceremony closed with the traditional feast, where the university heads and their examiners disposed of "confects and potables" at the expense of the young graduates.[4]

Two roads now lay open before him. He might become the head of a trivial school such as he himself had attended, or he might remain at the university as a lecturer and continue his studies. In fact, in the oath which preceded his graduation he had sworn to teach at Erfurt for a period of two years unless excused by the faculty of philosophy.[5] This obligation would not have prevented him from entering at the same time on preparation for a learned profession, as many a master had done before. He must have been regarded by professors and fellow students as a young man of unusual ability and promise. We have met one of the latter, Crotus Rubianus, who recalled his zeal for literary studies; and Martin's graduation as second in his class in the minimum period prescribed for the higher arts degree and at the minimum age of twenty-two point to excellent scholarly achievement. He had probably distinguished himself more by solid learning aided by a pow-

---

[1] The statutes provided that the graduates must present themselves for the examination at Epiphany. "Acten," VIII, II, 138, para. 79.

[2] *Ibid.*, p. 137, para. 75.

[3] *Ibid.*, p. 138, para. 77.

[4] *Ibid.*, pp. 153 f., Rubric XXVIII.

[5] *Ibid.*, p. 147, para. 128.

erful memory than through cleverness or originality in handling the tools of logic. The energy and fiery industry with which he flung himself into his tasks in later years must already have been impressive. We may also assume that the intolerance of opposition and the temperamental persistence in maintaining his own opinion which characterized him later on were already apparent to the masters and fellow-students in his *bursa*.[6] Undoubtedly he had matured greatly in the three and one-half years spent at the feet of Alma Mater and now looked out on life with the eager energy and ambition of one who feels his powers.

At this parting of the ways he took the course that led toward a legal career. Here the influence of his father came into play. Hans Luther was rising in the world and must have been aware of the promise in his son, for he was ready to push him along the road to wealth and distinction.[7] He must also have been impressed by Martin's enthusiasm for study and may have noticed in him a growing inclination to the religious life. He seems to have suggested to him the possibility of his marrying into a family of property and social standing, perhaps in order to drive from the mind of the young man any idea of devoting himself to a university career or to the Church.[8] Celibacy was usual in the semimonastic faculty of the university, and the pull toward the cloister frequently was felt by Martin's professors even in their advanced years. The pursuit of philosophy could not lead to civil position or wealth, for the material rewards of university scholarship were as modest in the sixteenth century as they are in modern times. Except in rare cases, public office was open only to those who prepared for it by study of one of the branches of the law, canon or civil. At that time the law school at Erfurt University was the largest of its professional schools. Its courses led into the intricate system of the Roman law which for a century or more had been spreading throughout Germany its web of statutes and procedures and which, with its sharp distinction of master and serf, had become a convenient means whereby the secular and clerical lords could suppress the rights of the free peasantry. Law studies were expanding, and they beckoned to ambitious men. A knowledge of the canon law also opened the way to remunerative office. As legal representative of a prince in Church

---

[6] See below, p. 87, n. 30.

[7] According to Valentin Bavarus, *Rhapsodiae et dicta quedam ex ore* . . . II, 752. This reference was not available to the writer for rechecking. According to Scheel, *Martin Luther*, I, 232, Hans showed his respect for the son's progress by dropping the familiar *Du* and addressing him henceforth with the more dignified *Sie*. See also *WA*, XLIX, 322, l. 12, where Luther says that his father, hearing he was to become a monk, calls him *Du*, while he formerly called him *vos*.

[8] Martin reminded his father of this in 1521. *De votis monasticis*, *WA*, VIII, 573.

relations or as administrator of the secular interests of a bishopric the gifted jurist could rise to high office.

While these prospects lay before Martin, the Easter vacation came and went. When the lectures began again in the faculty of arts,[9] it is possible that Martin was among the young masters of arts who ascended the teacher's rostrum, though there is no certainty that he did so. At any rate, a month later he had become a student in the school of law.[10] His studies, which were to be ended so suddenly midway in the semester by the most momentous decision of his life, may have begun either in the field of canon or of civil law. Later tradition has it that he undertook both.[11] The path for the learner who sought his way through the maze of the great *Corpus juris,* the source work for legal theory and precedent enriched with the accretion of learned interpretations, was as clearly marked out by the statutes of the juristic faculty as that on which the candidate was guided through the school of arts.[12] If Martin began with civil law, as seems probable, his first course would have been an introduction into the *Institutiones* of the Justinian code. Here he was required to memorize Latin titles in the same mechanical manner as he had four years earlier memorized the logical categories in Peter of Spain's treatise.[13] He was held to the regulations of life in the college as closely as heretofore. It is possible that he now took up residence in Porta Coeli College, which lay convenient to the law school, not far from the great cathedral.[14]

In what mood the young master of arts took hold of his studies we can only guess. In later years his contempt for the materialism of the legal profession was unbounded. The essential falseness of law procedures, the twisting about of the law to serve selfish ends, and the glorification of it in despite of all divine justice and human ethics are themes to which Martin

[9] Scheel, *Martin Luther,* I, 231, sets the day of beginning the lectures as April 24, the day following St. George's.

[10] Based on the procedure prescribed for the law faculty in 1425, Scheel, *ibid.,* I, 232, assumes that the opening was in the cathedral on the day of St. Ivo, i.e., May 19, 1505.

[11] For discussion, see *ibid.,* I, 234. The oft-repeated statement of biographers (Köstlin, *Martin Luther,* I, 45; Scheel, *Martin Luther,* I, 234) that Hans presented his son with the *Corpus juris,* and that as a young learner he had read in Accursius' notes on the great work, rests on a shaky foundation in the sources.

[12] "Acten," VIII, II, 79 ff.

[13] J. C. H. Weissenborn, "Die Urkunden zur Geschichte des M. Amplonius de Fago aus Rheinbergen," *Mitteilungen des Vereins für die Geschichte und Altertumskunde von Erfurt,* Vol. IX (1880), para. 25.

[14] The residence in the Amplonian college rests on a statement dated many years later, January 28, 1538, reported from Justus Jonas, who studied law at Erfurt in the next decade. Paul Tschackert, "Justus Jonas' Bericht aus dem Jahre 1538 über Martin Luthers Eintritt in das Kloster (1505)," *ThStKr,* LXX (1897), 577 ff.

comes back again and again in the *Table Talk* and which call forth some of his most resounding invective: "A pious lawyer is a rare bird!" [15] "It is hard for lawyers to go to heaven." [16] These are among the milder of his numerous attacks. The materialism which has rebuffed more than one student of philosophy entering on legal study must have made a painful impression on Martin when he contrasted it with the unselfish devotion to an ideal that he had observed among his professors in the philosophical faculty or among the clergy whom he had known in Magdeburg and Eisenach. "Just show me a jurist who studies for the sake of learning the real truth . . . they all study for profit and to attain great honor and wealth." [17] "The study of law is sordid and only for gain, and its final goal is money." [18] Much of the bitterness toward lawyers and their ways which echoes in these vigorous remarks of the middle-aged Luther to his table companions was based on later experience; much was no doubt rooted in his hatred of the canon law which became the object of his fiercest attack in the years of revolt. But his attacks point also to a period when, with the impatience of young manhood, he encountered the same conflict between tradition and justice and felt the same resentment at the rule of musty precedent over elemental human rights that young Goethe put into his *Faust*. There is no doubt that Martin's heart was elsewhere. Deep emotions had shaken him through the preceding year, and inner promptings toward the religious life would not cease. Early in July the trigger action came, and two weeks later he said farewell to the outer world and entered the cloister of the Augustinian friars.

The momentous step appeared to be sudden, but subconscious forces had been long at work preparing for it. Indeed, unless we disregard altogether the effect of environment and refuse to weigh Martin's actions in the light of his character as it develops later on, we shall have no difficulty in accounting for this turn to the cloister life. Only a determination to make his conversion appear as unpsychological and catastrophic as possible can overlook the powerful spiritual forces that had been drawing him to it.

Late medieval schools and universities were steeped in the religious spirit, and every move in the life of schoolboy and youth was surrounded with religious sanctions and ceremonies. As we have seen, Martin's imagination had been fired in childhood by the bright figures of Christian mythology and faith. The school at Mansfeld had nourished their mystic appeal in the child, and at Magdeburg this influence had been strengthened by the

---

[15] *TR,* I, No. 349, p. 143, l. 9.
[16] *TR,* II, No. 1340.
[17] *TR,* I, No. 349, p. 143, ll. 34 ff.
[18] *TR,* III, No. 2831.

touching example of the gentle Brethren of the Common Life. In school days at Eisenach the personal contact with religious men had softened the hardships of the young scholar. Vicar Braun of St. Nicholas, the devout Heinrich Schalbe, and the religious men of the little group on the side of the Wartburg became friends to whom he clung with an affection that outlasted schooldays. At Erfurt the temporal forms of late medieval religion arose around him in impressive grandeur.[19] On a little eminence near the university towered the great cathedral of Mary the Virgin, richly endowed with land and supporting numerous canons. Beside it stood the foundation of St. Severin and the fine episcopal palace and a little way beyond lay the rich Benedictine abbey of St. Peter. Every type of religious establishment lay about, and monks and nuns of every garb must have passed to and fro through the narrow streets. The mendicant brotherhoods were fully represented: members of "all the orders four," as Chaucer calls them, roamed about with their bags for alms.

It must have struck the eye of the observant young man that this army of clerical persons enjoyed privileges that set them apart from the secular world. The canon law put into the hands of the clergy the right to dispense justice wherever clerical interests were involved, and the sanction of the Church might also be expanded to include any breaches of the moral code among the lay population. Clerical industry and commerce competed without handicap of taxation with many branches of civic activity. No gift-tax interfered with the accumulation of rich legacies in cash and kind.[20] To find a parallel in our day for the wealth of textiles and vessels of silver and gold displayed within the sacred walls of the more important religious institutions, one must visit great Spanish churches like those at Segovia and Toledo. At public festivals such as that on Corpus Christi or on the occasion of the visit of an outstanding religious personality, colorful processions wound through the streets with all the pomp that the imagination of the later Middle Ages could suggest. On such occasions the university in academic dress, professors, masters, and students demonstrated the fealty of the academic world to the clerical. A recent great celebration had marked the visit of the papal legate Raymond Perault, cardinal of Gurk, on October 30, 1502. The magnificence of this occasion made a deep impression on con-

[19] See M. P. Bertram, "Der Erfurter Dorfpfarrer im Ausgehenden Mittelalter," *Zeitschrift des Vereins für Kirchengeschichte der Provinz Sachsen,* V (1908), *passim.* For reproduction of a sixteenth-century painting of Erfurt, see Scheel, *Martin Luther,* I, 120.

[20] Neubauer, *Frühzeit,* p. 84, gives an interesting inventory of the property and income in 1485 of the Servants of Mary at Erfurt, reputed to be one of the poorest orders in the city.

temporary chroniclers.[21] The young undergraduate from Mansfeld may have been one of those who trooped behind the waving banners and joined in the choral of litany and hymn.

These outer symbols of the solemn magnificence of the religious life could not have been without effect on an imaginative youth. Nevertheless, many another youth of similar character passed them by and went on to find his career in secular affairs. Young Martin would certainly have done the same had not an inner urge caused him to disregard parental wishes and throw overboard ambitious plans. Later on he liked to dwell on the suddenness of his decision,[22] and his friends, including classmates at the university like Crotus, were fond of comparing it with the transformation of Paul of Tarsus from an arrogant persecutor of the despised sect of Christians into one of its members.[23] Luther undoubtedly had a tendency to dramatize his inner life and to view it as a series of emotional crises. His later development, however, is sufficient proof that he must have reflected deeply on religion in school and university. In childhood animistic terrors and Christian mythology both gripped him tightly, and in the years after adolescence the reality of the supernatural world was kept constantly before him by his association with men of religion, some of them of profoundly ascetic character. All of this deepened earlier fixations.

As his studies progressed the Bible became more and more a subject of interest. Early in life he had learned to know the Psalms, Gospels, and Epistles from the liturgy, and his verbal command of these parts of the Scriptures, so astonishing in his mature years, must have written itself on the sensitive memory of youth before he came to Erfurt. He may have had in his hands in schooldays one of the "books of the evangels" containing the texts to be read during the church year that were in circulation in Germany at the end of the fifteenth century. At the university, then, he seems to have gotten hold of a copy of a Latin Bible or possibly one of the

---

[21] Konrad Stolle, "Memoriale thüringsch-erfurtische Chronik," ed. by R. Thiele, *Geschichtsquellen der Provinz Sachsen*, XXXIX (1900), 524 ff.

[22] *TR*, I, No. 881 (*ca.*1530); IV, No. 4707 (1539); V, No. 5373 (1540). These remarks, recorded by table scribes, the last of questionable validity, all date from more than a quarter century after the event. Like Melanchthon, *CR*, VI, 158, they reflect primarily the sudden and miraculous character of the experience. The unexpected nature of his decision is also emphasized by Martin in *De votis monasticis* in 1521, sixteen years after he entered the cloister. Father Heinrich Denifle (*Luthertum*) has made a general attack on the historical reliability of the later statements of Luther regarding his religious experiences. However, that Luther's conversion to the monastic life was a surprise to his associates is substantiated by Crotus, who was at that time a member of the university and one of Martin's intimates.

[23] *WAB*, I, 543, ll. 106 ff.

awkward German versions then in existence, and to have read it with keen interest.[24] The strenuous demands of academic study probably prevented his going further with this reading, but they could not kill the yearnings that began to arise for security amid the fears of the future life. Echoes of this reverberate in so many recollections of Luther's from later days that they cannot be overlooked.[25] "It is true that this extreme fear was not unknown to me from boyhood," he says a quarter of a century later in comforting a friend beset with uncertainties regarding his soul's salvation.[26] He affirms with a passionate declaration, recorded ten years later both in the *Table Talk* and in a sermon, that he did not rush into the cloister for the sake of his "belly" but in order to earn the gratitude of God by the fearful martyrdom of the monastic life.[27]

If we could lift the veil that shrouds the facts of these years we should certainly find a student of fiery energy and one possessed by an ardor for the spiritual side of life. Fellow students saw in him something unusual. At least one prophecy of future greatness clung to his memory from these university days.[28] We should also note that merry outbursts of youthful spirits made gay with the music of the lute alternated with fits of depression. In the vigorous and successful young man somber moods began to make their appearance, and fierce attacks of doubt regarding the future life beset him with the sinister forebodings that often come to natures

[24] A well-authenticated passage in the *Table Talk* reports that he got hold of a Bible and read the story of Samuel as a boy: "puer aliquando incidit in bibliam." *TR*, I, No. 116. A less well-authenticated statement says he found the Bible in the university library at Erfurt. *TR*, V, No. 5346. The latter statement is supported by Mathesius, *Das Leben Luthers*, pp. 2 f. A third passage in the *Table Talk* says that he discovered the Bible in his twenty-first year. *TR*, III, No. 3767, p. 598, ll. 9 ff. The question as to whether Martin's first acquaintance with the Bible as a whole came in school days or undergraduate years has been debated at length by Scheel, *Martin Luther*, I, 89 ff., and Kroker, *TR*, V, xiv ff. The testimony is conflicting. The strongest evidence for Martin's acquaintance with the Bible, far exceeding the selections in the postils, in the years before his entrance into the cloister, is his facility in citation throughout all periods of his life.

[25] It is quite impossible to unscramble satisfactorily memories of college days and those of early cloister life in the sources. Items of evidence for insecurity of soul at the university are individually not convincing: e.g., the often quoted passage in a *Sermon on Holy Baptism* (1534), *WA*, XXXVII, 661 (see also, *ibid.*, p. 274), where Martin refers to fears that drove him into the cloister (the text appears to be muddled; see Scheel, *Martin Luther*, I, 296, n. 8); the statement, *TR*, III, No. 3593, that doubts assailed him as a master of arts which reading the Bible did not alleviate; or such *disjecta membra* of experience as that quoted in Köstlin, *Martin Luther*, I, 48. Nevertheless, taken together with Martin's later development, these fragmentary recollections, despite chronological uncertainties, point conclusively to an intense emotional agitation in the later university years, in which fear played an important part.

[26] Letter to Gerhard Viscampius, Jan. 1, 1528, *WAB*, IV, 319.

[27] *TR*, IV, No. 4414 (1539); see also *WA*, XLIV, 782.

[28] *TR*, I, No. 223 (1532), ascribes the prophecy to the father of a fellow student; Mathesius, *Das Leben Luthers*, p. 3, credits it to an old priest.

such as his in the early twenties. Outer events familiar to the experience of the later Middle Ages deepened these fears. One of these nearly cost him his life. When Martin was a short distance out of Erfurt on his way to Mansfeld for the spring holidays in the company of a friend, he accidentally thrust his sword deep into his leg, severing an artery. He stopped the bleeding with his finger, but the leg swelled frightfully until a surgeon could be brought from the city. In his mortal anxiety the young man called on the Virgin for help and repeated the cry to the merciful Mother when the wound broke out again in the night.[29] The terror of sudden death which might bring him unshriven before the great Judge hung over him as it did and does over many a pious Catholic. Just as he was beginning his law studies, death entered his own immediate circle. A candidate for the bachelor's degree died, and a few weeks later the same fate befell one of Martin's fellow candidates for the master's degree.[30] About the same time a grim visitor came to the city and began to demand victims. It was probably the same form of typhus that ravaged German towns again and again in those unsanitary days; and it raged with fury among Erfurt's population the summer through.

Thus beset by fears and drawn hither and thither by conflicting urges, the young law student was ready for the spark which set off his overcharged emotions. In the latter part of June he made a visit to his home in Mansfeld. When he was returning to Erfurt a violent thunderstorm swept over him as he approached the city. The day was July 2, the Feast of the Virgin, and the traveler was not far from the village of Stotternheim when a terrific bolt of lightning darted past with a blinding flash and threw him to the ground. In his mortal anxiety he cried to the patron and protector whose name had been on his lips so often in childhood in the copper fields: "Dear St. Anne, I will become a monk!" [31]

The vow was made. It had been wrung from him by the terror of the moment and "in the agony of death." As the cloister years went by and his attitude regarding the Church and the spiritual orders underwent a revolution, the memory of those fears took possession of him to the exclusion of other memories and motives, and he declared repeatedly that he

[29] *TR*, I, No. 119; the event was probably early in his studies for the master's degree, possibly 1503; see Georg Buchwald, "Luther-Kalendarium," *SVRG*, XLVII, II (1929), 1.

[30] Oergel, *Vom jungen Luther*, pp. 34 ff., gives the names from the matriculation book of the Erfurt faculty of philosophy. The master's candidate is probably the case referred to by Melanchthon, *CR*, VI, 158.

[31] The circumstances are most reliably documented by Crotus, who was probably in Erfurt at the time. Letter of Oct. 16, 1519, *WAB*, II, 543. Luther confirms the event on its thirty-fourth anniversary. *TR*, IV, No. 4707. See also Oergel, *Vom jungen Luther*, p. 27.

carried out the vow against his will [32] and that he later regretted the step.[33] This feeling, however, did not begin to find expression until fifteen years after the event, when he was deep in the struggle against the hierarchy and when his determined individualism had revolted against the whole monastic system. In various remarks recorded in the *Table Talk* and in recollections communicated to friends like Melanchthon and intimate biographers touching his entry into the cloister it was quite impossible for Martin to recapture the mystic urges that must have ruled the will in his early twenties.

Nevertheless, the decision was a hard one and he delayed the step for two weeks. He had only just left his home and doubtless brought with him a keen memory of the hopes and ambitions which Hans, himself rapidly rising in prosperity, cherished for his gifted son. But Martin was no pliable youth. He was now twenty-two years of age and schooled by his university studies to independence of judgment. He had a tough will which yielded obedience only to the powerful surge of conviction. A resolution born of many motives and strengthened through many experiences carried him finally to the cloister gates.[34]

The decision was a shock to his friends. What had been going on in the soul of their impulsive and gay companion was hidden from them. Indeed, the full bearing upon his future of the adventure on which he was entering was probably blotted out for Martin himself by the general impression of miraculous suddenness. Its effect on the student circle is booked even by Crotus, who fourteen years later refers to the "lightning from

---

[32] *De votis monasticis, WA*, VIII, 573; *TR*, I, No. 623; IV, No. 4414; see also *ibid.*, No. 4707, and II, No. 2286.

[33] *TR*, IV, No. 4707; *WA*, VIII, 574. Considerable discussion has taken place regarding the binding nature of Luther's vow. Contributions to this have been made by Hartmann Grisar, a Jesuit, in his *Martin Luthers Leben und sein Werk*, p. 35 (see also his detailed analysis of fact and fancy with regard to Luther's cloister life in his *Luther*, Vol. III, chap. 37); by A. V. Müller, at one time a member of the Augustinian Order, in his "Beweggründe und Umstände bei Luthers Eintritt ins Kloster," *ThStKr*, XC (1917), 496 ff., and more fully in his *Luthers Werdegang;* as well as by certain Lutheran writers such as E. Hirsch, in his "Luthers Eintritt ins Kloster," *ThStKr*, XCII (1919), 307 ff., and Scheel, in his *Martin Luther*. These exchanges do little to explain Martin's persistence in his decision to enter the monastic life. The fulfillment of the vow is certainly comprehensible on psychological grounds, aside from any feeling of divine sanction attached to it. On the basis of a natural sensitiveness to religious emotions a tension of mind had developed in Martin that must have led him to reflect on the cloister long and often as a solution for his troubles. Such an attitude of emotional tension, leading at times to sudden and surprising decisions for life, is not incompatible with successful studies and a cheerful, even gay demeanor, as anyone can testify who has had much experience with younger university students.

[34] All sources agree that the father's opposition to Martin's step was bitter and persistent. Martin recalls this many times: e.g., in 1521 in *De votis monasticis, WA*, VIII, 573 f.; in 1533 in *TR*, I, No. 623; No. 855, p. 421, ll. 11 f.; and No. 881. His recollection on this point is confirmed by the family biographers, one of whom, Melanchthon, knew Hans personally.

Heaven" that threw Martin to the earth as a "second Paul." The friends tried to dissuade him, but without result. The events which preceded the crucial moment stamped themselves indelibly on Martin's memory. In the evening before the day on which his decision was carried out, he turned over his books to the bookseller, retaining only the dramas of Plautus and Vergil, intimates of hours of a budding enthusiasm for "good letters." [35] Some of his best friends joined him in a farewell banquet.[36] We may believe the family biographer Ratzeberger, who says that there was merry music on that occasion [37] and we may even hope that a second one of these scribes reports accurately when he adds that modest and virtuous maidens and married women were present, for this was to be Martin's last opportunity for association with the other sex except in the confessional for many years to come.[38] The next day friends marched with him to the gate of the Augustinian cloister and with tearful faces watched the heavy gates close behind him. It was on the Feast of St. Alexis, July 17, 1505.[39]

The gate and the great enclosure into which it led were well known to Martin. The cloister buildings, shut off from the life of the world by a high wall, were near neighbors to the college where he had spent his undergraduate years. They formed a massive religious island about which the life of the students and burghers flowed and eddied. The splendid Gothic chapel of the cloister was one of the decorations of Erfurt, and at the time when Martin entered the brothers were engaged in extending the institution, putting up a structure to house refectory, library, and lecture room.[40] Beside the wide area, bounded by three streets, the cloister also owned a number of houses in the city and throughout the surrounding country up to the foot of the Harz Mountains and drew a considerable income from this productive property, which was derived from legacies and other gifts showered upon the order in the centuries preceding. Within the great building dwelt seventy or more brothers, not including the novices, supplying theological teachers to the university and preachers to the pulpits of the city.[41] The Eremites of St. Augustine belonged to the mendicant orders,

[35] *TR*, I, No. 116.　　　　　　　　　　[36] *TR*, IV, No. 4707.

[37] Ratzeberger, *Handschriftliche Geschichte*, p. 46.

[38] Tschackert, "Justus Jonas' Bericht," p. 579. Jonas says the feast was in the Porta Coeli College.

[39] *TR*, IV, No. 4707.　　　　　　　　　[40] Oergel, *Vom jungen Luther*, pp. 46 ff.

[41] Kalkoff, *Humanismus und Reformation in Erfurt*, pp. 16 f., n. 3, thinks this figure, estimated by Oergel, too high. See T. T. Neubauer's attempt at a census of all religious persons in Erfurt at this period in "Die sozialen und wirtschaftlichen Verhältnisse der Stadt Erfurt vor Beginn der Reformation," *Mitteilungen des Vereins für die Geschichte und Altertumskunde von Erfurt*, XXXIV (1913), 27 ff. See also his *Frühzeit*, p. 85.

which had been founded as the result of the great wave of monastic reform that had swept over the Church three centuries earlier. Following in
the footsteps of St. Francis of Assisi, these men turned away from the
practices of early monasticism, which cultivated the religious life mainly by
prayer, meditation, and study, and devoted themselves to social helpfulness: the ministration to the sick and suffering and the care of the souls
of the masses from the pulpit and in the confessional. Thus, in spite of their
growing wealth and increasing materialism, the mendicant orders had grown
up with the German artisan and shopkeeper and their development was
interwoven with that of the city classes, among whom their influence was
often stronger than that of the parish clergy.

Established in Erfurt in the thirteenth century, somewhat later than the
Dominicans and Franciscans, the Eremites of St. Augustine had forged
ahead of these older orders both in wealth and influence. This eminence
seems to have been the expression of an inner vigor. The cloister had a
reputation for learning which put it in the van of the religious orders in
Erfurt: [42] like the Dominicans and Franciscans, it had a "general study"
whose leaders were regular professors in the university. Its vitality expressed itself also in the way in which it participated in the renewal of
spiritual life in the Augustinian order and the return to a severer discipline.

About the time Martin received his bachelor's degree, the leader of this
spiritual movement among the Eremites, Andreas Proles, had died, a godly
and energetic man who, as head of the Saxon-Thuringian province of the
order, had finally succeeded in bringing together thirty cloisters of the
province into a more rigid observance of the rule of St. Augustine in 1477.
Proles's successor, Johann von Staupitz, who was later to play so decisive
a rôle in Martin's development, drew up new statutes which might serve
as a pattern for the conduct of the monastic life in its daily round of self-
denial and brotherly service. The local chapter seems to have fallen into
line with enthusiasm for full conformity with these high standards.[43]

---

[42] Oergel, *Vom jungen Luther*, pp. 54 ff. See also Theodor Kolde, "Das religiöse Leben in
Erfurt beim Ausgang des Mittelalters," *SVRG*, LXIII, 15 ff. Benary, *Zur Geschichte der Stadt
und Universität Erfurt*, Part III, pp. 69 ff., casts doubts on Kolde's deductions regarding the
distinction of the Augustinians among the Erfurt orders, and adduces the fact that no member
was rector of the university nor dean of the faculty of philosophy prior to the Reformation.
This is by no means a convincing argument. It does seem, however, that the chapter had
passed the peak of its spiritual development somewhat before Martin joined it.

[43] *Constitutiones Fratrum Heremitarum Sancti Augustini ad apostolicorum privilegiorum
formana pro reformatione Alemanie* (1504). Manuscript in the university library at Jena. A
fine controversy over the severity of the Staupitz code as compared with the older statutes of
the order developed between Müller (*Werdegang*, pp. 25 ff.) and Scheel (*Martin Luther*,
II, 599 ff.). The revisions of Staupitz seem to have proceeded from a rational attitude of reform

Such an attitude was characteristic of the great reformatory zeal that gripped a considerable part of the mendicant orders in the last half of the fifteenth century. It called for a return to the early practice of monasticism. The order which Martin entered felt this influence strongly; indeed, an especially militant spirit seems to have characterized the Reformed Congregations of the Augustinians in Germany. In Italy also similar elements in the order moved in step to break up the stagnation among the Augustinians of the peninsula. One of these energetic leaders was Egidio of Viterbo, who attained to the generalship of the entire order two years after Martin's entry. A glance at his record shows that the awakening had penetrated into the high command under a modern and enlightened spirit. Egidio had sat at the feet of Ficino, the Florentine Neoplatonist. He read Greek with ease, spoke Latin with elegance, and composed verses in both Latin and Italian. Well known as a Hebraist, he was on intimate terms with Johann Reuchlin and took his part in the famous controversy over the burning of Jewish books, for like Reuchlin he was assured that the Jewish cabala contained proofs of Christianity. In spite of his association with the Platonists he was an ardent propagandist of the Christian faith, which he defined in sermons of genuine pietism and in a genial tone, sharply contrasting with the fanaticism of Savonarola. He strove with energy to reimpose the older practice in Italy: the strict life in common within the cloister, the rotation of prayers and the regulations for silence and for restricted intercourse with the outside world, but apparently with little success. Egidio was a warm friend of Staupitz and worked hand in hand with him for reform.[44]

Such, then, was the great institution to which Martin turned with all the self-sacrifice and zeal of youth. He must have felt a natural affinity for the Augustinian Eremites. His boyhood associations, beginning with the Brethren of the Common Life in Magdeburg and continuing with the little group of Franciscans at Eisenach, had been with men who interpreted the service of God in terms of service to fellow man. Dominicans and Franciscans and Augustinians all had professors at the university at Erfurt, and their "general studies" were interlocked with its faculty of philosophy. Indeed, the path from the university into the cloister of the Eremites seems to have been well worn. More than one master of arts had traveled in it

---

rather than an excess of severity. No one can read these statutes today without an impression that their hard ascetic prescriptions were intended to be controlled by a spirit of sympathy and fraternal support.

[44] Böhmer, *Romfahrt*, pp. 37 ff., gives a sympathetic account, with sources, of this interesting churchman and humanist.

in the preceding generation and attained distinction in the order. Among them was Johann Jeuser von Paltz, whose activity at Erfurt overlapped Martin's early studies in the cloister. Jeuser had risen to guide the theological studies of the Eremites. At the same time he held a chair of theology at the university. Another master of arts, Johann Lang, who was to become Martin's most intimate friend in his crucial years as friar, had taken the vow only a short time before, and later on Martin's heart was rejoiced when his professor of philosophy in the faculty of arts, the warm-hearted Arnold von Usingen, at fifty years of age forsook the academic life and followed him into the cloister, where he became a doctor of theology.

Arnold's enrollment among the Eremites points to another influence which beckoned Martin and his university associates thither, one very forceful on late medieval students. Their cloister promised a more congenial environment for those who had been trained in the school of William of Occam. The Dominicans, traditional adherents of orthodoxy and later to become Martin's first and most persistent opponents, were inclined to follow the "ancient way" out of fealty to their distinguished leader, Thomas Aquinas. The Franciscans were drawn with something of the same feeling to the apostle of Franciscan theology, Duns Scotus. The other mendicant order, Servants of Mary, was a rather unimportant group in Erfurt and was not represented in the university faculty. The friars of St. Augustine were without mortgage to the older scholastic tradition and had produced a number of scholars in the "modern way" of theology.

6

THE NOVITIATE YEAR

"LORD Jesus Christ, our leader and our strength, Thou hast set aside this servant of Thine by the fire of holy humility from the rest of mankind. We humbly pray that this will also separate him from carnal intercourse and from the community of earthly deeds through the sanctity shed from heaven upon him and that Thou wilt bestow on him grace to remain Thine." [1] Thus closes the long prayer with which the prior of the Augustinian convent received Martin among the brothers gathered in the cloister chapel. How soon after his entry into the cell this solemn act of reception took place we do not know. The statutes of the order required that a new initiate should be presented to the prior and then take up his abode in the guest house of the cloister, within its walls but outside of the real convent. Here he must remain during a probationary period which might extend for some weeks.[2] This was necessary in order that the brothers might be convinced that his spirit was of God, a warning incorporated into the Rule of St. Bernard from the First Epistle of St. John (4.1). Here Martin's sincerity was to be tested—thoroughly tested, if we may believe one of the legends that float down to us in the work of a not very trustworthy

[1] The prayer follows the formula for receiving novices given in the statutes of the Augustinian Eremites. This is an important source and has been used by many Luther biographers to recreate the conditions of his cloister life. The statutes then prevailing in the Erfurt cloister had been adopted by the member-chapters of the Reformed Congregation in convocation at Nuremberg not long before Martin's reception. They are available in several manuscripts. References that follow are to that in the university library at Jena, *Constitutiones Fratrum Heremitarum Sancti Augustini*. The statutes also help to verify certain recollections recorded in Luther's *Table Talk*. Some further information regarding the background of cloister life at Erfurt in Luther's day has been assembled by investigators of this period, notably Oergel, Scheel, Neubauer, and Benrath. A. V. Müller's writings deserve especial attention because of his experience as an Augustinian. It must be emphasized that the cloister *Constitutiones*, like the university statutes, give only a dim idea of actual cloister practice, although the reputation of the Erfurt convent for rigid observance of the rules is well documented.

[2] Oergel, *Vom jungen Luther*, pp. 71 ff., evidently finds six to eight weeks not an unusual period.

sixteenth-century biographer, Nicolaus Selneccer, that Martin's friends beleaguered the gates of the cloister for two days in the hope of recovering him.[3] It is also possible that this period was used for conference with his father who, as we know, hotly opposed Martin's course.

When and how Hans Luther learned of his son's momentous decision is uncertain. If we may believe the reporter of one of his sermons, Martin still recalled only two years before his death that his father "almost went wild" and in an angry letter formally withdrew his parental favor,[4] a statement that is confirmed by the contemporary scribe Bavarus.[5] The young man, who had reached a decision of such importance for his life after a hard struggle with himself, now confronted an agonizing dilemma: whether to carry out a vow wrung from his storm-shocked conscience or to fulfill the duty of obedience to his parent. According to a tradition that descends from the Wittenberg circle and bears a certain stamp of probability, his scruples were swept away by an act of Providence. At midsummer the plague, which had already beset Erfurt in the preceding February, swept throughout Thuringia, carrying off three of the candidates for the baccalaureate and sending professors and students in wild flight from the city.[6] This dread destroyer found its way into the home of the Mansfeld miner, as the story goes, and carried off two of Martin's brothers. It was even reported that Martin himself lay dead. Friends of Hans came to the grief-stricken parent and showed him the hand of God in these events, and he then gave his consent to Martin's reception into the cloister.[7] How unwillingly he gave up his ambitious plans for the gifted son is shown by the fact that even the pride of hearing the young friar say his first Mass two years later did not wipe out his disappointment nor his doubts as to whether Martin had taken the right course.

Perhaps comforted by even this grudging permission, the young candidate was regularly received into the fold. He had convinced the heads of the cloister of his sincerity and was ready to enter upon the period of novitiate.

---

[3] Selneccer, *Vitam Divi Lutheri*, p. 18; see Oergel, *Vom jungen Luther*, p. 71. Selneccer adds that no one was permitted to see Martin for a month, until after his father arrived from Eisleben.

[4] Second Sunday after Epiphany (January 20, 1544), *WA*, XLIX, 322.

[5] *Rhapsodiae*, II, 752 f. See Oergel, *Vom jungen Luther*, pp. 72 f.

[6] Probably due to the panic, the graduation ceremonies were advanced from Michaelmas to August 24. *Ibid.*, pp. 40 f. Eobanus Hessus recorded the exciting episode in his poem, *De recessu studentum* (1506).

[7] The story is told by Bavarus, *Rhapsodiae*, II, 752 ff. See Oergel, *Vom jungen Luther*, pp. 72 f. His statement that Hans visited Erfurt at this time and reminded Martin of the Fifth Commandment is quite likely to be true, even though Martin reports this admonition as made at the celebration of his first Mass. *WA*, VIII, 573 ff. See also below, p. 102, n. 57.

The formal step was taken in all probability toward the end of September.[8] After a general confession of his sins to the prior, the ceremony took place in the chapel.[9] Before the assembled convent he prostrated himself on the steps of the altar and listened as the prior recited the hardships of the life that lay before him: the surrender of his will, the meager fare, the coarse clothing, the watching by night and labor by day, the merciless chastisement of the flesh, the disgrace of poverty and the shame of begging, the weakness from fasting, the hateful exclusion from the world, all the self-destroying discipline that the life for God demands of those who follow the monastic rule. Declaring that he was prepared to do this with God's help so far as human weakness permitted, Martin bowed his head while the tonsure was shorn and then let himself be clad in the cowl and hood of the friar, beneath them the white scapulary that encircled his neck and was to be worn henceforth day and night as a perpetual emblem of the yoke of Christ.[10] Meanwhile the prior and brothers intoned a solemn liturgy. The ritual closed with hymn and prayer as the young novice lay before the high altar with arms stretched in the form of a cross.

A new life now opened before him and a test of the sincerity of his resolution began immediately. From the chapel he was led to his cell, in all probability the one still shown to visitors. Although the old cloister buildings at Erfurt were swept by fire in 1872, they still make it possible to recapture something of the loneliness and the hardships that surrounded the life of the young novice.[11] His cell was a tiny room, six feet by nine, bare of all except the most necessary furniture and unheated throughout the long North German winter, its one window looking out upon the arcade where the brothers found their last resting place. Only his name might remain the same. He did not need to lay it aside as many did on entering a religious life, for it was consecrated by the great father of Western monasticism, St. Martin of Tours.[12]

"Not he who begins but he who endures to the end will be saved." With

---

[8] Oergel, *Vom jungen Luther*, p. 73, suggests the second half of September, without, to be sure, very convincing reasons.

[9] *Constitutiones*, para. 15. See also Neubauer, *Frühzeit*, pp. 99 ff.

[10] Luther recalls in a sermon late in life that he could not lay aside the scapulary for a single moment. *EA*, XLIV, 347.

[11] See Biereye, *Die Erfurter Lutherstätten*. Oergel, *Vom jungen Luther*, pp. 87 f., thinks a cell was not assigned to Martin until after the "profession" that concluded the novitiate period. See, however, Scheel, *Martin Luther*, I, 301, n. 103.

[12] The statement in the lectures on Genesis that he received the name Augustinus is probably due to a scribe's error. Oergel, *Vom jungen Luther*, pp. 75 ff. If he received it, he did not use it in any source we have. He did at times during his friarhood sign himself "Augustinus," i.e., "the Augustinian," but ceased to do so after 1521.

these final words the prior put the young man in the care of the master of novices.[13] It was the duty of this older brother to initiate him into the rules covering the routine of life in common: the liturgical exercises and the personal bearing of a young religious. First of all he must learn by heart the Rule of St. Augustine and the main part of the statutes of the Eremites of St. Augustine, a code of fifty-one paragraphs that provided a system of iron discipline for controlling all the details of cloister life. These statutes had been drawn up by the general vicar of the order, Johann von Staupitz, and adopted by the cloisters of the Reformed Congregation not long before Martin's reception. The new statutes superseded an ancient code which had governed the Augustinian friars for more than two centuries and had been based on rules for the ascetic life growing out of a thousand years of monastic experience. Staupitz's revision reflects somewhat the severe spirit of the reform movement, but it certainly was written with no Draconian pen. Indeed, the body of rules under which Martin was to live for many years seems to the modern reader to be marked by a spirit of brotherly love and sympathetic understanding.[14]

Under this code Martin now took up the daily round of a young novice. He might not speak in choir, cell, or common work room; and it was a first duty to learn the language of gestures, which monastic experience had brought to the point where it took care of all the needs of intercourse. Until he had mastered this he might communicate in whispers, but for the most part the rules sealed his lips.[15] But if his lips were closed, his heart was to be opened wide to his superiors. He must confess at least once a week, laying bare every infraction of the cloister routine for reproof and penalty.[16] On Friday he assembled with the chapter to hear public confession by those guilty of breaches in the rules of the order.

Such was the life of renunciation and self-humiliation to which he was introduced. In the foreground of it all was the daily round of services in the chapel.[17] Soon after midnight the matins bell called the novice from

---

[13] *Const.*, para. 15.

[14] The relation between the Staupitz code and its predecessor, the old *Constitutiones* of the Augustinians, has been debated by Müller, *Werdegang*, pp. 25 ff., and Scheel, *Martin Luther*, II, 599 ff., without particularly enlightening results. The relative liberality of the two instruments respecting dispensations from certain ascetic requirements is a less significant question than that of the spirit in which the rules were enforced, for any real cloister reform depended less on statutes than on the attitude of the vicar and the prior and elder friars of individual chapters. Among the seven chapters of the Saxon Reformed Congregation, Erfurt seems to have enjoyed a good reputation for conformity.

[15] *Const.*, para. 17. See also paras. 11 and 48.   [16] *Ibid.*, para. 8.

[17] The Rule of St. Benedict sets the eighth hour for the awakening to the service of "vigils," about two o'clock. Sources for our knowledge of the cloister services are the so-called *Ordi-*

his slumber and the cloister day began. It was the duty of the master of novices to see that the sound sleep of youth did not hold him from his place in the procession that wound through the dark corridors toward the chapel,[18] that he did not fail to bow his knee and murmur a prayer when he passed before the altar and took his place in the choir, and that he joined properly in hymn and prayer and versicles. After the long matin service came the Lauds. This concluded the first of the seven "canonical hours" that summoned the cloister to prayer and praise throughout the day. Between matins and the dawn-service the brother might rest in his cell or use the silence of the night for study. At six the convent bell sounded for Prime, followed by the daily Mass;[19] at nine came Tierce; and at twelve Sext. Then the brothers, the prior at their head, marched to the refectory, where the young novice might break the fast which had lasted from the preceding evening. The ancient Rule of St. Benedict, which dominated all orders of strict observance, permitted only two meals a day. After an hour of rest the bell sounded for Nones, followed by the long vesper service. At six the cloister fraternity proceeded to their evening meal; then Compline, the final service, brought the end of the day of choral worship and permitted the novice to seek his bed of straw.

This was the round to which Martin now had to adapt himself. His severe training as a schoolboy must have made him a ready pupil for the liturgical services, and the hardships of life in the late medieval school and university had prepared him for the discipline of the convent. Nevertheless, the physical and mental burden of it lay heavy on the novice. Special services in choir and chapter-house were added to the demands of the canonical hours on certain saints' days and other holy days. Mass was said each Monday for departed members of the order. On Friday after Matins the brothers passed to the chapter-house for a penitential service. Here under flickering candles they prostrated themselves before the prior and made public confession of their sins. A few weeks after Martin's reception the festival of All Saints came around, opening the half-year of special services which was to last until Easter. Through Advent and Lent all religious activity was intensified and liturgical demands increased. The four to five hours of choral duty in the

---

narium of the Augustinian Eremites, prescribing the liturgical character of the several "canonical hours," the acts of the general chapters. See *Analecta Augustiniana*, the Nuremberg *Constitutiones*, and, of course, the Rule of St. Augustine. Scheel's reconstruction of Luther's day on the basis of the foregoing has been of help in my discussion. *Martin Luther*, II, 29 ff.

[18] *Const.*, para. 17.

[19] At certain times, notably in the Lenten season, Mass was statutory twice in the day. Scheel, *Martin Luther*, II, 41, and n. 4.

summer half-year were now extended, while the increased requirements of abstinence from customary food and fasting from all food must at times have made even the most devoted brothers feel that the days between Ash Wednesday and Easter dragged past with leaden feet.

The life on which Martin had entered was not a school for merely passive virtues. The psychology which the Augustinians applied for training the individual will to come to heel was the result of centuries of experience with human nature. The hours of service in the choir, where every slip in hymn or response or genuflection counted as a "fault" which must be atoned by a gesture of contrition and, if serious, by oral confession, called for unremitting attention on the part of the novice and absorbed his youthful energies. The memorizing of the rule and the statutes, the coaching by the master of novices made further demands. The ban on speaking, which was absolute for choir, cell, and refectory and might be broken only in emergency between the hours of Compline and Prime, forced the mind to turn inward and took away the stimulus to thoughts of the outer world that comes from conversation.

Thus while Martin's energies were fully occupied and routined, the outlets to the world were barred. His thoughts were given no leisure to run at large. At the silent table, when material desires might besiege the mind, an escape was provided through listening to the lector, who read from the lives of the saints and martyrs, particularly from the life and work of the great patron of the order, Augustine; from the rule and the statutes, and their interpretation. Virile energies were tamed by the program of abstinence and fasting which belonged to the cloister discipline.[20] Two meals a day can have been no great hardship for Martin, inured as he was to the somewhat Spartan life of the *bursa;* but the night vigils and the many services and studies until noon must have made the morning fast a real introduction to the ascetic life. Meatless days, of which there were two, perhaps three in the week, would not have made the refectory table less inviting than that of many middle-class households in late medieval Germany, especially as fish was admitted as a substitute; but in the season of religious festivals the demands for

[20] The *Constitutiones* adopted at Nuremberg give brief and general rules for abstinence and fasting, para. 20. The subject, which is important for Luther's early adaptation to cloister life, has been treated by Kolde, *Augustiner-Kongregation;* Müller, *Werdegang;* and Scheel, *Martin Luther,* II, 48 ff. and 610. The latter discusses at length the practices of the Eremites in respect to abstinence and fasting in the light of the older statutes of the order, those adopted at Regensburg in the thirteenth century and superseded for the Observant cloisters by Staupitz's code of 1504, and the *Vitae fratrum* of Jordanis of Saxony. It is impossible to say categorically what were the requirements at the Erfurt cloister at the time of Luther's entry, but its reputation for severity, confirmed by Luther himself, justifies the view that the Augustinian rules and practice were given a strict interpretation.

self-denial became much more severe. During Advent and Lent only one meal might be eaten—in the early afternoon—without meat, eggs or dairy products, supplemented by a ration of dry bread and wine in the evening.[21] Fasting did not extend to wine at any season; even brothers on leave outside the cloister, who were still bound by certain rules of abstinence, might drink wine.[22]

Like the university regulations, the statutes of the Eremites and the other acts and regulations of its general and provincial conventions give a cold and somewhat repellent picture. This would certainly be warmed into a more genial reality if we could see Martin as a companion of other eager novices amid older brothers, who were themselves subject to human frailties and whose hearts were certainly in many cases sympathetic with a beginner. In all the years of his struggle with the Church there is no evidence that Martin ever complained of ill treatment by the cloister brothers, though the many scribes who put down his recollections in the *Table Talk* and his lectures were more than willing to report strictures on monastic life in general. On the other hand, there are evidences that he carried through life a feeling of strong attachment and gratitude to certain of his associates among the Erfurt Eremites.

One of these was the master of novices. It was the duty of this official to instruct him in the rules of the order, and so far as possible to make the stony path of ascetic discipline into a road to peace of mind. Day by day he searched the soul of the young man and the memory of the sympathetic understanding of the "fine old man" clung to Martin long after he had turned with bitterness against all monkery.[23] A "true Christian," [24] as Luther called him years later, this preceptor seems to have played a fatherly rôle in the young man's life through the probationary months and afterwards in the restless days when the friar discovered that the cloister did not bring the contentment he had hoped for. It may have been that he also rejoiced Martin's heart by the gift of a copy of an ancient disputation in defense of the Trinity ascribed to Athanasius,[25] which the older brother had copied with

---

[21] Müller tends to emphasize the rigidity of fasting practice in the Erfurt cloister, *Werdegang*, pp. 30 f., while Scheel, *Martin Luther*, II, 48 ff., esp. p. 56, shows on the basis of extensive evidence from Augustinian regulations of the late fifteenth century that the humble evening refreshment was authorized. See also *Analecta Augustiniana*, VII, 346. Whether this was permitted at Erfurt is of course uncertain.

[22] *Const.*, para. 20.

[23] Letter from Luther to Elector John Frederick, June 10, 1540, *WAB*, IX, 133.

[24] Luther's Introduction to Athanasius' *Libri contra idolatriam gentium et de fide sanctae trinitatis* (1532), *WA*, XXX, III, 530.

[25] According to Enders, *Luthers Briefwechsel*, IX, 253, and n. 1, the author of the work to which Luther refers, *Dialogi III s. altercationes ab Athanasio contra Arium*, was Bishop Vigilius of Thapsus. See also *WA*, XXX, III, 530 f.

his own hand. On another occasion he shook the young novice out of a mood of despair with the question: "Don't you know that the Lord himself bids us hope?" [26] Perhaps in a similar moment of soul agony it was again the master of novices who urged Martin not to take the words of the creed, "I believe in the forgiveness of sins," too generally but to apply them to his own case.[27]

A man like this would surely have encouraged the novice to read the Bible. We have seen that Martin must already have had a copy of it in hand as a university student. The earliest statutes of the German Augustinians, dating from the thirteenth century, had expressly commanded that it should be "read eagerly, heard devoutly, and learned zealously," [28] and nothing regarding the history of the Erfurt cloister is better attested than the opportunity of a young friar to become acquainted with the Scriptures. Martin recalled that the cloister brothers gave him a copy, perhaps at his own request. The impression was a vivid one, for he remembered many years later that the book had a red cover. He plunged into the study of it with such zeal that he claimed afterwards that he was able to turn up the page and exact location of any verse from purely mechanical memory.[29] The enthusiasm that drove him to read and reread the Bible in those days, aided by a memory highly trained through the discipline of an age still so poor in books, gave him later on the extraordinary command of the Bible text which flows constantly into his lectures, sermons, and other writings. His statement that he knew the Psalms by heart is scarcely an exaggeration.

Legend has been woven thickly about Martin's early experiences with the Augustinian friars. How did he bear the burden of his first contact with

---

[26] *WA*, XL, ii, 412.   [27] Melanchthon, *CR*, VI, 156.

[28] Oergel, *Vom jungen Luther*, p. 82; Scheel, *Martin Luther*, II (1917), 336, n. 6.

[29] *TR*, I, No. 116, records merely that the brothers gave him a copy; *ibid.*, V, No. 5346, says that on his entry into the cloister he demanded the Bible and the brothers gave him one but took it away after his "profession" and gave him sophistical books instead. This remark belongs to a group of thirty-four passages in the *Table Talk* noted down by Rörer. Their reliability has been attacked by Scheel, *Martin Luther*, I, 91, and II, 601 ff., and defended by Kroker, *TR*, V, xiv ff., who seems in this case to have the best of the lively argument. There is certainly no contradiction in the two passages from the *Table Talk* just cited. The statement, *TR*, II, No. 1552, that, like Carlstadt, no doctor of theology in the first decade of the century owned a Bible and that it was astonishing when one was found ("ubi una erat, ibi erat monasterium" [probably an error for "monstrum"]), is not necessarily out of line with the other statements cited. The facts regarding the general accessibility of the Bible to the clergy and also the intelligent laity at the end of the Middle Ages are now so well known as to be out of the range of polemical dispute. See Reu, *Luther's German Bible*, pp. 8 ff., for a detailed statement of the opportunities available about the beginning of the sixteenth century in the form of Latin editions and German translations of the Scriptures, editions of the Psalms, pericopes of the Epistles and Gospels, and interpretative works, such as Bible concordances and dictionaries.

the ascetic life: its endless succession of choral exercises, its daily quota of private devotions from the breviary, its hymns and versicles, its lections and responses and orisons, many of which must have been already familiar to the former scholar of the trivial school, its unrelenting round of processions to choir and refectory, its ban on speech and laughter so natural to the healthy spirit of youth? In later years he looked back on his novitiate as a time when he was aflame with zeal; and as we shall see, he never ceased to view the early period of his cloister life as one of conscientious and even fanatical observance of all the rules. Nevertheless, the disciplining of so vigorous and combative a personality must have been a severe struggle both for the brothers and for Martin. In view of the characteristics he showed in later years we cannot wave aside the rumor reported by a contemporary, Johann Cochlaeus—to be sure a determined opponent in the later years of bitter strife—that at this early period the friars found that a conciliatory spirit was altogether lacking from his arguments and that he was "bold and violent in contradiction." [30] The readiness in giving expression to his opinions with vehemence and the impatience of opposition which he carried with him down to old age must have caused difficulties to the master of novices and his colleagues when they took the young graduate in hand. The well-tried school of discipline for a freshman in any organization is to put him to work at the humblest task. The friars seem to have applied this to Martin and set him at the dirtiest of duties, including cleaning the latrine.[31]

All of this Martin accepted as a part of the life which he had chosen. Living as he had for so many years in close neighborhood to the monastic life, he knew well its hardships before he entered the cloister. As a novice he was still free to withdraw at any time,[32] but such a retreat was far from his thoughts and he faced the tasks before him with fervid self-abnegation, even though his impulsive temperament may have found the discipline hard. Harder still must have been the rigid subjection to men who were his intellectual inferiors and even, in some cases, quite illiterate. In addition to menial tasks in the cloister, he had to beg alms with the "sack on his back."

---

[30] "Nusquam satis pacifice nixisse." *Ad semper victricem Germaniam paraklesis* (1524), fol. C2b. (Note that this work was not available to the writer for rechecking.) Further: "acer ingenio et ad contradicendum audax et vehemens." *Commentaria de actis et scriptis Martini Lutheri chronographice ex ordine ab anno Domini MDXVII usque ad annum MDXLVI inclusive fideliter conscripta* (Mainz, 1549), p. 2. See also "Chronik des Johan Oldecop," *Bibliothek des Litterarischen Vereins in Stuttgart*, CXC, 17 and 28.

[31] *TR*, V. No. 5375, again from a record of questionable reliability; but the passage is supported by Johann Mathesius, "Luthers Leben in Predigten," *Ausgewählte Werke* (1906), III, 20 f.

[32] *Const.*, para. 18.

The purpose of all this was certainly ascetic training rather than any advantage to the cloister. The Eremites of Erfurt had two classes of members. The lay brothers, who need not be able to read and write, conformed to the monastic vows and wore the garb of the order but were limited in their liturgical duty to the recital of memorized prayers. They did the lowly work of the cloister.

The other was the clerical class, and to this Martin belonged.[33] This might be regarded as the lowest grade of the priesthood. Its time was, as we have seen, filled with the duties of the choir, with private devotions, and study. Furthermore, the Erfurt cloister was well provided with gifts and endowments, so that the begging of bread required by statute of the mendicant orders was at this time rather a training in humility and the maintenance of a pious tradition than a necessity for support of the establishment. The collecting of alms and ministering at outside towns and villages, the "terminating" that played so large a part in the earlier life of the Augustinians as well as the other orders must have become irregular at this time, for the stations of the Erfurt establishment were all practically closed to this activity when Martin made the vows.[34] Nevertheless, bearing the beggar's sack was undoubtedly also a part of Martin's early discipline. Since the Magdeburg schooldays the figure of the pallid monk bowed under his heavy sack had been familiar to him. Now he himself, a brilliant graduate of the university, carried the same load through the familiar quarter, meeting former associates and teachers. In later years he looked back with resentment and contempt on the hostility to learning of those who put such hindrances in the way of young friars of intellectual promise: "If that brother studies, he will rule over us . . . and so a sack to his back!"[35] As the years of cloister life went by, the strong individualism that is such a striking characteristic of the great men of the Renaissance asserted itself in Martin, and he resented deeply the iron mold into which medieval practice tried to force all men: "It is an idle effort on the part of the monks to fit a shoe of one shape to all feet,"[36] and he quoted against them his favorite Augustine: "Not alike to all because ye have not all the same strength."[37] However, in those early days in the cloister he probably gloried in the rigid democracy of monastic

---

[33] The instruction which the master of novices gave him in his first year implies that he was already regarded as of the clerical order. *WA*, XXX, III, 530 ff.; also De Wette, *Dr. Martin Luthers Briefe*, IV, 427.

[34] Oergel, *Vom jungen Luther*, p. 52.

[35] *TR*, III, No. 3737, p. 580, ll. 6 f.; V, Nos. 5375 and 6039.

[36] *In primum librum Mose enarrationes*, *WA*, XLII, 641, ll. 1 f.

[37] *WA*, XLIII, 641, ll. 25 f. See also *WA*, XLIV, 705, ll. 35 f.

life and in its other humiliations and sacrifices as many later utterances by him attest.

The prior and the master of novices must have found his conduct fully satisfying, for when the period of probation was concluded he was received into the permanent ranks of the order. It is indeed possible that in view of his ready adaptation to the spirit of the order and his promise as a scholar the usual year of trial was somewhat shortened.[38] In any event this decisive step was taken by the end of the summer of 1506. The rites that marked it were even more impressive than those of the reception. On his knees before the assembled convent, he heard the words: "Now you have to choose one of two ways—either part from us, or renounce this world and consecrate and devote yourself entirely to God and our order." [39] When he had declared that he was ready to make this sacrifice of his own will for all time, he was clothed in the gray habit of the brothers, while prayers and hymns arose around him. Then, on his knees before the prior with his hand upon the statutes of the order, he swore the irrevocable oath: "I, Brother Martin, do make profession and promise obedience to Almighty God, to Mary the Sacred Virgin, and to you, the prior of this cloister as representative of the general head of the order of Eremites of the holy bishop of St. Augustine and his rightful successors, to live until death without worldly possessions and in chastity according to the rule of St. Augustine." The brothers filed in solemn procession into the choir, where the young initiate, kneeling before the altar with the consecrated candle in his hand, heard the prior make a final prayer imploring each of the Holy Trinity to aid the newly sworn to fulfill his oath with genuine humility and obedience.

"I received congratulations . . . from the prior, convent, and father confessor that I was now like an innocent child who had just come forth pure from baptism." [40] Thus Luther recalled many years later the words spoken to him as the brothers crowded around to give him the fraternal kiss. When he wrote this, he was, to be sure, far removed from the mood of that eventful day and could see it only through the dust of a fierce polemical struggle. Catholic theologians can find in the authorities on Church doctrine of that

---

[38] A. V. Müller suggests this possibility, basing it on an analysis of the course of Martin's studies for the priesthood, whose beginnings Müller advances to the spring of 1506. See *Werdegang*, pp. 37 ff., and "Nochmals Luthers Eintritt ins Kloster," *ThStKr*, XCIII (1921), 284. He would set the "profession" as early as the end of 1505. Oergel, *Vom jungen Luther*, p. 84, puts it at the middle of September, 1506, which implies the full year of novitiate. Scheel, *Martin Luther*, II, 611 stoutly waves aside any shortening of Luther's novitiate year. Such a shortening was, however, permissible under the Nuremberg *Constitutiones*, paras. 15 and 16.

[39] *Const.*, para. 18.

[40] *Kleine Antwort auf Herzog Georgen nächstes Buch* (1533), *WA*, XXXVIII, 147.

time no such implication in the monastic vow as that which Martin recalls. Yet the brothers, in congratulating him, may well have used words such as these, in which the proud self-consciousness of the order formulated its conception of its mission and privileges.[41]

[41] Luther's first charge that the "monastic baptism" was regarded as having the same purifying character as Holy Baptism is found many years earlier than the polemic cited. It occurs in *De captivitate babylonica* (1520), *WA*, VI, 539, and is reiterated in *De votis monasticis* (1521), *WA*, VIII, 596. See also the sermon of January 15, 1531, *WA*, XXXIV, 1, 92. A bitter discussion of this point was initiated by Denifle in *Luthertum* (1904), I, 223 ff., where he demonstrates rather conclusively that no such conception was to be found in theories of regeneration and forgiveness of sins set forth by any ecclesiastical writer of authority. Scheel, *Martin Luther*, II, 65, has shown, however, that at least one important Augustinian teacher, Johann Jeuser von Paltz, who was still living in the Erfurt cloister at the time of Martin's profession, did declare that entrance into the order and taking the oath was the same as coming from baptism. We are concerned here of course only with the reliability of Luther's recollections as indications of his feelings at the time of the profession. There is further confirmation of his attitude in the *Table Talk*, where he comments on the monks' view that profession was a new baptism. *TR*, IV, No. 3973, p. 48, ll. 17 ff.; VI, No. 6762, p. 171, ll. 28 ff. (from the Aurifaber collection, which is of questionable reliability). The statement occurs repeatedly in the sermons and works of the last decade of his life, e.g., *Auslegung des 3. und 4. Kapitels Johannis* (1539), *WA*, XLVII, 146; *Wider Hans Worst* (1541), *WA*, LI, 487.

7

BROTHER MARTIN OF
THE EREMITES

When the day of the "profession" was past and the young friar returned
from the evening service in the choir to throw himself on his bed of straw
in his cell, his heart must have been warm with pride and assurance. For
the moment, at least, the fears for salvation and the inner turmoil that
had driven him into the cloister were stilled. The congratulations of the
prior and the kiss of the brothers had sealed his entrance into a life where
the way to salvation was guarded by the most powerful sanctions of tradition. To win the grace of God had now become the goal and the profession
of his life.

The future seemed to lie clear before him. Until he should join the
brothers whose graves lay across from the window of his cell he must
endure hardship in the struggle against original sin which, in spite of
baptism and saving grace, still nestled down in the secret places of the
heart, and he must confront the temptations of the flesh and the wiles of
the devil. Nevertheless, he was now armed with sharper weapons than those
Christians who lived outside cloister walls.[1] These weapons he sought to

[1] The medieval conception of the peculiar character of piety attainable by the monk in comparison with that of the layman has been a subject of active discussion ever since the appearance
of Denifle's *Luthertum*. Catholic apologists contend that authoritative ideas in the Church
assured those who entered the cloister nothing essential toward the fulfillment of God's demands
that was not available also to every Christian outside; although obviously the superior opportunities of the monastic life for worship, self-denial, prayer, and meditation create a condition
more favorable to fulfillment. See Denifle, *Luthertum* (1904), *passim;* also N. Paulus, "Zu
Luthers Schrift über das Mönchsgelübde," *Historisches Jahrbuch,* XXVII (1906), 487 ff. Lutheran apologists, on the other hand, tend to stress ideas prevailing widely in clerical and lay
circles of the later Middle Ages that those who made the sacrifices demanded by the monastic
life and withdrew from the world might attain a qualitatively superior degree of perfection
than was possible for the best Christian in the world outside. See Scheel, ed., *Luthers Werke,*
Ergänzungsband II, 36 f., 45 ff., 90 ff.; Scheel, *Martin Luther,* II, 188 ff.; also Müller, *Luthers
theologische Quellen;* Holl, *Gesammelte Aufsätze zur Kirchengeschichte,* I, III, 16 ff. Luther's
views on this point are documented in his writings and in reports from him that belong to

use with all the energy of an ardent temperament. In later years he often spoke and wrote of the constant exercises by which he tried to appease a God of vengeance through mortification of the flesh. It is not safe, of course, to take his words at face value. In addition to expressing the natural tendency of middle age to exaggerate the hardships of youth, these remarks must be judged as those of a man suffering from the results of a sedentary life that had been filled with unremitting labors and nervous strain. In his eyes, the whole monkish order had become a religious crime. When he looked back at his experiences, he felt that as a friar he had lived in a world of delusion. "In the cloister I lost both the salvation of my soul and the health of my body," he declares, according to a scribe who took down one of his sermons in 1531,[2] and the same complaint echoes through sermons and lectures of the following years. He dwells on the rigors of his life and the zeal of his prayers. If he had not fasted so strenuously he would be a sounder man:[3] once for three whole days he did not touch a drop of liquid or a morsel of bread.[4] He was sure he had exceeded others in fasting:[5] "If I could have gotten to heaven by fasting I would have been there twenty years ago," he stated in 1532.[6] Everybody had wondered at the way he could stand cold and hunger.[7] He weakened himself so with prayer and fasting that he would not have lasted much longer had he stayed in the monastery:[8] the cold alone would have sufficed to kill him.[9] Recollections of this sort were caught up eagerly by the younger scribes who took down his sermons and lectures and *Table Talk* in the last decade of his life. With the approach of Martin's old age they rise to a crescendo of resentment and run through the whole list of ascetic experiences: disciplinary clothing, abstinence, fasting, exhausting liturgical exercises, fearful tormentings of the body, whatever the

---

the polemical period of his life, and they must be used with discretion. His attitude in the early cloister years was not dependent on fine-spun ideas of dogmatic authority but was derived from the current opinion of the value of monastic life prevailing among the laity and the brothers of his order. It can hardly be doubted that in his early years among the Eremites he felt that the monastic life gave especial assurance to those who fulfilled its vows, and he devoted himself with zeal to the sacrifices which they demanded.

[2] Aurifaber's transcript, Oct. 21, 1531, *WA*, XXXIII, 561.

[3] Sermon of Oct. 10, 1535, *WA*, XLI, 447; Sermon of Oct. 29, 1536, *ibid.*, p. 705.

[4] *TR*, IV, No. 4422 (1539).   [5] *Praelectio in psalmum xlv*, *WA*, XL, II, 574 (1532).

[6] *Ibid.*, p. 453. See also sermon of Oct. 22, 1536, *WA*, XLI, 702 f., and sermon on John 14, *WA*, XLV, 482 (1538).

[7] Sermon on Psalm 5, Jan. 17, 1535, *WA*, XLI, 15.

[8] Sermon on John 15, *WA*, XLV, 670 (1538). See also *Enarratio in Genesin*, *WA*, XLIV, 705 (1535); sermon of Nov. 29, 1545, *WA*, LI, 94 f.

[9] *WA*, XLV, 482. For citation of passages in Luther's works on this topic in chronological order, see Scheel, *Dokumente;* for a convenient collation of them, see Strohl, *L'Évolution religieuse de Luther*, pp. 78 ff.

conscientious and zealous monk can suffer from cloister discipline or self-imposed hardship.

Martin's tendency to exaggerate the hard experiences of youth was aided by the readiness for building legends on the part of amanuenses and other scribes who belonged to a generation ignorant of the usages of the old Church. Under the impulse of hero worship it was easy to dip the pen into lurid colors.[10] The urge to weave legends around the cloister experiences showed itself in Martin's opponents as well as his friends and with the former took on even more extravagant forms. Johann Cochlaeus, the Franciscan friar whose collision with Luther was one of the picturesque episodes of the struggle at Worms, relates in his *Commentary* published three years after Martin's death that once, during a reading of the Gospel passage in which Christ expels the devil from a deaf mute, the young monk fell suddenly in the choir, crying, " 'Tis not I! 'Tis not I!" Cochlaeus also repeats a statement of the cloister brothers that Martin had a secret devil with whom he was intimate.[11] Even stories like these cannot be neglected, as they throw light on the character of the friar. They indicate an emotional tension that might culminate in hysterical outbursts, and they strengthen the impression that fellow inmates of the cloister noted him as deviating from the normal type of monastic character. In an age so saturated with superstition, the belief that a dynamic personality of Martin's sort was subject to demoniacal passion was a natural habit of thought. Many years later a scribe reports that Luther recalled having visions of the devil during his cloister years; certain of these memories go back in all probability to Erfurt.[12] In later life Martin himself admitted that he had been marked as a peculiar man among the brothers,[13] some of whom he regarded as good and pious and ready for sacrifice.[14]

It is well to keep in mind, however, that usually only the mediocre are remembered as normal by their early associates. There is no reason to doubt that in the years of early monkhood Martin showed an eager zeal and gave himself up to the monastic life with all its demands. In the year following his

---

[10] Scheel, *Martin Luther*, II, 194 ff., discusses the exaggerations and interpolations of the early scribes and their effect on the Protestant tradition of Luther's martyrdom in the cloister. This analysis relieves Martin of much of the criticism that Denifle and Grisar directed against him.

[11] *Commentaria de actis et scriptis M. Lutheri . . .* , p. 2. The recollections gleaned by Cochlaeus evidently point back to the early Erfurt years. See also "Chronik des Johan Oldecop," *Bibliothek des Litterarischen Vereins*, CXC (1891), 18.

[12] *TR*, V, No. 5358a (1540). This text, from Rörer's MS, is not beyond question, as noted above, but it cannot be rejected altogether. See also *TR*, V, No. 5358b.

[13] *In epistolam ad Galatas commentarius* (1531), *WA*, XL, I, 134.

[14] *Wochenpredigt über Johannis VI–VIII* (1531), *WA*, XXXIII, 574 ff.

acceptance of the full burden of this life, when inviting friends to the celebration of his first Mass, he expressed himself with devout pride in the monastic profession and in the priestly office that he was about to assume. "I experienced in myself and in many others how tranquil Satan was wont to be in the first years of monkdom," he declared in the great revolutionary year of 1521.[15] Memories of the enthusiasm of these early days echo a decade later in the report of a Wittenberg lecture where the scribe has Martin tell of a certain shining pattern of holiness which hovered before his vision in those monastic days, that of a saint among the Eremites who lived on roots and cold water.[16] "If ever a monk could have got to heaven through monkhood, I wanted to do so. To that all the cloister comrades who knew me will testify." [17] That he had lived a pure life in his cloister days was a firm conviction that appears again and again in statements recorded by reporters in his mature years.[18]

The rules of the cloister were rigid, but the statutes of the Reformed Congregation which Martin memorized in his first year prescribed discretion in ascetic practice. From an early day monasticism in Catholic Europe was marked by a different spirit from that prevailing in the Near East and in Egypt, where the pillar saints and the anchorites of the desert practiced mortification of the body with truly Oriental fanaticism. The monks of the West had from the beginning looked upon the denial of the flesh as a means of checking the lusts of the body and not of killing the body itself.[19] Certain orders, to be sure, particularly the Carthusians, were noted for their rigid practices and some pathetic victims of this self-torture hobbled with weary limbs and pallid faces along the streets of Erfurt in Martin's cloister days.[20] But there were also ecclesiastical authorities of high standing, such as Jean Gerson, the famous chancellor of the University of Paris, who were resolute opponents of the idea that sin could be overcome by tormenting the body; and Martin knew of their arguments and warnings.[21] Nevertheless he flung himself earnestly into the religious life and carried it on under the lash

---

[15] *De votis monasticis, WA,* VIII, 660.

[16] *Ad Galatas commentarius* (1531), *WA,* XL, II, 103.

[17] *Kleine Antwort auf Herzog Georgen nächstes Buch* (1533), *WA,* XXXVIII, 143.

[18] *TR,* I, No. 518 (1533), p. 240, ll. 24 ff.; No. 121 (1531). See also *WA,* LVIII, I, 8 ff. for numerous examples.

[19] Denifle, *Luthertum* (1904), 361 ff. The rules of the Eremites warn directly against fasting to the point of injury to health. *Const.,* para. 22.

[20] See his recollection of their pallid faces (*Enarratio in Genesin* [1535], *WA,* XLII, 504), and that of a lame Carthusian who was obliged to use a crutch yet had no dispensation from the constant service in the choir (*Von den Konsiliis und Kirchen* [1539], *WA,* L, 612 f.). The Carthusians appear repeatedly as patterns of ascetic rigor in later lectures and *Table Talk.*

[21] *WA,* XLII, 504; see also *TR,* III, No. 3654.

of a sensitive conscience. To a character like Martin's there was always the urge to do more than the rules required and ever the haunting fear that some slip in the fulfillment of duty might bring mortal sin upon him.[22]

The life of the new brother was not without some distractions. In the spring of 1507 he took a trip to his old school town, Eisenach,[23] and at some time during the three cloister years before he left Erfurt for Wittenberg he visited the Thuringian city of Arnstadt.[24] He also made trips among the villages about Erfurt for begging and for clerical ministrations.[25] Even on such journeys he was bound by severe cloister regulations intended to safeguard the monks against any freedom of intercourse, especially with women. The master of novices instructed Martin that conversation with the other sex must be brief but kindly, otherwise a slip might be easy for both parties. The service of the mendicants to their order and to the community brought them into frequent contact with private homes, and their adventures play an important rôle in the erotic literature of the later Middle Ages. The authors of the regulations that bound the Augustinians were at pains to protect the reputation of the order and to safeguard the friars against temptations of the flesh. The constitution of the Eremites forbade the brothers to speak with a woman except by permission of the prior and in the presence of another brother; only with his mother and sisters might he converse out of hearing of others. On begging journeys exceptions might be made, but no long conversation was permitted; even when hearing confession, another brother must be present or near at hand.[26] In later years Martin insisted that he did his best to avoid even these official contacts with women, acting as confessor to none in Erfurt and to only three during his

---

[22] There seems to have been considerable difference of opinion at this period as to just what constituted a "mortal sin." A. V. Müller, *Luthers theologische Quellen*, pp. 46 f., calls attention to a commentary on the Augustine Rule, printed in Rome in 1482, which stamps as a *crimen* every omission of the Rule, even the carrying out of the Rule with less than the fullest observance (*minus bene*). In later years Luther has many bitter things to say about the classification of sins in the cloisters. He states that the monks, who were filled with pride, hatred, laziness, and all criminal desires, rated as deadly sins infractions like omitting to shave, forgetting to have a candle ready at Mass, or leaving the cell without the scapular, whereas whoring, adultery, and murder were simple sins. See *scholia* to the lectures on Isaiah (1534), *WA*, XXV, 197; also *WA*, XXXI, II, 177. These are obviously exaggerated statements. Nevertheless the ritualistic offenses were undoubtedly punished with severity and must have played an important rôle at the regular Friday "public confessions" of the Erfurt chapter. Particularly the insistence on wearing the scapular at all times stamped itself on Martin's mind. See the sermon on St. John, Aug. 12, 1531, *WA*, XXXIII, 435.

[23] Letter from Luther to Johann Braun, April 22, 1507, *WAB*, I, 11, l. 23.

[24] For the incident during this visit see *Kleine Antwort auf Herzog Georgen nächstes Buch*, *WA*, XXXVIII, 148 f.

[25] *TR*, IV, No. 3926 (1538), where he recalls his amusement when the village sexton struck up the Mass music on a lute, almost bringing an unholy burst of laughter from the young priest.

[26] *Const.*, para. 9.

monastic years in Wittenberg. In these cases he avoided looking at them, as he did not want to know their faces.[27] When seven years after his entry into religious life he was promoted to be district vicar of the reformed cloisters, he exercised his disciplinary duties with a sharp regard for the rules.

"In the first year of priesthood and monkhood, nothing seems more joyful than chastity." Thus fifteen years later Martin recalled his attitude and undoubtedly gave a faithful picture of his mood in the cloister.[28] Looking back on those days he remembered that he was as if "among the choir of angels." [29] Such memories clung to the celebration of his first Mass, when his soul floated high on the wings of mystical delight. The studies for the priesthood must have begun immediately after his profession, in the late summer or early fall of 1506. His selection for the dignity of the priesthood was a natural step in the development of a young friar. He had been a student marked for ability at the university and his dramatic entry into the religious life had undoubtedly riveted upon him the attention of the prior and perhaps even that of the general vicar of the order, Johann von Staupitz. The designation of candidates for promotion to the priesthood belonged to the superior officers of the cloister and to the prior,[30] who must have watched Martin's progress through the novitiate year with especial attention and called him for preparation for the priestly office very soon after his reception to full brotherhood.[31] He lacked as yet the minimum

[27] See the remark in *TR*, I, No. 121 (1531), a well-attested source. He even says that during his days in the order he neither saw nor spoke to any woman, "so to speak." *TR*, I, No. 518 (1531), p. 240, ll. 25 f.

[28] *De votis monasticis, WA*, VIII, 660.

[29] *Enarrationes . . . cap. IX Esaiae, EA*, XXIII, 401. He is speaking of the speculations regarding the character of the divinity of Christ in which he had indulged with eagerness in earlier days.

[30] *Const.*, para. 33. See also Müller, *Werdegang*, pp. 43 f.

[31] Kolde, *Augustiner-Kongregation*, pp. 247, 252, brings Martin into relationship with Staupitz at this time and ascribes his selection for the priesthood to the general vicar. Scheel, who discusses the matter at length, *Martin Luther*, II, 70 ff. and 615 ff., concludes that if Martin became acquainted with Staupitz before he was designated for the priesthood it must have been very casually, since the general vicar could scarcely have been in Erfurt between April, 1505, and June, 1506, and was then absent in Italy from the fall of 1506 until the spring of 1507, possibly until after the meeting of the general chapter in Naples on May 21 of that year. See also Kolde, *Augustiner-Kongregation*, p. 232. Müller, *Werdegang*, pp. 43 ff., is of the opinion that Staupitz did select Luther for study in preparation for ordination. Ernst Wolf, "Staupitz und Luther," *Quellen und Forschungen zur Reformationsgeschichte*, IX (1927), 133 ff., admits the possibility of a visit by Staupitz to Erfurt in the fall of 1506, but does not regard this necessarily as implying that he influenced Luther's career at this time. It is not impossible, however, that the vicar knew of Martin through correspondence with the convent, and his interest in the young friar may have been stimulated further by personal contact during the early days of Martin's studies for the priesthood. His consent to his ordination was expressly required by the rules of the Eremites.

age for the priest, twenty-five years, but the Augustinians were permitted by special dispensation to waive this,[32] and the young candidate advanced rapidly through the ranks of subdeacon and deacon to ordination in the early part of 1507.[33] Since these grades were necessarily separated by months, it is possible that Martin may have received his first consecration, that of subdeacon, permitting him to serve a deacon at the altar and to read the Epistle, in the month of his reception in the order.[34] In any event, his ordination, which elevated him to the office of priest of the Mass, must have taken place as soon as the preliminary studies allowed. He may also have begun regular studies in theology at the same time as those preparatory to the priesthood.[35]

During the fall and winter he threw himself with all the fire of his soul into the preparation for the duties of the priesthood. The basic work he used for this purpose was that of an eminent member of his order, Gabriel Biel, late professor at Tübingen, highly respected among the Augustinians as an authority in theology. Biel had died a dozen years earlier. Vicar Staupitz had been one of his students and also Brother Nathin, the head of theological studies in the Erfurt cloister, who was perhaps even then inducting Martin into the divine science. Biel's exposition of the canon of the Mass, either the full-length course of lectures which he gave at Tübingen or an epitome of these, served Martin as an introduction to this most solemn office of the priesthood.[36] One of these works Martin read at this time and it gave him keen delight. "My heart would bleed when I read in it," he recalled many years later.[37] This might well be, for Biel presented the great sacrificial work of the priest both in its mystical and its dogmatic character in a clearly organized but impassioned manner: "Oh truly heavenly indulgence! Oh cumulative grace! What super-excellent glory of the priest to hold and to dispense his God, distributing Him to others!" Here perhaps for the first time young Luther had an opportunity to look deeply into the nature of

---

[32] A privilege granted by Innocent VII in the bull of February 16, 1486, quoted by Scheel, *Martin Luther*, II, 77, n. 1. See also *Analecta Augustiniana*, IV, 233.

[33] Scheel, *Martin Luther*, II, 78. Müller, who sets the reception of Martin into the order at the end of 1505, would have him begin his studies for the priesthood early in 1506, thus extending these over a longer period than other authorities admit. See his *Werdegang*, pp. 53 f. Müller's chronology is somewhat doubtful.

[34] Oergel, *Vom jungen Luther*, p. 90, sets the date of consecration as subdeacon as September 19, 1506. The last possible date for this would have been December 19. See Scheel, *Martin Luther*, II, 79.

[35] This is Müller's hypothesis and may have been true despite Scheel's argumentation.

[36] Either the *Lectura super canone Missae* (Reutlingen, 1488) or the *Epithoma expositionis canonis Missae* (Tübingen, 1499) was used by Luther.

[37] *TR*, III, No. 3722 (1538), p. 564, ll. 3 ff., where he says that he still had the work in his library.

the Catholic faith. He learned the technical and formal procedure of the Mass, so intricate and difficult for the inexperienced, the symbolical meaning of the vestments and other objects and ceremonies which had been familiar to him as schoolboy, as student, and as youthful friar. Now the robes of the priest, the movements, gestures, and kneelings often observed in the bright candle-light of the altar took on new significance. He saw them as preparations for the solemn ceremony which memorializes and symbolizes the sacrifice of Christ for the redemption of man, a ceremony in which he himself would officiate. He learned the mystical significance of the sacred rites which set the believing soul free from deadly sins and wipe clean the slate of all lesser guilt. In the words of consecration with which the priest marks the transformation of the bread and wine into the body and blood of Christ, he saw the re-presentation before God of the death of His Son, the satisfaction of divine justice offended by the sins of mankind and the opening of the fountain of grace. To a young man of Martin's temperament the awesome responsibilities which the Mass imposes must have been a profound and overwhelming experience.

Most of all, his conscience must have been quickened by the warnings which Biel gives against entering on the service with an impure mind and carrying it out with anything short of the most rigid observances.[38] Following scholastic procedure, Biel distinguishes between the various "impediments" which may interfere with the proper celebration, and he catalogues the kinds and degrees of sins to which the officiating priest is liable. He warns also, to be sure, against timidity and encourages the hesitating soul who feels himself inclined to sin and yet has the will to fight against it.[39] Nevertheless, a sensitive conscience such as Martin's must have labored under the earnest warnings.

Hand in hand with these studies Martin received practical introduction into the administrations at the altar. First came his consecration as subdeacon, a formal act celebrated in the convent church by the prior of the convent or more probably by the bishop.[40] Martin had previously, perhaps even during his first year, been inducted into the lower order of ministrants, where candidates for the clerical office served as altar attendants or participated otherwise in liturgical exercises. As subdeacon he received the empty chalice, the paten for the consecrated wafer, and the book of Epistles, from which he might read in the Mass—all symbols of humbler services at the altar which he was now to perform. Later came his consecration to the

---

[38] Lecture VII.   [39] Lecture VIII.

[40] Müller, *Werdegang,* pp. 40 f., makes it seem quite probable that Martin's consecration as subdeacon and as deacon, as well as his ordination as priest, were by the suffragan bishop, Johann Bonemilch von Lasphe. See Oergel, *Vom jungen Luther,* p. 90.

deaconate, with the laying on of hands and the receipt of the Gospels. He was authorized now to assist the priest in celebrating the Mass. Finally, in the late winter or early spring of 1507, probably on April 3, he was ordained as priest.[41] With the words, the solemnity of which he remembered for years, "Receive the power of consecrating and sacrificing for the living and the dead," bread and wine were put into his hands, and the ceremony of unction and of clothing in the stole and chasuble, accompanied by prayers of consecration, sealed his entry into the priestly rank. The ordination took place before the main altar of the Erfurt Cathedral and was celebrated by the local suffragan bishop, Johann Bonemilch von Lasphe. Now twenty-three years of age, Martin had attained to the office which empowered him to stand as intermediary between God and the world of believers, to perform the full rites of the Mass, to consecrate its sacred elements before the kneeling congregation, and to dispense the body of Christ.[42]

Not long afterwards came the great festival which was to open his priestly career. The celebration of the first Mass, an event of such deep significance in the life of the young priest, fell on the fourth Sunday after Easter, Cantate Sunday, May 2. It was fixed by the convent to suit the convenience of his father. We can recapture something of Martin's feeling from two letters in which he bids friends of Eisenach days to come to the celebration. In a tone of proud humility, with phrases imitative of the sonorous Latin of Biel's lectures, Martin invites his friend of school days, Johann Braun, vicar of St. Mary's at Eisenach, and urges him to bring along Konrad Hutter, the kind patron of a decade earlier, and anyone else whom he may wish.[43] He begs the vicar to stay at the convent and ventures to suggest that he may convey an invitation to the "excellent men of the Schalbe Collegium." Shortly afterwards he asks another friend, probably his former teacher at Eisenach, Wigand Guldenapf, to come to the convent for the celebration.[44]

The months preceding had been a period of profound stirrings of the heart, and the Mass must have brought an excess of emotion. It was a doubly joyful occasion, for his father, who had looked with such hostile eyes

[41] The two possible dates of the ordination seem to be February 27 or April 3. Oergel, *ibid.*, p. 90, following the chronology which he worked out for Martin's consecration as subdeacon, argues for February 27. The later date seems, however, more probable, though by no means certain. See Buchwald, "Wann hat Luther die Priesterweihe empfangen?" *ZKG*, XXXVII (1918), 215 f.; Scheel, *Martin Luther*, II, 78 and 616 f.

[42] Scheel, *Martin Luther*, II, 80, has pointed out that the right to hear confession and assign penance could not have been attained by Martin until more than a year later, since he had not yet reached the age required by Augustinian procedure for this authority.

[43] Letter from Luther to Braun, April 22, 1507, *WAB*, I, 10 f.

[44] Letter of April 28, 1507, *WAB*, I, 15.

on the first day of his entry into the cloister two years before, now came to share in the festivity. The miner rode over from Mansfeld with twenty companions whose entertainment he paid, beside bringing twenty guilders as a present to the chapter. Years later Martin remembered that someone remarked to him: "You must have a great friend to make such an outlay for you."[45] It was indeed a thrilling occasion and remained for years a high point in Martin's memory. The celebration took place in the chapel of the cloister. His recollections of the event as recorded by his table companions and other scribes at Wittenberg show a tendency to dramatize it, and they are undoubtedly marked by exaggerations, due to the defective memory of the middle-aged Luther and to embellishments of younger associates. They record an attack of nervousness and fear which was something more than the stage fright to which any young priest might be liable. One record has it that when Martin reached the point where the priest bows at the altar with uplifted hands and eyes raised to God to receive the sacrifice suffered for the Church and reads the words, "To Thee, therefore, most merciful Father, supplicate through Jesus Christ, Thy Son,"[46] he was so terrified at speaking directly to God without a mediator that if the prior had not admonished him he would have fled from the altar before all the world.[47] Another report by an amanuensis of particular reliability, Johann Schlaginhaufen, makes Luther say that terror struck him as he was about to speak the words of the offertory, consecrating the Host, "To Thee, eternal living and true God."[48] Another statement, quoted in a transcript of one of the lectures on Genesis, expands the idea somewhat by having Martin say that he was horrified "at the words with which I addressed so great a majesty, when all ought to be terrified at beholding and at speaking with earthly lords."[49] This report adds that it was his preceptor who kept him from leaving the altar.[50]

[45] *TR*, II, No. 1558 (1532).

[46] This is the first prayer in the canon of the Mass: "Te igitur, clementissime Pater. . . ." Schott, *Das Messbuch der heiligen Kirche*, p. 20.

[47] *TR*, III, No. 3556A and 3556B (1537).

[48] *TR*, II, No. 1558 (1532). In this case Schlaginhaufen seems to have noted Luther's words from memory. As a matter of fact, the words he cites, "Aeterno vivo vero Deo," are found, not in the Offertory, as Luther says, but in the Silent Mass at the conclusion of the prayer "Memento Domine." Schott, *Messbuch*, p. 21.

[49] The sermon, *Enarratio in Genesin 25.21, WA*, XLIII, 382 (1540). Here Luther (or the scribe) has again made a slip, putting together the introductory words of the Silent Mass ("Te igitur, clementissime Pater") with a quotation in garbled form from the Offertory. The words Luther cites here, "Offerimus tibi vivo, vero et aeterno," seem to be a mixture of those found in the Offertory (Schott, *Messbuch*, p. 13) with the conclusion of the prayer, "Memento Domine." In the passage of twenty years Luther's memory of the *ordo missae* had become hazy, or else he was incorrectly quoted by the student who took down the Genesis lectures.

[50] The "preceptor" also appears in the account by Ericeus, *Sylvula Sententiarum*, p. 177.

13031

These accounts are colored by later experiences. At middle age Martin was bitterly intolerant of the old ceremonies and had stored away many memories of routine celebrations of the Mass which he had seen in Italy and elsewhere, by priests who could say Mass "rips, raps" as if doing a piece of sleight-of-hand.[51] When the breach came with tradition, one of his first objectives was the reform of the Mass. In the springtime of 1507 at Erfurt such thoughts were far from his mind. Nevertheless, the evidence of terror and quaking at his first Mass is too categorical to be overlooked. It may have been a mood of Sinai which made him tremble at his own unworthiness,[52] or it may have been the warnings of Biel that continued to ring in his mind despite the comforting assurance which that authority gives to those who approach the service of the altar with the right will, even though their performance be defective. Fears like these would have been in accord with the intense conscientiousness which is well attested for his early cloister years. Or it may have been only a nervous paroxysm resulting from long-drawn tension of studies and ascetic exercises. Whatever the cause, something made him hesitate, and he may well have needed the reassuring words of the prior or preceptor to carry him through the ordeal. To have an experienced assistant at hand was and still is customary at a first Mass. The scene gives further evidence that Martin's conscience was an imperious master and drove him to fulfill the demands of cloister life with eager zeal. As the moment approached when the prayer of consecration was to be read, when before the kneeling congregation of cloister brothers, friends, and relatives, he received from the assisting deacon the paten with the bread to be offered and with eyes directed upward was to speak the solemn words: "Receive, O sacred Father omnipotent and eternal this Sacred Host which I Thine unworthy servant offer to Thee, my living and true God, for my innumerable sins of commission and omission, and for all who are present and all faithful Christians living and dead, so that it may avail for their salvation in life eternal," when this solemn moment arrived Martin may well have been struck with fear and have required all of his own reserves of strength and the encouragement of those beside him to go ahead with the service.[53]

[51] TR, III, No. 3428. See also EA, XXI, 331.

[52] TR, IV, No. 4174 (1538).

[53] From the standpoint of the older brothers a momentary panic on Martin's part could have caused little surprise, though they may not have understood the mental perturbation that gave rise to it. Instances of hesitation and stage fright at a first Mass cannot be unusual, and for the conscientious ministrant the solemn passages in the Mass can never become mere routine. Luther recalled that he had seen many priests tremble and stammer at the words of consecration, even though it was a sin to hesitate with a single syllable. TR, IV, No. 4998 (1540). Luther's conscience kept him in terror of making any error in the service throughout his cloister years, if we may trust a remark in a sermon of Sept. 14, 1538, WA, XLVII, 108.

When the ordeal was past, the spirit of the young priest no doubt rebounded under the congratulations of friars, kinsmen, and friends. The first Mass was a festival of family and friendship. Martin once recalled that on such an occasion the young priest would lead off in a dance with his mother, if she still lived, amid the tears of the spectators, and if she were dead, he must free her soul from purgatory with his prayers.[54] Of Margarete Luther's presence on this joyous occasion nothing appears in the sources, and it is extremely unlikely, as all took place within cloister walls. Hans was there, however, as we have seen, and he remained for the banquet which, according to scholastic tradition, marked this event in his son's career. We may well believe a reminiscence of Luther, recorded near the end of his life, that certain doctors and masters of arts from the university also assisted in celebrating the beginning of his priesthood.[55] It was possibly at this banquet, as Dr. Ratzeberger records, that a memorable conversation took place between the young priest and his father.[56] The sturdy miner, now a man of growing affairs, seems to have made Martin's first Mass an occasion for a reconciliation, although he still regretted that his brilliant son had shut himself off from the world. Either in response to a remark of his son,[57] or according to another, less reliable source, in hot retort to the monks who had expressed surprise that he had resisted the entry of so gifted a son into the religious life, Hans burst out: "Don't you know that it is written, 'Thou shalt honor thy father and thy mother'?" [58] Martin, who had in all probability heard this scriptural admonition from Hans two years earlier, now found the latter still unconvinced that his son had taken the right step. Another remark of Hans, possibly on this occasion, struck deeper into his mind and, while disregarded at the time, did not cease to rankle so long as he remained a monk. In answer to the statement that his son had been drawn into the cloister by a heavenly vision, Hans replied: "I hope it was no illusion and trick of the devil!" [59] On one of Martin's sensitive imagination and deep mythological fixations these words must have fallen with peculiar force, and years did not dim the impression which they made. Fourteen years later, when he was about to lay aside the cowl forever, he

---

[54] *TR*, IV, No. 4174 (1538).   [55] *WA*, XLIV, 711 f.

[56] Ratzeberger, *Handschriftliche Geschichte*, pp. 48 f.

[57] *TR*, I, No. 623 (1533); No. 881 (middle of 1530s); III, No. 3556A and 3556B (1537). In the first of these records, Veit Dietrich, one of the most reliable scribes of the *Table Talk*, seems to imply that the conversation was solely between father and son. In *De votis monasticis*, *WA*, VIII, 573 ff., this also seems to be implied. See also the sermon of Jan. 20, 1544, *WA*, XLIX, 322. Lauterbach's report, *TR*, III, No. 3556, says it was the day following the Mass.

[58] *Enarratio in Genesin* (1544), *WA*, XLIV, 712.

[59] *De votis monasticis*, *WA*, VIII, 574.

quoted them, once in a letter to Melanchthon,[60] and two months later in the dedication to his father of his work *On the Monks' Vows*. "It drove roots into my heart," he declares, "as though God were speaking through your mouth." [61]

[60] Letter from Luther to Melanchthon, Sept. 9, 1521, *WAB*, II, 385, ll. 96 ff.
[61] *De votis monasticis*, *WA*, VIII, 574.

8

STUDENT OF THEOLOGY

MARTIN was now a priest, qualified for the service of the Mass and soon to be charged with the duties of a confessor of souls. If we may trust statements made after he had broken with the Church, he plunged into the new duties at the altar with ardent enthusiasm and performed them with more than usual zeal, becoming, he declares, a "slave of the Mass." [1] Thus he ministered at the chapels served by the Eremites in the country around Erfurt and in the convent church, and his heart swelled with pride when he had carried through the service to his satisfaction. [2] Still other duties of an absorbing nature came to fill the long convent day to overflowing. Even during the preparation for his ordination he may have entered on studies in theology; at any event, these must have begun no later than the fall of 1507. The statutes of the order required that the prior of the convent should constrain the brothers so far as possible to such studies. [3] The story of Martin's marvelous conversion had shed an unusual light on him; indeed, brothers from the convent carried reports of it to distant seats of the order. [4] Furthermore, his reputation as a gifted student at the university marked him as one who might well become a successful teacher among the Augustinians. Under such circumstances the prior can hardly have failed to enlist Martin for the study of theology at the earliest moment that accorded with cloister practice. In this case there could have been no necessity to "constrain" the candidate.

The convent at Erfurt was well equipped for theological training. The rules of the Observant Augustinians declared that "the order was founded

---

[1] "Ein Ertzpapist und viel hefftiger Messe knecht" (one of Luther's pet expressions, *Von seinem Buch der Winkelmessen, WA*, XXXVIII, 267 (1534).

[2] Lecture on Isaiah, perhaps Nov. 1528, *WA*, XXXI, ii, 154.   [3] *Const.*, para. 36.

[4] At least as far as the Rhine. See the report which his teacher of theology, Johann Nathin, took to the cloister at Mühlenhausen, in Dungersheim von Ochsenfurt's *Dadelung des obgesatzten bekenntnus oder untuchtigen Lutherischen Testaments* (1530), cited by Böhmer, *Romfahrt*, p. 57, n. 2.

on its studies," [5] and the Erfurt cloister was in this regard the most distinguished in the Saxon-Thuringian province.[6] Its "general study," which included philosophy and theology, had been founded long before the university; and when this institution came into being, the Erfurt convent, as we have seen, furnished it with a succession of able theologians and administrators. The interlocking of studies of theology between university and cloister attracted gifted young friars from other convents and swelled the number of cloister inmates.[7] The reforms of the fifteenth century, strengthening as they did cloister discipline, must also have had their effect on the discipline of study. Up to Luther's day the Eremites continued to supply teachers of theology to the university, and the cloister seems to have maintained a prestige for learning surpassing that of the other mendicant orders in Erfurt.[8]

The organization of studies in the cloister followed, at least in the lower stages, the general pattern of the university.[9] It was in the hands of a group of older brothers, "regents" for various subjects, but the requirements seem to have been safeguarded and normalized by regulations imposed by the general chapter. The award of degrees apparently depended on the approval of high authority in the order.[10] The so-called "particular" studies, which preceded those in theology, have an analogy to the undergraduate courses at the university in preparation for the bachelor of arts. They dealt with grammar and logic and included a certain amount of philosophy and metaphysics. At the end of four years the brother who had completed this basic course received the degree of *cursor* and might then go forward to studies in theology. At the end of a further period of three years the successful candidate became a *lector,* with the right to give instruction in the cloister school of theology.[11] The first course in theology might also be

---

[5] *Const.*, para. 32.　　　　　　　　　　[6] Oergel, *Vom jungen Luther,* pp. 53 ff.

[7] The Erfurt cloister was well equipped to care for a large monastic population. According to sources uncovered by Oergel, it was able as early as 1320 to entertain 200 brothers who crowded in from outside to attend the annual gathering of the order, a number far in excess of the capacity of other houses of the province. *Ibid.,* pp. 53 f.

[8] See above, p. 76, n. 42.

[9] The sources have been carefully studied by Oergel in *Vom jungen Luther,* and more recently by Scheel, *Martin Luther,* II, 119 ff., who assembled further information from the annals of the order, the *Analecta Augustiniana.* Still of importance are Kolde's *Augustiner-Kongregation* and, in spite of the author's lack of perspective, Müller's discussions in *Werdegang* and *Luthers theologische Quellen.*

[10] At least in some instances. The degree of *lector* was conferred on Andreas Proles, who carried through the reformation of the Augustinian chapters in Germany, by authority of the general of the order on conclusion of Proles's studies at Perugia. Kolde, *Augustiner-Kongregation,* p. 97, n. 2.

[11] The requirement for this first degree in theology seems to have been raised during the

undertaken at the university; and the statutes of the Erfurt theological faculty give a fairly clear idea of what was required of university candidates in the divine science. Such candidates, masters of arts of the university, advanced to the degree of "bachelor in the Bible" (*baccalaureus biblicus*), the statutes requiring a minimum of five years of study for this degree.[12] It is significant that the guardians of academic standards treated the *cursors* and other candidates from the monkish orders with greater liberality than their own masters of arts, demanding in cases of these religious persons who had been certified by the convent only that they should give proof of training in the disputation.[13]

These requirements are of some interest for the story of Martin's subsequent development, and the Erfurt statutes may therefore be permitted to engage our attention a little further. They give an interesting picture of the safeguards that the university faculty erected to prevent the sprouting of heresy among its young lecturers on the Bible. Every bachelor must work under the direction of a doctor of theology, and must submit to him in advance the notes and plans for his lectures.[14] He was permitted to lecture only on two books of the Bible, which were to be indicated by the faculty, one from the Old and one from the New Testament.[15] These he was to "set forth as a whole, with an explanation of important meanings," [16] in other words, to give lectures of the "survey" type. As an extra safeguard the candidate was forbidden to lecture outside of the university or behind a closed door.

After the young lecturer on the Bible had continued his studies two years longer, he was admitted to the degree of *sententiarius*. This entitled him to expound the great basic work of scholastic theology, the *Sentences* of Peter Lombard, a digest and summary in logical form of the dogmas of the Church. The path to this degree was also hedged by strict regulations.[17] Here, too, the monks were given special concessions, but the requirement of the disputation was laid upon all. The privilege of expounding the doctrines of the Church was jealously guarded and even after seven years of theological training at the university, or five years for those who had begun

latter half of the fifteenth century. See Scheel, *Martin Luther*, II, 120. The provision requiring seven years' study within the cloister was adopted at the general chapter in Rome in 1497. *Analecta Augustiniana*, VIII, 13.

[12] "Acten," VIII, II, 54, para. 53.   [13] *Ibid.;* see also p. 54, para. 51.

[14] *Ibid.*, p. 52, para. 37; p. 54, para. 48. I interpret *magister* as one possessing the highest degree in theology, i.e. *doctor*.

[15] *Ibid.*, p. 55, para. 55.   [16] *Ibid.*, para. 57.

[17] *Ibid.*, p. 55, para. 62.

these studies in the cloister, the academic theologian was not permitted to wander from exact prescriptions covering the manner of his exposition of Lombard. When, with careful observance of these, he had completed successfully the interpretation of two books of Lombard's great work, he became a *baccalaureus formatus*.[18] Before he might attain the next degree two years more must elapse, a period spent in further training in the disputation, in preaching, and maturing himself in the practice of Bible exegesis and interpretation of the *Sentences*. Finally, after passing an examination before the entire faculty and showing a mastery in the technique of the disputation, he might at last ascend to the highest rung of the theological ladder, the doctorate or *licentia magistralis*.[19]

The regulations governing the progress on this long road are marked by an emphasis on the development of practical qualities and a moral personality. The candidate must have a clear enunciation, and a ready command of spoken Latin. He was expected to be regular in attendance on the divine offices at the university and to show a moral bearing devoid of offense. Sincerity and reverence, a peaceful attitude, and a civil tongue toward opponents were demanded of masters and students alike. Beside these exhortations to self-restraint, the statutes urge the avoidance of any suspicion of heresy. In all public exercises the participants should begin with a preamble setting forth that the declarations which they are to make are not intended to contain anything contrary to the Catholic faith or the decisions of the sacred Mother Church, or anything making concessions in favor of, or condemned by, the articles of Paris, or anything contrary to sound doctrine or good morals, or anything offensive to pious ears.[20]

This was now the path on which the young priest entered. Apparently Martin combined studies in the cloister with those at the university. He came under the same teachers in both institutions, for the regents of theological studies of the Eremites were as a rule at this period also instructors in the university. One of his teachers, at least for a brief time, may have been the Johann Jeuser von Paltz,[21] who, like Martin, had turned

---

[18] *Ibid.*, p. 56, para. 72.

[19] *Ibid.*, p. 57, para. 75, and p. 58, para. 78. Erfurt, like other German universities, followed in general the pattern of Paris. "Just as at Paris and Bologna" appears repeatedly in the statutes of the theological faculty. *Ibid.*, pp. 53, l. 18; 54, l. 34; 55, l. 30. See also Denifle, ed., *Chartularium universitatis Parisiensis* (1889–97), III, 427, and Denifle's Introduction, I, xviii. Ritter's investigation points to the same general arrangement of courses at Heidelberg as that found at Paris. *Die Heidelberger Universität*, I, 208 ff.

[20] "Acten," VIII, ii, 53, para. 44.

[21] A long account of his work is to be found in Kolde, *Augustiner-Kongregation*, pp. 174 ff. For supplementary details, including a correction in the spelling of his name, see *WAB*, I, 26, n. 3.

to the religious life as a promising university scholar. Paltz represented a type of personality that had won for the Erfurt convent its reputation for spiritual devotion and high scholarship. At the time when Martin's studies began, this distinguished Eremite was just concluding his services at the cloister after nearly twenty years of activity as administrator and teacher of theology. He was a zealous and energetic reformer and undertook more than one tour of duty in order to bring other cloisters into line with strict observance. His fame as a preacher was considerable, particularly as a herald and defender of indulgences. A selection of his sermons dealing chiefly with this subject bears the promising title, "The Mine of Heaven." [22] Printed in 1502, it counts as an important contribution to the history of the dogmatic interpretation of indulgences. Paltz's zeal in this matter was of practical as well as spiritual aid to his cloister. One of the special indulgences which he was able to add to its store brought in sufficient income to complete the cloister library.[23] He may have initiated Martin into the study of the divine science, but he can scarcely have done more than that, for in the year of the young friar's ordination Paltz left Erfurt as the result of a discord and became the head of a sister convent on the Rhine.[24] Years later, in a fit of anger, Martin recalled the way in which the resentful doctor had poured out his wrath on the convent and, as it seems, also on a brother professor of theology there.[25]

The professor who remained in possession of the field was Johann Nathin.[26] He was evidently a less incisive personality, although no doubt a systematic and conscientious instructor. He had come into the Augustinian order a generation before, and was, like Martin, as it seems, a master of arts when he took the vows. After studies and teaching at Tübingen and Heidelberg, he returned to Erfurt, where he received his doctor of philosophy in 1493 and became professor of theology at the university and regent of studies in the cloister. Dr. Nathin was undoubtedly a conscientious interpreter of the scholastic learning. This is probably the reason why Mutianus, the humanist of Gotha, called him a barbarous and morose fellow,[27] a remark which is not to be taken too seriously, since the rationalistic canon

[22] *Coelifodina.* See Kolde, *Augustiner-Kongregation*, pp. 182 ff.

[23] *Ibid.*, pp. 206 f.

[24] Mühlheim (Thal Ehrenbreitstein). *Ibid.*, p. 175, and n. 3. See also the list of office holders of the Erfurt Eremites, where Paltz's name appears for the last time in 1506. *Ibid.*, p. 416.

[25] Letter to the Erfurt convent, June 16, 1514, *WAB*, I, 25.

[26] For information on Nathin, see Kolde, *Augustiner-Kongregation*, pp. 137 f., n. 4; Oergel, *Vom jungen Luther*, p. 104 and note.

[27] Letter from Mutianus to Urban, 1513. K. Gillert, ed., "Der Briefwechsel des Conradius Mutianus," *Geschichtsquellen der Provinz Sachsen*, XVIII, 1 (1890), 372.

had the tendency to overstatement characteristic of the sharp-tongued humanists. It is worth noting that Nathin guided the studies of young theologians at Erfurt during thirty years, and that when, as a result of Luther's revolt, the Erfurt cloister split asunder and vanished from the scene, this old scholastic, like Martin's philosophy teachers Trutvetter and Arnold, did not follow his former pupil out of the order. On the other side, it is also worth noting that in his *Table Talk* Martin never mentions Johann Nathin. He could have had neither the scholarship nor personality to cause his student to look back on him with the respect and affection shown to those who had been his teachers in the school of arts at the university.

It was under such men that Brother Martin began his theological studies. As these got under way, the days and hours must have been filled to the last minute, even though he may have received some relief from his liturgical duties in the choir. The demands of the lectures would certainly have interfered with some of these, and the rules of the order provided for concessions in such cases, although whatever might be thus omitted from the daily divine office in the choir must be made up in private prayers or else the neglectful brother would incur the risk of mortal sin. It was a characteristic of the Reformed Congregation, further emphasized in its new code of regulations, that strict observance and study must both go on without interfering with each other.[28]

Even if his early studies were carried on at the monastery, Martin was obliged to take part in disputations at the university, as provided in the regulations for all candidates for the first theological degree.[29] These requirements were imperative, and the disputations in theology were infused with a spirit quite different from those held under the faculty of philosophy, where preparation by the students often degenerated into the use of routine formulas based on an analysis of premises and arguments furnished by the presiding instructor.[30] In the theological faculty, the questions discussed revolved about such problems as the nature of divinity, of grace, and salvation, and although the number of disputational exercises required of the student of theology was probably less than in the faculty of arts, the preparation in which student and teacher cooperated was, obviously, much more serious and the clash of argument more decided.[31] Here, too, Martin was, of course, destined to encounter disputations leading into a field of purely formal

[28] *Const.*, para. 36.   [29] "Acten," VIII, II, 54, para. 53.

[30] See Gerhard Ritter, *Die Heidelberger Universität,* I, 182 ff., especially the discussion of the disputations in the faculty of arts, p. 187. Conditions at Erfurt can hardly have been different from those at Heidelberg.

[31] This is, in effect, Ritter's view of the situation at Heidelberg. *Ibid.,* I, 201 ff.

questions, occasionally quite hollow of any real meaning, but they also gave opportunity to confront problems of solemn importance.

In view of the statutes as outlined above it is probable that Martin began his studies leading to the *baccalaureus biblicus* with an exegetical course on one of the books of the Old and one of the New Testament. As we have seen, the young friar had probably begun to read the Bible with eagerness soon after his entry into the cloister,[32] and there seems little doubt that he had ready access to a copy of it in his cell, or at least in the cloister library.[33] When he began to hear "survey" courses on the Bible books, it is probable that he read the text of the Vulgate with renewed zeal. Contemporary biographers, followed by others of succeeding times, have set forth with varying degrees of detail and picturesqueness a collision at this time between the enthusiasm of the young Mansfeld priest for reading Scripture and the demands of cloister authority for the prosecution of dogmatic studies. Melanchthon declares that Martin continued to read in the "fountains of heavenly doctrine," that is, in the Bible, but he implies that it did not form a part of his theological studies.[34] A statement in the *Table Talk* of somewhat questionable authority has Luther say in 1540 that, having become an enthusiastic reader of the Bible in the cloister, the brothers took it away from him after his ordination and gave him "sophistical books" instead, but that whenever he could find time he hid in the library and read the Bible.[35] These reports stand on a somewhat shaky foundation. The evidence seems overwhelming that he heard courses on the Bible either in the cloister or at the university. It may be, however, that his enthusiasm for the first lessons in Bible exegesis and the discovery of the use of a commentary, which Erfurt required the instructor to employ so as to open further the meaning of Holy Writ,[36] may have made Lombard's formulas of dogmatic theology seem dusty and lifeless at the outset. From the modern standpoint, the Biblical lectures as delivered by the young bachelors would no doubt be arid enough. Contemporary material from Erfurt is lacking, but commentaries preserved at Heidelberg from the fifteenth century show that the dialectical enthusiasm of the age was fully reflected in these lectures.[37] In a commentary on

[32] See above, p. 86, and nn. 28 and 29.

[33] *Ibid.* [34] *CR*, VI, 159.

[35] *TR*, V, No. 5346. See above, p. 86, n. 29. The story finds support from at least one biographer of the generation following Luther; see Selneccer, *Historica Narratio* (1575). Oergel, *Vom jungen Luther*, pp. 106 ff., accepts these reports at practically full value. Scheel, *Martin Luther*, II, 133 ff., rejects them. The sources at this point are unreliable, but it does not seem unlikely that there is a kernel of truth in the story: Martin's repugnance for abstract theological studies on first acquaintance and his enthusiasm for reading the Bible.

[36] "Acten," VIII, 11, 55, para. 57.

[37] Ritter, *Die Heidelberger Universität*, I, 211 ff. See also *ibid.*, II, 497 f. Ritter's interest-

Matthew by the famous scholastic, Marsilius of Inghen, we have first a painful division of the text into subsections. These are to be read and interpreted; then the interpretation is to be attacked and defended by arguments pro and contra, and finally a solution reached. The method of analysis was that in use throughout Europe from Carolingian days: first, a historical exposition, then a dogmatic, then an allegorical. The treatment of a text in this manner might be stimulating when carried on by a master of the subject, but it must have become intolerably dreary in the hands of an unseasoned bachelor. To Martin, however, filled with ardor as he was and in the springtime of enthusiasm for the new Biblical studies, even the driest exposition would have been stimulating. He no doubt looked forward with eagerness to the time when he himself should become the expositor.

Whether he liked it or not, he was now, perhaps even in the year of his ordination, obliged to enter the thorny field of systematic theology. Here his guide was the most famous theological school book of the later Middle Ages, the *Sentences* of Peter Lombard.[38] The author of this work, an Italian by birth but, like Thomas Aquinas, identified throughout his creative life with Paris, where he was a bishop, belonged to the great movement toward the codification of orthodoxy which had set in with Abelard and reached its crest with the *Summa theologica* of Thomas. Lombard's work sets forth the whole range of Christian dogma by means of innumerable distinctions, subdivisions, and epilogues, beginning with the nature of the Trinity and ending with a discussion of questions of marriage. It abounds in examples from Biblical, patristic, and papal authority. Lombard's work has the pedestrian style and judicial restraint that are essential to pedagogical longevity. It balances carefully between opinions and treads deftly a middle ́path, so deftly indeed that both realists and nominalists accepted it. Whatever its defects, its author was gifted as a pedagogical writer, and his text dominated the schools in the later scholastic age. In this period many of the prominent theologians of Europe wrote commentaries on the *Sentences*. As we have seen, the exposition of this fundamental work was entrusted only to those who had had at least five years of theological training.

As a candidate for the baccalaureate in the Bible, Martin was required to hear at least one course of lectures on all four books of the *Sentences*.[39]

---

ing analysis of a Biblical lecture by Marsilius of Inghen is suggestive, but the pattern was of course remote from Martin's day. Marsilius, one of the greatest of German Schoolmen, gave his work a technical finish that was obviously beyond the reach of any Erfurt bachelor in the Bible.

[38] A convenient edition is that in J.-P. Migne, *Patrologiae cursus completus*, CXCII, 519 ff.

[39] "Acten," VIII, II, 54, para. 53. The same requirement prevailed at Paris, Denifle, ed., *Chartularium universitatis Parisiensis*, II, 698, para. 15.

We do not know certainly through how long a period these lectures extended, but the older statutes of the Erfurt theological faculty provided for an intensive course of one year, in which the lectures came every day during the university term, and also for a more leisurely course of two years with three lectures per week.[40] In any case, Martin heard Lombard's text explained word for word and interpreted from a strictly theological standpoint, since the *sententiarius* was warned against wandering in the fields of philosophical speculation.[41] His teachers in the cloister or at the university must also have given him suggestions for reading in commentaries, because a few years later, when he in his turn took the platform as lecturer on the *Sentences,* his notes show that he was familiar with a number of interpretative works. In the crowded days of the first year or two of study, however, filled as they were with liturgical duties and attendance on lectures and disputations, the time for reading must have been stolen from the hours of nightly rest, just as a few years earlier young Pellicanus, then prior in the Franciscan monastery at Tübingen, had taught himself Hebrew while others slept.

Dr. Nathin, or whoever lectured on the *Sentences,* was a follower of the "modern way," that of William of Occam, which was as supreme in the cloister school and among the university theologians as in the Erfurt faculty of philosophy. Whatever suggestion these instructors made regarding commentaries on Lombard, the first would have been that of the Tübingen professor, Gabriel Biel, whose work on the Mass had been of such importance for Martin. Nathin had studied under Biel, and a decade later Martin refers to the group of theologians at the Erfurt cloister as "Gabrielists."[42] This commentary must have come to his attention early and been read with diligence, for several years later, when he came to lecture on the *Sentences,* he knew it thoroughly. Perhaps one of his nominalist teachers was broadminded enough to direct his attention to the work on Lombard by the great realist Duns Scotus, since many years later Martin praised its third book;[43] other recollections in the *Table Talk* also point to a certain acquaintance with Scotus in the Erfurt period.[44] His knowledge of the great Franciscan can, however, hardly have gone beyond a general understanding of his

---

[40] "Acten," VIII, ii, 55 f., para. 64.   [41] Scheel, *Martin Luther,* II, 138, n. 5.

[42] Letter from Luther to Johann Lang, probably middle of October, 1516, *WAB,* I, 65.

[43] *TR,* III, No. 3722 (1538), p. 564, ll. 8 f.; also I, No. 280 (1532).

[44] *TR,* IV, No. 5009 (1540). Here Luther complains that in his cloister days the monks read Scotus instead of Augustine: "nos monachi non legimus eum, sed Scotum." This reference must have been to his earliest period of study, for Martin's marginal notes of 1509 already show some acquaintance with Augustine.

epistemological and theological position as refracted through the glass of nominalist prejudice. For an independent reading of Scotus, evidence is lacking.[45] There is somewhat more to show for a direct knowledge of the greatest summarist of Church theology and most famous successor of the master of the *Sentences,* Thomas Aquinas. Here also his instructors perhaps gave him only the general position of the Celestial Father; but it is probable that Martin dipped from time to time into the *Summa theologica.* There is a hint in the *Table Talk* that he drew material from it for his practice in the disputation.[46] He probably learned enough of the great summarist at this time to be impressed by the subtlety of his metaphysical method and the seductive skill with which he sets forth his scholastic position.[47] Whatever Martin's acquaintance may have been at this time with Scotus and Aquinas, we know that he studied Lombard intensively.

Melanchthon, probably more dependable in his statements about Luther's reading and theological equipment than concerning the stages in his religious development, says that Martin almost knew Lombard's work by

[45] Neither in earlier nor later years does Martin seem to have penetrated deeply into Scotus's ideas. References to him in the *Table Talk* are superficial characterizations such as might have clung to memory from any course in theology that he may have heard. See, for example, the definition of the position of Scotus, Thomas, and Occam respecting the generic character of man. *TR,* IV, No. 5134 (1540). In general Martin's references reflect the nominalist attitude toward the great Franciscan as a weaver of highly speculative ideas. See especially *TR,* IV, No. 4321 (1539), p. 222, ll. 12 f.; also *TR,* I, No. 651 (1533); No. 845 (first half of 1530s); II, No. 1745 (1532), p. 202, on Scotus's idea of the effect of baptism; Nos. 2544a and 2544b (1532); III, No. 3024 (1533); IV, No. 4118 (1538). Similarly a reference in the *Resolutions* for the Leipzig disputation of 1519 shows nothing more than a knowledge of Scotus's position in the history of dogma.

[46] "Cum essem iuvenis theologus et deberem facere ex una questione novem corrolaria, accipiebam haec duo vocabula: Deus creavit, da gab mir Thomas wol 100 questiones darauf." *TR,* I, No. 280 (1532). Martin goes on to say that Thomas's method was to accept at the outset statements by apostles and prophets, and then to interpret them according to Aristotle.

[47] Luther's knowledge of the *Summa theologica* is not easy to measure, and we shall have to return to it later on. The lectures and *Table Talk* swarm with references to the great systematist, although none that I have examined show anything more than a superficial acquaintance with Thomas. Father Denifle's *Luthertum* (1906), I, 523 ff., gives a detailed analysis of Martin's references and reaches the conclusion that his understanding of Thomas's ideas is to be rated at zero. Despite the bitter tone which disfigures Denifle's discussion, his arguments seem to be convincing. As in the case of Scotus, Martin's attitude toward Thomas bears throughout the stamp of nominalist prejudice. See the statement credited to him in the Genesis lectures, that he was repelled by Thomas's bringing political and economic questions into theological discussions, which is possibly an echo of criticisms by his nominalist teachers at Erfurt. *WA,* XLII, 486 (1537). When Martin became involved in the struggle with the Dominicans, the prejudice which he had acquired at Erfurt took on a bitter form: he does not know whether Thomas will be saved at last. *Rationis Latomianae . . . confutatio, WA,* VIII, 127 (1521). In later years Thomas, like "his master Aristotle," became a much-castigated symbol for the whole scholastic system of theology: "Thomas is not worth one louse; and it is the same with his writings: wash out the fur, but don't get it wet!" *TR,* II, No. 1721 (1532).

heart. From the early lectures which he heard in the cloister refectory and at the university he conceived a sincere respect for the judicially minded dogmatist. "Peter Lombard is a good enough theologian. He has no equal"; thus, twenty-five years after his initial acquaintance with the *Sentences*, Luther praises his first guide through the thorny field of the science of Christian theology.[48] He felt, to be sure, that the author had treated many useless questions, but his criticisms of the great dogmatist go no further than that.[49]

It is evident from the foregoing that, in addition to hearing lectures under baccalaureate instruction, the young theologian made a beginning with independent reading. Despite this full program, his progress toward the degree was more rapid than was permitted to the university masters of arts and must have been somewhat faster than that of the usual monastic student. Even though the chronology of events in his first years at the cloister is far from definite, it is most likely that his theological studies did not begin until after his "probation," probably not until the winter semester of 1506 at the earliest. He received his baccalaureate in the Bible in 1509, not more than three years and more probably about two and one-half years later.[50] In all likelihood, only two years of these studies were carried on at Erfurt, for, as we shall see, the fall of 1508 saw him called away to Wittenberg. Even in this period he may have had an opportunity to hear another type of lecture provided for in the regulations of the faculty, the so-called "magisterial" lectures, delivered by those scholars who had advanced to the degree of doctor of theology. While the Erfurt statutes give details regarding the competence and general preparation of the professors, they have nothing to say about their lectures.[51] It is possible that these dignitaries may have lectured also on the *Sentences*, but their real field seems to have been elsewhere. Such information as can be derived from other universities, mainly from Heidelberg, together with Martin's own practice less than a decade later when he had attained his doctor of theology and established himself as professor of the Bible at Wittenberg, leads us to believe that the magisterial lectures on the Bible were of an intensive character, quite different from the rapid surveys given by the bachelors.[52]

Time was apparently of little importance to the theologians of those days

[48] *TR*, I, No. 192 (1532).   [49] *TR*, III, No. 3698 (1538).

[50] As pointed out above (p. 89), it seems probable that Martin's novitiate did not end until September, 1506, but it is not possible to reject categorically A. V. Müller's theory of an earlier conclusion of this period. If Müller's chronology is correct, Biblical and theological studies, including the preparation for the priesthood, may have begun in the spring of 1506.

[51] "Acten," VIII, II, 58, 59, Rubrics 12 and 13.

[52] Ritter, *Die Heidelberger Universität*, I, 208 ff., 214 ff.

and to their hearers, as the heavy files of folio manuscript sheets in the Heidelberg and Vienna libraries testify. Some of these deal with a single Bible book or even a part of a book. A famous Viennese theologian of the fifteenth century, Heinrich von Langenstein, is said to have given a course on Genesis which ran through thirteen years, covering in that time only the first three or four chapters. Three vast folio volumes of his notes in the Vienna library deal with only three chapters.[53] This intensive treatment of their material seems to have been offset for the professors by a light teaching load. In Erfurt the duties of the doctors of theology were certainly not heavy; indeed, the statutes forbade them to lecture more than two or three hours a week.[54] Most of the professors' time was probably taken up with working out the disputation questions and supervising these exercises, and on special occasions taking part in them. Plans for the lectures were made far in advance: in Heidelberg an arrangement provided for three courses of twelve years each, one on the Gospels, one on the Epistles and Revelation, and one on the Pentateuch or the major and minor prophets. In general, the Heidelberg study for the doctorate covered twelve years, so that this arrangement fitted nicely with the requirements of such candidates as endured to the end.[55]

In view of this formidable array of evidence it is hard to see how the idea could have arisen and persisted throughout so many generations that the study of the Bible was neglected in the universities of the late scholastic period. As remarked, we have no information respecting courses of this kind at Erfurt. Judging by such data as we have, however, we are safe in conjecturing that the magisterial courses there proceeded slowly and covered a wide range of material, all the way from a meticulous discussion of the words of the text to the most important topics in systematic theology. The arguments of the lecturer were fortified by scholarly material drawn from the Bible itself, but more frequently from commentators as numerous as the scholarship and the energy of the professors permitted. Under his instructors Martin, therefore, must have had an opportunity to learn the technique of Biblical exegesis that had been developed by many generations of industrious Schoolmen. Within half a dozen years he was to take this in hand at Wittenberg and develop it to mastery.

The life of the young priest was obviously a busy one. Prayers, versicles,

---

[53] *Ibid.*, 214 f.; see n. 3. Ritter cites a story current in humanistic circles of another Viennese theologian of the fifteenth century, Thomas von Haselbach, who required thirty-two years to cover the first sixteen chapters of Isaiah, naturally with interruptions.

[54] "Acten," VIII, II, 51, para. 31.

[55] Ritter, *Die Heidelberger Universität*, I, 210.

and responses in the choir night, morning, and evening; lectures in the fore-noon and afternoon; visits to the village stations belonging to the cloister with celebration of the Mass there and on other occasions; making good the canonical hours in the breviary, which had been postponed when other duties required his absence from the choir; reading by the dim light of a fish-oil lamp or a wax-dipped rush in hours stolen from rest—thus the days and nights at the cloister were filled. These duties were, however, not enough to still the restlessness of the heart that throbbed under Martin's cowl. His rapid and orderly progress as student, teacher, and administrator in the service of his order and the picture which he drew in later years of his agitation of soul during his cloister life form a striking contrast, and the reconciliation of his outer and inner development is one of the major prob-lems for Luther biographers. There is evidence, to be examined in the next chapter, of truly extraordinary activity in the years directly following his ordination. Besides bearing the burden of ascetic life he flung himself with all the ardor of young manhood into the study of the intricate theories which generations of subtle thinkers had set up to explain the plan by which God saves or damns mankind. So far as the outer events of life are concerned, Martin continued to develop as should a gifted son of the cloister who brought to his work tireless industry and an intense devotion to the spiritual life. He rose through the varied grades of the theological profession with rapid step and attained within six years from the beginning of his studies, or perhaps a little longer, the ring of a doctor of theology and a chair in the faculty of Wittenberg. Such progress is evidence of the impression made by his scholarship and religious character on his academic teachers, the re-gents of studies at the cloister, and the provincial authorities of the order.

In none of the letters or other writings that have been preserved from this period has Martin anything to say of dissatisfaction with life in the cloister until more than a dozen years after his ordination; in fact, it is almost a quarter of a century before he begins to draw in lectures, sermons, and *Table Talk* the picture of grinding physical hardships, harrowing tor-tures of conscience, the fear of Christ as a stern judge, the horror of re-ceiving the Sacrament with an impure heart, fright at the celebration of the Mass, and other doubts and mental torments which a sensitive soul may suffer.[56] Like other great sons of the Renaissance, Martin was deeply in-

---

[56] With the exception of certain criticisms of monastic narrowness and pride, such as references to the theory of the reception into a religious order as a "new baptism," *De cap-tivitate Babylonica* (1520), *WA*, VII, 539, Martin's first attacks on the life and spirit of the orders occurs in *De votis monasticis*, *WA*, VIII, in 1521. It has been suggested that he had not yet at this time decided to leave the monastery, see *WA*, VIII, 565, but note his statement in his

terested in his own development and was acutely conscious of the part that the fifteen years spent under monastic vows had played in the great religious drama whose most important actor he was. But the path which his thinking had taken now made it difficult for him to recapture the moods and inner experiences through which he had passed in his twenties. The theological revolution begun when he became a professor and preacher at Wittenberg in 1512 wrought in the following decade so complete a change in his conception of monasticism that he came to regard the institution itself as contrary to God's command. In consequence, it is difficult to establish the chronology of Martin's recollections, for it is clearly impossible to isolate the experiences of soul which came to him in the Erfurt cloister from those belonging to later years in Wittenberg when he had come to grips with the Pauline theology. After the early battles of the revolt had been fought and he had attained the perspective of middle age, his whole life in the cloister seemed to him an experience filled with tormenting doubts and paralyzing fears, until at last the light suddenly broke upon him. The dramatization of this experience reached its crest in the autobiographical sketch written in the year before his death and prefaced to the first volume of his collected

letter to Wenceslaus Link, December 18, 1521, where the possibility is certainly implied: "Tu vero interim cum Hieremia in ministerio Babylonis maneris; nam et ego in habitu et ritu isto manebo, nisi mundus alius fiat." In *De votis* the laziness and self-indulgence of the monks is criticized, but only in passing. *WA*, VIII, 583. The main force of his attack is on the theological bases of monasticism, which, as he now feels, rests on a false conception of God's commands. This brings in its train a disregard of the commandment that children obey their parents, a loss of Christian freedom, a dethronement of faith, and in general a sacrifice of the spirit of religion for the form. The strongest protest is against the vow of chastity, and this phase of monasticism is the only one appearing in the work that suggests desperation and torment of conscience on the part of the cloister inmate. *WA*, VIII, 630 ff., 660. In the years immediately following, the monastic life serves to illustrate further Martin's theological position: it seeks salvation through works and not through faith. See as a typical instance the sermon on John 16, *WA*, XII, 543 f. (1523), where the monastic ideal of service is contrasted with his own. He looks back on the cloister life as a period of earnest but vain effort to fulfill the works necessary for salvation. See *Sommerpostille* (1526), *WA*, X, 1, Part 2, 436 ff.; sermon on Genesis 3 (1527), *WA*, XXIV, 91; lecture on Epistle of St. John (1527), *WA*, XX, 772 f.; and especially sermon on Acts 9.1 (1529), *WA*, XXIX, 49 ff. It is not until 1530 that we begin to find statements regarding sadness and unrest of conscience during his cloister days. See letter to H. Weller, Enders, *Luthers Briefwechsel*, VIII, 159 f. Then in the following years such reminiscences become numerous along with others emphasizing physical hardships and severe self-discipline as a part of his monastic experience. These are in the *Table Talk* as noted by all reporters; in the commentary on Galatians (1531), *WA*, XL, 1 and 11; the lectures on Psalms (1532), *WA*, XL, 11; in sermons of the years 1530–32, some striking instances in *WA*, XXXII, and 1535–38, *WA*, XLI, XLV–XLVII; in *Kleine Antwort auf Herzog Georgen nächstes Buch* (1533), *WA*, XXXVIII, and in the lectures on Genesis (1535–45), *WA*, XLII–XLIV. Scheel's *Dokumente* is useful for a general survey of these reminiscences, although it does not claim to be exhaustive and the citations in some cases do not supply the context necessary to a complete understanding of Luther's ideas. The user will not always agree with the editor's captions.

Latin works.[57] To a man of Luther's ardent temperament, it is inevitable that life, when viewed in perspective, should resolve itself into a series of violent experiences.

Not nearly so important as his own change in perspective, yet also deserving of consideration if one wishes to evaluate Luther's later utterances on his cloister life, is the doubtful authenticity of many reminiscences which have filtered down to us. These are for the most part recollections incorporated in lectures, sermons, and *Table Talk*. In the busy years that saw the foundation of the Evangelical Church, we have few manuscript texts of lectures or sermons in Martin's own hand, but are dependent on the notes and transcripts of students and associates. For these the customs of the monastic life and the religious attitude of the Catholic hierarchy were already a strange world. It is not safe for this reason to accept a single statement based on these sources at face value. Each must be examined for its validity as an expression of Martin's recollection of his development. The veil that hangs between us and the soul life of the youthful friar is therefore a heavy one, in spite of the wealth of autobiographical material that Martin furnished.

With these reservations in mind, we may now seek to discover so far as possible the nature of the inner conflicts which Martin underwent as the earliest cloister experiences receded into the past. Viewed in contemporary sources, so far as they exist, the period between his ordination in 1507 and his installation as professor in Wittenberg five years later appears as one of rapid and organic growth in scholarship and of ripening influence as a member of his order. He bore a heavy burden of ascetic life; he devoted himself to studies in the Bible, in systematic theology, and other theological literature; he began to lay the foundation for an independent approach to the sources of Christian dogma and for scholarly exegesis. Along with this development the friar was assailed by hours of restlessness and agonizing doubts. It is quite probable that this began to be the case early in his cloister life. "When I was first inducted into the monastery, it happened that I would always go about sad and depressed and could not shake off this melancholy," [58] is one of the recollections from his early middle age. There is reason to think, as we have seen, that fits of depression beset him before his entry into the cloister.[59] Certainly the monastic life must have brought many difficult hours to the mind of a young man of his active and energetic temperament and possessing the gifts which he showed for bestirring himself in the world of men. Once in later years he quotes the monks as saying

[57] *WA*, LIV, 185.

[58] Letter from Luther to H. Weller, 1530, Enders, *Luthers Briefwechsel*, VIII, 159.

[59] *TR*, III, No. 3593 (1537). There is no reason to doubt this statement, although the passage contains obvious errors.

that wherever there is a melancholy person a bath has been made ready for the devil.[60] The physical difficulties, too, for a young friar who submits himself fully to the discipline of monastic life, must be great. In Martin's case these were probably increased, for it seems likely that he went further than the regulations of the order demanded in fasting and other ascetic practices.[61] Nevertheless, though physical causes may have accentuated the attacks of depression, their source lay in his psychical personality and therefore far below the reach of the investigator's plummet. They play a large rôle in his reminiscences and undoubtedly began early in life, for they recur throughout the middle years. It was a part of the mythology implanted in childhood that he should have regarded these visitations as temptations of the devil. "It seems to me," he declares in 1521, "that from childhood Satan foresaw in me something of what he is now suffering from me. That is the reason he has raged against me with unbelievable tricks to hamper and destroy me, so that I have often wondered whether I was not the only one among mortals in whom he was laying his traps." [62] The attacks followed him through life, but with advancing age he worked out a system, based largely on the Scriptures, by which he gave himself successful treatment. The strife against mental depression, he concluded, is a struggle with the devil.[63] God is happiness and hates melancholy; the devil is melancholy,[64] and the Christian who fights off its attacks is resisting the devil.[65] At times Martin ascribes the cause to fasting and loneliness; [66] the treatment is prayer and conversation with pious friends.[67] Cases of mental disturbance among the younger inmates of the monastery cannot have been unknown, for Martin speaks of brothers who fell victim to acute mental disorders and in spite of all the resources of monastic clinical experience became hopelessly insane or were obliged to give up cloister life.[68] He himself seems to have escaped any real mental difficulty, but the tension of life showed itself in pronounced hyster-

---

[60] *TR*, I, No. 455 (1533); see also II, No. 1349 (1532) and IV, No. 5155 (1540). The proverb recurs in a number of passages in the *Table Talk*.

[61] At thirty-seven years of age he suffered acutely from constipation. See letters from the Wartburg, May 12, 1521, *WAB*, II, 333, ll. 34 ff.; also *ibid.*, p. 338.

[62] *De votis monasticis, WA*, VIII, 574.   [63] *TR*, I, No. 122 (1531).

[64] *TR*, I, No. 194 (1532); No. 676; see also No. 832.

[65] *TR*, I, No. 124; No. 676; No. 835; II, No. 1279; Nos. 2342a and 2342b.

[66] *TR*, II, No. 2456.

[67] *TR*, III, No. 2840b. Luther's discussions of melancholy are rich in psychological interest. As spiritual adviser he evidently had considerable experience with depressed and hysterical cases and this supplemented his own experience in the monastic life. See the story relating that a liberal feeding cured the sister of a bishop of the idea that she was eternally lost. *TR*, II, No. 2361b. Also the account of a hysterical case cured by suggestion. *TR*, III, Nos. 2889a and 2889b (1533).

[68] "Multos vidi factos amentes et sic factus fuissem." *Commentarius ad Galatos* (1531), *WA*, XL, I, 368.

ical symptoms which may be noted from time to time in the monastic years and tended to present themselves also, though less acutely, at middle age and even on the threshold of old age. These "temptations," as he calls them, brought him occasionally to the verge of despair. We have read the story of the fit in the cloister choir as reported to Johann Cochlaeus by certain Augustinian brothers. It bears marks of probability, for Luther himself records another instance of strikingly similar character which happened some years later, probably in 1515. Then, as he tells a scribe at table sixteen years after the event, he was struck with terror at sight of the sacrament borne by the vicar general, Dr. Staupitz, in the Corpus Christi procession.[69] His sensitivity to powerful attacks of depression is shown by several experiences recorded later but evidently belonging to the days when he was still in the Augustinian order. A vivid recollection of this kind comes down from the period of the struggle over indulgences and is found in the *Explanations on the Power of Indulgences* in 1518. Here, in a remarkable passage on the tortures of purgatory, he describes pangs of conscience which he had endured. "They lasted, to be sure, only a short while, but they were so hard and infernal that no tongue can express their power, no pen describe it, nor can anyone believe it who has never had the experience. If they should remain at their most extreme point for an hour, yes, even six minutes, the victim must quite perish and all his bones be turned to ashes." [70] About the same time at which these words were written, possibly two or three years later, he seems to have suffered severe attacks of despair, especially the feeling that he was hated of God. "I was beset by the most extreme temptations [fear of the wrath of God]; they devoured my body as with fire so that I scarcely remained alive." [71] Respecting a similar onset at the same period of life, he declares that no one could console him, so that he was

[69] *TR*, I, No. 137 (1531). Aurifaber's German translation of the passage builds up still further the impression of terror. Whether the attack was known only to himself or was apparent to others Luther does not disclose.

[70] *Resolutiones disputationum de indulgiarum virtute* (1518), *WA*, I, 557, ll. 34 ff. Scheel, *Martin Luther*, II, 635, raises a doubt as to whether Luther really refers to himself in this passage. Its introduction, "Sed et ego novi hominem, qui has poenas saepius passum sese asseruit," obviously is a rhetorical imitation of that of St. Paul in his recital of his heavenly vision in II Cor. 12.2: "Scio hominem in Christo ante annos quatuordecim. . . ." Luther's recital, however, follows a reference to cases of torment of conscience cited by Tauler, and this raises the possibility that Martin has here in mind another sufferer than himself. There is, however, a certain realism in the passage that bears the stamp of personal experience.

[71] *TR*, II, No. 1263 (1531): "Ante decem annos primum sensi hanc desperationem et irae divinae tentationem. Hab darnach rhue gehabt, ut etiam uxorem ducerem so gutte tag hett ich, sed postea rediit." This extract from Schlaginhaufen, one of the reporters of the *Table Talk*, agrees verbally, with trifling deviations, with a statement by Dietrich dated December 14, 1531, *TR*, I, No. 141 which was probably the first source. The association of his marriage with a period of cessation of the attacks is psychologically interesting.

obliged to ask: "Am I the only one to suffer the spirit of sadness? I saw so many apparitions. But ten years ago when I was alone, God comforted me with his angels to go on struggling and writing." [72] Ratzeberger adds a narrative which he assigns to be the "beginning of his struggle against the Pope." When Martin, who had scarcely taken food or drink for some time, locked himself in his room, his friends finally broke open the door and found him unconscious on the floor.[73]

Despite the need for caution in judging these utterances, as we have said, there is no reason to doubt that the afflictions, to which Luther was subject even in later years, came and went during the period following his ordination. Recollections of middle age forced happier memories of monastic days into the background and gave dramatic expression in lectures, sermons, and *Table Talk* to agonies of soul.[74] Yet the early soul experiences, even as they are reflected in the broken mirror of middle life, are too frequent and insistent to be without some factual basis. The existence of an inner restlessness in the Erfurt period, therefore, seems certain, though it is not likely that either Martin or his associates can have been as acutely aware of it

[72] *TR*, II, No. 1347 (January 1–March 23, 1532). Wolf, "Staupitz und Luther," pp. 142 ff., is of the opinion that Martin recalls here a different experience from that recorded in the reports discussed in the preceding note. His argument is scarcely convincing. In any case the memory of fierce attacks of depression in the crucial years of revolt, 1518–21, seems to have been vivid for Martin a decade later. Any attempt at dating these experiences more definitely or determining their precise nature would seek to do what probably lay beyond the ability of Martin himself a decade afterwards.

[73] Ratzeberger, *Handschriftliche Geschichte,* pp. 58 f. The author adds that after Martin came to himself he shook off his melancholy under the influence of the music of his friends: "Dan er befandt, so bald er Musicam hörete, dass sich seine tentationes und schwermut enderten."

[74] In his *Dokumente* Scheel assembles a large number of these recollections by Martin and others under the head of "Rückblicke (1513–1595)." To these he adds "Zeugnisse (1501–1519)," contemporary statements by Martin in lectures, letters, and sermons. It is only in the twentieth century that Luther biographers have become fully conscious of the difference between these two groups of sources. They have been at pains to identify various types of experience in the recollections and other source material, such as those due to the cloister environment with its ascetic demands and spiritual disappointments, those aroused by studies in scholastic theology, and those springing from dissatisfaction with the so-called juridical conception of man's relation to God as opposed to the Pauline ideas upon which Luther's theology is declared to have been based. This tendency to apply categories to the "tentationes," the term by which Martin at middle age designated every form of disturbance of mental and emotional life, may lead entirely away from human psychology, whose processes cannot all be forced into rational patterns but, especially in the case of genius, often follow original and spontaneous urges. We shall see that Martin on several occasions speaks of having acted intuitively and without his own volition. The student of his life must, therefore, be content to determine as clearly as the sources permit, the characteristics of individual experiences, and be willing to concede, *ignoramus!* The "tentationes" were inseparable from Martin's nature and varied only in emotional intensity under physical and intellectual stimulus, weakening with other biological forces when middle age came on. That such experiences occurred in the early cloister years, at least in the period immediately following his ordination to the priesthood, is widely held, at least by the Protestant biographers.

as later recollections would lead one to believe. The attacks to which he was subject were by no means merely the result of an interplay of physical and temperamental causes; nor were they solely the reactions of a body worn with fasting and loss of sleep, nervously overwrought by fulfillment of the exacting demands of the daily office in the choir and by an absorbing interest in study. The hardships of cloister life simply accented the crises which welled up from a nature extraordinarily sensitive to religious emotions and panting for a direct covenant with God. As we have seen, the complex causes of his conversion to the religious life included not only fears of God but the search for the security which he hoped to find on the path of self-renunciation. After his novitiate year, with his adaptation to the life of the friar, he became more and more absorbed in studies, first for the priestly office. Then the whole medieval theological system spread itself before him, as a metaphysical web to be unraveled. His studies must have stimulated powerfully the tendency of his mind to occupy itself with thoughts of sin and grace. At times he undoubtedly felt a happy security in the religious life. The Christian mythology of boyhood then took on a new vitality; the ritual of religious service and the lives of the saints now brought these shining figures directly to his side for protection and blessing. "St. Anne was my idol and St. Thomas my apostle." [75] In addition to the patron of the household at Mansfeld who had meant so much to his childhood, he clung to St. George, the bright figure who had looked down on him from altar or painted window in the Mansfeld church.[76] He declared that he called on three saints at every Mass;[77] indeed if we may trust recollections of middle life, he carried on the cult of sainthood with all the fanatic zeal of the time. In a conversation of 1539 he recalled that he selected twenty-one saints, invoking three each at the Mass: "Thus I came the round in a week." [78] The fears inspired by early beliefs also went with him into the cloister. One of these was that of Christ as his severe judge, which, as we have seen, probably arose from impressions derived in childhood from pictures familiar in late medieval iconography.[79] This became a source of unhappiness in the cloister to

[75] Sermon of December 22, 1532, WA, XXXVI, 388. A hostile tone toward his earlier reverence for the saints pervades many of his recollections. In a series of sermons on texts from St. John and St. Matthew (1537–40), he represents prayer to the saints as a form of idolatry. See especially, regarding prayer for intercession in the order: WA, XLVI, 663 (1537); ibid., 782 (1537–38); WA, XLVII, 109, 461 (1538); ibid., 589 (1539); "Est manifesta idololatria," WA, XLI, 654.

[76] WA, XLVII, 461. See also WA, XL, II, 285 (1532).

[77] EA, XXIII, 354 f. (1543–44). He names them as Barbara, Anne, and Christopher. WA, XLI, 393 (1535); see also WA, XXII, 174, 305; and WA, XLI, 654.

[78] TR, IV, No. 4422 (1539). According to another less reliable source, the number of these patrons was fourteen. TR, V, No. 5363 (1540).

[79] Sermon of November 1, 1531, WA, XXXIV, II, 410.

which he returns again and again in his recollections of experience there.[80] Here he refers frequently to his conviction that Christ was indifferent to human woes and must be won over through the intercession of his mother, the Virgin.[81] The picture of Christ sitting in judgment on the Last Day dwelt vividly in his mind, so that he could not shake off fears connected with it. "When I looked on Christ, I saw the devil: so [I said], 'Dear Mary, pray to your Son for me and still His anger.'" [82] He was the first of all the devils. Everybody fled from Him and hated Him.[83] Whenever he saw the picture of Christ he would cast down his eyes and was so minded that he would rather have seen the devil.[84] These pictures which he begins to draw two years after he had left the order recur in sermons and lectures through nearly a quarter of a century. They are, in fact, among his most persistent recollections of cloister ideology.[85] It is evident that there were times when the consciousness of sin lay as a crushing load upon him and a sensitive conscience sounded the alarm at every wandering thought. "When I was a monk I thought myself damned whenever I felt the desires of the flesh." [86] There were moments when all confidence in the possibility of his salvation deserted him. "My heart shivered and trembled as to how God could be merciful to me," he told his audience in a sermon at the end of the 1530s.[87] In a sharp polemical comment on the monk's baptism some four years earlier, there is a bitter memory of suffering in the cloister days: "Then I was the most miserable creature on the earth. Day and night there was nothing but horror and despair, and no one could give me help." [88] Perhaps the conception of the "justice of God" which was to play such an important rôle in his

[80] See *Kleine Antwort auf Herzog Georgen nächstes Buch* (1533), *WA*, XXXVIII, 148: "Denn ich kandte Christum nicht mehr denn als einen gestrengen Richter, für dem ich fliehen wolt und doch nicht entfliehen kundte. . . . ein zorniger Richter, ja, Hencker und Teuffel . . . inn unserm Hertzen." Particularly the later sermons swarm with references to this conception, prevalent in the cloister, of Christ as judge: he did not like to hear His name (*WA*, XLI, 197 [1535]); "schrecklicher Richter und Tyrann" (*WA*, XLV, 567 [1537]); poor stupid, timid hearts were more afraid of Christ than of the devil himself (*WA*, XXII, 305). See also *WA*, XLV, 153; XLVI, 8; XLVII, 99, 277, 576. Though these references fall in the later years, it is to be noted that the stress on this concept of Christ is also one of the early charges that Luther brings against the cloisters and universities after he has left his order. See the sermon of October 21, 1522, *WA*, X, III, 357.

[81] "Imo tantum iudicem Christum putavimus, sedentem in celis, non curantem res nostras." This appears in a sermon of 1523, *WA*, XI, 60. See also *ibid.*, p. 110. For similar expressions, see his commentary on Galatians, *WA*, XL, I, 561; also certain of his sermons, *WA*, XXV, 510 f.; XXXIII, 83 f. and 539 f.

[82] Sermon of May 21, 1537, *WA*, XLV, 86.

[83] Sermon on John 8.15 (1531), *WA*, XXXIII, 540.

[84] Sermon on Matthew 18 (1537), *WA*, XLVII, 310.

[85] It is striking that memories of this kind do not seem to appear in the *Table Talk*.

[86] Commentary on Galatians (1531), *WA*, XL, II, 92.

[87] *WA*, XLVII, 590.

[88] *Kleine Antwort auf Herzog Georgen nächstes Buch*, *WA*, XXXVIII, 148.

thinking when he undertook lectures at Wittenberg a few years later had already begun to plague him. He declares that when he first read in the Psalter, "Deliver me in Thy righteousness!" (*In iustitia tua libera me!*), he was frightened and hated the words, "For I had no other idea than that the righteousness of God meant his severe judgment. Would He save me from His severe judgment? I would be eternally lost." [89]

Amid these attacks he turned to his confessor in search of relief through this outlet for burdened souls. A certain verse in Proverbs, quite harmless-looking to the uninitiated but pregnant with symbolic importance in the mystical interpretation of the Middle Ages: "Know thou the state of thy flocks," frightened him so much that he laid before his confessor everything that he had done from youth up. For such excess of zeal his confessor finally punished him.[90] This overworking of the confession was natural to a sensitive soul, and Martin knew of many such cases. In one passage noted down in the *Table Talk* he tells of a friend, Dr. Hieronymus Schurf, a minor administrator in the Electorate of Saxony, who, after going to his confessor three and four times before the sacrament, felt obliged to whisper some neglected scruples in the ear of the priest at the altar.[91] Martin also remembered that on one occasion when he himself had come back to account for some forgotten sin, the confessor said, "God bids us hope in His mercy; go in peace!" [92] Sometimes he was driven by inner restlessness to think up sins which he had not committed.[93] It may have been in the early cloister years that he learned to know Jean Gerson, the "doctor consolatoris," whose prescription for lifting the burden from troubled consciences Martin held in high regard in later years.[94] It is quite probable that some brothers among the Eremites made sport of these over-stimulated consciences, and such treatment no doubt had its salutary effect. Others made short work of timorous souls. One of Martin's confessors, after listening to his "foolish sins," remarked, "You are a fool! God is not angry with you; you are angry with Him." "A magnificent expression!" Martin adds, "even though he spoke it before the dawning of the gospel light." [95] In the midst of these troubles, probably in Wittenberg, he put his case before the district vicar, Dr. Staupitz. This seasoned churchman, whose experience probably included

[89] *TR*, V, No. 5247 (1540).
[90] Proverbs 27.23: "Agnosce vultum pecoris tui." *TR*, I, No. 461, pp. 200 f.
[91] *TR*, V, No. 6017.   [92] *Ibid.*
[93] Sermon on Matthew 23, *WA*, XLVII, 441 (1538).
[94] *TR*, I, No. 141 (1531), p. 64, ll. 4 ff.; see also II, No. 1263 (1531), p. 15, ll. 24 ff.; I, No. 979 (first half of 1530s), and elsewhere. We shall see that Martin knew the great Paris theologian from several sides.
[95] *TR*, I, No. 122 (1531).

a great many storm-tossed cloister inmates, young and old, after listening to Martin's troubles of soul, remarked merely, "I do not understand it." "That was fine comfort!" Afterwards he went to another and it was the same thing. No confessor would have anything to do with it. Then he thought:

"No one has this temptation but you!" I felt like a corpse. Finally Staupitz remarked to me as I sat across the table from him, "Why are you so sad and cast down?" I answered: "What am I to do?" He said, "You do not understand how necessary it is. Otherwise no good would come of you." He himself did not understand, for he thought that I was a scholar and that unless I suffered these trials, I might become proud. I too accepted it like Paul: "There was given me a thorn that I should not be exalted overmuch. My power is made perfect in weakness." So I received this as the voice of the Holy Spirit consoling me.[96]

This interchange with the general vicar belongs in all probability to a period four or five years later than that which we are now considering. It is, however, of interest here, for it reveals the attitude of mind which enabled the young priest to combat the fears which beset him. As his reading widened, the fears at the thought of an angry God probably took on new color from his studies. "The justice of God" is one of the most persistent expressions in the *Table Talk*. It may have begun to occupy his mind soon after his ordination and hung more and more threateningly on the horizon as time went by and he assumed the responsibilities of a professor at Wittenberg. Here, then, it finally became the major problem that challenged his scholarship.[97]

To a mind beset by emotional crises, a single word or phrase may produce panic. On the other hand, it may jar open closed doors and let in reviving light and air. Melanchthon tells us in his brief biographical sketch that in a moment of anguish Luther found comfort with an old man who pointed out to him a passage in St. Bernard to the effect that when we say in the Apostles' Creed "I believe in the forgiveness of sins," each one must believe that his sins are forgiven.[98] There is some confirmation for the story in the lectures on Romans in 1516, where Martin quotes what is evidently the passage referred to in Bernard's sermon on the forgiveness of sins.[99] The practical mysticism of the great medieval preacher may well have furnished him with consolation in the Erfurt days, for he praises the saint repeatedly

[96] *TR*, I, No. 518 (1533), p. 240, ll. 13 ff.

[97] The bearing of the conception of *iustitia dei* on his development will be considered below. The comparison of its impact on the conscience to a bolt must have been a favorite one with Luther: the *Table Talk* reporters Schlaginhaufen, Lauterbach, and Cordatus all have it. *TR*, II, No. 1681; III, No. 3232a; IV, No. 4007.

[98] *CR*, VI, 159.   [99] Ficker, *Anfänge reformatorischer Bibelauslegung*, I, 197.

in later years in sermons and *Table Talk* as one who preached Christ even more than Augustine,[100] and as the most pleasing preacher of Christ.[101]

These spiritual agonies were compensated for by days of full happiness. Were the latter more numerous in Martin's monastic years? If one should trust the middle-aged professor in Wittenberg, the periods when contentment and happiness ruled in his soul were few, but on this point statements after 1530 are, as we have said, a particularly unreliable basis. It is possible, however, to find considerable evidence that despite all doubts and fears the years that followed immediately on his ordination to the priesthood were in the main a period of confidence in the guarantees of the religious life, of eager fulfillment of its liturgical duties, especially the duties of the altar, and of ardent enthusiasm for study. The most important evidence, as has been said, is the success that attended his efforts. Probably in the late fall of 1508, as we shall see, he was sent to Wittenberg as instructor in philosophy, and in the following spring received his baccalaureate in the Bible. We must see in this achievement a reflection of the opinion on the part of his elders in the order that his spiritual character was sound and his scholarship promising. In spite of his zeal for ascetic exercises and the hardships of cloister life, the sturdy constitution of the descendant of a race of hardy peasants was sound and vigorous. Once adapted to the round of life in the cloister he appears to have met the severe demands on limbs and eyes and nerves throughout the entire cloister period, for it was not until the very end was approaching that a relaxation of the daily service of prayer took place. The impression made by his personality at the Leipzig disputation in 1519 and two years later at the Diet of Worms was that of energy unimpaired by the preceding years of grueling mental strain. In the early cloister years at Erfurt ardor of temperament and fire of purpose must have glowed in him with all the vigor of youth. He devoted himself to the service of the altar with what we may believe was special zeal,[102] although the fear of slips in the ritual caused him anxiety in the early days of his priesthood.[103]

[100] *TR*, I, No. 872.

[101] *TR*, IV, No. 4772; see also sermons on Gospel of John, *WA*, XLVI, 782 (1537), and XLVII, 109 (1538).

[102] This zeal for saying Mass is one of Martin's most persistent declarations in later years concerning his priesthood. In *Von der Winkelmesse und Pfaffenweihe* (1533), one of his most bitter attacks on the Roman Church, he declares that he had said hedge Mass every day for fifteen years. *WA*, XXXVIII, 197. This, though obviously an exaggeration, is repeated many times in sermon transcripts and *Table Talk*. See the sermon of Aug. 1, 1535, *WA*, XLI, 393; also sermon on John 15.5, *WA*, XLV, 670. See also above, n. 1.

[103] "Wen ich ein Stuck in der messen nicht recht machete oder etwas darvon thette, ich muste verloren sein." Sermon on John 3.19 (1538), *WA*, XLVII, 108. See also references in preceding note.

We may well believe a statement of twenty years later that his heart beat high with confidence when the holy office had been discharged to his satisfaction.[104] Thus, with all the enthusiasm of young manhood, he pushed onward with the labors, joys, and pains of life devoted to high purpose. Eccentric and headstrong he may have seemed at times to prior and regents and definitors, as well as to the brothers, but they obviously also saw in him outstanding gifts. Certainly to the viewer of a later day his actions and thoughts bear the mark of genius struggling toward self-expression amid age-old traditions and hard-and-fast patterns of thought.

[104] "Missa una bene peracta, quantus mihi animus accessit." Lecture on Isaiah, probably late in 1528, *WA*, XXXI, II, 154. See also *TR*, III, Nos. 2935a and 2935b.

9

THE YOUNG LECTURER

DEEPLY immersed in his studies and bound to the requirements of the daily choir service, with its liturgical exercises and canonical devotions, Martin watched the church year roll around. On the cold, dark North German winter followed the Lenten season with its "quadrigesimal food" and other sacrifices, and on this the joys of Easter and the anniversary of his first Mass. Already the summer semester had opened at the university and if, as seems most likely, his studies were now in the faculty of theology rather than at the cloister, he continued to hear lectures on the *Sentences* and to attend disputations in the hall of the faculty, and perhaps also entered on a magisterial course in Bible exegesis. So the fall approached and now he might look forward to the attainment of his first degree in theology, that of bachelor in the Bible, when the winter semester should come to its end. At this moment an order arrived which opened a new episode in his life. Sometime in the autumn of 1508, probably before the opening of the winter semester, the cloister authorities directed him to leave Erfurt and go to the cloister of his order at Wittenberg. So unexpected was the command and so prompt the fulfillment that his most intimate friends scarcely knew of it, as he says in an apologetic letter the following March in answer to the complaints of his old friend Vicar Braun at Eisenach.[1]

In this letter Martin gives no hint of why he was transferred. It is probable that the cause had to do with the development of the university at Wittenberg. This had been founded six years earlier and was still in process of first growth. In connection with it the Augustinian cloister, hitherto of no great significance in the Saxon-Thuringian province of the order, was seeking to develop a "general study" similar to that in the Erfurt house. The relation of the university to the cloister in Wittenberg was, however, quite

---

[1] Letter from Luther to Johann Braun, March 17, 1509, *WAB*, I, 16 f. The letter is replete with unctuous monastic formulas and is marked in general by the same youthful *préciosité* as that to Vicar Braun two years before.

different from that prevailing in the Thuringian city. The statutes of the theological faculty in the new university were adopted in the year of Martin's arrival.[2] With the use of what economists now call "borrower's technique," the young institution took over the general framework of the traditional organization for theological study but gave it a simplified and modern form, omitting many requirements which had grown up through a century of scholasticism. Indeed, in their simplicity the Wittenberg statutes have something of the spirit of humanism. The relations of cloister and university were more intimate, for while the ancient Thuringian school was as independent as possible in an age when the Church dominated education, the young institution at Wittenberg, even in its faculty of arts, was largely supported by ecclesiastical funds. Here the little Augustinian cloister played an important rôle. Two lectureships had been set up from the cloister brotherhood, one in the Bible and one in moral philosophy, the former filled by the general vicar, Johann von Staupitz, so far as his frequent absences on official duties permitted, and the latter, according to a contemporary catalogue of the university, by another Augustinian.[3] It is probable that the responsibilities thus thrown on the Wittenberg cloister had proved too heavy for so small a group, and possibly as the result of a plan formed at the meeting of the provincial chapter which convened in Munich on October 18, 1508, seven brothers were drafted from various cloisters and sent to Wittenberg. As one of this delegation, Martin came to the city.[4] Whether his selection was due to the initiative of Staupitz or was the result of intellectual and spiritual characteristics which the Erfurt Eremites had discovered in him, cannot be said with certainty. We do know, however, that Martin continued to regard himself as a member of the Erfurt cloister, for he noted with his own hand in the faculty records of Wittenberg that his mother cloister would have to pay the fees for his promotion to the baccalaureate in the Bible.[5] Even though the exact time and the circumstances of his transfer remain

[2] They are conveniently accessible in W. Friedensburg, "Urkundenbuch der Universität Wittenberg," I (1502–1611), *Geschichtsquellen der Provinz Sachsen*, N.F. III (1926), 32 ff. For a comparison with the Erfurt statutes, see Oergel, *Vom jungen Luther*, p. 96.

[3] A certain Wolfgang Ostermayr of Munich. See *ibid.*, p. 110. Oergel's source, Christoph Scheurl's *Rotulus Doctorum Vittembergae profitentium* (1507), was not available to me. What became of Ostermayr when Martin came to Wittenberg is not known. Sources regarding the arrangements with the Augustinians may be found in Friedensburg, *Geschichte der Universität Wittenberg*, pp. 22 f., n. 1. Another theological professorship was filled by a Franciscan.

[4] Kolde, *Augustiner-Kongregation*, p. 252, n. 1, refers to the Wittenberg Album, p. 27, which attests the matriculation of the six other Augustinians who came with Martin. That the sending of the delegation of brothers was decided at the Munich general chapter is a hypothesis of Müller. See *Werdegang*, p. 49. See also Scheel, *Martin Luther*, II, 358, n. 6.

[5] "Nec faciet. Quia tunc pauper et sub obedientia nihil habuit. Solvet ergo Erffordia." Förstemann, *Liber decanorum*, p. 4, n. 3.

obscure, it is to be noted that the promising young scholar was immediately enlisted in the service of cloister and university as teacher of philosophy.

The city on the Elbe to which the mendicant came "in poverty and under orders," as the matriculation book records,[6] and which was later to become the pilot house of the religious revolution in Germany, could not have made a pleasant impression on Martin. He must have been struck by a painful contrast with the rich natural background and vigorous civic life of the Thuringian metropolis. Hostile observers of those days—and these include naturally the enemies of Luther—note the lack of the vigorous orchards so characteristic of the Erfurt region.[7] Even friendly critics among contemporaries like Friedrich Myconius[8] thought the town with its little ugly wooden buildings more like a village than a city. After many years of residence Martin expresses on more than one occasion his surprise that a university should have ever been established at Wittenberg,[9] and apparently agreed with a contemporary divine who called it a "flayer's yard."[10] In place of the swelling background of hills, framed in the south by the green heights of the Thuringian forest, he saw only the broad, featureless plain of the Saxon lowlands where the Elbe, most unpicturesque of rivers in its lower stretches, winds its lazy way through sandy soil, so sandy, indeed, that Martin once expressed his conviction that a villainous people must have dwelt there and left a curse on the land.[11]

These opinions were undoubtedly exaggerations. One is tempted to cite against them the roseate statements of university officials of the day, whose testimony is somewhat compromised, to be sure, by their evident desire to attract students to the new school. Of such kind was the opinion of a professor of law, Christoph Scheurl, who praises the mildness of the Wittenberg air.[12] An even more suspicious witness, Andreas Meinhard, brought out

---

[6] *Ibid.*

[7] Johann Cochlaeus, *Ein christliche vermanung der heyligen stat Rom an das Teutschlandt,* trans. by Johann Dietenberger (1524), cited by Scheel, *Martin Luther,* II, 314, n. 7.

[8] E. S. Cyprian, ed., "Historia Reformationis," in *Tentzels Historischer Bericht vom Anfang und Fortgang der Reformation Lutheri,* II, III, 27. Myconius was a Franciscan who spent his cloister years at Leipzig and Weimar.

[9] *TR,* III, No. 2871b (1533).

[10] *TR,* II, No. 2800b (1532): "Wir sitzen allhie Wittenbergae nur in einem schindeleich testante Domino Mellerstadt." According to Kroker's note, this sharp-tongued critic was probably Valentin Mellerstadt, son of the first rector of the university, Martin Pollich von Mellerstadt. Later on Luther had more biting things to say of the city and its people, which were faithfully recorded by the scribes at his table and in his lecture room. See, e.g., *TR,* IV, No. 4681 (1539). For sundry bitter criticisms in his sermons, see Buchwald, *Predigten D. Martin Luthers,* I, 20.

[11] Lectures on Genesis, *WA,* XLII, 358 (1536). In the *Table Talk* there are a number of references to the unfertile soil around Wittenberg.

[12] "Mira gaudet aeris temperie." Quoted by Strobel, *Neue Beyträge zur Litteratur,* III, II, 59 f.

at the invitation of the first rector a clever pamphlet of descriptive propaganda, a dialogue between an older student and a sub-freshman, in which Wittenberg is characterized as an earthly Paradise.[13]

The energetic descendants of the Low German and Flemish settlers, whom the Ascanian margraves of the thirteenth century had settled in the territory conquered from the Slavs on the north bank of the Elbe, had made of the sandy valley a country capable of producing enough grain and wine for the needs of its population. The city had been chartered more than two hundred years earlier at the crest of the great German push eastward. To the north and east it still faced an unbroken rural population of Slavic people, the Wends, and thus stood as an outpost of German culture and a citadel of German overlordship over the Slavic population. The despised Slavs possessed no civic rights within the city nor its suburbs, but tilled the soil round about or supported themselves as poor fishermen without the walls, paying serfage dues in labor and kind to their lords.[14] National and linguistic barriers separated this folk from the Germans, and the cleft widened as the years went by and the Reformation brought a religious separation of the Germans from their West Slavic neighbors.[15] The guilds, too, discriminated against them since they accepted no one of illegitimate birth and no one who had a grandparent not of the German tongue.[16] To the young monk as he crossed the great wooden bridge over the Elbe, a work of recent years,[17] and approached the city lying at this time half a mile from

[13] Republished in part by Haussleiter in *Die Universität Wittenberg vor dem Eintritt Luthers*. Meinhard's work, *Dialogus illustrate ac Augustissime urbis Albiorene vulgo Vittenberg dicte Situm Amenitatem ac Illustrationem docens Tirocinia nobilium artium iacientibus Editus*, printed at Leipzig in 1508, is a lively introduction to the new seat of the muses. In the dialogue between the two students town and university are passed in review, with especial attention to the Castle Church and its holy relics. The lengthy description of the hazing procedure (*depositio*) is especially interesting. A discussion in praise of celibacy gives a late-medieval flavor to this specimen of academic propaganda. There is a copy in the Jena University library. Of Meinhard not much is known. Haussleiter gives an analysis and summary of most of the material concerning him. For sources see N. Müller, *Die Wittenberger Bewegung*, pp. 300 ff.; Grohmann, *Annalen der Universität Wittenberg, passim*. See also G. Bauch, "Zur Cranachforschung," *Repertorium für Kunstwissenschaft*, XVII (1894), 426 ff. See below for Meinhard's catalogue of the relics in the Church of All Saints. Another work by him, *Elegantiarum rudimenta . . .*, is in the British Museum, listed in its *Catalogue of Printed Books*, XXXV, 239.

[14] O. Oppermann, "Das sächsische Amt Wittenberg im Anfang des 16. Jahrhunderts," *Leipziger Studien aus dem Gebiet der Geschichte*, IV, II (1897), 81.

[15] Luther reflects in the *Table Talk* this religious antagonism and also the intolerance of those living on a racial border line. "Sed pessima omnium natio ist die Wenden, da unss Gott eingeworffen hatt." *TR*, IV, No. 4997 (1540).

[16] Leopold, *Wittenberg und die umliegende Gegend*, p. 47. This work was not available to me for rechecking.

[17] It was begun by Elector Frederick immediately after he came to power in 1486. Meyner, *Geschichte der Stadt Wittenberg*, p. 98. Completed in 1490, the bridge survived many stormy years but fell a victim to the Thirty Years' War. *Ibid.*, pp. 98 f.

the northern bank, its modest walls and towers must have contrasted sharply with the powerful fortifications of Erfurt, which could not be taken "unless the Turks should besiege it."[18] In comparison with the great university and cloister buildings he had known, he found in Wittenberg few houses of respectable size.[19] The town was traversed by two chief streets following the main bearings of the compass. These must have seemed quiet indeed to one coming from the busy ways of a commercial metropolis.

Nevertheless the Wittenberg of Martin's younger years was no rural city, but had a well-organized civic life with the complicated stratification of society characteristic of the later Middle Ages. The municipality was dependent politically on the Saxon elector, who exercised a modified overlordship. Government rested on a sort of balance between the elector and the burghers. As in most cities of the time, the middle class was by far the largest,[20] and the city was governed with the orderliness characteristic of German urban life at all times. An important source of income was the brewing of beer, and this may explain the references by contemporaries to the drunkenness of the inhabitants and the tavern riots which play some rôle in the early history of the university.[21] Brewing, cloth-making, and other petty industries brought with them the picturesque guild system which was well developed in Wittenberg, although there was little export except to the immediate neighborhood.[22] The developments of the preceding century had not put Wittenberg under the rule of the artisans, like Augsburg and many other cities in the south and southwest. The propertied classes ruled its affairs. "Full burghers" were defined as persons "entitled to brew beer." The next class was the small house-owners.[23] With an electorate thus limited to the "optimates," the balancing of power with the elector was not difficult: the city enjoyed the usual rights of self-government, including the administration of justice. The population at the time of Martin's arrival

---

[18] *TR*, II, Nos. 2494a and 2494b (1532).

[19] When Martin came the burgher houses were of wood and stone construction, the lower story of stone, the upper of wood. Before his death the prospering citizens had replaced many of these with patrician houses of brick in a somewhat Gothic style, like the Melanchthon house, which was built in 1536–37. Edith Eschenhagen, "Beiträge zur Sozial- und Wirtschaftsgeschichte der Stadt Wittenberg in der Reformationszeit," *Jahrbuch der Luthergesellschaft*, IX (1927), 27.

[20] *Ibid.*, pp. 20, 87.

[21] Meyner, whose work claims to rest on archival sources, counts 172 breweries in the city in 1513. *Geschichte der Stadt Wittenberg*, p. 125. The local consumption must have been enormous, as the transportation facilities of the day did not permit the shipment of beer beyond the immediate vicinity.

[22] Due largely to Luther's great following after 1520 a new industry pushed forward, that of the printers and publishers. Among a group of eight wealthy citizens was the elder Cranach, the artist. Eschenhagen, "Wittenberg in der Reformationszeit," pp. 100 f.

[23] "Budellingen." Oppermann, "Das sächsische Amt Wittenberg," p. 84.

was over 2,000,[24] a figure which rose somewhat with the further development of the university.

Despite unpleasant contrasts with his former home, the young mendicant must have noticed at once evidences of the energy with which the elector of Saxony was pushing the development of a new Athens on the Elbe. At the western end of the city stood the electoral castle, the seat of the ruler on his visits to Wittenberg. The previous decade had seen the rebuilding of the castle and its attached chapel; and more recently, the Church of All Saints lying close beside and just within the western gate of the city had also been rebuilt at considerable cost. The church was not an impressive building; certainly it could not be compared with the great cathedral in Erfurt or the two religious buildings that flanked it. Nevertheless it was, as we shall see, richly endowed with indulgences and privileges, among others the right of perpetual freedom from the interdict, a privilege which it shared with the Augustinian monastery and which was at this time of greater traditional than practical importance.[25] No resources at the command of Frederick, the reigning prince, were withheld in the attempt to enhance the prestige of the city. Albrecht Dürer spent several months there at work on the historical frescoes in the castle. Lucas Cranach made it his home for life.

Wittenberg was, then, to be a northern center of culture. This meant, of course, an enhancement of its religious importance. At the opposite end of the long street from the castle church, the eastern end, lay the cloister of the Augustinians. When the young monk from Erfurt entered its gate at the end of his journey he found the building undergoing new construction at the expense of the elector. As yet, only the *dormitorium* was finished. The foundation of the new cloister church had been laid, but this was all. The old chapel was still standing. This modest structure, without decoration and with a pulpit of unpainted boards, could scarcely contain more than twenty persons standing. Its cheerless interior reminded a younger contemporary of Luther of the stall at Bethlehem in which Christ was born.[26] Here, four years later, Martin was to begin his career as preacher. One of his first visits when he had refreshed himself must have been to the Church of All Saints, which stands at the other end of Wittenberg's main street. The older student in Master Meinhard's dialogue tells the freshman at length about the wonderful caskets of silver purchased at an unheard-of price and

[24] Eschenhagen, "Wittenberg in der Reformationszeit," pp. 38 ff., estimates it at about 2,300.
[25] Meyner, *Geschichte der Stadt Wittenberg*, p. 88.
[26] Myconius saw the little building and remembered it clearly. See his vivid description in the "Historia Reformationis," ed. by Cyprian, pp. 24 f. Luther undoubtedly first preached in this structure. When it became too small for his audiences he was called to preach in the parish church.

other works of art with which the church was decorated. Throngs of worshippers came, especially on Misericordia Sunday, to see its great store of
sacred relics. If the young theologian reached Wittenberg before the last
day of October, he might still have crowded with hundreds of pilgrims
from near and far to look upon the sacred memorials of holy men and
women, most of whom had met the martyr's death.

The assembly of this impressive collection of relics had been a lifelong
task of Elector Frederick. On his accession to the throne in 1486 he had found
a great store from the time of his predecessors, among them, to be sure,
many of doubtful authenticity, even for the late medieval conscience, but
forming in their totality a chronological exposition of the entire history of
the Christian faith.[27] To increase this collection had been one of the prime
aims of Frederick's earlier years and he set systematically to work, bringing
to the task all the zeal of an ardent churchman and the imagination and
technique of a virtuoso in the collector's art. He had first enlarged his store
by a pilgrimage to Palestine; then he organized a regular drive to bring
in articles of faith. In the year preceding Luther's arrival in Wittenberg,
the elector had secured a letter from the Pope asking archbishops and other
Church dignitaries to turn over to him some of the relics at their disposal,
and with this in hand he set to work with untiring energy to add to his
sacred store. The results must have more than justified his efforts in the
mind of the age. Beginning with the year which brought Luther to the
scene, there exists an official catalogue of the various items in German, by the
same Andreas Meinhard who understood so well how to set forth the praises
of the city and university.[28] One would search long for a more vivid illustration of the late medieval imagination and the religious fervor that possessed
the masses in the early sixteenth century. For 1509 Meinhard's list announces
5,005 items, including 204 from the Innocents slaughtered by Herod, a piece
of the burning bush of Moses, various "particles" from the body of the
Holy Virgin, a part of the cradle of Jesus and fragments of the hay and
straw on which He was born, His swaddling clothes, and thirty-three fragments of the Holy Cross.[29] The treasures continued to pour in during

---

[27] Kalkoff, *Ablass und Reliquienverehrung,* pp. 53 ff.

[28] *Dye zaigung des hochlobwirdigen hailigthums der Stifft kirchen aller hailigen zu wittenburg*
(Wittenberg, 1509). A copy was used by me in the Munich Staatsbibliothek.

[29] Following an introduction in praise of Elector Frederick and his brother and co-regent John,
Meinhard gives a list of eight aisles (Gänge), classifying the relics exhibited in each. The relics
included two teeth of Saint Elizabeth, one each from St. Matthew and John the Baptist, and
other relics no less remarkable. Souvenirs of early German rulers of religious repute are also
listed.

Luther's early years as professor until in 1518 twelve corridors were necessary for the exhibition, which had grown to more than 17,000 items. Rich was the store of indulgences offered to the believing pilgrim, remarkable even in a period which carried the cult of the saints to the point of frenzy.[30] The church was likewise equipped with special indulgences, the most famous being the "Portiuncula," which had been bestowed on All Saints in 1398. This indulgence, which St. Francis was believed to have received directly from God, was shared only by the Church of Assisi and the cloister of St. Bridget at Vadstena in Sweden. It could be acquired at the festival of St. Francis and secured for the repentant believer the remission of all his sins.[31] It is not too much to say that at the time of Luther's arrival Wittenberg might justly claim to be the most important place of pilgrimage in North Germany.

The ambition of the elector was not merely to make his residence on the Elbe a place to which the eyes of the faithful might turn in religious devotion. He wanted also to make it a center of learning. The ancient patrimony of the house of Wettin, the Saxon dynasty, had been divided in 1485 into two parts, the one known as the Albertine branch receiving the ancient seat of the electors at Meissen as well as the cities of Dresden and Leipzig. The other, the Ernestine branch, retained the electoral dignity and the lands north of the Elbe, with the greater part of Thuringia. Of the ruler of Albertine Saxony, Duke George, we shall have much to say later on. His cousin, Elector Frederick, shared rule over the Saxon-Thuringian estates of the Ernestines with his brother, John. The university of Leipzig, a foundation of the days of the struggle with Huss and the seat of scholarship in Saxon lands for nearly a century, was now Albertine, and Frederick was eager to decorate his realm with an institution that might rival this ancient foundation on the Pleisse. On July 6, 1502, he obtained from the Emperor Maximilian a charter establishing the university at Wittenberg with the

[30] Kalkoff, *Ablass und Reliquienverehrung,* pp. 64 f., estimates that the more than 17,000 objects displayed in 1518 made up a grand total of possible indulgences of 127,799 years and 116 days.

[31] "Wie wol der löbliche Stifft so mit trefflichen und merklichen aplas und gnade von Bebsten Patriarchen Cardinalen Ertzbischoven und Bischoven versehen das sy mit wenigen schrifften oder worten zuermelden so ist doch unter vil anderm aplas in zaigung des hailigthumbs zu einem jeden gang hundert tag. Und von einem jeden stuck oder partickel desselben der uber etlich tausent seient hundert tag aplas geben. . . . So ist ouch die vilbemelt kirchen mit dem aplas vergebung Peyn und Schuld so zu Assias da sant Franciscus leyblich rastet des ersten tags Augusti zu der Capeln sant Marien de angelis Jehrlich ist zwen tag vor und nach allerheiligē tag von dem babst Bonifacio dem neunten gnediglich begabt und versehen. Welher aplas an wenigē orten darzu Assias un diser kirchē befunden." Meinhard, *Dye zaigung des hochlobwirdigen hailigthums,* pp. aiij ff.

usual rights and privileges, including the right to have its degrees recognized everywhere and entitling its doctors to teach not only within the German empire, but throughout the world.[32] These rights and privileges were confirmed by the papal legate, Cardinal Raymond Perault, on February 2 of the following year.[33]

No institution for general study in the later Middle Ages could hope to exist without drawing upon religious foundations for financial support as well as for the staffing of its faculties. Wittenberg was no exception, for here, as had been the case with all universities of the scholastic period, the foundation of a university meant primarily the bringing together of forces, intellectual and material, which were already on the spot, and their organization into a "general study." When the university was "enthroned" on October 18, 1502,[34] with the solemn festivities usual on such occasions, the professional and material support for its modest beginnings were supplied very largely by two institutions: the Church of All Saints, through its collegiate organization, and the Augustinian monastery, which the elector undertook to rebuild and expand at his own expense. Dr. Staupitz, who was shortly afterward to become provincial vicar of the Augustinian order, was made professor of the Bible and soon after dean of the theological faculty, and he threw himself heart and soul into the strengthening of the university by means of forces available in his order. The Augustinian house was the first place of instruction for the theologians, the city providing benches and desks. The Church of All Saints had certain outside parishes and, by degrees, others, including some rich livings, were added to these. The spiritual duties of these livings were discharged by vicars, while the income from them provided support for the teaching staff of the university. The university appointed the archdeacons, deacons, canons, custodians, and syndics of the collegiate church, and these were at the same time members of the various faculties.[35]

Thus set in motion, the university perfected its organization under the direction of the vice-chancellor, Martin Pollich of Mellerstadt, apparently a philosopher of the older scholastic type, who combined theology with medicine.[36] The organization had just been completed when Luther arrived. The inauguration of a new set of statutes in the semester in which he matric-

---

[32] Friedensburg, "Urkundenbuch," I, 1 ff.

[33] *Ibid.*, p. 5. The imperial charter was necessary also for the teaching of theology and canon law. Denifle, *Universitäten des Mittelalters*, I, 784.

[34] Entry in the deans' book. Förstemann, *Liber decanorum*, pp. 1 ff.

[35] Friedensburg, *Geschichte der Universität Wittenberg*, pp. 21 f.; *Oppermann*, "Das sächsische Amt Wittenberg," pp. 100 f.

[36] For Pollich (or Polich), see Friedensburg, *Geschichte der Universität Wittenberg*, pp. 10 ff.

ulated was the final step in the establishment of the institution. The most distinguished teachers in the new university, including the deans of the faculties of theology, law, and liberal arts, came from Tübingen, and it is not surprising that the Swabian university served as a model for this new seat of the muses.[37] As at Tübingen, the students were divided into faculties and not into nations as in the neighboring Leipzig and other German universities which followed the Paris model. As concerns its philosophical-theological direction, the authors of the constitution of the new school were evidently intent on avoiding the strife that had arisen in the western universities from a too-enthusiastic following of the "ancient" or the "modern" way, and they provided at the start for opening "the ways of the scholastic doctors without difference." [38] This liberal arrangement was carried into effect by the appointment of Andreas Carlstadt and Nikolaus Amsdorf to represent respectively the Thomist and Scotist "opinions," two varieties of the realistic theory. Beside these two men, who were both to play an important rôle in Martin's life, the young friar found his old professor from Erfurt, Trutvetter, who had been called in the preceding year to represent the nominalist direction.[39]

Thus organized, the university spared no effort to secure students. Free promotion for doctors seems to have been offered in the earlier years and energetic advertising, such as Meinhard's dialogue, was used. Nevertheless, after some initial success, the novelty of the new institution lost its drawing power, the plague arrived in 1506 to drive faculty and students into exile for some months, and in the semester when Luther seems to have entered only sixty-eight new students matriculated.[40] The situation of the institution brought it into competition with Leipzig and Erfurt, universities of great

---

[37] Gustav Bauch, "Wittenberg und die Scholastik," *Neues Archiv für sächsische Geschichte und Altertumskunde*, XVIII (1897), 299. Scheel, *Martin Luther*, II, 341, n. 5. Friedensburg, *Geschichte der Universität Wittenberg*, pp. 18 and 25 ff.

[38] "Vias scholasticorum doctorum absque differencia erigimus." Friedensburg, "Urkundenbuch," I, 20.

[39] Plitt, *Jodocus Trutfetter*, pp. 29 f.; Bauch, "Wittenberg und die Scholastik," p. 314. For a list of the faculty, see Friedensburg, "Urkundenbuch," pp. 14 ff.; see also Bauch, "Wittenberg und die Scholastik," pp. 311 ff. A very interesting innovation in German university organization were the so-called "reformators," a committee of four drawn from the doctors of the faculty which stood between the elector and the university and apparently had far-reaching initiative in the regulation of affairs within and without. It is worth noting as a matter of historical significance that the reformators also exercised a censorship over faculty publications. Friedensburg, "Urkundenbuch," pp. 22 ff. This institution was well known in the Italian universities and seems to have been borrowed from the practice at Bologna by the jurist Christoph Scheurl, who drew up the statutes. Scheurl, *Briefbuch*, I, 55, a source of considerable importance for Wittenberg and Luther's early years there. See also Friedensburg, *Geschichte der Universität Wittenberg*, p. 28.

[40] Förstemann, *Album academiae Vitebergensis 1502–1602*, I, 27 f.

prestige; and the Slavic country to the north was not a fruitful field for recruiting. Two years after the elector's new foundation came into being, a rival appeared to bid for the patronage of the German population in the northeast, for a university was established in the electorate of Brandenburg at Frankfurt-an-der-Oder.

In spite of the modest number of its students, the Wittenberg school developed a vigorous life, and its growth gradually brought a change into the little town on the "frontiers of civilization," as Luther calls it. The building and book-publishing trades felt the impulse. Taverns sprang up with a student atmosphere. The appearance of a "women's lane" and "women's house" in the record gives evidence of the moral level of the age.[41] Clashes between town and gown were not lacking, nor are acts of violence absent from the annals: in the year after Luther came the city was laid under the interdict by the Pope because students had made an attack on the servants of the bishop of Brandenburg, and four years later a student was executed for assassinating a rector of the university. Even the candidates for theological degrees were obliged to swear before their examination that they would not seek revenge in case of failure,[42] and it was strictly forbidden to bring weapons into lecture rooms. So far as the student body was concerned, the life of the new university was probably no better and no worse than that in its sister institutions and bore the same stamp of coarse vigor which marked them all on the eve of the ethical awakening that came in the following decades.

The faculty which the elector had brought together was not without distinction. Tübingen, as we have seen, furnished a number of scholars; theologians, jurists, and medical men came also from Leipzig; Erfurt and Cologne sent philosophers. More than one Italian found his way thither, including Peter Thomai of Ravenna, a distinguished exponent of the canon law, who remained, however, only three years.[43] Wittenberg went through the same experience as most new institutions: some of its faculty went away

---

[41] The municipal Frauenhaus was an established institution in Wittenberg as in other German cities of the time. It was rebuilt in 1516 and leased to a mistress, under the control of the superintendent of the market! Entrance was forbidden to married men and disorder was severely punished. Later Martin made a bitter attack on legalized prostitution, *An den christlichen Adel*, WA, VI, 467; see also p. 262. In 1521 entries regarding it in the Wittenberg archives cease. Eschenhagen, "Wittenberg in der Reformationszeit," p. 25. The university regulations forbade association with women of bad repute as well as public drinking, but they expressly permitted the academicians to drink in private "usque ad saturitatem." Friedensburg, "Urkundenbuch," p. 29. The municipal records allow the inference that the students availed themselves fully of this privilege.

[42] *Ibid.*, p. 34.

[43] "Petrus Ravennas," *Allgemeine Deutsche Biographie*, XXV, 533 f.

disappointed with their situation; others found the climate too severe and life in the city too primitive to suit their tastes; still others remained to give the university years of service and play a rôle in Luther's career. Evidences of the new spirit of humanism were not absent. Pollich of Mellerstadt, the medical scholar and theologian; Christoph Scheurl, the Nuremberg jurist; and Dr. Staupitz, the theologian, were not untouched by humanism. As a new institution, Wittenberg had a more liberal attitude toward classical studies than its scholastic sisters. The elector was well aware of the great importance of "good letters," as the humanists liked to call their subjects. An outstanding representative of their direction was Hermann von dem Busche, a roving scholar who for a time taught rhetoric and poetics at Wittenberg. He had studied in Italy and on the Rhine, had sat at the feet of Conrad Celtes and Rudolph Agricola, and was a facile writer of the Latin epistles and eulogies by which the humanists brought themselves to the attention of patrons. He had also all the wanderlust of the older generation of humanistic scholars and after a year's stay at Wittenberg went on to other fields of activity.

As yet, the adherence to the new learning was rather empty of realities, although there were a number of gestures in that direction. Scheurl, for example, inscribed in the statutes the provision that "poets laureate" might have a place immediately after the masters of arts at the session of the faculty.[44] The foundation for Greek studies had been laid by Nikolaus von Marschalk, who had come from Erfurt on the opening of the university. His stay was short, but the tradition of Greek instruction was established there, and a Greek grammar appeared the year of Martin's arrival, to be followed in the next decade by other works in Greek. Young men trailing humanistic names of Latin origin appeared in the first years of the university as poets and editors, and in 1509 Johann Grünenberg set up at Wittenberg the printing press which was later to become so important for Luther and his colleagues.[45] In the main, however, the faculties were still content to walk in the well-trodden paths of scholasticism. Professors in the faculty of arts and of theology were tagged with their philosophical "directions" and students to be examined must as a matter of course present themselves with similar tags.[46]

Such, then, was the institution which Martin found when, with his com-

[44] Friedensburg, "Urkundenbuch," p. 24.

[45] Bauch, "Wittenberg und die Scholastik," pp. 285 ff. Concerning Grünenberg, see Wustmann, *Aus Leipzigs Vergangenheit,* pp. 39 f.

[46] For schedule of lectures, see Friedensburg, "Urkundenbuch," pp. 15 f.; for conditions for promotion to degrees, *ibid.,* p. 34.

panions, he trudged through College Street from the Elbe gate and knocked at the door of the little Augustinian monastery. Here many and varied duties awaited him, so that he was not able to write his old friend, Vicar Braun, until the middle of March and even then was obliged to steal the minutes from his work to do so. He must have been detailed at once to join the group of Eremites represented on the faculty and also to continue his own theological studies. His duty as teacher was to give lectures on moral philosophy, probably to interpret the *Nichomachean Ethics* of Aristotle, the task with which his predecessor had been charged.[47] This was a work with which Martin must have become well acquainted four or five years earlier while studying for the master's degree at Erfurt, but he undoubtedly found that the conscientious teacher requires an altogether different sort of preparation from that of even the most studious scholar. In addition to these lectures he had also to supervise disputational exercises. He complains to Braun of the "violence of the studies, especially in philosophy."[48] He himself was deep in theological studies, which had entirely won his heart. He would like to have theology in place of philosophy, for it "searches out the kernel of the nut, the pith of the grain, and the marrow of the bones." He must have been greeted with pleasure by his old teacher Trutvetter, whose coming to Wittenberg was something of a triumph for the university. The modest scholar was promptly made rector, and later became dean of the theological faculty. Apparently, however, the atmosphere was uncongenial to a modernist, and in 1510 Trutvetter returned to Erfurt.[49]

Martin, whose training had been in the Occam "way," may have heard Trutvetter's lectures on theology. Just what else he heard we do not know. Thomists and Scotists were in the majority, and it is possible that Martin's enlistment for the university had been at the suggestion of Professor Trutvetter in the hope of strengthening the modernist philosophy.[50] It seems likely, on the other hand, that the young scholar may have taken advantage of this opportunity to widen acquaintance with Thomas and Scotus. Tartaret's interpretation of the latter was published by the university and seems to have enjoyed a vogue there. The most important exponent of the ideas of St. Thomas was the able and energetic Andreas Bodenstein von Carlstadt, whose learned interpretation of the great systematist was the first independent work of scholarship published by a Wittenberg theologian. His

---

[47] Wolfgang Ostermayr. *Ibid.*, p. 16. See also Oergel, *Vom jungen Luther*, pp. 110 f.

[48] *WAB*, I, 17. [49] See n. 39 above.

[50] This interesting possibility has been suggested by Bauer, *Die Wittenberger Universitätstheologie*, p. 10.

relations with Martin were to be of great importance, as we shall see, and led a dozen years later to one of the stormiest episodes of a stormy period.

In Wittenberg Martin found himself in a new cloister circle. He probably met a discipline less rigid than that to which he had been accustomed;[51] nevertheless, although as a heavily burdened teacher and student he was doubtless freed from some of the liturgical services, the canonical hours had to be performed privately if not done in the choir. Yet all demands were fulfilled, and on March 9 he was "admitted to the Bible."[52] He must now give a course on one of the books of the Bible, treating certain selected chapters, all under the same requirements for supervision by dean and masters in theology that we have learned to know in the Erfurt theological statutes. Martin had thus attained a goal toward which he had been driving with zeal, and it may be assumed that when the summer semester opened no Biblical bachelor ever faced his students with more intense earnestness. Nevertheless, his memories of his first stay in Wittenberg seem not to have been pleasant ones. He once referred to it as a "hazing."[53] If this was his feeling, the hour of delivery soon arrived. Wittenberg required of clerical students only one semester "in the Bible," for, like most younger institutions, it was more liberal in its demands.[54] When the summer semester had passed the young theologian applied for the degree as *sententiarius,* held his public disputation, and had already given his initial lecture when another sudden summons recalled him to the cloister in Erfurt.[55]

Notwithstanding these hardships, the Wittenberg year must have meant a long step upward toward independence of view in theological questions. His own teaching certainly showed him new resources in himself. Especially his lectures on the Bible stimulated further his absorption in the Vulgate text. Greater maturity and a wider range of acquaintance with the authorities in theology must have caused deep thinking, although the results were not yet assimilated. It is probable also that life in the little cloister at the end of College Street brought Martin into intimate contact with the general vicar, Johann von Staupitz, a man who was to have great influence

---

[51] This may be inferred from a passage in Martin's letter to Johann Lang, March 1, 1517, regarding a brother, Gabriel Zwilling, who was to be transferred from Wittenberg to Erfurt. He had been in Wittenberg five years but had not yet learned the "rites and customs of the order." *WAB,* I, 90.

[52] Förstemann, *Liber decanorum,* p. 4. See also Luther's letter to the faculty at Erfurt, Dec. 21, 1514, *WAB,* I, 30.

[53] *TR,* IV, No. 4714 (1539).

[54] "Quod stabo integrum annum in biblia, nisi fuerit religiosus, cui semestre deputamus." Friedensburg, "Urkundenbuch," p. 35.

[55] See below, pp. 146 f.

on his spiritual development. No one with whom Friar Martin was associated in his cloister years bulks so large in the autobiographical sources. Here he praises Staupitz repeatedly as the one who directed him toward peace of soul.[56] Some acquaintance with the character of the older man is therefore necessary for a closer view of Martin's inner development during his late twenties and early thirties.

As a result of the events of the next decade, the historical picture of Staupitz is strikingly incomplete when we consider the forcefulness of his character and the rôle that he played in the history of his order during critical years. Born of an old family of landed nobility in the Wittenberg region, his studies evidently began at Leipzig in 1485.[57] He appears later as a student at Leipzig and again at Cologne, where he seems to have received his master's degree about 1489. Like Martin, he then entered the Augustinian order, though it is not certain just where, nor do we know of his early theological studies. By 1497 his progress had been such that when he appears at Tübingen in that year it is as *lector* in the Bible. Shortly afterward he was made prior of the Augustinian convent, and from that time his progress as preacher and teacher in the order seems to have been rapid. From Munich, where he was prior of the convent in 1503, Staupitz was called to Wittenberg by Elector Frederick to aid in the development of the university and the expansion of the Augustinian monastery. About the same time the earnest churchman was chosen general vicar of the Reformed Congregation of the Eremites, for which, as we have seen, he prepared a new constitution.

Staupitz united in a marked degree the two ideals of his order, devotion to a strict observance of the rule of St. Augustine and enthusiasm for scholarship. Like his predecessor, the general vicar Andreas Proles, he was desirous of extending the strict observance to other convents and soldifying the organization of the reformed group. The immediate objective of the new

[56] Staupitz's relations with Luther have engaged the attention of many investigators, and his position in research has been strongly affected by confessional bias. Catholic historians blame him for weakness in permitting the Wittenberg heresy. After 1557 he was put on the "Index" in the first class. Reusch, *Index der verbotenen Bücher,* I, 279; see also 263. Lutheran apologists share the resentment which Martin felt at the failure of the vicar to support his cause. His character has varied directly with the persuasion of the biographer. With the rise of a more objective spirit on both sides, the picture of Staupitz has become clearer. For factual material on him Kolde's *Augustiner-Kongregation* is still most valuable. A very important contribution is Ernst Wolf's "Staupitz und Luther," *Quellen und Forschungen zur Reformationsgeschichte,* IX (1927). Here for the first time the Augustinian vicar is made the subject of a full-length study of scholarly balance.

[57] Kolde, *Augustiner-Kongregation,* pp. 211 ff. Wolf, "Staupitz und Luther," pp. 30 ff., and other studies of Staupitz correct and supplement Kolde's, for example, N. Paulus in Wetzer and Welte, *Kirchenlexikon,* XI, 746 f., and O. Clemen, in *Realenzyklopädie für protestantische Theologie und Kirche,* XVIII, 781 ff.

vicar, a union of the Reformed Congregation in Germany with the reformed convents of Lombardy, was blocked by political difficulties. Moves in that direction found a bitter opponent in the Augustinian general at Rome, Augustine of Interramna. When death had removed him, and his successor, Egidio of Viterbo, showed keen sympathy with the reform, Staupitz nevertheless saw his efforts toward expanding the observance shattered in Germany on the same rock of parochial narrowness and separatistic suspicion [58] that has brought destruction to so many fine plans in German history.

As a member of the old Saxon nobility, Staupitz was well fitted to stand at the right hand of Elector Frederick in the organization of the new university. As we have seen, he took over this task with zeal. The early faculty seems to have been largely of his selection, and it included a number of his former associates at Tübingen and Leipzig. St. Augustine, with the Virgin, became the official patron of the university, and the Augustinian order furnished one of the first deans of the faculties.[59] We have seen already that Martin was brought to Wittenberg in a further effort to mobilize the forces of the order for the university. Meinhard's student propaganda praises Staupitz as a "pillar of our new school."

In some respects the general vicar, who belonged to the student generation preceding Martin's, had built his theological ideals on a different foundation from that which the younger man laid in the Erfurt university and convent. Staupitz's works, consisting of sermons and devotional writings, nearly all in Latin, and echoes of his ideas in Luther's letters and works, are the sources for our knowledge of his thought.[60] His training in philosophy and theology seems to have been that of the "ancient way," and his ideas reflect a schooling in the work of Thomas Aquinas and a thirteenth-century exponent of the great systematist, Egidio Romano, the traditional orthodox theologian of the Augustinian order.[61] Staupitz, however, could not have qualified as a systematic theologian. His interest did not lie in the subtle analysis of problems of grace in the manner of the great Schoolmen. The goal of his thinking was the establishment of a personal and confidential relationship between a gracious God and the obedient soul, a relationship

---

[58] The difficulties in the order will be treated below. For an account of the affair based on a careful study of the sources, see Kolde, *Augustiner-Kongregation*, pp. 226 ff.; for Egidio's part in it, see Böhmer, *Romfahrt*, pp. 37 ff.

[59] Kolde, *Augustiner-Kongregation*, pp. 220 ff.

[60] Wolf assembles sources for Staupitz's theological ideas in "Staupitz und Luther," pp. 10 ff. An important addition to these is the text of thirty-four sermons on Job delivered at Munich and published from a MS in Munich by Buchwald and Wolf, *Tübinger Predigten des Joh. von Staupitz*.

[61] Wolf, "Staupitz und Luther," pp. 121 f. and *passim*. The difficulty encountered by Wolf in summarizing Staupitz's ideas shows the unsystematic character of the general vicar's theology.

that involves a life of pious service. In his work the idea of predestination shows a friendly face: the predestining grace of God makes us pleasing to Him and is the basis of all other acts of His grace.[62] A certain quietism marks his thought. His sermons and personality seem to radiate a truly medieval piety: we feel that here is one for whom the mystical union with God through the workings of divine love is a real experience. There is in his writings something of St. Bernard, something of the *devotio moderna* of Gerhard Groot,[63] the spirit of the Brothers of the Common Life. It is to be noted, however, that Staupitz does not reflect any of the ascetic technique of a Thomas à Kempis or an Ignatius Loyola.[64] He sets forth the practical demands of a pious life and dwells on the personal nature of man's relation to God, on the revelation of goodness and mercy that inspires men to good deeds.[65]

It is obvious that such a personality must influence a young scholar through his warmth of ideas rather than his abstract theological conceptions. Staupitz was indeed a preacher by nature. Luther remembered him many years later as a "disagreeable" preacher, to be sure, and declared that the people would rather hear a simple brother;[66] and one who reads the Tübingen sermons on Job can understand that such an exegetical treatment of the text with its heavy allegorical illustrations may have meant more to his cloister brothers than to stolid burghers and officials. In the convent he seems to have been regarded as a learned and eloquent expositor for a scholarly audience. Here the systematic construction of his sermons and his ready use of exegetical authorities from Father Ambrose down to Thomas Aquinas were duly appreciated.[67]

"Although I have certainly ceased to be agreeable and pleasant to you," Martin wrote the general vicar several years after the final parting of their ways, "nevertheless I ought not to be ungrateful to the one through whom the light of the Gospel first began to shine forth from the shadows into my heart." [68] Whatever this means, and generations of scholars have not been able to agree on that, it is certain that Martin never forgot his intimacy with the general vicar nor the rôle which the latter played in his inner life. No other contemporary of his cloister appears with anything like the frequency of Staupitz in the sermons, letters, and *Table Talk*, where Martin lives over

---

[62] *Idid.*, p. 59. Staupitz published a brief work on the subject, *Libellus de Executione eterne predestinationis* (Nüremberg, 1517), which was translated by Christoph Scheurl and warmly praised by Luther. *Ibid.*, p. 13.

[63] See Böhmer, *Luther im Lichte der neueren Forschung*, pp. 61 f.; *Der junge Luther*, p. 103.

[64] Wolf, "Staupitz und Luther," pp. 96 ff.   [65] *Ibid.*, pp. 118 ff.

[66] *TR*, V, No. 6404.   [67] Wolf, "Staupitz und Luther," pp. 23 ff.

[68] Letter from Luther to Staupitz, Sept. 17, 1523, *WAB*, III, 155 f.

again his early restlessness of soul.[69] For a time Staupitz was probably his most frequent correspondent.[70] Many of Martin's letters to him and all of those of the general vicar have been lost. If we had those written him by the younger man from the cloister we should undoubtedly be able to take a much deeper view into the nature of the "temptations" of which Martin complained. His confessions of indebtedness to Staupitz began in the year of the struggle over indulgences. In the covering letter to the *Explanations of Indulgences* he declares that Staupitz's definition of penance came to him like a voice sounding from heaven; [71] and testimonials of this kind continued down to the year preceding his death, when he writes to Elector John Frederick that Staupitz was the originator of his doctrine: "Dr. Staupitz, whom I must praise unless I am willing to be a damned ungrateful papal ass, was primarily my father in this doctrine and with Christ's help brought it into the world." [72]

The steps by which he followed this counselor cannot be traced. We do not know for certain when he first crossed Martin's path nor when their friendship developed into close intimacy; but even if the general vicar had seen him in his novitiate year or in his first year of study for the priesthood, the interest which he took in the bright young master of arts whom a miraculous thunderbolt had driven into the cloister can hardly have led to an intimacy of acquaintance until the winter and spring of 1508-9.[73] Here in the little Wittenberg cloister, perhaps "across the table," as Martin describes one conversation between them, the latter learned to know the sympathetic heart of the older man and to find peace for his throbbing conscience in the experience of Staupitz, who looked at the religious life with the clear view of a practical realist, in spite of his mystical preaching. His reserve sometimes stung Martin to resentment: "Cold he is, as always, and lacking in ardor," was his criticism on looking over a devotional work of

---

[69] Wolf counts sixty-eight passages in Luther's *Table Talk* that mention Staupitz and over fifty in his letters, sermons, and other writings.

[70] *TR*, VI, No. 6669.

[71] *WA*, I, 525.

[72] "Dr. Staupitz, welchen ich rhümen mus (wo ich nicht ein verdampter undanckbar Bepstlicher Esel sein wil), das er erstlich mein Vater ynn dieser lere gewest ist und ynn Christo geborn hat." Letter from Luther to the elector, March 27, 1545. Enders, *Luthers Briefwechsel*, XVI, 202.

[73] The possibilities regarding their early acquaintance have been canvassed many times since Kolde unlocked the sources respecting Staupitz. The arguments are summarized by Wolf, "Staupitz und Luther," pp. 131 ff. Two periods offer the greatest possibility of intimate association, from the summer of 1508 to that of 1509 at Wittenberg and from the spring of 1512 to October of that year, again in Wittenberg. That is as far as the sources take us. As we shall see, the chronology of Martin's life from the spring of 1511 to the following spring is very uncertain.

Staupitz's published after the latter's death.[74] This very characteristic of spiritual withdrawal may have made the vicar an ideal comforter and adviser for the headlong and headstrong young friar in his struggles with his conscience and the patterns of cloister life and with the scholastic theological tradition. It is certain that the general vicar pulled him out of the slough of despond at critical times. As Martin wrote many years later, "If Dr. Staupitz, or rather God through Dr. Staupitz, had not helped me then, I would have drowned in them and been in hell long ago."[75] Based on a long clinical experience with such difficulties, Staupitz had, as we have seen, pointed out the necessity of just these doubts and fears for spiritual development,[76] a theme on which he had dwelt in his sermons.[77]

It is probable that before the end of the Wittenberg year Martin had found encouragement with the vicar. It is scarcely likely, however, that the discussion of theological problems went further at this time. As Martin's studies ripened in the years that followed under the stress of teaching Lombard's system to Erfurt students, other difficulties arose on which the general vicar was especially equipped to give helpful advice. The question of predestination [78] and of a true understanding of the "justice of God" in its relation to repentance [79] were subjects on which Staupitz had written and concerning which his training as a Thomist enabled him to take a more genial view than that of Martin's nominalist teachers. We shall see some effect of his influence four years later, when Martin struggles with his first professorial lectures in Wittenberg and comes to close grips with the scholastic theology.

In October Martin was back in the mother convent at Erfurt. His return, although probably not so sudden or unexpected as his departure for Wittenberg, must have been a surprise to the young teacher and can hardly have been a pleasant one.[80] It came in response to a summons received from his

---

[74] *Von dem heiligen rechten Christlichen glauben.* See letter from Luther to Link, Feb. 7, 1525, *WAB*, III, 437.

[75] Letter from Luther to Albrecht von Mansfeld, 1542, Enders, *Luthers Briefwechsel*, XIV, 189.

[76] Martin's letter to H. Weller from the Veste Koburg, July (?), 1530, *WAB*, V, 519; see also *TR*, I, No. 141 (1531), p. 62, ll. 1 ff.; *TR*, II, No. 1263 (1531), p. 13, ll. 25 ff.; also I, No. 518 (1533), p. 240, ll. 12 ff.

[77] Wolf, "Staupitz und Luther," pp. 158 ff.

[78] *Ibid.,* pp. 168 ff., i.e., Part II, chap. 2. This question occupied Martin's thought especially when preparing the lectures on Romans in 1515, and we shall return to it in that connection.

[79] See the covering letter to his *Resolutiones disputationum de indulgentiarum virtute, WA,* I, 525 f.; also Wolf, "Staupitz und Luther," pp. 228 ff., 240 ff. Wolf (p. 250) finds a reflection of Staupitz's ideas on repentance in Luther's marginalia on Augustine, *ca.*1510. This seems highly doubtful. The chronology of Martin's absorption of the general vicar's ideas seems quite out of the reach of investigation.

[80] Sources covering Martin's return and his stay at Erfurt from 1509 to 1511 or 1512 are few, and they were long overlooked. The Erfurt university sources for the period have been lost or are

cloister [81] at a critical time; he was about to obtain the degree of *sententiarius* at Wittenberg.[82] It is highly probable that the prior and definitors at Erfurt who had loaned him to Wittenberg were anxious to recover a promising teacher for their "general study." There seems reason to think, however, that there were those in the theological faculty at Erfurt who did not approve of so speedy a promotion. Older universities are apt to be autocratic in their attitude toward younger institutions and Wittenberg, as we have seen, was eager for students and less bound by tradition. Probably certain of the Erfurt scholars felt that the new university was dangerously liberal in the granting of degrees. Erfurt held its bachelors in the Bible to two years of lectures on the Scriptures before recognizing them as eligible for the degree of *sententiarius*. Martin, who had left his alma mater as a simple student of theology, now returned after scarcely a year of absence and claimed the higher degree. The matter was finally adjusted and he was promoted to *sententiarius,* but the picture which he draws of this ceremony two years later seems to indicate that at least Professor Nathin felt that there was an irregularity to be overcome.[83] The usual oath not to take the next higher degree elsewhere than at Erfurt seems to have been omitted on this occasion, and this was to have an embarrassing influence on the young lecturer's relations with the faculty five years later.

The preliminaries, however, were disposed of, and the new *sententiarius* began his exposition of Lombard. Absorbed though he was, he must have noticed speedily that Erfurt was not the same city as when he left it. Conditions in the Thuringian metropolis had changed greatly for the worse in the year of his absence, and even within the sanctuary of cloister walls he felt the repercussion of outside events. An economic crisis, not uncommon in the German cities at this period, was complicated by political convulsions. The city was deeply in debt. Taxes had risen to unheard-of figures and retarded the whole machinery of trade. As elsewhere in Germany at this time, the rapid development of the capitalist class had lifted a few of the artisans into this group but had depressed the great majority, along with all of the journeyman workers, into a helpless and embittered proletariat which now vented its discontent on the city council.[84] The agents of the

---

defective. Oergel, *Vom jungen Luther,* p. 113. We are dependent on entries in the Wittenberg *Liber decanorum* and on two letters from Martin written in 1514 referred to below.

[81] "Vocatus Erphordiam." Förstemann, *Liber decanorum,* p. 4.

[82] The situation is described in Martin's letter to dean and theological faculty at Erfurt on December 21, 1514, *WAB,* I, 30; and to the Erfurt convent on June 16, 1514, *ibid.,* p. 25.

[83] Nathin interrupted the proceedings by reading the graduation requirements from a "large sheet." *WAB,* I, 30, ll. 21 f.

[84] For sources regarding the Erfurt revolt, see above, p. 36, n. 24. In addition, for an

archbishop of Mainz, with whom the council had carried on a long struggle for administrative independence, fanned the flames of revolt and the secular clergy and religious orders were not inactive on the same side. The Saxon elector interfered and the entire year 1510 was one of disorder, with riots and bloodshed. The rage of the populace turned against members of the council. The chief of the influential "Council of Four," Heinrich Kellner, was done to death, and his four-year-old son was held in the Augustinian cloister as a hostage against reprisals on the part of the injured family.[85] Other prominent citizens were driven into exile and as the "mad year" went by the disorders culminated in a serious blow to the university. On August 4 a riot broke out between students of the Old College and men-at-arms of the city guard. Hard pressed by their half-disciplined opponents, the students barricaded themselves in the college building. This was carried by storm and overrun by a mob of guards and townsfolk who drove the students to flight, plundered the building, and burned it with its library. While the mob vented its fury against other colleges, the theological faculty in its sanctuary of church and convent seems not to have been disturbed. We have no contemporary writings from Martin in which the affair might appear. As members of the clergy, his cloister probably sympathized with the anti-council party, but Martin, who had been in Wittenberg in association with Staupitz, probably felt bound by cords of sympathy to the elector of Saxony.[86] The impression made by an unleashed mob remained with him, however, and its results appeared years later when the peasant uprisings reached a climax. In 1525 Erfurt was again in revolution and Martin's memory of the excesses of the earlier outbreak echo in a published attack on the citizens for permitting everything to be turned upside down.[87]

The young instructor's new work in the faculty of theology must have seemed to him far more important than anything that went on outside. By direction of the faculty, he began his lectures on the *Sentences* of Peter Lombard at some time in the fall. We do not know whether they were delivered in an auditorium of the university or the refectory of the cloister. His method followed the hard-and-fast prescriptions that governed the work

---

important study of the economic life of the city at the time, see T. Neubauer, "Die sozialen und wirtschaftlichen Verhältnisse der Stadt Erfurt vor Beginn der Reformation," *Mitteilungen des Vereins für die Geschichte und Altertumskunde von Erfurt*, XXXIV (1913), 31 ff., and "Zur Geschichte der mittelalterlichen Stadt Erfurt," *ibid.*, XXXV (1914), 4 ff.

[85] Luther refers more than once to Kellner's brutal execution in the *Table Talk*. *TR*, I, No. 487 (1533); II, Nos. 2494a and 2494b (1532); II, No. 2709b (1532).

[86] In later years his sympathies were naturally on the elector's side. See n. 85 above, also *TR*, II, Nos. 2800a and 2800b.

[87] *An den Rat zu Erfurt* (1525), *WA*, XVIII, 539.

of the theological faculty. The text of the four books of the Master of Sentences must be read word for word and its difficulties explained. He seems to have prepared for this by making notes on the margin of the copy of Lombard's work in the cloister library. The volume has been preserved and his marginalia give us our first idea of his method as a lecturer.

Annotating books was common practice in the late medieval monasteries, as many theological incunabula and volumes from the early sixteenth century remain to testify. That a studious friar should add his own interpretations to those of the author in the cloister library appears not to have been resented by his brothers; indeed, subsequent users found these glosses and discursions, interlined or entered on the broad margins, of so much interest that they not infrequently annotated the annotations with as much zeal as the original text.[88] Martin made full use of this privilege and added his own ideas in a number of volumes in the cloister library at Erfurt and afterwards at Wittenberg. Several of these are preserved in the Zwickau Municipal Library: two volumes of Augustine and Lombard's *Sentences,* in which the notes were made in 1509 and the years immediately following, and one volume of Johann von Tritheim's *Liber lugubris de statu et ruina monastici ordinis.*[89] Among these groups of marginalia two claim our special attention, those in a volume of the briefer works of Augustine [90] and in the one containing his works *On the Trinity* and *The City of God,*[91] and especially those in the *Sentences* of Lombard,[92] for they all undoubtedly belong to the period of his Erfurt lectures on the *Sentences*. Here the lecturer after two or three years of study opens to us his intellectual laboratory. Here in his own careful hand he sets forth, with the intention that they may be read by later users, ideas suggested by the text before him. Here he shows what his reading has been in other books and the method whereby he tries to

[88] This occurred in Martin's case. The text of Augustine's *De civitate Dei* which he used (see below) had been previously annotated and he comments on these notes. Copies of early theological works with carefully written notes by scribes of several generations are not unusual; that of Biel's canon of the Mass (Tübingen, 1499) in the library of the Union Theological Seminary from a cloister library in Halberstadt is freely glossarized by at least two hands. Martin also made notes freely in a privately owned volume. His notes on Tauler's sermons were made in a copy belonging to Johann Lang, which Martin seems to have kept in his possession half a dozen years. *WAB,* II, 548, n. 3.

[89] *WA,* IX, 104 ff. The Zwickau group was brought together by Andreas Poach, a zealous transcriber of Luther's sermons. Two volumes containing Martin's annotations formerly in Poach's possession are missing. *WA,* IX, 1 f. In addition there are marginal notes on two works of Biel in Luther's hand in the seminary library at Wittenberg, and a few glosses in a copy of Faber's edition of the Hebrew psalms (Basel, 1500), dating probably from 1516–20 in the municipal library at Frankfort.

[90] *Opuscula plurima* (1489).

[91] *De trinitate* and *De civitate Dei* (Basel, 1489).

[92] *Textus Sententiarum cum conclusionibus ac titulis questionum sancti Thome* (Basel, 1489).

clarify in his own mind the ideas of the authors and to present the results to his students. These early notes are therefore a mine rich in information regarding his intellectual and spiritual state at the beginning of his theological career, and although they do not yield all of the material for an understanding of his development that eager investigators have sought to press out of them, they are nevertheless of the utmost importance for judging the stage of progress which he had then attained.[93]

With the full enthusiasm of a young philologian he assembles for his task of interpretation all the wisdom that he has garnered from his reading. His scholarly training has taught him that the first duty of the exegete is to watch his text. He certainly had in hand other editions of the *Sentences* than that which he was annotating, for here and there he makes comparisons in order to establish the correct reading. Evidently also he was at pains to check his author's Bible citations, and he cannot altogether conceal his astonishment when they occasionally diverge from the Vulgate text.[94] The interlinings and marginal notes are in Latin, of course, although on at least two occasions he helps himself out with a German word, a hint that the pedantry of the young scholar did not keep him from turning to the vernacular when necessary to clinch a definition.[95] Here also we have the first evidence that he had made a beginning with the study of the two original languages of Holy Scriptures, Greek and Hebrew. Where and when he took his first steps in Greek we do not know. As we have seen, there is little likelihood that it was in the school of arts at Erfurt; and the first years in the cloister were so much occupied that he could hardly have found time for breaking into a new language. At Wittenberg, to be sure, there was a rising interest in Greek, but Martin's absorption in lecturing and theological study was there, if anything, more complete than at Erfurt. After his return to the mother cloister he made or renewed contact with at least one brother among the Eremites who could be of help to him. This was Johann Lang, who, as we have seen, probably began Greek studies under Marschalk. After Lang took his bachelor's degree he followed Martin into the cloister, where he

[93]All serious Luther students have used the marginalia since their publication in 1893 and have drawn a wide range of deductions. See the résumé of these in Rommel, *Über Luthers Randbemerkungen*, pp. 1 ff. Rommel goes further than Scheel, *Martin Luther*, II, 442 ff., in a denial of non-Occamist ideas in the marginalia and a refusal to recognize distinctly humanistic innovations. In much of the literature on the subject there is a tendency to force the meager material into rigid patterns of thought. In such circumstances the nontheological student can steer his course only by common sense and such scholarly experience as he has.

[94]"Incredibilis et multum mirabilis diversitas est a nostra translatione papae," *WA*, IX, 27.

[95]"Jerlich (annatim)," *WA*, IX, 18, l. 6; "Teutonice achtung (estimationem)," *ibid.*, p. 30, ll. 29 f.; "Kuntschafft, signum (argumentum)," *ibid.*, p. 91, ll. 14 f.

continued his studies for the master's, which he finally achieved at Wittenberg after the mature preparation of nine years.[96] It is altogether likely that
when Martin returned to Erfurt Lang gave him help with Greek.[97] Printed
assistance was also at hand. He mentions in the Lombard marginalia a
medieval dictionary of Greek words from the thirteenth century, the
Catholicon,[98] which he classes years later among the "mad, useless, harmful
books of the monks." [99] This may possibly have been the source of his
knowledge of the few Greek words which he writes into the marginalia.
They are written in part with Latin characters,[100] but in a few cases he
shows that he knows the Greek alphabet, for he inserts words in this text.[101]

If his acquaintance with Greek seems still to have been in its early stages,
his knowledge of Hebrew was apparently even slighter. He recalls many
years later that he bought a copy of Reuchlin's *Rudiments* in the early
days of his studies at Erfurt.[102] Here he came into possession of the first
Hebrew grammar published in Germany, for three years earlier Reuchlin
had opened the door to the language for students in the cloister and
university. Martin knows the Hebrew letters and their pronunciation and
also some words which he probably took from the dictionary attached to
Reuchlin's work.[103] It is, however, half a dozen years later before evidence
appears of real progress with the language of the Old Testament. Though
his equipment in these languages was slight, he was ready to use it. He also
gives other evidence of philological schooling in his efforts to explain some
of Augustine's words by etymological analyses.[104]

This philological enthusiasm may point to the influence of humanistic
friends. There seems to be some further evidence of this in the marginal
notes. He not infrequently interlards his discussions with references to
classical mythology and literature with here and there stilted phrases and

---

[96] Burgdorf, *Johann Lange*, pp. 10 ff. See esp. pp. 11 and 16.

[97] The assistance was not altogether one-sided, as Lang confesses some years later to his
friend Mutianus in a letter of May 2, 1515. Karl Gillert, ed., "Der Briefwechsel des Conradius
Mutianus," *Geschichtsquellen der Provinz Sachsen*, XVIII, II (1890), 149 f.

[98] "Sic allegat Catholicon," *WA*, IX, 68, l. 14.

[99] *An die Ratsherren aller Städte* (1524), *WA*, XV, 50.

[100] *WA*, IX, 10, l. 38; 24, l. 6; 62, ll. 37 ff.

[101] *WA*, IX, 24, l. 7; 25, l. 25; 26, l. 34. A line from Plato on the inside cover of Augustine's
Opuscula (*ibid.*, p. 16) may not have been written at this time.

[102] *De rudimentis hebraicis*, 1506. See letter from Luther to Lang, May 29, 1522, *WAB*,
II, 547: "Lexicon Hebraicon . . . quod olim Erfordiae emeram ab initio."

[103] *WA*, IX, 26, ll. 11 ff.; also p. 32, ll. 15 f. Burgdorf, *Einfluss der Erfurter Humanisten*,
pp. 58 f., would refer the beginning of Hebrew studies to Marschalk's instruction or to a
printed introduction by this teacher. It is certain that Martin worked with Lang on Hebrew,
probably in 1515. *WA*, IX, 115.

[104] "Hisionis a niti," *WA*, IX, 21, l. 31; "suscus, cudis, suscudes sunt tabellae," *ibid.*, p. 25,
ll. 33 f.

images from ancient sources, such as those with which the humanists liked to decorate their style.[105] Aside from such conventional ornamentation, to be sure, this apparent interest in the new studies as well as his acquaintance with classical literature does not exceed what he had acquired at the Erfurt school of arts. The Eclogues of Baptist the Mantuan, which he had studied diligently on the university benches, are still fresh in his memory.[106] Nevertheless, one may assume that the friendship with Lang was widening his knowledge of the humanistic ideals of the time. It brought him into touch with at least one other enthusiast for the new learning, Peter Eberbach, a member of a scholarly Erfurt family, who on more than one occasion in the years immediately following sends his greetings to Luther and asks the prayers of the earnest young friar.[107]

Nevertheless, the notes with which he covered the blank spaces in the cloister volumes offer no evidence that he shared the ideals of the humanists, except perhaps their enthusiasm for a scholarly interpretation of the sources. On the other hand, they show that he bristled with anger at an attack on his order from the humanistic side, that of the great Alsatian, Jakob Wimpfeling.[108] This eminent pedagogue had opened his campaign with strictures on the spirit prevailing among the secular clergy and monks while Martin was still in the Erfurt school of arts. The belligerent humanist, who was throughout his life a storm center of literary feuds, finally brought out in the year of Martin's profession his *Little Book on Purity*,[109] which attacked particularly the moral and religious life of the clergy both within and without the cloister. Wimpfeling's *Little Book* is a sharp arraignment of worldliness, self-indulgence, and ignorance scarcely excelled in bitterness either by Geiler von Kaisersberg or Erasmus, or Luther's polemics of later years. As a humanist and secular priest, the Alsatian reformer was hostile to the orders, particularly the mendicants, and the Augustinians more than any others felt the sting of his attack. Like other humanists, he had a natural affinity for Augustine and for that reason exerted himself to show that the Bishop of Hippo was not himself a monk or the founder of the order that bore his name. The *Sermon to the Eremites* attributed to Augustine, favorite reading in the Eremite cloisters, was not, Wimpfeling declared, his work, but that of the missionary to the Anglo-Saxons. Angry replies to his attack exploded

---

[105] Rommel, *Über Luthers Randbemerkungen*, p. 15, suggests that Martin might have derived such classical references mainly from Trutvetter.

[106] *WA*, IX, 24, l. 15.

[107] Oergel, *Vom jungen Luther*, pp. 116 f., 133. For Eberbach, see Burgdorf, *Einfluss der Erfurter Humanisten*, pp. 40 ff.

[108] *Ibid.*, pp. 63 ff.   [109] *De integritate libellus* (Strassburg, 1505).

from the clerical side, and Wimpfeling, a skilled and relentless controversial-ist, did not turn the other cheek. Humanistic sympathizers rallied to his support [110] and the affair continued to reverberate until the strife over the burning of Hebrew books and the resulting Reuchlin controversy gave the clerical and humanistic opponents a more pressing cause for dispute and led the way to the biting satires in the *Letters of Obscure Men*.

Doubtless Martin had heard much and lively discussion of the matter even before his departure for Wittenberg and on his return to the Erfurt cloister must have found the brothers still agitated. Lang's relations with at least one of the critical spirits, Eberbach, may have given an especial realism to the affair in the Erfurt chapter.[111] The young lecturer reacted against the criticisms of the Alsatian humanist with unbridled resentment. It was especially the attempt to deprive the order of its great patron that called him to defense. This was to be expected. On many solemn occasions he had joined his brothers of the cloister in singing the consecratory hymn, "Great Father Augustine." Memorizing the Rule of the saint had been one of his first experiences as a novice, and ever since his reception he had listened to reading from his works in chapter house and refectory. Undoubtedly the *Sermon to the Eremites in the Wilderness* was one of the selections fre-quently read. This was no more than routine acquaintance with Augustine. It gave place to real discovery when Martin himself began to read his works. Some years later he declares that Augustine did not enjoy the least favor with him until he came upon his books.[112] Now when he begins to go through these with pen in hand he feels himself drawn to Augustine with deep admiration. This must have begun well before he undertook the annotation, since he feels sufficiently sure of his acquaintance with the writer to reject one of the works before him as not of his authorship be-cause of its wordy style, and to assign certain others to him with definite-ness.[113] It is, then, with a bitter tone that he commends the reading of Augustine's *On the Life and Manners of the Clergy* to Wimpfeling, the "chattering bleater and critic of the fame of the Augustinians," with the advice that he first "recall his reason" which has been driven far afield under a long affliction of obstinacy and envy, and put spectacles on his "mole's eyes." Why does this "aged and distracted scarecrow" overlook the testimony

---

[110] Letter from Eberbach to Lang, Sept. 5, 1508, Burgdorf, *Einfluss der Erfurter Humanisten*, pp. 124 f.

[111] See Burgdorf, *Einfluss der Erfurter Humanisten*, pp. 104 ff., especially p. 115, where he argues that Wimpfeling's book gave Martin a shock respecting the monastic ideal.

[112] Letter from Luther to Spalatin, Oct. 19, 1516, *WAB*, I, 70, ll. 17 ff.

[113] *De cognitione verae vitae. WA*, IX, 6, ll. 10 f.; 14, ll. 22 ff.

of Hugh of St. Victor to Augustine's authorship of the *Sermon to the Eremites?* "Why do you correct the Church of God? Why do you tell such dirty lies?" [114] He cannot restrain his enthusiasm for the eloquence of the great author.[115] A certain passage in the *City of God* is worthy of Augustine alone, "whose praise can never be high enough." [116]

The notes on Augustine, which revolve about specific passages in the text, are brief though spirited. In those in Lombard's *Sentences* Martin gives himself much greater elbow room. They vary from mere word glosses to long *scholia* in which he seeks to epitomize and discuss certain of the master's "Distinctions" as a whole. For the author of the *Sentences* Martin has all the enthusiasm of a young discoverer: "Read a thousand scholars," he declares regarding Lombard's remarks on the freedom of the will. "None solves this problem better"; Scotists, modernists and followers of the ancient way, "they do not know what they are talking about." [117] His notes are concerned chiefly with the early part of the work, which discusses the nature of God, the Trinity, and the major problems of sin and redemption. His studies had provided him already with a considerable range of knowledge, which his unusual memory put within ready call, and from time to time he slips in a name of authority to buttress his argument. Lombard regarded Augustine highly and Martin greets with satisfaction the harmony of thought between the two great authorities.[118] The name of Augustine appears on almost every page in his notes on the *Sentences* as the first and greatest source of knowledge. Other witnesses are summoned as needed. Hugh of St. Victor, the mystic and one of the fathers of Scholasticism, was called on, as we have seen, to testify against Wimpfeling. Fathers and early theologians of the Church, Dionysius the Areopagite, Chrysostom the Golden-mouthed, Jerome, Ambrose, and Hilary appear. It need not be supposed that his reading of this formidable array of authorities had gone far; perhaps he knew them only from his university lectures, perhaps from an anthology in the cloister library. A young lecturer's readiness with scholarly references need not be taken too seriously. The material that Martin knows thoroughly is that of the school in which he had been trained by Trutvetter and Arnold von Usingen in his formative years, and the marginal notes show how fully the modernist ideas had been absorbed. Occam's epistemology is set forth with precision and applied with assurance again and again to Lombard's ideas. Martin does not doubt that the universal is a collective idea, and the species abstracted from the individuals.[119] He does not fail to

114 *WA*, IX, 12, ll. 7 ff.   115 *Ibid.*, p. 7, ll. 26 f.   116 *Ibid.*, p. 29, ll. 5 f.
117 *Ibid.*, p. 62, ll. 19 ff.   118 *Ibid.*, p. 29.   119 *Ibid.*, p. 45, ll. 11 ff.

note the error of the realists in ascribing unity to things which are distinct entities.[120] As a matter of course Augustine is appropriated for the modernist conception.[121] Martin deduces its basic formula regarding the universal quite neatly from one of Augustine's propositions [122] and praises Occam for a clever adjustment of his ideas to those of the African Father,[123] whose Neoplatonism with its recognition of the reality of ideas he seems to have overlooked entirely.[124]

All of this he had received from Trutvetter and Usingen and these scholars had also inoculated him quite thoroughly with modernist conceptions of theology. The impotence of the reason in measuring the idea of God, the superiority of revelation to human reason, these are the ground tones in his discussion of Lombard whenever he approaches fundamental ideas. His contempt for the realists is formulated in the abusive terms of which he made such liberal use in later years. "The stinking rules of the logicians" lie concerning the infinite breadth of divinity.[125] A proposition of Augustine convicts their "whole stupid philosophy." [126] Theology is unattainable by the laws of reason. Martin says in effect:

Note this, reader, whoever thou art, even though it be observed by a blockhead. The smoke of earth has never succeeded in lighting up heaven but rather in shutting off light from the earth. I mean by that, theology is heaven, or rather the kingdom of heaven; man and his speculations, earth. This is the reason for the great difference among scholars. Observe that the sow could never teach Minerva, even though she ventured to try, nor can wild lions and bears, or even birds, be caught with spider webs.[127]

He marvels greatly that even some of his own school are bold enough to declare that Aristotle does not differ from the Catholic truth,[128] and he lifts Augustine high above "the story-teller Aristotle" with his "frivolous defenders," "falsifiers and destroyers of the true faith." [129] A long introductory note to the *Sentences* is a paean of praise for the prudence of Augustine and an invective against philosophy, whose devotees are caught in a labyrinth of error. "The world is full of . . . chimeras and hydras." [130]

---

[120] *Ibid.*, p. 83, ll. 8 ff. See also his fling at the "formalities" of the Scotists, p. 56, ll. 19 f.

[121] "In re tamen idem dicit quod moderni" (concerning the nature of time), *ibid.*, p. 9, ll. 17 f.

[122] *Ibid.*, p. 45, ll. 9 ff.

[123] "Satis ingeniose concordat et exponit verba b. Augustini," *ibid.*, p. 33, ll. 30 f.

[124] For contrary opinions on Luther's views, see Rommel, *Über Luthers Randbemerkungen*, pp. 2 ff.

[125] *WA*, IX, 47, ll. 6 f.; see also p. 48, ll. 4 f.

[126] *Ibid.*, p. 13, l. 20.   [127] *Ibid.*, p. 65, ll. 11 ff.   [128] *Ibid.*, p. 27, ll. 22 ff.

[129] *Ibid.*, p. 23, ll. 6 ff.   [130] *Ibid.*, p. 29, l. 13.

Despite Luther's claims later in life that he knew the chief works of Thomas as a student, his notes do not mention this most famous interpreter of the *Sentences* at all. Those commentators whom he does cite are William of Occam; Gregory of Rimini, an Italian Augustinian; Pierre d'Ailly, the brilliant French theologian of the preceding century who at Martin's age had written an exposition of the *Sentences* [131] of nominalist tendency; and Gabriel Biel. Whether he had examined personally the books of the first three is doubtful, although it is probable that they were in the cloister library. The work upon which he leaned most heavily was the commentary of the great Tübingen modernist, Gabriel Biel, whose *Canon of the Mass* had meant so much to him three years before. Biel's *Summary of the Sentences,*[132] based directly on Occam's commentary, was a systematic and definitive presentation of nominalist theology. Undoubtedly this sturdy work, for which even Catholic theologians of the present day testify their respect,[133] was well known to Martin's teachers and almost certainly the young lecturer read in it diligently. Some years later when he had attained a more independent position in Wittenberg he got hold of a copy of a later edition of Biel's *Summary* and filled its margins with critical and sarcastic comments.[134] In the Erfurt days such an attitude was far from him. He finds in the master of nominalism the same theology which his teachers at university and cloister had impressed upon him. He has now mastered it and applies its precepts to the great dogmatic problems in Lombard. Quite in the footsteps of Biel,[135] he winds off a syllogism to prove that sin is a pure negative and seeks his way, though somewhat unsteadily, along abstract paths toward a formula differentiating good and evil.[136] With

[131] First printed at Brussels in 1478. Severely condemned by orthodox Catholicism. See Vacant and Mangenot, *Dictionnaire de Théologie Catholique,* I, 651.

[132] *Epithomata et collectorium pariter collectorium circa quattuor Sententiarium libros* (Tübingen, 1499). Hain, *Repertorium Bibliographicum,* No. 3187. Various reprintings followed. Probably Martin used the Tübingen edition of 1501, a copy of which is in the library of the Union Theological Seminary.

[133] "Et certes, jamais le nominalisme ne fut présenté dans une exposition plus claire." Vacant and Mangenot, *Dictionnaire de Théologie Catholique,* II, 816.

[134] See H. Degering, *Luthers Randbemerkungen zu Gabriel Biels Collectorium.* The editor concludes that the volume, which was used by the present writer in the library of the theological seminary at Wittenberg, once belonged to the Augustinian monastery there, and that the many marginalia, including Luther's, were written here in 1515–19. He is of the opinion that this was the first copy of Biel's commentary that Martin had seen and that the notes in the Lombard at Erfurt derived their knowledge of Biel from the lectures of Trutvetter and Usingen. The argument is far from conclusive, for it is hardly likely that the young *sententiarius,* who read so diligently in Augustine, should not have made personal acquaintance with a work of the prestige of Biel's. Furthermore, the many parallels with the *Collectorium* set forth by Rommel can hardly have rested on second-hand information.

[135] *WA,* IX, 73, ll. 6 ff.

[136] *Ibid.,* p. 56, ll. 5 ff.; 61, ll. 16 ff. Cf. Rommel, *Über Luthers Randbemerkungen,* pp. 41 f.

equal diligence he follows his school in explaining the entry of original sin as a corollary to the liberty of the will, which destroyed the harmony of soul that God bestowed on man.[137] He traces the fateful course of hereditary evil in its passage down the ages in the form of concupiscence, rebegotten in fleshly lust from generation to generation.[138] He follows his teachers in their abstruse scholastic differentiation between the "formal" side of sin which baptism destroys, and the "touchwood" (*fomes*) of lust of the senses which it cannot eradicate.[139] Like them, he defines sin as a "defection from the fire of love," [140] and seeks its essential nature in the inner man and not the outward act.[141]

The notes evidence that the young expositor of the *Sentences* was seeking to clarify his own mind respecting the major problem of theology, the method by which salvation comes to man. The scattered entries do not, of course, attempt to formulate a system of his own; instead, he continues to rely on the system already received from his theological teachers, though he must have pondered on it deeply in the notes on their lectures and in his reading concerning it in Biel. He now tries to adapt his thinking on the subject to Lombard and puts down some of the results here and there as suggested to him by a phrase in the text or by the general contents of one of Lombard's "Distinctions." These remarks are scattered among syllogisms and definitions and dialectical formulas such as he had learned to use in the disputational exercises. Now and then he attests his dexterity in the treatment of theological subtleties, such as the question whether the angels have free will. There are, however, a number of notes which show that Martin had seized and assimilated the conceptions of grace which his school of theology held. These were a part of the dogmatic structure which many centuries of subtle thinkers had put together. The great problem in this construction was of course the adjustment of the relation between divine purpose and the human will. This has engaged the thought and imagination of man at every period and history shows an unceasing oscillation between ideals of determinism by outer forces and autonomy of the individual. A rhythmic movement of this kind is observable throughout the development of medieval Christian theology. The struggle with the question became for Martin as the years went by a matter of supreme importance, and it is therefore necessary to examine briefly the form in which he first approached it.

St. Augustine, the great thinker of the early Church, whose views were so

---

[137] *WA*, IX, 69, ll. 11 ff.   [138] *Ibid.*, p. 74, ll. 30 ff.
[139] *Ibid.*, p. 75, ll. 11 ff.; see also p. 79, ll. 2 ff.
[140] *Ibid.*, p. 88, l. 15.   [141] *Ibid.*, p. 81, ll. 4 ff.

influential on succeeding generations, emphasized the necessity of a divine grace freely given to men for the work of salvation. The infusion of grace begets a supernatural love without which no effort of man can bring him to the heavenly bourne. However, Augustine makes one great reservation: even· if man's works are sanctified by grace, another gift is necessary, the predestinating choice of God. As the centuries went by, it was inevitable that this view of arbitrary action by divine power should gradually become weaker under the pressure of rationalizing tendencies and that in the minds of Augustine's successors compensating emphasis should be placed on the participation of free will in the winning of God's favor. Father Anselm showed the way; the influx of Aristotelian ideas in the twelfth century brought a certain spirit of Greek humanism, and the scholastic age incorporated this into the intricate theory of "infused grace" which the scholars of the period rounded out so skillfully. The conception of a natural disposition to good in man forced its way to the fore and elbowed the Augustinian ideas further to one side, though the theological systematists of the full Middle Ages, like Thomas Aquinas, were well aware of the danger that lay in too generous an adoption of this theory and worked diligently for a compromise that should avoid the Pelagian heresy which would make man capable of obtaining his salvation by natural forces, a belief against which Augustine had fought with such vigor. They held fast to the conception of a divine infusion of grace, but opened the door definitely to human cooperation. Moral conduct creates a natural disposition of the will— they called it the *habitus* in imitation of Aristotle—which prepares it for grace. To make possible the infusion of grace, however, another stage must be passed. This is effected by a special grace, which is freely given (*gratia gratis data*) and which creates a second *habitus*. With the disposition thus acquired, it is then in man's power to mobilize the will and do his utmost to achieve salvation (*faciens quod in se est*). The good works thus performed have a certain merit in God's eyes, they are agreeable to Him (*merita de congruo*), but they are not sufficient for salvation. This requires the infusion of the supernatural grace (*gratia gratum faciens*), which justifies man before God and makes his works truly meritorious for salvation (*merita de condigno*).

This subtle adjustment between the will and grace was attacked by Duns Scotus. As we have seen, the great English Franciscan led the way toward a more robust conception of the power of the human will. He belittled the "freely given grace" and thus automatically enforced the importance of the disposition acquired by man through his own natural powers. William of

Occam followed Scotus in rejecting the intermediate stage. The Occamist theologians who were Luther's teachers and the great systematizer of modernist theology, Gabriel Biel, stressed the importance of the natural powers.[142] Martin shows in his first Wittenberg course of lectures that he understood quite fully these conceptions.[143] The metaphysicians of the modernist direction had need of all the logical skill for which they were famous to establish and defend their position on free will. It did not occur to the Erfurt professors or Biel, to be sure, to regard the will in action as inclined to anything other than evil. The "touchwood" for sin remains after baptism, though it is modified, as we have seen in Luther's notes. The modernists therefore did not recognize the works of the will without grace as effective for salvation even though the commands of God were fulfilled in substance. Here was, however, a subtlety of distinction that was, indeed, finespun. Martin does not grapple with it in the Lombard notes. Perhaps he overlooked it because of the fervor with which his school proclaimed the supremacy of revelation over speculation, perhaps because of the energy with which his teachers had impressed upon him the necessity for an arbitrary act of God to bring grace into the heart. Nevertheless, this acceptance of the natural powers of man for good clung to his thinking and comes strongly to the fore years later when he breaks with the whole system.[144]

These were, then, the ideas which Martin absorbed, partly through his reading in Biel's interpretation of Lombard, but mainly, without doubt, from lectures which he had heard at Erfurt and Wittenberg. He accepted them wholeheartedly and reproduced them as best he could in his notes. Hence his quarrel with the "philosophers," meaning the metaphysicists of the Thomist and Scotist persuasion. Hence his emphasis on the contrast between reason and revelation and his insistence on the scriptural text, and hence also the careful distinction which he draws between works done before the infusion of divine grace and those that follow it.[145] He knows the Occamist position regarding the freedom of the will.[146] He knows that

---

[142] Scheel, *Martin Luther*, II, 164 ff., gives a lengthy and careful analysis of the modernist position in its differentiation between the good works performed through the natural powers of the will and those done in a state of grace.

[143] *Dictata super Psalterium* (1513–16), *WA*, IV, 262. The modernist theory is set forth in the terminology of the school with clearness and conviction.

[144] *Resolutiones Lutherianae super propositionibus suis Lipsiae disputatis* (1519), *WA*, II, 401.

[145] *WA*, IX, 72, ll. 27 f. See Rommel, *Über Luthers Randbemerkungen*, p. 57, n. 5, for Biel's influence here. He quotes a verse ascribed to Albertus Magnus (*WA*, IX, 72, l. 27):

Quidquid habes meriti praeventrix gratia donat.

Some years later he cites this again in his notes on Tauler's sermons, but in another sense. *WA*, IX, 99, ll. 26 f.

[146] *Ibid.*, pp. 31 and 62.

grace cannot be forced upon man. Predestination seems not to cause him any difficulty: he seeks to explain the difference between preknowledge and pre-destination, as no doubt his teachers did, by a metaphysical device, a demonstration of the inapplicability of human ideas of time to eternity.[147] He knows that the natural will is "polluted" and ever inclined to evil.[148] He knows the subtle difference between the faith that is acquired by natural powers of man and that which diffuses itself through him on the receipt of divine grace.[149]

This first look into the workings of his mind finds him, then, a faithful follower of the scholastic learning as he had received it. It is highly doubtful if one may find in the notes any departure from this ideology. They do, however, give abundant testimony to the energy and persistence with which he had attacked and assimilated the resistant material received on the university benches or read in the heavy volumes of Augustine and Biel and perhaps other texts of Church Fathers and medieval interpreters. His presentation still treads the path of the scholastic exposition in definition and syllogism, but where he gives himself elbow room he is vigorous and begins to show signs of readiness to attack contesting authorities with the violence that was one of the scholastic traditions in which he afterward attained mastery.[150] The notes are marked by all the self-assurance of youth. Their style already bears the stamp of personality. He shakes off something of the medieval Latin formalism without borrowing any of the preciosity of humanism.[151]

[147] *Ibid.*, p. 59, ll. 2 ff.   [148] In a long analysis. *Ibid.*, p. 79, ll. 10 ff.

[149] *Fides acquisita* and *fides infusa. Ibid.*, p. 90, ll. 10 ff. Rommel thinks that Martin does not follow Biel here. It should be noted that many scholars find that the conception of faith in the marginal notes goes further than that of the Occam school. This applies particularly to Martin's discussion of the three "theological" virtues, faith, hope, and love, which he regards as inseparable although qualitatively unequal. Rommel, *Über Luthers Randbemerkungen*, pp. 77 ff., finds that while he has misunderstood earlier writers to some extent, Martin is nevertheless in general harmony with Occam's position. However, in the treatment of faith as a transition from the natural to the supernatural world, there is an interesting anticipation of the conception set forth eight years later in the lectures on Hebrews.

[150] H. Grisar, *Luther,* I, 16, finds the language of the notes "self-conscious and daring." See also his *Luthers Leben und sein Werk,* p. 45.

[151] In 1516 Lang writes Mutianus that Martin avoided this *ex industria*. Gillert, "Mutianus," II, No. 490 (p. 150). See also Burgdorf, *Einfluss der Erfurter Humanisten,* p. 58.

I O

THE JOURNEY TO ROME

FOR the two years or more following the course of lectures on the *Sentences* contemporary sources regarding Martin's life are silent. No letters or cloister records are at hand. No university annals permit us to follow his work in the faculty of theology. Presumably he went on giving lectures after the winter semester of 1509–10, either on Lombard or on the Bible or both for at least a part of these two years, and there is a probability also that he served the Eremites as subregent of studies at the cloister in association with Professor Nathin. In 1512 he appears again in Wittenberg, sufficiently mature in scholarship and personality to look forward to the doctor's degree and a professor's chair at the university. Within this period an episode occurred about which his memory brightened as middle life approached, and which became a focus of many picturesque statements in the *Table Talk,* sermons and lectures: the journey to Rome.[1]

"I would not take one hundred thousand florins for having seen and heard Rome." This declaration of Martin's more than a quarter of a century after the visit indicates the importance which his stay in the Eternal City had assumed in his mind and emphasizes his consciousness of its dramatic character in any account of his own life.[2] Succeeding generations of biographers have fully exploited its colorful possibilities; the vivid contrast suggested by the presence of the future antagonist of the Roman Church in the citadel of its power and abuses has stimulated much spirited writing and a great deal of patient research. Nevertheless contemporary sources of primary value are few and a knowledge of the persons and circumstances of the journey is limited to

---

[1] Luther's recollections after 1531 are the only direct source for knowledge of his visit to Rome. To the collateral evidence regarding the circumstances that brought it about very little has been added since the appearance of Kolde's *Augustiner-Kongregation* in 1879. A great deal of information has been assembled pertaining to the time and especially to things touched on in Martin's reminiscences. This has added to the historical picture without throwing further light on the biographical problem.

[2] *TR*, III, No. 3478 (1536); for a similar idea, though more mildly put, see No. 3582A (1537). The account in Heydenreich's text says "1,000 florins." *TR*, V, No. 5484 (1542).

the recollections of the aging Luther, which in this case are perhaps more strongly colored by his polemical attitude than in any other, and to collateral material for the most part of little pertinence.[3] It cannot be said with certainty just when he set forth on the journey, who accompanied him, nor when he returned. Circumstantial evidence points to the late fall or winter of 1510, but it is not impossible that his trip to Italy occurred a year later.[4] Regarding the causes which sent him, his recollections are silent except for a casual statement that he went on business of the order and its conflict with Dr. Staupitz.[5] The family biographer Mathesius, too, gives "cloister business" as the reason for the journey.[6]

The order of Augustinian Eremites had indeed at this time reached a crisis in its affairs. The reform of the cloister observance and the respiritualization of the order had been carried through in Germany, as we have seen, by Andreas Proles. He had brought a great number of cloisters under the strict observance, binding them to full submission to the rule of St. Augustine. The general objective of the observance was a full performance of the daily choir services and other disciplinary and devotional phases of the common life and the submission by the brothers to a spirit of self-denial and humility characteristic of the highest ideals of the monastic order. Seventy of the observant cloisters were brought together into one congregation independent of the four German "provinces," with Proles at their head as general vicar. When he died, in 1503, Staupitz succeeded him and drew more tightly the lines that bound the German congregation by means of the new constitution, which had just gone into effect when Martin entered the cloister. His first step to ensure perpetuity and progress to the reform was an effort to free the congregation from the general of the order and bring it, like the Lombard group of observant cloisters, from which the movement for reform had come into Germany, directly under the pope. We have seen that these efforts at autonomy for the reformed cloisters were blocked by the general, Interramna, and that his death and the succession of a new general brought

[3] Apparently the visit did not attain significance in his mind until two decades after it was made, but this is no reason for denying that it influenced his thought and attitude during the intervening years. Nevertheless, it remains a puzzle that recollections of his contact with Rome did not emerge in his sermons and lectures during the critical years of his struggle against the hierarchy, 1520–21, nor for a decade longer. Evidently he realized with the retrospective years that the Roman visit had been a factor in his development.

[4] Melanchthon, CR, VI, 156, gives 1511. Mathesius, Ausgewählte Werke (1906), III, 23, gives 1510. See also Böhmer, Romfahrt, p. 3. Martin himself seems to have been quite uncertain as to the year. He gives both 1509 (TR, II, No. 2717) and 1510 (TR, V, No. 6059).

[5] "Anno . . . nono Romam profectus sum causa contentionis Staupitii." TR, II, No. 2717 (1532).

[6] "Ins Klosters geschefften." Mathesius, Ausgewählte Werke (1906), III, 23.

a man into office who was thoroughly in harmony with Staupitz's plans for reform.[7] Egidio of Viterbo was a son of the Renaissance, but like many another of the great Italians of that age, an ardent and spiritually minded churchman, one of those who gave evidence of the widespread longing felt in every Christian country for a renewal of church and religion. With such an auxiliary Staupitz might count on success. The unreformed convents of the Saxon lands, twenty-five in number, petitioned the papal legate, Carvajal, to attach them to the Reformed Congregation, and in a papal bull of December 15, 1507 they were brought together with thirty-four observant cloisters into one chapter under one head, at once the "provincial" and the general vicar.[8]

In this office Staupitz was then confirmed by the general of the order on June 25, 1509.[9] In the meantime, however, he had begun to experience difficulties, the most serious of which arose from the strongly independent spirit of the self-governing German imperial cities. The Nuremberg council, in its pride of civic autonomy, became alarmed at the political complications which might result from the union of its cloister with others under the provincial of Saxony and interposed forcible restraint on the Nuremberg Augustinians, shutting off their drinking water.[10] Other cloisters of the congregation seem also to have opposed the union, fearful lest the rigidity of their observance might be impaired by association with so many conventuals as yet unreformed. Delays ensued. Nevertheless Staupitz proceeded with his plans on a visit to Rome in the spring and early summer of 1510. On June 26 of that year he was again confirmed in his office [11] and on September 30 the bull of almost three years earlier was published in Germany, giving to the new union all the sanction of canonical law.[12] This did not, however, still the opposition of the seven protesting cloisters. Among these Erfurt was distinguished as a model in fulfillment of strict observance, and Erfurt seems to have assumed an active rôle in opposition to the proposed consolidation.

In this affair Martin undoubtedly played a part. What his personal opinions were regarding the question at issue we have no way of knowing, but we do know his zeal for the sanctity of the observance as it is reflected in letters which followed his elevation to the office of subvicar of the Saxon-

---

[7] Kolde, *Augustiner-Kongregation*, pp. 231 f.

[8] For the text of the bull, see Böhmer, *Romfahrt*, pp. 161 ff.

[9] *Ibid.*, p. 55.

[10] Kolde, *Augustiner-Kongregation*, pp. 235 f.; Böhmer, *Romfahrt*, p. 55.

[11] Ant. Höhn, *Chronologia provinciae Rheno-Suevicae ord. F.F. Erem. S.S. Aug.* (1744), p. 154, cited by Böhmer, *Romfahrt*, p. 31, n. 1.

[12] *Ibid.*, pp. 141 ff.

Thuringian province in 1514.[13] It is quite probable that Martin, ardent in ascetic exercises and ready to speak his mind without reserve, was put forward to defend what the Erfurt brothers held to be sacred interests. This probability is strengthened by the fact that he was sent with the head of theological studies at Erfurt, Nathin, to Halle to ask that the cathedral provost there intervene with the archbishop of Magdeburg against the papal bull of union.[14] It is, then, likely that when, in the fall of 1510, the seven cloisters concluded to appeal to the Vatican, Martin was chosen to represent Erfurt.

The mission consisted of two brothers. It must have left Germany in November, for in January it appeared before the general procurator in Rome. A year or more later, when it became evident that the opposition to the plan of union was too strong to be overcome, Staupitz himself sent another mission to the Eternal City. The chief of this, the so-called *litis procurator,* was the learned Augustinian, Johann von Mecheln.[15] To one of these missions Martin certainly belonged. Although the evidence is contradictory, it seems to point, as we have seen, to that of 1510.[16] In any event, the summons to go must have been welcomed with eager heart by the young friar, whose theological studies made him all the more anxious to see the great center of the Church's earthly power. Here he could stand beside the place where Paul met a martyr's death and Peter founded the visible Church. Many years afterwards he asserted that there was another reason for his journey. He wished to make a general confession and "become pious." [17] So overwhelming were the impressions of the trip, both sacred and profane, that they seem to have effaced from his mind all memory of the plea of his convent, which must have lain very close to his heart at that time. In all probability he went along, not as the leader of the mission, but as a "companion of the journey" (*socius itinerarius*) in accordance with the requirement of the constitution of the Eremites and monastic practice generally.[18]

---

[13] E.g., letter from Luther to Georg Mascov, May 17, 1517, *WAB,* I, 97 f.

[14] Heinrich Dungersheim recalls having heard of this visit to Adolf von Anhalt, at that time provost in Halle and later, as bishop of Merseburg, to become one of Martin's early opponents. *Dadelung des obgesatzten bekenntnus oder untuchtigen Lutherischen Testaments* (1530), fol. 14, quoted by Böhmer, *Romfahrt,* p. 57.

[15] N. Besler, "Vita Nicolai Besleri Augustiniani ab ipso conscripta," *Fortgesetzte Sammlung von alten und neuen theologischen Sachen* (Leipzig, 1732), pp. 356 ff., 363; Kolde, "Innere Bewegungen unter den deutschen Augustinern und Luthers Romreise," *ZKG,* II (1878), 468; also Scheel, *Martin Luther,* II, 548 and n. 1.

[16] See above, n. 4. Recent biographers favor 1510: Böhmer, *Romfahrt,* pp. 3 ff.; Scheel, *Martin Luther,* II, 488, n. 2. Nevertheless, the evidence is not altogether convincing.

[17] *TR,* III, Nos. 3582A and 3582B (1537). The passage is, to be sure, bitterly polemical.

[18] *Const.,* para. 20.

Whether his chief was the eminent Johann von Mecheln or some other, we do not know, but it was undoubtedly a brother with experience in Roman ways. Martin's contact with the affair in Rome can only have been slight.

Our only knowledge of the facts of the journey is gathered, as has been remarked, from scattered statements of much later years. All date from a time when Rome and its associations had become anathema to Martin. Nevertheless many observations and experiences of the pilgrimage had stamped themselves enduringly on his mind; and while it is not possible to follow his itinerary in detail nor outline with exactness his experiences in Rome, the impressions and many of the events of the memorable trip to the south are preserved in sermons and *Table Talk* with something of the intensity of the days when, as a mendicant wayfarer, he planted his staff along the rocky mule trails of the Alps and laid his head in the dust before the sacred relics in St. John Lateran. Even through the strongly colored views of advanced years, there appear in his memories of Rome many characteristics of the young friar.

The two mendicants set forth on foot, quietly, one following behind the other as the monastic rule required. The credentials of their cloister assured them food and rest by the way; indeed they could scarcely fail to find an Augustinian monastery at the end of even a short day's journey. In Tuscany alone fifty-three cloisters of their order were to be found. The distance before them from Erfurt to Rome might, in view of pilgrim standards and the pace of Martin's journey to Augsburg seven years later, have been covered in six weeks. The sources offer no means for determining which road the Eremite brothers followed. Two well-won pilgrim routes lay open to them for crossing the Alps, one through Switzerland, where the roads led to Verona or Milan, the other through the Tyrol to Verona. Martin recalls passing through Milan [19] and refers with some definiteness to Innsbruck; [20] it is therefore probable that he went and came by different roads. He recalls that the journey took him through Augsburg, but whether going or returning we do not know. He probably also visited Ulm, for his subsequent references to the great cathedral there seem to show that he had seen this splendid structure with his own eyes.[21] The season was fall, as he remembered eating ripe pomegranates on the way.

The eyes of the friar, turned inward by ascetic and scholastic training,

[19] *TR*, IV, No. 4760.

[20] *TR*, V, No. 6392, a reference to the style of houses in Innsbruck. Its collocation with remarks regarding cities which Martin knew well implies that he had also been in the Tyrolese capital.

[21] *TR*, III, No. 3781 (1538).

gradually lifted to observe the world that lay around him. Familiar from boyhood with the farm and its products, he did not fail to take notice of the country through which he passed, although his view remained a limited one. The aesthetic charms of the Swiss and Italian scenery made no impression, nor did the wild Alpine landscape awaken other reflections than amazement at its unproductive soil and its good roads.[22] The Swiss seemed a very sturdy people, but the land they inhabited was good for grazing alone.[23] Despite such realistic observations, Martin viewed nature in most cases only through monastic eyes. The lemon tree with its glossy leaves, greeted with such joy by northern travelers, serves only to point a devout simile: bearing ripe and green fruit together, it reminds us that Christ provides that one defender of the faith will always succeed another, "so that the voice of the Gospel is heard and the eternal patrimony is harvested for the Son of God." [24] The Italian olives growing among the flinty stones illustrate passages in Psalms and Matthew.[25] The rich Lombard plain and the valley of the Po is a human paradise where only man is vile.[26] The countryside that awakened such sober reflections in the monk also brought physical discomfort, for, like many German pilgrims to Italy, Martin and his companion caught malaria from sleeping with open windows, so that their heads were filled with fog and they could go only one German mile the next day; but they cured this, he states, by eating pomegranates.[27]

For the people on the way the eyes of the friar were keener. He recalled at middle age the hospitality and generosity which the Swabians and Bavarians showered upon the travelers.[28] The long trail gave him abundant opportunity to test the manner and sincerity of monastic life in the many convents where they found food and lodging. He recalled the lavish expenditure for guests in the great cloister of St. Benedict on the Po, where he found "right honorable" treatment.[29] As a Northerner, he was struck with amazement by the divergent usage of the Ambrosian missal,[30] which kept

---

[22] Ibid., Nos. 2871a and 2871b (1533).　　[23] Ibid., No. 3621 (1537).

[24] TR, V, No. 6242.　　[25] TR, III, Nos. 3578A and 3578B (1537).

[26] Ibid., No. 3717 (1538); see also II, No. 1327 (1532), where Aurifaber's transcript shows particular bitterness against the Italians. The Po valley made a deep impression on the northern pilgrim, TR, IV, No. 4573; V, No. 6142.

[27] TR, II, No. 1327. A decade earlier the Franciscan Pellicanus, who was headed for Rome in the train of Cardinal Perault, was not so easily cured and was obliged to turn back to Switzerland.

[28] TR, III, No. 3473 (1536). He adds some sarcastic observations regarding the uncivil behavior of the Saxons, and particularly the Wittenbergers, toward strangers.

[29] TR, V, No. 6042. Böhmer, Romfahrt, p. 82, thinks this was San Benedetto Po near Mantua. Scheel, Martin Luther, II, 499, decides for the San Sisto in Piacenza.

[30] TR, IV, No. 4760; V, No. 6360; Kurzes Bekenntnis vom heiligen Sakrament (1544), WA, LIV, 166.

him from saying Mass in the diocese of Milan. This contact with foreign peoples must have quickened his national feeling, another of the results of the journey that was not to develop until later years. He never learned to understand Italian, and as the Italian priests at that time were not usually able to talk Latin, he was shut off from their ideas and could only judge by what he saw.[31] Vivid pictures that come back from those impressionable days show that he had his eyes open for cultural deviations from the German pattern. He praises the cut of Italian garments in contrast with the short coats in which the Saxon "hops around like a magpie." [32] He notes the urbane manners of the Italians [33] and has complimentary remarks to make about their self-restraint in drinking, again a moving contrast to the Germans.[34] Like most Germans, he notes with amusement the vivacity of the Italians in speech and gesture [35] and pours contempt on certain naïve street customs, "like those of dogs," which required the setting up of an image of St. Anthony as a protection against the defilement of buildings.[36] He was struck by their nonattendance on Mass and cites the contemptuous expression with which they decorated a poor, weak-minded person as a "good Christian." He had warm enthusiasm for public institutions in Italy, the hospital and the foundling asylum in Florence, the famous Santa Maria degli Innocenti, whose façade was already decorated with the charming *bambini* of Luca della Robbia. The "royal" equipment of these foundations, their excellent administration, their medical agencies, abundant food, scientific treatment of the sick, and the self-denying labor of volunteer nurses [37] all clung fast in memory from the days when he walked about the city and talked with German mendicants on the highway or in the cloister. His severe arraignment of the Italian people for lying, unbelief, frivolous blasphemy, treachery, and unnatural sins may have had its beginning in similar contacts with Germans in Italy. In later days these ideas were intensified by the religious conflict and developed into the savage criticisms that are scattered through the *Table Talk*. The humanists had already begun to raise the standard of nationalism in Germany, but it was not until the Italian war of Maximilian that this feeling swelled in violence against the land to the south. In Ulrich von Hutten's bitter satires of 1519 and Martin's fiery appeals a year later to the German pride of independence Rome appeared as a national enemy.

Whatever road the two pilgrims followed across the Lombard plain,

---

[31] See *Enarratio in Genesin, WA*, XLII, 414, where he notes that the inability to understand each other's language was a mutual cause of "rage and hostility."

[32] *TR*, V, No. 6237.   [33] *WA*, XLIII, 330.   [34] *TR*, IV, No. 4948 (1540).

[35] *TR*, V, No. 5198 (1540).   [36] *TR*, III, No. 3718.   [37] *TR*, IV, No. 3930 (1538).

they probably turned at last into the ancient Aemilian Way. On this they climbed the Apennines in the cold and wet of early winter and descended into the valley of the Arno and to Florence, which Martin certainly visited either going or returning. Thence the great road, trod by so many generations of yearning souls, pointed straight through Siena toward Rome. It was on a wintry day that he first caught sight of the Eternal City, perhaps from the Monte Mario, whence pilgrims during so many centuries have greeted the towers and churches framed by the hills that overlook the valley of the Tiber; or perhaps it was on emerging from the low ridge that borders the northern Campagna along the ancient Via Flaminia. Wherever it was, Martin hailed the city of his desire with an outbust of emotion. He declared years afterward that he threw himself on the earth, crying "Hail, sacred Rome, sanctified in truth by the holy martyrs with whose blood thou wast drenched." [38] The longed-for day had come. The way of the two pilgrims now led over the Ponte Molle, which marked the site where once Constantine had seen the cross in the heavens. Beyond this, just inside the Porta del Popolo, lay the great Augustinian monastery where the brothers must have found lodging during their stay.[39]

For four weeks Martin remained in Rome. So much he recalled in later years, but he gives no connected account of his experience. Like the journey to and from the city, the days spent there appear only as a series of brief flashes of memory, fragments scattered through sermons, lectures, and *Table Talk,* beginning a few years after his return and continuing until his death. These recollections cover a wide field, from chance remarks on social conditions to arraignments of all that pertained to the city of the pope. Nearly all are marked by emotional outbursts and polemical bitterness. Even as early as the second magisterial course of lectures at Wittenberg, that on the Epistle to the Romans, which began in 1515, he warns against the vices which walk abroad in Rome. His bitterness grows in sermons and pamphlets after 1518, as the struggle with the hierarchy opens; and it then develops further and reaches a crescendo two years later with a denunciation of the luxury of life of the cardinals and the greed of the papal court, so that he feels there is greater need of the apostles in Rome at the present time than when they first came to the city.[40] From that time on the city becomes a synonym for all that is rotten in the Church. It is possible, however, by

---

[38] *TR,* V, No. 6059.

[39] The Observant friars had been expressly directed by the general chapter of 1497 to stay at "Sancta Maria de Populo" when they were in Rome. *Analecta Augustiniana,* VIII, 12.

[40] *An den christlichen Adel* (1520), *WA,* VI, 437. He goes on to say that pilgrimages to Rome make the pilgrim progressively a worse Christian.

comparing these later remarks of Martin's with observations by other pilgrims of the second decade of the century, pious Catholics without any trace of heresy, to check the accuracy of his statements and indeed to reproduce a number of his experiences as well as something of the spirit with which the young friar gathered the store of impressions upon which he was to draw during his lifetime.[41]

Whatever business the two delegates had to perform, it must have been their first undertaking. If, as seems most probable, the commission on which they were dispatched was that of the winter of 1510–11, the request that the chapters be permitted to appeal directly to the Curia was laid before the procurator of their order and was refused, as shown by the records of the general of the Augustinians.[42] The business of the papal court was highly organized; it is the one aspect of the papal system of administration which Martin held in respect in later years.[43] Possibly this impression was a memory from conversations with litigants in the refectory of Santa Maria del Popolo or some hostelry for German pilgrims; certainly not from Martin's own experience, since the young mendicant who was only the traveling companion of the bearer of a mission relatively slight in importance, could hardly have come into personal contact with the legal machinery of the Vatican.

For a devout and eager student of divinity, the days in Rome must have been crowded with precious experiences. He ran, he said afterwards, through all the churches and crypts of the city, like a crazy saint.[44] He must have had at hand one of the many guide books which were well thumbed by generations of pilgrims since the high Middle Ages. These go back to a celebrated collection of wonders of the twelfth century, the *Mirabilia Urbis Romae*, which he probably had in his professor's library at Wittenberg, for a number of his later statements have been traced to the medieval archetype.[45] These handbooks had little to say about the ancient city. When Martin came this had lain for four centuries buried under its ruins. The palaces which once crowned the Caelian and Aventine hills had given place

[41] See Böhmer, *Romfahrt,* pp. 142 ff., for an array of witnesses, Italian and foreign. It is to be remembered that as a Wittenberg professor, beginning certainly as early as 1520, Martin came into contact with a number of Germans, clerics and laymen, who had been in Rome and were sharply critical of conditions there. For a list of those, see *ibid.,* pp. 155 ff.

[42] G. Kawerau, "Aus den Actis generalatus Aegidii Viterbiensis," *ZKG,* XXXII (1911), 604.

[43] *TR,* III, No. 3700 (1538).

[44] *Der 117. Psalm ausgelegt* (1530), *WA,* XXX, 1, 226.

[45] Parallels have been investigated by Hausrath, *Martin Luthers Romfahrt nach einem gleichzeitigen Pilgerbuch.* For a quotation from one of these texts, see *Der 117. Psalm ausgelegt, WA,* XXXI, 1, 226 and n. 6.

to monastic establishments. Rubbish filled the whole first story of the Coliseum. The site of the baths of Diocletian was a game preserve and the Circus Maximus enclosed a vegetable garden. Heaps of debris covered the once busy markets where the patrician ladies of the day of the Antonines had made their purchases, and acres of vineyards and gardens spread over once splendid quarters of the imperial city. According to contemporary plans, only a third of the area enclosed by the Aurelian wall still had the appearance of a city. When the Franciscan pilgrim, Pellicanus, visited Rome in 1517, he walked through districts altogether deserted all the way from the Piazza del Popolo to his quarters in the Franciscan monastery of the Arcoeli on the Capitoline hill.[46] Martin noted the ravages that had leveled the ancient monuments and followed the traditions of his day in charging them to the Goths.[47]

Few pilgrims visited these deserted areas. Desperate characters infested the unpeopled districts, and although Martin praises the iron justice of the captain of the papal gendarme who patrolled at night and the short shrift he gave to criminals and suspicious characters,[48] he recalls that he was in the greatest danger when wandering through the uninhabited parts of the ancient city.[49]

When viewed from the Janiculum and other heights west of the Tiber, the city had then an essentially medieval appearance. The houses of the great families were fortified castles, with towers and ramparts. On every height rose the walls of churches and convents, many of them falling into ruins. Only when he approached the bridges leading over the river did the pilgrim come into scenes of business activity like those with which he was familiar in the swarming streets of the German cities. Even here the relics of former monuments lay far beneath the life and travel of his day. On the approach to the bridge of San Angelo rubbish lay two lances deep.[50] Active life gathered in the Rioni, where the Tiber bends below this bridge, and here a considerable part of the approximately 40,000 inhabitants of Rome found their living.[51] Not a few of these were drawn to the city by the great finan-

---

[46] Pellicanus, *Die Hauschronik*, p. 61. Pellicanus notes that the Capitol had been restored "in barbaric style" after its destruction by the Goths.

[47] ". . . das alte Rom, optima aedificia a Gottis plane esse solo aequata." *TR*, III, No. 3479a (1536); see also III, No. 3766.

[48] *EA*, LXII, 439.

[49] *TR*, III, No. 3479. The text in Aurifaber's collection is questionable; see however No. 3479a.

[50] *TR*, III, No. 3700 (1538).

[51] Von Pastor, *Die Stadt Rom zu Ende der Renaissance*, pp. 31 f. Regarding population statistics, see *ibid.*, p. 2.

cial enterprises of the Curia, among them Germans attached to the banking houses of Fugger and Welser-Vöhlin of Augsburg.[52] In this section were also the swarm of prostitutes whose presence in the city of the popes kindled fiery resentment among the pious pilgrims and even aroused the indignation of humanists like Wimpfeling and artists like Michelangelo.[53] The ravages of syphilis showed themselves everywhere and unnatural vice stalked abroad. It cannot be denied that a strong religious feeling throbbed in the artists of the Renaissance, but it is also certain that they gilded vice with a splendor and refinement that made it doubly seductive. Raphael painted his mistress under the halo of the Virgin, and is even said to have glorified the most celebrated of Roman prostitutes in his day, Imperia de Cugnatis,[54] whose palatial home was visited by cardinals of the Church, as the beautiful Calliope in one of his paintings in the Vatican Stanze. The nearer one drew to the papal palace the thicker grew the swarm of diplomatic and political agents, the financial go-betweens, the seekers for benefices, and petitioners of every description.

Of all this the young friar must have made mental notes which were to be interpreted by the reflection and experience of later years. None of the remaining impressions are aesthetic. The great art works of the Renaissance were, to be sure, just coming into existence. Michelangelo was then at work on the ceiling of the Sistine Chapel and Raphael on the walls of the Stanze; but the frescoes of Pinturicchio were already open to view, and the great work of Bramante, the dome of St. Peter's, was arising. No recollection of all this clung to Martin's mind. If the beggar monk failed to notice them, he was no different from the learned humanists of his day. Erasmus was twice in Rome, but his letters and works contain no hint that he saw there or elsewhere in Italy anything of the great art of the time. Martin was indeed awed by the size of the city,[55] but stresses its wickedness rather than its grandeur.[56] He marveled at the size of the Pantheon and the round hole in the roof.[57] The building evidently made a strong impression, for he uses

[52] Heading the Fugger interests in Rome at that time was Johann Finck, who was later to influence Martin's career directly by his commercialization of indulgences on a grand scale of high finance. See Schulte, *Die Fugger in Rom.*

[53] Regarding the moral conditions in Rome at the time, see Von Pastor, *Geschichte der Päpste,* III, 94 ff., and the abundant contemporary references cited by Böhmer, *Romfahrt,* pp. 100 ff.

[54] For literature concerning her, see Böhmer, *Romfahrt,* pp. 101 f.

[55] He estimates the Rome he saw at slightly under five miles (one German mile) in cross-section. *TR,* III, No. 3517 (1537).

[56] *TR* II, No. 2494b; V, No. 5506; see also III, No. 3478.

[57] *TR,* I, No. 507 (1533). Aurifaber's rendering in *TR,* I, 232, ll. 22 ff., is probably expanded but in the main reliable.

it in his sermons to illustrate the victory of Christ over the heathen gods whose images once stood in the rotunda.[58] He had no eyes for the great paintings of the Renaissance, but he recalled a Madonna in the cloister where he stayed, which had been painted by St. Luke himself.[59]

His heart aflame with zeal, the young friar set out to see and worship at the holy places of which he had heard and read. His first duty was a general confession which, as we have seen, was one of his objects in making the journey. With burning heart he descended into the catacomb of St. Calixtus. Long after he had become sarcastic about the sanctuaries and sanctions of the Church he still spoke with reverence of the "many thousands" of martyrs buried in the catacombs.[60] The churches and chapels must have attracted his steps from the moment of his arrival. Great was the number of those whose rich store of relics drew the pious visitor.[61] Foremost among these for sanctity were the seven great basilicas and it is likely that Martin followed the pilgrim's round and heard Mass in all these in one day, but we have evidence that he visited many other churches as well. "There I . . . ran through all the churches and crypts and believed every dirty lie that was told." [62] We have no reason to think that this is an exaggeration. He had been raised in an atmosphere of unquestioning veneration of holy relics and some of those displayed in the Church of All Saints at Wittenberg made just as severe demands on faith as any he mentions in Rome. He declares that he climbed the Scala Santa on his knees in the faith that if he did this and said a pater noster at every step he could free a soul from purgatory. He hoped thus to redeem his grandfather: "But when I got to the top I thought, who knows if it is true?" [63] Obviously, this is a question which might well have occurred to the mind of even the most pious pilgrim, and does not of itself indicate that his faith was seriously shaken.

[58] Sermon of Jan. 31, 1546, WA, LI, 156.

[59] Sermon of June 30, 1539, WA, XLVII, 817.

[60] TR, III, No. 3479a: "Multa milia martyrum." TR, II, No. 2709b (1532) apparently follows a pilgrims' guide in making the number of martyred popes 40, that of martyred saints 76,000. The version in TR, V, No. 6447, increases the saints to 176,000.

[61] See "Nikolaus Muffels Beschreibung der Stadt Rom," ed. by W. Vogt, Bibliothek des Litterarischen Vereins in Stuttgart, CXXVIII (Tübingen, 1876).

[62] Der 117. Psalm ausgelegt, WA, XXXI, 1, 226. For the various churches mentioned: St. Peter: TR, III, p. 611; IV, p. 537; WA, XLII, 466, l. 12; St. Sebastian: WA, XXXIX, 1, p. 150, ll. 2 ff.; St. Calixtus: TR, V, No. 6463; St. Pancreas and Maria Araceli: TR, III, No. 3479a; WA, LIV, 223; St. John Lateran: WA, XXXI, 1, 226.

[63] Sermon of Nov. 15, 1545, WA, LI, 89. This recollection was embellished by Martin's son Paul in 1582 with the quite impossible statement that the Pauline citation from Habakkuk, "The just shall live by faith" (Rom. 1.17), occurred to his father at the top of the Sacred Stairs and brought him to a recognition of the true gospel. See Reu, Thirty-five Years of Luther Research, p. 126.

One means by which he could avail himself of the great opportunities offered by Rome was through the saying of Mass in especially famous churches. This made a particular appeal to his zealous spirit. He declares repeatedly that in Rome he said many and heard many.[64] "I was sorry at the time," he adds on one of these occasions, "that my parents were still alive for I should have liked to free them from purgatory with my Masses and other excellent works and prayers."[65] There were many altars in Rome where this happy result was thought to attend the saying of a Mass.[66] One of these drew him especially, that before the grating of a chapel of the Holy of Holies in St. John Lateran, where the Mass, to be effective, must be said on Saturday: "Blessed is the mother," he recalls in the language of the pilgrims' guide, "whose son celebrates a Mass at St. John on Saturday."[67] However, the crowd was too great and he was obliged to give it up. When he had broken with the Church, he made a long list of charges against the Roman clergy, whose ignorance and laziness and frivolous attitude toward their sacred duties, whose abuse of the faith of the worshippers called forth the indignation of the many visitors, including Erasmus.[68] The routine and casual performance of the holy office was a rude blow to the conscience of the devout friar. He claimed many years afterwards to have seen seven priests celebrate Mass in St. Sebastian's Church in one hour.[69] He found the Roman clergy weak in Latin as did other German pilgrims.[70] He recalled that the Italian priests had finished the Mass before he reached the Gospel and rushed him away from the altar with a *"Passa, passa!"* ("Come on, come on!").[71] Indeed he claimed to have heard crude, blasphemous jokes across the table from clerical profiteers, who made sport of the way the holy office was performed by certain of their number, saying over their bread and wine,

[64] *Von der Winkelmesse und Pfaffenweihe* (1533), *WA,* XXXVIII, 211; *TR,* III, No. 3428 (1533), p. 313.

[65] *WA,* XXXI, 1, 226 (1530).

[66] "Muffels Beschreibung der Stadt Rom," pp. 10, 37.

[67] *WA,* XXXI, 1, 226.

[68] Böhmer, *Romfahrt,* p. 150, n. 4, cites an Italian traveler who noted in Germany and the Netherlands a slower and more reverent Mass service and consequently a greater reverence on the part of the congregation and a more regular attendance at the celebration. See also Ludwig von Pastor, "Die Reise des Kardinals Luigi d'Aragona durch Deutschland, die Niederlande, Frankreich und Oberitalien, 1517 bis 1518, beschrieben von Antonio de Beatis," *Erläuterungen und Ergänzungen zu Janssens Geschichte des deutschen Volkes* (Freiburg, 1905), IV, IV, 122 and 107 f.

[69] *WA,* XXXIX, 1, 138 ff., Argument VI; see also *TR,* V, No. 5484, where Martin says the Italian finished six or seven Masses before he read one.

[70] *TR,* IV, No. 4195 (1538); III, Nos. 3582A and 3582B. Seven years later Pellicanus and his associates took an interpreter along on their visit to Rome, since the Italian brothers could not speak Latin with them.

[71] *WA,* XXXVIII, 212. See also *TR,* III, No. 3428.

"Bread thou art and bread thou wilt remain: wine thou art and wine thou wilt remain," a frightful parody of the sacred words of transsubstantiation. He recalled it with horror for he was a "serious pious" monk in those days.[72]

"Whoever came to Rome bringing money got forgiveness of his sins. Fool that I was, I also carried onions to Rome and brought back garlic."[73] This is the keynote of the impressions of the city as viewed in retrospect more than a quarter of a century later. Even at the time of his visit Martin could not have been more blind than his contemporaries to what was going on at Rome. Twenty years earlier Savonarola had attacked the city with all the fire of his eloquence. Since then one indignant voice after another had been raised to denounce the viciousness of the Romans and to predict the destruction of the city.[74] At the time of Martin's visit the air was filled with forebodings: twenty years more and the fulfillment came when the German mercenaries of Charles V scaled the walls and drove the pope into the Castello San Angelo. Martin recalled that he had heard it said on the streets of Rome, "If there is a hell, then Rome stands upon it."[75] He remembered that a certain office-seeker at the papal court had said to him: "It cannot go on this way. It must break down."[76] "But the papacy was due to collapse, as they themselves acknowledged when I was at Rome. For in those days it was called a fountain of justice, but I heard it was a whore."[77] He must have observed the desolate condition of many cloisters and churches in the city whose income had been appropriated by the pope and the cardinals, for he refers to this frequently in later years.[78] He certainly heard some of the sinister though greatly exaggerated stories still current in the city regarding the dissolute life of the late Pope Alexander, the Borgia—that he was a Jew and an atheist, that he and his son Caesar were guilty of incest and other crimes, and that Alexander had died of poison prepared for the cardinals of the Church.[79] The ruling pope, the energetic and warlike Julius II, Martin

[72] See the foregoing note. Von Pastor, *Geschichte der Päpste*, III, 125, thinks the condition of the clergy no worse in Rome than in other Italian cities. Venice he holds to have been the worst.

[73] Sermon on Matthew 21.12 ff., *WA*, XLVII, 392 (1538).

[74] See Von Pastor, *Geschichte der Päpste*, III, for the activity of the mendicant preachers (pp. 127 ff.) and the predictions of various "prophets" (esp. p. 159).

[75] *Wider das Papsttum zu Rom, vom Teufel gestiftet*, *WA*, LIV, 220 (1545); also *TR*, III, Nos. 3201a and 3201b (1532), and *WA*, XXVI, 198.

[76] *WA*, XXVI, 198.

[77] "Sed ruere debuit papatus, id quod ipsi fassi sunt, cum Romae essem. Ea enim tum temporis vocata erat fons iustitiae, sed ego audivi eam esse meretricem." *TR*, IV, No. 4937 (1540).

[78] Sermon at Merseburg, *WA*, LI, 20; *Wider das Papsttum*, *WA*, LIV, 219 f.; *Enarratio in Genesin*, *WA*, XLIII, 421; *TR*, V, No. 6463.

[79] *TR*, II, No. 1611 (1532); V, No. 6453. For an evaluation of these stories, see Von Pastor, *Geschichte der Päpste*, III, 366, 375 ff., 473 ff.

did not see, for he was away campaigning against Venice. If, as seems likely, he talked with German residents, members of his own or other orders in the city, he discovered on the part of these too a profound uneasiness at the state of affairs. There were many Germans in office about the Vatican, and it was probably from them that he heard stories of the libertinism of certain cardinals, stories which came again to memory when he opened his attack on the hierarchy a decade later.[80] Even then it may have been known to him that the general of his own order, Egidio, shared the feeling of deep concern over Roman affairs.[81]

Thoughts like these may have revolved in his mind as he and his companion plodded the long, long path back to northern Germany. Five years later his impressions and experiences at the seat of the papacy were to give realism to the criticisms of Roman luxury and corruption in his Wittenberg lectures.[82] For the moment critical thoughts were probably of slight importance compared with the spiritual elation that came from his visit to the Eternal City. Among the many experiences which must have crowded his memory, the reality of the sacred heart of Christendom was doubtless the dominant one. So it continued for years to come. The historical unity of the Church had revealed itself in the holy monuments and relics of the ancient city. Nearly two years after his battle with the powers of the Church had begun, Rome was still for him a site enjoying special favor with God. The incompetence and shameful behavior of the popes, Martin insists, would never warrant tearing oneself loose from the Church whose seat had been hallowed by the blood of St. Peter and St. Paul, forty-six popes, and many hundred thousand martyrs.[83]

In the chill damp of late January or early February the brothers wandered northward. What route they took is as uncertain as the road they had followed southward, whether to Florence and thence over the snowy Apennines to Bologna and so toward the eastern passes of the Alps, or westward to Genoa and across one of the western passes. In either case the long trail led over many an icy, windswept ridge and through many valleys deep in snow before it descended to the mountain forelands of Swabia or Bavaria.[84] Even

---

[80] *Enarratio in Genesin, WA,* XLIII, 57 (1535–45).   [81] *TR,* II, No. 2174 (1531).

[82] Ficker, *Anfänge reformatorischer Bibelauslegung,* I, esp, pp. 310, 319. Böhmer, *Romfahrt,* pp. 142 ff., has collated a number of attacks on the papal court and Roman hierarchy from Luther's earlier and later works. The list is by no means complete.

[83] *Unterricht auf etliche Artikel* (1519), *WA,* II, 72 f.

[84] Grisar, "Lutheranalekten," *Historisches Jahrbuch,* XXXIX (1918–19), has developed the theory that Martin returned through southern France by way of Avignon and Lyon, and thence eastward up the Rhone through Switzerland to Lake Constance. His argument, resting on unpublished material, is not convincing.

here Martin found cause for thought on the matter of pious frauds, for Germany also had its share of them. One such he encountered at Augsburg, where he may have stopped in the course of his homeward journey. He visited a certain Anna Laminit, who dwelt in the odor of sanctity, being supposed to live solely from the sacrament. To the believing eyes of the young friar she seemed surrounded by a heavenly aura, and he ventured the question whether she did not wish to die and go to heaven at once. "By my troth, no," she answered. "How things go up there I do not know, but how they are here, I do know." [85]

If doubts were aroused in Martin's mind on this occasion, they could hardly have been insistent ones. Neither here nor in Rome, so far as we have evidence, did any doubts he may have had concern fundamental points of the teaching of the Church or impair his veneration for its institutions. When the journey of six weeks over wintry mountains and through lonely valleys had separated him from the center and heart of the hierarchy, he no doubt felt disillusioned and to some extent disheartened by much that he had seen and heard. Far more of error flourished among the princes of the Church than he had imagined. Sin walked abroad even in the highest places. Especially the greater reverence of the Germans for the sanctity and dignity of the Church and its offices must have come to him with a flash of national pride as he trudged through the Frankish valleys and listened to the myriad bells of church and monastery. Nevertheless the great fabric of faith as represented by pope and cardinals, sacred relics and indulgences, Mass and sacraments, the theory of salvation and system of monastic life, remained unshaken in his heart.

The end of the struggle over the observance apparently left as slight an impression on Martin's memory as its beginning and progress. Its importance for him did not end, however, with the journey to Rome, for in the month of January, 1511, in which the procurator of the order at Rome refused the plea of the seven convents to be permitted to appeal to the pope, the general of the Augustinians made another attempt to bring them into line by dispatching a German brother to Staupitz, and two months later took the matter up with the Emperor Maximilian, both by letter and through

[85] TR, IV, No. 4925 (1540); also a detailed account in the Aurifaber collection, TR, VI, No. 7005. For a full account of this impostor, who was finally executed in 1518, see F. Roth, "Die geistliche Betrügerin Anna Laminit von Augsburg," ZKG, XLIII, N.F. VI (1924), 355 ff.; also Albert Büchi, "Das Ende der Betrügerin Anna Laminit in Freiburg i. Uechtland," ZKG, XLVII, N.F. X (1928), 41 ff.

a diplomatic messenger.[86] Egidio's efforts were vain, owing in considerable part to the determined opposition of the Nuremberg council.[87] Apparently a compromise proposal finally emerged from a conference of the objecting convents with Staupitz in Jena in 1511.[88] However, the Nuremberg city fathers, who had caused an appeal to be sent directly to the general on April 2 alleging that union with the nonobservant Saxon provinces would destroy the reform, stood by their guns, put the case of the observant cloisters forcefully to Staupitz,[89] and repeated their appeal on April 26, 1512, to the Augustinian chapter of reformed cloisters.[90] In the meantime, however, the general and Staupitz had begun to see the impossibility of carrying the union through to success. The former dispatched Johann von Mecheln to Rome the following winter. As has been pointed out, it is just possible that this was the mission which took Martin to the Eternal City. After it returned, a chapter of the Reformed Congregation met in Cologne on May 5, 1512, and buried Staupitz's plan forever.[91]

The meager correspondence and other sources indicate that the whole dispute was conducted on the part of Staupitz and others of the German congregation in a spirit of brotherhood and closed in peace and amity on both sides.[92] It can hardly, however, have passed without some lasting bitterness in those convents which felt that their reforms were endangered. It is not possible to judge Martin's attitude toward the affair in all of its bearings. His mission to Halle makes it probable that at the beginning he shared the standpoint of his cloister, and he may well have gone to Rome with the

---

[86] The documents were published by G. Kawerau, "Aus den Actis generalatus Aegidii Viterbiensis," ZKG, XXXII (1911), 603 ff.

[87] For documents, see Böhmer, Romfahrt, pp. 166 f.   [88] Ibid., pp. 60 ff.

[89] Letter of Sept. 19, 1511, published by Th. Kolde, "Innere Bewegungen unter den deutschen Augustinern und Luthers Romreise," ZKG, II (1878), 470 ff.

[90] Böhmer, Romfahrt, p. 167.   [91] Kolde, Augustiner-Kongregation, p. 242.

[92] Another interpretation of the attitude of Staupitz in the struggle to bring the observant cloisters into line has been set forth. This was initiated by Grisar (finally developed in Luthers Leben und sein Werk, pp. 59 ff.) and has found acceptance by other investigators. A. V. Müller, "Der Augustiner Observantismus und die Kritik und Psychologie Luthers," ARG, XVIII (1921), 1 ff., finds in Staupitz's efforts after 1507 an ambitious attempt to divorce the German province from the authority of the general (ibid., p. 14). After making peace with Egidio at Rome in 1510 Staupitz, according to Müller, was forced to yield to the seven cloisters (ibid., pp. 21 f.). This picture of the general vicar is essentially different from that of Lutheran apologists. It represents Staupitz as a schemer whose moves were mostly stupid ones. Luther, in Müller's opinion, was moved by strict loyalty to the general of the order. The matter has been discussed at length by Scheel, Martin Luther, II, 658 ff. Despite the obscurity that surrounds the motives and to some extent the actions of Staupitz in the affair of the observance, the charges against the sincerity of his character do not seem to be sustained by the facts of his life so far as these are known to us. That he showed more zeal than judgment in his effort to extend the reform may well be true.

feeling that he was representing the righteous cause of reform. The contemporary historian and biographer, Johann Cochlaeus, claims to have heard from Luther's brethren of the convent that he "fell away to his Staupitz"; [93] and in view of the gratitude which Martin so often expressed for Staupitz's help in spiritual matters, it does seem probable that, in the later stages of the controversy, he went over to the side of the general vicar. If so, this may have led to a difference of opinion with the Erfurt brothers that caused Martin's final transfer to Wittenberg.[94] This is just what happened to his friend Johann Lang, who left Erfurt for Wittenberg in August, 1511.[95] We have enough evidence about Martin's character to know that he was accustomed to speak his opinion in a vigorous manner and without regard to the feelings of others. His correspondence with the Erfurt cloister three years later has a certain acidity of tone that seems to indicate previous disagreements and justifies the inference that when he left both sides were in a bad humor. It is probable that the young teacher became a member of the Wittenberg convent and university as early as the fall of 1511.

In spite of the unimportant rôle played by the dispute over the cloister union in Martin's memory, it was undoubtedly of significance for his development. It may well have given him opportunity to deepen the impression of vigor as a scholar and force as a man which he had previously made on Staupitz and the Augustinian convents, for the chapter held at Cologne gives evidence that he had become a prominent and trusted member of the order. The brothers there assembled elected him subprior of the Wittenberg cloister.[96] Then, or soon afterward, the general vicar directed him to apply for the degree of doctor of theology.[97] Martin was himself present at Cologne, for he recalls in later years the impression made on him by the cathedral and also the strong taste of the Cologne wine.[98]

[93] Cochlaeus, *Ad semper victricem Germaniam paraklesis,* fol. C2. See also "Die Chronik des Johan Oldecop," *Bibliothek des Litterarischen Vereins in Stuttgart,* CXC, 17, concerning Luther's presumably unfriendly departure from Erfurt.

[94] That the final transfer to Wittenberg was the result of the struggle over the union is a view widely held both by apologists and critics of Luther. See Böhmer, *Romfahrt,* pp. 64 ff.; Scheel, *Martin Luther,* II, 545 f.; Grisar, *Luthers Leben und sein Werk,* p. 50; also his *Luther,* I, 28 ff.

[95] Arnold von Usingen, cited by Oergel, *Vom jungen Luther,* p. 132, calls Lang's departure an "exile."

[96] Kolde, *Augustiner-Kongregation,* p. 243.

[97] Letter from Staupitz to the Erfurt cloister, Sept. 22, 1512, *WAB,* I, 18.

[98] *TR,* III, No. 3781 (1538); comment on Proverbs 27 (1539), *WA, Deutsche Bibel,* IV, 29.

I I

PROFESSOR AND PREACHER
AT WITTENBERG

"ONCE Staupitz was sitting absorbed in thought under the pear tree which still stands in the middle of the yard of my house. Finally he said to me: 'Master, you must take the doctor's degree; that will give you something to do.'" [1] The place and the mood in which the younger brother heard this program for his future dwelt vividly in his mind twenty years later. We do not know the time of the conversation, but it was probably in the spring or summer of 1512. Perhaps, if Martin shared Lang's exile from the Erfurt cloister for taking the side of Staupitz, he may have joined the Wittenberg cloister in the preceding winter. His abilities, his spiritual experiences, and Staupitz's friendship made him a marked man among the Augustinians, and many must have looked at him with interest when he appeared among the representatives of reformed cloisters at the Cologne conference of 1512. The administrative duties of subprior at Wittenberg which were put on him at this conference could not occupy fully the energies of so dynamic a personality. It soon became apparent that Staupitz intended him for an office that would call forth all his reserves, since becoming a doctor of theology would bring with it two serious tasks: he would have to preach and to take the place of the general vicar as Biblical professor. The latter entailed giving a series of formal and formidable magisterial lectures on those books of the Old and New Testament which lent themselves to dogmatic interpretation. The former meant standing before his brother friars and his teachers—quite another matter than facing an uncritical group of theological students. It was the call to preach that made him hesitate, he declares later, and the reports of his remarks on this subject are so categorical that they attest a deep and genuine feeling of uncertainty and even fear. On one occasion two decades later, standing under the same pear tree, he talked to a young

[1] *TR*, II, No. 2255a (1531).

brother who was in anxiety about preaching: "I was probably just as much afraid of the pulpit as you . . . Oh, how frightened I was . . . I had fifteen arguments to support my objections to Doctor Staupitz under this pear tree, but none of them were of avail. When I said: 'Staupitz, you will kill me; I won't live three months through it,' he answered, 'All right, our God has great affairs in hand; he needs clever people up there.' " [2]

Martin had by no means undergone the training usually required of one called to such a responsible office. His alma mater, Erfurt, set the minimum for the doctorate in theology at ten years of study in that subject, and cases occur in the records of candidates who studied eighteen years before promotion to the highest degree.[3] In Heidelberg the master of arts had to study twelve years before he might advance to the final degree in theology; in Paris studies lasted a few years longer.[4] Wittenberg, a younger university, had a more liberal policy in such matters and the faculty of theology was authorized to make concessions in the case of religious persons, with the reservation that it should promote no one "disgracefully weak in letters and reflecting discredit on the standing of the university." [5] Andreas Carlstadt, who came to Wittenberg in 1504, slipped into theology by the back door of philosophy and attained the doctorate after only five years of the divine sciences. He was now dean of the faculty.[6] In form at least Martin had been a student and teacher of theology five and a half years when he took his doctorate. Contemporaries, as he recalled, were astonished at his youthfulness, twenty-eight years, when, "compelled by Staupitz," he received the coveted degree.[7] "At Erfurt," he declares, "only men of fifty years of age were promoted to be doctors of theology."

Two ceremonies distinguished the event, and the records of the Wittenberg faculty enable us to reconstruct them in some detail. The first, the awarding of the "license" [8] by the vice-chancellor, was set for October 4. This was a ceremony of much dignity. The candidate was required to swear a long oath, promising fidelity to the university and pledging himself to re-

[2] *TR*, III, No. 3143b (1532); see II, No. 2255a; V, No. 5371 (1540); see also Johann Mathesius, "Luthers Leben in Predigten," *Ausgewählte Werke*, III (1898), 24.

[3] Oergel, *Vom jungen Luther*, p. 96.

[4] Ritter, *Die Heidelberger Universität*, I, 199 f.

[5] See statutes of the theological faculty in W. Friedensburg, "Urkundenbuch der Universität Wittenberg," I (1502–1611), *Geschichtsquellen der Provinz Sachsen*, N.F. III (1926), 34.

[6] Friedensburg, *Geschichte der Universität Wittenberg*, pp. 66 ff.; Barge, *Andreas Bodenstein*, Vol. I, chaps. 1 and 2.

[7] *TR*, IV, No. 4091 (1538); see II, Nos. 2739a and 2739b, where he reckons his age at twenty seven.

[8] That is, the permission to apply for the doctorate, the *licentia magistrandi*. See Förstemann, *Liber decanorum*, p. 12.

frain from setting forth vain and strange doctrines condemned by the Church or offensive to pious ears. It concluded with a pledge of obedience to the Church of Rome.[9] Then followed on October 18 the promotion to doctor of theology, a ceremony calling forth all the formal circumstance commanded by the university, but also accompanied by the frolicsome humor in which the scholars and students of the Renaissance so delighted.

The function opened with a vesper service.[10] This brought together the members of the university and many distinguished guests under the presidency of Dean Carlstadt to listen to academic disputations, the center of every university festivity. The debates on the first evening between the bachelors of arts as well as masters and doctors were an *hors d'oeuvre* for the more serious exercises [11] which were to fill the greater part of the following day. Early in the morning the clanging of the great bell called professors and guests to the Church of All Saints. Here the candidate swore again a long promotion oath, binding him to obey dean and faculty, to serve the welfare of the university, not to take the degree elsewhere, not to teach false and improper doctrines and to denounce anyone teaching them, in short, to preserve intact the customs, rites, and privileges of university and Church. He then received the symbols of his new powers, the open and closed Bible and the silver doctor's ring. The latter, which Martin treasured and wore throughout life, is still preserved in the city museum at Brunswick. Thus inducted into office, the new doctor ascended the pulpit and gave his first address.[12] Then followed the disputation, which went off under circumstances of great solemnity. Two academic questions carefully defined and limited were debated. In the final clash, the new doctor, flanked by assistant champions or "cocks" (*galli*), had room for a full display of his dialectical powers. The two seconds who stood beside Martin at this academic duel are worthy of our notice. They were Wenceslaus Link, prior of the Augustinian convent, and Nikolaus Grünberg, the priest of the Wittenberg parish church.[13] Four

[9] Friedensburg, "Urkundenbuch," pp. 34 ff.; text of oath, *ibid.*, pp. 35 f. See also P. Steinlein, "Luthers Doktorat," *Neue kirchliche Zeitschrift* (*Luthertum*), XXIII, 11 (1912), 760, n. 2.

[10] Förstemann, *Liber decanorum*, p. 13. For an account of the ceremonies, see Steinlein, "Luthers Doktorat," pp. 761 ff.

[11] Academic tradition demanded that the "vesperial" should be concluded by the presiding officer with a witty speech "crammed with jokes and full of quips, without, however, insulting anyone." Förstemann, *Liber decanorum*, p. 146. The vesper prelude was probably a good deal more hilarious than the statutes indicate. Like many another merry feature of the late Middle Ages, this jovial session had to retire in the serious decades that followed on the break with the Church. Melanchthon's revision of the theological statutes at Wittenberg put an end to the "inept vespers." Friedensburg, "Urkundenbuch," p. 156.

[12] Probably in praise of the Holy Scriptures; at least, such was the custom at Paris. Steinlein, "Luthers Doktorat," p. 764, n. 1.

[13] Förstemann, *Liber decanorum*, p. 13.

days later the "Reverend Father Luder" was admitted to the university senate after swearing anew "with the help of God and the sacred evangelists," an oath of loyalty to the theological faculty and its statutes.[14]

As may be imagined, the costs of these festivities were not light, and according to academic usage they must be borne by the candidate. Each of the officiating participants received a fee. Their shares, conscientiously set forth in the statutes,[15] run to the impressive total of more than forty florins.[16] Even a much smaller sum would have been beyond the power of the mendicant monk. Staupitz had, however, appealed to Elector Frederick, the patron of the university, and the money was put in Martin's hands from the princely purse, a fact which he recalled repeatedly in later years.[17] A note in the accounts of the court chamberlain records that Staupitz assured the elector that Martin would become life occupant of the lectureship on the Bible which the general vicar had held.[18] Leipzig, the nearest commercial center, was also the center for transaction of the financial business of the Ernestine Electorate, and from there the money had to be fetched. According to the family biographer, Mathesius, the young candidate went to collect it himself, covering the hundred miles of the round trip afoot and lingering at Leipzig until the customary official red tape had been unwound.[19] If Martin took this trip, he must have wandered among the booths of the great semi-annual fair which was then bringing its crowds to the city. At all events, the receipt which he gave the electoral chamberlain's agent has been preserved, and is the first document that we have in his writing, the fine cursive script of a late medieval hand: "I, Martin, brother of the monastic order at Wittenberg, do acknowledge with this my hand on behalf of the Prior at Wittenberg that I have received from the Honorable Degenhart Pfeffinger and Johann Doltzer, chamberlains of my gracious Lord, fifty guilders, Sunday after St. Francis' Day [October 9], 1512." [20]

The promotion set the capstone on a successful academic preparation and opened a career brilliant with promise for the order. It had, however, one

[14] Friedensburg, "Urkundenbuch," p. 32; Förstemann, *Liber decanorum*, p. 13.

[15] Friedensburg, "Urkundenbuch," p. 49.

[16] Steinlein, "Luthers Doktorat," p. 774, n. 5.

[17] Dedication to Elector Frederick of the *Operationes in psalmos*, April, 1519, *WA*, V, 19 ff. For sources and details, including the legend told by Kilian Leib, prior at Rebdorf, see Steinlein, "Luthers Doktorat," pp. 774 ff.

[18] From a note in the Weimar archives. Scheel, *Martin Luther*, II, 556, n. 3.

[19] Mathesius, "Luthers Leben in Predigten," p. 24. Sources for the trip to Leipzig are examined by Georg Buchwald, "Ist Luther am 9. Oktober 1512 in Leipzig gewesen?" *Beiträge zur sächsischen Kirchengeschichte*, Vol. XXXVI (1927).

[20] Facsimile in Scheel, *Martin Luther*, II, 557; for transcription, see Enders, *Luthers Briefwechsel*, I, 9.

bitter sequel. It brought to a head the bad feeling that had already shown itself in the Erfurt cloister against the stubborn and argumentative young brother. Three years earlier Erfurt had accepted the Wittenberg credentials of the *sententiarius* with difficulty, as Martin was well aware. It will be recalled that while the oath which he should have taken at that time included the usual promise to take the doctorate only in Erfurt, Martin was insistent that he did not hear or swear this oath,[21] for the dean was interrupted by Professor Nathin, who began to read from a large sheet, setting forth the requirements and duties of the lecturer.

This sounds very much like sophistry on Martin's part. The pledge not to take the higher degree at another university was so far routine in the faculties at this time that a candidate could hardly have been ignorant of it. Nevertheless the public mind at the time set much store on formal "rights" in the whole social structure, and Martin's excuse that he had slipped by without an oath would, therefore, probably have been acceptable in university opinion. Furthermore, the restriction on the freedom of change to another university may have been waived on occasion.[22] In this case, however, the Erfurt faculty was not willing to overlook the matter. They could not be indifferent to the loss of a promising scholar, and it is likely that the Augustinians among them were nursing bruised feelings on account of Martin's attitude in the observance affair.

The record of the interchanges on the subject is defective. Apparently after some delay the theological faculty in Erfurt made resentful protests. We have neither their communication nor Martin's first two replies, addressed to the Erfurt cloister, which in this case he identified with the university faculty. On September 22, 1512, after he had been summoned by Staupitz to take the doctorate, Martin had addressed a flowery letter to the prior and convent at Erfurt, inviting them to attend his promotion.[23] His tone shows no indication that he suspected the presence of smouldering fires in the cloister or among the theological faculty. When and how these broke out is not certain. The first letters by Martin, which have been lost, were apparently very bitter. The two that we have date from two years later, when the professor had begun to regret his violence toward his alma mater. In the first, June 16, 1514, he appeals in heated language to the prior and brothers against the behavior of Professor Nathin, who had been charging him with perjury and infamy, particularly with breaking an oath which he had never taken.

---

[21] Letter of Dec. 21, 1514, *WAB*, I, 30 f. Oergel, *Vom jungen Luther*, p. 130, gives the oath which the candidate was supposed to take.

[22] *Ibid.*

[23] *WAB*, I, 18.

He had been obliged to appeal to a convention of the order which put a check on these slanders for a time. He censures the Erfurt faculty for not having reminded him in time of his obligation: he would then have had an excuse for rejecting Staupitz's suggestion that he take the higher degree. Six months later his anger had cooled. On December 21, he addressed the mother convent again, this time in a spirit of profound humility, taking on himself any guilt that he might have unconsciously incurred in breaking the statutes at Erfurt and asking forgiveness for any wrong that he might have done "without intent or knowledge." [24]

"I was forced to be a preacher. First I had to preach in the refectory before the brothers. Oh, how I feared the pulpit." [25] Staupitz's quiet but decisive words under the pear tree meant, as we have seen, a call to the pulpit as well as to the professor's chair. The causes for Martin's fear of preaching can only be a matter of speculation. We have already spoken of the audience of fellow brothers and teachers whom he would be required to address. Other factors may also be suggested to explain his hesitation. Possibly his experiences in the debates over the union of the convents and his parting from the mother convent at Erfurt had brought a fit of low spirits. Perhaps hard study and ascetic exercises had resulted in temporary ill health. Or it may be that the return to conventual life after the journey to Rome had plunged him into a fresh struggle with the "temptations" which figure so prominently in his recollections of cloister life, and it is not unlikely that the new responsibilities were urged on him by Staupitz during one of these periods of spiritual depression. One must also take into account the possibility that Martin had already made attempts at preaching, perhaps unsuccessful ones, in the Erfurt cloister, for the statutes of the theological faculty there required that the *sententiarius* have practice in the art before he could be licensed to apply for the doctorate. Two sermons have been preserved which their sixteenth-century transmitter, Andreas Poach, claimed to have found in the library of the mother convent at Erfurt.[26] Whether this was the scene of Martin's first attempt at preaching or whether that came in the Wittenberg refectory is uncertain; in later years he himself was quite hazy on the subject.[27]

[24] "Extra dolum et conscientiam." *WAB*, I, 31, ll. 43 ff.

[25] *TR*, III, No. 3143b. The three passages in the *Table Talk* which refer to the conversation with Staupitz do not mention the obligation to preach in connection with the call to the doctorate. However, the question of promotion may have been discussed in more than one conversation, probably in a number.

[26] *WA*, IV, 587 ff. (introduction), and 590 ff. These were discovered in the Zwickau Ratsschulbibliothek by Buchwald, who inclines to ascribe them to 1512. See *WA*, XXII, pp. xlvii ff. Erich Vogelsang, "Zur Datierung der frühsten Lutherpredigten," *ZKG*, L, 3. Folge, 1 (1931), 114 ff., leaves undecided the question as to whether they belong to 1510 or 1512.

[27] See the contradictory statements cited by Vogelsang, "Lutherpredigten," p. 114, n. 1.

Wherever he started his pulpit career, it is not improbable that his first effort was a disappointment and perhaps a humiliation, and that this brought on a shyness which only the full authority of Staupitz could overcome. In any event, though he resisted the call to higher duties to the point of "offense against authority," the mood of inferiority must have passed quickly after he received his doctor's degree, the crowning honor of late medieval scholarship.

Like other forms of religious expression at that time, preaching enjoyed great popularity in Germany.[28] Since the days of her first outstanding public preacher, the Franciscan Berthold of Regensburg, a succession of pulpit orators had appeared, some learned and emotional, like the mystics Suso and Tauler; others philosophical and scholastic, like Albertus Magnus and Meister Eckhart; still others were fiery reformers, like Geiler of Kaisersberg. Whatever the quality of German sermons in the later Middle Ages, there can be no doubt as to their frequency. For Westphalia alone, between 1378 and 1517, one hundred manuscript volumes have been listed, along with ten thousand individual sermons which were printed in approximately fifty years after the invention of the art.[29] The Germans must indeed have been patient listeners in those days. Preaching was usual throughout the year, not merely in the Advent and Lenten seasons, as Ignatius Loyola found when he visited Rome in 1538,[30] and in contrast with this city where people were astounded when anyone but a member of the orders ascended the pulpit, the secular clergy in Germany also preached frequently. Nevertheless, in Martin's cloister days the Mass priest was not likely to be a preacher, for in general the preaching cleric belonged to one of the mendicant orders.[31] Within these the steps to the public pulpit, far from being open to all the brothers, were safeguarded by formal requirements. The preacher must have the right training in the knowledge and application of Scripture, he was expected to command a fluent style and a ready use of the elaborate allegories that were an important part of pulpit oratory, and above all it must be certain that his orthodoxy could be depended on. The constitution of the Augustinian Eremites did not entrust the selection of a brother for preaching to the

---

[28] Despite an increasing pettiness in the content of the sermon (Grisar, *Luther,* I, 60), nothing about religious life in the early sixteenth century is more fully documented than the enthusiasm for preaching. See Cruel, *Geschichte der deutschen Predigt,* p. 651, and the impressive list of evidence summarized by Kiessling, *Early Sermons of Luther,* pp. 13 ff.

[29] F. Landman, *Das Predigtwesen in Westfalen in der letzten Zeit des Mittelalters* (Münster, 1900), cited by Kiessling, *Early Sermons of Luther,* pp. 17 ff.

[30] Böhmer, *Romfahrt,* p. 107, n. 2.

[31] See Rodriguez, *De origine Societatis Jesu,* p. 499, for the astonishment aroused in Rome by the frequent sermons of the Jesuits: "Nos procul dubio putabamus a monachis haberi conciones posse." Quoted by Böhmer, *Romfahrt,* p. 107, n. 3.

individual convents, but reserved this for the decision of the general vicar.[32]

Once entered on these duties, Martin must have discovered soon that they were decidedly to his liking. His audiences responded and his own enthusiasm doubtless rose with his success. From the refectory of the cloister he probably moved to the tiny chapel where his first lectures were also given, and where he now might count among the hearers of his sermons a few burghers and officials of Wittenberg along with his brother friars. After little more than a year, toward the end of 1514, he was called to face a larger audience. The pastor at the parish church, St. Mary's, had fallen ill and the city council invited Martin to become his assistant and substitute. The first sermon which he is known to have preached in St. Mary's was on the day of St. John the Apostle, December 27.[33] The church became from now on the chief scene of his preaching, although he did not give up the cloister pulpit. The hesitation he had felt two years before was quickly forgotten when the circle of his hearers widened to include a popular audience, and he flung himself into the work with fiery enthusiasm and great freedom of utterance. For this we have evidence both from his hearers and in the transcripts that have come down to us.

Like the actor and others on the public forum, the popular preacher can leave but few and unconvincing traces of the enthusiasm once aroused among his hearers. The magic of personality conveyed by a powerful voice which awakens the will of the hearer or moves him to tears can never be recaptured in the printed word. Like those of the great Berthold, who had thrilled open-air audiences in South Germany three centuries before, Martin's sermons have not been transmitted as they were delivered; indeed, among the two thousand or more published in the Weimar edition there is no single one of which it can be said that it was delivered by Luther in the form in which it is printed.[34] Of the texts that have come down from

---

[32] *Const.*, ch. 31.

[33] In *WA*, I, 37, n. 2, it is assumed that the sermon for the day of St. John the Apostle (December 27) which Löscher records as preached in the parish church, belongs to 1514. Böhmer, *Der junge Luther*, p. 118, accepts this and thus fixes the date for Martin's earliest preaching in St. Mary's. Vogelsang, "Lutherpredigten," pp. 121 ff., who made a very careful analysis of the individual sermons in the Löscher MS, presents cogent evidence for assigning this sermon to December 27, 1517, or even 1518. The dating of the sermon as 1514 is an example of the loose chronology that has prevailed in Luther's biography.

[34] The sermons of the period now under consideration are preserved in four sources: the Zwickau MS, formerly in the Erfurt cloister; a MS now lost, but published in 1720 in *Ref.-Act.*, Vol. I, by Löscher, containing seven sermons and a number of introductory addresses (*Exordien- predigten*) to the sermons on the Decalogue (1514–17), *WA*, I, 18 ff.; the lectures on Psalms (1513–16), in which nine sermons are mentioned and partly analyzed, *WA*, Vol. III; and a group of 47 sermons (1515–20), collected by Stephan Roth, in a MS now in Zwickau, *WA*, IV, 590 ff. The Stephan Roth group, together with the collection by Johann Poliander, *WA*, IX, 314 ff.,

the earlier years, the only one in Martin's handwriting is a discourse on martyrs, probably given in the spring of 1514 and woven into the text of his lectures on Psalms. We can, however, feel sure that in the earliest years of his preaching he worked vigorously to bring his ideas into order for the approaching Sunday or feast day, and despite indirectness of transmission, it is probable that the texts that we have for this period correspond to his own drafts. At the beginning he may have written them out beforehand; later on it is more likely that he drew them up after delivery. As experience brought self-assurance, he restricted himself to outlines or to drawing up lists of topics.[35] Before long, eager students in Wittenberg or brothers in his cloister began to take down his sermons as best they could. Where they were in Latin this was not difficult, for a rudimentary form of Latin shorthand was widely practiced. In German no such system was then available. It was natural, therefore, that the cloister and university scribes, from whose pens Latin flowed readily, should translate Martin's words into Latin while he was speaking and preserve them in that form.

It is certain that he soon began to preach in German. The burghers and officials in the pews at St. Mary's could not have followed him in the language of the academy. Nevertheless, true to the scholarly tradition, his outlines and summaries have come down to us in Latin. The earliest of these show him feeling his way anxiously, following the scholastic pattern. The scriptural text is interpreted in a threefold manner as allegory, as dogma, and as a mystical prophecy of final events. With "firstly," "secondly," "thirdly," and so on, his thoughts are strung together in the style that certain preachers have continued to practice down to modern days. He analyzes the law of love, graphing a sort of multiple scholastic equation to demonstrate the responsibilities of the Christian.[36] Preaching on a text taken

---

belongs with few exceptions to the period *following* the opening of the struggle over indulgences. See the listing in Vogelsang, "Lutherpredigten," pp. 137 ff.; also Buchwald's complete register of Luther's sermons in *WA*, XXII, pp. xli ff., which, unfortunately, follows the order of Scripture texts instead of a chronological sequence. Aside from minor variations, authorities now agree on the dating, save that of the nine sermons which Böhmer found referred to in the lectures on Psalms. "Luthers erste Vorlesung," *Berichte über die Verhandlungen der sächsischen Akademie der Wissenschaften zu Leipzig,* phil.-hist. Klasse, LXXV, 1 (1923), p. 7, n. 7, and pp. 21 ff. Buchwald lists only that for which the text appears, viz. the Sermon on Martyrs, *WA*, III, 342 ff. For the five years preceding Martin's attack on indulgences we have, then, texts or partial texts for approximately 42 sermons, of which 32 are introductory discourses preceding the sermons on the Ten Commandments. This maximum is based on Vogelsang's careful analysis. It should be noted, however, that a number of question marks must accompany it.

[35] It is hardly probable, as Kiessling seems to think, *Early Sermons of Luther,* p. 56, that Martin had reached this point when he began to preach in St. Mary's.

[36] *WA*, IV, 592.

from the Gospel for Whitmonday, he rolls up the heavy artillery of university logic to establish the certainty of punishment of sin and redemption through grace.[37] It is noteworthy that among his weighty deductions and corollaries he can reel off a couplet from Ovid's *Ex Ponto:*

> Nescio quo natale solum dulcedine captos
> Ducit, et immemores non sinit esse sui.[38]

But there follows then the ascetic application: Homeward from this vale of tears![39]

The scholastic pattern furnished the frame. Scholastic thought provided also much of the content of his sermons in the first four or five years. The painstaking use of these traditional tools is evidence of the effort it cost him to put his earlier discourses together. Enumerations of the "doctors" and their quarrels; the setting up of abstract logical categories, like those of the days under Professor Trutvetter at Erfurt; [40] the diligence in producing fantastic allegories of a kind which were a stock in trade of the late medieval preacher—all these point to scholastic models. The homiletical textbooks of Luther's day and the practice of the pulpit built the approved sermon on two foundations: documentation in Church authority and interpretations by means of allegories.[41] In his earlier transcripts Martin shows readiness and dexterity in providing the material needed, and lets his imagination wander unrestrained in the inviting field of allegorical fancy.

In the Sermon on Martyrs he takes his text from Psalms 60.8, "Moab is my washpot." This he understands as "cooking pot," [42] and this humble vessel opens the way for a long succession of allegories joined one to the other. The pot represents the persecutors of the Church; its legs, the lusts of the world; the Christian souls are the game which is put in the pot to boil. This game must be hunted down by the preacher in the forest of sin, killed with the weapons of God's word, boiled by Christ in sin and sorrow, while the prayers of the seething souls wreathe upward in steam. Thus, whenever he sets forth in pursuit of a metaphor, he stumbles across another and makes it the starting point for branching off into a new field of fancy. Martin must have showered scriptural quotations on his hearers, for the transcripts are full of them, and these are twirled about so as to show us several hidden meanings. The stone which the builders rejected is

---

[37] *Ibid.*, pp. 595 ff.   [38] *Ex Ponto*, I, iii, ll. 35 f.

[39] *WA*, IV, 603, l. 23.   [40] *WA*, I, 26.

[41] For an extended discussion of the late medieval practice, see Kiessling, *Early Sermons of Luther*, pp. 33 ff.

[42] This is his understanding of *olla* in the Vulgate. The sermon is imbedded in the lectures on Psalms: Ps. 60.8, *WA*, III, 342 ff. See Kiessling, *Early Sermons of Luther*, p. 71.

held up as the soul.[43] Then we see the builders as the troubles of life which in God's marvelous way hew the sufferers into foundation stones. Thus he leads his hearers through a maze of inner meanings concealed in his Bible quotations; indeed, he develops an untiring dexterity in fitting incidents of the Biblical narrative to dogmatic ideas and also in applying its didactic and proverbial material to the experiences of real life. He appeals constantly to scriptural authority. In comparison, the sermons up to 1517 draw little on patristic and legendary sources or on the supernatural tales of the animal world which furnished so much material to the clergy of the later Middle Ages.

The pallid outlines of these early texts can give little idea of what Martin's vigorous personality must have meant to convent brothers or burghers. As samples of his early preaching we may cite two sermons of approximately this period. One of these he seems to have written for a brother cleric, Georg Maskov, provost of the Premonstratensian monastery at Leitzkau in Brandenburg. This sermon, which was in all probability intended to be delivered at a meeting of the district synod of the order in the spring of 1515, was evidently put together by Martin with care, as the manuscript was to be read by another.[44] Here, in a well-rounded discourse, free from allegories, although not from late medieval coarseness, Martin denounces the materialism of the clergy, its wealth, self-indulgence, and worldly lusts, and pleads for a conquest of these evils. The sermon closes with a spiritual and sonorous peroration.

The serious tone of this sermon is also found in one delivered at the district meeting of the Augustinians just referred to, held at Gotha on May 1 of the same year, but it lacks the reserve and dignity of the sermon written for Maskov.[45] Whether the text as we have it came from his pen or from that of some eager listener, it has the stamp of dynamic and unrestrained vigor in denunciation and exhortation which is one of Luther's

---

[43] *WA*, I, 89, ll. 17 ff. See also the fantastic game of hide-and-seek played with Samson's riddle, Judges 14.14: *WA*, I, 58.

[44] *WA*, I, 8 ff. The assumption that this sermon was delivered in connection with the synodal gathering held at the Brandenburg episcopal palace at Ziesar on June 22, 1512, appears *ibid*. This rests on a series of hypotheses, and the date seems quite incompatible with the reformatory tone of the sermon and its maturity and self-assurance. Inner evidence that it was addressed to a clerical gathering and its tone indicate that it was prepared after Martin's elevation to district vicar, which occurred at the Augustinian conclave at Gotha, beginning April 29, 1515. A district synod of the diocese was held on May 21, 1515, and this may have been the occasion of the sermon. See *WAB*, I, 59.

[45] *WA*, I, 44 ff.; IV, 675 ff. A brief variant appears in the lectures on Psalms, *WA*, IV, 221 ff., inserted as a sort of plan for a sermon. Vogelsang, in his "Lutherpredigten," p. 118, marks out here a combination as a criterion for the chronology of Luther's lectures on Psalms and Romans.

characteristics in mature years. Still within the form of a scholastic discourse, it blazes with fury against a besetting sin of the cloistered life, whether in the monastery or at the university, the sin of slander and back-biting. He attacks those who thus corrupt souls with all the resources of the late Latin vocabulary of abusive terms, illustrating their deeds and the certainty of their punishment by a wealth of scriptural phrase. Here and there, where the Latin vocabulary of invective, so enriched by late medieval theologians and humanists, does not suffice, he breaks into German to picture the slanderers as pitiless tyrants, traitors, deserters, thieves, murderers, robbers, devils, who are the cause of every kind of misfortune, desperation, and despair. The preacher waxes more and more furious and reaches the climax with a quotation from Job's description of the Behemoth. In a transport of indignation he unrolls one after another pictures of astounding foulness paralleled only in the dialogues and other farces with which professors and students beguiled idle hours at the humanistic university.[46] Despite the indifference of that age to offensive terms, the modern reader is tempted to see in this sermon evidence of a certain neurotic attitude resulting from the stress of the monastic life on a personality like Martin's. The sermon was talked about widely outside of the cloister. Mutianus heard of the "sharp preacher," and inquired of Lang about him.[47] The tone of the discourse must have been an impressive one and apparently the Augustinian brothers were not offended by it, for it was this gathering that elected Martin district vicar in charge of ten convents.

The first duty of the professor was to take over the "magisterial lectures" on the Bible. This was a heavy responsibility and no doubt contributed to the perturbation of soul with which he greeted Staupitz's command to proceed to the doctorate. When the mood of hesitation had been overcome, he threw himself into the work with energy and industry and grew rapidly in self-assurance. The regulations of the Wittenberg theological faculty demanded the interpretation of the Psalms and Epistles, and in a little more than five years after he put on the doctor's gown, Martin had delivered four courses, those on the Psalms and on the Epistles to the Romans, on the Galatians and on the Hebrews, and had begun a second course on the Psalms. All of these have come down to us either in his own hand or in those of his

[46] See the "Quaestiones fabulosae" or Jakob Hartlieb's *De fide meretricum in suos amatores,* a fit predecessor to Dedekind's *Grobianus.* See Zarncke, *Die deutschen Universitäten im Mittelalter,* I, 48 ff. and 67 ff.

[47] See Lang's reply to Mutianus, May 2, 1515, in the latter's correspondence. "Der Briefwechsel des Conradius Mutianus," ed. by Karl Gillert, *Geschichtsquellen der Provinz Sachsen,* XVIII (1890), II, 149 f.

students.[48] A first task was an exegetical interpretation of the Psalms.[49] This was an entirely different undertaking from the cursory lectures of earlier years, and the professor took hold of it with all the fire of youth and a dynamic character. "You would not believe how much intensive study one verse caused me," he says of his second course of lectures on the Psalms a few years later,[50] but that was an easy undertaking compared with the first. He must have begun work soon after his appointment, studying and writing in the refectory until far into the night. Sometimes, as he remembered, the silence of the cloister was broken by a persistent scraping in a great chest. This he ascribed to the devil, and when he heard it he would put up his writing and go to bed.[51] Specific references in the sermons of 1513 to works employed in interpreting the Psalms and the careful working out of these sources in the lectures [52] show how anxiously he ground away at the material for his course. The meticulous care with which he put together his notes is further evidence of his thoroughness in preparation. He had a Wittenberg printer, Grünenberg, print the text of the Latin Vulgate, about a hundred quarto leaves with wide margins, for the use of his students. One set he used to enter interlinear and marginal glossaries, explaining individual words and phrases in the style of the medieval exegetes, and this has come down to us in his own hand.[53] Late medieval exegesis, how-

[48] The chronology of Luther's early lectures still has some dark spots, but it is in the main clear in outline. See Johannes Ficker, "Luther als Professor," *Hallische Universitätsreden,* Vol. XXXIV (1928). Böhmer, "Luthers erste Vorlesung," p. 9, note, works out the following, based on university records and data inferred from contemporary sermons: first lecture on Genesis (*ca.* October 25, 1512, to *ca.* July 12, 1513); Psalms (mid-August, 1513, to mid-October, 1515); Romans (early November, 1515, to *ca.* September 7, 1516); Galatians (October 27, 1516, to March 13, 1517); Hebrews (March 16, 1517, to March 27, 1518); second course on Psalms (April 12, 1518, to March 29, 1521). The course on Judges, *WA,* IV, 529 ff., was probably not by Luther. A course on Titus, formerly ascribed to him, was probably given by Johann Lang in 1517 at Wittenberg. See Meissinger, *Luthers Exegese in der Frühzeit,* p. 4. As will be noted below, Böhmer's chronology for the lectures on Romans differs somewhat from that of Ficker and others. This is one of the questions concerning the chronology of the early lectures which is still unsettled.

[49] Böhmer's suggestion, "Luthers erste Vorlesung," p. 4, that Martin began a course on Genesis in October of 1512, just three days after receiving the doctorate, rests mainly on a statement by Luther in 1539, *Von den Konziliis und Kirchen, WA,* L, 519. If such a course was given, it must have remained a fragment; it has vanished without a trace. See Johannes Ficker, "Luthers erste Vorlesung—welche?" *ThStKr,* C (1927–28), 348 ff., and Hans von Schubert and Karl Meissinger, "Zu Luthers Vorlesungstätigkeit," *Sitzungsberichte der Heidelberger Akademie der Wissenschaften, phil.-hist. Klasse,* IX (1920), 8 ff.

[50] *EA,* II, 319. Ficker, "Luther als Professor," pp. 33 f., cites many similar remarks regarding the trouble the Psalms caused him.

[51] The vivid account in Aurifaber's collection of the *Table Talk, TR,* VI, No. 6832, is somewhat questionable as to reliability.

[52] See Ficker, "Luthers erste Vorlesung—welche?" p. 352.

[53] Böhmer, "Luthers erste Vorlesung," pp. 10 ff., gives the results of an intensive examination of the two Luther holographs published by Kawerau, *Dictata super Psalterium, WA,* Vols. III, IV, an edition marked by many defects in text and arrangement. The two sources are

ever, did not pause here, and Martin followed long tradition in preparing also a series of *scholia* or notes for free treatment of the content of the Psalms on a wide range of theological and moral topics. These notes too have been preserved in great part, also in Martin's hand. It is more than probable that the long task of preparation was far from complete when he stepped to the professor's chair at the opening of the fall semester in August, 1513.[54] Much must have been written during the progress of the course. At the same time he worked under great stress after the close of the long monastic day of service in the choir on academic duties such as preparing and presiding over the disputations of his students. In addition, he was called on more and more frequently for sermons in the cloister or parish church. The rules permitted only limited dispensation from spiritual exercises for university duties. To be sure, Wittenberg, like other theological schools, did not burden its professors with many lectures. In accordance with the easy-going academic ways of the time, Martin probably lectured only twice a week. Nevertheless, he must have worked diligently, and like modern professors who are pursued by administrative duties he must often have gone before his students with the ink still damp on his manuscript. The results show in the irregularity of his notes. Sometimes he dwells persistently on a single word. Thus in seeking to plumb the meaning of *somnus,* he lines up fifteen parallel expressions.[55] To support his explanation of another passage he marshalls five scholarly authorities, from Cassiodorus down to the contemporary Hebraist Reuchlin.[56] Sometimes every word in a psalm is explained, as in the case of Psalm 98; in other cases he skips hastily through an entire psalm.

The sources at his elbow included probably all the texts and exegeses that he found in the cloister library or could borrow elsewhere. First, the Bible text in the Vulgate, which he reveres above all others. He quotes it constantly, probably often from memory, as there are many false references, some of which go so far astray as to confuse books of the Bible.[57] Next came a Latin translation by St. Jerome, which he found in the *Five-fold Psalter* of a contemporary Paris theologian, Jacques Lefèvre d'Étaples, best known by his humanistic name of Faber Stapulensis.[58] Like all beginners,

---

the glossary referred to, now at Wolfenbüttel, and the so-called Dresden Psalter, which contains the *scholia.* This MS, of 297 sheets, lacks one third to one fourth of the original. Böhmer, "Luthers erste Vorlesung," p. 17.

[54] Evidence *ibid.,* pp. 19 ff.   [55] *WA,* III, 398.

[56] *WA,* IV, 26 ff.

[57] Held, *Luthers erste Psalmenvorlesung,* pp. 8 and 25.

[58] *Psalterium Quintuplex, gallicanum, romanum, hebraicum, vetus, conciliatum* (Paris, 1509).

Martin attached himself to one work for formal guidance. His selection was Faber's commentary, which had appeared only four years earlier in Paris. The copy he used, in the Dresden Library when examined by the present writer, shows with what intensity the youthful exegete labored over it. In accordance with the practice of the time and his own manner of work he filled the pages of Faber with marginal notes, probably at the time that he was working on his lectures.[59] Faber prescribes the method, but other massive commentators of earlier centuries lay on his table: Cardinal Hugo of St. Cher,[60] Nicholas of Lyra,[61] Archbishop Paul of Burgos,[62] and their authoritative associate Peter Lombard, along with Reuchlin's *Rudiments of Hebrew*. Of all the exegetes, however, Augustine stands at the head in furnishing ideas for discussion. The commentary on Psalms by the African Father appears repeatedly in the lectures. Martin mentions Augustine 270 times and borrows verbally from him twenty-five times without mentioning his name.[63]

Thus equipped he began the weighty subject on a mid-August day in the little auditorium of his convent. Besides the group of students, probably mostly brothers of the order, others must have gathered to hear him: colleagues of the theological faculty like Carlstadt and Nikolaus Amsdorf, perhaps the rector, Matthias Beskau,[64] along with other friends from the faculty, and electoral officers. It was seven o'clock in the morning, the hour of freshman professors.[65] When he opened his notes, the candle or oil

---

Faber (1455–1536), a profound student of Aristotle and later under attack for heresy (the charge was evoked by his translation of the New Testament into French in 1523), presents five Latin texts: the Gallic, now in the Latin Bible and breviary; the Roman, Jerome's first translation, still in use in the Roman missal; the Hebraic, Jerome's third rendering; the pre-Jerome *Itala;* and a collation of these. Wetzer and Welte, *Kirchenlexikon*, XII, 1127 ff., and V, 2017 ff.

[59] Published as *Adnotationes Quincuplici Fabri Stapulensis Psalterio manu adscriptae, WA*, IV, 466 ff.

[60] Hugo's work of the thirteenth century was probably used by Martin in a Basel edition, *Repertorium Apostillarum*, 1509.

[61] *Postillae perpetuae in universam S. Scripturam*, the first Biblical commentary to be printed. *Catholic Encyclopedia*, XI, 63 f. Nicholas (1270–1340), a professor at the Sorbonne, strives for a literal interpretation and against the traditional drowning of the text in mystical interpretations.

[62] Paul (Solomon ha-Levi, 1351–1435), was a converted Jew who rose to high office in the Church. His *Additiones* to Nicholas of Lyra's *Postillae* contribute much rabbinical material to scriptural interpretation. See *Catholic Encyclopedia*, XI, 588.

[63] Held, *Luthers erste Psalmenvorlesung*, pp. 12 f.

[64] Förstemann, *Album Academiae Vitebergensis* I, 48.

[65] See Friedensburg, "Urkundenbuch," p. 37, for the statute providing that lectures in the winter semester should begin at this hour. For the course on Romans two and one half years later Martin was allotted a "convenient" hour, viz., one o'clock, immediately following the midday meal. *Ibid.*, p. 77.

lamp which flickered in the dimness of the early morning must have lighted a face tense with earnestness; and on this first day the requirement of the faculty that a lecture must be read "from the beginning to the end of the hour in a clear and intelligible voice" can hardly have been fulfilled. Any embarrassment he may have felt probably vanished with his dictation of the glossary. This was the customary practice so that the hearers might enter on their copies of the text what he had put down on his own copy. Later, when he came to the *scholia* for a wider interpretation, he was able to speak more freely; and it is likely that as he swung into the spirit of the mighty Word his dynamic nature found expression in a free, impromptu rendering, of which his notes give a very feeble picture.

"I feel, indeed, how heavily this burden weighs on my neck, a burden which I have long resisted and to which I have at last yielded under the compulsion of my superiors." [66] With this remark the lecturer opened his course. It was truly a formidable task and he must have felt his insufficiency for it as he plowed into the text. As yet he knew little Hebrew. He had, to be sure, Reuchlin's print of the seven penitential psalms before him in the language of the original [67] and many references and explanations in the works of Lyra and the convert Paul of Burgos, and from these he often takes over such material in a quite uncritical way. In his inexperience he is obliged to follow his guides, chiefly Faber,[68] rather mechanically. Like them, he believes in the prophetic character of the Psalms. It is Christ who speaks in the name of David. Divine inspiration has guided the interpreters and it is therefore possible to bring all translations and interpretations into accord.[69] He sets out to seek the meaning by the fourfold approach sanctioned by scholastic tradition, which had developed this method of probing for hidden meanings beneath the scriptural text. In addition to its literal significance, the psalm is to be explained as an allegory for the doctrines of faith, as a moral law for the conduct of human life, and in an eschatological sense to reveal the mysteries of the world and God's final judgment.[70] By this means any passage can be made to mean anything. "When

---

[66] *Praefatio, WA*, III, 14, apparently written in 1513 as an introduction to the *scholia*. Böhmer, "Luthers erste Vorlesung," p. 20.

[67] *Ibid.*, p. 45.

[68] *Ibid.*, pp. 45 f. Böhmer thinks Martin would better have followed Lyra.

[69] *WA*, IV, 43, l. 27.

[70] This fourfold approach, literal, allegorical, tropological, and anagogical (eschatological), finds illustrations in German literature as far back as Otfried's *Messiad* (867–68). It was formulated in the scholastic mnemonic verse:

> Litera gesta docet, quid credas allegoria,
> Moralis, quid agas, quid speres anagogia.

See Bauer, *Die Wittenberger Universitätstheologie*, pp. 17 f.

I was a monk I was a skilled workman with allegories," Martin declared many years later;[71] "I used to allegorize everything; I even allegorized the privy." In the style of his day he plays with allegory like a juggler with colored balls. When the Psalmist mentions the sea, he means the peoples of the world; the mountains stand for the Apostles; day and night signify prosperity and adversity; a river is morality; dogs are demons.[72] Later on he seeks primarily the figurative or tropological sense, for it tells of Christ in His relation to man. He illustrates his method at full length by Psalm 78, which sets forth God's mighty works for the Children of Israel and His guidance in spite of their unfaithfulness. Literally, these wondrous works were done in the person of Christ; figuratively, in the soul against flesh and the devil; allegorically, by the Word against evil men; eschatologically, in heaven and in hell.[73] Nowhere in his interpretation of the Psalms does the literal meaning really come to the fore, except when it is brought in to illustrate the figurative meaning.[74]

This complicated network envelops both glossary and *scholia*. Nevertheless, the emotional earnestness of the lecturer shines through it everywhere. "With my whole heart have I sought Thee, not with half of it, like those who seek by means of the intellect, as the philosophers do," he explains in the glossary to Psalm 110.[75] "It is experience that most often teaches us all these things." [76] The scholastic path is the ancient way on which to seek the truth and he reveres it, but the finely written and at times chaotic notes vibrate with emotional conviction. After all, he was not writing a commentary, but preparing to explain the divine word to hearers. The vigor with which he must have enforced his ideas shows itself throughout the preparatory material. The worldliness and arrogance of the clergy stir him to vehement denunciation. Prelates who study the canon law and Aristotle instead of the Bible;[77] priests who lay aside their sacred duty and pursue money and women;[78] the luxurious dress of the nobility and their drunkenness;[79] the pride, boastfulness, greed, and neglect of duties on the part

---

[71] *TR*, I, No. 335.

[72] See Held, *Luthers erste Psalmenvorlesung*, p. 7.

[73] *WA*, III, 532 f. Böhmer, "Luthers erste Vorlesung," pp. 54 f., notes that in the *Adnotationes* Martin calls the literal sense the principal one and that in the course of the Psalms lectures he turns from allegorizing to a prevailingly tropological explanation. Böhmer finds this change between Psalm 30 and Psalm 31. It is probable that the turning away from allegorical subtleties to a more practical application to the problems of the Christian soul was due to a growth of independence on the part of the young exegete; possibly Lyra's procedure also influenced him. See n. 61 above.

[74] See Bauer, *Die Wittenberger Universitätstheologie*, pp. 18 f.

[75] *WA*, IV, 282, ll. 8 ff.   [76] *Ibid.*, p. 213, l. 15.

[77] *WA*, III, 422 f.   [78] *Ibid.*, p. 308, ll. 15 f.

[79] *Ibid.*, p. 428, l. 3.

of the religious orders;[80] the hypocrisy of the observance;[81] the eternal juggling with subtle distinctions by Thomists and Scotists [82]—all of these come in for bitter arraignment. The *scholia* are couched in a vigorous medieval Latin which has a genuine personal ring. At times, in the fervor of his exposition he breaks into German—German of the earthy sort that was to appear more frequently in the succeeding courses of lectures. Undoubtedly he made many explanations in the mother tongue when he expounded his notes. Here and there these admit a German word to help out the understanding of a technical term. We have contemporary evidence of the vigor with which he was wont to express himself in the vernacular in a series of footnotes scribbled on the margin of a "Rosary of the Virgin" [83] in the period of the Psalms lectures. These marginalia, mostly in German, consist of forceful and often sarcastic remarks about the pious tales in this work of recent origin which pretended to be old. A statement that St. Bernard had prayed through this psalter with "wondrous wisdom and devotion" he glossarizes, "Brother, this is too big a lie!" [84] Of a similar remark concerning St. Bernard he notes, "Keep on lying in the name of all the devils! Have you no limits?" Where the pious author says that praying fifteen times a day through the entire year is to pray through all the wounds of Christ, he cries, "The devil! Where do all these many and various lies come from?" Christians are taught "to be justified by stupid work," he exclaims. This is, in fact, a basic complaint which runs through the notes on the Rosary.

The lecture course on Psalms shows that the professor-friar was at grips with a wealth of traditional material and by no means clear as to his own standpoint. Quite obviously he feels himself drawn in various directions. In the long series of tangled and often obscure notes Occamistic ideas of grace are supplemented by those of Augustine. Here and there the African Father's Neoplatonic conceptions creep into Martin's expositions. As a whole, he stands on traditional theology; he recognizes the store of merit accumulated by the saints and believes in satisfaction through good works.[85] On the other hand, in an underscored passage he pushes aside justification through merit and extols "the unique grace and mercy of God as freely

---

[80] *Ibid.*, p. 421, ll. 16 f.   [81] *Ibid.*, p. 155, l. 8.

[82] *WA*, IV, 369, ll. 5 f.; cf. also *WA*, III, 218, ll. 15 ff.

[83] Marcus von Weida, *Der Spiegel hochloblicher Bruderschaft des Rosenkrantz Marie* (Leipzig, 1515). Martin's notes were published by G. Kawerau, "Luthers Randglossen zum Marienpsalter 1515," *ThStKr*, XC (1917), 81 ff.

[84] *Ibid.*, p. 84.

[85] The Catholic theologians Denifle and Grisar agree that the notes as a whole show no actual heresy.

given." [86] The problem as to the way in which the soul attains justification, for which the scholastic age had spun a series of subtle explanations, had to be laid bare before his students and he bores into it again and again, but no clear solution is yet visible. "Oh God of my righteousness!" (Psalms 4.1): here was an idea on which he sought light with eagerness and found it for the present in the traditional conception of the identity of justice and mercy. "In so far as He has mercy upon me, He makes me just. For His mercy is my justification." [87]

The occupation with the idea of the justice of God becomes intensive during the lectures. Before their conclusion there is evidence that at last he had begun to discern that the conception was not what he had thought it to be, but meant the justification which grace achieves in the sinner, making him just before God.[88] In his old age Martin recalled this discovery

---

[86] *WA*, III, 42, ll. 18 ff.

[87] "Quod enim mihi miseretur, eo ipso me iustificiat. Eius enim misericordia est mea iustitia." *WA*, III, 43, ll. 9 ff. The word *iustitia* in its active and passive meaning causes the translator difficulty, since it contains the quality of God as "just" and likewise the result of the "justification" which brings the sinner into line with God's will. This double semantic character of the word was the very stumbling block which Luther finally surmounted, as we shall see.

[88] The acceptance of the idea of *iustitia dei* in this passive sense, which initiated a revolutionary change in Martin's theological ideas, has been the source of a flood of literature, mobilizing a wealth of dogmatic history. It has led to intensive examinations of the manuscripts of Martin's notes for the Psalms lectures. The idea of a startling change in his conception of grace, which proceeded from the autobiographical sketch (see nn. 89 and 90 below) and long dominated biographers, has now paled somewhat, but still remains among Lutheran scholars. Some have felt that it was necessary to point out the exact year of this transformation. Denifle's devastating attack on the tradition that hardships and shams of cloister life were responsible for Luther's reorientation has done much to destroy this theory. That the conception of an angry God faded before that of a God of mercy and brought a revival of the Pauline and Augustinian ideas of grace seems well documented. This has stimulated a search for such a turning point in Martin's early lectures, where it is assumed that the interpretation of the *iustitia dei* furnishes one index for the change. Hence the insistent demand for a better methodological basis for investigation than the edition in *WA*, III and IV. Thomas, *Zur Würdigung der Psalmenvorlesung Luthers*, made an ineffectual beginning; see Böhmer, "Luthers erste Vorlesung," pp. 42 ff. E. Hirsch, "Initium theologiae Lutheri," in *Festgabe für J. Kaftan* (Tübingen, 1920), showed the lack of sequence in the chronology of the Dresden MS of the Psalms lectures; Böhmer made this discovery conclusive. Vogelsang, *Die Anfänge von Luthers Christologie*, followed with an exhaustive study. Scheel, *Martin Luther*, II, 664 ff., reviewed the evidence of these investigations. It appears that the inconsistencies in Martin's exposition of the *iustitia dei* are due in part to a revision of his manuscript in preparation for printing. He was engaged in this in September, 1516. Letter from Luther to Spalatin, Sept. 9, *WAB*, I, 56. To the revised portions belong the *scholia* to Psalms 1 and 4 (Böhmer, "Luthers erste Vorlesung," pp. 38 ff.), where he shows evidence of a new light on the "justice of God." These ideas then appear quite definitely in the preliminary summary of Psalm 31 (*WA*, III, 171, 172), which stresses the importance of faith. Vogelsang, *Die Anfänge von Luthers Christologie*, pp. 31 ff., sets the final turn in Martin's ideas with the interpretation of Romans 1.17—in the *scholion* to Psalms 70 and 71. Here appears the complete identification of *iustitia dei* with faith: "Iustitia dei . . . tropologice est fides Christi. . . . Et ita est frequentissimus usus in Scripturis . . . Corollarium. . . . Suavissimae sunt istae orationes in psalmis." *WA*, III, 466, ll. 26 ff. In view of the findings of Böhmer, Scheel, and Vogelsang, it can scarcely be doubted

as a vivid experience. In an autobiographical sketch penned a year and a half before his death, he recites his hardships and fears in the cloister, then tells of the blood-curdling terror with which he had dwelt on the passage in Romans 1.17, "Therein is revealed the righteousness of God," and asserts that the phrase "justice of God" had been interpreted by all scholars as the justice with which God punishes sinners. Thus pondering on it he began to understand that it means "the justification to which man attains through the gift of God"; "that is, the justice with which a merciful God makes just through faith, as it is written, 'the righteous shall live by faith.' . . . Straightway I felt myself reborn and entering the open gates of heaven." [89] The sketch is marked by a confused chronology which reflects the weakened memory of age. Nevertheless, it cannot be overlooked that here, as on other occasions in later years when he talked about his religious development, he brought this powerful experience into connection with the study of the Psalms.[90] The conception that a new light broke upon him in a flash was part of a constant tendency in his later years, already noted, to dramatize the stages of his religious development. In a well-attested remark to his students he even goes so far as to point out the exact spot where the enlightenment came. This was the tower of the great cloister in Wittenberg, and in all probability the workroom or refectory where he had carried on his study of the Psalms. "But God be thanked, when once I was pondering in this tower and workroom on these words, 'The just shall live by faith' and 'the justice of God,' it occurred to me: If the just are to live by faith and the justice of God is to be for the salvation of every believer, then it will not be our righteousness but the mercy of God. So my soul was lifted up. For the justice of God is that by which we are justified and saved through Christ. Then I felt a greater joy in these words. The Holy Ghost revealed the Scriptures to me in this tower." [91]

---

that Martin was progressing toward a new understanding on this critical point during the course of the lectures on Psalms, even though the sources offer no evidence of a catastrophic experience such as the aging Luther recalled.

[89] Preface to the Wittenberg edition of his works, March 5, 1545. *WA*, LIV, 185 f.

[90] In the autobiographical sketch in the preface referred to above, he connects it with his second course on Psalms, which began to go to the printer in March, 1519. *WA*, V, 1 ff. See also *TR*, V, No. 5247 (1540); *ibid.*, No. 5553; No. 5693. In the first two passages he quotes directly from Psalm 30.2: "In iustitia tua libera me."

[91] *TR*, III, Nos. 3232a and 3232b; see also II, No. 1681 (1532), where the word *cloaca*, instead of *hypocaustum*, seems well attested. Schlaginhaufen's MS of the *TR* reads *"cl."* E. Stracke, "Luthers grosses Selbstzeugnis 1545 über seine Entwicklung zum Reformator," *SVRG*, XLIV, 1 (1926), 121 f., n. 2, interprets it as *clarissima* and makes this refer to the passage Romans 1.17. *Hypocaustum* was used for a common heated room. See Du Cange, *Glossarium mediae et infimae Latinitatis*, Vol. IV, where *hypocaustorium* is defined thus. *Cloaca*, "privy," has caused

We have observed earlier that Martin's emotional nature was subject to severe crises and that certain of these burned indelibly into his memory. Such had been the vision that called him to the cloister life. Such, too, was that in the tower in the early years of his professorship. In later days this took the form of a flash of enlightenment from above scarcely less extraordinary and material than the blinding lightning in the Thuringian forest which showed him the way to the cloister. As the years passed by the catastrophic character of the experience increased in his mind, and the gradual steps by which his ideas had matured through the passing years as the new theology emerged all telescoped in memory into one great soul-shaking moment.[92] Many keen-eyed students have searched the yellowed leaves of the notes prepared for the lectures on Psalms and have not hesitated to put their fingers on the year and even the month when this revolutionary idea of passive justification swept away his fear of divine justice.[93] It is certainly probable that many deep emotional experiences shook Martin's soul in 1513 and the following year. He was wrestling with resistant material in the traditional methods of exegesis, and many questions presented themselves urgently for clarification to his own mind and that of his students. Of these the problem of the meaning of *iustitia* was the most important. In hours of mental and physical exhaustion above all, doubts and fears must have assailed him as to his own position when confronting an angry God. The Psalms themselves offered abundant opportunity for a discussion of the "temptations" to which a sensitive soul is exposed, and Martin's notes show

---

much perturbation to Luther biographers. See Scheel, *Martin Luther*, II, 569 f., n. 6. The privy was probably located in the tower which was removed shortly after Martin's death. H. Voigt, "Die entscheidendste Stunde in Luthers religiöser Entwicklung," *Zeitschrift des Vereins für Kirchengeschichte der Provinz Sachsen*, XXIV (1928), 32 ff. A reference to the privy in this connection would not have been out of line with the realistic speech of Martin and his time.

[92] The conversion of Luther and its corollary, the birth-hour of the Reformation, is a dramatization of history which few apologetic biographers have been willing to forego. These have followed Martin's sketch in presenting the sudden vision as an escape from a tormenting conscience. In essence it was rather a crisis in the development of theological ideas, although for any dynamic personality every decisive point in scholarship is an emotional experience.

[93] Böhmer, *Der junge Luther*, pp. 110 ff., locates it through the summary of Psalm 31 in April or May of 1513; Vogelsang, *Die Anfänge von Luthers Christologie*, p. 57, in the fall of 1514; Scheel, *Martin Luther*, II (1917), p. 321, between the winter of 1512 and the summer of 1513, and in his *Martin Luther*, II (1930), pp. 571 f., between the autumn of 1513 and that of 1514; H. Wendorf, "Der Durchbruch der neuen Erkenntnis Luthers im Lichte der handschriftlichen Überlieferung," Parts I and II, *Historische Vierteljahrschrift*, Vol. XXVII (1932–33), between 1512 and 1513; Stracke, "Luthers grosses Selbstzeugnis," before 1515. See H. Hermelink, "Die neuere Lutherforschung," *Theologische Rundschau*, VII (1935), 131 ff., for a survey of these theories. Others, like Bauer, *Die Wittenberger Universitätstheologie*, tend to refer the "tower experience" to the realm of imagination. See also Iwand, *Rechtfertigungslehre und Christusglaube*.

that he had much to say to his students on this topic.[94] Years afterwards he remarked to his table comrades that the Holy Psalter was "full of temptations." [95] Many phases of such doubts and scruples which he rehearses later deal with the fear of the law and of God's justice,[96] and with Christ as a judge.[97] The burden of sin and the insufficiency of penitence which remained as a source of anguish may well have visited him in the anxious days of his first course of university lectures.[98] Martin recalls that in troubled moments of this sort the fear of the unforgivable sin of blasphemy seized him. This sin, which no one understands and for which no one knows a remedy, was far more tormenting than the fleshly thoughts which were a persistent attendant of the celibate mind and which had caused St. Benedict to roll his naked body in the thorns. At such times, Martin states, the devil always stands in the background with his sardonic grin.[99]

How far these vivid experiences beset the lecturer at this time we do not know. Certainly he was much occupied with setting forth the theological and monastic ideas regarding the tribulations of the sensitive soul, and he clearly shows a wide knowledge of them. A further and related problem, perhaps the knottiest of all those which a theologian can attack and the richest source of anguish for many generations of religious minds, caused him great perturbation—the problem of predestination. Undoubtedly real crises of spirit came as he twisted and turned in an effort to attain a satisfying view as to the certainty of salvation, for no other question echoes more persistently in his later recollections as a cause of despair. "No one could help me," he declared years later in speaking of this lack of assurance.[100] The idea persisted as an ever recurring torment. In middle life he admits that when he thinks of it he arrives at the conclusion that God is a "villain." "There the *laudati* stops and the *blasphemati* begins." [101]

[94] *WA*, III, 162, l. 27; 187, l. 14; 265, l. 8; 299, l. 26; IV, 91, l. 6.

[95] *TR*, V, No. 6305.

[96] See the lay discussion in *TR*, I, No. 141, pp. 61 ff.; No. 590, pp. 275 ff., and No. 612, pp. 288 ff.; see also the Galatians commentary of 1531, *WA*, XL, ii, 14 ff.

[97] *TR*, II, Nos. 2393a and 2393b (1532), and the numerous examples collated in Scheel, *Dokumente*.

[98] The character of these "temptations," including their relation to the lectures on Psalms, has been examined carefully by Ernst Wolf, "Staupitz und Luther," *Quellen und Forschungen zur Reformationsgeschichte*, IX, 139 ff., who, however, becomes somewhat smothered in the sources.

[99] *TR*, IV, No. 5097 (1540).

[100] *TR*, I, No. 518 (1533), p. 240, l. 9. See also *TR*, IV, No. 3933 (1538); V, No. 5886; and lectures on Romans, ed. by Ficker, *Anfänge reformatorischer Bibelauslegung*, Vol. I. See esp. his introduction, pp. 50 f., for a survey of Luther's basic ideas and problems in this work. See Braun, *Bedeutung der Concupiszens*, pp. 34 ff., for occurrences of the idea of predestination in Luther's works.

[101] *TR*, II, Nos. 2654a and 2654b (1532); also No. 1490 (1532); and the sermon *Von der Bereitung zum Sterben* (1519), *WA*, II, 688.

"I was freed from this cogitation by Staupitz, otherwise I would have been long burning in hell." [102] " 'If you are inclined to weigh the matter of predestination,' he said, 'begin by reflecting on the wounds of Christ and there will be an end of it. If you keep on arguing about it, you will lose Christ, the Scriptures, the sacraments, and everything.' " [103] The path that the general vicar pointed out was the same one which Ignatius Loyola and many others followed in order to escape from the maze of scholastic subtleties into a world of religious activity. It made a deep impression, for Martin passes on the advice early in 1516 to a troubled brother in another convent [104] and frequently later to his students. [105] On another occasion, Martin recalls, he stumbled over the Occamist ideas of the arbitrary will of God, and turned to Staupitz to make his confession. [106] The seasoned churchman told him that these very doubts were a necessary part of his development. [107] With all his monasticism, Staupitz was a practical Christian who had himself fought his way to peace of soul and who knew how to take a morbid brother out of the vicious circles of his own thought. He also knew the dangers of entanglement in the refinements of the Schoolmen on the subject of grace. In 1518, when Martin faced his conflict with the scholastic tradition on this question, he recalled that it was Staupitz who had pointed out the fallacy in the scholastic conception that the soul finds its way through to the selfless love of God by a series of steps, and had shown him that God does not offer man salvation thus hesitatingly and bit by bit, but that the love of God stands at the beginning of repentance. These words Martin declared "stuck in me like a sharp arrow," [108] and after that nothing was more pleasant to him than repentance. In the "heavenly tones" of his spiritual father he heard the comforting assurance that it was useless to agonize over God's acceptance of the contrite soul. They taught him rather to see in God a friend and helper who followed him with His love.

[102] *TR*, V, No. 5658a. The remark is reported from 1542.

[103] *TR*, II, Nos. 2654a and 2654b. Predestination was a theological theme of constant interest, especially to the Occamists. Biel gives much attention to it, and Martin was undoubtedly familiar with his discussion. Wolf, "Staupitz und Luther," pp. 168 ff. It becomes more prominent in his lectures on Romans in 1515 and 1516. For his gratitude for Staupitz's help with the problem, see letter from Luther to Albrecht von Mansfeld, Feb. 23, 1542, *WAB*, IX, 626 ff. For the attitude of Staupitz toward the subject, see Wolf, "Staupitz und Luther," pp. 201 ff., who finds a turning away from doctrinary nominalism.

[104] Letter from Luther to Georg Spenlein, April 8, 1516, *WAB*, I, 35, ll. 24 ff.

[105] For the first of many examples, in the lecture on Romans, see Ficker, "Scholien," *Anfänge reformatorischer Bibelauslegung*, I, 226, ll. 6 ff.

[106] *TR*, I, No. 518 (1533), p. 240, ll. 12 ff.

[107] *TR*, I, No. 141 (1531), p. 62, ll. 1 ff. This was a subject on which Staupitz dwelt in his sermons. See Wolf, "Luther und Staupitz," pp. 158 ff.

[108] *Resolutiones disputationum de indulgentiarum virtute* (1518), *WA*, I, 525, l. 15.

It is natural, therefore, that in a recollection twenty years after he opened his course on the Psalms, Martin places Staupitz at the threshold of his theological revolt: "Staupitz used to say to me, 'You have to look at the man, that is, Christ.' Staupitz began that doctrine." [109] A decade earlier in a sort of farewell letter to the general vicar, then retired from the religious strife to the isolation of a Salzburg convent, he had also recalled that the impulse for the new theology came from Staupitz.[110] There is no reason to doubt that his influence prompted the development of Martin's new theological ideas. Staupitz's religious views as well as his practical experience equipped him to provide the guidance which the younger man needed. His Thomistic training, shown in his sermons, tended to soften the effects of the doctrinal mechanism which had been inculcated on Martin; and although the dynamic nature of the young professor must have lain beyond the range of Staupitz's understanding, his sensible approach to Martin's problems obviously helped the latter more than once when the effort to clarify dogmatic problems for his students stirred the depths of his being. By whatever path the gentler conception of God came into Martin's soul, it is clear that it had begun at this time to grind away the hard edge of nominalist ideas which he had found in Gabriel Biel and heard expounded by his Erfurt teachers. He has begun to be aware that God's will is free and arbitrary, to be sure, but that He is reasonable and purposeful in His attitude toward man and that His mercy balances His justice. God is, therefore, no capricious despot but the father of a family. When Martin comes to prepare his next course of lectures, he has found the way to build up some defense against the fierce attacks of the idea of predestination.

[109] *TR*, I, No. 526 (1533).
[110] Letter from Luther to Staupitz, Sept. 17, 1523, *WAB*, III, 155 f. See p. 146, n. 79, above.

I2

INTERPRETER OF AUGUSTINE
AND PAUL

WHEN Martin finally brought the course of lectures on Psalms to an end is not certain. Perhaps it was with the Easter holiday in 1515, perhaps not until the October following that the long series was completed.[1] He had now been three years in Wittenberg and had won the respect of his colleagues for spiritual earnestness and energetic scholarship. In spite of the impulsive violence of language and intolerance for many highly regarded scholastic authorities which grew as he gained confidence in his own conception of the truth, the Augustinian brothers both in Wittenberg and in the neighboring convent showed their trust in his ability and character. When he took over Staupitz's Biblical chair he was also appointed subprior of the convent, and in 1515 he was made director of its higher studies. In the same year, at a convocation of the order held in Gotha on April 29, he was, as we have seen, elected district vicar for a term of three years. This was a position of heavy responsibility, for it brought under his supervision the cloisters of the Meissen and Thuringian districts, eleven in all, including his mother cloister at Erfurt and important houses at Dresden, Gotha, and Magdeburg. Dr. Staupitz often traveled far in pursuit of his administrative duties, and as second in command for a part of the cloisters many burdens must have pressed heavily on Martin's shoulders. At the moment when these new responsibilities came to him he was deep in the preparation of his second course of magisterial lectures, that on the Epistle to the Romans.

The duties of district vicar called for prudence as well as administrative zeal. This appears in letters which Martin wrote to the various convents under his charge. In one he begs for the return of a runaway brother who

[1] Böhmer, "Luthers erste Vorlesung," *Berichte über die Verhandlungen der sächsischen Akademie der Wissenschaften zu Leipzig,* phil.-hist. Klasse, LXXV, 1 (1923), 8 f., n. 1, argues for October 20 as the approximate date of the final lecture on the basis of a shrewd, but unconvincing, combination of data.

had found refuge in Mainz; he will seek to lead the wandering sheep back into the right path.[2] In another he gives careful directions to a newly appointed prior at Erfurt, his old friend Johann Lang, regarding the entertainment of guests at the convent.[3] In still another he directs that admission be refused a brother from another order without the written permission of his former associates: "according to the prescribed law and decrees of the superior fathers."[4] In a tone of kindness, but very frankly, he reduces the prior of Neustädt to the ranks for his failure to suppress dissension in the cloister; Martin is willing to admit that his intentions have been good, but they have not led to peace.[5] In such letters to the convents and their heads there is a genuine anxiety lest a rigid adherence to the Augustinian constitution may be neglected, a fear that the brothers may become too proud, or that a prior may be too bitter and vindictive in punishment of offenses; and there are many earnest pleas that mutual tolerance and gentleness may rule in the convents and that a wise spirit of forbearance may ward off interconventual jealousies and fears. We have several letters from 1516 which show that his warm interest in the spiritual welfare of the brothers springs from the feeling that their problems are very like his own. "The Cross of Christ is over the whole world; everyone gets his part," he writes to a troubled friar in Erfurt; "insults, persecutions, sorrows and hatred of men, the just as well as the wicked, are sacred relics which Christ blessed and consecrated."[6] Through the pious phrases there breaks the impulsive personality which here, as in sermons and lectures, infuses real pathos into the conventional monastic clichés.

The duties of this office also required him to undertake journeys of visitation, some of which can be followed by contemporary references.[7] They took him as far as Dresden in the east and westward through the Thuringian towns to his old cloister at Erfurt. Tiresome as it must have been to plod the muddy roadways of late December from Erfurt to Wittenberg as he did in 1515, these outings were no doubt a joy to the vigorous friar at other seasons, for they broke the monotony of cloister life and brought him into contact with practical things in which the cloister had an interest, such as, for example, the tithing of fish in the neighboring village of Leitzkau.

[2] Letter from Luther to Johann Bercken, Dresden, May 1, 1516, WAB, I, 39.

[3] From Langensalza. Letter from Luther to Lang, May 29, 1516, WAB, I, 41 f.

[4] Letter from Luther to Michael Dressel, June 23, 1516, WAB, I, 46.

[5] Letter from Luther to Michael Dressel and the Augustinian cloister at Neustädt, Sept. 25, 1516, WAB, I, 57 f.

[6] Letter from Luther to Georg Leiffer, April 15, 1516, WAB, I, 37 f.

[7] Mainly in Luther's letters. See G. Buchwald, "Luther-Kalendarium," SVRG, XLVII, II (1929).

There is nothing in contemporary sources to show how his relation to colleagues in the Wittenberg faculty was developing, but one may conclude that valuable associations were being formed. The most gifted of his colleagues, Carlstadt, shared Martin's interest in Augustine and was carrying on active studies in the African Father's works. Another fellow-theologian, Nikolaus Amsdorf, of the same age as Martin but a man of cooler temperament, seems to have stood aloof from the lecturer in these first years. With another associate, however, Georg Spalatin, Martin welded a friendship in the early Wittenberg days that was to last through life and prove of the highest importance for Luther's biographers. It will therefore be worth while to pause for a moment and examine Spalatin's personality.[8]

Born into the artisan class of Nuremberg, a city where civic culture had reached its highest development, Georg Spalt was almost of an age with Martin. He entered Erfurt University at fourteen and promptly Latinized his name. He became a bachelor of arts in the following year. Drawn to humanistic studies by Marschalk, he followed the latter to Wittenberg the year after Martin came to Erfurt, and he received his master's degree there. In 1515 Spalatin was back in Erfurt, where his interest in the new learning brought him friendship with Mutianus and the Gotha group of humanists. In the cloister of the neighboring Georgenthal, where Spalatin taught, he was consecrated priest the year after Martin's introduction into the sacred office and by the same bishop. A year later he became attached to the family of the elector of Saxony as instructor of the young heir, John Frederick, and he later mounted in the service of the elector to become librarian, chaplain, and secretary. As time went by Spalatin won the complete confidence of Frederick, who entrusted him with his correspondence and lent a willing ear to his advice. A rather slight figure, Spalatin was a man of great intellectual energy and had the Renaissance gift for historiography. He was not without pedantry, and he had a tendency toward worry, for which his position brought many opportunities; but he seems to have been quite lacking in egotism. A true scholar, he avoided the active collisions of life. On the other hand, he kept his head in a crisis, as will appear in our narrative, and he often laid a restraining hand on Martin when his headstrong will drove him to radical action.

---

[8] Spalatin's relations to the period were so important that it is strange that he has not yet found a suitable biographer. Berbig's *Spalatin und sein Verhältnis zu Martin Luther* exaggerates the force of his personality but does not place him adequately in the history of the time. Paul Kalkoff in his various works shrinks the electoral chaplain into a minor figure devoid of color and without real influence on events. An examination of the sources from 1517 to 1525 shows that the mild humanist was by no means a mere go-between, but a level-headed counselor and active intermediary in these critical years.

When Martin first made the acquaintance of the man who was to become in critical years his most valued friend and adviser, the sources do not reveal. Probably it was not until Martin entered on the professorship at Wittenberg. From that time on their friendship grew. The electoral chaplain was a man of deep piety who had an eager interest in theological questions, and he soon learned to put absolute confidence in Martin's spiritual character and Biblical scholarship. As we shall see, Spalatin followed the development of Luther's ideas with nervousness and hesitation at times, but in general with full acceptance, and he kept the friar-professor informed of the changing color of the elector's mind, thereby doing much to guide the course of affairs in the stern days from 1517 to 1521. Martin, on the other hand, found in Spalatin a friend to whom he could unbosom himself fully. Like many a man of a powerful emotional nature, he required an outlet such as Spalatin furnished for his ideas, and his letters to the chaplain are the richest contemporary source for a knowledge of Martin's inner development. Fortunately, Spalatin had the intuitive feeling of the historian for archival values. From the earliest years of their acquaintance he preserved Martin's letters carefully. Not many seem to have disappeared. He had all the humanistic lust for letter writing and carried on an active correspondence with many scholars. Mutianus once said that Spalatin's letters were like a shower of rain. Unfortunately Martin lacked the instinct of the archivist and few of the many communications of Spalatin to him have been preserved.

Luther's correspondence as we have it is therefore one-sided but rich in biographical material. Of the 2,500 letters and formulas from his hand contained in the thirteen volumes of Enders's edition, 430 are addressed to Spalatin. The latter lived for the most part at the electoral court in Torgau, a few miles up the Elbe from Wittenberg, but he was often in the university town at the electoral castle. There can be no doubt that he and Martin were often together and that the letters are only a very small part of their interchange of confidences. Beginning in 1514, the letters increase in number until 1519. Occasionally Martin writes twice on the same day. Even when the friend is in Wittenberg the eager friar cannot wait for a meeting, but rushes to put into writing his ideas on a theological question or some crisis of the moment. The letters cover every subject of spiritual and monastic life as well as university policy and matters of state. While they are sometimes touched by a crude humor, their tone is generally reserved. Like other theologians and humanists of the sixteenth century, Luther was ready to pass along personal scandal and was by no means above obscenities in his correspondence, but the age admitted no sentimental glow of friendship such as marks the interchanges of the eighteenth century. Martin did not have in his nature the possibility of that kind of expression. Furthermore, the electoral chaplain was separated from the temperamental friar by a certain difference of character which admitted no effusive friendship and relatively few expressions of gratitude. Plainly Martin felt his own spiritual and intellectual superiority, but had great respect for the learning and judgment of his friend. All of his outpourings of soul have to do with serious questions of religious life.

Another friend who drew close to him in the early Wittenberg years was the associate of Erfurt days, Johann Lang. Lang's assistance in the study of Greek and Hebrew must have been active in the first three years of Martin's professorship, but these studies find slight echo in their correspondence, which begins in May, 1516, after Lang's removal to Erfurt. Here the sturdy humanist and earnest friar was to be of active assistance when the crisis drew near in Martin's relation to the hierarchy. Martin's letters to him have much to say of cloister affairs and associates in the order. He keeps Lang in touch with the progress of his own work and occasionally asks for advice on points of classical scholarship. The letters are such as one would write to a cloister friend and companion in arms.

It was through this old friend that Martin and Spalatin had their first approach. The exchange sprang from the great conflict then agitating all humanistic circles, the attempt of the scholastic group at the Cologne University to crush Johann Reuchlin for his defense of Jewish books.[9] Reuchlin had replied vigorously to the charge of heresy hurled against him by his opponents, and the affair reached a climax by the end of 1513 when, in response to an invitation of the Cologne theologians, the faculties at Louvain, Mainz, and Erfurt condemned Reuchlin's *Mirror* as heretical. It was perhaps this action of their alma mater that moved Spalatin to ask Martin's opinion. This he did through Lang.[10] Martin's reply, addressed directly to Spalatin, is a vigorous acquittal of the "learned Doctor Reuchlin," whom he holds in high regard. There is not the least danger to faith in his book. The Cologne crowd, instead of attempting to cleanse the Church within, devote their zeal to supposed enemies outside. If they are allowed to go on, they will soon be stamping the very orthodox as heretics. Reuchlin had protested against the proposal to burn the books of the Jews. Martin declares that we have God's word for it that the Jews are bound to abuse and blaspheme Christ and if we

[9] For convenient guidance through the history of this controversy and the abundant literature on the subject, see Aloys Bömer's edition of the *Epistolae obscurorum virorum*, Vol. I.

[10] Letter from Spalatin to Lang, *WAB*, I, 20.

take away what they have written they will simply write worse things.[11] As the year 1514 progressed, the strife between the Cologne heresy hunters and humanists reached an acute phase when both parties appealed to Rome and Pope Leo X appointed a high ecclesiastic as judge. City councils here and there in Germany felt called upon to take sides, influential personalities aligned themselves for and against Reuchlin, and the voices of the disputants grew shrill with rage. One of the Cologne spokesmen, Ortwin Gratius, attacked Reuchlin in a particularly arrogant pamphlet,[12] to which Spalatin called Luther's attention. The latter replied in the earliest letter that we have in his own handwriting.[13] It bristles with abusive superlatives and such comparisons of the Cologne scholar to members of the lower animal kingdom as those with which embattled humanists of the day were accustomed to decorate their opponents: dog, ravening wolf, pretended lion showing his asinine nature, crocodile. Martin ends with a prayer for Reuchlin. His resentment against the heresy hunters of Cologne was genuine, but in defending the humanist he plainly took his cue from his friend Lang, who was on intimate terms with the group in Erfurt and Gotha.

Two years later Lang exerted himself to bring about a personal friendship between Martin and the retired sage at Gotha, Mutianus. The year before Mutianus had heard echoes of the bitter sermon against slanderers at the Augustinian convention in Gotha, and through the intervention of Lang he received a copy of the text and was delighted at its stinging castigation of monastic sins.[14] Plainly Martin was flattered by the interest of the widely known humanist. It is highly doubtful whether he met Mutianus personally, but in May of 1516, while pausing in Gotha on his journey of visitation, he sent the canon a letter excusing his failure to call on him.[15] The letter is in humanistic style: calling himself a "rustic Corydon" and a barbarian accustomed to cry out among geese, the younger man salutes Mutianus as a scholar of the most profound learning. These are well-oiled phrases of the time. The episode was of importance, however, since it marks Martin's

[11] Letter from Luther to Spalatin, Feb. (?), 1514, *WAB*, I, 23.

[12] Gratius, a Latinization of Van Graes, was to become a target for Crotus's satire in the *Epistolae obscurorum virorum* as a type of the clerical obscurantist. As a matter of fact, the Cologne scholar was a very competent theologian according to the standards of the scholastic age. His satirical attacks on Reuchlin were certainly no more bitter or tactless than the counterthrusts of the Swabian Hebraist. Regarding the work of Gratius which stirred Luther to rage, see Bömer, *Epistolae*, I, 15 f.

[13] Letter from Luther to Spalatin, Aug. 5, 1514, *WAB*, I, 28 f.

[14] Letter from Lang to Mutianus, May 2, 1515, in Gillert, "Der Briefwechsel des Conradius Mutianus," *Geschichtsquellen der Provinz Sachsen*, XVIII, II (1890), 149 f.

[15] Letter from Luther to Mutianus, May 29, 1516, *WAB*, I, 40,

closest approach to the humanistic group which was at this time, through his student acquaintance Crotus and the fiery Ulrich von Hutten, engaged in exploding the bitterest and most successful satire of the age against scholastic ignorance and pride. These *Letters of Obscure Men,* however, mark the split between humanism and theological reform. After the appearance of this work, Martin threw his whole effort into the religious field, and the battle for "good letters" ceased to be of interest to him except in so far as it contributed to a direct knowledge of the sources of the Scriptures.

This humanistic passage at arms was also of importance because it brought his first contact with Spalatin. Martin's defense of Reuchlin evidently pleased the chaplain greatly, and probably early in the spring of 1515 he commends the professor to Lang as a "very learned and earnest man" and "what is also very rare, a man of the most discerning judgment."[16] Shortly afterwards, according to Lang, Spalatin had come to honor the professor as an "Apollo" and to take him into counsel.[17] Evidence of this appeared immediately after Luther's return from his spring visit to the Thuringian cloisters in 1516. Elector Frederick had apparently determined to press the appointment of Staupitz to a bishopric, and Spalatin, somewhat in doubt whether to urge the general vicar's acceptance, writes to Martin for advice. Martin's letter has been preserved, and it is a vigorous argument against the proposal.[18] He intends to write to Staupitz and try to persuade him not to accept. He will do this even in spite of Spalatin and the elector: "For many things please your prince and shine mightily in his eyes which are displeasing to God and are foul in His sight." He declares he does not say these things in a corner, but is ready if opportunity offers to speak them in public. In these days the ambitions and efforts of the bishops are not those of the ancient leaders of the Church and even the best of them carry on wars and build private fortunes with insatiable greed. He fears lest Staupitz, far removed as he is from such views, may be drawn into these turmoils.

In the meantime the professor had given fresh evidence of exegetic scholarship. Hardly had the course of lectures on Psalms been brought to an end when he began a new course, on Paul's Epistle to the Romans.[19] Either

---

[16] Enders, *Luthers Briefwechsel,* I, 13. The date of Spalatin's letter is highly questionable. Enders puts it at March 3, 1512. In *Luthers Correspondence,* I, 32, ed. and trans. by Smith and Jacobs, it is dated March 3, 1515, on the basis of a reference to Erasmus. It seems reasonable to connect it with the judgment of Luther on the Reuchlin affair.

[17] See letter from Lang to Mutianus, May 2, 1515, in Gillert, "Mutianus," II, 149 f.

[18] June 8, 1516. *WAB,* I, 44 ff.

[19] The date of beginning the lectures on Romans is by no means certain. Basing on statements by Oldecop, "Die Chronik des Johan Oldecop," (*Bibliothek des Litterarischen Vereins in*

just after Easter, 1515, or in the following term he stepped to the lecturer's desk to begin a series which was to demonstrate the full maturity of his powers as an exegete, both in content and technique. As he looked over his manuscript for the course on Psalms, he was well aware of its defects. "Trifles, quite worthy of the sponge," he wrote to friend Spalatin in September, 1516, in response to the chaplain's suggestion that the manuscript be turned over to a Leipzig printer.[20] Staupitz also had been urging publication of the lectures,[21] but they do not yet seem to Martin fit material for good types and typesetters, and he does not expect that the printer can have them until the beginning of Lent in the following year. Martin never carried out the task of bringing the notes on Psalms into order, but contented himself, as we shall see, with trimming into shape the portion on the seven penitential Psalms and sending these to the press just about the time he had promised.

In comparison with the vast mass of notes on Psalms intended only for his own eye, Martin's manuscript of the lectures on Romans was prepared with extreme care. The orderliness of the *scholia* shows, in part at least, that he made a fair copy from earlier notes.[22] His original manuscript of the Romans lectures, now in the National Library in Berlin, is a remarkable example of the calligraphic traditions of the late medieval university. This time also he had the text of the Vulgate printed by a Wittenberg press, with wide interlinear spaces and broad margins.[23] The philological care of his procedure is reflected in his treatment of the Latin text,[24] which he amended here and there with the help of the edition of Paul's epistles published a few years before by the French humanist Faber,[25] whose commentary on Psalms had been at his elbow through the preceding year. On one of the printed sheets of the Vulgate the lecturer then wrote his glossary, crowding

---

Stuttgart, CXC, 45). Ficker sets the opening of the course at Easter, 1515 (*WA*, LVI, xii), and most scholars seem to accept this dating. Nevertheless, Oldecop's statement is not categorical, and Böhmer, "Luthers erste Vorlesung," p. 9, note, finds evidence in the lectures for a later beginning, approximately November 3, 1515.

[20] Letter from Luther to Spalatin, Sept. 9, 1516, *WAB*, I, 56. There is a difference of opinion regarding the date of this letter, but Böhmer's view seems conclusive. See "Luthers erste Vorlesung," pp. 8 f., n. 1.

[21] This seems the natural interpretation of Luther's *coactus praecepto*, *WAB*, I, 56, l. 7.

[22] See *WA*, LVI, xviii ff., especially xxiii.

[23] For a description of the MS and an account of its interesting history, see *WA*, LVI, xiii ff. It was first published by Ficker in his *Anfänge reformatorischer Bibelauslegung*, Vols. I (1908) and II (1929), and again by the same scholar in *WA*, LVI (1938), in both cases with full textual and other scholarly apparatus. There is a German translation by Eduard Ellwein.

[24] The basic text of the Vulgate used was the *Biblia latina* (Basel, 1509), published by Froben.

[25] Ficker finds that the Paris editions of both 1512 and 1515 were used by Luther. *WA*, LVI, xv ff.

the blank spaces with explanatory words and sentences. Then followed the *scholia,* a many-leaved manuscript containing long excursuses suggested by the text, all marked with critical care. In addition to this manuscript, where the vigorous handwriting of the professor permits us to recapture something of the ardor and rush with which he attacked the problems of Pauline theology, there is in the Vatican library another version, a copy made under the direction of one of Luther's amanuenses of later years, Johann Aurifaber. This came into the hands of the great Protestant Maecenas of the sixteenth century, Ulrich Fugger, passed thence into the electoral library at Heidelberg, and with the rest of that priceless collection was presented to the Vatican by Elector Max of Bavaria as a part of the booty which he seized when he occupied the Palatinate in 1619.[26]

It was with a sense of increased power and self-assurance that Martin entered on the new course. His transition from Psalms to Romans was a natural one, for as we have seen, Paul's ideas through Augustinian interpretation had thrust themselves repeatedly to the fore when Martin was explaining the Psalms. Even if he began the course as early as Easter, 1515, as seems most likely, his preparation must have reached far back into the preceding winter months. From the first he demonstrates how great his progress has been in the past years in clarity of inner vision, originality of view, and reliance on his own ideas. The careful glossary shows in graphic form with what penetrating vision he dwelt on every word, indeed every letter, of the original. Verbal explanations, synonyms, punctuation, and the other minutiae necessary to a clear understanding of the text attest the conscientious scholar. In fact, the lecturer constructed his own text with the use of a shelf of exegetical authorities: the so-called *Glossa ordinaria,* comprising a text grown up under the hands of a series of medieval commentators, and especially the edition of Faber and probably also the commentary of Thomas Aquinas. When he had passed the half-way mark, the original Greek text came into his hands in Erasmus's edition of the Greek New Testament with a Latin interpretation by the great humanist.[27] Martin seizes it with eagerness and makes constant use of it for the remaining chapters. He even ventures to insert a few words in Greek script,[28] for thanks to Lang's help, Greek was no longer an unknown language. At his side were the Greco-Latin

---

[26] For a full account, see Ficker, *Anfänge reformatorischer Bibelauslegung,* I, xxv ff. See also Stauber, *Das Haus Fugger,* pp. 119 ff.

[27] The *Novum instrumentum cum annotationibus* probably came from the press in Basel in March, 1516, and may have reached Luther very soon afterward. His first reference appears to be in the glossary. *WA,* LVI, 89.

[28] *WA,* LVI, 95 and 152.

lexicon published in Paris in 1512 with a foreword by Aleander, and the Greek dictionary published by the Aldine press in Venice in 1497. Reuchlin's Hebrew lexicons, too, were at hand. As the work proceeds he becomes more and more independent in the use of these sources and confronts even Faber and Erasmus with his own emendations and interpretations.

Thus armed with an increasingly adequate equipment, he takes up the text of the Apostle and shows a scholar's technique in observation and in the use of his grammatical and logical apparatus. Above all, he commands the scholar's greatest asset, a powerful memory, whose astonishing facility in quotation could only be the product of an age poor in books. Every page literally swarms with citations from the Bible. Next in importance are Augustine and the Church Fathers. Then come Latin writers, classical, post-classical, and modern, like Vergil, Catullus, Ovid, Perseus, Juvenal, Seneca, Aesop, Baptist the Mantuan; historians like the elder Pliny; Hellenistic and medieval mystics like Dionysius the Areopagite, St. Bernard, and Johannes Tauler; Schoolmen like Scotus, Occam, and Biel; university teachers like Aristotle; early medieval ecclesiastics like Bishop Cyprian of Antioch and Gregory the Great; theologians like Lombard; historians like Polybius and Suetonius; and pietists like Gerhard Groot.[29]

Of all these sources it is Augustine who stands most constantly at his elbow; Augustine, who in the *Confessions,* as Martin recalled many years later, ascribed his conversion to a verse in Romans (13.13), "not in reviling and drunkenness and not in chambering and wantonness." It is Augustine's work on the *Spirit and the Letter* which chained Martin's attention and which, as he declared in the year before his death, had contributed to his discovery of the Gospel.[30] The eloquent language of the African Father echoes here and there in the Latin text of the professor's manuscript.[31] The fourfold medieval framework for exegesis which he used so painstakingly in the course on Psalms has well-nigh disappeared. At times he drops back into a tropological or allegorical interpretation, but in the main the whole scholastic framework is swept aside to make room for a literal and direct presentation of the thought of the Apostle.

Throughout his lectures the recurrent theme is the Apostle's attitude toward sin. "The sum and substance of this Epistle is to scatter and destroy

[29] See Ficker's register, *WA*, LVI, introduction.

[30] Strohl finds Augustine cited 124 times in the lectures; *De spiritu et litera* is cited 26 times. *L'Épanouissement de la pensée religieuse de Luther,* p. 100. Ficker registers more than 200 citations and references. *WA*, LVI, li.

[31] Ficker notes especially the influence of the *Confessio* on Luther's language in the *scholia. Anfänge reformatorischer Bibelauslegung,* I, lxii.

all of the righteousness and wisdom of the flesh and on the other hand to establish, augment, and magnify sin and nothingness, so that finally Christ and his righteousness may enter into us in place of those things which are wiped out." [32] Thus the first lecture begins and the reality and danger of sin runs through all that follows. When he turns to describe God's attitude toward the sinner his pathos has the stern accents of a Jeremiah. God does not desire sin, but wills that it take place in order to manifest to man the sublimity of His nature. Sin remains ineradicable, even for the faithful believer. The saints themselves are unjust as well as just. "For behold, every saint is a sinner and prays for his sins. Thus the righteous man begins with the accusation of himself." [33] With solemn insistence he pursues the analysis of sin throughout the earlier chapters of the Epistle. It is reiterated that the inclination to sin is incurable: "It is an error to think that this evil is cured by works, since experience proves that in spite of all our good works the desire for evil endures and no one is free from it, not even the child a day old. But such is the mercy of God that, although this evil persists, it is not counted as sin for those who call upon Him and demand their deliverance with sighs. . . . Thus we are sinners and nevertheless we are accounted righteous by God through faith." [34] The contrast between the law and faith, which Paul draws with an eye on the Christian community in Rome where Jewish converts played an important rôle, opens the way for a long discussion. Martin has convinced himself that the scholastic ideas derived from Aristotle collide with the teaching of Augustine. In the conception that love of God may bring sinful man to wish and will the good lurks a fatal error, the idea that the natural powers of man can create this love. At the bottom of it all is the false conception of the powers of the human will for good, Pelagianism. "For even though none are Pelagians by profession and name, nevertheless the most are such, perhaps ignorantly, in their real essence and opinion," he declares toward the close of the series on Romans. "They think with security and boldness that when they conceive a good intention they will inevitably obtain grace." [35]

A tone of gloomy pathos sounds throughout the earlier chapters of Martin's course. The shadow of the soul crisis arising from his study of the Occamist philosophy lies upon him. Only a faint ray of the inexhaustible grace of God and His kindly guidance of the human soul lights up the dark picture. Augustine's deeply mystical conception of the relation of God to man has

---

[32] *WA*, LVI, 3.

[33] "Sic justus in principio est accusator sui." *Ibid.*, p. 270. This idea, taken from Jesus Sirach, chap. 29, is a favorite with Luther at this period. See the lectures on Psalms, *WA*, III, 29, l. 16.

[34] *WA*, LVI, 271, ll. 24 ff.   [35] *Ibid.*, p. 502, ll. 14 ff.

possession of him, and it is from Augustine that he draws his ideas of the impotence of the human will:

Those reason most dangerously that take from philosophy their arguments concerning good, since God will turn it into evil. For even if all good things are truly good, nevertheless none are good for us in themselves, and even if none are in any way evil, nevertheless all are evil for us. . . . So we ought to flee from the good and take on ourselves the evil, and this not merely in words and with a pretended willingness of heart, but heartily show and desire to be lost and damned. Because just as any man behaves who hates another, so we ought to behave toward ourselves. For whoever hates, not feignedly but seriously, is eager to destroy and kill and damn him whom he hates. If we then sincerely destroy and take vengeance upon ourselves and offer ourselves to hell for the sake of God and His justice, we have truly satisfied that justice and He will have mercy on us and set us free. If we judge ourselves, we shall certainly not be judged by the Lord. For such seek only to wash away their guilt and reconcile the grace of an offended God. They do not seek the kingdom, they are prepared never to be saved, they are willing to be damned. Nevertheless, with the grace of an appeased God they do not fear punishment, but only the displeasure of God.[36]

This struggle against scholastic ideas reaches its crescendo when the lecturer comes to the eighth and ninth chapters of Romans. Here Martin declares that the conception that the human will can play a part in man's salvation bears its fruits in reliance on works done under the law. The only way to salvation lies in abject humiliation, the only merit man can claim is the fear of God. Paul's summary of the racial history of Israel,[37] an elaborate justification of God's choice of the Gentiles, Martin bends to fit those of his own time who do not know the nature of grace and redemption:

Why is man proud of his merit and his works, which in no wise please because they have merit or are good, but because they have been chosen by God from eternity that they should please Him? Therefore we have no good works except the search for grace, because our works do not make us good, but our goodness, or rather the goodness of God, makes us and our works good. They would not be good in themselves unless God reckoned them as good, and they only amount to as much as He counts or does not count them. Therefore what we reckon or do not reckon is nothing. Whoever understands this is always in terror, and always fears and awaits the reckoning of God. He cannot, therefore, be proud or contentious,

---

[36] *Ibid.*, p. 393, ll. 21 ff.

[37] Grisar, *Luther*, I, 156, points out that Catholic authorities interpret the passage in a different way. They assume that Paul does not refer to the individual soul, but to the Jewish people: having received the promise without desert, they are now excluded from it as a race and people because of their wickedness.

as are those haughty men who claim to be justified and are confident of their good works.[38]

The necessity of fear as a constant companion in the Christian life is a basic chord in the *scholia:* "Happy is the man who is always in terror," he quotes from Job.[39] "Who can tell me whether my good intention is from God? How am I to know that what I do or what is in me pleases God?"[40] Once again he brands as a Pelagian error the scholastic declaration, passed down through Biel, that God will infallibly infuse His grace into him who does what lies in his power.[41] Let not the man who goes to confession believe that he is rid of his burden. Sin remains to exercise us in the life of grace, to humble our pride and check our presumption. The only path to grace is the broken will and the humble heart that is ready to accept what God imposes. Works are of no effect, for the supreme will of God has decided that we are not to be saved by our righteousness, but by the imputed righteousness of Christ. We must submerge ourselves in nothingness and thus placate God and receive the righteousness of Christ: "in our ignorance justified, in our knowledge unjustified; sinners in fact, but righteous in hope."[42]

The nominalist ideas of the arbitrary will of God imbibed at Erfurt have intertwined themselves with Augustine's conception of sin and of the worthlessness of the human will. The eloquence of Paul's presentation of the inscrutable will of God infects Martin and echoes throughout the lectures, but Paul's profound idea of the liberating power of faith still escapes him, though he ascribes a high place to it in comparison with works. The problem of predestination still causes him anxiety, and the uncompromising position of the Apostle as Martin interprets him on this subject plainly confuses the lecturer. At one point he extricates himself from the contradictions inherent in the conception of predestination by a dialectical explanation. It is impossible that one who conforms fully to the will of God should remain in hell. "Because he wishes what God wishes, therefore he pleases God. If he pleases God, then he is loved. If he is loved, then he will be saved."[43] Earlier, however, he states that it is certain that all the elect will be saved, but no one can be sure that he is chosen.[44] Paul's wish that he himself might be

---

[38] *WA*, LVI, 394, ll. 27 ff.

[39] *Ibid.*, p. 502, ll. 28 f., following the Vulgate, Job 9.28. The English translators rendered this quite differently.

[40] *WA*, LVI, 502, ll. 30 ff.   [41] *Ibid.*, p. 503, ll. 1 ff.

[42] *Ibid.*, p. 269, l. 30.   [43] *Ibid.*, p. 391, ll. 14 ff.

[44] "Deus vult omnes homines salvos fieri . . . semper haec dicta intelliguntur de electis tantum." *WA*, LVI, 385, ll. 23 ff. This interpretation goes back of course to Augustine. See *Enchiridion ad Laurentium*, in Migne, *Patrologiae cursus completus*, XL, 231 ff.

accursed for the redemption of his fellow Israelites perhaps suggests to Martin the drastic demand for self-effacement and humility, already mentioned above, which he directs at those who love God for the sake of their security and eternal happiness or from the fear of hell. Perfect love must go to the point where the soul is willing to embrace eternal damnation if that is the will of God: "For such offer themselves to the will of God in all things, even to hell and eternal punishment if God wishes, in order that His will may be fully satisfied." [45] This complete negation of the will to love seeks expression in mystical antitheses:

For our good is mysterious and so profound that it is hidden under the opposite: thus our life under death, our love under our hate, our glory under ignominy, our safety under destruction, our rule under exile, heaven under hell, wisdom under folly, justification under sin, virtue under weakness. And as a whole, all our affirmation of good lies in the negative so that faith may have a place in God, who is negative essence and goodness and wisdom and justice; nor can He be possessed or touched except by the negation of all our affirmatives. [46]

Here, as elsewhere in his interpretation, he borrows age-old ideas and even language from the Neoplatonic mystic, Dionysius the Areopagite, whose theology he had at hand. [47]

The somberness of the lectures in their presentation of sin and justification not only reflects the gloom of medieval asceticism. It is also a product of the clash between convictions dating back to studies of nominalistic theology at Erfurt and the ideas of Augustine. This accounts for uncertainties in his theological position as regards predestination. The intense eloquence and lurid flashes of temperamental vehemence in his pictures of man's lost state and the possibilities of justification give us some idea of the severity of the experience that racked his soul in these days. Furthermore, life in the cloisters, with its spirit of pride and tendency to self-satisfaction, was a constant irritation in contrast with the ideas that he found in Augustine and Paul. This echoes in a letter of the time to a brother friar, Georg Spenlein, an uneasy soul who had been an intimate of Martin's at Wittenberg and was transferred to a Bavarian convent, perhaps early in 1516. Martin writes him on April 8 of that year, criticizing the presumption of those who try to stand before God through the strength of their own efforts and merits instead of trusting in the righteousness of Christ. "You were of this opinion, nay rather in this error. I was also, but now I am fighting against the error, though even

---

[45] *WA*, LVI, 391, ll. 9 ff.   [46] *Ibid.*, p. 392, ll. 28 ff.

[47] *Ibid.*, p. 299, ll. 28 ff., and Ficker's note. In the lectures on Psalms Luther had referred to the Areopagite's "mystical shadows" and his ladder of negations. *WA*, III, 124, ll. 32 f.

yet I have not subdued it." [48] In the attacks on good works in the lectures he puts some of his own inner experiences into theological costume. "Experience," he declares, "is necessary in the law. . . . How much more in theology." [49] After all, the religious development of Paul bore a strong resemblance to his own. The fearful despair, the power of the Evil One and the impotence of human effort against it, the struggle for certainty and the swaying back and forth between certainty and uncertainty of salvation—all of these are taken directly out of his own soul history. Throughout it all rings a tone of resolute combat against diabolical foes within him. "We are not called to ease but to labor against our passions." [50] The law of our life, he feels, is combat.

Important for Luther at this time too, is the influence of the mystics. His acquaintance with the works of Bernard of Clairvaux, Bonaventure, and Gerson dated back to his early theological studies in Erfurt. In these writers he found a refuge from the round of cloister ritual and ascetic self-denial in another side of monastic devotion, the appeal for humility of soul. That these teachers must have affected him strongly is shown by his frequent references to them in later years. The eloquent appeals to the devout soul in St. Bernard made a deep impression, and the great French mystic is called on frequently as a witness in the Romans lectures. Bonaventure's urge to a union of the soul with God through "mental prayer" led Martin to spiritual exercises by which he tried to fuse mind and will into a unity of effort.[51] This profound effacement of the soul before the majesty of God is of only minor importance in the lectures on Psalms.[52] It is the keynote throughout the course on Romans.

Compared with this practical mysticism, the metaphysical mysticism of the Neoplatonic writers seems to have had little influence. Martin had, to be sure, known some of the works of Dionysius the Areopagite while a student at Erfurt, and, as we have seen, he echoes the visionary language of this late Hellenic writer in his interpretation of Romans. Some years later he recalled that the ecstatic dreamings of the Neoplatonists had stimulated him to

---

[48] *WAB*, I, 35 f.   [49] *WA*, LVI, 447, ll. 21 f.   [50] *Ibid.*, p. 350, ll. 8 f.

[51] See Scheel, *Martin Luther*, II, 627 f. Bonaventure is not mentioned in the lectures on Romans, but Luther declares many years later that reading the saint had "set him wild." *TR*, I, No. 644 (1533). In a lecture on Psalms he tried to define "mental prayer" by means of the mystical symbolism of the circle. *WA*, IV, 671, ll. 21 ff. Cf. E. Hirsch's interpretation, "Luther über die oratio mentalis," *Zeitschrift für systematische Theologie*, VI (1929), 136 ff.

[52] Braun, *Bedeutung der Concupiszens*, esp. pp. 273 ff., tries to demonstrate mystical ideas in the lectures on Psalms. Also A. W. Hunzinger in his brief study, "Luther und die deutsche Mystik," *Neue kirchliche Zeitschrift* (*Luthertum*), XIX (1908), 972 ff., claims to find an influence of Augustine's Neoplatonism in these lectures. I have not been able to discover there anything more than an acquaintance with Neoplatonic vocabulary.

speculations that led nowhere.[53] Fired by their writings, for the time, however, his emotional nature had moments of elation in which he believed that he had found a direct path to God. In a sermon of 1523, he remembers that he was then "carried into the third heaven." [54] Toward the end of his life he recalled that while engaged in exercises to attain spiritual unity with God he had felt himself to be in the "chorus of angels." [55] After his break with the Church, these ideas vanished into thin air, and when he looked back on his spiritual life he recognized that he had never had any real taste for such speculations.

Nevertheless, in the years of his early lectures certain mystical ideas possessed him strongly. Here Staupitz wielded an influence that was both restraining and stimulating. As a practical man, the general vicar knew how to draw the line between the morbid and the wholesome. Martin recalled later that when Staupitz compelled him to a life of theological scholarship, he rescued him from losing himself in visions like those of St. Bridget.[56] On the other hand, there was, as we have seen, a vein of mystic piety in the nature of Staupitz and the influence of this on Luther was certainly important. Staupitz's writings teem with appeals to the Christian soul to free itself from the speculations of philosophers, so dangerous to morality, to submerge itself in God with a humble hope for mercy, and to recognize that suffering is a necessary companion of the Christian throughout life. It must have been an echo of conversations with Staupitz that led Martin two years after he had finished the Romans lectures to thank the spiritual father for having warned him not to dwell on sacramental grace, but to seek inner grace, and especially for having pointed out the insignificance of the sacrament of penance as compared with the contrition of soul which must precede it.[57] Perhaps it was Staupitz who, noting the painful concentration of Martin on works of scholastic theology, called his attention to the writings of the youngest of the great German mystical fathers of the later Middle Ages, Johannes Tauler.

It is uncertain when the sermons of Tauler came into Martin's hand.[58] It is probable, however, that it was while he was midway in the *scholia* for

---

[53] "Expertus loquor." *De captivitate Babylonica, WA,* VI, 562, ll. 5 ff. Cf. *TR,* I, No. 644; also his rejection of "gefährliche Prediger" in the sermon of May 14, 1531. Buchwald, *Die Predigten D. Martin Luthers,* II, 267.

[54] Sermon of May 25, 1523, *WA,* XI, 117, ll. 35 f.

[55] Sermon on Isaiah IX, *EA,* XXIII, 401. The sermon was written up after Luther's death for publication and is textually unreliable.

[56] Lectures on Genesis, *WA,* XLIII, 667.

[57] Dedicatory letter to the *Resolutiones disputationum de indulgentiarum virtute, WA,* I, 525.

[58] The first mention of Tauler is in a letter to Lang, belonging probably to the middle of 1516, *WAB,* I, 65. Preserved Smith, in Smith and Jacobs, *Luther's Correspondence,* I, 41, thinks that the influence of Tauler appears as early as the preceding April in a letter to Lang.

the lectures on Romans and therefore early in 1516 that he began to read
the text of the eloquent Dominican who had thrilled the Alsatian cloisters in
the preceding century with his appeals for a life free from self through the
fusion of the soul of the believer with the perfect soul of God. It was not
long before the language of the mystic threw its spell over him and found
an echo in his lectures. In his impassioned discussion of the eighth chapter of
Paul's epistle, Martin refers to Tauler's mystical passage regarding the long
suffering of the brooding spirit of God.[59] From this time on, the ideas of
Tauler mingle with the quietism of Staupitz in shaping Martin's thought.
In his own personal conflict with the conception of the law and his struggle
for a theological position respecting God's justice Tauler, like Staupitz and
Gerson, brought comfort, for Tauler had also known these "torments." [60]
From the middle of the Romans lectures on the glowing eloquence of the
mystic is echoed. "I have never," Martin writes to Spalatin soon after the
conclusion of the Romans course, "either in Latin or in our language, seen
a theology which was saner and more in accord with the Evangelists." [61] A
copy of the sermons of Tauler marked with comments and notations,
probably in the year 1516, formed a permanent part of Martin's library.[62]
Many of the passages in the lectures on Romans in their sharply sketched
pictures of the struggling soul suggest the influence of this father of German
prose. Here Martin found a pattern for his eloquent exposition of the
futility of our endeavor to please God which appears in his sermons of the
time as well as his lectures:

> Whatever thine of merit, the grace of God endows;
> Nought does he crown within us save gifts which he bestows.[63]

In Tauler also he found an inspiration for his impassioned descriptions of
the passivity of the will in receiving God's spirit:

For the reception of the first grace as well as of the full glory, we must hold ourselves ever passive like a woman at conception. For we are the bride of Christ; so
before grace comes we should pray and implore, but when it comes and the soul

---

[59] *WA*, LVI, 378, ll. 13 ff.

[60] *Resolutiones disputationum de indulgentiarum virtute* (1518), *WA*, I, 557, ll. 25 ff. See
also *Operationes in Psalmos* (1521), *WA*, V, 202 ff., and the *Adventspostille*, 1522, *WA*, X, 1,
Part 2, 105, for similar references to Tauler.

[61] Letter from Luther to Spalatin, Dec. 14, 1516, *WAB*, I, 79.

[62] *Sermones . . . Johannis Taulerii*, Augsburg, 1508. The notes of Luther are published in
WA, IX, 95 ff.

[63]   Quidquid habes meriti, praeventrix gratia donat:
            Nil deus in nobis praeter sua dona coronat.

The couplet, ascribed to Albertus Magnus, is cited in the marginalia on Lombard's *Sentences*,
probably 1510. *WA*, IX, 72, and again in the notes on Tauler, *ibid.*, p. 99.

is penetrated by the spirit we ought neither to pray nor exert ourselves, but only to remain passive. This is, in truth, difficult, and causes us violent affliction, for when the spirit surrenders all understanding and wishing, it takes flight into the shadows and, as it were, passes into perdition and destruction. Then the soul seeks with all its power to escape and so it often happens that it is robbed of the finest gifts.[64]

Tauler was, however, no quietist. A vigorous ethical tone runs through his sermons calling to activity in the Christian life. This appeal echoes in Martin's later *scholia,* in the discussion of the chapters where St. Paul summons his readers to the practical fulfillment of the law of love. To build on good works is, to be sure, a foundation of sand, but for those who recognize this, the Christian's path is nevertheless one of self-sacrifice. "Life does not consist in repose, but in progress from good to better." [65] This he illustrates by the Aristotelian formula of progress from nonexistence up to action and suffering which he had learned from his Erfurt teachers. Good works are necessary, but they are to be done with humility of spirit; then God will not reject the least of them.[66] Thus Martin laid hold on the essential ideas of German mysticism and held them tightly in the crucial year that followed. Throughout 1516 and 1517, when his theological ideas were taking shape for explosion against the hierarchy, there is evidence from letters and sermons that Tauler was at his right hand.[67] He recommends him to Spalatin for reading by anyone who loves a pure and solid theology and one most like that of the early time.[68]

During the preparation of the lectures another mystical work of the fifteenth century had come into his possession. Sometime in 1516 he got hold of a manuscript of the so-called *German Theology,* a tract by a writer from the springtime of German mysticism known to posterity only as "The Frankforter." [69] This, like other mystical writings, had been much copied and revised, and apparently the first form that came into Martin's hands was an abbreviated version. The work is a model of stylistic simplicity, and the quaint, archaic flavor of its German must have been as sweet on Luther's palate as the language of John Bunyan to a reader of the twentieth century. He assumed at once that the book was by Tauler, devoured with eagerness

---

[64] *WA,* LVI, 379, ll. 1 ff.   [65] *Ibid.,* p. 441, ll. 16 f.   [66] *Ibid.,* p. 428, ll. 8 ff.

[67] See particularly the sermon of Feb. 15, 1517, *WA,* I, 137 f.

[68] Letter from Luther to Spalatin, Dec. 14, 1516, *WAB,* I, 79; also letter of May, 1517, *ibid.,* p. 96, ll. 21 f.

[69] See H. Hermelink, "Text und Gedankengang der Theologia Deutsch," in *Aus Deutschlands kirchlicher Vergangenheit: Festschrift zum 70. Geburtstag von Th. Brieger* (Leipzig, 1912).

the devout rhapsodies concerning the nature of God and the life in Him, and published it early in December, 1516, with an enthusiastic introduction in German.[70] Two years later he came across another and more extended version, and this he also published.[71]

The *German Theology* was Martin's first published work, and there can be no doubt that he felt a powerful affinity for its contents as well as for its mystical language. "The German theologians are undoubtedly the best theologians," he declares in his introduction to the second version.[72] Like Tauler, "The Frankforter" opened to him another view than the one he had found in the rationalistic dialectics of the nominalists and the stern, uncompromising conception of sin and God's righteousness in Augustine. In "The Frankforter," too, as in Tauler, Martin found the idea that the soul prepares a way for a complete union with God only by filling itself with a sense of its own nothingness, and that the very state of terror, which he himself knew so well, is a forerunner of the dawning light of faith. These writers, with their eloquent German, also form an important counterbalance to the limited humanistic style which might have contracted Martin's work within the academic Latin of an Erasmus. Thus far his theological authorities had been clothed in the learned language of scholarship. Here he found deep religious thought clothed in vivid German.

It is not, therefore, extraordinary that during the period of his occupation with these works German finds its way more and more into the dictation of his lectures on Romans. In their text the tendency to use German words increases as the course goes on. Most often they appear as further definitions of an obscure word or phrase; sometimes a pithy German popular saying is flashed on the thought; and once at least the lecturer finds the Latin vocabulary of abuse insufficient to express his anger at a scholastic conception and stamps those who believe in the existence of natural goodness in man as *Sawtheologen,* "sow theologians." [73] Undoubtedly he used the vernacular much more freely in his oral explanations. "The students liked to hear him, for no one else had been heard there who translated so boldly from the Latin word," remarked Johan Oldecop of Hildesheim, later a bitter enemy of Luther, who came to Wittenberg just in time to hear the course on Romans.[74]

---

[70] Luther's introduction, *WA,* I, 153.

[71] *Ibid.,* pp. 378 ff. Both manuscripts have been lost. There is no mention of the *Theologia Deutsch* in the lectures on Romans. Some students, e.g., A. V. Müller, are of the opinion that Luther's knowledge of this work goes back to the early Wittenberg period. I can find no evidence for this.

[72] *WA,* I, 379.   [73] *WA,* LVI, 274, l. 14.

[74] "Die Chronik des Johan Oldecop," p. 28; see also p. 45.

The text of the lectures probably gives a very insufficient idea of the vigor of their presentation and the violence with which he attacked scholastic authorities and ecclesiastical dignitaries. Medieval Latin was rich in terms of abuse. The mixture of unbridled revilings with profound religious and ethical maxims, the interweaving of a vocabulary of envenomed characterizations of opponents with scriptural quotations, was the habit of an age which did not distinguish in thought or life between the bizarre and the grandiose. Like his contemporaries, Martin saw no inconsistency in an intolerant denunciation of the intolerance of others, such as that which he launches against the Cologne heresy hunters:

On the other side are many who burst forth in their marvelous stupidity and call the Jews dogs, curs, or whatever they please, when they themselves without knowing it are indeed such in the face of God. These have exploded with blasphemous agnominations when they ought to have sympathized with them and feared a like fate. On the other hand, as if they were sure of themselves, they rashly declared themselves blessed and others cursed. Such are the Cologne theologians who, with stupid fanaticism in their articles or in their silly and unintelligible productions, are not ashamed to call the Jews accursed. Why? Because they themselves have forgotten that the next chapter says: "Bless and curse not." . . . They want to convert the Jews by violence and cursings. But may God resist them.[75]

The same tone of popular appeal rings in Martin's unrestrained, earthy language in these lectures that we have seen in his sermons. At times a crude obscenity comes to the fore: nauseating pictures in which biological functioning is used to illustrate a spiritual truth.[76] Some of this certainly belongs to the popular idiom of a century which found delight in the stories about Till Eulenspiegel. The modern student of Luther's cloister life, however, cannot avoid the conclusion, as we have stated previously, that to some extent the vividness of the coarse pictures shows the effect on Martin of the frustrations of monastic life, which diverted the imagination to find satisfaction in dwelling upon the obscene.

In spite of such stylistic and psychological limitations, the lectures on Romans show that Martin looked on the whole ecclesiastical situation with a certain bold independence and originality. He turns a critical eye on the monkish observances. The office of the Church is sublime, but it is filled with corruption. The pope and the chief prelates of the Church, enriched by wealth from indulgences, seduce Christian folk from the true worship of

[75] WA, LVI, 436, ll. 13 ff.
[76] See the offensive references to infantile filth, ibid., p. 516, ll. 3 ff., or the long allegorical interpretation of Zipporah's circumcision of her son (Exodus 4.25) in a sermon of Jan. 1, 1517, WA, I, 120, ll. 35 ff.

God.[77] The pope and bishops are more cruel than cruelty itself, refusing to grant for God's sake indulgence for sin which they have received gratis from God. He formulates a vigorous description of contemporary themes of highest interest in Germany, the conflict between the civil and the canon law and the abuses arising from use of the ban of excommunication in prosecuting the claims of the hierarchy to property and privilege.

One must wonder at the thick darkness of our time. Spiritual persons, these devourers of temporalities on a grand scale, indeed bear nothing with greater difficulty than any disturbance of the liberties, rights, and powers of the Church; in such a case they speedily let loose all the lightnings of excommunication, proclaim the offenders heretics and brand them with astounding boldness as enemies of God, the Church, and the Apostles Peter and Paul . . . Thus they declare obedience and faith to consist in the safeguarding, extension, and defense of temporal things.[78]

Again and again he returns to attack the sordid materialism of the clergy: "Those stupid and godless ecclesiastics who strut about with the goods which they have received from the laity and think they are doing enough when they mutter a few prayers on behalf of their benefactors." He is of the opinion that it would be safer if the temporal affairs of the clergy were also placed under the secular power.[79]

Such complaints filled the air at the time. Martin incorporates them in bitter and vituperative language in his course of scholarly exegesis. He goes further and illustrates his anger at conditions in the Church by citing conflicts which were then agitating the public mind. The council of Strasbourg was seeking to bring a criminal canon before civil justice, apparently in opposition to the bishop: "Bishops thirst for revenge, brand the doer, and deserve much more to be branded themselves." Similarly the chronic struggle over financial questions between the bishop of Martin's diocese, Brandenburg, and the city of Wittenberg, the rivalry between Elector Frederick and Cardinal Albert of Brandenburg in the acquisition of sacred relics, the local traffic in indulgences, these and many other contemporary situations he lays before his students to enforce his attack on abuses in the Church. Especially the sale of indulgences was becoming an acute question in Wittenberg and involving Martin's own monastery, whose new buildings were rising in the year of his lectures on Romans. Two indulgences were authorized by papal bulls at this time, one for the construction of St. Peter's in Rome and the other for the completion of the Church of All Saints in Wittenberg. As a result indulgences flooded the city and the vicinity.

[77] *WA*, LVI, 417, ll. 27 ff.   [78] *Ibid.*, p. 476, ll. 28 ff.   [79] *Ibid.*, p. 478, ll. 25 ff.

I3

THE FINAL BREAK WITH
SCHOLASTICISM

I HAVE need of two scribes or amanuenses. I do almost nothing all day but write letters, so that I do not know whether I repeat what I have said before. I am lecturer at the convent, reader during meals, I am also called from day to day to preach in the parish church, am regent of studies at the convent and subvicar, which means prior of eleven convents, have to collect fish at Leitzkau, administer the affairs of Herzberg at Torgau, lecture on Paul, edit my lectures on the Psalms, and besides am loaded down with writing letters which, as I have said, take the greater part of my time. I really do not have time for the prayers in the breviary or for saying Mass. Besides all that, I have to contend against the temptations of the world, flesh, and the devil. You can see how much leisure I have.[1]

This outburst gives a vivid picture of Martin's busy life in the fall of 1516. Students were streaming into the Wittenberg theological school, and the new buildings of the Augustinian cloister were becoming overcrowded with brothers sent from other cloisters to study.[2] At the end of October the Eremites at Wittenberg were housing forty-one religious persons. In addition, the plague had broken out in the neighborhood in September and soon after invaded the city. It killed the son of the blacksmith just across the way from Martin's convent and prostrated a second son. Martin states that he is resolved to send the brothers away should the disease spread further, but he refuses to accept Lang's invitation to flee to Erfurt and is determined not to leave the city unless the general vicar insists on it: "Not that I shall not be afraid of death, for I am not the Apostle Paul, but only a lecturer on him, but I hope God will lift me out of my terror."[3] Despite his busy life, he has his attacks of depression, and at the end of September writes to his friend Maskov, prior of the convent of another order at Leitzkau, in a tone which

---

[1] Letter from Luther to Lang, Oct. 26, 1516, *WAB*, I, 72.
[2] Luther to Lang, Oct., 1516, *WAB*, I, 65.
[3] Luther to Lang, *WAB*, I, 73; see also *ibid.*, p. 58.

contrasts strongly with the ironical character of some of his letters to Lang: "My life draws nearer and nearer to hell. Day by day I become worse and more wretched." [4]

In general, however, the mood shown in his letters as 1516 inclined to its close is strong and self-reliant and points to a life filled with absorbing duties and a mind clear as to the future. By the early part of September the lectures on Romans were brought to an end and he had set himself to put the earlier course, on the Psalms,[5] in shape for the printer. As regards the world without, he had won for himself a position of influence in academic circles and had begun to attract the favorable attention of Elector Frederick. Before the end of the year this patron of the University sent him his first recorded gift, a cowl of material "too good for a cowl." [6]

Martin's ideas were still undergoing development and on many points he was yet uncertain. He had, however, gained a feeling of conviction on certain important points which broke with the views of his teachers of theology: on justification and its problems of merit, good works, and the power of the human will to do things pleasing to God. The conception of grace was not clear to him in some of its implications. In his mind these ideas still took the form of academic propositions, but his struggle with Biblical and other sources reached deep into his emotional life. We have seen evidence of this in letters of the spring of 1516 which echo his Pauline studies. He criticizes those who seek through good works to stand before God, "decorated, as it were, in their virtues and merits," but adds that he has not yet succeeded in expelling this error from his mind.[7] In the tone of one still unsure of himself, he urges an Augustinian brother at Erfurt to appeal to his former teacher Arnold for relief from temptations, reminding him that all our problems come from the wisdom of our own minds. "This still gives me trouble." [8]

Six months later, after the conclusion of the lectures on Romans, his tone had grown self-confident. Works performed outside of faith, he writes Spalatin, "taste as little of righteousness as sorb-apples of the fig." [9] He was convinced that he had found a system of justification and was prepared to defend it with all vigor. The lectures on Romans show that Martin was a preacher rather than a systematist. His presentation in the *scholia* is emotional and eloquent, never rational and categorical. Nevertheless, he has put

---

[4] Letter from Luther to Georg Maskov, Sept. 26, 1516, *WAB*, I, 60. The date of this fragmentary letter is not beyond question.

[5] Letter from Luther to Spalatin, Sept. 9, 1516, *WAB*, I, 56.

[6] Luther to Spalatin, Dec. 14, 1516, *WAB*, I, 78, l. 11.

[7] Luther to Georg Spenlein, April 8, 1516, *WAB*, I, 35 f.

[8] Luther to Georg Leiffer, April 15, 1516, *WAB*, I, 37.

[9] Luther to Spalatin, Oct. 19, 1516, *WAB*, I, 70, ll. 26 ff.

together the framework of a theological structure which is now all but complete. Because of its crucial importance in Martin's development it is well to review it once more. Despite his attack on the Schoolmen its foundations were laid on the doctrine of the powerful, irrational will of God as he had learned it from the Erfurt nominalists. From his reading in Augustine he had developed his ideas about the fusion of faith and will. Tauler had inspired him with a vision of the suffering soul humbled before God. St. Paul contributed the concept of God as a personification of love and faith. In his theological system, therefore, Martin pictures God as mysterious and terrible but at the same time as a God of love. His majesty surpasses our intelligence; and Martin rails at those who treat God as the shoemaker does his leather.[10] He is also a God of mercy who overwhelms us with His kindness, "for His glory consists in His graciousness towards us." [11] The chief of His mercies is that He does not charge our sins to us. Through contact with Him man experiences a work of healing which is to go on through life. God picks up the contrite soul as the good Samaritan did the sufferer by the wayside. It is through our suffering in the school of temptation that we find Him. The terrible thought of predestination drives us always back to God for safety. It destroys man's presumption, and but for this refuge it would leave him in absolute despair. Sin is the greatest reality in life and the human will can make no headway against it. To believe that it can is heresy, and Martin is convinced that the ruling theologians are tainted with it, for they lead men to trust in natural goodness and forget their own unworthiness. He is still uncertain as regards assurance of salvation, though he discusses it at great length; but he points out that faith and hope are inseparable and that God's promises inspire hope.[12] To this reasoning the German mystics contributed their influence, particularly on the later *scholia* of the Romans lectures. Martin did not absorb the philosophical attitude of German mysticism with its egotistical tendency toward self-analysis and its emotional metaphysics. A certain natural realism kept him from that. He was, however, prepared through his reading in Bernard and Bonaventure and others to accept the seductive pattern of humiliation which Tauler set. The love of God without self-interest, and the resignation of the will, appears in the Romans lectures and persists for several years in Martin's writings.[13]

[10] *WA*, LVI, 185, l. 32.   [11] *Ibid.*, p. 520, l. 20.

[12] *Ibid.*, p. 387, ll. 20 ff. K. Holl, "Luther," in *Gesammelte Aufsätze zur Kirchengeschichte*, I, III, regards the certainty of salvation as clearly implied in the Romans lectures. His arguments are too finespun to hold against the quite definite language of the *scholia*.

[13] This will be pointed out below in the *Sermon von den guten Werken* and particularly in *Von der Freiheit eines Christenmenschen*. In anticipation, attention may be called here to A. V. Müller, *Luther und Tauler*, who regards these ideas of Tauler as the *Leitmotiv* of the latter work. See also Strohl, *L'Épanouissement de la pensée religieuse de Luther*, pp. 120 ff.

This theology did not, obviously, develop all at once in the course of the lectures. For years Martin had struggled with all the ardor and enthusiasm of his nature to master and adopt the rigid abstractions of the Schoolmen. In the late Erfurt and early Wittenberg years Augustine came to his support. In a second stage, which followed the lectures on Psalms, the German mystics brought aid to the African Father. These, then, united with the Pauline conception of justification through faith in God's love to establish the ideological structure we have in the lectures.

With his ideas thus clarified, it is understandable that a feeling of self-confidence gives the tone in the letters to his two most intimate friends, Spalatin and Lang. To both Martin now writes like one who is sure of his ground and ready for an aggressive propaganda. Striking confirmation of this appears soon after the conclusion of the lectures on Romans. In a letter of October 19 to Spalatin he attacks the interpretation of the Pauline attitude in the fifth chapter of Romans which he had found in the notes of Erasmus. It is too historical, and Martin contrasts with it the spiritual interpretation by Augustine. He puts the African Father far ahead of St. Jerome, and he begs Spalatin as a Christian to intervene with Erasmus.[14] In spite of a humanistic bow of modesty in the direction of the highly esteemed scholar, the tone of Martin's letter shows that he is ready to stand up against the highest authorities both in theology and letters. After due consideration, Spalatin passed on Martin's anxieties to Erasmus, wrapping the implied criticisms in a thick covering of obsequious phrases.[15] A few months later Martin makes a more categorical attack on Erasmus in a letter to Lang. Though he recognizes the service of the great scholar in branding the selfish, ignorant clergy, he declares, "The more I read him the less I like him." To know Greek and Latin does not make a Christian: "Jerome with five languages did not come up to Augustine with one." [16]

Outspoken in his letters, Martin was equally ready to express his opinion face to face with students and colleagues. The criticisms of the clerical life which abound in the manuscript of the Romans lectures must have stung, even though charges of formalism, worldliness, laziness, and smug self-satisfaction had been ringing in monastic ears through many generations. Martin's fellow friars may have shrugged off his strictures as the effusions of an eager temperament, but the theologians at Wittenberg and Erfurt resented his attacks on the traditional ideas of the school. There is contemporary evidence, credible even though from a hostile camp, that he had

---

[14] Letter from Luther to Spalatin, Oct. 19, 1516, *WAB*, I, 70.

[15] Allen, *Opus epistolarum Erasmi*, II, 416 ff.

[16] Letter from Luther to Lang, March 1, 1517, *WAB*, I, 90.

left Erfurt with a reputation for obstinacy and a tendency to quarrel in the disputations.[17] The attacks on Aristotle, to be sure, had their foundation in his student days, when Trutvetter and Arnold taught him to distrust the great philosopher as a religious guide; but now a real iconoclasm begins to appear in Martin's attitude toward him. In the lectures on Psalms he had charged him specifically with leading all the theologians to stress man's proud and vain works in preference to grace. "Does not the disposition, metaphysics, and philosophy of Aristotle lead astray our theologians, following after human tradition?" he asks his readers when dwelling on the same topic in his lectures on Romans.[18] Aristotle is the first scholastic ideal to be crushed. "I am panting for nothing so much," he writes to Lang toward the end of the winter, "as to put that mountebank to public shame"; and he declares that now he is occupied with a little commentary on the first book of Aristotle's *Physics* [19] which will expose the cunning deceitfulness of its author.

Soon after the conclusion of the lectures on Romans he took advantage of an academic disputation to confront the theological faculty with his ideas. One of his students, Bartholomäus Bernhardi of Feldkirchen in Württemberg, was to be promoted to *sententiarius* on September 25,[20] and the usual public disputation was staged for that occasion. Here the candidate defended a number of theses on the "powers and will of man without grace," [21] a proposition inspired by Martin and founded on the idea which had now taken possession of him, that man is absolutely unable to obey the commands of God through his own effort. The theses show clearly the stamp of the professor's thinking in their attack on the ruling scholastic theology, which they brand as tainted with Pelagian heresy. Martin presided at the disputation and wrote gleefully to Lang soon afterward that the Erfurt Gabrielists would probably be astounded at the proposition, since those in Wittenberg were mightily astounded.[22] He has done this in order to stop the mouths of those who are chattering against his lectures. Some of the Wittenberg faculty, including the dean, Carlstadt, were indeed deeply offended that Martin had presumed to declare that Augustine was not the author of the work *On True and False Repentance* traditionally ascribed to him.[23]

---

[17] "Die Chronik des Johan Oldecop," *Bibliothek des Litterarischen Vereins in Stuttgart*, CXC, 28: "Martinus wolde do rede in allen disputationen recht hebben und sankede gern."

[18] *WA*, LVI, 349, l. 22.

[19] Letter from Luther to Lang, Feb. 8, 1517, *WAB*, I, 88.

[20] Förstemann, *Liber decanorum*, p. 19. [21] The theses are listed in *WA*, I, 145.

[22] Letter from Luther to Lang, mid-October, 1516, *WAB*, I, 65, ll. 18 ff.

[23] Martin's opinion is said to have been derived from the humanist Trithemius. It seems

In the midst of these trials and triumphs he begins on October 27 a new course of lectures, on the Epistle of St. Paul to the Galatians.[24] The choice was a natural progression in the exegetical series. Through the studies for the lectures on Romans he felt that he had a grip on a new theology, and he must have found a personal experience in Paul's message to the converts at Galatea, harassed by sticklers for observance of the Hebrew ritual. "The Epistle to the Galatians is my epistle, to which I have plighted my troth. It is my Käthe von Bora," he declared fifteen years later when he came to lecture on the subject again.[25] When the course opened, the plague hung over the city and two hundred students fled.[26] This may have caused interruptions, but in any event he was through by the end of the winter semester, March 13, 1517.[27] This was fast work, even with a brief Epistle. His notes must have been made in haste and lacked the finished form which marked his preparation for the lectures on Romans. More than two years later, in September, 1519, Martin published the lectures on Galatians in a strongly revised form.[28] His original manuscript for the course has disappeared; what we have is a transcript written down from the professor's dictation by an intelligent though not always attentive student.[29] After an earlier edition by Hans von Schubert, the manuscript was finally incorporated into the Weimar edition in 1939.[30]

In his second course on St. Paul the lecturer prepared the way for his students in his accustomed manner by furnishing them with the printed Latin text on which to enter the interlinear and marginal glossaries.[31]

---

now to be the view of competent critics generally. See Migne, *Patrologiae cursus completus*, XL. IIII ff. and 1113 ff.

[24] Letter from Luther to Lang, Oct. 26, *WAB*, I, 73.

[25] TR, I, No. 146 (Dec. 14, 1531–Jan. 22, 1532).

[26] W. Friedensburg, "Urkundenbuch der Universität Wittenberg," I (1502–1611), *Geschichtsquellen der Provinz Sachsen*, N.F. III (1926), p. 82.

[27] *WA*, LVII, v. See also Von Schubert, "Luthers Vorlesung über den Galaterbrief," *Abhandlungen der Heidelberger Akademie der Wiss., phil.-hist. Klasse*, V (1918), vi.

[28] *In epistolam Pauli ad Galatos M. Lutheri commentarius* (1519), *WA*, II, 443 ff. Cf. *WAB*, I, 506, l. 20. In August, 1523, he issued a second edition, further revised in content and form, see *WA*, II, 437. For the later course (1531) we have the notes of Georg Rörer, published as a commentary under Luther's supervision in 1535. *WA*, XL, 1 ff. See also G. Schulze, "Die Vorlesung Luthers über den Galaterbrief von 1531 und der gedruckte Kommentar von 1535," *ThStKr*, XCVIII–XCIX (1926), 18 ff.

[29] K. A. Meissinger in the preface to the edition in *WA*, LVII, of *Die erste Vorlesung über den Galateerbrief, 1516–17* rehearses some hypotheses regarding the student scribe (p. vii) and has much to say in criticism of his work. All defects in the transcription are, however, insignificant in comparison with the achievement of this young theologian, to whom Luther owes many things. Among these obligations, his beautiful handwriting should not be overlooked.

[30] See the three preceding notes. For the analysis of the MS, Meissinger made full use of Von Schubert's notes.

[31] The edition of the Vulgate which he used has not been determined. In any case it was

Viewed through the imperfect glass of the copy, the Galatians lectures show that Martin continued to tread the well-worn path of medieval exegesis. As in his earlier lectures, we have a brief interlinear analysis, a broader treatment of the thought on the margin of the Biblical text, and then a presentation of his ideas at some length in *scholia*. How much of the emotional style of the *scholia* was caught by the flying pen of the scribe we do not know, but he has given us enough to show that Martin still followed the late medieval method of interpretation with its series of propositions, objections, answers, summaries, and corollaries. Paul's reference to the allegory contained in the Old Testament story of the sons of Abraham (Gal. 4.24 ff.) opens the way to an application of the fourfold pattern of scholastic exegesis in order to illustrate Augustine's contrast between letter and spirit.[32] Well-tried helps to the understanding, such as the *Glossa ordinaria* and Faber, were evidently at hand. He calls in Jerome to help explain points in the text and frequently cites him and others of the Fathers for the interpretation of Paul's meaning, although he does not hesitate to differ with Jerome in his understanding of the Pauline idea.[33] Other early Christian sources appear as witnesses. One is the Pseudo-Ambrose, another is Eusebius of Caesarea, whose *History of the Church* was to become a support two years later in the attack on the papacy. Although it is plain from the transcript that the scholastic method has not been altogether rejected, even though it has lost something of its reality, the conscientious textual studies of the humanists have risen well above the horizon. Erasmus's Greek text, now a well-thumbed volume, moves to the fore in the struggle for an understanding of Paul.[34] Interesting is the frequent pairing of Jerome with Augustine. While the spiritual character of the latter's interpretation evidently appeals strongly to Martin, he occasionally declares his preference for the interpretation of the great scholar of the early Church,[35] and notes on the margin of the Vulgate print, "In this whole Epistle Jerome pleases me more than Augustine." [36] This is indeed surprising in view of his dislike for Jerome's historical attitude toward grace, referred to in the letter to Spalatin of the preceding October. When he concentrated his attention on the text,

---

not the Basel print of 1509 on which the Romans text was based. See Von Schubert, "Luthers Vorlesung," p. x, and n. 1.

[32] *WA*, LVII, 95, ll. 23 ff.

[33] *Ibid.*, p. 16, ll. 16 ff., and 79, ll. 4 ff., are cases in point.

[34] Erasmus is mentioned only once, but Von Schubert finds his trail throughout. See his index, "Luthers Vorlesung," p. 72.

[35] "Argumentum Jeronimi forcius Augustino," *WA*, LVII, 71, l. 5; see also p. 64, ll. 26 f.

[36] *WA*, LVII, 29, l. 15.

respect for the penetrating vision of the great Biblical scholar overcame his suspicion that Jerome's interpretation exalted the letter of Scripture above its spirit.

With the lectures on Galatians, then, Martin falls into line with humanistic scholarship. Here at last he renders tribute to the great masters who had unlocked the sources for a full comprehension of Holy Writ. Jerome and Erasmus are the pillars on which he rests his understanding of Paul's words. Nevertheless, it is Augustine who plumbs their spiritual depth, and Augustine's interpretations run throughout the *scholia*. Scriptural quotations, literal or paraphrased, fill the student's transcript, and are interwoven with the lecturer's remarks. In a method that had become habitual Martin pours them upon his students in an unceasing stream, from Genesis to St. Paul. A bold confidence enforces his condemnation of good works as a means of salvation. It is no longer the tone of the seeker that we hear, but of one who feels that he has arrived. The conception of freedom from the law which Paul set forth to instruct and comfort the little community at Galatea has developed into a triumphant thesis of faith as the liberator. "For sins are destroyed by faith," the scribe notes on the margin.[37] "Therefore faith is the universal justification," he summarizes in the *scholia*.[38] Sin is reduced to unbelief; belief in Christ is our freedom and assurance. Mystic tones from the *German Theology* echo repeatedly in the transcript. "To know God, or rather to be known by God": in this simple phrase lies a profound theology. "For all our works are rather our sufferings and the works of God." [39]

Nearly three years later, as we have seen, the lectures on Galatians appeared in print under Martin's name in the revised form of a commentary.[40] Shorn of all direct personal appeal to the hearer, they are expanded into a polemical tractate, "salted" [41] with the controversial experience of many battles. They present the matured results of his development of the theology of faith following the lectures on Romans and the full sum of his indebtedness to humanism.[42] The *Commentary on Galatians* was greeted by his colleagues and followers as the definitive formulation of the new theology and has remained a foundation stone of the Lutheran creed. How far other Wittenberg theologians, notably Carlstadt and Amsdorf, contributed to this new program remains doubtful, but the stylistic character of the *Commentary* suggests the gifted hand of one of the group, Philip Melanchthon.

[37] *Ibid.*, p. 18, l. 25.   [38] *Ibid.*, p. 70, l. 5.
[39] *Ibid.*, pp. 89 f., ll. 21 ff.   [40] See n. 28 above.
[41] See letter from Luther to Spalatin, Sept. 22, 1519, *WAB*, I, 508, l. 10.
[42] Meissinger, *WA*, LVII, xi ff., gives a systematic textual comparison of the two forms, lectures and commentary.

This brilliant great-nephew of Reuchlin came to Wittenberg in 1518 and brought a training that fitted him well to lend the ideas of the older colleague a Latin form befitting what was to become a theological classic for the Lutheran world.[43] Whoever framed or revised this later work, however, it gives no such picture of Martin's throbbing soul as was caught by the unknown student to whom we owe the transcript from the troubled autumn and winter of 1516–17.

How fully Martin had absorbed Tauler appears in a series of sermons which he delivered in the parish church of St. Mary's in the second half of 1516 and the first two months of the following year. Their preparation shared the fall and winter with that of the Galatians lectures. Following the custom of the time, he preached a double sermon at the morning service, dealing in the first half with the Gospel for the day, in the second part developing a series on the Ten Commandments.[44] The discourses on the Gospel were, like Martin's other early sermons, directed at the Wittenberg community, though, as we have seen, they have come down to us only in Latin transcripts.[45] Nevertheless, the German in which they were spoken breaks through the learned language again and again.

These discourses reflect something of the trend toward the mystical that we have found in the lectures on Romans. Suffering is considered a necessary part of the education of the Christian. Denunciation of pride and an appeal for genuine humility of soul take on a richer coloring than the professorial language of two years earlier in the lectures on Psalms. Real humility drives us to "recede" from God.[46] Man knows himself to be nothing and abandons to God all that is good. Without wealth, help, or power is the soul "that seeks God alone, so that it looks upon whatever it says, hears, and feels without God as suffering and misery," [47] and does this also in times of prosperity. Martin borrows and expands well-worn similes from the German mystics to illustrate the helplessness and passivity of the soul. Christ is the hen that spreads her protecting wings.[48] The soul, like a well-broken horse, submits itself to be ridden whithersoever God directs it and goes ahead through water, mud, storm, and snow. It is acted upon rather than acting.[49]

[43] *WA*, LVII, xvi ff.

[44] The series on the Decalogue began at the end of June, 1516 and continued to February 24, 1517. A series on the Lord's Prayer followed through Lent, 1517. See Kiessling, *Early Sermons of Luther*, pp. 78 ff.

[45] For the sources of our knowledge of the early sermons, see above, pp. 186 f., n. 34.

[46] Sermon of July 27, 1516, *WA*, I, 63, ll. 23 ff.

[47] Sermon of Aug. 10, 1516, *WA*, I, 74, ll. 18 ff.

[48] Sermon of Dec. 27, 1516, *WA*, I, 117, ll. 4 ff.

[49] Sermon of Aug. 3, 1516, *WA*, I, 73, ll. 17 ff.

Beside this destruction of self stands faith. The preacher has bitter words for the belief that justification comes from works. This is a "perversity" for which Aristotle is to blame.[50] The conception of the nonimputation of sin is the ground tone in many sermons of this fall and winter.[51] In his eagerness to defend the idea of perfect faith the preacher occasionally unfolds abstract concepts that must have flown far over the heads of the burghers in his audience. He erects an ascending scale on whose topmost rung faith dwells—"so absolute a sphere" that it believes more than could possibly be shown by any signs or wonders and receives all things as flowing from God alone: "and by its very rotundity refers everything to Him, ready to do whatever He wishes in all things with all things." [52] The German mystics had infected Martin not only with their ideals of humility and passive yearning, but also with their theosophy. Underlying these abstractions, however, there is a basis of realism such as we noted in the lectures on Romans, and this must have been even more apparent in Martin's delivery than in the transcript of our academic scribe. The plague then raging in Wittenberg gives vigor to the exposition of the Christian's cross of suffering. Here justification means the surrender of everything. When all has gone from us, when every emotion that haunts the soul has been expelled, then God lifts us up.[53] At this point Martin cites a verse which was to become a slogan of the Reformation period: "The righteous shall live by faith" (Romans 1.17). He who has faith must hang on the cross so that he may nowhere touch the earth for support.[54]

Whatever difficulty his abstract analysis may have caused the unlearned among his hearers, the parish church was crowded with those who came to listen to the now distinguished professor as he set forth his convictions on the uselessness of good works and the redeeming power of faith. They certainly heard many things which were unusual in contemporary sermons. One concerned the veneration of saints. Early in the gospel sermons Martin raised a warning finger at those who cultivated the saints as patrons of their own pride and avarice, and in a discourse on the feast of St. Bartholomew he ridiculed certain stories of apostolic miracles and scoffed at the legend that depicts Bartholomew in the robes of a king: "I am astonished that he is not described as wearing yellow trousers and spurs." [55] A few weeks later

[50] Sermon of Jan. 1, 1517, *WA*, I, 119, ll. 30 f.
[51] For a characteristic passage see sermon of Sept. 21, 1516, *WA*, I, 85 f.
[52] Sermon of Oct. 5, 1516, *WA*, I, 88, ll. 23 ff.
[53] Sermon on St. Andrew's Day, Nov. 30, 1516, *WA*, I, 101 ff. The sermon winds an allegory in medieval style about the boat and the net which St. Andrew left to follow Christ.
[54] *Ibid.*, p. 102, ll. 39 f.: "Justus enim ex fide vivit, credere autem non potest nisi nihil videat aut sentiat aut tangat intus et extus."
[55] *WA*, I, 80, ll. 10 f. See letter to Spalatin, probably Aug. 24, 1516, *WAB*, I, 50.

he formulates his ideas on the subject in one of the Latin theses for the Bernhardi disputation, declaring that it is a superstition to assign aid in this or that matter to the saints, since all good things are possible through Christ.[56] It is probable that he had treated the question of prayers to the saints in sermons on the First Commandment during the summer, but we have only a revised version of 1518, and not the form in which they were delivered.[57] In any event, the subject was one of those uppermost in his mind during the fall and winter and came to spirited expression in a sermon on the day of St. Barbara, December 4.[58] In this discourse on the legendary martyr, whom artists delighted in portraying as a virgin of surpassing beauty, Martin concedes that it is proper to pray to individual saints for particular benefits, but warns against the peril to the soul in turning to them only for physical and temporal welfare. Some people ascribe to the holy saints a power that is in the hands of God alone, and thus actually worship an idol or a devil as did the ancients with Neptune, Hercules, or Aesculapius. He repeats this view in his correspondence. Martin's stand on the cult of saints in the Bernhardi thesis and possibly also that in his sermons on the subject had reached the attentive Spalatin, and he asked for a fuller explanation. In his reply, on the last day of 1516,[59] the professor hastens to deny that he shared the Bohemian heresy which held prayers to the saints for material things to be a superstition. He meant to condemn only those who seek needs of the body exclusively and neglect those pertaining to the soul's salvation. Though Martin has obviously not yet clarified his position in his own mind, it is evident that these ideas fall into line with a conception that runs through all his public and private utterances after the lectures on Romans, the necessity for a respiritualization of religion in thought and practice. They touch a chord of reform that sounded nearly a decade before in a work well known to the Wittenberg preacher, Erasmus's *Enchiridion,* a manual for the Christian soldier.

As we have seen, the Gospel discourse was followed regularly by a second

---

[56] *WA*, I, 150, ll. 4 ff.

[57] *Decem praecepta Wittenbergensi praedicata populo,* especially *WA*, I, 411–26.

[58] *WA*, IV, 639 ff. The editor sets the date tentatively at Dec. 4, 1517. E. Hirsch, "Randglossen zu Luthertexten," *ThStKr*, XCI (1918), 118, note, argues for 1515. So far as we can follow the development of Luther's ideas on the subject, the contents of the sermon point to 1516. See the following note.

[59] *WAB*, I, 82 f. The date of the letter is not beyond question. Enders, *Luthers Briefwechsel,* I, 135, sets it a year later, Dec. 31, 1517, but the argument of Clemen, editor of *WAB*, I, for 1516 seems conclusive. It is to be noted, however, that the expression "pro corporalibus," which Luther uses here, quoting Spalatin's question, does not occur in Bernhardi's thesis, but points to a knowledge on Spalatin's part of the references to prayers to the saints in Martin's Gospel sermons.

sermon dealing with the Ten Commandments. This series no longer exists in contemporary form,[60] and for our knowledge of Martin's exposition we are dependent on a Latin tractate which he published two years later.[61] If the original transcript of the sermons by his hearers or the German version which he prepared soon after delivery were at hand, we would know how far controversial questions such as the condemnation of the extravagant cult of the saints had already taken form in Martin's mind in 1516, and how far the treatise published in 1518 reflects the emotional reactions to excesses in religious life that swell to such proportions in the intervening months.[62]

For a series of sermons on the Lord's Prayer which followed that on the Decalogue, we have, fortunately, contemporary evidence. These were delivered during Lent in 1517 and taken down by a hearer, Johann Agricola, who published them in the following year as *An Explanation and Interpretation of the Lord's Prayer by Dr. Martin Luther*.[63] A brief Latin sketch on this subject, probably dating from 1516 and not published until 1929,[64] gives the keynote of these sermons. It echoes a theme which was heard from Martin so often in that year, mystic submission to God's will and the necessity for placing all our hopes for salvation in His hands. Over against this spiritual interpretation he sets the attitude of those "perverse persons"

[60] The Latin manuscript containing the sermons on the Decalogue in transcript by an auditor seems to have been in Löscher's possession early in the eighteenth century, but it has now vanished. See *WA*, I, 394.

[61] *Decem praecepta Wittenbergensi praedicata populo, WA,* I, 398 ff.

[62] The sermons on the Decalogue involve one of the knotty questions in Lutheran chronology. Connections between these and the Gospel series are evident, and a calendar for the delivery of the Decalogue group has been set up by Vogelsang, "Zur Datierung der frühsten Lutherpredigten," *ZKG*, L, 3. Folge, I (1931), 138 ff. Martin sent them in Latin and German versions to Lang on September 4, 1517 (*WAB*, I, 103), whether in manuscript or in print we do not know, but probably in the former. Most Lutheran students seem to assume that the ideas expressed in the print of 1518 were essentially the same as those heard by the congregations in St. Mary's Church in the summer and fall of 1516, but this seems to me very unlikely, particularly with regard to Martin's attitude toward prayer to the saints, which is treated at length in connection with the First Commandment, *WA*, I, 412 ff. That he was thinking on this subject has been shown in our discussion, and Clemen, the editor of *WAB*, I, has pointed out parallels in the letter to Spalatin of December 31, 1516, with the *Decem praecepta*. See *WAB*, I, 81 f. Even these, and acceptance of the same editor's dating of this letter as 1516, do not justify the conclusion that Martin's ideas on this topic had developed so early into the polemical form they show in the published work. On the other hand he may have been stimulated to a clear and extensive formulation of his views by Spalatin's question and perhaps by similar questioning from other members of the Wittenberg circle. It is worthy of note that he does not go into misusages connected with the saints in either the course on Romans or that on Galatians, although both offered suggestive material for a discussion of this subject.

[63] *Auslegung und Deutung des heiligen Vaterunsers* (Leipzig, 1518). *WA*, IX, 123 ff. For bibliography, see *WA*, II, 75 ff.

[64] O. Clemen, "Das lateinische Original von Luthers 'Vater-Unser vorwärts und rückwärts' vom Jahre 1516," *ZKG*, XLVIII, N.F. XI (1929), 198 ff.

who pray without heart and seek only satisfaction of self. Sometime later this brief Latin discourse was put into German and found its way to an Augsburg press. Here it was issued with the label, "Not for scholars." [65] In this earnest little tract Martin visualizes with all the concreteness of the early woodcut the positions of those who repeat the Lord's Prayer. Those who spiritualize the prayer say it "in front"; those who repeat the words without uplifting of the heart, say it "behind them."

Young Agricola, who was later to become a leader in the revolt against the Church, confesses with due modesty that he has "elucubrated" the sermons. He need not have been ashamed of his performance. He exerted himself to bring the ideas of the preacher into a scholastic pattern of petitions, deductions, and conclusions, but his simple German reflects Martin's strong feeling throughout. Here again are the ideas that had agitated the professor's mind in the months preceding. In the language of Tauler, he pictures the pious soul as a wanderer in strange lands; "the deeper human nature is plunged into shame, the greater its consolation." [66] "The kind little lamb, Christ," hangs on the cross, inviting the sinner to Him. The contrast between the Crucified One and the erring soul flows in a stream of adjectives which exhaust the list of virtues and vices.[67] Augustine again confronts Aristotle. "They have dreamed it out of Aristotle," those learned teachers of theology,[68] with their doctrine of voluntary inclination of the sinner to God.[69] This German "explanation and interpretation" found eager readers: five editions of Agricola's pamphlet appeared in 1518 and 1519. It did not please Martin, however; and before the end of 1518 he set himself to prepare a new version. Working on it amid a whirl of interruptions, he was not able to bring it out until April of the following year. When his *Interpretation of the Lord's Prayer for Simple Laymen* finally appeared, the mystical tone had faded out before a bitterly polemical one.

"Not for scholars!" This was the unexpressed motto of another work which occupied Martin during the Lenten months, an interpretation of the seven penitential Psalms. It was now almost two years since he had brought to a conclusion his long struggle for a scholarly interpretation of Psalms. Now he devotes himself to a group of these which breathe a spirit of humility and sacrifice of self. The seven—Psalms 6, 32, 38, 51, 102, 130, and

---

[65] *Eine kurze und gute Auslegung des heiligen Vaterunsers vor sich und hinter sich.* Text in *WA*, VI, 21 f.; bibliography, *WA*, II, 78. Dated 1516 by Clemen (see note 64, above); 1520 seems more probable.

[66] *WA*, IX, 138, ll. 19 f.   [67] *Ibid.*, p. 149, ll. 8 ff.

[68] *Ibid.*, p. 140, l. 2.   [69] "Dispositiones de congruo." *Ibid.*, p. 148, l. 24.

143—are wont to be a part of the Good Friday office of the Church.[70]
Martin prefaces his interpretation with a free translation of each Psalm in
the informal rhythm of the original Hebrew.[71] Apparently he had some
misgivings regarding both translation and explanations, and the criticisms of
Lang, to whom he sent the manuscript, seem not to have been favorable.
It was Martin's first essay at connected translation from the Bible; and despite whatever pedantic objections may have been made, he persisted in
publication: "If they please no one else, they please me." [72] Two months
later, when they had become known through Staupitz to the humanistic
critics at Nuremberg, the author makes apologies, though not without
sarcasm. "They were not put out for the Nurembergers; that is to say, highly
sensitive and sharp-nosed souls," he writes to Dr. Christoph Scheurl, a cultured lawyer of the southern German center of good letters, "but for rude
Saxons, the kind you know, for whom Christian erudition can never be
chewed fine enough"; and he begs this scholarly friend to keep the book
out of sight of the learned.[73]

In his preface Martin confesses that, beside Father Jerome, Reuchlin's
translation had helped him much in rendering the Hebrew text. To the
modern reader, his version seems to approach well the pathos of the Psalmist. His German is reminiscent of the eloquent pleading in the King James
Bible and has much of the sonorousness of the Vulgate. His interpretation
follows the text phrase by phrase and drives the lesson of penitence into
the reader with deep emotion. Here is no mere analysis, but a series of
exhortations to those prostrate in sin: the gates of eternal damnation lie
at the end of the path of sin, but God's love beckons the repentant soul to
the gates of Paradise. Underlying his thought is the traditional dualism of
the medieval preacher, the emptiness of all the joys of flesh and blood. To
the contrast of body and spirit comes another which has now taken full
possession of him: on the one hand the futility of the human will and the
helplessness of the soul that trusts in works, and on the other the firm
assurance of him who persists in hope and the belief that God will not withhold His grace. In his exegesis of these Psalms, particularly of Psalm 132,
there echoes something of the mystic passivity that he had absorbed from
Tauler and the *German Theology*, something of the helpful grace which

---

[70] The numbering follows Luther's and that of the English Bible. The Douay version numbers one less after Psalm 6. See *Catholic Encyclopedia*, XII, 543.

[71] *Die sieben Busspsalmen mit deutscher Auslegung nach dem schriftlichen Sinne. WA*, I,
158 ff.

[72] Letter from Luther to Lang, March 1, 1517, *WAB*, I, 90, l. 13.

[73] Letter from Luther to Scheurl, May 6, 1517, *WAB*, I, 93 f.

has no name and can bear none, that comes to the soul which surrenders it-self helpless to the will of God.[74] He clothes his ideas in a style of trans-parent simplicity and drops rarely into formulas of scholasticism. His con-demnation of self-righteousness and good works never descends to angry polemics, nor does it disturb the deeply devotional tone of the work.

"The fact is, I do not want you to have them. They have not been pub-lished for refined minds, but for the rudest sort." So Martin excuses himself for not sending the learned Spalatin a copy of his Seven Penitential Psalms.[75] Such "thrice-chewed food" was not for a tender humanistic palate, as he had also said to Scheurl, but for those who were weak and ignorant of the testimony of the Scriptures. The little book marks a trend of major influence in his development, for with the exception of the brief introduction to the German Theology, it was the first of his works to go into print. For the moment the Latin-trained monk was somewhat embarrassed by his own boldness in putting his ideas into simple language and his native speech, but the impulse to interpret his new convictions on faith and grace for such an audience as that which gathered before him in St. Mary's Church was to grow powerfully.

The Wittenberg colleagues were beginning to fall into line with his views. Dr. Carlstadt,[76] the most active spirit among them and a learned follower of the scholastic theology, had watched the growth of Martin's ideas with discontent and resentment. According to a somewhat apocryphal source, he told the junior colleague to his face on one occasion that he was talking heresy.[77] During the winter, however, Carlstadt took to a diligent reading of Augustine and this brought on an emotional crisis from which he emerged to find himself in line with Martin's interpretation of justifica-tion.[78] In April he made an open avowal of his new position by posting 152 Latin theses setting forth ideas on law and grace, sin and predestination in full accord with those he found in Augustine, and denouncing the mingling of Aristotle and theology.[79] Martin read the theses with delight and for-warded them to his Nuremberg friend, Scheurl, terminating a fine outburst

---

[74] WA, I, 208, ll. 15 ff.

[75] Letter from Luther to Spalatin, early in May, WAB, I, 96, ll. 13 ff.

[76] See Barge, Andreas Bodenstein, I, 69 ff.; also TR, IV, No. 4187 (Dec. 12, 1538). For a summary of Carlstadt's early relations to the new theology at Wittenberg, see Bauer, Die Witten-berger Universitätstheologie, pp. 45 ff., which does more justice to Martin's colleague than most Lutheran writers have done.

[77] The story comes from Veit Dietrich. Enders, Luthers Briefwechsel, I, 98, n. 7.

[78] See Carlstadt's confession in the introduction to his incomplete edition of Augustine's De spiritu et litera. Barge, Andreas Bodenstein, II, 533 ff. See also ibid., I, 90 f.

[79] Ibid., I, 75 ff.

of humanistic pyrotechnics with "Blessed be God, who maketh light to shine anew out of darkness." [80] A few days later he wrote to Lang: "Our theology and Saint Augustine prosper and rule at our university by the help of God; Aristotle is going down little by little, headed for final destruction." He added that whoever hoped for hearers at Wittenberg would have to lecture on the new theology.[81]

In his enthusiasm for propagating his theories Martin did not halt at the gates of the little city on the Elbe, but sought to infect his old teachers at his alma mater. Early in February, he had sent Lang a letter for Trutvetter, "filled with blasphemies and maledictions against Aristotle, Porphyry, and the commentators on Peter Lombard, who swallow everything without a squeak." [82] He is eager to have Lang "smell out" Trutvetter. Apparently the latter did not disclose his ideas; but a year later Martin discovered that his old teacher, to whom he owed his first suggestions of the unreliability of Aristotle in matters of Christian theology, would not follow him on the path of revolt.

There were signs that the lectures and sermons of the past year were carrying Martin's reputation into other parts of Germany. Early in January, he received a letter from Christoph Scheurl, whose correspondence with Martin was mentioned above. One of the leading humanists of Nuremberg, Scheurl asks formally for his friendship on the basis of their mutual admiration for Staupitz.[83] Some weeks later Martin accepted the proffered hand with cordiality. Modestly waving aside Scheurl's compliments, he proceeds to put himself in the right position with his new friend by an earnest homily on Christian humility, interspersed with some phrases of compliment and many citations from the Bible.[84] The establishment of this connection with the Nuremberg jurist opened the door to South German humanism.[85] Scheurl was just the man for that, as he had a wide and ever expanding acquaintance with the scholarly world. Born of a well-to-do merchant family in Nuremberg with distinguished patrician connections, he had studied at

---

[80] Letter from Luther to Scheurl, May 6, 1517, *WAB*, I, 94, l. 26.

[81] Letter from Luther to Lang, May 18, 1517, *WAB*, I, 99.

[82] Letter from Luther to Lang, Feb. 8, 1517, *WAB*, I, 88. Martin's letter to Trutvetter has not been preserved.

[83] Letter from Scheurl to Luther, Jan. 2, 1517, *WAB*, I, 84 f.; Scheurl, *Briefbuch*, II, 1 f.

[84] Letter from Luther to Scheurl, Jan. 27, 1517, *WAB*, I, 86 f.

[85] The most informative work on Scheurl is that of Wilhelm Graf, "Dr. Christoph Scheurl von Nürnberg," *Beiträge zur Kulturgeschichte des Mittelalters und der Renaissance*, XLIII (1930). The Scheurl archives in Nuremberg contain unpublished material, however, which still awaits careful study. It includes an autobiography, an extract from which was published by G. Bauch in "Christoph Scheurl in Wittenberg," *Neue Mitteilungen aus dem Gebiet historisch-antiquarischer Forschung*, XXI, 1 (1901), 33 ff.

Heidelberg and spent seven years in Italy, chiefly as a student of law at Bologna. Here his colleagues included many young Germans who were later to become legal officials in cities and territorial states; and he also made friends with a considerable circle of Italian humanists. He was called to Wittenberg in 1507, where he served as lecturer and dean of the law faculty, and did much to further the progress of the young institution. After five years at the Saxon university, he returned to his native city as legal adviser to the council, and speedily came to play an influential rôle in the many activities of this powerful body, both within the city and in other parts of Germany. In Nuremberg he took his place in the group of patrician officials, artists, and scholars who made up the cultural life of the city in the earlier decades of the century. Willibald Pirckheimer and his sister Charitas, abbess of the nunnery of St. Claire; Albrecht Dürer, whom Scheurl had known since his student days in Italy; Lazarus Spengler, and Johann Cochlaeus were among his intimates. In addition he found time for a wide correspondence with humanistic acquaintances from Cologne to Vienna, and like Erasmus, he saw to it that his letters were preserved for posterity.[86] Unlike Erasmus and certain other humanists whose interests lay in the exploration of early Christian sources and Church reform, Scheurl turned to theology and devotional literature in such time as he was not engaged in legal and diplomatic duties. He corresponded zealously with theologians, including Trutvetter. He continued to take a keen interest in the Wittenberg university and kept well informed as to what was going on there. In Nuremberg he renewed acquaintanceship with Staupitz, and gathered his friends about the inspiring and lovable personality of the general vicar whenever Staupitz visited the city. The little group, which included a number of distinguished men, developed into a kind of "sodality," such as the German humanists delighted in forming, and Scheurl regarded himself as the leader of this group of patricians [87] and clerics. He translated into German [88] Staupitz's sermons on predestination and was untiring in his efforts to bring the general vicar into contact with the secular and religious personalities of the city.

It was probably Staupitz who brought the first news of the startling development of Martin to Scheurl's attention, and the latter sought quickly

---

[86] The *Briefbuch*, in two volumes, contains 282 letters, only a part of those in the Scheurl archives, and only letters written by Scheurl. In the years 1510–18 there are twenty-nine letters to Trutvetter.

[87] See Scheurl, *Briefbuch*, esp. II, 35 f.

[88] They were published in Latin and German in January and February, 1517. E. Wolf, "Staupitz und Luther," *Quellen und Forschungen zur Reformationsgeschichte*, IX (1927), 13.

to establish relations with so promising a theologian. He was an active gatherer of personal and political news items, and he found that these were always welcomed by those immured in the cloister; in return he sought persistently for advice on religious matters. He was well suited by nature to become a friend and an intermediator among friends. Compliments in humanistic style flowed readily from his pen. After the first exchange with Martin, the new friendship grew rapidly. Early in May, Martin sent him Carlstadt's theses [89] and at the end of the summer Scheurl visited Wittenberg. On this occasion, Martin invited Spalatin to bring the visitor to dinner at the monastery and also some wine for the party.[90] After Scheurl's departure Martin wrote him a letter studded with humanistic clichés, enclosing a set of theses which he had just prepared and which were to be forwarded to the famous South German theologian, Dr. Johann Eck. Evidently Martin was pleased at the opening of a window toward the south, and his letter closes with warm greetings from Wittenberg colleagues, including a mutual friend, the local barber! [91]

In the meantime the summer semester had brought a new course of lectures in the Biblical series. This was to be the last of Martin's exegetics according to the traditional scholastic pattern and a further step on the path of his new theology. The lectures on Hebrews probably opened just after the Easter holiday and extended through the summer and winter to Easter, 1518.[92] Now, as the leading personality in the faculty, he could claim the most coveted hour on the program, twelve o'clock, following the early cloister dinner. At this hour, two days in the week, students crowded the lecture room to hear his exposition of the third Epistle in his series. It is to one or more than one of these eager hearers that we owe our knowledge of the course, for Martin's original notes have been lost and a Vatican manuscript, written a generation later and the main source for study, is a transcript by one of his youngest disciples, Johann Aurifaber, from notes that had been made by hearers. After reposing nearly four centuries in the libraries of Germany and Italy, the lectures were finally published twice in the summer of 1929.[93] Although the text comes to us through a second or perhaps

---

[89] Letter from Luther to Scheurl, May 6, 1517, *WAB*, I, 93 f.

[90] End of August. *WAB*, I, 103.

[91] Letter from Luther to Scheurl, Sept. 11, 1517, *WAB*, I, 105 f.

[92] Hans von Schubert and Karl Meissinger, "Zu Luthers Vorlesungstätigkeit," *Sitzungsberichte der Heidelberger Akademie der Wissenschaften, phil.-hist. Klasse*, IX (1920), 9 ff., 21. See also *WA*, LVII, p. xix. Böhmer, *Der junge Luther*, p. 121, figures the dates as March 16, 1517, to March 27, 1518. Hirsch and Rückert, *Luthers Vorlesung über den Hebräerbrief*, pp. xxv f., would date the course March 16, 1517, to March 26, 1518. See n. 93 below.

[93] After the discovery of the manuscript, Palatina 1826, in the Vatican in 1899 by Johannes

a third hand, it was carefully put together and undoubtedly represents the lectures as Martin delivered them, so far as the hurrying pens of the students could put them on paper. Manifest errors are not lacking, to be sure, and obvious gaps exist in the transcript, but these are defects that are characteristic of student notes and do not impair the general picture.

With these lectures Martin laid his course for the last time along the path of scholastic interpretation. Once again he had the Bible text reprinted from the Vulgate and put this before his hearers.[94] Once more he divides his interpretations and exposition into glossary and *scholia,* although he shows an increasing tendency to merge the two and thus approach the type of free commentary which became his habit later on.[95] The commentaries of Lyra, Paul of Burgos, and others are still at hand. Nevertheless, scholastic traditions drop into the background in comparison with the apparatus of humanism, and emphasis on humanistic authority marks this course of lectures even more than those of the preceding winter on Galatians. Erasmus's Greek text as well as his Latin translation and Faber's rendering are at his elbow. The Epistle to the Hebrews, with its numerous citations from the Old Testament, opened the way to philological exercises that testify to the intensity of Martin's studies in Greek and Hebrew. The transcription indicates that he now wrote Greek characters with facility and was not afraid of trying his hand at Hebrew, including the diacritical symbols.[96] He makes his own translations from both these languages, argues freely with Erasmus and Faber, and occasionally pushes both aside to give an individual interpretation.[97] He makes many linguistic suggestions of his own and plays with bold etymologies. Beside Jerome, another patristic author comes to

---

Ficker (see *Anfänge reformatorischer Bibelauslegung,* I, viii ff. and xxv ff.), he published extracts from it in 1918 in "Luther 1517," *SVRG,* XXXVI (1918), and a complete edition in 1929 in *Anfänge reformatorischer Bibelauslegung,* Vol. II. In the same year the text was published by Hirsch and Rückert in *Luthers Vorlesung über den Hebräerbrief.* Both editions contain extensive commentaries. Finally Ficker incorporated the lectures with those on Romans and Galatians into Vol. LVII of the Weimar edition (1939). For his two editions Ficker also used a manuscript in the Anhalt Staatsbibliothek at Dessau, containing a transcript of *scholia* I–V. It seems probable that the Palatine text was copied, in part by Aurifaber himself, either from Luther's original manuscript, or, as appears more likely, from transcripts made by several auditors. The Dessau fragment was written apparently from Martin's dictation in the lecture room. See *WA,* LVII, xvi ff. The lectures have been translated into German by E. Vogelsang, "Luthers Hebräerbrief-Vorlesung," *Arbeiten zur Kirchengeschichte,* XVII (1930) and by Helbig, *Martin Luthers Vorlesung über den Hebräerbrief 1517/18.*

[94] There is evidence of this in the transcript, although the edition of the Latin Bible used has not been identified. Ficker, *Anfänge reformatorischer Bibelauslegung,* II, xxx; Hirsch and Rückert, *Luthers Vorlesung über den Hebräerbrief,* p. xxi.

[95] Ficker, *Anfänge reformatorischer Bibelauslegung,* II, xxix.

[96] *WA,* LVII, 69, l. 21; 119, ll. 15 f.; 172, l. 12.　　　　[97] *Ibid.,* p. 119, ll. 2 ff.

the fore, Chrysostom, whose widely known work on Hebrews had been translated by Mutianus. Martin makes use of this translation repeatedly and at great length.[98]

With the lectures on the Epistle to the Hebrews, then, he finally crosses the line that divides scholastic traditions and methods from the patterns and enthusiasms of humanism. The deep respect of the humanists for first sources and their skill in the play of philological weapons have now become a real experience and are enlisted in the service of his theological ideas. This does not mean, to be sure, that he aligns himself with the humanists. One feels, rather, a half-concealed resentment at the scholarly objectivity of a man like Erasmus, such as Martin expressed under the seal of confidence in a contemporary letter to Spalatin.[99] "Vain is all boasting about erudition, wisdom, and knowledge, for they do not make anyone better, even though they may be good and laudable gifts of God," he tells his students.[100]

Martin's ideas as formulated in the lectures lack the forceful swing of the two earlier courses on the Epistles of St. Paul. The earlier chapters on Hebrews are presented with deliberate scholarship, but when the fall semester opened the controversy over indulgences was already upon Martin, and there are evidences of increasing haste when he approaches the conclusion.[101] It is probable that he now had time only for the hurried preparation of notes. In the main, however, the Latin *scholia* flow smoothly, and critical exposition is rarely interrupted by stormy passages. Some of this reserve may be ascribed to the Epistle itself, which is marked by a tone of rational argument, since its author was seeking to win pious Jews for the Christian faith. In contrast to Erasmus, Martin repeatedly voices doubt as to Paul's authorship of the Epistle,[102] but he notes and echoes the tone of deep piety that pervades it. He passes lightly over its prophetic character, and makes use of it as a basis for expounding his ideas on Christian theology. The mystery of the hidden God and the revelation of Christ as unity of the divine and the human which finds such trenchant expression in the Epistle open the way to more than one eloquent passage in the lectures. Citations

---

[98] Later Martin said that as an interpreter of Hebrews, Chrysostom had left him "sticking in the mud." *TR*, I, No. 188 (1532); II, No. 2544a (1532).

[99] Letter from Luther to Spalatin, Jan. 18, 1518, *WAB*, I, 133.

[100] *WA*, LVII, 109, ll. 19 f.

[101] Ficker, *Anfänge reformatorischer Bibelauslegung*, II, xxvii ff., thinks that the first five chapters were treated in the summer semester, thus leaving three fourths of the epistle for the winter.

[102] *WA*, LVII, 10, ll. 20 ff.; 13, l. 9; 52, ll. 20 f. Later, in translating the New Testament, he denied that Paul was the author.

from the Old and New Testaments are intertwined with vivid metaphors to interpret the mystery of the synthesis of God and man in Christ and the sacramental character of His suffering, and to illustrate the quality of faith as the "total substance of the new law and of its justice" [103] and the "glue" which binds the sacred Word to the human heart.[104]

The sharp outbursts against the scholastic ideas of grace which marked the earlier lectures are less frequent in these. To be sure, there are occasional outbursts of anger against clerical ignorance and intolerance, such as that exemplified in the cruel persecution of the Jews, who, a few years before, had been the victims of a mass slaughter in Berlin. The lecturer summons to repentance in sackcloth and ashes the clerical instigators whose hands had been consecrated for the Sacrament:

But now these sacred hands and anointed fingers are stained with all the poison of wild fury and proceed to attack with swords and firearms the very Sacrament, that is, the kind Father's beloved children in Christ. Boiling with rage and panting with piety, they rush out to burn certain Jews for having stabbed the Host with daggers or cut it with knives. They themselves, however, have murdered, not the Sacred Host, but the very Sacrament itself [*rem ipsam*], not with daggers, but with artillery and every kind of din and assault of arms. In all this they do not understand Christ's warning to the Jews, or they would note that they themselves are seven times more deserving of fire and death of every kind who proceed in such wild and infernal fury against the Sacrament itself.[105]

The scribe, or scribes, who followed Martin's lectures noted few of such explosions of feeling. Before he had finished the course in the early spring of 1518, he had already locked horns with the Dominican defenders of indulgences, but there is little in the lectures to indicate an approaching crisis. Attacks on the "hypocrites who labor with perverse zeal for grace through works," thrusts at the "inexhaustible flow of decrees, decretals, and statutes," [106] and other polemical interpretations are rare as the lecturer follows the path which leads from the ancient faith of the Hebrews to its fulfillment in the God-manhood of Christ.

[103] *Ibid.*, p. 114, ll. 2 f.
[104] *Ibid.*, p. 157, l. 1.
[105] *Ibid.*, p. 168, ll. 1 ff.
[106] *Ibid.*, p. 230, ll. 20 ff.

14

THE ATTACK ON INDULGENCES

"I WAS completely dead to the world until God deemed that the time had come; then Junker Tetzel excited me with indulgences and Dr. Staupitz spurred me on against the pope." [1] In these words, more than twenty years later, Martin epitomized the conflict that had carried him out of the narrow world of cloister and university into the foreground of history. He was thirty-four years of age and had reached full maturity of intellectual power and creative energy. To those who knew him at Wittenberg and Erfurt and had followed his career during his five years in the chair of Bible exegesis it must have been clear that the convictions of the man backed by so forceful a will and such tremendous power for work would eventually take him into a larger arena than that bounded by the Saxon university. No one, however, would have predicted that within a year this arena would include also the highest officials of the Roman Church and the German Empire, nor that the name of the mendicant monk and Bible exegete would have found its way into the correspondence of the greatest chancelleries of Europe. Least of all did Martin himself anticipate any such result when he prepared and published his theses against indulgences. There is, on the other hand, abundant evidence in the correspondence during the months following his protest that he looked around with something like consternation at the unexpected uproar aroused by what he regarded as only a challenge to the academic guild.

The stage on which he sought to present his ideas, that of the disputation, was the usual one in the late medieval university. The rising conviction that he had found a new theology in his studies of Augustine and the Pauline Epistles and the forceful individualism that made him resent the control of scholarly tradition and hierarchical discipline had already shown themselves in an urge to bring his ideas into full collision with the scholastic theologians. We have seen how he did this through theses on the "powers and

[1] *TR*, IV, No. 4707.

will of man without grace," defended by Bartholomäus Bernhardi in September, 1516, and have noted the glee with which he hailed the astonishment aroused by this attack on the Biel tradition at his mother university and at Wittenberg. Now, a year later, another of his students, Franz Günther, came up for promotion to the baccalaureate in Bible and was made the spokesman for a much stronger expression of Martin's convictions.

The "disputation against scholastic theology" was held on September 4.[2] Martin presided, and the audience must have recognized at once that the candidate was defending his professor's ideas with the aid of his professor's scholarly equipment. The 97 theses, calling on Augustine as their authority, attacked sharply what their author considered scholastic Pelagianism. With equal vigor they launched against Aristotle the same kind of attack that Martin had been hurling at him in lectures, sermons, and correspondence ever since his Erfurt days. Though the theses ended with the routine pledge that nothing in them was inconsistent with Catholic doctrine and the teaching of the Church, they are a vigorous arraignment and an open defiance of the theological system as set forth by Biel, d'Ailly, and other authorities of the later Middle Ages, all highly respected in Martin's order.[3] He was particularly interested in the shock the theses would give to his alma mater, and he sent them off posthaste to Lang in Erfurt with an offer to defend them there in public.[4] He also sent them to Scheurl, who had just left Wittenberg, and that busy intermediary passed them around to many, including Professor Trutvetter and Professor Johann Eck, then dean of the theological faculty at Ingolstadt and a redoubtable master in the disputation.[5]

"It was the boldness and ignorance of these people, I confess, that drove me not to give way to fear; except for that no one would ever have known me outside of my corner," Martin states in excusing himself in a letter to his bishop when the debate on indulgences was rising to a crisis.[6] As a matter of fact, the opening of a fight on this time-honored institution was the next logical step for a man who had reached his conception of justification and whose naturally combative impulses were fired by an urge to redirect what he believed to be the erring theology of the time. In the great body of ecclesiastical abuses upon which his eyes had become fixed during

---

[2] *Disputatio contra scholasticam theologiam. WA*, I, 224 ff.

[3] For an analysis of the theses, see C. Stange, "Die ältesten ethischen Disputationen Luthers," *Quellenschriften zur Geschichte des Protestantismus*, I (1904), foreword and pp. 34 ff.

[4] Letter from Luther to Lang, Sept. 4, 1517, *WAB*, I, 103.

[5] Scheurl, *Briefbuch*, II, 30; *WAB*, I, 107.

[6] *WAB*, I, 140. The date of this letter to Bishop Scultetus has been much debated. See introduction by Clemen, who sets it at February 13, 1518.

the years since he became a doctor of theology, events combined to bring this one immediately before his vision just at this time.[7]

It is quite certain that in the fall of 1517 many aspects of indulgences as a problem in theology were not clear to Martin. Nor is this surprising, since some of the brightest minds, both Catholic and Protestant, have striven unsuccessfully through the succeeding four centuries to attain an unambiguous and mutually acceptable position on the question. In the sense handed down by tradition, although not unanimously recognized in Luther's day, forgiveness of sins was supposed to follow confession, and indulgences could free the penitent only from physical punishment or such penitential burdens as his confessor laid upon him. It was understood that the guilt which only God can forgive remained to be atoned for in purgatory. Nevertheless, from the end of the fourteenth century, these acts of remission were also called "indulgences of punishment and guilt" (*poena et culpa*); and the laity, whose minds were untrained in theological distinctions, were thus led to assume that they were receiving for their payment of money a remission not merely of the punishment imposed by the priest but also that to be imposed by God. This was then extended to include the remission of punishment yet to be undergone by the souls of the dead in purgatory. Further confusion was wrought in the public mind when the so-called "plenary indulgences" were issued remitting the sins of all Christendom. Here the relation of penitence and confession became quite unclear, and the door was opened to the agent entrusted with the sale of indulgences, thus confusing still further the mind of the ordinary man.[8]

Under these conditions the spiritual aspect of the plenary indulgence tended to disappear from view, and this evil grew with the growing worldliness of the papacy during the Renaissance. There were men of authority in the Church who recognized the danger and tried to safeguard the popular mind against misunderstanding, but they carried on a difficult fight. In pursuance of the famous bull of Leo X of March 31, 1515, providing indulgences for the building of St. Peter's at Rome, the instructions of the archbishop of Mainz to the commissioners appointed for the sale set forth

[7] The literature on the theory and history of indulgences would fill a library of some dimensions. Those who are interested in the topic would better begin by consulting one of the great religious encyclopedias, where they will find abundant references. It need hardly be said that all discussion has been more or less under confessional influences. A painstaking examination of the situation in the Renaissance period is that of Brieger, *Das Wesen des Ablasses am Ausgange des Mittelalters.*

[8] For the text of the most important bulls of indulgence from the eleventh century down to 1518, see W. Köhler, "Dokumente zum Ablassstreit von 1517," *Sammlung ausgewählter kirchen- und dogmengeschichtlicher Quellenschriften*, 2. Reihe, Heft 3 (1902).

distinctly, to be sure, that absolution applied only in the case of such sins as had been confessed with repentance or where the penitent had at least the intention of confessing, but they also contained the words "full remission of sins" and provided that the purchaser might present the indulgence to a priest of his own choosing once in a lifetime or in the hour of death and receive therefore general absolution.[9] The connection between the payment of money and the remission of sins, especially when this had to do with the freeing of a loved one from purgatory, was so direct that the average mind overlooked the subtle distinctions involved. Furthermore, the zealous purveyors of indulgences had a great deal less to say about penitence and confession than about forgiveness and remission.

Indulgences played so important a rôle in religious practice and theological discussion in the later Middle Ages, and particularly in the early sixteenth century, that Martin must have come into contact with the question on many occasions. There is evidence that he gave much earnest thought to it during the preparation of the lectures on Romans when he was revolving in his mind the whole matter of justification. As we have seen, he referred with some bitterness in this course of lectures to the sale of forgiveness of sins by those prelates who had received it gratis from God. At this time the papal indulgence of 1515 had already made its appearance in Saxony and its sale was carried on actively in the neighboring area of Meissen by the Dominican, Johann Tetzel, a subcommissioner of the archbishopric of Mainz.[10] On All Saints' Day, October 31, 1516, Martin delivered the festival sermon in the Castle Church and devoted himself to the question of indulgences,[11] a matter of importance for this church whose great store of sacred relics was weighted with papal concessions of this kind. The subject was therefore a delicate one and evidently Martin had made up his mind to tread carefully. He was at pains to say that the intention of the Pope as set forth in the bull was right and proper. Nevertheless, he was deeply concerned over the seductive display in the aisles before him and the trumpeting that was going on in the neighborhood. Penitence, he felt, must be from the heart, since selfish fear of punishment is hateful to God.

At the end of the following winter he came back to the subject again. Tetzel was now fully commissioned and carrying on a lucrative campaign in the neighboring territory of Brandenburg. In the last of his prefatory dis-

---

[9] The text of the bull of 1515 and the *Instructio Summaria* to the commissioners are to be found in Köhler, "Dokumente zum Ablassstreit," pp. 83 ff. and 104 ff.

[10] Cf. E. Stracke, "Luthers grosses Selbstzeugnis 1545 über seine Entwicklung zum Reformator," *SVRG*, XLIV, 1 (1926), 18 f.

[11] *WA*, I, 94 ff.

courses to the series on the Ten Commandments, on February 24, 1517, Martin thunders a solemn warning to his Wittenberg audience in the parish church.[12] This pouring out of indulgences is really an exhortation to sin and a license for banishing the cross of Christ. "Oh, the dangers of our time! Oh, the snoring clergy! . . . How securely we rest in the worst of our dangers!" [13] Later in the year he devotes another discourse to an attack on the agents who are recommending the indulgences for sale, and here he tries to explain the limitations of temporal punishment.[14] The pope, whose prayers arise through the merits of the entire Church, has a right to remit from punishment on earth and his prayers may sway God in favor of the penitents. Nevertheless, no one can be certain of this. On the other hand, the preacher concedes that indulgences have their use, despite the behavior of those who dispose of them. The end of the long argument is that the satisfaction of punishment through indulgences must not produce a feeling of security or a moral relaxation. This sermon, more than the others on the same subject, shows an inner conflict, reflected in the hesitation of the preacher. He desires to defend the traditional theological position, but the abuses that have grown out of the archbishop's instructions make him anxious, for he cannot reconcile them with his own belief in the necessity for an inner transformation of the sinner. He seeks to keep his feet on ancient ground, but feels that it is slipping away beneath him.[15]

One must do all honor to an audience, whether composed of theologians or townspeople, that was able to follow the subtleties of Martin's discussion, punctuated as it is here and there by confessions of ignorance and doubt. On the other hand any Wittenberg resident was quite able to appreciate his arraignment of the behavior of the agents who had charge of the distribution of the indulgences. It was, indeed, an old story throughout Christendom and certainly familiar enough to the Saxons. The bull issued by Pope Leo in 1515 was nothing extraordinary in view of the record, certainly not for Saxony. The bridge over the Elbe at Torgau had been built by the income from an indulgence, renewed in 1512, permitting the consumption of butter,

---

[12] *Ibid.*, pp. 138 ff.   [13] *Ibid.*, p. 141, ll. 37 ff.

[14] *Ibid.*, pp. 65 ff.

[15] The sermon, which is one of those found in the Löscher collection, has been associated with the exordial series to the Decalogue and dated July 27, 1516. Both Buchwald and Vogelsang accept this. G. Krüger concludes from a MS of the text in the archives at Darmstadt that it was not a sermon at all, but a tractate written by Luther about the same time as the Ninety-five Theses—late October, 1517. See his "Luthers Tractatus de Indulgentiis," *ThStKr*, XC (1917), 507 ff. This seems unlikely, as the tone is more restrained than that of the Theses. On the other hand, its contents point rather to a later date than the Decalogue series, perhaps the second half of 1517. See Kiessling, *The Early Sermons of Luther*, pp. 100 f.

milk, and cheese during Lent. This rested on an agreement between Rome and the elector whereby the money seems to have been divided equally between the Saxon court and the Vatican. The financial results must have been disappointing, for the elector showed much concern lest a number of his subjects should eat the forbidden food without paying and urged the bishops to call the attention of the faithful to the ensuing danger to their souls.[16] Frederick's attitude was quite in line with the policy of the German princes, who sought to keep out indulgences for foreign purposes but to get all possible income from them for German religious establishments. Frederick the Wise and his brother John, co-rulers of the state, had, in fact, been especially active in pushing indulgences, and Martin's attacks had no immediate effect on their efforts. In addition to those which the Church of All Saints at Wittenberg already enjoyed, Frederick secured another in 1518 for which he had been working for more than six years. To be sure, the distribution of the indulgences of March, 1515, had been banned in the principalities of both Ernestine and Albertine Saxony, but this was undoubtedly done because neither state shared in the proceeds.

This realistic attitude of the German princes was no doubt known to Martin, but he was unaware of the financial transaction that lay behind the distribution of the indulgences now in circulation. This involved Prince Albert of Brandenburg, Archbishop of Mainz, and the great South German banking house of Fugger, which acted as fiscal agents for the Vatican at that time in Central Europe and Scandinavia. Albert, the young prince of the House of Hohenzollern, who already ruled as bishop of Magdeburg and administered also the diocese of Halberstadt, sought in addition the vacant archbishopric of Mainz, regarded as the major Church dignity in the empire. Such a concentration of ecclesiastical offices had begun to be notable in Germany before the end of the fifteenth century, and had now become an ecclesiastical abuse that awakened strong resentment.[17] For his consecration as archbishop, the Curia, which since the last crusade had used just such occasions to get financial support for its widening diplomatic and military program, required of him 21,000 ducats as *pallium* fee and an additional 10,000 ducats for permitting the accumulation of ecclesiastical offices in his hand. These enormous sums were advanced by the Fuggers.[18] Through the arrangement with Rome, reimbursement for the second of these fees was to

---

[16] Paul Kirn, "Friedrich der Weise und die Kirche," *Beiträge zur Kulturgeschichte des Mittelalters und der Renaissance*, XXX (1926), 121.

[17] Janssen, *Geschichte des deutschen Volkes von dem Ausgang des Mittelalters*, I, 703.

[18] The contract belongs to the best-known episodes of this period. Schulte, *Die Fugger in Rom*, chap. V, gives details of the transaction. See also Grisar, *Luther*, I, 282 ff.

be provided to the banking house by the sale of the indulgences in the territories of the archbishopric of Mainz, Albert's North German diocese, and that of Brandenburg, half of the proceeds going to Rome directly for the construction of St. Peter's and the other half to the Fuggers for liquidation of Albert's account. The distribution of the indulgences was, as we have seen, brought painfully close to Wittenberg by the vigorous campaign of Johann Tetzel, who, as subcommissioner and later as commissioner under Albert's authority, set about his task with the energy of an aggressive personality and methods derived from a strong business sense and wide experience in finding purchasers for indulgences.[19] Tetzel had special sermons printed in preparation for his journey, and according to contemporaries was received with solemn ceremonies in the towns through which he passed, where, amid waving flags, pealing bells and resounding organs, the papal banner and the purveyor's cross were escorted into the churches. Under these conditions the summons to repent and buy indulgences found lucrative response.[20]

In the spring of 1517 the energetic indulgence preacher swung around through the neighboring towns in the dioceses of Brandenburg and Magdeburg. Martin had learned of Albert's instructions to the commissioner and in all probability began to find in his confessional persons who in spite of their lives of persistent sin demanded absolution on the strength of the new indulgences.[21] He must have been aware that Elector Frederick had forbidden their sale in his territories and that George, duke of Saxony, had warned Tetzel away from Leipzig.[22] He heard stories floating about, which probably lost nothing in retelling, regarding blasphemous statements made by the purveyor, and in later years he declared that Staupitz had asked him to turn his pen against the evils of the institution.[23] Under these circumstances, his resolution hardened as the months went by, and at the end of October he strode to action. The path he took was, as we have said, the traditional one for discovering the formulas of truth, the academic disputation. This time it was not to be behind the mask of a student but through theses defended by Luther himself. For making these public he chose one of the most important academic occasions of the Wittenberg year. All Saints' Day saw the celebration of the great annual festival when the Castle Church

---

[19] For an account of Tetzel's activities and a well-balanced résumé of the man's character, see Paulus, *Johann Tetzel.*

[20] The more colorful reports are of course from Lutheran sources; e.g., that of a younger contemporary, Friedrich Myconius. See his *Historia Reformationis 1517–1542,* reproduced in the Cyprian edition, II (Leipzig, 1718), pp. 10 ff., esp. p. 15.

[21] *Wider Hans Worst* (1541). *WA,* LI, 539 f.

[22] See F. Gess, "Luthers Thesen und der Herzog von Sachsen," *ZKG,* IX (1888), 590 f.

[23] *TR,* IV, No. 4707.

with its store of sacred relics was visited by crowds. On the preceding day, October 31, the university, as was its wont, held a special service, and this was the occasion which Martin used. He had prepared his theses with great care, and probably had them printed in advance in accordance with his usual method. Possibly he discussed them with colleagues of the theological faculty; [24] when the day arrived, however, he did not consult even his most intimate friends, but posted them in broadside form on the doors of the church, prefaced by a declaration that he would defend them.[25] On the same day he sent a copy to the person most immediately concerned, Archbishop Albert, with a covering letter.[26] Another copy went to Hieronymus Scultetus, who as bishop of Brandenburg was the immediate ecclesiastical superior of the Wittenberg cloister and university.[27] Copies were probably also sent to churchmen of importance in Wittenberg and its vicinity.

The routine form in which the Ninety-five Theses hung that evening on the great doors of All Saints' Church and their ecclesiastical Latin and academic phraseology could not mask the powerful and explosive nature of their contents from the eager eyes of faculty members and theological students. First prints of the *Disputation in Explanation of the Power of Indulgences* exist no more, but copies are still to be found in the familiar folio form of the sixteenth century, probably from presses in Leipzig and Magdeburg.[28] The theses open in measured tones, with a definition of the inner, lifelong repentance demanded by Christ, and show that the moral change which He requires must lead to a transformation within the sinner which differs in its nature from that produced by any punishments demanded by the Church. They then proceed to draw a similar line of difference between the canonical punishments imposed by the pope and the purgatorial punishments which lie beyond his power and are necessary for cleansing the soul, and brand as

[24] Johannes Luther, *Martin Luthers 95 Thesen*, pp. 6 ff., seeks to show that the subject matter of the theses was debated in advance in the theological faculty. All the evidence, however, points to a sudden and personal decision on Martin's part. Immediately following the posting of the theses he explains to Spalatin that he was intent that no one at court should know anything about the theses in advance, lest it be thought that they were issued with the connivance of the elector in order to attack Archbishop Albert. *WAB*, I, 118, ll. 9 ff. See also p. 146, ll. 80 ff., and pp. 245 and 355 ff.

[25] For the difficult question of the first prints and distribution of the theses, see Otto Clemen, "Beiträge zur Lutherforschung," *Aus Deutschlands kirchlicher Vergangenheit. Festschrift zum 70. Geburtstag von Th. Brieger* (Leipzig, 1912), pp. 21 ff.; also in summary in *Luthers Werke*, ed. by Clemen (Bonn, 1925), I, 1 ff., and in J. Luther, *Martin Luthers 95 Thesen*.

[26] *WAB*, I, 110 ff. (October 31, 1517).

[27] The letter has been lost. The sources attesting that Luther wrote it are given in *WAB*, I, 113.

[28] Copies in *Placat* style are in the British Museum and the Berlin Staatsbibliothek. *WA*, I, 233 ff.

error the claim of the preachers that indulgences bring the remission of any and all sins.[29] "Who knows," Martin asks in the tone of the German mystics, "whether all the souls in purgatory want to be set free?"[30] He is careful to distinguish between the institution of indulgence and its interpretation by the agents. Indulgences themselves are not to be despised, for they are a valuable declaration of divine forgiveness,[31] but he points out how difficult it is to extol their virtues without relaxing the demand for true contrition. Half way through the theses his tone rises to powerful feeling in denouncing the instructions to the preachers of indulgence. If the Pope knew of the sharp dealings of these purveyors, "he would prefer to have St. Peter's collapse into ruins rather than build it with the skin and flesh and bones of his sheep."[32] A powerful and imaginative style marks the later theses and strains visibly here and there at the bonds of academic Latin. The real treasure and "keys" of the Church are the merit of Christ; indulgences are merely used to angle for the treasure of the rich. If for the sake of ruinous money the Pope can free so many souls from purgatory, why does not he for the sake of love and justice evacuate purgatory altogether?[33] In conclusion, the theses strike a chord so often heard in Martin's sermons and lectures of these years, a mystical plea for suffering as the gateway to heaven.[34]

Martin's attempt to bring this institution of the Church into the limits of academic discussion bears the stamp of a powerful emotional experience. He burns with eagerness to defend his hard-won ideas. In something like symphonic form the Ninety-five Theses open with notes of a restrained and serene presentation, rise then to stormy passages where the solemn introduction, repeated in nine successive theses,[35] *Docendi sunt Christiani!* ("Christians must be taught!") resounds in its sonorous Latin like a series of mighty trumpet blasts, and ends with an emotional adagio. Nevertheless he was evidently not aware that he was taking a more revolutionary step than in his previous efforts to set up academic supports for his ideas of regeneration through grace. "Paradoxes," he calls the theses when sending them a few days later to his friend Lang at Erfurt,[36] paradoxes which will no doubt bring on him again the charge of boldness and pride. Later, when the clouds of the rising storm begin to appear, he repeats to his bishop,

[29] Theses 20–21.   [30] Thesis 29.   [31] Thesis 38.

[32] Thesis 50.   [33] Thesis 82.

[34] Attempts at a topical grouping and analysis of the theses are not numerous, and they are usually marked by a polemical coloring. See that of Theodor Brieger, "Die Gliederung der 95 Thesen Luthers," *Studien und Versuche zur neueren Geschichte, Max Lenz gewidmet* (Berlin, 1910).

[35] *WA*, I, 235.   [36] Letter from Luther to Lang, Nov. 11, 1517, *WAB*, I, 121.

Scultetus, that he merely wanted to dispute about the whole matter until the Church should determine what was to be believed.[37] Again, in a similar vein, he writes Scheurl a little later that he regarded the theses as tentative and only sought to discuss them with a few in Wittenberg and round about before sending them further, as some things in them were still unclear to him.[38]

Although the Wittenberg professor was surprised and not a little aghast at the storm which rose from outside cloister walls, he could hardly have failed to expect a bitter struggle when the theses should become known in theological circles. He was still feeling his way, to be sure, but he writes to Lang in a defiant spirit; and the fact that he had the theses printed and sent them at once to eminent officials of the Church shows that he was fired to the point of vigorous action and prepared to go to the utmost bounds in academic defense of his position. At the same time he had evidently measured just as little as had his friends and opponents the tremendous power for combat that lay coiled within him.

Indeed, the situation soon developed to a point where all his energies were to be called into play. Probably through the mediation of friends to whom early copies had been sent, the theses were speedily reprinted in Leipzig, Magdeburg, Nuremberg, and Basel, in German as well as in Latin. Martin's statement a quarter of a century later that they ran through the whole of Germany in two weeks is a little exaggerated,[39] but his lectures and disputations must already have carried his name far in academic circles, and there is proof that the propositions regarding indulgences spread with amazing rapidity among German and Swiss scholars. A well informed contemporary writing a few years later declares that within four weeks they raced through all Christendom "as though the angels themselves were messengers." [40]

The echoes were not long in reaching Wittenberg. Some of these cheered the author in an hour of uncertainty, such as messages from Nuremberg friends, or a comforting letter from an aged Franciscan, Dr. Johann Fleck, a distinguished preacher, who was prior of the cloister near Bitterfeld.[41] Soon after the appearance of the theses, Scheurl was busy distributing copies to humanistic friends.[42] Possibly through this Nuremberg correspondent Martin received during the winter a gift from the great South German artist,

---

[37] Letter from Luther to Scultetus, Feb. 13(?), 1518, *WAB*, I, 138 ff.

[38] Letter from Luther to Scheurl, March 5, 1518, *WAB*, I, 152; see also letter to Scultetus, p. 139, ll. 46 ff.

[39] *Wider Hans Worst. WA*, LI, 540.

[40] Myconius, *Historia Reformationis*, chap. IV, p. 23.

[41] *TR*, II, Nos. 2619a and 2619b (1532); V, No. 5480.

[42] Scheurl, *Briefbuch*, II, 39 ff.

Albrecht Dürer, perhaps one of the series of that master's religious wood engravings. On the other hand, members of the Wittenberg circle were deeply concerned at what they heard from without. Years later, Luther recalled that the prior and subprior of his cloister came to him and begged him not to bring their order into shame, and that the leading light in the juristic faculty, Dr. Hieronymus Schurf, gave him a solemn warning not to write against the Pope.[43] It was already being reported that the theses had been inspired by the Saxon elector as an attack on the Hohenzollern archbishop, and Martin hastened to forestall any resentment on the part of his prince by a letter to Spalatin.[44] As the sky grew darker, he exerted himself also to absolve the university from any responsibility for the sensational theses.

It was not long before the wheels of the hierarchy came into motion. The letter which Martin forwarded to Albert of Brandenburg with the theses was deeply submissive in tone, as became a humble scholar from a mendicant order in addressing one of the greatest Church dignitaries of Central Europe.[45] Albert, altogether without ecclesiastical training, had leanings toward humanism: he was on terms of friendship with Erasmus, who lost no opportunity to attach the threads of his correspondence to the thrones of the mighty. With his humanistic dilettantism the archbishop united a Renaissance love of display, and in general showed himself the type of the pliant opportunist not infrequent in a period when ecclesiastical and temporal politics were a tissue of trickery. In spite of the apparent humility of its tone, Martin's letter to Albert is marked by the aggressive boldness that from now on comes to be characteristic of his correspondence. He calls attention to the misunderstandings which the common people draw from the sermons of the indulgence preachers and repeats from reports some of the most drastic statements ascribed to Tetzel, such as the blasphemous claim that forgiveness might be assured even to one who had violated the Virgin Mary herself, or the notorious doggerel promising immediate release from purgatory to those whose redemption-money had been paid:

> When clinking coin the cash-bell rings
> The soul from purging fires springs.[46]

---

[43] TR, III, No. 3722, p. 564, ll. 16 f.; also EA, XLI, 37.
[44] WAB, I, 118.   [45] WAB, I, 110 ff.
[46] Martin paraphrases in Latin, of course; WAB, I, 111, ll. 20 f. The oft-recited jingle runs in German:

> Sobald das Geld in Kasten klingt,
> Die Seele aus dem Fegefeuer springt.

Paulus, *Johann Tetzel*, p. 139, concedes that this crude formulation was in line with Tetzel's preaching, but contends that the idea is not so objectionable as Lutheran tradition assumes.

Statements like these, he declares, have led ignorant people to the belief that the indulgence alone will insure their salvation. This error was confirmed by the archbishop's instructions, which, Martin politely assumes, were drawn "without your knowledge and consent."

When the letter came to the notice of the archbishop he promptly took steps against the "rash monk of Wittenberg," as Martin is called in the archdiocesal documents. On December 1 he turned the theses over to the theologians and jurists of the university at Mainz for study.[47] While awaiting their decision Albert took counsel with advisers at his court and before the middle of the month forwarded the papers to Rome as basis for an "inhibitory process" which should put a stop to Martin's activities. By thus passing on responsibility for punitive action, the wily churchman sought to avoid direct complications with the Saxon electorate and the powerful Augustinian order. At the same time he could not overlook Martin's charges against the indulgence preachers nor his threat to give the matter further publicity. The procedure at Rome might be long delayed, and the archbishop was eager to put out the fire before it had time to destroy the financial edifice that had been built on the distribution of indulgences. Therefore, at the same time that he sent the charges to the Pope, he referred the affair to the council of his North German dioceses at Halle with an urgent letter.[48] Waving aside contemptuously the defiant behavior of the "obstinate monk" in respect to himself, the episcopal prince expressed his sharp displeasure with the pomp and expense attending the sale of the indulgence and the general attitude of the commissioners. He urged his council to intervene with Martin through Tetzel and gave instructions for a more severe control over the income from indulgence sales.

What action the Saxon councilors took does not appear in the sources, but it seems probable that they did nothing. The administrative heads representing the dioceses of Magdeburg and Halberstadt were likely to be as little concerned with the theological aspects as their master and were probably much less disposed to exert themselves to secure profits for the archepiscopate of Mainz. On the other hand, the tone of Martin's attack was so bold that it

---

[47] Two letters from Albert to the faculty, December 1 and 13, in the Mainz Stadtbibliothek are reproduced by F. Herrmann in "Miscellen zur Reformationsgeschichte," ZKG, XXIII (1902), 265 f. Other published works of Martin, possibly the Günther theses, may have come into the archbishop's hands at this time. Theodor Brieger, "Kritische Erörterungen zur neuen Luther-Ausgabe," ZKG, XI (1890), 114 ff., and Paul Kalkoff's long discussion, "Zu Luthers römischem Prozess," ZKG, XXXI (1910), 48 ff.

[48] Original from the Magdeburg archives in Hennes, Albrecht von Brandenburg, pp. 59 ff. This letter is also the source for establishing Albert's complaint to the Pope concerning Luther's doctrines.

pointed to support by the patron of his university, Elector Frederick. If any drastic action was to be taken against the obstreperous monk, they may well have preferred not to participate in it.

The faculty at Mainz showed equal unwillingness to interfere. The scholars proceeded with the usual academic deliberateness, and when, after further prodding, they concluded their debates, their report to the archbishop sidestepped any decision on theological questions involved in the theses and advised that the matter be referred to Rome, since Luther's statements implied a restriction on the power of the pope.[49] Thus by unanimous consent the German representatives of the hierarchy most concerned hastened to clear their skirts and shift the responsibility to the papal court.

For the Curia, the path of religious discipline lay open. How far the matter came to the personal notice of Pope Leo is not certain. It is, however, doubtful whether the cultured Medici, whose interest was absorbed in the building of the great church and the decoration of the Eternal City with the art works of the Renaissance, gave even routine attention to what would have seemed to him merely an academic dispute between dusty-brained theologians. Many years afterwards Martin remarked that he had heard that Leo pronounced the theses the work of a drunken German who would feel differently when he sobered up,[50] and this, whether true or not, seems well in accord with the Pope's temperament. Nevertheless, it was under the authority of the triple crown that the machinery of Roman discipline began to move. It took the same direction as that employed two decades earlier by Pope Alexander VI against another monastic offender, the Florentine Savonarola, namely the enlistment of the head of the order to which the offending cleric belonged. On February 3, Pope Leo called the attention of the newly chosen general of Augustinian Eremites, Gabriel Venetus, to a monk of his order who was starting disputes in Germany, and directed him to "soothe and quiet" the man, reminding him that it is not hard to quench a fire just as it has broken out, while nothing is so dangerous as delay.[51] Venetus seems to have acted promptly, writing to Staupitz to ask him to call the brother to account.

News of the proceedings on the part of the archbishop as well as Rome probably filtered through to Wittenberg in the course of the winter. It seems likely, however, that it was not until March and through Staupitz that Martin learned of the bad impression which his theses had created at the papal court. As for an exchange between the friar-professor and his spiritual

[49] Herrmann, "Miscellen," pp. 265 ff.   [50] *TR*, II, Nos. 2635a and 2635b (1532).
[51] Kalkoff, *Forschungen*, p. 44, gives the source.

father, the general vicar, we have only a letter of Martin's written on the last day of March.[52] This is a brief but sturdy defense. He knows well that he is in bad odor for his condemnation of routine prayers and good works, but he cannot cease on account of the evil impression made by his writings; and he defends himself by authorities like Tauler and the general vicar himself. It was not to win fame or infamy that he began, nor will either cause him to cease. Scholastics swell with hate against him, but he cares nothing for these spooks. If the greatest masters of scholasticism disagreed among themselves, why should he not be allowed to defend his opinion?

At Wittenberg in the meantime, life in cloister and university had brought again its round of lectures and religious duties. Letters and a few sermons remain to document the life and thinking of Martin in the months that followed the posting of the Ninety-five Theses. We must assume that the eyes of faculty and students now turned to him with increasing attention. In an address to the students at the opening of the winter semester, his colleague Carlstadt paid Martin a ringing tribute for the learning and eloquence of his lectures;[53] and despite hesitancy among certain members of the faculty, there is little doubt that the unruly scholar had many adherents in Wittenberg who were willing to follow him through thick and thin, including a number who knew little about theological questions but were attracted by his spiritual power, rugged eloquence, and boldness.

There are signs that Martin viewed his situation with growing independence. He seems to have felt increasingly the weight of cloister poverty, and there is evidence that he did not accept with humility this demand of monastic life on himself and his brothers.[54] Money derived from the sale of Staupitz's works which had been sent to Wittenberg by Scheurl in the summer months was retained by Martin for the poorer brothers and himself, "for I have never known anyone poorer than I am."[55] The year before, the elector had promised him a new cowl; in a letter which is an adroit mixture of humility and urgency, the friar reminds him of the promise and gets the robe a few days later through Spalatin.[56] More than once during the winter he sends thanks to the elector for gifts, and we may assume that this generosity was due to the suggestions of the electoral chaplain. The latter has come to have a deep respect for the Wittenberg professor as an authority in spiritual matters and calls on him repeatedly through the winter for help

[52] WAB, I, 160.   [53] Barge, Andreas Bodenstein, II, 535 f.

[54] He reported to Lang, in a letter of Oct. 5, 1516, that the general vicar had been unable to leave Munich on an important mission to the north on account of poverty. WAB, I, 61.

[55] Letter to Scheurl, Sept. 11, 1517, WAB, I, 106.

[56] Letters of early Nov., 1517, WAB, I, 118, 120, 124.

in theological problems. Martin analyzes for him a scholastic problem, interprets obscurities in the Gospels, or sets forth a program for Bible students. In his letters to the chaplain he gives expression to opinions he would not have confided even to Carlstadt or Amsdorf. He tells him, for example, that he has the highest praise for Erasmus in recognition of his service to the cause of "good letters," but, swearing Spalatin to secrecy, he declares roundly that the great scholar lacks much as a Christian; Jerome, too, stands at the top in ability, but something more than ability and effort is necessary in order to have the knowledge of Christ and His grace found in Ambrose and especially in Augustine.[57] Here, as in the lectures, he follows the humanists as scholars but realizes that his life-objective differs from theirs. He does not point out their weaknesses more strongly for fear of encouraging their obscurantist enemies on the scholastic side. Plainly, the spirit of humanistic satire is getting on his nerves. His nature will not permit him to attack the mysteries of the Church with laughter, as Erasmus does in his "Julian Dialogues." These things are not to be ridiculed, he feels, but lamented.[58]

The new theology was of deep concern to Spalatin and he sought aid repeatedly from both Carlstadt and Luther. In February, he puts two questions to them: the proper attitude for those who attend Mass and perform good works, and the limitations of indulgences. Regarding the latter question, Carlstadt, who stood somewhat aloof from Luther's theses, promises light in a book which he has now on the stocks. As concerns the preparation for grace, he discourses with a wealth of citations from the Scriptures, Ambrose, and Augustine, whose work *On the Spirit and the Letter* he was just about to publish. All good works must come from God and not from man's efforts; human knowledge and wisdom are filthy rags, and dialectics are not necessary for theology. Amid unctuous clichés Carlstadt does not forget to insinuate a plea that the elector contribute thirty florins for paper in order to bring out his book.[59] In contrast, Martin's answer to Spalatin's questions has nothing stereotyped.[60] Touching the sacrificial attitude and the performance of good works, he gives a classical formulation of the mystical spirit of humility and self-condemnation that we find in the lectures on Romans and in the sermons. "The just man is his own accuser": only he can be justified who anticipates God's judgment and bows his will to God. As concerns indulgences, Martin still regards the general question as open, but he is ready to declare privately to his friends that he looks upon them as an illusion

[57] Letter from Luther to Spalatin, Jan. 18, 1518, *WAB*, I, 133 f.
[58] Letter from Luther to Spalatin, early in Nov., 1517, *WAB*, I, 118.
[59] Letter from Carlstadt to Spalatin, Feb. 15, 1518, *WAB*, I, 142.
[60] Letter from Luther to Spalatin, Feb. 15, 1518, *WAB*, I, 144 ff.

of no value except for indolent souls.[61] It was the love of truth that drove him to enter this labyrinth and stir up six hundred minotaurs. On one point he is entirely clear, that charity and helpfulness to one's neighbors is vastly better than indulgences, and he intends to make his position clear in a documented work to which he has been driven by the raging denunciations of hatred that are directed against him and the university. He is especially grieved at those who try to involve Frederick in the affair and stir up the elector of Brandenburg to hostility against him.[62]

In the midst of these thoughts and occupations he finds time for discussing problems in Greek vocabulary with Lang,[63] and he follows with eager interest the appearance of new humanistic works. His circle of correspondents has now widened to include Wolfgang Capito, scholarly adviser and proof-reader for the publisher Froben in Basel. Martin's mouth waters in anticipation of some of the books that are coming from this great humanistic press, such as More's *Utopia* and Erasmus's latest contribution to his controversy with Faber over the translation of a mooted passage in Hebrews. The rising wave of humanistic studies at last promised to bring reforms in the curriculum at Wittenberg and thus enforce the movement against scholastic theology. In the previous spring Martin had rejoiced at the decline of Aristotelian studies and those in Lombard's *Sentences*. Carlstadt went hand in hand with him in the opposition to dialectics; and early in March, 1517, they worked out a plan for a new curriculum which Martin laid before Spalatin with the hope that the elector would be willing to grant funds for a wide increase in scholarship and the elimination of "general barbarism." [64] The plan threw overboard such scholastic ballast as the logic of Peter Hispanus and Aristotle, and brought in their stead a three-language program of Latin, Greek, and Hebrew, as well as lectures on Pliny, Quintilian, and mathematics. Despite the elector's reputation as tight-fisted in academic matters, the reform program was approved, and on March 21 Martin reports with jubilation to Lang that it is being considered in the electoral council.[65]

It is likely that heresy proceedings on the part of the archbishop of Mainz and his Magdeburg councilors were prevented by the fear of offending the elector rather than by the active interposition of that prince. Undoubtedly

---

[61] *Ibid.*, p. 146, ll. 4 ff.

[62] Letter to Spalatin, Feb. 22, 1516, *WAB*, I, 149.

[63] Letter from Luther to Lang, Feb. 19, 1518, *WAB*, I, 148.

[64] Letter from Luther to Spalatin, March 11, 1518, *WAB*, I, 153 f.

[65] Letter from Luther to Lang, March 21, 1518, *WAB*, I, 155.

the sympathy and protection of Staupitz obstructed energetic steps against Martin within his own order. Other attacks came, however, particularly those by members of the Dominican Order, as Martin was soon to discover. Indeed, it is probable that these attacks, more than anything else, hurried him along the path of development. As was to be expected, Tetzel lost no time in replying to Martin. On January 20, before a large convention of Dominican brothers at the university in Frankfort, he defended a series of theses on indulgences. These had been prepared by Konrad Wimpina, a distinguished professor at the university who presided at the disputation.[66] About the middle of March, a bundle of the theses was brought to Wittenberg, but before they could be distributed they were snatched from the hands of the messenger by excited students and publicly burned on the market place. Martin hastened to disclaim to his friends and the public any connivance with this act, which he felt would certainly be reported to his damage.[67] The riot was portentous of things yet to come, and every wind from the Dominican quarter brought new threats. The indulgence preachers, Martin writes to Lang on March 21, cannot find names horrible enough to call him, and they are promising that he will be burned in a fortnight or a month. He has, however, assurances that the elector has taken him and Carlstadt under his protection and that he will not permit them to be dragged to Rome.[68]

Luther had, in fact, girded himself for the struggle. The months following the fateful October 31 of the preceding year were indeed such as to call for the last reserves of a body worn with study, lecturing, preaching, and letter writing. The latter alone, in view of the considerable remains of his correspondence preserved from the winter and spring, must have been a physical burden hardly measurable by those who live in a machine age. He was still district vicar of his order, and conferences with students and their preparation for academic promotion must have been insistent. Yet his will was indomitable and was steeled by the deepest soul experiences. Courageously he rejects the charge of rashness and presumption. "Without arguments, at least without the appearance and suspicion of contentiousness, nothing new can be brought forward," he had declared to Lang when he sent him his Ninety-five Theses. Thus it was with Christ and the martyrs. They were regarded as arrogant and as despisers of old and famous wisdom.[69]

---

[66] See Paulus, *Johann Tetzel*, pp. 49 f.

[67] Letters to Lang, March 21, 1518, *WAB*, I, 155, and Trutvetter, May 9, *WAB*, I, 170; also the Latin postscript to the sermon of March 18, *WA*, I, 277.

[68] Letter to Lang, March 21, *WAB*, I, 154 f.

[69] Letter to Lang, Nov. 11, 1517, *WAB*, I, 122.

"A dissipation of the soul, useless except for those who snore and dawdle on the way to God." [70] This was his private view of the work whose plan he confided to Spalatin in the middle of February. He was not yet ready, he says, to put it before the world, but something must be said to justify himself. The wide distribution of the theses, various reactions that they had caused in Germany, the uncertainty of his friends in Wittenberg, and particularly the Wimpina-Tetzel counterthrust, drove him to make clear his standpoint, at least before the academic world. This he planned to do in a scholarly paper in Latin addressed to the same kind of audience as that for which his theses had been intended. These "explanations and proofs" he forwarded to his bishop, Scultetus, before the middle of February, asking him to reject or approve.[71] With becoming deference to episcopal authority he defends his proposal to debate a question which has not yet been decided by the Church. No confidence should be put in the opinions of scholars, he declares, so long as they are only opinions: "It is disgraceful for a jurist to speak without a text and much more disgraceful for a theologian." The only sources which he trusts are the Scripture, Church canons, and the Fathers. Since no one has appeared to dispute with him on the theses, he is now forced to publish explanations and proofs. It is a mistake to think that everything in the theses is an assertion: he is still doubtful on some points, ignorant about others, others he denies, but he makes no obstinate assertions and is willing to submit everything to the Church and its judgment.

However firm his purpose, it is plain that he felt the weight of responsibility for his university and his order. Perhaps he had reason to expect that the bishop would give him encouragement,[72] but the prelate cautiously withheld a decision. While the Latin manuscript lay thus week after week unpublished, Martin, with one of those sudden resolutions characteristic of him, decided to make his position clear in a German discourse, which he hopes will "suppress the quite indefinite theses." [73] The *Sermon on Indulgence and Grace* came speedily from the press and was circulated about the end of March. Either proof sheets or an early copy fell into the hands of Bishop Scultetus, who seems to have been shaken into an immediate re-

[70] *WAB*, I, 146.

[71] *WAB*, I, 138 ff. The date of this letter has been much disputed. Although Clemen's arguments for Feb. 13 (*ibid.*, pp. 135 ff.) are not conclusive, they offer the best solution.

[72] Some later references to Scultetus might be interpreted in this way, especially *TR*, IV, No. 4446 (1539), and No. 4358, p. 257, ll. 17 ff. The statement in *TR*, II, No. 2474 (1532), that the bishop advised him to keep quiet, probably refers to a later time. The passage in *TR*, IV, No. 4016, charging the "episcopus Brandenburgensis" with pride and heavy drinking, probably does not refer to Scultetus, despite the editor's note.

[73] Letter from Luther to Scheurl, March 5, *WAB*, I, 152.

sponse. Sometime about the end of the month, Martin was surprised to receive a visit from the abbot of Lehnin, who brought a letter from the bishop requesting him to postpone for a little while the publication of his Latin "proofs and similar lucubrations." The bishop was not pleased with the German tractate and asked that it be withheld from the public.[74] Martin assented, a little abashed and flattered by this distinguished intervention, and gave his promise, but shortly afterward the bishop released him from it.

The *Sermon on Indulgence and Grace*[75] was probably never heard from the pulpit but was written down in order to initiate the laity into the questions at dispute. In this effort, however, Luther goes somewhat further than in the theses in declaring that indulgences are not commended, not even advised, but simply permitted for the sake of imperfect Christians. Their only effect is to take the place of wholesome suffering which the repentant sinner should willingly undergo. "It is my desire and . . . advice that no one should buy indulgences. Let lazy and sleepy Christians buy them and go your own course." With a slap at the scholastic doctors, he declares flatly that he does not believe that indulgences can free souls from purgatory. As for those who charge him with heresy, "I pay little attention to that kind of chatter, for no one does that but a few blockheads who never smelled the Bible [or] read a word of Christian doctrine."[76] The little pamphlet traveled fast and far, for laymen also were eager to learn about the much-advertised indulgence question, and Martin's argument with its twenty points set forth in clear and homely German ran through the country from Wittenberg to Basel in thirteen or more prints before the end of the year and carried his protest far and wide into circles untouched by the Ninety-five Theses.[77] This the anxious author could not have foreseen. In spite of encouragement in the attitude of Wittenberg colleagues and the friend at court, the early spring days were tense with anxiety. There is a time when every bold spirit realizes that he faces his enemies alone, and as Easter approached Martin was, indeed, aware of the seriousness of his position.

A week after Easter, the much harried professor left Wittenberg to attend the triennial convention of Augustinian chapters at Heidelberg.[78] In ac-

---

[74] Letter from Luther to Spalatin, *WAB*, I, 162. The date of the abbot's visit and its relation to the publication of the *Sermon on Indulgence and Grace* present difficulties, but the sequence of events given above seems the most probable.

[75] *Ein Sermon von dem Ablass und Gnade. WA*, I, 243 ff.

[76] *Ibid.*, p. 246, ll. 12 ff., and 31 ff.   [77] See Knaake's list, *WA*, I, 240 ff.

[78] Apparently Martin left Wittenberg on April 9. See his letter to Spalatin, *WAB*, I, 165; see also Karl Bauer, "Die Heidelberger Disputation Luthers," *ZKG*, XXI (1901), 233 ff., where the sources are examined in detail. For a general account, see Kolde's *Augustiner-Kongregation*, pp. 313 ff.

cordance with custom, this gathering was to be enlivened by a learned disputation, and the choice of protagonist fell on the Wittenberg scholar whose vigorous presentation of ideas of justification by grace had been so widely debated. In spite of the distinction which he now enjoyed in the order and an obviously wide sympathy with his views, the journey forebode danger, for his bitter and unsparing manner of attack had made him many foes. Spalatin brought this to the attention of the elector, and at his suggestion Martin addressed a letter to Frederick, asking for protection.[79] He had reason to feel, as he stated to Lang some days earlier, that the patron of the university would not put him in the power of his enemies.[80] Frederick found the situation threatening enough to send a warning to Staupitz, cautioning him to see that Martin was not "carried off or restrained." [81] He also gave Martin a safe-conduct, in reality a flattering letter of recommendation,[82] providing him also with introductions, including one to the bishop of Würzburg.

A brief but vivid outline of the stirring weeks of his absence is found in Martin's letters to Spalatin during the journey and after his return. Proceeding southward on foot as mendicant poverty demanded, and accompanied by a cloister brother, he meets the Saxon councilor Pfeffinger in the Thuringian village of Judenbach, and he smacks his lips over the good dinner which that official provides.[83] With rueful humor he complains that it is a sin for him to go on foot, but since he is fully contrite and has made complete satisfaction he does not need any indulgence. Faring thus through the most beautiful of Thuringian valleys and over the ridge to Coburg, he turns eastward into the Main country and stops in the ancient episcopal town of Würzburg, where kind-hearted Bishop Laurentius talks with him "face to face" and speeds him on his way.[84] Here in the Main metropolis, where, with an eye practiced in rural economics, he notices that the Franconians expect a good wine harvest, he meets old friends from Erfurt who give a welcome rest to his tired feet in their wagon and carry him up the

---

[79] This seems a fair interpretation of Martin's letters to Spalatin, written around Easter Day, April 4, *WAB*, I, 164 and 165. Kalkoff, whose major thesis is a close relationship between Luther and the elector after the posting of the Ninety-five Theses, contends for a deep personal interest on the part of Frederick in the fate of the professor at this time. See especially "Zu Luthers römischem Process," *ZKG*, XXXI (1910), 407. This is a somewhat violent treatment of the sources.

[80] Letter from Luther to Lang, March 21, 1518, *WAB*, I, 155.

[81] Frederick's letter is reprinted in Kolde, *Augustiner-Kongregation*, p. 314, n. 1.

[82] Sources in Bauer, "Die Heidelberger Disputation Luthers," pp. 241 f. See also letter from Luther to Spalatin, April 15, 1518, *WAB*, I, 166.

[83] *Ibid.*

[84] Luther to Spalatin, April 19, 1518, *WAB*, I, 168.

Rhine valley to the famous university town on the Neckar. He arrived probably on April 21 [85] and was cheered by a warm welcome from Palgrave Wolfgang, the brother of the Palatine elector, who had been a student and an honorary rector of the university of Wittenberg. With Staupitz and Lang he is treated to a bountiful dinner and shown the church treasures and the wonders of the great Heidelberg castle,[86] then still a medieval fortress.

So far as the sources show, the meetings of the Augustinians passed untroubled by any public mention of disciplinary moves against Martin. Staupitz was reaffirmed in his position as general vicar, and Martin's nearest cloister friend, Johann Lang, was selected to succeed the Wittenberg professor as district vicar. It seems hardly possible that the moves against the offending scholar were altogether unknown among the representatives of the cloisters, and one may assume that the attacks of the Dominicans on Martin had bound together the brethren of the Reformed Congregation in sympathy with his difficulties. The disputation, which passed off without demonstrations, was evidently attended by an unusual number, including not only friars and professors but people from the court and burghers of the city. When it took place on April 26 Martin, who presided, felt that he had a tolerant audience. As defender of his theses he had brought along Leonard Beyer, a young Augustinian from Wittenberg, and he and his professor must have rehearsed their rôles carefully during the journey through the fields and forests of Thuringia. Various Heidelberg theologians took part, and although they were opposed to his views, he found them kindly disposed, except one, a junior doctor, who aroused a laugh when he exclaimed, "If the peasants heard this, they would certainly stone you to death." [87] The affair had, then, its lively passages, but in general went off quietly and seems to have ended in something like personal triumph for Martin.

The Heidelberg theses include twenty-eight propositions from theology and twelve from philosophy.[88] They developed still further the ideas of justification and grace that had appeared in the Bernhardi and Günther disputations, but they are couched in a bolder style, with the inclination to

[85] Bauer, "Die Heidelberger Disputation Luthers," p. 241.

[86] Luther to Spalatin, May 18, 1518, *WAB*, I, 173.   [87] *Ibid.*, ll. 28 f.

[88] Contemporary prints of the theses seem not to exist. They were published in the first collected edition of Luther's works, *Probationes conclusionum quae in capitulo Heidelbergensi disputatae sunt* (Jena, 1545). *WA*, I, 355 ff. Here the theological theses are defended briefly by Martin; it is not clear when these notes were written. See *ibid.*, pp. 350 ff. For an analysis of the philosophical and theological significance of Luther's positions, see Carl Stange, "Die ältesten ethischen Disputationen Luthers," *Quellenschriften zur Geschichte des Protestantismus* (Leipzig, 1904), I, 50 ff.

paradox which was one of the growing characteristics of Martin's imaginative mind. More incisively than before, they present the total emptiness of man's will and works. Not these but belief in Christ makes a man righteous: one must not work, but believe. Once more the mystical conception of the destruction of self finds expression, and so far as the crispness of academic Latin permits, we hear again an echo of the burning eloquence of Tauler's warning that the soul must pass through annihilation in order to arrive at the certainty of salvation. The philosophical theses reflect the friar's theological studies and marshall against the old enemy, Aristotle, ideas of Plato and those attributed to Anaxagoras and Pythagoras.

The university professors, guardians of the scholastic tradition, were against him, but one auditor, at least, was captivated by Martin's vigor of mind and directness of speech and attached himself to the Wittenberg leader as a lifelong disciple. This was Martin Bucer, a fiery young Dominican who was later to become an eloquent preacher in Strasbourg and a defender of the Wittenberg theology in the upper Rhine country. Immediately following the lively day in the Augustinian hall he sought an interview with Martin, and a few days later poured forth his enthusiasm in a letter to a humanistic friend in Basel.[89] The Wittenberg professor has delighted him "with his incomparable forbearance in listening" and his method of disputation in which one recognizes the keenness of Paul, not of Scotus. Young Bucer was also favorably impressed by Martin's free and open manner of exposition in comparison with Erasmus who "merely insinuates." He followed the argument with attention and sends his friend a detailed analysis of Luther's defense of a number of the theses. At the same time, another auditor, Palgrave Wolfgang, dispatched a letter to Elector Frederick, in which he sang the praises of the Wittenberg scholar with all the enthusiasm of an alumnus.[90]

Returning with members of the Erfurt chapter, Martin spent the time in debate with his old friend and teacher, Arnold von Usingen, but left him astonished and unconverted.[91] To Spalatin he confesses that he now sets his hopes only in the younger generation: "As Christ turned to the heathen when the Jews rejected Him, so now let His true theology, which these deluded old men reject, betake itself to the young." [92] A decade of in-

[89] Letter from Bucer to Rhenanus, May 1, 1518, in *Briefwechsel des Beatus Rhenanus,* ed. by Horawitz and Hartfelder, pp. 106 ff.

[90] Cyprian, "Nützliche Urkunden," I, 1, 330 ff.

[91] Letter from Luther to Spalatin, May 18, 1518, *WAB,* I, 173, ll. 40 ff.

[92] *Ibid.,* p. 174, ll. 45 ff.

dependent development lay between him and the orthodox nominalism of his old teachers at Erfurt, but in spite of his resentment at their opposition to his views he still retained an affection for them and an admiration for their ability. With unusual pathos he notes that Arnold will not go with him on the new path. "The best comforter and adviser that one can have among men," he had called him two years before in writing to a troubled brother in Erfurt. Even more painful was the alienation from his old teacher of philosophy, Trutvetter. This sturdy theologian, deeply grieved by his pupil's course, had written him a letter of severe rebuke, charging him with ignorance of dialectics and theology.[93] On the way through Erfurt, Martin tried to see him, but received a rebuff. The following day he wrote him a letter, marked by the deep respect due to a former teacher and colleague, but vigorously independent.[94] With gratitude he confesses that he owes everything to him, but his tone hardens as he sets forth his conviction that no reform of the Church will be possible unless it begins at the bottom and roots out canons, decretals, scholastic theology, philosophy, and logic, putting in their place the Bible and the holy Fathers: "A resolution from which neither your authority, although it is certainly of the greatest weight for me, much less that of any others, can turn me aside." Before he left his alma mater he caught Trutvetter for a face-to-face talk, but heard only the same attacks.[95]

On May 15 he is back in Wittenberg. He did not have to return afoot, and reports to Spalatin that the good food and drink had so cheered him that some people find him stouter than when he left.[96] Either immediately after his return or perhaps just before his journey southward, he sent to Grünenberg's press a bulky Latin manuscript containing the "explanations and proofs" which were to defend his theses on indulgence in the eyes of the learned world. Printing dragged, and it was not until the end of August that he was able to forward the completed work to Spalatin.[97] Probably at Heidelberg he had received from Staupitz further news of the attack which had been made on him at Rome; and in place of the dedicatory epistle which he had intended for his bishop, he decided to preface the work with one addressed directly to the head of Christendom, Pope Leo himself. This

[93] *Ibid.*, p. 173, ll. 30 f. See also Martin's letter to Link, July 10, 1518, *WAB*, I, 186, ll. 49 f.

[94] Letter from Luther to Trutvetter, May 9, 1518, *WAB*, I, 169 ff.

[95] Letter from Luther to Link, July 10, 1518, *WAB*, I, 186, ll. 49 ff.; see also letter from Luther to Spalatin, May 18, 1518, *WAB*, I, 173, ll. 33 f.

[96] May 18. Letter from Luther to Spalatin, *WAB*, I, 173, ll. 10 ff.

[97] Probably only the proof-sheets. See Clemen, ed., *Luthers Werke*, I, 15; see also letter from Luther to Spalatin, Aug. 28, 1518, *WAB*, I, 190, ll. 31 ff.

remarkable document is dated May 30, and on the same day he prepared a covering letter to Staupitz.[98] To the vicar general he justifies his position in a tone of sincere affection, like a son explaining his actions to a sympathetic father. Staupitz it was who first made the word penance charming and pleasant to him with his explanation of true penance as beginning with love of righteousness and of God. Later on his studies of Greek had taught him that the word in the Greek New Testament for repentance means no less than a transformation of disposition and of love. That is why he ventured forth from his corner. He does not want to draw Staupitz into danger but begs him to send the work to the Pope. "For the rest," he declares, "I have nothing to answer my threatening friends except a remark of Reuchlin's: 'Whoever is poor fears nothing, for he can lose nothing.' Possessions I neither have nor desire . . . only one thing is left to me, my poor weak body, worn by continual hardship. If they destroy it through violence or trickery, . . . perhaps they will make me poorer by one or two hours of life. Sufficient for me is my sweet Redeemer and Mediator, Jesus Christ, whom I will praise my life long. If, however, any one does not care to sing with me, what do I care? Let him howl for himself if he will." [99]

The dedication to the Pope is both in tone and content a careful presentation of Martin's side of the case. There is some evidence that at least one draft was cast aside before the letter reached its final form.[100] In a tone of deep respect and seriousness the monk sets forth to the father of Christendom the excesses of the purveyors of indulgences, the resulting damage to the reputation of the clergy and to papal prestige, his own righteous resentment, and his private warnings to those in power before his final recourse to a disputation in exercise of his rights and duties as a doctor of theology. He claims that he is still puzzled as to why so usual an academic proceeding, which offered no dogmas but only questions for disputing, should have become known to everyone. What is he to do now? He cannot call back his theses; an attempt to explain them is his only recourse. With diplomatic cleverness he touches a chord that might ring pleasantly in the humanistic ears of Leo by a reference to Cicero, and in laying the matter before the Pope for decision he does not forget to hint that he is backed by the elector and his university. "Prostrate at the feet of Your Holiness, I offer myself and all that I am and have . . . Your voice I will recognize as the voice of

---

[98] *WA*, I, 525 ff.

[99] *Ibid.*, p. 525, l. 15 and p. 527, ll. 6 ff.

[100] There are fragments in Luther's hand in the Stuttgart Landesbibliothek, possibly from an early, and widely differing, draft. *WA*, IX, 173 ff., and Steiff's introduction, pp. 171 ff.

Christ, who rules and speaks in you. If I have deserved it I shall not hesitate to die." [101]

If Cicero knocks elbows with the Old Testament in the dedicatory epistle, the *Explanations of the Disputations on the Power of Indulgences* [102] are recast in the traditional method of scholasticism. Step by step and with academic detachment the author traverses the ground of each of his Ninety-five Theses and sums up his conclusions. In an initial series of "protests" he declares that he intends to recognize no authority except the Scriptures, the sacred Fathers, the historians of the Church, and the canon law and papal decretals. So far as scholastic authorities are concerned, he feels free to use his own judgment to accept or reject them all, from Thomas Aquinas down. The many pages of the "explanations" which follow swarm with Biblical citations and learned references. Augustine and Chrysostom, Bonaventure and Bernard play a somewhat minor rôle; the papal decrees as included in the canon law are brought up again and again to define and support the orthodoxy of his position. Old authors in his library give place to a new group of astonishing range, writers from the thirteenth to the fifteenth centuries who support his analyses of the nature of indulgences. Evidently in the tense days of the past winter he had thumbed over many a hitherto unopened volume. He writes for theologians, but not only for these, for he evidently had an eye also on the humanistic group who stood on the margin of theology and whose respect for original sources he himself had learned to share. With great care he seeks to clarify the various kinds of punishment for sin and to narrow and define the realm in which the pope's power of forgiveness is efficacious. [103] Especially when he attacks the question of purgatory (Thesis 20) and the power of the keys of Peter (Thesis 26) he is aware that he walks on dangerous ground and places his feet with care. The dogma of purgatory he still holds fast. To the power of the keys he devotes the longest of his "conclusions" (Thesis 26) with numbers and sub-numbers, objections and responses. The thesis runs: "It would be best should the pope give remission for souls by his prayers and not by the power of the Key (which does not profit any)." While Martin defends this stoutly and at length, he again withdraws behind the academic shield: he does not intend to pronounce a dogma, but to discuss. [104] His task is to define the apostolic power of the pope as symbolized by the gift of the keys

[101] *WA*, I, 529, ll. 23 ff.
[102] *Resolutiones disputationum de indulgentiarum virtute. WA*, I, 529 ff.
[103] *Ibid.*, pp. 534 ff.
[104] *Ibid.*, p. 574, ll. 16 ff.

to heaven and hell and the power of the pontiff through his prayers as head
of Christendom. Some of his arguments are as subtle as any in the scholastic
tradition, but the conclusion is clear: the power of the keys does not extend
to the souls in purgatory; it is prayer and not jurisdictional power that
comes to the aid of the souls that are being purged.[105]

However completely Martin put himself in the Pope's hands in the
dedicatory letter, the *Explanations* are marked throughout by a tone of bold
assurance that the logical structure he has built is impregnable. He cites the
declaration of a Paris theologian that the pope had been pleased by an argument that souls could be freed from purgatory by the power of the keys,
and answers: "I do not care what pleases or displeases the pope. He is a
man like other men. There have been many popes inclined to errors, vices,
and even very strange things." [106] He demands respect for the pope and
pays a high compliment to Leo X, "whose integrity and learning are a joy
in the eyes of all good men," [107] but recalls the evil deeds of Alexander VI
and Julius II. He is not clear regarding the boundary between papal and
civil authority; nevertheless he ventures a jest on the nature of the "gift" of
Constantine, the traditional source of the pope's temporal authority.[108] He
denies that a ban of excommunication when unjust has any power over the
conscience.[109] He builds on the authority of the decrees, for now he evidently
thought it good policy to hold back his full opinion of their unreliability.

Underlying the work is the urge for a reform of the Church. Against
distressing conditions in the hierarchy he had already struck more than one
blow in his lectures, and they fire him now to an open declaration. "This
many-headed monster, this inferno of simony, licentiousness, pomp, murder,
and other abominations in the Church," [110] drives him to a bitter arraignment. Attempts at reform have been made, but in vain. "Rome itself, yes,
Rome, chief of all, today ridicules good popes. For in what part of the
Christian world do they ridicule the popes more than in that genuine
Babylon, Rome?" [111] With equal bitterness he turns against the papal
courtiers, those legal and financial officials of the Curia, whose cupidity and
injustice in the distribution of Church funds had been the subject of complaint in Germany for generations. "The Church needs a reformation, but
that is not the affair of a single man, nor of many cardinals, as the most
recent councils have shown, but of the whole world, or rather of God
alone!" [112]

---

[105] *Ibid.*, p. 579, ll. 25 ff.   [106] *Ibid.*, p. 582, ll. 19 f.   [107] *Ibid.*, p. 573, l. 18.
[108] "Palea quaedam, sine tamen grano." *Ibid.*, p. 615, ll. 3 ff.
[109] *Ibid.*, p. 621, ll. 18 ff.   [110] *Ibid.*, p. 620, ll. 19 f.   [111] *Ibid.*, p. 573, ll. 23 ff.
[112] *Ibid.*, p. 627, ll. 27 ff.

The measured though tense tone of his argument becomes vehement when he turns to the peddlers of indulgences. The stories he has heard of their crude appeals and their blasphemies he does not vouch for, and hopes they are not true, but they are having a deplorable effect on the laity. Even if indulgences are authorized and helpful, the fact that they are misused is sufficient reason for abolishing them; the indulgence peddlers themselves go crazy about money. These are the people who charge him with heresy, these and our "dear friends," a title which he reserves for theologians like Wimpina and Eck. He quotes from the archbishop's instructions to the purveyors of indulgences and then lays aside his pen lest he should "rave at them according to their merits." [113]

The *Explanations,* like the Theses, rise and fall with the intensity of the attack. Sharp irony and abuse are not absent: polemics against the Wimpina-Tetzel theses; condemnation of the outworn studies of Aristotle, on whom so many of the brightest minds in so many universities have labored for three hundred years without understanding him, yet scattering their misunderstanding throughout the entire Church; attacks on the hypocritical motives behind many pilgrimages; a somewhat affected bow of deference to humanistic authority—these are overtones in a work whose leading motif is a solemn call to forsake the illusions of scholastic theology and turn to the theology of the Cross, "that is, of the crucified and unfathomable God." [114] Within a rigid and academic framework the *Explanations* formulate an inner experience which had now become a conviction and which was driving him with powerful urge to shake off the shackles of traditional authority without, as he had already shaken them off within.

[113] *Ibid.,* pp. 589 f.   [114] *Ibid.,* p. 613, ll. 23 f.

15

IN BATTLE WITH THE
DOMINICANS

EVEN before the Augustinian professor opened the question of indulgences, his career must have drawn the attention of other religious orders. The aggressive tone of his polemics against Aristotle and the Thomistic tradition can hardly have escaped notice elsewhere nor failed to kindle resentment among conservative theologians. It was quite to be expected that when his criticism of scholastic traditions in lectures and sermons developed into an open attack in the earlier Wittenberg disputations, and especially when the theses on indulgences made their appearance, he would draw fire at once from the great brotherhood which since the thirteenth century had occupied the foremost trenches in defense of Catholic dogma, the learned Order of Preachers of St. Dominic.[1] The university at Frankfort on the Oder was a North German stronghold of Dominican theology, and something more than a hint of lively rivalry between Wittenberg and this institution appears here and there in Martin's correspondence before the struggle about indulgences, such as his acid criticism of a work by the Frankfort theologian Wimpina, *Concerning God's Providence,* in 1517.[2] It was at Frankfort, as we have seen, that Tetzel defended Wimpina's theses against Luther. When Martin's *Sermon on Indulgence and Grace* appeared, Tetzel hastened to reply in a lengthy German *Refutation,* in which he called attention to the dangers to faith and practice inherent in Martin's work:

---

[1] For a running account of the early procedure of the Dominicans against Luther, see Kalkoff, "Zu Luthers römischem Prozess," *ZKG,* XXXI (1910), 368 ff., and XXXII (1911), 218 ff. Like Kalkoff's other studies, these are rich in source materials but on occasion unreliable in their "combinations" and conclusions. From the standpoint of a Dominican, Nikolaus Paulus presents the other side in "Die deutschen Dominikaner im Kampfe gegen Luther, 1518–1563," *Erläuterungen und Ergänzungen zu Janssens Geschichte des deutschen Volkes,* Vol. IV, I–II (Freiburg, 1903).

[2] In a letter to Spalatin, May 6, 1517 (Clemen's dating) Luther says that Carlstadt shared his opinion. *WAB,* I, 96 f.

"for everyone will believe what pleases him."[3] These propositions were speedily followed by a series of fifty theses in which Tetzel, pushing aside the question of indulgences, made a strong defense of the pope as supreme in ecclesiastical affairs, supreme therefore over a council of the Church.[4] Even before he went to Heidelberg, Martin saw clearly the camps where his enemies were gathering. Three days after his return he sent to Link the manuscript of his reply to Eck's *Obelisci* for forwarding to Ingolstadt, so that he might see "how dangerous it is to condemn works of others, especially when he does not understand them."[5] About the same time he wrote directly to the recreant friend a sharp letter of offended pride, offering him peace or war.[6] Nevertheless, his admiration for Eck's learning was genuine, and after having shown his displeasure he allowed himself to be mollified. During Luther's absence in Heidelberg his colleague Carlstadt had come to his defense in a series of some three hundred and eighty theses.[7] These took a position well in advance of Martin's in respect to the authority of the Scriptures, demanding that they be interpreted by the entire Church as representing the unity of believers, and going so far as to state that the declaration of a scholar backed by canonical authority is weightier than a declaration by the pope.[8] In the forceful presentation of his position concerning the inability of the human will to open the way to saving grace Carlstadt seconded the view of Luther, but in implications respecting the freedom of the individual conscience he pointed the way toward an acceptance of humanistic ideas which his colleague followed only later and with hesitation. These revolutionary theses were defended in disputations by Carlstadt's students.[9] They took Eck's attack as their springboard, and Martin seems to have greeted them without enthusiasm. He was not eager to add the redoubtable Ingolstadt scholar to his open enemies, and he accepted Scheurl's mediation.[10] Eck also was far from willing to enter into public controversy with the Wittenbergers,[11] and although Martin could not restrain his colleague, a truce was agreed upon between Eck and himself, and Martin's *Asterisks* remained unpublished.[12]

With the enemies at Frankfort it was different. When he saw Tetzel's

---

[3] *Vorlegung . . . wyder eynen vormessen Sermon von tzwentzig irrigen Artikeln.* In *Ref. Act.*, I, 484 ff. Cf. Paulus, "Dominikaner gegen Luther," p. 4.

[4] *Ref. Act.*, I, 517 f.; cf. Paulus, "Dominikaner gegen Luther," pp. 5 f.

[5] *WAB*, I, 177. The affair will be discussed in detail in a later chapter.

[6] *Ibid.*, p. 178.   [7] Barge, *Andreas Bodenstein*, I, 117 ff.

[8] *Ibid.*, p. 119.   [9] *Ibid.*, p. 118.

[10] Letter from Luther to Scheurl, June 15, 1518, *WAB*, I, 183.

[11] See letter from Eck to Carlstadt, May 28, *Ref. Act.*, II, 64 f.

[12] See below, pp. 335 f., n. 50.

refutation and new theses, Martin's heart swelled to the conflict and he gripped his weapon shorter. His counterthrust appeared early in June from a Wittenberg press as *Freedom of the Sermon on Indulgence and Grace*.[13] The brief pamphlet, scarcely ten pages, is in a coarser tone than anything we have yet seen from his pen. In Tetzel's work he can find only a tissue of abuse, and he repays this with interest. In spite of many scriptural references his answer is a repetition in rugged German of previous arguments. The Dominican's charge that he was undermining papal authority is met only by the remark that worse things are now tolerated in Rome.[14]

By the middle of May Luther saw himself surrounded by a well defined circle of enemies. Through Staupitz and Spalatin news may have come to him that the Frankfort Dominicans were taking steps to press his case upon the Roman authorities.[15] The ban of excommunication might appear on the horizon at any time, and it was with emotions thus aroused that he ascended the pulpit on the Sunday following his return from Heidelberg and preached his sermon on the powers of excommunication.[16] The misuse of the ban and the interdict for selfish and political purposes was one of the outstanding grievances against the Church in Germany. The air in Wittenberg was becoming electrical. The preacher's words were noted down and passed around by both friends and enemies. The question was an important one in Saxony, where the ban was taken seriously, and any attempt to stay the arm of Church officialdom in its employment of this weapon in defense of its rights and privileges was certain to arouse resentment in high places. During the summer, reports of Martin's remarks floated far and wide. As usual, he wanted to arrange a public disputation on the subject, but Bishop Scultetus, whose use of the Church's sanctions was a sore subject in Wittenberg and elsewhere, again interfered through a messenger, and Martin cancelled his plans.[17] His opponents wove selected passages from the sermon into a series of theses, which they printed and, as we shall see, used with damaging effect in the highest quarters. Under these circumstances, Luther wrote out the sermon from his notes and published it in the last week of August.

[13] *Eine Freiheit des Sermons päpstlichen Ablass und Gnade belangend. WA*, I, 383 ff.

[14] *Ibid.*, p. 392, ll. 21 ff.

[15] Kalkoff, "Zu Luthers römischem Prozess," *ZKG*, XXXII, 232 ff., suggests that a report denouncing Luther's heresy may have been forwarded to Rome by the Dominican provincial in January. I can find no evidence for this.

[16] For this dating see Clemen, *Luthers Werke*, I, 213.

[17] Letter from Luther to Link, July 10, 1518, *WAB*, I, 186, ll. 39 ff. A series of fourteen rather mild theses on the subject, *De excommunicatione, WA*, IX, 310 ff., discovered by Kawerau in Lübeck, seems to have been defended by Martin in a routine university disputation of the following year.

Whether a warning from the elector really came too late, as he alleges to Spalatin,[18] or whether Martin persisted in spite of it, cannot be said with certainty. In any event, the much advertised discourse found eager readers and appeared in five editions through the fall.[19]

Martin was sure that this *Sermon on the Power of Excommunication* [20] would find favor even among those "who have joy in this tyranny." [21] Certainly the brief tractate as it lies before us in published form contains nothing that deviates from the ancient doctrine that when excommunication is unjustly imposed it does not exclude the sufferer from the inner spiritual life of the Church.[22] To endure such a ban is the noblest service. There appears, however, a fundamental distinction which was slowly emerging in Martin's mind between the Church as a hierarchic organization and the spiritual life of the believer. An idea emerges also which was later to appear as the basis of Luther's attitude toward the political powers: those who wield the weapons unjustly, like Caiphas and Pilate, use a power which God has given into their hands. Their acts are unjust, but their power comes from God.

Whatever Martin may have said to his Wittenberg audience, certainly nothing that had yet come from him fed the rising flame of passion as much as the sermon on the ban, for it touched the authority of the canon law in civil life, a question which was afloat on the surface of the public mind. In midsummer Martin visited the Dresden cloister with the new district vicar, Lang, and was invited to preach on July 25 in the ducal church before George, duke of Saxony, and his court. It was the Feast of Saint James the Greater, and the now distinguished professor, taking his text from the gospel of the day, "Ye know not what ye ask," discoursed on the folly of certain types of prayer and the true object of Christian prayer.[23] There is no other record of what he said, and our knowledge of the affair is based on Martin's account in a letter to Spalatin six months later. It is clear that he faced an unsympathetic audience, and that those who were hostile to him and the development at Wittenberg found much to criticize. The prior of the Augustinian cloister wrote him afterwards that many at court found fault with him for ignorance and arrogance and that parts of his sermon had been misinterpreted. The Wittenberg visitor had an

---

[18] Letter from Luther to Spalatin, Aug. 31, 1518, *WAB*, I, 191, ll. 4 ff.

[19] *WA*, I, 636 ff.

[20] *Sermo de virtute excommunicationis. WA*, I, 638 ff.

[21] *WAB*, I, 192, ll. 6 ff.   [22] Grisar, *Luther*, I, 273.

[23] Luther to Spalatin, Jan. 14, 1519, *WAB*, I, 302, ll. 40 ff. In this letter Martin gives the detailed account of his experiences in Dresden reproduced in the text below.

opportunity to feel the hostile atmosphere at a dinner given by a former Erfurt teacher, Hieronymus Emser. Here Martin fell into an argument with a Leipzig master of arts who had found his attacks on St. Thomas and Aristotle offensive. The dispute seems to have been marked by violent and exaggerated statements on Luther's part and much shouting on the part of his opponents. Later on he learned that a Dominican who was listening outside the door was so angered by his attacks on the great father of scholastic theology that he could hardly restrain himself from rushing in and spitting in the face of the offender. In the bitter polemic which arose between Martin and Emser two years later, there are charges and denials as to warnings which Emser gave to Martin, and fiery and in part unintelligible replies are ascribed to the latter. From his own account of the affair and from the obscure atmosphere of attack and counterattack in his subsequent exchanges with Emser, it appears clear that the Augustinian came into bitter collision with scholastic clerics and that the feeling against him was intensified by his aggressive and defiant attitude.

While the *Explanations of the Disputations on the Power of Indulgences* was dragging its way through the press, the Dominicans at Rome had launched an attack that was calculated to bring the offender promptly to the bar. The intervention of the Augustinian general in February had brought no results except to incite the rebellious friar to a further attack. After the Heidelberg conference it was apparent that no effective steps could be expected from the German Eremites. The Curia therefore moved against him both on theological and political paths. An acceleration of its procedure was probably due to Dominican initiative, possibly as a result of the presence at Rome of representatives of the Brandenburg diocese, which included the university at Frankfort.[24] The proceedings brought into action traditional machinery for the extirpation of heresy. They were initiated by the papal procurator fiscal, who raised a formal charge of suspicion of disseminating heresy. In accordance with canon law, the Pope then commissioned the auditor of the Sacred Palace, the bishop of Ascoli, to summon Martin for a personal hearing and at the same time directed the commissioner of the Sacred Palace, Sylvester Prierias, to draw up a statement of the theological aspects of the question. The auditor, who was entrusted with judicial as well as financial functions, was not a theologian of standing; Prierias, like all the commissioners of the papal palace, was a Dominican

---

[24] Kalkoff, "Zu Luthers römischem Prozess (Schluss)," *ZKG*, XXXIII (1912), 1 ff.; also his *Forschungen*, pp. 50 ff., for a chronological arrangement of the steps at Rome. K. G. Müller, "Luthers römischer Prozess," *ZKG*, XXIV (1903), 46 ff., gives a clear analysis of the sources.

scholar. By virtue of his office he was censor of all books appearing in Roman territory and therefore to some extent a recognized judge in matters of faith. A man of about sixty years of age, Prierias had published three years previously a *Summa Summarium* of theology. This Roman scholar seems to have had before him the Ninety-five Theses and perhaps also those which Martin had prepared for Bernhardi and Günther, and he had made some study of Martin's propositions. He now brought to completion within three days a Latin dialogue, *Against the Presumptuous Theses of Martin Luther concerning the Power of the Pope.*[25] The papal theologian had neither time, learning, nor inclination to go deeply into the question of indulgences, but concentrated on a defense of the papistic theory accepted by the Lateran Council of 1515, the theory which held that the pope as head of the Church was vested with authority above cardinals or council. His pamphlet is couched in the current humanistic phraseology and marked by the self-conceit typical of humanistic controversy. It attacks the presumptuous monk mercilessly and does not hesitate to employ the type of invective current in contemporary polemics, such as, "I am afraid your father might have been a dog"; or "Just as the devil smells of his pride in all his works, so you . . . smell of your malevolence."[26]

The dialogue with its prefatory letter was printed in Rome and reached Wittenberg, perhaps through Spalatin, early in August.[27] It must have been the first evidence to come before Martin's eyes that the Curia had focused its attention upon him, and in spite of all previous warnings, it was undoubtedly a shock. Fifteen years later he recalled that the Pope never hurt him so much as when he glimpsed the words "Commissioner of the Sacred Palace" in the title of this work and realized that now the matter had actually come to the Pope's attention. When he read the frivolous and careless work, however, his fear turned to laughter.[28] To answer such an opponent was no difficult task for a Wittenberg doctor seasoned in the hard knocks of the academic disputation. Here he was on his own ground, and he punned sarcastically to Spalatin on the "Sylvestrian" name of his "very suave" opponent.[29] Mocking the Roman theologian, he claims to have prepared his answer in two days; and in the latter part of August, which saw also the appearance of the *Explanations of the Disputations on*

---

[25] *R. P. Fratris Silvestri Prieriatis . . . in praesumptuosas Martini Lutheri Conclusiones de potestate Papae Dialogus.* Reproduced in *EA,* XXXII, 344 ff.

[26] *Ibid.,* pp. 370 f. and *passim.*

[27] The date of its reception in Wittenberg is not certain, but may have been in advance of the citation of Martin to Rome. See letter from Luther to Spalatin, Aug. 8, 1518, *WAB,* I, 188.

[28] *TR,* I, No. 491 (1533), p. 216, ll. 1 ff.   [29] Letter of Aug. 8, *WAB,* I, 188.

the Power of Indulgences and the *Sermon on Indulgence and Grace*, he brought out his *Response to the Dialogue of Sylvester Prierias on the Power of the Pope.*[30] At the same time he had the dialogue of Prierias reprinted without preface or remark.[31] In a tone as insolent and even more aggressive than that of the Dominican, he sets about the defense of his theses and takes his stand against the papistic theology. He recognizes the Church as existing only in Christ, its representative only in the council.[32] He does not allege that the opinions of the pope in matters concerning faith and morals may be wrong, but he recalls the bloody crimes of Julius II and the tyrannies ascribed to Boniface VIII, and reasserts his ideas regarding the enslavement of the human will and the character of true penance, which sees only its beginning in the sacrament. The *Response* is as rich in references to Church authority and the Scriptures as that of Prierias was lacking in these respects. The old opposition to Aristotle blazes forth anew, and Martin pours on the theological school of his adversary a violent wrath. The spirit of resistance to hierarchical authority is evident, in spite of repeated expressions of deference to papal power. It is clear that he hopes the Pope and council will agree with him, but equally apparent that he is so thoroughly persuaded of the justice of his position that his conviction will remain, no matter what their decision is.

Whatever exultation he may have felt at his apparently easy victory in this exchange was dampened by a summons which reached him on August 7 from the bishop of Ascoli, demanding that he appear in Rome within sixty days and answer for his acts and words.[33] The juristic member of the papal commission had worked with a celerity equal to that of his theological colleague. Before the end of June the former had addressed a letter to the Augustinian general vicar, Venetus, regarding the charges against a member of his order.[34] We do not know the contents of this second communication, but it must have been sharp. The citation to Rome, "those Lernian forests with their hydras and portents," [35] can have caused Martin no great surprise, for he was scarcely ignorant that efforts were being made against him there. Nevertheless the blow had fallen, and the letter which Martin writes to Spalatin, now in Augsburg with the elector in attendance on the Diet, gives evidence of deep anxiety. Despite the almost unanimous backing of his university and the sympathy of friends elsewhere, he felt alone

---

[30] *Ad dialogum Silvestri Prieratis de potestate papae responsio. WA*, I, 647 ff.
[31] *WA*, I, 644 ff.   [32] *Ibid.*, p. 656, ll. 36 f.
[33] *Acta Augustana. WA*, II, 25; see also p. 38. The probable form of the summons has been reconstructed from Pope Leo's letter to Cajetan on August 23 by Müller, "Luthers römischer Prozess," 59 ff.
[34] Kalkoff, *Forschungen*, pp. 51 f.   [35] *WAB*, I, 188, ll. 12 ff.

in the face of the immense power of Rome, which was armed with all the temporal forces subservient to the Church and the eternal yesterdays of a mighty tradition. Only the elector could save him. Once in Rome, he must expect, if not the fate of John Huss, at least an enforced and perpetual silence.

How long the professor of Bible had been in the elector's eye during the years of his development in Wittenberg is impossible to say, but as we have seen, much indicates that Frederick had followed his career with growing interest. The elector had never seen him, but Spalatin, Martin's closest friend, was a firm link between court and cloister. In November of the preceding year, a letter from Martin to Frederick, the first direct communication extant, points to a certain confidence on the part of the writer regarding his relationship to the prince. The letter is marked by a tone of independence that is surprising in an age so heavy with deference to the great. After reminding the patron of the university of an unfulfilled promise of a new cowl, Martin proceeds to warn him quite frankly against putting into operation certain new taxes that were impending.[36] Obviously Martin's confidence was well founded, for there is no evidence that Frederick resented his famous professor's views on saints and good works, despite the fact that they implied criticism of Frederick's ruling passion, the collection of relics for the Castle Church at Wittenberg. Nor does he appear to have taken amiss Martin's attack on indulgences, although the church was, as we have seen, richly equipped with widely advertised and attractive indulgences, which Frederick was seeking to increase. Indeed, as noted above, the professor had received assurances in March that the elector would not allow him to be dragged off to Rome, and Frederick had intervened directly to ensure that Martin's journey to Heidelberg should be without molestation or hardship.

Now Martin appeals to him urgently. His letter of early August has been lost,[37] but we know that it asked the intervention of Frederick to bring about the hearing of his case in Augsburg. Two weeks later he still had no news from the elector but his temper has grown more assured: "I have no fear," he writes to Spalatin, ". . . for I am confident that everything that they are attacking comes to me from God." [38] He has learned that his affair is to occupy the greatest persons in Christendom, since the

---

[36] *Ibid.,* p. 120.

[37] It was probably written on August 7, immediately after Martin received the citation. See his letter to Spalatin, Aug. 8, *WAB,* I, 188, ll. 5 ff.

[38] Letter from Luther to Spalatin, August 28, *WAB,* I, 190, ll. 13 ff. Enders, *Luthers Briefwechsel,* I, 218, dates the letter August 21, but Clemen's argument in *WAB,* I, seems conclusive.

Pope has commissioned his legate, Cardinal Cajetan, "to set in motion the hearts of emperor and princes" against him. He is sorry that his name and affair have grown so great. The days are flitting past, and now his only hope is that the elector will relieve him of the journey to Rome by refusing to give him a safe-conduct. A few days after this he is completely at peace with himself and able to write Spalatin enthusiastically about the splendid impression made by the new professor of Greek, young Philip Melanchthon, and to pun again on the name of his "sylvan" opponent, Prierias.[39] About the same time, he tries to soothe the anxieties of Staupitz with the assurance that neither the citation to Rome nor threats can move him in the slightest. He boils with resentment against Roman arrogance, and promises that if attacks continue he will really unleash his pen and show the Romans that the Germans understand their tricks.[40]

In the meantime papal diplomacy was drawing the net more closely, and a political game was in progress at Augsburg whose stakes included also the safety of the Wittenberg professor. At the head of his opponents now stood Rome's highest representative in Germany and its most distinguished theologian Thomas de Vio, called Cajetanus, Cardinal of San Sisto and general of the Dominican order. Cajetan had left Rome for Germany early in May as apostolic legate, bearing Leo's instructions to endeavor to put an end to the Hussite heresy and win the Germans to the proclamation of a war against the Turks, who were then threatening to overrun Austria.[41] The cardinal and his train were held up long in the Tyrol and Bavaria by the endless official formalities that marked the progress of a high Church dignitary as well as by the personal jealousies which beset the Roman hierarchy in its dealings with the empire.[42] Finally, on July 2, he passed through the gates of Augsburg amid all the ceremonies due the personal representation of the head of Christendom. The Diet, which was awaiting his arrival, immediately convened, and the papal ambassador plunged at once into the difficult task of securing funds from the reluctant princes for

---

[39] Letter from Luther to Spalatin, August 31, *WAB*, I, 192, l. 32.

[40] Letter from Luther to Staupitz, Sept. 1, 1518, *WAB*, I, 193 f.

[41] Papal letter of instruction in C. Baronio and O. Rinaldi, *Annales ecclesiastici*, XXXI, 209 f.; see also *Ref. Act.*, II, 310 ff. The mission of Cajetan is discussed at length by Kalkoff in *Forschungen*, pp. 94 ff.

[42] The Venetian representative in Rome explained Cajetan's delay as due to the insistence of Matthäus Lang, Cardinal of Gurk, that he should also be named as papal legate, and the necessity of awaiting the papal bull of appointment. Sanuto, *I Diarii di Marino Sanuto*, XXV, col. 460. The Venetians mistrusted Cajetan as a Neapolitan and hence a dependent of the Spanish crown, and they had worked against his appointment in Rome. See *ibid.*, col. 367. It is also possible that Maximilian held back Cajetan's arrival in order to delay the opening of the Diet. Kalkoff discusses the question at length in *Forschungen*, pp. 102 ff. See also Von Pastor, *Geschichte der Päpste*, IV, 1, (Freiburg, 1906), 167 and n. 4.

the Turkish campaign. Cajetan had not come with empty hands. Emperor Maximilian received a consecrated hat and sword. Albert, Archbishop of Mainz, was elevated to the cardinalate. To Frederick, the most powerful territorial prince in the empire, Cajetan held out in immediate prospect a long-coveted papal decoration, "The Golden Rose of Virtue," and further indulgences for his church in Wittenberg.

It cannot have been long before the case of the unruly Augustinian came to the attention of the legate. There seems little doubt that the North German Dominicans found a way to approach him, and it is possible that it was they who were responsible for the circulation of the distorted form of Luther's *Sermon on the Power of Excommunication* referred to above. At all events, "theses" of the ill-reputed friar on this subject were circulating in Augsburg and arousing bitter feelings, especially an epilogue in the form of a verse attacking the avarice of the Romans.[43] This came into the hands of the legate. Dominican diplomacy was actively at work at the imperial court. It was no doubt due to its efforts that on August 5, 1518, Maximilian forwarded a letter to the Pope wherein he promised his support in executing the papal judgment against Luther throughout the empire.[44] The letter contained more than one reference to powerful patrons who had been led astray by Luther's error, an obvious thrust at Elector Frederick. Aside from diplomatic motives, it is hardly likely that the aging Maximilian, burdened with a severe political crisis, regarded the affair of Luther as other than a petty academic quarrel.[45] Nevertheless, his attitude toward Frederick at the time was one of resentment, since the elector maintained an unshakable opposition to his efforts to have his grandson, Charles, who had just succeeded to the throne in Spain, elected king of the Romans and thus assured of the imperial crown.[46] Whatever may have been the circumstances which impelled Maximilian to write to Rome, the political situation demanded that he keep a severely neutral position between the Church and the estates.

As usual when the Diet met, the quarters of the territorial princes buzzed with political negotiations. When Cajetan had measured the feeling of the representatives of the estates, he reported to Rome that the Germans must not be provoked at this time.[47] The situation that confronted the Church

[43] Letter from Spalatin to Luther, Sept. 5, 1518, *WAB*, I, 201, ll. 33 ff.

[44] *EA*, XXXIII, 350.

[45] In the *Table Talk* Luther is credited with a statement that Maximilian told the Saxon councilor Degenhard Pfeffinger at Augsburg that the theses on indulgences were not to be despised. *TR*, V, No. 5343, a passage of doubtful authenticity.

[46] Maximilian's efforts to gain the support of the elector Frederick for Charles's succession had been actively in progress since December, 1517. *DRA*, I, 67 ff. Frederick's refusal seems to have been made quite categorically. *Ibid.*, p. 94 and n. 3.

[47] Letter of Sept. 8, 1518, cited by Kalkoff, *Forschungen*, p. 127.

in Germany was a difficult one, for the long roll of ecclesiastical abuses came constantly to the fore, and it was only the selfish interests of the various princes that enabled Roman diplomacy to forestall a concerted demand for relief through a council of the Church. The list of "burdens" had already been compiled and was extensive: the accumulation of Church offices in the hands of one person, the incorporation of parishes under monasteries, the leasing out of ecclesiastical offices, the ever recurring disputes between clerical and urban authorities over exemptions from taxation on Church property and commerce, the interference of the diocesan officials in order to make effective the canon law in civil cases—all these and many other complaints had now reached a point where reform seemed only a matter of time.[48] In addition to other causes of resentment against Rome, the record of Leo's predecessors in raising money through indulgences for a crusade against the Turks and its subsequent expenditure for political aggrandizement of the papacy dwelt in bitter memory among the estates since the days of Julius II. Under conditions such as these the two papal delegates, Cajetan and the German cardinal of Gurk, Matthäus Lang,[49] faced their task, which, in addition to securing support for the war against the Turks, consisted in checking Maximilian's ambition for the election of his successor.[50]

Thus, in a manner of which he could have had no conception, the Wittenberg professor's fate was tossed back and forth on political waves. He himself saw his opponents only in the rival religious order which was pressing the charge of heresy against a lowly son of the Church for teaching in conformity with what he considered its unpolluted traditions. At all events, the wheels of the machinery at Rome were now turning swiftly. It is not certain whether the *Explanations of the Disputations on the Power of Indulgences,* sent to Staupitz in manuscript on May 20, went to Rome

---

[48] The economic burdens of clerical privileges were an especial source of irritation in the cities. See A. Störmann, "Die städtischen Gravamina gegen den Klerus," *RgST,* XXIV–XXVI (1916), 160 ff.; also, for a general historical review, G. von Below, "Die Ursachen der Reformation," *Historische Bibliothek,* XXXVIII (1917), *passim;* see also Von Pastor, *Geschichte der Päpste,* IV, 1, 169 ff.

[49] Letter from Spalatin to Luther, Sept. 5, 1518, *WAB,* I, 201. Lang, who was of lowly origin, was much disliked by the German princes for this reason and because of his persistent and successful pursuit of Church offices. Already bishop of Gurk and a cardinal, he added to these offices and honors the archbishopric of Salzburg in 1519. He was for many years a trusted adviser of Maximilian, to whom he remained loyal through many crises. If he influenced the negotiations at the Augsburg Diet, it was in support of imperial rather than papal interests, and he was probably a hindrance rather than a help in Cajetan's efforts.

[50] Ulmann, *Kaiser Maximilian I,* II, 713 ff., gives a running account of the negotiations at the Augsburg Diet. The sources respecting the emperor's effort to secure the succession for his grandson, Charles, and the counter-intrigues of the King of France are to be found in *DRA,* I.

in that form, but Martin's letter to Pope Leo certainly was not long delayed, and it no doubt accelerated the citation for suspicion of heresy. The garbled form of the *Sermon on the Power of Excommunication* and reports of forthcoming publications of Martin also found their way to Rome, and these together with the pressure from the Dominican side speeded up action by the papal inquisitors. The examination of the papal commission had now shown that Martin had attained "notoriety as a heretic," and the judicial official of the Curia felt it necessary to secure his person.

This was attempted in two ways. The general of the Augustinians, Venetus, had been apprised of the citation, and on August 25 he sent a letter to the head of the Saxon province, commanding him to proceed against Martin as a rebel and enemy of the Cross of Christ, to have him seized, manacled hand and foot, and put behind bars at the disposal of the Pope. The authority of the Pope was attached to this procedure, which included the right of interdict and excommunication in case of interference.[51] In turning to the head of the nonreformed cloisters, the general indicated that his own authority had been defied by the Eremites. Two days before Venetus acted, the papal authorities had directed similar instructions to Cardinal Cajetan in a breve of August 23, ordering the legate to declare the monk a notorious heretic and to summon him into his presence, calling on the empire and the estates for help. If, then, Martin did not recant, he was to be held pending further orders from Rome. If he did not obey the summons, he and his followers were to be excommunicated.[52] In case of opposition from religious or secular quarters the document armed the cardinal with powers of excommunication and interdict, sanctions which lost nothing of their terror in the sonorous periods of the papal secretary, Sadoletus. On the same date the Pope wrote to Frederick, conjuring him by his faith and that of his fathers to have this "child of evil" turned over to the legate.[53]

An escape from the tightening meshes of the net lay only through the interference of Elector Frederick. At this juncture the diplomatic situation had put the Saxon ruler in a position of strategic power. From Paris, Francis

---

[51] The text of Venetus's communication, discovered by Kolde in an Augustinian codex in Munich and published in "Innere Bewegungen unter den deutschen Augustinern und Luthers Romreise," *ZKG*, II (1878), 476 ff., seems incontestable. Luther appears to have heard of the mandate, which was probably passed on to the Augsburg chapter of his order. *WA*, II, 17, l. 34.

[52] Text in *Ref. Act.*, II, 437 ff.; *WA*, II, 23 ff. K. G. Müller analyzes the judicial procedure involved in the summary process and the canonical justification for the papal instruction in "Luthers römischer Prozess," *ZKG*, XXIV, 64 ff. Kalkoff discusses the papal breve at length in "Zu Luthers römischem Prozess," *ZKG*, XXV (1904), 273 ff., reaching practically the same conclusion.

[53] *Ref. Act.*, II, 443 f.; *EA*, XXXIII, 352 ff.

I was spinning golden threads to the electoral courts in furtherance of his ambition for the imperial crown, and as long as the succession remained unsettled Maximilian could certainly not proceed against the most powerful and respected prince in Germany for the sake of a theological dispute. For the Vatican also, things did not go well at Augsburg. The answer of the estates to the request for tithes and troops for the Turkish war was a repetition of grievances over ecclesiastical abuses, and the legates encountered stiff opposition to collective action by the Diet.[54] Despite his shrewdness, however, Frederick was under heavy pressure. Martin feared that this was on his account, and wrote in anxiety to Spalatin that he wished it to be known that he alone was responsible and that his opponents would find him ready to show or be shown.[55] A few days later the situation looked better, and the troubled professor must have been greatly cheered by an optimistic letter from the electoral chaplain. The legate was showing himself much more conciliatory than had been expected. In addition Spalatin was evidently deeply impressed by the courage and scholarship shown in the *Explanations of the Disputations on Indulgences,* which now lay before him, and by the interest of others in the embattled friar. He urges him, therefore, to have the courage of a theologian, but to be careful not to stir up any more hornets' nests with sermons and disputations.[56]

It is clear that the elector and his advisers sympathized with Martin's insistence that his case be heard in Germany and regarded his offer to submit himself to impartial judges in a neutral place as a fair proposal.[57] The astute Saxon prince discussed the matter personally with the legate, who then forwarded to Rome the request that he himself be permitted to hear and terminate the matter.[58] On September 16 Martin writes Lang that the elector has informed him that the legate has asked Rome to permit his case to be heard in Germany.[59] The news from Augsburg in the first week of September was of a nature to move the Pope to concessions, for just about that time the papal court must have received information from Cajetan

---

[54] See Ulmann, *Kaiser Maximilian I,* II, 716 ff.

[55] Letter from Luther to Spalatin, Sept. 2, 1518, *WAB,* I, 195 f.

[56] Spalatin to Luther, Sept. 5, *WAB,* I, 200 f.

[57] "In loco non suspecto, iudicibus non suspectis." *Ibid.,* p. 201, ll. 15 ff. In a letter written by Spalatin on commission of Elector Frederick to the imperial councilor Renner (*Ref. Act.,* II, 445), the latter is urged to persuade Maximilian to intervene with the Pope to allow Luther's case to be heard by the bishops of Würzburg and Freisingen and any unbiased university, specifically excepting Erfurt, Leipzig, and Frankfort. The letter was probably written in the latter part of August.

[58] Kalkoff, *Forschungen,* pp. 57 ff., reconstructs Cajetan's phrasing of this request from a papal breve in reply to the legate, probably dated September 11, published in garbled form in Fontana, *Theatrum Dominicarum,* p. 346.

[59] *WAB,* I, 203.

about the resistance of Frederick to the election of young Charles. That the Saxon elector should adhere to this resolution in the face of continued pressure from Maximilian was greatly desired by the Medicis, and they opened a chest of long-desired favors. On September 10 young Karl von Miltitz, a Saxon attached to the Curia, wrote to Spalatin that he had in his hands the Golden Rose of Virtue for delivery to Frederick, as well as the bulls of indulgence and full confessional privileges for the Castle Church in Wittenberg.[60] On the following day a papal breve was addressed to the cardinal legate, in which he was authorized to have Martin brought before him in Augsburg, and having heard and examined him, to pronounce absolution or condemnation.[61] This authorization reached Augsburg in time for Cajetan to inform the elector before the departure of the Saxon court on September 22. On the next day the Diet adjourned, referring the Turkish question to the decision of the individual states [62] and leaving undecided the confirmation of Maximilian's successor.[63] The possibility that Frederick himself might finally be a successful compromise candidate for the imperial crown must have occurred to many.

Martin was to be heard in Augsburg, but it became clear later that the legate and the elector differed in their interpretation of the procedure to be followed.[64] Both, to be sure, understood that the Augsburg hearing was to be conducted by the cardinal "with fatherly kindness." [65] They differed as to the treatment of the defendant in case he should refuse to recant. Frederick, as will appear below, looked upon the hearing rather as a conference for adjustment, which in case of failure would be followed by a full hearing before neutral judges. The cardinal as the representative of the papal authority was obliged to regard a refusal to recant as leading inevitably to condemnation.

It is probable that the first news of the arrangement came back to Saxony with the electoral party, reaching Martin in the last week of September. In the meantime, his friends both within and without the order knew

[60] E. S. Cyprian, "Nützliche Urkunden zur Erläuterung der ersten Reformationsgeschichte," in *Tentzels Historischer Bericht vom Anfang und Fortgang der Reformation Lutheri*, I (Leipzig, 1717), II, 53 f.

[61] *WAB*, I, 203.   [62] Ulmann, *Kaiser Maximilian I*, II, 718 f.

[63] On September 1 four electors and the proxies of the kings of Bohemia and Poland signed a document pledging themselves to vote for Charles as Maximilian's successor. Saxony and Trier remained aloof. *DRA*, I, 110.

[64] After K. G. Müller's analysis, "Luthers römischer Prozess," pp. 65 ff., Kalkoff clarified the situation further, *Forschungen*, pp. 53 ff. and 152 ff. See also Von Pastor, *Geschichte der Päpste*, IV, 1, 254 f.

[65] ". . . paterne tamen, non iudicialiter," Luther's version of Cajetan's assurance to him in initiating their conference. Letter from Luther to the elector, Frederick, Nov. 21(?), 1518, *WAB*, I, 233, ll. 42 f. See also *WA*, II, 16, l. 28.

nothing of these moves but heard the most alarming reports. Martin's tendency to impulsive action was well known, and some feared a sudden violent outbreak against his enemies that would make his case hopeless. In Basel, where Wolfgang Capito was preparing an edition of Luther's works, this industrious scholar was beside himself with anxiety and he urged Martin by the example of the Apostles to proceed with circumspection against the citadel of Church tyranny.[66] The university at Wittenberg naturally felt itself exposed to fire, and rector and faculty joined to defend their now famous colleague in two letters, evidently drafted before the news of the elector's arrangement with Cajetan had reached their city. With due humility the faculty supports Martin's petition that he be dispensed from the journey to Rome on account of weak health and the dangers of the route. Admitting that he may indeed have disputed "somewhat more freely" than he should have, they testify to his orthodoxy.[67] On the same day the faculty addressed to Karl von Miltitz a plea to use his influence with the Pope in Martin's defense, adding emphatic assurances of their colleague's erudition and piety, and charging Miltitz as a fellow countryman and a German to stand by another German in his difficulties.[68]

Amid these events the summer of 1518 came to an end and the day of Luther's departure for Augsburg approached. Some years later in his *Table Talk*, Martin recalled vividly his fears:[69] "I clearly saw my grave ready and kept saying to myself, 'What a disgrace I shall be to my dear parents!'" Even now that the hearing had been transferred to German soil, examples of the treatment of former protesting sons of the Church must have assailed him day and night. Little more than a century before, John Huss, a scholar better supported than he by the temporal power, had gone to the Council of Constance under a safe-conduct of Emperor Sigismund and had perished amid faggots piled by Dominican hands. In July, Lang had passed on to him a warning from Albert, count of Mansfeld, not to leave Wittenberg because certain persons of influence were preparing to have him strangled or drowned.[70] Faced by an encirclement of hatred, Martin speaks with the resigned spirit of one prepared for the last sacrifice:

Only one thing is left, a weak and miserable broken body. If they take that away they will cut me off perhaps from one or two hours of life, but the soul they cannot

---

[66] Letter from Capito to Luther, Sept. 4, 1518, *WAB*, I, 197 f.

[67] *EA*, XXXIII, 363 f.   [68] *Ibid.*, pp. 361 f.

[69] *TR*, II, Nos. 2668a and 2668b (1532).

[70] Letter from Luther to Link, July 10, 1518, *WAB*, I, 185, ll. 13 ff. The date of the letter has caused discussion, but both Enders and Clemen set it at July 10. It is probable that Martin was planning at that time the journey to Dresden which he made with Lang in the last week of July.

take . . . I know that from the beginning the word of Christ has been such that whoever wants to present it in the world must necessarily, like the Apostles, renounce everything and expect death at every hour. If it were not so, then it would not be the word of Christ. It was bought with death, it has spread abroad with manifold death. With manifold death it must be preserved or brought back again.[71]

[71] *Ibid.*, ll. 27 ff. See also his words to Staupitz, *WA*, I, 525 ff.

16

THE HEARING AT AUGSBURG

"LET the will of the Lord be done. In Augsburg, even in the midst of his enemies, Jesus Christ rules. May Christ live even though Martin and every sinner perish." [1] To the Wittenberg friends, many of whom had tried to dissuade him from the journey, the professor sends this solemn greeting from the road, perhaps from Nuremberg. He was facing a great crisis in a career rich in dramatic moments. The appearance before Cajetan lacks, to be sure, the theatrical interest of the climax attained three years later in his appearance before the emperor and the Diet at Worms. In some ways also it does not awaken the deep psychological interest of his memorable journey to South Germany in 1530, when, forbidden as a public outlaw to approach Augsburg, he dwelt for months among the jackdaws on the eerie heights of Castle Coburg and followed with tense anxiety the efforts of the Wittenberg group to consolidate Church reform in conference with representatives of the old faith and the reformers from southern and eastern Germany. Nevertheless, the interview with Cardinal Cajetan opened the rift with the authority of Rome and thus put to a more severe test than any later occasion his resolution to accept no compromise affecting his theological position.

The interview with the papal legate was, in another respect as well, a great milestone in his career. Here, in an imperial city, the friar and cloister teacher made his entry on the world stage. A little more than seven years earlier he had paused in Augsburg, an unknown young monk returning from his journey to Rome, his mind filled with veneration for the Church, its traditions, and its hierarchy. Now, a widely known scholar, supported by a powerful prince and bearing the sympathies and hopes of many hearts, but suspected or hated by many others, he saw himself an object of universal attention. He knew that emperor and Pope had made him the subject of

[1] Letter from Luther to Wittenberg friends, Oct. 3 or 4, 1518, *WAB,* I, 208.

official correspondence, but he could not guess at that time how far other high chancelleries of Europe had been occupied with his name.[2]

There is evidence that he started on his momentous journey fully aware of the importance of his position. It is clear also from his letters, as we have seen above, that any feelings of pride were stilled by the thought that this might be his last look at the hills and valleys of his native Thuringia.[3] The memory of his fears and his feeling of physical weakness during the journey remained vivid for many years.[4] He could not look into the cards of his opponents nor know how far the influence of the elector would avail to save him, and his spirit was shaken by the fears of his friends, who believed that he was going to his death. In this mind he set forth, just as September drew to its close, traveling, as the rules of the order demanded, with an Augustinian brother, apparently Leonard Beyer, his colleague at the Heidelberg disputation.[5] On the 29th he paused at Weimar and preached in the church of the ducal castle.[6] According to an early biographer, Myconius, he spent the night and said Mass at the Franciscan cloister, where the steward warned him that the sly Italians would burn him. To this Martin is said to have answered, with the sort of morose humor that marks so much of his *Table Talk*, that if his cause was lost, the shame would be God's.[7] In later years he recalled that the elector gave him twenty guilders for the journey;[8] even so, as a mendicant he had to make the journey on "the feet of the Apostles." When he reached Nuremberg he borrowed from his Augustinian brother, Link, a better cowl to replace his shabby one. Ex-

[2] An echo from Rome in the letter of September 4 from the Venetian representative at the Vatican to the Signoria is worth quoting: "Il Papa ha deliberato di mandar la rosa . . . al duca di Saxonia, desiderando con il suo mezo extirpare una secta che de li è nasuta per il predicar di uno frate di l'ordene di Predicatori [a lively memory of Savonarola, perhaps!] che danna la vita si observa al presenta, et non vole che le indulgentie a questo modo date siano di alcun valore; la qual cossa li a Roma è tenuta per grande eresia." Sanuto, *I Diarii di Marino Sanuto*, XXVI, col. 18.

[3] Letter to Spalatin, Oct. 10, 1518, *WAB*, I, 210, ll. 59 ff.; letter to Melanchthon, Oct. 11, *WAB*, I, 213.

[4] *TR*, I, No. 509 (1533); II, Nos. 2668a and 2668b (1532).

[5] Letter from Luther to Spalatin, *WAB*, I, 210, l. 53. *TR*, II, No. 2668b; V, No. 5349 (1540), p. 78.

[6] Some three months later he reproduced the sermon from memory at Spalatin's request. Text in *EA*, XXXII, 226 ff. See also Luther's letter to Spalatin, late December, 1518, *WAB*, I, 284 f., and that to the same friend a few days earlier, *WAB*, I, 282. In this form it is a bitter attack on hypocrisy in Church office, probably considerably strengthened in invective as a result of his Augsburg experience.

[7] E. S. Cyprian, "Nützliche Urkunden zur Erläuterung der ersten Reformationsgeschichte," in *Tentzels Historischer Bericht vom Anfang und Fortgang der Reformation Lutheri*, II (Leipzig, 1718), II, 31.

[8] *TR*, II, Nos. 2668a and 2668b; V, No. 5349. In both of these reports the account of the journey is confused, and the second report is of doubtful authenticity.

ceedingly weary of foot and plagued by constipation,[9] the disorder which was probably the cause of so many physical crises in his later years, he welcomed the help of a wagon when he was three miles from his goal, and so rode into the ancient capital of the Lech Valley on October 7. Christoph Scheurl was absent from Nuremberg and could not accompany him as legal adviser, as the careful elector had requested,[10] but Link came along, and in Augsburg Martin found two councilors of the Saxon court waiting to guide him with advice. At the cloister of the Carmelites he found hospitable care at the hands of the prior, a former Wittenberger,[11] and the distinguished humanist Konrad Peutinger gave him a dinner. The emperor was absent, but the court officials were polite and helpful. Under such circumstances his mood rose and the will to fight burned strongly. Four days after his arrival he writes his young colleague Melanchthon that he will die rather than recant and thus help the enemies of scholarship to destroy the "best studies." [12]

The situation soon clarified. In certain respects fortune was on his side. In his favor was the absence of Maximilian and of the German legate *a latere,* the cardinal of Gurk, Matthäus Lang. Behind him stood the seasoned councilors of the Saxon court to see that he made no false moves. They would not let him see the cardinal at all until he had secured a safe conduct from the emperor and the city.[13] On the other side stood the papal legate, armed with all the prestige which the Roman court could provide and attended by a group of astute Italians. The national contrast could not have been absent from the minds of the German officials and burghers in Augsburg; it was certainly not absent from that of Martin. His first collision came the second day after his arrival in a visit from one of the Italians, Urban of Serralonga, a young aristocrat in attendance on Cajetan, who had visited Frederick's court the year before on a diplomatic mission on behalf of Margrave William of Montferrat and was known to the Saxons as the "orator of Mount Ferrat." [14] He made a formal call on Martin and tried to persuade him that he should return to the Church and avoid all further disputation, warning him especially not to attempt any dialetical jousting with the legate. Martin declared his willingness to recant if it could be

---

[9] Letter from Luther to Spalatin, Oct. 10, 1518, *WAB,* I, 209, ll. 6 ff.

[10] *Ibid.,* p. 211, n. 16. See also Scheurl, *Briefbuch,* II, 50 f. and 53 f. (letter from Scheurl to Spalatin); p. 57 (letter from Scheurl to Otto Beckmann).

[11] Roth, *Augsburgs Reformationsgeschichte 1517–1527,* p. 54 and note.

[12] Letter from Luther to Melanchthon, Oct. 11, 1518, *WAB,* I, 213, ll. 12 ff.

[13] Letter from Luther to Elector Frederick, Nov. 1518, *WAB,* I, 237, ll. 27 ff. and 37 ff.

[14] We have only Martin's account of the interview with Urban. See his letter to Spalatin, Oct. 10, 1518, *WAB,* I, 209 ff.; to Frederick, Nov. 21(?), 1518, *WAB,* I, 236 f.

shown that he had said anything except what the Church recognized as true. In the responses of the Italian he heard only a cynical defense of lying for profit and persistent arguments for the absolute supremacy of the pope in matters of faith. He recalled that Urban asked him sarcastically if he believed that the elector would take up arms for him.[15] To the suspicious monk, this go-between was just a representative of Roman trickery: "In brief, he is and remains an Italian," he comments to Spalatin.[16]

Three days later, on October 12, Martin entered the presence of the legate.[17] The imperial safe-conduct had finally been granted with the consent of the cardinal, who was much irritated at this lack of confidence on the part of Elector Frederick.[18] Flanking the Wittenberg professor stood his host, the Carmelite prior, and certain monks from that cloister, as well as two Augustinian brothers, Link and probably Beyer. Facing him Martin saw the Italian prelate and behind him Urban and several Italians, who now crowded forward with looks of curiosity. Among them was the papal nuncio, Marino Caracciolo; the others were probably Italian cavaliers in the cardinal's train.[19]

The man who formed the center of this group was in scholarship a character fully worthy of the honors which the Church had bestowed on him.[20]

---

[15] *TR*, III, No. 3857 (1538).   [16] *WAB*, I, 209, l. 32.

[17] It is possible that a preliminary visit to the cardinal had taken place on October 10. Martin forecasts this in a letter to Spalatin that day, *WAB*, I, 209 ff., and in a statement to the same correspondent on October 14, "Dominus legatus iam quarto die mecum . . . agit," *WAB*, I, 214, l. 9, he implies that it took place. On the other hand, all his other accounts of the hearing make the impression that the meeting of October 12 was his first confrontation of the legate. Clemen, however, interprets otherwise. See *WAB*, I, 215, n. 1.

[18] Letter from Cajetan to Elector Frederick, Oct. 25, 1518, *WAB*, I, 233, ll. 1 ff. The imperial safe conduct was forwarded to the Augsburg council on October 11.

[19] Cajetan's notarial affirmation of the papal bull on indulgences, made at Linz in Austria on December 13, 1518, includes the names of two Italian aristocrats as witnesses (*EA*, XXXIII, 433), but whether these were present at the Augsburg hearing, as Kalkoff assumes in Luther, *Ausgewählte Werke*, I, 410 f., is uncertain. Luther evidently did not know them. See *Acta Augustana*, *WA*, II, 7, l. 40.

[20] No satisfactory biography of De Vio exists. Cossio, *Il cardinale Gaetano e la Riforma*, I, is regarded as ill informed, according to Kalkoff, "Zu Luthers römischem Prozess (Schluss)," *ZKG*, XXXIII (1912), 240, n. 1. The work of Giovanni Battista Flavio, who came into the cardinal's service as secretary in 1518, has the form of a memorial address: *Oratio de vita sanctissimi viri maximeque Reverendi D. Thomae de Vio Caietani, cardinalis S. Xysti*, probably published in 1534. It is extremely rare, but available in *Thomae de Vio, D. Caietani Opera omnia, quotquot in Sacrae Scripturae expositionem reperiuntur*, Vol. I, where Vita and Carmen have no paging. Flavio's brief work is a wholehearted defense of the cardinal's life and character. As representative of Rome's political policies, 1518-20, Cajetan was unpopular with reformers and humanists like Hutten, whose bitter satires against him will be considered below, and the tone of Lutheran writers in the intolerant centuries was equally unjust. Luther evidently respected his sincerity, and modern Lutherans seem inclined to do him justice. See Kalkoff, in "G. B. Flavio als Biograph Kajetans und sein Bericht über Luthers Verhör in Augsburg," *ZKG*, XXXIII, 11; and in Luther, *Ausgewählte Werke*, I, 409 f. See also bibliography

In Thomas de Vio, Dominican theology found a truly classical exponent. Born in the coastal town of Gaeta, near Naples, from which derives the name Gaetano (Latin: Cajetanus), most frequently given him by historians, he entered the Dominican order at sixteen years of age and trod the usual paths of learning in philosophy and theology, becoming a teacher of these subjects in the general studies of Dominican cloisters in Naples and northern Italy and later at the universities in Padua, Pavia, and Rome. An intensive student and an able teacher and theologian, devoted to the scholastic tradition, he won high prestige in Dominican circles and became general of the order in 1508. True to its ideas he appeared as champion of the supreme authority of the pope at the time of the pseudo-council at Pisa in 1511–12 and at the Fifth Lateral Council of 1512–17. In the struggle against the University of Paris in its efforts to establish the authority of the council, the writings and eloquence of the great churchman gave learned support to the papal cause, and in 1517 he was made cardinal of San Sisto. His scholarship was widely recognized and he was vigorous in promoting the studies in the Dominican institutions. In rigid performance of religious duties and ascetic simplicity of life he was "a guardian of the ancient usage," as his secretary testifies,[21] and in this respect a striking contrast to many higher officials under Julius II and Leo X. An openhanded generosity to dependents and subordinates kept him poor throughout life. His criticisms of ecclesiastical abuses were almost as severe as Luther's, particularly his strictures on plurality of office and greed among Roman officials. For his failure to carry out the Medician policies in Germany in 1518 he fell into disfavor at the papal court, but became again a trusted councilor of their more spiritually minded successor, Adrian VI. He seems to have been regarded as the chief dogmatic authority by Pope Clement VII, who commissioned him to examine the claim of Henry VIII to an annulment of his marriage with Catherine of Aragon. The conscientious churchman upheld its validity. Contemporaries felt that he would have succeeded to the papal crown had he outlived Pope Clement.[22] His series of commentaries on Thomas Aquinas, to which he devoted himself for fifteen years, fills nine great

---

in Lauchert's edition of De Vio's *De divina institutione pontificatus Romani pontificis*, in *Corpus Catholicorum*, X, vi ff. See also Lauchert, "Die italienischen literarischen Gegner Luthers," *Erläuterungen und Ergänzungen zu Janssens Geschichte des deutschen Volkes*, VIII, 133 ff.

[21]
        Et priscos mores, mandataque prisca relinquent
        Quae veterum ad normam Xystus servare coegit.

"Carmen," in Flavio, *Oratio de vita . . . Caietani*, I [p. 16].

[22] Flavio, *Oratio de vita . . . Caietani*, I [p. 15]; see also *Catholic Encyclopedia*, III, 146.

volumes of the Vatican edition of the Angelic Doctor and is regarded as a classic by the Church of Rome.[23]

The cardinal received Martin in a fatherly manner and, except for occasional outbursts of anger, his attitude remained kind throughout.[24] Nevertheless, his demands were categorical. Martin must recant his errors and promise to refrain in the future from these and from anything else that might disturb the peace of the Church. When the Augustinian asked to be shown his errors, the cardinal formulated them with dialectical clearness: the thesis which denied that the merit of Christ and the saints was the foundation of indulgences, and the statement in the *Explanations of the Disputations on the Power of Indulgences* that the force of the sacrament was dependent upon the faith of the communicant. An argument then followed which was a collision between two methods of theological thought so widely divergent that the participants unconsciously ceased to speak the same language. On the one side, scholastic interpretations and the principle of supreme papal authority; on the other, the Holy Scriptures, which Martin poured forth with his usual fluency and accompanied with his own interpretations. The discussion revolved first about a bull of Clement VI of 1343, incorporated into the canon law; then traversed the position of the pope in relation to the Scriptures, the Church, and the council, and passed on to Gerson's belief in the importance of a Church council and the pending appeal of the University of Paris to such a council against the absolute authority of the pope. The stage was certainly unfavorable for an understanding. Martin's attempts at a rebuttal of the Clementine bull by means of scriptural authority were overwhelmed with assertions drawn from the scholastic arsenal by an expert in Thomistic literature, authorities which the Wittenberg professor had come to regard as enemies of the true faith. "He is perhaps a famous Thomist, but a vague, obscure, and unintelligible theologian or Christian and therefore as unsuited to understand and judge in this matter

---

[23] *S. Thomae Aquinatis op. omnia*, Vols. IV–XII (Rome, 1888–1903).

[24] The sources for our knowledge of the three conferences are detailed, although rather one-sided. Luther's vivid accounts in two letters dashed off in the Carmelite monastery, to Spalatin and Carlstadt, *WAB*, I, 213 ff., are supplemented by his formal pleas to Cajetan at Augsburg, *WAB*, I, 217 ff., and his review two months later in the *Acta Augustana*, *WA*, II, 6 ff. Finally, he reviewed the affair in the summary of his life prefaced to the Wittenberg edition of his works in 1545, *WA*, LIV, 179 ff. A secondary source of value is Spalatin's report, which was undoubtedly based on conversations with Martin. Walch, *Schriften*, XV, 679 ff. From Cajetan there is only the letter of arraignment to Frederick. *WAB*, I, 233 ff. His secretary, Flavio, seems not to have been present, but the latter's account was no doubt derived from the Italians who were there. It is vivid, but does not go into the theological discussion. A brief memorandum by the Saxon councilor Johann Ruel, who was present at one of the sessions, is no more than a factual statement colored by strong admiration of Martin's attitude. *EA*, XXXIII, 365.

as an ass to play the harp," he wrote to Carlstadt after the conferences ended.[25] Spalatin reported, doubtless basing on the impressions of the Saxon councilors, that "as soon as the legate opened his mouth, the whole talk was of nothing but Thomas, notions, and scholastic matters," and that when the cardinal declared that the pope had power over everything, Martin broke in with *Salva Scriptura!* (except the Scriptures!).[26] The first conference ended as it had begun, with the demand that Martin recant, and with a "gracious oration" from the cardinal. Martin then withdrew with a plea for time for consideration.

When he reached the convent he found that Staupitz had arrived and was awaiting him there. On the next day the general vicar accompanied his younger friend to the cardinal. With him went the Augsburg patrician, Peutinger, the Saxon chancellor, Von Feilitzsch, four imperial councilors, and a notary. Thus flanked by spiritual and legal counsel, Martin read a brief formula [27] which declared that he followed the Church in all its past, present, and future commands, but in answer to the demands of the cardinal he insisted that he could not be forced to a recantation until he had been heard and proved in error. He was ready to set forth in public his views and await the decision of the faculties of Basel, Freiburg, Louvain, and of Paris, "which from ancient days has been regarded as the most Christian university and most excellent in Holy Scriptures."

On the third day, accompanied this time only by the two Saxon councilors, the friar appeared again before the cardinal [28] and solemnly presented his written justification.[29] This document, prepared in haste but with great care, is a curious mixture of sophistical reasoning and sincere argument. In fifty-six paragraphs bristling with Scriptural quotations he defends his attitude on the two points which the cardinal had condemned, denying the efficacy of the accumulated merit of the saints for forgiveness of sin and contending for the necessity of faith to justification. The exigencies of the argument against the bull of Pope Clement have now driven him to an unequivocal statement regarding the papal power, and he declares that he can recognize the truth of the decree only if it squares with Holy Scriptures. He begs the legate to have sympathy with his conscience and show him the truth and not to force him to a recantation, for, "so long as the passages of the Scripture

---

[25] Letter from Luther to Carlstadt, Oct. 14, 1518, *WAB*, I, 216, ll. 39 ff.

[26] Walch, *Schriften*, XV, 681. [27] *WA*, II, 8 f.

[28] Letter from Luther to Spalatin, Oct. 14, 1518, *WAB*, I, 214, l. 9. There is some discrepancy in Luther's dating of the third, and last, conference, but it seems clear that it took place on Thursday, October 14. See Clemen's discussion, *WAB*, I, 247 ff.

[29] Reproduced in the *Acta Augustana*, *WA*, II, 9 ff.

stand, I cannot do otherwise. . . . It would be my greatest joy to see the truth victorious." [30]

The cardinal promised to send the "justification" to Rome, but again he faced the friar with an imperative *Revoca!* The interview, as Martin described it that evening in his letter to Spalatin, developed into a violent argument over the bull of Clement in which both shouted at the top of their lungs amid excited gestures and mocking laughter. The Wittenberg professor, whose theological training had included many a hard-fought disputation, drove the legate to an outbreak of temper. Thus aroused, the cardinal dismissed him: "Go and do not return unless you are ready to recant!" [31] When he was back in the Carmelite cloister Martin relieved his feelings in letters to Spalatin and Carlstadt: "I will not become a heretic by contradicting the opinion with which I became a Christian: I will rather die, be burned, exiled, accursed." [32]

The Saxon councilors were delighted at the skill with which their scholar defended himself and chuckled with national pride over the discomfiture of the Italians.[33] On reflection, however, neither side seems to have felt that all hope of a satisfactory ending was yet lost. According to Flavio, Cajetan's secretary, the cardinal was of the opinion that Martin was held back from a recantation by shame rather than by inner conviction.[34] Before the close of the fateful day the legate summoned Staupitz and Link in another effort to adjust the matter.[35] In a fatherly manner he assured them of his friendship for Martin and urged them to persuade him to recant. Martin did not yet know of the stern instructions of the Pope in his breve of August 23, but the Saxon group had learned that something drastic was in the wind and probably advised extreme caution. At any event, several days later [36] the professor addressed a humble letter to the legate asking pardon for his lack of respect and offering to keep silence if his opponents could be silenced. As concerns a recantation, he avoids a flat refusal, but asks that the matter be referred to the Pope in order that he may obey the judgment of the Church.

It is not clear what the friends intended to advise; but one alternative they considered may have been a refuge for the friar at the University of Paris,

[30] *Ibid.*, p. 16, ll. 10 ff.
[31] Letter from Luther to Spalatin, Oct. 14, 1518, *WAB*, I, 214, ll. 38 f.
[32] Letter from Luther to Carlstadt, Oct. 14, 1518, *WAB*, I, 217, ll. 59 ff.
[33] Spalatin, in the Wittenberg edition of Luther's works (1551–69), Vol. IX, pp. 35v. and 36r.
[34] *Oratio de vita . . . Caietani*, I [p. 9].
[35] Luther to Cajetanus, probably October 17, *WAB*, I, 220, ll. 5 ff. See also Luther's letter to Carlstadt, Oct. 14, 1518, *WAB*, I, 216, ll. 25 ff.
[36] Probably October 17. *WAB*, I, 220 ff.

the center of opposition to papal absolutism, and it is possible that they tried to raise money from sympathetic Augsburg friends of Martin for this purpose.[37] There was certainly reason for fear. Despite the safe-conduct, forceful measures might be taken at any moment by the imperial officials, and the Augustinians who were with Martin seem to have been in a state of panic, for both Staupitz and Link left Augsburg in haste the day following Martin's letter of apology. Before he went, the vicar-general, whose influence on Luther in crucial moments had been so important, comforted him with the words: "Remember that you have begun this affair in the name of our Lord Jesus Christ." Like many other remarks of Staupitz, this clung to the mind of the younger man and rose to memory again when he faced another great crisis, the departure for Worms.[38]

Martin was now convinced that nothing more could be done with the cardinal, in whom he saw only the peculiar Dominican attitude. His statement many years later, that if Cajetan had shown himself a little more moderate matters would not have gone so far,[39] failed to recognize how widely his own attitude of mind had now separated him from the directive authority of the Church. He was extremely anxious about the fate of his university and bitter against the tyranny of the Dominicans; and his resentment extended to Pope Leo himself, whom he held responsible for the action of the Fifth Lateran Council in condemning the Council of Basel. On the day of his brothers' departure, and with their help and that of a canon lawyer, Martin prepared a solemn appeal "from the ill-informed" to the "better-to-be-informed Pope." [40] This was attested before a notary and witnesses. In formal legal language the document reviews briefly his complaints against the preachers of indulgences and his objections to the commissioners selected to examine his case, both of them Dominicans and Thomistic theologians. The journey to Rome to which he has been cited is impossible on account of his weak health and his poverty, and because he is persuaded that "sword and poison" would threaten him. He submits himself to the Pope as to the voice of Christ. In spite of caustic references to the Dominicans, he speaks politely of the cardinal and again declares that he wishes to say nothing which cannot be proved "in and out of the Holy Scriptures, Church Fathers, and sacred canons." On the following day he once more addresses himself to the cardinal, enclosing the appeal to the

---

[37] Cf. "Christoph Scheurls Geschichtbuch der Christenheit von 1511 bis 1521," in *Jahrbücher des deutschen Reichs und der deutschen Kirche,* ed. by J. K. F. Knaake, I (1872), 125.

[38] Letter from Luther to Staupitz, Jan. 14, 1521, *WAB,* II, 245, ll. 3 f.

[39] *TR,* III, No. 3857 (1538), p. 662, ll. 12 ff.

[40] Probably printed first with the *Acta Augustana* by Froben. See *WA,* II, 28 ff.

pontiff with a humble and urgent request that it be graciously received and forwarded to the Pope. He has not been able to answer the objections of his friends: "What will you recant? Will you with your recantation set up a law of faith for us? Let the Church first condemn, if there is anything to be condemned, and follow its judgment."[41]

The day passed without any word from the legate, and when on the following day nothing was heard, the silence became ominous. On the night of October 20 the friar fled from the city, leaving the letter of appeal in the hands of friends for delivery to Cajetan. Two days later the appeal was posted on the cathedral door, apparently by Martin's directions.[42] Whether the danger threatened most from the imperial officials or the clergy, or as Martin afterwards is reported to have said, from some riotous conduct in the city,[43] it appeared very real to the Saxon councilors and his other friends and it was on their advice that he hastened northward.[44] Once more in Nuremberg, he found himself in a circle of influential friends. There he received a letter from Spalatin that enabled him to estimate fully the dangers that had threatened him. It enclosed a copy of the papal breve of August 23 and possibly also the order of the Augustinian general to the Saxon provincial for his arrest. The breve Martin at once pronounced to be a forgery;[45] but we may doubt the sincerity of this statement, which he repeated again and again later in the year. For the moment it strengthened his cause against the Dominicans to be able to regard his affair as still under judgment. On October 31, 1518, one year after the posting of the momentous theses on indulgences, he again passed through the gates into his cloister.

"I exhort and beseech Your Highness that you take counsel of your conscience and either send Brother Martin to Rome or drive him out of your country."[46] This urgent plea from Cajetan to the elector followed northward close on the heels of the returning friar. In his letter the cardinal reviewed the Augsburg conference in a dignified and injured tone, rather patronizing toward Martin but contemptuous of Staupitz, and directed a thinly veiled threat against the elector himself. With due deliberation, Frederick forwarded the letter to Wittenberg, where it found Martin quite

---

[41] *WAB*, I, 222 f.

[42] To Spalatin, Oct. 31, 1518, *WAB*, I, 224 f. and n. 3. Later Martin reported that it had been posted by the notary as a result of efforts by the prior of the Carmelites. Spalatin's account says that wise friends had advised him against a personal delivery to the cardinal. See Wittenberg edition of Luther's works, IX, 38v.

[43] *TR*, V, No. 5375C (a confused and poorly attested passage).

[44] *TR*, I, No. 1203 (first half of 1530s); see also *TR*, V, No. 5349. Spalatin adds that when Martin reached the village of Moheim he fell exhausted in the straw beside his horse.

[45] Letter from Luther to Spalatin, Oct. 31, 1518, *WAB*, I, 224 ff.

[46] Letter from Cajetan to Frederick, Oct. 25, 1518, *WAB*, I, 234, ll. 76 f.

sure of himself and clear of all scruples. He had come back from the battle full of joy and peace, as he states to Spalatin, and with two purposes in mind: to publish his answers to Cajetan and to appeal to a Church council, in line with the action of the Paris faculty, in case Pope Leo "in the fullness of tyranny" should refuse his plea.[47] In answer to the cardinal's letter, Martin now presents his side to the elector at full length.[48] Again he urges that the case be transferred to Germany, reminding his prince that his prosecution would open the way to the destruction of the university by the "furies of the Dominican order." His long commentary on the cardinal's charges is not wanting in deference toward the legate, but rings with absolute confidence in his own opinions. He tries to put the case "large and plain." With a mixture of sarcasm and diplomacy he reminds the prince, who knows well "the Italian and Roman sharp practices," that he is being invited to become a Pilate, and suggests that he answer the cardinal's charges of heresy as follows: "Show me the evidence for this. Put it in writing, do not be afraid of the light of publicity. When that has been done I will send Martin to Rome. Yes, I will imprison him and put him to death myself." [49] Martin claims to have left nothing undone but the six letters: *Revoco!* He begs the elector to insist that his enemies show him where he is wrong. "They have paper and pens in Rome. They have innumerable notaries . . . it will cost less to instruct me in my absence than to put me to death by trickery on the spot." [50] The tone of his plea rises at times to passionate denunciation of the unfairness of the procedure against him; at others it drops into a pathos cleverly adjusted to the elector's self-esteem and his sensitive feeling of personal honor. As concerns the cardinal's threat against the elector, Martin offers to go into voluntary exile:

For what hope can I cherish, wretched and humble monk? Yes, what dangers have I not to fear, what violence may I not anticipate from those who hate me, since they do not even hesitate to hurl such extraordinary insults at Your Sublime Highness, so great a prince, so great an elector of the Holy Roman Empire and so great a promoter of the Christian faith, in that they threaten you with I know not what disasters if you do not send me to Rome or drive me from your lands?

As with other men of courage, Martin's spirit rose to the conflict when an enemy stood before him, but the fear of unseen forces preyed on his nerves. Thus it was in the days that followed. The ban of excommunication might come at any moment and the future was dark. He set his house in order,

---

[47] Letter from Luther to Spalatin, *WAB,* I, 224, ll. 10 ff.

[48] Letter from Luther to Frederick, *WAB,* I, 236 ff. The date of the letter is uncertain. Clemen sets it about November 21.

[49] *Ibid.,* p. 243, ll. 286 ff.　　　　　　[50] *Ibid.,* p. 244, ll. 350 ff.

ready, like Abraham, to go, "I know not whither, or rather, I do know whither, for God is everywhere." [51] For a time Frederick seems to have wavered as to his course. At a meeting in Lichtenburg, to which Martin was summoned, as it appears, after the receipt of Cajetan's letter, the electoral chaplain seems to have told him that Frederick preferred to have him go away, but advised against his going to Paris. [52] The friar came back to Wittenberg in uncertainty as to what he should do, but was resolved to leave Saxony if his presence there was to cause the elector to suffer. [53] In a sermon early in December he bade a pathetic farewell to his congregation in case they should not see him again. [54] He had heard of serious threats in the event that he should leave the protecting walls of the city; the Nuremberg friends were grieved by a report that he was already in flight and unprotected. [55] On December 2 a letter from the electoral chaplain finds him still ready for departure. [56]

A week later, the wind changed at court, and Martin seems to have received a reassuring message. Possibly this was due to the arrival from Rome of Karl von Miltitz, who had undertaken the rôle of mediator, though he had at that time not yet met with Frederick. From some cause Frederick's anxious diplomacy had now found its way to firmer ground, and at last, about December 8, the elector answered the cardinal legate in a tone of unconcealed resentment. [57] No one in his lands, he declares, has found the monk's teaching heretical except those whose interests have been damaged thereby. He encloses Martin's comments on the cardinal's charges and awaits proof of the professor's heresy. When this rebuff came into Martin's hands, it warmed his heart. His only fear was that the Italians would not be able to see the full force of it. "Let him [the legate] learn that the temporal power is also from God and that he who has it cannot be trodden under foot, especially by him who has received his power only from man." [58]

[51] Letter from Luther to Spalatin, Nov. 25, 1518, *WAB*, I, 253.

[52] Letter from Luther to Staupitz, Nov. 25, *WAB*, I, 258, ll. 18 ff. Enders dates the letter December 13, but the evidence for the earlier date seems conclusive.

[53] *WAB*, I, 236 ff. See esp. p. 245.

[54] Letter from Luther to Spalatin, Dec. 9, 1518, *WAB*, I, 264, ll. 18 ff. Luther says it was not a farewell, but his remarks as he cites them belie this.

[55] Letter from Scheurl to Staupitz, Dec. 10, 1518, Scheurl, *Briefbuch*, II, 63. Letter from Scheurl to Luther, Dec. 19 or 20, *WAB*, I, 272.

[56] *WAB*, I, 260. Two rather confused reports in the *Table Talk* supplement the record with a picturesque account of the arrest of Martin's departure by a letter from Spalatin delivered at a farewell banquet to his university colleagues. *TR*, I, No. 1203, p. 598, ll. 8 ff.; V, No. 5375c.

[57] Letter from Frederick to Cajetan, probably December 7 or 8, *WAB*, I, 250 f. Miltitz and Frederick met at Altenburg on December 28, as we shall see later.

[58] Letter from Luther to Spalatin, Dec. 20, 1518, *WAB*, I, 281, ll. 31 f.

When he arrived in Wittenberg on his return from the conference at Augsburg, Martin had already resolved to publish his side of the controversy, including his appeal to Rome. He had also planned, as we noted, to appeal his case directly to a council of the Church. In the early days of November he put together the documents and provided them with an introduction and a bitter postscript, and by November 12 copy was already in the press.[59] The elector, then still reflecting on his response to Cajetan, objected to a publication of the Augsburg record;[60] but the monk, who saw his days at Wittenberg drawing to a close, was intent on putting before the public a statement of the positions he had defended, before exile and possibly imprisonment should seal his lips. He seems, therefore, to have gone ahead with the printing, although he blacked out a passage intended to support his argument that the papal breve of August 23 was a falsification. There is no evidence that this concession to the feelings of the cardinal and the other officials at Rome was due to any other reason than his own second thought or the advice of friends.[61] Interest in the forthcoming pamphlet was feverish, and the folio sheets were sold at the printing office as fast as they came off the press. When a second and peremptory mandate from the elector reached Wittenberg, only the last folio was still unfinished, but the author let it go forth, and before December 9 the complete work was in the hands of eager readers.[62] In response to what seems to have been a sharp reproof from court, the author made excuses which in the light of the record appear to be rather lame.[63]

Before the end of the year the *Acta Augustana* were flying from presses in Wittenberg and Leipzig, and from those of Froben in Basel, who had begun to distribute Martin's works in southwest Germany and abroad.[64] In a tone of defiance, with more than a trace of sarcasm, the injured scholar arraigns his critics as the same unfair and prejudiced group that had attacked Reuchlin in the preceding decade. It was in his discussion with the

[59] Letter to Spalatin, Nov. 12, 1518, *WAB*, I, 228, l. 22.

[60] Letter from Luther to Christoph Langenmantel, Nov. 25, 1518, *WAB*, I, 256, l. 31.

[61] The text of the blacked-out passage is reprinted in *WA*, IX, 205, from an unmutilated copy in Zwickau. It is an attempt to demonstrate the falsification of the papal breve by citing trivial deviations from the customary diction of the Vatican chancellery. See Kalkoff's interpretation in Luther, *Ausgewählte Werke*, I, 402 ff.

[62] Letter from Luther to Spalatin, Dec. 9, 1518, *WAB*, I, 263, ll. 4 ff.

[63] On November 25 Luther informed Spalatin that the work was in press. He knew of the elector's objection at that time (see letter to Langenmantel, *WAB*, I, 256), but he says nothing about it in his letter to Spalatin of December 2. There seems no other interpretation than that in the stress of these crucial days he resolved to disregard the opposition of the electoral court.

[64] Froben also published the appeal from Cajetan to the Pope, which Luther omitted from the *Acta Augustana*. See *WA*, II, 27.

legate, he declares, that he heard for the first time the claim that the pope was superior over council, Scriptures, and the whole Church, and that this then raised a new cause of contention. He repeats that he has never alleged anything which was not in agreement with the Scriptures, the Fathers, and the papal decrees properly interpreted, and offers again to submit himself to the judgment of the Church under arbitrament of neutral universities. He declares that the cardinal legate never advanced a single scriptural authority against him. Finally, he condemns the much discussed bull of Clement VI and denies again, as he had done to the legate, that the Roman Church stands above all other Christian churches, and flatly contradicts the claim that the merits of Christ are under control of the pope. In the *Acta* are also included copies of his "justification" to Cajetan and the papal breve of August 23, the terms of which Martin regards as so unfair that he is inclined to consider it spurious.

As an immediate sequel to his recital of the events at Augsburg he issued his appeal to a general council of the Church. When he returned from South Germany he had already determined on this bold step, and in the tense days that followed he put the document into legal form. On November 28, in the Corpus Christi chapel of the parish church at Wittenberg,[65] he certified to it before a notary and witnesses. It then went at once to the printer, ready for posting in case the papal ban of excommunication should arrive. By the end of the first week of December, however, the broadside had come into the hands of avid readers far and wide. When Spalatin reproached him for this, Martin protested his own irritation at the greed of the printers, which had caused a breach of their contract.[66]

The appeal touched a problem which had agitated the clerical world since the great councils of the preceding century, that of the supremacy of pope or council in the spiritual affairs of the Church. The claims to sovereignty of the pope, which reached a climax under Boniface VIII in 1300, met tenacious opposition in the following century. This opposition was rooted in a theory descended through the ages from the old Roman conception of the sovereignty of the people in the Church over that of the bishops, the theory that the council represented the universal Church and was supreme over the pope. The approval of this theory by the councils of Constance and Basel aroused strenuous opposition on the part of succeeding popes, and the papal position was set forth repeatedly in bulls of condemnation prohibiting appeals to a council. Nevertheless, the conciliar idea, which had been so ably presented by the great French theologian, Jean Gerson, per-

---

[65] *WA*, II, 36 ff.   [66] Letter from Luther to Spalatin of Dec. 20, *WAB*, I, 280.

sisted in the Paris university. The Fifth Lateran Council approved a concordat negotiated between the French king and Pope Leo, but on the 27th of March, 1517, the Paris faculty, defying both temporal and spiritual lords, appealed to a future council and petitioned the archbishop of Lyon to call a French national council. In June, 1518, the Pope retorted with a bull condemning the faculty for its arrogance.[67] This was the conciliar question which was debated by the two opponents at Augsburg.

It was, then, the pattern of Paris that the professor followed, but he followed it as an individual and alone. In backing the idea of theological democracy and academic freedom the young university at Wittenberg would have been insignificant in prestige as compared with the great mother of northern scholarship on the Seine, and however warmly Luther's colleagues may have gathered about him in defense of the Wittenberg theology, Martin stood by the determination he had repeatedly expressed not to involve his order and its political patron in his own fate. In his appeal he followed closely the cumbrous theological-legal form of the Parisians,[68] declaring, like them, that the pope is a man and therefore can sin, and that he is not to be obeyed against the commands of God. Like them, he turns from Rome and appeals his case to a future council of the Church as the supreme authority in matters of faith. In expectation of its verdict he traverses briefly his theological position concerning indulgences and the procedure of the Curia and its representative, the cardinal legate.

Throughout the struggles of the months gone by, the safety and progress of his university had shared Martin's heart with the theological question. There is abundant evidence in his letters that he felt that reform in university studies and reform in the Church were inseparable. The dead weight of scholasticism still clung to the feet of young theologians and must be cast aside. In the previous February he had expressed the conviction that dialectics had no value for religion, however useful it might be for the mental training of youth.[69] He and his friends were unanimous in the opinion that they themselves had had no profit, indeed that they had been harmed by their study of philosophy and dialectics; and he classes the whole of Porphyry's categories as merely "valuable for old women and a dream of the sick." The eerie edifice which the scholastic fathers had built on this scholar and Aristotle has become unreal to him, and he now understands why the "captives" of these philosophers, like Professor Trutvetter, cannot compre-

---

[67] See Von Pastor, *Geschichte der Päpste*, IV, 1, 588.
[68] For the Paris text, see *Ref. Act.*, I, 553 f.
[69] Letter from Luther to Spalatin, Feb. 22, 1518, *WAB*, I, 149, ll. 10 ff.

hend or teach a chapter of Scriptures. The drive against Aristotle had gained headway throughout the past year; "stupid lectures" on Peter Hispanus' logic and Tartaretus' commentaries were to be swept from the Wittenberg program. In the new winter semester the program was well under way: "Thomistic physics" and the "Thomistic logic" are to be abandoned, and the instructor who had been lecturing on the latter was now busy with Ovid's *Metamorphoses*. There was hope that before long the Scotist philosophy and logic would follow into the discard.[70]

Ovid to replace Aristotle, the sources to become the foundation of useful scholarship instead of dry commentaries and sterile dialectics—this was the fresh wind of humanism that was now clearing Wittenberg of scholastic mist. The university theologians had ardently desired well-trained teachers of Greek and Hebrew in order that the increasing interest in Bible study might rest on a sure basis of acquaintance with the sources. In April the elector had asked the great Swabian humanist, Reuchlin, to suggest a man for the chair of Greek, and Reuchlin's great-nephew, Philip Schwarzerd, called in the jargon of the humanists "Melanchthon," was recommended. The young scholar arrived on August 25, 1518, and straightway won Martin's heart. "Most erudite, most humane," he describes him to Spalatin and Lang,[71] "a boy in years but one of us in all the rest." The humanistic conception of scholarship had now taken full possession of Wittenberg's professor of the Bible. For the physics of Aristotle, the fountain from which he had drawn useful knowledge of the outer world, he has now nothing but bitter words. "God ruled in his anger that the human race should be occupied for so many centuries with these trifles," [72] but the time is now fulfilled; and he fumes with impatience that a genius like Melanchthon has to lecture on this stuff. In place of Aristotle's theorizing Martin would put the observation of nature as found in Pliny, and he shares the enthusiasm of the humanists for the rhetorician Quintilian. "One who makes the best men," [73] he declares. With the arrival of Melanchthon, Greek courses assume an increasing place in Martin's mind. He buys a Homer in order to become a Greek,[74] and his studies with the younger colleague are reflected in the rapidly increasing use of Greek expressions in his letters.

The younger generation responded with a will to the call of the new learning. So many students flooded in with the new liberal spirit that some

[70] Letter to Spalatin, Dec. 9, 1518, *WAB*, I, 262.
[71] Letter to Spalatin, *WAB*, I, 196, l. 40; letter to Lang, *WAB*, I, 203, ll. 11 f.
[72] Letter to Spalatin, March 13, 1519, *WAB*, I, 359, ll. 11 f.
[73] Letter to Spalatin, Nov. 29(?), 1519, *WAB*, I, 562 f.
[74] Enders, *Luthers Briefwechsel*, IV, 120, and n. 8, p. 121.

Wittenberg scholars opposed the reorganization of the curriculum on economic grounds. How were all these new masters of arts going to live? Stipends which were needed for strengthening the faculty were now so heavily mortgaged to the new graduates that Martin began to fear the university would soon turn into a poorhouse, and he reminded Spalatin that the poor have to be fed in some other way. Poverty was, as we have seen, a duty of the Augustinian brothers; and we have noted how the habit of living from charity showed itself in Martin in a mendicant aggressiveness that to modern minds contrasts strangely with his defiant independence as scholar and theologian.

Academic poverty had its compensations, however, even in a monastic university. After the tense concentration of the early Wittenberg years, Martin's vigorous social nature comes more and more into view and asserts itself against cloister restrictions, though he acts in the best tradition of the cloister when he practices the virtue of hospitality. We hear, for example, that the professor of Bible invites a number of friends to share his meager fare, among them Spalatin, who is asked to bring along venison from the elector's store, remembering that he comes from the court to the cloister and not from the cloister to the court.[75] Melanchthon's ascetic temperament lacked the full-blooded vitality of his colleague, and Martin chides him for his absence from a doctor's banquet, as "not acquainted with the Muse and with Apollo." [76]

[75] Letters from Luther to Spalatin, Nov. 12, 1518, *WAB*, I, 228, l. 20; Nov. 13, *ibid.*, p. 230, l. 8.

[76] Letter from Luther to Melanchthon, Nov. 22, *WAB*, I, 252.

17

AN ATTEMPT AT COMPROMISE

LUTHER did not leave Wittenberg. We do not know whence came the rift in the threatening clouds which had been gathering around him so thickly that even the elector felt that he could give him no guarantee of safety. Whatever the cause, the decided ring of Frederick's reply to Cajetan on December 8, 1518, marks a new self-assurance on the part of the elector, and the fact that the brief and sturdy document was at once given circulation in Germany both by the prince's secretary and by Martin himself [1] indicates that the Saxon ruler felt his position assured enough to come into the open in claiming a hearing for the professor.

The political game between the German princes and Rome was becoming more and more intertwined with Luther's struggle against Roman authority. At the Augsburg Diet the princes had, as we have seen, presented their *gravamina* against the Church, and Spalatin, reporting on Frederick's action in this body, records with satisfaction that his prince opposed an indulgence suggested by Cajetan for a war against the Turks. In December, 1518, the elector and Duke George met in Jena to consider Cajetan's request for a tax to support the same cause, and Spalatin writes to Martin to inquire whether such a war might be approved on the basis of Scripture.[2] Martin, therefore, who three years earlier had intimated to Spalatin that he regarded the elector "seven times blind" in spiritual matters, although the wisest of men in temporal affairs,[3] evidently draws new courage from Frederick's attitude about the turn of the year. His letters bear the stamp of increasing self-confidence, which at times finds vigorous expression.[4]

---

[1] See letter from Luther to Spalatin, Jan. 10, 1519, *WAB*, I, 297 f.

[2] Spalatin, *Friedrichs des Weisen Leben und Zeitgeschichte*, ed. by Neudecker and Preller, pp. 50, 159. See also Enders, *Luthers Briefwechsel*, I, 318, 332 f., and 334, n. 1; *WAB*, I, 249, 282 f.

[3] On June 8, 1516, *WAB*, I, 44, ll. 20 ff.

[4] Letter to Spalatin, Dec. 9, 1518: "Appellavi etiam ad futurum concilium. Atque quo illi magis furiunt et vi affectant viam, eo minus ego terreor. Ero adhuc liberior aliquando in

When the *Replica* of his once-feared Dominican opponent, Sylvester Prierias, reaches him, he shows his contempt for its childish and effeminate character by having it printed with a few sarcastic words of recommendation and circulating it among his friends without other reply.[5] It causes him amusement when he hears that in a collection of his briefer works which appeared in Basel toward the end of the year a printer's error entitles his Italian critic *magirus,* "cook," instead of *magister.*[6] His life is running over with activity. Day after day, he writes to Spalatin in March,[7] he interprets the Lord's Prayer to children and then preaches. He is getting ready his commentary on the Epistle to the Galatians, and besides that he has the prescribed prayers of his order and must give his lectures. He does not mention the immense mortgages of his controversy with Rome and the writing that went with it. He nevertheless finds time to prepare, possibly for the Lenten instruction referred to, his *Interpretation of the Lord's Prayer for the Unlearned,* which had been put together and printed a year earlier by one of his younger associates at the university, Johann Agricola.[8]

All the fiery energy which found outlet in so many activities was soon to be called into play for a new round in the struggle against Rome. The Curia was not resting in its effort to curb the captious monk. With a skill born of experience with many heretical zealots it advanced to the struggle with new weapons. Hitherto Martin had been able to give strength to his attacks on indulgences by arguments from many Church authorities. Henceforth this ground was to be cut from under his feet. In a papal decretal issued on November 9 and published by Cajetan on December 13 in Linz, the successor of St. Peter makes a definite and clear declaration regarding indulgences, "in order that no one may pretend ignorance of the doctrine of the Roman Church." The Pope now formally declares the right of Christ's vicar on earth through the power of the keys to remit "punishment which is due according to divine justice for actual sins," whether the sinner be in this life or in purgatory, through indulgences from the treasure of merits of Christ and His saints.[9] Luther is not mentioned by name, but

---

Romanas istas lernas." *WAB,* I, 263 f., ll. 15 ff. See also letter to Egranus, Feb. 2, 1519, *WAB,* I, 313, ll. 11 ff.

[5] *Replica F. Sylvestri Prieratis . . . ad F. Martinum Luther. WA,* II, 50 ff. See letter from Luther to Scheurl, Jan. 13, 1519, *WAB,* I, 299; and letter from Luther to Spalatin, Jan. 14, *WAB,* I, 303, ll. 85 ff.

[6] Letter from Luther to Staupitz, Feb. 20, 1519, *WAB,* I, 344.

[7] *WAB,* I, 359.

[8] *Auslegung deutsch des Vaterunsers für die einfältigen Laien. WA,* II, 80 ff.

[9] The decretal *Cum postquam* is dated at the Vatican, November 9, 1518. See Mirbt, *Quellen zur Geschichte des Papsttums und des römischen Katholizismus,* p. 256, No. 416. See also *EA,* XXXIII, 428 ff. Cajetan remained in Augsburg until December and must have pre-

excommunication is threatened against anyone holding and preaching other-wise. Plainly this was Cajetan's reply to Martin's arguments at Augsburg. Circulated as it was from an out-of-the-way place the bull did not reach Luther's notice until the middle of January, 1519. In the meantime he pre-pared for a serious attack on Roman errors: "For thus far I have only played and jested with the Roman affair." [10] His threat had, however, to wait more than a year for fulfillment.

Cajetan's failure had in the meantime, as we have said, brought a new intermediary on the scene in the person of a young Saxon chamberlain of the Pope's household, Karl von Miltitz.[11] His efforts at compromise, which form an interesting episode in Luther's struggle with the Roman power, were to extend over more than a year and bring Martin directly into con-tact with the ambitions and policies of both the Vatican and the Saxon chancellery. The papal courtier took up the task of winning Martin back to obedience largely on his own initiative, but he was not without ability for this work of conciliation. Miltitz had studied canon law at Cologne and at Bologna, where he probably received his master's degree.[12] He seems to have been intended for the Church, but he never became a priest. His family connections were distinguished, and he had some diplomatic talent. He sought employment at Rome, where he became chamberlain, notary, and count of the Lateran, and was presented for various German benefices. These he enjoyed of course *in absentia,* as was customary with servants of the Roman See.[13] Through his association with the younger Medicis Miltitz

---

pared the decretal for transmission to Rome soon after Martin's departure. See Paul Kalkoff, "Die von Cajetan verfasste Ablassdekretale und seine Verhandlungen mit dem Kurfürsten von Sachsen in Weimar den 28. und 29. Mai 1519," *ARG,* IX (1911/12), 142 ff.

[10] Letter from Luther to Lang, Feb. 3, 1519, *WAB,* I, 315, l. 9.

[11] The sources regarding Miltitz have been examined by Seidemann, *Karl von Miltitz,* and more recently by Creutzberg, *Die Jugend des Karl von Miltitz,* and Kalkoff, *Die Miltitziade.* These authorities come to widely different conclusions as to his personality and the nature of his commissions from the Curia. That he proceeded independently of his instructions there can be no doubt, but it is equally evident that he was something more than a messenger. His efforts to bring Luther to a compromise were, as matters lay, foredoomed to failure; but both Luther and Frederick took Miltitz and his mission seriously, and the letters of Martin as well as those of the Saxon court show that the young nobleman must have had considerable charm of personality and diplomatic tact as well as tenacity. He certainly was not without skill in judging a confused situation, and if his procedure was at times devious and insincere, the same may be said of that of all others concerned in the episode, including Luther's and Frederick's, and was quite in accord with the diplomatic practice of all periods. His personal character was that of the scheming and pliant papal courtier of the Medician era.

[12] Creutzberg, *Die Jugend des Karl von Miltitz,* p. 6.

[13] *Ibid.,* p. 10. Kalkoff, who regards Miltitz's position at Rome as of slight importance, contends that the title "cubicularius secretus" had not the significance of "chamberlain." See *Die Miltitziade,* pp. 59 ff. He also thinks that the young papal courtier's success in securing German benefices was slight. *Ibid.,* pp. 64 ff.

was in a position to sue for papal favors,[14] and he seems to have represented both the elector and Duke George in certain Roman affairs.[15] If his own statements may be trusted, he had striven three years to secure for Frederick special indulgences for the Castle Church and the coveted Golden Rose from the Pope. He was also in a position to supply the Curia with important information regarding Saxon affairs. No one could seem better suited to win over the Saxon prince and possibly secure Luther's person.

It appears that Miltitz's mission was somewhat loosely defined, but it was certainly as much concerned with the crafty moves of papal family politics as with the question of Luther. The end of Maximilian's life was approaching and the shadow of Habsburg world-dominion in the person of young Charles of Spain loomed on the horizon as a threat to the pretensions of the Medici. For this and other reasons as we have seen, it was of prime importance for the Florentine clan at this juncture to win the powerful support of the Saxon elector. On September 3, 1518, the consistory of the cardinals approved the award of the Golden Rose to Frederick,[16] and a week later Miltitz received the decoration for delivery, though it had to be deposited at Augsburg for the present. At the same time he obtained for Frederick the promise of special indulgences for the Castle Church.[17] On the same day, as was stated in a previous chapter, he notified Spalatin that he was setting forth at once to bring to the elector these much desired favors.[18]

The policies of Rome and Saxony had been reckoned without the Wittenberg monk, and another year was to pass before the papal favors came into Frederick's possession. We cannot follow the progress of Vatican diplomacy in all its details in the months which succeeded, but the tireless investigations of Paul Kalkoff have made it possible to trace in general outline the sequence of events. Some of these have been mentioned in previous chapters, but may be recalled here. In June the regular judicial procedure against Luther was broken off and in its place a new and summary process inaugurated. As a result of this, on August 23 a papal breve was sent to

---

[14] See Miltitz's letter to the elector, reproduced in E. S. Cyprian, "Nützliche Urkunden zur Erläuterung der ersten Reformationsgeschichte," in *Tentzels Historischer Bericht vom Anfang und Fortgang der Reformation Lutheri*, I, 1 (Leipzig, 1717), 415 ff.; see also Creutzberg, *Die Jugend des Karl von Miltitz*, p. 9.

[15] *Ibid.*, pp. 14 ff. Kalkoff finds no evidence of this, but his argument is far from conclusive. See his *Aleander gegen Luther*, p. 15, n. 2, and *Die Miltitziade*, pp. 72 ff. In addition to the documents quoted by Creutzberg, however, it is to be noted that when Wittenberg University petitioned the Vatican to transfer Luther's examination to Augsburg, it asked the friendly intervention of Miltitz. That this was done on the motion of the elector is merely Kalkoff's guess. *Forschungen*, p. 60.

[16] See the document cited by Kalkoff, *Forschungen*, p. 56.

[17] *Ibid.*, p. 58.   [18] See above, p. 285, n. 60.

Cajetan, in which the legate was instructed to call Luther before him; in case he should refuse to appear of his own free will, or to recant, Cajetan was to have him seized and brought to Rome. Should Luther not appear at all, Cajetan had the power to declare the monk and his followers "heretics, excommunicates, anathemata, and accursed," and call upon all clerical and secular authorities to deliver them up for punishment. At the same time Leo wrote to the elector demanding the surrender of Luther as a "son of evil" and, through Venetus, the Augustinian vicar general, set in motion the machinery of the order for bringing Luther to Rome. The receipt of the papal letter had been followed by Frederick's intervention with Cajetan on Luther's behalf. Meanwhile Miltitz was detained in Rome, in all probability because of the report of the elector's action.[19]

In the meantime the Curia had found it politically convenient to accept Frederick's offer to produce Luther in Augsburg, and Cajetan had been instructed in a breve of September 11, 1518, to examine him and condemn him if he should remain obstinate and refuse to recant, the Pope reserving to himself the formulation of the excommunicatory sentence. The Golden Rose and the bulls containing special privileges for the Wittenberg church were then given to Miltitz on October 1 for delivery to the legate,[20] but Cardinal Medici informed Cajetan that since Frederick had made so many conditions in Luther's case he should receive the Golden Rose only in case he delivered Luther to Miltitz.[21] Cajetan's report of the interview with Luther was forwarded to Rome on October 25, and Miltitz must have left the Eternal City about the middle of November. Though his mission appears not to have been clearly circumscribed, it seems unlikely that it included negotiations with Luther, who had been condemned and whose punishment was now awaited as soon as Cajetan should find it expedient to release the bull of excommunication, which the young papal nuncio possibly brought with him from Rome.[22] Whatever his powers, it is certain that Miltitz soon realized the necessity for winning over Luther. When he arrived in South Germany he found an excited state of public opinion and a strong sentiment

[19] See Kalkoff, *Die Miltitziade*, p. 7, who assumes that it was originally intended that the decoration should be given to Frederick in Augsburg. Cajetan's report from Augsburg, dated September 5, sets forth the violent opposition of Frederick to Charles's election as successor to Maximilian. At the same time the legate may also have reported his negotiations with the elector regarding Luther's case. The evidence is to be found in Kalkoff's *Forschungen*, pp. 57 ff.

[20] *Ibid.*, pp. 62 ff. See also letter from Scheurl to Staupitz, in Scheurl, *Briefbuch*, II, 63 and 78.

[21] The instruction quoted in Kalkoff, *Forschungen*, p. 61.

[22] Miltitz's formal commission from the Vatican, dated October 15, covers simply the mission to Frederick. The final delivery of the papal favors to the elector is made to depend upon Cajetan's decision. Cyprian, "Nützliche Urkunden," I, ii, 56 ff.; *Ref. Act.*, II, 554 f.

for Luther's cause and person.[23] Martin recalled many years later that Miltitz told him that if he had 25,000 armed men he would not guarantee to take Luther to Rome.[24] Certainly he was well equipped with appeals from the spiritual to the temporal arm, bringing letters of introduction[25] to Frederick, to Pfeffinger and Spalatin, and to the military and civil heads of the Wittenberg city government, as well as the authorities of a number of other cities.

When the first collisions with German public opinion had shown the futility of making use of this machinery for seizing Luther's person, Miltitz began to set diplomatic wheels in motion. In Bavaria he had enlisted the help of Frederick's trusted councilor, Degenhard Pfeffinger. In Nuremberg he appealed to the group of humanists whom Martin counted among his stanch friends. Three letters from Christoph Scheurl went off to Wittenberg in rapid succession at the end of the year,[26] all evidently the result of Miltitz's adroit efforts. At great length and with the labored learning of a monastic lawyer, Scheurl tells of Miltitz's mission and his conversations with him, in which the nuncio dwelt on the importance of submitting to the Pope. Luther's *Sermon on Indulgence and Grace* had made a worse impression in Rome than all his disputations and resolutions, and the Nuremberg friend warns Martin to be careful and advises against a flight to France, where the king would not support him three days against the Pope. After all, order must be maintained and the elector himself may fall away from him. "Rome fears you!" Not in ten years has the Curia had a more difficult, tormenting, and humiliating affair than this. Pfeffinger thinks that he might have a bishopric or some other honor if he would but recant. The hesitant and cautious Scheurl is plainly appalled at the possibility of further violence on Luther's part. He begs him to modify his letter to the cardinal and to answer Prierias's *Replica* with reserve, and finally to think of the interests of his order.

Owing to the delays in South Germany, it was near the end of December[27] before the nuncio arrived in Altenburg, where the elector was spending the Christmas season. In the meantime the diplomatic situation had reached a deadlock. Luther's publication of the *Acta Augustana* and the

[23] This is reflected in his conversations with Scheurl in Nuremberg, where he spent several days. See Scheurl, *Briefbuch*, II, 69 f.

[24] *WA*, LIV, 184, l. 18. See also *TR*, III, No. 3413.

[25] Printed in Cyprian, "Nützliche Urkunden," I, ii, *passim;* also in *Ref. Act.*, II, 555 ff.

[26] Scheurl, *Briefbuch*, II, No. 182, pp. 70 ff.; No. 186, pp. 75 f.; No. 190, p. 81; these letters are dated, respectively, December 20 and 22, 1518, and January 1, 1519.

[27] December 28 (*Die Innocentum*). See "Chronicon sive Annales Georgii Spalatini," ed. by Mencke, in *Scriptores rerum Germanicarum*, II, 593.

elector's refusal to accede to Cajetan's demand that the recalcitrant monk be banished had been followed on December 13 by the legate's publication of the papal decretal which, to be sure, was as yet known in Saxony only through report. Frederick's language to Miltitz cannot have been less categorical than to Cajetan. He understood the situation thoroughly, however, and was well aware that Rome would not give him the long-desired Golden Rose unless a compromise could be brought about that would enable Cajetan to report Luther's recantation.[28] Perhaps Miltitz's diplomatic arts might succeed where the austerity of Cajetan had failed.

Under these circumstances the young diplomat set to work on his difficult task. His first move was to summon Tetzel before him. The Dominican friar, appalled at the development of events during the past year, excused himself from appearing because of the tremendous feeling which Luther had aroused against him throughout Central Europe.[29] A few days later Luther appeared. The meeting between the papal nuncio and the monk-professor lasted two days, apparently January 5 and 6.[30] It seems that Spalatin and Feilitzsch were present during a part of the discussion, which took place in Spalatin's quarters. At the end of the first day Martin sent the elector a detailed report.[31] After listening to Miltitz's arraignment Martin is ready for concessions. He is prepared to write to Pope Leo acknowledging that he has been too violent and to publish a work of the same tenor urging obedience to the Church. He proffers for the elector's decision a suggestion from Feilitzsch that the matter of his appeal to the council be referred to the bishop of Salzburg. To the insistence of the nuncio that he recant, he opposes a categorical refusal.

So deep seems to have been the effect of Miltitz's urgent pleading that the perturbed monk, possibly on the same evening, drafted a letter to Pope Leo

---

[28] In a contemporary letter to Duke George written the day after Miltitz's arrival, the elector describes Miltitz's powers of process against Luther as wide: "Und mocht wol die sache seyn das man mir die rose nicht wolld geben, ich vorjagete dan den müynch und sprech auch, er were ain keczer." Gess, *Briefe und Akten*, I, 51 f.

[29] Cyprian, "Nützliche Urkunden," I, 1, 374 ff.

[30] The Altenburg edition of Luther's works to which Enders refers in *Briefwechsel*, I, 258, has a memorandum in defense of his attack on indulgences which Enders (*ibid.*, I, 341 ff.) and other authorities held was drawn up by Martin in preparation for the conference with Miltitz. In this brief document the chief blame for the dispute is laid on Pope Leo for having forced Archbishop Albert into the trade in indulgences by the heavy charges for investment. The real guilt, according to this document, does not lie with the simple, goodhearted Pope, however, but with his Florentine relatives, whose greed and lust for money is "as insatiable as hell." The arguments are in accord with Martin's attitude at this time, but the German form is certainly not in his style and its connection with the Altenburg conference is uncertain. See Kalkoff's note in Luther, *Ausgewählte Werke*, I, 416 f.

[31] On January 5 or 6. *WAB*, I, 289 ff.

in defense of his behavior. What is probably the original of this draft has been preserved,[32] and even in its mutilated form it is a highly important revelation of Martin's state of mind at this time. He was deeply moved by Miltitz's recital of the anxiety which he had caused the Church, and his reply is marked by a pathos and humility which are absent from his other writings at this time and are indeed rare in any period of his life. As the lowliest of men and the dust of the earth he entreats the Holy Father to listen to the "bleating" of one of his sheep.[33] He is deeply grieved that his honest and faithful service has been interpreted as an effort to bring dishonor and disgrace on the Church of Rome when his intention had been to defend its honor and dignity. But what shall he do? He would be willing to recall his theses, but the opposition and oppression on the part of his opponents have brought it about that his writings have gone so far abroad and sunk so deeply into many minds that a recantation would only open the mouths of all for an attack on the Roman Church.

It is they, it is those opponents, Blessed Father, who have brought insult and infamy among us upon the Church of Rome. It is those whom I have striven against who with their futile and foolish teachings in the name of your Holiness, have practiced only shameful greed and have befouled the holy place with the filth of Egypt; and [now] lest evil enough should not be done, arraign me before your Holiness as the cause of their audacious conduct, although I have striven with all my might against their outrageous behavior.

He calls God and every creature to witness that he has never wished to attack or diminish the power of the Roman Church or the pope and declares his faith in that Church as having power over everything in heaven and earth save only Jesus Christ. He offers again to keep silence regarding indulgences if only those on the other side will withhold their idle boastings. He is willing to circulate a work among the common people to further the honor of the Roman Church and to hold in check the excessive bitterness which he formerly directed against the Church of Rome in his attacks on

[32] In the Gotha Codex A, 379, fol. 1, where it breaks off without conclusion. *WAB*, I, 291 f. The early prints date it "Altenburg, March 3." This is evidently an error, as Luther was not in Altenburg on that day. The tone and contents of the document are so incompatible with Martin's attitude in early March that its origin at that time seems out of the question. On the other hand, its spirit of concession and self-criticism point to the softening impression of the first meeting with Miltitz. Strangely enough, Lutheran partisans have felt it necessary to defend the letter as due to the elector's influence. In reality it bears the marks of spontaneity and of the struggle with his conscience which are striking traits of Luther's spiritual life and are reflected throughout his correspondence.

[33] "Quare paternas ac vere illas Christi vicarias aures huic ovicule tue interim clementissime accomodare dignetur Beatitudo tua et Balatum meum hunc officiose intelligere." *WAB*, I, 292, ll. 4 ff.

empty-headed opponents.[34] His sole aim has been to save that Church from the stain of greed and to save the people from putting indulgences before the love of brother.

It is certain that this plea was never sent to Rome. It adds, of course, nothing to what had been proposed in his conference with Cajetan and fails to offer the only thing which the Pope must insist upon and which Martin would not give, an unconditional recantation. Its tone was no doubt due in part to a desire to conform to the wishes of the elector, whose political plans made it desirable to allay the irritation of the Roman See as speedily as possible. In addition, as Luther well knew, Frederick was a loyal son of the Church and bound by faith and tradition to a deep respect for Roman authority in religious matters. Nevertheless, no one can read the draft without an impression of its profound sincerity. It voices a yearning for a solution which would bring peace to a troubled conscience. The traditional reverence for the head of the Church still laid its restraining hand upon him, and the inborn dread of the name of schismatic and heretic must at times have been a leaden weight upon his conscience. He had not yet begun the systematic study of papal history which was in the next few months to destroy his faith in the historical claims of the Roman See. Cajetan's arguments had added fuel to the fiery spirit of theological combat; Miltitz had touched another and gentler chord which drove him to make one more attempt to bridge the chasm which he saw widening between himself and the head of his Church.

On the second day of the conference a spirit of compromise prevailed, and apparently the papal nuncio dropped his demand for an immediate revocation. It was finally agreed that both parties to the controversy should be prohibited from preaching, writing, or going further into the matter under dispute, and Miltitz promised to ask Pope Leo to refer to a "learned bishop" the question as to which of Luther's articles should be revoked. Luther on his side agreed that when he had been shown his error he would recant it.[35]

It is evident that the clever young Saxon exerted all his arts to bring about an arrangement, and it is probable that he played with skill and success on Martin's fears that the elector would leave him to his fate. On the other hand, his pliant manners did not deceive the monk, whose eye for human indirection had been sharpened by a year rich in experience with diplomatic fencing. Outwardly they parted as good friends. Miltitz told

---

[34] "Meam acrimoniam . . . adversus Ecclesiam Romanam, qua ego usus sum, immo abusus et excessi adversus balatrones istos." *WAB*, I, 293, ll. 42 ff.

[35] Luther to Frederick (second letter), Jan. 5 or 6, 1519, *WAB*, I, 293 f.

Luther as German to German that the "Romish Romans" would rather have given ten thousand ducats than have the matter go on.[36] He had expected to meet an elderly, dusty-brained theologian and did not conceal his surprise when he was faced by a vigorous and resolute personality. So the affair closed with a happy repast marked by real German *Gemütlichkeit*. But neither the ingratiating remarks and "Italian tricks" nor the "crocodile tears" and "Judas kiss" of the young diplomat [37] could make Martin forget that Karl had come to Germany armed with more than seventy apostolic letters in order to bring him a captive to the "murderous Jerusalem," and that the reason why he did not try to carry out his purpose of delivering him to the "Babylon clothed in purple" was because two thirds of those with whom he had talked in Germany were opposed to Rome.[38]

After the meeting at Altenburg Miltitz was received by the elector at Lochau.[39] At the latter's request he put into written form the steps which should now be taken to bring the controversy to a peaceful end.[40] The obsequious language of his memorandum does not conceal the categorical nature of these demands. Luther must humble himself before the Roman Church and fulfill his promise to disclaim any irreverence toward its dignity and that of the pope. In case of refusal he is to be forbidden to preach "for all time to come." With reference to Martin's appeal to a council, the elector is reminded that nine cardinals, an emperor, and many kings once sought through a council to oppose the pope, but that the Holy Church triumphed over them all. Finally the nuncio presents certified copies of the decretal of November 9 on indulgences, through which Pope Leo has settled the question for all time. Among these statements Miltitz inserts for the elector's consideration the polite suggestion that if Luther were then present he would hope with the help of the prince to bring about an arrangement which

---

[36] Letter from Luther to Egranus, Feb. 2, 1519, *WAB*, I, 313, ll. 20 ff.

[37] "Ac sic amice discessimus etiam cum osculo (Judas scilicet), nam et inter exhortandum lacrymabatur. Ego rursus dissimulabam has crocodili lacrymas a me intelligi." *Ibid.*, p. 313, ll. 16 f. See also letter from Luther to Staupitz, Feb. 20, *WAB*, I, 344, ll. 20 ff.

[38] See the letters cited in n. 37. For Luther's later recollections of Miltitz's mission, see *TR*, I, Nos. 156 and 1203; III, No. 3413; also the fragmentary autobiography, *WA*, LIV, 184.

[39] Letter from Luther to Spalatin, Jan. 19, 1519, *WAB*, I, 309. The date of this meeting cannot be fixed.

[40] The document in Cyprian, "Nützliche Urkunden," I, ii, 134 ff., seems to belong here, although the sequence of events is disputed and Kalkoff, in "Die von Cajetan verfasste Ablassdekretale," pp. 161 f., and n. 3, would place the communication of the demands by Miltitz and Spalatin's answer to these (see below) at the end of May, when Miltitz joined the electoral party at Weimar. Neither of the documents is dated, but Martin's reply to Miltitz's memorandum, though also undated, seems to belong between January 13 and 19, 1519. See *WAB*, I, 305 f., where the chronology is examined at length. This would locate the two documents in question somewhere within the fortnight following the Altenburg conference.

would be agreeable to the Church, perhaps through the selection of an
umpire acceptable to Martin. In outlining a reply Spalatin presents what are
no more than a series of lawyer's objections and arguments.[41] Martin must
first know what he is to recant. He is ready to lay the matter before the
universities of Freiburg, Louvain, Basel, and Paris [42] or to refer it to a group
of learned Italians, Frenchmen, and Germans.

The plan of the Saxon chancellery was evidently to gain time in the face
of the critical political situation. Luther, even though on intimate terms with
the elector's secretary, probably knew little of the political moves that were
being made. He must have felt, however, that he was playing a dangerous
game with the elector, of whose support he could not be sure. Nevertheless,
his temper had hardened since he talked with the persuasive young Saxon
at Altenburg and reflection had strengthened his impression of Miltitz's
lack of sincerity. When Spalatin sent him the memorandum of the nuncio,
therefore, his reply to Frederick is stiff and combative.[43] Point by point he
answers Miltitz's demands. With all honor to the Roman Church, he is
ready to recant if his opponents will show him his errors, but will not revoke
all he has said merely on this peremptory demand. Preaching and teaching
bring him neither joy nor wealth nor honor, but he can only obey God's
command. As umpires he nominates three eminent German churchmen,
the bishops of Trier, Salzburg, and Naumburg.[44] To Miltitz's reference to
the cardinals and others who had sought to array the council against the
pope, Martin answers that it is a pity these efforts to improve the Church
were not successful, but he still hopes that Rome will no longer tolerate the
wretched trade in indulgences. As for the new papal decree, he voices his
astonishment that this pronouncement and those which had gone before
were not based on a single sentence from Holy Scripture nor the Fathers
nor canon law. Mere words he can not accept as the "satisfying and just
doctrine of Holy Church," but must remain true to God's word. Again, as in
the Altenburg draft of the letter to Pope Leo, his refusal to recant is enforced
by the proud, intellectual independence of humanism: "Since in our day
Holy Scriptures and the old teachers are reappearing and people everywhere
in the world begin to ask not what but why this and that was said, were I

---

[41] Cyprian, "Nützliche Urkunden," I, ıı, 137 ff.

[42] The reference of the dispute to the universities as umpires was entirely in accord with
the practice of the later Middle Ages and the Renaissance. It seems to have been Luther's
first suggestion, for in Frederick's reply to Cajetan of November, 1518, *WAB*, I, 251, ll. 35 ff.,
the elector had quoted an offer from Martin to refer the matter to universities for arbitration.

[43] About mid-January, 1519. *WAB*, I, 306 ff.

[44] In a contemporary letter to Spalatin, January 19, he adds a layman, Palgrave Philip. *WAB*,
I, 309.

to accept these mere words and recant, my recantation would find no belief but would be looked upon as a mockery. . . . For what it [the decretal] says without any basis would not be established by my recantation." [45]

Miltitz had evidently succeeded in impressing the elector with his arguments, for he obtained from Frederick a promise to write to the Pope in a spirit of conciliation and obedience. In fulfillment of this the elector drafted a letter to Rome in which he reviewed the negotiations with Cajetan and the nuncio.[46] Although washing his hands of responsibility for Luther's actions ("wiewol ich mich des Doctors gantz entschlagen gehabt"), he defends him as a well reputed scholar, who will now without doubt show himself an obedient son of the Pope. This letter, intended as a plea for compromise, was never sent. Instead, Frederick writes to Councilor Feilitzsch that to intervene with Rome at this crisis might bring on serious difficulties, including the interdict, and thus prevent a peaceful solution of the matter.[47] At the same time the elector informs Miltitz that he has reconsidered writing to the Pope and will now do nothing further, in order to avoid the suspicion of harming the Church.[48] Frederick's policy may have been influenced by the political crisis which was approaching. The Emperor Maximilian's death had been expected, and it occurred on January 12, 1519. Thus the struggle over the succession would soon enter an acute stage. Frederick, who had steadily avoided committing himself to any candidate, may have had in mind the possibility of receiving papal support for himself as against the two powerful aspirants, Charles and Francis. His defense of Luther at this juncture and in the following months was to be one of passive resistance, for which the proposition of an umpire furnished an admirable device. Also, the elector was well aware of Martin's rapidly growing popularity, and in the draft of his letter to the Pope expressed the fear that an uprising might follow unless the matter was adjusted. He was no lover of disorder and felt a heavy responsibility for the maintenance of peace not only in Saxony but throughout the empire.

In fulfillment of his promise to Miltitz, Luther, on his part, now sets to work to draw up a plea to the people not to misinterpret his attack on indulgences as an attack on the Roman faith. This appeal, couched in simple German, he calls his "apology in his native language." [49] In plain and

---

[45] *Ibid.*, p. 308, ll. 54 ff.

[46] Reprinted in *Ref. Act.*, III, 14 ff. Löscher dates the letter "etwa am 8. Jan."

[47] *Ibid.*, pp. 17 f. Dated January 12.   [48] *Ibid.*, pp. 18 f.

[49] "Bis monuisti, mi Spalatine, ut de fide et operibus, tamen de obedientia ecclesie Romane in apologia mea vernacula mentionem facerem." Letter from Luther to Spalatin, March 5, 1519, *WAB*, I, 356. The *Unterricht auf etliche Artikel*, *WA*, II, 69 ff., a small pamphlet, seems to have been published late in February.

vigorous style his *Instruction regarding Certain Articles Which Are Ascribed to Him by His Opponents* interprets for the average man his attitude toward six questions: intercession of saints, purgatory, indulgences, the commands of the Holy Church and God's commands, good works, and the power of the Roman See. The pamphlet may be called a plea for the spirit against the letter and marks in its simple brevity an important stage in the professor's progress. While the old traditions maintain themselves, a new moral content has been poured into the ancient mould. The monk still believes in the miraculous works done beside the graves and through the good works of the saints, yet warns his hearers that these wonders are wrought, not by the power of the saints, but through their intercession, and that we should pray to them for spiritual gifts more earnestly than for material ones. He still believes in purgatory, but rejects all dogmatic statements regarding it and repudiates emphatically any interference through indulgences with the divine work of satisfaction or purification. The question of indulgences he reserves for scholars; the simple man should know, however, that indulgences can never be a substitute for works of charity. He does not oppose the demands of the Church for fasting and prayer and honor to the saints, but he reminds his readers that an adulterer, murderer, or robber can also fulfill these. Even if there were no commands of the Church we could do right through God's command: one makes of the Church's commands a "shameful cover for iniquity" if one puts them before the commands of God. He has never preached against good works but has only held that God judges of the heart and that we are dependent on His boundless grace and mercy and not on our good deeds.

As regards the Roman Church, Luther's standpoint is now interesting, for it indicates a decided movement away from the position assumed in the *Explanations* and in the *Acta Augustana*. There he had declared that the Eastern Church in the early centuries, although belonging to the Church of Christ, had not stood under the Roman power. Now, though he appeals for spiritual unity and can see no cause great enough to produce a schism, he declares that the welfare of souls does not depend on the power or supremacy of Rome, which is after all a matter for the learned to discuss. He values the Roman Church as representing a temporal and exterior side of religion, one of those things which, like earthly goods and art, come from God. In other words, the papacy has become in his mind a convenient function in human affairs and is devoid of spiritual rights. The claim to supremacy, about which the divinely inspired Council of Nicaea and the Church Fathers knew nothing, cannot rest upon divine law. These ideas, which appear dimly in the *Instruction Regarding Certain Articles*, stand forth more and more clearly in Martin's letters as the spring goes by and the great disputation with Eck approaches. It is obvious that his diligent examination of the decrees of the popes was leading him to an ever more definite conviction that the acts of the papacy were temporal in character and without divine inspiration.

Before turning to the great contest which was to consolidate Luther's attitude of independence with respect to Roman claims, let us follow the progress of Miltitz's efforts at compromise through the tangled course of Roman and imperial politics in the months succeeding the Altenburg conference. The papal nuncio must have sent to Rome an optimistic report of his meeting with the recalcitrant professor, for on March 29 Pope Leo, through his secretary Sadoletus, addresses a gracious letter to Martin.[50] In gentle tones he tells the "dearly beloved son" of his gratification at the news from Miltitz that Luther did not intend to go as far as he had gone in his attack on indulgences and that he is now suffering "bitter anguish of heart" and is ready to recall all that he has written and to refrain from similar errors in the future. The refusal to recant before Cajetan is condoned as due perhaps to the too severe attitude of the legate. Now, thanks be to God, the heart of the erring one is illuminated and the faithful will no longer be led into grave and pernicious errors! With an implied compliment on Martin's learning, the letter summons him to come to Rome and make his revocation to the Pope, "in order that we may rejoice in you as an obedient son and you may be happy to find in us a devoted and merciful father."

In all probability the letter was forwarded to Cajetan, but there is no evidence that Luther ever saw it, for when it was received it had become plain that Miltitz's optimism regarding Luther's readiness to recant and refrain from further action was not justified by the events.[51]

The letter is, however, important as marking a change in policy on the

---

[50] Text in *WAB*, I, 364 f. See also Kalkoff, *Forschungen*, p. 69.

[51] Paul Kalkoff, "Luthers Antwort auf Kajetans Ablassdekretale (30. Mai 1519)," *ARG*, XI (1914), 166 f., n. 2, assumes that the Pope's letter was sent to Frederick by Cajetan, accompanied by a severe arraignment of Luther, and that Luther was then informed. This energetic investigator of the relations between Rome and the Saxon chancellery goes so far as to reconstruct Cajetan's letter to the elector. Further evidence of this correspondence is found by Kalkoff in a passage in Luther's letter to Johann Lang, April 13, *WAB*, I, 369, l. 52, announcing receipt by the elector of "another letter" from Cajetan concerning him. This Martin characterizes as containing "crazy ideas" and evidence of "Italian impudence" (Italitatem rudissimam). The original of the Pope's letter, now lost, was in the hands of Lutheran scholars in the early eighteenth century and the text is well certified. How it came into their possession is a riddle. No copy is now in the papal archives. See Kalkoff, *Forschungen*, pp. 9 ff. It seems certain that if Luther had known of Leo's letter, some mention of it would have found its way into his letters to Spalatin, four of which have come down to us from April 28 to May 24.

part of the Roman See. The death of Maximilian in January and the approaching election of his successor had brought a crisis which the Roman diplomats had been long expecting. Both of the candidates for the imperial crown, Charles of Spain and Francis of France, had claims and pretensions in Italy which would endanger the papal state in case they should be backed by the power of a German emperor, but those of the Habsburg aspirant, as heir to the Sicilian throne, were far more threatening, and Leo's advisers and agents worked with feverish energy throughout the spring to prevent Charles's election. By the terms of the Golden Bull the choice lay with the electoral princes of Germany, and of these Frederick of Saxony, because of his political sagacity and conservative character and his prestige as administrator of the empire (*Reichsverweser*), was the most influential. We should recall that in the preceding year Frederick had refused to pledge support to the election of Charles, and he was now therefore the strategic center for opposition to Habsburg success. Ten days after Maximilian's death Leo instructed Cajetan to oppose in every way possible the election of a powerful emperor, particularly of Charles, and to further the choice of one of the electors, a goal which would probably be most easily attainable in the case of the elector of Saxony.[52] This was followed by letters from Rome to Frederick and the other electors, urging them to support the choice of an emperor who would not disturb the peace of the Church and the Holy See,[53] to which Frederick returned the diplomatic answer that he would fulfill his duty toward God and the empire.[54] This was the situation following the conference of Luther with Miltitz and explains the suspension of the prosecution, since no steps could be undertaken against the rebellious professor in the papal chancellery while the Pope was working frantically to win the support of Martin's protector.

Meanwhile Miltitz was busy with his plan for arbitration. He wrote Frederick from Augsburg reporting that he had sent a letter to the Pope as the elector had commissioned and praying that Martin be allowed to take no further steps until the return of the nuncio to Saxony.[55] In response Frederick gave a curt assurance that Luther would undertake nothing further unless he was driven to it by the acts of his opponents.[56] Luther

---

[52] *DRA*, I, 148 f.; see Paul Kalkoff, "Zu Luthers römischem Prozess," *ZKG*, XXV, 406 ff.

[53] February 10 and March 2. *DRA*, I, 223 and n. 1; 333 f. This was followed by a special message which Robert Orsini, papal nuncio, was to deliver to Frederick in person. *Ibid.*, pp. 557 f.

[54] April 6. *Ibid.*, p. 525. Kalkoff, "Zu Luthers römischem Prozess," *ZKG*, XXV, 407 f., has made it seem probable that at just about the time of the papal letter to Luther the Curia had received information which pointed to the growing probability of Charles's success.

[55] Cyprian, "Nützliche Urkunden," I, 1, 382 f.   [56] *Ibid.*, pp. 391 f.

himself, when he received Miltitz's warning from the elector, declared that
it had been his firm intention to remain silent in accordance with the agreement, and that he had gone so far as to make no reply to Prierias's last attack
in spite of the mockery of his opponents and the advice of his friends. But
if his mouth is to be closed and those of all others opened, the elector can
well see the disgrace that will fall upon him. If his enemies do not remain
silent, he begs his prince not to take it ill of him if he defends the truth,
even though it affects the position of the Holy See.[57]

As the weeks passed and Miltitz received no reply from the Pope, he became nervous for fear of the impression which this delay might make on the
Saxon court. On March 20 he excuses himself to Frederick, ascribing the
silence of Rome to the illness of the Pope and explaining that he has not yet
been able to meet the papal legate.[58] He is hopeful that letters will soon
arrive from His Holiness concerning Luther. Finally on May 3 he overtook
Cajetan in Coblenz and on the same day dispatched three letters, to Frederick, to Luther, and to Spalatin. To the elector [59] he apologizes again for
delay in hearing from Rome but asserts that Cardinal Rangone has informed
him that three of his letters regarding Martin's case have been turned over
to the Cardinals Pucci and Accolti for answer.[60] The legate is now quite
ready to forget and forgive and asks no apologies. It is Cajetan's wish that
Luther come at once to Coblenz in order that the archbishop of Trier and
the legate may judge the case jointly: "Whatever the Bishop of Trier does,
the legate will not dispute." As yet nothing has been said to the archbishop,
but Miltitz is sure that he will consent to act as judge and that Martin will
be safe with him in life and limb. Apparently the chamberlain has some
misgivings as to Cajetan, whom he describes as "hot-tempered" (*colericus*),[61]
and in a postscript he advises the elector to write to the archbishop asking
him to judge the case alone.

The letter to Frederick is in a subservient tone. That to Martin is respect-

---

[57] Letter from Luther to Frederick, March 13, 1519, *WAB*, I, 357 f.

[58] See Cyprian, "Nützliche Urkunden," I, i, 431 ff., where we learn that Miltitz had set out
to join the legate at Linz on the Danube, where the latter had spent the winter, but was
detained by illness in Landshut. He was obliged to follow Cajetan to the Rhine. Kalkoff,
"Zu Luthers römischem Prozess," *ZKG*, XXV, 400 f., n. 1, advances evidence to show that the
illness of Leo was an invention of Miltitz to gain time.

[59] *WAB*, I, 377 f.

[60] Kalkoff, "Zu Luthers römischem Prozess," *ZKG*, XXV, 410 f., and n. 2, regards the
reference below to the appointment of a court of arbitration by the Pope as another lie of the
nuncio to gain time. While no evidence has been found that Leo ever approved the plan
for arbitration, the papal court may have played with the idea for three months as a device
to avoid a drastic decision at this crucial period.

[61] *WAB*, I, 379, l. 72.

ful but more urgent.[62] In a highly baroque Latin and an unctuous style, Luther is addressed as "Your Paternity" (*Tua Paternitas*) and learns that Cajetan is well disposed toward him if he will only "deport himself better." He is urged to come at once to Coblenz, since the legate will certainly require nothing of him except what the archbishop agrees to. If Luther does not come, the matter may become more difficult, as he has heard from Rome that the Pope wishes to add other bishops as judges. To Spalatin, Miltitz repeats the same arguments.[63]

Luther read the letter with surprise and contempt. The softened mood of Altenburg, when Miltitz, probably with the support of Spalatin and Feilitzsch, had urged the necessity of composing his difficulties with the Roman Church, had now again given place to a feeling of embitterment toward his enemies and a defiant resolution to face the worst, if need be, in defense of his convictions. Within a week after the meeting with Miltitz he told Scheurl that "unless God intervenes, nothing will be done, especially if they begin to press upon me with that new decretal." [64] This refers to the papal pronouncement on indulgences of November 9, which he has not yet seen; but he has heard that it affirms a fullness of powers without authority of Scripture or canons, "and that certainly is something I will not concede even to the most ancient decretal."

Martin's attitude had by this time become one of profound distrust. In the past three months he had waited in vain for any word from Pope Leo authorizing the appointment of an arbitrator. In the meantime he had observed that Johann Eck, against whom his resentment grew day by day, was arming himself for a great public attack. More than that, Martin had been devoting himself to an intensive study of the history of the papacy as set forth in its decrees, and had become persuaded that the supremacy of the Roman pontiff rested on no divine authority. In this state of mind he receives Miltitz's invitation to Coblenz and finds it ridiculous. It is not the archbishop but Miltitz who is summoning him before Cajetan. "Are these people insane?" he asks.[65] In another letter he concludes that Miltitz is a smooth fellow who takes him for a blockhead.[66]

It is in this mood that Martin takes up his pen to reply to the nuncio.[67] The tone of his letter shows that he had ceased to ascribe importance to

---

[62] *Ibid.,* pp. 374 f. [63] *Ibid.,* pp. 376 f.

[64] Letter from Luther to Scheurl, Jan. 13, 1519, *WAB,* I, 300, ll. 17 f.

[65] Letter to Spalatin, May 16, 1519, *WAB,* I, 394, l. 7.

[66] Letter to Lang, May 16: "Homo suavis, simul confitens, se nondum ex Urbe recepisse mandatum et sperat me tam crassae naris esse, ut non vocatus nisi sua temeritate veniam." *WAB,* I, 399, ll. 19 ff.

[67] May 17, 1519. *WAB,* I, 402 f.

Miltitz or to regard the prospects of mediation as worthy of serious consideration. He can see no reason, he says, for further conferences; even the Altenburg meeting was unnecessary since his books contain all that is requisite in order to point out his errors and assign reasons for their revocation. He would be foolish to accept Miltitz's invitation without Rome's approval. Besides that, he is without safe conduct and without funds for the journey. In addition, a great disputation is impending, where the matter can be more diligently examined than before any archbishop or cardinal. His hostility to Cajetan explodes in denunciation of the learned representative of papal supremacy: "I do not want him to be present, nor is he worthy, since he sought at Augsburg to turn me aside from the Christian faith. I doubt whether he is a Catholic Christian." If he ever has the leisure, he will arraign him before pope and cardinals. "I grieve that there are legates of the Apostolic See who seek to abolish Christ." As regards the judges, he is quite willing that Pope Leo should appoint ten; in fact, in his books he has already put his case before the whole world. With bitter sarcasm he tells Miltitz that he more than half believes that a shady character who has recently been driven out of Wittenberg was a spy in the service of the nuncio. If Miltitz is obliged to see him, let him come quickly in God's name. He has himself too much to do to waste time on the journey.

As has been pointed out, Pope Leo's policy was in dire need of Frederick's help. Two days after Miltitz's urgent letters to Saxony, the papal legate Cajetan himself writes to the elector, informing him that the nuncio is coming at once to deliver the Golden Rose.[68] A few days later a letter from Miltitz follows, stating that he now has orders from Rome to bring the Rose and papal indulgences and is setting forth in great haste to execute this commission and discuss other matters with him.[69] The archbishop of Trier has consented to act as arbitrator and the nuncio begs that Luther be kept at Wittenberg until his meeting with the elector. What the important matter was that caused a change in Cajetan's policy is nowhere stated, but it is highly probable that he now employed Miltitz to convey to Frederick the Pope's proposals, either in support of Francis at the coming election or for

[68] *DRA*, I, 756 f., n. 4. In his reply from Würzburg on June 8 the elector reminds Cajetan tartly that the chamberlain has been promising to bring the decoration for some time without result and adds that he expects to continue to serve the Roman See in such a manner as the duty of an elector of the Holy Roman Empire demands, without hope or promise of fame. Cyprian, "Nützliche Urkunden," I, II, 109 ff.

[69] *Ibid.*, I, I, 402 ff. Miltitz explains that the rose has been deposited with the Fuggers in Augsburg, and he asks the elector to have it fetched from there, since his private commission to Frederick does not admit of delay.

the furtherance of the candidacy of the elector himself.[70] The latter supposition finds a certain support in the fact that shortly before this Leo had authorized the legate, in case such action was necessary, to promote an election which would be favorable to Christendom and "to confirm and approve" by means of the plenary power of the pope choice of an emperor by three electors.[71] Whether Miltitz had an opportunity to discuss matters with Frederick we do not know, but he came to Weimar and it seems probable that he met the elector there and traveled with the electoral party toward Frankfort the week following.[72]

When in the last week of June the electors gathered in the Frankfort cathedral for the final act, the choice of the Spanish Charles as Roman King and emperor-to-be was already a foregone conclusion.[73] Habsburg diplomacy and power won the day in a contest which for more than two years had reeked with bribery, double dealing, and deceit; and the young successor to the throne of the medieval emperors came in with a storm of bells and great national acclaim. Leo fought almost to the last against what was undoubtedly the choice of an overwhelming majority of the German princes and people, and Miltitz was employed as a go-between by the papal emissary, Archbishop Orsini, the archbishop of Trier, and the French ambassador in a final effort to win Elector Frederick to the support of the French king, or failing that, to persuade him to come forward himself as a candidate.[74] The record of the crucial sessions of the electoral college is

[70] Kalkoff puts together the evidence and concludes that the cardinal's proposition was really for the support of Frederick himself. "Zu Luthers römischem Prozess," ZKG, XXV, 412 ff.

[71] DRA, I, 656 f. One inference from the papal instruction is that the case might arise in which Frederick could be chosen emperor through his own vote and that of the archbishop of Trier and the elector of Brandenburg.

[72] Frederick was in Weimar from May 26 to 30. Kalkoff, "Die von Cajetan verfasste Ablassdekretale," 161 ff.

[73] The sources for the long negotiations which preceded the famous event and for the exciting Wahltage, June 27–28, are to be found in DRA, I; they are carefully considered in the light of other evidence by Bernhard Weicker, "Die Stellung der Kurfürsten zur Wahl Karls V im Jahre 1519," Historische Studien, Vol. XXII (1901). They picture the first grandiose international crisis of modern history and form a chronicle of greed and treachery on the part of most of the parties in the controversy, clerical and secular, which throws a weird light on the diplomacy of the time. Kalkoff, in various studies, notably those in ZKG, XXV, 417 ff. and passim; ZKG, XLIV, N.F. VII, 216 ff.; and ARG, XXI, 133 ff., interprets the sources from the standpoint of a strong partisan of Frederick.

[74] Frederick declined a meeting with Orsini, the papal nuncio, when en route to Frankfort. DRA, I, 765 f. On June 7, Leo sent an urgent message to Orsini for further intervention with Frederick, ibid., pp. 822 ff., and on the 21st Orsini, on his own behalf and that of the French embassy, sent the elector a message through Miltitz, ibid., pp. 823 f.; see also Spalatin, Friedrichs des Weisen Leben und Zeitgeschichte, pp. 40 f. and 58 f. In this message Orsini urged the elector to vote for Francis, in which case he should become permanent administrator

incomplete and it is not certain whether the Saxon prince, who had accepted no bribes and kept himself clear of promises and entanglements throughout, could have won the prize or, as some students of history believe, was actually for a brief time the choice of a majority of the electors.[75] In any event, he showed himself in this crisis fully deserving of the appellation "the Wise" which history has bestowed on him, since opposition to the powerful national forces arrayed on the Habsburg side would certainly have provoked immediate and bloody civil strife. Whatever ambitions he may have nourished, he appears in the sources as the single patriotic and incorruptible figure in a group that was untrustworthy, egotistical, and venal. Hesitant and over-timid he certainly was, but concerned always for the peace and welfare and dignity of the empire.

When the summer had passed with its exciting events, Miltitz finally appeared in Altenburg on September 25 to deliver the papal favors to Frederick. In spite of all that had happened, the elector received with satisfaction the Golden Rose and the special indulgences for the Wittenberg church, and directed that two hundred guilders be given to Miltitz, together with a promise of employment in his service for three years. The nuncio was by no means satisfied with this as a reward for so many months of effort, and reminding the elector of his unremitting service on his behalf, asked for another two hundred.[76] Now free from the control of

---

of the empire under the ruler, and the Pope would permit him to nominate some one of his friends for the cardinalate. In case Frederick should regard Francis's choice as impossible, however, it was the wish of the Pope and the French embassy that he should himself accept the crown. In that case they promised him full support. A similar offer was also made by Admiral Bonnivet, a representative of the French king. DRA, I, 827 f.; see also Weicker, "Die Stellung der Kurfürsten," pp. 349 ff.

[75] The authority for Frederick's election and immediate abdication is a statement ascribed by the Venetian ambassador to Richard Pace, the representative of Henry VIII in the electoral campaign. See DRA, I, 828, n. Kalkoff accepts it as proven in "Die Kaiserwahl Friedrichs des Weisen (27. Juni 1519)," ARG, XXI (1924), 139. Similarly he interprets Leo's promise of a cardinal's hat to one of Frederick's friends as the offer of this honor for Luther himself. "Kleine Nachträge zu 'Luthers römischem Prozess,'" ZKG, XLIV, N.F. VII (1925), 216. A possible confirmation of this has been found in a letter from Cardinal Giovanni Salviati, dated at Torchiara, to the Cardinal of Ravenna, reproduced by Drescher in Lutherstudien, pp. 283 ff. Salviati reports the news that there is to be a creation of cardinals "of little enough honor" (assai poco honorevole), and further, "on the best authority" that "there is thought of adding Martin Luther and another of those heretics" (ho inteso, et di bonissimo luogo, che pensava di aggiungnere Martino Luther et un altro di quelli heretici, con li quali intendo ha pratiche molto strette et pensa ridurli, et con danari et con permesse di capelli a ridirsi). Salviati reasserts that he has good authority for his statement. The letter bears the date of November 12, 1539, but Drescher is of the opinion that the date should be 1519, since there could have been no thought of an offer of this character to Luther in 1539. If this is true, it would support Kalkoff's premise.

[76] Cyprian, "Nützliche Urkunden," I, 1, 414 ff.

Cajetan, he added an apology for any threats of papal discipline which may have escaped him and asked that Luther be instructed to meet him again for conference in order to complete arrangements with the archbishop of Trier as umpire in his cause,[77] forwarding with his letter a friendly invitation to be delivered to Martin.[78] On the eve of his departure from Frankfort, though hurried because of the outbreak of the plague, which robbed him of his most trusted councilor, Degenhard Pfeffinger, Frederick had found time to confer with the archbishop and receive the latter's promise to see Luther when the elector should bring him along to the next Diet, which was to be held at Frankfort in the following spring. Frederick therefore accepted Miltitz's suggestion and through Spalatin bade Luther arrange a meeting.[79]

Martin promised himself nothing from another conference with Miltitz. "I know the fox," he tells Staupitz.[80] The controversy with Eck had put him in no mood for parley with adroit and slippery opponents, and he tells the elector that he sees through Karl's pretenses better than the latter thinks.[81] Nevertheless, he could not refuse to set a date for the meeting, and this took place on October 9 at the village of Liebenwerda near Wittenberg. Again Miltitz showed himself clever and conciliatory and the conference seems to have passed off with good feeling on both sides. Luther, who forwarded a memorandum to Spalatin immediately afterwards, notes that the meeting closed with a brief discussion of the power of the pope, in which Miltitz finally remarked, "We would soon reach an agreement." [82] Martin's report is tinged with sarcasm, which hardened into anger and contempt when he learned that the nuncio had reported to Frederick a promise on Martin's part to accompany him to see the archbishop of Trier.[83] Luther indignantly denied this and declared that Miltitz had stated that he himself was now going directly to Rome, since his task in Germany had been accomplished.[84] The nuncio in turn protested that this was untrue.[85] Luther, who had held throughout to his Altenburg proposal of an umpire and was ready to accompany the elector to Frankfort,[86] had no intention of going anywhere with Miltitz. He had learned that the papal chamber-

---

[77] Ibid., pp. 417 ff. [78] September 26. WAB, I, 510.
[79] Cyprian, "Nützliche Urkunden," I, II, 129 f.
[80] Letter of Oct. 3, 1519, WAB, I, 513, l. 12.
[81] Letter of Oct. 1, 1519, WAB, I, 512, ll. 10 f.
[82] The letter is undated, but it must have been written on October 9 or 10. WAB, I, 525.
[83] Letter from Miltitz to Frederick, Oct. 10, 1519, WAB, I, 525 ff.
[84] Letter from Luther to Spalatin, Oct. 13, 1519, WAB, I, 529.
[85] Letter from Miltitz to Frederick, Oct. 14, 1519, WAB, I, 527 f.
[86] Letter from Luther to Frederick, Oct. 15, 1519, WAB, I, 535.

lain was not taken seriously in Rome, and he was of the opinion that the "wretched" man would eventually become an object of ridicule in Germany also.[87] The conference at Liebenwerda brought an end to Miltitz's rôle, so far as Martin was concerned. As an intermediary between the electoral court and Rome, however, the young Saxon, who was now living from Frederick's largess, had still some part to play during the months that followed.[88]

[87] Letter from Luther to Spalatin, Oct. 13, 1519, *WAB*, I, 529, ll. 28 f.

[88] See letter from Miltitz to Frederick, Dec. 8, 1519, transmitting new admonitions from the papal court, in Cyprian, "Nützliche Urkunden," I, 1, 408 ff. Miltitz's fears of the interdict on Saxony and other severe ecclesiastical sanctions were taken seriously by the electoral councilors, as is evidenced by documents preserved in the archives, i.e., a memorandum of minutes of the council's discussion at Torgau, Cyprian, "Nützliche Urkunden," I, 11, 148 ff., and a carefully organized memorandum to the elector for reply to Miltitz, *ibid.*, pp. 142 ff. See also Spalatin's preliminary draft, *ibid.*, I, 1, 411 ff.

18

THE LEIPZIG DISPUTATION
THE PRELUDE

THE Leipzig disputation throws full light on Luther's personality for the first time, so that it is possible to see the man in action as viewed by his contemporaries.[1] It also brings to the front of the stage other men whose rôles in his life were to be of importance for years to come. His companion in arms on this occasion, Carlstadt, has already claimed our attention more than once. Later on he became one of Martin's most determined opponents, remaining a troublous element in the latter's life and work throughout the crucial years of the Reformation. Andreas Bodenstein of Carlstadt[2] is one of those contemporaries with whom Luther's biographers have dealt no more gently than with others who opposed the ideas and obstructed the purposes of the Wittenberg reformer. Like Thomas Münzer and the Catholic opponents, Carlstadt has had to wait until the twentieth century for a fair judgment of his part in the struggle against the scholastic ideals and his attempt to find new formulas for the future. Some of his unpopularity with the witnesses of his period was certainly due to temperamental difficulties of the man, whose character bears marks of self-seeking and a certain unsteadiness of purpose.

Andreas was several years Luther's senior.[3] He was a son of the chief official of the quiet little town of Carlstadt in Franconia, and like Luther began his studies at Erfurt. After receiving his bachelor's degree in 1502, Carlstadt went to Cologne to continue his studies.[4] Here he entered the

---

[1] The sources for the Leipzig disputation are, in addition to Luther's letters, those of Carlstadt, Melanchthon, Eck, Johann Cellarius, Nikolaus von Amsdorf, Peter Mosellanus, and Johann Rubeus, all in the year 1519; and the recollections of Sebastian Fröschel, written nearly half a century later.

[2] See Barge, who in his *Andreas Bodenstein* draws on rich source material.

[3] His birth date cannot be fixed definitely. See *ibid.*, I, 2.

[4] The facts have been carefully collated by Gustav Bauch, "Andreas Karlstadt als Scholastiker," *ZKG*, XVIII (1898), 37 ff.

citadel of Thomistic philosophy in Germany and undoubtedly learned to know the archrepresentatives of scholastic theology who were a dozen years later to become the target for the satiric attacks by the authors of the *Letters of Obscure Men*. In the year when Luther entered the monastery Carlstadt transferred to Wittenberg, where he soon after received the degree of master of arts and two years later, in 1507, appeared as lecturer on Thomistic philosophy and Aristotle's metaphysics.[5] In the same year, while Luther was still engaged in theological studies in Erfurt, Carlstadt brought out the first original scholastic work which the new Saxon university had yet produced, a defense of the philosophy of St. Thomas.[6] Thomistic in tone and diffuse in method, his analysis of the principles of logic must nevertheless have excited the admiration and gratitude of the university, for in the year of its appearance he was made dean of the faculty of arts and in the following year Christoph Scheurl, orator of the university, praised him in All Saints' Church as "important as a philosopher, more important as a theologian, most important as a Thomist. . . . If we had many Carlstadts we should easily, I think, be able to rival the Parisians." [7]

In the meantime Andreas had dedicated himself to a theological career, the final port of most philosophically minded students. He passed rapidly through the lower degrees and attained that of doctor of philosophy in 1510.[8] Material rewards which came to him showed that the university appreciated the ability of so productive a young scholar. In 1510 he was made archdeacon of the Church of All Saints, the most important clerical position in Wittenberg, and this brought him to the altar and the pulpit of the electoral church on all important occasions in the Christian year. His prestige in the university is indicated by its official records, which note his election as rector as early as 1511 and as dean eight times in the decade after 1512.[9] In the meantime his studies had broadened to include the philosophy of Scotus. A concordance to canon and civil law and one to Thomas and Scotus and a drill book on Aristotle's *Metaphysics* give evidence of his energy.[10] The year in which Luther began his lectures on Romans his ambitious colleague went to Rome for further studies in law, and in

---

[5] See the list of Wittenberg professors and their lectures in the summer semester of 1507 in Kaufmann, *Geschichte der deutschen Universitäten*, II, 576.

[6] *De intentionibus opusculum . . . compilatum ad Sancti emulorum Thome commoditatem.* See Barge, *Andreas Bodenstein*, I, 9; Bauch, "Karlstadt als Scholastiker," p. 40.

[7] Quoted by Barge, *Andreas Bodenstein*, I, 28 f., n. 95.

[8] Förstemann, *Liber decanorum*, pp. 3, 4, 8, 9; see also Barge, *Andreas Bodenstein*, I, 30.

[9] Förstemann, *Liber decanorum, passim.*

[10] *Questiones in libros Metaphysicae Aristotelis.* Barge, *Andreas Bodenstein*, I, 46, gives the sources for our knowledge of this early period in Carlstadt's career.

March, 1516, the university at Siena conferred on him the doctorate in both canon and civil law.[11]

Here are indisputable evidences of productive energy. His subsequent development also shows that he was not lacking in courage and zeal. On the other hand, the sources also give indications of flaws in character and temperament which boded ill for the future. Carlstadt became involved in disputes with the chapter of the collegiate church to which he was attached, conflicts which can scarcely be interpreted otherwise than as the result of a tendency to contentiousness on his part, and they led to complaints against him from the administrative board of the chapter.[12]

In the meantime, Carlstadt seems to have shown a spirit of fairness and a commendable openness of mind in his relationship with Luther.[13] According to the testimony of Martin, given many years later, his colleague at first opposed him and then was won over to Luther's views by a study of St. Augustine.[14] When the Bernhardi disputation took place Carlstadt was much offended that Martin had denied to Augustine the authorship of one of the works commonly attributed to him,[15] but the following year Andreas's views had undergone a change and he accepted Martin's judgment of the Schoolmen.[16] He bought Augustine's works, and the acquaintance with the African Father which followed so stirred his soul that he was filled with shame and awe.[17] In reviewing later the spiritual crisis through which he passed in turning away from scholastic self-righteousness, he declares that he was frightened for his own salvation and suffered penance through bitter years.[18] How far this change was due to association with Martin cannot be said. Carlstadt himself declares that he was turned from his scholastic ideas to the Church Fathers through reading a sermon by Staupitz; then Augustine's work *On the Spirit and the Letter* came into his hands and he found in the book "the handle and the threshold to every theology." [19]

The revolutionary changes thus wrought in his views took the form

---

[11] *Ibid.*, p. 52.   [12] *Ibid.*, pp. 49, 53.   [13] See *ibid.*, II, 535 f.

[14] *TR*, IV, No. 4187 (1538), p. 188, ll. 16 ff.: "Carlstadt und Petrus Lupinus waren in der Erste, da das Euangelium anging, meine heftigsten Widersacher; aber da ich sie mit Disputiren beschloss und uberwand sie mit den Schriften Augustini und sie denselben gelesen hatten, waren sie viel heftiger in dieser Sache denn ich."

[15] Letter from Luther to Lang, Oct., 1516, *WAB*, I, 65, ll. 24 ff.

[16] See Carlstadt's introductory letter to Staupitz, November 17, 1517, prefixed to his edition of Augustine's *De spiritu et litera*. Barge, *Andreas Bodenstein*, I, 72, and II, 533 ff., Anlage 5a. At first he was influenced against accepting Luther's views by the latter's youth: "Mouebar Martini iuuenta ac magis subtilitate atque multitudine scholasticorum." *Ibid.*, II, 534.

[17] *Ibid.*, II, 534.

[18] Quoted from Carlstadt's *De impii justificatione* by Barge. *Ibid.*, I, 74.

[19] *Ibid.*, II, 534 f.

common to the academic life of the time, the issuance of a series of theses. As we have seen, he seized the occasion of the celebration of the relics in the Castle Church on April 26, 1517, to put forward 152 propositions, whose Latin text rings with the sincerity of conviction.[20] Here we find many of those ideas of St. Augustine which Luther was soon afterwards to put into even more ardent language. The sin which always remains in the heart, the ineradicable concupiscence, stands forth in contrast with the boundless grace of God. Plainly Andreas had now broken with Scotus's ideas of the participation of the sinner in the work of regeneration. A further stage on his new path is marked by his notes on Augustine's great work *On the Spirit and the Letter,* most of which were written in the same year.[21]

What was the relation of this man to Luther, whose theological ideas kept pace so closely with his in this crucial year? The sources do not permit us to say with exactness nor to determine to which of the two belongs the primacy in the condemnation of Aristotle. Luther's sharp attack on Aristotle's influence on theology, found in his letters at this time and in the disputation of Franz Günther in September, 1517, had its counterpart in the compact sentences of Carlstadt's theses earlier in the same year.[22] In any case, there appears thus far no difference of opinion between the two theologians. In the introductory address to his interpretation of Augustine's great mystical work Carlstadt praises Martin's ability in interpreting not only the Latin text but also the Greek and Hebrew Scriptures,[23] and he proclaims the impotence of the human will and the futility of self-righteousness in the same style which Martin employs in his Ninety-five Theses. Others of his ideas in the essay, too, such as the criticism of the exaggerated cult of saints, find their parallel in Martin's views.[24] It is not surprising, therefore, that the latter's interest in his colleague's edition of *On the Spirit*

---

[20] Text in Theodor Kolde, "Wittenberger Disputationsthesen aus den Jahren 1516 bis 1522," *ZKG,* XI (1890), 448 ff. See also Barge, *Andreas Bodenstein,* I, 463 f.

[21] *Sanctissimi Augustini de spiritu et litera liber magne theologo commoditati. Cum explicationibus sive lecturis.* For this work of Carlstadt's, the most extensive which is preserved from his pen, see Barge, *Andreas Bodenstein,* I, 90 ff. It did not come from the press until 1519.

[22] See *ibid.,* pp. 79 ff.; Barge follows Kolde, "Wittenberger Disputationsthesen," p. 449, in placing Carlstadt's theses at the very beginning of the theological reform and in stressing their revolutionary character. This idea has been strongly combatted. It is perhaps fair to say that while Luther's thinking on Augustine may have been clarified by association with Carlstadt, Martin assimilates Augustine's ideas in an entirely natural and organic manner. See further, Barge, *Andreas Bodenstein,* I, 86, and *passim.*

[23] *Ibid.,* II, 536, Anlage 5b.

[24] Carlstadt's attack on the cult of the saints developed in the interpretation of Augustine's work into a bold arraignment of false relics and saint-service. Barge, *Andreas Bodenstein,* I, 105 ff.

and the Letter was so keen that he sent the sheets of the first part of the work to Lang soon after their appearance.[25] Early in 1518 he calls Andreas "a man of incomparable zeal," [26] and although signs are not lacking that the two men did not continue to see eye to eye when the great combat approached in which they were to be brothers in arms,[27] their common enthusiasm for the ideas of Augustine in his great mystical work still held them together in the spring of 1519. This then was the man with whom Martin was to share the great disputation and whom he was finally to displace as Wittenberg's chief protagonist.

What manner of man was the opponent who summoned the two to decisive conflict? Johann Eck, at the time when he came to conclusions with Martin at Leipzig, was perhaps the most feared disputant of the German academic world. Protestant historians have repaid Eck for the relentlessness with which he pursued Luther and his followers by four centuries of abuse. They have pointed to his well-attested greed in seeking further ecclesiastical offices in addition to the professorship and parish and canonate which he held.[28] They have charged that he was in the pay of the Fuggers as an advocate of the practice of collecting interest,[29] and that he urged upon the Pope unceasingly claims to a reward for publishing the bull against Luther.[30] They have pointed to the boastful character of the letters with which he proclaimed his victory over the Wittenberg scholars. His Protestant contemporaries decorated him with a selected list of the insulting epithets which the theologians of the sixteenth century used so liberally. "Assophist," "ass's head," "dunce head," "fool," "quarrelsome bully," "greedy hypocrite," "liar," "blasphemer," "heretic," are among the printable ones. Carlstadt denounced him as "a fierce-tempered goat," Spengler called him "Doctor Filth," and even Melanchthon claimed to hear in "Eck! Eck!" the cry of the coarse-voiced raven. After the disputation Martin joined with full throat in this chorus of abuse and salted his epithets with a savage humor, including an unending series of puns on the name of his antagonist.[31]

---

[25] Letter from Luther to Lang, March 21, 1518, *WAB*, I, 154. Barge points out (I, 102) that in 1525, in his pamphlet *Wider die himmlischen Propheten,* Luther develops ideas closely resembling those which Carlstadt had expressed in his interpretation of Augustine's work.

[26] "Homo studii incomparabilis." Letter from Luther to Spalatin, Jan. 18, 1518, *WAB*, I, 134, ll. 48 f.

[27] See Barge, *Andreas Bodenstein,* I, 109.

[28] See especially Kalkoff in Luther, *Ausgewählte Werke,* I, 340.

[29] Paul Kalkoff, "Die Bulle Exsurge," *ZKG,* XXXVII (1918), 107.

[30] *Ibid.,* p. 118.

[31] Eck's own fluency in the use of abusive epithets is also fully attested. As a by no means drastic example may be cited his letter to the duke of Bavaria of November 23, 1527, de-

These attacks cannot be dismissed as noisome products of an age reckless in personal insult. They spring from a bitterness of feeling which marked the desperate nature of the conflict on which the religious world had now entered. The grim implications of the charge of heresy were sufficiently understood to give a savage turn to any theological discussion. After 1521 Eck himself repeatedly sat in judgment on the followers of Luther and helped to expedite to a fiery end more than one sincere opponent of the old order.[32]

Catholic scholars of recent days have shown that in spite of his self-advertising tactics Eck was a man of sound scholarly attainments and great productive energy in the field of scholastic theology.[33] He was born three years after Luther, of a rural family in Bavaria, and received the usual scholastic education at Heidelberg, Tübingen, Cologne, and Freiburg in Breisgau. At sixteen years of age he became a lecturer at Freiburg and was initiated there into the study of Greek and Hebrew. He showed more than the usual precocity of the times, becoming master of arts at fourteen and dean of the college of liberal arts at twenty-two. The next year he became a priest and a year later professor of philosophy, transferring in 1510 to Ingolstadt where he was speedily promoted to be dean of the faculty of theology, and at twenty-six years of age was chosen rector of the university. By nature and training a follower of the scholastic theology, Eck was, however, far from lacking independence of character. His *Chrysopassus prae-destinationis* (1514) [34] is an energetic and well-balanced presentation of the

---

nouncing Pastor Konrad Sam of Ulm, whom he accused of heresy, as "einen ertzketzerischen, ungelehrten, ungeschickten, verführerischen, teuflischen, verderblichen Menschen, einen Seelendieb, Seelenmörder, hergelaufen Buben." Quoted by Wiedemann, *Dr. Johann Eck*, p. 261. Heinrich Schauerte, "Die Busslehre des Johannes Eck," *RgST*, XXXVIII/XXXIX (1919), 56 ff., gives a selection from Eck's personal attacks on Luther: "Lügner"; "Lügenprophet, der den Teufel zum Vater hat"; "Diener, Organ, Jäger und Jagdhund des Teufels"; "Saitenspieler"; "Sophist"; "dentata bestia"; "giftige Spinne, Esel, sächsisches Kalb"; "Bastard"; and so on. On the other hand, I cannot find that Eck ever descended into sexual obscenity for his comparisons as Luther did. Those who are interested in this subject may consult Denifle's *Luthertum* (1906), I, 813 ff., where a truly appalling list of invectives has been brought together. The theologians of the Middle Ages found a rich vocabulary of abuse in the Old Testament and the humanists supplied notable additions from classical antiquity. Reuchlin in his *Defensio* applies a well selected list of epithets to his critics: "rams," "sheep," "goats," "swine," "horses and mules," "devil's pupils," "comrades of the underworld." He concludes by saying that people will be surprised that he treats them so mildly! See Geiger, *Johann Reuchlin*, pp. 276 ff.

[32] He sat among the judges of Leonard Käser in the Bavarian town of Schräding in 1527. Käser was a pastor who was burned for heresy. See Wiedemann, *Dr. Johann Eck*, pp. 201 ff.

[33] Theodor Wiedemann's work on Eck is far from unbiased, but it is nevertheless a sturdy attempt to understand the man by a study of the sources. The works of later Catholic scholars, Greving, Schauerte, and others, are more judicial in tone.

[34] See Joseph Greving, "Johann Eck als junger Gelehrter. Eine literar- und dogmengeschicht-

doctrine of predestination, marked by wide scholarship and an eager desire to interpret the subject with clearness. An examination of the work shows that Eck was familiar with the classical writers of both the pagan and Christian eras, with clerical authorities and humanists of Germany and Italy, and even with some of the representatives of Jewish and Arabic learning.[35] His *Doctrine of Penance* shows highly developed dialectical command of his subject, and in spite of its thoroughly scholastic attitude, a keen understanding of the evils which had grown up around the system of indulgences. His *Parish Book of the Church of Our Lady at Ingolstadt* indicates a sense for practical administration.[36] Always sure of himself and incurably addicted to self-praise, overbearing and frequently insulting in his polemics, Eck's writings nevertheless index a mind sincere in its orthodoxy, and they are not lacking in expressions of proud humility of faith. He was quite without a trace of sentimentalism in life or work. His thoroughgoing rationalism is indicated by his lack of belief in current astrological superstitions. In Italy he called Pico della Mirandola his friend, and his standing as a scholar was unquestioned throughout German lands. In the four years preceding the Leipzig disputation he issued commentaries on the *Logic* of Petrus Hispanus and several of the works of Aristotle. He had an active and productive interest in geography.[37] The great humanist Reuchlin visited him in 1519 and again in 1520. Melanchthon, undoubtedly the best qualified judge of scholars in the whole group which listened to the Leipzig disputation, testified that most of those present regarded Eck with admiration on account of his varied and distinguished intellectual powers.[38]

The tireless energy of the man, which could not exhaust itself in profes-

---

liche Untersuchung über seinen Chrysopassus Praedestinationis aus dem Jahre 1514," *RgST*, I (1906).

[35] Greving, "Eck als Gelehrter," pp. 19 ff., examines the long list of authorities which the young author cites (Eck was only twenty-eight when he wrote the *Chrysopassus*) and shows that he was at least as careful as his contemporaries in the use of scholarly sources. In spite of the abundant source material which he uses, Eck relies mainly on Scotus and Bonaventure in developing his view of predestination. Schauerte, in "Die Busslehre," traverses a great array of scholarly sources for Eck's doctrines of penance; see his summary, pp. 48 ff. Certain it is that in the confusion caused by Luther's attack the scholastic ideas of penance found in Eck a well-trained opponent who did much to open the way through his polemics for the formulation that took place at the Council of Trent. His ability as exegete and his service in the development of the post-Tridentine dogma are gradually coming to light through the active work of Catholic savants whose republications of Eck's works in the *Corpus Catholicorum* enable us to draw a more just picture of the man's ability and productive energy.

[36] Joseph Greving, "Johann Ecks Pfarrbuch für U. L. Frau in Ingolstadt. Ein Beitrag zur Kenntnis der pfarrkirchlichen Verhältnisse im 16. Jahrhundert," *RgST*, Vols. IV, V (1908).

[37] Greving, "Eck als Gelehrter," pp. xi ff.

[38] Letter from Melanchthon to Oecolampadius, July 21, 1519. Quoted by Seifert, *Die Reformation in Leipzig*, p. 48.

sorial and religious duties, in constant visits to libraries and scholars, and in the writing of sermons, exegetical and devotional works, and countless letters, sought a further outlet in the disputation. Taste and training drew him early in life to these exercises, which had moreover an especial attraction for one of his egotistic nature. When he crossed Luther's path, his fame as a disputant had already resounded throughout Central Europe. Supported by the Fuggers, he had publicly defended in Germany the lending at interest at 5 percent, and debated the same thesis in a famous disputation held in Bologna in 1515, where he also defended theses on predestination and questions of logic and physics.[39] In Vienna two years afterward he challenged the entire theological faculty, which after many attempts at escape finally yielded to the command of the emperor and gave its redoubtable antagonist an opportunity to boast of a mighty victory.[40] Nine years after his encounter with Luther, in company with Thomas Murner and Faber, he faced the learned Swiss reformer Oecolampadius and others in a disputation at Baden in Switzerland that lasted nineteen days and was of the highest importance for the future religious history of the Helvetic Confederation.[41]

This then was the man who called Martin into the lists. The importance of the occasion was blurred in Luther's mind at the time by indignation at what he regarded as unfair treatment on the part of his opponent and the Leipzig theologians. Even in the summary of his life drawn up the year before his death he does not emphasize the significance of the disputation in his development, merely remarking in general of the period concerned (1519) that he had at that time attained his first definite knowledge of the faith of Christ.[42] Indeed, neither in 1545 nor a quarter of a century earlier when reporting on the disputation to his friends does Luther seem to realize the radical change which the disputation wrought in his attitude toward pope and council. At the time of the disputation he was overwhelmed with resentment because the meeting to which he had looked

[39] Wiedemann, *Dr. Johann Eck,* pp. 53 ff.

[40] *Ibid.,* pp. 63 ff. Eck's theses for the disputation, together with related material, were published in his *Disputatio Viennae Pannoniae habita* (1517); republished by Therese Virnich in *Corp. Cath.,* Vol. VI.

[41] The disputation, which took place from May 19 to June 8, 1526, was organized by the city of Berne. Eck and his companions had expected to face Zwingli on this occasion, but the Zürich city council, probably concerned for his safety, would not allow him to attend. On receipt of Zwingli's invitation Eck had refused him the greeting "which is usual in letters": "dz ich dich erkenn als ein verworffen, abtrinnigen vom glauben, vermaledeiten ketzer und gotzlesterer." Wiedemann, *Dr. Johann Eck,* p. 251.

[42] "Deinde primitias cognitionis et fidei Christi hauseram." *WA,* LIV, 183.

forward as a scholarly discussion had become an occasion requiring him to call up all his reserves of courage and self-restraint.

In order to trace the beginnings of the historic meeting it is necessary to go back a year to the early repercussions of Luther's theses on indulgences. Eck was probably one of those who received the theses through Christoph Scheurl, who, as we have seen, was active in distributing them; and they aroused immediately the zeal of the Ingolstadt theologian for combat. Scheurl reports less than two months after their appearance, "Eck replies that he would go ten miles to dispute about them." [43] Several weeks later, about the middle of February, Eck wrote a series of comments and sent them to Gabriel von Eyb,[44] the bishop of the neighboring See of Eichstädt. These the author termed "Adnotationes" (Comments), but the name which Martin gave them, "Obelisks" (Daggers), has clung to them.[45] Eck contended persistently that the "Obelisks" were never intended for printing but for private circulation only,[46] and Luther himself refers to them as "privately written." [47] They came into Luther's hands at some time between March 5 and 24, probably through one of Eck's numerous enemies, Bernhard Adelmann, an Augsburg humanist who sent them to the Nuremberg chapter of Augustinians and thence to Martin by way of his friend Wenceslaus Link.[48] Martin's reply, which the author entitled "Asterisks," was written down in great haste, possibly in the tense days of his self-defense at Heidelberg, and is six or seven times as long as the attack which called it forth.[49] Apparently after some weeks of delay it was sent to Link and thus found its way into Eck's hands.[50] Martin's tone is in the highest degree

---

[43] Letter from Scheurl to Kaspar Güttel, Jan. 8, 1518, Scheurl, *Briefbuch*, II, 43 f.

[44] See Joseph Greving, "Johannes Eck, Defensio contra amarulentas D. Andreae Bodenstein Carolstatini invectiones (1518)," in *Corp. Cath.* I, 7 f. See also Luther's repeated sneer that Eck's "Obelisks" were written in the "meatless days" (i.e. Lent). *WA*, I, 281, l. 28; 309, ll. 35 ff.

[45] The "Obelisks" were first printed along with Luther's reply in the Wittenberg edition of 1545. *WA*, I, 281 ff. As concerns the text, see *WA*, IX, 770 ff., and Greving, "Eck, Defensio," pp. 8 ff.

[46] See the introduction to his *Defensio* in Greving's edition, p. 37; also Eck's letters: to Carlstadt, May 28, 1518, *Ref. Act.*, II, 64 f.; to Matthäus Lang, *WA*, IX, 207, ll. 12 f.; and to Kaspar von Wessobrunn and Johann von Polling, March 14, 1519, *Ref. Act.*, III, 560 ("privatim factas").

[47] Letter from Luther to Scheurl, June 15, 1518, *WAB*, I, 183, l. 9.

[48] Letter from Scheurl to Eck, May 14, 1518, Scheurl, *Briefbuch*, II, 47. F. X. Thurnhofer is of the opinion that the "Obelisks" came to Link through Bernhard Adelmann. See his "Bernhard Adelmann von Adelmannsfelden, Humanist und Luthers Freund (1457–1523)," *Erläuterungen und Ergänzungen zu Janssens Geschichte des deutschen Volkes*, II, 1, 60. Clemen's hypothesis, *WAB*, I, 153, n. 9, that Luther knew of the "Obelisks" when he wrote to Eck before March 5 seems quite untenable.

[49] *Asterisci Lutheri adversus obeliscos Eckii* (1518). *WA*, I, 278 ff.

[50] See Luther's letters: to Eck, May 19, 1518, *WAB*, I, 178, ll. 17 ff.; and to Link, *ibid.*,

irritated and aggressive. He traverses Eck's arguments one by one and replies to them. He makes a vigorous defense of his orthodoxy against the charge that he is a "Bohemian heretic" and calls on his opponent to read Augustine's work *On the Spirit and the Letter* for better instructions. The tone of Eck's "Comments" was coarse, to be sure, but was after all directed rather against Luther's theses than against their author, and the epithets he employs were the traditional vocabulary aimed at anyone who smelled of heresy. The tone of Martin's reply is personal and has the flavor of the monastic polemics which seek to overwhelm the opponent with repulsive analogies. Yes, he declares, the statement that the will rules in the soul like a king in his kingdom really means "like the landlady of a brothel in the brothel. . . . For the will alone is always a whore and has all the qualities of a whore." [51] With supreme contempt he brands Eck as full of blasphemy and bitterness: [52] "He stinks again of his goat Aristotle." [53] After this savory exchange the opponents were both of a mind to let the matter rest. They were like veteran fighters who respect each other's powers, somewhat more than willing to withdraw from combat if it can be done with dignity. Martin, as we have seen, contented himself with a letter full of reprimands and threats but containing the assurance that the "Asterisks" were not meant for public knowledge. [54]

Eck, especially, regretted his attack, and Scheurl mediated between the two men, whose friendship he had sought to establish by correspondence. [55] Andreas Carlstadt, however, even more irascible and belligerent than Luther, felt himself called upon to take up the cudgels on behalf of the Wittenberg theological faculty, of which he had recently been made dean for the fourth time, [56] as well as to defend the new ideas of penance and grace that he had begun to develop in the preceding year. While Luther was absent at the Heidelberg disputation, Carlstadt prepared 379 theses, which we have seen to be a more radical formulation of the new theology than Martin had yet attained, and declared that he would have his students dispute on them in the course of the summer. [57] They were printed in part in order to prepare for the first of the new semester's disputations on May

---

p. 177. Apparently Link had already received a copy from another source. Clemen suggests that a transcript had been made at Heidelberg from Martin's manuscript without the author's knowledge. *Ibid.*, pp. 176 f.

[51] *WA*, I, 283, ll. 20 f.   [52] *Ibid.*, p. 305, ll. 23 f.   [53] *Ibid.*, p. 291, l. 16.

[54] Letter from Luther to Eck, May 19, 1518, *WAB*, I, 178, ll. 20 f.

[55] Letter from Luther to Scheurl, June 15, 1518, *WAB*, I, 183.

[56] Barge, *Andreas Bodenstein*, I, 44.

[57] The "Apologeticae Conclusiones" in *Ref. Act.*, II, 78 ff.

14.[58] They review the questions of the freedom of the will, predestination, indulgences, and the general charge of heresy which Eck had launched against the Wittenberg theologians. When the news of the theses came to Ingolstadt, Eck speedily wrote a conciliatory letter to Carlstadt in an effort to halt their publication, but too late.[59] On hearing of this Luther hastened to assure Scheurl that his brother professor had printed the theses against his will and without his knowledge, and he begged the Nuremberg friend to intervene with Eck. At the same time he entreated the Ingolstadt professor to answer Andreas with restraint.[60] Carlstadt, however, was bent on forcing a quarrel and answered Eck's plea for an armistice in the aggressive and insulting tone of the scholastic cocks-of-the-walk. He upbraids him for his attack on Luther and closes with a "vivat" for Martin, "who has given the occasion to extract the very marrow from the Law of God!" [61]

Carlstadt's *Apologetic Conclusions,* now grown to 405, finally came from the Wittenberg press in July.[62] Only a part (112) were directed against Eck's "Obelisks," three of which were selected for attack, but these struck at the heart of Luther's position on indulgences, and Carlstadt's rebuttal unfolds a full definition of the Wittenberg theology concerning true penance and the limitations on the papal power to forgive sin. The result was to arouse all the combative instinct of the disputatious Dominican. Eck issued at once his *Defense,* a systematic reply to Carlstadt's theses point by point.[63] To his opponent's quotations from scholastic authors Eck opposes other quotations, and arrays Anselm, Boethius, and Augustine against Carlstadt's assertions of the incapacity of the human will, closing with the scholastic proposition which the Wittenberg theologians had denied categorically and repeatedly: that God cannot withhold grace from him who does the best he can. In spite of the bombastic and egotistic tone which marks so much of Eck's writing, the pamphlet ends on a conciliatory note with the suggestion that the propositions be laid before the Apostolic Chair or the universities of Rome, Paris, or Cologne.[64]

Carlstadt had no thought of reconciliation. The same day, August 28, that he received Eck's *Defense* he set to work on a detailed reply.[65] His

[58] Barge, *Andreas Bodenstein,* I, 118.
[59] See letter from Eck to Carlstadt, May 28, 1518, *Ref. Act.,* II, 64 f.
[60] Letter from Luther to Scheurl, June 15, 1518, *WAB,* I, 183. Luther's letter to Eck is lost.
[61] Letter from Carlstadt to Eck, June 11, 1518, *Ref. Act.,* II, 649 f.
[62] See *WA,* II, 154. For the number of theses see *Corp. Cath.,* I, 21.
[63] Reprinted by Joseph Greving in *Corp. Cath.,* Vol. I.
[64] *Ibid.,* p. 81.
[65] *Defensio . . . adversus eximii D. Johannis Eckii, theologiae doctoris et ordinarii Ingolstadtensis monomachiam* (1518). *Ref. Act.,* II, 108 ff.

own *Defense* grew to considerably greater length than Eck's and was finally completed on September 14.[66] It is a vigorous championship of Luther's proposition that the whole life of a Christian consists of penance, and a strong attack on Eck's belief in the freedom of man to do good.[67]

Both sides were eager for a disputation when Luther went to Augsburg in October to appear before Cajetan. Here he met Eck,[68] and it was agreed that the quarrel, which had assumed the characteristic appearance of a scholastic feud, should be settled by a regular disputation between Eck and Carlstadt. That the meeting with Eck was in no way a hostile one is shown by the friendly tone of Luther's letter to Ingolstadt some weeks later.[69] Martin rejected the Dominican's suggestion that the decision should be given at Rome on the ground that it was too far away and the expense of the journey too great; and after various places for the disputation had been discussed it was finally agreed that either Erfurt or Leipzig might be chosen. The decision was left to Eck, who naturally selected the Saxon city, where the Dominican influence on the university was stronger than at Erfurt, the alma mater of both Carlstadt and Luther and largely under Augustinian control.[70]

Finally, early in December, both Luther and Eck asked the Leipzig theological faculty and the duke of Saxony for permission to hold the disputation at the university.[71] The Saxon theologians had no desire to be drawn into a question which might open the door to a long quarrel, particularly one concerning which a papal commission had already been appointed. In a long and adroitly worded letter to Duke George[72] the faculty pointed out the disagreeable results which might arise from popular excitement over the matter and referred guardedly to the complications that loomed for them and for the duke through Elector Frederick's well known patronage of the Wittenberg theologians. The Saxon duke did not share these anxieties, but called the attention of the faculty to the "praise and honor" that would come to the university as scene of the disputation, and he also informed Eck of his approval.[73]

---

[66] It seems not to have been printed until October (before October 20). *WA*, II, 154.

[67] See Barge, *Andreas Bodenstein*, I, 127 ff.

[68] See Luther's letters: to Eck, Nov. 15, 1518, *WAB*, I, 231; to Egranus, Feb. 2, 1519, *WAB*, I, 314, ll. 33 ff.; to Carlstadt, early in February, 1519, *WAB*, I, 316, ll. 3 ff.

[69] *WAB*, I, 231.

[70] See letter from Luther to Spalatin, Dec. 3, 1519, *WAB*, I, 565. Eck's letter fixing on Leipzig is lost.

[71] Luther's letters have both been lost, as has Eck's letter to the faculty. The letter from Eck to George is reprinted in Gess, *Briefe und Akten*, I, 48 f.

[72] *Ibid.*, pp. 49 ff.   [73] *Ibid.*, pp. 52 f.

Before Eck had learned of this answer he seems to have assumed that the disputation was as good as settled and proceeded to put his lance in rest against a more distinguished opponent than Carlstadt. On December 29 he published the twelve theses that he was prepared to defend at Leipzig. These were printed in the usual placard form for posting and a month later were in Martin's hands.[74] When he read them, Martin saw at once that they were not directed against Carlstadt but against himself. Without naming Luther, Eck attacks specifically his declarations on penance, indulgences, merit, and purgatory as he had done in his "Obelisks" and his *Defense:* penance is not a lifelong affair, and the just man, if he remains just, cannot be considered to be in mortal sin; souls in purgatory may be freed by the merit of others, and the merit of Christ is a treasure of the Church; the pope can free souls from purgatory through indulgences. The theses culminate in a declaration that the pope is the successor of Peter and the general vicar of Christ, and in this connection Eck denies that this supremacy dates from the time of Pope Sylvester, who was said to have received the gift of the temporal power from Constantine. This was a direct reference to Luther's declaration in the *Explanations of the Power of Indulgences* and had nothing to do with the propositions of Carlstadt, which attacked the freedom of the will and its value for human salvation [75] and touched on the papal power only in so far as it related to the forgiveness of sin.

This complete clarification of Eck's position brought Luther for the first time into the fray. That this was bound to happen might have been foreseen, for Martin's letters after his return from Augsburg had shown an increasing readiness to face the consequences of his attack on indulgences, and Eck's polemics had been directed from the first against Luther's position. Indeed, six months before, in his letter of June 11 to Eck, Carlstadt had spoken of his own theses as an "apology" for Luther.[76] That Eck had in mind a disputation with Luther from the very beginning of his

[74] *Contra novam doctrinam Scheda disputatoria. In studio Lipsiensi disputiat Eckius propositiones infra notatas contra D. Bodenstein Carlestadium Archidiaconum et doctorem Wittenbergensi.* The theses, which are accompanied by a letter to Bishop Matthäus Lang, were printed in Augsburg and reached Martin by way of Pirckheimer on or before February 2. See letter from Luther to Egranus, *WAB,* I, 314, l. 41.

[75] In his *Resolutiones,* "Conclusio XXII," *WA,* I, 571, Luther had declared that the Roman Church at the time of Gregory the Great did not stand above the Greek Church. In the *Acta Augustana* he held that the pope stood not over but under the Scriptures. *WA,* II, 11, ll. 2 ff. Eck's thesis reads, "Romanam Ecclesiam non fuisse superiorem aliis Ecclesiis ante tempora Sylvestri, negamus. Sed eum, qui sedem beatissimi Petri habuit et fidem, successorem Petri et Vicarium Christi generalem semper agnovimus." *Ref. Act.,* III, 211. Thus in his arraignment of Luther's position he makes it somewhat more anti-papal than it was.

[76] "Monomachiam seu potius Apologiam contra aliquos tuarum conclusionum ediderim." *Ref. Act.,* II, 649.

quarrel with Carlstadt is improbable in view of the sources which we have traversed. It was Carlstadt who forced the fighting. In a letter to a friend at this time Luther declares, however, that some assert the Dominicans "suborned" Eck to the attack on him,[77] and it is not improbable that the moves of his order in Rome eventually persuaded Eck to endeavor to bring the more widely advertised of the Wittenberg professors into the arena.

Meanwhile the arrangements for the disputation continued to encounter difficulties. The Leipzig theologians had, as we have seen, no desire to find themselves squeezed between Luther's powerful patron on the one side and the Church authorities on the other. While pleading with the Saxon duke,[78] the dean and doctors of theology of the university sent a cry for help to their ecclesiastical superior, Adolf of Anhalt, bishop of Merseburg and chancellor of the university.[79] Adolf wished nothing less than to see centered in his diocese a theological dispute which was growing more and more bitter, and he responded immediately with letters to both the duke and the university, disapproving of the disputation on the grounds that it might produce confusion and injury and was in direct opposition to the order of Pope Leo.[80] The university authorities, who seem to have looked on the matter more favorably than their theological faculty, asked the duke for advice.[81] The Saxon ruler was not long in replying. Besides his keen interest in theological affairs, George saw an opportunity to bring prestige to his university, and on January 17 he replied to the bishop in a long autograph letter of vigorous and homely phrase in which he charged the theological faculty with laziness and fear of exposing its ignorance, and reminded him that disputations had often been held in Leipzig concerning all the articles of faith.[82] Two days later he informed the university that he favored the disputation between Carlstadt and Eck.[83] The bishop remained firm, however, and twice urged the duke to send a confidential agent to him to discuss the matter. George sent his councilor, Cäsar Pflug, but this did not move the bishop, who never withdrew his opposition. On February 1 the university had already informed the duke that they consented to Eck's request.[84]

These exchanges between Leipzig, Merseburg, and the ducal court spun out through January. In the meantime Martin had met Miltitz at

---

[77] Letter from Luther to Egranus, Feb. 2, 1519, *WAB*, I, 313.
[78] Letter of Jan. 4, 1519, Gess, *Briefe und Akten*, I, 53.
[79] See Seckendorf, *Commentarius historicus*, I, 126, para. 57.
[80] January 11. Gess, *Briefe und Akten*, I, 54 f.
[81] January 15. *Ibid.*, pp. 55 f.   [82] *Ibid.*, pp. 60 ff.
[83] *Ibid.*, pp. 63 f.   [84] *Ibid.*, p. 66.

Altenburg and his indignation grew as the crafty nuncio continued to beset Elector Frederick with plans for umpiring the case. At this juncture Martin received Eck's twelve theses, and he prepared at once to enter the ring, for Eck's broadside seemed to him a direct breach of the armistice pledged to Miltitz. In an open letter to Carlstadt he attacked Eck as a vain boaster who had called up the indulgence question again out of Orcus.[85] He will not now permit Carlstadt, his "teacher and superior," to dispute the subjects which Eck had set forth, "for your talents and disputation are too worthy to condescend to these trifles of the sophists and mine, that is, indulgences, or rather, in truth trash and nonsense." [86] He begs Carlstadt to join him in an appeal to Duke George and the Leipzig senate to provide a place for a disputation with notaries in order that the results may be sent to the Pope, the bishops, and all Christendom.

Accompanying the letter are twelve theses which he proposes to defend against Eck. Eleven reformulate the ideas of penance and forgiveness which had been set forth again and again by Carlstadt and himself. The twelfth is revolutionary. In the strongest language that he has yet used publicly against Rome he attacks the historical claims of the papacy: "That the Roman Church is superior to all others is shown by the insipid decrees which the Roman popes have put forth during four hundred years; against these are the historical evidence of fifteen hundred years, the text of Divine Scriptures, and the decree of the Council of Nicaea, the most sacred of all." Letter and theses went immediately to press and by the end of the first week of February were speeding in all directions.[87]

Luther's injection of himself into the controversy aroused the Leipzig university to protest. They knew the unhesitating character of their neighbor in Wittenberg and were wary of him. The senate wrote at once to Duke George urging that Luther should not be allowed to dispute without the duke's consent,[88] and at the same time directed a reprimand to Martin for seeking to undertake a disputation at Leipzig without permission of the university.[89] To the Wittenberg professor this seemed unfair treatment.[90] He may also have felt that the patronizing tone of the letter conveyed an assumption of superiority towards his university as the younger institution

---

[85] Luther to Carlstadt (open letter), *WAB*, I, 315 ff. The exact date of the letter has been debated. See Seidemann, *Die Leipziger Disputation*, pp. 27, 28. See also *WA*, II, 155 ff. It belongs somewhere between February 4 and 7.

[86] *WAB*, I, 316, ll. 24 ff.

[87] *Disputatio et excusatio . . . adversus criminationes D. Johannis Eccii*. See *WA*, II, 158 ff.

[88] February 15. Gess, *Briefe und Akten*, I, 69 ff.

[89] *WAB*, I, 338 f., probably Feb. 16, 1519. See also Gess, *Briefe und Akten*, I, 73, n. 1.

[90] See letter from Luther to Staupitz, Feb. 20, 1519, *WAB*, I, 345, ll. 39 ff.

in Saxony. The protests which he made to the rector and the dean of the theological faculty at Leipzig are missing, but they were evidently effective. In the meantime Eck had accepted the challenge and agreed that it was Luther, not Carlstadt, whom he was to regard as his chief antagonist.[91] At the same time he wrote to the Leipzig faculty setting June 27 as the date for the disputation.

Nevertheless, the field was not yet clear. The new combatant had still to deal with the duke, who seems to have opposed his entry into the fray. The acquaintance between the two and the disfavor of the duke probably went back to the preceding summer, when Martin's sermon in the Castle Church in Dresden met with disapproval and misinterpretation.[92] In his open letter Luther had asked Carlstadt to join in the petition for his admission to the dispute. It seems probable that his colleague did not altogether welcome this turn in affairs. Carlstadt's lines for the disputation were already laid down and he could not entirely approve of Luther's declaration regarding the papacy.[93] Luther then addressed himself directly to the duke[94] and after considerable delay was told that he must come to an understanding with Eck.[95] Although the Leipzig university now supported his petition for permission to take part in the disputation,[96] the months of March and April went by without any assurance from the Dresden court; and on April 28, after an impatient letter to Eck had brought no result,[97] Martin wrote again urging the duke to give him safe conduct for the journey.[98] George's reply of May 7 was a curt reiteration that Luther should arrange matters with Eck.[99] With rising impatience Martin saw the disputation approaching without any guarantee that he would be allowed to take part in it. An urgent letter to Duke George on May 16 begs for permission to dispute even if he cannot reach an understanding with Eck beforehand.[100] This evoked only a cold reply from the duke on May 23, stating that he had nothing against Luther, that Eck has made a request for him, and that if he can agree with Eck, George will consent to his appearance. The duke expresses surprise that Luther insists on the disputation

[91] *Ibid.*, p. 343.   [92] See above, pp. 275 f.

[93] See letter from Carlstadt to Spalatin, Feb. 24, 1519, *Ref. Act.*, III, 90 ff. Luther assigns a more selfish motive in his letter to Lang of April 13, 1519: Carlstadt feared to lose his benefice by offending the Pope. *WAB*, I, 368, ll. 19 ff. In view of Carlstadt's record for courage, this seems an undeserved insult. See Barge, *Andreas Bodenstein*, I, 143.

[94] *WAB*, I, 341.   [95] March 4. Gess, *Briefe und Akten*, I, 76 f.

[96] *Ibid.*, pp. 77, 79 f.

[97] Letter from Luther to Eck, April 5, *WAB*, I, 366.

[98] *WAB*, I, 373.   [99] Gess, *Briefe und Akten*, I, 84.

[100] *WAB*, I, 400 f.

in the face of the opposition of the theological faculty.[101] Up to the last George continued to regard Carlstadt as Eck's real opponent and the only notice which he took officially of Luther's coming to Leipzig was to make the safe conduct that he sent to Carlstadt include "those whom he might bring with him." [102] From the tone of Martin's letters we may guess with what bad grace he accepted this humiliating solution.

In the meantime Martin's correspondence with Eck left no doubt that Carlstadt was to play a minor rôle in the disputation. On February 18 Luther formally declared the friendship with Eck at an end and brands his opponent as "hardheaded and cloudy-brained," a man who does not know how to distinguish subject from predicate.[103] Two days later he tells Scheurl that thus far he has been playing, but now he intends to proceed in earnest against the Roman pope and Roman arrogance.[104] To Pirckheimer at Nuremberg he writes on the same day a letter filled with joy in the approaching combat, which was to be against the unholy corruption of the Holy Scripture. "The Lord draws me and I follow not unwillingly." [105] Everybody fears that he is going to come off badly with his twelfth thesis, he writes to Lang in April, but even if he cannot hope to capture the slippery sophist he will hold up his end, "so help me Christ!" The Leipzig theologians are rending him in pieces, especially Ochsenfurt, that "bull, ox, ass," and are trying to stir up hatred in Leipzig against him. Some clergy there, he has learned, have asked young students in the confessional whether they own Martin's writings and have punished those who admitted to having them.[106] In mid-March he writes to Frederick touching a chord to which the prince was especially sensitive: he wanted to defend the honor of Wittenberg University. His opponents wished to close his mouth and open that of his enemies. In accordance with the usages of the disputation he is obliged to take the position of an opponent of the pope; at the same time, he makes reserve of submission and obedience for the Roman See.[107] This last, the product perhaps of some residual doubt concerning the justice of his stand, was obviously intended to soothe the anxiety of the Saxon ruler, whose negotiations with Miltitz were still under way and who was still firmly attached to the dogma of papal suprem-

---

[101] Gess, *Briefe und Akten*, I, 85 f.   [102] June 10. *Ibid.*, pp. 86 f.
[103] Letter from Luther to Eck, *WAB*, I, 340, ll. 7 ff.
[104] *WAB*, I, 346, ll. 17 f. See also Luther's letter to Spalatin, Feb. 7, 1519, *WAB*, I, 325, ll. 18 ff.
[105] Letter from Luther to Pirckheimer, *WAB*, I, 348, ll. 16 f.
[106] Letter from Luther to Lang, April 13, 1519, *WAB*, I, 369 ff.
[107] Letter from Luther to Frederick, March 13, 1519, *WAB*, I, 357 f.

acy in the Church, even though he felt free to oppose the diplomatic moves of the Pope. On the same day, March 13, Martin writes to Spalatin: "I am busy with the papal decrees for my disputation, and (for your ear alone) I don't know whether the pope is Antichrist himself or his apostle, so wretchedly is Christ, that is, the truth, twisted and crucified by him in the decrees." [108]

This study of the papal decrees was by no means the beginning of Luther's doubts as to whether papal supremacy was justified by the historical sources. His independent attitude goes back at least as far as the lectures on Romans, where he scores in forceful language the rottenness of those who are in high places in the Church. In the intervening years his view had dwelt increasingly on the shams and worldliness of the Roman hierarchy. The journey to Augsburg and the defiance aroused in his mind by what he experienced there armed and enforced his growing doubts.[109] Eck's keen eyes had not overlooked the trace of anti-papal heresy in the theses against indulgence. Now when Eck's theses, particularly the last one, come under Martin's eye, the latter's mind is made up: the supremacy of the Roman Church is contradicted by the findings of history for fifteen hundred years. This conviction, which finds expression in his twelfth thesis, is reenforced by the further conviction that Rome is the seat of the corruption which infects the Church, a thought which appears again and again in explosive language in his letters. "Rome, the destroyer of Scripture and the Church; Rome or better, Babylon." He denounces the city of the papal power as "this animal." [110] His twelfth thesis had been "forced from him by Eck," and now he devotes himself to an intensive study of the historical question and finds in the decrees of the popes a confirmation of all his skepticism.

Two months earlier at Altenburg Luther had prepared a letter to Pope Leo filled with protestations of loyalty and submission. It is possible, as we have seen, that this letter, which was never sent, was the result of a softened mood due to the appeals of Miltitz, who had awakened in him a desire to try once more to bridge the gap between himself and the Church. But the mood was destined to pass. His statement to Spalatin that he suppressed much against the Roman "Babylon" on account of the elector

---

[108] *WAB*, I, 359 ff. It was not until a year later that Martin got hold of Laurentius Valla's pamphlet on the Donation of Constantine published by Hutten as a refutation of the papal claims: *De donatione Constantini quid veri habeat, eruditorum quorundam iudicorum*. For the problem of dating, see *WAB*, II, 48, ll. 20 ff., and p. 51, n. 14. The pamphlet was not published until late in 1519. See Kalkoff, *Huttens Vagantenzeit und Untergang*, pp. 223 f., n. 1.

[109] Letter from Luther to Link, Dec. 18, 1518, *WAB*, I, 270, ll. 12 ff.

[110] "Haec belua." Letter from Luther to Spalatin, Feb. 24(?), 1519, *WAB*, I, 351, ll. 16 ff.

and the university might, to be sure, indicate that some hesitancy still remained.[111] But if Martin's battles with himself were not yet over, his studies were bringing him increasing certainty. He was beginning to see also what an abyss yawned before him. He had come to the point where he was ready to express himself freely to friends and proclaim his convictions in an academic disputation, and felt the hour approaching when he would tear away once for all the halo with which his early training had surrounded the Vicar of Christ. He plunged forward on the way upon which he had started, "more acted upon than acting," as he declared in later life.[112]

In the meantime Eck had returned to the attack. Stung by Martin's open letter to Carlstadt, which must have reached him early in March, he issued on March 14 a revised set of theses for the disputation.[113] Again he makes use of the broadside form and accompanies the theses with a letter to two South German churchmen, Abbot Kaspar of Wessobrunn and Johann Zinngiesser, official of the cloister at Polling, written in the tone of feigned modesty characteristic of humanistic dedications. His own reserve, he declares, has been great in the face of the violence of his two adversaries. He has challenged Luther as his chief opponent and followed him to the gates of his native land, where like a degenerate and timid soldier he wants now to hide behind fortifications. He defends himself against the charge of having been false to Luther: "They may abuse me as freely as they will provided they do not deny me the title of a believer and a Christian." The letter, bristling with quotations from Church Fathers and medieval authorities, is important as a full-length defense of his course of action. In order to meet Luther's charge that his theses were directed against him alone, Eck now adds to the twelve that had been published three months earlier a thirteenth, on the freedom of the will, aimed at Carlstadt's position.

Carlstadt was by no means pleased with Luther's theses, but he had had his own quarrel with Eck. Before the end of March he had sought to make the Dominican scholar ridiculous by publishing a picture, possibly by Lucas Cranach the Elder, representing two wagons, one bearing a cross and taking the right way to heaven, the other on the false road of scholasticism and free will.[114] Such pictorial satires were common in the humanistic

---

[111] *Ibid.*, p. 351, ll. 15 ff.

[112] *WA*, I, 649, l. 28; see also *WA*, VII, 272, ll. 32 ff.

[113] *Disputatio et excusatio Domini Johannis Eccii adversus criminationes F. Martini Lutheri ordinis eremitarum.* Reproduced by Clemen from a contemporary print, *WAB*, I, 320 ff. The new thesis is intercalated as seventh in the series.

[114] No copy of the picture seems to be preserved, in spite of the fact that it was widely distributed. It was apparently in existence at the end of the seventeenth century, and it is

period in Germany. This one was greeted with derisive laughter by Eck's many enemies, but aroused especially bitter feelings among the Leipzig theologians, who felt it directed against themselves. The eagerness with which the broadside was seized on in various parts of Germany is an evidence of wide interest in the impending disputation. The picture was followed by an interpretation, which was Carlstadt's first German paper.[115] Here the Wittenberg theologian defends the common layman's understanding of religious matters and makes a plea that the Scriptures be given to the unlearned in the German language. Before the end of April, Carlstadt followed with seventeen theses against Eck.[116] The covering statement to these *Conclusions* has a sharply abusive tone. Eck is charged with confusing the laity by his sophistry and laying traps for the unscholarly. "It is a shame," Carlstadt declares, "to tell such coarse and obvious lies"; his opponent is only a "miserable stentorian howler." After this blast of defiance, he sets forth his theses, which contain a restatement of the Wittenberg doctrine: the human will serves only to produce sin before grace is poured into it, for while seeking the law of righteousness, it sets up its own righteousness. In the last thesis he declares that Eck "judaizes" when he talks of man's fulfilling the canons or winning salvation through the efforts of his own will.[117]

Martin followed the *Conclusions* of Carlstadt with a restatement of his own position. His *Explanation of the Thirteenth Proposition concerning the Pope's Power* was printed June 22 in preparation for the disputation and reprinted after its close.[118] It runs through fifty-eight quarto pages in the Weimar edition and sheds an important light on Luther's position at this time. As a reasoned analysis of his attitude toward the papacy it stands halfway between the *Explanations of the Power of Indulgences* (1517), and the *Letter to the Christian Nobility* (1520), but it differs from both in that the arguments are enforced by a strongly personal tone, now

---

described in *Ref. Act.*, II, 104 f., where its appearance is set in 1518. This is probably erroneous; see Seidemann, *Die Leipziger Disputation*, pp. 23 ff. Barge, *Andreas Bodenstein*, I, 465, discusses the matter in detail and advances arguments for Cranach's authorship. Eck took deep offense at the picture and still more at the satirical verses which accompanied the figures. Twice in the following months in his letters to Duke George he comes back to the insult thus put upon him. *Ref. Act.*, III, 607, 627.

[115] Dated April 18. See Barge, *Andreas Bodenstein*, I, 147.

[116] *Conclusiones Carolostadii contra D. Johannem Eccum, Lipsiae, 27. Junii tuendae. Ref. Act.*, III, 284. See also Barge, I, 144 ff.

[117] "D. Joannis dicens salutem ita in canonibus consistere, si quispiam ex liberi arbitrii facultate fecerit quae iubent, Judaisat, et sectando legem iustitiae, suam iustitiam constituit." *Ref. Act.*, III, 291.

[118] *Resolutio Lutheriana super propositione sua tertia decima de potestate papae. WA*, II, 181 ff.

rising to a ringing appeal for confidence in individual faith, now sinking to scurrilous epithets.

Martin begins with an apology for his attitude toward his critics, but says that he has to use a hard wedge for a hard stone. His opponents have made the temple of God into a den of thieves. He resents keenly the name of heretic, but comforts himself with the thought that the Jews charged Christ with being possessed of a devil. He then proceeds to array arguments in defense of the thesis attacking the supremacy of the Roman Church. The primacy of the pope was set up to check heretics and schismatics, but the decrees and proofs which have been used to support it lack any foundation in Scripture. We may suffer the power of the pontiff patiently even though unjust, but this is because like other powers set up by man and strengthened by God, it is accepted by a consensus of the faithful. He examines the proofs alleged from the Bible and rejects both these and the papal decrees. A reference to the command of Christ to Peter, "Feed my sheep," calls forth a bitter attack on the pope and all the bishops for the greed and selfishness with which they have preyed upon Christians; instead of feeding Christ's sheep they have shorn and slaughtered them. Evidently Martin was exerting himself to set forth his position in calm and measured language, and it is with a restrained tone that he passes in review the papal decrees. He does not altogether reject them, but will not accept them as the only interpretation of Scripture. The Church at Rome has no right, but a privilege, and that only in so far as it is built on the rock of faith. "Therefore, wherever the word of God is preached and believed, there is the true faith, there the immovable rock; wherever faith, there is the Church; . . . there is everything which belongs to the Bridegroom." Faith includes all: keys, sacraments, power, and everything else.[119] God's word is misused when the pope claims the sole right to consecrate bishops, a right which was never asserted by Peter himself. To the famous declaration that the greater and lesser of the heavenly lights symbolize the papacy and the empire, he opposes a symbolism of his own:

It is to be regretted that with such jests and frivolities the words of God (as they claim) are falsified in order to establish such serious things. . . . For the meaning of these words is this: Christ is the sun; the Church, the moon; the heavens, the apostles; and the stars, the saints. The power of the empire belongs to the Church just as little as do other things of earth.[120]

The historical claims of the Roman Church are the result of the struggle of a thousand years to establish these claims. Never, at any time, has

---

[119] *WA*, II, 208, ll. 26 ff.   [120] *Ibid.*, p. 224, ll. 31 ff.

the Church of Rome ruled over all the churches of the world. Antichrist stands in the midst of the temple.

The vigorous argumentation in the *Explanation of the Thirteenth Proposition* is backed by all the historical knowledge which Martin commanded at that time. It appeals from the pope to the Nicene Council and the Church Fathers, and extends the circle of witnesses to include all Christians dwelling in the Greek and African world who refuse to subject themselves to the pope's power.

19

THE LEIPZIG DISPUTATION
THE COMBAT

MEANWHILE the date fixed for the disputation was approaching. No city in Germany could have been better situated than Leipzig to give resonance to this historical clash of argument. The crossing point of five great highways leading through Germany and equally distant from such peripheral points of the empire as Basel and Danzig, Breslau, and Frankfort, Leipzig lay at the heart of German-speaking lands. The scene of great commercial fairs since the second half of the twelfth century, the city was famed no less for its trade than for its celebrated university, and it enjoyed all the trappings of civic power and culture.[1] Martin shared the Wittenberg tradition of hostility which had been aroused by the opposition of the older university at Leipzig to the younger university on the Elbe, a feeling which continued to rankle in his mind throughout the years to come. "The leaders look down on Wittenberg with the old hatred," he warned Link, two decades later, when the latter was considering an invitation to Leipzig.[2]

[1] Luther's contemporary, Johann Cochlaeus, who knew the most famous cities in Germany and Italy, calls Leipzig "urbs et mercatu et Universitate insignis." *Commentaria de actis et scriptis Lutheri* (Mainz, 1549), p. 13. Elsewhere he states, "eine Stadt dan freilich im gantzen Reich kein Fürstenstat . . . yr gleich ist, in gebewden, in Bürgerlichem Regiment und Wesen, in Gottisdienst, in der Universitet, in kaufhendeln." *Auf Luthers Trostbrieff an etliche zu Leipzig* (Dresden, 1533), 1b. (This work was not available to the author for rechecking.) Luther's dislike of Leipzig lasted through life, and in his correspondence both university and citizens are decked with many abusive epithets. He accuses the former of persistent envy and hatred of Wittenberg and denounces the place as a seat of arrogance, greed, and usury. Even after the new theology triumphed there his private opinion remained the same. He calls it a "Sodom, the filthy pool of usurers and evil ones." Letter to Link, Oct. 26, 1539, *WAB*, VIII, 579. "I hate the Leipzig people . . . as I would hate nothing more under the sun." Letter to Lang, May 15, 1540, De Wette, *Dr. Martin Luthers Briefe*, V, 283. In the last year of his life he still regards the city as "the greediest, haughtiest, and worst Sodom of all." Letter to Amsdorf, Jan. 8, 1546, *ibid.*, p. 773. Many other passages in his letters are equally bitter. See also *TR*, III, No. 3683 (1538), p. 528, ll. 4 ff.; IV, No. 4168.

[2] Letter to Link, Oct. 26, 1539, *WAB*, VIII, 579, ll. 5 f. For the rivalry between the two universities, see Felician Gess, "Leipzig und Wittenberg. Ein Beitrag zur sächsischen Reformationsgeschichte," *Neues Archiv für sächsische Geschichte*, XVI (1895), 43 ff.

Some of this resentment may well have extended to Duke George [3] who had opposed with such vigor Martin's admission to the disputation. As has been pointed out, it was Eck who finally secured the safe conduct which enabled Martin to take part.

When the Wittenbergers rode into the city on June 24 they found Eck already present. He had arrived three days earlier accompanied by the duke of Bavaria and by the Fuggers, with whom he was on terms of friendship, having supported their claim to receive interest in the disputation in Bologna in 1515. The Dominican challenger and his party were received at once by Duke George himself. From an eye-witness, Sebastian Fröschel, we have a colorful account of the arrival of the Wittenberg delegation: [4] the two disputants, Luther and Carlstadt, accompanied by the rector of the university, Duke Barnim of Pomerania, together with Melanchthon, Johann Lang, and Nikolaus von Amsdorf, and a group of jurists and theologians. Beside the wagon ran two hundred Wittenberg students armed with halberds and spears. Amid a crowd of spectators the cavalcade passed through the Grimma gate and into the narrow main street of the ancient city. Here, in front of the Pauline Church, Carlstadt's wagon came to grief and the dignified theologian was thrown to the ground, an omen which was not forgotten by the spectators and three years later served an opponent, Hieronymus Emser, as occasion for a sarcastic reference.[5] Just as the Wittenbergers arrived in the market place, a messenger of Bishop Adolf was posting on the door of the city hall a proclamation forbidding the disputation. The Wittenbergers took up their quarters in the house of the publisher Melchior Lotter, father of the Wittenberg printer.[6]

Long and wearisome negotiations on the rules of the disputation followed. Nevertheless the duke was determined to see it through despite the opposi-

---

[3] In later years George was a persistent defender of the old faith, and Martin exchanged many attacks with the sturdy old prince, whom he came to regard as a "devil's apostle." See Luther's letter to the Leipzig Christians, April 11, 1533, *WAB*, VI, 449. See Seifert, *Die Reformation in Leipzig*, pp. 18 ff., for the hostility between the duke and the Wittenberg reformers. George, like his cousin Frederick, was a devout character, but more conservative and more interested in theological matters. See Hans Becker, "Herzog Georg von Sachsen als kirchlicher und theologischer Schriftsteller," *ARG*, XXV (1928), 161 ff., for the duke's religious poems and polemics.

[4] Fröschel was a young student of theology at Leipzig at the time of the disputation. He did not write down his account of what he saw and heard until fifty years later, *Ref. Act.*, III, 276 ff., and his credibility has often been attacked. His story is vivid and in the main seems to be trustworthy. See Oskar Germann, "Sebastian Fröschel, sein Leben und seine Schriften," *Beiträge zur sächsischen Kirchengeschichte*, XIV (1899), 10 ff.

[5] *Vor antwurtung auff das ketzerische buch;* Preface of April 2, 1522. Quoted by Barge, *Andreas Bodenstein*, I, 151, n. 62.

[6] Wustmann, *Aus Leipzigs Vergangenheit*, pp. 44 f.

tion of the diocesan bishop. When he received the proclamation of Adolf he returned it with an angry note written in his own hand and instructed his councilors to see that the program was not interfered with.[7] Two days after his arrival Carlstadt was summoned to the ducal castle, the ancient Pleissenburg, where he met Eck and a group of officials and masters and doctors of the university under the chairmanship of the duke's chancellor, Johann Köchel. Eck's reputation for cleverness in dialectical clashes was so well known that Carlstadt, in agreement with Luther, insisted on the appointment of notaries. Nevertheless, greatly to his dissatisfaction, Martin was forced to concede that the publication of the notarial report should be delayed until after the umpires had rendered their decision.[8] It was the understanding of the Wittenberg contestants that Eck had previously agreed with Luther to a "free disputation," which implied that the arguments should be made public at once. After the Leipzig meeting Eck alleged that the condition regarding delay in publication was forced on him by the duke's officials.[9] The contract providing for four notaries and for preparing a true copy of the proceedings was drawn up and agreed to by Eck and Carlstadt at the conference of June 26.[10] The arrangement covering the debate between Eck and Martin was not concluded until July 4. In the meantime Martin's participation became so doubtful that a report was widely circulated that he would not dispute.[11] He held out for a week, and when he yielded it was with the reservation that the papal court should not judge the disputation. His insistence on a "free disputation" may have been due to the fear that his thirteenth thesis was too radical to find a hearing from any judge that might be selected. Possibly also his hesitation arose from resentment at being forced to debate after Carlstadt, a humiliation he could not forget.[12]

The controversy as to who should be the judges of final victory in the debate dragged along and revolved around fine points, each side wary of

[7] Gess, *Briefe und Akten*, I, 90.

[8] Seidemann, *Die Leipziger Disputation*, pp. 42 ff., gives the sources for the negotiation. Martin had agreed with Eck that each party should bring two notaries. Letter from Luther to Carlstadt, Feb., 1519, *WAB*, I, 318, l. 75.

[9] See the passage in the long letter which Eck wrote to Frederick on Nov. 8, 1519, *WAB*, I, 491. Luther resented any judgment before publication as a breach of faith: "Das ist convenient, dass die Disputation, durch die Notarien verfasst, nicht soll vor dem Sentenz gedruckt werden. Dahin uns Dr. Eck sampt den Leipzigern mit Gewalt gedrungen wider sein eigen Geschrift, Siegel, Zusagen und ersten Pakt. Wir wollten ein freie Disputation in die Federn sprechen und an das Licht für alle Welt geben. . . ." Letter from Luther to Frederick, Aug. 18, 1519, *WAB*, I, 477.

[10] For text see *WAB*, I, 428 ff.

[11] Seidemann, *Die Leipziger Disputation*, pp. 43 f.

[12] *TR*, IV, No. 4187 (1538). See also Seidemann, *Die Leipziger Disputation*, p. 52, n. 1.

giving the other the slightest advantage in the selection. The paragraph relating to this was not signed until July 14. These negotiations were a bitter experience for Martin. He now began to feel that Eck and his backers were more interested in winning a decision than in penetrating to the core of the theological questions involved.[13] He did not fail to notice also the eyes of hatred with which the Leipzig theologians looked upon him.[14] Finally Eck and Martin agreed on the Universities of Paris and Erfurt, Eck and Carlstadt on Erfurt alone. They left to Duke George the decision whether the whole faculty or only the theologians should render the verdict. To this agreement, lacking in unanimity, the three doctors affixed their seals.[15]

Meanwhile the disputation between Carlstadt and Eck got under way. The opening was surrounded by all the colorful trappings which the late medieval university could summon, enriched in this case by the assistance of the highest ducal officials. Early on the morning of June 27 the university faculty with the city officials, important clergy and nobility, clerics and citizens, assembled at the university to be addressed by Professor Simon Pistorius of the law faculty in a flowery Latin speech. All then marched in solemn procession to St. Thomas's Church, the Leipzig and Wittenberg masters of arts walking together two and two. The old church, already famous for its music, heard a mass sung by twelve voices, then an unprecedented effort. A grand procession followed with banners and trumpets, marshalled by the civic guard, which policed the disputation.[16] Recollections of this procession remained vivid in the mind of at least one witness half a century later.[17] The train swept into a hall decked with fine tapestries at the expense of the duke. Here from their elevated desks Eck and his successive opponents were to look down upon their audience. Spectators noted that the tapestry decorating the desk of Eck bore the picture of St. George, the knightly hero of Christianity, while on that of Carlstadt and Luther was the charitable St. Martin.

That the antagonists stood under the sign of rising humanism was shown by the introductory speech delivered by the professor of Greek,

---

[13] In succeeding months Luther complained that Eck did not want to find out the truth, and came back to the charge several years later in his controversy with Hieronymus Emser. See *Auf des Bocks zu Leipzig Antwort, WA*, VII, 272, l. 14.

[14] Two years afterwards he recalled that Emser had breathed "threatenings and slaughter" against him in the hall of disputation. Letter from Luther to Staupitz, Jan. 14, 1521, *WAB*, II, 245, ll. 21 f.

[15] Seidemann, *Die Leipziger Disputation*, pp. 72 f., and document No. 28, pp. 137 f.

[16] Mosellanus's account, *Ref. Act.*, III, 245. See also n. 21 below.

[17] Sebastian Fröschel. *Ibid.*, p. 279.

Peter Schade Mosellanus. This distinguished young humanist droned away for almost two hours,[18] rolling out his periods in Erasmian Latin, but in such a low tone that his hearers were in doubt as to whether he was speaking or reading.[19] The exordial oration with its pompous tone and labored attempts at humor followed the usual style of such academic efforts, whether of the sixteenth century or the twentieth. The speaker called the roll of the distinguished persons who had assembled to hear the renowned representatives of the two universities, who like famous knights would now advance to the contest, each accompanied by his followers. With flowery compliments they are urged to curb all boasting and abuse and to remember the solemn nature of a theological disputation. The orator called up before his audience a list of the great theological clashes of the past, those of Peter and Paul, Jerome and Augustine, Gregory and Basil, and finally the memorable debate of Erasmus and Faber, which gave him an opportunity to praise the Christian spirit of the great Dutch humanist. The combatants were exhorted not to forget that they were under the eyes of all Christendom and to observe due modesty in order that Christian concord might grow out of the struggle. When the oration finally came to its end the musicians played three times *Veni Sancte Spiritus,* and the assembly adjourned for dinner.[20]

The disputation began on the afternoon of the same day. Our information regarding its progress is singularly detailed. Indeed, there is no episode in the life of Luther for which the record is so complete, not even his dramatic appearance two years later before the Diet at Worms. One may go further and doubt whether there is in the history of the sixteenth century any other meeting for which the events, the carriage and appearance of the actors and their words and gestures, and even the interruptions of the bystanders are preserved for posterity with such faithful accuracy as is found in the well-attested minutes that have come down from the fateful seventeen days that began on June 27 when Eck and Carlstadt mounted

[18] For the oration, see *ibid.,* pp. 567 ff. Mosellanus was well known in Wittenberg. Spalatin favored him for the chair of Greek there the year before the disputation. Ludwig Geiger, "Mosellanus," *Allgemeine Deutsche Biographie,* XXII, 359.

[19] See the dispute between Johann Cellarius and Petrus Suavenius Pomeranus as to whether Mosellanus's speech was read from manuscript. *Ref. Act.,* III, 655, 657, 659; Seidemann, *Die Leipziger Disputation,* p. 50, n. 1.

[20] The introductory speech was to have been delivered by a boy representing "Pure Theology," *Ref. Act.,* III, 511 f. and 579. In view of its length, however, and the illness of the substitute, the author had to deliver it himself and was apparently not a little pleased at his success. *Ibid.,* p. 245. George had read it beforehand and was much surprised to learn that theologians were so godless as to need the advice which it offered. Seidemann, *Die Leipziger Disputation,* p. 49 and n. 3.

their rostra in the ancient Pleissenburg. In addition to the three chief participants five eye witnesses recorded their impressions while fresh in memory during the months that followed, and these were supplemented by the report of still another, Sebastian Fröschel, who recalled vividly nearly half a century later in a naïve but straightforward and convincing manner his recollections of the great contest.[21] Of these witnesses two, Melanchthon and Amsdorf, were Wittenberg professors and of course saw the affair with the eyes of their colleagues; two others, Cellarius, a Leipzig professor of Hebrew, and Rubeus, a Leipzig student, took the side of Eck. Mosellanus, the author of the longest account, claims to be nonpartisan. In addition, four sworn notaries struggled to put down the arguments; and if we may believe the first publisher of a verbatim report, which came from an Erfurt press in December, 1519, more than thirty other persons also noted down the speeches and sent them to various parts of the world.[22]

Among these accounts, that of Mosellanus is the most specific and vivid. This Leipzig scholar, who had something more than the usual self-esteem common in this period of rising humanism, fully appreciated his rôle as speaker of the prologue to the widely heralded disputation. Although a member of the theological faculty, he had looked forward to the contest with the amused interest of a detached observer. In a letter to Erasmus early in the preceding January he announced the forthcoming battle between Carlstadt and Eck as a collision between two rival orders and predicted that the whole affair would end in a great noise, so that "ten Democrituses will have something to laugh at." [23] A few months after the memorable contest Mosellanus writes a long account of it to a Saxon nobleman of his acquaintance.[24] Here he describes Eck as he saw him ascend the rostrum: a tall

---

[21] A list of the contemporary reports, for the most part in private letters, is to be found in *Ref. Act.*, III, 215 ff., where, however, the number is erroneously stated. Among others it includes the following letters: Eck to Jakob Hochstraten, July 24; Luther's dedicatory letter to Spalatin prefixed to the *Resolutiones super propositionibus*, Aug. 15; Melanchthon to Oecolampadius, July 21; Johann Cellarius to Wolfgang Capito in Basel, end of July; Nikolaus Amsdorf to Spalatin, Aug. 1; Petrus Mosellanus to Julius Pflug, Dec. 8; and a report from the Franconian student in Leipzig, Johann Rubeus, the introduction to which is dated August 13. For Sebastian Fröschel's account, see *Ref. Act.*, III, 276 ff.

[22] "Plus triginta exemplaria sint illic excepta et in diversas orbes partes emissa." *WA*, II, 252 (from the introduction to the first print of the *Disputatio . . . Johannis Eccij et Andreae Carolostadij. . . .* The author makes this statement in defense of his publication of the minutes against the agreement made by the disputants. Theodor Brieger, after an intensive examination of the evidence, comes to the conclusion that this first print is itself not a copy of the notarial transcript but a draft by one of the self-appointed secretaries, and that the Freiburg MS in the Bibliothek des Gymnasium Albertinum used by Löscher, *Ref. Act.*, III, 292 ff., is likewise taken from such an independent record. Brieger, "Über die handschriftlichen Protokolle der Leipziger Disputation," in *Beiträge zur Reformationsgeschichte*, pp. 37 ff.

[23] Letter of Jan. 6, 1519, Allen, *Opus epistolarum Erasmi*, III, 470.

[24] *Ref. Act.*, III, 242 ff.

and powerful man with a coarse, genuinely German voice, suitable for a tragedian or a herald, his whole face and appearance that of a butcher or a hardy soldier rather than a theologian. The Ingolstadt champion has a splendid memory, reports Mosellanus, and if he had an intelligence equal to it he would be a masterpiece of nature. He piles up reasons, cites from the Scriptures and brings in other quotations, all in a muddle without rhyme or reason. His method is to call up a host of authorities and thus to dazzle the audience. He is very clever, however, and when he sees that he is about to be caught he promptly turns to something else. Sometimes he takes over the opinion of his opponents and proclaims them as his own, and turns his own ideas upside down in such a manner that he appears as wise as Socrates.[25]

More hostile witnesses, like Amsdorf, branded Eck a sophist who had learned his lines well and spoke them with great solemnity and impressive gestures but merely in order to win praise for his memory and to defend the teachings of his sect, not to discover the truth.[26] According to the Italian fashion, Amsdorf continues, Eck would produce nine or ten arguments at once. The spectators always hold as the victor the one who shouts the loudest and gets in the last word, and for that reason the Leipzig people award the crown to Eck. Amsdorf admits that Eck surpassed Carlstadt in memory and delivery, but contends that he was not to be compared to Luther in doctrine or art, "any more than one can compare a stone or filth with the most beautiful and purest gold." According to Amsdorf, the Wittenberg party would have come away disgraced if the whole proceedings had not been written down.[27] Luther, in reviewing the disputation several weeks later, records an impression similar to that of Mosellanus and Amsdorf, adding that Eck, like a Proteus, would accept everything which in the beginning he had opposed with great violence and then would hasten to boast that he had brought Carlstadt to his way of thinking.[28]

When he faced the powerful Dominican, Carlstadt made a poor impression. Short of figure and sallow of countenance, with a hollow and uncertain voice, he appeared to observers no match for his opponent.[29] Indeed the disputation had not gone far when Eck's experience in rough-and-tumble conflicts was put to use. Carlstadt had brought notes and books with him and read from these, a method of disputing which was not to Eck's fancy,

[25] *Ibid.*, pp. 248 f.   [26] *Ibid.*, p. 239.
[27] *Ibid.*, pp. 240 f.   [28] *WA*, II, 393 f.
[29] Mosellanus gives the only description of Carlstadt which has been preserved. *Ref. Act.*, III, 248. See also Barge, *Andreas Bodenstein*, I, 153, n. 67, who quotes Eck's statement regarding Carlstadt's unpleasant voice.

and he demanded that they follow the Italian custom of speaking without notes.[30] A lively scene ensued,[31] and the ducal umpires finally decided against Carlstadt, to the murmured approval of the audience, as Luther noted.[32] Carlstadt was now badly handicapped, and his aggressive opponent took full advantage of his embarrassment and uncertainty to carry off a victory before the crowd.[33]

Since all accounts of the disputation are colored at least to some extent by partisan feeling, we must seek the clash of argument in the record of the scribes.[34] In spite of the physical and temperamental difficulties with which he had to contend, Carlstadt made his position quite clear by denying that the human will has a part in the work of salvation. Eck, on the other hand, was apparently not yet fully armed with theological weapons to defend ideas respecting free will and grace. He quoted a passage from St. Bernard which both Luther and Melanchthon show to have been beside the question; he brought up Cicero to defend Aristotle; he cited the common sense of mankind to enforce his plea for the activity of the human will in preparing the way for grace, and summoned Bernard again to prove that free will and grace work together for man's salvation.

When Carlstadt came back to the rostrum after the scene just described he demanded that Eck tell him how it was possible that an entire effect

[30] Luther found the bringing in of books quite proper if the truth was really to be established. See his dedication to Spalatin, Aug. 15, 1519, of the *Resolutiones Lutherianae super propositionibus suis Lipsiae disputatis. WA*, II, 393, ll. 25 ff. According to one account, Carlstadt brought a whole cartload of books with the excuse that his memory had suffered as the result of a loss of blood. Seidemann, *Die Leipziger Disputation*, p. 52, n. 3. See also Otto Clemen, "Litterarische Nachspiele zur Leipziger Disputation," *Beiträge zur sächsischen Kirchengeschichte*, XII (1897), 59 f.

[31] Described in *Der authentische Text der Leipziger Disputation*, ed. by Otto Seitz, p. 33.

[32] *WA*, I, 394, l. 2.

[33] See Eck's letter to Georg Hauer and Franz Burckhard, July 1, 1519, written just after the event and before the beginning of the disputation with Luther. Text in Joseph Schlecht, "Briefmappe II," *RgST*, XL (1922), 91 ff. Apparently Eck was impressed with his own courage in facing the Wittenbergers, who had appeared in such numbers ("At ego solus aequitate comitatus, astabam"; letter to Hochstraten, *Ref. Act.*, III, 223), and was delighted to be able to throw Carlstadt into confusion. In a pamphlet issued the following December, *Contra Martini Ludder obtusum propugnatorem Andream Rodolphi Bodenstein Carlstadium*, he recounts Carlstadt's humiliation and outburst of temper. Barge, *Andreas Bodenstein*, I, 153 f.

[34] The best text of the disputation is that of Otto Seitz, which takes as its basis a print covering the disputation between Luther and Eck copies of which Seitz found in the Predigerum in Wittenberg, in the Bibliothèque Nationale in Paris, and in the British Museum. This he thinks corresponds closely to the vanished protocol. In addition he makes use of the Freiburg MS, written down by a self-appointed scribe at the disputation. Seitz, *Der authentische Text der Leipziger Disputation*, p. 6; see also Brieger, "Über die Protokolle." Seitz also uses the Erfurt print of 1519, which he thinks was derived from another private script. For convenience, references to the debate between Eck and Luther are made to the Weimar edition, which uses the Erfurt print but excludes the Eck-Carlstadt exchanges. *WA*, II, 254 ff.

should be brought about by two causes working separately. Eck met this with a dialectical parry: grace and free will may each perform the good work in its entirety (*totum*) yet not entirely (*totaliter*). Although Melanchthon stamps this as a classical example of dealing in sophistry,[35] Eck's position is interesting from an epistemological standpoint and was by no means merely a debater's evasion. Nevertheless, it was not difficult for Carlstadt to show that such a compromise between the activity of the will and grace was not in line with the thought of Eck's scholastic authors. It is plain that the Ingolstadt disputant, who had begun with the thesis that the will rules in man's soul freely as a king in his kingdom, had been forced into a compromising position.

The learned Dominican was, however, far from conceding that his position had been shaken in any way. Indeed, when at the end of four days the disputation with Carlstadt was adjourned, Eck and the majority of his hearers were clearly of opinion that the champion of free will was well in the lead. At this stage Eck wrote to two colleagues at his university that Carlstadt had no memory and had disgraced himself by reading from books, and that he had to admit finally that free will had an influence on good works. "At that I did not want to dispute any further because I had brought him to the true Christian doctrine." [36] Eck entertains no fear of the final result, although he concedes that the Wittenbergers hate him and are in such numbers that a guard has had to be posted to ward off an attack by them and by the Bohemian heretics from Prague who were present.

It was then a champion flushed with a feeling of triumph whom Martin faced when he ascended the rostrum on July 4. The monk-professor must have welcomed in his very soul the opening of a contest to which he had looked forward through so many months. Admission to take part had been made difficult for him and was in fact uncertain up to the last. It was only on that morning that he had finally signed the agreement which permitted him to enter the disputation. His refusal to accept the conditions imposed on Carlstadt, that the disputation should not be made public until after the decision of the judges had brought about an *impasse,* which was broken only when Martin finally yielded to the solicitation of friends in order, as he

---

[35] *Ref. Act.,* III, 217 f. In general Melanchthon was disgusted with the violence of the argument. He contrasted such a debate with the work of the spirit, which takes possession of our hearts in silence and comes to those who are not ambitious but desirous of knowing the truth. Eck defended his position later on in a pamphlet directed against Melanchthon. Regarding the polemic between the two men, see Wiedemann, *Dr. Johann Eck,* pp. 501 ff.

[36] Letter from Eck to Georg Hauer and Franz Burkhard, July 1, 1519, in Schlecht, "Briefmappe II," pp. 91 ff.

says, to save his university from disgrace.[37] As we have seen, he made the reservation that the Roman Curia should not be the judge, and the discussion as to who should be the final arbitrators went on during the ten agitated days that followed.

From the beginning of the preparations for the meeting the Leipzig theologians had given Martin continuous evidence of their hostility. He resented their jealousy of Wittenberg and felt a growing indignation as the disputation drew near.[38] In reviewing the disputation after its conclusion Martin complains that his party were treated like enemies during their entire stay, while their opponent was overwhelmed with invitations to banquets.[39] The Dominicans were especially hostile. Once when Luther went into their church the officiating priests caught up the sacred vessels and rushed into the sacristy. On the other hand, the local clergy sent Eck invitations to preach and he delivered several sermons during the course of the disputation.[40]

Although the church pulpits of the city were not open to Luther, he found occasion to preach one memorable sermon. It was on the day of Peter and Paul, June 29. The invitation had come from young Barnim, duke of Pomerania, who was the honorary rector of the Wittenberg university and had accompanied the university's delegation.[41] The sermon was set for the ducal chapel, but such a crowd assembled at the Pleissenburg that it was necessary to adjourn to the hall where the disputation was held. Martin seized the occasion to review the two burning questions under discussion, the question of grace and free will and that of the bestowal of power on St. Peter, "to the great displeasure" of the Leipzig group. As published, the sermon is designed for the guidance of the average man and does not take up directly the thirteen theses which Martin was shortly to defend. Instead it seeks to show how good works arise not from man's natural self, but grow inevitably out of the despair over our innate evil condition and our faith in God's grace to save us. Martin then interprets for his audience the gift of the keys to Peter as conferring no personal power or privilege but as an office to administer for the Church of Christ.

---

[37] Letter from Luther to Spalatin, July 20, 1519, WAB, I, 421, ll. 35 ff.: "Haec omnia odiosissime et malignissime jactata et interpretata, ita ut et amicissimos quoque omnes subverterent, et jam Universitati nostrae ignominia perpetua erat in promptu."

[38] Letter from Luther to Lang, May 16, 1519, WAB, I, 399, ll. 16 f.

[39] Letter from Luther to Spalatin, July 20, 1519, WAB, I, 423, ll. 106 ff.

[40] See Schlecht, "Briefmappe II," p. 94. Eck claims to have preached three times. Letter from Eck to Elector Frederick, Nov. 8, 1519, WAB, I, 493, l. 533.

[41] WAB, I, 423, ll. 125 f. The sermon was afterwards published as Ein Sermon gepredigt zu Leipzig auf dem Schloss am Tag Petri und Pauli (Leipzig, 1519), with a half-length picture of Luther as a frontispiece. See WA, II, 241 ff.

The sermon in published form gives no adequate idea of the power with which the ardent monk must have set forth his position. One hostile witness, Emser, declared that he had never in his life heard such an "impudent preacher," [42] and Eck denounced it as "Hussite" and clearly erroneous.[43] The Dominican professor was put up at once to reply and did this in two sermons in St. Nicholas' Church. Evidently the university theologians were determined that the Wittenberg radical should not have the last word.

This was then the tense situation when Martin ascended the rostrum. He found an adversary armed and heartened for victory and an audience composed of anxious friends, angry opponents, and umpires who were sorely concerned lest his unbridled tongue bring religious and social confusion. Mosellanus, who eyed him closely, noted a man of medium height, so gaunt from anxiety [44] and study that one might count his ribs, yet vigorous and of clear and penetrating voice. It became apparent at once that here was a different man from Carlstadt. Profound scholarship and an instant readiness with scriptural quotations as well as a command of Greek and Hebrew in interpretation impressed the scholarly observers and must have had their effect on the audience also in that day of flowering humanism. A vigorous and flowing power of language made him master of the situation. Mosellanus noted his cheerful countenance and manner. His readiness to jest in the face of threats gave men a feeling that he had divine support, while his courteous and genial bearing on the rostrum formed a striking contrast to the aggressive and blustering carriage of his opponent and must certainly have been rare in a theological disputation in that era. The Leipzig theologians were not accustomed to hear the gravest subjects treated with cheerfulness and observed with sour looks that the bold and temperamental monk brought flowers to the rostrum with him and smelled them from time to time during the momentous passage at arms.[45] On the other hand, when Martin was aroused the scholarly audience was shocked by the biting and insolent tone with which he went to the assault. This seemed to theological minds an indecent method of presenting new propositions, and Mosellanus remarks in a tone of youthful arrogance that this is the way of all who have been called to their learning somewhat late in life.[46] Thus Martin

[42] *Auff des Stieres tzu Wiettenberg wiettende replica.* See Ludwig Enders, "Luther und Emser. Ihre Streitschriften aus dem Jahre 1521," *Neudrucke deutscher Literaturwerke des XVI. und XVII. Jahrhunderts,* II, 30.

[43] See letter from Eck to Hochstraten, July 24, 1519, *Ref. Act.,* III, 224.

[44] "Curis." *Ibid.,* p. 247.

[45] Letter from Luther to Spalatin, Oct. 13, 1519, *WAB,* I, 530, ll. 54 ff.

[46] *Ref. Act.,* III, 247 f. Cf. also Theodor Brieger, "Einiges über die Leipziger Disputation

stands before us as seen by his contemporaries: no dry-as-dust scholar such as one was accustomed to see under the doctor's beret, no shouting and hairsplitting win-at-any-cost, but a vigorous, original personality; in the cool but not unfriendly eyes of attentive observers a handsome man, from whose bold face a pair of "falcon eyes" shone upon opponents and on-lookers.[47]

The two disputants went at once to the heart of their argument and began to debate the thesis relating to the supremacy of the pope. The discussion opened coolly enough. Martin protested his respect for the pope and the Church. He voiced his regret that he had been driven to put forward his thirteenth thesis by Eck's attack, and he expressed the wish that "those libellous inquisitors" (i.e., his Dominican adversaries in Rome) who had made charges of heresy against him were not present.[48] Eck replied that it was only Luther's claim that the papal supremacy began with Sylvester which had forced him to bring the question to an issue.[49] Both then pro-ceeded to fortify their positions with liberal citations from Scripture and from patristic and scholastic authority. On the second day the contest warmed when the Dominican charged Luther with repeating the condemned beliefs of Wyclif and the "pestilential errors" of John Huss.[50] In bringing in the name of Huss, Eck could not have been unaware that he was touching a chord to which the audience was peculiarly sensitive. It was more than one hundred years since the great Bohemian heretic had been burned at the Council of Constance, and the Hussite wars which had gone on intermit-tently through the century succeeding had been a vital question for the Saxon duchy. The Leipzig university owed its foundation to the resistance of Bohemian Germans to the rise of Czech nationalism under the leadership of Huss, and the arms of the resentful followers of the arch-heretic had more than once ravaged the lands of the ducal line and brought almost to the walls of the university city the abhorred banner embroidered with the chalice, symbolizing the heretical demands for communion in both kinds. Thus Huss and Hussitism might well send a thrill of political as well as theological anxiety through the hall of the old Pleissenburg. Luther hastened to deny passionately any association with the iniquitous Bohemians, who sought to destroy in the Church the unity which rested on the sovereign divine command of unity and love: "Never in all eternity will I agree to

von 1519," in *Die Universität Leipzig 1409–1909. Gedenkblätter zum 30. Juli 1909* (Leipzig, 1909), pp. 39 ff.

[47] Erasmus Alberus, quoted by Seidemann, *Die Leipziger Disputation,* p. 54 and n. 1.

[48] *WA,* II, 254.   [49] *Ibid.,* p. 255.   [50] *Ibid.,* p. 275.

any schism," [51] he declared. What he attacked was the claim that the foundation of the Roman Church was coincident with that of the Apostolic Church. Once more he put forward his arguments drawn from historical and patristic sources, and in conclusion he implored Eck earnestly not to insult him by classing him with the Bohemian heretics, whom he had always hated.[52]

It can hardly be doubted that thoughts of Huss and his attitude toward the papal question had been much in his mind in the months preceding the disputation when he was studying the papal decrees and the historical aspects of the papal claims to supremacy. In his early cloister years the memory of the Bohemian heretic still lived in all the religious orders, where his great learning was generally conceded. If there were doubts of Huss's guilt, they were suppressed [53] or put forth furtively.[54] There is no evidence that Martin shared these, for in lectures and sermons he had joined in the general chorus of attack on the Bohemian heretics and their leader. The charge of "scattering Bohemian poison" had been raised by Eck in his first assault on Martin's theses concerning indulgences,[55] and this part of the attack was the one which most aroused Martin's anger and which must have come to his mind often during the period of preparation for the defense of his thirteen theses. He must have faced at that time the analogy between his position and that of the Bohemian theologian, and the vigor with which he repelled Eck's charge may indicate a sensitive conscience.[56]

When the disputation continued after the noon hour it was clear that Martin had had time for reflection. He did not, he said, wish to defend the Bohemian schism, but, he added: "This is certain, that among the articles of John Huss or the Bohemians there are many that are plainly very Christian and evangelical which it is not possible for the universal Church to condemn." Among these was the statement that it is not necessary to salvation to believe that the Roman Church is superior to others:

Whether it be of Wyclif or Huss, I do not care. I know that Gregory Nazanzenus, Basil the Great, Epiphian the Cyprian, and innumerable other Greek bishops were

---

[51] *Ibid.,* p. 275, ll. 37 ff. "Nunquam mihi placuit nec in eternum placebit quodcunque schisma: inique faciunt Bohemi, quod se auctoritate propria separant a nostra unitate, etiam si ius divinum pro eis staret, cum supremum ius divinum sit charitas et unitas spiritus."

[52] *Ibid.,* p. 278, ll. 32 ff.   [53] See *TR,* IV, No. 4922 (1540).

[54] Later he claimed to have heard an older monastic colleague say that Huss had been condemned without having been shown to be wrong. *Von den neuen Eckischen Bullen und Lügen* (1520). *WA,* VI, 591, ll. 12 ff.

[55] *Obelisci,* No. 18, *WA,* I, 302.

[56] He felt, however, that the charge of being a "Bohemian" was not used as an argument so much as a demagogic appeal to prejudice on the part of his opponents. This is shown by many bitter references in letters of the following months.

saved, who nevertheless did not believe in this article, nor is it in the power of the Roman pope or the inquisitors into heresy to found new articles of faith but to judge according to those already established. It is not possible for a faithful Christian to be constrained beyond Sacred Scripture, which was properly established by divine law, unless a new revelation has been established.[57]

Eck now saw his opening and charged Luther with confusing the holy Greeks with heretics and calling the "most pestilential errors" of the Hussites "very Christian." Martin interrupted with an impassioned objection: "I protest before you all and publicly that the excellent doctor in speaking thus about me is an impudent liar!"[58] Eck went on with relentless logic adducing patristic and scholastic authorities and pressing home the charge that Luther in pronouncing certain articles of Huss most Christian and evangelical had spoken against the sacred Council of Constance and was a defender of the condemned Huss. The excited monk interrupted these charges with repeated denials and branded the last as "a most shameless lie!"[59]

It must have been an excited audience which adjourned from the memorable session, and the following night was doubtless an anxious one for the Wittenbergers. Clearly Eck's tactics had been to bait Luther into a denial of the inspiration of the Council of Constance, which had enjoyed great prestige in Germany during the preceding century. When he mounted the rostrum the next day Martin registered a solemn protest against being stamped as a heretic in violation of the agreement and the duke's will, and challenged his opponent to name the "pestilential" Hussite articles which he had called "most Christian."[60] He then went on to defend the Christians of Greece and the Orient who were not subject to Rome before the Council of Nicaea. As for the Bohemians, he complained that instead of following Paul's fraternal procedure with the recreant Galatians and seeking to win back these erring souls with kind words and concessions, their opponents had assailed them with abuse. The Council of Constance had not condemned all of Huss's articles as heretical but had labeled some as rash, seditious, offensive to pious ears, and the like, which did not mean necessarily that they were false. The article which held that the belief in the superiority of the Roman Church to all others was not necessary to salvation had never been shown

---

[57] *WA*, II, 279, ll. 11 ff.

[58] "Protestor coram vobis omnibus et publice, quod egregius d. d. hoc mendaciter et impudenter de me loquitur." *Ibid.*, p. 280, ll. 35 f.

[59] *Ibid.*, p. 284, l. 1. Mosellanus says that Martin was most eager to deny the Bohemian heresy. *Ref. Act.*, III, 247.

[60] *WA*, II, 285 ff.

to be heretical.[61] So excited were the disputants, and probably also their partisans in the audience, that the presiding umpire, Cäsar Pflug, thought it necessary at the following session to admonish them in the name of the duke and the assembled masters to abstain from recrimination and abuse.[62]

The disputation now went forward more quietly for a time, but the inevitable clash recurred very soon. The debate continued to revolve about the divine right of the pope, which Eck insisted was confirmed by innumerable Church Fathers and popes and by the Council of Constance. Facing the mixed audience Martin dropped Latin for the moment and spoke German: "For I know that I am getting a bad reputation among the common people." He declared that he did not wish to assail nor could any Christian assail the primacy of the Roman Church or deny obedience to it; nevertheless he was obliged to assert that this primacy was not divinely established, but, in the same manner as the imperial power among the Germans, could not be rejected, although it was not founded in Sacred Scripture.[63] Resuming Latin, he declared that the Hussite article denying that Christ's words to Peter, "Upon this rock," established the supremacy of the Roman Chair had never been shown to be heretical. Eck's reply drew the inference with dialectical clearness. The article was condemned as heretical by the Council of Constance. Luther accepts the article, therefore he holds for truth a condemned and rejected article.[64] Obviously Martin was being driven into a corner. There was much citation and counter-citation of Church Fathers and interpretation of passages from the Evangelists regarding Christ's words to Peter, but Eck came back persistently to Huss and the Council of Constance. Thus beset Martin declared finally that no council could give divine sanction to anything that had not been divinely sanctioned and therefore nothing is heretical unless it is against the law of God.[65] He challenged Eck to prove that a council has not erred and cannot err. When his turn came, Eck replied: "I will tell you, honored father, if you say that a council, properly convoked, can err and has erred, you are for me a heathen and a publican." [66]

Plainly Luther would have been glad to avoid the question of the Council

---

[61] *Ibid.*, p. 288, ll. 8 ff.

[62] Seitz, *Der authentische Text der Leipziger Disputation*, p. 102.

[63] The protocol translates his words into Latin. *WA*, II, 299.

[64] *Ibid.*, p. 305, ll. 36 f.

[65] "Non movebor odiosissimis inculcationibus huius articuli, donec egregius d. d. probaverit concilium non posse errare, non errasse aut etiam non errare, cum concilium facere ius divinum non possit ex eo, quod natura sua non est ius divinum. Ideo neque hereticum est nisi quod contra ius divinum est. Haec pro isto articulo." *WA*, II, 308, ll. 29 ff.

[66] *Ibid.*, p. 311, ll. 18 ff.

of Constance and to dwell instead on the interpretation of Biblical passages, defending his position with the authority of the Council of Nicaea and the orthodoxy of the Greek Fathers. It is doubtful whether he had thought through to an end the full consequences toward which the studies and reflections of the preceding months were leading him. In reviewing this passage at arms a few days later he complained that Eck "puffed up like an adder, exaggerated my crime, and acted almost like a madman." [67] Eck knew his audience, and in spite of Martin's disclaimer, the strong-voiced Dominican exploited to the full the opportunity for linking his opponent's denial of papal supremacy by divine right with the Hussite heresy. Martin did not fail to hear the tittering with which Eck's partisans greeted their champion's denunciations. One of the auditors recalled that at Luther's declaration that not all of the Hussite articles were heretical, Duke George burst out loudly, "Plague take it!" [68]

The two contestants had now faced each other for almost five days and had debated only one thesis. Finally on the afternoon of July 8 they turned to the one regarding purgatory and two days later passed to a discussion of indulgences, penance, and the forgiveness of sins. Here the clash of argument was slight indeed. Martin set forth once more the ideas which he had formulated a year before in his theses and *Explanations of Indulgences* and was surprised to find in Eck a mild and conciliatory opponent. On the indulgence question, to which he had expected a great part of the debate to be devoted, little difference of opinion developed; indeed, Luther declared a few weeks later that if the preachers of indulgences had talked as Eck did at Leipzig, "perhaps no one would ever have heard Luther's name." [69] For both Eck and the audience the high point in the disputation had evidently been passed with the discussion of the supremacy of pope and council. At the end of eleven days of disputing Martin was so wearied with the endless repetition of his opponent's arguments that he did not avail himself of his right to a final reply. In a last outburst he charged Eck with coming back ever and again like a ridiculous lute player to the same old tune, to which Eck retorted that Luther had violated the decencies of a theological disputation. With this exchange both consigned the matter to the judges. [70]

[67] *WAB*, I, 422, ll. 73 f. [68] Fröschel. *Ref. Act.*, III, 279 f.

[69] Prefatory letter to the *Resolutiones . . . super propositionibus suis Lipsiae disputatis*, *WA*, II, 396, l. 15. In 1520, in a pamphlet in defense of the Council of Constance, Eck criticized the abuse of indulgences quite frankly. "Gegen Martin Luthers Anklage wider das Konzil von Konstanz in Sachen des Johannes Hus und des Hieronymus von Prag," *Corp. Cath.*, XIV, 10.

[70] *WA*, II, 382, ll. 11 ff.

Carlstadt now ascended the rostrum and for two days debated with Eck the well-worn subject of free will and grace. It was probably to the relief of disputants and audience that on July 15, the hall being needed for the entertainment of a ducal guest, the disputation came to a somewhat lame conclusion. Johann Langius Lambergius, a former rector of the university, made a long address[71] to nearly vacant seats and the cantor of the Thomas School led the choir and city musicians in a final "Te deum laudamus."[72]

Thus the great disputation ended with deep embitterment on both sides. From both parties the usual charge of fouls was heard. The Wittenbergers were particularly resentful of the attitude of the Leipzig theologians and the ducal umpires. Amsdorf noted that the Leipzig "Sophists" put up on a board a passage from Isaiah (61.1) which they had found in a Bible concordance and which in their opinions applied to indulgences. This Eck saw and used, dictating it to the notaries.[73] Eck, on the other hand, maintained that the Wittenberg group had supported their colleagues with notes and whispering,[74] and that armed partisans of Luther had threatened him and made such a noise before his lodgings at night that the city council had to give him a guard.[75] The taverns resounded with the tumult of the opposing parties and the air was full of sinister rumors. Luther heard that it was said he carried a devil with him in a box.[76] The silver ring which he wore aroused suspicion.[77] Those who came to visit the Wittenbergers did so secretly.[78] They were, to be sure, offered the "Ehrenwein" on the conclusion of the disputation, but no other gifts. The duke invited them to dinner; but he sent for Luther alone and discussed his works with him, telling him that the Bohemians expected many things of him and that his

---

[71] *Ref. Act.*, III, 580 ff.

[72] The disputation had not been without amusing as well as exciting features. According to the account of Chancellor Pfeifer, one of those present was Duke George's one-eyed court jester, who caused great amusement by an outburst against Eck, whom he accused of making fun of him. Walch, *Schriften*, XV, 1441. Such diversions were no doubt welcome during the eighteen days of the disputation, for some of the Leipzig doctors became so weary that they fell asleep and had to be wakened in order not to miss dinner. Fröschel's report, *Ref. Act.*, III, 280.

[73] Letter from Amsdorf to Spalatin, *Ref. Act.*, III, 239; see also *ibid.*, p. 447. Eck really used the passage. *WA*, II, 352, ll. 12 ff.

[74] According to Rubeus, Eck seems to have thrown this charge against Melanchthon during the disputation. See *Ref. Act.*, III, 270.

[75] Letter from Eck to Frederick, Aug. 8, *WAB*, I, 492, ll. 475 ff.

[76] Letter from Luther to Frederick, *WAB*, I, 474, l. 326.

[77] Eck records this. *WAB*, I, 494, ll. 566 f. Luther made sport of the charge. See *Ein Sermon gepredigt zu Leipzig, WA*, II, 245, l. 4.

[78] Letter from Luther to Spalatin, July 20, 1519, *WAB*, I, 423, l. 113. This letter is also the source for the statements which follow in our text.

sermon concerning the Lord's Prayer had brought confusion to many hearts.

In contrast with this treatment, which made it seem that they were "among the worst enemies in the world," the Wittenberg group observed that Eck received royal treatment by the Leipzig people. He was dined and wined and at the end of the disputation was presented with a coat of fine stuff. While they took their departure promptly, the Ingolstadt professor continued to enjoy the Leipzig flesh-pots for eleven days,[79] received a testimonial from the university, and finally left in the company of the duke for Annaberg. These flattering attentions swelled Eck's feeling of triumph. Before the conclusion of the debate with Carlstadt he boasted of having made an impression on those who had formerly been partisans of Luther, among whom he included most of the court crowd and the majority of the citizens. When he had finished with his opponents he sent to a fellow Dominican, Professor Hochstraten at Cologne, a detailed account of the proceedings and a denunciation of Luther's heretical denial of papal supremacy and defense of the Bohemian articles.[80] He boasted of not having read from any memorandum during the entire disputation when he stood alone against a host of Wittenbergers, armed only with his good cause. He urges the Cologne scholar to support him in case the affair is referred to his university for decision, for it is certain that the "grammarians" are infiltrating errors into the Church.[81] More neutral observers like Mosellanus took another view of the affair. That humanistically inclined professor does not like this theatrical manner of disputing, he writes to Willibald Pirckheimer in Nuremberg;[82] and a few months later he concludes that Eck's triumph is conceded only by those who know as little about it as the ass about lute playing, while the victory of Martin and Carlstadt is recognized only by the few learned.[83]

Luther went back to Wittenberg filled with profound disappointment and weariness.[84] He was deeply embittered over Eck's behavior and the

---

[79] See Eck's boastful letter to Christoph Tengler, Aug. 26, 1519, in which he rehearses the various honors conferred on him. In *Notizenblatt: Beilage zum Archiv für Kunde österreichischer Geschichtsquellen,* IV (1854), 500. These included disputations which the theologians arranged for him and where he carried off easy victories. See Fröschel's account of one of these in which Eck sadly confused his opponent, whom he accused of "reeking of Luther." *Ref. Act.,* III, 281.

[80] On July 24, 1519. See *Ref. Act.,* III, 222 ff.

[81] This was a clever touch, as Cologne was still smarting from the attack of the humanists in the *Epistolae obscurorum virorum.*

[82] Quoted by Seidemann, *Die Leipziger Disputation,* p. 79.

[83] Letter from Mosellanus to Julius Pflug, Dec. 8, 1519, *Ref. Act.,* III, 247. This seems to have been the opinion also of some competent nontheologians, e.g., the Leipzig city official Heinrich Stromer; see his letter to Spalatin, July 19, 1519, in Kolde, *Analecta Lutherana,* p. 9.

[84] Some months later, in a letter to the elector, Eck claimed that he had so wearied Luther

treatment which he had received from the Leipzig theologians. A few days later, on July 20, he wrote from the convent a long letter to Spalatin in which he gave a detailed account of the disputation. Again and again his rage boils over when he recalls the duplicity of Eck and the hostility of Eck's Leipzig partisans, who, as he well knows, are exulting in triumph with his opponent. The whole thing began badly and finished badly, for he is convinced now that the other side never sought the truth but only fame for themselves. "I have experienced hatred before, but never more shameless or impudent. There you have the whole tragedy."

---

at the conclusion of the disputation that he would not stand longer on the rostrum. *Ref. Act.*, III, 640; Walch, *Schriften*, XV, 1571.

20

THE LEIPZIG DISPUTATION
THE AFTERMATH

THE great disputation was past, but its echoes continued to reverberate throughout the theological world and beyond. Martin came back to Wittenberg smarting under a sense of unfair treatment and determined to put his case before a less prejudiced audience than that which had faced him in when Eck scored a point, all are set forth in detail. Throughout the letter to Spalatin which Martin wrote on July 20, within a day or two after his return to his cell, a letter in which moods of sarcastic humor, anger and firm determination succeed each other.[1] Eck's blustering and unfairness, the breach of contract which forced the Wittenbergers to submit a sacred cause to judges for decision, the mocking exultation of the Leipzig crew when Eck scored a point, all are set forth in detail. Throughout the letter there sounds a tone of frustration. An occasion which was intended to establish truth and bring about harmony between Wittenberg and Leipzig had turned out to be a noisy academic fracas. For Duke George, Martin brought away a certain feeling of respect, although he grieved to see him lend an ear to the violent ideas of others; but for his opponent and especially for the representatives of the rival university, who tittered when Eck denounced him as a heretic and a friend of the Bohemians and who grudged him an opportunity to preach in their city, he nourished the deepest resentment. "Although I put a certain restraint on myself, I can not [refrain from] vomiting out all of my dissatisfaction, because I am a man of flesh and blood and the shameless hatred and malignant injustice were too great in so sacred and divine a matter."[2] Nothing, he declares, was discussed in a worthy manner except his thesis on the papal power. He is therefore determined to issue to the world a new series of "Explanations" covering

[1] *WAB*, I, 420 ff.

[2] *Ibid.*, p. 424, ll. 149 ff. The sentence is incomplete, probably because of the writer's excitement.

all his disputation theses. The letter was plainly intended also for the eye of the elector, who had just returned from the exciting combat of force and diplomacy at the Frankfort election.

If Martin found the disputation barren of results as concerned the establishment of truth and the settlement of the controversy, he expected even less from a decision of the judges. In consenting to submit the case to a jury he had explicitly reserved the right to maintain his appeal before a council.[3] When he signed the contract at last, he agreed that his dispute with Eck was to be referred to the universities of Erfurt and Paris, but he had objected strongly to putting the decision into the hands of the theological faculty alone.[4] He knew the spirit of the theological schools and had little hope that those who had been brought up in an atmosphere of Thomas, Scotus, or Occam, or who felt themselves bound by the papal decree against indulgences, would give his arguments an objective hearing. Nevertheless, Duke George, a man of sturdy though narrow religious attitude, wanted an authoritative settlement of the vexing question at issue and ruled that only theologians were competent for this.[5] Accordingly he forwarded the papers to Erfurt and Paris and waited impatiently for an answer.[6]

Martin professed indifference as to the decision. Nevertheless he looked forward to the result with ill-concealed nervousness.[7] As the weeks passed and nothing was forthcoming, he complained to Lang that the Leipzig people were circulating a report that Erfurt would decide against him, and warned him that if this should be the case, he intended to send out an answer both in Latin and in German that would proclaim the injustice and ignorance of the Erfurt colleagues to the entire world. "I shall be innocent of your blood, for it is not my intention to leave a single syllable of our theses undefended. God's will be done!"[8] Like other men of powerful will and deep conviction of their right, he was unable to envisage the possibility of any fair and informed judgment that did not support his views. In December he notes that Erfurt still delays its decision and that thus far the only gain from the disputation is that it opened the way for speaking against the Roman Antichrist.[9] In the meantime the text of the Leipzig

---

[3] *Ibid.*, p. 429, ll. 29 f.

[4] Luther's memorandum for George gives his reasons. *WAB*, I, 431. Seidemann, *Die Leipziger Disputation*, pp. 149 f., prints Eck's counterargument.

[5] For the text of his decision, see Gess, *Briefe und Akten*, I, 94.

[6] The letter to Erfurt is lacking in the Saxon archives, see *ibid.*, p. 113, n. 1; that to Paris was dispatched on Oct. 4, 1519, *ibid.*, pp. 100 f.

[7] See letters from Luther to Lang, Sept. 3, *WAB*, I, 506, and Dec. 18, *ibid.*, p. 597, l. 20.

[8] Letter to Lang, Oct. 16, 1519, *WAB*, I, 539, ll. 10 ff.

[9] Letter to Lang, Dec. 18, *WAB*, I, 597, ll. 20 ff.

contest as prepared by the notaries had found its way into print.[10] It appeared probably in Erfurt, where it is possible that Lang, as a member of the university faculty, had access to the document and put it into the press.[11] In any event this friend was in a position to keep Martin informed of what was going on and possibly to prevent decisive action.

Finally, on December 29, Erfurt sent an answer to Duke George.[12] Politely but firmly the university refused to render a verdict on the ground that there had been a difference of opinion on the part of the contestants as to which faculties should participate in the judgment. Furthermore, the Erfurt colleagues declared themselves unwilling to exclude their learned brethren of the Dominican and Augustinian orders from a share in the matter. George wrote again urging a reconsideration of this action,[13] but after further delay the papers were returned to him without a judgment.

With Paris the duke had little better success. In all probability Martin suggested the French university because of its long tradition of opposing papal claims to supremacy over a council, a tradition firmly established by its famous rector, Jean Gerson. George had written to Paris on October 4, 1519, but nothing came of it. He repeated his request a year later when the effect of Luther's revolutionary works of the summer and fall of 1520 had shaken his conservative nature with alarm.[14] At last the Paris theologians appointed a committee to examine Martin's works. Its report, which appeared on the minutes of the faculty in the following spring, condemned certain of Luther's ideas as pernicious, but carefully avoided giving judgment on the Leipzig disputation.[15]

In the meantime friends of both parties had hastened to claim the victory, but the shouts of triumph of Eck and his followers drowned out the more modest protests of the Wittenbergers. Within a month after the meeting a Leipzig student of theology, Johann Rubeus, published an account which proclaimed the Ingolstadt professor as a Hercules and Samson of the academic arena and gloated over the defeated Wittenbergers, whom he abused roundly for ignorance of the Scriptures, the Church Fathers, and scholastic authority.[16] Stung by this attack, a teacher

---

[10] See above, p. 354, n. 22.

[11] That Lang was connected with the publication may be concluded from Luther's letter to him of December 18, 1519.

[12] Gess, *Briefe und Akten*, I, 113.

[13] On January 9, 1520. *Ibid.*, p. 114.

[14] On November 10, 1520. *Ibid.*, pp. 144 ff.

[15] Dated April 15, 1521. Quoted *ibid.*, p. 145, n. 1.

[16] *Solutiones ac responsa Wit. Doctorum in publica disputatione Lipsica contra fulmina Eckiana parum profutura, tumorque adventus et humilitas eorum recessus, per Jo. Ru. Longi*

at Wittenberg, Johann Montanus, took up the cudgels and replied in a pamphlet, which for boastfulness and absence of ideas somewhat outdid the effusion of Rubeus.[17] In answer the latter brought out a poem in the doggerel verse characteristic of German satirical literature of the baser sort in those decades.[18] The affair had degenerated into the kind of inter-university squabble in which humanists of the age delighted to exhibit themselves. Martin dismissed Rubeus as "an ass,"[19] but another Leipzig protagonist now took the field. Johann Cellarius, not without honor in the annals of humanism, came to the defense of his university as a seat of the new science. He waved aside Rubeus and his arguments as of no consequence and pledged the fealty of his faculty to Aristotle alone.[20] Montanus responded to the attack of this champion also, and so the affair went on with duplique and replique, having long since lost any importance for the theological controversy.

The efforts of these pamphleteers had no more serious purpose than winning the applause of their academic colleagues and expressing the boundless egotism that was so marked a characteristic of Renaissance scholars great and small. In the meantime, a Wittenberg representative armed with infinitely greater scholarship and good sense had come to the assistance of his colleagues. Philip Melanchthon sent to Johann Oecolampadius, his friend and former teacher at Basel, an objective and reasoned account of the disputation which acknowledged Eck's versatile and striking gifts but concealed neither the author's admiration for Luther nor his dislike for the sophistry and the noisy and theatrical manner of his opponent.[21] The letter was published immediately. Eck saw it before he left Leipzig and straightway made answer.[22] With contemptuous

---

comparata. See text in *Ref. Act.,* III, 251 ff. The dedication to the bishop of Würzburg (Rubeus was from Franconia) is dated August 13.

[17] *Neminis Wittenbergensis Encomium Rubii Longipolli apud Lipsium in errores, quos pueriliter commisit, adversus Wittenbergenses.* See *Ref. Act.,* III, 785 ff., where it is stated that Montanus was from Hesse and taught privately in Wittenberg.

[18] *Eyn neu buchlein von d'loblichen disputation, offentlich gehalten vor fursten und vor hern vor hochgelarten und ungelarte yn der werde hochgepreysten stat Leyptzick . . . 1519.* See Weller, *Repertorium typographicum,* III, 153, No. 1264. See also *Ref. Act.,* III, 272. Luther heard from Staupitz in December, 1519, that Eck had had this printed in Augsburg at his own expense. *WAB,* I, 572 and n. 3.

[19] Letter from Luther to Lang, Oct. 16, 1519, *WAB,* I, 540, l. 4. His first intention seems to have been to reply to Rubeus, see letter to Spalatin of Sept. 22, *WAB,* I, 508, l. 13; he then probably decided that Montanus could take care of the Leipzig champion.

[20] Text in *Ref. Act.,* III, 799 ff. See also *ibid.,* p. 804.

[21] The letter is dated Wittenberg, July 21, 1519, and is reprinted in *Ref. Act.,* III, 215 ff. Oecolampadius published a bitter satire on Eck in December.

[22] *Excusatio Eckii ad ea, quae falso sibi Phil. Melanchthon Grammaticus Wittenb. super Theologica Disputatione Lipsica adscripsit. Ref. Act.,* III, 591 ff.

flings at Melanchthon as a "grammarian" who has dared to mix in matters of theological scholarship, he replies to the Wittenberg professor's criticisms of his arguments. Before the end of July, Melanchthon returned with another open letter, marked by a conciliatory tone.[23] He denies that he has any wish to anticipate the decision of the judges or to wound Eck, and proceeds to a careful analysis of the sources and arguments of the Dominican disputant in order to justify his condemnation of Eck's sophistical devices and the rash manner in which Eck interprets the Scriptures and the Fathers. The young humanist, who had none of the pugnacious temperament of contemporary scholarship, claims to have been driven to reply by his Wittenberg colleagues.[24] He is at pains to pour oil on troubled waters and concludes his letter with an apology for interfering in a theological question: even a common Christian who does not hate theological studies may feed a little upon its "holy delights." [25] None could have surmised that a decade later this "common Christian" would be obliged to take the place of Luther and lead the defense against Eck in the momentous days of the Augsburg Diet.

A spirit like Melanchthon's was foreign to Eck and to theological polemics in general in those warlike years. The energetic and combative Dominican did not delay a moment in pushing to completion what he regarded as a victory over the Saxon enemies of the Church. Before leaving the scene of the disputation he addressed a letter to Elector Frederick that was intended both as an apology and a denunciation.[26] He had not wished, he declares, to attack the prince's university nor his scholars. Only loyalty to holy faith had driven him to take up the challenge of Carlstadt, who had heaped public contempt on him, and that of Luther, who was endowed with great gifts, to be sure, but had set himself against the opinion of the Fathers and saints of the Church. Martin had pronounced Christian and evangelical many articles of Huss and the Bohemians, to the ultimate joy of all heretics, and had denied the supremacy of Peter. Eck reminds the elector of his sacred obligation to Christ, to Christian faith, and to his own land. Though a poor priest, he has borne his own expenses at the disputation and he is now ready to dispute with Luther at Cologne, Louvain, or Paris. Frederick referred the letter at once to his two theologians for reply.[27] Carlstadt, nervous and

---

[23] *Defensio Philippi Melanchthonis contra Johannem Eckium Theologiae Professorem. Ref. Act.,* III, 596 ff.
[24] *Ibid.,* p. 598.   [25] *Ibid.,* p. 604.
[26] Letter from Eck to Frederick, July 22, 1519, *WAB,* I, 459 ff.
[27] Letter from Frederick to Eck, July 24, 1519, *WAB,* I, 463.

irritable as always, sent an answer within a week.[28] Later he and Martin will respond in detail, he promises, but now he is in haste to explain and justify his use of books at the disputation and denounce Eck's dishonesty. As evidence he cites his opponent's use of a quotation from St. Jerome which he was unable to verify.

After several weeks of preparation the joint reply is ready.[29] Although Carlstadt's name is signed first to the letter it is written in Martin's hand.[30] In its tone of profound conviction, enforced by a picturesque style that is tinged here and there with a sarcastic humor, it bears throughout the stamp of Martin's authorship. It is the earliest long letter in German which has been preserved from his pen and it shows him for the first time in full control of the vigorous style that lifts him above all save a very few masters of German epistolary prose. It was not the Wittenbergers, he tells Frederick, but Eck who began the quarrel, for in his "Obelisks" he had denounced Martin as a Bohemian and a heretic. He then meets Eck's attack point by point with sarcastic references to his pettifogging and sophistical tricks. He makes a spirited defense of his statements regarding the articles of Huss, the possibility that a Church council may err, and papal supremacy as derived from human law. His formulation of these views is frank and categorical and culminates in an unequivocal statement that the Scriptures, even in the mouth of a layman, take precedence over pope and council when unsupported by scriptural authority.[31] This is a highly significant statement, his first plea for the right of the simple Christian to interpret for himself his duty to God and man, an idea which was to be expanded in eloquent terms a

---

[28] Letter from Carlstadt to Frederick, July 31, 1519, WAB, I, 463 ff.

[29] August 18. WAB, I, 465 ff.

[30] This on the authority of Seckendorf, who saw the original in the Weimar archives. See Enders, Luthers Briefwechsel, II, 127, n. 2. This seems now to have disappeared. The brief covering letter forwarded to the elector with the longer document, WAB, I, 501 f., is in Carlstadt's handwriting. Enders, Luthers Briefwechsel, II, 128. The original is in the Gotha archives. In style and contents it is unlike Luther. Its purposes seem to have been in the main to excuse the publication of Luther's forthcoming Explanations and to call Frederick's especial attention to Eck's campaign against Wittenberg University.

[31] "Das wöll Gott nimmermehr, dass ein frumm Christenmensch ein Spruch der Geschrift recht verstand und in sich bildet und sollt denselben darnach umb etlicher irrigen Verstands willen verwerfen, unangesehen seinen rechten Verstand. Darüber sollt man Papst und Concilia verleugnen zur Rettung der heiligen Geschrift, denn wo dieser Artikel ketzerisch gescholten wird, so muss Evangelium, Paulus und Aug[ustinus] untergehen. Ehe ich das tu, will ich meiner christlichen Freiheit brauchen und sagen also: Ein Concilium mag irren (wie alle Lehrer der Gschrift und Rechten schreiben) und hat etlich Mal geirret, wie die Historien beweisen und das jetzige letzte Römisch angezeigt wider das Costnitzer und Baseler. Also irret in den Artikeln das Costnitzer auch. Oder bewähre du, dass es nicht geirret habe. Sonderlich so man mehr einem Laien sollt glauben, der Geschrift hat, dann dem Papst und Concilio ohne Geschrift, ut supra." WAB, I, 472, ll. 251 ff.

year later in the revolutionary treatise *On the Freedom of a Christian.*
The letter is no mere theologian's argument but an appeal to the sound
sense of a practical statesman who might well agree that lawyers, physicians,
and masters of arts, in short, men like the elector himself, could be
counted on for a more objective judgment of these affairs than cloistered
theologians. "I want to have the whole university and not the theologians
decide, for Dr. Reuchlin's case taught me how learned theologians are
and how they judge." [32] Eck had made a final suggestion that the elector
should have all Luther's books burned. "That's the real Eck!" exclaims
Martin. "A letter like his should have a postscript like that! That is something that does honor to a theologian, not to have looked at a book and
yet condemn it to the fire." [33]

The letter is plainly keyed for the elector's ear. In spite of its frankness it does not overlook a telling *argumentum ad hominem* in the repeated
charge that Eck and the Leipzig crowd are trying to injure Frederick's
university. But Martin was not content to convince the elector of the
righteousness of his cause. From the time of his return to Wittenberg he had
in mind an appeal to a larger audience with a clear statement of his
position on those topics which had to his mind been discussed so inade-
quately in the Leipzig turmoil.[34] Some days before he forwarded to the
elector the joint reply to Eck, he prepared a long letter to Spalatin.[35]
This was evidently intended to be published and was printed, at first
separately and then as a preface to his *Explanations by Luther of his
Theses Debated at Leipzig,* the complete statement of his side of the disputation.

It is, in fact, as an introduction to this longer work that the letter is
to be read. Eck and his partisans are crowing victory everywhere and
singing songs of triumph. The disputation itself was a loss of time and not
a search for truth, for "Eck and his crew in their search for fame pretend

---

[32] *Ibid.,* p. 477, ll. 421 ff.   [33] *Ibid.,* p. 478, ll. 438 ff.

[34] Letter from Luther to Spalatin, July 20, *WAB,* I, 423, l. 105. The reference here is not
to a new edition of the *Resolutio super propositione sua decima tertia,* as Enders assumes,
Luthers Briefwechsel, II, 88 f., n. 17, but to the *Resolutiones Lutherianae,* see n. 35 below.
There is no evidence that Luther personally reissued the former work, although several
editions appeared in 1519 and 1520. See *WA,* II, 181 ff.

[35] Enders, *Luthers Briefwechsel,* II, 81 ff.; see also *WA,* II, 391 ff. The evidence for the
previous publication of the letter rests chiefly on a note of Melanchthon's transmitting Luther's
letter to Spalatin and on a separate print of the letter. Eck claimed to have seen this letter
as early as August 15 in Nuremberg. The bibliographical data are discussed at length by
Clemen, *WAB,* I, 435 f., who argues for August 10 or thereabouts as the date of Luther's
letter. The Weimar edition publishes letter and *Explanations* from the joint issue which came
from Grünenberg's press in the second half of August, *Resolutiones Lutherianae super
propositionibus suis Lipsiae disputatis.*

one thing and feel otherwise in their hearts." It was a tragedy or a comedy, "or if you prefer, a satire." [36] Again he passes the whole affair in review: the hostility of the Leipzig scholars, Eck's breach of contract, and his numerous self-contradictory statements and shifts in position. He defends his statements regarding the Council of Constance. Since a council can err, let it rather be that of Constance than more sacred councils like the Nicaean or the African Council. Councils do contradict and reject each other. He promises to observe the agreement not to print his notarial copy of the disputation, but he has never promised not to write about it. One thing he owes to the disputation and it is of momentous importance: in this affair the false theology at last came to grief.

It is enough for me that the tormentor of consciences, that false theology [theologistria] to which I owe all my suffering fell to the ground in this disputation. For in earlier years I learned that the merit that makes man acceptable [meritum congrui] is one thing, that which makes man worthy [condigni] is another; that man can do what is within him for obtaining grace; that he can remove obstacles to grace but cannot interpose obstacles to it; that he can fulfill the commands of God according to their substance although not according to the intention of Him who commands, that the free will can work in contradictory directions; that from its purely natural powers it can love God above everything; from its natural powers demonstrate love [actum haberi amoris] and friendship— those and other monstrosities of that kind which are set forth as the first principles of scholastic theology, and have filled the books and ears of all.[37]

Thus he declares himself free from the theology of his youth. The theory which he characterizes so bitterly is that of Occam's school as taught him by Trutvetter and others at Erfurt. This, in retrospect, he now regards as the source of all his unhappiness in the cloister and the early years of university teaching, and he is convinced that its day is fulfilled; the Leipzig disputation has shattered the whole airy, metaphysical structure.

Probably before the end of August this letter appeared again as the introduction to Luther's *Explanations . . . of His Theses Debated at Leipzig*.[38] Three months earlier Martin had published the theses, but included a systematic defense of only the thirteenth, that dealing with the supremacy of the pope.[39] Now he takes up all his propositions and presents them

---

[36] *WA*, II, 392, ll. 4 ff. and 37 ff.   [37] *Ibid.*, p. 401, ll. 20 ff.

[38] *Ibid.*, pp. 403 ff. The pamphlet was on sale in Wittenberg on September 3, as Luther writes to Lang. *WAB*, I, 506, ll. 15 f.

[39] *Resolutio Lutheriana super propositione sua decima tertia de potestate papae (per autorem locupleta)*. *WA*, II, 183 ff. All the theses, with a preface but without argument, had been printed in May as *Disputatio et excusatio F. Martini Luther adversus criminationes Dr. Johannis Eccii*. *WA*, II, 158 ff.

as "conclusions," supported by such arguments as he would have put forward at Leipzig, where some "were not touched with a single syllable, others were only imperfectly discussed." It is no longer Eck with whom he is arguing at this time, but the great audience of theologians and laymen who have been roused to thought on these subjects. It is before them that he unfolds his confession of faith on the matters that have caused so much argument. Here is no personal invective but a vibrant expression of profound conviction, won through many years of struggle. This leads again and again to eloquent denunciation of the scholastic conceptions regarding man's will and its powers, of theological tradition and papal decrees as a substitute for scriptural teaching, and of the doctrine of venial sins and the whole theory of indulgences. Through the entire discussion we hear ever and again the monk's earnest plea for a recognition of the evil that nestles down in men's hearts, eternal and ineradicable without the miraculous cleansing power of God's grace.

Martin begins the defense of his position with an apology for differing with the philosophy of the schools. God spoke through the mouth of an ass what he had hidden from a prophet, and revealed to the child Samuel the truth which he had withheld from a priest of Israel. Scotus and Occam introduced new ideas; why might not he do so? That the Council of Constance condemned the view in his first proposition, that every deed of man is good or evil, does not frighten him. "I regard myself as a Christian theologian who dwells in the kingdom of truth. It is therefore my duty not only to affirm the truth but also to insist on it and defend it by blood and death." [40] The Council of Constance contradicted itself. It declared that a council was above the pope and yet it condemned Huss's statement that the pope does not rule over all churches by divine right. Councils have contradicted each other. Thus the Roman Council abrogated the decree of the Basel Council and declared that the pope was above the council. Condemnation fell upon articles of Huss which were most true. So let them now cry out on him as a patron of the Bohemians; it is his duty in the face of all the din about words,[41] titles, reputation, and dignity to speak the truth and oppose falsehood.

The first and second "conclusions" deal with the inherent incompetence of man to do good. Martin advances scriptural texts and arguments from the Fathers to prove that every deed of man is either good or evil and that our good works turn into evil works in God's sight through our own guilt. The just man is a rusty tool which cuts poorly until God

[40] *WA*, II, 404, ll. 11 ff.   [41] *Ibid.*, p. 406, ll. 31 ff.

has polished it. Things like this he did not learn in the theology of the schools: "I lost Christ then; now I have found him again in Paul."[42] Even where the impeachment for sin (*reatus*) is quashed, concupiscence remains and must be succeeded by love, which can not exist where concupiscence is. This exposes the fallacy of the theory of venial sins, which the theologians claim do not offend God or offend Him but little. To be sure, the Council of Constance ruled against the thesis that all deeds are good or bad, but the Thomists must have had the upper hand there.[43] A Pelagian heretic is he who claims that a good work or penitence can begin before the love of righteousness, which is a gift of God's grace and not of nature.

The next three conclusions deal with the nature of penitence and punishment and formulate Martin's position with a clarity not hitherto attained. Only God himself can transform eternal punishment into temporal punishment. Every penitent is entitled to absolution from guilt and punishment and the priest sins who does not absolve him. It is the bishops and the pope who keep priests from doing this.[44] As regards purgatory, it is perhaps true that souls must do penance there, but it can not be shown that God requires more from man than a willing death.[45]

The seventh thesis comes back again to freedom of the will and denies that the will is lord over our deeds for good or ill. Before works must come justification through faith. The statement in the Epistle of St. James that faith without works is dead has been cited against him. Evidently the passage caused Martin considerable uneasiness. He counters it with the remark that this Epistle in point of style is quite beneath the "apostolic majesty" and is not to be compared with the Pauline Epistles.[46] After all, he adds sophistically, dead faith is no faith, but an opinion, while Paul is speaking of the living faith. Pettifogging theologians hold to this passage alone and quite disregard the fact that all other Scripture commands faith without works.

Once more he condemns indulgences with bitter words. With the papal bull of the preceding November in mind, he declares that neither Church nor pope can create new articles of faith nor laws regarding morals and good works. These are all taught sufficiently in Scripture. The papal sycophants without letters or morals proclaim things out of their own heads as if the Holy Spirit were guiding them.[47] The Church has not been

---

[42] "Ego Christum amiseram illic, nunc in Paulo reperi." *Ibid.*, p. 414, l. 28.

[43] *Ibid.*, p. 421, ll. 3 ff. [44] *Ibid.*, p. 423, Conclusio V.

[45] *Idem.*, Conclusio VI. [46] *Ibid.*, p. 425, ll. 11 ff.

[47] *Ibid.*, pp. 427 f.: "velut certi, quod spiritus sanctus eos regat."

abandoned by the spirit of Christ, but it is not the pope nor the cardinals nor even the council which make up the Church, as he understands it. To say that indulgences are good for the Christian is raving madness.[48]

Finally he comes back to another defense of his position regarding the pope. This was the proposition which had seemed so scandalous "to pious ears," that is, to the ears of "pride and hatred." [49] For these and others he sums up briefly his most telling arguments: It can be shown from Scripture that every state is entitled to its own bishop; distant Christians can not depend on Rome for the Roman bishop can not care for all; the Council of Constance deposed a pope, which would have been an heretical act had the pope been superior to all by divine right; and lastly, the assertion that the pope is pope by divine right is a new dogma of which the ancient Fathers of the faith knew nothing. In conclusion, he assures his readers in solemn tones that it is not his adversaries whom he hates as the cause of these evils but "Behemoth," the Prince of Evil, "whose shadow I see; he wants to frighten me and if he can, to use me as an instrument to drive truth out of his kingdom." [50]

The *Explanations* are a restatement of Luther's entire theological position. With reserve but with great vigor of style he once more denies the freedom of man's will to do good. Our good deeds are evil in God's sight unless we first turn in love to God through faith and receive grace; every priest must absolve any penitent; faith must precede works and works then appear as the natural fruit of justification; purgatory may cleanse the sinner, but no one can say what change takes place within the soul after death; indulgences are stumbling blocks to Christians, for neither pope nor priest can dispose of the merits of Christ or the saints; the primacy of the pope rests on human law and convenience. With prophetic conviction Martin concludes the work, in which he has looked beyond his opponents at the greater audience outside the confines of the academic world, by laying his case before the judgment bar of generations yet unborn.

> Bad is the judgment of the present,
> The verdict of posterity will be better.[51]

In the meantime Eck had seen in Nuremberg the printed copy of Luther's prefatory letter of August to Spalatin and immediately prepared a reply. This *Vindication of Eck from Brother Martin Luther's Charges* [52] came

[48] *Ibid.*, p. 428, Conclusio XI.   [49] *Ibid.*, p. 432, ll. 23 f.   [50] *Ibid.*, p. 435.
[51] Praesens male iudicat aetas,
    Judicium melius posteritatis erit.
[52] *Expurgatio Joan. Eckii Theologi Ingolstadiensis adversus criminationes F. Martin Luther*

from the press on the heels of Martin's *Explanations*. It opens with an account of the disputation by Professor Cellarius. This was written under the immediate impression of the stirring events, as we have seen, and while the author claimed to give an objective account of proceedings, he showed unmistakable admiration for Eck's powers.[53] Eck then takes up Martin's letter and answers his charges point by point, defending especially his own views of the freedom of the will. He repeats now in print the charge which he had made in the disputation and his letters, that Luther was a friend of the Hussites. Apparently the pamphlet did not come into Martin's hands until late in October. When it did, it called forth an acrimonious personal reply.[54]

Before he saw Eck's pamphlet, Luther had given further evidence of his earnestness and the fierce resentment which had grown up within him against the man who was now hounding him in private correspondence and through the press with constantly reiterated charges of heresy. A pamphlet entitled *Defense against the Malicious Indictment of Eck*, which appeared scarcely four weeks after his *Explanations,* was Luther's reply to another attack by his Dominican enemy.[55] It grew out of a controversy that had its roots in the rising opposition to the Wittenberg theology and illustrates Martin's sensitiveness and the unrestrained character of his polemics in this year of bitter struggle.

Franz Günther, whom we have met as a student of Martin's at Wittenberg, was now parish priest at Jüterbog, a few miles farther north. In the spring of 1519 he became involved in a dispute with the head of the Franciscan monastery in his town regarding statements which he was alleged to have made in his sermons,[56] statements which reflected certain of Luther's teachings in an exaggerated and distorted form. Günther denied these charges and two witnesses were summoned in his favor from among the Wittenberg Augustinians, one of them a university lector in theology. Their visit only increased the feeling of hostility that was plainly expanding

---

Vuittenbergen. ordinis heremitarum. See Wiedemann, *Dr. Johann Eck,* pp. 505 ff. Eck dates the dedication September 2.

[53] Cellarius's account appeared at the end of July in the form of a letter to Wolfgang Capito in Basel. *Ref. Act.,* III, 225 ff. As the result of an uncomplimentary reference to his colleague Mosellanus, Cellarius became involved in a lively controversy with one of Mosellanus's students, Petrus Suavenus of Pomerania, which only the most fanatical student of humanistic vapidities could find interesting. See *ibid.,* 653 ff.

[54] *Ad Johannem Eccium M. Lutheri epistola super expurgatione Ecciana.*

[55] *Contra malignum Joh. Eckii iudicium . . . defensio. WA,* II, 625 ff.

[56] See *WA,* II, 621 ff., and Enders, *Luthers Briefwechsel,* II, 36 f., for the circumstances which initiated the controversy, based on the *Articuli per Fratres Minores contra Lutheranos.*

against Luther and his colleague.[57] Provoked by certain informal statements of the lector, the Franciscans drew up a list of fourteen points which
they regarded as heretical. Günther affirmed his belief in seven of them.
Soon afterward he fell under the censure of the bishop of Brandenburg
and suspended his preaching, but made matters worse by selecting as his
substitute Thomas Münzer, who had just been expelled from Brunswick.
This radical theologian, a stormy petrel of the coming religious conflict in
Germany, aroused the Franciscans still further by attacking the Pope for
his failure to convene a council with regularity.[58] Forthwith the guardian
of the Franciscan convent and its lector lodged a formal appeal with the
diocesan vicar of the Brandenburg bishopric, Jakob Gropper, rehearsing
the dispute and formulating their charges, with an arraignment of Günther
for heretical statements, including contemptuous remarks which he was
charged with having made about indulgences.[59] These charges, dated May 4
and 5, named Luther as the author of the destructive errors which they
condemned.

The appeal to his diocesan superiors came promptly into Martin's
hands. It arrived in the trying hour when he was fighting off Miltitz
and struggling for admittance to the Leipzig disputation. On May 15
he addressed to the convent a letter that even for the period is unusually
sarcastic and menacing in tone.[60] Why, he asks the Franciscan brothers,
have they not taken the matter up with him beforehand as the Scripture
directs? Now they must retract the slur on his name or he will make a
public and humiliating exposure of their ignorance. Franciscan ignorance

[57] These Wittenberg Augustinians were the prior and a lector in theology of the university.
At a collation which took place after the hearing, the lector made a number of informal
statements (Luther refers to it as a "private disputation," *WAB*, I, 390, l. 35) which the
Franciscans regarded as heretical and summed up under fourteen headings.

[58] In the Franciscan charges, as published later, the heretical preacher bears the name
of "M. Thomas." It is evident that Münzer is meant.

[59] Complaint was first made orally, then in the form of two addresses, both written by
the Franciscan lector Bernhard Dappen. One is addressed to the vicar, on behalf of the
lector himself, the other in the name of the Franciscan cloister to the bishop of Brandenburg.
See Knaake, ed., *WA*, II, 622, who uses the printed form of the charges, *Articuli per Fratres
minores de observantia propositi Reverendissimo domino Episcopo Brandenburgen. contra
Lutheranos*. This now rare pamphlet was published at Ingolstadt, probably by Eck. It appears
to have come from the press in October, at the same time as Eck's *Ad criminatricem Martini
Luders . . . offensionem . . .* ; see n. 83 below. Karl Schottenloher, "Magister Andreas Lutz
in Ingolstadt, der Drucker der Bulle 'Exsurge Domini' (1519–1524)," *Zentralblatt für Bibliothekswesen*, XXXII (1915), 256, gives the title from a copy in the Munich Staatsbibliothek and
dates the printing "Ende 1519." There is no evidence that Martin saw the *Articuli* in other
than manuscript form before his reply to Eck's attack in *Contra malignum Joh. Eckii iudicium
. . . defensio.*

[60] *WAB*, I, 389 ff.

was a target for humanistic gibing throughout the whole period from Erasmus to Rabelais, and Martin does not let the opportunity escape him. Their order, he remarks, has always shown a contempt for study and entertained its audiences with visions and its own cogitations. His doctrine has been set forth for three years at Wittenberg and discussed before the most learned men without condemnation. Now it is branded as heretical in the fiery test of a petty convent "by one or two snoring brethren who perchance have some time seen a master of arts but have never known one personally." In answering the charges against the Wittenberg theologians he accompanies his exposition with continual gibes at Franciscan limitations. "You never read anything, much less do you understand anything, and yet you claim to judge of doctrines." They pronounce the most sacred teachings of the Fathers, which they have never read, "pestiferous, absurd, and foreign to Catholic doctrine. Is not this blasphemy against the Holy Spirit?" [61] He is ready to proclaim categorically that the pope is vicar of Christ on earth only by human law and invites the convent to read St. Jerome and certain inscriptions on the Latern church at Rome, which he interprets as a confirmation of his assertion.[62] In closing he threatens that if they do not bow to the truth, he will expose to everyone their "marvelous wisdom."

Here the matter rested until after the Leipzig disputation. At this point Eck came into the dispute. Before leaving the Saxon city he received from the bishop of Brandenburg, Hieronymus Scultetus, who was passing through, the charges of the two Franciscans and was asked to give an opinion on the matter.[63] This the Dominican scholar did with speed, according to his own statement "in the space of two hours." [64] His memorandum formulated fifteen heretical articles as set forth in the statements credited to the "Lutherans" and added notes to these justifying his findings. Eck's memorandum came to Luther's ears by August 15, possibly through the bishop, and he promises a worthy treatment of the author as soon as he has the latter's "progeny" in hand.[65] Martin was deeply incensed to find that Eck classes him with the Manichaeans, with Huss, Wyclif, and all kinds of heretics. His indignation extends to Bishop Scultetus,

[61] *Ibid.*, pp. 390 ff., ll. 25 f., 90 f., 104 ff., and 145 f.

[62] See Enders, *Luthers Briefwechsel*, II, 44 f., n. 26, for the inscriptions, still legible in the seventeenth century. Luther interprets these as establishing papal authority by human law.

[63] Wiedemann, *Dr. Johann Eck*, p. 508, and n. 5. The arrival of Joachim, elector of Brandenburg, had brought the Leipzig disputation to a close. The prince summoned Eck and had an account of the disputation from him. Scultetus was traveling with the elector.

[64] Eck's dedication to Leonard von Eck, quoted by Wiedemann, *ibid.*, p. 508 and n. 6.

[65] Enders, *Luthers Briefwechsel*, II, 119.

who had hitherto shown himself friendly and tactful and now without giving Martin a hearing, lends authority to Eck's lies.[66] Although the pamphlet in answer to Eck's memorandum is silent regarding the part played in the affair by Scultetus, Luther did not restrain his feeling of resentment in private letters. Evidently hostile talebearers had been at work, for Martin heard that the bishop said he would not be able to rest till he had thrown Luther like a firebrand into the fire, and he complains bitterly to Staupitz. The man's arrogance is to no avail, like Moab's (Isaiah 16.6), Luther states. After all, he is only a wretched bladder blown up by Eck's wind.[67] The tense atmosphere was filled with other rumors, too, which did nothing to soothe Martin's combative mood. He hears that the Franciscans have been saying at a convention of their order that he has preached against the stigmata of St. Francis. He himself professes to be indifferent to the fact that they even go so far as to invent charges against him, but regrets that their ignorance is making their whole profession ridiculous. In this mood his answer to Eck is written and forwarded to Leipzig for publication. Before it was issued, however, the provincial head of the Franciscan order heard of it and sent a deputation of brothers to Wittenberg asking for peace. Luther was evidently touched by their plea and agreed that if they would indemnify the printer for his costs he was willing to "pass a sponge over" the book.[68] But intervention had come too late, and a week later Martin sent a copy of the printed pamphlet to Günther in Jüterbog.[69]

In this pamphlet, *Defense against the Malicious Indictment of Eck*,[70] Martin lets off easily the authors of the original controversy. He has even forgotten his bitter communication of the preceding May, and declares that he sent only a friendly warning to the Franciscan convent and invited them to come to Wittenberg and dispute and defend their errors. It is against Eck that his reply is now directed for seizing this opportunity of attacking him behind his back. He contrasts his own method of argument with that of his opponent, who adduces self-contradictory things "merely in order to spit out the great store of saliva that he has collected." [71] He then takes up the fifteen articles in which Eck had set forth his heresy. Martin's denials and declarations cover familiar ground and seek to define precisely his position. He has not refused to accept the councils of the

[66] Letter from Luther to Spalatin, Aug. 18, *WAB*, I, 503, ll. 23 ff.
[67] Letter from Luther to Staupitz, Oct. 3, *WAB*, I, 514, ll. 44 ff.
[68] Letter from Luther to Spalatin, Sept. 22, *WAB*, I, 509, ll. 28 ff.
[69] Letter to Günther, Sept. 30, *WAB*, I, 511.
[70] *WA*, II, 625 ff.   [71] *Ibid.*, p. 626, ll. 28 f.

Church, but has said that some councils have erred. He has not denied that the pope is Christ's vicar, but holds that the papal office is based on human law alone. Against the papal claims of spiritual succession to the Apostle Peter he alleges the unspiritual character of papal acts. Eck has argued for the primacy of Peter and Peter's successors by citing Christ's command to the Apostle to "confirm" his brethren. Whoever is to fullfill this duty, returns Luther, must be first converted and have an indestructible faith. "It follows therefore that either the pope must have faith and exercise the office of encouraging [the faithful] or he can have no profit whatever from these words [to Peter] and can not be regarded as Peter's successor. But where will the popes then be, since now for many years they have not encouraged the brethren but, themselves devoid of faith and voice, have only wrought destruction with their thunderbolts and eaten up the substance of the brethren with wars, penalties, and condemnations, worse than tyrants."[72] Luther reinterprets the passage in Luke (22.32) and shows Eck, the "despiser of grammar," that Peter received this office to strengthen the brethren not as a mere honor but as a duty, and only in case he has unflinching faith. Here and there the old technique of the monkish disputant comes to the fore. Eck's arguments are far-fetched and Luther's reply, though picturesque in language, moves on the same level of scholastic quibbling, seeking to pile up as many rejoinders as possible, with a dialectical pettifogging that is empty of results.[73] On the other hand, when he shakes off the scholastic yoke a tone of genuine eloquence rings through the long arraignment of Eck for defending the power of the successor of Peter and saying nothing about the spiritual duty which Christ laid on the apostle, "assuredly the heaviest and most dangerous, that of teaching the word and of dying for souls."[74]

Important as a herald of the ideas which were to appear a year later in the *Address to the Christian Nobility* is Martin's declaration regarding the canon law. Four years earlier in his lectures on Romans he had called attention to the abuse of this code which set the clergy apart from other men. Now he denies that canon law has any basis in divine law. If it is

[72] *Ibid.*, p. 632, ll. 21 ff.

[73] See Luther's arguments in rebuttal, that the popes as successors of Peter should pay tribute to the temporal princes, *ibid.*, p. 633, or the discussion of St. Bernard's figurative interpretation of Peter's walking on the water, *ibid.*, p. 634. Barge, *Andreas Bodenstein*, I, 168 f., has called attention to a similar, although much more pronounced tendency to wander in the arid field of dialectics in Carlstadt's pamphlet written in the same period, *Epistola adversus ineptam et ridiculam inventionem Joannis Eckii*. Plainly neither of the Wittenberg theologians had yet brushed off the dust of scholasticism.

[74] *WA*, II, 635, ll. 31 ff.

supposed to establish the discipline of the Church, where was this discipline in the days of Cyprian and the Nicene Council? It is the fault of the Roman tyrants that canon law and reserved cases are nothing more than snares of greed. When money is given, then canon law and everything else is for sale.[75]

Important further for the revolutionary works of the following year is the statement about confession. Secret confession is not of divine institution, only public confession. "Nevertheless I do not condemn that secret confession, but I do lament that it is turned into a torment, so that people are forced to confess and make scruples out of things in which there is no sin, not even a venial sin." [76] The priests are wrong, he feels, in inflicting torture of conscience by their lists of sins for confession (*confessionalia*), "with their descendants, offspring, species, and kinds of sins," when only the conscience should be consulted in these matters. Nothing in the Church needs reform as much as the trade in confession and penance, for here laws, force, tyranny, and error rage most violently. Of these things the popes take too little heed, but leave them to the "sophists and tormentors of souls." [77]

Assured that he has cleared himself of Eck's fifteen allegations of heresy, Martin draws up twenty-four of his own against his opponent. These he deduces from Eck's statements and brands them as "pestilential and blasphemous." Eck, the heretic hunter, is guilty of holding that the most sacred councils of ecclesiastical history were heretical in their acts, the Church Fathers heretics, and the pope, the whole clerical world, and the Church Universal all heretic except Eck and his brothers alone. Some day, he warns, his opponent is going to arouse the sleeping dog in him and the abuse of his patience will then come to an end.[78] Thus the pamphlet, which began with a reproof of the Franciscans for misrepresenting Luther's ideas, ends with a threat of worse treatment for the arch-accuser who has taken the prosecution out of their hands. Martin finds that no terms are too severe to characterize Eck's arguments and attitude. His superlative stupidity makes Sylvester Prierias and his followers seem learned men; [79] he is a childish theologian; [80] he and his followers are pseudo-prophets,[81] and a "brood of vipers." [82] In spite of these rough words and the dialectical baggage in his arguments, the formulation of Luther's attitude toward the subjects he deems vital is clear and streams forth with a vigor breathing unshakable conviction and unbending purpose.

[75] *Ibid.*, p. 643, ll. 7 f.   [76] *Ibid.*, p. 645, ll. 22 ff.   [77] *Ibid.*, p. 646, ll. 1 ff.
[78] *Ibid.*, p. 654, ll. 34 f.   [79] *Ibid.*, p. 635, ll. 10 ff.
[80] "Bulla theologus." *Ibid.*, p. 644, l. 35. Luther obviously puns on "bulla dignus."
[81] *WA*, II, 651, l. 15.   [82] *Ibid.*, p. 649, l. 19.

As was to be expected, Eck took up the challenge which Luther had thrown down in his pamphlet. His reply, *Answer to the Defamatory Attack of Martin Luther* was issued at Ingolstadt about October 19.[83] The author congratulated himself a little later on having given "magnificent" treatment therein to an "accursed, blasphemous, impious heresy." [84] In nineteen quarto pages he discusses Luther's preface and the charges and countercharges of heresy and seeks to refute the arguments advanced by his opponent. As was his wont, the pugnacious Dominican emphasizes the one brief "little day" which the preparation of this reply demanded of him. The gentle reader must not take amiss his style as being "somewhat too pungent," for in giving the lie direct to heretical articles he has only followed the example of Saints Cyprian, Augustine, and Jerome. The work indeed bristles with epithets like "pseudo-prophet," "sycophant," "filthy monk," and other, even more insulting, terms such as the humanistic age loved to forge together from Latin roots and endings in order to decorate a hated opponent. Luther is assured that if he would go to school to Eck for two years he might become a good theologian. "All know Eck, all know how little malice he bears, but you sweat with hatred, as is indicated by your livid face and unseemly appearance. It is from wickedness that you dare to inflict your hatred so often on me; but because you are crazy and beside yourself, poison must be administered to you until you recover." [85]

Whether Luther saw this pamphlet, which even Eck's apologist, Wiedemann, describes as "rather coarse," is not certain. At all events he seems not to have made a reply to it. About the time it was issued, the *Vindication* which Eck had launched against Martin's letter to Spalatin of August came to Luther's attention [86] and he set to work to uncover the "pretenses" of the man and the Leipzig people for whom he speaks. On November 1 his pamphlet is already in press; a week later he sends a copy to Spalatin and promises a further reply when Eck shall have produced all of his impious hypocrisy.[87]

The answer to Eck, which is cast in the form of a letter to the Ingolstadt enemy,[88] is even more aggressive in tone than the reply two months earlier

---

[83] *Ad criminatricem Martini Luders Vittembergen. offensionem super iudicio iustissimo facto ad articulos quosdam per minoritas de observantia . . . Reverendissimo Episcopo Brandenburgensi oblatos Eckiana responsio.* See Wiedemann, *Dr. Johann Eck*, p. 507, and n. 59 above. It was dedicated to Leonard von Eck, Oct. 19, 1519.

[84] In his pamphlet against Carlstadt, *Contra Martini Ludder obtusum propugnatorem.* . . . Wiedemann, *Dr. Johann Eck*, p. 508, n. 8.

[85] Quoted *ibid.*, p. 509.

[86] Letter from Luther to Spalatin, Nov. 1, 1519, *WAB*, I, 548.

[87] Letter from Luther to Spalatin, Nov. 7, 1519, *WAB*, I, 551.

[88] *Ad Johannem Eccium Martini Lutheri epistola super expurgatione Ecciana. WA*, II, 700 ff.

to Eck's championship of the Franciscans. Gone is the humor which occasionally softened the sarcasm of the earlier stages of the polemic and in its
place we have an invective, direct and personal, against the man who once
pretended friendship but is now following him with constant abuse. Like
the ostrich which tries to conceal itself by putting a twig on its neck, Eck
seeks to appear as a model of humility and love. However, he is no longer
on the Leipzig stage, and Luther is no longer his captive but is now in his
own arena of combat.

Martin is especially incensed that Eck has forgotten that in the midst of
the disputation he admitted the truth of Carlstadt's theses regarding the
sinful nature of the free will before grace appears.[89] Through that admission Carlstadt won the debate, in Martin's opinion. The only path on
which Eck could escape from the dilemma of either admitting his defeat
or returning to Ingolstadt as a confessed Pelagian heretic was by inventing
a new vocabulary which classifies the works of the free will that are done
before grace as not meritorious and yet not sinful: "O accursed is the
day on which I was born, to speak with Jeremiah, that I should behold
such impudent tricks." [90] Henceforth let Eck desist from seeking the truth
in theology and return to his deceiver Aristotle, the most sinful hypocrite
among theologians, "who never was willing to seem to say what he did
say: Here is a master most worthy of you." [91] One thing he begs of him, not
to have anything more to do with Luther. Now it is clear why Eck wished
no notaries: he wanted to publish a decision by his own faction. "Do you
not believe, wretched man that you are, that aside from your Leipzig
supporters and borrowed donkeys (for not all scratch you), there are not those
in the world who know what it is to be a sincere and frank searcher for
truth, among whom these effusions about your sincerity are more noxious
than a stinking cesspool?" [92] He has heard of Eck's letter written during
the disputation to the two Ingolstadt professors, "a foul and filthy epistle," [93]
in which Eck claimed to have brought Carlstadt to an acknowledgment
of the effective activity of free will and regretted that he had allowed the
confused Wittenberg scholar time to prepare a reply during the night.
What would then have happened to Eck, Martin asks, if the disputation

---

[89] *Ibid.*, p. 703. It may be pointed out that Eck's attitude toward the relationship of free
will and grace was no more uncertain than that of other theologians of his time and after.
Even the Council of Trent expressed itself with great reserve on this topic. See Barge, *Andreas
Bodenstein*, I, 159, n. 80. The Wittenberg theologians had developed their own system on
this point to a degree of definiteness which was lacking in contemporary schools of theology.

[90] *WA*, II, 703, ll. 23 ff.   [91] *Ibid.*, p. 704, ll. 25 ff.

[92] ". . . nec enim omnes te scabunt." *Ibid.*, p. 705, ll. 22 ff.

[93] *Ibid.*, p. 706, l. 15.

had been carried out in a way to seek truth alone as Duke George had intended? Finally he summarizes the matter: either Eck must acknowledge that Carlstadt defeated him or he is a convinced Pelagian.[94] "The day is drawing near when it will be clear whether you with your followers through the prince of darkness Aristotle, whom indeed you do not understand, or I have done more to injure the Church. . . . Farewell and may the Lord Jesus make sound your soul in eternity. Amen." [95]

This resounding answer was Luther's final public reply to Eck. In the meantime the militant Dominican was drawing up an answer to his opponent's letter of August 18 to Elector Frederick, in an effort to put his case conclusively before the patron of Luther's university. Frederick seems to have delayed forwarding Luther's letter to Eck, possibly in the hope that the bitter mood of controversy might pass, so that it was not sent until October 12.[96] Evidently the Ingolstadt disputant saw no reason to delay his reply, which was prepared within four weeks.[97] Although he apologizes for the haste in preparation, he sets forth at great length the questions at issue between himself and the Wittenberg scholars, from the "Obelisks" down to the present. He replies in detail to the charges made by his opponents, not even neglecting Luther's criticism of himself and the Leipzig group for circulating the report that Martin carried the devil about with him in a box. Eck denies responsibility for any such remark but calls attention to a little chain and a silver ring which Luther wore at that time and which caused much talk. Here, as elsewhere in the discussion and in the intellectual life of the sixteenth century in general, the petty and burlesque are mixed with the profound and serious. For Eck's letter, although bearing the marks of haste, shows a diligent assembling of material from the Bible, the Christian Fathers, from popes and founders of ecclesiastical orders and bishops, in defense of the primacy of Peter and the authority of the pope. A genuineness of conviction speaks in his plea for the unity of the Church as symbolized in the pope and in his denunciation of Luther's "blasphemous" statements about the Council of Constance. He promises to issue a full and detailed discussion of the primacy of Peter, and he repeats and emphasizes his former suggestion that Luther's book on this matter be publicly burned. Finally he adjures the elector by his responsibility to God to spare no costs in order to have Martin's doctrine judged by scholars and by the provincial synods.[98] Al-

---

[94] *Ibid.*, p. 707, ll. 23 ff.   [95] *Ibid.*, p. 708, ll. 2 ff.
[96] See letter from Frederick to Eck, *WAB*, I, 478.
[97] Dated November 8, 1519. Published in *WAB*, I, 479 ff.
[98] *Ibid.*, p. 500, ll. 770 ff.

though unsparing in condemnation of the arguments of "Brother Ludder," the letter is not marked by personal abuse. It shows, rather, a profound conviction on Eck's part that he has been called to throw himself with all his power against the growth of the Wittenberg heresy.

The theological controversy with Eck became less important for Martin as the former's personal activity against him at Rome and elsewhere grew more threatening. But although his argument with Eck is closed, his resentment against the energetic and relentless opponent flares up again and again in letters of the fall and winter. When he sees Eck's response to the elector he declares: "Such as he was as disputant at Leipzig, so he is as a letter writer. For his whole fury is . . . effective in this one respect: to stir up hate." [99] He is only awaiting Eck's threatened publication concerning the papacy in order to expose his tricks clearly and publicly.[100] From Staupitz he learns of Eck's activities against him in Augsburg. The "sophist" has threatened the elector in such a tone that "you would think that God Almighty was speaking."[101]

In the meantime Eck had taken up the cudgels for Hieronymus Emser, with whom Luther's controversy had begun in the fall.[102] Nevertheless, when Carlstadt, stung by an attack in Eck's pamphlet, *Against Martin Luther's Weak Champion Andreas Rudolf Bodenstein*,[103] prepared immediately to publish a reply to be entitled "Against the Very Stupid Ass and Arrogant Doctorling . . . ," Luther urged Spalatin to restrain his colleague's unreflecting anger.[104] Yet Martin can scarcely contain himself at the im-

[99] Letter from Luther to Spalatin, Dec. 3, 1519, *WAB*, I, 565, ll. 7 ff.

[100] Letter to Spalatin, Dec. 8, *WAB*, I, 570.

[101] Letter to Lang, Dec. 18, 1519, *WAB*, I, 597, ll. 17 ff.

[102] Letter to Spalatin, Dec. 25, 1519, *ibid.*, p. 600.

[103] *Contra Martini Ludder obtusum propugnatorem Andream Rodolphi Bodenstein.* The dedication was signed December 3, 1519. See Wiedemann, *Dr. Joh. Eck*, pp. 512 ff. This was in reply to Carlstadt's *Epistola adversus ineptam et ridiculam inventionem Joannis Eckii*. See Barge, *Andreas Bodenstein*, I, 168.

[104] *Contra brutissimum asinum et assertum doctorculum.* . . . Letter of Feb. 5, 1520, *WAB*, II, 30, ll. 15 f. Carlstadt's polemics against Eck in the months following the disputation are discussed by Barge, *Andreas Bodenstein*, I, 168 ff. A nervous and highly sensitive scholar, Carlstadt lacked the self-control and physical reserves that enabled Luther to carry on an intellectual combat, with violence and vituperation to be sure, but without falling into incoherent abuse. Judging from a remark of Martin's in a letter to Spalatin, Aug. 20, 1519, *WAB*, I, 504 f., his colleague's condition of nerves following the Leipzig disputation was deserving of sympathy. The *Confutatio*, Carlstadt's reply to Eck's pamphlet of December, was modified somewhat in response to Spalatin's intervention, but this answer, published probably in March, remains a real "Schimpflexikon." "Die ganze Schrift Carlstadts setzt sich aus persönlichen Invektiven zusammen." Barge, *Andreas Bodenstein*, I, 178 f. Later the author wrote an apologetic letter to Spalatin. Partly due no doubt to his excited condition, his attitude toward Luther had become distrustful, foreshadowing the divergence which was to come between the colleagues. Letter from Luther to Spalatin, Feb. 5, 1520, *WAB*, II, 30, ll. 22 f.: "ut est homo infirmatus suspicionibus."

pudence and baseness of Eck's attack on his colleague. He tells Spalatin that he has begun to despise the man as he never despised anyone. His anger was fanned by reports from his friend Link about the efforts of his opponent in South Germany to bring him into disrepute and destroy his influence. The suggestion which Eck had made to the elector, to burn Luther's books, the determined theologian now urged on the priors of the convents and sought to carry out himself in Ingolstadt. On New Year's Day, 1520, the stage was set for this typical sixteenth-century drama, and Luther's works together with a pamphlet by Oecolampadius, the reply of the "Ignorant Canons," were piled ready for the torch; but at the last moment the Ingolstadt faculty stepped in, on Reuchlin's advice, as Martin heard, and halted this auto-da-fé. Eck's enemies, of whom he had many both within and without his university, chuckled at his public humiliation.[105]

Particularly the humanists bore Eck a grudge for his intolerance and violence. One of this group, the Nuremberg patrician Willibald Pirckheimer, a friend of Martin's, launched in February an anonymous satire against him entitled *The Purified Eck*.[106] The pamphlet is a clever one, surpassing most of the humanistic satires of the period in its adroitness and the thinness of the allegorical costume in which it drapes its attack on the hated defender of scholastic ideas. In spite of his feelings against his implacable opponent, Martin could not approve of this method of exposing him. For him the whole question had a deadly earnestness that demanded an open confutation and refutation of the errors which Eck represented. For he was well informed that while the Nuremberg and Augsburg humanists were amusing themselves with skits like this, his determined

---

[105] Letter from Luther to Spalatin, Feb. 8, 1520, *WAB*, II, 36, ll. 6 ff. See also the description of the affair by a hostile humanist, Thomas Venatorius, to Willibald Pirckheimer, Jan. 7, 1520. In *Bilibaldi Pirckheimeri. . . . Opera*, ed. by M. Goldast, p. 332.

[106] *Eccius Dedolatus Autore Joanne francisco Cotta Lembergio, Poeta Laureato*, which appeared in Bonn, Dresden, Strasbourg, and elsewhere, is one of the most famous antischolastic pamphlets of that time. A critical edition by Max Herrmann and Siegfried Szamatolski may be found in *Lateinische Literaturdenkmäler des XV. und XVI. Jahrhunderts*, Vol. II (Berlin, 1891). Here Eck's vices and errors are removed by a surgical operation. In general it is a highly amusing attack on theological narrowness and self-conceit, although the modern reader will find some of the images revolting. It belongs to the same kind of ruthless persiflage as the *Epistolae obscurorum virorum* which had appeared five years earlier. It was published anonymously, but both Luther and Eck recognized Pirckheimer at once as the author. See Wiedemann, *Dr. Johann Eck*, p. 148, n. 11; also letter from Luther to Spalatin, March 2, 1520, *WAB*, II, 59: "Dialogus ingenium olet Bilibaldi, meo iudicio." Recent investigators have questioned Pirckheimer's authorship. Merker, who examined the question at length in *Reformationsdialoge*, came to the conclusion that the author was Nikolaus Gerbel, a well-known humanist of Strasbourg. It must be said, however, that despite the mass of material which Merker assembles, his thesis remains unproven in the face of the opinion of Luther and humanistic intimates of the Nuremberg patrician.

enemy was already in Rome lighting anew the fires of Dominican opposition.[107]

"Behold the fruit of the Leipzig disputation!" [108] With this weary exclamation Martin in February looks back on half a year of polemics, attacks, and counterattacks. The violence of the personal invectives which had flown back and forth between him and Eck was in part no doubt the product of the antipathy which had developed in the hot exchanges in the Pleissenburg, but it was not due to this clash alone. It was rather the costume which an age, accustomed to dress its arguments in vituperation and to color them with personal vindictiveness, draped about a sharp collision of views. It cannot be too strongly emphasized that Luther was concerned not with the man Eck but with his defense of his own sincere beliefs. When he prepared himself for the disputation and when he set forth his arguments from the rostrum and restudied and reformulated them in the following months, he was absolutely convinced that his position was the orthodox and necessary position of every intelligent Christian. Nor can it be doubted that this was likewise the conviction of his friends in the theological faculty at Wittenberg, of Spalatin, and also of Frederick, so far as he was able to follow the discussion. That is why Martin resented so deeply the charge of heresy and continued to resent it.

This was true especially with respect to the relation of the Church to the Roman pontiff. It is not clear how far Martin as a student and young professor of theology had made himself familiar with the struggle which had gone on in the great Church councils of the first half of the preceding century over the supremacy of pope or council.[109] It is certain, however, that in spite of the victory of the curial party and the quiescence of this question in the two generations preceding Martin's entry on theological studies, there were many in Germany, especially among statesmen and lawyers, who held fast to the principle that a general council of the Church was superior to the pope. The Lateran Council, which had expressly confirmed the supremacy of the Curia, had few German representatives and its

[107] Eck departed from Ingolstadt for Rome after February 10. See his letter to Cuspinian on that day: "Iam Romam peto." Hans von Ankwicz, ed., "Zwei unbekannte briefe Johann Ecks an Johann Cuspinian," *Mitteilungen des Instituts für österreichische Geschichtsforschung,* XXXVII (1917), p. 76. According to Kalkoff, Eck was not in the Eternal City before the middle of March. "Zu Luthers römischem Prozess," *ZKG,* XXV, 580, n. 3. On February 26 Luther had news of his journey. See letter from Luther to Spalatin, *WAB,* II, 55, ll. 6 f.

[108] *WAB,* II, 36, l. 23.

[109] For an interesting discussion of the relationship of Luther to the conciliar ideas of the preceding century, especially the possibility of his having been infected with these in Erfurt, see Wendorf, *Martin Luther, der Aufbau seiner Persönlichkeit,* pp. 89 ff.

conclusions were not highly regarded north of the Alps. In view of Martin's attitude at Augsburg when he faced Cajetan, a scholar who was powerfully entrenched in the curialistic position, it is not possible to believe that he was entirely ignorant of the arguments which the theologians and jurists had advanced a century before in defense of the council as the supreme arbiter in matters of faith. As early as August, 1518, in his reply to Sylvester Prierias, Martin, taking issue with the declaration of his Dominican opponent that penalties inflicted by God could be remitted through the authority given to Peter, had declared that the mere act of the Church was not sufficient for him, "because both the pope and the council can err." [110] He states further that he does not recognize the Church in essence (*virtualiter*) save in Christ. As its representative he recognizes only a council, and he calls attention to the monstrous deeds of a Boniface VIII or a Julius II as arguments against the recognition of the pope as "virtually" the Church universal. Arguing with Cajetan, Martin was, as we have seen, in a quandary. Desirous of peace, he found himself facing a representative of ideas respecting the papacy which he believed to be unorthodox. If the sources concerning the discussion are reliable, the stern defender of ultra-curial doctrine drove him at first to a declaration of lack of faith in the papal decrees. Yet on the following day Martin declared that he subjected himself to the "legitimate holy Church," [111] and in his written statement of October 14, while bringing up scriptural evidence against Cajetan's authority, the bull "Unigenitus" of Pope Clement, he nevertheless declared himself ready to submit if the Pope pronounced him in error.[112] He states subsequently that he yielded to the persuasion of friends in this.[113] A month later in the *Acta Augustana* he takes the unambiguous and categorical position that popes and papal decrees can err and laments that there are those who subject everything to the pope. The appeal to the council follows on November 28. He had, in fact, planned it when he went to Augsburg, in the event the legate should try force on him.[114]

Throughout the following spring the belief that the papal power was not of divine origin had become firmly established in his mind by a

[110] "Nec satis ibi esse credo etiam factum ecclesiae . . . quia tam Papa tam concilium potest errare." *WA*, I, 656, ll. 30 ff.

[111] "Nihilominus tamen sum homo potens errare, submisi me et etiam nunc submitto iudicio et determinationi sanctae Ecclesiae et omnibus melius sentientibus." *WA*, II, 9, ll. 1 ff.

[112] To Cajetan, Oct. 14, *ibid.*, p. 12, ll. 33 f. For a well-balanced discussion of Luther's uncertainty at Augsburg on this subject, see Kolde, *Luthers Stellung zu Concil und Kirche*, pp. 32 f.

[113] Letter from Luther to Cajetan, Oct. 18, 1518, *WAB*, I, 223, ll. 39 ff.

[114] Letter to Spalatin, Oct. 10, 1518, *WAB*, I, 210, ll. 59 ff.

study of the historical sources. He knew now that he was advocating a cause which had been defended by a long line of theologians and jurists, and as his opinion took form in his cell he marshalled arguments from Scripture, from the practice of the Church Fathers and the great council of the inspired age, and from the beliefs and usages of the non-Roman Christians into what he held to be an irresistible phalanx of truth with which to attack the pretensions of Rome.

His belief that the papacy grew out of the practical demands of humanity and not from divine institution was fully established when he entered the Leipzig arena. Its formulation then and afterward was no dialectical device, even though the phraseology and the symbols with which he clothed his ideas on this topic grew in definiteness and picturesqueness as he addressed himself again and again to the task of making his views clear to the elector and Eck and to the theological and lay world beyond them. He felt that he represented the opinions of the great majority of intelligent theologians, so far as these were not blinded by subservience to scholastic tradition, and of the great number of intelligent laymen, for whom the ever increasing opportunity for access to the scriptural and other sources of religious knowledge had opened the way to an insight into the basis of their faith and a personal attitude toward questions of Church organization.

Despite his firm convictions it is hard to say whether Martin was aware what the full consequence of his stand on the papacy would be. Eck, Emser, and others had, in effect, appealed to him to uphold the papacy as a symbol of the unity of the Church and a necessary condition to its continued existence. Later in life he showed himself open to such pleas for order and tradition in both Church and state. Why he did not listen to them in this crisis is not easy to determine. No doubt it was in part his sympathy with the growing body of public opinion, lay and theological, that impelled him onward. He himself, in looking back on the struggle over indulgences, felt that he had been driven forward by more irrational forces—the will of God, or the relentless action of his enemies.[115] Something of this sense of inner compulsion probably also derived from the powerful authority with which the scriptural word was clothed for him at this time, an authority arising from the experiences and studies out of which his theological attitude had crystallized at the beginning of 1518.[116]

---

[115] *WA*, I, 649, l. 28; *WA*, VII, 272, ll. 32 ff. See also the examples in *Wider Hans Worst*, *WA*, LI, 469 ff. and *passim*.

[116] At no time, however, had Luther taken the radical position regarding the authority of the Scriptures which we find in Carlstadt's theses against Eck of May, 1518. *Ref. Act.*, II, 80; see also Barge, *Andreas Bodenstein*, I, 119. Here Carlstadt declares (Thesis 12) that the text of the Bible is not only to be preferred to one or several doctors of the Church, but also to

Another set of more tangible experiences was also undoubtedly of great influence in determining his attitude toward the papacy and masking from him the consequences of the course on which he had entered. The discontent over the selfish policy of the Curia that had been voiced at many German national diets and by many German princes and cities had sounded in his ears for a long time and had echoed in the Romans lectures in 1516. The scandal of papal politics under Julius II and now under Leo, the evils of papal nepotism, the greed of the Roman courtiers and their German allies and tools, the strife and the moral disintegration of the clergy which flowed from the canon law—all these were abuses that occupied the minds of intelligent laymen and many churchmen, and were to have forceful expression a year after the Leipzig disputation in Martin's *Address to the Christian Nobility*. They must have blocked the path to any appeal to abandon for the sake of unity and order his theological and historical position respecting the papacy, and they certainly armed his attacks with virulent force.

The position which he took at Leipzig respecting the divine right of the pope was therefore attained as the result of a long and organic development. This was not true, however, of his statements regarding the authority of the council and the right of the Church as composed of individual Christians. The struggle against Eck brought more clarity in his ideas as to the basis of faith. In his *Explanation of the Thirteenth Thesis* Martin had set up the Church universal against the claims of the Roman Church to be the representative of Christ, the Church universal, which exists wherever God's word is preached and believed: "Wherever faith is, there is the Church." [117] Whither this conception was shortly to lead him he could not have been aware when he entered the Leipzig arena, but his position became clearer under Eck's fire. This drove him to the declaration that one must accept the decision of a council in matters of faith, even though a council

---

the authority of the whole Church, and he goes on to say (Thesis 14) that the dictum of a single scholar supported by canonical authority is to be believed in preference to a papal declaration. In comparison with this radical position Luther's views regarding the Scriptures as the final authority in matters of debate developed slowly and seem to have kept pace with his studies of the sources of papal power. The belief in the ultimate authority of Scripture is expressed with some reserve in the letter to Cajetan: "Decretales Romani Pontificis tanquam vocem Petri oportet audire, ut dicitur dist. XIX, tamen hoc ipsum intelligitur de hiis solum [ut dicitur ibidem], quae consonae sunt sacrae Scripturae." *WA*, II, 10, ll. 8 ff. It appears more clearly in the defense of his position in a letter to Hieronymus Dungersheim. *WAB*, I, 601 f., ll. 32 ff.

[117] "Quare ubicunque praedicatur verbum dei et creditur, ibi est vera fides, petra ista immobilis: ubi autem fides, ibi ecclesia; ubi ecclesia, ibi sponsa Christi; ubi sponsa Christi, ibi omnia quae sunt sponsi." *WA*, II, 208, ll. 25 ff.

can err and has erred, more especially in matters that do not belong to faith.[118] The general thesis that a council can err Martin had begun to put forward a year previously and had repeated. This might have passed, but when Eck drove him to the admission that the Council of Constance had erred in a specific case, that of four articles of Huss, Martin made himself guilty of categorical heresy, as was generally recognized by his hearers. We have seen the strenuous efforts he made to free himself from the charge and set his position clear. For the first time he seems to have recognized the point to which his studies and thinking had led him.

In the months that followed Martin concentrated his attacks on Eck about the question of grace and free will and the primacy of the pope. Nevertheless the question of conciliar authority was one which he could not overlook, even had his opponents permitted him to do so. He admits to Spalatin his statements regarding the Council of Constance,[119] but a month later in his *Explanations* he asserts his faith in this council, although he shows its errors and affirms and reaffirms the superiority of the Nicene Council. In a work of late September, 1519, it is the Scriptures which are the final arbiter.[120]

Plainly Martin's ideas regarding the ultimate source of Christian faith and authority on earth were still in process of growth. But the great disputation which crystallized his ideas regarding the papal claims had also given them a mighty impulse in the direction of independence with regard to Church authority over the individual Christian. This development was to be furthered and accelerated in the following months by the storms of other polemical struggles and a new attack from Rome.

---

[118] He adds, however, that a council cannot set up new articles of faith. That there is a contradiction here with the preceding statement is pointed out by Kolde, *Luthers Stellung zu Concil und Kirche,* pp. 49 f. That the keen ears of Eck did not catch this and exploit it was probably due to self-satisfaction at having just brought Luther to a heretical declaration.

[119] Letter of July 20, *WAB,* I, 422, ll. 70 ff.

[120] "Non potestas Papae aut alicuius Episcopi in Ecclesia dominatur, sed verbum dei." *Ad aegocerotem Emserianum M. Lutheri additio. WA,* II, 676, ll. 34 ff.

21

A BATTLE OF POLEMICS

THE year 1519 had opened on a note of reconciliation. After casting down the glove of defiance to the papal party and the defenders of indulgences in the *Acta Augustana,* Martin had listened to the pleas of Miltitz and for the moment seems to have believed that a way might be found to reconcile his views with obedience to Rome. But this belief, if it really guided his pen at Altenburg, faded as soon as he learned that Eck's attack on Carlstadt was actually launched against himself; and with the passing of the early spring his blood surged ever more hotly against the aggressive opponent and the claims of the Roman party. Theological ideas had always taken a concrete personality in his mind; again and again in his life he strove with theological error in corporeal form as with the Archfiend himself. His bitterness toward Aristotle and Thomas and Scotus and other authorities of the scholastic theology in which he had been trained burns in his letters and writings with the naïve fury of a combatant who looks into the eyes of a tricky and hated enemy. How much more hotly must this rage have flamed when he heard what he believed to be error defended by the mouth of an opponent or read the written and printed attacks of living men on positions which he held as sacred. The vigorous eloquence and unrestrained tone of his polemics against Eck and the Franciscans are outbreaks of a powerful will enforced by a profoundly emotional temperament. The flame of resentment spread to include all of those who placed themselves across the path of his ideas. As time went by theological opponents who at first resisted these ideas without acrimony became infected with the spirit of violence, so easily transmitted in a century of ardent polemics, and gave back his attacks with equal venom, though without Martin's elemental force and picturesque naturalness of style. Even when, as in the collision with Cajetan, a prudent regard for the welfare of his university and the opinion of his prince held him back from a public expression of his bitterness, Martin laid no restraint on his pen when writing to his *alter ego,* Spalatin, or to his old comrade of

Erfurt days, Johann Lang. It is not surprising, then, that especially after the Leipzig disputation, fresh opponents arose armed with increasingly virulent pens.

As might be expected, the Leipzig faculty led the way in theological attack. The combat was opened by its most learned scholar, Hieronymus Dungersheim,[1] and began as a gentle postlude to the disputation. Born at Ochsenfurt in Franconia nearly two decades before Luther, Dungersheim passed through the various academic grades at Leipzig and received his early theological training at Cologne, returning to the Saxon university to lecture on the *Sentences* of Lombard and to pursue a life of productive scholarship as interpreter of Lombard and Thomas. He had been the Leipzig representative at the inauguration of the new university at Wittenberg and the dedication of the Augustinian church there by the papal legate, Cardinal Perault. His scholarship was stimulated by travels and studies in Italy, where the university at Siena made him a doctor of theology. His colleagues and Duke George evidently held him in high regard, delegating him on several occasions to represent the university at episcopal celebrations in central Germany. His success as a teacher of theology is attested by three reprints of his *Epithemata,* an introduction to Lombard's great work on dogmatics. As a preacher he filled important pulpits in Saxon lands.[2]

Whether Martin had crossed the path of this well-equipped scholar before the Leipzig disputation is not certain, but there is evidence that he counted him among his opponents as the debate drew near. In a letter to Lang on April 13 denouncing the jealous theologians who were stirring up feeling against him he marks out for especial attack "that bull, ox, and ass," probably a play on Dungersheim's birthplace, Ochsenfurt.[3] When repercussions of the disputation had become most acute, perhaps early in October, Martin received a long-drawn argument from the learned theologian directed against statements of his concerning papal supremacy.[4] Martin's statements

---

[1] The facts regarding Dungersheim have been brought together by Seidemann in the *Allgemeine Deutsche Biographie,* V, 473 f., and by Streber in the *Kirchenlexikon,* IV, 14 ff. The *Catholic Encyclopedia* does not give him a special article.

[2] Dungersheim's persistent defense of the old Church made him an unpopular figure with Luther's followers, and they seem to have played up a local tradition that he was a miser; at least Michael Lindener satirizes him for this in his "Katzipori," *Bibliothek des Litterarischen Vereins in Stuttgart,* CLXIII, 97 f.

[3] *WAB,* I, 369, ll. 43 f.

[4] *WAB,* I, 518 ff. Dungersheim's letters, first published in 1531, are without dates. Enders sets the first on January 18, 1519. In his "Bemerkungen zum Briefwechsel der Reformatoren," *ThStKr,* LXXIII (1900), 268 ff., Joachim Knaake argues for October 7 and revises the chronology of the interchanges quite radically. His arrangement has been accepted by Clemen and I follow it in the main, although quite aware that uncertainties exist.

were based on the attitude of the Nicene Council, and documented by quotations from the church history of Eusebius of Caesarea in the Latin translation by Rufinus. Dungersheim calls this an untrustworthy source, and after this methodological refutation proceeds to array a long series of authorities, from the Fathers of the Nicene Council and St. Athanasius down through the two centuries that followed, all in support of the apostolic authority of the papacy. He asks an answer by bearer and Martin apparently lets him have it.[5] It is courteous though crisp in tone and brief in content. It congratulates the distinguished scholar on the diligence with which he has scraped together so many arguments from works which Martin knew very well already. It is probable, the writer believes, that Eck will bring forward precisely these as well as additional arguments; and inasmuch as Martin is preparing to reply to him in detail, he begs that the forthcoming answer to Eck may serve for both critics. He does, however, anticipate something of his future rebuttal with a dialectical refutation: since the papal decretals admitted certain statements regarding the Nicene Council which Dungersheim also does not reject, either the authority claimed by the pontiffs is not divine or they and the Fathers of the Council have been themselves guilty of heresy. But, he adds, this countering of argument with argument is not the real foundation for his position, which rests on the words of the Gospel.

Dungersheim had no intention of awaiting the issue of Luther's controversy with Eck, but returned promptly to the attack with a long and learned epistle.[6] The pedantic scholar was in his element, and he entered on a discussion of the sources of the Nicene Council with gusto. Now that he has fully warmed to the task of exposing the errors of the Wittenberg colleague, he chides him for his exegesis of a passage in St. Paul's letter to the Philippians (2.5 f.), in his *Sermon on Twofold Righteousness* of the preceding winter.[7] Here he overwhelms Martin with a flood of quotations from patristic and other sources ranging from Chrysostom to Bernard of Clairvaux. Again he begs for a reply by bearer, promising then an even more extended discussion of the subjects at issue. Again Luther sends him a prompt response.[8] He is awaiting Eck's attack and must be concise, and he formulates his position respecting the pope in a few words. He acknowledges the supremacy of the Roman pontiff and the dignity and honor which are due him, but he is unwilling to admit that a bishop may not exist or

[5] *WAB*, I, 567. Clemen dates Luther's letter early in December, 1519, on very unconvincing grounds.

[6] *WAB*, I, 574 ff. The date is again uncertain, possibly before the end of October.

[7] *WA*, II, 143 ff. Probably printed in 1519, though attributed to 1518. See *ibid.*, p. 141.

[8] *WAB*, I, 601 ff. Again the date is uncertain, possibly in November, 1519.

anything be done in the Church without the pope's authority. To ascribe divine authority to him would be to make heretics of the most sacred Fathers from Jerome to Gregory and of all the bishops of the Eastern Church. Furthermore, no Scripture can be alleged in support of the Roman power, and it is Scripture which must be examined, not the interpretation of the Fathers, who intended only to point us to Scripture itself. Like Augustine and Bernard, he is himself trying to follow the brooks of inspiration to their sources. So far as his interpretation of the Philippian passage is concerned, he is giving it according to Erasmus's text independently, with no fear of sinning because he deviates from the Fathers. It is just this kind of effort to make all exegesis agree, Martin declares, that befuddles instructors in dogmatics. What theologians need in the conflict with Satan is just plain common sense.

The Leipzig theologian was not discouraged by the brevity of Luther's trenchant replies, but responded a month later with a third letter almost as long as his second.[9] In a serious tone he takes Martin to task for his freedom of speech regarding the pope, and for the concern which he has expressed lest the Church by its quibbling debates deprive itself of arms in the combat with heresy. Saint Augustine has shown the way to deal with heretics. Against those who will not listen to arguments and insist on spreading error the temporal arm is to be invoked. Quite clearly and with great dignity the earnest theologian sets forth his position on the relation of the Fathers to the Scriptures. He can find no conflict. The Fathers are to be used because under the guidance of God they interpret the Scriptures in a Catholic sense. It is not a question of twisting Scripture to agree with the Fathers or of twisting them to conform with one's own ideas. There has never been a heretic who did not claim to have the Scriptures on his side.

In this letter Dungersheim rises above the pedantry of his earlier efforts to something like the dignity of a defender of the faith. Plainly he understands Luther's position, and his knowledge of the history of the Church supplies him with enough examples to show whither the course of the Wittenberg professor must lead unless it is resisted. His statement of the position of the Church with respect to the importance of tradition lends support to a remark of Ludwig von Pastor that the debates engendered by Luther's attacks led those theological scholars who remained in the Catholic

---

[9] *WAB*, II, 2 ff. Knaake, "Bemerkungen zum Briefwechsel der Reformatoren," dates it about the middle of January.

faith to a clarification of doctrinal points in their own minds and opened the way for the doctrinal formulas of the Council of Trent.[10]

Arguments like those of Dungersheim made no impression on Martin. He was firmly convinced that the heretics were to be found in the opposite camp, and this conviction was growing day by day as he armed for the contest with Rome. He could only feel that Dungersheim's long letter was an intrusion on time which was needed for a much more serious cause. He responds with but a few words of acknowledgment to the "very learned doctor" and promises a further answer to his letter, "nay, rather a volume!" [11]

Dungersheim was eager to continue the debate and looked forward impatiently to a full-length reply. When none came after several weeks of waiting, he sent Martin a verbal reminder and followed it with an urgent letter.[12] Again Martin's answer was brief.[13] He has far more to do than his opponent, and an understanding between them is hopeless since his correspondent rests his faith on the authority of the Fathers whom Martin can not accept save with the concurrence of Scripture. "It is enough if the Sacred Fathers are defended from the charge of heresy; from error and a violent distortion of Scripture no one can or ought to defend them." The inevitable reply came a few weeks later, for Dungersheim was in deadly earnest and in accord with the polemical convention, he could not permit his opponent to have the last word.[14] The letter brought nothing new. In a serious though kindly tone the middle-aged theologian marshals a host of authorities to combat Luther's interpretation of the passage in Philippians and his position regarding the pope. Luther now considered it best to end the exchanges. It was June, and the storm of Roman anger had grown black on the horizon, but he felt it necessary to make a full restatement of his attitude toward the authority of Scripture and the Fathers.[15] He formulates his views in short sentences which no one can fail to understand. His opponent is ever crying, "Church, Church, heretics, heretics!" and is not willing to try all things, as the Apostle commands. He points out that Dungersheim insists on misunderstanding his words, something which may be a part of the Leipzig attitude of mind. He has, he admits, shown Dungersheim's letters to others and he is quite willing that his opponent

---

[10] "Theologie und Philologie bei den Katholiken," in Johannes Janssen, *Geschichte des deutschen Volkes seit dem Ausgang des Mittelalters*, VII, 536 f.

[11] *WAB*, II, 23.   [12] Possibly late in May, 1520. *WAB*, II, 112.

[13] *WAB*, II, 113.

[14] Enders prints the entire letter. *Luthers Briefwechsel*, II, 141 ff.

[15] *WAB*, II, 125 ff. Clemen, the editor, dates the letter mid-June, 1520.

should retaliate. But he urges him to reflect how much the Wittenbergers are suffering from his party and warns him not to carry the matter too far if he wishes to avoid strife. Through the letters runs a tone of bitter resignation. He feels that the teeth of the ravening wolves are all directed against him. Finally he suggests that Dungersheim desist from writing to him further about this matter: "I understand your opinions sufficiently; make an effort to understand mine."

Apparently this warning did not halt the tireless opponent. With considerable sharpness he accepts Luther's invitation to publish his views.[16] These took the form of a dialogue between the two correspondents in which the various points in Luther's last letter appear with responses from Dungersheim's arsenal of argument.[17] Like the other letters from both sides, this dialogue did not see the light of publicity until 1531,[18] when Luther had long since passed the stage of controversy with representatives of the old Church on points of dogma.

Martin's replies to the aggressive theologian were marked by a restraint that reflected Dungersheim's tone of dignity. At the same time letters to his friends show resentment at these attacks from the rival faculty. This was deepened when another blast came from the same direction. Its author, Augustin von Alfeld, to whom we shall refer again in a later chapter, was a lector in the Franciscan cloister at Leipzig and the first member of that order to enter the lists publicly against the Wittenberg heretic.[19] Early in April he sent Martin a note of defiance and followed this a month later with a pamphlet in defense of the apostolic rights of the papacy.[20] When this came to the attention of Martin, who had slight respect for Franciscan learning, as we have seen, he was convinced that the new antagonist was only a straw man for the "ox," Dungersheim. Under this impression he delegated others to make reply.[21]

---

[16] Enders, *Luthers Briefwechsel,* II, 166 f. The date of the dialogue is uncertain, but it is probably in May of 1520.

[17] For Dungersheim's side of the dialogue see *ibid.,* II, 168 ff.

[18] In *Aliqua opuscula magistri Hieronimi Dungersheym . . . contra Martinum Lutherum edita* (Leipzig, 1531). Enders, *Luthers Briefwechsel,* I, 355 ff.

[19] See Leonhard Lemmens, "Zur Biographie des P. Augustin von Alfeld," *Franziskanische Studien,* V, 131 ff.; also "Pater Augustin von Alfeld," *Erläuterungen und Ergänzungen zu Janssens Geschichte des deutschen Volkes,* Vol. I, Part IV. Alfeld's writings, of which Lemmens cites fifteen titles, are important for their polemical sincerity and popular appeal rather than for scholastic learning. Linguistically his German *Flugschriften* have considerable value. See his *Wyder den wittenbergischen Abgot Martin Luther* and *Erklärung des Salve Regina,* in *Corp. Cath.,* Vol. XI.

[20] *Super apostolica Sede an videlicet divino sit jure nec ne . . . Declaratio.* Leipzig, 1520.

[21] Letter from Luther to Spalatin, May 5, 1520, *WAB,* II, 98, ll. 8 ff. See also Lemmens, "Pater Augustin von Alfeld," p. 8.

The controversy with Dungersheim had been carried on with a show of friendliness to the end, although at last Luther's temper became brittle under the persistent repetition of arguments by his opponent which he considered already disposed of. Toward another Saxon scholar, Hieronymus Emser, he showed an animosity that equaled if it did not exceed that which pointed his attacks on Eck. The acquaintance with Emser dated back to a personal contact of Martin's student years. Half a dozen years Luther's senior, Emser came from a good family of the Ulm neighborhood and began his studies in the Swabian university of Tübingen, then in the earliest stage of its development.[22] He received his two academic degrees at Basel [23] and soon afterward became attached to the papal legate Raymond Perault, in whose train he traveled widely in Germany, probably taking orders during this period.[24] In 1504 he lectured for a few months at the University of Erfurt on the Latin drama *Sergius* by the famous humanist Reuchlin, and, as we have stated, claimed to have had Luther among his hearers.[25] His contacts in Italy and South Germany had inoculated him with humanistic enthusiasms and he lectured on humanistic topics at Leipzig; here he continued his studies and received his bachelor of theology.[26] His knowledge of Greek and Latin was considerable and, like other young humanists of the age, he looked to Erasmus as leader, developing a facility in Latin which was marked even in a day when every young student could reel off pseudo-classical verses.

Abilities like these, joined to publicistic energy,[27] were much sought after

[22] See Gustav Kawerau, "Hieronymus Emser. Ein Lebensbild aus der Reformationsgeschichte," *SVRG*, LXI (1898), 1 ff.; Franz X. Thurnhofer, "Hieronymus Emser," *Corp. Cath.*, IV (1921), 9 ff. Some obscurity veils Emser's birth and parentage. It is, however, probable that he was born in the village of Weidenstetten (see *ibid.*, p. 9, n. 4) on March 26, 1478, the son of Johannes Emser, who at the beginning of the following century was chancellor of a Benedictine monastery in Augsburg.

[23] As a student at Basel, Emser's humanistic cleverness got him into trouble with the city authorities. A Latin epigram sharply critical of the Swiss fell into the hands of the local councilors and aroused the ire of those worthies, who showed themselves as unable to take a joke as the officials of another Swiss canton three centuries later, when another young Swabian, Friedrich Schiller, was disciplined for a slurring remark in his *Die Räuber*. Emser's offense was reported to the representatives of the Swiss confederation and there was talk of cutting off his head. Finally, however, he was permitted to leave Basel after three months' imprisonment and a solemn recantation. *Ibid.*, p. 10, and Kawerau, "Hieronymus Emser," pp. 3 f.

[24] *Ibid.*, pp. 4 f.; Thurnhofer, "Hieronymus Emser," p. 10.

[25] "Acten," VIII, II, 235. See also Ludwig Enders, "Luther und Emser. Ihre Streitschriften aus dem Jahre 1521," *Neudrucke deutscher Literaturwerke des XVI. und XVII. Jahrhunderts*, II, 179.

[26] See Kawerau, "Hieronymus Emser," p. 10.

[27] For a list of Emser's works, see Mosen, *Emser, der Vorkämpfer Roms gegen die Reformation*, Anhang, pp. 59 ff. In the style of the humanists he was active chiefly as editor and translator, his own compositions consisting of verses introducing his text. Among his

by princes of the humanistic period, and on Perault's recommendation Duke George took the young cleric into his service.[28] For six years Emser employed his pen and diplomacy as secretary of the duke, mainly in seeking to effect the canonization of Benno, bishop of Meissen in the eleventh century. Missions connected with this took him through Saxony, Bohemia, and as far as Rome. His efforts were not successful, but he won the favor of the duke and was rewarded with prebends in Dresden and Meissen. He was now free to spend his time in cultivating scholarship and literature. The power of the man lay plainly in his unflagging industry and in facility with his pen rather than in sound scholarship, of which his work gives little evidence. In one respect he merits comparison with Luther. Unlike most humanistic contemporaries, he turned readily to the use of German, and before he crossed swords with Luther he had employed the vernacular in a satire, a version of his Latin life of Benno, and an essay on Plutarch. In the years of controversy following the Leipzig disputation he showed full recognition of the importance of putting his arguments before readers ignorant of Latin. His contribution to the popularization of the Saxon usages as the norms of German speech are, next to Luther's, the most important in the decade that saw the spread of German as a vehicle for serious and scholarly discussion, and his translation of the New Testament, although it leans heavily on Luther's, is certainly not without original elements and characteristics of style far removed from the pedantry of his humanistic contemporaries.

The early relations between Emser and Luther seem to have been friendly. It is possible that brief contacts of Luther's student days had been followed by others for which documentary evidence is lacking. When Martin preached in the court church in Dresden on July 25, 1518, his former tutor invited him to his house. It will be recalled that Luther's sermon on this occasion was sharply criticized, and that the social gathering at Emser's developed into a heated argument between Martin and other guests.[29] It is probable that Martin's sermon on the ban was one of the subjects discussed, and Emser seems to refer to this occasion three years later when he quotes Luther as saying that the pope's ban meant nothing to him: he had already made up his mind to die in it.[30] Emser himself appears to have taken no part in the violent scene and later apologized to Martin for the bad ending

---

productions was an edition of Erasmus's *Manual of a Christian Soldier* and a Latin life of Bishop Benno (1512), introduced by a description of Meissen which has some historical value. *Ibid.*, p. 61.

[28] Gess, *Briefe und Akten,* I, 23, n. 3. [29] See above, pp. 275 f.

[30] Enders, "Luther und Emser," II, 32.

of the party,[31] but he asserted afterwards that before Martin left Dresden he reasoned with him, urging him to speak with more discretion to the folk of lesser understanding lest he should deprive them of all religion and make unbelievers of the Germans.[32] When the disputants at Leipzig met to arrange the conditions Emser seems to have played an active rôle in these preliminaries. According to his statement two years later he took occasion at that time to warn Martin again solemnly to "spare the poor people, who are distressed by this," and he declares that Luther retorted, "The devil take it! The affair was not begun on God's account, neither shall it end on God's account!" [33]—a reply which moved Emser deeply and which he did not forget. Throughout the disputation he was in steady attendance, and noted with anxiety Martin's statement concerning the orthodoxy of certain articles of Huss, fearing that this would defeat negotiations then in progress with the Bohemians, which were to bring these "lost sheep" back to Mother Church.[34] He found Luther's manner of speaking during the disputation "haughty and proud, bold and presumptuous," [35] and it is not surprising that at the conclusion of the debate he regarded Eck as the victor.[36]

Especially Luther's reference to the Bohemians stuck in Emser's mind. He feared that the orthodox Christians in Bohemia might misinterpret these statements, and this feeling of anxiety increased when he heard that the Bohemians were offering public prayers for Luther's success in the debate.[37] Accordingly on August 13 he addressed to Provost Johann Zak of Leitmeritz, a prominent Bohemian churchman, a letter in which he sought to clear Luther of the imputation of Hussite views. Publicity was obviously Emser's intent. The letter appeared at once in print and was widely distributed.[38] It is ostensibly both an apology for Martin and a defense of the orthodox position against the Bohemian heretics. After congratulating Zak on his courageous struggle against the Hussites, Emser points out that these erring ones are not to rejoice in Martin as a patron of theirs, because he explicitly condemned their defection from the Church and their opposition to the pope. Luther's assertion that no one has sought to convert these heretics by argument was clearly disproved by Eck. Martin also declared that certain of the articles of Huss which were true were condemned by

---

[31] Letter from Luther to Spalatin, Jan. 14, 1519, *WAB*, I, 302, ll. 35 f.

[32] Enders, "Luther und Emser," II, 5.

[33] "Da schlag der teuffel tzu, Die sach ist umb Gotes willen nith angefangen; sol ouch umb Gotes willen nith auff horen." *Ibid.;* see also p. iii.

[34] *Ibid.*, I, 134.   [35] *Ibid.*, II, 30.   [36] *Ibid.*, p. 31.

[37] *De disputatione Lipsicensi*, ed. by F. X. Thurnhofer, in *Corp. Cath.*, IV, 32 ff.

[38] *Ibid.*, pp. 15 f.

the Council of Constance, but after all, that was the manner of heretics, to mix up the true and the false. As to the assertion that the papacy is of human origin, that is still to be judged, and Martin will not be so obstinate as to refuse to yield when he hears better arguments, for he admitted that the rule of the pope is necessary. Emser then adds reasons of his own in support of papal authority. In its flowing style the letter is a characteristic humanistic production, padded with references to classical mythology and decorations from Cicero, Horace, Vergil and other classical writers, and concluding with an ode in Sapphic meter in praise of reconciliation through divine mildness.

In spite of these humanistic flourishes, the letter is entirely serious in purpose. The Dresden canon was by no means blind to flaws in the Church. Two years later he makes formal admission of the greed and shamelessness of the indulgence preachers and draws a realistic picture of the sad condition of the temporal and spiritual world,[39] where the fear of God and the love of the brethren are so completely extinguished that it has "never been worse with any people, Jews, heathen, Turks, or Tartars, so that if things are not changed by a new and thorough reformation, the Day of Judgment must come necessarily." [40] But if Emser approved of Martin's first attacks on indulgences, he soon became highly nervous over his outspoken criticisms of the Church, and the ambiguity of his references to Luther in the letter to Zak shows disapproval of Martin's cause and an uncertainty as to his orthodoxy. He does, to be sure, praise him as a man of rare erudition and doctrine,[41] but his references to Eck are more flattering and more decided in tone. The reader cannot avoid the impression that the main purpose of the letter was to force Luther to a categorical abjuration of the Bohemian heretics and their views.[42]

Emser's letter was dated August 13. It must have come to Martin's attention at a time when, having finished his *Explanations* of the Leipzig disputation, he was at work on his reply to Eck's defense of the Franciscans of Jüterbog. He was, therefore, in no mood to brook new criticism of his

---

[39] Enders, "Luther und Emser," I, 57. He credits these evils, however, to the "greedy commissioners, monks and priests," and absolves the pope from blame.

[40] *Ibid.*, pp. 17 f. It must be noted, of course, that this was written in 1521, after Luther's severe arraignment of the preceding year.

[41] Thurnhofer, ed., *De disputatione Lipsicensi, Corp. Cath.*, IV, 33.

[42] In one passage Emser's Latin is phrased with great care to this end. Speaking of the prayers of the Bohemians for Luther, he says, "O miserum Lutherum, si execrandis et abhominabilibus istorum piaculis confisus ac non potius iugi scripturarum meditatione . . . fretus cum fortissimo theologorum Ecchio pugnam ineat." *Ibid.*, p. 32. The use of the present instead of the pluperfect subjunctive was a stroke worthy of Erasmus.

position, even though pleased by praise of his scholarship. Furthermore, the Dresden humanist had touched him on the sorest spot which the disputation had left, his defense of the articles of Huss, for here the skill and persistence of Eck had driven him to a declaration which he must have known was plain heresy in the minds of his hearers. Moreover it involved a position regarding the authority of a general council of the Church on which his own mind was not yet clear. Irritating, too, was the fact that this was no cloistered argument like that of Dungersheim, but a public declaration. Even so, it is hard to understand the violence of Martin's reaction to Emser's letter. Possibly the Leipzig meeting had given him some visible proof of his critic's partisanship for Eck which, added to Emser's repeated warnings, persuaded him that the former friend was disloyal and hostile in spirit.

However that may have been, he quite lost control of himself and at the end of September gave to the press a reply which is one of the most savage of his polemical writings. *Luther's Addition to Emser's Wild Goat* [43] takes its title from a woodcut on the published letter to Zak, representing Emser's coat of arms, a group of heraldic emblems surmounted by a long-horned goat,[44] and contains many noisome references to this symbolic beast.[45] The author begins by congratulating Emser sarcastically for rescuing him from Hussite heresy. He then turns savagely to picture the Dresden canon as a Joab who treacherously slew Abner and Amasa; a Judas who betrays with a kiss; a coward who fears to face an opponent frankly and openly. If he now kept silent, he would acknowledge himself a Bohemian heretic and a protector of heretics. Scornfully he waves aside the Judas kiss of Emser's praise. Why not call him a Jew, since he has much in common with the faith of the Jews? "O ye unhappy and impotent theologians and world-idols, who, ignorant of the Sacred Scriptures, cannot defend the opinions of the Church with other weapons than by fear, rage, and suspicion, like women and boys, not otherwise than [by declaring] that the dogmas will give pleasure to heretics!" [46] In Leipzig he had said to Eck that he did not care what the Bohemians thought of him; now he hopes, prays, and is rejoiced to have his doctrines please the Bohemians, "Yes, Jews and Turks and

---

[43] *Ad aegocerotem Emserianum Martini Lutheri additio. WA*, II, 658 ff. The work was still under way on September 22. See letter from Luther to Spalatin, *WAB*, I, 508, ll. 11 f.

[44] See the reproduction in *Corp. Cath.*, IV, 27.

[45] In truly humanistic wise the contemporaries were quick to forge a new title for Emser, "Bock Emser." In the following spring "Emseranus Capricornus" plays a rôle in "Eccius Dedolatus Autore Joanne francisco Cotta Lembergio, Poeta Laureato," *Lateinische Litteraturdenkmäler des XV. und XVI. Jahrhunderts*, II, 17 and 32. For other instances see Kawerau, "Hieronymus Emser," pp. 99 ff.

[46] *WA*, II, 662, ll. 24 ff.

also you and Eck, so that you might give up your impious errors." [47] Let Emser show him any false doctrine of his which the Bohemians praise, for his teaching, true or false, is to be judged by its contents and not by the opinion of the Bohemians. There is something else—and here he is convinced that he has caught the "goat": what Emser really intends is to oppose his thesis about the pope. Alternately he scoffs at and answers Emser's arguments in support of the papal power. He is more than skeptical that the Bohemians ever offered prayers for him. "My whole intent was to remain in my corner. Now, however, since I have been caught by a single disputation broadside as by the skirt of my coat and dragged forcibly into public view, in the belief that this happened through God's will I shall fear neither your very brave and very noisy Eck, nor you, most feeble man, nor any other very ignorant opponent." [48]

Once more he voices his disgust with the Leipzig disputation. The whole of it could have been disposed of in one hour if he had not had to listen to Eck's recital of all the mess and filth of the scholastic writers. With an ironical application of what he calls Eck's and Emser's method of exegesis, he demonstrates that Matthew, and before him Judas, the purse-bearer, was chief among the apostles. Sarcasm and irony give way to a calmer tone when he once more comes to defend his contention that the papacy is not of divine right, but merely an office to serve the Church. If the latter were the prevailing view, if the popes were responsible to every Christian, the criminal and the godless would not desire to be heads of the Church by any right, human or divine. The power of the pope and the bishops is a power and office to serve and not to rule. The mistake he made in the disputation was in casting pearls before swine. He summons Emser to pray with him that what happened there to harm the Church and bring it into disrepute may be turned by God's mercy to the destruction of envy and vainglory. It is his wish to dispute with those who seek the truth rather than their own glory, but if he should be sent out among wolves, he will pray God to put kindness into his heart that he may preserve the harmlessness of the dove with the wisdom of the serpent. Emser can scarcely imagine what sarcasms, what mockeries, what scoffings the old Adam had put into his mind against him, but these Christ had suppressed. How long, he groans, will he have to waste time on indulgences and the power of the pope, things which have nothing whatever to do with faith in God and salvation; and he compares himself to Reuchlin, who was also obliged to waste many years over an unimportant matter. "I have often wished to keep silent among the peaceful,

[47] *Ibid.*, p. 663, ll. 22 ff.   [48] *Ibid.*, p. 672, ll. 29 ff.

but against noisy and furious opponents I have thus far had a vigorous and confident spirit, thanks to the gift of Christ! It is my desire to love all and fear none." [49]

Having launched his attack, Martin waited eagerly for Emser's reply. Before it came Eck took up the cudgels on behalf of the Dresden scholar. Emser's case was also his own. On October 28, ten days after he had dedicated his reply to Luther's attack on him for championing the criticisms of the Franciscans (*Defense against the Malicious Indictment of Eck*) and while he was still ruminating on his answer to Luther's and Carlstadt's letter to Elector Frederick he issued a *Response for Hieronymus Emser to the Insane Hunt of Luther,* couched in the form of a letter to the bishop of Meissen, Johann von Schleynitz.[50] With his accustomed vigor he attacks Luther as the persecutor of an innocent man with "slanders and lies," [51] and repeats his charge that Bohemians were secretly present at the Leipzig disputation. He is still counting on the decision of the university at Paris, the "Athens of Christendom." [52] With little argument and much abuse he traverses Luther's reply to Emser. He is willing to dispute with Luther at Rome, Naples, Bologna, Paris, Toulouse, Louvain, Cologne, or Vienna. He is particularly pleased to have confirmation in Martin's own hand of his mildness toward the Hussites, and he now advances a new charge: he has evidence of the Wittenberger's neglect of religious duty; at least after careful inquiry at Leipzig he can not find that during the entire disputation, a period of three weeks, Martin said a single Mass.[53] As far as he is concerned, he prays that Luther's prayers may not do him any harm. Martin is weak in scholarship but strong in biting and abusing. He is a liar and a Hussite.

Eck's attack, like several others in the months following the disputation, probably reached Martin about the middle of December,[54] apparently some weeks after the reply by Emser. Eck's defense of the Leipzig canon seems not to have made much impression; it merely added one more to the series of attacks, and Martin decided to reserve his ammunition until Eck's often promised work on the primacy of the pope should appear. He dismissed the pamphlet as an "offspring worthy of its parent, a mess of foul language," and its author, Emser's champion, as a "worthy patron of such a client." [55] He was more interested in Emser's forthcoming reply. In the

[49] *Ibid.,* p. 679, l. 20.
[50] *Joannis Eckii pro Hieronymo Emser contra malesanam Luteri Venationem responsio.* Wiedemann, *Dr. Joh. Eck,* pp. 509 ff. Walch, *Schriften,* XVIII, 1090 ff.
[51] *Ibid.,* p. 1091. [52] *Ibid.,* p. 1113. [53] *Ibid.,* p. 1103.
[54] Letter from Luther to Spalatin, Dec. 25, 1519, *WAB,* I, 600.
[55] *Ibid.*

middle of October he heard that the canon was preparing whole "Iliads of war" against him,[56] or, varying the figure, was about to bring an elephant into the world with the help of the Leipzig group as midwives.[57] Martin is anxious that the expected attack should not appear in Wittenberg and even thinks that his university might intervene with that at Leipzig. He would himself write to Duke George, only he has had too much experience with the Dresden chancellor, Cäsar Pflug.[58]

Finally, early in November, Emser's answer appeared, entitled *Freeing the Wild Goat from Luther's Hunt*.[59] The author employed the dialogue, a popular form among the humanists and one which he was to use repeatedly in his controversy with Luther two years later. The work was prepared with great care and shows Emser as no mean humanist in Latin style and in wealth of classical allusions. It is larded with quotations from Cicero, Horace, and Vergil, and Erasmus is frequently summoned to illustrate his points. The pedantic canon is at pains to balance his antitheses neatly [60] and to give his sentences a rhythmical swing. Luther had censured him for a wrong ending. Emser refuses to accept the correction and takes his opponent to task for ignorance of the proper use of the superlative, "Which even schoolboys know." [61] The dialogue, characterized by humanistic preciosity, is largely a plea in self-defense. The temptation to assume an air of injured innocence was too strong to be resisted. As regards Martin's appeal to the council, he can never permit to Luther what Peter permitted to Paul: "Of Paul we know that he was the chosen vessel to preach the Gospel to the Gentiles. Of Luther we do not know yet whether he is of Christ or of the other party." [62] A reform of clergy, monks, and laity is necessary, to be sure, but it can come only by the combined effort of the emperor and the Catholic princes, together with the pope.[63] With a classical reference especially dear to the humanists, Emser warns his antagonist that the die is now cast between them,[64] and urges him to pause in his career, mindful of the fate of Phaëthon and of Icarus.

When the reply of Emser came into Martin's hands it found him in a

---

[56] Letter to Spalatin, Oct. 15, 1519, *WAB*, I, 534.

[57] Letter to Lang, Oct. 16, *WAB*, I, 540. [58] *Ibid.*, p. 534.

[59] *A venatione Luteriana aegocerotis assertio*. Edited by F. X. Thurnhofer, in *Corp. Cath.*, IV, 45 ff.

[60] For example, see *ibid.*, p. 80, ll. 11 ff.

[61] *Ibid.*, p. 83, ll. 10 ff. In spite of his ability in Latin, Emser was by no means secure against humiliating slips. He was obliged to reprint his paper against "20 adlige Studenten" in Leipzig in 1521 because in a distich at the beginning he had the ictus fall on a short *i* in *Stilus*. Kawerau, "Hieronymus Emser," p. 120, nn. 89a and 89b.

[62] *A venatione Luteriana, Corp. Cath.*, IV, 87, ll. 20 ff.

[63] *Ibid.*, p. 90, ll. 20 ff. [64] *Ibid.*, p. 97, l. 2.

mood of self-restraint.[65] He can not imagine a better opening for making sport of this "mole" and his Leipzig friends, but concern for his own name and the fear of Christ hold him back.[66] Apparently he was somewhat ashamed of the violence of his attack on the Dresden canon and after a month's reflection we find him resolved not to answer because, as he tells Lang, Emser has conceded everything and brought nothing pertinent to the case, only a furious noise.[67] Two months later in an outburst against Spalatin for chiding him for his violence, he declared that his patience with Emser and Eck had been a cause of new attacks on him.[68] Later, in 1521, he reminds the Dresden opponent that he is not to feel safe just because he has received no answer to his lies.[69] At the end of 1520, when Martin lit the memorable fire before the Elster gate in Wittenberg, he cast into the flames Emser's pamphlets against him along with the Pope's bull and the papal decrees and canon law. Thus he arrayed among the enemies of Church and faith the Dresden humanist who had through a clever subterfuge tried to force from him a declaration regarding the Bohemian heretics. In the meantime Emser had now found his mission in life and he set himself to it with an intensity that shook off the dress of humanistic egotism. Luther's revolutionary tractates of 1520 awakened him from all pedantic dreams to an earnest defense of the faith. In a series of German works he assailed the Wittenberg heretic with a vigor and ruthlessness equal to Luther's own. A discussion of this controversy must await a later chapter.

In Emser's letter to the head of the Bohemian orthodox Catholics Martin had seen an effort to conceal hostility under a neutral mask, and this conviction of the duplicity of the Dresden scholar barbed his attack with special resentment. Some of his bitterness was due no doubt to surprise that one who could make no claim to learning in theology should sit in judgment on his actions. He could not foresee the energy which this dilettante in theological matters would develop in the years to follow. In Martin's eyes his chief opponents were in the religious order to which Cajetan and Prierias and Eck belonged, the order which had won for itself a unique position as defender of orthodoxy and particularly of papal claims. The citadel of Dominican activity in Germany was at Cologne. Here Dominican scholars controlled the theological faculty of the university. Their major prophet was Jakob Hochstraten, who had been for many years head of the

---

[65] Letter from Luther to Spalatin, Nov. 19, 1519, *WAB*, I, 555.
[66] Letter to Spalatin, Nov. 20, *WAB*, I, 556 f.
[67] Letter from Luther to Lang, Dec. 18, 1519, *WAB*, I, 597, ll. 28 ff.
[68] Letter to Spalatin, middle of February, 1520, *WAB*, II, 43, ll. 13 ff.
[69] Enders, "Luther und Emser," I, 150.

studies of the order in Cologne and professor of theology at the university, and as prior of the convent was chief inquisitor in the country lying along the middle Rhone and the Moselle.[70] In this position he displayed great energy and delivered at least one backsliding heretic to the temporal arm and a fiery death.[71] Among the humanists he was in ill-repute for fanatical intolerance, particularly because of his leadership in the attack on Reuchlin in 1511. Preceding this widely advertised affair, Hochstraten had, in agreement with the Cologne university, condemned to destruction the Talmudic books of the Jews, and he thus became the storm center of one of the most intense quarrels in the history of humanism. Through his writings, issued in Germany and Italy, and in his activity as inquisitor, he led the fight against the Swabian scholar and humanistic allies such as Hutten, Crotus, and Hermann von dem Busche. In the spring of 1519 he published an attack on Reuchlin's work on the cabala,[72] a work drawn from Hebrew sources and marked by a spirit which to scholastic churchmen appeared confusing to Christian minds and destructive of faith. In dedicating this pamphlet to Pope Leo, Hochstraten urged the Pope to a defense against heresy and quoted from Luther's thirteenth thesis against the papal power. "Arise," he exhorts the pontiff, "arise with the spirit of a lion and drive out the disturber of the Christian faith!" [73]

Although Luther's name was not mentioned, the reference was unmistakable and aroused Martin to action. His answer was probably circulated as a broadside.[74] Just when it appeared cannot be said, but in sharpness of tone it reflects the mood of Luther immediately after the Leipzig disputation.[75] It is a caustic attack on this "new enemy" who has been "raised from an old one," "the master of heretics." In the year preceding Martin had expressed his sympathy with Reuchlin, but disapproved of the sarcasm in the attack on scholasticism in the Letters of Obscure Men; now he himself proceeds against the leader of the scholastics as one who has "consumed and

---

[70] For a somewhat partisan discussion of Hochstraten, or Hoogstraeten (he was born in Hoogstraeten, near Antwerp), see N. Paulus, "Die deutschen Dominikaner im Kampfe gegen Luther 1518–1563," Erläuterungen und Ergänzungen zu Janssens Geschichte des deutschen Volkes, IV, 1–11, 87 ff.

[71] Hermann von Rysswick, in 1512. Ibid., p. 94.

[72] Destructio Cabale seu Cabalistice perfidie. See letter from Reuchlin to Michael Hummelberg, June 29, 1519, in "Johann Reuchlins Briefwechsel," Bibliothek des Litterarischen Vereins in Stuttgart, CXXVI (1875), 315, ed. by Ludwig Geiger. See also Geiger, Johann Reuchlin, p. 199, and Paulus, "Dominikaner gegen Luther," p. 98.

[73] Quoted in WA, II, 384.

[74] For the text of this work, the Scheda adversus Jacobum Hochstraten, see ibid., pp. 386 f.

[75] Knaake, WA, II, 384 ff., supposes that Luther published the Scheda by posting before the end of the Leipzig disputation. This can be only a pure guess.

wasted all his days in dialectics." Sarcastically he reproves the Cologne theologian for making a "beast" (lion) of the Pope. If whoever acts against the Scriptures is heretical, as the Cologne professor asserts, then David must have been a heretic because he was an adulterer. The only real heretics, Martin insists, are those who assert and defend their errors with persistence. The short paper bristles with the same abusive vocabulary which Hochstraten had heard from Reuchlin and Hutten. The heretic hunter is himself a "pestilential and impudent heretic," "one who feeds on Christian blood," "a cruel parasite" "thirsting for the blood of the brothers," "an ignorant ass," and he is warned that if he tries anything against Luther the latter will show that there has not been a more dangerous heretic in forty years than Hochstraten himself.[76]

The Cologne Dominican was too fully occupied with the Reuchlin affair, which reached a final crisis in 1520, to make a reply,[77] and it was not until after the Diet of Worms that he entered the lists with a direct attack upon Luther.[78] In the meantime, however, he was not inactive for, if we may believe Erasmus, it was he who induced the Cologne university to condemn Luther's works.[79] This verdict fell on August 30, 1519, and was followed by similar action on the part of the Louvain faculty on November 7.[80] The condemnation by the universities, to which we shall return in a later chapter, seems not to have become known in Wittenberg until the following spring.[81]

In the midst of these attacks Martin was comforted by the support of many friends. This was not confined to the Wittenberg faculty or students, whose sympathy and eager championship at the Leipzig disputation and in the days that followed were abundantly in evidence. It extended to colleagues of the order at Erfurt and Nuremberg and to humanistic groups, both clerical and lay, throughout Germany. Luther was soon to receive evidence that political figures of importance on the Rhine and in Franconia were also watching his struggle against papal power with warm interest and

---

[76] The bitterness of Luther's *Scheda* is evidence of his feeling at this time that he and the Reuchlin party were fighting against a common enemy. It may have been accentuated by a knowledge of Eck's appeal to the Cologne Dominican to use his influence with the Paris faculty for a decision in Eck's favor. *Ref. Act.*, III, 222 ff. Eck's letter is dated July 24 from Leipzig, and in accordance with the custom of the time was probably published at once. See Wiedemann, *Dr. Johann Eck*, p. 501.

[77] Paulus, "Dominikaner gegen Luther," pp. 98 f.

[78] . . . *Jacobi de Hochstraten cum divo Augustino Colloquia* . . . (1521), and others. See Paulus, "Dominikaner gegen Luther," pp. 103 ff.

[79] Letter from Erasmus to Matthias Kretz, March 11, 1531, *Erasmi Opera omnia*, III, 1361.

[80] See *WA*, VI, 174 ff.

[81] Letter from Luther to Spalatin, March 19, 1520, *WAB*, II, 72.

a growing desire to help. Many members of the clerical orders, particularly Franciscans in North and South Germany, had come to see in him a champion of long-needed reforms and were following the work with ardent hope.[82] Beginning with the Leipzig disputation, however, observers with keener vision discerned behind the vigor of his attacks on the papal power and Church abuses and the earnestness of his sermons a theological attitude that was moving steadily further away from scholastic dogmas and must finally lead to a wide rift in the Church. Naturally the Dominican scholars who were trained in the detection of heresy were the first to discover these tendencies in the Wittenberg theology and to take arms against them. To the great majority of churchmen the full significance of Luther's ideas did not become clear until more than a year after the disputation, when Luther's attack on the sacraments showed the width of the chasm that separated him from time-honored dogmas of the Roman Church.

It is evident from what we have learned of Martin's position after the great disputation that those who felt the approach of what Eck called "a new theology" did so more clearly than he himself. It is equally clear that the many persons who testified their approval of his course had a great variety of reasons—political, social, and spiritual—for their support, and that it was only in the Wittenberg group that a real understanding of his theological position was to be found. With his ideas concerning the nature of the Christian Church and his own ultimate purposes not yet fully developed, and facing a growing circle of enemies, it is natural that Martin welcomed any assurances of support and did not seek to analyze the motives of those who gave him words of comfort. Nevertheless he could not overlook, and there is evidence that he began to note, that his course was taking him toward a break with orthodox tradition. This seems to have impressed him when early in October, 1519, he received two letters from Bohemian clergymen, pastors of a utraquist church in Prague and therefore followers of one of the Hussite groups. These were Johann Poduška and Wenzel von Roždalowsky,[83] who wrote on July 17 through the chancellery of Frederick. The letters were therefore much delayed and had been opened in transit. Both contained warm expressions of admiration and sympathy in his contest with Eck. Poduška, who claimed to find in Luther's writings the true doctrine, congratulates him on teaching the pure law of Christ and the Fathers uncontaminated by man's invention, and begs him to continue

[82] For evidence see Lemmens, "Pater Augustin von Alfeld," I, i, pp. 7 f.

[83] WAB, I, 417 ff. Poduška was pastor of the church "am Tein" in Prague, and Roždalowsky was an ecclesiastical official in that city. Both died in the following year.

to oppose the adversaries of God although he will certainly be classed as a heretic for so doing. There are many in Bohemia faithful to God, the writer states, who support him day and night with their prayers. Roždalowsky rejoices at the news from Leipzig of the victory over Eck. He has learned that Luther wants Huss's books, and sends him the Bohemian martyr's little treatise, *On the Church*.[84] Luther is now in Saxony, he declares, what Huss was in Bohemia. Both letters are in excellent Latin and particularly that of Poduška is filled with scriptural quotations.[85]

Luther seems to have read these letters with mixed emotions.[86] Their warm tone and deeply religious feeling must have cheered him at a time when the full force of Eck's hostility and Emser's criticisms was making itself felt. On the other hand, the letters came very near to confirming Emser's information that public prayers were being offered for him in Bohemia, a statement which he had denounced as an invention of the Dresden canon.[87] He had expressly condemned the Bohemian departure from the Church and resented deeply at Leipzig and afterward Eck's effort to associate him with these heretics. Whatever his private views regarding the great Bohemian,[88] he had been careful at Leipzig and was still careful not to endorse the ideas of Huss, and had recorded both at Leipzig and afterwards his disapproval of the Bohemian schism.

Nevertheless, his hesitation in this respect did not deter him from replying cordially to the greeting of the Bohemian clerics. A short time after the receipt of the letters, a Bohemian visited Wittenberg, making the impression of a man of culture.[89] The theologians received him cordially and entrusted him with a reply to the Bohemian clergymen. In view of the Erasmian Latin of these correspondents, Melanchthon was commissioned to draft a letter, which was probably no more than a warm acknowledgment on the

[84] Whether Huss's work was sent in print or manuscript is not clear. In 1520 it circulated widely in published form and aroused great interest throughout Germany. See Köhler, *Luther und die Kirchengeschichte*, p. 200, n. 1.

[85] Roždalowsky says that his information regarding the Leipzig events came from a certain "Jacobus organarius," *WAB*, I, 419, l. 4. This would be evidence confirming Eck's statement that Bohemians were present at the disputation and showed their satisfaction at Luther's declarations.

[86] This appears in the tone of Martin's announcement of the receipt of the letters to Staupitz on October 3. While praising the knowledge of Scripture shown by the writers, he declares, "Erasmisant miro modo quam sensu quam stylo." *WAB*, I, 514, l. 31.

[87] *Ad aegocerotem Emserianum. WA*, II, 664, ll. 39 ff.

[88] A year later in an attack on Eck, Luther declared that before he ever thought of becoming a priest he heard from his master of novices, Johann Greifenstein, "a learned and pious man," that Huss had been secretly condemned by ignorant tyrants and that it had never been shown that he was wrong. *Von den neuen Eckischen Bullen und Lügen, WA*, VI, 591.

[89] Letter from Luther to Spalatin, Oct. 15, *WAB*, I, 534.

part of the Wittenberg faculty. To this reply Martin added the gift of his works. That the greetings from Prague and perhaps the sending of Huss's work *On the Church,* which Martin declares he had not previously read, were not without their effect, is indicated a few weeks later by a parenthetical remark in Martin's reply to Eck's account of the Leipzig disputation for Elector Frederick. Accepting as "most Christian" a certain article of Huss, he injects: "And I now hold many more of his [articles] than I held at Leipzig, as I shall show at its own good time." [90]

[90] *Ad Johannem Eccium M. Lutheri epistola super expurgatione Ecciana. WA,* II, 703, ll. 2 f.

22

HUMANISTIC FRIENDS
AND ALLIES

STANDING outside theological circles was a group that watched the rising conflict with especial interest. These were the enthusiastic followers of classical studies, long engaged in an intense struggle against the defenders of scholasticism and now ready to applaud any attack on clerical arrogance. Luther's relations with the humanists during his Erfurt and early Wittenberg years have been discussed above. It may be repeated here that for this period in his life, evidence of contact with the men who were rapidly undermining scholastic studies at the universities is very inconclusive. It is highly probable that Johann Lang gave him instruction in Greek, and it was to the same friend that Martin owed his acquaintance with Konrad Mutianus in Gotha. This must in any case have been slight,[1] for Luther's interest in these years was concentrated in the theological field, where his struggles with the ideas of Occam took him far away from humanistic interests except as they furnished material for his exegetic studies. The rise of the new spirit in scholarship, however, stirred up a strife which penetrated even the cell and lecture room of one for whom theology was the all-absorbing passion. Luther's letters in the autumn of 1516 give evidence that he was following the conflict between Reuchlin and his Dominican opponents in Cologne with interest, though, as we have noted, he criticized the frivolity and intemperate tone of the *Letters of Obscure Men*.[2]

The year following the publication of the Ninety-five Theses altered his

[1] The letters to Lang, Zasius, and Spalatin in 1516 and 1520 reflect a languid interest in Luther. See Karl Gillert, ed., "Der Briefwechsel des Conradius Mutianus," *Geschichtsquellen der Provinz Sachsen*, XVIII, II, *passim*. After June, 1521, Mutianus complains of the hostile attitude of the Wittenbergers. *Ibid.*, pp. 280 ff., 296 ff.

[2] Letters from Luther to Lang, Oct. 5, 1516, *WAB*, I, 61, and Oct. 26, 1516, *WAB*, I, 73. See also his letter to Spalatin of Oct. 5, 1516, *WAB*, I, 63 f. Two years earlier, at the height of the controversy, Luther had expressed his sympathy with Reuchlin in a letter to Spalatin, *WAB*, I, 23.

relationship to humanistic scholars as it did to many others in the world outside the cloister. The correspondence with Scheurl shows the sympathy which the liberal spirits of Nuremberg, the richest center of civic culture in Germany, felt for Luther. The impression of a common cause with the South German humanists must have been strengthened by Martin's visit to Nuremberg when on his way to Augsburg, and particularly when he found refuge and sympathy among friends there after his battle with Cajetan. The bond became still closer when Philip Melanchthon joined the Wittenberg faculty. He had laid the foundation in student days at Tübingen for a profound knowledge of the classical languages, and before he came to Wittenberg had already become the friend and correspondent of several South German scholars of humanistic tastes. It was at his suggestion that Luther wrote a letter to Reuchlin in December, 1518, congratulating him on a happy turn in the investigation that the Cologne heresy-hunters were pressing against him on account of his *Augenspiegel*.[3]

When 1518 had passed and the following year brought the disputation with Eck, Luther's circle of friends widened still further beyond the guild of theologians. Although much of the correspondence of the time has undoubtedly been lost, enough letters have been preserved to show a wide expression of sympathy with the bold opponent of Eck on the part of men interested in reform in education as well as in religious affairs. With the group of Nuremberg friends and others in South Germany, personal antipathy to the aggressive Dominican undoubtedly played a rôle. Here, as in other conflicts of the time, there is, however, no question of a solid front of humanism against scholasticism. That had not even been attained in the struggle against the "Obscure Men,"[4] and after all, Eck could have qualified as a humanist as well some of Luther's South German supporters. There is enough evidence, however, that the bullying attitude of the Ingolstadt theologian had made him unpopular among men of independent minds. Essentially he represented the same arrogant assumption of the right of conservative theologians to sit in judgment on the findings of scholarship that men of humanistic training had resented so deeply in the attack of the Cologne scholars on Reuchlin.

Even before the controversy over indulgences one of these South German

[3] Letter from Luther to Reuchlin, *WAB*, I, 268. Reuchlin seems not to have answered the letter, although some months afterward he sent greetings to Luther through Melanchthon. Ludwig Geiger, ed., "Johann Reuchlins Briefwechsel," *Bibliothek des Litterarischen Vereins in Stuttgart*, CXXVI (1875), 357.

[4] See Gerhard Ritter, "Die geschichtliche Bedeutung des deutschen Humanismus," *Historische Zeitschrift*, CXXVII (1923), 405.

reformers had identified Luther with the cause of Reuchlin. Willibald Pirckheimer, the foremost humanist of Nuremberg, in his translation of Lucian's dialogue, *The Fisher,* published in defense of Reuchlin in August, 1517, names Luther along with Erasmus, Eck, and a number of others as a defender of the true theology.[5] Pirckheimer was outstanding among the group with which Martin had come in touch through Christoph Scheurl. After seven years' study in Italy he had cultivated scholarship and literature in the best humanistic style. As a member of a distinguished patrician family and a councilor of the city for many years, he enjoyed great prestige in political as well as scholarly circles. He was probably the most learned man in Germany in the classical tongues, and he counted among his correspondents almost the whole aristocracy of the new learning throughout Central Europe. That he exchanged letters with Luther in the year following the theses on indulgences is probable, though not certain. In any event, he had seen Luther's "Asterisks," the reply to Eck's critical notes on the Ninety-five Theses, in the hands of the Augustinian prior, Wenceslaus Link, and it was Pirckheimer who had sent to Wittenberg the broadside containing Eck's theses in February, 1519. Martin thanks him a few days later in a letter of appreciative friendship and tells him of his purpose to attack the papal decrees.[6] After the disputation he sends him a report of the affair, with a formal claim of victory for Carlstadt.[7]

Pirckheimer was never a severe critic of the Roman Church. It is probable that he heard in Eck's attack on Luther an echo of the intolerance of the Cologne Dominicans toward Reuchlin and in the Leipzig disputation a continuation of the battle between scholarship and obscurantism. But the dignified patrician was no fanatic. In his defense of Reuchlin he did not allow the latter to pass without criticism for his violence and abuse of his opponents.[8] When he learned of the quarrel between Emser and Luther he expressed deep regret and censured both parties for lack of self-control, preserving a neutrality which both seem to have resented.[9] Two years later Pirckheimer showed himself no more willing to tread the path of martyrdom than his humanistic contemporaries, and he renounced all community with

---

[5] See Drews, *Pirckheimers Stellung,* p. 32.

[6] Letter from Luther to Pirckheimer, February 20, 1519, *WAB,* I, 348.

[7] The letter apparently has been lost, but Luther refers to it early in November in the *Epistola super expurgatione Ecciana, WA,* II, 701. Knaake's note 2 is an error, as the only letter from Luther to Pirckheimer is that of February 20, 1519.

[8] Drews, *Pirckheimers Stellung,* p. 22.

[9] See Franz X. Thurnhofer, "Willibald Pirkheimer und Hieronymus Emser," *Beiträge zur Geschichte der Renaissance und Reformation. Festschrift für J. Schlecht,* pp. 343 ff. Pirckheimer heard that Luther did not approve his dedication to Emser of a Latin translation from Lucian.

the Wittenberg theology. Nevertheless, he maintained friendly relations with Melanchthon to the end of his life.[10]

In the months following the disputation Luther certainly had reason to count Pirckheimer as a powerful ally. When the *Purified Eck* appeared in the spring of 1520, Martin at once credited the clever thrust at the Dominican professor to the satirical pen of the Nuremberg humanist. Pirckheimer denied authorship, and when in October, 1520, he learned that he was included in the bull of condemnation just published by Eck in Meissen, he felt that this was due as much to revenge for his support of Reuchlin as to Eck's resentment at the biting pamphlet.[11]

A more outspoken enemy of the Ingolstadt champion was another South German of humanistic interests, Bernhard Adelmann of Adelmannsfelden. Although by no means so highly regarded for scholarship as Pirckheimer, Adelmann had a wide acquaintance in humanistic circles. Born of a pious and cultivated noble family in Swabia, he had sat on the university benches at Basel with Sebastian Brant, the great Strasbourg satirist, and had begun there a friendship with Reuchlin which was to last until the latter's death.[12] He had traveled through Europe from Rome to London as a diplomat in the service of the bishops of Eichstätt. Now on the threshold of old age, he lived in Augsburg as a canon at the cathedral, devoting his life to scholarship and benevolence.[13] As friend and correspondent of Reuchlin, he criticized vigorously the papal delay in permitting the commission appointed in his case to reach a decision.[14] Adelmann was a bitter enemy of Eck and gave free expression to his contempt for the motives and methods of the Ingolstadt doctor, attacking with especial vigor the latter's defense in the Bologna disputation of lending at interest.[15]

Adelmann's acquaintance with Luther began, as it appears, through Martin's *Sermon on the Ten Commandments* and his attention was riveted on him further by reports of his scholarship and ascetic life.[16] He was a warm friend of Pirckheimer, who may have informed him of Wittenberg affairs.

---

[10] See Drews, *Pirckheimers Stellung*, p. 41 and notes.

[11] *Ibid.*, p. 46.

[12] See F. X. Thurnhofer, "Bernhard Adelmann von Adelmannsfelden, Humanist und Luthers Freund (1457–1523)," *Erläuterungen und Ergänzungen zu Janssens Geschichte des deutschen Volkes*, II, 1, 20.

[13] Thurnhofer notes that in 1513 Bernhard established at Eichstätt a refuge for sufferers from syphilis. *Ibid.*, pp. 35 f., 136.

[14] *Ibid.*, pp. 20, 46 ff.

[15] *Ibid.*, pp. 53 ff. One of Thurnhofer's sources is the correspondence of Adelmann and Pirckheimer published by Heumann in *Documenta litteraria varii argumenti* (Altdorf, 1758) a work not accessible to me.

[16] Thurnhofer, "Bernhard Adelmann," pp. 56 f. and n. 3.

With joy he greeted Martin's arrival in Augsburg, where both he and his brother Konrad showed cordial friendship to the monk in the trying days of his hearing before Cajetan.[17] Correspondence which would mark the friendship between Luther and Bernhard in 1519 has been lost. At this time the question of indulgences came up in the dioceses of southeastern Germany, and Adelmann stands on common ground with Martin in resentment over the abuse of the people's trust in the Church.[18] His enthusiasm for Luther and anxiety for his safety find expression in letters to Pirckheimer and others and must have come to Martin's knowledge more than once during the preparation for the Leipzig disputation. The warm-hearted canon takes at face value a report from Oecolampadius that Henry VIII has invited Martin to England and that Duke George is trying to win him and Melanchthon for the Leipzig University.[19] He secures Luther's latest works from Wittenberg and passes them on to friends. With great eagerness he looks forward to Martin's reply to Eck's "Obelisks"; indeed, he it was who brought these to Martin's attention through Link.[20] After the disputation he listened to Eck's boasting with deep indignation and without hesitation decided against Emser when the dispute arose between him and Luther. In his defense of Emser, Eck had inserted the marginal remark that only a few "ignorant canons" held with Luther. This innuendo stung the aging humanist to action, and before the end of December he had put into the press the manuscript of the sharpest attack on Eck which the controversy brought forth, the *Response of the Ignorant Lutheran Canons to Johann Eck*, written by Adelmann's friend Oecolampadius.[21] At once Luther's keen eye recognized that it must have come from an abler pen than that of Adelmann.[22] Eck, on the other hand, held the Augsburg canon to be the author, and so fierce was the mutual hatred of the two churchmen that under the stimulating influence of a New Year's Eve celebration they seem to have come close to physical conflict.[23]

---

[17] *Ibid.*, p. 57.   [18] *Ibid.*, pp. 58 f.

[19] Letter to Pirckheimer, March 2, 1519. Heumann, *Documenta*, quoted in Thurnhofer, "Bernhard Adelmann," p. 59.

[20] See above, p. 335, n. 48.

[21] Text in *Ref. Act.*, III, 935 ff. See Wiedemann, *Dr. Johann Eck*, pp. 140 ff.; Thurnhofer, "Bernhard Adelmann," pp. 63 ff.

[22] In answer to a question of Spalatin's, Luther writes on February 8, 1520, that judging by the style the satire was written either by Oecolampadius or Konrad Adelmann, Bernhard's brother, "qui mihi valentior pleniorque videtur Bernhardo." *WAB*, II, 36, ll. 7 f. A few weeks later he learns from Melanchthon that Oecolampadius had confessed himself the author. Letter from Luther to Spalatin, Feb. 27, 1520, *WAB*, II, 56, l. 7.

[23] Adelmann's account of the scene is quoted by Thurnhofer, "Bernhard Adelmann," p. 67, from Heumann's *Documenta*.

With Eck's departure for Rome, Adelmann's anxiety for Luther rose and found vivid expression in letters to his friends in Nuremberg: "For that villain of a Geck [fop] will soon arrive with the bull and will have everything his own way." [24] In view of all of this, it is certainly not surprising that when Eck received the bull and with it authority to insert among the condemned persons the names of those whom he regarded as the most important followers of the new doctrine, he hastened to put Adelmann down among the enemies of the Church.

In Oecolampadius Luther found a more gifted, even if less enthusiastic supporter than the temperamental canon. Johann Huszgen who clothed himself in this unwieldy, Grecized name, was in these years preacher at Augsburg's cathedral church. A Swabian by birth, he was almost of an age with Luther. His training and association might have been envied by any ambitious scholar and were a fitting preparation for the part which he was destined to play beside Ulrich Zwingli in the reformation in Switzerland. He had sat at Reuchlin's feet as a brilliant pupil in Hebrew, on the recommendation of Wimpfeling he had become the assistant of Erasmus in preparing the first and second editions of the Greek New Testament, and in 1520 he published a Greek grammar. Like Adelmann he had heard of Luther through the *Sermons on the Ten Commandments* and the Ninety-five Theses. He had himself scored certain practices of the clergy from his pulpit. When Oecolampadius received a report of the Leipzig disputation from Melanchthon, he published in December, 1519 his response of the "ignorant canons" against the bullying of the Ingolstadt professor.[25] The *Response* stands high above the other polemical offspring of the Leipzig debate in spirited earnestness of tone and in the quality of its Latin. It arraigns Eck for pride and vindictiveness and breathes warm admiration for Luther, whose sermons and devotional works and high courage bind the unlearned clergy to him. The attack seems to have caused Eck more chagrin than anything else published against him. It was one of the works that he piled for burning at Ingolstadt. To Martin it gave deep satisfaction, as is shown by repeated references in his letters.[26]

[24] Letter from Adelmann to Pirckheimer, June 11, 1520. Heumann, *Documenta,* p. 200, quoted in Thurnhofer, "Bernhard Adelmann," p. 69.

[25] Oecolampadius also published the papers in the Melanchthon-Eck controversy (Augsburg, 1519), with a brief, neutral preface in the most flowery humanistic style. See Staehelin, ed., *Briefe und Akten zum Leben Oecolampads,* I, 99 f.; also Otto Clemen, ed., "Melanchthons Briefwechsel I," *Supplementa Melanchthoniana,* VI, 71.

[26] In later years Luther never shows toward Oecolampadius the bitterness that marked his attitude toward the other humanists. In the *Table Talk* his many references to the Swiss theologian are in a tone touched with pity and regret, in sharp contrast to the vindictiveness shown toward the martyred Zwingli.

Among those from whom the disputation brought expressions of sympathy and support was a humanistic friend of Martin's Erfurt days, Crotus Rubianus. Two letters from him reached Wittenberg late in the fall of 1519 and must have awakened in Luther vivid recollections of student years before the cloister gate had closed on him. The first letter bears date at Bologna, October 16, and Martin received it seven weeks later from the hand of Jakob Hess, who was returning to North Germany from studies in Italy.[27] The second letter has been dated October 31 by editors since Seidemann although not altogether convincingly.[28] In any event, it was written soon after the preceding letter and must have followed it over the Alps at no great interval.

Crotus was one of the cleverest and most acid-tongued of the German humanists. He was several years older than Martin and had preceded him somewhat in the academic career at the Thuringian university. Crotus recalled that they had been members of the same college, probably that of St. George.[29] Then their ways parted. Crotus went on to cultivate humanistic interests and to play an active part in the Reuchlin controversy as one of the chief contributors of the stinging satires in the *Letters of Obscure Men.* Since 1517 he had been at Bologna and Rome as tutor in a wealthy German family.

Both letters ring with a tone of warm friendship. In the first Crotus recalls their comradeship at Erfurt in the study of "good letters" and voices admiration for Martin as a defender of "right godliness." He has followed his Ninety-five Theses and the *Acta Augustana* and his controversy with Prierias, and assures him of his sympathy in the struggle against the "conspiring Dominicans." He has had to keep silence in the face of these attacks on Luther but approves of his appeal to a council, which has stirred up great hatred on the part of the Florentine party. Crotus's nimble pen runs on in bitter denunciation of Prierias's hierarchical arrogance and pedantry and fulsome praise of Martin's pious courage. Martin is indeed a "father of his country," worthy of a statue of gold and annual festivals. He recalls the miraculous conversion of his university friend, like that of "another Paul," and urges him to persist in the course which he has begun. He is destined to convert Germany, but he must accomplish it, not in the arena of the disputation, but by his pen. He has heard through Lang and Melanchthon

---

[27] *WAB*, I, 541 ff.; see also letter from Luther to Spalatin, Dec. 7, 1519, *WAB*, I, 568.
[28] *WAB*, I, 545 ff.
[29] See Johannes Biereye, "Über die Wohnung Luthers und einiger zeitgenössischer Humanisten in Erfurt," *Beiträge zur thüringischen und sächsischen Geschichte: Festschrift für Otto Dobenecker*, p. 260.

of Luther's success at Leipzig and promises to defend him so far as safety permits.[30]

This letter, as stated above, was followed by another, probably written some weeks later.[31] Here Crotus announces that Rome is celebrating the triumph of Eck, but he warns the joyful ones that this may turn out to be as bad a slip as was the premature assurance of the election of Francis as emperor. Through a physician at the papal court he has learned of a letter from Eck to the Pope,[32] attacking Luther especially for his approval of Hussite errors, condemning the poets and students of literature, particularly Ulrich von Hutten, and emphasizing the danger arising from the study of the classics. Delay, Eck has warned, may cost the Pope Thuringia, Meissen, Brandenburg, and other regions. Crotus begs Martin to hold this confidential until he himself shall have gotten back to Germany, where he can snap his fingers at the "pseudo-apostles who are devouring us." Recently Sylvester Prierias showed him three books that he had written against Luther. These give Crotus occasion for some characteristic jokes at the boastful Dominican.

Thus when the exciting summer gave place to an equally exciting fall and the North German winter came on with its dark and chilly days, the monk-professor in his little cell beside the Wittenberg moat must have received many letters of cheer. It is remarkable what a range his name and fame had taken among German scholars in the two years since the publication of the Ninety-five Theses. Although the correspondence and other records that have survived more than four centuries can offer only a very incomplete picture, the sources give abundant evidence of the mobilization of humanistic opinion on a wide front in the year following the Leipzig disputation. From Prague and Nuremberg and Augsburg and from Rome itself came demonstrations of encouragement and support. Capito in Basel,[33] Bucer in Heidelberg,[34] Jonas in Erfurt, just turning from law to theology, and Zasius in Freiburg [35] are among those who in 1519 and early in 1520 sent letters of sympathy, even though some of them and doubtless many others whose communications have been lost, counseled gentleness and restraint. These

---

[30] Crotus claims to have sent a letter to Luther at Augsburg, which was not delivered. *WAB*, I, 543, ll. 111 f. Some confirmation of this appears in a letter from Luther to Spalatin, Nov. 25, 1518, *WAB*, I, 253. See, however, Clemen, *WAB*, I, 254, n. 2.

[31] Letter from Crotus to Luther, *WAB*, I, 545 ff.

[32] Luther had already learned of this letter, as he mentions it to Spalatin on October 13. *WAB*, I, 530.

[33] *WAB*, I, 335 f.; II, 70 f.   [34] *WAB*, I, 614 ff.

[35] September 1, 1520, *WAB*, II, 181 ff. Already on December 1, 1519, Zasius had written Mutianus that while he did not approve Luther's attack on the papal decrees, he regarded him as the "most sincere of men." Gillert, "Mutianus," II, 256. See also n. 1, above.

men were leaders in the new learning and saw in Luther a champion, like Reuchlin, in the struggle against obscurantism and for freedom of personality. What was the attitude of the man, who, a greater scholar than any, had in earlier years pointed the way toward reform among the clerical classes, the man to whom all humanists looked still for leadership, the great Erasmus?

When Luther first became acquainted with the work of the great humanist cannot be said with assurance. Erasmus's international reputation began with the publication of the *Praise of Folly*, which appeared in Paris in 1511 [36] and by 1515 had carried his name throughout all intellectual circles of Europe. Whether Luther was among those whose attention was first drawn to him by his brilliant satire is not known.[37] It is possible that Spalatin was the intermediary,[38] for the elector's secretary was thoroughly familiar with the works of Erasmus and bought them for the electoral library in Wittenberg, where some appeared as early as 1512.[39] Among these was the *Praise of Folly*. This work seems to have been known to Martin when he was preparing his lectures on Psalms probably early in 1515; at least there is one reference toward the end of the manuscript which points in that direction.[40] A year or so later he works over the lectures on Romans with Erasmus's Greek text of the New Testament before him. We have seen that with the

---

[36] See Preserved Smith, *Erasmus*, pp. 123 ff., for a bibliography of the *Encomium moriae*. It was reprinted at Strasbourg in August, 1511, and Jakob Wimpfeling probably had this reprint before him when he wrote to Erasmus on August 19, 1511, from that city. Allen, *Opus epistolarum Erasmi*, I, 462 ff. A copy of the *Moriae* came to the Wittenberg library in the following year.

[37] A quotation in Luther's marginal notes on Lombard's *Sentences* (1509 or 1510) of the proverb "sus Minervam" may have been suggested by Erasmus's *Adages*. *WA*, IX, 65, ll. 17 f. See Smith, *Erasmus*, p. 213, n. 3.

[38] Spalatin's translation into German of Erasmus's famous letter on peace of March 14, 1514, to Anton of Bergen would point to an early acquaintance between Erasmus and Luther's close friend and correspondent. The translation was published without date, but probably appeared in 1514. See Allen, *Opus epistolarum Erasmi*, I, 551. Luther's earliest letter to Spalatin that has come down to us is the one referring to the Reuchlin dispute, and belongs no later than the early part of 1514 (see n. 2, above), or possibly late in 1513.

[39] Spalatin was after 1512 in charge of the ducal library in the castle. See Ernst Hildebrandt, "Die kurfürstliche Schloss- und Universitätsbibliothek zu Wittenberg 1512–1547," *Zeitschrift für Buchkunde*, II (1925), 39. Luther calls Spalatin "ducali bibliophylaci et philobiblio." *WAB*, I, 82. Bills for books received show that these included at Michaelmas, 1512, the "Opera Erasmi Roterodami" and at Easter, 1513, the "Moria erasmi." Georg Buchwald, "Archivalische Mitteilungen über Bücherbezüge der kurfürstlichen Bibliothek und Georg Spalatins in Wittenberg," *Archiv für Geschichte des deutschen Buchhandels*, XVIII (1896), 8, 10. See also Smith, *Erasmus*, p. 214, n. 2. Many of Spalatin's journeys to Wittenberg during more than thirty years of his activity at the electoral court were concerned with the library. See Georg Buchwald, "Zu Spalatins Reisen, insbesondere nach Wittenberg in Angelegenheit der Kurfürstlichen Bibliothek," *Archiv für Bibliographie*, II (1929), 92 ff.

[40] *WA*, IV, 442. See *ibid.*, p. viii, "Nachträge."

ninth chapter he begins to use it in interpreting the Vulgate version and employs it afterwards for both glosses and scholia.[41]

This must have been in the spring of 1516. In August he is awaiting Erasmus's edition of the letters of St. Jerome, which had just appeared from the Basel press.[42] By the autumn he has been giving much thought to the notes (*Adnotationes*) which Erasmus appends to his New Testament and, as we stated earlier, he already finds grounds for differing with the exegete. He tells Spalatin that the "most learned man's" interpretation of Romans stirs him to protest, for Erasmus understands the Apostle's remarks concerning the justification by works of the law or by human righteousness as referring only to outer, ceremonial observances.[43] Furthermore, as regards original sin, although Erasmus accepts it, nevertheless he does not give full expression to the testimony of the Apostle. Luther then cites Augustine and a whole series of Church Fathers to support his conception of Paul's meaning. "I at least do not hesitate to differ from Erasmus in this case, because I put Jerome just as far below Augustine in interpreting the Scriptures as he puts Augustine in everything behind Jerome." Martin goes on then to formulate the idea which occupied him at that time so constantly, the worthlessness of good works except as an expression of faith.[44] In conclusion he begs Spalatin to communicate this to Erasmus, for he fears that this scholar of so outstanding a reputation may be regarded as a supporter of the literal and dead interpretation used by almost all commentators except Augustine.[45] He excuses himself for his boldness and closes with a classical reference which may have been suggested by one of the *Adages* of the great scholar whom he is criticizing.

In spite of the respect for Erasmus that is voiced repeatedly in the letters of 1517 and 1518,[46] Luther becomes more critical of his ideas as his knowledge of his works deepens. In March, 1517, he confesses to Lang that day by day he likes Erasmus less.[47] He approves, to be sure, his attacks on the

---

[41] Luther's marginal notes in the fourth edition of the Greek New Testament are further evidence of his intense occupation with Erasmus's text. See Ernst Thiele, "Die Originalhandschriften Luthers," *Luther-Studien zur 4. Jahrhundertfeier der Reformation,* ed. Karl Drescher, p. 244; also Smith, *Erasmus,* pp. 182 ff.

[42] Letter to Spalatin, August 24, 1516, *WAB,* I, 50.

[43] Letter of Oct. 19, *WAB,* I, 70.   [44] *Ibid.,* ll. 26 ff.

[45] Spalatin passed on Luther's criticism almost word for word in a letter to Erasmus on December 11, 1516, saying that it came from "a friend." Erasmus apparently made no reply. Allen, *Opus epistolarum Erasmi,* II, 417 ff.

[46] He rarely mentions his name without a flattering adjective: "homine eruditissimo," *WAB,* I, 70; "summis laudibus semper offero," *WAB,* I, 133, l. 19; "Longe quidem superat Erasmus et melius loquitur, sed etiam acerbius" (i.e., than Faber Stapulensis), *WAB,* I, 134. He has Erasmus's Greek Testament constantly at hand. See letter to Spalatin, Dec. 20, 1517, *WAB,* I, 130; letter to Lang, Feb. 19, 1518, *WAB,* I, 148.

[47] *WAB,* I, 90.

priests for their laziness and ignorance, but he fears that he does not put forward sufficiently Christ and the grace of God, thoughts that may have been suggested by reading Erasmus's *Manual of a Christian Soldier.* He hesitates to express such an opinion about him, but in these dangerous times one must not forget that a good Grecist or Hebraist is not necessarily a good Christian. Jerome with his five languages does not equal Augustine with one. He falls out particularly with Erasmus's ideas respecting Jerome. In common with other humanists Erasmus held the Biblical father in high esteem, far higher than St. Augustine.[48] In the beginning of 1518 Luther again comes back to this attitude and takes issue with it in a letter to Spalatin, where he gives advice as to the best helps for a study of the Scriptures.[49] He insists that he is not moved by the prejudices of his order when he holds up St. Augustine against Jerome. He opposes Erasmus with hesitation, since he has always extolled and defended him, "although there are many things in Erasmus that seem to me far removed from a knowledge of Christ." He adjures Spalatin, however, not to reveal his judgment of Erasmus in order not to give assistance to those who are exerting themselves in raising a scandal against classical scholarship. Luther takes issue not only with the humanistic enthusiasm of Erasmus that exalts the great scholar Jerome above the great theologian Augustine. In a letter to Spalatin, written the day after the posting of the Ninety-five Theses, he expresses his impatience at the Erasmian spirit that constrains us to laugh at the evils and miseries of the Church of Christ when every Christian ought to lament them with groanings before God.[50] It is the dialogue *Julius and Peter* that he probably has in mind here;[51] later when he is preparing for the Leipzig

[48] In a letter to Eck of May 15, 1518, in reply to the latter's criticisms of his New Testament edition, Erasmus puts forward at great length his position respecting the superior merits of Jerome over the African Father: "Plus me docet Christianae philosophiae unica Origenis pagina quam decem Augustini. Et praeter Originem tam multos praeceptores habet Hieronymus . . . Ipse olim adolescens in ea fui sententia in qua tu nunc es . . . Mutavi sententiam, non quod minus praeclare sentiam de Augustino . . . sed quod propius contemplatus sim Hieronymum." Allen, *Opus epistolarum Erasmi*, III, 337, No. 844.

[49] *WAB*, I, 133 f.

[50] Letter of early November, 1517. The dating is Clemen's, but his argument for it is not conclusive; *WAB*, I, 117 f. In later years Luther became convinced that Erasmus's satires welled up from a heart altogether without reverence. Of all the bitter attacks which are sprinkled through the *Table Talk* there is none more frequent than the charge that Erasmus is an Epicurean who mocks at sacred things. The following is characteristic, "Wenn ich Erasmus hertz sollt aufschneyden, so wollt ich lachende meuler finden de trinitate, sacramenta . . . Es ist eitel gelechter mit ihm." *TR*, I, No. 484 (1533).

[51] The work bears various titles in the several editions, the most common being *Julius exclusus*. It is a bitter satire on Pope Julius and the Roman court. In a dialogue between the guardian of the gate of heaven and the Rovere pontiff, Julius sets forth to the astonished Apostle the papal claims to power in the most extreme form and lays bare with cynical frankness all the evils that were the object of contemporary attacks on Rome. The satire was written in 1513 soon after the death of Julius and seems to have been passed around in

disputation he sees the dialogue with a different eye. He finds now that it contains solid material if one reads it with serious mind, and he regrets that it cannot become well known in Rome, since it reveals so fully the monstrous behavior of the papal court.[52]

The contrasts in temper and interest between the two men thus become plain when one examines Luther's letters in the two years following his first contact with the thought of the older scholar, though as yet Martin acknowledges these differences only with hesitation and to his most intimate friends. Nevertheless he occupies himself increasingly with Erasmus's works, especially through the year 1518. Capito writes him from Basel—and he is interested enough to pass the news to Lang—that a new and enlarged edition of the *Adages* has come from Froben's press,[53] as well as the *Complaint of Peace,*[54] the *Dialogues of Lucian*[55] and *Apology to Lefèvre d'Étaples,* with whom Erasmus differed on the reading of a Pauline passage.[56] Martin's interest in Erasmus's works is keen and he is eager for the latest editions. His intensive reading of the *Adages* at this time is attested by his ready use of phrases and illustrations borrowed from them in the letters of 1518 and 1519.[57] He is familiar with the group of Erasmus's letters which Froben

---

manuscript, and possibly print, before its publication in 1517. Böcking gives the text of the earliest print (somewhat emended), with a full bibliography, in Hutten, *Opera,* IV, 422 ff.; Stange, *Erasmus und Julius II,* reproduces the same print photographically, with a careful examination of the relationship among the editions.

Like other anonymous pamphlets of the Renaissance, *Julius exclusus* is a nut on which many antiquarians have tried their teeth. Students of Erasmus, like Allen, *Opus epistolarum Erasmi,* II, 419 f., J. B. Pineau, *Érasme et la Papauté,* and Johan Huizinga, *Erasmus,* are convinced that he was the author. Wallace K. Ferguson includes the *Julius exclusus* (Böcking's text) in Erasmus's works, *Erasmi opuscula,* pp. 62 ff. Stange in his stout volume on the subject, *Erasmus und Julius II,* argues strongly against this conclusion. He stresses the French, proconciliar attitude of the author and joins Böcking and Von Pastor in ascribing it to Faustus Andrelinus, an Italian humanist residing in Paris.

Martin seems to have received the dialogue from Scheurl first. Letter from Scheurl to Spalatin, Sept. 30, 1517, Scheurl, *Briefbuch,* II, 25. He found it in the Erasmian style: "id est omnino Erasmice." *WAB,* I, 118, l. 5 (probably mid-November, 1517).

[52] Letter to Scheurl, Feb. 20, 1519, *WAB,* I, 346: "Multam sane continet frugem, si serio legatur. Doleo, eum non fieri in Urbe celebrem." Some years later he feels differently: "In morendo habet [Erasmus] spiritum et sunt verba calidissima, ut in Moria et suo Iulio; in docendo est frigidissimus." *TR,* II, No. 1319 (1532).

[53] Letter of Feb. 19, 1518, *WAB,* I, 147, and p. 148, n. 2. The edition he refers to is *Erasmi adagiorum chiliades iam tertium ab ipso . . . recognitae,* November, 1517. See Panzer, *Annales Typographici,* VI, 207, No. 236.

[54] *Querela pacis undique gentium ejectae profligataeque . . .* Froben, December, 1517. Panzer, *Annales Typographici,* VI, 201, No. 194.

[55] Froben, 1517. *Ibid.,* p. 202, No. 196.

[56] Froben, February, 1518. *Ibid.,* p. 204, No. 214.

[57] Preserved Smith in his *Erasmus,* p. 213, counts seventeen such references, but it is doubtful whether all of these need have been drawn from the *Adagia.* "Winged words" of this character might come to a scholar at this period from other humanistic sources.

published in August, 1518, containing the reply to Eck's criticism of the Greek New Testament text,[58] and he knows the *New Farrago,*[59] the edition of letters which followed in October of 1519.

The influence of Erasmus on the lectures on Galatians has been noted above. This was, however, only one factor in the general trend toward a humanistic treatment of the sources observable in Martin's exegeses after 1516. Were we sure that the lectures on Galatians in the edition of 1519 came from Martin's hand, we should have striking evidence for the effect of the Erasmian style of interpretation. The Galatians lectures in this revised version are marked by a kind of scholarly impersonality; their structure is simple and lucid, and allegory and dialectics have given way to philology. These are all characteristics for which Erasmus's *Notes on the New Testament* gives the pattern. We have seen, however, that the humanistic coloring here points to another hand than Martin's, possibly that of Melanchthon.[60]

Anyone who looks through the lectures and letters written in the years before the Leipzig disputation, then, sees the importance for Luther of Erasmus as a textual critic and exegete and as an interpreter of the gnomic wealth of classical literature. As an interpreter of theological truth, on the other hand, Martin found him incompetent to fathom the profound meaning of Pauline thought. As a reformer of religious life Martin was disposed to resent the method which attacks ills by making them laughable. To one as deadly serious as he in his struggle against indulgences, the irony of the *Praise of Folly* seemed too frivolous in the face of the awful wickedness which was to be dethroned. As regards the other great reformatory work of Erasmus, however, the *Manual of a Christian Soldier,* its spirit moved on another ethical plane and there is evidence that it was not without effect on Martin's development of a reform program.

This great plea for a moral life which Erasmus launched into the world at the early flood tide of his powers was aimed directly at men of the universities. The little book shows that the author was truly a religious personality.[61] In a restrained and objective though intensely serious manner he sets forth man's purpose in the world as a struggle to maintain a righteous

[58] *Auctarium selectarum aliquot epistolarum Erasmi.* Luther refers to it in his *Epistola super expurgatione Ecciana, WA,* II, 706, l. 11, which was sent to Spalatin at the end of October, 1519. Enders, *Luthers Briefwechsel,* II, 216, n. 8.

[59] *Farrago nova epistolarum Desiderii Erasmi,* Froben, Basel, October, 1519. See letter from Luther to Spalatin, March 26, 1520, *WAB,* II, 78.

[60] It is worth noting that the many references to Erasmus in the lectures on Galatians of 1519 (*WA,* II, 452, 476, 508, *inter alia*) were eliminated in the edition of 1523, along with those to other contemporaries. See Knaake, *WA,* II, 437.

[61] See Lezius, *Zur Charakteristik des religiösen Standpunktes des Erasmus,* pp. 15 ff. An incisive presentation, although marred by a strong bias against the Erasmian ideas.

life. Building on an idea common in the Church since Paul's letter to the
Ephesians, he summons the Christian to a warrior's loyalty in the service of
his great Leader. The conception of the Christian life which the work thus
unfolds is widely at variance with the monkish ideal. Piety and morality are
not the monk's privilege, but an unworldly heart may be found also under
the dress of a layman or the corselet of a soldier. In any class or rank the
Christian can find salvation. He wins this reward by his inner attitude and
and not by outer observances. No clearer and more stimulating challenge to
the moral life could have been addressed to the intelligent young men of the
first decade of the century than that which furnishes the keynote of the
Enchiridion.[62] Nevertheless, it is easy to see the point of collision with
Martin's hard-won ideas, and the monk must have recognized early the difference of accent between this identification of morality with religion and
his own deep sense of sin and fear of an angry God. The contrast between
the religious experience of the two reformers has been analyzed frequently
and need not be dwelt on here.[63] Erasmus's life does not appear to have been
marked by religious crises, and his attitude toward monastic Christianity
was that of the observant and reflective moralist. Rewards at the end of his
period of service are constantly held up before the soldier of Christ, and
the idea of the aid of accumulated merit finds its place in Erasmus's scheme
of salvation.

Nevertheless, these conflicts with his own thinking evidently did not
provoke Luther to an early protest. On the other hand, the arraignment of
the narrow, legalistic attitude in the Church which he found in the
Enchiridion gave support to his own attack on the prayers to the saints for
material benefits and to the belief in the equality of monks and laity, of
bishop and civil magistrates that were beginning to find expression in his
sermons and in the lectures on Romans.[64] Later on Luther's eloquent
declarations in *The Freedom of a Christian* that all Christians are equal,
whether in the monk's cowl, in the burgher's gown, the priest's cope, or the
soldier's armor, closely parallel some of the formulas in the *Enchiridion.*
From his earliest days in Wittenberg the justice of Erasmus's severe criti-

[62] The attitude of Catholic scholars toward the *Enchiridion* seems to be decidedly cool. See
Gustav Schnürer, "Warum wurde Erasmus nicht ein Führer der kirchlichen Erneuerung?"
Historisches Jahrbuch, LV (1935), 339: "A very roundabout way by which, after long studies,
a few could come to the goal."

[63] See Lezius, *Zur Charakteristik des religiösen Standpunktes des Erasmus, passim;* Richter,
Die Stellung des Erasmus, pp. 10 ff.; Smith, *Erasmus,* pp. 209 ff.

[64] In the sermons on the Ten Commandments at least one passage on the prayers to the
saints, *WA,* I, 420, ll. 33 ff., resembles strongly those in the *Enchiridion,* waiving the differences between Erasmus's finished style, with its subtle yet recognizable undertone of satire,
and Luther's powerful and indignant protest, where "every word weighs a pound."

cism was brought home to Martin day after day in the museum of venerated relics in the electoral church. In spite, then, of the consciousness of fundamental differences between Erasmus's views and his own that begins to be reflected in Luther's letters as early as 1517, it is evident that he felt himself in agreement with the reformatory ideas of the author of the *Enchiridion* and the *Praise of Folly*. What was the attitude of Erasmus?

At this time Erasmus occupied a position that for personal prestige and influence has never been attained by any other scholar in the history of Western Europe. His works were known and admired by progressive minds in all the universities and chancelleries. In the two years during which Luther's reputation was spreading abroad, Erasmus counted among his correspondents not only most of the distinguished humanists north of the Alps but rulers like Pope Leo, Albert of Brandenburg, Philip of the Palatinate, Frederick, elector of Saxony, and George, duke of Saxony. Men saw in him the leader who was to bring about the longed-for reformation of everything in state and Church. His attention was probably first directed to Luther by the appearance of the Ninety-five Theses.[65] These he forwarded from Louvain in a letter to his friend Thomas More in March, 1518, without comment;[66] but early in May, Wolfgang Capito wrote to Martin that Erasmus had expressed sincere admiration for the Theses.[67] In the October following, Erasmus himself tells Lang that these had given general satisfaction, except the few regarding purgatory. He adds that he has seen Prierias's *Dialogue,* which he regards as extremely silly, but he doubts whether it is expedient to touch upon the ulcer of the Roman chief priest and fears that the princes who should move against it are conspiring with the pontiff for a part of the spoils. He had heard that Eck is moving against Luther and wonders what has come over the Ingolstadt scholar that he should undertake such an attack.[68]

Direct communication between the great humanist and Luther seems to have been effected through Melanchthon. The scholarly young Swabian must have come to Erasmus's notice very early, for in 1516, as a budding master of arts engaged in editorial work in Tübingen, Melanchthon composed some laudatory Greek verses in Erasmus's honor,[69] and in the following year Oecolampadius assured the latter of Philip's admiration and

[65] Kalkoff suggests that Erasmus may have had some earlier knowledge of Luther through Augustinians from the Netherlands who had studied at Wittenberg. See his "Erasmus, Luther und Friederich der Weise," *SVRG*, CXXXII (1919), 57.

[66] Allen, *Opus epistolarum Erasmi*, III, 239, No. 785.

[67] December 5. *WAB*, I, 197 f.

[68] October 17. Allen, *Opus epistolarum Erasmi*, III, 409 f., No. 872.

[69] Letter from Melanchthon to Erasmus, August 20, 1516. *Ibid.*, II, 319 f.

added that the young man gave promise of becoming his successor.[70] In the difficult hour when Martin was engaged in negotiations with Miltitz and the disputation with Eck loomed threateningly on the horizon, Melanchthon addresses a letter to Erasmus in which he mentions Luther as his admirer.[71] In the meantime Erasmus was kept in touch with Luther's affairs,[72] and about the same time as the Melanchthon letter Mosellanus sent him from Leipzig a sarcastic account of the fluttering in the theological pigeon house that preceded the great disputation.[73]

Finally, on March 28, 1519, Luther lays his cause before the leader of humanistic scholarship.[74] He begins with a humble reference to the supreme position of Erasmus in letters ("Whom does not Erasmus teach?") and to his own unworthiness to address a letter to so great a man. He has learned from Capito that his name is not unknown to Erasmus and has noted in the most recent edition of the *Enchiridion* [75] that his trifling ideas (*fabulamenta*) have been accepted by Erasmus. The reference is to a passage in a prefatory letter to Paul Volz,[76] in which Erasmus indicated that good deeds are more to be trusted than papal pardons, and services to family and generosity to the poor are to be preferred as evidences of true piety above pilgrimages to Rome, Jerusalem, and Campostella. In deferential and humble tones Martin now asks Erasmus to recognize him as "a little brother in Christ" who is devoted to him. To this appeal for friendship, couched in an awkward Latin, he adds a request that Erasmus intervene with Melanchthon lest he break himself down with overwork.[77]

Erasmus was at this time in correspondence with the elector Frederick, to whom, with Duke George, he had in 1517 dedicated his edition of the history of Suetonius.[78] Frederick's letter of acknowledgment has been lost, but a letter from Erasmus to Luther's protector, dated April 14, 1519, has

[70] "Si quisquam Germanorum, Erasmum praestabit." March 27, 1517. *Ibid.*, II, No. 524.

[71] January 5, 1519. *Ibid.*, III, 467 f., No. 910. The date is assigned by Allen on rather slight grounds, but cannot be far wrong. See Smith, *Erasmus*, p. 220, n. 3.

[72] See letter to Capito of Oct. 19, 1518 (?). Allen, *Opus epistolarum Erasmi*, III, 415, No. 877.

[73] January 6, 1519. *Ibid.*, 470, No. 911.   [74] *WAB*, I, 361 ff.

[75] This had appeared in August, 1518.

[76] Allen, *Opus epistolarum Erasmi*, III, 372, ll. 405 ff.

[77] The letter may have been carried to Antwerp by Justus Jonas, who was the bearer of the letter from the elector to Erasmus, discussed below. See Kalkoff, "Erasmus, Luther und Friedrich der Weise," pp. 32 ff. Kalkoff's suggestion (*ibid.*, p. 32) that Luther may have forwarded at the same time his lectures on Psalms, a part of which had just appeared (see *WA*, V, 4 f.), is one of those colorful hypotheses which this diligent scholar insinuated into Luther biography and which he afterwards repeated as an accepted fact. See Luther, *Ausgewählte Werke*, I, 338.

[78] *Historiae Augustae Scriptores*, published by Froben in June, 1518. See dedicatory letter of June 5, 1517. Allen, *Opus epistolarum Erasmi*, II, 579 ff.

been preserved.[79] In this Erasmus devotes some lines to Luther. He notes that Luther's arraignment before Cajetan has caused exultation on the part of those who now confuse Luther with the cause of humanism.[80] Luther is quite unknown to him and he has not read his productions except here and there, but Martin's character is regarded everywhere as above suspicion. Erasmus is enraged that men are always ready to cry "heretic" and urge on to violence. He is at pains to convince Frederick that he has no personal interest in Luther's cause. What they think in Rome of Luther he does not know, but in Antwerp, whence he writes, the professor's books are read eagerly by the best men. Erasmus's statement that he had not read Luther's books sounds like a subterfuge in order to avoid expressing an opinion regarding them, but it is a position which he maintained for a considerable time. On April 22 he repeats the same disclaimer to Melanchthon.[81] Frederick's reply, a month later, has the tone of reserve which marked his attitude toward the Wittenberg professor at this time. It testifies to the general respect in Saxony for Martin's character and learning but is careful to state that his approval and protection are for the cause rather than the man.[82]

The desire of Luther for some assurance of support from the powerful humanist was strongly backed by his academic friends. Justus Jonas, rector of the Erfurt university, who visited Erasmus at Antwerp at this time and remained through the month of May, doubtless put Martin's case with a strong plea for aid.[83] It seems clear that Erasmus was for the moment pulled in opposite directions by two strong influences: a sympathy with Luther's independence and with his protest against clerical pretensions, and a fear lest he himself might be held responsible for the reckless attacks by the

[79] *Ibid.*, III, 527 ff., No. 939. Kalkoff's assumption that this letter is a reply to one from Frederick asking Erasmus's support of Luther at Leipzig is altogether without authority in the sources. See his "Erasmus, Luther und Friedrich der Weise," pp. 19 ff. Four days after the letter just cited, which is in Latin, Erasmus followed with a letter in German to the Saxon elector from Louvain. According to Allen, *Opus epistolarum Erasmi*, II, 527, this unpublished letter, a copy of which, in Spalatin's hand, is in the Weimar archives, does not mention Luther.

[80] *Ibid.*, III, 529 ff., No. 939. [81] *Ibid.*, p. 540, No. 947.

[82] May 14. *Ibid.*, pp. 577 f., No. 963.

[83] Jonas had just been elected to this office. He was accompanied by Kaspar Schalbe, a member of the family whose acquaintance with Luther went back to school days at Eisenach. Kalkoff, "Erasmus, Luther und Friedrich der Weise," pp. 34 ff., with his customary enthusiasm, builds up a theory that Frederick and Erasmus, beginning with the visit of Jonas, entered into an alliance for Luther's protection. This is a very questionable deduction from the sources. It seems more likely that Frederick, who never showed sufficient interest in Luther to meet him personally, was less concerned with Martin at this time than with the elimination of evils in the Church and the welfare and independence of his university at Wittenberg, of which he was very proud. He was doubtless much influenced by Spalatin and the court councilors, who became strong supporters of the monk after the hearing at Augsburg.

fearless Wittenberger. As an undercurrent to all of his remarks on the subject runs the feeling that the new learning may be harmed by the temperamental violence of men like Reuchlin and Luther, whom the opponents of humanism identified with the cause of "good letters." [84] It was for this reason that Erasmus advised Froben, the Basel publisher, who brought out a volume of Luther's writings in October, 1518, against any further printing of Luther's works.[85] It was also for this reason that he repeated to Wolsey that Luther was entirely unknown to him and protested that he had never read nor approved nor disapproved of any of his writings.

Finally at the end of May he answers Luther's letter.[86] It is a cordial and friendly epistle. He calls attention to the difficulty he has in driving from the minds of people the idea that Luther's works were written with his help and that he himself was the standard bearer of this movement. He complains that the whole affair is giving fresh excuses for an attack on the new learning, an attack formulated in the usual kind of violent expressions. He is moved to suggest a friendly warning against violence, citing his own experience and the examples of Christ and Paul. As one who loves peace, he adds that it is better to attack those who abuse the papal authority than the popes themselves, and certainly better to direct the schools to more serious studies than to heap contumely on them. At the end he puts in a warning against anger and hatred and any desire for glory, which is accustomed to insinuate itself even into the heart that strives for uprightness. These hints are conveyed with tact and the skill of his incomparable epistolary style and are accompanied by the statement that he has looked into Luther's commentaries on the Psalms and found them excellent.

We have no way of knowing the immediate effect of this letter on Martin, who at the time of its receipt was about to mount the rostrum for the great disputation at Leipzig. It fell into the hands of Mosellanus, the scholar who introduced the combatants on that occasion, and he published it together with certain other documents.[87] This was an indiscretion for which Luther seems to have expressed regret,[88] and which caused Erasmus serious embarrassment, since the letter was immediately seized upon by Hochstraten and

---

[84] Letter to Wolsey, May 18, 1519(?). Allen, *Opus epistolarum Erasmi*, III, 590, No. 967.

[85] Letters to Albert of Brandenburg, Oct. 19, 1519 (*ibid.*, IV, 100, No. 1033); to Campegio, Dec. 6, 1520 (*ibid.*, p. 406, No. 1167). Froben's edition in three volumes (1518–19) included Luther's *Sermon on Penance, Sermon on Indulgences, Sermon on the Ban*, and *Sermons on the Ten Commandments*. See Smith, *Erasmus*, p. 218. According to Pellicanus, *Das Chronikon*, p. 75, it was Beatus Rhenanus who prepared the work for the press.

[86] May 30. Allen, *Opus epistolarum Erasmi*, III, 605 ff., No. 979.

[87] See *WAB*, I, 410 f.

[88] Luther's letter is lost. See Allen, *Opus epistolarum Erasmi*, IV, 122, l. 46 and note.

waved aloft as proof of Erasmus's sympathy with Luther. As a result the hard-pressed humanist felt obliged to make a public statement [89] protesting his neutrality: "If I am called upon, I would answer even a Turk." [90]

Luther's eagerness for Erasmus's support was shared by his friends as the disputation with Eck drew near. Capito, who had assured Martin in February of the success of the Basel edition of his works,[91] wrote urgently to Erasmus imploring his help for Luther.[92] Indeed, Erasmus could not avoid feeling that he and Luther were engaged against the same adversaries, but he was wary about committing himself on the coming conflict. He recognized Luther not as a protagonist of the new learning, but rather as a disciple of the scholastic age.[93] The growing interest in the disputation drove him to increasing complaints that he was being charged with connivance in the authorship of Luther's works, although, he declares, the writer is as unknown to him as the greatest stranger.[94] He continues to reiterate that he has not read Luther's books [95] and that he does not want to be involved in the affairs of Reuchlin and Luther. "It is always the same," he says. "Whatever book appears at this time showing a little more than wonted license, they lay it to me"; [96] and he continues to express the hope that Luther, whose freedom of expression finds such favor, might lay some restraint upon himself in order that the affair may not lead to dispute and disorder.[97]

About the disputation itself Erasmus has nothing to say, although Melanchthon sent him Eck's *Excusatio* and his own *Defensio,* which referred to Erasmus as the "head of pious studies." [98] Three months later Erasmus wrote a long letter to Albert of Brandenburg in which he set forth his position regarding Luther and Reuchlin.[99] This letter, which was destined to play an important rôle in the relations of Erasmus and Hutten, was one of a series in furtherance of the program on which Erasmus was engaged at this

---

[89] Appended to the *Colloquiorum formulae.* See *ibid.,* IV, 120 ff. In the autumn of 1519 Erasmus then published the letter himself, with certain alterations. See *WAB,* I, 411 f.

[90] Letter to the reader, November(?), 1519, Allen, *Opus epistolarum Erasmi,* IV, 121.

[91] *WAB,* I, 336.   [92] Allen, *Opus epistolarum Erasmi,* III, 527, No. 938.

[93] Letter from Erasmus to Mosellanus, April 22, *ibid.,* p. 544, No. 948.

[94] To Cardinal Campegio, May 1, 1519, *ibid.,* p. 574, No. 961.

[95] See letter to Priccard, July 1, 1519, *ibid.,* IV, 2, No. 993; to Albert of Brandenburg, Oct. 19, 1519, *ibid.,* p. 100, No. 1033; and to Campegio, Dec. 6, 1520, *ibid.,* p. 405, No. 1167. Erasmus continued to pretend ignorance of Luther's writings long after the camouflage had become transparent. In September, 1521, when he met with the papal legate Aleander in Brussels, he asked his permission to read Luther's works. He reports that Aleander referred him to Pope Leo. See letter from Erasmus to Bombasius, Sept. 23, 1521, *ibid.,* IV, 586, No. 1236. One can well imagine the sarcastic tone in which the crafty diplomat gave this advice.

[96] Letter to Campegio, May 1, 1519, Allen, *ibid.,* III, 574, No. 961.

[97] Letter to Lang, May 30, *ibid.,* p. 609, No. 983.

[98] *CR,* I, 119.   [99] Allen, *Opus epistolarum Erasmi,* IV, 99 ff., No. 1033.

time, the defense of the new learning against the hostility of the Church orders.[100] In bringing before the archbishop of Mainz the cause which he had been pleading for a dozen years, Erasmus writes with the tone of a man who expects a sympathetic hearing, and he speaks of the abuses of the indulgences with a frankness that does credit to his courage, when we consider that it was addressed to the greatest profiteer from these. It is rather casually that he takes up Luther's case, as that of one who, he reiterates, is entirely unknown to him and whose books he has only dipped into here and there. While thus emphasizing his own neutrality, he has severe words for those theologians who, without correcting Luther, attack him with the bitterest abuse, who without knowing his books burn them as heretical, and who condemn doctrines in Luther's works which have always been regarded as orthodox and pious in the works of Bernard and Augustine. Plainly then, although he will not abate anything of his claim to neutrality in theological affairs, Erasmus dwells upon Luther's case with interest and sympathy as evidence in support of the plea which he is making against the intolerance of his own enemies. His continued assertions that he does not know Luther's works are of course an exaggeration, and are contradicted by at least one passage in his letter to Albert, where he shows himself familiar not only with Luther's arguments in his *Sermon on Penance,* but with their bearing on the history of dogma.[101] In spite of the fact that he was nothing of a systematic theologian and was always disinclined to theological controversy, Erasmus was fully able to understand the force of Luther's reasoning with respect to grace and merit as found in his *Explanations of the Power of Indulgences* and in his sermons of 1518. Within three months the letter to Albert had been printed and circulated throughout Germany and Switzerland in a number of editions,[102] an indiscretion which Erasmus charged to Hutten, who sent it to the press with what Erasmus called "Punic perfidy." [103] In the exciting summer and autumn of 1519 Luther seems to have thought little about Erasmus, and references to him become sporadic. In October someone passes on to him a remark of the Dutch scholar that he fears Martin will fall a victim to his own uprightness.[104] When Erasmus's

[100] See letters to Pope Leo, August 13, 1519, *ibid.,* pp. 52 f., No. 1007; to Wolsey, Feb. 1, 1520, *ibid.,* pp. 157 f., No. 1060; to Campegio, Feb. 5, 1520, *ibid.,* pp. 180 ff., No. 1062, among others.

[101] *Ibid.,* IV, p. 101, ll. 77 ff. See also Allen's note.

[102] Letter from Erasmus to Albert of Brandenburg, Oct. 19, 1519, *ibid.,* pp. 96 ff.

[103] This passage was inserted in a letter to Albert of Oct. 8, 1520, when this was prepared for publication. See *ibid.,* IV, p. 361, No. 1152.

[104] Letter from Luther to Staupitz, Oct. 3, 1519, *WAB,* I, 514, ll. 38 ff.

letter to Albert fell into Luther's hands in the following January, he found it "excellent," noting the Erasmian dexterity with which the letter came to his defense without seeming to do so.[105]

[105] Letter to Lang, *WAB*, I, 619, ll. 14 ff. In later years Luther has bitter words for Erasmus's cleverness in avoiding direct statements: "rex amphiboliarum, ein Meister geschraubter Wankelwort und Reden." *TR*, III, No. 3392b (1534).

23

GROWTH AS TEACHER
AND PREACHER

THE autumn of 1519 was passed in the midst of absorbing activities. The "busiest and most sinful of your brethren," Martin signs himself to Lang on September 3.[1] Eck is scattering "triumphal wreaths," assisted by the "innumerable frogs of Leipzig." Martin's reply to the Jüterbog Franciscans is in the hands of the printer. He is occupied putting a new commentary on Psalms through the press, from which that on Galatians has just issued.[2] A task suggested by Spalatin, a consolatory tractate for the elector in his illness, claims such time as he can spare for it. Autumn goes by with no lessening of nerve-racking occupations. The struggle with Eck continues, and Emser is now added to his opponents. A further importunity of Miltitz takes him away for a week to a conference at Lochau and Liebenwerda. The persistent Dungersheim still drags at his cowl with a constant reiteration of the same pedantic arguments. Ideas born of experience with the cure of souls in the Wittenberg parish and ripening thoughts on the sacraments urge for expression in sermons and tracts, which must be carefully prepared. It is well that he is "swift of hand and ready in memory," as he says a few months later,[3] so that whatever he writes "flows from him rather than that it has to be forced." As the year nears its end, he sums up his activities to Spalatin: "The Psalter requires a whole man; a whole man the series of sermons, for which I am working through the Gospel [Matthew] and Genesis; a third whole man, the prayers and services of my order; a fourth, the work of exegesis, not to speak of writing letters and the occupation with other people's affairs, including the meeting with good friends—I cannot call it feasting—which steals away much of my time."[4] The elector's chaplain,

[1] *WAB*, I, 506.
[2] Printing was completed at Leipzig on September 3.
[3] Letter from Luther to Spalatin, February 8, 1520, *WAB*, II, 36, ll. 34 f.
[4] *WAB*, I, 594, ll. 10 ff.

who knew well enough Martin's harassed state, had tried to divert him from "bitter and turbulent things" by urging him to "sacred and peaceful studies," the preparation of a series of sermons, the form to be a running commentary on the Gospels and Epistles of the Sundays and feast days. In spite of his occupations [5] Martin sets about the task,[6] but as the months go by amid "snarling and violent writings," he yearns in vain for an opportunity to devote himself to it. In the winter, indeed, each month, almost each week, brings a peremptory demand for reply to attacks or for the clarification of his position in sermons or in letters to friends and opponents. Early in February, 1520, in response to Spalatin's urging that the commentary be expanded to include the scriptural readings for Lent, Martin exclaims, "Give me two or three days for each day and it will scarcely be enough." [7] The number of new students at Wittenberg had doubled since the momentous day when he fastened his theses to the door of the Castle Church.[8] Even at the opening of the summer semester of 1519 Martin reported "floods of them," [9] and emphasized the excellence of their quality.[10] A year later their number had risen to a fourth part of the total population of the little city and it had become impossible for a new professor to find a dwelling.[11] On the other hand, Leipzig was devastated in the fall of 1519 by one of the periodical attacks of plague that swept over German cities in those years. When Martin learned of the anxiety of the faculty there lest their students should go to other universities, he exclaimed, not without a certain satisfaction, "How busy and yet how unlucky is hatred!" [12] At Wittenberg theology was flourishing, and he rejoiced in the prospect which such an influx promised for letters,[13] but the responsibility of lecturing to perhaps 400 hearers in a year was great.[14]

---

[5] March 7, 1521, in the preface to his Latin postil, *Enarrationes epistolarum et evangeliorum*, *WA*, VII, 463, Martin reviews the origin of the series.

[6] Letter to Spalatin, Nov. 7, 1519, *WAB*, I, 553, ll. 3 ff.

[7] Letter to Spalatin, Feb. 8, *WAB*, II, 36, ll. 31 f.

[8] See Förstemann, *Album Academiae Vitebergensis*, I, 66 ff., for reports on new registration of students from 1517 to 1520. F. Eulenburg, "Die Frequenz der deutschen Universitäten von ihrer Gründung bis zur Gegenwart," *Abhandlungen der sächsischen Gesellschaft der Wissenschaften*, XXIV, 11 (1904), 55, gives an average total registration at Wittenberg in the five years following 1516 as 600 per year.

[9] "Sicut aqua inundans." Letter to Spalatin, May 24, 1519, *WAB*, I, 407, l. 10.

[10] Letter to Spalatin, May 22, 1519, *WAB*, I, 404, l. 15.

[11] Letter from Luther to Spalatin, May 1, 1520, *WAB*, II, 96, ll. 8 ff.

[12] Letter to Spalatin, May 31, 1520, *WAB*, II, 111, ll. 7 ff. From August to the end of November 2,360 people died in Leipzig. O. Clemen, "Kleine Beiträge zur sächsischen Gelehrtengeschichte in der Reformationszeit," *Neues Archiv für sächsische Geschichte*, XXIII (1902), 137. Seifert, *Die Reformation in Leipzig*, p. 53, is of the opinion, however, that there was no real migration of students to Wittenberg.

[13] Letter to Spalatin, May 5, 1520, *WAB*, II, 98.

[14] Spalatin estimates that this number heard Luther toward the end of 1520. See Seifert, *Reformation in Leipzig*, p. 52.

At the same time he was actively engaged with Melanchthon in reforming the curriculum.[15]

University and cloister, townsmen, students and correspondents made constant demands on his time and sympathy. A widow, in a burst of generosity, has given her home to the Castle Church and now in distress pleads for its return. Luther urges her case repeatedly on the electoral authority, against the scruples of the narrow-minded legalists in the chapter.[16] On more than one occasion he has to intervene diplomatically to prevent suffering and injustice, "lest I should see greed on the part of those charged with the care of Church property." Poor petitioners who seek his intervention at court find a ready hearing and a warm response, as the correspondence with Spalatin shows.[17] From his native city of Mansfeld the vicar asks his opinion as to behavior during an onset of the plague. Martin writes him an answer full of sympathy for the weak who flee from danger, but insists that it is the duty of the priest under such circumstances to care for the sick who have been deserted by all.[18] Wider circles begin to seek his advice. The Regensburg city council turns to him in a dispute with the bishop of the diocese over funds derived from certain pilgrims.[19] Martin has doubts whether the pope has the power to make grants of this kind; he can only give advice "as from a theologian," that the bishop and council come to a friendly agreement in the sense of the adjuration in the Sermon on the Mount: "To him who taketh away thy cloak, give him thy coat also."[20]

Younger men especially looked to him for counsel. This is reflected in a set of "Rules for Life for the Clergy."[21] Here he lays down maxims such as he must have given often to theological candidates. When they were written is uncertain; possibly in 1518. In the informal Latin of monastic lecture room and refectory he sets forth the principles that should guide the personal life of a conscientious priest: moderation in food and drink, humility and zeal in Scripture study, love and charity in social intercourse, constancy in prayer, self-forgetfulness at Mass, with a final exhortation to deal gently with the sinner, all buttressed with many quotations from Scripture and at least one reminiscence of the *Adages* of Erasmus.

[15] Letter to Spalatin, *ca.* Nov. 24, 1519, *WAB*, I, 562 f.; also Melanchthon to Spalatin, *CR*, I, 127, and Friedensburg, *Geschichte der Universität Wittenberg*, pp. 111 ff.

[16] Letters to Spalatin: Nov. 19, 1519, *WAB*, I, 555; Dec. 8, 1519, *WAB*, I, 570. This case was on Luther's mind for at least a year.

[17] See letter of Feb. 26, 1520, *WAB*, II, 55, ll. 4 ff.

[18] Letter to Martin Seligmann, Oct. 14, 1519, *WAB*, I, 532 f.

[19] Letter to Thomas Fuchs, Dec. 12, 1519, *WAB*, I, 573.

[20] Letter to Fuchs, Dec. 23, *WAB*, I, 599.

[21] Reproduced from an eighteenth-century print as an appendix to a letter to Spalatin of May 16, 1519, *WAB*, I, 396 ff.

Amid all the fightings and fears of this momentous year, he slashes unceasingly at his enemies. In polemics against Eck and Emser and the Leipzig
faculty his resentment often rises to shrill abuse of his tricky opponents,
lighted now and then by flashes of sarcastic humor. Only here and there,
beneath obstinate insistence and passionate defiance, we see, as if arising
from subconscious depths, a flash of doubt and a yearning for the sustaining
hand of a friend. Thus in a dream his heart turns in agony to his old teacher
Staupitz. "Last night I dreamed of you," he writes. "It seemed as if you
were going away from me and that I was weeping and lamenting bitterly.
But you waved your hand and said that I should take courage and that you
would return to me." [22]

Escape from the vexations of the struggle in which he was engaged lay in
his work as preacher and teacher in the Wittenberg community and in his
concern for the great community outside that caught up eagerly whatever
came from his pen. More and more he addressed this wider audience in their
own language, writing increasingly, as his style developed, in the idiom
natural to a dynamic personality. It was, to be sure, not until the summer of
1520 that his controversial writings turned finally from Latin to German;
and only from the beginning of 1519 do the devotional and interpretative
writings appear almost exclusively in German, in a style whose directness
and warmth pulses in the outworn scholastic framework of his presentation.
As early as 1517, however, as we have seen, Martin had already sought to
reach the common people in the vernacular in his interpretation of the seven
penitential Psalms and the Ten Commandments. In the next year he sought
the same audience in his sermon *On Indulgence and Grace,* an effort at
popularization which met with outstanding success,[23] and in his *Freedom of
a Sermon touching Indulgence and Grace.* Latin still remained for him the
language of lecture and disputation, theological formulation and discussion,
but in the summer of 1518 he broke with the tradition that prescribed Latin
as the language of scriptural exegesis by preparing a German interpretation
of one of the Psalms.[24] The year before, Scheurl had asked him for "something personal" for an admirer of Martin's, the Nuremberg patrician
Hieronymus Ebner,[25] and Luther found time in the busy months before
the Augsburg hearing to write a brief treatise on Psalm 109, which he

---

[22] October 3, 1519, *WAB,* I, 515.

[23] Otto Clemen, in *Luthers Werke in Auswahl,* I, 10, points out that twenty contemporary
editions of this sermon are known as against only three of the Ninety-five Theses.

[24] *Auslegung des 109. (110.) Psalms, WA,* I, 689 ff., from the Wittenberg edition of 1518;
also published from Luther's MS, *WA,* IX, 180 ff., which deviates widely from the printed
text.

[25] Letter from Luther to Scheurl, Dec. 11, 1517, *WAB,* I, 126, ll. 16 ff.

dedicated to Ebner. Not he, but Spalatin, sent it to a press at Augsburg,[26] whence it apparently issued in mutilated form.[27]

In simple and direct German, which shows considerable progress in freedom of style as compared with his earlier attempts, Martin puts before his readers the ideas suggested by the eight verses in which the exultant Psalmist proclaims the coming of Israel's great Liberator. His interpretation tries to clarify the wording and unravel the allegory which medieval mysticism had woven about the Psalm. He waves aside, to be sure, the glosses of the "dear Fathers" of olden time, who were wont to do violence to the Biblical text so as to emphasize the dignity of Christ against heretics; [28] yet for him, as for his predecessors, the Psalm still revolves about the person of Christ, whose coming it proclaims, and he is at pains to show how this prophecy has worked out in the history of the Church. Though he spins out a long exegesis within the traditional limitations of the allegory, he draws freely on the proverbial phrases of the common man. It is interesting that in these pre-Leipzig days the Hussites are still outside the fold for him. They are "blind neighbors" [29] of the Germans, "Jews in spirit and miserable heretics," setting their own wisdom above that of Christ: "Dear God, our Father, take pity on this miserable, erring people and do not lay up their blasphemy as sin against them." [30]

In the tense months that preceded the first collision with the hierarchy at Augsburg he turned with enthusiasm to an academic task. This was to be a second course on the Psalter. All his efforts to bring his first lectures into form for publication had been vain.[31] They were now outdated in ideas and content. The years since he had begun his struggle with Biblical exegesis had clarified his theological views and widened greatly his knowledge of Hebrew. He took up the old task with new enthusiasm and opened the course, as it seems, in the early days of 1518.[32] Some preparation for it had doubtless been made, but as new demands crowded on his time, he must have brought freshly written and incomplete notes to his auditorium, and these were then

---

[26] WA, I, 687 f.

[27] The manuscript, which appears to be Martin's original draft, did not turn up until the 1880s. WA, IX, 176 ff.

[28] Ibid., p. 200, ll. 33 ff.

[29] Ibid., p. 187, l. 10.

[30] Ibid., p. 188.

[31] See above, p. 210.

[32] It is uncertain when he began the lectures. Böhmer, in "Luthers erste Vorlesung," Berichte über die Verhandlungen der sächsischen Akademie der Wissenschaften zu Leipzig, phil.-hist. Klasse, LXXV, 1 (1923), 9, sets the date at April 12, 1518. Ficker, in "Luther als Professor," Hallische Universitätsreden, Vol. XXXIV, and especially Von Schubert, argue more convincingly for an earlier beginning. Cf. Hans von Schubert and Karl Meissinger, "Zu Luthers Vorlesungstätigkeit," Sitzungsberichte der Heidelberger Akademie der Wissenschaften, phil.-hist. Klasse, IX (1920), 12 f. After Psalm 5 it is probable that lectures and printing went along concurrently.

expanded under pressure for the benefit of his audience of readers. The initial sheets, with a dedication to the elector in the fulsome style of humanism, came from the press in March of 1519; two weeks later he sent the first installment of the commentary to Johann Lang in Erfurt, his counselor in Hebrew studies.[33] Soon afterward the great Erasmus voiced his approval.[34] Waiting readers snatched up the sheets as they came from the press. Thus spurred to effort, Martin worked feverishly amid the interruptions of the great disputation and the polemical battles of the fall and by the end of 1519 ten Psalms were already in print. Then the work slowed down; and as each month brought him nearer to the break with Rome, the lecturer seems to have lost interest in the course, until finally, when the crisis at Worms approached, he brought it to an abrupt conclusion with Psalm 21.

The *Commentary on Psalms* strikes a gentler note than that which sounded in the preceding lectures. Polemical tones are seldom heard. The few attacks on Roman arrogance,[35] the injustice of the papal court,[36] or the scholastic theologians never rise to angry explosions. The struggle for his theological position is over, and he sets forth his views with full confidence. Jerome and other authorities reappear to enforce textual interpretations, but the scholastic pattern of glosses and scholia has gone to join the scholastic theology, and the exegesis is subordinated to a discursive treatment, which flows on in an even stream of robust and sonorous Latin. His interpretation revolves continually about a central theme, the supremacy of faith.[37] He says a last farewell to the "inflated and showy science" of Neoplatonic mysticism,[38] but reverts time and again to the exalted language of Tauler. With serene assurance he dismisses once for all the theologians who trouble the soul with doubts of salvation: God bids us hope; "the Cross alone is our theology." [39] This is the basic idea and it appears in countless variations and illustrations in the nearly two hundred closely printed quarto pages devoted to the first ten Psalms.[40] It takes more time to write a short book than a long one, and Martin was pressed for time. The present-day reader does not know whether to wonder most at the tremendous energy that enabled the hard-driven teacher to produce this mass of material or at the

---

[33] *Operationes in Psalmos. WA,* V, 1 ff. Dates of publication are not precisely known; the dedication to Frederick is dated March 27, 1519, and part of the print was sent to Lang by Melanchthon on April 3. Martin followed this with another part on April 13. See letter to Lang, *WAB,* I, 370, ll. 69 f. and n. 30, p. 371; cf. also *WA,* V, 3 ff.

[34] Letter from Erasmus to Luther, May 30, 1519, *WAB,* I, 413, ll. 48 f.

[35] *WA,* V, 57, ll. 13 ff.   [36] *Ibid.,* p. 116, ll. 5 ff.   [37] *Ibid.,* p. 159, ll. 19 ff.

[38] *Ibid.,* p. 163, ll. 9 ff.   [39] *Ibid.,* p. 176, ll. 32 ff.

[40] A tenth of the whole deals with a single verse, Psalm 5.12.

enthusiasm with which contemporary clerics in cloisters and universities seized the sheets when still damp from the press.

Throughout all the stressful and harassing months he continued to occupy the pulpits of the parish church on the market place and in the little chapel and the refectory at the cloister. Here on Sundays and feast days and through the Lenten season he put his ideas into burning words of remonstrance or entreaty or consolation. Ever since the memorable day under the pear tree in the cloister court when Staupitz wrung from him consent to undertake the preaching office, the friar had thrown himself with increasing zeal into this duty; and as the struggle over indulgences and the whole question of faith and grace went forward, he had put these and other questions of reform before his hearers. Wittenberg was used to much preaching: Sundays, three festival days each at Christmas, Easter, and Whitsuntide, numerous saints' days and the Advent and Lenten seasons—all brought one or more sermons. There were also times when sermons were heard on Wednesdays throughout the entire year.[41] Judging by what is known of Martin's practice in later years, his Sunday and holiday sermons were regularly based on the Gospel and Epistle of the day, and he may have formed early the habit which he had later, of preaching without a specific Biblical text.[42]

We cannot be sure that a single one of Luther's sermons has survived the centuries in the form in which it was delivered. As we stated previously, eager auditors, colleagues, and students, took them down as he poured them forth, often turning into rough and ready Latin the German in which they were delivered. These transcripts then found their way into the hands of the public through the Leipzig press, on which the Wittenberg professor had no influence, at times in a form that brought him great humiliation.[43] This kind of piracy at the expense of a popular preacher continued into the eighteenth century. In such cases Martin's only defense was to prepare his own manuscript for publication. Beside the printing thus enforced, he sent many sermons to the press voluntarily, often in greatly expanded form.

[41] Wedermann, *Luthers Wittenberger Gemeinde*, pp. 23 ff.; Buchwald, *Die Predigten D. Martin Luthers*, I, Introduction.

[42] Werdermann, *Luthers Wittenberger Gemeinde*, p. 173.

[43] "Mea ignominia haec est"; see letter to Lang, April 13, 1519, *WAB*, I, 370, l. 77, regarding the unauthorized publication of the *Sermo de duplici iustitia* and the German *Vom ehelichen Leben*. Here a comparison of the unauthorized with the authorized version shows, however, that the former was very carefully taken down. See *WA*, II, 145 ff.; see also Knaake's introduction, pp. 143 f., and his notes. The financial rewards reaped by the printers must have been very great. On the basis of lists in the Weimar edition, Kiessling, *The Early Sermons of Luther*, pp. 53 f., reckons that down to 1522 over thirty printers in twelve cities were publishing volumes containing Luther's works. Certainly the Leipzig presses were among the heaviest profiters.

In addition to the earliest collection of sermons, which has already been discussed,[44] two other groups lie before us, ascribed to Martin by editorial tradition and covering all together the six or seven years preceding the Diet of Worms. With exception of two early discourses, which claim to be copies of Martin's own manuscripts,[45] all of these are probably transcripts made by hearers. The sermons of the earlier of these two groups found in the Municipal Library at Zwickau, whither so many of the early records of Luther's life and work have drifted,[46] are all in Latin. Their structure, too, is the traditional one. It was evidently only by degrees that the preacher shook himself free from the scholastic method which arrayed virtues and vices in parallel categories and expounded the text in the conventional form current in the dialectical practice of the schools. In evidence from the first, however, is a command of Scripture that made him always ready to whip out a quotation to illustrate his point, quite obviously from memory and hence often inexact, but always suited to his purpose. More and more the proverbial sayings which give such color to his later writings find their way into these sermons. His illustrations show the coarse taste of a generation that took no offense at foul images, a characteristic that we have noted in the earliest group of sermons.[47]

The other collection is preserved in a great codex of the Municipal Library at Königsberg.[48] It covers the period from 1519 to 1521 and affords a deep look into his manner of preaching in these momentous years.[49] Here from the busy pen of a visiting Leipzig instructor, Johann Poliander, and those of Johann Agricola and others, possibly including Melanchthon,[50] we have a large number of Latin and German sermons, comprising no less than 417 quarto pages of manuscript. The reader is astonished at the great wealth of thought contained in these notes, which summarize the development of Martin's ideas as they poured forth in an inexhaustible stream.[51] Equally overwhelming is the impression of the time and effort that must have gone into the preparation and delivery of such discourses during these active years. To the final months of 1519 alone the editor assigns twenty-four Latin

---

[44] Cf. above, pp. 186 f., n. 34.   [45] WA, IV, 590 ff.

[46] Ibid., pp. 587 ff. Kiessling, Early Sermons of Luther, pp. 154 ff., gives a convenient checklist of the sermons that appeared in contemporary prints.

[47] Especially the Sermo contra vitium detractionis (1515), WA, I, 44 ff., which fairly reeks with coarse epithets and obscene suggestions.

[48] What the present fate of this codex is it is impossible to say.

[49] WA, IX, 329 ff. See also Thiele's introduction, pp. 314 ff.

[50] As early as 1519, Agricola was associated with Melanchthon in writing down Luther's addresses. CR, I, 82.

[51] See the classification by Thiele in WA, IX, 316 ff. See also Kiessling, Early Sermons of Luther, pp. 50 ff.

sermons, largely on the Gospels for the day. Before this series had been finished he had already begun another, on Matthew, carrying on at the same time still another series, on Genesis.[52] Throughout 1520 he continued to preach on Sundays and feast days. Fifty-four sermons from this period have been preserved, mainly in the scholarly notes of Melanchthon,[53] while another group of thirty-seven, largely in German, extends through the early months of 1521.[54] The great series on Genesis, delivered to the burgher folk and university men attending the parish church, was begun at the end of 1519 and extended up to the time Luther left Wittenberg for the great adventure on the Rhine.[55]

Brief as the notes are in Melanchthon's analyses, incomplete and unorganized as they appear in the mixture of Latin and German or in the abbreviated German of Agricola and others, they nevertheless enable us to gain an intimate idea of the character of his thought in this period. Although he stands in the vortex of bitter controversy, he leads his hearers through the Gospel story or expounds to them the entrance of sin into the world. Dialectical subtleties persist, to be sure, and the old allegories are still there. The three wells which Isaac dug in the desert represent a threefold prophecy: the advent of Moses, of Elijah, and of Christ.[56] In Rachel and Leah appear two sides of Christian life, the cheerful and the sad. The account of the leprosy and paralysis which attack the centurion (Matt. 8. 1 ff.) leads to an interpretation of these afflictions as significant of weakness in faith and good works.[57] Now and then, however, the preacher widens his application to include reformatory ideas. The purification of Mary introduces a disquisition on the liberty of the Christian. Jacob's betrayal in his suit for Rachel brings an arraignment of the abuses of the canon law covering marriage. The rules of the Church on fasting are criticized, and here as in the *Commentary on Psalms* he discourses at length on justification through faith.

"There is a great difference whether a matter is put forth with the living voice or in dead letters." [58] Thus Luther introduces one of his sermons to print in 1519; and the transcripts we have can certainly give little idea of the vigor and earthy phrase of the impassioned monk. Nevertheless, something of the force of Martin's language was caught by the attentive ear of the scribes, and their transcripts presage the sermons of later years when his preaching had shaken off all scholastic trappings and went straight at the

---

[52] *WA*, IX, 322.   [53] *Ibid.*, pp. 444 ff.   [54] *Ibid.*, pp. 516 ff.

[55] Letters to Spalatin: Dec. 18, 1519, *WAB*, I, 594; Feb. 8, 1520, *WAB*, II, 36. See also Thiele, *WA*, IX, 320 f. This series is not to be confused with a later, memorable group of sermons on Genesis delivered 1523–24. See *WA*, Vol. XXII, for an index by texts.

[56] *WA*, IX, 387, ll. 4 ff.   [57] *Ibid.*, p. 557.

[58] *Sermon von dem ehelichen Stand, WA*, II, 166.

heart of the common man. The infiltration of German words increases and reflects the growing simplicity of his appeals. From the first, Latin must have been used in the refectory and chapel of the cloister, German in the parish church; but we have seen that even before 1518 the sources attest the use of the barbaric mixture of Latin and German that was the jargon of monastery and university for informal intercourse and that appears in rich variety in Luther's *Table Talk*. There is, in fact, evidence of an early use of the vernacular for his sermons also before monastic audiences. Despite second-hand transmission and the uncertain chronology of the sermons between the Leipzig disputation and the journey to Worms, we may see proof in them of an increasing use of a homely, vigorous German. Proverbial expressions in increasing number, rough-and-ready etymologies, personal experiences and stories caught up from daily contacts, all echo a direct approach to the imagination of plain people.

Martin's experience in cloister and pulpit prescribed the sermon as the form in which to bring his ideas before the public. As his audience widened, he sped his messages to readers in the same form and the same intimate, personal tone as when he stood face to face with cloister brethren or city folk. Thus, as time went on, he gave the title of "sermon" to many treatises which he never delivered from the pulpit.

As a son of the humanistic age, Martin felt the urge to a constant use of the printing press. Before the end of 1518 his ideas on devotional as well as controversial subjects had been carried by Basel prints throughout Western Europe and echoes had begun to come to the Wittenberg monastery from across the English Channel and the Pyrenees. The following year brought a demand from Central and Southern Germany for all that the Wittenberg and Leipzig presses could furnish from Martin's pen and the circulation of his devotional and exegetical writings rose to impressive figures; indeed, the constant reprinting of his sermons and tractates at Wittenberg, Leipzig, Nuremberg, Augsburg, Strasbourg, and Basel through 1519 and 1520, largely in Latin, shows the amazing strength of the appeal which the burning exposition of forgiveness and faith was making to laymen as well as to those in cloisters and universities. The *Sermon on the Worthy Preparation of the Heart for Receiving the Eucharist* and the *Sermon on Penance,* both belonging to the months immediately after the opening of the struggle over indulgences, were each printed eight times in Latin in 1518 and 1519, and the Latin treatise *On Confession* which appeared in March, 1520, went into press eight times in that and the following year.[59] The number of reprints in the

[59] *Confitendi ratio. WA,* VI, 157 f.

vernacular indicates an even greater circulation among an audience that could not read the language of scholarship.

His audience widened rapidly. Nature and experience combined to make him a virtuoso in mass appeal. It is quite plain that it was not only the note of protest that attracted readers. An even larger number greeted those writings that met the needs of the soul asking the way to peace and salvation. Two tracts of this character are striking examples. One, an earnest appeal for a softening of the heart hardened by sin, *On the Contemplation of the Holy Suffering of Christ,* written and sent to press when the disputation with Eck lay before him, was reprinted twenty-five times in that and the following year; [60] another pamphlet, marked by a warm feeling of Christian confidence, *On the Preparation for Death,* which came from his pen just after the close of the first chapter of his controversy with Emser, has been preserved in nineteen separate printings, all within three years of its first issue.[61] Whether in Latin or German, whether addressed primarily to theologian or to simple believer, all these treatises ring with the same vivid, personal tone that marks the responses to Prierias and Eck, but their message does not draw on historical or theological speculations. It echoes his experience as teacher and confessor in contact with men and women perplexed and terrified in a maze of popular usages and Church teachings and practices. To souls like these he speaks with an intimate understanding of their problems.

This is apparent in a Latin commentary published in July, 1518, entitled *Sermons on the Ten Commandments Preached to the People of Wittenberg,*[62] a reworking of a series of introductory discourses in the parish church in the years preceding. From the early days of Christianity the Ten Commandments had been the basis for catechizing and confession, and lists of sins attached to the several Commandments fill a long chapter in the literature of the medieval Church.[63] This apparatus for confession was a thorn in Martin's side, and he attacked it in the first of his Ninety-five Theses.

---

[60] *WA,* II, 131 ff.

[61] *Ibid.,* pp. 680 ff. The number of copies in an edition must have varied widely, and any estimate of the total circulation of a given work can be only a guess. Heinz Dannenbauer, "Luther als religiöser Volksschriftsteller, 1517–1520," *Sammlung gemeinverständlicher Vorträge und Schriften aus dem Gebiet der Theologie und Religionsgeschichte,* CXLV (1930), 30, n. 65, calculates on rather insufficient data that by 1520 more than 250,000 copies of works by Luther were in circulation in German lands.

[62] *Decem praecepta Wittenbergensi praedicata populo. WA,* I, 398 ff. For the relation between the sermons of 1516, 1517, and the commentary, see above, p. 235, n. 62.

[63] For an interesting example of the "confession book" based on the Commandments, see that of Johannes Wolff (1478) in "Drei Beichtbüchlein nach den zehn Geboten," ed. by Franz Falk, *RgST,* Vol. II (1907).

While he was preaching on the Decalogue in 1516 he felt moved to prepare a brief explanation of the Commandments, and in the Lenten days of 1518 he printed it in German and in Latin.[64] Except for its simplicity and vigor of style, this manual for Lenten devotions follows the conventional pattern. The commentary, *Sermons on the Ten Commandments,* also has much in common with older literature. In analyzing sins against God's law the medieval preacher was wont to interrupt stern warnings and penitential prescriptions by excursions in the field of colorful allegory and hair-raising narratives. Martin's approach is similar, and his appeal to the popular imagination is as vivid as that with which Geiler of Kaisersberg had thrilled his Strasbourg hearers in the preceding generation, though Martin lacks the satirical grimaces of the Alsatian. Characteristic, too, is the fact that Martin's commentary swarms with quotations from Scripture in place of the pedantic formulas so common in the confessional sermons of the later Middle Ages. With a dextrous hand he weaves the usages of contemporary life into the frame of the Decalogue. The First Commandment opens the way for a long discussion of popular superstitions and unrolls a picture of medieval magic as weird as that in the *Witches' Hammer.*[65] Weapon magic, love charms, black art practiced with consecrated candles or holy water, baleful spells cast on children and cattle, divination by the cries of birds, crowd each other in a long procession of popular beliefs and diabolical practices. Many of these are waved aside as delusions. Such is astrology: "The stars have no power over the wise but only over fools." [66] He is quite sure that the baleful power of witches is among the devil's tricks but he hesitates at stories of old women riding goats and broomsticks, and he is even more skeptical about house spirits. The long recital of the devil's interference in the affairs of men shows how deeply the stories heard in boyhood still nested in his mind and how earnest was his effort to hold these terrors at arm's length and convince himself and his hearers that such works are possible only because God permits them as punishment for man's lack of faith. "Alas, alas! We are so sure of ourselves today, learned and unlearned, as if the devil were dead. . . . Our evil deserves that we should be given up." [67]

Reformatory and revolutionary ideas also come to the fore in this work.

[64] *Eine kurze Erklärung der zehn Gebote. WA,* I, 250 ff. The first print has not been found and its form cannot be determined with accuracy. See *ibid.,* pp. 247 ff. It was intended for catechetical use. Reu, *Dr. Martin Luther's Small Catechism,* p. 7, regards it as the first germ of Martin's Catechism. Luther republished the *Kurze Erklärung* in revised form in 1520.

[65] See Klingner, *Luther und der deutsche Volksaberglaube.* Some valuable notes on Luther's interpretation of popular mythology and its medieval sources are found in *Luthers Werke für das christliche Haus,* IV, 41 ff.

[66] *WA,* I, 405, ll. 26 f.   [67] *Ibid.,* p. 411.

We have seen how the cult of the saints stirred Luther to criticism in the sermons of 1516. The commentary on the Decalogue, published on the eve of his journey to Augsburg, finds him ready for a comprehensive statement on the saints. The simple hearts of believers have distorted these witnesses of God's power into magical instruments for curing bodily ills or for material gain. St. Christopher, "whose legend is most questionable," hangs on the wall as an image for divine honor. St. Anne, honored as patron of Hans Luther's craft, is debased into a means of bringing wealth or power. More than once, Martin is at pains to say that it is not prayer to these sublime figures that he condemns, but the sordid motives behind it. It would be better to give up saints' festivals, even to forget their names, better to sit at home and drink in moderation and invite in the poor, better do some useful work than to celebrate saints' days in the present fashion. So it is with other abuses in religious life: show and spending at the consecration of churches, wasteful pilgrimages, so attractive to women. Whoever has a wife or servant desirous of going on a pilgrimage should take a stout oaken cross and effect a cure with blows on her back.[68]

Thus in images drawn from everyday life he interprets the demands which the Commandments impose. The form is the Latin of the cloister, but the tone is that of one accustomed to advise the common man in distress of soul; the homely illustrations lend realism to the preacher's definitions of sin and enforce his solemn appeals for an alignment of daily conduct with divine law. The long commentary on the Commandments [69] is a milestone in the development of the Wittenberg teacher. Its bases are theological ideas ripened in the cloister; its undertone is the call for faith as the foundation of religious life. The conviction that falsity and sham pervade the Church and block the path of the Christian has crystallized and become a basic motive for his teaching.

It is easy to find in the sermons traces of the growth of ideas, spiritual and ecclesiastical, that we have seen reflected in the lectures and polemical writings after 1516. A sermon On Threefold Justice,[70] for example, formulates the basis for Christian confidence that appears so reassuringly in the lectures on Galatians. It was probably preached late in 1518, and the first print dates from that year. In scholastic formulas it analyzes three classes of sin and the means of justification which are to be sought: the sin against human laws, the taint of sin in which we are conceived and born as Adam's seed, and finally the sins that develop out of the congenital spark of evil

---

[68] *Ibid.*, p. 423, ll. 30 f.   [69] In the Weimar edition 123 quarto pages.
[70] *De triplici iustitia. WA*, II, 43 f.

within us. As compensation, many would offer the merits attained by their good works; against these Martin holds up again the thesis of the "new theology": faith is our only merit, for it is faith in Christ that works a transformation in the whole inner man and gives merit to his works. Thus, with careful step, he arrives at a synthesis of faith and works. He returns to the same idea a few months later in a sermon *On Twofold Justice*,[71] but treats it somewhat more conservatively. The *iustitia dei,* which had become the doorway to trust and confidence, is now identified with Christ. Beside this justification, based on Him and infused in us without our acts and through grace alone, stands that which is attained by works of mortification of self, of humility, and inner self-abasement.

In 1519, as one crisis after another drew Luther deeper into the polemical struggle, the demands on him for guidance in religious life became incessant. For devotional writings, scholastic and monastic tradition gave the form; the ideas that he poured into them are a simplified and easily intelligible theology; the style, Latin or German, vigorous and deeply emotional. Thus he writes three times in this year of violent polemics on a time-honored theme of pulpit and cloister, the right attitude toward suffering and death. The first work, *On the Contemplation of the Holy Suffering of Christ*,[72] is a prelude, a sermon prepared for the Lenten season. Beginning with the somber thought that the sufferings of Christ show the depth of God's wrath against sin, he leads the Christian soul along the path of passion and death to the Easter morning of joy in God's love. From this contemplation of Christ's sacrifice he then takes the reader by careful steps to the practical lesson, the duty of active and unceasing conflict with sin. In its simple and earthy German the little tractate sped far afield; it was printed twenty times within less than two years.

The second work on the lessons of suffering grew from a long tradition whose outstanding representative is the famous *Ars moriendi—Arte and Crafte to Knowe Well to Dye,* as Caxton calls it in his early print.[73] In the making of this medieval handbook for clergy and laity many pious hands played a rôle, from Heinrich Suso or Seuse, the German mystic, to the practical soul physician, Jean Gerson. Its popularity in the century before Luther is attested by many manuscripts and prints, particularly in Germany, where the macabre taste of early artists of the woodcut found

---

[71] *Sermo de duplici iustitia*, printed in March, 1519. *WA,* II, 145 ff.

[72] *Ein Sermon von der Betrachtung des heiligen Leidens Christi. Ibid.,* pp. 136 ff.

[73] See the comprehensive work on the *Ars moriendi* by Sister Mary Catharine O'Connor, *The Art of Dying Well.* Of interest for Luther's contributions is Helmut Appel's "Anfechtung und Trost in Spätmittelalter und bei Luther," *SVRG,* LVI, 1 (Leipzig, 1938).

inspiration for a realistic portrayal of the dying man confronted by devils, theologians, saints, and symbolical figures. Martin must have known the work in early cloister days. Both text and woodcuts seem to have clung in his mind, where they fused with the ideas of Tauler and borrowed mood and illustration from Staupitz.

Martin was well suited for the task of consolation. The optimism of a vigorous personality that was bearing him through so many storms, must have made him a magnetic pole for distressed souls. Of the many from town, university, and convent that unquestionably came to him for comfort and guidance, the records are silent; but their fears can be read in the writings dedicated to a few outstanding persons. Frederick, just returned from the exciting election of the new emperor at Frankfort, was stricken by what seemed to be a mortal illness, and Martin wrote for him a little work which he called *Fourteen Consolers for the Troubled and Burdened*.[74] Held back by the polemics that filled the weeks after the Leipzig disputation, he did not finish it until the summer's end; and when the manuscript went to Spalatin on September 22, accompanied by a letter of dedication to the prince,[75] the latter was quite well again. Possibly because the tractate had thus lost its personal application, more likely because its form might stir up further attacks by his enemies,[76] Martin delayed publication; but on December 18 it was in press,[77] and in February a translation into German by Spalatin also appeared.[78] In deep gratitude Martin dedicates to his prince its fourteen chapters as a substitute for the fourteen saints whom "our superstition" calls defenders from disease.[79] For his consolatory essay he borrows from the old "Art of Dying" the idea of contrasting groups beside the bed of the sinner, but the way in which he treats it is an original and truly classical example of allegorical ingenuity. He holds up to the gaze of the sufferer two tablets of pictures or images: the first seven show the evils under which mankind groans; the

---

[74] *Tessaradecas consolatoria pro laborantibus et oneratis. WA*, VI, 99 ff.

[75] *Ibid.*, pp. 104 ff.; *WAB*, I, 507 and 508.

[76] "The kind of writing which savors of Christ is most hated by the sophists." Letter to Spalatin, Dec. 7, 1519, *WAB*, I, 568. Modern Catholic opinion seems to approve the work: "Abgesehen von der Tendenz bietet es schöne und katholische Gedanken." Leonhard Lemmens, "Pater Augustin von Alfeld," *Erläuterungen und Ergänzungen zu Janssens Geschichte des deutschen Volkes*, I, IV (1899), 5, n. 4.

[77] Letter from Luther to Spalatin, *WAB*, I, 594 f. See also his letter to Spalatin of Feb. 5, 1520, *WAB*, II, 30.

[78] Walch, *Schriften*, X, 2130–2203; see also *WAB*, II, 38, n. 1.

[79] The cult of this group of saints had a long history in Germany, and several great churches had been dedicated to them. The names vary somewhat but all were martyrs from the early Church. See "Nothelfer," *Kirchenlexikon*, ed. by Wetzer and Welte, IX, 515 ff.

other seven the ways in which these are softened by the mercies of God. Within the panels he classifies in scholastic manner the evils that beset us: the evil within, our vanity and insincerity, which God in His mercy hides from us by the suffering He sends; the evil before us, death, which comes to all but is preferable to the sin that surrounds us; the evil behind us, which teaches the abounding care of God; the evil beneath us, eternal punishment, from which we are mercifully spared, although so many lie in hell's torments who had not a thousandth part of our sins, so many unbelievers, heathen, Jews, and infants, who would now be in heaven if they had had our opportunities; [80] the evil to the left, the torments of conscience which sinners must undergo while we are free; the evil to the right, our friends who, like the saints, undergo suffering as a part of heaven's discipline; and, finally, the evil above us, the crucified Christ who by death opened the door to life. "O, that we might look upon the heart of Christ, as He hung on the cross, so that He might destroy and debase death! With what ardor and sweetness He embraced death and torment for timid men, who tremble at death and pain, and how gladly He pledges this chalice to the sick, so that we, too, may not dread to take it, for we see through the Resurrection that no evil, but only good, came to Him. . . . Without any doubt, that noble myrrh dropping from the lips of Christ and commended by His words would become most delicious and sweet for us, like the fragrance and form of lilies." [81]

In contrast with those evils which he has recounted, the author now turns to the other panel and holds up seven images of good. He opens with something of the pride of the Renaissance reflected in Hamlet's bitter soliloquy: "What a piece of work is man! how noble in reason! how infinite in faculty! in form and moving how express and admirable! in action how like an angel! in apprehension how like a god! the beauty of the world! the paragon of animals!" Martin too counts off the gifts of body and mind that man possesses, not forgetting the high qualities that fit the male sex for noble deeds which women cannot perform—a truly monkish touch! [82] The greatest of gifts is faith in Christ, a blessing which, could we appreciate it fully, would at once transfer us from earth to heaven. Before us lies a common hope, death, which brings an end to the "whole tragedy of the evils of this life" [83] and an end to the vices and sins of the body.

---

[80] *WA*, VI, 113. [81] *Ibid.*, p. 119, ll. 6 ff.
[82] "Primo corporis dotes quantae sunt! forma, robur, valetudo, vivacitas sensus, quibus in masculo accedit nobilissimus sexus, quo multis rebus tum privatis tum publicis gerendis et egregiis facinoribus idoneus est, a quibus mulier aliena est." *WA*, VI, 119.
[83] *Ibid.*, p. 122, l. 33.

For the faithful, death is dead; it is only an apparition and a specter. Behind us we see that God has led us through our lives. In the stern tones of the Psalmist he exalts the justice of God. "We ought to love and praise His justice, and thus rejoice in God even when He destroys evil men in evil body and soul, because His supreme and inexpressible justice shines forth in all of these things. Thus hell is also full of God and of supreme good, no less than heaven. For the justice of God is God himself; God, in truth, is the highest good. Therefore, just as His mercy, so also His justice or judgment is to be loved and praised and preached most earnestly." [84] Again, he echoes the stern joy of the Hebrew Psalmist over the death of the sinner. "In this sense David says, 'The righteous man shall rejoice when he sees vengeance; he will wash his hands in the blood of the sinner,'" [85] grim words that enemies in his own and later generations did not forget to lay up against the author. Looking to the left of us, we may contrast our blessings with the hollow happiness of the evil-minded. Sweet are the disciplinary uses of adversity! To our right stands the great community of believers, whose support gives joy in tribulation. We need only lift our eyes to behold the horsemen and chariots of fire that surrounded Elisha. Above us is Christ, the King of Glory, arising from the dead. "Since therefore it is impossible that Christ in His justice should not please God so it is impossible that we should not please Him through our faith by which we cling to that justice. Thus it comes about that the Christian is all powerful, lord of all, possessing all things, accomplishing all things, utterly without sin." [86]

The *Fourteen Consolers* is a truly remarkable expression of Luther's complex personality. Marked at the beginning by the Stoic spirit which pervades a certain type of monastic Christianity in the later Middle Ages, it develops into a synthesis of Old and New Testament ideas respecting the attitude of man toward suffering and death. Dominating the whole is a conception of the reality and frightfulness of sin and the glorious triumph of faith. The dignity and freedom of the individual soul, so grandly conceived by the Bohemian nobleman Johann von Saaz a hundred years earlier in the *Bohemian Peasant,* is here fused with the conception of the Christian freeman, bound and yet free, slave and yet master, which was to find eloquent expression a year later in Martin's *Freedom of a Christian.* The *Fourteen Consolers* is more than a tractate of consolation for those in distress, like *The Art of Dying,* with which it has much in common: it is a declaration of independence from fear made by one who

[84] *Ibid.*, p. 127, ll. 34 ff.   [85] *Ibid.*, p. 128.   [86] *Ibid.*, p. 133, ll. 36 ff.

has now emerged triumphant from doubts and uncertainties. All of Martin's dynamic personality applies itself to the solution of the greatest of human problems, man's relation to evil and his conflict with the harms and sorrows of life and the terrors of death. The slight allegorical structure all but collapses under the weight of his pleading, now grim with bloody images from prophet and psalmist, now lyrical in ecstatic contemplation of the victory of Christ over death. All smug contentment of the soul which feels itself secure in a system of rational ethics, like that in Erasmus's *Enchiridion,* is here buried fathoms deep under a powerful flood of dualistic conceptions. Indeed, for a profound realization of sin and its consequences, for a picture of the soul rising triumphant over the fearful realities of suffering and death, the *Fourteen Consolers* is no unworthy successor to Paul's great song of victory in the sixth chapter of the second epistle to the church at Corinth. Even Erasmus, at a time of active opposition to Luther, found the work worthy of praise.

Death, particularly sudden death, was girt about with peculiar horrors, and echoes of these are to be found in Martin's earliest recollections. A councilor of the electoral court and a friend and benefactor of the Augustinian monastery in Wittenberg, Markus Schart, had sought comfort against such distressful thoughts, and Martin felt there was need of a work which should bring help to souls tormented by the awful vista of eternal retribution. The conflict with Eck and Emser delayed it, but finally on the first day of November the sermon, *On Preparation for Death,* published in German form, was sent to Spalatin.[87]

Here arrangement and contents follow closely the old pattern.[88] Like the *Art of Dying,* the discourse marks off the stages of preparation for death and braces the sufferer against temptations to despair as he measures the burden of his sins and looks into the yawning jaws of hell; but the scholastic accessories of earlier works of consolation give place to a wealth of scriptural quotations and Martin's heartening counsels have the realism of personal experience. It is not in mystical tones or with the lofty resignation of the *Bohemian Peasant* that he guides his patient to the supreme crisis,

[87] *Ein Sermon von der Bereitung zum Sterben. WA,* II, 685 ff. See also letter to Spalatin, *WAB,* I, 548. The Latin edition came in 1520.

[88] Sister Mary O'Connor, in *The Art of Dying Well,* pp. 190 f., points out characteristics in Luther's sermon which may be traced to the old version of the *Ars moriendi.* Martin's references to the devil beside the bed of the dying man may reflect impressions derived from illustrations in the block-books. See the reproduction in Appel "Anfechtung und Trost," pp. 112 ff. and 121 ff. He discusses at some length the relation of the *Sermon von der Bereitung zum Sterben* to the *Ars moriendi.* For influences of Staupitz, see Scheel, *Martin Luther,* II (1917), 206.

but with the assurance of one who has himself struggled with those terrors and overcome them. Death is, like birth, the entry into a wider life. In life we should open our minds willingly to reflections on death; but when it draws near, we must drive thoughts of it from us and dwell only on God's mercy. From a persistent experience of his own he warns that it is the trickery of the archfiend which makes us doubt whether we are really chosen to be saved: "You must then allow God to be God and to know more about you than you do." [89] He still puts trust in the intercessory prayer of the Holy Virgin and the saints, and throughout he dwells on the real and symbolic importance of the sacrament for the dying: "Trust just as firmly in the absolution of the priest as if God had sent you an especial angel or an apostle, yes, as if Christ himself absolved you." [90] It is possible to see in the consolatory works of 1519 traces of the new theology in their emphasis on humble self-destroying faith and on Scriptural rather than scholastic foundations. For an understanding of Martin's character they give further evidence of the strong currents of devotional life that were flowing within him in days when he was heaping invectives on his opponents in public prints and private letters.

Another practical side of the cure of souls is reflected in Martin's attitude toward prayer. The abuses incident to the great out-door festival which opens the summer called forth a sermon *On Prayers and Processions in Corpus Christi Week*,[91] preached on one of the late spring days of 1519, shortly before the clash at Leipzig. It opens on a note which we have heard in his lectures and early sermons: the sinfulness of prayer offered without faith and with trust in self-righteousness. Those who participate in the celebration should either do so with the proper attitude in prayer or remain at home. He then goes on to condemn the drunkenness and disorder that have become associated with the village processions. To the prayers commonly said at this time, which is also the planting season, he would add others that the fruits of the fields may not poison us: "For whence come the pestilences and other plagues except that the evil spirits poison the air and thereafter the fruits of the fields, wine and grain, so that through God's ordaining we eat and drink death and torment on our own land." [92] With equal fervor we should pray to be free from pestilence of the soul. The present age is sunk in sin; when God grants the Corpus Christi prayers and the fields bring forth sufficiently, man's response is drunkenness, idleness,

[89] *WA*, II, 690, ll. 16 f.   [90] *Ibid.*, p. 694, ll. 14 ff.
[91] *Ein Sermon von dem Gebet und Procession in der Kreuzwoche. WA*, II, 175 ff.
[92] *Ibid.*, p. 178, ll. 26 ff.

and unchasity. What prayer can help against such a "deluge of sins"? "God help us all to come to our senses and in right faith turn aside His vengeance." [93]

In this year prayer and its forms were much on his mind. Early in 1519 he had, as we have seen, revised and published in German a series of sermons on the Lord's prayer, originally preached in 1517 and printed from notes by his famulus, Agricola.[94] The little work found success, but Martin was not content to see his ideas reflected in this way, and found time in the uncertain days following the Augsburg hearing, when flight from Wittenberg was perhaps more than a possibility, to begin his own version for the press. In this *Interpretation of the Lord's Prayer in German for Simple Laymen* [95] the seven petitions serve as texts for an arraignment of the hollowness and futility of stereotyped prayer, patterned mechanically by clergy and laity. The little tract became a real "folkbook," making its way through Central and South Germany in a dozen editions in the following year. Its tone must have been unwelcome to many earnest churchmen: Duke George said to Martin at Leipzig that the pamphlet had turned people away from prayer. On the other hand, the mingling of eloquent spiritual appeal and violent denunciation of clerical hypocrisy penetrated circles which intellectuals like Erasmus could not reach.

Briefer and attuned to youthful understanding is a series of prayers which Martin issued late in 1519: *A Short Way to Understand and Say the Lord's Prayer for Young Children.*[96] Here he turns the petitions into the language of the peasant and wandering artisan and specifies with rugged eloquence the terrors that trail their footsteps, from hail and lightning to bloody encounters and syphilis. At almost the same time he made use of the Lord's Prayer to frame a little pedagogical satire. *A Short and Good Interpretation of the Lord's Prayer Forward and Backward* [97] is a very brief analysis of the several petitions that make up the prayer, followed by the reverse interpretation put on them by those who pray with the mouth and not with the heart. The work seems to be fragmentary, and Martin had probably intended to develop more fully under each petition the patterns of conduct that mark the selfish man. It is chiefly of interest as showing how eagerly the press snatched up his every writing, however incomplete and informal. Somehow or other an Augsburg printer got hold

---

[93] *Ibid.,* p. 179, ll. 31 f.   [94] See *WA,* IX, 123 ff.
[95] *Auslegung deutsch des Vaterunsers für die einfältigen Laien. WA,* II, 80 ff.
[96] *Eine kurze Form, das Paternoster zu verstehen und zu beten für die jungen Kinder. WA,* VI, 11 ff.
[97] *Eine kurze und gute Auslegung des Vaterunsers vor sich und hinter sich. WA,* VI, 21 ff.

of the manuscript and printed it along with the earlier tract, *The Lord's Prayer for Simple Laymen.*

The trend of events after the posting of the Ninety-five Theses brought a constant widening of contacts with life outside the walls of cloister and university. Social questions appear more and more on Martin's horizon and reflect themselves in sermons and correspondence. In that day most of secular life lay under religious sanctions and was subject to the workings of canon law. For the Wittenberg monk and teacher, Church and society were infected with the same ills and equally in need of reform. Foremost on the list of social problems was that of marriage. This came directly to Martin's vision through his experience as confessor, and early in 1519 called forth a sermon, *On the Married State.*[98] In connection with the gospel for the day, Martin preached in January on the wedding at Cana in Galilee, a topic dear to pulpit literature and to sacred and profane art in the Renaissance. A month later an unauthorized version appeared at Leipzig, written down by an auditor, and in May Martin put his own version into press.

His approach to the marriage problem in this work gives the first glimpse of the peculiar mixture of monastic fixations and secular piety that marks his many utterances on this subject throughout his life. Marriage was a divine institution, Martin states, but through Adam's fall it has become a "hospital for incurables" in order that men may not fall into worse sin. Learned men have discovered benefits in marriage: resistance to fleshly lust, bonded loyalty, and the gift of children. Parents should so raise their children that the latter will seek a mate according to the judgment of their elders, and children should not betroth themselves without their parents' consent. Martin broaches here a theme which was later to play a large part in his social teaching. The proper rearing of children, who are to him the end and chief office of marriage, is a service to God far better than pilgrimages to Rome or Campostella, building churches or founding Masses. Children are the real churches, altars, and Masses that we leave behind us. There is no easier way to deserve heaven than through one's children.[99]

Another problem of secular importance which arrested his attention was the thorny one of lending at interest. As an ethical and legal question, the discussion of interest began in the ancient world and engaged the minds of Christian theologians from the early days of the Church. The canonical

---

[98] *Ein Sermon von dem ehelichen Stand. WA,* II, 166 ff.
[99] *Ibid.,* p. 169, ll. 38 f. to p. 170, ll. 1 ff.

prohibition of taking interest, founded on Hebrew law in the Old Testament and on the commands of Christ to his disciples, was evaded more and more with the disintegration of medieval economy. Here theory tended to keep in step with practice.[100] Thomas Aquinas supported the prohibition in the main, but defined as an important exception cases where the lender assumed part of the risk. This opened the way for a more liberal interpretation; and in spite of the resistance of conservative churchmen, a left wing of scholastic dialecticians worked out a theory, the so-called "triple contract" (*contractus trinus*), which permitted the taking of interest at a restricted rate with no guarantee from the lender to share in any loss.[101] This was in step with economic changes that brought rulers and cities increasingly into the borrowing market and from the middle of the fourteenth century promoted the rapid accumulation of capital. Johann Eck belonged to the party favoring interest, and it will be recalled that he won fame and a golden reward for his defense of the advanced position at Bologna in 1515. With the support of the Fuggers the doughty theologian continued to uphold the practice in disputations and in print.

In a small city like Wittenberg Martin could see many harmful results of rising capitalism. Undoubtedly cases of extortion and other injustice came under his eye. He knew as little of contemporary economic trends as any other begging friar, but he shared the distrust of money lenders felt by the master artisans and peasant proprietors, and he was intolerant of any relationship between money and the religious life. His standards of conduct were built on a literal interpretation of the Scriptures and the "natural law" of ethics. As a popular teacher he felt the urge to protest, and he set forth his views in a *Sermon on Usury,* which came from the press late in 1519.[102] Several months later he expanded this into a larger tract.[103] Ten reprints of the latter work, appearing within a year from presses in Wittenberg,

[100] Theological conflicts on interest fill a long chapter in Church history and one that has by no means reached its end. Those who care to pursue these subtleties will find abundant material in Knoll, *Der Zins in der Scholastik,* and in the incomplete though valuable *The Church and Usury* by P. Cleary. For the development of theory and practice in Germany, see Neumann, *Geschichte des Wuchers in Deutschland.* The literature on the subject would fill a library of some dimensions.

[101] For the *contractus trinus* see Knoll, *Der Zins in der Scholastik,* pp. 70 ff. It became the basis for various sophistic devices to shelter the economic demands of the later Middle Ages and Renaissance from canonical censure. It was one of the varieties of the triple contract that Eck supported (*ibid.,* pp. 144 ff.). These disputes were particularly active in Dominican and later in Jesuit circles, and in spite of various papal bulls on the subject, differences of theological interpretation still exist.

[102] *Kleiner Sermon von dem Wucher. WA,* VI, 3 ff.

[103] *Grosser Sermon von dem Wucher. WA,* VI, 36 ff.

Leipzig, Augsburg, and Basel, testify to the timeliness of the subject and the wide interest in this first public effort of Luther to apply Christian ethics to economic life.

As was to be expected, he approached the question from Scripture. Christ commanded His followers to suffer violence and to give the cloak also to him who takes the coat. It is, he insists, a categorical command laid upon all and disobedience to it has brought violence and strife into the Christian world, so that "lawsuits and disputes, judges, notaries, officials, lawyers and that kind of ignoble rabble are as thick as flies in summer." For a debt of three or four florins some poor Christian is summoned many miles away from home and family, or even driven out and banned. It is only fair, therefore, that he who demands back all that belongs to him must pay to judges, clerks, and lawyers, "into the devil's service," twenty, thirty, and forty florins because he was unwilling to forgive a neighbor a small debt for the sake of God and eternal reward. Yet though we are commanded to give freely to anyone who asks, Martin does not overlook the fact that this command has been abused by the Church in seeking money for churches, cloisters, organs, towers, or for the endowment of Masses and prayers. The living members of the Church of Christ are neglected, and while so-called "alms" are given for stone, wood, and painted objects, so costly that help for providing them has to be sought from "bulls and parchments, lead, tin, cords great and small, and wax, green, yellow, and white," all to purchase indulgences from Rome. With a bitter reference to St. Peter's at Rome, then just lifting its vast cupola, he demands that Church authorities or a council call a halt to indiscriminate begging for building in the papal city. It is surprising, he states, that the Romans are so stupid as not to charge even higher prices for the creation of saints, the investiture of bishops, and their bulls and charters, "so long as such fat German fools continue to come to their fair." [104] After this vigorous digression on a theme which he was to treat at full length a few months later in his *Address to the Christian Nobility,* he brings together the passages from the Old and New Testament that forbid lending at interest and proclaims Christ's command (Luke 5.34,35), "Ye shall lend and not receive again," as binding for each and every Christian.

Having thus defined the proper attitude of the Christian toward worldly possessions, he turns to the burning question of capital investment in business and in cultural undertakings. This is a new invention "in this recent dangerous time, when nothing good is brought to light any more

[104] *Ibid.*, p. 46, ll. 28 f.

and all man's mind and thought is an unbridled striving for wealth, honor and lust." [105] It is the direct opposite of Christian love that the lender is always intent only on his own advantage to the damage of the borrower. Whether usury or not, the gains from interest are, like the winnings from gambling, prostitution, or fraud, earned by means of sin. The piling up of income from interest and its reinvestment "so that one interest drives on another like the water the wheel" is open and shameless greed. In Latin they call it "interest"—"The noble, dear, tender little word!" [106] This pest makes it possible to earn money by just sitting still, even though the lender be an invalid, a child, or a woman, while others lose. He is familiar with the "triple contract" for commercial enterprises, with unconditional repayment, and regards it as an affair of sharpers, thieves, and robbers, for it is nothing else than buying the luck associated with money, a thing which is in the power of no man.

Historically, Martin stands precisely on the position of Thomas Aquinas,[107] and follows the Angelic Doctor in making only one exception, where the lender accepts a share in losses "from God's hand," such as illness, death, water, fire, hail, or from evil animals or evil men, an arrangement which he contends is in accord with reason and natural law. Where lender and borrower have a mutual need of each other, he would limit the interest to 4, 5, or 6 percent: "the smaller the percentage, the more godly and Christian the loan." [108] The excuse offered by churches and clergy that they lend at interest in order to use the income for God's service, is a disgrace. "If you want to serve God . . . , do it without damage to your neighbor and in fulfillment of His command." [109] The whole business has a dangerous side that is little noted: the gaining of money in idleness through the labor and risk of others. That is against God's command, "for when you seek advantages from your neighbor that you will not permit him to have, then love has vanished and the law of nature is rent asunder." [110]

The year 1519, which saw a growing urge to publicize his views on the relation of Church and society, also brought a rapid expansion of Martin's conception of the office and function of the Church in meeting the needs of the individual soul. The conviction that faith is supreme in the work of salvation was obliged to drive him sooner or later to an examination of the rôle of the sacraments. In the last months of the year he devoted to this topic

---

[105] *Ibid.*, p. 51, ll. 23 ff.   [106] *Ibid.*, p. 53, ll. 11 ff. and 22.

[107] See Knoll, *Der Zins in der Scholastik*, pp. 13 ff. In later years Martin made some concessions. See Luther, *Ausgewählte Werke*, VII, 334 ff.

[108] *WA*, VI, 58, ll. 15 ff.   [109] *Ibid.*, p. 59, ll. 18 f.

[110] *Ibid.*, p. 60, ll. 7 ff.

three tracts which he put speedily into press.[111] Several persons in Wittenberg asked him to dedicate some devotional work to the Duchess Margaret of Brunswick and Lüneburg, a woman of deeply religious character with whom he seems to have had some personal acquaintance.[112] It is to her, then, that the memorable series is inscribed. It begins on a note of revolutionary significance. The three sacraments to which he devotes himself are penance, baptism, and the Eucharist. There is no other that he will accept, he declares to Spalatin, "until someone shows me by what passage I can prove it," [113] and he promises his friend something more regarding the "things that are fabricated about the seven sacraments." This fateful declaration marks off a rapid step forward, for we recall that only two months earlier in his tract *On Preparation for Death* he made an impassioned plea for faith in the sacrament for the dying.

In his first sermon, *On the Sacrament of Penance*,[114] Martin comes at once to a theme on which he had been dwelling with insistence since the memorable Theses of two years before: faith as the only door for rescue from sin. No pilgrimages, no indulgences can avail to cleanse the guilty heart; no good works can drive out sin. Faith alone gives validity to absolution; faith in Christ's word brings the gift of grace, which does not stand within the power of priest, bishop, or pope. No priest may doubt one's penitence nor refuse absolution; indeed, in the category of sins there is none greater than to doubt the article on the forgiveness of sins. Once more he defends the thesis that the keys of St. Peter do not confer power but impose service and that the right of absolution was given not to St. Peter alone but to every Christian. Once more he comes back to an idea which appeared four years earlier in the lectures on Romans: the difficulty of distinguishing between venial and mortal sins. This is a distinction which no learning can define; one should therefore confess all sins each month. Throughout the sermon rings a faith which sets free from all fears: a confidence that the sacrament establishes a direct relation between man and God, a relation in which the intervention of priest and prelate dwindles and vanishes.

The same note dominates the second treatise, *On the Holy Sacrament of Baptism*.[115] In the ceremony of immersion he recognizes the form which

---

[111] The first probably appeared in October, the second on November 9, and the third was in press at the end of that month. See *WA*, II, 709 f.; and Clemen, *Luthers Werke in Auswahl*, I, 174. See also letter to Spalatin of Nov. 29, *WAB*, I, 563 f.

[112] See letter from Luther to Margaret, Nov. 4, *WAB*, I, 549; letter to Spalatin, Dec. 25, *WAB*, I, 550, n. 1. Concerning the duchess, see *WAB*, I, 550, n. 1.

[113] Dec. 18, 1519, *WAB*, I, 594 f.

[114] *Ein Sermon von dem Sakrament der Busse. WA*, II, 714 ff.

[115] *Ein Sermon von dem heiligen, hochwürdigen Sakrament der Taufe. WA*, II, 727 ff.

represents most fully the indwelling symbolism of the baptismal act: the driving out of the old man and the birth of the new. For Martin, as for all whose ideology was rooted in the Middle Ages, the symbol of baptism had a realism that the modern mind can hardly recapture. He is profoundly moved by the deep meaning of the sacrament as an enduring force throughout life in man's struggle against sin and his rise after defeat to a renewal of the covenant. Once more the monk is possessed by the conception of sin as a living enemy, and he finds cheer in the thought of death, bitter and horrible as it is, since it will bring freedom from sin. The way of escape is not through fasting nor excessive practices of self-torture: only so much of these are admissible as are necessary to complete the work of baptism. Cleric and layman carry out the task, each in his own way; as with men traveling to a city, the goal is the same even though one takes the footpath and another the highway. Both travelers have hardships peculiar to the path which they follow, although the clerical life by its self-imposed abstinence and suffering leads to a more speedy fulfillment of the baptismal sacrament. The tract was evidently prepared with more than usual care. It offers no new idea, but is a vigorous restatement of that which Martin had set forth in learned and popular form since 1517: the independent responsibility of the Christian for the progress of his soul. Drawing again on his own harrowing experiences, he seeks to guide his readers along the difficult path that leads between useless, tormenting fear and the illusory feeling of security.

When he comes to discuss the Eucharist he again throws himself earnestly into the task of making clear to his hearers the difference between the symbol and the faith from which its fufillment derives. The sermon *On the Holy Sacrament of the Eucharist and on the Brotherhoods* [116] opens with the dangerous question of the two forms of communion, bread and wine. Here he measures his step, but it leads in a new direction. He points out that councils of the Church have declared repeatedly that the sacrament may be given in two forms, and that is what he himself prefers in order to carry out most fully its symbolic character, just as in the sermon *On Baptism* he preferred immersion to other forms. The Eucharist symbolizes the union of all citizens of God's city, joined in duty, in joy and in pain, one body with Christ—an idea that fires him to lyrical, mystic phrase reminiscent of Tauler and the *German Theology*. Bread and wine, transformed into the "genuine, natural" body and blood, are symbols and evidence that the Church shares in Christ's suffering. Brushing aside all the metaphysical

---

[116] *Ein Sermon von dem hochwürdigen Sakrament des heiligen wahren Leichnams Christi und von den Brüderschaften. WA, II, 742 ff.*

interpretations that clustered so thickly about the Eucharist, he emphasizes above all the necessity for being certain that Christ and all the saints associate themselves with us in the sacrament. It is in faith that all the power of the sacrament lies, and it is more important that we concentrate our attention on the spiritual than on the natural body of Christ. He brands as a scholastic subtlety the theory that the sacrament is pleasing to God in itself, even when those who share in it do not please Him. Not as "a work that is done" (*opus operatum*) does it please, but as "the work of the doer" (*opus operantis*), a work done with faith. Metaphysical refinements like this grow out of too much concentration on the natural body of Christ: "Who could repeat all the frightful misuses and misbelief that increase day by day about this blessed sacrament!" [117]

In the main a sturdy realism marks the sermon on the Eucharist. Martin avoids entanglement in the metaphysical subtleties of the medieval scholastics and leaves the dogma of transubstantiation unimpaired. A dozen years later he was to set up a theory on the subject that is as scholastic as those he condemns. As a pendant to the treatise he attached another of quite different tone, possibly just for convenience of publication. This returns to the abuses in the lay brotherhoods which had called forth the Corpus Christi sermon earlier in the year. Founded for the cultivation of fraternal religious life, the German brotherhoods were active in the endowment of Masses and the establishment of altars and chapels and organization of pilgrimages. They showed many of the defects of the social religious life of the time, and Martin does not let any of these escape him. It would be better if there were no brotherhoods, and he is sorry for the saints whose names they carry on their banners. "If you put up a sow as the patron of such a fraternity, I don't believe she would endure it." [118] He is sharply critical of the selfishness which limits to the members of a brotherhood all the treasure of merit accruing from their good works: "These partisan brotherhoods have one register, one Mass, one kind of good works, one time, one money, and as things are now, one beer, one gluttony, and one guzzling." [119] He closes his denunciation, which has the lurid vocabulary of his polemical style, with an appeal for a spirit of selfless, fraternal love.

[117] *Ibid.*, pp. 751 f.
[119] *Ibid.*, p. 756, ll. 27 ff.
[118] *Ibid.*, p. 754, l. 35 to p. 755, l. 1.

24

THE RISING TIDE
OF REVOLT

"ALL Switzerland, Constance, Augsburg and a good part of Italy depend on Luther." Thus wrote the Freiburg jurist Ulrich Zasius to Konrad Mutianus at the beginning of December, 1519.[1] For half a year the energetic Froben had been diligently sending out his first edition of Luther's Latin works from the Basel press. Early in the year six hundred copies had gone to France and to Spain; the book had also become widely known in the Netherlands and England, and a Pavia colleague of Froben's had undertaken to distribute it among Italian scholars.[2] By February, 1519, the edition was almost exhausted, and before the end of May an augmented second edition, issued in that month, was already sought in vain on the Basel bookstalls.[3] A year later Konrad Pellicanus, then guardian of the Franciscan convent in the Swiss city and later an associate of Zwingli, writes to Martin that reprints of his German writings are appearing there,[4] and that brothers of the Order of St. Francis are translating his exposition of the Ten Commandments into German and making it the subject of sermons to appreciative audiences. While he does not sympathize with Erasmus's indiscriminate attacks on monasticism, Pellicanus urges Luther to persist in his criticism of its abuses.

The Swiss cleric was only one of the earlier witnesses to the widening of Luther's contacts as the spring of 1520 opened. The spread of his fame brought a rapid expansion in the circle of his correspondents, which included clerics in Constance, Ulm, Augsburg, Breslau, the East Mark, his childhood home of Mansfeld, far-away Paris, and, before summer, representatives of the knightly class. His interchanges with the humanists Crotus, Erasmus, Wolfgang Capito, and Ulrich von Hutten became active, and though unfor-

---

[1] Karl Gillert, ed., "Der Briefwechsel des Conradius Mutianus," *Geschichtsquellen der Provinz Sachsen*, XVIII, ii, 256.
[2] Letter from Johann Froben to Luther, Feb. 14, 1519, *WAB*, I, 332.
[3] *Ibid.*, p. 335, n. 18.   [4] March 16, 1520. *WAB*, II, 65, ll. 26 ff.

tunately some of the correspondence from both sides has been lost, the professor's progress can be traced in the unbroken flow of letters, notes, and memoranda to Spalatin, his *alter ego*.

While the letters that have been preserved and the references to others which have been lost, furnish evidence of the widening contacts, it is only here and there that we have a glimpse of the increasing number of visitors that found their way into the refectory or into Martin's cell to have a word with the monk whose writings were penetrating the farthest limits of Catholic Europe. Influential laymen like Wilhelm Reiffenstein, steward of the North German lords of Stolberg,[5] scholars and clerics bearing letters of introduction [6] knock on Martin's door; and social invitations from persons within the little city are so numerous that the hard-driven professor suspects them to be an invention of Satan to disturb his work.[7] In addition, there was the procession of new students, whose number caused a serious embarrassment at the opening of the summer semester of 1520: "Good Lord, how many stream together here; what a promise for letters this flood of men brings us!" [8]

Increasing fame brought the usual envy and slander, fraught with all the venom that belonged to theological discussion in this revolutionary age. Strange tales regarding his parentage and education were passed about and came under his eye,[9] monstrosities like those circulated some years later by his enemies: that he was begotten by a devilish incubus, or that he was born in heretical Bohemia and received in youth the doctrines of Wyclif,[10] so that Martin felt moved at last to give Spalatin a little sketch of his birth and baptism,[11] of his Eisenach relationships, and so on, and to cite the counts of Mansfeld as confirming witnesses. At the same time increasing evidence of support from friends and strangers stiffened his will. A Constance canon, Johann von Botzheim, well known for his ascetic life, hails Luther as the "most vigilant reawakener of sacred learning" and rejoices that fate has permitted him to see this revival of holy and profane letters by a hand that deals out a potent remedy for the healing, not only of scholarship but also of souls suffering from the disease of scholasticism.[12] In similar inflated style, a young North German pupil of Erasmus, Hermann Humpius of

---

[5] Letter from Luther to Spalatin, May 5, 1520, *WAB*, II, 101.

[6] See letter to Spalatin, June 29, 1520, *WAB*, II, 131.

[7] Letter to Spalatin, May 5, 1520, *WAB*, II, 101.

[8] Letter to Spalatin, May 5, 1520, *WAB*, II, 98; also see letter to Spalatin, May 1, 1520, *WAB*, II, 96.

[9] Letter to Spalatin, Jan. 10, 1520, *WAB*, I, 608, l. 9.

[10] See *ibid.*, pp. 608 f., n. 2.   [11] January 14. *WAB*, I, 610.

[12] March 3, 1520. *WAB*, II, 60 f.

Emden, writes from Paris, assuring Martin of his support and undertaking to print, if need be at his own expense, the resolution of the Louvain faculty condemning Martin, along with certain marginal "annotations" of his own, for which he seems to have mobilized all the humanistic muses.[13]

Through the winter and spring Martin's position was not without personal danger. In spite of the elector's protection, he had reason to think that men were abroad who sought his life. He heard through Melanchthon that the clergy at George's residence in Meissen, Emser among them, were so enraged against him that they thought he could be slain without incurring sin.[14] In April he received a solemn warning through friends in Halberstadt that a certain doctor of medicine, who had the power to make himself invisible, was commissioned to kill him and that the deed was set for the next public showing of the holy relics at All Saints' Church.[15] It was therefore a comfort when early in May a student from Franconia arrived with a message from his father, the knight Sylvester von Schaumberg, offering Martin a haven of refuge if his perilous course should bring any danger to the elector.[16]

No threats served, however, to daunt or tame the embattled spirit, and Martin rose with ever increasing vigor to meet his enemies as the winter came and went. Stung by the attacks on his birth and parentage and the constantly reiterated charge of Bohemian heresy, he waves aside Spalatin's advice to teach theology without offense to the pope. He has committed his cause to God and defies those who would slay him or blast him as a heretic: "The more fiercely they set upon me, the more they amuse me. For I am resolved to be afraid of nothing whatever in this matter. . . . And if I did not hesitate to involve the elector in the affair, I would publish so complete a defense as to provoke these furies still further and make sport of their stupid rage against me." [17] So long as Eck continues to raise his voice he may not withhold his hand, but is obliged to commit the affair to God and like a ship give himself up to tide and waves. "I have the idea that an extraordinary storm is coming on me unless God halts Satan. . . . What difference does it make, the word of divine justice could never be set forth without turmoil, uproar, and danger . . . therefore in this affair we have to despair of peace and tranquillity or the Word will be set at naught." [18]

Throughout the later winter and the spring a fierce resentment burns in

[13] March 14, 1520. *WAB*, II, 62 f.
[14] Letter from Luther to Spalatin, Dec. 25, 1519, *WAB*, I, 600.
[15] Letter to Spalatin, April 16, 1520, *WAB*, II, 83.
[16] Letter to Spalatin, May 13, 1520, *WAB*, II, 103. The offer was repeated in a letter some weeks later.
[17] Letter to Spalatin, Jan. 14, 1520, *WAB*, I, 611, ll. 59 ff.
[18] Letter to Spalatin, *ca.* Feb. 14, 1520, *WAB*, II, 41 f., ll. 12 ff.

the letters to Spalatin, and every attack by Eck and his Leipzig followers is met by an acrimonious counterattack. Directly after the great disputation his Dresden enemies began to align Martin with their heretical neighbors to the southeast, and it was reported to Duke George, probably not without foundation, that Hussite visitors had found their way to Martin's cell.[19] These suspicions of watchful defenders of the faith were confirmed by the appearance of Martin's sermon on the sacrament, which bore on its title page a woodcut showing two monstrances, one with the holy wafer and the other with the chalice.[20] George's eye fell on the pamphlet and picture very soon after printing [21] and he sent at once complaining letters to his cousin, the elector, and to the bishops of Meissen and Merseburg, stamping the sermon as "almost Prague in spirit" and adding that he had credible reports of an increase of 6,000 among Bohemian utraquists as a result of Luther's action.[22] The zealous churchman had dipped into the sermon, and was fully persuaded of Martin's agreement with the Bohemian heretics. Frederick declined politely to interfere; and Bishop Adolf of Merseburg, whose efforts to stop the Leipzig affair had only brought a reprimand from the duke, contented himself with a general promise to try to prevent vexation. The bishop of Meissen, however, who sat close to the ducal elbow, took more vigorous action and on January 24 ordered confiscation of the sermon.[23]

In the interval Luther had wind of George's letter, probably through a correspondent in Leipzig, and claimed to recognize the work of his enemies there in befooling the untheological mind of the duke.[24] To Spalatin he insists that he does not wish to declare for the sacrament in two forms, and he repeats this assurance four days later.[25] He was bitterly incensed against the Leipzig crowd, especially the persistent Dungersheim, whom he suspected of having circulated the defamatory reports about his birth. In this state of mind he yields to the wish of friends and prepares an answer to the charge of utraquism. This was printed and enclosed in a letter to Lang on January 26.[26] His *Explanation of Certain Articles in His Sermon on the Sacrament* [27] opens with a sarcastic apology for answering critics whose

[19] See letter from George to Frederick, Dec. 27, 1519. Gess, *Briefe und Akten*, I, p. 111.

[20] The use of this cut by the Wittenberg printer probably had no significant relation to the reference in the sermon to the sacrament in two forms. The block used was one that had been prepared originally by Lucas Cranach for his woodcuts illustrating the collection of relics at Wittenberg, in *Dye zaigung des hochwirdigen hailigthums der Stifft kirchen aller hailigen zu wittenburg* (1509). *WA*, VI, 76, n. 1.

[21] December 24. Gess, *Briefe und Akten*, I, 110 f.

[22] December 27. *Ibid.*, pp. 110 ff.   [23] See *WA*, VI, 135.

[24] Letter to Spalatin, Jan. 10, *WAB*, I, 608.   [25] January 14. *WAB*, I, 610, ll. 9 ff.

[26] *WAB*, I, 619.

[27] *Verklärung D. M.L.'s etlicher Artikel in seinem Sermon von dem heiligen Sakrament. WA*, VI, 78 ff.

noise he regards no more than the rattling of a dried pig-bladder. He denies that the Roman Church has ever held the giving of the sacrament in two kinds as heresy or condemned those who did so as heretics. Both the Bohemians and those who attack them are wrong: the former for deviating from the general practice of the Church, and the latter for stigmatizing utraquist usage as heretical; and he calls for a compromise, or at least a peaceful disagreement. He answers the charges of Bohemian birth and training with a miniature autobiography, and declares that he has never been nearer Bohemia than Dresden. As for visits from Bohemians, he welcomes them as he would welcome Jews, Turks, or heathens; yes, he adds, if he were as wise as his slanderers think themselves to be, he would go to Bohemia and try to bring some of these schismatics back under the Roman See instead of abusing them.

Meanwhile it is probable that Spalatin or other electoral councilors had intervened to stem the tide of criticism that was associating Luther with the Hussites. At any rate, Martin drew up letters of explanation and defense to Archbishop Albert of Brandenburg and the bishop of Merseburg and submitted them to Spalatin for approval and forwarding.[28] The tone of the letters is conciliatory but independent. Martin presents himself once more as one who seeks to teach only Christ and His commands without hope of earthly reward or glory. He repeats the offer to recant if it can be shown that he is in error. Surely, he states, it can be no personal profit that he seeks, for his course has brought him condemnation in place of reward, shame in place of glory, censure, violence, death instead of protection and life. It is only envious people who have condemned his works, which have found support and approval from neutral judges of the highest ability and scholarship, a verdict which he is sure the bishop will endorse if he can find time to examine his arguments. As for what has been charged against him in respect to the papal power and the sacrament in two kinds, he is confident that in their own conscience his opponents support his views.[29] Albert he addresses as an outstanding man in good letters, and urges his own claim for protection as that of one who had been born and brought up in the diocese of this Hohenzollern prince.[30] The letters are marked by a certain proud humility and are cordial in tone; but it is noticeable that Martin makes no attempt to justify himself regarding the points on which the charge of heresy was concentrating: his attack on the papal claims and his ambiguous attitude toward Bohemian utraquism.

[28] February 5, 1520. *WAB*, II, 30.
[29] Letter to Bishop Adolf of Merseburg, *WAB*, II, 26, ll. 60 ff.
[30] Letter to Archbishop Albert of Mainz, *WAB*, II, 29, ll. 60 ff.

Both prelates responded without delay. Albert maintains the same attitude of diplomatic aloofness from the conflict as marked earlier moves by this easy-going Hohenzollern.[31] He waives any decision on Luther's writings in favor of those above him, observing that such questions as those of the divine right of the pope and freedom of the will are trifles (*nugamenta*) in comparison with the vital demands of Christian life. He warns against violent discussion as tending to incite men to resist the established authority of the Church, and points out the danger of bringing to the ears of the people the question of the sacrament in two kinds.[32] In contrast with the friendly and suave tone of the archiepiscopal chancellery, the reply of Adolf of Merseburg is brief and stern. He regrets that Martin's sermon on the sacrament has brought scruples to the conscience of simple people,[33] censures its author for his bold and embittered attacks in the papal question, and suggests that he moderate his tone. Finally he holds out vaguely some prospect of giving the monk a hearing.

In the meantime, Martin was again giving evidence that conciliation was far from his mind. Just as he dispatched to Spalatin for forwarding the letters addressed to the two Church dignitaries, there came into his hands the mandate of the bishop of Meissen for suppressing his sermon on the sacrament.[34] In a tone of stern admonition it warns the diocese against Luther's published sermon, since its claim that a Church council had commanded the sacrament to be given to all Christians in both kinds, that is, not partially, but wholly,[35] is in conflict with the acts of the Lateran Council. The bishop therefore orders the sermon confiscated and sequestrated, and the people taught that in accord with the view of the Church as expressed in a general synod the sacrament should be administered to communicants in the single form of the bread, and that taking it in two kinds is "bold, presumptuous, scandalous, seditious, and disturbing of an ecclesiastical rite and in consequence conducive to eternal damnation."

Martin flew to arms. He felt that he had been cruelly misrepresented and promised an immediate answer to this "offspring of great hatred and greater ignorance." [36] Half a day suffices for writing his response in German, and a few days later he sends to Spalatin the printed form of his *Answer to the*

---

[31] Letter from Albert to Luther, Feb. 26, *WAB*, II, 53 ff. The letter was written from the archiepiscopal residence near Magdeburg. For a suggestion as to authorship, see Kalkoff, *Die Miltitziade*, p. 45.

[32] *Ibid.*, p. 54, ll. 36 f.   [33] *WAB*, II, 52 f.

[34] Text in *WA*, VI, 151 ff. The mandate was issued from the bishop's chancellery at Stolpen, near Meissen, under the seal of the "official" of the bishop.

[35] "Non parcialiter seu per partes sed integre." *WA*, VI, 152, ll. 4 f.

[36] Letter to Spalatin, Feb. 5, *WAB*, II, 31.

Proclamation of the Stolpen Official.[37] The electoral chaplain had warned against starting a new conflagration, but his monitions came too late, Luther excusing himself, as often in such cases, by declaring that the work was already published.[38] His mood was one of grim exultation in the conflict. Neither God nor he is to blame if his enemies rage: "Who knows whether they may not be predestined as the occasion for revealing the truth?" News comes from Oschatz that sarcastic remarks had been scribbled on the bishop's proclamation there, and Martin is sure that God's hand is in the matter.

Martin's answer begins with a polite subterfuge: he does not believe the bishop personally responsible for a document so filled with lies and insults.[39] His answer follows in the sarcastic and aggressive style that marks the polemics of the times. He derides the author of the mandate for citing in support of the sacrament in one form the authority of the Lateran Council, whose rating in Germany is very low. Were he a Bohemian, he would think the Germans were drunk, as usual. By misquoting him, his enemies seek to rouse the mob against him, as Caiphas did against Christ. He bids "Doctor Malicious" (Neidhart), the author of the proclamation, to follow the example of the Cologne adversaries of Reuchlin, who had burned the books they did not like, for where one cannot resist truth, fire is the best protection against books and death against their author. In this way one may become more learned than "Doctor Luther," indeed, "the most learned of men." [40]

The tone of the reply, which is reported to have brought even suspicious Duke George to hearty laughter,[41] caused serious uneasiness at the electoral court. The following week Luther makes answer to Spalatin's anxieties with a declaration [42] in language swollen with emotion. His one fear is that he may write what is pleasing to men instead of to God. God is his witness how sternly he must hold himself in check not to say things which "those blockheads" ought to hear. "Nothing more poisonous, pestilential, malignant, mendacious has ever been written against me, nay, not against me, but against God's word!" Spalatin knows how little he regards the possible consequences of his action—exile, departure from his place, or whatever has to be endured—and he implores the chaplain to remember that the word of God is

[37] February 8. *WAB*, II, 36, ll. 33 ff.

[38] Letter to Spalatin, Feb. 12, *WAB*, II, 39, ll. 7 ff.

[39] *Antwort auf die Zettel, so unter des Officials zu Stolpen Siegel ist ausgegangen. WA*, VI, 137.

[40] *Ibid.*, p. 141.

[41] From a report of Karl von Miltitz to the elector, Frederick, from Scharfenberg, Sunday before Shrovetide, 1520. E. S. Cyprian, "Nützliche Urkunden zur Erläuterung der ersten Reformationsgeschichte," in *Tentzels Historischer Bericht vom Anfang und ersten Fortgang der Reformation Lutheri*, I, i, 430.

[42] *Circa* February 16. *WAB*, II, 43 ff.

a sword, is war, ruin, scandal, perdition, and poison. It is God who sweeps him along. Who can know what He intends to do with him? Whatever may come of it, he has no thought of gain or loss for himself. Having somewhat vented his feelings, Martin admits that he is more violent than he should be, but his enemies know his temper and should not stir up the dog. Such an indignity against himself and God's word would move a temper of stone, how much more a hot-blooded man, who, he adds, wields no blunt pen. In excuse he cites the vigorous names which Christ and Paul applied to the Jews. Everybody asks self-restraint of him, especially his enemies, who themselves show no trace of it. At least he is frank and straightforward, wherein he differs from his insidious critics.

A day or two of reflection softens his temper, and he promises the reproachful Spalatin that a Latin rejoinder to the bishop which he has in hand will be in a gentler tone, and agrees to send the chaplain a copy for approval before printing.[43] The reply was already under way, emerging from the press "with obstetrical pressure" and the help of Melanchthon.[44] The tone of this Latin *Answer to the Prohibition of the Sermon on the Sacrament of the Eucharist* [45] is more serious in tone than his German polemics, to be sure, but abates nothing of sarcastic vigor of argument and does not spare abusive words. "I will not suffer an error condemned in God's Gospel to be pronounced even by all the angels in heaven," he declares to Spalatin,[46] "still less by the idols of an earthly Church"; and he begs the chaplain to do his enemies the favor of writing to any who will listen, warning them to proceed as prudently as possible against Luther. In his Latin *Answer* he still refuses to regard the bishop as the author of the prohibition but ascribes it to two or three canons, branding them ignoramuses who may be able to manage the rules of school dialectics but who in theology can scarcely distinguish the devil from Christ.[47] The statement ascribed to him that communion in one kind does not contain the whole Christ, he denies most vigorously. It is necessary to recognize certain rules and usages of the Church, even though the results are deplorable. Who is there among the best men, he asks, who in view of the present dangers and scandals does not desire that priests be allowed to marry, as the Greek priests do? He waves aside the Lateran Council as a laughing-stock in Rome and throughout almost the

---

[43] February 18. *WAB*, II, 46.

[44] Letter to Spalatin, Feb. 12, *WAB*, II, 39. It is not certain that the work was completed at that time, as assumed by Knaake, *WA*, VI, 142.

[45] *Ad schedulam inhibitionis sub nomine episcopi Misnensis editam super sermone de sacramento eucharistae M. L. Augustiniani responsio. Ibid.*, pp. 144 ff.

[46] Letter to Spalatin, Feb. 18, 1520, *WAB*, II, 46.

[47] *WA*, VI, 147, ll. 4 f.

whole world. If the Bohemians are to be refuted, it must be on the authority of the Scriptures and the Church Fathers, and not by means of the latest rubbish of men. He had declared in his sermon that it would be proper if the form or symbol of the sacrament were not limited to one part, but given as a whole;[48] now his enemies twist this statement around and charge him with alleging that communion in one form is only partly (*partialiter*) given. Those who cannot follow the distinction between the sacrament partly given and the body of Christ partly given should be feeding pigs instead of writing mandates for popular enlightenment.[49]

For the moment the controversy ended with the publication of Luther's Latin pamphlet.[50] When his German reply fell into Duke George's hands, that solicitous defender of the faith at once sketched off for publication a letter stating that his bishop was to clear up all uncertainties by accepting personal responsibility for the mandate and then appealing to the decision of neutral judges.[51] Martin expected a counterattack and was ready for it: "Let them come on," he writes to Spalatin.[52] But there is no evidence that the matter went any further. Martin's stinging rebuttal did more than to bring the episcopal chancellery to silence, for the episode seems to have made clear to him that he had reached a new stage in his thinking. He became aware, suddenly as it seems, that there was no difference between his convictions and those which a century before had sent another theologian to the flames. In the preceding October, as we have seen, he had received from the Prague correspondent a copy of Huss's little work *On the Church*,[53] and he seems to have read it and pondered on it in the months that followed. He now realizes that it is the doctrines of the Bohemian heretic he has been expounding, and in a letter written in the midst of the dispute with the Meissen episcopate he declares that he and Staupitz have been teaching the ideas of Huss: "In short, we are all heretics without knowing it." Indeed, "Paul and Augustine are Hussites word for word."[54] He is appalled that the plain truth of the Gospel which was burned a hundred years before at Constance is still condemned and not permitted to exist. A month later he sends a new edition of Huss's book to Spalatin with a burst of admiration for its wonderful

[48] *WA*, II, 742, l. 30: "nit stucklich eyns teyls, sondern gantz."

[49] *WA*, VI, 151, ll. 14 ff.

[50] Possibly by the end of February. Spalatin apparently received a copy on February 24. Letter from Luther to Spalatin, Feb. 24, *WAB*, II, 48.

[51] Probably on February 17. The text is in George's own hand. See Gess, *Briefe und Akten*, I, 117. The duke calls attention to the contrast between the abusive language in Luther's *Answer* and the pious advice in the *Fourteen Consolers*, which had just come from the press.

[52] February 24, *WAB*, II, 48, ll. 5 f.

[53] See letter from Wenzel von Roždalowsky to Luther, July 17, 1519, *WAB*, I, 419 f.

[54] To Spalatin, *ca.* Feb. 14, *WAB*, II, 42.

spirit and scholarship.[55] The deep impression which the little work made on his mind was reflected half a year later in an open letter to Eck, where he makes confession to his complete agreement with Huss and calls the latter's *On the Church* the best book in four hundred years.[56] In the lectures on Psalms, on which he was working at the same time, he says that it was only in this book that he was able to see how wholly Christian in thought were the articles which the Church had condemned.[57]

About the same time another work fell into his hands that opened his eyes to a striking coincidence between his own ideas and those of another great critic of the Church. This was the famous *Donation of Constantine* by Laurentius Valla, containing a sharp attack on the claims of the papacy to temporal power.[58] More than half a century before, this Florentine nationalist, whose merciless disregard of tradition and realistic criticism have won him the title of the "Voltaire of humanism," issued a destructive analysis of the legend of the bestowal of temporal power on the pope.[59] This work had just been republished by Ulrich von Hutten, and a clerical friend in Nuremberg now forwarded it to Martin. It was prefaced by Hutten with an introductory letter to Leo X, demanding that the Pope free himself from the "thieves and robbers" surrounding him.[60] Valla's vigorous arguments and his recital of the crimes of the papal court made such a deep impression on Martin that he could scarcely control himself. He is overcome, he declares to Spalatin, that the darkness and deceit of the Romanists, their stupidity and impudent lies have become a part of the articles of faith. It has now come to such a pass that he has no doubt that the pope is the real Antichrist whom the world expects.[61]

---

[55] March 19, *WAB*, II, 72.

[56] *Von den neuen Eckischen Bullen und Lügen. WA*, VI, 587 f., ll. 21 ff.

[57] *Operationes in Psalmos. WA*, V, 452, ll. 3 ff.

[58] *De falsa credita et ementita Constantini donatione* (1477). Valla was, of course, not alone in stamping the so-called "Donation of Constantine" as a falsification. Arnold of Brescia, Nicolas Cusanus, and Reginald Peacock also protested against the document, which had been incorporated into the canon law. See *WA*, L, 65.

[59] For a full characterization of Valla's brilliant attack, see Von Pastor, *Geschichte der Päpste*, I, 17 f. For his great importance in the history of humanistic criticism, see Mestwerdt, *Erasmus*, pp. 29 f.

[60] Hutten's prefatory letter, *Opera*, I, 155 ff., to Valla's *De donatione Constantini quid veri habeat, eruditorum quorundam iudicium* is dated at Stechelberg, 1517; it seems, however, that the work, which bears no date, was not published until the end of 1519. In spite of Böcking, who dates it 1518 (*ibid.*, p. 18), one may agree with Kalkoff's arguments for a later issue without accepting his theory that Hutten falsified the date of the dedication to Leo. See *Huttens Vagantenzeit und Untergang*, p. 223, n. 1; see also Paul Joachimsen's review of that book in *Historische Zeitschrift*, CXXXVI (1927), 339.

[61] February 24. *WAB*, II, 48. Many years later Luther bases on Valla a bitter attack on the Constantine legend, his *Einer aus den hohen Artikeln des päpstlichen Glaubens. WA*, L, 65 ff.

While Luther was consolidating his revolutionary views the forces marshalled by his scholastic opponents were beginning to concentrate against him. The decision of the universities on the Leipzig disputation was still outstanding; in spite of urgent letters from Duke George, both Erfurt and Paris kept silent. The conservative theologians of the lower Rhine country, however, the tireless prosecutors of Reuchlin, could not overlook this new enemy arising out of the very bosom of theology. The Basel volume of Martin's Latin works, the *Lucubrations,* had come to the attention of the Louvain theological faculty immediately after its issue in 1518, and they forwarded it promptly to their colleagues at Cologne.[62] Several months later representatives of the two faculties brought certain heretical passages in it to the attention of Cardinal Cajetan at Coblenz. According to Martin Bucer,[63] who had it from a friend, the learned Italian replied that the statements, while erroneous, could not be called heretical.[64] This dash of cold water, perhaps, held up action by the faculties until after the Leipzig disputation. Then came the appeal from Eck to his Dominican colleagues in Cologne, and this was followed shortly by the bitter diatribe which Luther launched against the Cologne heretic-hunter, Hochstraten. The Rhine theologians now took the offensive, and on August 30 issued a condemnation which made a general arraignment of Martin's *Explanations of Indulgences* and sermons as full of scandals, errors, and heresies, and worthy of being suppressed and burned, and declared that the author should be forced to recant.[65] The faculty at Louvain, although the first to raise the question, was longer in reaching a decision, and it was not until November 7 that it issued its condemnation.[66] The doctors went carefully to work and cited a number of assertions from Luther's sermons and his writings of 1518, chiefly from the *Explanations of Indulgences,* the *Sermon on Penance,* and the *Sermons on the Ten Commandments.* These ideas they branded as false, scandalous, heretical or smelling of heresy, and condemned the Basel print

[62] As early as February 22, 1519, according to P. F. X. de Ram, "Disquisitio historica de iis quae contra Lutherum Lovanienses theologi egerunt," *Nouveaux Mémoires de l'Académie Royale . . . de Bruxelles,* XVI (1843), 3. He gives no sources.

[63] Letter from Bucer to Beatus Rhenanus, Heidelberg, July 30, 1519. *Briefwechsel des Beatus Rhenanus,* ed. by Horawitz and Hartfelder, p. 166. See also Paul Kalkoff, "Die Anfänge der Gegenreformation in den Niederlanden," *SVRG,* Vol. XXI, no. 79 (1903), pp. 104 f. and n. 19.

[64] "Sint errores, non haereses."   [65] See *WAB,* II, 72, n. 4.

[66] According to Erasmus, whose letters furnish an interesting, although far from impartial, commentary on the events of this time, it was Hochstraten who pushed the Louvain faculty into action. See letter to Kretzer, Dec. 22, 1531, where Erasmus states that Hochstraten left no stone unturned to help the Dominicans stir up Paris, Cologne, and Louvain. See *Opera Omnia,* III, 1361. This has, however, been questioned and is certainly questionable. See De Jongh, *L'Ancienne Faculté de Théologie de Louvain,* pp. 215 f.

to the fire and its author to recantation. It is possible that Martin was not without defenders at Louvain, as he heard afterwards;[67] and before proceeding to publication the faculty sought backing from a former colleague, Cardinal Adrian of Utrecht, Bishop of Tortosa, an influential figure in the Church who was later to ascend the papal throne. The cardinal added his approval to their condemnation of the "rude and palpable heresies" in Luther's work, and his letter together with the acts of the two universities was published at Louvain in February, 1520. It must have come under Martin's eye very soon thereafter, for on March 19 he reports that he has in hand a reply to the "Cologne and Louvain asses,"[68] and two days later this is in press.[69] He prints the attacks of his critics and addresses his response to a colleague, Christoph Blanck, the dean of All Saints' Church.[70]

The brief document is a biting attack on the narrow-mindedness and ignorance of the theologians rather than an attempt to defend again the basic ideas which they have branded as heretical. Martin feels that he has his opponents in a corner because their charges against Reuchlin had been thrown out of court by a papal commission,[71] and he exploits to the full the storm of hatred which the fanatical attacks on Reuchlin by the Cologne school had aroused among the humanists. The condemnation by the faculties, which is accompanied by no proof, can only mean, "whatever we may say is gospel and whatever we condemn is heresy."[72] Antichrist must indeed be at hand when men can thus elevate themselves above the work of God and consign to present and future fires anyone who denies the justice of their claims. He calls the roll of scholars who suffered condemnation from the universities only to be extolled later by the same authorities: Occam, Pico, Valla ("also charged with the crime of ignorance by those who are in no way worthy to hand him a chamber-pot"), Reuchlin (who, according to Martin, brought them into ignominy from which they are now trying to redeem themselves on Luther), Johann of Wesel, Faber, Erasmus. No one can stand out in scholarship without being attacked at once by these ignoble

[67] *WA*, VI, 182, l. 29. Possibly Martin Dorp, a friend of Erasmus at this time, spoke up for him. See letter from Martin Dorp to Erasmus Nov. 28, 1519. Allen, *Opus epistolarum Erasmi*, IV, 128, No. 1044. Note however that Dorp was later summoned by the faculty to retract the statement that the action was not united and harmonious. See De Jongh, *L'Ancienne Faculté de Théologie de Louvain*, pp. 214 f.

[68] Letter to Spalatin, *WAB*, II, 72.

[69] Letter from Luther to Lang, *WAB*, II, 74.

[70] *Responsio Lutheriana ad condemnationem doctrinalem per magistros nostros Lovanienses et Colonienses factam. WA*, VI, 181 ff.

[71] He could not foresee, of course, that this verdict was to be upset and the Cologne attacks definitely supported by a papal decision.

[72] *WA*, VI, 181, l. 30.

drones.[73] They debase philosophy by contradicting merely with words: "it is," "it is not," "it is thus," "it is not so." [74] He has studied diligently their philosophy for more than twelve years, and no one can now persuade him that their chattering about the Aristotelian categories of matter, motion, and so on, is a real philosophy, for it brings no help for the mind or the affections or usual customs of mankind, but leads only to strife. Until the faculties can disprove his assertions by Scripture he will pay no more attention to their condemnation than to the ravings of a drunken man. He repeats, in ringing words, the statements which they have condemned, rising at one point to an expression so harsh that on second thought he eliminated it from the text, and thus leaves us in ignorance of this pearl from his rich store of abusive terms.[75]

The tractate is indeed as full of hard words as any humanistic attack of the period. Martin treats his critics with a sarcasm that he must have felt would win applause from the humanists who had defended Reuchlin against these intolerant scholastics. Confirmation that the same "obscure men" of Cologne were at his heels came through a letter from Martin Dorp, one of the Louvain faculty, who was friendly with Erasmus.[76] Erasmus himself forwarded a copy of the *Response* to Hutten, who showed it to Crotus Rubianus, then visiting in Bamberg on his way north from Italy. This early friend and admirer, whose correspondence with Luther in the preceding year will be recalled, now sent Martin a long letter of fulsome congratulation,[77] well backed by scriptural allusions, classical figures, and many sarcastic flings at the Rhenish theologians reminiscent of Crotus's language in the *Letters of Obscure Men*.[78] Erasmus, that "he-goat caught by the horns in the bushes," as Luther calls him, also expressed approval, though in measured tones.[79] He is himself facing the same foes at Louvain, but he puts in a word for greater civility and moderation.

In Crotus the rising wave of Dominican resentment awakened memories of bloody work by the arch-inquisitor Hochstraten, which had come to his

[73] *Ibid.*, pp. 183, ll. 26 ff.; 184, ll. 1 ff. and 27.
[74] *Ibid.*, p. 187, ll. 32 ff.
[75] "Rogo vos crassos [. . . pene effluxisset], desiste Lutheriana aut iudicare aut tractare." *Ibid.*, p. 192, ll. 31 f.
[76] Letter from Luther to Martin Seligmann, March 25, 1520, *WAB*, II, 76.
[77] April 28, *WAB*, II, 87 ff.
[78] *Ibid.*, p. 89, ll. 78 ff.: ". . . iudicio omnium damnatus es tu non doctrinaliter, sed Lovanialiter, quemadmodum et multis incutitur pontificis fulmen Romcanaliter, non Christionaliter."
[79] Letter from Erasmus to Melanchthon, Louvain, *ca.* June 21. Allen, *Opus epistolarum Erasmi*, IV, 287, No. 1113. The letter was intended equally for Luther. See letter from Erasmus to Spalatin, July 6, 1520, *ibid.*, p. 298, No. 1119.

knowledge a few years before at Cologne.[80] Such thoughts were not absent
from Luther's mind as his enemies gathered about him. He read accounts
of flaming omens in the sky seen at Vienna, and recalling the lightning that
many years before had hurled him from the plotted course of life into the
path of monkdom, he remarks to Spalatin that these fiery rays aloft may
also contain his fate.[81] That the ban of excommunication hung over him by
a thread and might fall at any time he was well aware. He had faced this
danger since the summer of 1518, and his bold sermon on the ban [82] had
aroused much criticism both before and after its publication. Now again,
probably just before the end of 1519, Martin put his ideas on this subject into
a sermon which he issued in German early in 1520 and which speedily reappeared in many prints.[83] Here he examines the dreaded weapon of the
Church from the standpoint of a member of the communion of saints such
as he had pictured in his sermon on the Eucharist, and comes to the conclusion that nothing but lack of faith can really exclude the soul from the group
of Christian believers. Bishop and pope control only the outer organization
of the Church. He details to his hearers the various degrees of the ban: the
little ban, excluding from the sacraments; the greater ban, shutting off from
association with men; and finally, the extreme ban, which mobilizes the
temporal power with fire and sword. He points out that the proper use of
the ban is to improve the sinner, and he decries the increasing abuse of this
weapon for private vengeance or from temporal causes. The ban makes no
one better or worse and, unrightly used, brings more danger to him who
wields it than to him who is banned. We must treat the temporal power with
respect even though we are ruled by young, unintelligent, and inexperienced men, and must rest assured that God will punish evil and take care
that injustice does not harm us. He who dies under an unjust ban for the
sake of the truth renders a great and noble service to God, who will bestow
on him the eternal crown. The measured tone of Martin's reasoning reflects
the solemn mood in which he faces the dread weapon of Church authority.
He recognizes and accepts its reformatory value for the individual and the
Church, but finds comfort in the thought that it does not touch the inner
relationship between man and God. This relation rests upon faith, and
remains unbroken by the anathema of the Church. Though the victim is kept

[80] Letter from Crotus to Luther, *WAB*, II, 88, ll. 31 ff. Possibly a reference to the burning
of the Dutch doctor, Hermann von Rysswick, in 1512. See Kalkoff, *Die Reformation in der
Reichsstadt Nürnberg*, p. 80.
[81] Letter to Spalatin, March 19, *WAB*, II, 72. Also Klingner, *Luther und Volksaberglaube*,
pp. 95 f.
[82] *De virtute excommunicationis. WA*, I, 638 f.
[83] *Ein Sermon von dem Bann. WA*, VI, 63 ff.

from the sacrament of the altar, he may still, by faith, enjoy sacramental union with Christ in his own soul.

Braced by thoughts like this, Martin awaits what may come. He is stirred to sarcasm by false reports that Eck has turned back from his journey to Rome;[84] but late in February he learns that his relentless opponent is really on his way southward, "to stir up against me the abyss of abysses."[85] Nevertheless, as the weeks pass tense with waiting, he is resolved to face the consequence without flinching. "Rome is also subject to Christ . . . who, if I am worthy, will act for me there; if not, I should not wish Him to act for me here."[86] About the middle of April a warning comes from Nikolaus Demuth, provost of the Augustinian canons at Neuwerk, near Halle, that a new undertaking is on foot against him,[87] and by the end of the month rumors become numerous that Pope Leo is preparing dire things.[88] Crotus, in the letter from Bamberg referred to above, reminds Martin that he is in danger of joining Huss and increasing the number of Christian martyrs. In spite of this warning, the letter from the friend of Erfurt days must have strengthened Martin's hand, for it brought assurance that there were many who shared his heresy, and that even though he seemed to be alone, others were willing to enter the fire with him. One passage in Crotus's letter opened a vista that could not be other than alluring to the hard-pressed monk: escape, if worst comes to worst. This is an invitation, passed on to Crotus by Hutten, to take refuge with Franz von Sickingen, the powerful Rhenish knight, whose great stronghold on the Stechelberg in the Moselle hills was a center for political plots and mercenary operations. Here, Crotus pictures to him a refuge from the snares of his enemies, a place of tranquillity, a house for his studies, attendance, food, and all the needs of life in abundance. As another assurance of support Crotus promises a copy of Erasmus's letter to the archbishop of Mainz, with its commendation of Luther. Such reassuring messages must have been supplemented by many others, for much of the correspondence of this time has undoubtedly perished.[89] The encour-

---

[84] Letter from Luther to Bucer, early February, *WAB*, II, 33, ll. 37 ff.

[85] Letter to Spalatin, Feb. 26, *WAB*, II, 55. Eck had left Ingolstadt on February 10. See *WAB*, II, 34 f., n. 14, for sources.

[86] Letter from Luther to Lang, March 21, *WAB*, II, 74.

[87] Letter from Luther to Spalatin, April 16, *WAB*, II, 83.

[88] See letter from Melanchthon to Hess, April 17, *CR*, I, 160; see also letter to Lang, *ibid.*, p. 163.

[89] On May 5 Luther mentions that letters had been written to Hutten, Erasmus, and Fabritius. Letter from Luther to Spalatin, *WAB*, II, 98. None of these appear to have been preserved, nor are contemporary letters from these correspondents to be found. Other humanists, like Adelmann and Pirckheimer, would almost certainly have written to Luther in the days when reports of Eck's activity in Rome must have come with every cleric returning to the South German cities.

agement which they brought is reflected in the tone of defiance that appears in Martin's own letters and writings throughout the spring. Most important of all, he now feels certain, through assurances from Spalatin, that the elector is going to see the matter through.[90]

[90] See the references to a lost letter from Luther to Bucer in the latter's letter to Beatus Rhenanus of April 2, *WAB*, II, 32 f. The editor, Clemen, dates this lost letter early in February, but it seems more likely to have been written several weeks later. See Enders, *Luthers Briefwechsel*, II, 364.

25

THE ATTACK ON THE SACRAMENTS

IN the midst of the excitement of the late winter and early spring, Martin found time to give form to his mature convictions on the subject of the forgiveness of sins. This he did in two sermons, prepared with unusual care, *On the Manner of Confession* and *On Good Works*. Both set forth ideas that had been ripening in his mind ever since the Romans lectures, had appeared in the course on Galatians, and were now finding their way into the commentary on Psalms.

The sermon on confession goes back to a request of Spalatin, who had, as it appears, asked him repeatedly for a formula of confession. In January, 1519, in the interval between the early negotiations with Miltitz and the preparation for the duel with Eck, Martin wrote out in Latin a simple formula,[1] from which a German extract, *A Brief Instruction for Confession*, appears to have been made and published by Spalatin. Here, after a short introduction, Martin lists under each of the Ten Commandments the offenses which might be committed and should be confessed. These traverse the thoughts and actions of a man of his day, both in social relationships and in the laboratory of the soul's imaginings and desires. The First Commandment, for example, is broken when we have conferences with magicians or consult astrologers, when we make a league with the devil or divine the future by means of stones and herbs, as well as when we seek from the saints only temporal blessings or trust in our own righteousness. The Commandment to honor our parents requires that we should hold in honor princes, lords, and councilors, whether they be good or evil; that against murder is broken when we fail to pray for our enemies; that against stealing when we lend money at interest.

This German sketch found its way into the press and circulated widely

[1] Sent to Spalatin on January 24. See *WAB*, I, 311; see also Enders, *Luthers Briefwechsel*, II, 297, n. 3.

in reprints from several cities.[2] A year after writing it, Martin asked Spalatin to return the Latin manuscript.[3] His Augsburg friend, Bernhard Adelmann, had suggested that it might be printed as a whole, and Martin felt the urge to set forth his ideas on the subject at full length. Almost simultaneously with his answer to the faculties of Louvain and Cologne, the enlarged sermon came from the press in Latin form.[4] *On the Manner of Confession* [5] subjects to a fundamental analysis the nature and manner of confession as a work of purification for the Christian soul, and like other tracts and sermons of the period, it rejects forcefully the traditional forms and formulas and makes a vigorous demand for inner experience of sin and forgiveness. He opens on this chord: the purpose of confession is not to "provoke" God to forgiveness through our own exertions, but to accept His promise of forgiveness. Martin warns against the pretense of those who confess to a hatred of sin and then, secure in their absolution, go back to live as before. Unless one is seriously resolved upon a better life, he ought to abstain from confession, despite the command of the Church; but man should not try to carry out this resolve by his own powers: he can only cast himself down, broken and contrite, before God's mercy.

The so-called venial sins cannot be avoided; perhaps they are tests to strengthen the soul. He is uncertain whether hidden sins of the heart really belong to the sacrament of confession, but he suspects that confession of them is an invention of greedy and curious prelates: "It is like interfering deeply with the judgment of God and violating His court of justice." [6] In any case, he is opposed to searching the heart for imaginary sins: if any secret sins are to be confessed, it should be "only those which the sinner himself has found in his heart in violation of the divine command," not merely inclinations springing from an ardent physical desire, however improper. Loose thoughts are aroused by the world, the flesh, or the devil and one cannot avoid them. He again condemns the classification of sins as venial and mortal: such distinctions are an insanity of theologians, for God desires us to glorify His mercy, not through our righteousness but because of our sins and miseries. Most harmful of all and utterly useless are the cataloguing and classifying of sins and the numbering of virtues, of sacraments, beatitudes, and gifts of the spirit; these dull the gnawings of conscience and give joy in absolution,

---

[2] *Eine kurze Unterweisung, wie man beichten soll. WA*, II, 57 ff.

[3] January 18, 1520, *WAB*, I, 612.

[4] Letter from Luther to Spalatin, March 25, *WAB*, II, 75.

[5] *Confitendi ratio. WA*, VI, 157 ff. The dedication to a member of the elector's court, which was omitted from the first printing, is dated March 26, possibly as a misprint for March 21. See *WAB*, II, 76, n. 1.

[6] *WA*, VI, 161, ll. 12 f.

not because they free from the burden of tormenting sins, but because they bring an end to a tormenting confession. The sacrament of confession was meant to tranquilize, not to confuse the conscience.

The demand for a spiritual experience in confession leads now into well-known reformatory and polemical paths. A careful distinction must be drawn between sins against God's commands and those against the statutes of man. This has to be kept in mind because of the insanity which rates more heavily offenses against the papal decrees than those against God. There are priests and monks who hold that hesitation or repetition by the priest officiating at Mass is a monstrosity, while no regard is paid to hypocrisy and slander in his heart after performing the holy office. Omission of the canonical hours is an unremittable sin, but fornication and the omission of studies are easily excused, and Martin, whose monastic bonds were rapidly growing loose, is particularly bitter against those who contend that the daily prayers of the breviary may not be anticipated or made up afterwards without sin, even in order to serve the dire necessities of one's neighbor, though the performance of such an act "is six hundred times as meritorious as their feeble and well-nigh damnable prayers." [7] It is a popular idea that eating butter or eggs on fast days is heretical, while no one calls adultery heretical, and fornication is held to be a minor sin. Let those who have scruples of conscience go to the altar even if they have not confessed some petty sin or other; and when mortal trial or terror of death recalls to them hidden and unconfessed sins, let them be ready to trust in the mercy of God. This is not contempt of the sacrament, but an assurance for the tender conscience that it may trust in God and not tremble at every rustling leaf. Often the result of confession is to do away with trusting, so that we learn to confess much and to trust little.

Finally he comes to the so-called "reserved cases," particularly heinous offenses which can be absolved only by the highest clergy. Here he treads with caution. He is not clear whether the remission of guilt can be reserved, although the penalty certainly can; but, he adds, excommunication is a penalty, not a sin, and when expiation has to be put off on account of the long journey to Rome, the priest should nevertheless give absolution from all sins in the face of God and conscience, on the promise of the offender that he will satisfy later whatever penalty shall be imposed upon him. Reverting to an old complaint, he urges the popes and their advisers to check the tendency to vows and pilgrimages, fastings and prayers. Far better is the fulfillment of the baptismal vows and the performance of service at home

---

[7] *Ibid.*, p. 165, ll. 17 f.

to neighbor, wife, children, servants, and masters, he states, and he again has sharp words for the mechanical attitude toward vows. God judges works not according to their greatness or their multitude, but according to the spirit of the doer. He finds many traps and heavy penalties in case of so-called "incest," that is, sexual intercourse between persons of forbidden relationship. "The fact is," he concludes, "that this most helpful sacrament of penance has become nothing but a mine of plenty for tyrants, a vice and an increase of sins." [8]

Before the text of this work had left the press, Luther had in hand a sermon which was to be a reasoned statement of his entire position regarding man's search for heaven. He had once promised in a sermon to discourse on good works, and in February Spalatin reminded him of the promise.[9] Martin was then so absorbed in his clash with the authorities in Meissen that he waved the matter aside, with the excuse that there was danger of flooding the market with his writings. When his mind was relieved by his answer to the Meissen attack he recalled his promise,[10] and before the pamphlet on confession had left the press, was hard at work on a German tractate which he felt was going to be the best thing he had ever published.[11] It grew under his hand into a "little book," the first part of which seems to have been already in print before the last pages of the manuscript left his cell.[12] Early in June the pamphlet found its way to the reading public.[13]

On Good Works [14] was the longest German work that Martin had yet produced. From the awkward prose of his earlier writings in the vernacular he had come far on the road toward control of a vigorous and personal German. *On Good Works* does not yet pulse with the rhythm and naturalness of his Latin style; nevertheless it sets forth in glowing language a problem of interest to every thoughtful soul and moves along with elastic tread, little hampered by the shackles of "chancellery German." People have charged him, Martin declares in his dedication to John, duke of Saxony, with writing little books and sermons for the simple laity; he wishes now that he had devoted all his efforts to this cause. He has lost patience with weighty books

[8] *Ibid.*, p. 169, ll. 11 ff.

[9] Letter from Luther to Spalatin, Feb. 24, 1520, *WAB*, II, 48.

[10] Letter to Spalatin, Feb. 26, *WAB*, II, 55, ll. 11 f.

[11] Letter to Spalatin, March 25, *WAB*, II, 75.

[12] Letter to Spalatin, May 5, *WAB*, II, 101. See also letter from Melanchthon to Johann Hess, *CR*, I, 160.

[13] On June 8 Melanchthon sent a copy to Hess. *CR*, I, 201. See also *WA*, VI, 196 f.

[14] *WA*, VI, 202 ff. Luther's original manuscript, at one time in the municipal library at Danzig, shows some unimportant variations from the print of May–June, 1520. It is printed in *WA*, IX, 229 ff. See Clemen, *Luthers Werke in Auswahl*, I, 227 ff.

and the learning of the schools and feels no shame in addressing the simple man in language which he can understand.

Again he builds on an analysis of the Ten Commandments and their fulfillment in practical life. The greater part concerns the first three Commandments, which define man's relationship to God. The noblest of works is faith in Christ, and all other good works depend upon this. He then goes on to expand a favorite idea in recent sermons: good works include the duties and pleasures of daily life, not simply prayer and fasting. Indeed, if one does it with faith in God, even lifting up a straw is a good work. No Christian needs to be taught good works, but knows of himself what he has to do and does it freely and with happiness. In passionate tones Martin exalts the faith that continues to see God even in mortal suffering and to believe that God is pleased with us amidst the worst torments of conscience, even though He may turn His face away. In vivid contrast is the teaching of false prophets in sheep's clothing who tell us that men can buy God's grace by their works, "as if He were a peddler or day laborer," [15] and can fulfill the First Commandment by saying Mass, playing organs, founding churches, and cloisters, and collecting jewels, rich clothes, and other treasures. It is this contrast between such works and the faith within that has moved him and others to cast aside all the papal bulls, seals, and indulgences.

From the exaltation of faith he passes to an idea that had developed rapidly in the sermons of the preceding year: the freedom of the Christian. Faith is like good health, which must pervade the limbs of the patient before their movements can be healthful. The reason for ceremonies in churches and holy places lies in the varying character of men. Some require no law; others misuse the freedom that faith gives; still others must be restrained; at the same time there are those who, like children, have to be enticed into the right path by prayers, fasting, and music. We must bear with the weak, but the main point is that works and all things are free to the Christian through his faith and that all that he does is pleasant in God's sight. We are not to look down with contempt on others in their use of many ceremonies, but to endure them and lead them onto the right path.

The old question which had tormented him in earlier years, "How can I know that my works please God when I sin so much?" he now answers with full assurance: faith cancels all our daily sins.[16] Just as all the members of a healthy body are healthy, so good works are not different in quality, since faith works in all. The highest and noblest of all works is to honor and

[15] *WA*, VI, 210, l. 21.   [16] *Ibid.*, p. 215, ll. 17 ff.

praise the name of God, and the poor man who does this in his own humble home with faith in time of adversity does more to honor God than those who fast, found churches, and go on pilgrimages. After all, how does it help a man if he does everything that is good, hastens on pilgrimages to Rome and other holy places, buys indulgences, and builds churches and monasteries, yet neglects the truth, which is itself the name and honor of God? [17] Resistance to heresy is also a good work, but God tests us by requiring us to choose between heresy as measured by deviation from His Word and heresy as defined by those in the Church who uphold their own teachings. If we meet this test the papal ban will fall on us in vain. How few are ready to step forth and attack those of power and reputation, like the prophets of old who raised their voices and hands against sin, whether the offender was "big Jack or little Nick": [18] "it is high time that we pray God with earnestness to hallow His name. It will cost blood, and those who rejoice in the inheritance of the holy martyrs and are saved through the martyrs' blood will themselves have to produce martyrs." [19]

The Third Commandment opens the way for an attack on social abuses and clerical formalities that had drawn Martin's fire increasingly during the past three years: the idleness, gluttony, and drunkenness of "holy days"; the sermons of the time, which "go promenading among useless stories" and forget Christ; prayers which consist in turning over many pages and counting many beads. Reform in prayer is a prime need: like singing, it is getting worse in the churches every day. It must be made in faith and is itself a training in faith, in hope, and in love. The neglect of real prayer is a theme which Martin had treated with many variations and with which he now deals at length. If he has a broken leg or is in danger of death, man is willing to pray in the full belief that God will hear him, but he is unwilling to pray for the greater need of faith, hope, love, humility, and obedience: "in illness of the body we run to God; in illness of the soul we run away from Him and do not want to return until we are well." [20] The united prayer of a Christian congregation is so irresistible that the devil is in terror of it, even though it be offered under a straw roof or in a pigsty. What wonder that churches are set on fire by lightning when prayer in them is turned into mockery! When the Turks destroy cities and lay waste lands and churches

---

[17] *Ibid.*, p. 227, ll. 15 ff.

[18] "Der grosse Hans odder klein Nickel." *Ibid.*, pp. 228 f.

[19] "Es ist hoch zeit, das wir got mit ernst bitten, das er seinen namen wolt heiligen, es wirt aber blut kosten, und die in der heiligen martern gut sitzen, und mit ihrem blut gewonnen sein, mussenn wiederumb selbs marterer machenn." *Ibid.*, p. 229, ll. 11 ff.

[20] *Ibid.*, p. 237, ll. 20 f.

we think that great damage has been done to Christendom, but when faith perishes and love grows cold, the popes, bishops, and priests themselves become leaders of the enemy, like Judas when Christ was taken prisoner.

From spiritual prayer, Martin turns to consider the spiritual Sabbath, attained through the school of sin and suffering. In language reminiscent of Tauler and the *German Theology* he points out the way to this Nirvana of the soul, where, under God's discipline and guidance, reason and happiness and unhappiness and all the works of men are destroyed and room is made for God's works.

The six Commandments which cover the duty of man to man give the text for a review of the moral ills of the time and the need of an ethical reformation which must thrust its roots deep into the nourishing soil of religious faith. Parenthood leads the way. Those who spoil their children through excessive lenience or who rush off on pilgrimages instead of setting good examples of an active charity and a pious, industrious life, show that the easiest way for parents to earn hell is by means of their offspring. However, disciplining children is in vain unless it is done with the help of faith and divine grace, for many heretics have brought up their children beautifully, and yet love's labor has been lost. Obedience to the spiritual Mother, the Church, has fallen lower still, but then this Mother has played the harlot: greed sits in the seat of power and the clergy are more worldly than the worldlings. Nowadays nothing comes from Rome except trafficking in spiritual gifts, which are bought and sold openly and shamelessly: indulgences, parishes, cloisters, bishoprics, provostries, and benefices, so that not only is all money and all property in the world drawn and driven to Rome— that would be the least of ills—but parishes, bishoprics, and prelacies are torn asunder, abandoned, wasted, and in this way the people are neglected, God's word, name, and honor perish, and faith is destroyed, so that finally the religious foundations and offices fall not only into the hands of the ignorant and incompetent, but for the most part into those of Romans, the chief villains [21] of the world. The result is that what was founded for God's service, to teach, rule, and improve people, now goes to serve horseboys and muleteers; yes, to Roman whores and villains.[22] Therefore we are under obligation to resist, as children resist a parent who has gone insane.

For the councils of the Church Martin has very little respect, and declares that the so-called Reform Synods of the fifteenth century, those of Constance and Basel, only made things worse because Rome obliges the kings and princes beforehand to lock the door to the Holy Ghost, who would bring

[21] "Buffen" (Buben). *Ibid.*, p. 257, l. 18.   [22] *Ibid.*, ll. 9 ff.

about reform. The only recourse Martin sees is an appeal to the temporal powers to uphold the first three Commandments. To be sure, it is not only the clerical leaders who have gone astray; the worldly powers also have betrayed their trust by injustice to the poor, a net that catches the little flies and lets the millstones go through. He scores the officials of the bishoprics for greed in their treatment of the poor, and the cities for permitting houses of prostitution. Nevertheless, these worldly offenders can only harm body and goods but not the soul, for they have nothing to do with preaching and faith or the first three Commandments. The spiritual power, on the other hand, does harm not only because of its wrongs but also because men follow it as the path that leads to God. Here for the first time Martin draws a line between the provinces of Church and state: one must resist the spiritual power when it is not in the right, but must not resist the temporal power even if it is wrong.

In concluding his long analysis of offenses against the Third Commandment, Martin launches a final review of the decay of social life in Germany, a theme which swelled in the literature of clerical protest and satirical attack, in step with the economic inflation that followed the opening of the New World. Luther was ignorant of the basic cause of the changes, but he felt that a disintegration of social morality was taking place and arraigned the trend with vivid protest: the excesses in eating and drinking, the rising desire for fine clothes, the lending at interest, which "everywhere destroys land, people, and cities." [23] He attacks the artisans for disorders and the serving classes for illoyalty and disobedience, "truly a plague of God." [24] He demands that the wife be obedient to her husband, "as her ruler," ready "to give way and be silent and admit that he is right"; and he warns the husband to refrain from too great sharpness.[25]

The last five Commandments are treated briefly. Here man has to contend with his own desires and lusts, and the battleground and field of victory lie within us. "Thou shalt not steal" means that we are to train ourselves in kindly thought toward our enemies. "Thou shalt not commit adultery" points to a lifelong struggle with a fiery and furious enemy that dwells in heart and eyes and ears and mouth and feet, a struggle which Martin, following the great patron of his order, St. Augustine, calls the fiercest of all that beset the Christian, and in which it is only faith and prayer that can purify the inner sources of conduct. "Thou shalt not kill" he translates into a command of charity toward the ungrateful and the hostile; the command

---

[23] *Ibid.*, p. 262, l. 8. [24] *Ibid.*, p. 263, ll. 17 f.
[25] *Ibid.*, p. 264, ll. 10 ff.

against false witness means an unterrified confession of truth, "at the risk of your coat or your life, be it before pope or king." [26]

Among all of Luther's briefer writings, the sermon *On Good Works* stands out as a sort of summary of practical theology. Though not balanced in its parts, it is at once an epitome of his theology and an exposition of the duty of man toward God and his neighbor. It is dominated by the two basic ideas of his mature theology: the desperate wickedness and helplessness of human nature and the power of faith as an anchor and reliance amid the storm of sin and death. In the background lies the struggle with his opponents, and the resentment that was burning within him thrusts itself again and again to the fore when his theme suggests the greed and worldliness of the clergy. In the main, however, he strives to lift the religious life of man into a spiritual realm. As Martin looked at the world about him, it seemed to labor under a profound misunderstanding of the nature of Christianity, and to this misunderstanding he ascribes the ills that affect Church and state.

During the previous winter and spring Luther had thought much about the sacrament of the Mass, and it continued to occupy his mind after completion of the sermon on the Holy Sacrament, which brought him, as we have seen, a sharp attack from the episcopal authorities at Meissen. In that sermon and again in his sermon on good works Luther had taken a strong position against the conception of the Mass as a sacrifice. He looked upon it rather as a festival of gratitude which should warm the heart with love, and he censures those who remain cold at heart and do not accompany the invocation with thankfulness or love or praise. He promised his readers a further discussion of the subject,[27] and this took the form of another sermon, which he delivered in German and which Melanchthon rated so highly that he made a Latin abstract of it for forwarding to a friend.[28] Very soon afterwards Martin sent it to the press,[29] whence it seems to have issued late in April.[30]

Written as it was in the interval between reformatory sermons and polemical pamphlets, the *Sermon on the New Testament or the Holy Mass* [31]

---

[26] *Ibid.*, p. 275, ll. 10 f.   [27] *Von den guten Werken. WA*, VI, 231, ll. 14 f.

[28] Letter from Melanchthon to Johann Hess, April 17, 1520, *CR*, I, 159.

[29] Letter from Luther to Hess, April 27, 1520, *WAB*, II, 86.

[30] See Clemen, *Luthers Werke in Auswahl*, I, 299. The date of issue is not certain. Martin does not mention the work again until August 3, when he forwards a copy to a member of his order in Magdeburg, Johann Voigt, *WAB*, II, 162, with instructions to pass it on to Lang, at this time district vicar of the Augustinians. It is probable that the work was overshadowed by the much more detailed sermon on good works and later by the attacks on Alfeld and Prierias and by the astounding furore created by the *Address to the Christian Nobility*. However, eleven printings of the *Sermon on the Mass* appeared before the end of 1520.

[31] *Ein Sermon von dem Neuen Testament, das ist von der heiligen Messe. WA*, VI, 353 f.

does not appear to have struck fire from contemporaries as did the works which preceded and followed it, although it did attain a very wide circulation in the succeeding months. It is marked by the same repetitions and digressions that encumber the thought of the earlier works of this year, yet it is forceful in presentation and temperate in tone, as befitted the discussion of so solemn a topic. Luther had come a long distance in the thirteen years since the days when, with the Mass book of Gabriel Biel in hand, he had prepared himself for his first administration of the sacred office. The world, he now declares, has too many laws and too many sects. Christ established the Mass as a simple service, but it has grown through accretions until the chief object of the service has been lost to view and only the additions remain. Rich dress and music, song and decorations, pomp and prayers, elevation and laying down, are all without value: the whole Mass lies in the words of Christ, which we must accept with a full assurance that God thus becomes gracious to us. We cannot climb up to God, but can only seize hold of the promise which He gives in such clear and definite language—the promise of Christ, finally sealed by His death. In the bread and wine are contained the true body of Christ, for God must live and the sacrament is a symbol of His life, and it must be received with a faith which awakens hope and a love that leads us with joy to the new life and drives sin away from our hearts. "Let others pray, fast, confess, and prepare themselves for the Mass and the sacrament as they will. You may do that also, if you recognize that it is all foolishness and deceit unless you accept the words of the Testament and awaken within yourself faith and a desire for it." [32] This is the faith that drives out all fear of unworthiness. The sinner presents himself as a beggar to whom a great fortune has been bequeathed and who now demands that it be given him, not for the sake of his own worthiness, but on account of the great generosity of the giver. But the Mass has been sadly distorted. With masterly craft the devil has stolen the heart away from it. Why should not the Germans hear the Mass in their own tongue as the Romans and the Greeks do? Without the words, the sacrament is like a body without a soul, the jewel without a case. "It is of the nature of the sacrament that it is not a work, but an exercise in faith alone." [33]

The worst misuse of the sacrament is making it a sacrifice. It must be separated from the prayers which were added to it by the Church Fathers. It is a sacrifice only in so far as we sacrifice ourselves. It is not the priest alone who offers himself before God, but all are priests who have faith in Christ as their mediator and have no doubt in their hearts that their sins are for-

---

[32] *Ibid.*, pp. 360 f., ll. 32 ff.   [33] *Ibid.*, p. 364, ll. 30 f.

given. Here Luther touched upon a question that he had revolved in his mind with earnestness during the preceding months: the proper office of the priesthood. It was the holy service of the Mass that more than anything else gave to the priest his exalted position and placed him in a different relationship to God from that of the layman. In his early days at the altar Luther must have shared the feeling of his contemporaries that the priest who blesses the bread and wine and by his prayers invites the sacrifice of Christ, participates in a miracle of grace that transports him to holy ground and raises him into a zone above the believers who kneel before the rail. In proportion, however, as Martin's ideas on the hierarchy became more critical, the priestly office shrank to humbler dimensions. About a year earlier, in a memorandum of instructions for young clergymen, he had warned them against approaching the altar with trust in their own fitness for the sacrifice.[34] As time went by and the nature of the sacrament occupied his mind more and more, the idea seems to have taken root that the priest as a servant of Christ differs in no way from the layman except in the duties of his service. "I am ignorant concerning the duties of the priest," he writes to the questioning Spalatin on December 18, "for no matter how much I reflect on it, I find nothing to say except what concerns ceremonies." He bases this on the words of Peter and John. In nothing does the priesthood seem to differ from the laity except in the administration of the sacrament and in preaching. "If you take away the ceremonies and human statutes, all else is equal." [35] At the end of April he is ready to declare to his friend Hess, who is about to be consecrated a priest, that in the use of the Mass there is no difference between priesthood and laity.[36] Now, in the *Sermon on the Mass,* he asserts that faith is the real priestly office; therefore all Christians are priests, whether man or woman, young or old, lord or servant, wife or maid, scholar or layman.[37]

As regards the Masses for freeing souls from purgatory, he speaks with some hesitation. The Mass demands faith: God Himself can do nothing good for man unless man believes in Him, and he is sure that the endowment of so many Masses for the dead cannot be without its abuses. Even though he may invite the charge of heresy by the statement, he declares that if we gather at the Mass and pray for souls without doubt that we are heard, the souls will be released through faith. As for the wine at the sacrament, Martin now speaks out more decidedly than a few months earlier. He still

[34] *WAB*, I, 397, ll. 52 ff.
[35] Letter to Spalatin, Dec. 18, 1519, *WAB*, I, 595.
[36] Letter to Hess, April 27, 1520, *WAB*, II, 86.
[37] *WA*, VI, 370, ll. 25 ff.

does not look upon the administration of the wine to the laity as a matter of the highest importance, since the words of the Mass are greater than the symbol, but he feels that to withhold it is an evil sign in a dangerous time. "They say that the pope has power to do this. I say . . . that he has not a hair's breadth of power to alter what Christ commanded, and in so ordering he behaves like a tyrant and an Antichrist." [38] Martin does not want to raise a tumult respecting the withdrawal of the wine from the laity, but says it is a crime that we are urged not only to endure what is wrong, but also to extol it as right and beneficial. "It is enough that, with Christ, we allow our cheek to be struck; but it is not possible for us to praise it, as if one had done us a favor and earned a divine reward by it."

Martin finally passes in review the abuses by which the Mass has been transformed into an act of magic. Here faith, like Christ, is sold by greedy Judases. He criticizes especially the pressure upon priests in the cloisters to say annuals, often without faith or form; and he closes with the lament that while Christ laid on the Church only a few laws and works and offered it many pledges in return for faith, we have reversed His command and thus we seek grace in vain.

[38] *Ibid.*, p. 374, ll. 27 ff.

26

THE BREAK WITH ROME

"I AM disturbed, Martin, disturbed at the quarrel that has been stirred up by the wretched Dominicans, who with many others are plotting against your life." [1] In these words the humanist friend of Erfurt days, Crotus Rubianus, warned Martin from the Eternal City in mid-October, when chronicling the intensified attack of Luther's opponents, whose temper was now to be inflamed still further by triumphant reports from Eck. It was not long, indeed, before the machinery of the Curia, which had been halted by the diplomatic exigencies of the imperial election, was to be set again into motion against Luther and his protector, the Saxon prince.[2] Just when the wheels began to move cannot be said with certainty. Cajetan was back in Rome at the beginning of September,[3] and while it seems that his reception was courteous and that he continued to enjoy the confidence of the Pope, he

---

[1] "Movet enim me, Martine, movet controversia, quam tibi concitarunt cum multis aliis in caput tuum conspirantes Dominicistae." *WAB*, I, 541, ll. 11 f.

[2] The sources for the renewal of the Roman attack have been so thoroughly explored by a number of scholars that it is not likely that new documents of importance will come to light from the Vatican collections or elsewhere. To the earliest systematic investigation, Karl G. Müller's "Luthers römischer Prozess," *ZKG*, Vol. XXIV (1903), Aloys Schulte added important source studies in his "Die römischen Verhandlungen über Luther 1520," *Quellen und Forschungen aus italienischen Archiven und Bibliotheken*, Vol. VI (1904). Finally, Paul Kalkoff's researches, extending over a number of years, have traversed the period so minutely that the story shows few gaps. See his *Forschungen zu Luthers römischem Prozess*, which includes a chronological survey, and the studies "Zu Luthers römischem Prozess" published in the *Zeitschrift für Kirchengeschichte*, Vols. XXV (1904), XXXI (1910), XXXII (1911), and XXXIII (1912).

Kalkoff's tireless investigation is unfortunately marred by poor organization and tedious repetition. These are, however, minor defects compared with the partisan and subjective way in which he treats the sources. It is necessary to examine every one of these at first hand and check each of his statements in order to determine whether the basis is contemporary material or some hypothesis or interpretation of Kalkoff's which may be set forth without any reservation or indication that it is the result of his own "combination." Often these hypotheses are truly astounding. This method, which mars all of the work of this industrious and self-denying scholar, has added greatly to the difficulty of reaching objective conclusions regarding this period. Fortunately the contemporary sources, such as official documents, minutes, and various letters, are nearly all available in reliable forms.

[3] See Kalkoff, "Zu Luthers römischem Prozess," *ZKG*, XXV, 426, n. 1.

stood in no favor with the younger Medicis and their followers.[4] Hutten's dialogue, *Fever I*, which had appeared in February,[5] attacked the legate with biting sarcasm for his love of Italian luxuries and his contempt for the Germans and their ways; and another dialogue, *The Observers*, followed in April, 1520,[6] picturing Cajetan as an arrogant and boastful exponent of Roman greed. These scathing attacks on the learned and faithful cardinal must have become known very quickly in Rome and strengthened the impression that his failure with Luther had been due to tactlessness in his treatment of the Germans. Although his scholarship continued to be employed by the Vatican, the lack of success in his diplomatic efforts created an unfavorable atmosphere that affected his subsequent career throughout the Medici regime.[7] Eck, whose letters had aroused hopes of victory among the Romans before the disputation,[8] followed this contest with communications proclaiming his triumph,[9] and, as we have seen, sent to the papal court a warning of the rapidly spreading heresy and a prediction that, unless it was checked promptly, it would lead to the loss of Thuringia, Meissen, Brandenburg, and other regions. This threat, which seems to have been treated confidentially at the court,[10] aroused the Curia to action. Hope still lingered that the elector might be induced to proceed against the troublesome professor, and a warning and threat were sent to him through Miltitz. The latter was now in Frederick's service, and he transmitted the papal message to the elector early in December.[11] The Pope is growing impatient, he says, at the way the matter drags on. Certain bishops may also have written to Rome,[12] and Miltitz fears that the affair may be put in the hands of another

---

[4] *Ibid.*, p. 425.

[5] *Febris Prima.* Hutten, *Opera*, I, 36 f.

[6] *Inspicientes*, which appeared with the *Trias Romana. Ibid.*, p. 48.

[7] Kalkoff, "Zu Luthers römischem Prozess," *ZKG*, XXV, 425 f. According to Luther, *TR*, IV, No. 4937, Cardinal Campeggi declared at Augsburg in 1530 that Cajetan had spoiled everything by his threats of force, certainly an unjust criticism in view of the legate's instructions from the Pope.

[8] See the letter from Johann Hess in Rome to Johann Lang, Nov. 19, 1519, in Kolde, *Analecta Lutherana*, pp. 9 f.

[9] Letter from Crotus to Luther, Oct. 31(?), 1519, *WAB*, I, 545.

[10] Crotus writes Luther that besides the Pope only a small group saw this letter. "Misit Heckius epistolam Romam praeterquam Pontifici et duobus theologis paucissimis visam." *Ibid.*, p. 545. See also *ibid.*, p. 546, ll. 25 ff.

[11] E. S. Cyprian, "Nützliche Urkunden zur Erläuterung der ersten Reformationsgeschichte," in *Tentzels Historischer Bericht vom Anfang und ersten Fortgang der Reformation Lutheri*, I, 1, 408 ff.

[12] Kalkoff, who is biased against Miltitz, regards this as an invention of the latter. "Zu Luthers römischem Prozess," *ZKG, XXV*, 437. However, it may well have been true; Luther at least seems to have believed it. See letter from Luther to Lang, Dec. 18, 1519, *WAB*, I, 597, ll. 34 f.

and an interdict eventually laid upon the electoral lands.[13] The volatile young Saxon was aroused to new activity and ran busily back and forth,[14] seeking to expedite the hearing before the archbishop of Trier; but in spite of the earnest exhortation which Miltitz claimed to have received from the Pope to get the matter settled before the meeting of the Diet, the archbishop, who may himself have been awaiting an order from Rome, preferred to postpone the hearing until the estates should come together.[15] Luther, who was well aware of what was going on, thought at the time that he might go to Trier if a safe-conduct could be arranged.[16]

Part of Miltitz's activity was inspired, no doubt, by the elector. Frederick was intent that the question should be laid before the archbishop for his decision, and had in October reminded that dignitary of his promise to give a hearing to Luther at the next meeting of the Diet.[17] In the meantime, he seems to have been fully aware of the seriousness of the situation and made ready to meet it with the prudence that marked his character. The question of a reply for the Pope was submitted to his councilors and the record of their deliberations has been preserved in three forms: the agenda by Spalatin for the discussion,[18] the memorandum of the council to the elector, showing point by point how Miltitz's letter was to be answered,[19] and finally, the elector's instructions for the reply.[20] Frederick's letter is diplomatically clever, but registers no change in his attitude since the preceding January. Again he prefers not to address himself directly to Rome, but to deal with the papal court through its agent, Miltitz. Again, in traversing the history of the affair, he dissociates himself from Luther's case, as he had done two years earlier with Cajetan and the year before with Miltitz. He reminds the latter that Luther had offered to leave Saxony, but had been detained at Miltitz's request, for fear that if he went elsewhere the affair might become more difficult and attain wider scope. He lays on Miltitz's shoulders the responsibility for the delay in a decision by the archbishop of Trier, before

---

[13] Kalkoff, *Forschungen,* p. 70, assumes that Miltitz received two letters from the Pope, in November and December, but the evidence of address is not conclusive.

[14] Letter from Luther to Spalatin, Dec. 18, *WAB,* I, 594 f., and n. 1.

[15] See Miltitz's letters to the archbishop as reflected in the latter's replies. Cyprian, "Nützliche Urkunden," I, 1, 395 ff.; also 393 ff.

[16] Letter to Lang, Dec. 18, *WAB,* I, 597.

[17] Walch, *Schriften,* XV, 903 ff. Kalkoff is strongly of the opinion that the elector was using the archbishop's suggestion merely as an excuse, but it appears to have been meant sincerely. Luther evidently thought so at this time. It seems, however, quite unlikely that the archbishop ever received any other authorization from Rome than was implied in a perhaps verbal commission from Cajetan. Kalkoff, "Zu Luthers römischem Prozess," *ZKG,* XXV, 440 f., n. 3.

[18] Cyprian, "Nützliche Urkunden," I, II, 148 ff.

[19] *Ibid.,* I, 1, 411 ff.   [20] *Ibid.,* I, II, 142 ff.

whom Luther is ready to appear whenever he shall receive a safe-conduct. For the rest, he states, Luther has only defended himself against attacks. In view of his own actions, Frederick protests vigorously against interdict or censure.

In the meantime, Eck was busy at Nuremberg, Augsburg, and elsewhere in South Germany, and finally crossed the Alps, doubtless on a summons from the Pope, and arrived in Rome sometime before the end of March. The Curia had not, however, awaited his coming before proceeding to more vigorous action. In a public consistory on January 9, an Italian attached to the papal court delivered an arraignment of Luther and his protector, Frederick. The name of this fiery protagonist is not known, but a young Swiss lawyer who was present records that the orator urged the Pope to direct his auditor of the chamber to proceed at once against these "heads of the hydra," and require that they declare their faith or be proclaimed and rated as heretics.[21] This demand found an immediate response from Leo, and although his procedure was delayed by the red tape of the canon law and the disputes of theologians, so that five months were required for its completion, the final goal was never lost to view.

Perhaps due to the energetic impulse that set it in motion, papal action appears to have made a false start. About February 1, a congregation of Franciscan observants came together under the leadership of Cajetan and Cardinal Pietro Accolti, who bore the reputation of a learned and careful jurist, and it forthwith condemned certain of Luther's propositions.[22] Apparently this action, which consumed only a few days, met with opposition [23] on the part of those who felt that weighty theological issues were concerned demanding a procedure that could be defended from every attack; and the question was then referred to a congregation evidently composed of various learned representatives of the monastic orders, including probably the generals of the powerful Augustinians, Carmelites, and Conventual Franciscans.[24] This group, which the head of Luther's order [25] described as in-

[21] Report of Melchior von Watt, in Schulte, "Die römischen Verhandlungen," pp. 174 f. See also Kalkoff, "Zu Luthers römischem Prozess," ZKG, XXV, 95 ff., and his Forschungen, pp. 15 ff. Kalkoff suggests reasons for thinking that this Italian may have been Hieronymus Aleander, who played the rôle of prosecuting attorney against Luther at Worms.

[22] Sanuto, I Diarii, XXVIII, 256 f. See also Schulte, "Die römischen Verhandlungen," pp. 44 f.; also Kalkoff, "Zu Luthers römischem Prozess," ZKG, XXV, 99 f., and his Forschungen, p. 72, where he substitutes Pucci for Cajetan (but cf. Schulte, "Die römischen Verhandlungen," p. 46).

[23] The Venetian observer Marco Minio notes criticism of the manner in which the affair was handled. Schulte, "Die römischen Verhandlungen," p. 43.

[24] Ibid., pp. 36 f. and 44.

[25] Gabriel della Volta. Sanuto, I Diarii, XXVIII, 376. See also Kalkoff, "Zu Luthers römischem Prozess," ZKG, XXV, 101, n. 4.

cluding "all the theologians in Rome," reached conclusions strikingly in agreement with the remark which Cajetan is reported to have made two years earlier to the Louvain and Cologne theologians: that Luther's propositions were errors, but not necessarily heresies. According to the Augustinian general, a part of Martin's doctrines were regarded by the theologians as heretical, a part as "scandalous." The congregation recommended that a papal declaration (*Extravagante*) should be issued in which Luther's doctrines should be "reproved" [26] without, however, naming the offender, and that Luther should be summoned by a special breve to recantation and, in case of contumacy, be proceeded against as a heretic.[27] The mildness of this action on the part of the Roman theologians was not approved by the Pope, and it seems natural to assume that Eck, who must have arrived in Rome before the end of March, argued for uncompromising procedure against his Saxon opponent. In any event, Eck reports on May 3 to a friend in Germany [28] that a group consisting of the Pope, the two cardinals, a Spanish scholar, and himself held a long conference on the matter, each giving his opinion, and that from this discussion the bull emerged. It had been laid before the Pope on the preceding day, and now the matter would be brought before a consistory for approval.[29]

It has been suggested that the long delay in the procedure was caused by the absence in Florence of the papal vice chancellor, Cardinal Medici, the chief driving force in the Vatican's affairs. It is likely, however, that the main cause was a difference of opinion between Eck and the Romans as to whether Luther's propositions should be condemned as a whole, or whether a distinction should be made between those plainly heretical and those to be regarded merely as erroneous. It is very probable that the discussions in Rome and at Marliana, the papal country seat, found Eck opposed to Cajetan who, as a competent theologian, was intent on discriminating between that which was manifestly in opposition to the decrees of the Church and that which conflicted only with theories not as yet incorporated into the body of recognized doctrines. It must be remembered that much that later found recognition by the Council of Trent was still unfixed and debatable. Under these circumstances, whatever was condemned in the writings of Luther would assume a great importance for the future,

---

[26] "Hora se dice che si cavarà una extravagante, per la quale ditte sue false oppositione saranno reprobate, non lo nominando." Sanuto, *I Diarii*, XXVIII, 376.

[27] For the succession of events, see Kalkoff, "Zu Luthers römischem Prozess," *ZKG*, XXV, 580 f., n. 3, where sources not available to Schulte are cited.

[28] Published from the Jena edition of Luther's works (1556) in *EA*, XXXV, 256 ff.

[29] See Wiedemann, *Dr. Johann Eck*, p. 151. Other sources may be found in Kalkoff, "Zu Luthers römischem Prozess," *ZKG*, XXV, 102 f. and n. 3.

since the Church would by this action bind itself to certain doctrines.

The importance of the aggressive Ingolstadt professor in formulating the bull *Exsurge domine* comes to light if one compares that document in its final form with the action of the Louvain and Cologne faculties. There is considerable identity between the propositions condemned,[30] but one of the points mentioned in the bull is notably absent from the Louvain indictment, although it occurs in that of the sister university at Cologne,[31] namely Luther's attack on the supremacy of the pope. Here the sturdy German Dominican, who had just come to the defense of the papal power in a forceful argument, *On the Primacy of Peter,* which he had brought to Rome with him,[32] must have found a supporter in Cajetan, for this was one of the points that the learned cardinal had put into the forefront of his arraignment of Luther at Augsburg. It was probable also that this point was responsible for some of the violent discussion in the consistory,[33] where the opposition was evidently led by Cardinal Carvajal, a representative of the belief, still latent in the Sacred College, in the supremacy of the council over the pope.

How the forces lined up when the draft of the bull went to the cardinals for their consideration cannot be said, but the sources show that the question was on the agenda of four consistories,[34] held in rapid succession toward the end of May. It is also clear that when the bull received final approval, it was in a form which had been little altered after its presentation. Whatever the disputes were regarding theological refinements or major questions of Church government, the lines of control over a free expression of opinion within the Church were growing taut and an era of aggressive action on the part of Rome against its critics in Germany was about to be opened. This became apparent when the Pope finally set aside the decision of the bishop of Spires and the German commission which had supported Reuchlin in his controversy with the Cologne Dominicans. Reuchlin was now condemned and Hochstraten, the leader of his opponents, was thus confirmed in his powers as inquisitor.

In the consistory, victory lay with those who would condemn Martin's

---

[30] *Ibid.,* pp. 107 f.; see also Wiedemann, *Dr. Johann Eck,* p. 152.

[31] *Condemnatio Facultatis Theologiae Coloniensis. WA,* VI, 180.

[32] *De primatu Petri adversus Lutherum.* See Wiedemann, *Dr. Johann Eck,* p. 517.

[33] If we may trust the statement of Erasmus, doubtless received from friends and correspondents who were present. See *Acta academiae Lovaniensis, EA,* XXXV, 311 f. See also Kalkoff, "Zu Luthers römischem Prozess," *ZKG,* XXV, 120 f.

[34] May 21, 23, 25, and June 1. Schulte, "Die römischen Verhandlungen," p. 33; Kalkoff, "Zu Luthers römischem Prozess," *ZKG,* XXV, 112 ff. Kalkoff adduces sources to show that the decisive action took place on May 25. *Ibid.,* p. 119 and notes.

doctrines as a whole, without decision as to their degree of deviation from the Church's norms: forty-one propositions were voted on severally and condemned as "heretical or scandalous or offensive to pious ears." [35] Eck's victory was complete, in spite of the fact that his manners seemed to have caused general amusement among the Italians.[36] "It was well," he had written to his friend in Germany during the drafting of the bull, "that I came to Rome at this time, because the others were too little acquainted with the Lutheran errors." [37] The objective of his journey was fully attained when, on June 15, 1520, the bull was finally engrossed in the papal chancery, and shortly afterwards in accordance with its provisions, the books of Luther were publicly burned in the Piazza Navona.[38] According to the reports which Luther received about this time, Leo had shown the German Dominican a special honor, "to the profound astonishment of everyone." [39] Early in July Eck received his traveling expenses from the papal exchequer [40] and soon afterwards was on his way northward, eager to publish the bull in southern and middle Germany. Following him, the Pope speeded another emissary toward the lower Rhine,[41] Hieronymus Aleander, schooled in the humanistic methods of philology and hard-baked in the oven of Roman diplomacy. Less of a theologian than Cajetan and Eck, Aleander was greatly their superior in the diplomatic treatment of public men and well adapted to assume leadership in the coming duel with the German revolutionaries.

Before either of these emissaries bore the bull along the well-worn paths toward the north, the papal court had formulated its last grave warnings to Luther's protector. Early in April old Cardinal Raphael Riario, the dean of the Sacred College, had addressed to Frederick a long letter, courteous in its official and personal tone, which charged Luther with deceiving and turning aside many from the zeal for religion, "with hope and eagerness for a false and empty glory," and dwelt upon the misery that was caused by this misuse of his high gifts.[42] The cardinal, with many a scriptural

---

[35] "Tanquam . . . hereticos seu scandalosos aut . . . piarum aurium offensivos." Erasmus pretended to find the failure to differentiate as to the character of Luther's errors proof that this bull was not genuine. *Acta academiae Lovaniensis, EA*, XXXV, 312. For Martin's attitude toward such mass condemnation, see *Adversus execrabilem Antichristi bullam. WA*, VI, 601 f.

[36] According to the report of Melchior von Watt. Schulte, "Die römischen Verhandlungen," p. 176.

[37] May 3, 1520. *EA*, XXXV, 256.

[38] Kalkoff, "Zu Luthers römischem Prozess," *ZKG*, XXV, 129.

[39] Letter from Luther to Hess, June 7, 1520, *WAB*, II, 118.

[40] Schulte, "Die römischen Verhandlungen," p. 176.

[41] See Kalkoff, "Zu Luthers römischem Prozess," *ZKG*, XXV, 131, for sources.

[42] Text of the letter, which is dated April 3, is reproduced by Kalkoff; *ibid.*, pp. 587 f.

figure and quotation, exhorted the elector by the fame of his illustrious ancestors to force Luther to a revocation, for it depended altogether on his will whether one man should be permitted to sow tares and thorns in the garden of the Lord. Somewhat later, another letter was forwarded by Valentin von Tetleben, an agent of the elector in Rome, who was also attached to the court of the elector of Mainz.[43] This was apparently also written under a papal commission. It called attention to the trouble which Luther was causing in Rome, and waiving all judgment as to the correctness of Martin's views, warned the elector against giving an opportunity for the growth of the Lutheran party under any pretense.[44]

These two letters did not reach the electoral court until the beginning of July.[45] Before their arrival Eck and Aleander had each been equipped with a letter to Frederick from the Pope which repeated in a categorical form the warnings that were incorporated in the bull. Both these letters bore date of July 8. Only that which was entrusted to Eck reached the elector's hands.

The bull *Exsurge domine,* prepared after so many months of discussion, took a form closely following that of the letter of authority to Cajetan which had been drawn up in August two years earlier.[46] "Let the Lord rise and his enemies be scattered!" Thus it begins with a call to battle in defense of the faith, and the same solemn tone rings through the long document. It condemns 41 propositions of Luther's, as we have seen, forbids the books containing these, and commands that they be burned immediately. The earlier stages in the affair are reviewed, and it is noted that Martin has been under censure for contumacy for more than a year and that he has appealed to a council, an offense which two popes had declared subject to punishment for heresy. He and his supporters are now warned to renounce their errors and burn their writings within sixty days after the posting of the bull at St. Peter's and at the chancelleries and cathedrals of Brandenburg, Meissen, and Merseburg. Luther must forward his recantation or appear at Rome personally. Otherwise he and his supporters are declared notorious and obstinate heretics, whom every spiritual and temporal power is obligated to deliver to Rome.

Kalkoff's hypothesis (*ibid.,* p. 452, n. 1) that the letter was intentionally predated by six weeks, seems poorly substantiated.

[43] Dated May 20. See *ibid.,* pp. 591 f., for text.

[44] "Ne christianae reipublicae sub dissimulatione quadam erroris ansam aliquando praestitisse videatur."

[45] *Ibid.,* p. 450.

[46] For the relationship of the bulls *Exsurge* and *Decet Romanum* (Jan. 3, 1521) to the breve of August 23, 1518, see Karl G. Müller, "Luthers römischer Prozess," *ZKG,* XXIV (1903), 63 ff., and Kalkoff, "Zu Luthers römischem Prozess," *ZKG,* XXV, 276 ff.

The spring had passed and the early summer days had come in Wittenberg without bringing to Luther anything more than indistinct rumors of the storm brewing against him beside the Tiber. The atmosphere surrounding Martin had, to be sure, grown more tense as the May days passed, and a warning had come now and again from Halle or from Bamberg; but so far as the sources show, he had obtained no definite information respecting events at the Roman court. Offers of support had come to him, certainly none more welcome than that from his old adviser, Staupitz, who encouraged him with prayers and hopes for his cause.[47] Thus his ship was tossed about between hope and fear, but his mind was clarified and his resolution fixed.

In the meantime, there was no halt in polemical activity, which had now introduced a new enemy. This was Augustin von Alfeld, a lecturer on the Bible in the Franciscan cloister at Leipzig. The powerful order of the Franciscans had shown themselves favorable to Luther in other centers, notably in Basel, where Martin's works were interpreted in conventual sermons, and the brotherhood was later to furnish many adherents to the Reformation cause. The criticisms by the Jüterbog cloister, which had called forth such a stinging rebuke from Luther in the previous year, had been disapproved by the provincial head of the order, and disciplinary measures were promised against those responsible for the attack.[48] Alfeld, whose earlier career is unrecorded in the available annals of the time,[49] was a native of the Hildesheim region, and demonstrated later in more than fifteen polemical writings in support of the Church against the Lutheran movement that he had undergone considerable training in theology. Well versed in the Bible as well as in the humanistic lore of the day, his linguistic competence included some knowledge of Greek and Hebrew as well as Latin. Like most of those who turned their guns against Luther in these early days, however, his argumentation followed scholastic patterns. His knowledge of history was defective, and his undoubted courage and persistence in facing the sarcasm and filth which Luther's followers flung at him was supported neither by power of logical presentation nor gift for popular appeal.

This sturdy brother was called into the lists by the bishop of his diocese, Adolf of Anhalt, the prelate who had offered such strenuous resistance to Luther's appearance at the Leipzig disputation.[50] Some time in the previous

---

[47] Letter from Luther to Spalatin, May 1, 1520, *WAB*, II, 96.
[48] Letter from Luther to Spalatin, Sept. 22, 1519, *WAB*, I, 509.
[49] See Leonhard Lemmens, "Pater Augustin von Alfeld," *Erläuterungen und Ergänzungen zu Janssens Geschichte des deutschen Volkes*, Vol. I.
[50] Lemmens, "Pater Augustin von Alfeld," p. 3.

year, Alfeld set out to write a defense of the supremacy of the pope,[51] and on April 7 heralded its appearance by a letter of defiance addressed to Luther, promising in the blustering tone characteristic of the time that he would attack him "with spirit and with truth." [52] He followed this threat a few weeks later with the publication of a Latin pamphlet *On the Roman See*.[53] Starting with a comparison of Martin to Wyclif, Huss, and other heretics, the Leipzig theologian proceeds to defend the rights of the pope on the basis of history and Scripture, and decorates his treatise with abusive characterizations of the heresies in Luther's work.[54]

Martin had been expecting the attack. When he had read it he called it "mush," and declined to waste any time in replying.[55] He found in all features of the work a striking resemblance to the "ox," Dungersheim, with whom his debate was slowly dragging its weary length; and he turned it over to his famulus, Johann Lonicer, for answering. This young Augustinian entered on his task with zeal, and following a plan which Martin furnished,[56] had his reply in print at the end of the month. The pamphlet, *Against the Romanist Brother Augustin von Alfeld*,[57] was the maiden effort of the young bachelor of arts and is marked by the characteristics of a beginner in theological tilting. He starts by calling his opponent "more stupid than a Boeotian sow," and ends by dubbing him a "blasphemous ox." He does not overlook Alfeld's linguistic and other defects, and adds the satirical spice that was so beloved of the humanistic polemicists. At least one other supporter from the Wittenberg circle, Bartholomäus Bernhardi of Feldkirchen, joined in the attack with a *Confutation*.[58] But Alfeld's work also found support, to the astonishment of Luther, who regarded it as "in every syllable silly and stupid," so that words failed him with which to characterize it.[59] It was looked upon with especial favor by certain persons with legal and official connections in Saxon lands, and Luther asks, "I implore

---

[51] See his letters to Miltitz, Tuesday after Cantate, 1520. Cyprian, "Nützliche Urkunden," I, II, 160 ff.

[52] *WAB*, II, 79 f.

[53] *Super apostolica sede, an videlicet divino sit iure nec ne.* Lemmens, "Pater Augustin von Alfeld," pp. 3 and 100; see also the letter from Alfeld to Miltitz, Cyprian, "Nützliche Urkunden," I, II, 161 f.

[54] Lemmens, "Pater Augustin von Alfeld," pp. 10 ff. and 16 f. Alfeld's pamphlets have not been available to me for examination.

[55] Letter to Spalatin, May 5, 1520, *WAB*, II, 98.

[56] Letter to Spalatin, May 13, *WAB*, II, 103.

[57] *Contra Romanistum fratrem Augustinum Alveldem* . . . dedicated May 12. *WA*, VI, 279 f. See also Lemmens, "Pater Augustin von Alfeld," pp. 22 f.

[58] *Confutatio inepti et impii libelli F. Augustini Alfeld.* . . . See *ibid.*, p. 17; see also *WA*, VI, 280. For the continuation of the controversy between Alfeld, Lonicer, and others, see Lemmens, "Pater Augustin von Alfeld," pp. 24 ff.

[59] Letter from Luther to Spalatin, May 13, 1520, *WAB*, II, 103.

you, is it not strange that men of that sort have no nose?" [60] He was thinking of a reply when the belligerent Franciscan, who persisted in his attacks in spite of opposition within his own order,[61] brought out about the middle of May, possibly on the advice of Miltitz, a German work entitled, *A Very Fruitful and Useful Little Book on the Papal See and Saint Peter and the True Lambs of Christ*.[62] Here he formulates briefly, in stilted and somewhat inconsequent manner, arguments in defense of the papal power.

The appearance of this book, with its appeal through the vernacular to the common man, brought Luther into action. At the end of May his reply is in process of birth,[63] and comes from the press before the end of the following month.[64] *On the Papacy at Rome against the Famous Romanist at Leipzig* [65] presents once more, but in sharper form, ideas that had been expressed throughout the previous year in the Leipzig disputation and in the exchanges with Eck and Emser. Martin urges again the necessity of an appeal to the temporal estates, such as we noted in his *Sermon on Good Works*. He passes in review his opponents—Cajetan, Eck, Emser, and the Cologne and Louvain theologians—and observes that others have now entered the lists. It is not the poor, untrained, barefoot monk whom he means, but persons higher up who have put Alfeld forward because they do not venture into battle themselves. For himself, Martin asserts, the affair is profoundly serious, but since he has been attacked with satire and mockery, he is unfortunately obliged to reply in the same tone. He gives indeed full expression to his contempt for the "miserable, blind Romanist" and his "foolish book." Martin's work is marked by the same rambling style characteristic of the polemical writings and sermons which he so hastily threw together in these stirring months, and the arguments show his tendency to make points by means of the sophistical devices common in the disputational skirmishing of university and cloister. Nevertheless, Martin's heart is in the effort to bring his ideas on the subject of the Roman claims to power into such simple form as can be understood by the lay reader, who must be reached through plain German and whose feelings will respond only to forceful appeals.

The question he considers is whether the papal power, which all recog-

[60] Letter to Spalatin, May 17, *WAB*, II, 104.

[61] See his letter to Miltitz. Cyprian, "Nützliche Urkunden," I, II, 161 f.

[62] *Ein gar fruchtbares und nützliches Büchlein von dem päpstlichen Stuhle und von Sankt Peter und von den wahrhaftigen Schäflein Christi.* See Lemmens, "Pater Augustin von Alfeld," pp. 33 ff. and 100.

[63] Letter from Luther to Spalatin, May 31. *WAB*, II, 111.

[64] Letter to Spalatin, June 25, *WAB*, II, 130.

[65] *Von dem Papsttum zu Rom wider den hochberühmten Romanisten zu Leipzig. WA*, VI, 285 ff.

nize, is derived from God or man. Are all Christians who do not buy the
privilege of having their bishops confirmed at Rome, such as the Russians,
Greeks, and Bohemians, to be called heretics, even though they have
the same faith and baptism as ourselves, but will not allow themselves to
be flayed and disgraced like the "drunken Germans"? He declares that
they are not heretics, and supports his view by an indictment of the abuses
at Rome, where a "good Christian" is synonymous with a fool and where
greed for gain and the "divine order" are one and the same. It is because of this greed that the Romans have not replied to his arguments
respecting more important questions in theology but have stuck to a defense of indulgences and the papal power. That he has paid no attention
to their "growling and grunting" has broken their hearts.[66]

Martin dismisses the Leipzig champion of the pope with the charge that
Alfeld has attacked him with abuse but without bringing forward any
proof. Rising above sportive and sophistical play with the arguments of
his rather helpless opponent, however, Luther declares his independence of
all spiritual leadership by the pope and the Roman hierarchy. The realm
of Christendom, he states, is not to be compared with any earthly kingdom.
It is a union of all hearts who accept the Christian confession and live in
faith, hope, and charity. The kingdom of God is within us and not in
Rome, and he denounces as a blasphemous lie against the Holy Ghost the
claim that union under the Roman power is by divine command. We belong to Christendom, not with our bodies, but with our souls; and all
classes and ranks are equal members of the Christian community, where
the clergy are distinguished from others only by sermons, garb, and kind
of service; indeed the hierarchy that rules in Christendom may contain many
who are not really members of the spiritual Church. As often before, Martin
objects to the use of the terms "churchly" and "ecclesiastical" as designations
of law or property.

It is on these lines that he then proceeds to attack Alfeld's arguments from
the Old and New Testament. Over against the Franciscan's rather unwieldy comparison of Aaron and the pope, he points to Christ as the spiritual
high priest between God and ourselves. Again he sets forth, with the
homely illustrations of which he had so rich a command, the equality of all
the apostles as heirs of Christ, repeats with variations his interpretation of
the method by which Rome feeds Christ's sheep, and asks with bitterness
to be shown a pope who has had the love that Christ demanded of those
who were to perform the shepherd's service. He is charged with having been

[66] "Runzen und grunzen." *Ibid.*, p. 289, ll. 22 f.

vicious and vindictive, but he fears he has done too little: "I ought to have laid hold of the ravening wolves more vigorously." [67] He sums up with the declaration that he will not permit men to add new articles to faith nor to stamp as a heretic everyone who will not subject himself to the pope; and he claims the right to judge by sacred Scripture everything that the pope does. The Roman villains have introduced a new definition of faith in substituting for the Pauline "assurance of things unseen" a belief in Roman supremacy that is visible to everyone. "May God forbid that the pope come to that point: then I would say frankly that he is the real Antichrist of whom all the Scripture speaks. . . . Let him who will set up a pope as an idol; I will not worship him." Finally he would like to summon the kings, princes, and nobles in order that they might put a stop to Roman greed. "Thus, you red harlot of Babylon, as St. John calls you, you make out of our religion a mockery before the whole world, yet you claim to make a Christian of everyone." [68]

In conclusion, Martin offers his apologies to the university and city of Leipzig. He intends no insult to them; the author of the "apish book" would have been beneath his notice if he had not written in German to mislead poor people: "for the coarse miller's pack-mule can't even sing his 'Ika, Ika,' and yet interferes in an affair which the Roman See itself has not been able to carry through in a thousand years with the aid of all its bishops and scholars." [69] If he permits such blockheads as this to run at large, the bath maids will soon be writing against him.

Martin's pamphlet ran speedily through a dozen printings in South Germany and Switzerland.[70] His opponent lost no time in replying, but his answer, which came from the press in the following month,[71] like a work later in the year attacking Luther's sermon on the Mass, brought no response from Martin. The latter was occupied with a far greater task, a call to action against Rome that was to be addressed, not to an audience intent on theological and historical issues, but to the nobility of Germany itself. The famous *Address to the Christian Nobility of the German Nation* had long been brewing in Luther's mind, and the ideas it contains had already forced themselves into view during the preceding year. The contrast between Roman claims to rule by God's command and Roman greed and sharp practice received, no doubt, a personal coloring from the knowledge

---

[67] "Ich solt den reyssenden wolffen bass in die wolle griffen haben." *Ibid.*, p. 320, ll. 28 f.
[68] *Ibid.*, p. 322, ll. 17 ff. and 37 ff. [69] *Ibid.*, p. 323, ll. 30 ff.
[70] *Ibid.*, pp. 281 f.
[71] *Sermon darin sich Bruder Augustinus von Alveld beklaget. . . .* See Lemmens, "Pater Augustin von Alfeld," pp. 40 and 101.

that his own fate lay at this time on the conference table of the Curia. How appalling a gulf yawned between his views and those of the defenders of the papal authority was evident to him when he took up the arguments of the Leipzig Franciscan. This must have struck him even more forcefully when there fell into his hands, about this time, a work by the official defender of the papal prerogative, Sylvester Prierias. The palace theologian, who had launched the first Roman attack on Luther two years before, had waited longer to renew the battle than was the custom of the day, so long, in fact, that Luther seems to have crossed him off the list of his opponents.[72] The Dominican official was, however, diligently at work, and in June of the preceding year had laid before the Pope the manuscript of his defense. Crotus had written from Rome in October that Prierias was showing around among his Dominican brothers a lengthy work on Martin's heresies.[73] It was indeed a ponderous volume when it finally appeared, nearly three hundred quarto pages of *Errors and Arguments of Martin Luther, Enumerated, Exposed, Repelled, and Fully Ground to Pieces.*[74] The zealous defender of the faith did not wait to issue the entire work, but before the end of 1519 put forth at Perugia an *Epitome of the Answer to Martin Luther,*[75] containing what he called "a list of his weapons." This is nothing less than an exact summary of the first books of his forthcoming great work. Apparently this epitome came into Luther's hands through Nuremberg friends early in June,[76] and it appeared to him so blasphemous that, as he said, the reading of it almost killed him.[77] Everyone at Rome, he writes under the first impression, has become "crazy, foolish, raging, mad, fools, sticks, stones, hell, and devil," since they allow this "infernal work" to go out into the Church. He promises to republish the book with little comments of his own; and in spite of his other occupations, he reports to Spalatin on June 13 that "Sylvester's insanity" is already in press.[78] A fortnight later it appeared, on the same day as his reply to Alfeld.[79]

In his treatment of the work Martin follows the same procedure as with the former book of that author, publishing the work with an introduction and conclusion of his own, and margining Prierias's arguments with

---

[72] Letter from Luther to Spalatin, Oct. 13, 1519, *WAB*, I, 529.
[73] Letter from Crotus Rubianus to Luther, Oct. 31(?), 1519, *WAB*, I, 546.
[74] *WA*, VI, 327.
[75] *Epitoma responsionis ad Martinum Lutherum. Ibid.*, pp. 328 ff.
[76] Letter from Luther to Spalatin, June 7(?), 1520, *WAB*, II, 120.
[77] Letter to Hess, June 7, *WAB*, II, 118.   [78] *WAB*, II, 122.
[79] Letter to Spalatin, June 25, 1520, *WAB*, II, 130.

sarcastic notes.[80] The introduction is brief, but it bristles with invectives. It is the sharpest attack that Martin had yet launched against the Roman power. The wretched man, he says, has repaid his leniency in the treatment of his earlier works by putting out a book that is so filled from top to bottom with blasphemies that it might have been published in the middle of hell by Satan himself. If the Pope and cardinals approve of these things, he feels free to say that Antichrist is enthroned in God's very temple. The best refutation then is to publish the book itself. If Rome believes these things, then happy is Greece, happy is Bohemia, happy are all who have separated themselves from the midst of this Babylon; and he is ready to abjure the Church, with pope and cardinals, now that the abomination of desolation stands in the holy place.

Now, farewell, you unhappy, lost, and blasphemous Rome: the wrath of God has come upon you at last, as you have merited, for in spite of all the prayers that have been said for you, you have become worse each day. We would have healed Babylon, but she is not healed. Let us forsake her then to become a dwelling place of dragons, evil spirits, goblins, and witches, and her name an eternal confusion, filled to the brim as she is with the idols of greed, with traitors, apostates, beasts, (cynaedis), lechers, thieves, and simoners, and an infinity of other monsters, something new in the way of a pantheon of iniquity! [81]

Following a peroration so strongly compounded of Old Testament and humanistic epithets, Luther provides the text of Prierias with caustic notes, in which he attacks ever and again the claim of the papacy to be regarded as the foundation of the laws of the Church, a claim advanced in exaggerated form by the palace theologian. To the assertion that the pope as head of the hierarchy is a judge from whom there is no appeal, Martin remarks, "Not for Luther, foul sycophant!" [82] and when Prierias outlines what the pope has to do when he acts as pope, his editor comments that he acts as pope when he is borne aloft and offers his blessed foot to be kissed, then absorbs the whole world and destroys souls for greed.[83] In his concluding address to the reader, Martin casts an eye back over the appalling claims asserted for the papacy by this "organ of Satan," and finds that no remedy remains except that the emperor, the kings, and the princes attack this "pest of the world" and render a decision, not with words but with iron. "If we punish thieves with the gallows, robbers with the sword, and heretics with fire, why should we not all the more assail with arms these masters of

---

[80] Ad dialogum Sylvestri Prieratis . . . responsio. WA, I, 647 ff.
[81] WA, VI, 329, ll. 17 ff.   [82] Ibid., p. 336, l. 35.
[83] Ibid., p. 337, ll. 35 ff.

perdition, these cardinals, these popes, the whole dregs of the Roman Sodom, who have been corrupting the Church of God without intermission, and wash our hands in their blood, so as to free ourselves and those under our care from the conflagration that threatens to overwhelm all"—words that have been cited innumerable times as evidence of Martin's intolerance and violence [84]—and he concludes: "I have published and I do declare, basing on the words of Peter and of Christ, that if the leaders, the bishops, and all other loyal followers do not admonish, arraign, and accuse the erring pope, whatever may be his crimes, and hold him as a heathen, they are all blasphemers of the way of truth and deniers of Christ, and are, with the pope, to be eternally damned. I have spoken." [85]

With this glossary on Prierias's work, wherein Martin's denunciation of the claim of the pope to divine authority over the Church rises in fury to the point of incoherence, he reaches the end of a long path. When, as an obscure monk and professor, he faced Cajetan nearly two years before, uncertain as to whither his course was to lead him, he offered to subject himself to Pope Leo's decision, although denying the justice of a decree of one of Leo's predecessors. Already two months later, in his declaration in the *Acta Augustana,* he had begun to lament that people put everything in the hands of the pope; and shortly afterward, in his response to the first attack by Prierias, he had arrived at the conviction that a council alone can represent the whole Church. The exchanges with Eck brought him to a complete denial of the divine authority of Rome, and in the succeeding months the belief grew within him that the papal power as exercised through the machinery of the Curia and the canon law was responsible for all the fearful abuses which were threatening the life of the Church in Germany and elsewhere. With this there had grown up in Martin a conviction that the system could be overthrown only by mobilizing the political forces in German lands. This conviction was now to take the form of an appeal that should be addressed, not to theologians or churchmen, but to the whole nobility of Germany.

---

[84] *Ibid.,* p. 347, ll. 22 ff.

[85] *Ibid.,* p. 348. As has been pointed out by many Lutheran apologists, Martin is paraphrasing, in his usual free way, the psalmist's denunciation of those who deceive Israel: "The righteous shall rejoice when he seeth the vengeance: he shall wash his feet in the blood of the wicked" (Ps. 58.10). For a typical apologetic treatment of this statement by Luther, see Kalkoff's *Ulrich von Hutten und die Reformation,* pp. 16 f.

27

APPEAL TO THE SECULAR
CLASSES

THE *Address to the Christian Nobility of the German Nation* [1] was the final step by which Luther brought his case before the bar of public opinion. Although he deals mainly with religious abuses, Martin does not now approach them as a critical theologian or an aroused preacher but as a public reformer. Historically viewed, Luther's attack is a chapter in a struggle for reform which had been going on in the Church since the thirteenth century and which did not come to an end until the Council of Trent took up the task of eliminating many of the evils he sets forth.[2] Diet after diet had seen a long list of complaints of this character on its agenda. Cajetan, like many papal envoys before him, had been obliged to listen to a formidable document of *gravamina* when he came to Augsburg in 1518 to seek the aid of the German states in a crusade against the Turks. Immediately afterwards and in the following year Cajetan was attacked in a series of Latin dialogues by the Franconian humanist, Ulrich von Hutten,[3] whose clever pen, sharpened through a dozen years of satirical practice, was now fully devoted to the cause of a national struggle against Rome.

[1] *An den christlichen Adel deutscher Nation von des christlichen Standes Besserung. WA,* VI, 404 ff.

[2] The sources for Luther's arraignment are thoroughly canvassed by Köhler in his *Die Quellen zu Luthers Schrift "An den christlichen Adel deutscher Nation."* For a brief résumé of the historical background, see Georg v. Below, "Die Ursachen der Reformation," *Historische Bibliothek,* Vol. XXXVIII (1917).

[3] Hutten's character and historical importance have been bitterly attacked by Kalkoff in a series of investigations which also traverse the relations of Luther to Hutten. The most important are *Ulrich von Hutten und die Reformation* and *Huttens Vagantenzeit und Untergang.* A sturdy defense of Hutten has been made by Fritz Walser, "Die politische Entwickelung Ulrichs von Hutten während der Entscheidungsjahre der Reformation," *Historische Zeitschrift,* No. 14 (1928). See also Werner Kaegi, "Hutten und Erasmus," *Historische Vierteljahrschrift,* Vol. XXII (1925). Kalkoff set out to destroy the romantic figure of Hutten in David F. Strauss's biography *Ulrich von Hutten.* His researches have added greatly to knowledge of the field, but his views of Hutten bear everywhere the marks of bias, and the resultant historical picture is somewhat of a caricature.

Ulrich von Hutten was born five years after Luther, a member of an ancient and vigorous family of knightly lineage in the Hesse-Nassau hills. Apparently destined by his family for the monastic life, he developed gifts of energy and talent that took him at seventeen away from the great Benedictine abbey at Fulda and led him for half a dozen years among as many German universities, where he studied the humanities and formed personal associations with the protagonists of "good letters" in Erfurt and Mainz. He became skilled in the usual fields of Renaissance poetic art. In Italy, whither he wandered as a student amid the wild wretchedness of the Franco-Imperial war, he developed power as an epigrammatist, and speedily found his way to the satirical dialogue in the style of Lucian. In this he made himself a master of picturesque and biting satire, rising at times to powerful denunciation. His Latin style was distinguished. In spite of all the misery of the wandering scholar's life, along with the torments of syphilis and its barbarous treatments, in spite of alienations from his family and dire poverty, he had the will and infinite patience to achieve the command of a verse that has charm and grace, and a forceful prose with power for stinging sarcasm and relentless invective.

Just when the feeling of resentment against Rome began to take form in the mind of the young humanist it is impossible to say. As a councilor in the service of the elector of Mainz he obtained the latter's assistance in going to Italy for further studies. A stay in Rome at this time probably laid the foundation for the opposition to Roman pretensions and greed that was soon to become Hutten's master passion. A series of epigrams addressed to Crotus Rubianus, which gives full-throated expression to this feeling, may have been written at this time.[4] In any event, by 1517 he is ready to turn against the Roman court the full power of satire that he had shortly before brought to the support of Reuchlin in the *Letters of Obscure Men*. In the midst of journeyings here and there, a bitter literary feud against Ulrich von Württemberg in defense of the Hutten family honor, and the usual humanistic literary occupations, Ulrich found time, as we noted previously, to publish the *Donation of Constantine* by Lorenzo Valla, in which that brilliant representative of religious enlightenment in Italy had demonstrated nearly a century before the falsity of the document by which Constantine the Great was supposed to have endowed the popes with temporal power.[5] This publication Hutten had dedicated to Pope Leo himself with a remarkable

[4] *Ad Crotum Rubianum de statu Romano. Epigrammata ex Urbe Missa* (1518). Hutten, *Opera*, III, 278 ff.; see also *ibid.*, I, Index, pp. 34 f.

[5] Regarding the dating, see above, p. 472, n. 60.

introduction,[6] in which formal professions of respect and devotion are offered in a tone of subtle and persistent irony. Assuming that the Pope will be grateful to him for showing that the claims of his predecessors to temporal rule were false, the fiery-tongued knight recites a long list of abuses which this power has brought with it and summons Leo to divest himself of it without delay. In case he does not, the princes will be justified in dividing out the papal state.

Thus in the fateful year when Martin opened his battle against indulgences, Hutten turned his attention away from the "obscure men," the scholastic theologians of Cologne and their following in university, monastery, and diocesan chancellery, and began to concentrate his fire on Rome itself. In an address *On the Turkish War,*[7] circulated among friends in advance of the meeting of the Augsburg Diet of 1518, he supports the Pope's call to arms against the foes of Christendom and the German nation, but he interweaves such trenchant and sarcastic references to the greed of the papal court for power and money that his friends seem to have taken alarm and the address was withheld from the press. The meeting of the Diet, so fateful in the life of Martin, brought Hutten to Augsburg in the train of his protector, Albert, elector of Mainz. Not long after, his hatred of Roman evils led Hutten to launch a sharp attack on the unpopular legate Cajetan in the first dialogue called *Fever.*[8] The clever personal satire in Hutten's peculiarly reckless tone broadened here into an attack on the luxurious life of the religious orders and the dissoluteness of the Roman Christians.

Step by step the Frankish knight came to look upon the Roman court as the enemy of the German people. Like most of his humanistic contemporaries, he seems to have hailed with enthusiasm the election of Charles as Emperor.[9] The elevation of a young monarch to the throne held a promise for those who hoped for a renewal in letters and scholarship, and there was an impulse to greet him as a national leader. While Luther was fighting rear-guard engagements after the battle with Eck at Leipzig, the pen of Hutten was at work in Mainz on *The Roman Triad,* a satire against all the evil for which Rome stood in Germany.[10] It appeared to him now that the successors of the defeated Roman general, Varus, were sitting on the papal throne and that the struggle against the Romanists was a continuation of the war which Arminius had waged on the banks of the Weser fifteen cen-

---

[6] Hutten, *Opera,* I, 155 ff.

[7] *Ad principes Germanos ut bellum Turcis inferant exhortatoria.* Hutten, *Opera,* V, 97 ff.

[8] *Febris.* Hutten, *Opera,* IV, 29 f. See also *ibid.,* I, Index, pp. 36 f.

[9] See the dialogue *Fortuna* (1520). *Ibid.,* IV, 92, ll. 4 ff. See also *ibid.,* I, Index, pp. 48 f.

[10] Letter to Eobanus Hessus and Peter Aperbach, Aug. 3, 1519, *ibid.,* I, 302.

turies earlier. Early in 1520 three of his dialogues appeared,[11] *Fever II, The Roman Triad,* and *The Observers,* showing a sort of ascending scale of nationalism. The first devotes itself to the vices of the clergy, the second to the greed and luxury of Rome, while the third calls the Germans to patriotic unity.[12]

The Roman Triad found its way to Wittenberg late in April, and in all probability Luther read the savage satire with eager interest. Its enumeration of clerical vices, its denunciation of wrongs done to the Germans and other nations by Rome, have much similarity with passages in the *Address to the Christian Nobility.* Hutten's tone, however, is more drastic; it is that of the soldier who is accustomed to an immediate appeal to arms. His indictment of Rome is clothed in a series of triads reminiscent of the pithy sentences of ancient Germanic folk law: "Three things are for sale in Rome: Christ, priesthoods, and women"; "three things are well dressed in Rome: priests, mules, and prostitutes"; "three things all wish for: short Mass-services, good coin, and a lustful life"; "only three things may bring Rome back to order: the severity of the princes, the impatience of all Christians, and the harshest scourge of the Turks."

Whether this work of "the most audacious of all men," as a contemporary humanist calls Hutten,[13] lay before Luther when he was preparing his *Address to the Christian Nobility,* is still a subject of debate.[14] Martin's attack on the sins of Rome in this work was not, however, the result of a sudden resolution nor was its style begotten of a moment. Both content and method of attack may be observed in uninterrupted development in the letters and polemical writings through more than a year preceding. Yet Hutten's bold sarcasm may have stimulated Martin to go a step further than the Frankish knight and, throwing aside all Latin, drive his message home to the hearts of the landed and noble classes in the mother tongue.

The momentary union of the efforts of monk-professor and cavalier-humanist for the purpose of reform has a dramatic aspect. Ulrich had marked

---

[11] *Ibid.,* Index, I, 48 f.; for text, see Vol. IV, 103 ff. The exact time of writing is not clear; the publication was announced by Cochlaeus to Pirckheimer on February 8, 1520 (*ibid.,* I, 321 f.), and by Hutten to Melanchthon on February 28 (*ibid.,* pp. 324 f.). It had not reached Cochlaeus on April 5. See letter from Cochlaeus to Pirckheimer on that day; *ibid.,* p. 335.

[12] The relation of Hutten's work to a collection of German "Triads," assigned by some scholars to Crotus Rubianus, has been fully discussed by Kalkoff, "Die Crotus-Legende und die deutschen Triaden," *ARG,* XXIII (1926), 113 ff. This article is marked by a strong anti-Hutten bias.

[13] Letter from Beatus Rhenanus to Zwingli, March 19, 1519. *Briefwechsel des Beatus Rhenanus,* ed. by Horawitz and Hartfelder, p. 144.

[14] Discussed innumerable times. For a careful analysis of the parallelisms between the *Roman Triad* and Luther's pamphlet, see Kohlmeyer, *Die Entstehung der Schrift Luthers An den christlichen Adel deutscher Nation,* pp. 47 ff.

the rise of the struggle of Wittenberg against indulgences with a mild interest, as showing a tendency toward self-criticism within the Church.[15] Writing to his humanistic friend Pirckheimer [16] he refers to the monastic dispute with a certain glee. But the duel with Eck at Leipzig [17] awakened him to the seriousness of Martin's efforts, and on October 26, 1519, he wrote to Eobanus Hessus in Erfurt in a thoroughly altered frame of mind,[18] though he does not venture to enlist Luther in the attack which he is preparing against the "papal tyrants," because of Elector Albert's fear of becoming involved.

Before the end of 1519 Hutten and his humanistic colleagues had the satisfaction of seeing the Cologne Dominicans forced to compensate Reuchlin for attacks made five years earlier. The pressure to pay this award came from the iron hand of Franz von Sickingen, Hutten's friend, a knight of the Moselle region and a reckless mercenary intent on military adventures. Early in the new year Hutten writes to Melanchthon [19] as to Luther's closest friend, offering on behalf of Sickingen a similar support to Luther against his enemies in case Martin sees no other solution. A month later this was followed by a still more urgent offer.[20]

Just when Luther received these encouraging promises and how they affected him, is not clear in the sources. In April Hutten was in Bamberg with Crotus, and the latter wrote to Martin, as we have seen, urging again the invitation of Sickingen.[21] Luther's answer to Hutten has been lost and the gaps in the sources make it impossible to say why it was not sent earlier. The difference between the two men in their whole attitude toward life must have been apparent to Luther even at this stage, and it was certainly felt also by Hutten. The latter had conceived a plan of seeking to win young Ferdinand, brother of Emperor Charles, as leader of the anti-Roman party; and on the eve of a journey into the Netherlands for this purpose he writes to Martin regarding his plans.[22] His opening salutation, "Long live freedom!" gives the dominant tone of feeling at this time. He has heard of Luther's excommunication, one of the reports which must have floated north from Rome in advance of the event. "How great, how great you are, Luther, if this be true!" He hears that Eck is returning, laden with livings and

---

[15] Letter to Count von Neuenar, April 3, 1518. Hutten, *Opera*, I, 167.

[16] October 25, 1518. *Ibid.*, p. 216.

[17] The account was sent him on September 22 by Dr. Heinrich Stromer. See Clemen, *Beiträge zur Reformationsgeschichte*, I, 24 ff., and Kalkoff, *Hutten und die Reformation*, pp. 160 f.

[18] Hutten, *Opera*, I, 313.   [19] January 20, 1520. *Ibid.*, pp. 320 f.

[20] February 28. *Ibid.*, pp. 324 f.

[21] Letter from Crotus to Luther, April 28, 1520, *WAB*, II, 91; see also letter from Luther to Capito, April 30, 1520, *WAB*, II, 94.

[22] June 4, 1520. Hutten, *Opera*, I, 355 f.; see also *WAB*, II, 116 f., for the same letter.

money. Hutten feels himself in danger, for snares are being laid for him also, but he will be ready to meet force with force. He evidently makes an effort to adapt his tone so as to win Luther's confidence. Scriptural quotations float uneasily on his vigorous Latin. He declares that he has always agreed with Luther in so far as he understood him. They are defending a common liberty, the long-oppressed freedom of the fatherland. He repeats Sickingen's urgent invitation that Martin take refuge with him.[23]

Thus the atmosphere about Martin was electrical with the approaching storm of attack and the encouraging voices of those who were willing to stand by him in defense. Before he received Hutten's impassioned words of cheer, he had outlined to Spalatin his plan for an appeal to emperor and nobility.[24] Not long afterward he must have received a letter from Sylvester von Schaumberg, written in the sturdy German of the period, repeating the offer of protection and asylum previously made:[25] the rumor has reached the Frankish knight that Martin is going to be obliged to flee to the Bohemians; he himself and one hundred noblemen of his neighborhood are ready to come to his aid.

Amid such strain and excitement Martin set himself to prepare a broadside appealing to Charles and the German nobility.[26] Two weeks later he sent it to his colleague Nikolaus Amsdorf with a dedication, saying that he is now going to speak to the laity, disregarding all criticism that may come for addressing himself to those of high degree: "For once I have undertaken to play the court fool."[27]

The temper in which the *Address to the Christian Nobility* was composed is reflected in the savage tone of a letter written by Martin at this time to the persistent Dungersheim.[28] The work went forward slowly. Now and then we hear in his letters an echo of charges against the Pope that are being included in the general accusation.[29] Not until August 3 do we hear that the work is in press.[30]

---

[23] Kalkoff's suggestion that Hutten was driven by fear of the bull to seek to share Luther's defenses seems unfounded in view of the tone of Ulrich's letter. Walser, "Die politische Entwickelung Ulrichs von Hutten," pp. 30 f.

[24] Letter from Luther to Spalatin, June 7(?), *WAB*, II, 120.

[25] Dated at Münnerstadt, June 11, 1520. *WAB*, II, 121 f.

[26] "Est animus publicam schedam edere ad Carolum et totius Germaniae nobilitatem adversus Ro. Curiae tyrannidem et nequitiam." Letter from Luther to Spalatin, June 7(?), 1520, *WAB*, II, 120.

[27] "Auch ein mal hoffnarr werden." *WA*, VI, 404, l. 25.

[28] Middle of June, 1520. *WAB*, II, 125 f.

[29] See Martin's reference to the Pope's interference with reformatory efforts on the part of the bishop of Strasbourg in a letter to Spalatin of June 25, *WAB*, II, 130 and n. 4. He promises to treat the tragedy "in its proper place," and afterwards makes it an item in his arraignment of Rome. *WA*, VI, 422 f.

[30] Letter from Luther to Johann Voigt, *WAB*, II, 162.

For this delay in publication, so unusual with Martin, the cause is to be found in the work itself. The *Address to the Christian Nobility* did not flow from his pen in one powerful stream like the sermons and polemics of the preceding year. There are seams and repetitions in it that show that it was put together of parts separate in origin. The first part, the broadside, was apparently written in June.[31] Stung and alarmed by Alfeld's and Prierias's proclamation of papal absolutism, Luther writes a nationalistic denunciation of the pope's claim to temporal and spiritual supremacy and sets up against this the idea of the universal priesthood of the Christian laity. To this he attaches the demand that a council, free of Roman domination, be called together by the temporal powers, and he submits a list of abuses on the part of the hierarchy that should come before this council.[32] There follows then a second part containing a long series of propositions for reforming the Church in its government and its relations to German society.[33] Here Martin repeats and expands and exposes fully the evils of Roman rule. It is probable that following his custom, he began to send the work to the printer as fast as it flowed from his nervous fingers.[34] What slowed his hand and caused the original broadside to grow into the longest pamphlet that Luther published?

Early in July there came to the elector the two letters from Rome conveying the final call to revocation. These communications from Cardinal Riario and Dr. Tetleben were, as we have seen, conciliatory in content[35] but none the less categorical and definitive in their demand that Frederick force his professor to recant. On July 9, three days after their arrival, Martin has read them and writes to Spalatin in burning tones of resentment, not unmixed with sadness.[36] It is probable that in this mood Martin resolved to make the appeal to the political estates more forceful and conclusive, and therefore brought together from all available sources the material for an exhaustive arraignment of Roman abuses and practical suggestions for their removal. Thus the work marched slowly toward completion. The deliberateness of its progress must have allowed the radical character of the pamphlet

---

[31] A discussion of the genesis of the work, whose lack of unity is obvious even to the casual reader, is found in all the editions of *An den Christlichen Adel*, and in the special works treating it. The theory of a double origin seems now generally accepted, although opinions differ as to just how much the original broadside contained. See Kohlmeyer, *Die Entstehung der Schrift An den Christlichen Adel*, pp. 8 ff., and a somewhat different view by Kalkoff in Luther, *Ausgewählte Werke*, II, 250 f.

[32] This corresponds to the edition in *WA*, VI, pp. 405–27.

[33] *Ibid.*, pp. 427 to conclusion.

[34] Letter from Luther to Link, July 20, *WAB*, II, 146.

[35] Both printed by Kalkoff in "Zu Luthers römischem Prozess." *ZKG*, XXV, 587 ff.

[36] Letter from Luther to Spalatin, July 9, 1520, *WAB*, II, 134 ff. See also *ibid.*, p. 136, n. 1.

to become widely known, for on August 18 the Wittenberg printer had already taken 4,000 copies from the press, and Martin wrote to alarmed and protesting friends of the Augustinian group that their intervention was too late, as the matter was no longer in his hands.[37]

The work which created this astounding impression was the result of a determination that had been long maturing. The conviction had been growing upon him, and, as we have seen, had found expression in the preceding months, that only the emperor and the political estates could check the pretensions and greed of Rome. This conviction expresses itself with explosive force in the *Address to the Christian Nobility*. He begins his summons to the contest with a warning to the princes that if they rely upon their own powers, the young emperor will suffer the same fate as his predecessors on the imperial throne and be trampled under the feet of the pope. It is only humble confidence in God that can make the attack succeed. The Romanists, like Tartarus in Vergil's *Aeneid,* are girt about with three walls: the claims that ecclesiastical power is superior over the temporal, that the pope alone can interpret the Holy Scriptures, and that he alone can call a council of the Church. Against these defenses Martin sounds the advance, with the prayer that God may give him one of the trumpets of Jericho.

The arguments with which he makes his attacks have all appeared in his earlier works: here they are concentrated in a closely knit array and are followed by suggestions for improvement. All Christians belong to the spiritual class; priests and laymen are distinguished only through their service. The temporal power is appointed by God and the interposition of the canonical law to protect the religious classes is an impertinence, a Roman fiction. "If a priest is slain, the land is put under an interdict: why not also if a peasant is slain?"[38] The monstrous assertion of Prierias that the pope could not be deposed even if he were to lead all souls to the devil, was, Martin exclaims, inspired by the chief of all devils. Against the claim that the pope cannot err on matters of faith he advances the words of Paul and Christ that all Christians are taught by God. Instead of confessing our belief in one holy Christian Church, we would in such case have to say, "I believe in the pope at Rome." Any faithful member of the body of the Church, he declares, can bring about a proper and free council. No one can do that so well as the temporal power, which shares spiritual office and spiritual rights. Any citizen may summon help in case of a fire in the city without waiting for the orders of the burgomaster. Martin urges his readers

[37] Letter to Lang, Aug. 18, *WAB,* II, 167; letter to Link, Aug. 19, *WAB,* II, 168.
[38] *WA,* VI, 410, ll. 16 ff.

to flout all bans and to regard no miraculous sign or plague that may testify for the pope: all of these come by the devil's aid.

Luther now lays before his readers the matter which should come before a council: the luxury and pomp of the pope, with his triple crown; the cardinals, created only to hold bishoprics; the resulting ruin of cloisters, dioceses, cities, and lands. So it has been in Italy and so it is now to follow in Germany, for the "drunken Germans" will not understand what is going on until they have no spiritual office and not a penny left in their possession, receiving in return for the hundreds of thousands of guilders paid to Rome only mockery and shame. He passes in rapid review the means by which Rome has enriched itself at the expense of Germany: the annates; the "papal months"; the income from livings, improperly claimed for the papal followers; the sale of the pallium; the commends and the simony; the employment of the Fuggers as bankers for trade in all these things. These abuses are rehearsed as they had been frequently during the preceding decade by patriots like Jakob Wimpfeling, in memorandums laid before the Diet, and more recently by Ulrich von Hutten; in Martin's work, however, they do not appear in humanistic Latin or legal phrase, but in forceful German with simple illustrations. At times his deep earnestness flames into bitter resentment: "If we are justified in hanging thieves and decapitating robbers, why should we let go free the greed of Rome, which is the greatest thief and robber that has ever come on earth or can come, all in the holy name of Christ and St. Peter?" [39]

What is the cure for all of these evils? Martin proceeds to set forth his ideas for reform under twenty-six headings. One should refuse to pay the annates to the pope, refuse to permit him to name successors to livings, and if a papal courtier turns up and persists in claiming one of these, he is to be ordered to jump into the Rhine, taking the papal ban with him.[40] No bishop is to fetch his pallium from Rome. No temporary case is to be referred there for decision, but is to be settled by a general synod with judicial powers, to be elected in Germany. No claims for German livings are to be raised in Rome; no pious priest is to be cited thither by the treachery of the papal courtiers. "Reserved cases," petty matters of discipline which are a source of papal income are to be abolished, papal offices are to be reduced or swept away; the formal investment of the bishop is to cease; the political claims of the pope on the emperor and Italian cities and states are to be canceled. The splendid ceremonies, the foot-kissing, the bearing aloft, the service of the Mass by a kneeling cardinal, are to come to an end: "May

[39] *Ibid.*, p. 427, ll. 18 ff. [40] *Ibid.*, pp. 428 f.

God help a free council to teach the Pope that he also is a man and not greater than God, as he makes bold to be." [41]

Turning from the relations of the Church to the hierarchy, Martin proceeds in vigorous and homely language to discuss social abuses that have grown up in religious life. He demands the suppression of pilgrimages to Rome, where only bad examples and vexation await the visitor, and cites the proverb "the nearer Rome, the worse Christians." [42] Like Erasmus in his *Praise of Folly,* he condemns the man who spends his money on a journey to Rome that no one has demanded of him and lets his wife, child, and kin suffer in poverty. It is interesting that whereas Martin would forbid pilgrimages as supposed good works, he would permit them to those driven by curiosity to seek out a foreign land. No new cloisters are to be built for the mendicant orders; new sects and orders should be forbidden and the old reformed; indeed, he would like to see the orders of the Church freed from compulsion, so that any Christian could enter and withdraw from them at will, thus making them into training schools in the Bible and Christian discipline. To any parish priest he would concede the right to marry. To demand of every candidate for consecration the pledge of chastity is a "diabolical tyranny." [43] The choice of taking a wife or not he would leave to the conscience of the individual. His deep sympathy is aroused by the situation of many otherwise pious priests who are living with a woman in devoted and loyal union. Such couples he advises to regard themselves as married in the eyes of God. His own experience in the cloister prompts him to come to the rescue of tender consciences tormented by secret mortal sins which they are afraid to confess to abbot or prelate of the order as is required, and he advises them to disregard the statutes of their order and seek a brother or sister and receive absolution in peace. He protests against the many anniversary Masses and other commemorative services as an excuse for greed, guzzling, and gluttony; and against the interdict, the ban, and other punishments under the canon law. As in the *Sermon on Good Works,* he demands a reform of the Church festivals, so conducive to drinking, gambling, and idleness: it does more honor to a saint to turn his holiday into a working day. He demands that a change be made in the canon law to cover the many prescriptions regarding forbidden degrees of consanguinity in marriage, a "golden cord and ecclesiastical net" [44] of the pope. Dispensations of this character he would leave to the local clergy; freedom to fast or not, to the individual Christian. All indulgences and similar privileges sold

---

[41] *Ibid.,* p. 436, ll. 37 f.   [42] "Yhe ner Rom, yhe erger Christen." *Ibid.,* p. 437, ll. 6 f.
[43] *Ibid.,* p. 441, l. 34.   [44] *Ibid.,* p. 446, l. 36.

by the pope should be swept away: "If you are to ride to heaven on his wax and parchment your wagon will soon break down and you will fall into hell."[45] He advocates the abolition of begging and the introduction of systematic poor relief, and demands the restriction of the mendicant orders, which to the number of five or six lay cities under tribute half a dozen times in a single year.

Such abuses, as well as the traffic in indulgences and the various dispensations in return for money, furnish proof for Martin of the suspicion which he had long been expressing in his letters that the pope is the real Antichrist.

Listen, Pope—not most holy but most sinful! May God from heaven speedily pull down your throne and sink it into the abyss of hell. Who gave you power to raise yourself above your God, to break and to loosen His commands and to teach the Christians, especially the German nation, extolled in all histories as faithful and constant, to be unreliable, to be perjurers, traitors, villains, faithless? . . . O Christ, my Lord, arise and let your Day of Judgment dawn and destroy the devil's nest at Rome.[46]

Then, passing in review the oaths broken by the pope or with papal consent, he solemnly declares: "If that is not Antichrist, then may someone tell me who he is."[47]

With the Bohemians Martin no longer hesitates to express full sympathy. They are justified in their resentment, he finds, because of the breach of the papal and imperial safe conduct issued to Huss and Hieronymus of Prague. One should honor a pledge of this character even if the world perish, all the more when it is a question of getting rid of a heretic. In the articles of Huss he declares he has found nothing mistaken. The Pope should recognize the Bohemians and permit them to choose their own archbishop. He denies that it is necessary to believe that the bread and wine are not essential and natural in the sacrament. This declaration is a delusion of St. Thomas and the Pope.

Martin next takes up the necessity for reforming the universities, and explodes in wrath against the "blind heathen master" Aristotle. His physics and metaphysics, his works *On the Soul* and his *Ethics* would be banished entirely, if Martin had his way. With these Aristotle has led Christians astray and deceived them long enough. Martin claims that he himself knows the Greek philosopher better than St. Thomas or Duns Scotus did. As for the canonical law, he would like to see it wiped out from the first letter to the last, for all its decisions are subject to the caprice of a pope. Regarding theology he protests against the practice that allows a mere bachelor at the university to lecture on the Bible, while the *Sentences* of Lombard can be

---

[45] *Ibid.*, p. 450, ll. 11 f.   [46] *Ibid.*, p. 453, ll. 12 ff.   [47] *Ibid.*, p. 454, ll. 14 f.

interpreted only by a doctor of theology and a priest. Reading of the Bible should come first in every school, high and low, for girls as well as boys, and he laments the ignorance and neglect of the Scriptures in cloisters, schools, and universities: "I am in great anxiety lest the universities become open doors of hell, if they do not give training in the Holy Scriptures and drive them into young people." [48]

Finally he turns to examine the relation of the papacy to the German Empire. He admits that the popes took the imperial title from the Greeks and gave it to the Germans, but the latter are only the servants of the trickiest tyrants bearing title and trappings of empire, while the pope has the treasure and the power. But he regards the claim of Germany to imperial rule as justified by God's will: "So help us God . . . to show the Romans some day what we have received from God through them. They boast that they gave us the empire; all right, so be it; then let the pope give us Rome and all he received from the empire . . . let him give us again our freedom, power, property, honor, body and soul." [49]

In conclusion Martin turns against his own countrymen and censures them for a multitude of social and moral failings. Luxury in clothes and lavish expenditure for foreign food, lending at interest—the greatest misfortune of the nation—these threaten to bring the Germans to the point where they will be devouring each other. Restraint must be laid on the Fuggers and their kind, for it is against divine law that in one lifetime such wealth should be accumulated. The temporal power must interfere against guzzling and gluttony and houses of prostitution. Much unchasteness and social degeneration can be prevented, he finds, if young people are not permitted to take vows of chastity in their early years.

Martin closes his address with the admission that he has "sung in a high key," demanding what seems to be impossible and attacking at times too sharply. But he cannot do otherwise. They can do no worse than take away his life. He has frequently offered peace to his opponents, but through them God has constrained him to open his mouth still wider. Now Martin threatens his enemies with "another little song of Rome and of them." "May God give us all a Christian understanding, and especially to the nobility of the German nation courage of the spirit to do their best for the poor Church." [50]

"I am beyond injury. Whatever I have done and do, I do under constraint, ever ready to keep quiet if only they do not demand that the truth of the

[48] *Ibid.*, p. 462, ll. 9 ff.   [49] *Ibid.*, p. 464, ll. 34 ff.   [50] *Ibid.*, p. 469.

Gospel be quiet." With this offer Martin returns to Spalatin the letters from the Italian cardinal and the German intermediary in Rome.[51] His reply is intended for Roman eyes and was used by Frederick's chancellor in preparing the formal answers dispatched a month later, setting forth the position of the elector regarding Luther's case.[52] Luther prepares, therefore, a definite statement of his cause, such as might appeal to the elector and at the same time meet the attack of enemies who, as he notes, praise the genius and acumen of his writings although they declare they have not read them. He has not sought the quarrel and has wished for nothing else than to live apart in a desert place. "Let him have my office who will; let him burn my books [53] who will; what more can I do?" But of one thing he will not be guilty: the unforgivable sin of silence. He is pleased that the elector does not intend to turn away from him, and he hopes that Frederick will write in such a manner as to make these Roman heads understand that the Germans have been held down not by their own national barbarism [54] but, through the mysterious judgment of God, by that of the Italians.[55] The next day he follows with another letter,[56] enclosing the offer of protection from Sylvester of Schaumberg, so that the prince may call attention to the fact that there are those in Germany who will protect him against all the "lightnings" of the cardinal. Such defenders as this would carry on a more vigorous war against Rome than he could wage in his public office as teacher. The thought of the support which he now has fires him to an expression of defiance. For him the die is cast, and he despises Roman fear and favor. "Let them condemn and burn my writings: I, for my part, unless I can get hold of no fire, will condemn and burn publicly the whole law of the papacy, that serpent of heresy." He has reached the end of his humanity and of the self-restraint by which he sought in vain to avoid inflaming further the enemies of the Gospel. In a postscript he suggests for the elector's answer to Rome the statement that the Luther doctrine has spread and rooted itself in Germany and that it will not be safe to arouse the well-known ferocity of the Germans. The latter can be controlled only by the Scriptures and by reason, especially now when letters and linguistic knowledge rule and the laity has begun to know things.[57]

The conviction that he has found support throughout Germany is re-

---

[51] Letter to Spalatin, July 9, *WAB*, II, 135, ll. 41 ff.

[52] Kalkoff, "Zu Luthers römischem Prozess," *ZKG*, XXV, 455. See also *ibid.*, pp. 593 ff. For the text of Frederick's reply to Tetleben, see *EA*, XXXVI, 7 ff.

[53] "Mea." Letter to Spalatin, July 9, *WAB*, II, 135, ll. 24 ff.

[54] "Ruditate." *Ibid.*, p. 136, l. 55.   [55] *Ibid.*, p. 136.

[56] Letter to Spalatin, *WAB*, II, 137 f.   [57] *Ibid.*, pp. 137 f.

flected again in a letter written at this time to a correspondent in the Netherlands, the rector of the school of the Brothers of the Common Life at
Zwolle.[58] Martin regrets that he has wasted the past years in unhappy strife;
nevertheless, he is consoled by the feeling that while all the evil beasts are
trying to win laurels by attacking him, and Rome is preparing threats, Germany is finally beginning to understand the hypocrisy of the papists.

"I am overwhelmed with men and affairs and conversation." [59] Despite
this complaint in a letter to Johann Lang, the end of July finds him well
enough in body and mind, "save for my sins," as he tells a Breslau correspondent.[60] He takes the time to write words of strong cheer and comfort
to the bishop of Breslau, then lying at the point of death; [61] he intercedes
with the elector for cases of poverty in Wittenberg and for the placement of
former students in parishes; he busies himself with the marriage of Melanchthon and with university matters.[62] His fiery temperament leads him into
a conflict with his colleagues at the university over demonstrations by the
students against the journeymen of the painter Lucas Cranach and the city
folk. These excesses had begun in February, and by the middle of July they
took a form that threatened the bloody results so common in town and gown
riots at that time. Luther was angered by the attitude of the faculty, "who
are worse than the students," and appealed to the elector against the rector
of the university as an "insane man." [63] Luther believed that the conflict had
been forecast by a vision in the Netherlands of which he had heard, and on
July 16 he delivered a sermon on the subject that aroused sharp antagonism.
He credits this to the devil, who, having been unable to accomplish anything
against him in Rome, now seeks to damage him from within, and he fore-
sees sedition and disorder as great future perils.[64] The affair evidently
affected Martin deeply, for he writes that the danger of the crisis in Wittenberg was equal to that which had confronted him in Augsburg and Leipzig.[65]
University friends like Amsdorf took the part of the students, and criticisms
of Luther seem to have gone to Spalatin. Martin pretends not to care, and
recalls that no one was ever more unrelenting in the condemnation of evil

[58] Letter to Gerardus Listrius, July 28, *WAB*, II, 149 f.
[59] Letter from Luther to Lang, July 29, *WAB*, II, 151.
[60] Letter to Michael Wittiger, July 30, *WAB*, II, 153 f.
[61] Letter from Luther to Johann Thurzo, July 30, *WAB*, II, 152 f.
[62] See his letter to Lang, July 29, 1520, *WAB*, II, 150 f., and two letters of Aug. 5 and Aug.
10, 1520 to Spalatin, *WAB*, II, 163 f. and 165.
[63] Letter to Spalatin, July 14, *WAB*, II, 142 f.
[64] Letter to Spalatin, July 17, *WAB*, II, 144.
[65] *Ibid.*, p. 145.

than the prophets: "In our age we have become unused to hearing the truth about ourselves."[66]

If Martin could not avoid making enemies, the warlike spirit that burns so brightly in the *Address to the Christian Nobility* also attracted support on many sides. The full story of the encouragement that came to him in these summer days cannot be put together from the meager sources, but enough echoes from contemporaries have been preserved to show that Martin had reason to look on himself as the champion of a large section of Germany. When the belligerent radical Thomas Münzer gets into trouble with the Franciscans at Zwickau, the city council advises him to appeal to Luther, "a pattern and lamp of the friends of God," as Münzer calls him in his letter.[67] The juristic humanist, Ulrich Zasius, although unable to agree with Martin's position regarding the pope's power in the controversy with Eck, calls him nevertheless the phoenix of theologians and assures him that almost all scholars follow him.[68] The greatest of humanistic scholars, Erasmus, was, however, growing alarmed by the rising tide of conflict. His letter of the preceding October to Albert had been published, as we have seen, and straightway brought an attack from the archenemy of humanism, Hochstraten.[69] Throughout the following spring the letters of the perturbed humanist show an increasing nervousness over what seems to him the unnecessary stirring up of bad blood.[70] Early in the summer he sends compliments to Luther through Melanchthon, but adds that Martin's supporters wish he had written with more restraint.[71] Soon afterwards he tells Spalatin that he prays Christ may temper Martin's head and heart: it would have been better if he had discussed only Gospel matters.[72] Luther has preached many things brilliantly; "would that he had done it more civilly."[73] Now, at the beginning of August, he sits down to write a long letter to Luther himself. After a lengthy prelude regarding his own controversy with Edward Lee and an attempt by his enemies to convict him of heresy before the king and queen of England, he deftly adds a report on a royal audience with King Henry, in which the English sovereign, after listening to Erasmus's praise

[66] Letter to Spalatin, August 5, 1520, *WAB*, II, 164.

[67] "Specimen et lucerna amicorum Dei." Letter from Münzer to Luther, July 13, *WAB*, II, 141, ll. 95 f.

[68] Letter from Zasius to Luther, Sept. 1, *WAB*, II, 181 f.

[69] Letter from Erasmus to Martin Lypsius, November(?), 1519, Allen, *Opus epistolarum Erasmi*, IV, 119, No. 1040.

[70] See the letter to Lypsius, February(?), 1520, *ibid.*, p. 193, No. 1070.

[71] *Circa* June 21, 1520, *ibid.*, p. 287, No. 1113.

[72] July 6, *ibid.*, p. 298, No. 1119.

[73] Letter from Erasmus to Louis Platz, July 31, 1520(?), *ibid.*, p. 319, No. 1127.

of Luther, expressed the wish that Martin had written about certain things
with greater prudence and modesty. This, says Erasmus, is the wish of
Luther's friends. He adds many warnings against raising a storm that may
get beyond control and begs Martin in the future not to mix "hatefully"
in his writings Erasmus's name and those of his friends, as he had done in
his answer to Louvain and Cologne. In conclusion, he expresses the wish that
Luther may devote himself wholeheartedly to the treatment of some part of
divine Scriptures until the uproar should cease, and finally bestows a somewhat reserved compliment on Martin's *Lectures on the Psalms*. Evidently
this clever and flattering letter made a favorable impression on Luther. His
answer has been lost; but later in the year he explains to a friend that he has
never felt vexed with Erasmus and is happy to omit his name from his
writings.[74]

This rather casual attitude toward the great humanist, like the character of
Luther's works at this time, shows that the appeal to a large popular
audience of laymen has, for the moment at least, dulled Martin's interest
in the work of scholarship. The commentary on Psalms slows up and he
begins to regret that he has ever undertaken it, because of the difficulty and
obscurity of the material,[75] obstacles which two years earlier in preparing
the Galatians commentary were accepted enthusiastically as a challenge to
his skill in exegesis. In this state of mind the offer of support by the Franconian knights must have been a greater source of joy and courage throughout the summer[76] than Erasmus's cautious advice. Hutten's promise that
Sickingen would protect him may well have kindled hopes of enlisting this
powerful leader in the cause for which Martin was now appealing in his
Address to the Christian Nobility, and he writes twice to Sickingen during
the summer.[77] We have seen how closely this work was related in spirit to
the program that Hutten had been developing in his satires. Late in the
summer Martin received a passionate letter from the Frankish knight,
written from Sickingen's castle of Ebernburg, "burning against the Roman
Pope," whom Hutten is now attacking "with letters and arms." The Pope,
he asserts, is laying plots against him with dagger and poison and has
ordered the archbishop of Mainz to send him bound to Rome, while the

---

[74] Letter from Luther to Spengler, Nov. 17, *WAB*, II, 217.

[75] Letter from Luther to Listrius, July 28, *WAB*, II, 149 f.

[76] Letters to Spalatin, July 10, *WAB*, II, 137 and July 17, *WAB*, II, 145. Letters to Link,
July 20, *WAB*, II, 146; and to Voigt, August 3, *WAB*, II, 162.

[77] Both letters are lost. See, however, the letters from Luther to Spalatin, June 29, *WAB*, II,
131, and August 31, *WAB*, II, 179. See also Sickingen's letter to Luther from Cologne, Nov. 3,
WAB, II, 208.

latter has forbidden the sale and reading of Hutten's books against the Pope on pain of excommunication. Martin suspects that his own works are also covered by this prohibition, and he promises that if the archbishop refers to him by name, he will join with Hutten and exculpate himself in a letter that will not make the prelate of Mainz happy.[78]

[78] The letter is lost. Luther informs Spalatin of its contents on September 11. *WAB*, II, 184 f.

28

THE FINAL BREAK WITH CHURCH TRADITION

A SPIRIT of haughty self-confidence marks Luther's letters as the summer of 1520 fades. Perhaps it was an echo of the tremendous success of the *Address to the Christian Nobility*. The revolutionary character of this appeal was evidently well known in advance, and at least two interested hands tried to stop its appearance, as we have seen. But before their intervention reached Martin, the "blast, frightful and fierce," as Luther's friend Lang called it,[1] had already started on its way in thousands of copies.[2]

Papal Commissioner Miltitz felt that the crisis called for a renewal of his efforts. He wrote to the elector that if Luther would delay issuance of the work he hoped to help him out of his "error and disfavor." [3] A convention of the Augustinian Eremites had been summoned to meet at Eisleben on August 26, in order that a successor might be chosen to take over the vicarship from the weary hands of Luther's old friend Staupitz. Here Miltitz, who did not consider the affair as black as the priests made it, presented himself and delivered a Latin address "clothed in the Italian pronunciation," as Luther learned.[4] Frederick had replied to Miltitz's letter politely, with the usual excuse that he was not in touch with these matters, but added that if he had received his letter earlier he would have done what he could to delay the appearance of Luther's book.[5] At Eisleben the Augustinian

---

[1] "Classicum . . . tam atrox et ferox." Letter from Luther to Lang, Aug. 18, 1520, *WAB*, II, 167.

[2] Otto Clemen, editor of Volumes I and II of *Luthers Briefwechsel*, supposes that Spalatin, alarmed at the violence of Luther's attack, had informed Lang of its character. See *WAB*, II, 164, n. 6, and 169, n. 6. It is likely that the nature of the book was known to the whole electoral court before its publication.

[3] From Halle. E. S. Cyprian, "Nützliche Urkunden zur Erläuterung der ersten Reformationsgeschichte," in *Tentzels Historischer Bericht vom Anfang und ersten Fortgang der Reformation Lutheri*, I, 1, 435.

[4] Letter from Luther to Spalatin, Sept. 1, 1520, *WAB*, II, 180.

[5] Cyprian, "Nützliche Urkunden," I, 1, 436 f.

brothers made an equally evasive answer, disclaiming any connection with Luther's doings and any knowledge of his plans.[6] They finally appointed two brothers, however, to confer with Martin. These were Staupitz and Wenceslaus Link, who had been chosen as successor to the vicarship.[7] Preceded by an urgent letter from the young commissioner, in which Miltitz assured Luther that he was his "unique friend," [8] the two old associates arrived at Martin's cell on September 1. As a result, Luther agreed with them to write to the Pope stating that he had never undertaken anything against him personally.[9] This he claims is the truth, and he intends henceforth to avoid writing "too wildly" against the papal chair and cause. Nevertheless, he adds that his letter "will be sprinkled with salt." The agile Miltitz now joined the elector, who was just setting forth to attend the coronation of the new emperor at Aachen in October. On the way, Miltitz was cheered by favorable reports from the two Augustinians on their interview with Luther.[10] Events were now impending in Saxony, however, that called for all of his energy and optimism. On September 21, the redoubtable Eck, who had probably given Miltitz notice of his coming, arrived in the episcopal city of Meissen, bringing with him the much-heralded bull of condemnation.[11]

How far the contents of this formidable instrument were known in advance to the electoral court and to Luther is not altogether clear. That definite action had been taken by the Pope and cardinals could hardly have been doubtful after the receipt of the two letters of warning early in July. Nevertheless, suspense as to the nature of the action seems to have continued throughout this summer, and Martin, who three weeks earlier had yearned to see the "famous and ferocious" bull,[12] hears at the beginning of August that Eck has thus far accomplished nothing in Rome.[13] A few days later he regards the reports of Eck's arrival in Meissen as "fables." [14] Although he makes no reference to the bull itself in such sources as remain to us, he must have learned its general tenor before the arrival of Eck, for this was ap-

---

[6] Letter from Luther to Spalatin, Sept. 1, *WAB*, II, 180.

[7] Letter to Spalatin, Sept. 11, *WAB*, II, 184.

[8] Letter from Miltitz to Luther, Aug. 29, *WAB*, II, 171.

[9] Letter to Spalatin, Sept. 11, *WAB*, II, 184, ll. 12 f.

[10] Staupitz's letter was delayed and did not reach him until after Miltitz had had a conference with Link at Erfurt. See Miltitz's letter to Frederick, in Cyprian, "Nützliche Urkunden," I, 1, 438 ff.

[11] Kalkoff suggests that Miltitz had planned to go to Rome at this time, but remained in Saxony to observe Eck's actions. "Zu Luthers römischem Prozess," *ZKG*, XXV, 521, n. 1.

[12] Letter from Luther to Spalatin, July 10, 1520, *WAB*, II, 137.

[13] Letter to Voigt, Aug. 3, *WAB*, II, 162.

[14] Letter to Spalatin, Aug. 14, *WAB*, II, 166.

parently known to Hutten by the middle of September.[15] We cannot rule out the possibility, therefore, that knowledge of the bull influenced Luther in preparing a defense before the emperor. On the other hand, the impulse may have been given by Frederick, who, in preparation for his journey to the coronation, may have desired to equip himself with material that he could use in support of his position and especially for an intervention with Emperor Charles. For this purpose Martin prepared two drafts, which he seems to have forwarded to Spalatin for revision on August 23:[16] a formal "Offer" ("Erbieten") and a letter to Charles himself. A week later, having apparently gotten them back with Spalatin's corrections, Martin sends to the latter the "Offer" in printed form, together with the letter to Charles,[17] adding, as it appears, a letter for delivery to Sickingen.[18] The need for allying himself with other opponents of the Pope led Martin also to send to the elector, along with the two documents, a draft of a letter to Carvajal, cardinal of the Holy Cross, a Spaniard whose strong ideas with regard to conciliar supremacy have already been referred to. Reports may have reached Wittenberg, as they did Erasmus,[19] that this sturdy churchman had opposed Martin's condemnation in the consistory at Rome. Luther now suggests to Frederick that although the cardinal has little reputation in the world, a letter should be sent him, asking his intervention as an umpire.[20] He offers peace, although without recantation [21] or the stigma of heresy, and on condition that he retain his liberty to teach.[22] There is no further trace in the sources that the letter was ever sent to the independent cardinal at Rome.

Martin's appeal to Charles came to the monarch's attention in the following February with dramatic results, as we shall see.[23] The tone of his letter is one of deep humility, though touched with humanistic conceit. He justifies

[15] See Hutten's letter to Frederick from the Ebernburg, September 11. Hutten, *Opera*, I, 383 ff. See also Kalkoff, "Zu Luthers römischem Prozess," *ZKG*, XXV, 523 f.

[16] "Elogion et literas ecce mitto corrigenda." *WAB*, II, 169. That these were the "Offer" and the letter to Charles is more than likely.

[17] August 31, *WAB*, II, 179. Luther does not say here that the letter was also printed. See the editor's note 5 to this passage, *ibid*.

[18] See Sickingen's reply to Luther, Nov. 3, *WAB*, II, 208.

[19] Kalkoff, "Zu Luthers römischem Prozess," *ZKG*, XXV, 120 f.

[20] "Sequestrum." Letter from Luther to Spalatin, Aug. 23, 1520, *WAB*, II, 169.

[21] "Palinodia." *Ibid*.

[22] Clemen is of the opinion that this letter was to be sent by the elector. *WAB*, II, 170, n. 3. Kalkoff ("Zu Luthers römischem Prozess," *ZKG*, XXV, 512 ff.) thinks that Luther was to send the letter as from himself. There is no evidence that it was forwarded to Carvajal.

[23] Whether the temperamental outburst of Charles on February 6, 1521, followed the *first* delivery of Luther's letter is not certain, and all hypotheses seem useless. See letter from Rafael de' Medici to Vice-Chancellor Medici, Feb. 6 and 7, 1521, in Kalkoff, "Briefe, Depeschen und Berichte über Luther vom Wormser Reichstage 1521," *SVRG*, LIX (1898), 38. See also *WAB*, II, 174 f.

his boldness in addressing himself to the "king of kings and lord of lords" with the statement that it is a question of the eternal truth of the Gospel, which is worthy of being brought before the throne of heaven itself. Thus he prostrates himself, a weak and destitute man, before the seat of majesty, a most unworthy instrument in a worthy cause. His little books which have aroused the hatred of many were written unwillingly, for it would have been his eager desire to remain hidden in his corner. By the witness of his own conscience and the judgment of the best men, he has set forth nothing save the truth of the Gospel over against the superstitious traditions of men. It is for this that he has now for three years been exposed to continual abuse, dangers, and all the evils that his enemies could devise. In vain he has offered to keep silence—it is nothing less than the destruction of himself and the universal Gospel that has been sought. Now, like Athanasius, he invokes the aid of imperial majesty and begs humbly the chief of earthly kings to take under his protection himself and the cause of truth until the victory shall be decided by reason. He does not ask for any protection if he shall be found to be a heretic, but simply that neither truth nor error be condemned unheard. It will bring honor to the emperor's reign and age if he does not permit the unjust to devour the just.[24]

The "Offer" is a brief and formal exposition of his situation.[25] What appears to be its original form is in a humble yet passionate style.[26] Martin recalls how for three years he had prayed without success to be allowed

[24] Two forms of the letter are available: one a contemporary MS by an unknown hand, now in the British Museum; the other derived from two contemporary prints, marked by minor variations. *WAB*, II, 172–75. Clemen, after an intensive study of the sources, regards the manuscript text (A) as the draft which Luther forwarded to Spalatin for revision on August 23, 1520. To the present writer the style of the London copy, although strained and artificial in places, seems more spontaneous than that in the published forms, and I have used it in my analysis. The so-called "non-Lutheran" expressions may be explained by the unique character of the task which Martin faced in addressing so exalted a personage. He was not, like Erasmus, accustomed to exchange letters with royalty.

[25] It has many points in common with the answer which he had returned to the letters of Cardinal Riario and Dr. Tetleben six weeks earlier and which had been used by Spalatin for his draft of the elector's reply. It also has much in common with the letter to the emperor, mentioned above. Kalkoff was of the opinion that the "Offer" was planned at the time these letters were drafted. "Zu Luthers römischem Prozess," *ZKG*, XXV, 505 ff.

[26] The original form of the "Offer" is said still to have existed in Luther's handwriting in the eighteenth century. It was published by Cyprian in 1717. "Nützliche Urkunden," I, i, 493 ff. See *WA*, VI, 476 f. It shows decided marks of the personal attitude of Luther in the summer of 1520 when compared with the version printed in broadside form, *ibid.*, pp. 480 f. Here the text appears to have been cut down and formalized by Spalatin or some other courtly hand before publication. This broadside print then reappeared again in October, 1520, in *Martini Luthers mancherley büchlin und tractetlin, ibid.*, p. 479. A Latin translation, *Oblatio sive protestatio, ibid.*, p. 482, was printed soon afterward, together with the Latin letter to Charles, and was forwarded by Luther to the elector on January 25, 1521. Letter from Luther to Frederick, *WAB*, II, 253 ff.

to defend his case in a disputation and had offered to submit it to the judgment of several universities. Nevertheless trickery continued its unceasing
attacks upon him. On his conscience he declares that he would never have
attacked the papal power had not envy and ambition sought to win laurels
by attacking him. Now his opponents have turned to abuse and charge him
with violence and vengefulness. He protests that he has not sought publicity
or fame. As he now sees, the devil used his humility to damage his teaching. He is not made of stone [27] and it is no wonder that so many ravening
wolves have forced him to bark and bite. Now he offers peace, but let no one
undertake to make war upon him: "My God-given spirit is such that I am
confident that I can sooner tire out the whole world. My rock on which
I build stands fast. It will not totter nor sink under me though all the
gates of hell may fight against it. Of that I am sure." [28] He rejects the
charge of pride and ambition. In their day Christian truth depended solely
on Saint Paul, Athanasius, and Augustine: "Who knows what God intends
to accomplish through us?" Finally he begs everyone not to ascribe hatred
to him as his temper is not of that sort: his eyes and his heart are fixed
upon truth alone and he begs for pardon if he has been too free and
eager.[29] In its note of defiance this first draft of the "Offer" breathes, as
few documents do, the spirit of Luther at this time. Apparently through
Spalatin's criticism, it was converted before publication into a more formal
and measured statement.

About the middle of August the *Address to the Christian Nobility* was
also on its way to readers throughout the country. A week later the publisher, Melchior Lotter, was already planning a second edition.[30] In this
Martin inserted a new passage regarding the pope's transfer of the Roman
Empire to the Germans, thus bringing to a climax the political and national
tendency of the work.[31] The impulse for this may have come from a hostile
source. A pamphlet by a Lombard Dominican, Isidorus de Isolanis, *A Revocation of Martin Luther to the Sacred See*,[32] came to Luther's attention
during the summer.[33] This appeal, written in November of the preceding
year by a teacher of theology at Bologna, contained little besides a preface

---

[27] ". . . auss keynem felss gesprungen." *WA*, VI, 477, ll. 22 f.
[28] *Ibid.*, p. 477, ll. 31 ff.   [29] *Ibid.*, p. 478.
[30] Letter from Luther to Spalatin, August 23, *WAB*, II, 169.
[31] Section XXVI, *WA*, VI, 462–65. The passage is inserted, not very pertinently, at the end
of the arraignment of spiritual conditions, before the discussion of the social weaknesses of
Germany.
[32] *Revocatio Martinii Lutheri Augustiniani ad sanctam Sedem*, published at Cremona, with
the date 1520, *WA*, VI, 486. See Kalkoff, "Zu Luthers römischem Prozess, Fortsetzung," *ZKG*,
XXXII, 49 f., concerning the date; see also *WAB*, I, 558 f.
[33] Letter from Luther to Lang, July 29, 1520, *WAB*, II, 150.

and conclusion,[34] in which the author makes an earnest plea to Martin to recant. The little work did not bear its author's name. On reading it, Luther remarks that it was written to show him that "Italy too is not without asses," and declares that he does not intend to answer "the barbarous and most ignorant man."[35] On reflection, however, he feels that the Italian may have acted without malice, and was probably moved less by a desire to bring about his revocation than to please the French and the Pope.[36] Nevertheless the work was not without effect on Martin, for the Bologna professor had reminded the Germans that they owed to the pope the transfer of imperial power, and it is probable that this repetition of an old papal claim stung Luther to insert a reply in the new edition of this work.[37]

The pamphlet of Isidorus de Isolanis may also have contributed its mite to the ripening of another plan in Martin's mind. While the *Address to the Christian Nobility* was still in the making, there are hints in his letters that his next step will be a final reckoning with the theology of the Roman Church. He had already shown his independence of the commonly accepted canon of the Scriptures by rejecting Second Maccabees in the Leipzig disputation and by questioning the apostolic origin of the Epistle of Saint James, which collided so directly with his ideas on the power of faith and works for the attainment of salvation. In his three great sermons on the sacraments of the previous winter he had emphasized baptism and the Eucharist as the chief of these sacred observances. At that time he had promised Spalatin to take issue with the "chatter about the seven sacraments."[38] Now only some impulse was needed to crystallize his conceptions of the sacramental structure of the Church. This impulse seems to have come from another work of the Leipzig enemy, Alfeld, against whom, together with his university, Martin nourished deep resentment. He had heard that the Dominicans were for the present under orders to write nothing against him. In place of the representatives of the learned order of Cajetan, Prierias, and Eck, therefore, he now faced the Franciscan theologians,[39] for whose learning he entertained a contempt as profound as that which was a few decades later to barb the satire of Rabelais. In the second half of July, in the midst of his labors on the *Address to the Christian*

---

[34] Text of both parts in *WAB*, I, 559 f.

[35] Letter to Lang, July 29, *WAB*, II, 151. See also Luther's letter to Voigt, Aug. 3, *WAB*, II, 162.

[36] *De captivitate Babylonica ecclesiae praeludium. WA*, VI, 501, ll. 26 ff.

[37] A suggestion of Knaake, following Kolde. See *WA*, VI, 397.

[38] Letter to Spalatin, Dec. 18, 1519, *WAB*, I, 595.

[39] Letter from Luther to Wittiger, July 30, *WAB*, II, 154.

Nobility, he learns that the Leipzig "ass" has published a new attack on him, "a new number filled with blasphemies," and that he is planning to reply to Luther's *On the Papacy at Rome.*[40] Alfeld's work on the *Sacrament in Two Kinds* [41] seems to Martin one of the "tragedies" which his enemies in Leipzig are performing under cover of the Franciscans, and he decides not to answer it, but to make it an excuse for irritating the vipers still more.[42] At the end of August the work is in press, but progress is slow. Three contemporary disputations, however, for which we have only the list of theses,[43] show his active occupation with the question of the sacraments and form a prelude to the great work that was under his hand.

It was not until October 3 that the *Prelude concerning the Babylonian Captivity of the Church* [44] came from the press and was forwarded to the absent Spalatin.[45] This second great work which helped to make complete the religious schism in Germany was a more radical break with the usages and traditions of the Church than any of its predecessors. It was quite different in grain and spirit from the *Address to the Christian Nobility.* The latter work was in German and was addressed to the politically thoughtful members of the ruling class. The *Babylonian Captivity* is in Latin and directs itself primarily to churchmen and theologians. Not since the *Explanations of the Power of Indulgences* of 1518 had Martin given such care to the form of his arguments. In spite of its breathless, hasty style and the frequent tautologies, the *Babylonian Captivity* marches in carefully organized array toward clearly defined goals. Here is no effort to pile up bitter accusations and run off into violent polemics, though vehement terms of condemnation increase as the work approaches its end. Rather, it is a considered review of early Church history and usages, and an attempt to find clear formulas for his conception of the ministry to souls through the sacred offices of the Church, now enmeshed in a web of hierarchical and traditional accretions.

The work, dedicated briefly to Hermann Tulich, a master of arts of Wittenberg University,[46] opens with a retrospect. Martin looks back on the

---

[40] Letter from Luther to Spalatin, July 22, *WAB,* II, 147.

[41] *Tractatus de communione sub utraque specie* (July, 1520). See Lemmens, "Pater Augustin von Alfeld," in *Erläuterungen und Ergänzungen zu Janssens Geschichte des deutschen Volkes,* I, 45.

[42] Letter from Luther to Spalatin, Aug. 5, *WAB,* II, 164.

[43] *Questio circularis de signis gratiae, WA,* VI, 470 f.; *De baptismate legis, ibid.,* pp. 472 f.; *De sacramentis, WA,* IX, 313.

[44] *De captivitate Babylonica ecclesiae praeludium. WA,* VI, 497 ff.

[45] Letter from Luther to Spalatin, Oct. 3, 1520, *WAB,* II, 191.

[46] For Tulich, see Enders, *Briefwechsel,* II, 489 f. See also Gustav Bauch, "Zu Luthers Briefwechsel," *ZKG,* XVIII (1898), 404 f.

polemical road along which he has traveled from the day when he first began alone his effort to turn "the boulder" of superstition. He owes it to Sylvester Prierias and others that he has now advanced far from his early position on indulgences and has come to regard them as wicked ideas of Roman flatterers.[47] Thanks to Eck and Emser, he is now convinced that the papacy is the kingdom of Babylon and the vast hunting ground of a mighty Nimrod, the Roman bishop. He has been attacked for defending the sacrament in two kinds by a certain Italian of Cremona and by a German from Leipzig, Alfeld, who has criticized his plea in the *Sermon on the Mass* that a council of the Church might establish the administration of the sacrament in both kinds. He brands the arguments of these opponents as sophistical and inconsistent, and sarcastically waves aside Alfeld and his kind as merely seeking to win a reputation by attacking him:

> This I know in sooth, that if I fight against filth,
> Victor or vanquished, I shall ever be filthy.[48]

While these champions are enjoying their triumph over one of his assumed heresies, he now hastens to commit a new one. He will seek to show that it is sinful to deny to the laity the sacrament in either form. That he may do this the more convincingly, he offers this "Prelude" concerning the fetters which the Roman Church lays upon men. In this the very learned papists will find many things to conquer.

After this blast of defiance, Martin states his thesis. Of the seven sacraments he denies all save three: baptism, penance, and the Eucharist; all the rest are a part of the "captivity" to which the Roman Curia has condemned the Church. As concerns the Eucharist, when he wrote his sermon on that subject he still clung to the general usage. Now let the papists laugh or weep in one grand chorus, for he finds in the Gospels the definite command of Christ that all drink of the cup. Godless it is, therefore, to deny the cup to the laity, "even if an angel from heaven should do it." [49] One could as well take baptism or penance away from them. Who can deny that when Christ said, "My blood which was shed for you and for many for the remission of sins," he meant to include laymen? It is this concept of the Eucharist that has kept Martin from condemning the Bohemians, who, whether they are evil or good, certainly have the word and deed of Christ on their side. "If any are to be called heretics and schismatics, it is not the Bohemians or the Greeks, because they follow the Gospel, but you Romans . . . who presume to set your own conviction against the plain writ-

---

[47] *WA*, VI, 497. [48] *Ibid.*, p. 501. [49] *Ibid.*, p. 503, l. 25.

ings of God." [50] In fiery language he arrays witnesses, Paul and Cyprian, to prove his charge. As on many occasions before, he pits the Council of Basel against the Council of Constance. The priests, he declares, are not the lords of the sacrament but its servants. This, then, is the first imprisonment in which the Church languishes. It would be well,[51] he continues, if a general council should return to the believer his Christian liberty, his freedom in this sacrament as in that of baptism and penance.

The second imprisonment concerns the nature of the sacrament itself. Here Martin knows that he is going to be blasted as a Wyclifite heretic. Nevertheless he asserts that the bread and wine are actually present in the sacraments and not merely "accidents," as the "Thomistic" and "Aristotelian" Church has ruled. This ruling is an opinion of the theologians, not an article of faith. If Wyclif was a heretic, those who hold this opinion are tenfold heretics and sophists. For twelve hundred years men had the right belief until Aristotelian philosophy began to run wild in the Church,[52] bringing a subtle idea of "substance" and "accidents" which no layman can understand. Speaking in a familiar image, Luther states that God dwells in the bread and wine like the fire in hot iron. Over against the subtleties of Aristotelian metaphysics concerning "subject" and "object" he points to the simple man's naïve power to comprehend the mystery: "Even if philosophy does not understand it, faith understands it." [53]

A third imprisonment is the belief that the sacrament is a good work. Thus it is made a matter of contract and has brought about all the abuses of brotherhoods, accumulated merit, pilgrimages, and practices of that sort. He knows well enough that the food of the monks depends on these things. But the sacrament must be stripped of all the splendor that has been hung about it. Rich garments, decorations, songs, prayers, perfumes, lights, all these are men's additions to the simple words of Christ in which the whole nature of the sacrament lies: a testament, a promise of the forgiveness of sins depending on faith alone. The meaning of this testament is obscured by the priest, who speaks so that the laity cannot even hear the words of consecration, "as if they were too sacred to be delivered before the common crowd." [54] It is faith on which all depends, and how can we have faith if we do not hear?

After analyzing the nature of the promise contained in the sacrament, he finds that two things stand in the way of our receiving the real fruits of the

[50] *Ibid.*, p. 505, ll. 21 ff.   [51] "Pulchrum." *Ibid.*, p. 507, l. 28.
[52] "Grassari." *Ibid.*, p. 509, l. 30.   [53] *Ibid.*, p. 511, l. 38.
[54] *Ibid.*, p. 516, ll. 18 f.

Mass: the feeling that we are sinners and unworthy and the belief that we are by nature too weak to desire or hope for the fulfillment of such great things. But the beggar receives a great inheritance through no worthiness, simply through the right of bequest. It is ignorance of this fact that gives rise to the belief that the Mass is a good work. We can no more transfer the benefit of the Mass to another than we can transfer baptism or penance or final unction. If he is asked whether he wants to overthrow all the Masses that have been endowed, he answers that that is just what has driven him to write this work. "What do I care about the number and high position of those who are in error? The truth is stronger than all of them." [55] He is speaking strange things, of that he is quite aware. Prayers are good works or good deeds only if they are offered in faith, which is strengthened or increased by the Mass. The priests have ascribed to the Mass what really belongs to prayer. The benefits of the prayers of the believer may extend to everyone, but no one receives any benefit from the sacrament except through faith. Again he traverses the arguments set forth in his *Sermon on the Mass* against regarding the Mass as a sacrifice. The elevation of the Mass developed from a Hebrew gesture of gratitude for that which is received, and it is intended only to awaken faith. He wishes that the accompanying words of the Testament might be pronounced in a language that would more actively arouse this faith. "For why may the Mass be performed in Greek or Latin or Hebrew and not also in German or any other language?" [56] In every Mass, including those said in private, the idea of sacrifice lies in the prayers that are said, whether for the living or the dead, and not in the sacrament itself.

The Mass is no less a testimony and a sacrifice when received at the hands of godless priests. Even when celebrated by the most godly it is not the performance of the holy office but the prayer that demands faith. Finally he draws a line between Mass and prayer, between sacrament and work, testimony and sacrifice. The former come from God through the ministry of the priest and demand faith, while the latter arise to God through the priest from our faith and demand that He hear us. "Faith is the sole peace of the conscience; unbelief the only confusion of the conscience." [57]

Martin next turns to an analysis of baptism, which he finds has also fallen a victim to the tyranny of greed and superstition. Almost no one remembers that he has been baptized, but all look for other ways of getting free of sin and getting to heaven. Baptism also depends on faith, and without faith it harms rather than helps throughout life. Penance is not just another

---

[55] *Ibid.*, p. 522, ll. 2 f.   [56] *Ibid.*, p. 524, ll. 33 ff.   [57] *Ibid.*, p. 526, ll. 32 f.

board on which the shipwrecked soul may find a rescue. Sin does not destroy the power of baptism: "This one ship remains, solid and indestructible, and will never go to pieces."[58] He attacks Peter Lombard and other dogmatists who emphasize only the material and form of the sacrament and leave its spirit untouched. Faith in the sacrament of baptism will of necessity be followed by good works. He waves aside all disputes over the forms and formulas of baptism: faith is the important thing and in this regard there is no difference between the ceremonies described in the Old Testament and in the New. The dogmatists do not understand the sacraments, because they overlook the faith and promises which belong to them and emphasize merely the sign and symbol. With much repetition and at great length, he continues to argue that the fruits of baptism cannot be destroyed by sin. It is through its power alone that we return to grace. The happiest period in the history of the Church was when the martyrs went to their death like sheep to the slaughter, for then faith in baptism had its full power.

"This knowledge of baptism is today a captive, and to whom can we ascribe this fact save to the single tyrant, the Roman pontiff?"[59] Thus he introduces a long denunciation of the pope for the forms and ceremonies which have destroyed the power and knowledge of baptism and hindered the faith in Christ. This climaxes in a fierce accusation of the papacy, which is "nothing but the dominion of Babylon and the true Antichrist." The pope himself is the "man of sin and the son of perdition, who sits in the Church like God and by his doctrines and statutes increases the sin of the Church and the destruction of souls."[60] With deep indignation he turns against those who hold that the infant is unable to receive a baptism of faith. He demands the abolition of vows taken so easily for the fulfillment of religious works, so that men may return to the vow of baptism, in which enough has already been promised. He attacks the belief that entrance into a religious order is a new baptism and counsels the heads of the Church to withhold approval of all vows. In case they fail to do so, he urges all, particularly young persons, to refrain from any vows, especially those that bind for all the future. No one entering an order should have the idea that the work of the clergy differs from that of the farmer or of the woman who attends to her household. The pope has no more right than any other Christian to dispense from vows or to dissolve a marriage: "No pope made this decree but an ass changed into a pope."[61] The pope has no right to dissolve a

---

[58] Ibid., p. 529, ll. 24 f.   [59] Ibid., p. 535, ll. 27 ff.   [60] Ibid., p. 537, ll. 25 ff.
[61] Ibid., p. 541, ll. 31 f.

marriage in order that one party may enter a convent. It is ridiculous and stupid when parents consecrate their offspring, sometimes still unborn or in infancy, to a life of chastity.

Martin now comes to the sacrament of penance. Here he finds that no trace of a sacrifice or of penance has been left. Through a denial of any necessity for faith in this sacrament, Rome has extinguished faith. It has sundered it into three parts: contrition, confession, and absolution. By inventing the idea of a certain "attrition" for the godless it has done away altogether with repentance. In contrast to these scholastic subtleties, he pictures with profound emotion the truth of God's promises as they reveal themselves to a contrite heart. God does not look upon our sorrow or lamenting, but upon our faith alone: "All other things are the works and fruits which follow of their own accord upon this and do not of themselves make a man good, but are done by one who has been made good through faith in the truth of God." [62] He praises confession heartily, especially secret confession, as a source of help to the troubled conscience, but finds that it has now become an instrument of tyranny and extortion, particularly when it deals with secret and trivial sins. The whole web of degrees and grades of sin should be torn away. "Among Christians there is one thing alone—the brother has sinned." [63]

Turning away now from the three sacraments which he would retain, Luther goes on to show why he rejects the remaining four. He does not condemn the seven sacraments, but he denies that they can be established from Scripture. All that is left of the apostolic laying on of hands is the sacrament of confirmation, which has been devised in order to add to the prestige of the office of bishop. What is a bishop other than an idol, if he does not preach or care for souls? Confirmation is only a form of sacramental ceremony, not a sacrament itself.

Similarly he finds no scriptural authority for the sacrament of marriage. The heathen have a true and valid marriage, and likewise the unbelievers who dwell among Christians. He expresses horror at the practice of the "Roman tyrants," who sever or command marriage at will, illustrating from a book of some standing, the *Summa Angelica* of Angelus Carletus, "put together from the dregs of all human traditions," [64] which gives eighteen obstacles to marriage. Based on the canon law, the work had currency for the instruction of clerical confessors as furnishing a manual of impediments

[62] *Ibid.*, p. 545, ll. 29 ff.   [63] *Ibid.*, p. 548, l. 10.
[64] *Ibid.*, p. 553, ll. 29 f.

which justified the prevention or dissolution of marriages. Through these restrictions the Romans have been able to set up a regular commerce in "private parts and stinking corpses." [65]

The reward is certainly very worthy of these most sordid and base traffickers in greed and sin. For there is no impediment today which the intercession of mammon does not legitimize, so that these laws of man seem to have been produced for no other reason than that such avaricious men and rapacious Nimrods should have snares for money and nooses for souls, and that in the Church, the sacred place of God, there should stand that abomination which sells publicly the secret parts of both sexes, or as the Scripture says, shame and villainy, which in advance they have stolen by their own laws. O worthy trade for our followers of the pope! [66]

To find a remedy he looks to the character of the civil authority rather than to laws and restrictions:

I know this: that no state can be governed happily by laws. If the government is prudent, it will govern more successfully by following the lead of nature than by laws; if it is not prudent, it will promote nothing except evil by laws, since it does not know how to employ them or temper them to the occasion. . . . If wisdom in the law of God is associated with natural prudence, it is obviously superfluous and harmful to have written laws. But above all let charity never be lacking in respect to any law. [67]

This leads to the conclusion that a marriage, unless expressly forbidden in Scripture, should be confirmed by the Church despite all human laws. Marriage is a divine institution, and if pope or bishop or Church official dissolves any marriage which is against human law, he is Antichrist and a sinner against divine majesty. That a spiritual confraternity, such as that of god-parents, is a hindrance to marriage, is only a human superstition.

Also to be condemned is the interpretation by which the theologians have created other obstacles to marriage, such as the fourth degree of cousin-hood. This is a robbery of freedom through superstition and ignorance. If the pope makes dispensations for the sake of money, why cannot I make dispensations for the sake of my own salvation or that of my brother? He goes further and advises a woman with an impotent husband who does not wish to go through the publicity and legal difficulties of divorcing him, to divorce herself, even without the will of her husband, and cohabit with another, an unmarried man or a single brother of her husband, in secret marriage, raising the children of this union as if they were those of her husband. Such a woman is in a state of salvation and free according to divine law. Under such circumstances he even regards a wife as justified in

---

[65] *Ibid.*, p. 554, l. 11.   [66] *Ibid.*, p. 554, ll. 11 ff.   [67] *Ibid.*, p. 554, ll. 24 ff.

deceiving her husband. "What other counsel can be given to one continually struggling against the dangers of desire?" [68] If the husband refuses divorce, he deserves to be required to rear the children of another. As to divorce, Martin says that he abhors it so that he would prefer bigamy,[69] though he does not dare to say whether this is permissible.[70] When divorce has been permitted, he does not understand why the man is forced to remain unmarried. Cases where husband or wife has disappeared trouble him greatly and he would like to refer them, not to the pope, but to the decision of two pious men.

The sacrament for creating a priest he does not hold to be justified as the Church cannot set up new divine promises. Consecration of priests or monks is simply the preparation of tools or vessels for service. This sacrament was invented merely to increase the distance between the clergy and laity and to give the hierarchy a privileged position, "while the brotherhood of Christians is perishing." [71] We are all equally priests in so far as we are baptized. This leads him to attack those who only say the canonical hours and offer Mass, without preaching, as "horal or Mass priests" and "living idols." [72] After denouncing the canon law which makes incompetent for the priesthood those who have entered on marriage and interposes no such barrier to those who dishonor women outside of wedlock, he cries,

Oh you popes, worthy of this venerable sacrament of ordination! Oh princes, not of the Catholic Church, but of the synagogues of Satan, rather of darkness. . . . Oh shame on the Church of God which you have loaded with these priestly monostrosities! Where are the bishops or priests who even know the Gospel, not to say preach it. . . . The priest's office is to preach, and if he does not do it he is as much a priest as a picture of a man is a man. . . . I almost burst when I think of the most godless tyrannies of the criminals who play with and ruin to such a degree with jests and childish trifles the liberty and glory of the Christian religion.[73]

The final sacrament, that of extreme unction, Martin traces to a passage in the Epistle of St. James, and takes occasion to repeat his denial that the Epistle was really by the apostle. Whoever the writer was, his words have been twisted in interpretation so that "were it not so serious, who could keep from laughing?" [74] The instruction for a free and daily oiling of the sick has been turned into a last unction for those without expectation of recovery. He finds this interpretation peculiarly mad because the oiling is

[68] *Ibid.*, p. 558, ll. 35 ff. [69] "Digamiam." [70] *WA*, VI, 559, ll. 20 ff.
[71] *Ibid.*, p. 564, ll. 3 f. [72] *Ibid.*, p. 564, l. 28. [73] *Ibid.*, pp. 565, ll. 20 ff.
[74] *Ibid.*, p. 568, l. 36.

coupled with a prayer of faith for the recovery of the sick and yet it is given only in cases where death seems certain. He does not condemn the sacrament in itself, but denies that it is a divine institution.

In his summary Martin justifies the existence of only two sacraments as divine institutions, baptism and the Eucharist. It is only in these that the divinely instituted symbol is joined to a promise of the remission of sins. He has heard that bulls and "papistic portents" are prepared against him urging him to revocation and declaring him a heretic. He now offers this little book as a part of his "revocation" and promises in the near future another part such as the Roman See has not yet seen nor heard.[75] He closes with a verse from an old Latin hymn:

> Wretched enemy Herod,
> Why dost thou fear Christ's coming?
> He who bestows kingdoms in the skies
> Does not seize those of earth.[76]

[75] A reference to his pamphlet *On the Freedom of a Christian.*

[76] Hostis Herodes impie,/Christum venire quid times?/Non arripit mortalia,/Qui regna dat coelestia. Caelius Sedulius, "Hymnus acrostichis, totam vitam Christi continens," in Wackernagel, *Das deutsche Kirchenlied,* I, 45 f.

29

THE BULL AND THE COUNTERATTACK

"I DO not know anything about Eck up to the present, except that he has come barbed, bulled, and provided with money." Thus wrote Luther to a friendly canon in Merseburg on September 28.[1] It was true. The hostile Dominican had arrived in Saxony with the bull and had hastened to post it on the cathedral doors in Duke George's city of Meissen, with the observation of all the formalities required by the canon law.[2] Within another week he had repeated this ceremony at the Saxon episcopal see in Merseburg and at the capital of Luther's own diocese in Brandenburg. Thence he returned to Leipzig and prepared for further publication. Spalatin was away in the Rhineland with the elector in attendance on the coronation festivities of the new emperor. This probably explains why, in spite of the fact that the text of the bull had been posted on three sides of him within a radius of fifty miles, Martin seems to have remained in ignorance as to what definite points in his doctrine were condemned until several weeks after Eck opened his campaign in Saxony.[3]

[1] Letter to Günter von Bünau, Sept. 28, 1520, *WAB*, II, 187, l. 29.

[2] On September 21. Kalkoff refers to Eck's letter to William, duke of Bavaria, on December 11. "Zu Luthers römischem Prozess," *ZKG*, XXV, 534. See also Riederer, *Beytrag zu den Reformationsurkunden*, pp. 109 ff.; also Joseph Greving's introductory comments in "Briefmappe. Erstes Stück," *RgST*, XXI/XXII (1912), 196.

[3] The general tenor of the bull was known to humanistic circles in Western Germany by the middle of September. See Hutten's letter to the elector on September 11 from the Ebernburg, in Hutten, *Opera*, I, 383 ff. I cannot follow Kalkoff ("Zu Luthers römischem Prozess," *ZKG*, XXV, 523) in assuming that Hutten was necessarily acquainted with the contents of the bull when he wrote this letter. Erasmus, especially, appears to have had inside sources of information at Rome that promptly communicated to him matters in progress at the Vatican. Aleander, papal delegate at Worms, complained bitterly to Medici of spies at the Roman court who were in contact with its enemies in Germany, so that every word of his dispatches was promptly reported back. Theodor Brieger, "Aleander und Luther, 1521," *Quellen und Forschungen zur Geschichte der Reformation*, pp. 27, 41; Kalkoff, *Depeschen*, pp. 50, 59. He says also that the bull was printed in Germany before it had been published at Rome. In view of Luther's ignorance of the text until October 11, it does not seem at all likely that the bull had been printed on the Rhine a month earlier.

When the news comes to him of his enemy's arrival with the new weapon, his first reaction is to ridicule the bull or "bubble," as he calls it,[4] with a pun that reappeared frequently in those days on the Latin words *bulla* and *ampulla*. As the days go by, however, the matter begins to appear to him in a more serious light. On the first of October he has heard that Eck, the "organ of Satan," is at Leipzig trumpeting forth his bull with great fame and glory, but he is certain that He who sits in heaven caring for all things foresaw from eternity the beginning and progress of this affair to the expected end.[5] Two days later he passed on to Spalatin a suggestion for a counterattack which had been made by friends: that the elector secure an imperial edict forbidding his condemnation or the prohibition of his books until he should be convicted by Scriptures.[6] He admits that his books are confused and inelegant, and he could wish that they might all perish. With satisfaction, he learns that Eck is not safe in Leipzig and that he has taken refuge in the Dominican cloister.[7] Martin does not want him to be killed, but hopes that his counsels will come to naught.

The hated opponent found time, however, to push the attack on Luther in the field of polemics. In the exciting days in Leipzig, where he found himself, a pursuer, pursued by public opinion, Eck brought out a pamphlet in which he took Martin severely to task on an old point of difference concerning which he had brought him to a significant declaration in the disputation: the question of the Bohemian heresy and Luther's admission that the Council of Constance had erred in condemning its authors. Eck now had in hand a much more categorical declaration on the subject in Luther's *Address to the Christian Nobility,* and he rushed forward with a pamphlet in defense of the council's action.[8] Martin did not delay with his reply, which he wrote while awaiting the full force of the papal attack directed

---

[4] Letter to Günter von Bünau, *WAB*, II, 188.

[5] Letter from Luther to Konrad Sam, *WAB*, II, 189.

[6] Letter from Luther to Spalatin, Oct. 3, 1520, *WAB*, II, 191.

[7] Public opinion in Leipzig had now, in fact, turned against Eck, no doubt stimulated by visiting students from Wittenberg. Miltitz wrote to the elector that there were fifty of them in Leipzig, "die sich unnütz machen uff In." E. S. Cyprian, "Nützliche Urkunden zur Erläuterung der ersten Reformationsgeschichte," in *Tentzels Historischer Bericht vom Anfang und ersten Fortgang der Reformation Lutheri,* I, 1, 440. Placards were posted against him in the streets. One of them was an appeal by Melanchthon to the Germans. See "Melanchthons Briefwechsel I," *Supplementa Melanchthoniana,* VI, 115 ff. Miltitz also reported to the elector that Eck had been driven by threats to take refuge in the Pauline cloister, and that in spite of the intervention of the official of Duke George, from whom Eck had a safe-conduct, the threats increased: "They have made up a song against him and sing it on the streets." Cyprian, "Nützliche Urkunden," I, 1, 440.

[8] *Des heiligen Concilie tzu . . . Costentz . . . entschüldigung das in bruder Martin Luder mit unwarheit auff gelegt, Sie haben Joannem Huss und Hieronymum von Prag wider Babstlich Christlich Keyserlich geleidt und eydt vorbrandt . . .* Forwarded by Miltitz to the elector. *Ibid.*

against him by Eck. *On the New Bulls and Lies of Eck* [9] came from the press in the middle of October. It is written in the same tone of satire and savage resentment as the polemics against Eck a year earlier, but now Martin speaks with far greater clearness. The days of uncertainty regarding the Constance Council are past. He opens with a bitter prelude against Eck for falsifying ideas set forth in his sermons *On Baptism* and *On Penance*. His enemy is guilty of venomous lies when he charges him with wanting to exclude the nobility from religious foundations and with raising himself above doctors and councils. In reply to Eck's taunt that he is cowardly and fears to be burned as a heretic, Martin points out that the Ingolstadt professor fled to a Leipzig cloister from fear of a popular attack. Heretics are burned, Martin suspects, because of the fear that they cannot be overcome in argument. Eck cannot interpret three lines of Scripture in a Christian manner, yet distributes everywhere praise and blame. It is not true, Martin says, that he has attacked the person of the Pope or that he wishes to destroy the mendicant orders. It is true that he opposes the war against the Turks. The nobility should use the sword to put down those who set the pope above the Scriptures. He asserts again that fasting should be left free to believers, so that they may do it or not, as they wish. "For God's sake, my dear Eck, what is the use of such public lies, when you know very well that the matter stands differently? Do you think that I am afraid of your lies?" The Leipzig disputation should have taught him that lies get one nowhere. In that memorable encounter he did not reject *all* the doctors but only those who had erred. He stands upon the Scriptures first and forever. Eck may boast of his modesty: he himself will boast only of Holy Writ.

Following this prelude, Martin proceeds to answer Eck's justification of the betrayal of Huss at Constance. His position now is different from that which he held at Leipzig, for then he had not read Huss; otherwise he would have defended all the articles condemned by the council. This he now does, since he has read the Bohemian scholar's "highly intelligent, noble and Christian little book," [10] the like of which has not been written for four hundred years.[11] He wishes to God that he himself had been worthy to be burned for these articles, which were not from Huss but from Christ, Paul, and Augustine. He does not want to make a martyr of Huss and concedes that the guilt for his death did not lie with the pope but with the German emperor and nobility. They were, however, bound and deceived by the lying Roman sophists, and he repeats his demand for a free council,

---

[9] *Von den neuen Eckischen Bullen und Lügen. WA*, VI, 576 ff.
[10] *De causa Boemica*, published in 1520.   [11] *WA*, VI, 587, ll. 24 f.

where honorable and experienced princes, nobles, and laymen may also sit. He follows with an examination of Eck's defense of the breach of safe-conduct that brought death to Huss, and contrasts this way of dealing with heretics with that of Augustine and Hilarius. Terroristic methods, such as these and the scattering of Huss's ashes in the Rhine, have never kept the truth from coming to the fore. "Even if the bladders of all priests were to burst, the stones will yet cry out against the murderers of Huss." [12] He recalls that even in his early days in the cloister he had heard from his teacher,[13] Johann Greifenstein, "a learned and pious man," that Huss had been secretly condemned by the votes of ignorant Junkers and executed without instruction, proof, or conviction.[14] Murmuring about Huss has gone on now ever since his death, and twenty thousand Ecks cannot show why he was condemned.

Martin now returns to the report that Eck has brought a bull with him from Rome full of lies and errors,[15] like Eck himself. Reverting to a policy familiar to us in his dealings with Rome in the preceding year Luther declares that he will not believe that this is the Pope's work or that there is really such a bull for several reasons: he has appealed to a council and is therefore not dependent on the Pope; his case has been referred to the arbitrament of the archbishop of Trier on motion of the elector, Frederick; and furthermore he will not believe that the Pope would give such a commission to Eck, who is so filled with hatred against him. Finally, he must see the original before he credits any bull. He sticks to his previous declarations that the breve brought by Cajetan two years earlier and the bull of 1518 approving indulgences were forgeries. He must see these documents: wax, cord, signature, confirmation and all, with his own eyes: "Herewith I want to warn everybody, lest basely deceived by Roman tricks and by Dr. Eck, he may attack me, and especially I warn those who undertake to execute the bull, lest they get a slap. . . .[16] If violence has to come and further complications with it, . . . I am ready to risk it in the name of Jesus Christ." [17]

"At length the Roman Bull has arrived," Luther writes to Spalatin on the morning of October 11, just before he leaves for Lichtenburg several miles away for the conference with Miltitz. At last the text of the Pope's condemnation had reached him, through the rector of the university.[18]

---

[12] *Ibid.*, p. 590, ll. 13 f.   [13] "Institutor." *Ibid.*, p. 591, l. 18.   [14] *Ibid.*, ll. 12 ff.
[15] Nothing in the work indicates that Luther had as yet seen the text of the bull.
[16] "Schlaffen."   [17] *WA*, VI, 593, ll. 28 ff.
[18] Letter to Spalatin, Oct. 11, *WAB*, II, 195. The chronology is somewhat confused. Miltitz,

Martin's first reaction is a renewed defiance toward what he calls an impious and lying document. Christ himself, he maintains, is condemned in the bull. He is resolved to take the position, which he maintained throughout the fall, that the bull is a fictitious and forged one, but asserts his personal belief that it is a genuine creation of the papists.[19] However, he fears nothing for himself: "Let God's will be done." He is inclined to think that if he and his friends show no anxiety the bull will collapse of itself. "If these things prevail, then it is all over with faith and the Church." He confesses, however, to a feeling of relief, for now he is certain that the pope is Antichrist and the papal See manifestly that of Satan. Probably after reflecting on the matter during the journey to Lichtenburg, he resolved to renew his appeal of two years earlier to a council. He would prefer to have the bull proceed against him, but he hesitates because he must think

---

who was evidently keeping a close watch on Eck, wrote to Frederick that he had seen Eck and received a report of the publication of the bull in Meissen, Merseburg, and Brandenburg. He forwarded with the letter a certified copy of the Roman print of the bull that Eck gave him. Cyprian, "Nützliche Urkunden," I, 1, 439 f. At the same time Eck sent a similar copy to the Wittenberg university. For Eck's letter to the rector see Walch, *Luthers Schriften*, XV, 1874. This Wittenberg copy was the one Luther saw. Why there was a delay of a week in the transmission from Leipzig to Wittenberg, only fifty miles away, can only be surmised. In the night of October 3, Eck, who had received many threats, left Leipzig by stealth for Freiberg, a neighboring Saxon town. See Wiedemann, *Dr. Johann Eck*, p. 154. The delay in forwarding the bull to Wittenberg was possibly due to his sudden flight. See Otto Clemen in *WAB*, II, 193 f. Luther's letter to Spalatin, cited above (*WAB*, II, 195), is dated October 13, although certainly written on October 11 before he left for the conference with Miltitz. Possibly the date and the two final sentences were added after his return.

[19] Luther's position was the one taken officially by the Wittenberg university in defending itself. See Martin's letter to Spengler on November 17: "We still hold that it was not properly formulated"; *WAB*, II, 217 f. The secrecy attending the transmission of the bull to Germany, and the fact that it was brought by Eck, who besides being a bitter enemy of the Wittenbergers was also highly unpopular in various quarters, cast doubt on the genuineness of the bull. Most of all, suspicion was aroused by the authority that it gave to Eck to add to the name of Luther the names of others guilty of heretical doings. In a period when great importance was attached to legal formulas and when the means of communication were few and slow, the omission of any step in the legal routine caused delay. In the case of the bull "Exsurge" the authorities were mostly reluctant to act and welcomed any excuse that gave an avenue for escape. For the care which Eck observed in publication, see *inter alia*, Kalkoff, "Ein neuaufgefundenes Original der Bulle 'Exsurge Domine,'" *ZKG*, XXXIX (1921), 134 ff. Erasmus believed, or feigned to believe, that the bull was a counterfeit. "Acta academiae Lovaniensis," *EA*, XXXV, 312. See also Kalkoff, "Die Vermittlungspolitik des Erasmus," *ARG*, I (1903), 7 f., 29 f., 36, 77. Nuremberg, two of whose leading citizens were condemned in the bull, called attention to various errors in technical form. See Kalkoff, "Zu Luthers römischem Prozess," *ZKG*, XXV, 536 f. George, duke of Saxony, complained to Aleander of the lack of solemnity, notaries, and witnesses in the publication of so important an instrument. Eck was finally driven to issue a statement on November 12, 1520, to the bishop of Bamberg, showing by his commission and instruction from the Pope that he had authority to act as he did. Riederer, *Beytrag zu den Reformationsurkunden*, pp. 79 ff. See also Eck's letter to the bishop of Bamberg on December 5, 1520, and that to the bishop of Augsburg on October 29, 1520, Greving, "Briefmappe. Erstes Stück," *RgST*, XXI/XXII (1912), 220 f., 209 ff. See also *ibid.*, pp. 201 ff.

of the two colleagues whose fate Eck has now interwoven with his by including their names in the bull.[20]

When Martin rode off to Lichtenburg to meet once more with the agile papal messenger, Karl von Miltitz, he did so without enthusiasm and only because the elector had commanded it.[21] The meeting took place at the cloister of the Antonites and seems to have been brief. So little optimism as to its success was felt by well-informed officials that the preceptor of the monastery, Reissenbusch,[22] absented himself for fear of being implicated in a failure. Evidently Miltitz showed his usual cleverness, for Martin, who had canceled his promise of a month earlier to write to the Pope, out of resentment over the coming of the bull, now agreed to publish a letter to Leo in Latin and German. In this epistle he was to say that he had never attacked the Pope's person and was to throw the whole blame on Eck, offering silence as humbly as possible, if only the others will be silent.[23] This was obviously an effort to take the wind out of Eck's sails and to permit the ever optimistic Miltitz to try further negotiations with Rome.[24] It was agreed that the letter and a "little book," which Luther intended should go with it, were to be dated back to September 6, two weeks before the publication of the bull at Meissen, lest it appear as though the Dominican and his party had forced Martin by means of the bull to write the letter.[25] Miltitz himself was now ready to proceed to Rome, where he hoped to have a limit set upon the operation of bull and ban. For this he needed only traveling money from the elector.[26] His enthusiastic letter to Frederick contrasts strongly with Martin's reserved brevity in his letter to Frederick's secretary. Martin declares his readiness to do what he can. However the matter turns out it will be well, since it will be God's will.

The letter to the Pope and the "little book," *On the Freedom of a Christian,* must have been written speedily in fulfillment of Luther's promise. Apparently both were prepared first in Latin and then in German, these versions coming from the press about the end of October.[27] The letter to

[20] Evidently Carlstadt and Johann Dölsch. See *WAB*, II, 196, n. 14.
[21] Letter from Luther to Spalatin, Oct. 11, 1520, *WAB*, II, 195.
[22] He bore responsibilities to the elector as well as to the Church and feared that a trap was being laid to get him into trouble. See letter from Reissenbusch to Feilitzsch, in Cyprian, "Nützliche Urkunden," I, 1, 444 ff.
[23] Letter to Spalatin, Oct. 12(?), *WAB*, II, 197.
[24] See the letter from Miltitz to Frederick in Cyprian, "Nützliche Urkunden," I, 1, 433 ff.
[25] Letter from Miltitz to Frederick, *ibid.,* pp. 449 f.
[26] *Ibid.,* pp. 449 ff.
[27] The date of the issue is not known as, strangely enough, there are no references to these important records in the correspondence of Luther or others during the succeeding months. On November 16 Miltitz sent a copy of the letter to Pirckheimer in Nuremberg; Riederer,

Leo [28] strikes a tone of manly independence. Beginning with a dignified expression of respect for the Pope's person, the writer seeks to justify his appeal to a free council over the head of the Roman See. It has been asserted, Luther continues, that Leo himself was the object of his attack. On the contrary, he has always said the most honorable and best things about the person of the Pope, although in other respects he has called him a Daniel in Babylon. He admits that Leo has a good reputation in all the world. It was not on account of their evil lives that he has attacked his opponents, but for their evil doctrines. Against these he has not spared hard words. Christ and Paul and the prophets did not spare them: "Of what use is the blade of a sword if it does not cut sharply?" [29] Leo himself must confess that the Roman court is worse than Sodom or Gomorrah or Babylon. In the name of the Pope and the Roman Church the poor people of the whole world have been deceived and harmed. This is what has aroused him, and although he does not hope to bring about the reform of Rome, he is determined to do his Christian duty of warning. In the tone of an intimate counselor he calls the Pope to witness how the Roman Church has become a "den of thieves," "a supreme house of villainy," [30] "a head and dominion of sin, death, and damnation," and he asks what the Pope, a sheep among wolves, can accomplish with the help of three or four scholarly and pious cardinals against such a crowd without falling a victim to poison. It is all over with the Roman See; it cannot avoid the fate of its mother, the whore of Babylon. He is sorry that good Leo has become pope at this time and he wishes that he might resign an office worthy of Judas Iscariot. The Roman See is Leo's prison, yes, his hell! His own studies in the Holy Scriptures have been interrupted by the evil spirit who awakened the ambition of Johann Eck, the "prime enemy of Christ and truth." [31] In a disputation this great and boastful hero seized on one of his words about the Roman See, became swollen with the idea that he was the foremost theologian of the world, and assumed that he could win honors by a victory over Luther.

In reviewing his case, Martin denounces the treatment he had received

---

Nachrichten, I, 170. See *WA*, VII, 1 f. The Latin forms, *Epistola Lutheriana ad Leonem* and *Tractatus de libertate christiana*, were issued together, seven printings appearing during the year. In the German form the letter and the tractate appeared separately, but apparently at the same time. In both cases the Latin form is the clearer in picture and more incisive in statement, as will be pointed out below.

[28] *Sendbrief an den Papst Leo*. The analysis above follows the German form, *WA*, VII, 3 ff. The differences from the Latin are slight.

[29] *Ibid.*, p. 4, ll. 34 f.   [30] *Ibid.*, p. 5, l. 29. See also p. 44, ll. 16 f.

[31] *Ibid.*, p. 7, ll. 15 f.

from Cajetan, whose criminal and arbitrary demands for a recantation aggravated a matter which might have been halted at that time. What he has now resolved is not his fault, but the cardinal's. Again, the affair was on the way to arbitration through the efforts of the elector and Miltitz when Eck stirred up the disputation at Leipzig and by his lies and secret tricks lighted a great flame. Thus the Pope and all may see what an enemy and flatterer can do: "The name of the Roman court is now an evil stench throughout the whole world." Martin's rage against Eck knows no restraint: "He whinnies after fame like a prancing, lustful stallion." [32]

Finally, Luther prostrates himself at Leo's feet and begs the Pope to restrain the flatterers who feign a love of peace but are actually its enemies. He will not recant his doctrines. He will not allow God's word to be led captive. With all humility he begs the Pope not to listen to the sweet words of those who tell him that he is not a man but compounded of man and God. The servant of all the servants of God, Leo is in a wretchedly dangerous position, as is well known throughout the world. "Don't be deceived by the liars and hypocrites who tell you that you are lord of the world . . . that you have power in heaven, hell and purgatory. They are your enemies and seek to ruin your soul." [33] The vicar of Christ in whose heart Christ does not dwell is not the regent of Christ but is an Antichrist and an idol. With a last apology for forgetting the Pope's majesty in order to do his fraternal duty, which is not that of a flatterer but of a friend, he presents himself with his little book, "the gift of a poor man," a spiritual work containing the whole sum of the Christian life.

This poor man's gift, *On the Freedom of a Christian*,[34] is one of the most original of Luther's works. In vigor of thought and natural eloquence it is among the most remarkable books of that age. It seems to have come from the press about the same time in Latin and in German form. As might be expected, the Latin version is in dialectical character more precise and complete than the German—it is about one-fourth longer—and its conclusions are logically more impressive, but the German text is marked by a warmth and a conviction that has given it a high place among the prose monuments of that language.[35] Twelve reprintings at the Wittenberg and Leipzig presses and elsewhere within a year of its appearance testify to the interest which contemporaries took in the work.

[32] *Ibid.*, p. 8, ll. 38 ff.   [33] *Ibid.*, p. 10.

[34] *Tractatus de libertate christiana, ibid.*, pp. 49 ff.; and *Von der Freiheit eines Christenmenschen, ibid.*, pp. 20 ff.

[35] As stated above, my analysis follows mainly the German form, but the Latin has been kept in view wherever it gives a more complete exposition of Luther's ideas; e.g., *WA*, VII, 54, l. 30 to 55, l. 33.

For at least two years Martin had been thinking much about the relation of the individual to the Church, and his thoughts had dwelt on the social as well as on the religious aspect of this relationship. Liberty from the law through faith was one of the ideas which he had clothed in sonorous and powerful Latin in his theses against indulgences. Beside this there had sprung up during the past year doubts of hierarchical privilege and the conviction that the layman had a right to judge his own actions. In the little work on Christian liberty he sums up these ideas, and by a series of logical steps seeks to show that the Christian is subject only to the law of faith and love. At the beginning he places two theses: the Christian is lord over everything and subject to no one; the Christian is servant in everything and subject to everyone. This apparent contradiction he explains from the double nature of man, the spiritual and the physical. The inner freedom of the spirit is quite independent of such things as health or disease, freedom or imprisonment of the body. Friedrich Schiller later incorporated the same conception, from the standpoint of eighteenth-century idealism, in his *Three Words of Faith*. So-called pious works, Luther declares, are of no value to the soul, which needs only faith and trust in God's word. Once more he takes his stand on the old promise in Romans 1.17, "The righteous shall live by faith," and supports himself by means of a long array of scriptural passages. Once more, and with a logical consequence scarcely attained in any of his preceding works, he sets forth the liberating power of faith. All Scripture is divided into commands and promises. The commands are imposed merely to show man the futility of his efforts. One may see here Martin's own experience in the battle against despair: the struggle to fulfill the impossible and the ever-present dread of eternal condemnation. So too one may trace his liberation by means of the promise that through faith God's commands are fulfilled. "Command and fulfillment! He alone commands; He alone fulfills also." He then goes on to show how faith brings unity and harmony into the spirit. The divine promises suffuse the soul, as iron is heated to a glow through union with fire.[36] Thus the Christian has enough if he possesses faith; he needs no other work and is free from all commands and laws. But, he hastens to say, this does not mean idleness or evil doing. Faith establishes a mutual relation of sincerity and confidence and honor between God and man. In a mystical and poetic flight that is rare with him Martin shows how the soul unites with Christ in a sharing of virtues and of sins. Using the age-old imagery of David of Augsburg and Henry Suso he symbolizes the union

[36] *Ibid.*, p. 24, ll. 19 ff.

of Christ and the soul in the bridal ring of love and the dowry of faith. "Is that not a happy arrangement when the rich, noble, and pious bridegroom Christ takes in marriage the poor, despised, wicked little whore and frees her from all evil and decorates her with wealth?" [37]

This then is the spiritual kingdom of Christ. His priesthood is also spiritual and consists of prayer and teaching. Each Christian receives this great spiritual priesthood through faith and thus becomes a spiritual lord over all things that tend towards salvation. Through the infinite dignity and importance of this spiritual priesthood the Christian may appear before the face of God for himself and for others. He even has power over the commands of God. In contrast to this Christian freeman, he that would be saved by good works is like the dog in the fable who drops the piece of meat in order to snap at its reflection in water. While Scripture makes no difference between the priest and the laity, save that the former are servants of the Gospel, these servants have now taken away all Christian freedom and made the Christians their servants.

The freedom which Martin has described belongs to the inner man; but the outer man must perform the services required of a Christian. The body demands its discipline of fasting and prayer in order to make it serve its spiritual lord. Purity of soul and love of God call for purity of the body, and so man practices good works, not for his own justification but in order to please God. Nevertheless, the freedom of the spirit remains: everyone may set the measure of the chastisement that is necessary for his own discipline. Like Adam everyone is established in Paradise and must work in order to avoid idleness and for the preservation and hardening of the body. Like the tree in Christ's parable, man must be good or evil before he can do good or evil works. "A good or bad house does not make a good or bad carpenter, but a good or bad carpenter makes a good or bad house. No work makes a master, . . . but as the master is, so is his work." [38] Again and again he illustrates this from the Bible. Once more he condemns the "seductive, diabolical teaching" [39] which dwells on the necessity for penitence, confession, and satisfaction without going on to teach the promise of grace. Penitence flows from God's commands; faith from His promises.

Having established man's spiritual service to God, he now turns to discuss his service toward his fellow man. The Christian willingly takes it upon himself to serve his neighbor in gratitude for the mercy of God toward himself and in order to please God. This then is the sum of Christian ethics: "Toward my neighbor I will be a Christian as Christ was to me

---

[37] *Ibid.*, p. 26, ll. 4 ff.   [38] *Ibid.*, p. 32, ll. 18 ff.   [39] *Ibid.*, p. 34, l. 11.

and do nothing to him save what I see is for his need, his use, and his salvation, since through my faith I have enough of everything in Christ." [40] So from faith flow love and joy in God and from love a free and happy life in the service of our neighbor. Priests and cloisters of every rank and order are called upon to do this work for the help of others, for discipline of the body, and as an example to all. Thus the Christian is permitted to fulfill the innumerable commands and laws of spiritual and temporal rulers, not because he needs to do them for his own salvation but to give an example of service and suffering. The demands of tyrants are certainly wrong, but they do no harm to the Christian so long as they are not against God's commands. Martin pauses to dwell on the uselessness of works that are not of service to others and voices the fear that very few religious foundations are really Christian. God's blessings flow from one to another, each sharing them with his neighbor; so too each must take upon himself the sins of his neighbor as if they were his own.

In bringing the Latin form of the work to an end Martin draws a contrast between two types of Christians, the obdurate "ceremonists" who want nothing to do with true liberty, and the simple and weak in faith who cannot appreciate liberty. We cannot get on in this life without ceremonies and works; especially ardent and inexperienced youth needs to be defended and preserved by these bonds. These ceremonies, however, are like the scaffolding that the carpenters prepare for building a house; they are not an end in themselves.

"It is a little booklet so far as paper is concerned, but if its meaning is understood, it contains the whole sum of a Christian life." [41] In the few pages of this work Martin has indeed summarized his whole theology as it had developed during the preceding six years: the uselessness of struggling to fulfill the law, the necessity for the submission of self and for the passivity of the will which had come to him from Occam as well as the mystics,[42] and a liberation through faith. The first part recalls his struggle with the inner devils of doubt and despair and his triumphant emergence into peace and confidence. The second part is an attempt to formulate the ethics of the Christian in his social contact, and shows the monastic ideals that still dominated Martin's thinking. Not as in the *Address to the Christian Nobility* does he seek here to meet contemporary situations with practical proposals for reform, but he lays the foundation for all the relationships of

---

[40] *Ibid.*, p. 35, l. 34 to p. 36, l. 2.   [41] *Ibid.*, p. 11.

[42] See D. M. Rade, "Luthers 'De libertate christiana' mystisch?" *Zeitschrift für Theologie und Kirche*, XXIII (1913), 266 ff. See also W. Köhler, "Die Mystik in Luthers 'Freiheit eines Christenmenschen,'" *ibid.*, pp. 399 f.

life in an attitude of mind which is in its essence unworldly and other worldly. The behavior of man in his relation to the Church and to his neighbors is based on the monastic and medieval conception of the world as an enemy against which one must arm himself. Especially in the latter portion of the Latin form, the work is a symmetrical and harmonious formulation of the ascetic ideals of the later Middle Ages.

After his return from Lichtenburg Martin found time to study the bull, and he was appalled. "Did Satan ever speak so impiously against God from the beginning of the world?" he exclaims to Spalatin a few weeks later. The "Satanic bull" torments him so that it almost reduces him to silence. "The greatness of the horrid blasphemies of that bull overcomes me, and no one notices it. In truth I am convinced by many a powerful argument that the last day is on the threshold. The reign of Antichrist is beginning." [43]

The bull *Exsurge Domine* is indeed a forcible instrument. It contains no theological exposition or argument, as Luther and his contemporaries pointed out, but it is unsparing in threats and denunciations uttered in the solemn and sonorous phraseology that was the traditional form for the thunders of the Vatican against heresy.[44] "O God, arise and defend Thy cause!" Thus the formidable document begins, and then bids Peter, Paul, the saints, and the whole Church of God to come forward against a fox in the vineyard, a wild swine, a new Porphyry who has attacked and torn all the holy popes of the preceding age. Anxiety and pain hardly permit the Pope to specify these heresies. Some of them have already been condemned by councils. Others are heretical or false or vicious or offensive to Christian ears or such as to lead simple souls astray. They have arisen in the German nation, to which the Roman Church transferred the empire from the Greeks, those Germans, hitherto the severest enemies of heresy, from whom Leo and his predecessors have selected governors and protectors of the Church. The heretical opinions which are now to be condemned are those of the Hussites and Wyclifites and of Hieronymus of Prague. They have been rejected by the universities of Cologne and Louvain, those most sturdy and godfearing cultivators of the divine field.

On this introduction follows a list of the erroneous doctrines which contain this "deadly poison." At its conclusion the Holy Father brands anew the heresy contained in them as "pestiferous or pestilent," "an eating cancer, . . . condemned by the most learned ministers, teachers, and masters," and

---

[43] Letter from Luther to Spalatin, Nov. 4, 1520, *WAB*, II, 211, ll. 32 ff.

[44] For a German translation of the bull by Spalatin, made at Cologne in October, see Kalkoff, "Die Übersetzung der Bulle 'Exsurge,'" *ZKG*, XLV, N.F. VIII (1927), 384 ff.

denounces it as unchristian or against the teaching and interpretation of the Holy Catholic Church. All orders, spiritual and lay, all clerical and temporal office-bearers are warned against proclaiming or accepting these errors on pain of losing all their rights and privileges. At the end of the long list of officials, institutions, and political estates and organs that are thus reminded of their duty the name of a "certain Martinus Luther" appears as one whose writings contain these errors and many others. Finally all are forbidden to read, declare, preach, praise, print, publish, or defend the books in Latin or other languages in which these errors are found, and all officials are summoned to burn them publicly in the sight of clergy and laymen.

With pathos the Pope then recites the efforts he has made to have Martin recant, the latter's refusal to obey the citation, and his criminal appeal to a council. This makes him a heretic and liable to condemnation as such, but out of kindness the way back into the bosom of the Church is still held open. He and his followers are exhorted to cease to disturb the peace and unity of the Church, and in case of obedience, love and gentleness are promised to them. A limit of sixty days is set within which Martin must recant formally or come to Rome, otherwise he and his supporters are condemned as public and obstinate heretics. In the meantime they must refrain from all preaching, all defense of their actions or issuance of books, and they must burn those books which contain their errors. All are then forbidden to support or in any way make public Luther's works, even those which do not contain error, "so that his memory may be wiped out from the community of Christian believers." [45] All lay and clerical persons are summoned to seize him and his supporters and to hold them subject to the Pope's orders or send them to Rome. All of those who fail to do this are liable to expulsion from office and honors. Cities and countries harboring him are threatened with the interdict. In conclusion, all clerical authorities are commanded to publish the bull, and Brandenburg, Meissen, and Merseburg are directed to post it on the doors of the diocesan cathedral and the episcopal chancellery.

In the face of this blast Martin's confidence in himself hardens. "I am never prouder nor more full of fire [46] than when I hear that I am displeasing to these people. Are they doctors, are they bishops, are they princes, what difference does it make? If the word of God were not attacked by them, it would not be the word of God." Thus he writes to a friend, a member

---

[45] *Ibid.*, p. 396.
[46] "Animosior." Letter to Michael Muris, Oct. 20, 1520, *WAB*, II, 201, l. 6.

of the Cistercian order at Leipzig University;[47] he adds that he despises his Satanic enemies and, if he were not detained in Wittenberg, he would go further than Rome in despite of Satan and all the furies. "What if they slay me? I am not worthy to suffer anything in so happy a cause." In the meantime discouraging news had evidently come from Spalatin in Cologne regarding the possibility of support from Emperor Charles.[48] "Put not your trust in princes," Martin had written several weeks earlier.[49] He had heard through a letter from Erasmus that the court was filled with dictatorial beggars.[50] Now in sending the text of the bull to the elector's chaplain, Martin voices his satisfaction that Spalatin has ceased to depend on the judgment of men.[51] Luther was evidently aware of the diplomatic struggle which, as we shall soon see, was at the moment going on between the elector and the Roman agents Caracciolo and Aleander in the Rhenish city, but he is unwilling to make any concession. "It is hard to set oneself against princes and potentates, but there is no other way to escape hell and divine wrath." Probably Spalatin had suggested that Martin write privately to the princes. He declines to do this. Instead he determined to prepare an appeal to the public, a plan which he was to carry out two weeks later in renewing his appeal to a council. "For the Gospel is not such that it is propagated or preserved by the rulers of the earth, else God would not have called fishermen." It is probably in reply to complaints passed on to him by Spalatin from high personalities in Cologne that Martin is led to declare himself independent of temporal allies: "See to it that those who take offense at my bitterness are not such as consider the cause of the Lord insignificant and have human plans."[52] Among the princes he bears an especial grudge against Duke George and proposes to reckon with him and the bishop of Merseburg in an "anti-bull" which he is putting forth, not because he hopes "to be able to soften their refractory spirits, but to redeem my conscience in revealing to them their danger."

The "anti-bull," *Against the Accursed Bull of Antichrist*, which was forwarded on November 4 to Spalatin, was dashed off in this mood of burning resentment. It came from the press toward the end of October,[53] and

---

[47] *Ibid.*, pp. 201 f.

[48] See letter from Luther to Spalatin, Nov. 4, 1520, *WAB*, II, 210 f.

[49] Letter to Spalatin, Oct. 11, *WAB*, II, 195.

[50] "Mendicotyrannis." *Ibid.*, l. 25. See Erasmus's letter to Melanchthon, June 21, Allen, *Opus epistolarum Erasmi*, IV, 288.

[51] Letter to Spalatin, Nov. 4, *WAB*, II, 210.   [52] *Ibid.*, pp. 210 f.

[53] Peter Burchard sent a copy to Lazarus Spengler on October 29. See *WA*, VI, 595. In sending the Latin form, *Adversus execrabilem Antichristi bullam*, to Spalatin on November 4, Luther says that the German version is in process of publication: "cuditur et eadem vernacula." *WAB*, II, 211.

must have been written down about the same time as the open letter to Pope Leo and the *Freedom of a Christian*. Its spirit and style have little in common with the profoundly mystical tone of the great work on Christian ethics. *Against the Accursed Bull of Antichrist* is sharply satirical. Martin's object is to hold the bull up to ridicule and especially to show that its authors have made no attempt to establish the heresy of his ideas. He follows his declared policy, and assumes that the bull is a falsification on the part of Eck, a man made up of "lies, pretenses, errors, and heresies." [54] If, however, Leo and his learned councilors are really its authors, Martin declares that it is his eager desire never to be absolved or reconciled or to have anything in common "with that most unlearned, impious, and furious Antichrist." [55] He would return joyful thanks to God for a happy death if he might perish in this affair. Whoever is the author of the bull, Martin regards him as Antichrist and his reply is therefore directed against Antichrist.

After this defiant introduction he proceeds to state his position. Before Christ and the sacred evangelists he reasserts his belief in the condemned articles and curses the bull as sacrilege and blasphemy. Why does Antichrist assume that he can overcome Scripture with mere words? Perhaps the condemnation was borrowed from the faculties of Louvain and Cologne. "But Luther, accustomed to struggles, is not frightened by bulls and knows how to distinguish between useless paper and the omnipotent word of God." [56] In the bull his errors are classified as "respectively" heretical or scandalous or false or offensive to pious ears and as tending to lead astray simple minds. With much sarcasm and some sophistry Martin demands why no attempt has been made to separate the errors in these groups. "I do not want to be instructed 'respectively,' but absolutely, and with assurance." For he, who is of Occam's faction, condemns everything that is "respective" [57] and regards everything as absolute, like the jester in Erasmus's *Praise of Folly*.[58] At the Leipzig disputation Eck, foaming at the lips, branded him repeatedly as a heretic because he praised the condemned articles of Huss, but was not able to identify any of them as heretical and had to confine himself to an indiscriminate condemnation, like that in the bull. In the style of the academic disputation Luther analyzes and plays on the word "respectively" and urges the papists to write soberly: "For this bull seems either to have been begotten miserably among whores at a nocturnal banquet or to have been jumbled together in the raging dog days." [59] The finest

---

[54] *WA*, VI, 597, ll. 19 f.   [55] *Ibid.*, p. 598, ll. 5 f.   [56] *Ibid.*, p. 599, ll. 18 f.
[57] "Respectus."   [58] *Ibid.*, p. 600, ll. 10 ff.
[59] "In canicularibus furiis confusam." *Ibid.*, p. 602, ll. 12 ff.

thing about it, he adds derisively, is the sinful contradiction revealed in the hearts of the authors of the bull, who brand men as heretics, though they themselves condemn all truth.

The end of the argument is that the bull is none other than Antichrist, the enemy who embraces all the worst enemies, "impiety, blasphemy, ignorance, imprudence, hypocrisy, lying." [60] A weakness of the bull is revealed in its demand that even those books in which there are no errors should be burned. Did not the "bull-producers" [61] of Antichrist fear that stones and logs would sweat blood for horror over such infamy and blasphemy? [62] After calling on Emperor Charles and kings, princes, bishops, and doctors to proceed against this game of Satan, Martin summons down the wrath of God upon the papistic enemies of the cross of Christ and the truth of God. If the bull was issued in Leo's name and with his knowledge, he will use the power conferred on him through baptism as a son of God and a brother of Christ to warn the Pope to lay aside these diabolical blasphemies and impieties; otherwise he will curse him as the chief enemy of Christ and will not only bear his censures with joy but will also condemn him and his associates to bodily destruction,[63] along with the bull and all the decrees of Satan. He is, to be sure, not yet persuaded that the bull is the Pope's and not that of Eck, who with his fellow Dominicans is singing, "Like Sheol let us swallow him up alive and whole, as one that goes down into the pit" (Proverbs 1.12). With particular bitterness Martin refers to the statement in the bull that at Augsburg money and a safe conduct had been offered him to go to Rome, a lie which he ascribes to the notoriously penurious Cajetan. If they want to send him money, let them do so, but it must be enough so that he may go to Rome accompanied by twenty thousand foot and five thousand horse. "In this manner I will guarantee that faith is kept with me,[64] and this on account of Rome, which devours its inhabitants, never having kept faith nor keeping it now, where the most sacred fathers kill their beloved sons for the love of God, and brothers destroy brothers in obedience to Christ, as is the Roman custom and style." He denounces the small group of cardinals, priors, and doctors, in all scarcely thirty men, for calling themselves the "Church universal," and points to Christians east, north, and south, who do not follow Rome and are therefore burned as heretics, although Rome itself is the chief

---

[60] *Ibid.*, p. 603, l. 11.
[61] "Bullati," from "bulla," a bubble, a further play on the double meaning of the word.
[62] *WA*, VI, 603, ll. 26 f.
[63] "Ad interitum carnis." *Ibid.*, p. 604, l. 36.
[64] "Qua arte mihi satis fidei parabo." *Ibid.*, p. 606, l. 16.

source of all schism. He pauses to denounce further the arrogance of the Roman See, which seeks to be regarded as the seat of all power, sends out stupid and impious bulls, and outside of all doctrine and all sanctity of life presumes to decide for men what they shall say and do, as if through the power and glory of the Spirit.

Briefly Martin then takes up six of the condemned articles drawn from works of two years earlier, chiefly the *Explanations of Indulgences* and the *Sermon on Penance*. These have to do with his attacks on indulgences and deal with scholastic problems of sin and repentance. He defends his position briefly in each case and arrives at the conclusion that the authors of the bull do not understand his ideas nor see what he has sought to do in his books. He has now put his enemies to flight.[65] Everything the bull has condemned he declares to be Catholic dogma, as has been clearly shown in his books. If there is no other way to resist this wordy and empty condemnation, he will risk his name, his life, his blood. It is better that he should be killed a thousand times than revoke a single syllable of these condemned articles. "And just as they excommunicate me on account of sacrilegious heresy of their own, I in my turn excommunicate them for the sake of the truth. Christ, the judge, will see which excommunication has the most value with Him." [66]

The German "anti-bull" [67] is a very different work from the Latin version. Addressed to the common people, it strikes a forceful popular note with its ready use of a well-practiced vocabulary of denunciation. Martin is intent, he says, on showing to the common folk the deceit of the papists, who have tried to persuade them that the errors which they have introduced into the Church are unassailable truths of Christianity. The universal Church of Christ, that is, all the Christians in the world, cannot err; but the supporters of the pope have substituted an erring pontiff for an unerring Christendom. The error of papal infallibility is at the bottom of the tricks by which people and lands have been destroyed. Now the same deceivers are attacking his books, forbidding and burning them. He would be quite willing to see them burn if an understanding of the Scriptures could take their place; but he warns everyone against being driven from the truth by the swollen words of this bull which has just now come from Rome. He touches again what he knows is a popular chord when he declares that the bull justifies his resistance to the preachers of indulgences, for Rome never punishes them, but as soon as the Romans are themselves attacked

[65] *Ibid.*, p. 611, l. 36.   [66] *Ibid.*, p. 612, ll. 21 ff.
[67] *Wider die Bulle des Endchrists. Ibid.*, pp. 614 ff.

they mobilize heaven and earth with bulls and bans. "It would not be strange if the princes, nobility, and laity . . . chased pope, bishops, priests, and monks out of the country. . . . What Christian heart can suffer or listen to an out-and-out command to burn the truth and follow error, such as this cursed, shameless, devilish bull does?" [68]

Finally, he assembles the heresies charged against him and adds others to them. In place of the six condemned articles which he had defended in the Latin "anti-bull" he now sets forth twelve, with an earnest effort to make his theological position clear to ordinary laymen. The discussion is shot through with savage criticism of the authors of the bull, who "dare to enter heaven with the tinder of original sin and the old Adam, so that they may be sure to have some filth to make them stink in heaven." The inexhaustible abusive vocabulary of the age runs through his denunciation of the "cursed and damned" bull, begotten of "a thousand furies," "a most ignorant, blasphemous, and anti-Christian" document; its authors "Roman villains," "insane, raging priests," "soul murderers." Finally the readers of the German work are told that the papal instrument deserves to be trampled under foot by all true Christians and sent home to the Roman Antichrist and Doctor Eck, his apostle, with fire and sulphur.[69]

"It is impossible for those to be saved who promote this bull or do not reject it." [70] It is with this absolute conviction that Martin follows the efforts of Eck to put Rome's condemnation into effect. The energetic Dominican was indeed driving forward with furious vigor and courage in the face of passive resistance on the part of clerical and lay authorities and violent opposition by German students.[71] After the publication of the bull in Saxony and Brandenburg, he was obliged, as we have seen, to flee from Leipzig, where unfriendly observers believed his life to be in danger.[72] He now directed appeals to the universities, which, together with the bishops, were especially charged with the publication of the bull. Eck did not venture to go to Wittenberg himself, but set out for Erfurt, where his entry into the city was halted by a group of armed students, stirred up to action by Luther's friend in the theological faculty, Justus Jonas.[73] Martin's old

---

[68] *Ibid.*, p. 621, ll. 10 ff.   [69] *Ibid.*, p. 629, ll. 10 ff.

[70] Letter to Spalatin, November 4, *WAB*, II, 211, ll. 49 f.

[71] Kalkoff has made a painstaking investigation of the progress of Eck's efforts in "Die Bulle Exsurge," *ZKG*, XXXV (1914), 166 ff., and XXXVII (1918), 89 ff.; and "Die Vollziehung der Bulle Exsurge," *ZKG*, XXXIX, N.F. II (1921), 1 ff. Any examination of the evidence will show how important a rôle Eck played in stemming the rising tide of enthusiasm for Luther in the period just before the Diet at Worms. No one of less energy and will power could have accomplished it.

[72] See the letter from Milititz to Elector Frederick, Cyprian, "Nützliche Urkunden," I, 1, 453.

[73] Kalkoff, "Die Stellung der deutschen Humanisten zur Reformation," *ZKG*, XLVI, N.F. IX (1928), 192.

university was strictly conservative, as in the days of his study there. The year before it had received Eck with applause on his triumphant return from the Leipzig disputation,[74] and six months later, during the critical days of the Worms Diet the conservative members of the faculty turned against Jonas and Lang, Luther's most active supporters among its members.[75] In addition to these two warm friends, however, the students here as at Wittenberg and Leipzig were easily aroused against what must have seemed to them an attack on the progress of "good letters" and on the freedom of university teaching. They seized the printer's copies of the bull and threw them into the river, hailing the floating paper as a "bubble," the humanistic pun on *bulla* so often exploited by Luther and his friends.[76]

Martin heard the news of these popular demonstrations against his enemy with obvious satisfaction.[77] Nevertheless he had to deal with an antagonist convinced to the point of fanaticism that the Wittenberg professor was an enemy of the Church and was undermining the entire fabric of Christian dogma.[78] The great difficulties overcome by Eck in the campaign which he was obliged to wage at Augsburg against the hostile clergy testify to his energetic persistence in the face of relentless enmity.[79] By the middle of October he was back in Ingolstadt, whence on October 14 he issued a categorical summons to the bishops demanding that they publish the bull through all grades of their clergy, have Luther's books burned, and after the sixty-day period denounce his refractory followers.[80] The resistance which his demand encountered arose perhaps less from sympathy with Martin's theological ideas on the part of the autocratic and indifferent princes of the Church than from the opposition of their humanistically inclined vicars and officials, who saw in Eck an intolerant obscurantist. It

[74] Kalkoff, "Die Erfurter theologische Fakultät gegenüber der Bulle 'Exsurge,'" *Historisches Jahrbuch*, XLVII (1927), 353 f.

[75] Kalkoff, *Humanismus und Reformation in Erfurt*, p. 62 and *passim*.

[76] See *WAB*, II, 207, n. 4.

[77] Letter from Luther to Spalatin, Oct. 3, 1520, *WAB*, II, 191, ll. 31 ff. See also his letter to Gräfendorf, Oct. 30, 1520, *WAB*, II, 207.

[78] Eck asserted repeatedly that he had undertaken the publication of the bull against his will. See his letter of Oct. 29, 1520 to Bishop Christoph of Augsburg, in Greving, "Briefmappe," 209 ff. Protestant historians have called attention to his greed for ecclesiastical office. In temperament he was vindictive and unforgiving: his Catholic biographer Wiedemann, *Dr. Johann Eck*, p. 170, declares that the inclusion in the bull of the six humanists not mentioned in the Roman document was an act of private revenge. The sources show, however, that he had full papal authority for this action. See his letter of November 12 to the bishop of Bamberg, in Riederer, *Beytrag*, pp. 79 ff. The student of history will find it hard to see how Rome could have opposed Luther in this crisis without granting Eck very wide powers. Obviously he could not have made headway against Martin without trying at the same time to terrorize the latter's supporters.

[79] Karl Schottenloher, "Magister Andreas Lutz in Ingolstadt, der Drucker der Bulle 'Exsurge Domine' 1519–24," *Zentralblatt für Bibliothekswesen*, XXXII (1915), 249 f.

[80] Kalkoff, "Die Bulle Exsurge," *ZKG*, XXXVII, 91 ff.

arose, too, from fear of popular demonstrations of sympathy, which assumed threatening form at the episcopal residences throughout northern and central Germany. How deeply Martin's widely disseminated pamphlets had stirred up feeling among followers of the new learning and the popular classes becomes manifest in the obstructions thrown in Eck's path by episcopal chancelleries and university faculties all the way from the Baltic to the Sava.[81] In almost every Saxon town the bull was greeted with insult. Throughout North Germany the bishops delayed and made difficulties. The general vicar of the bishop of Bamberg expressed the wish that "someone would drown the rascal Eck." [82] Several authorities, like the dukes of Bavaria, asked for a suspension of the bull. At the universities the progress in execution was no easier. The case of Erfurt has been noted. At Ingolstadt, Eck's university, the publication of the bull and the book-burning were duly carried out, but in Vienna the rector of the university and the civil governor locked horns with the theological faculty, and it was only the decision of Emperor Charles several months later in favor of the faculty that opened the way to the execution of the bull in the Danube capital.

In spite of fierce opposition, the efforts of Eck finally brought about the execution of the bull throughout northern, eastern and southeastern Germany. The news of all this must have filtered through to Wittenberg in the fall and winter, but little reference to it appears in such correspondence of Martin as has been preserved. Naturally his interest was fixed upon his own university, which was one of the prime objects of Eck's attack. After the latter's return to Germany he had by papal authority included six others besides Luther for condemnation in the bull. The names were carefully selected and included the best-known supporters of Luther.[83] Two of them, Willibald Pirckheimer and Lazarus Spengler, prominent city councilors of Nuremberg, had given Martin aid and support when he made his appearance before Cajetan at Augsburg two years earlier. Another name was that of Bernhard Adelmann of Adelmannsfelden, the Augsburg canon. Two other "destroyers of the faith" were members of the theological faculty of Wittenberg, and as we have seen, one of Eck's early moves was to send a copy of the bull to that university with a demand that no one be allowed further to teach the condemned articles under penalty of a withdrawal of its privileges.[84] The rector, Peter Burchard, sent copies im-

---

[81] *Ibid*. See also Wiedemann, *Dr. Johann Eck*, pp. 153 ff.

[82] *Ibid*., p. 166.

[83] Not merely enemies of Eck, so far as we know. See Kalkoff, "Zu Luthers römischem Prozess," *ZKG*, XXV, 532, n. 3.

[84] The text of Eck's letter to the university is printed in Walch, *Schriften*, XV, 1874.

mediately to the elector in Cologne and to John, the co-regent of Saxony, at Coburg, meantime withholding the bull from publication.[85] Eck had come provided with letters from the Pope to these two Christian rulers, and Martin soon had in his hands a copy of these "apostolic or apostate letters," as he calls them.[86]

To Luther these attacks were part of a plan long nourished by his Leipzig enemies and Duke George to drive him from the university and to destroy Leipzig's rival institution in Wittenberg. His suspicions, which he repeatedly expresses in his letters to Saxon dignitaries,[87] no doubt were also those of his Wittenberg colleagues and served to crystallize opposition to the bull and support of Martin among the elector's associates and servants. Sympathy came to him in the crisis from more than one influential quarter. Barnim, duke of Pomerania, who had been present among the Wittenbergers at the Leipzig disputation, writes him congratulations on his courage.[88] More inspiring still must have been a letter which arrived at this time from a very young man who was later to hold the fortunes of the little Saxon state in his hands, Crown Prince John Frederick of Saxony, a son of John and a nephew of the elector, the heir to their joint estates and powers. With the impulsiveness of youth the prince, who was at this time only seventeen years of age, wrote words of cheer to Martin and also intervened with his uncle, the elector, for his support.[89] There are many indications indeed, even in the very meager sources of the time, that Martin was receiving constantly increasing expressions of sympathy, such as unflinching courage always commands. His *Babylonian Captivity*, the work which burned the bridges between him and orthodox Catholicism, was not yet fully known; but the *Address to the Christian Nobility* had made him a national champion among those who, like Hutten, saw in the struggle against Rome an affair of national honor. From theologians,[90] from humanists like Crotus, from

[85] Cyprian, "Nützliche Urkunden," I, 1, 476 ff. See *EA*, XXXVI, 248, n. 3. See also Hans von Schubert, "Die Vorgeschichte der Berufung Luthers auf den Reichstag zu Worms 1521," *Sitzungsberichte der Heidelberger Akademie der Wissenschaften, phil.-hist. Klasse*, VI (1912), 19 f.

[86] "Exemplar literarum apostolicarum seu apostaticarum." Letter to Johann von Gräfendorf, Oct. 30, 1520, *WAB*, II, 207. One was left for Duke John by Eck on his return through Coburg and was forwarded by the duke to the Wittenberg faculty with a request for suggestions as to his conduct. See *WAB*, II, 194.

[87] See Luther's letters: to John Frederick of Saxony, Oct. 30, *WAB*, II, 205; to Von Gräfendorf, *WAB*, II, 206 f.; to Spalatin, Nov. 4, *WAB*, II, 211.

[88] Letter from Barnim to Luther, Oct. 20, *WAB*, II, 203 f.

[89] The letter has been lost. See, however, Martin's reply, Oct. 30, 1520, *WAB*, II, 205 ff. A further letter came from the young duke on December 20, 1520. *WAB*, II, 237 f.

[90] See the very *précieuse* letter from Sebastian Hofmeister, a Franciscan doctor of theology in Konstanz, *WAB*, II, 209.

members of the lower nobility like Hutten, there were offers of support and ardent appeals to him to go forward in the struggle. He must have been touched even more deeply by evidences of personal devotion which came to him from those nearer his own circle. Such was a legacy of one hundred florins which he received from Heinrich Schmiedberg in the early November days when he was suffering under the first impact of the bull. Schmiedberg, chancellor of the bishop of Naumburg and Freising, was one of those officials who now had to choose between the demands of Eck for the publication of the bull and those of his own conscience, backed by popular feeling in the diocese. In his desperation of soul Schmiedberg, who had been one of the sympathizers with Martin at the Leipzig disputation, arranged for a conference with him at nearby Eilenburg. Death overtook him before this meeting. The legacy, concrete evidence of his sympathy, made a deep impression on Luther, who contrasts this gift with that which Duke George had made to Eck in the preceding year "in contempt of God's order." [91] What delights Martin most is that his enemies will now be tormented by the thought that Dr. Schmiedberg, who died in the Christian faith, had by this act publicly commended his teaching. "You see then," he adds in informing Spalatin of the affair, "the presence of Christ."

One of the first methods of counterattack that suggested itself to Luther was an appeal to a council of the Church. Soon after the bull arrived in Wittenberg Martin turned to the city council with a request that it support a renewal of his appeal of two years before.[92] The elector was away on the Rhine and the prudent officials delayed action. On November 4 Martin rejects Spalatin's suggestion that he write privately to the princes and declares that he will repeat his appeal to the council in a public broadside, inviting all Germans to join with him.[93] Two weeks later this appeal came from the press, both in Latin and in German.[94]

In the formal style of a juristic document Luther calls attention to his previous appeal. The Pope continues his tyranny and has now condemned him and his books; he therefore renews again his demand for a council of the Church. Solemnly he arraigns Leo, who without hearing him has pronounced him a heretic and an apostate and has commanded him to deny that faith is necessary in the sacraments. The Pope is himself a heretic for

[91] Letter from Luther to Spalatin, November 13, *WAB*, II, 214.

[92] See the letter of the Wittenberg council to the electoral councilors, Cyprian, "Nützliche Urkunden," I, 1, 474, and the answer of the latter, *ibid.*, II, 186 f.

[93] Letter to Spalatin, *WAB*, II, 211.

[94] *Appellatio . . . ad Concilium a Leone X. denuo repetita et innovata. WA*, VII, 75 ff. There is no evidence that the formalities of certification and posting were fulfilled, as had been done on Luther's return from Augsburg in November, 1518.

putting forward his own empty words against those of sacred Scripture, for contempt of the sacred Church of God, for blasphemy, for pride, and for denying the authority of the council. The emperor, electors, princes, nobility, and Christian officials of Germany are called upon to support the appeal and oppose the incredible insanity of the Pope, thus postponing the execution of the bull until a council shall have been convoked. In conclusion Martin declares that he has now freed his conscience in the face of all who persist in obeying the Pope and is prepared therefore to confront the judgment of God on the Last Day.

In addition to the Latin text, a somewhat briefer and less formal version was prepared in German for the laity.[95] This was printed eight times within the two months following, at Wittenberg, Augsburg and Strasbourg presses, so great was the keenness of popular interest in Martin's defense.

[95] *Appellation oder Berufung an ein christlich frei Concilium von dem Papst Leo und seinem unrechten Frevel verneuert und repetirt. WA,* VII, 85 ff.

30

BOOK-BURNING ON
RHINE AND ELBE

"O WOULD that Charles were the man to attack these Satans in defense of Christ!"[1] This pessimistic cry of Martin's when at last he has the text of the bull before him shows that he has now no hope of support for his cause from the young emperor, who was just in the midst of preparations for his coronation at Aachen. "Put not your trust in princes!" This warning comes from Martin again and again during the autumn days, when he must have been following the negotiations between the German princes and the imperial councilors as closely as was permitted by letters from Spalatin (now lost) and information received through the electoral officials in Wittenberg. The scene of these negotiations was Cologne, where Frederick and the other electors were awaiting the coronation festivities and anxiously taking counsel lest something hinder imperial confirmation of the "electoral capitulation" that had been a condition of their support of Charles and was now to be reaffirmed before the crown of Germany should decorate the head of the young sovereign. " 'The heathen rage,' " Martin writes, " 'and the people imagined vain things. The kings of the earth set themselves together and the princes plotted against God and against His anointed.' Here you have the office and effort of princes, kings, and bishops toward the word of Christ. . . . The affair of God is secret and spiritual. It is not a matter for the public as these are."[2] It is no wonder that anyone who looks at the matter according to office and honor should cry out today, he writes Spalatin early in November,[3] perhaps after receipt of a letter setting forth the political situation in Cologne. He himself commits the whole affair to God. A few days later he notes as an old story that no hope is to be expected from Charles's court.[4] On November 28 Elector Frederick is back in Eilenburg,

---

[1] Letter to Spalatin, Oct. 11, 1520, *WAB*, II, 195.
[2] Letter to Michael Muris, October 20, *WAB*, II, 201 f.
[3] *WAB*, II, 211.
[4] Letter from Luther to Spalatin, November 13, *WAB*, II, 213.

and Martin, like others of his subjects, feels renewed hope from his return.[5]

In the three months of the elector's absence the storm center of Luther's struggle had moved to the Rhine.[6] There the tempest was to increase in violence and reach its crest when the April days of the following year brought Martin into the brilliant spotlight of the German political stage. Again, as two years before at Augsburg, the fate of the monk and his work was entangled in the skein of European politics, but now the circle of his opponents was greatly widened and the struggle was certain to be a protracted one. At Augsburg Luther was known only as a monkish rebel against theological dogmas. At Worms he was to appear as the champion of a reform whose political and social aspects were recognized everywhere by prince, knight, and burgher.

Among the German electoral princes and their councilors gathered in Cologne in late September, there could hardly have been anyone who doubted that the next few months must bring to explosion the great conflict between Habsburg and Valois. None could have foreseen that this conflict, which was to fill Europe for a decade with its thunders, would coincide with a religious schism in Germany which should divide Christendom for centuries, or that the monk who must have appeared to all except Elector Frederick merely as a peculiarly refractory and troublesome theologian with a gift for exciting the popular mind, was creating a rift in the German people that generations could not avail to close.

Young Charles had come to the realm of his ancestors as an unknown figure. He still lacked some months of his twenty-first birthday. He bore certain characteristics of face and feature that distinguished the Habsburgs before and since.[7] An acute sufferer from adenoids, he experienced a difficulty in breathing which gave to the lower part of his face a weakness that did not belong to his character. He was well trained in the sports and graces of that romantic knighthood whose revival had been a passion of his grandfather Maximilian. He had the capacity for resolute action that characterized another ancestor, Charles of Burgundy, and the reserve that might have been expected from the descendant of two Spanish royal houses. In training the young man to whom Luther's case was now to be submitted was in no way either Spanish or German. The first great ruler of

[5] See Luther's letter to Lang, November 28, *WAB*, II, 218 f. and Clemen's note, *ibid.*, p. 219, n. 1.
[6] Frederick had left Lochau late in August and after a deliberate journey through his Thuringian territories had arrived at Cologne a month later, remaining there until November 7. Spalatin, "Chronicon sive Annales," in Mencke, *Scriptores Rerum Germanicarum*, II, 602 ff.
[7] See the vivid description of him by Francesco Cornaro quoted by Kalkoff, "Briefe, Depeschen und Berichte vom Wormer Reichstag 1521," *SVRG*, LIX (1898), 20 ff.

Germanic and Romance peoples since Charlemagne was in his meager intellectual culture a son of the French-speaking Netherlands. Commanding little Spanish and not a word of German, he had been surrounded from youth by members of the Walloon aristocracy, like William of Croy, Lord of Chièvres, and Jean Carandolet, bishop of Palermo. From earliest youth he grew up amid the traditions of the house of Burgundy, and it was by means of personalities and methods of administration of the Burgundian court that he initiated and carried on his foreign policies after he had attained to his great Spanish and Austrian inheritance. Later on Charles was to develop into a statesman of great originality and daring. At the moment when the crown of Charlemagne was placed on his head he was still a pupil of the astute De Croy, the instructor of his youth, and of Gattinara, his clever chancellor.

The men who surrounded Charles when he became emperor were, in the main, churchmen, but solely because the custom of the day made the Church a convenient source from which rulers might take power and wealth to reward their advisers. Charles was himself, however, of a strongly devout nature which remained unaffected by his diplomatic and military conflicts with the Roman hierarchy. No traces of a mystical or reformatory character seem to have entered into the religious training of this heir of the Catholic kings. His zealous fulfillment of religious forms made an impression on Italian and German observers. When at Worms the Roman legates worked on the young ruler through his Franciscan confessor, Glapion, his response to appeals to put down the rising heresy was spontaneous and immediate. The difficulties encountered by the policy of Rome in its attack on Luther were due to a statecraft which originated with the imperial advisers and to which Charles made only the most necessary concessions.

This then was the youthful ruler in whom Hutten and the humanists and to some extent Luther himself had placed their hopes. When after a long struggle with the estates of Aragon and Castile and the diplomatic chess move of a brief visit to England the young sovereign landed at Flushing, he was still almost an unknown quantity to his German subjects. He was met by high expectations from the empire, where the great potential power of its chosen ruler had already shown itself a unifying influence. Attempts at dissension which arose after his election had been checked.[8] Even Elector Frederick, discontented with the delay in summoning the Diet and disappointed because Charles's sister, the promised bride of the heir of Saxony, had not arrived,[9] was mollified by the conciliatory attitude

[8] *DRA*, II, 1 f.   [9] *Ibid.*, p. 32, n. 1.

of the emperor's representative, and his delegates were among those Germans
who crowded the court at Brussels to greet the young ruler.[10] Apparently
some mistrust remained in the minds of the Saxon court, but the tactful
efforts of the imperial councilors brought Frederick to join the other electors
at Cologne in the last week of September. Here a fear of the plague and
an attack of the gout prevented his attendance at the coronation,[11] which
was held with great pomp at Aachen, but he saw Charles soon afterward
in Cologne and was received with much respect by the emperor and his
courtiers.[12]

In the meantime, however, another figure had appeared on the scene,
one destined to play a leading rôle in the effort of the Church to crush
the new heresy. This was Hieronymus Aleander, the papal nuncio.[13] As
bearer of a commission similar to Eck's, he had set forth about the same
time as the Dominican to carry the Roman bull of condemnation into
Western Germany. Of the two clerical enemies who came to direct the
papal fulminations against Martin, Aleander was by far the most dangerous.
While he lacked the wide learning in theology and the furious and vindictive sincerity of the Ingolstadt professor, he had all the urbane culture of
Italian and French humanism and the supple diplomacy trained in a long
experience at episcopal and papal courts. Joined to these was an unusual
objectivity in the judgment of men and events and an ability to recognize
the realities of a situation and the means necessary to meet the crisis. More
clearly than his contemporaries he foresaw what the Lutheran revolt would
mean to the Church unless checked at the beginning, and he was keenly
aware of the basic evils that afflicted the relations of the Roman See with
Germany.[14] He had none of the *furor theologicus* of his day, and his treatment of Erasmus showed that he was not disposed to persecute a defeated
enemy. Aleander's keen intelligence and the adaptable temper that enabled
him to attain his goal, the mobilization of the imperial forces against Luther,
when Cajetan and Eck had failed in reaching theirs, did not suffice for an

---

[10] *Ibid.*, pp. 66 ff.   [11] *Ibid.*, p. 86.   [12] *Ibid.*, p. 102.

[13] For the earlier sources regarding Aleander, see Kalkoff, *Depeschen*, pp. 2 f. The dispatches
of Aleander to the papal court, written in Italian interspersed with Latin, are not available,
but copies derived from preliminary drafts, in part corrected by Aleander himself, are preserved
in the Vatican library. These were published by Balan in *Monumenta Reformationis Lutheranae
ex Tabulariis secretioribus S. Sedis 1521–1525,* and by Theodor Brieger in his "Aleander und
Luther 1521," *Quellen und Forschungen zur Geschichte der Reformation,* Vol. I. Brieger's
arrangement follows a more careful chronological order and was used by Kalkoff in his
German translation of the dispatches published in *Depeschen des Nuntius Aleander.* I have
used Brieger, checking his text from Balan where doubt arises. The *Deutsche Reichstagsakten*
uses the Vatican codices.

[14] Brieger, "Aleander," pp. 30 f. and 43, and Kalkoff, *Depeschen,* pp. 48 and 63.

understanding of Luther's character and efforts. Like many Italians of his day he had a native, although well concealed, contempt for German coarseness and violence, and like his fellow Italians, for the most part, he failed to understand the profound ethical and religious forces that gave such power to the movement initiated by Luther. In the history of the German Church the results of Aleander's efforts were, like Alba's in the Netherlands, negative rather than positive. Nevertheless he is entitled to be called a father of the Counter Reformation.

The papal envoy was filled with a whole-hearted desire to stamp out the Lutheran heresy by the full enlistment of the temporal power. In seeking to do this, Aleander showed a keen delight in the game itself, the playing upon the keys and stops of faith and prejudice and greed. His dispatches to the papal court show the concentration of interest in the human actor that is so marked a characteristic of the Italian Renaissance. With great skill he draws and then touches and retouches with lingering pen the portraits of the princes and clergy with whom he has to deal. Plainly he desires to impress the Medici with his grasp of the situation. He shows, too, the dialectical power that has been an Italian intellectual inheritance since St. Thomas and Dante. Despite these gifts, however, he was often obliged to work in the dark, as his mandate made him subordinate to the other papal nuncio, Marino Caracciolo,[15] a wily diplomat with three years' experience in Germany, whither Aleander now came for the first time. At first Leo's advisers seem to have had no great confidence in the discretion of their humanistic emissary. Of the political negotiations by which Leo tried to play off the French king against the emperor, Aleander was told nothing, although a knowledge of these was of critical importance in the struggle against Luther's protector Frederick. An effort to gain light on such moves evoked an immediate rebuff from Rome and the limitations of his mission were brought sharply to Aleander's attention. His supply of papal privileges and gifts, such as benefices, titles, and offices, for the purchase of cooperation by the clergy was far more limited than that of his colleague.[16] Gradually as his dispatches gave the Pope's advisers a clearer insight into the danger of the German situation, they moved to give the harassed envoy full cooperation.

Along with rare qualities, this attorney for Martin's foes had a training

[15] See Paquier, *L'Humanisme et la Réforme*, pp. 148 f. and notes; see also *ibid.*, pp. 368 ff.; see also Kalkoff, *Aleander gegen Luther*, p. 9.

[16] See Kalkoff, *Forschungen*, pp. 62 f. and 180 ff. For Aleander's commission of July 16, see Kalkoff, *Aleander gegen Luther*, pp. 17 f. The request on the part of the nuncio that his armament of privileges be increased was refused. See also Balan, *Monumenta*, pp. 10 f., and Kalkoff, *Aleander gegen Luther*, pp. 11 f., 14 f.

that fitted him well for his task.[17] Born three years before Luther in a middle-class family at Motta, near Venice, Aleander seems to have attained as a boy in his native city and the neighboring Padua a recognized competence in Greek, for he became proofreader and editor to the firm of Aldus, which was at that time bringing out its great editions of the classics. During Erasmus's first visit to Italy in 1508, the two humanists lived together and Aleander worked closely with the Dutch scholar at the Aldine press. As a rising young scholar he was called to the university at Paris, where his lectures enjoyed wide popularity and where five years later he became rector. His contribution to the rise of Greek studies during his teaching at the Collège de la Marche entitle him to be called one of the founders of humanistic scholarship in France.[18] His erudition and ready although somewhat stiff Latin style brought him service under the bishop of Paris, then vice-chancellor of France. This administrative and diplomatic experience was extended when he became chancellor of Eberhard de la Mark, the vigorous and rapacious bishop of Liége. From this office he returned to Rome in 1516, where his talents found speedy recognition at the Vatican. He was appointed secretary to the Pope's nephew and vice-chancellor, Julius de Medici, and he later became papal librarian. His course of life was marked by the same indifference to the oath of chastity that characterized other Italian clerics of high degree in the Renaissance period.[19] His selection as nuncio to bring the bull of condemnation to Western Germany was due no doubt to his acquaintance with influential persons, lay and clerical, in the Netherlands and to his relations with university men in this region, for in Rome, as in Germany, the struggle against Luther's aberration was recognized as an affair in which the universities must play an important part. In this field the attitude of Hutten and other humanistic followers of Reuchlin was recognized by the papal councilors as a great source of danger.

Armed with the bull and bearing the papal instructions and safe conduct, the nuncio came northward. He was directed to go straight to Charles and gain his intervention with the German princes and bishops.[20] He was especially warned to resist efforts to give the Wittenberg heretic a public hearing.

[17] See Paquier, *L'Humanisme et la Réforme*.

[18] See Jovy, *François Tissard et Jérôme Aléandre. Contribution à l'histoire des études grecques en France*, Vol. III. Jovy lists fourteen scholarly works edited or written by Alexander during his second stay in France, in 1511–14, including a Greek grammar and a Greek dictionary. *Ibid.*, pp. 195 ff. For the high opinion of Aleander's scholarship, see *ibid.*, pp. 5 f.

[19] He was the father of at least two children and greeted with personal interest Hutten's work on a cure for syphilis, *De Guaiaci medicina et morbo Gallico*. Kalkoff, *Aleander gegen Luther*, pp. 143 f.

[20] Balan, *Monumenta*, pp. 4 f., 8 ff.

Cooperation in this campaign was to be assured by a close liaison with Eck and frequent reports to Rome. After a long delay, probably in Florence in attendance on the papal vice-chancellor Julius,[21] and a brief detention by the French authorities, Aleander arrived in Antwerp on September 26. Here he found the young emperor deep in negotiations with the Brabant estates and surrounded by a crowd of officials and foreign envoys. In spite of this, the energetic nuncio succeeded two days after his arrival in opening the doors to the presence of Charles, where he and his colleague Caracciolo presented the bull and the Pope's letter and met a cordial response.[22]

The delighted Aleander received at once an order valid in Burgundy and the Low Countries for the confiscation and burning of heretical books.[23] The nuncio seems to have had high hopes of lighting the flames under Luther's works in Antwerp on the following day,[24] but legal formalities prevented it,[25] and Martin's books were burned for the first time in solemn form on the market place of the university town of Louvain. Here Aleander came into contact with Erasmus, his old associate in the labors of humanism. As we have seen, the latter had now been for three years in Louvain as a member of the theological faculty and had carried on there a constant warfare with the enemies of the Trilingual College and of humanism generally. Brief armistices interrupted the strife,[26] but it broke out ever anew against the acid-tongued scholar. One of Erasmus's chief enemies was Jakob Hochstraten, and this tireless persecutor of heretics and his associates were quick to connect the hated humanist with Luther's work.[27] The publication of Erasmus's letter to Luther of May, 1519, and especially his letter of October, 1519, to Albert of Mainz, had given color to this charge.[28] Erasmus had seen the storm approaching and had sought to keep his cause separate from

[21] This is Kalkoff's hypothesis in "Die Anfänge der Gegenreformation in den Niederlanden," *SVRG*, XXI (1903), No. 79, p. 8 and n. 4.

[22] See Aleander's letter to Rome, late September, 1520, in Friedensburg, *Quellen und Forschungen*, I, 150 ff.; see also his letter to Copis from Aix, Oct. 24, 1520, *DRA*, II, 456, n. 1.

[23] Letter from Aleander to Leo X, Oct. 23, 1520, *DRA*, II, 454 f.; Kalkoff, *Depeschen*, p. 19.

[24] See n. 22, above.

[25] Paquier, *L'Humanisme et la Réforme*, p. 153.

[26] Kalkoff, "Anfänge der Gegenreformation," pp. 65 ff.; letters from Erasmus to William Blount and Cuthbert Tunstall, Oct. 16, 1519, in Allen, *Opus epistolarum Erasmi*, IV, 90, 91.

[27] For references to Erasmus's enmity with Hochstraten see the following letters, reproduced by Allen: to Hochstraten, Aug. 11, 1519, *ibid.*, pp. 42 ff.; to Ortwin Gratius, Oct.(?) 15, 1519, pp. 85 f.; to Martin Lypsius, Nov.(?), 1519, p. 119. For some of the many references in Erasmus's correspondence to the accusation that he was connected with Luther's work, see his letters to Albert of Mainz, Oct. 19, 1519, *ibid.*, p. 102; to Jodocus Jonas, Nov. 11, 1520, p. 375; and to Richard Pace, July 5, 1521, p. 541. See also the letter to Campegio, May 1, 1519, *ibid.*, III, 574.

[28] *Ibid.*, p. 605; IV, 96 ff.

that of the aggressive Wittenberg professor,[29] an arrangement which, as we have seen, Luther willingly accepted.[30] Whatever position Erasmus might assume, however, his enemies had no intention of permitting him to evade responsibility. They knew only too well his great prestige among the humanists. Zeal for the faith was joined in their hearts with a desire to seize the opportunity for revenge on the hated leader of a hated group. By the fall of 1520 Erasmus was well aware that the Dominicans and Carmelites in Louvain were seething with hostility against him.[31] With the arrival of Aleander this feeling reached a climax.

The burning of Martin's books, along with the writings of others, took place at the hands of the public executioner on October 8 on the market square of the university town. The papal nuncio rubs his hands with satisfaction in reporting to Rome this auto-da-fé, which was witnessed by distinguished representatives of the imperial court and of foreign powers.[32] Erasmus, if we accept him as being the author of the biting satire, the *Acts of the Louvain Academy*,[33] gives a very different account of the proceedings. According to this, the theological faculty tricked the university into giving consent to the burning.[34] Other sources friendly to Luther report that the students pressed forward and threw on the fire well-known works of scholastic pedagogy and that considerable rowdyism followed.[35] The public act of condemnation awakened a powerful repercussion among the Rhenish humanists; and the Louvain theologians, who had sent a delegation to assist at the conflagration, began to become nervous at the responsibility they had assumed.[36] Whatever pressure it may have been necessary to exert

[29] For this reason Erasmus was distressed that his letter to Albert had been published, by Hutten as he thought. According to Kalkoff, Jakob Wimpfeling had the letter printed and sent it to the bishop of Basel, begging him to intervene with the Vatican. See Kalkoff, "Die Stellung der deutschen Humanisten zur Reformation," ZKG, XLVI, N.F. IX (1928), 170 f.

[30] See Clemen's introduction to the letter from Erasmus to Luther, Aug. 1, 1520, WAB, II, 155.

[31] Letter from Erasmus to Albert of Mainz, Oct. 8, 1520, in Allen, *Opus epistolarum Erasmi*, IV, 361. See also Kalkoff, "Anfänge der Gegenreformation," p. 74 and n. 27.

[32] Letter from Aleander to Leo X, Oct. 23, 1520, DRA, II, 455; Kalkoff, *Depeschen*, p. 20.

[33] Published in 1520. See EA, XXXV, 310 ff., for text. See also Kalkoff, "Die Vermittlungspolitik des Erasmus und sein Anteil an den Flugschriften der ersten Reformationszeit," ARG, I (1903–4), 29.

[34] Erasmus was not invited when the bull was laid before the theological faculty at the house of Rosemund, its dean, and he was excluded from subsequent meetings. The three months following were filled with attacks by his opponents. Allen, *Opus epistolarum Erasmi*, IV, 375, 398. In the meantime Erasmus delivered a counterattack in his bitterly sarcastic *Axiomata* and in the *Acta academiae Lovaniensis*, which is in all probability his work.

[35] EA, XXXVI, 238 ff.; see also Kalkoff, "Anfänge der Gegenreformation," p. 22 and n. 37, and Enders, *Briefwechsel*, II, 534, n. 6.

[36] Latomus declared that the theological faculty had only "permitted" the burning ("passi

at Louvain, in Liége, where Aleander was fully at home, the task was easier,[37] for here he needed only a mandate from his patron and friend, the bishop, in order to burn Luther's books. This took place on October 17. The mandate of the clerical despot against Luther and his followers was so thoroughgoing that Aleander held it up as a model for all future edicts.[38]

On October 28 the nuncio arrived at Cologne with the imperial party and at once sought out the arch enemy of heretics and humanists, Hochstraten.[39] Aleander had already delighted the Dominican theologian on his passage through Cologne a month earlier by the presentation of the papal edict canceling the decision of the commission favorable to Reuchlin and restoring Hochstraten to his inquisitorial office. The first effort of the two papal envoys was of course directed at the elector of Saxony, who had been in the Rhenish city for more than a month in conference with his fellow-electors on the state of the empire. Now that Emperor Charles was at Cologne, Frederick, who had not taken a personal part in the coronation, had an opportunity to greet him for the first time. It is hardly likely that Luther became a subject of discussion in the midst of the many affairs occupying the emperor and the electors.[40] It is however possible that Frederick took this opportunity to deliver to the imperial court the letter and the "Offer" which Martin had prepared at his request two months earlier.[41] In view of the careful nature of Frederick's diplomacy and the emphasis which the age laid upon the meticulous assertion of rights and privileges, it is probable that the presentation of these two documents was regarded by Luther and his advisers as a formal assertion of the legal right to a hearing. The "Offer" was at this time

---

sumus"). Kalkoff, "Anfänge der Gegenreformation," p. 80 and n. 38. See also letter from Crotus to Luther, Dec. 5, 1520, *WAB*, II, 227, ll. 43 ff.

[37] See Kalkoff, "Anfänge der Gegenreformation," p. 25. Aleander's brother was now secretary to Bishop Eberhard, Aleander's former patron. *Ibid.*, pp. 34 f.; see also Paquier, *L'Humanisme et la Réforme*, pp. 275 ff. and n. 4.

[38] Letter from Aleander to Leo X, Oct. 23, 1520, *DRA*, II, 456; Kalkoff, *Depeschen*, p. 21.

[39] Letter from Aleander to Leo X, Oct. 30, *DRA*, II, 459; Kalkoff, *Depeschen*, p. 25; see also Kalkoff, "Anfänge der Gegenreformation," pp. 82 f.

[40] Kalkoff assumes that it did and that the emperor made at this time a verbal promise that Luther should be given a hearing. "Zu Luthers römischem Prozess," *ZKG*, XXV, 548 f., 583 f. The only evidence we have of a meeting between Charles and Frederick is a letter from Frederick to Duke John on October 31, in which it is stated that they met after Mass, in the sacristy of the church, and that the emperor agreed to convene the Diet at Worms. *DRA*, II, 136.

[41] Kalkoff, *Die Entstehung des Wormser Edikts*, p. 32, note, assumes that the presentation of the *Oblatio* or "Offer" by Luther was the first necessary legal step in obtaining the course of justice. See also his statement concerning the importance of Articles 17 and 24 of the *Wahlkapitulation* as guarantees of the right of a subject to be tried in the empire and as a protection against the imperial ban until he should be heard. "Zu Luthers römischem Prozess," *ZGK*, XXV, 543 ff., 553 f.

posted on a public placard in Cologne.[42] What went on between Frederick and the emperor was of course unknown to Aleander, but his sources of information were adequate to show him the difficulties that lay in his way. He knew that the Saxon councilors were friends and supporters of Luther and can hardly have been unaware that Erasmus was on terms of friendship with Frederick.[43] He must have known also that among other visitors to the lodgings of the elector was Franz von Sickingen, now in high favor with the emperor and still the protector of Hutten. The latter loomed more and more threateningly on the horizon. He published further installments of his furious attack on the Roman court,[44] and after his arrival in Cologne Aleander was shown a bitter letter from the Frankish knight addressed to Charles.[45] A personal encounter between Hutten and Hochstraten had taken place near Louvain a month before,[46] and the terror of the Dominican at this meeting gave the humanists material for malicious joy.[47] The nuncio watched with growing nervousness the doings of this restless guest at Sickingen's neighboring castle of Ebernburg.[48]

It was therefore in none too optimistic a mood that the two Roman envoys finally broke through the barriers of ceremonious defense with which German princes, and particularly Frederick, were surrounded, and caught the elector on his way to church at the Franciscan monastery.[49] The result of this first interview left Aleander somewhat encouraged. His dispatch reporting a second conference with Frederick has been lost,[50] but it seems probable

[42] Letter from Sickingen to Luther, Nov. 3, *WAB*, II, 208.

[43] On November 5 Erasmus was summoned by the elector to give his advice. Spalatin, *Annales Reformationis*, Cyprian ed., II, 28. On this occasion he is said to have made the famous answer that Luther had committed two sins in that he had touched the crown of the pope and the bellies of the monks. Later on he wrote for Spalatin his *Axiomata* (*EA*, XXXVI, 241 f.), approving Luther's offer to go before impartial judges. Luther in the following decade confirmed the report of Erasmus's interview with Frederick. He says that the elector gave the humanist on that occasion a damask coat ("damaskgatt"), but afterwards remarked to Spalatin, "Qualis ille vir est? Weiss man doch nicht wie man mit im dran ist." *TR*, IV, No. 4899

[44] The *Dialogus Bulla*, Hutten, *Opera*, IV, 332 ff., and the *Epistola Udelonis Cymbri Cusani de Exustione Librorum Lutheri, ibid.*, III, 460 f.

[45] Published in Hutten, *Opera*, I, 371 ff. See Aleander's letter to Leo X, November 6, *DRA*, II, 460; Kalkoff, *Depeschen*, p. 26.

[46] Kalkoff, *Ulrich von Hutten und die Reformation*, pp. 234 ff.; "Zu Luthers römischem Prozess, Fortsetzung," *ZKG*, XXXII, 65 f.

[47] Letter from Crotus to Luther, Dec. 5, *WAB*, II, 227.

[48] A report that Hutten had made an attack on Aleander and Caracciolo reached Wittenberg about the middle of November, bringing pleasure to Luther, who wished that the knight might have captured these enemies. Letter from Luther to Spalatin, Nov. 13, *WAB*, II, 213.

[49] Letter from Aleander to Leo X, Nov. 6, 1520, also the Saxon report, Nov. 4 and 6, *DRA*, II, 461 ff.; Kalkoff, *Depeschen*, p. 28.

[50] *DRA*, II, 461, n. 4.

that he took this opportunity to hand to the elector the papal letter, perhaps a duplicate of that sent by Eck to Duke John.[51] A brief official report of the interview from the Saxon side [52] tells us that after a plea by Aleander for the execution of the bull, the elector promised to take the matter under consideration. Two days later, on November 6, Frederick made a formal reply consisting of a diplomatic complaint against the action of Eck and a defense of Luther on the lines of the latter's "Offer." The elector asks that the legates exert themselves to have Luther's case brought before a just tribunal.[53] In their reply the legates pointed out that the Pope had made efforts to bring Luther into the right path and insisted that His Holiness was the only judge in matters of faith. They declared that no other course was now open to the elector and his colleagues than to have Luther's books burned. Aleander added that the Pope did not wish "to make his hands greasy with Luther's blood." [54]

Before his meeting with the elector, Aleander had already set into motion machinery for a second solemn burning of Luther's books. A conference was held with representatives of the Cologne university and of the city guilds and four days later the bull was brought before the faculty of the university.[55] In view of the attacks of Erasmus on the validity of the proceedings in the Louvain faculty, precautions were taken at this conference to have the bull carefully checked and certified, with the observance of all formalities. The members of the faculty present, whose authority to act for the entire body did not pass unquestioned, referred Aleander to the archbishop and the civil authorities for burning the condemned books,[56] and the rite was then carried out in the presence of representatives of the archbishop. Warned by their experience at Louvain, Aleander seems to have staged this act of faith without publicity. Two weeks later an attempt at the execution of the bull at the archiepiscopal seat of Mainz turned out a fiasco and gave material to humanistic pens, whose satires had already irritated the temper and made more difficult the task of the envoys. Aleander was charged with

---

[51] Published in Walch, *Schriften*, XV, 1666 f.

[52] Probably prepared by Spalatin; published in Latin (*EA*, XXXVI, 243 ff.) and in a somewhat briefer form in German (Walch, *Schriften*, XV, 1919 f.). Both forms were printed and circulated during the meeting of the Diet at Worms. See *DRA*, II, 462. The official character of the report is attested by the fact that during his journey home the elector sent copies to the rector of the university at Wittenberg, where Luther saw it. See Luther's letters: to Lang, Nov. 28, *WAB*, II, 218 f.; to Spalatin, Nov. 29, *WAB*, II, 221.

[53] *DRA*, II, 465.   [54] *Ibid.*, p. 466.

[55] Letter from Aleander to Leo X, Nov. 6, 1520, *DRA*, II, 460; see also Kalkoff, *Aleander gegen Luther*, p. 37 and n. 1.

[56] For the minutes of the university faculty see *EA*, XXXV, 182 ff. See also Kalkoff, *Aleander gegen Luther*, pp. 39 f.

being a Jew and a traitor to the cause of good letters.[57] The humanists of Cologne, who especially resented his alliance with Hochstraten, composed dialogues against him and posted insulting songs on academic doors. Aleander even feared for his life and was assured by many well-informed persons that Hutten was laying traps for him.[58]

Still more humiliating, then, was the collapse of the auto-da-fé which had been set for November 28 in Mainz. The emperor had left the city and there was no shock battalion of scholastic theologians as in Louvain and Cologne to deliver the attack. As pictured from the humanistic side,[59] the first attempt to burn Luther's works was a failure, as the executioner refused to light the fire, and Aleander just escaped being stoned. On the next day the archbishop and cathedral canons intervened and some books were burned on the market place by the city flayer. A humanist who was present [60] reported that these were not Luther's books but those of Eneo Silvio, Prierias, and Eck. In the following night a "hateful poem" was posted on Aleander's door and elsewhere. The affair gave Hutten material for his satire: *Lament over the Lutheran Burning at Mainz*.[61] In spite of these protests and the conviction that he had as his enemies the nobility of the region, the unterrified nuncio regarded the effort to burn the books of this "heretic worse than a thousand Ariuses" [62] as worthy of all his efforts on account of its effect on the laity.

The news of these events must have come through to Luther slowly. Two weeks after the burning of his books in Cologne he writes to friend Lang of the affair, briefly and without passion, enclosing at the same time the "learned and sharp" reply of the elector to Aleander, which has come

[57] See the letter from Aleander to Medici, Dec., 1520, Brieger, "Aleander," p. 28. See also p. 623, n. 41 below.

[58] Letter from Aleander to Leo X, Nov. 6, *DRA*, II, 460 f.

[59] See the letter from Beatus Rhenanus to Amerbach, Jan. 7, 1521, from Mainz, in *Briefwechsel des Beatus Rhenanus*, ed. by Horawitz and Hartfelder, pp. 266 f.; see also letter from Hedio to Zwingli, Dec. 21, 1520, in Hutten, *Opera*, I, 438. Hutten seems to have had the news of the fiasco on the day of its occurrence. See his letter to Bucer, Nov. 28, *ibid.*, pp. 428 f.; see also letter from Hutten to Luther, Dec. 9, *WAB*, II, 232.

[60] Hedio. See n. 59 above.

[61] *Eyn Klag über den Lutherisch Brandt zu Mentz*, Hutten, *Opera*, III, 455 ff. Earlier in the fall Hutten had published a Latin pamphlet, *In incendium Lutherianum exclamatio, ibid.*, pp. 453 ff., called forth by the book-burning at Cologne. Also other humanists began immediately to issue pamphlets in protest, e.g., Franciscus Faber (1497–1565), "Silva de incendio Lutheranorum." See Ellinger, *Geschichte der neulateinischen Literatur Deutschlands im sechzehnten Jahrhundert*, I, 478.

[62] ". . . più che mille Arii." Letter from Aleander to Medici, dated "fortasse 12. Januar 1521" by Balan, *Monumenta*, p. 24, and December 14, 1520, by Kalkoff. The Trient MS, on which Brieger's text is based, omits the comparison. See Brieger, "Aleander," p. 18. Kalkoff mistranslates it in *Depeschen*, p. 30.

to the university.[63] One of the published attacks of the humanists directed against the nuncio has also come to Luther's attention, and he remarks on this too without passion. Unfortunately a letter to Spalatin which might afford a deeper insight into Martin's feelings at this time has been lost.[64]

There are signs which indicate that Frederick grew wary after leaving Cologne. The bold mood which had dictated the reply to the papal nuncios gave way, and the natural caution of his character again came to the fore. Other events may well have caused him to hesitate. His plans for a politically significant marriage for his nephew and heir had thus far met with little success.[65] The importance of another international match for his nephew, that with the sister of Charles, now loomed greater than before.[66] The general staff at the Vatican may also have used more than one avenue to send Frederick reminders of his duty to the faith of his fathers. One of these pleas reached him soon after his return to Saxony, voiced in two letters from the Italian Urban of Serralonga, whom Luther had encountered two years before at Augsburg.[67] Apparently Spalatin saw how the wind was blowing at court and urged Martin to moderation, a piece of advice which Luther seems to have received in good part.[68] To Frederick's advisers, permeated with the spirit of formality and legality that pervaded every court, Martin's powerful *Against the Bull of Antichrist,* in both its Latin and German forms, must have seemed very incomplete as a rebuttal of the errors listed against him in the Roman bull. At Frederick's request, then, or that of his ministers, Martin undertook to answer these charges systematically and definitely and to defend the condemned articles one by one. The defense was begun in Latin toward the end of November,[69] and by December 3 Spalatin is able to report to Frederick that the "unterrified" Dr. Martinus has it one sixth finished.[70] As usual the printer

[63] November 28, 1520. *WAB*, II, 218 f. See Clemen's note 3, *ibid.*, p. 219.

[64] See Luther's letter to Spalatin, Nov. 29, 1520, *WAB*, II, 220, l. 3.

[65] See *DRA*, I, 121 f., 241, and *passim.*

[66] See Spalatin, *Friedrichs des Weisen Leben und Zeitgeschichte,* ed. by Neudecker and Preller, pp. 58 ff.; Johann G. Droysen, "Über das Verlöbnis der Infantin Katharina mit Herzog Johann Friedrich von Sachsen 1519," *Berichte über die Verhandlungen der königlich sächsischen Gesellschaft der Wissenschaften zu Leipzig, phil.-hist. Klasse,* V (1853), 151 ff.

[67] Cyprian, "Nützliche Urkunden," I, II, 168 ff.; see also Kalkoff, "Zu Luthers römischem Prozess," *ZKG*, XXV, 568 f., n. 2.

[68] Letter from Luther to Spalatin, Dec. 7, *WAB*, II, 229. See Spalatin's letter to the elector, Dec. 3, in Otto Waltz, "Epistolae Reformatorum," *ZKG*, II (1878), 121; and that of the end of November, 1520, in Muther, *Aus dem Universitäts- und Gelehrtenleben,* pp. 429 f. See also Paul Kirn, "Friedrich der Weise und die Kirche," *Beiträge zur Kulturgeschichte des Mittelalters und der Renaissance,* XXX (1926), 141.

[69] Letter from Luther to Spalatin, Nov. 29, 1520, *WAB*, II, 220.

[70] Waltz, "Epistolae Reformatorum," p. 121.

followed closely on Martin's pen. The warm relationship between the Wittenberg professor and the court is attested by Luther's dedication of the work to the elector's councilor Fabian von Feilitzsch. This minister died while the first sheets were still damp from the press, but Martin allowed his inscription to stand as to one "who now lives more than ever." [71] In the midst of many occupations the work dragged and it was not until the middle of January that the *Assertion concerning All the Articles* [72] finally appeared. The preparation of the German form of the work Luther reserved for himself, as he found Spalatin too constrained and timid for such a task. [73] The printing of the edition in the vernacular, *Reason and Cause of All the Articles,* [74] began before the end of the year, but it also came along very slowly and the entire work did not come from the press until early in March. [75]

The Latin form of Luther's defense is a scholarly appeal to the reader interested in theology. In the dedication to Feilitzsch, however, Martin says expressly that it is to the laity who have embraced the truth condemned in the bull that he is addressing his defense of writings burned by incendiaries like those at Cologne and Louvain. He has undertaken the work to meet the wishes of friends. It is, indeed, a time when one should not only know Christ but also defend Him with the sword. He records, first of all, his protest against the interpretation of sacred Scriptures by means of the writings of the holy Fathers instead of the Scriptures themselves. Nowadays men are immersed in human doctrine and attribute the right to interpret Scripture to one man alone, the Roman pontiff, who is hedged about by the most ignorant sophists. Following the method of the university disputation, Luther now sets forth his arguments for the interpretation of the Scriptures in their own spirit. This was the way of the early Church, which as yet had no Augustine or Thomas, but sought the truth in the sacred writings themselves. Augustine and the Fathers are often at odds with each other and no conclusion can be proved from them. "Let no one set up against me the authority of the pope or of any saint unless it is supported by the Scriptures." [76]

Following this defense of his method of seeking the truth, Martin now

---

[71] Letter from Luther to Spalatin, Dec. 7, *WAB,* II, 229 f.

[72] *Assertio omnium articulorum. WA,* VII, 94 ff.

[73] Letter from Luther to Spalatin, Nov. 29, *WAB,* II, 220.

[74] *Grund und Ursach aller Artikel. WA,* VII, 308 ff.

[75] On January 21 he sent Spalatin the first six sheets; on February 17 and 27, further installments. In March came the remainder. See his letters to Spalatin on these days, *WAB,* II, 251, 266, 270, 275, respectively.

[76] *WA,* VII, 98, ll. 35 f.

applies it to the condemned articles. One by one he cites the declarations attributed to him and with scriptural authority defends his position as evangelical and free from heresy. Many of his arguments are merely a repetition of those contained in previous works, such as the Ninety-five Theses, the *Explanations of Indulgences* of 1518, the *Sermon on Penance,* and the great series of sermons of the winter and spring of 1520, as well as in the *Babylonian Captivity.* A few are drawn from the propositions defended at Leipzig. All of these he traverses once more and summarizes his entire theological position in measured terms, more measured and reserved indeed than at any time in the preceding two years. Once more he takes occasion to pass in review the controversies of the past three years. Once more he pushes aside the scholastic refinements that have grown up about the processes by which grace comes to the human heart: the subtle distinction between "attrition" and "contrition," the shadowy character of the *fides acquisita,* the metaphysical attempt to differentiate between "sin" and "defect," [77] the nature of that which remains of sin after baptism, the "tinder" [78] containing the spark of new sin. These superrefined distinctions and featherweight differences are swept aside and again, as four years earlier in the lectures on Romans, Martin lifts up sin into a position of lurid and grandiose importance. How he abominates the word "satisfaction," as if anyone could "satisfy" God for any sin! [79] Faith steps again into the foreground: forgiveness is the transformation which takes place within the believer himself, "with a great concussion of soul." [80] This retracing of his own inner experience brings memories of earlier years in the cloister. The discussion of the second condemned article, that dealing with the remains of sin after baptism, brings up for Martin tormenting memories of the lingering thorn of "concupiscence." Here is a battle that was waged by means of labors and watchings, fastings and prayer, with the help of "all the spiritual machinery," by St. Jerome against the claims of carnal desire, by Cyprian against anger, shamelessness, greed, and ambition. Once more it is Augustine who brings the solution, with his "most beautiful" declaration that sin is not remitted in baptism as if it had not been, but is not imputed to the sinner.

In the light of the condemnation of his theology, Martin examines anew the foundation stones of the new theology. The basic error of the scholastic system, that which had occupied him and Carlstadt for so long, the belief that man can by his own efforts prepare the way for the entry of grace

---

[77] *Ibid.,* p. 108.
[78] "Fomes." *Ibid.,* p. 110, l. 23.
[79] *Ibid.,* p. 113, ll. 16 ff.
[80] *Ibid.,* p. 117, ll. 6 f.

into the heart, comes to the fore again and again as Martin takes up the articles in which his sternly Augustinian attitude is condemned. Earlier, in the *Explanations of the Power of Indulgences* and the *Sermon on Penance,* he had still held himself in leash on this question; now he speaks in ringing and unequivocal tones. Any spark of sin that remains, even if there is no active sin, will restrain the soul from entering heaven. Again he declares the "wretched free will" to be impotent for any good. Man is flesh, flesh is evil, evil are all the things which the free will does when it does all that it can (*quod in se est*).[81] Will and the wisdom of the flesh—these things are death, "For how can man prepare himself for good, when it is not in his power to prepare himself for evil?"[82] He turns as an illustration to the papal bull, whose authors work with all the force of the free will against him and yet, he finds, have delivered themselves in blind ignorance to all errors and heresies. In these scholastic ideas Pelagianism continues to live. His argument on this point is long, he confesses, but he excuses himself on the ground that the truth has been crushed by scholastic authors for more than three hundred years. So infected have men's minds become with these errors that he can now find no allies to stand and carry on the struggle with him.

Here and there Martin professes his willingness to revoke his previous statements, but when he comes to do so, they give place to declarations still more radical and uncompromising. This applies to his view that indulgences are a "feigned and false satisfaction."[83] They are not, as he himself has called them, "pious frauds of the faith," but the "most impious frauds and impostures of the most villainous popes and impostors."[84] He demands that everything he has said previously on this point be burned, and begs his readers not to believe that the rod of divine punishment will be spared, even if the angels should teach it, "still less if the blasphemous dragon of the Roman court roars otherwise."[85] Again, with sarcastic pleasure, he revokes his statement in the disputation with Eck regarding the Council of Constance. He has been charged with saying that some of the articles of Huss condemned by the council were most Christian. Now he withdraws this statement and makes instead of it another declaration: "Not some but all the articles of John Huss were condemned at Constance by Antichrist and his apostles, brought together into a new synagogue of Satan from among the most criminal sophists. In your face, most holy

---

[81] *Ibid.,* p. 142, l. 24.
[83] *Ibid.,* p. 113, ll. 4 f.
[85] *Ibid.,* p. 126, ll. 23 ff.

[82] *Ibid.,* p. 144, ll. 33 f.
[84] *Ibid.,* p. 125, ll. 5 ff.

vicar of God, I say freely that everything by John Huss that was condemned was evangelical and Christian; all your declarations, on the other hand, are impious and diabolical. This is the revocation which your bull demands. What more do you want?" [86]

Thus he willingly confesses his "heresy." He is ten times more of a heretic than Huss, who began to reveal the truth. "If Saint Peter were today to preside at Rome, he would deny that the Roman bishop was pope." [87] Huss and Wyclif had held the papal decrees to be apocryphal; he calls these decrees impious and swollen with the spirit of Satan. No Church of Christ, he declares categorically, has ever burned heretics, but heretics have burned true Catholics, and to this company of martyrs, in addition to Huss and Hieronymus of Prague, he now admits Savonarola.[88] In an equally confident and categorical manner he clarifies his position with regard to the heretical Bohemian demand that the Eucharist be administered to the laity in two forms, declaring the position of the Bohemians and Greeks to be most evangelical.[89] Once more he states the case against the primacy of the pope, with the boast that he derives his arguments from Huss, especially from his *De Ecclesia*. Once more, as repeatedly during the year, and especially in his October pamphlet *On the Freedom of a Christian,* he dethrones the hierarchy and elevates to the dignity of the priesthood every Christian believer—"even if it be a woman or a boy."

The *Assertion,* like Luther's other Latin works written after the arrival of the bull, is marked by clarity of expression and by a spirit of defiance which at times closely approaches truculence. Like the *Babylonian Captivity,* it begins with a measured tone and grows in vigor and violence as the author proceeds, rising at the end to strident denunciation. The pope and all who follow that "Roman idol" are heretics and schismatics; the pope is the Roman Antichrist who does not fear to state his own impious and blasphemous ideas as if they were those of heaven itself, a son of perdition and a man of sin; his followers are villainous blood-suckers of the people of God, the most Turkish of Turks. Rome itself is the seat of the beast, the abomination of desolation in the mystical Babylon, the very abomination of sin and perdition. "O Satan, Satan, Satan, woe to you, with the pope and your papists, who make sport so impudently in such serious affairs of the Church and put to death souls and bodies." [90] The final blast is reserved for Eck, "that paraclete of the pope," who, he adds ironically, "is as slow to tell lies as he is unwilling to speak."

[86] *Ibid.,* p. 135, ll. 17 ff. [87] *Ibid.,* p. 136, ll. 2 f. [88] *Ibid.,* p. 139, l. 23.
[89] *Ibid.,* p. 123, ll. 3 ff. [90] *Ibid.,* p. 140, ll. 15 ff.

Regarding the charge that he had wished to abolish the mendicant orders he exclaims: "Farewell, wretched abomination! You speak so stupidly and at the same time so impiously that you are unworthy of so many words and show plainly in this remarkable article in what spirit you have excreted this cursed bull." [91]

The *Reason and Cause of All the Articles* is the German form of Luther's reply to the bull.[92] He preferred this version to the Latin,[93] in which he says he was obliged to intersperse "some salt for Latin stomachs." [94] Modern writers will find, as in the case of the essay on *The Freedom of a Christian,* that the German is less clear in presenting the theological arguments, but goes more directly to the heart in its sturdy warmth of style which occasionally swells into a furious outburst of denunciation.

While the *Assertion* was under his hand, Martin planned and carried out another counterattack on his opponents. On December 3 Spalatin, who had come to Wittenberg on the preceding day, wrote to the elector: "Dr. Martin . . . humbly agrees to follow your gracious counsel and to write henceforth with greater restraint." [95] In the same letter, however, Spalatin informs his patron that Luther was making ready to burn publicly the papal decrees and the bull.[96] Just a week later the electoral chaplain received a note from Wittenberg which ran as follows:

Hail! In the year 1520, on the tenth of December, at the hour of noon at the East Gate of Wittenberg next to the Church of the Holy Cross, there were burned all the books of the pope: decree, decretals, the *extravagantes* of Sixtus and Clement, and the most recent bull of Leo X, also the *Summa Angelica,* the *Chrysopassus* of Eck, and other works of the same author and of Emser and of certain others, which were thrown on by other persons, so that the papist incendiaries may see that it requires no great force to burn books which they cannot refute.[97]

Five months earlier, while still awaiting the arrival of the bull, Martin had threatened to condemn and burn the whole law of the popes, "that hydra of heresy." [98] When the news came that his works had been thrown on the flames in Louvain and Cologne, he expressed no concern.[99] Never-

[91] *Ibid.,* p. 150, ll. 31 ff.
[92] *WA,* VII, 308 ff., gives Luther's original manuscript and the first print on opposite pages.
[93] Letter from Luther to Spalatin, Jan. 21, 1521, *WAB,* II, 251.
[94] Letter to Spalatin, Jan. 16, *WAB,* II, 249.
[95] Waltz, "Epistolae Reformatorum," p. 121.
[96] *Ibid.,* p. 122. Luther's first plan was to burn the bull in the pulpit.
[97] *WAB,* II, 234.
[98] Letter to Spalatin, July 10, 1520, *WAB,* II, 137.
[99] Letter from Luther to Lang, Nov. 28, *WAB,* II, 219. See also *WA,* VII, 94, ll. 25 f.

theless the injury must have rankled, all the more because Martin was expecting a similar ceremony from his hated enemy Eck in Leipzig.[100] Just what brought about the final action, we do not know. Perhaps it was reports of the burning of his books at Halberstadt and by the Franciscans at Kottbus, which reached him about this time,[101] that ripened his resolution into the deed.

The pyre which Luther set aflame early on that December morning was of such a dramatic nature that it has drawn the attention of many generations of students.[102] At least one eye witness, an enthusiastic follower of Luther with an appreciation of humor, was at pains to record the events in detail.[103] On the day preceding Melanchthon had posted a brief Latin notice on the doors of the parish church summoning all who held to the evangelical truth to be present at nine before the Church of the Holy Cross, when according to the ancient custom of the apostles, the godless books of the papal laws and the scholastic theology would be burned. "Pious students" were especially invited to attend these "pious exercises." [104] The "whole student body" went in a crowd to the place of the burning, now a historical spot, just outside of the Elster gate. Luther, having laid the papal decrees on the fire, followed with the papal bull, saying, "Because you have condemned the truth of God, He also condemns you today to the fire, amen." [105] After this Luther returned, accompanied by a great number of doctors, masters, and other candidates in letters. The enthusiastic students were, however, by no means satisfied, and they celebrated the last rites of the papal decrees with the singing of *Te deum laudamus*. In the afternoon they organized a celebration of their own of a mock heroic character similar to that which was usual in hazing university freshmen.

---

[100] See Spalatin's letter to Frederick, n. 95 above.

[101] Letter from Luther to Spalatin, Dec. 15, *WAB*, II, 236.

[102] The sources have been conveniently assembled by Johann Luther and M. Perlbach in "Ein neuer Bericht über Luthers Verbrennung der Bannbulle," *Abhandlungen der preussischen Akademie der Wissenschaften* (1907), 95 ff. See also Otto Clemen, "Über die Verbrennung der Bannbulle durch Luther," *ThStKr*, LXXXI (1908), 460 ff.; Heinrich Böhmer, "Luther und der 10. Dezember 1520," *Jahrbuch der Luthergesellschaft*, II/III, 7 ff.; Hartmann Grisar, "Lutheranalekten," *Historisches Jahrbuch*, XLII (1922), 266 ff. The chief contemporary sources are the broadside of Melanchthon, Luther's letter to Spalatin, and the *Exustionis Antichristianorum decretalium acta*, written by a student and follower of Luther, and a note by Johann Agricola, an eye witness. The report of the bishop of Brandenburg is less reliable.

[103] *Exustionis Antichristianorum decretalium acta, WA*, VII, 184 ff.

[104] See Melanchthon's invitation to the students, *ibid.*, p. 183.

[105] The version in the *Exustionis . . . acta, WA*, VII, 184, seems to be garbled. See Clemen's hypothesis, based on Agricola's recollection, in "Über die Verbrennung der Bannbulle." Böhmer thinks that the burning of the bull was an afterthought and that Luther's first intention was to burn only the papal decrees. "Luther und der 10. Dezember 1520," pp. 30 f. See also Clemen, in *WAB*, II, 235, n. 1.

A procession of maskers drew in a cart an immense effigy of the bull, followed by symbolical floats, in the preparation of which the masters of arts seem to have collaborated. To the accompaniment of wild music the train wove out to the place of burning. There the flames shot up again and consumed the bull and such of the papal books, volumes by Eck and other "sophistical" works as the crowd of onlookers could contribute. After the singing of the *Te deum,* "O Thou Poor Judas," and other songs and the flinging about of the scattered leaves of the hated books, the crowd departed.

A month later Luther confessed to his old master, Staupitz, that he burned the books and the bull at first with trepidation and prayer; now he was more happy about it than any other action of his life.[106] It was indeed a momentous act, although the flames that destroyed the decrees of Rome were no hotter than the words which he had directed against them in the *Babylonian Captivity* and half a dozen other works of the preceding months. To this destructive criticism he had now added the symbolical destruction of the canon law. On the children of his age, for whom the symbol so greatly exceeded in importance any abstract presentation, the events of December 10 were bound to make a profound impression. Their influence on Luther himself as well as on later happenings in Germany and at Rome cannot be overlooked.

For the moment no "trepidation" is to be found in such expressions of Martin as the sources have brought down to us. His report to Spalatin is as terse and objective as that of any annalist chronicling a happening in which he has no personal interest. Nor can any excitement be noted in the contemporary account of his address in the parish church on the following day.[107] Warning his auditors against the commands of the pope, he declares that the burning did not go far enough and should have included the See of Rome itself. Those who do not dissent wholeheartedly from the papal rule are in danger of losing their souls. It would be better to see no one at all in the monastic life than to see men in the kingdom of that Antichrist; and he warns all Christians that they now confront a choice that may involve the forfeiting of life here and hereafter. For his part, he prefers to run a risk in this life rather than to bear on his conscience the burden of lost souls.

The need of justifying himself before a wider public than that which he could reach from the pulpit impelled Martin to undertake a published

---

[106] Letter from Luther to Staupitz, Jan. 14, 1521, *WAB,* II, 245.
[107] *Exustionis . . . acta, WA,* VII, 186, ll. 4 f.

defense of his action. Very soon after the burning of the papal books, perhaps beginning on the following day, he wrote the pamphlet, *Why the Books of the Pope and His Disciples Were Burned by Dr. Martin Luther*.[108] The work was caught up with great eagerness by readers, and ten printings appeared within the month,[109] while a Latin edition came out speedily at Wittenberg and in the following month at Worms.[110] At the end of January, Cuthbert Tunstall, the English ambassador, sent it to Cardinal Wolsey, reporting that the work was known all over Germany.[111]

Martin's defense opens with the justification of book-burning as a custom established in the Acts of the Apostles. Moreover, as a Christian, a sworn doctor of the Scriptures and a preacher, it is his duty to destroy false, seductive, and unchristian doctrine. His spirit, armed by God's grace with the necessary courage, cannot follow the passive example of others. In spite of the fact that their errors have been demonstrated by him, the Pope and the papists continue to condemn and burn the doctrine of Christ and to uphold their own anti-Christian, demoniacal teaching. He hopes that the books of Leo's predecessors which have been burned do not please the Pope, but it makes no difference whether they do or not. He declares that he has definite evidence that the burning of his own books at Louvain and Cologne was accomplished by bribing imperial officials. Since the burning of his books may cause harm to the souls of simple people, he has burned the books of his opponents. In conclusion, he urges everyone not to allow himself to be blinded by the prestige of the papal books, but to examine them for himself and to note especially the poisonous and frightful teaching of the canon law.

Martin then takes up this system of clerical laws and analyzes the errors in it and in other papal books under twenty headings. In only two cases does he go further than a simple categorical statement. His study of the papal decrees during the past two years enables him to draw up a long list of papal claims which he bans as erroneous: independence of God's command, superiority of the spiritual power over the temporal, superiority

---

108 *Warum des Papstes und seiner Jünger Bücher von Dr. Martin Luther verbrannt sind*, WA, VII, 161 ff.

109 *WA*, VII, 154 ff. In view of the large number of printings in 1520, it may be assumed that this work came from the press very soon after the burning of the books, but there are no indications in the sources as to the time of composition.

110 The editors of Volume VII of the Weimar edition, Joachim K. F. Knaake and Paul Pietsch, do not think that the Latin translation was by Luther. *WA*, VII, 154. Kalkoff credits it to Hermann von dem Busche in *Der Wormser Reichstag*, p. 234 and n. 4.

111 See Kalkoff, "Briefe, Depeschen und Berichte vom Wormser Reichstag," *SVRG*, LIX (1898), 32.

of the Church over the councils, control over all law, the right to the oath of fealty from the bishops, freedom for even the most evil popes from judgment and punishment, the claim that the power of God rests in the Roman See, which is beyond all legal control, the claim to supremacy based on the papal succession to the Apostle Peter, to whom Christ's priesthood was transferred, the right to make laws for the Christian Church, and so on. To this he adds another list of papal claims that have to do with the daily usages of the Church, such as the right to prescribe feasts and the demand that the clergy remain unmarried. In addition he lists the political claims that Rome bases on the supposed Donation of Constantine: the legacy of power from the Roman Empire, the right to dethrone kings and to release from oaths and political obligations, the right to remit religious vows, the elevation of the canon law to equality with the Gospels, and the papal claim to be the sole interpreter of Holy Scriptures.

On one papal claim the author dwells at length: that the pope is above all human judgment and that he has the right to judge all men. This, he states, supports the entire fabric of canon law and is the source of all misfortune in the world. Over against it he sets up the demand that spiritual power rest not on exterior authority but on humility. The proposition that the Scriptures have their authority only from the pope makes not only man, but God and all the angels subject to him. The canon law declares the pope to be a God on earth over all divine, earthly, spiritual, and temporal things, so that no one may ask him what he is doing. Here Martin finds the fulfillment of the eschatological vision of Christ, Paul, and John. The pope is identical with Antichrist. The greatest evil has arisen in the holiest places: Lucifer is revealed in heaven; Christ was crucified in Jerusalem and Rome produces the Antichrist. The pamphlet closes with an oft-repeated threat of worse attacks yet to come, for thus far he claims only to have jested and played with the papal affair. The pope has never yet overthrown anyone with the aid of Scripture or with argument but has attacked with the ban, with violence or trickery. Because of these deeds of darkness, this fear of the light, he would not put confidence in him even if he were an angel. "For all this I accept full responsibility before anyone," he concludes, justifying himself with the words of Samson: "As they did unto me, so have I done unto them."

"I begin to regard the papacy, which has thus far been held up as impregnable, as something which can be overthrown beyond the hope of all, or else the last day is at hand." [112] Thus, five days after the burning

[112] Letter to Spalatin, Dec. 15, 1520, *WAB*, II, 236.

of the bull, the monk looks forward with ardent hopes to the downfall of his opponents. He has just had in hand Hutten's pamphlet, *Complaints*.[113] Here in a series of letters to the emperor and German princes the knight calls the rulers of Germany to arms against the Roman party. Hutten's first poem in German, *Arraignment and Condemnation*,[114] came to Martin's cell during December.[115] Since then the pen of Luther's valiant ally, dipped in the vitriol of humanistic polemics, had poured forth a stream of letters and dialogues against the Roman party. Not long after the burning of the bull Martin received a letter [116] from Hutten enclosing a savagely satirical attack on the bull, fresh from the press at Mainz.[117] He promised further Latin and German satires on the Mainz book-burning fiasco.[118] Hutten's letter shows an eagerness to join forces with the Saxon professor and through him to win the support of the Saxon elector. Sickingen is his chief defense, and as Hutten takes pains to point out, he has now won his patron over to Luther's works, which he causes to be read to him at every meal.[119] Sickingen, who had the temper of a mercenary soldier and led a mobile force of hirelings in the middle Rhine country, enjoyed the favor of Charles at this time; and Hutten, who himself had little trust in the new emperor—"for he has around him great troops of priests" [120]—had much confidence in Sickingen, who, he says, may play a great part in the approaching conflict and counts for much with the emperor.

Martin showed an active interest in Hutten's writings.[121] There is, however, no evidence that he had any sympathy with the political plans of the knight, who evidently looked forward to the coming war against France with the hope that it would find Rome on the side of Germany's enemies. There is certainly no proof of any kind that Luther intervened with Spalatin in furtherance of Hutten's effort to win the support of the elector for a violent solution of the Roman question, as Hutten requests. There was indeed a deep chasm between the philosophies of the two men. The fiery theologian and the fiery nationalist had a common enemy; but to

---

[113] *Conquestiones*, in Hutten, *Opera*, I, Index, pp. 56 f.

[114] *Klag und Vermahnung, ibid.,* pp. 65 ff.

[115] Letter from Hutten to Luther, December 9, *WAB*, II, 232. See also n. 17, p. 233.

[116] See note 115 above.

[117] *Bulla decimi Leonis contra errores Martini Lutheri*, Hutten, *Opera*, I, Index, pp. 61 f.

[118] *Ibid.,* pp. 62 f. and 64 f.

[119] Sickingen's interest in Luther's works is thus attested. That he had any real understanding of them is very improbable in view of his character. The legend of his championship of Luther's ideas was, however, widely spread. The *Neu-Karsthans*, one of the *Flugschriften* of the following years, makes the ambitious mercenary a champion of Reformation ideas and has him quote Scripture and interpret as learnedly as Luther himself.

[120] Letter to Luther, *WAB*, II, 231, ll. 38 f.

[121] He forwarded copies to Spalatin on December 15, 1520 and on January 16, 1521 with his letters on these dates. See *WAB*, II, 235 and 249 respectively.

Martin, who was first of all an eager scholar and an ardent preacher and teacher, it must have become clear that in religious questions he could have little in common with Hutten, who in one and the same letter begs him to "strengthen himself and stick to the truth with constant mind" and asks his intervention with the elector for armed aid to accomplish a "fine deed" [122] in case occasion arose for it in his dominions.

Whatever Martin may have thought of Hutten's plans for an appeal to arms, he must have been cheered by the enthusiasm of the knightly humanist, whose energy and courage throb in this letter. It showed him that he had allies; and the assurance that his works were highly regarded in the Rhineland and that many were ready to defend them from book-burnings gave him fresh spirit. Humanistic pens were, indeed, busily at work [123] from the lower Rhine to the hills of upper Alsace, where out of the widely known school of the Brothers of the Common Life at Schlettstadt and under the leadership of the great humanist Jakob Wimpfeling a spirit of nationalism had been awakened against Rome. We see the rising of the first tide of broadside and pamphlet literature that was to roll in a great flood during the next two years. The cause of reform was sweeping all kinds of advocates into a sort of alliance, and a feverish enthusiasm seized many of the humanists.[124]

Hutten represented one aspect of German humanism, which counted in its ranks many sturdy and courageous characters as well as some bullies. On the other hand, there was another group which, with Erasmus, feared the "tumult," and like many scholars past and present was willing to play with revolution but afraid to face its violent outbreaks. When these showed themselves to be inevitable, such men drew back to seek, even at the cost of peace of mind, the tranquillity that is necessary for the cultivation of "good letters." Even in these days Martin had a presage of the disappointment that he was to suffer from men of this sort. It came to him in letters from two representatives of the new learning, his university friend Crotus, and the scholar from the upper Rhine, Wolfgang Capito. Crotus's letter, written on December 5 from Erfurt,[125] shows a great contrast with one from the same correspondent the previous spring,[126] when he had just returned from Italy and hastened to cheer Martin on to further

---

[122] "Ad pulchrum facinus." *WAB*, II, 232, l. 75.

[123] See Kalkoff, *Ulrich von Hutten und die Reformation*, pp. 39 f., for a list of authors of satires in support of Luther, beginning with the fall of 1520.

[124] For the rôle played by the humanists in these *Flugschriften*, see Gottfried Blochwitz, "Die antirömischen deutschen Flugschriften der frühen Reformationszeit," *ARG*, XXVII (1930); also Kalkoff, "Die Stellung der deutschen Humanisten zur Reformation," *ZKG*, XLVI, N.F. IX (1928).

[125] *WAB*, II, 226 f.   [126] *WAB*, II, 87 f.

efforts, even if they demanded the supreme sacrifice. Now he is the rector of Luther's old university at Erfurt. Here it is constantly reported to him that Martin has no fear, and he has become concerned lest the world be endangered by his "sacred alacrity." With many saws and proverbs from the ancients and the Bible he warns him to take care of himself. Crotus has heard a sturdy captain declare in public that it would not be hard to kidnap Martin Luther and deliver him into the Pope's hands.[127] The university rector is impressed by the promises of ecclesiastical honors that have been made to those who write against Luther. This is confirmed by Erasmus himself, who had written a friend three months earlier that he could have had a bishopric if he would do this.[128] Plainly Crotus considers Luther to be in great danger and is depressed that the old enemies of humanism in Cologne, of whom he retains bitter memories for their behavior in the Reuchlin struggle, are raising their heads again. The chief of all these "tenebricious" ones, as he calls them, is Hochstraten: "He will not be quiet so long as his wretched soul struggles in his lost body." [129] At a recent encounter Hutten only spared Hochstraten, Crotus states, because he considered him unworthy of death by a generous hand.

Despite its chatty and loyal character this letter from Crotus reveals that he, like Erasmus, fears the passions that Martin has aroused. A similar note is touched in the letter of Wolfgang Capito, now in the service of the elector of Mainz.[130] He is one of those councilors of the archbishop whom Aleander suspected and was watching closely.[131] Capito was well aware of this. In a Latin that is both bombastic and *précieuse* he gives Martin an inside account of affairs in Mainz: the reception of a bitter satiric dialogue on Hochstraten, *The Triumph of Hochstraten;* the attacks on Aleander, and the jokes that were circulated against him in connection with the book burning; the issue of two books by a Strasbourg Franciscan directed against Martin. Capito is sharply satirical of Luther's enemies, but his letter is evidently meant to lay the hand of restraint on the too ardent reformer. He represents public opinion as divided, and with many platitudes and much humanistic palaver he advises Martin to be patient and to work for peace.

---

[127] Letter to Luther, *WAB*, II, 227, ll. 25 ff. See Kalkoff, "Die Crotus-Legende und die deutschen Triaden," *ARG*, XXIII (1926), 128, n. 1.

[128] Letter to Geldenhauer, Sept. 9, in Allen, *Opus epistolarum Erasmi*, IV, 340, ll. 30 f.

[129] *WAB*, II, 227, ll. 40 ff.   [130] Letter to Luther, Dec. 4, *WAB*, II, 222 ff.

[131] Letter to Medici, Feb. 6, 1521, in Brieger, "Aleander," p. 45; see also Balan, *Monumenta*, p. 49; Kalkoff, *Depeschen*, p. 68.

31

PRELUDE TO THE DIET
AT WORMS

A FEW days after Frederick's departure from Cologne the papal nuncio Aleander had brought about the burning of Luther's books at the episcopal seat there, and by the end of November he had succeeded in carrying out a similar rite at Mainz. When the news of these "acts of faith" reached Frederick in Saxony it seems to have aroused a feeling of resentment and to have stiffened his support of the now famous member of his university faculty.[1] The elector had evidently departed from Cologne with the hope that Luther would not be condemned unheard and on his way home had brought the matter to the attention of the imperial councilors, Chièvres and Henry of Nassau.[2] Charles's advisers were looking forward to a sharp diplomatic struggle with the estates of the empire at the forthcoming Diet, and in this the Saxon elector would certainly play an important rôle. Policy demanded, therefore, that he be conciliated. Consequently, on November 27, the emperor's councilors communicated to Frederick the intention of Charles to invite him to bring Luther to Worms,[3] and on the very next

[1] Kalkoff builds on a rather slight foundation a theory of a carefully arranged plan by Frederick and Erasmus for the protection of Luther by means of a hearing before impartial scholars. See his "Erasmus, Luther und Friedrich der Weise," SVRG, CXXXII (1919). He assumes that Frederick had communicated to Charles personally in Cologne Luther's "Oblatio" or "Offer" and received a guarantee that the heretical monk would be heard in his own defense before condemnation. On this theory Frederick would have been justified in regarding the burning of Luther's books as a breach of contract. See Kalkoff, "Zu Luthers römischem Prozess," ZKG, XXV (1904), 548 ff., and his "Erasmus, Luther und Friedrich der Weise," pp. 98 ff. Here again Kalkoff's thesis goes too far. If Charles was informed of the contents of Luther's "Offer" by the elector, why the formal presentation of the document to him by the Saxon councilors early in February and the dramatic rejection? It is certain, however, that Martin's protest was well known in Cologne, where it was posted at this time. See WA, VI, 478, and WA, IX, 801. See also the letter from Sickingen to Luther, Nov. 3, 1520, WAB, II, 208. It also seems possible that the "Offer" was given to the emperor's councilors in Cologne. See DRA, II, 471, n. 3.

[2] This letter is now lost. See DRA, II, 466, n. 2.

[3] E. S. Cyprian, "Nützliche Urkunden zur Erläuterung der ersten Reformationsgeschichte,"

day the emperor addressed a letter to Frederick, saying that in order to prevent further "improper behavior on the part of Dr. Martin Luther" the elector should bring him along to Worms, so that he could be heard by learned persons and no wrong be done him. In the meantime he urged that Luther be prevented from writing or publishing anything further against the pope.[4] The letter from the imperial councilors reached Eilenburg on December 7. The elector's answer a week later, referring to Martin's "multiple protest and offer" and to the report of the burning of his books, gives a rather broad hint that the professor is planning some sort of retaliatory act.[5] On December 20, Frederick has the imperial invitation in hand and replies to it with a diplomatic but positive refusal.[6] As usual, he waives all responsibility for Martin's writing and preaching. It was in the interest of the truth that he had asked through the imperial councilors that Luther should not be condemned unheard. Since, however, Luther's books have been burned "unheard" and Luther "may have done something in reply," he begs to be excused from bringing him to Worms.

Three days before Frederick's letter of declination was sent, Charles had already recalled the invitation. This reversal of policy was due to the energetic and determined intervention of Aleander. When the emperor's invitation went forward, the resourceful nuncio was still in Mainz engaged in the difficult task of executing the bull against Luther's books in the face of a hostile group of clerics and humanists. When on November 30 he rode into Worms and surveyed the situation in this city, which was to be the scene of papal defeat or victory, he was appalled at the prospect. There was a mood of opposition, the cause of which he could not fathom. "Today in Worms," he writes to Medici with true humanistic *préciosité*, "through some cause or other our serene sky is somewhat overclouded and the fortunate course of our sailing is a little retarded."[7] He is now able to survey his opponents and auxiliaries and hastens to give the papal court a picture of the contending forces. In the emperor he has full trust, but Councilor Chièvres and the grand chancellor of the empire, Gattinara, have a political game in hand. They must conciliate the Germans so as to assure support for an imposing march to Rome, where the emperor is to

---

in *Tentzels Historischer Bericht vom Anfang und Fortgang der Reformation Lutheri*, I, II, 190 f.

[4] *Ibid.*, I, 489 f.; see also *DRA*, II, 466 and 468 ff.

[5] Letter of Dec. 14, *DRA*, II, 466, n. 2; also Cyprian, "Nützliche Urkunden," II, 193 ff.

[6] *Ibid.*, I, I, 489 ff.; *DRA*, II, 470 ff.

[7] See Aleander's letters to Medici, middle of December, Brieger, "Aleander und Luther, 1521," *Quellen und Forschungen zur Geschichte der Reformation*, I, 19 and 23 ff.; and Kalkoff, *Depeschen*, pp. 29 ff. and 37 ff.

be crowned in the city of St. Peter. Other councilors of Charles from abroad must be watched and their support assured by papal favors. Of the German electors and bishops, some are reliable; others, like the Count Palatine, may be won by tactful treatment or by honors from Rome. The influential archbishop of Mainz, the hereditary chancellor of the empire, has good intentions, but he is surrounded by anti-Roman councilors. Elector Frederick has been seduced by his advisers, who are all scholars of Luther, and he bears a deep grudge against the Curia. As for the Germans of lower degree, they are all against him [Aleander]: the lawyers, civil and canon, the poor German nobility, and the crowd of humanists; yes, the embitterment extends even to Aleander's former students at the university at Paris. Great is his wonder to discover that except for the parish priests all the lesser clergy, even the monks of orders other than the Augustinians, are arrayed among his enemies. The masses follow recklessly without any real understanding of Luther's doctrine, confusing matters of faith with their blind hatred of Rome. Hutten sits a day's journey away at the castle of Ebernburg, under the protection of Franz von Sickingen, and pours forth German attacks in prose and verse, watching for a chance to ambush the nuncio as soon as he leaves the protection of the city. The tender Italian, uncertain in health, laments that he must shiver in unheated and stinking lodgings on the banks of the "icy Rhine." [8]

Bleak though the prospect is, the nuncio does not lose hope that all may yet turn out for the best. His great objective is to bring about the issue of an edict for the empire, ordering the execution of the bull against Luther's person and works, like that which he had secured for the emperor's dominions in the Netherlands. The imperial councilors opposed this, however, pointing out that the imperial constitution, initiated by agreement with the estates in the preceding year, included an article binding the emperor to put no one under the ban without a hearing, without "regular process and a due decree of the Holy Roman Empire." [9] Of this guarantee Aleander learned to his disgust, and this increased greatly when he heard that Frederick had been invited to bring Luther to the Diet.[10] The nuncio began immediately to advance counter arguments.

He is determined that if Luther must come, it shall be only after recantation in the form demanded in the papal bull.[11] Backed by the

[8] Brieger, "Aleander," p. 29, l. 14, and Kalkoff, *Depeschen*, p. 46.

[9] See the "Wahlverschreibung," *DRA*, I, 871, 873.

[10] Brieger, "Aleander," p. 19, and Kalkoff, *Depeschen*, pp. 33 f.

[11] See the letter probably addressed to Lorenzo Pucci, middle of December. Brieger, "Aleander," p. 34, and Kalkoff, *Depeschen*, p. 52. Concerning the date, see Brieger, "Aleander," p. 33, n. 1; see also *DRA*, II, 769, n. 1.

intervention of his patron, the bishop of Liége, he obtains an interview with Chièvres, who hears him sympathetically and invites him to lay the case before the German council on the following day, December 14. To the bishops and other councilors there assembled, the nuncio sets forth all his arguments, based, not on the theologians, as he writes to his superiors at Rome, but on historical documents which he had rummaged out in German libraries and archives. In these the pope was acknowledged as "pontifex of the Church universal." In Aleander's address to the Germans he dwells especially on an original document which he discovered in a church at Worms, wherein the Greek emperor, John VI, nearly one hundred years earlier had accepted the supremacy of Rome and thereby brought the Eastern Church into a union under the pope.[12] The versatile Italian was well pleased with the effect of his address, and his report to Rome lingers with satisfaction on the triumph of the arguments with which he held up the heretical iconoclasm of Luther's *Babylonian Captivity* before the terrified eyes of the princes of the Church. So sure was he of the effect that he ventured to propose to the council the immediate issuance of an imperial edict. Reckoning from the date of Eck's transmission of the bull to the Wittenberg faculty, the sixty days' grace allowed Luther had now expired. Against the opposition of the chancellor, Gattinara, the nuncio threw himself with a determined rehearsal of arguments. These he repeats to the vice-chancellor Medici, spicing them with denunciations of the "Mahomet," the "Satan," whose coming he was endeavoring to prevent.[13]

The envoy's intervention was of immediate effect. On December 17 the emperor wrote to the elector withdrawing the invitation to bring Luther to Worms. Martin is now under the papal ban, Charles declares, and any city that harbors him becomes liable to the interdict. If Luther will withdraw all he has written against the pope and the acts of the council and will submit himself to the Papal See, Frederick is to bring him to Frankfort or some other convenient place, where he may await a decision. Whether he comes, or refuses to come, Charles will discuss the matter with the elector personally.[14] Aleander approves the letter and speeds it to the "Saxon basilisk."[15] He has the threads now in his hands and urges that the Pope support him by letters to the emperor, chancellors, and cardinals, and begs that his own limited powers for distributing papal offices and favors be

---

[12] The document in question is a bull of the council of Florence, 1439. For an analysis of this from the Saxon standpoint, see *DRA*, II, 501, n. 1. See also Kalkoff, *Depeschen*, p. 53, n. 1.

[13] Brieger, "Aleander," p. 21, and Kalkoff, *Depeschen*, p. 36.

[14] See *DRA*, II, 468 ff. for text.

[15] Letter from Aleander to Medici, Dec. 18(?), Brieger, "Aleander," p. 40, l. 12, and p. 42; Kalkoff, *Depeschen*, p. 61.

extended to meet the emergency.[16] Medici saw to it that a letter to Charles was forwarded immediately, but declined to entrust Aleander with increased powers, directing him instead to send his requests for papal favors to Rome.[17]

Before the emperor's letter reached Saxony, the elector had, as we have seen, refused to bring Luther along. Frederick was, in fact, already on the road to Worms, where he looked forward to a personal discussion of the matter with Charles. Aleander hastened to spin a web before his arrival, though he was much troubled by reports that Elector Frederick had said of his own knowledge that the Pope would give Martin an archbishopric and a cardinal's hat if he would recant,[18] and by evidence of Luther's popularity among the common people, who bought pictures of the monk decorated as a saint, his head surmounted by a dove and begirt with an aureole.[19] On December 29 the full imperial council met and drew up an edict condemning Luther's doctrines.[20] Nevertheless the nuncio saw his goal receding into the distance. The execution of the mandate was halted, as Aleander reports, because of the hesitation of the archbishop of Mainz, who was under the influence of the Saxon elector, and because of the general feeling against Rome. Instead, a commission was appointed to visit Frederick, and was furnished with long and detailed instructions for meeting arguments and persuading the elector to withdraw his support from Luther.[21] With the arrival of Frederick in Worms this attempt at mediation seems to have been abandoned. It is plain that while Aleander's fiery appeals to loyalty to the Church and to fears concerning the effect of heresy on the hierarchy might sway Charles and his bishops, the hardheaded advisers of the emperor were not ready to offend the most influential of the electoral princes and his friends at this critical moment. So in spite of long and intensive negotiations, no headway was made with the question of Luther's condemnation before the meeting of the Diet.[22]

[16] For the commission of Aleander, see Balan, *Monumenta*, Nos. 3, 4, and 5.

[17] Letter from Medici to Aleander, Dec. 3, Balan, *Monumenta*, pp. 10 f.

[18] He claims to have heard this from the archbishop of Trier, who maintained that he had heard it directly from Frederick. Letter of December 18(?), Brieger, "Aleander," p. 40, and Kalkoff, *Depeschen*, p. 58.

[19] Letter from Aleander to Medici, Dec. 18(?), Brieger, "Aleander," pp. 40 f., and Kalkoff, *Depeschen*, pp. 58 f.

[20] See Aleander's letters to Medici on February 8 and 27, Brieger, "Aleander," pp. 49, 75, and Kalkoff, *Depeschen*, pp. 72, 100. See also Aleander's letter to Eck, Feb. 16, Balan, *Monumenta*, pp. 58 f.

[21] *Ibid.*, pp. 87–97. See *DRA*, II, 474 f., n. 1, and pp. 640 ff. See also Kalkoff, *Depeschen*, p. 34, n. 1. The instructions were probably drawn up by Aleander.

[22] Lazarus Spengler writes to Pirckheimer from Nuremberg on January 10 that, according to news received the day before from Worms, the court was almost exclusively occupied with negotiations regarding Luther. *DRA*, II, 890, n. 2.

In the meantime, the disturber of the ecclesiastic and temporal peace went about his accustomed duties at Wittenberg with even temper. The old contrast between faith and works remains in the foreground of the problems with which he concerns himself. Somewhere about this time there appears a group of Latin theses for a "Disputation Whether Works Aid in Justification."[23] The twenty propositions are paradoxical in character, setting forth the relationship between faith and good deeds in a sharply dialectical style like that of the treatise *On the Freedom of a Christian*. As a whole, they present a framework into which a disputant could put the essence of Luther's revolutionary doctrine. As there can be no justification except through faith, so also there is no sin except through unbelief; faith is no faith and does not justify unless it is altogether without works; it is impossible that there be faith without constant, many, and great works; one born of God does not sin and cannot sin; if adultery could be committed in faith, it would not be a sin; if one adores God in unbelief one is committing an act of idolatry; it is not permitted to do evil so that good may come; evil is never done nor does it come into being so that good comes of it; and the final, often-repeated thesis that faith and justification do not proceed from works but works from faith and justification.

It was not only the theological structure of faith that occupied Luther's mind and pen. Now in a moment of calm before the storm, as in the tense weeks following the first appeal to the council and those after the fiery debate with Eck, Luther turns from the arena of theological dispute to find relief in teaching the simple, basic truths of Christianity and the lessons suggested by the revolving Christian year. For children and lay folk he publishes a short form of the Ten Commandments, Apostles' Creed, and Lord's Prayer.[24] Here Martin's style of popular presentation reaches full development. In 1516 and 1517 he had discussed the Ten Commandments and the Lord's Prayer in a series of sermons, and these, as we have seen, had appeared in print in 1518, the former in Latin,[25] the latter in German, through the hand of young Johann Agricola,[26] and then in Luther's own edition.[27] In 1518 and the following year he had also published brief German interpretations of both formulas.[28] His little introduction to the Command-

---

[23] *Quaestio, utrum opera faciant ad iustificationem. WA*, VII, 230 f. The date is somewhat uncertain, probably late in 1520.

[24] *Eine kurze Form der zehn Gebote, Eine kurze Form des Glaubens*, and *Eine kurze Form des Vaterunsers. WA*, VII, 204 ff.

[25] *Decem praecepta Wittenbergensi praedicata populo. WA*, I, 398 ff.; *WA*, IX, 780 f.

[26] *Auslegung und Deutung des heiligen Vaterunsers. WA*, IX, 123 ff.

[27] *Auslegung deutsch des Vaterunsers für die einfältigen Laien* (1519). *WA*, II, 80 ff.

[28] *Die zehn Gebote Gottes mit einer kurzen Auslegung ihrer Erfüllung und Übertretung*

ments, the Creed, and the Lord's Prayer is a fine example of the style that Martin had now attained for bringing religious ideas to the understanding of lay readers. The three formulas are like medicine for a sick man: the Commandments tell what his illness is, the Creed shows him where to seek physic for it, and the Lord's Prayer how to ask for this relief. In accordance with ecclesiastical traditions the Commandments are grouped as on the two tablets of Moses, and each is set between a little introduction and a list of transgressions drawn directly from the experience of practical life. The author shows that he is still bound by the conventions of the Middle Ages: his analysis of the various types of sin follows the classification of the scholastics.[29] Thus the little tractate of 1518 on the Commandments has been expanded into a sort of guide for penitents. It has, however, also its positive side, for on the list of infractions follow directions of ways in which the Commandments are to be fulfilled. In his explanation of the Creed, Martin breaks with tradition in dividing it into three articles instead of the usual twelve, following the three persons of the Trinity, an arrangement which he was to perpetuate later in his shorter catechism.[30] As a whole, this little work is fresh with the morning of Luther's early vigor of presentation. It clothes the ancient forms in a garment made of the vital experience of common men, without obscuring their deep spiritual significance. The work was an instant success. In 1520 and 1521 it was issued eleven times from the presses of Wittenberg, Augsburg, Nuremberg, and Leipzig, and appeared in Italy as well.[31]

The sources for a knowledge of Luther's sermons are, as has been pointed out, very incomplete, and in most cases their texts cannot be relied upon. Yet even the fragmentary records justify a belief that his preaching was never more earnest and spiritual than in the crucial days that intervened between the polemics against the bull and the opening of the Diet where his fate was to be decided. A series of sermons which seem to have been preached on Christmas Day, 1520, and one of the days following gave Martin an opportunity to discourse with great tenderness and warmth on the text in the second chapter of Luke.[32] Like many of his sermons, these have come down to us as they were caught fleetingly and imperfectly by the hand of an auditor, possibly Luther's famulus, Johann Agricola,[33] in any case, by one who preserves something of the fervor and immediacy of

---

(1518). *WA*, I, 250 ff. *Eine kurze Form, das Paternoster zu verstehen und zu beten* (1519). *WA*, VI, 11 ff.

[29] See *WA*, VII, 207 ff.

[30] *Ibid.*, p. 194.

[31] *Ibid.*, pp. 195 ff.

[32] *WA*, IX, 516 ff.

[33] See *WA*, IX, 319 f.

the preacher's appeal. Twice on Christmas Day, in the morning in the parish church and in the afternoon in the chapel of the cloister, and on the following Sunday as well,[34] Martin set forth the mystery of the incarnation, interpreting it in the manner of late medieval homiletics as a symbol of the entry of Christ into a heart empty of all human lusts and earthly pride. One of these sermons, that delivered on Christmas morning, was published. It appeared three years later at Wittenberg, in all probability with the use of Martin's own notes.[35] In the editing that it has undergone as compared with the rapidly sketched text of Luther's auditor in a mixture of Latin and German, the Christmas morning *Sermon on the Birth of Christ* has lost none of its ardent and direct style.[36] Tenderly the preacher sets forth, as the supreme miracle of the incarnation, the belief of Mary that such a thing could take place within her. Each one must repeat in himself this miracle of purification and holiness, he declares, a thought that rings again and again through the whole series of Christmas sermons. With deep emotion he dwells on the joy that comes with the discovery that Christ is born in the heart. For this the heart must be passive and desolate; all of its own virtue must be cast out, the old skin quite thrown off, if the King of Kings is to reign there. This emptiness of soul is found only in those who have suffered. Throughout the sermons that deal with the incarnation something like a spirit of mystical humility rules; and nothing in the little series indicates that they were preached at a time of deep concern over the approach of the great crisis. Rarely does the scribe who noted them down record any reference to the struggle of the day, to the tyranny of temporal and spiritual powers, the destruction of faith and the glorification of works by the pope and the bishops.

When the feast of the Nativity was past, however, Martin showed in other sermons that he was ready to use the pulpit to carry on the struggle against the pride of the Church hierarchy and its belief that merit could be attained through good works. Out of the fragmentary sources two sermons stand forth in this period as eloquent presentations of the contrast between faith and works. Both are suggested by the feast of the Three

[34] Georg Buchwald, "Luther-Kalendarium," *SVRG*, XLVII, II (1929), 17.

[35] See *WA*, VII, 188 ff.; *WA*, IX, 498. Another sermon of this group, that of Sunday, December 30, was printed at Erfurt in 1523, apparently from an auditor's copy and without revision. *WA*, IX, 531 ff.; see also *ibid.*, pp. 499 f. It develops further the ideas expressed in the Christmas morning sermon and closes in the style of the medieval allegory with a lengthy mystical interpretation of the swaddling clothes, the crib, the ox, and the ass. Possibly it was these scholastic trappings, which Luther was outgrowing at this time, that deterred him from publishing it. They are lacking in the sermon of Christmas morning.

[36] See *WA*, VII, 187 f. for information regarding editions of this sermon.

Wise Men. Apparently on Epiphany, 1521, Luther preached twice, both times in the refectory of the convent, if we may trust a somewhat doubtful manuscript notation. Both sermons were printed soon afterward.[37] One of them, *On the Kingdom of Christ and of Herod,* may have been preached originally in Latin, although it was published in German.[38] Luther begins with a contrast of Herod and Christ as kings: the former outwardly mighty and wise, but quite wretched at home with wife, sister, and child; the latter wretched and poor in the eyes of the world, but inwardly full of joy, comfort, and courage. The Three Wise Men, who left all human works and help behind and followed the star with confidence in God, lead the preacher to his familiar argument that the soul must trust in God's promises and first enter into God's Kingdom before it can become righteous. The Kingdom of Christ gives no gold or silver, but a serene conscience: "It will not help you to eat up and swallow the pope and all his bulls and thus feast yourselves until you are crazy and foolish." [39] Herod's people cannot endure to hear that works alone will not save them and so they come with the thunder and lightning of the ban. Popes, bishops, and prelates can do nothing but pile up works, and they resent any other preaching: "They fear that their beggar's bag will lose something, for if people really learn that works will not save, then they will leave the pope with his secretaries; and parchments, red cords, wax and seals, and trickery like that will not be so valuable at Rome." [40] To Herod, who claimed that he wanted to worship Christ but intended to cut His throat, Martin compares the learned doctors, who claim to pray to Him and yet throttle the dear Child, and preach "their damned decrees and human law." Over and over again he emphasizes that faith is the chief work; its effect is to bring forth works of fasting, prayer, labor, and church-going, "not in order to become pious or earn anything in heaven, but just to tame the lazy ass, for the old Adam wants to be driven and spurred and chastened, the lazy rascal, so that he will follow the soul. That is the only reason for doing good works, the subduing of our lustful flesh." [41] It is dangerous to oppose the papal preachers, for just as soon as one attacks good works they cry, "Into the fire with him!" Before one can plant Christ in men's hearts, one must first root out the pope and his dominion. Every real Gospel preacher must walk among wolves and look forward to the cross and a cruel death at any hour. Yet it is better to burn an hour in this world for the truth than

[37] See *WA,* VII, 237.
[38] *Sermon von dem Reich Christi und Herodis* (Jan. 6, 1521). *WA,* VII, 238 ff. See also *WA,* IX, 501 ff.
[39] *WA,* VII, 241, ll. 9 ff.   [40] *Ibid.,* p. 241, ll. 31 ff.   [41] *Ibid.,* p. 243, ll. 1 ff.

to burn eternally with those who want to drive out Christ under the cover
of spiritual power. One stroke of the thresher's flail counts for as much
before God as a whole Psalter sung by a Carthusian monk. In conclusion,
Martin summons his hearers to pray for such fearless preachers of the
Gospel as those he has described. The Church was never so well off as when
many preachers were slain for the sake of God's word.

The sources which preserve for us the second sermon on the festival
of the Three Wise Men declare that it was preached in the afternoon in
the convent, probably before the evening meal.[42] This *Sermon Preached on
Epiphany,* January 6, 1521,[43] was evidently popular. It was printed soon
afterward in Wittenberg, Augsburg, Breslau, and Strasbourg. Three festivals,
as Luther points out, those of the Magi, John the Baptist, and the Miracle
of Cana, fall on this day. As in the morning sermon, he sets up the Wise
Men as representatives of faith. They are also benefactors of the poor and
examples of those who disdain the world's glittering sham. This leads him
again to speak of the futility of showy observances and devices: anniversaries, vigils, brotherhoods, altars, temples and chapels, monstrances,
banners and organs. All of these make a display in the world and contrast
with the work of Christ. The latter would mean applying charitable gifts
not only to our own family, but to the poor priests, so that they might "the
better devote themselves day and night to the Bible . . . not that they
may become lazy squires or street rovers. . . . What would it help to give
a golden monstrance for an altar and at the same time let a houseful of
children suffer and die in hunger, anxiety, and distress?"[44] With skillful
eloquence he weaves quotations from the Prophets and the Gospels and
his own words together into a running arraignment of the doctrine of
good works. He contrasts the poverty of the infant Christ and the true
Christian life with the pride of the haughty Christians, "the splendor,
decoration, and adornment, the tonsure ("blatten"), capes, and crowns of
the pope, the bishops, priests, and monks."[45] The adoration and offering
by the Three Kings symbolizes the sacrifice of the dominion of our will,
which must perish or nothing can live in us. To follow one's own will is
a burning hell, while the acceptance of suffering is the incense by which
we pay honor to God. The mighty myrrh which the Wise Men offered is

---

[42] *Ibid.,* pp. 237 and 246.

[43] *Ein Sermon gepredigt am Obersten. WA,* VII, 248 ff. A widely deviating version is
found in the Poliander MS, *WA,* IX, 548 ff. For the relation between the two texts, see *WA,*
IX, 547. The version printed soon after Luther's delivery bears much more definitely the impress
of the spoken word, especially in its polemics, though it contains some clearly non-Lutheran
expressions.

[44] *WA,* VII, 250, ll. 20 ff.   [45] *Ibid.,* p. 252, ll. 17 f.

a symbol of the powerful faith that Christ has conquered death. In contrast Luther attacks those who give money to priests for vigils and anniversaries in order that one may call out their names from the pulpit, "as one calls out a wine."[46] The priests and bishops cheat the laity out of what they should give them for nothing and the laity cheat the poor priests out of what they should have.[47] He dwells on the great grace of baptism as something which is now forgotten. It is necessary to build upon the promise of Christ that through baptism we are fellow citizens with Him and the angels.

The sermon is long and highly repetitious in style. It is, however, intensely earnest in tone, despite the use of the symbolical interpretations which Luther inherited from the medieval tradition.

We do not know when the busy monk received the news of the invitation to Worms and of its rejection by the elector. There can be no doubt that he desired to go. When Spalatin, weighing the possibility of a direct summons by the emperor after the elector's arrival in Worms, asks what Martin's attitude would be toward such a call, the monk declares: "So far as lies in me, if I am summoned, I will go, even though I am sick."[48] If there is to be violence, he places his case in the hands of God, who saved the Hebrew children in the fiery furnace. His own head is a small matter and his one fear is that the Gospel may become the plaything of the wicked and that they may glory if he fails in the courage to shed his blood for what he had taught. If he is to perish, he would rather do so at the hands of the Romans than have the young emperor begin his reign by staining his hands with blood and thus incur the fate of the Emperor Sigismund and his family for the execution of Huss. Martin assures Spalatin that one may expect everything from him except fright or recantation.

When the emperor's letter recalling the invitation is sent him, he expresses his regret.[49] All is chaos, he declares; matters are fermenting in tumultuous confusion.[50] Perhaps this heralds the approach of the great flood which had been predicted for 1524,[51] a forecast then causing tremors to

---

[46] Ibid., p. 256, ll. 13 ff.

[47] "Da lügen die pfaffen und Bischoff auf, was sy uns laien umbsunst geben, hinwiederumb lügen auff die layen, was sy den armen priestern umbsunst geben." Ibid., p. 256, ll. 22 ff.

[48] Letter from Luther to Spalatin, Dec. 29, 1520, WAB, II, 242 f.

[49] Letter to Spalatin, Jan. 16, 1521, WAB, II, 249.

[50] "Ora pro verbo, videns rem tumultuosissimo tumultu tumultuantem." Letter from Luther to Link, Jan. 14, 1521, WAB, II, 248.

[51] See Clemen's comment, WAB, II, 248, n. 8. In the following year Luther was convinced that great disturbances in nature were in the offing. See WA, X, 1, Part 2, 108.

many, high and low, throughout Western Europe. He is prompted to write to his old teacher, Staupitz, now withdrawn from the administration of the order and living in retirement with the Dominicans at Salzburg. Perhaps he had seen a letter to Link from Staupitz, saying that the "roar of the lion" (Leo X) had been heard in his retreat, for the Pope was seeking to force him to denounce Luther's doctrine as heretical.[52] Martin reminds Staupitz that two years earlier, in the fateful days at Augsburg, the vicar had bidden him remember that he (Luther) had begun these things in Christ's name and that unless God finished the matter it could not be concluded.[53] Now Martin says he does not believe that matters can be settled until the Last Day. God knows what will happen. A month later, in reply to a letter from Staupitz in which the old friend seems to have recommended more humility, Martin chides him, not without kindness, but in a tone of solemnity that echoes the depth of his resolution and the uncompromising position that he has taken.[54] In response to the summons of Leo, the vicar is to give an example of the martyrdom which he had preached. Staupitz had sought escape from the dilemma of recantation or approval of Luther's articles through a declaration that he himself was not their author. This evasion was evidently a deep disappointment to Martin, since it condemned everything that Staupitz "had thus far taught and understood of the mercy of God," and Martin now exhorts his friend to pride, as Staupitz had exhorted him to humility. He repeats that the affair has become very serious. Now that one makes sport of the Saviour in the whole world, should we not offer our heads for Him? "My father, the danger is greater than many think. Here the words of the Gospel come into effect: Whoever confesses me before men, him will I confess before my Father; he who is ashamed of me before men, him will I be ashamed of before my Father." Any compromise is now impossible, and he warns Staupitz against getting caught midway between Christ and the pope, when it is apparent that these are opposite poles.

Together with a stern resolution to carry through to the end, which speaks in all his letters during the winter, there is interwoven the same spirit of fatalism that we observed earlier. "I am carried along, rolled over by the waves," he writes to Staupitz in the middle of January.[55] Early in that month death had struck down one of the most shining examples of political and religious favoritism, young William of Croy, a member of a

---

[52] Quoted by Clemen, *WAB*, II, 246, n. 2.
[53] Letter from Luther to Staupitz, Jan. 14, 1521, *WAB*, II, 245.
[54] Letter of Feb. 9, 1521, *WAB*, II, 263 f.
[55] "Ego fluctibus his rapior at volvor." Letter of Jan. 14, 1521, *WAB*, II, 246, l. 32.

powerful Netherlands family, who at twenty as bishop of Croy had been promoted to be cardinal and archbishop of Toledo, and thereby primate of Spain and archchancellor of Castile. Martin marvels at the boldness of Christ, who without fear of the Pope or his creature had slain this outstanding figure in the midst of his comrades.[56]

Evidences of the loyalty of friends bring him comfort. Money comes to him: in addition to the legacy of one hundred florins from Heinrich Schmiedberg already mentioned, he received a gift from another friend, Markus Schart.[57] Martin begins to fear that God is trying to reward him in this world; so he gives half of the legacy to the rejoicing prior of his cloister.[58] Early in March he receives another bequest, this time from the estate of the councilor Fabian von Feilitzsch, a gift which arouses the displeasure of the bishop of Meissen;[59] and a present from a Nuremberg admirer, which Luther acknowledges through a counter gift of books.[60]

He has become a public personality, and his cell attracts others than theologians and monastic brothers. Indeed he is an object of curiosity to one of the highest persons in Germany. Joachim, elector of Brandenburg, faring through Wittenberg toward Worms with other princes, summons him to an audience;[61] and on February 3, Bogislav, duke of Pomerania, also bound for the Reichstag, stops over to dine with him and hear his sermon.[62] News of the spread of his influence comes to cheer him from time to time. A young Bohemian humanist presents him with a book showing, although as Luther admits, "without proving his point," that St. Peter was never in Rome; and he receives translations into Czech of his group of Latin sermons on the Ten Commandments and his German translation of the Lord's Prayer.[63] Student sympathies break out into a violent anti-hierarchical demonstration. The youngsters carry around a ludicrous effigy of the pope and bombard with missiles figures of the cardinals and bishops, amidst great uproar. Luther reports the outbreak to Spalatin with stern approval. "The enemy of Christ was worthy of this scoffing, for he makes sport of the highest King, yes, of Christ himself,"[64] and it is with a similar feeling that he chronicles desecrations of the bull at Torgau

[56] Letter from Luther to Spalatin, Feb. 3, 1521, *WAB*, II, 260; see also *ibid.*, n. 1.
[57] See *WAB*, I, 382, n. 7.
[58] Letter from Luther to Spalatin, Jan. 16, 1521, *WAB*, II, 249.
[59] "Male habet." Letter to Spalatin, March 6, 1521, *WAB*, II, 275, l. 14.
[60] Letter to Link, March 7, 1521, *WAB*, II, 282.
[61] Letter to Spalatin, Jan. 16, 1521, *WAB*, II, 249.
[62] Letter to Spalatin, Feb. 3, 1521, *WAB*, II, 260.
[63] *Ibid.*, p. 260, and pp. 261 f., nn. 9, 10, 11.
[64] Letter to Spalatin, Feb. 17, *WAB*, II, 266.

and Döbeln.[65] Nevertheless he disclaims any wish to carry on the struggle for the Gospel with violence and murder. It is by the Word that the world is to be won and the Church preserved and reformed and by the Word that Antichrist is to be destroyed.[66] It is in this spirit that he writes to Hutten "very fully" (*copiosissimas*) a letter which apparently never reached the Ebernburg.[67] Hutten's relentless attacks on the bull and his pamphlet denouncing the burning of Luther's books are in Martin's hands and he sends them to Worms with a definite statement dissociating himself from the knight's program of violence.[68]

In the meantime attacks by his enemies go on. Before the end of January, his books were burned publicly at Merseburg by his old opponent Bishop Adolf, whom Martin, in reporting the news to Spalatin, dubs sarcastically, "a holy man, a servant of the Pope." [69] Ten days later he adds that "cartloads" of his books are being burned in Merseburg and Meissen.[70] Emser has written against him again, at the command of Duke George, as Martin thinks; Alfeld, the other Leipzig enemy, "the ass of the Barefooted," cannot worry him any more.[71] New opponents join the old ones. One of these, Thomas Murner, who was later to ridicule the Lutheran movement in the most successful of contemporary satires, had taken the field against him. This uneasy Franciscan of Strasbourg, whose sermons and satires in verse place him second to Sebastian Brant as an interpreter of contemporary social weaknesses, had issued in December two German pamphlets, one a defense of the papacy and the other a mild though sturdy attack on Luther's *Address to the Christian Nobility*.[72] Before the end of December a reply to them appeared, in which the author, probably a Strasbourg humanist, sprang to the defense of the "Christians of the Cross," [73] who might call themselves "Lutherani" after their champion. Attached to this polemic are three letters, one of which, signed "Petrus Francisci," is addressed to Luther. Here the writer urges Martin to reply to Murner's books and array this opponent among the immortals as he had Prierias and Eck, Emser, and Alfeld: "Do something for the sake of your friends." [74] Except for a few, he continues, there is no one in Strasbourg

---

[65] Letters of March 7 to Link and to Spalatin, *WAB*, II, 282 f.

[66] Letter to Spalatin, Jan. 16, 1521, *WAB*, II, 249.

[67] Letter to Spalatin, Feb. 17, *WAB*, II, 266; see also that of Jan. 16, *WAB*, II, 249.

[68] *Ibid.*   [69] *WAB*, II, 266; see also n. 11, p. 267.

[70] Letter to Spalatin, Feb. 27, *WAB*, II, 270; letter to Lang, March 6, *WAB*, II, 277.

[71] Letters of Jan. 14 to Staupitz and to Link, *WAB*, II, 245 ff.

[72] *Von dem babstentum* and *An den Grossmechtigsten und Durchlüchtigsten adel tütscher nation*. See *WA*, VII, 615.

[73] *Defensio Christianorum de cruce*.

[74] Probably December 25, 1520, *WAB*, II, 240 f. See also Clemen's introductory comments, *ibid.*, pp. 238 f.

who does not applaud him as a true Christian, from the common people up
to the magistracy. The writer exhorts Luther to good courage as a soldier
of Christ and assures him that he will triumph. This encouragement and the
ardent appeal from his admirer must have reached Martin in January, just
as he was arming himself against a new attack by his old enemy Emser. He
resolved to reply to the two adversaries, Emser and Murner, in the same
work.

Since the last encounter, Emser had been silent, but Luther and his Witten-
berg friends watched him with suspicious eyes. When the *Address to the
Christian Nobility* appeared it called forth an immediate answer from a
Roman theologian, Thomas Rhadinus,[75] which was reprinted in October in
Leipzig on the initiative of Eck. Luther and Melanchthon accredited it at
once to Emser.[76] On January 14, Martin has learned that Emser, induced by
Duke George, is writing a book against him in German, and he resolves to
attack the "beast."[77] A few days later Emser's work *Against the Un-
Christian Book of Martin Luther, the Augustinian, to the German Nobility*,
came from a Leipzig press.[78] In some way Martin got hold of a sheet containing the first four pages of this work while it was still on the press,
and without waiting for the completion of the book, prepared his reply.[79]

Luther's brief pamphlet *To the Goat at Leipzig*[80] is nothing more than
a blast of defiance. He declares that he is not afraid of the horns of this goat;
he does not fear even those who have more sense in one horn than Emser
in his whole body and soul. It is Emser's first German work, and Martin
derides the "crazy goat" for asserting that he can interpret Scripture according to the spirit when his German is so ragged. Emser is a "licentiate"
in the canon law and a "prohibiate" in Sacred Scriptures.[81] The Leipzig
cleric has always hated him, Martin asserts. He reviews their controversy

[75] *Oratio . . . ad . . . principes et Populos Germaniae in Martinum Lutherum* (Rome,
August, 1520). See Friedrich Lauchert, "Die italienischen literarischen Gegner Luthers," *Erläuterungen und Ergänzungen zu Janssens Geschichte des deutschen Volkes*, VIII, 177 f.

[76] "Stilus et saliva consonat." Letter from Luther to Michael Muris, Oct. 20, 1520, *WAB*,
II, 202. See also Luther's letter to Spalatin, Nov. 13, *WAB*, II, 214, and Melanchthon's to
Spalatin, *CR*, I, 273; see also "Melanchthons Briefwechsel, I," *Supplementa Melanchthoniana*, VI,
ed. by Clemen, pp. 116 ff., for a list of letters related to Rhadinus's work. See further *WA*,
VII, 259 f.

[77] Letters of Jan. 14 to Staupitz and to Link, *WAB*, II, 245 ff. See also Luther's letters to
Spalatin, Jan. 16 and 21, *WAB*, II, 249 ff.

[78] *Wider das unchristliche Buch Martini Luthers Augustiners an den Teutschen Adel aus-
gangen. Vorlegung Hieronymi Emser an gemeyne Hochlöbliche Teutsche Nation.* See *WA*, VII,
260.

[79] Emser resented bitterly this reply based on a fragment of his work. See Ludwig Enders,
"Luther und Emser. Ihre Streitschriften aus dem Jahre 1521," *Neudrucke deutscher Literaturwerke des XVI. und XVII. Jahrhunderts*, II, 4.

[80] *An den Bock zu Leipzig.* *WA*, VII, 262 ff.

[81] *Ibid.*, p. 262, ll. 33 f.

and declares that Emser's book against him was such that "all scholars became your enemies, . . . so many lies and whole wagon-loads of abuse" did it pour out.[82] In the Rhadinus book, Martin states, his opponent launched another attack, and now is preparing a third. But Martin will not permit him to defile Holy Scripture with his goat's muzzle. His own object in writing is merely to assure Emser that he is going to answer him, and it will be an answer that will wake him up. "Go on, take up the small and the great sword; you are responsible for three books and several letters, especially several impious lies. . . . I will undertake to turn loose my spirit on you. So don't imagine, Dr. Goat, that you are the only one in the field!" [83]

Luther's little work called forth immediately a brief answer from the infuriated Emser, *To the Ox at Wittenberg*.[84] It was sent to Martin possibly by Haugold von Einsiedel, one of Frederick's councilors. Martin must have replied very speedily, though it is not quite clear when his reply, *To the Leipzig Goat's Answer,* was published.[85] At any event it was written before he had received all the sheets of Emser's attack on his *Address to the Christian Nobility.*

Luther's reply is, if anything, more furious and sarcastic than his preceding onslaught. In its vigorous German, charged with proverbial expressions and popular turns of speech, it sounds a singularly personal note. At times Martin flies at the throat of his opponent with taunts and threats. He declares that he has been advised not to answer Emser's reply because it is the work of a plain liar and blasphemer. Nevertheless he has decided to do so, so that "the sow may not grow too large a belly." [86] He scorns Emser's assertions that Luther attacked him with hatred, envy, and lies, and shows him what kind of bird he really is.[87] Reverting to the Leipzig disputation, he fairly boils under Emser's accusation that he began the quarrel: "I can boast and prove that I have never begun any of these affairs with anyone; I have always been pulled along and driven against my will." [88] He promises, however, that his enemies shall pay for their shameful treatment of him. "They are not going to put a damper on me that way, as I hope to God; and before ten years are up, Emser, Eck, and the Pope with all their liars and seducers will see whether I have begun in God's name, even though they may burn my books and me along with them." [89] He is especially infuriated over Emser's misinterpretation of a remark which he had

---

[82] *Ibid.*, p. 263, ll. 14 ff.   [83] *Ibid.*, p. 264, ll. 33 ff.
[84] *An den Stier zu Wittenberg.* *WA*, VII, 266. See Enders, "Luther und Emser," II, 3 ff.
[85] *Auf des Bocks zu Leipzig Antwort.* *WA*, VII, 271 ff.
[86] *Ibid.*, p. 271, l. 10.   [87] *Ibid.*, p. 272, l. 8.
[88] *Ibid.*, ll. 32 ff.   [89] *Ibid.*, p. 273, ll. 8 f.

made at Leipzig to the effect that the disputation was not begun in God's name, and he brands Emser as a shameful and intentional liar. Emser had also charged him with indifference to the common people. This, too, Martin denounces as a lie, and brands his opponents, "the Ecks, villains, Emsers, goats, wolves, serpents, and other senseless raging beasts," as Annas, Caiphas, Herod, Judas, Pharisees, and Scribes.[90] "Because I do not humble myself before your raging, blood-thirsty tyrants and accept your lies and poison, I must be called proud. So according to the Jews, Christ and John were possessed of the devil." [91]

As for his own person, he has repeatedly said that anyone may attack him who will: "I do not set up to be an angel." He will not permit his teaching to be touched, however, because it is also God's teaching. He calls the Wittenbergers to witness that they and his correspondents from many countries have warned him against being so approachable to everyone and have criticized his too humble spirit. Never before has he been charged with pride. The vast burden of his work alone would have kept his spirit humble. Bitterly he denies Emser's charge that he has forbidden obedience to the pope and civil authorities. He refuses to believe that Emser is not the author of Rhadinus's work: if there had been more knowledge in it he would not have laid it to his account. He puts no faith in Emser's admissions that abuses exist among the clergy. Why is he silent about the frightful misuse of indulgences and Roman villainies? He reminds his opponent and others of the Judgment to come and assures them that he will not revoke anything, but is ready to risk his life.

With a long series of scriptural quotations he compares Emser to the Scribes and Pharisees, and illustrates the malignant stupidity of his opponent with many proverbial citations. He might have shown his hatred by attacking Emser's life, he states, but his concern is with doctrine, not with personality, for an evil life is harmful chiefly to him who lives it, while evil doctrine does the greatest harm on earth, because it leads troops of souls to hell.[92] He protests his humility before God, at whose feet he lays his doctrines for acceptance or rejection. "But you insolent, bold hero, far above St. Paul and all the saints . . . you are quite independent of God's Last Judgment; you do everything in His name and without hatred." [93] Continuing with savage sarcasm he declares that when Emser goes through the streets of Leipzig, all the bells should ring and roses be strewn under the feet of this new saint.

In conclusion he suggests that Emser forbid God to judge him, for he

---

[90] *Ibid.*, p. 274, ll. 9 ff.   [91] *Ibid.*, ll. 27 ff.
[92] *Ibid.*, p. 279, ll. 1 ff.   [93] *Ibid.*, ll. 24 ff.

has judged himself as fit to wear the crown of crowns. He would better stick to writing beggarly verses, as God's word is too sublime for him. Emser has charged his doctrine with having brought dispute into every house: Martin rejoices that it has found opposition. The Gospel must arouse strife, dispute, and uproar. It was just for making an uproar that Huss and Hieronymus of Prague were burned at Constance, where the cardinals condemned them, not because these two men defended the sacrament in two forms, but because they wanted to reform the Church. Martin recalls also that Cajetan would have found a way of escape for him at Augsburg, if he had only recanted on indulgences. For himself he is willing to give up Aristotle if they will only leave him Huss, now awakened from the dead and tormenting the pope and papists more than when he was alive: "Even if the pope and all the liars of the pope burst with anger, they must hear John Huss say to their faces, 'You murderers of Christ are able to spill innocent blood but you will never bring the matter to silence.'" [94] Finally he threatens Emser anew with many books, but invites him to revocation and peace.

When at last, early in February, Luther had seen "Goat" Emser's whole work, he declared that it was one lie from beginning to end.[95] Now that Emser has "vomited his poison to win the favor of Duke George," [96] he feels that he must respond, for it is the duke who has inspired the goat's insanity. This was to be no fiery denunciation but a carefully prepared argument, and the writing went forward slowly. On March 6 it was "in birth," [97] and three weeks later he sends a copy to Lang.[98] To this reply Luther also attached his answer to Thomas Murner. Martin was inclined to treat this opponent with silence, declaring to Spalatin [99] that he despised Murner. Later, however, he resolved to answer, and it was this reply which he appended to his work against Emser. The *Answer to the Superchristian Book of Goat Emser* [100] must have had considerable circulation, as it was printed four times within the year.

Luther introduced his attack with a gibe at the illustration on the title page of Emser's *To the Ox at Wittenberg,* representing a soldier with spear and sword. He compares his opponent with the monk who, when he had seen a shoemaker cut leather, thought that he could do so as well, but only succeeded in destroying all the leather. After reviewing Emser's statements and interpretations of his *Address to the Christian Nobility,* Martin comes to

---

[94] *Ibid.,* p. 282, ll. 19 ff.
[95] Letter to Staupitz, Feb. 9, 1521, *WAB,* II, 263.
[96] Letter from Luther to Spalatin, Feb. 17, *WAB,* II, 266, l. 12.
[97] Letters of March 6 to Spalatin and to Lang, *WAB,* II, 275 ff.
[98] Letter to Lang, March 29, *WAB,* II, 293.   [99] January 21. *WAB,* II, 251.
[100] *Auf das überchristlich . . . Buch Bocks Emsers zu Leipzig Antwort. WA,* VII, 621 ff.

the conclusion that intolerable hatred has made the goat as crazy as Hecuba. It was with lies and impossible interpretations like this that Christ, St. Stephen, and Huss were attacked by their enemies. While all kinds of lies and foolishness are overlooked in his opponents, even the deviation of a hair's breadth on his part is branded as heresy. Thus he stands alone, surrounded by a ring of enemies. The time has now come to drag into the light the evil spirit that has never ceased through Emser's mouth to blaspheme and deny the truth.

After this introduction, angry and contemptuous in tone, Martin proceeds to answer Emser systematically. He first defends his thesis of the universal priesthood of believers. Priest and bishop, he declares, are really the same, and the latter has no such status in the Scriptures as he enjoys in the hierarchy. "If tonsures, sacraments, anointings, clothes made priests and bishops, Christ and the apostles would never have been priests or bishops." [101]

Emser had formulated his attack under the head of three symbols: spear, dagger, and sword, and Martin responds under the same figures. To Emser's "spear," a defense of tradition and custom, Martin opposes Holy Scriptures and the articles of faith, to show that the priesthood is an office of service to the whole body of believers, since all are priests without the consecration of a bishop. The priest is an official, like a dean or cantor, who may be put into office and put out again. If the priesthood rests upon custom, another custom may be instituted to do away with it. Pope and priesthood have to be endured and honored in the same manner as we endure and honor the power of the Turks or any unjust power. If the custom that established pope and consecrated priest were Christian it would have some authority in Scripture, but as a mere custom it is a Shrovetide play. He begs pardon for his jokes, but "who can make use always of courageous seriousness against the childish, foolish, blind heads who undertake everything and accomplish nothing?" [102] It is proper to mock those who make sport of God's word and work, as Elijah mocked the prophets of Baal. As for the followers of Aristotle, they are a ridiculous guild who do not know their own handicraft.

He next directs himself against Emser's "dagger," the necessity for interpreting the Scriptures by means of the Church Fathers. His opponents are afraid of the Scriptures because they do not know them, and therefore bring the Fathers against him. Like the frogs in the fable, his goatish enemies swell up against the ox with their own breath. Now he proposes to tread upon them with the ox's foot of Scripture so that they will squeal. The Scriptures are the sun from which the Fathers and all others receive their light and the

[101] *Ibid.*, p. 631, ll. 32 f.   [102] *Ibid.*, p. 637, ll. 2 ff.

Fathers interpreted them by means of Scripture itself. As for him, he takes his stand with Paul and believes that the Scriptures need no man's interpretation. It is indeed a new discovery of the pope and his sect in the universities that one must arrive at the meaning of the Scriptures not through the Bible itself but through patristic interpretation. They are up to their ears in the heresy of the Manichaeans, who had declared that the Holy Ghost was promised in order to teach more than was in the Scriptures. St. Augustine showed that everything necessary to be taught was fulfilled and written by the apostles with the aid of the Holy Ghost. The laws of the pope and of men should rule where they do not collide with faith and with God's word; but it is distressing that everyone is damned as a heretic who does not keep these laws, even though he may observe all the articles of faith. The pope has sworn to Christ to teach and act, not according to his own words, but according to those of Christ. If he does not do this he is a thief and murderer, as Christ himself said (John 10.1,8). Popes have often been heretics and scoundrels. Emser had recalled Luther's wish that the laity might wash their hands in the blood of the priests. Martin answers that this was the kind of lies that might be told if he himself were dead. The remark, which he had made in his reply to Prierias, was merely a hypothetical statement. On the other hand, the threats of burning and banning make it look as if Emser and his associates wanted to bring a new Bohemia upon themselves. They will soon find out whether they can stop the game that is going on. No one can destroy the pope except his own creatures. "Tell me, Doctor Emser, if you may write that it is necessary and right to burn heretics and if you think that you do not thereby stain your hands with Christian blood, why should it not be right to destroy you and Sylvester [Prierias], along with the pope and all your sects, in the most shameful manner; since you are permitted to write, not merely in the manner of a heretic, but in the manner of Antichrist, and say things that all the devils are not allowed to say: that the Gospel is confirmed by the pope and its power depends on the authority of the pope, and that what the pope does the Church does? What heretic has ever condemned and destroyed God's words all at once so abysmally? So I say, 'If heretics have deserved the stake then you and the pope should be killed a thousand times'; nevertheless I do not want it to be done."[103] In spite of their errors, heretics were honest men and met argument with argument. On the other hand, his persecutors now drop the case against him and like rascals, devote themselves solely to lies.

He then turns against Emser's interpretation of the difference between the

[103] *Ibid.,* p. 646, ll. 16 ff.

letter and the spirit. He confesses that he was once in the same error and thought that Scripture had two meanings, an apparent and a spiritual one. With drastically realistic examples he now points out the unreality of the "spiritual" meaning, so common in the exegesis and preaching of the Middle Ages, summoning to his assistance St. Paul, with whom Emser agrees "as much as the ass with the nightingale." [104] Nothing definite can be proved about this spiritual meaning: "One must allow Aaron to remain plain Aaron, in the simple sense"; [105] but this does not mean to exclude figures of speech. It is just one of these when he says, "Emser is a rude ass," although he has neither long ears nor four feet. [106] Nor does he exclude the mysteries revealed in the Scriptures through the Holy Ghost. The difference between spirit and letter is the difference between the Old Testament and the New. It is the "sophists" who teach only the dead letter, with their summaries and their confessionals, tormenting people with penance and good works. Quoting from Augustine, he defines the letter as the law without grace and the spirit as grace without the law; and he dwells on the thought that the spirit of God is freedom. With much sarcasm he asks Emser whether the pope now preaches the spirit or the letter with his canon law, consecrated salt, holy water, washings, Masses, and other jugglery. If such usages as tonsures and clerical garb were done away with, where would the pope be? Emser need not array against him St. Augustine, Benedict, Francis, Dominic, and more "such cousins"; for him, God's word is more than all angels, saints, and creatures. He must be vanquished by the Scriptures and not by the uncertain doctrines of men. Emser, he says, is a bad poet, and fits the rôle of philosopher and theologian as an ass would that of a bagpiper. [107] He has raised a hue and cry against him for the sake of his Antichrist chief at Rome; Martin now raises one against him for the sake of the Chief in heaven, since Emser has implied that the Holy Ghost and Christ had not told us enough without additions to their teachings. This makes him the worst blasphemer that ever lived. "Who ever heard more blasphemous, poisonous, diabolical, heretical, tyrannical, and stupid words than those which Emser here pours out of his poisonous hell-jaws, thus bringing a stench into heaven?" [108] "I say these things just so that you, dear Goat, can see that if nothing but raising a loud alarm and holding forth in a fury can strengthen your cause, I can strengthen mine much better in that way." [109] He adds, however, that his case does not need this, as it is founded on the Scriptures. If Emser will only admit that the pope is a tyrant and that pope and papists are thieves,

---

[104] *Ibid.*, p. 649, l. 20. [105] *Ibid.*, p. 650. [106] *Ibid.*, p. 651, ll. 25 ff.
[107] *Ibid.*, p. 666, ll. 11 ff. [108] *Ibid.*, p. 668, ll. 4 ff. [109] *Ibid.*, ll. 16 ff.

robbers, wolves, and seducers, Luther offers to endure the papal laws as Christ bore the cord and cross to which Judas, the pope's predecessor, brought him. His conscience must, however, remain free. If he has to confess that such things are right, then, as long as he has breath he will cry, "No!" He is willing to suffer injustice from the pope and to obey his laws, because Christ teaches suffering, but he protests that he does it unwillingly, for with these laws the pope drives souls into hell and is therefore a man of sin and a son of perdition. He does not wish to be free from human laws and doctrines, but only to have his conscience free, otherwise he would be in continual sin. "Woe on you, you abominable abomination! Come, Lord Jesus, and deliver us from the Antichrist; thrust down his See into the abyss of hell, as he has deserved, in order that sin and destruction may cease, amen!" [110]

Another argument of Emser's bases on the claim of a thousand years' standing that St. Peter was bishop at Rome for twenty-five years. By an analysis of the chronology of the early Church Martin seeks to show that this is impossible. He himself believes that St. Peter was in Rome, but it cannot be proved, and it is certainly not an article of faith. God did not put anything about St. Peter's visit to Rome in the Scriptures because He foresaw that the papists would build the papacy on it, and so He let them lay their foundation in mud and sand.

In reply to Martin's advice of marriage to a clergyman who is living with a woman and is the father of her children, the Leipzig theologian had sung a paean of praise to chastity. Luther now defines his position, saying that he would exclude from marriage the canons, the vicars, and those evil priests who live with prostitutes. Against Emser's "lily white chastity" he appeals to St. Paul and finds in the Apostle's First Epistle to Timothy (4.3) divine authority for regarding the prohibition of marriage a doctrine of the devil. "Scriptures, Scriptures, Scriptures, don't you hear them, you deaf goat and coarse donkey?" [111] He asks whether Christian priests should obey the devil and his apostle, the pope, and follows with a string of sarcastic remarks, becoming almost unintelligible in his resentment and defiance. He argues the case with this "licentiate in the sacred law that has been burned," [112] showering him with a wealth of ironical Latin definitions borrowed from the vocabulary of the legal disputation. Martin is mightily pleased with his word-play and continues the scintillating comedy with a glossary for Emser, in which *deus* means pope and *demones* the Church. In the matter of marriage the priests owe it to their soul's salvation to choose their own course

[110] *Ibid.*, p. 671, ll. 13 ff. [111] *Ibid.*, p. 675, ll. 2 f. [112] *Ibid.*, l. 30.

and to resist the pope as they would the devil himself, tearing up the oath that was forced upon them. All bishops and priests who follow the papal command are the devil's messengers and helpers. In debating Emser's arguments from the Fathers against the marriage of the clergy, Martin assigns the pope a place among all the heretics whom the Romans gathered together in their pantheon. He asks sarcastically whether Emser learned his logic from Malmsey wine or from Leipzig brown beer. Finally he repeats his advice to the "poor crowd of fallen clergy," and declares again that the papal command of invariable celibacy proves the pope to be Antichrist and a son of perdition.[113]

Martin now takes up the charge of Emser and Murner that he had attacked the sins of the clergy alone. He has not left the worldly classes uncensured. He did not set forth to arraign the vices of either clergy or laity, but to attack those vices which the papists regard as virtues. The evil customs and deeds of the papists are, however, only a trifle compared with the false doctrine and superstition in which the clergy are drowned. The trouble is that they are accustomed only to praise, and have punishments only for other people.

Emser's book has helped him, he declares, in four respects. It has shown the author's complete incapacity to prove him wrong by the Scriptures; it has charged him with errors which had first to be invented by Emser; it has confessed that Luther did not offend against the articles of faith or the Scriptures, something which Martin regards as the highest praise; and it has admitted that Emser's own case depends on the doctrines and customs of men.

Luther then turns to answer Murner, and falls into a somewhat gentler tone.[114] The Strasbourg Franciscan has issued a friendly warning, and Martin does not regard him as a liar like Emser, although Murner too places his confidence in human doctrine and custom and not in the Scriptures. Murner treats him like a child by advancing obvious platitudes as arguments, and Luther ridicules this by throwing Murner's method into the form of a syllogism where the disputant has to defend only the major proposition. When Luther hits him on the head, Murner bandages up his feet. Murner has threatened to write many books against him. Why does he not argue with his idle companions or with a sharp-tongued woman instead of Luther? It would be easier for the Rhine to dry up than for Murner to fall short of words, but if he had to deal with Scripture one sheet of paper would more than suffice. He shall have blow for blow if he makes a serious attack upon him. Murner has taken issue with Luther's assertion in the

[113] *Ibid.*, p. 678, ll. 15 ff.   [114] *Ibid.*, pp. 681 ff.

Address to the Christian Nobility that the Christian Church is a spiritual unity. With many scriptural citations Martin defends the idea of an invisible Church. He also interprets again his distinction between this spiritual kingdom of God on earth and earthly things that are a necessary part of the Church but do not belong to it, like martyrdom, persecution, death and sin: "Your cowl may well not be free from lice; are the lice therefore a monk's cowl?" [115] In a tone of serious sarcasm, Martin develops then his idea of the spiritual Church. The Christian Church is not bound to place, person, or time: "Our citizenship is in heaven" (Philippians, 3.20). One does not believe in the things that one sees or feels; in this the pope and his bishops and followers do not have nearly so much knowledge as a coarse peasant or a child. A contrast between the whole Church of Christ and the "mad church of the popes" is a contrast between the spiritual and the visible and tangible. The result is that nowhere are there so many sects as in Rome.

Luther takes leave of Murner with a few doggerel verses against the latter that had been sent to him from the Rhine.[116] To Emser he bids farewell with a final denunciation of his lies. To both he recommends repentance. "The Scriptures are coming to light, men's eyes are waking up; you will have to guide your affairs otherwise or the bright light will bring you to disgrace. I warn you in all sincerity."

This reply to Emser is one of the most vigorous and personal of all of Martin's polemical writings. A spirit of exuberant energy has possession of him, now rising in strident tones of bitter hatred and violent abuse, now sinking to solemn pathos as he pours forth his ideas on the sovereignty of the Scriptures, the pitiful condition of the laity, or on the invisible Church of God. A sort of wild humor comes to the fore which plays with word meanings or clothes itself in proverbial sayings and homely figures that are at times vulgar and obscene. Supremely confident in the security of his position, occasionally arrogant and at times sophistical, Luther bombards his opponents with the roughest missiles from the polemical arsenal of humanism and medieval theology. The whole is pervaded by a defiant spirit and an assurance that he stands firmly on a foundation of divine inspiration.

The soul of Luther will always remain a riddle. One may attempt to account for his actions as one pleases, whether as a result of the conflict between monastic medievalism and the rising individualism of the Renaissance, or as an outgrowth of his experiences in the cloister life and in the debates of humanism, but in the end certain elements of his character remain un-

---

[115] *Ibid.*, p. 684, ll. 8 f.   [116] According to *WA*, VII, 616.

fathomable by any rational plummet. No critical formulation can embrace the spiritual depth of his thought, the almost demoniacal energy of his will, the vast surge of passion, and the earthy quality of imagination that reveals itself in rhapsodical flights into the realm of the spirit, in vigorous analyses of scholarly problems, and violent outbreaks of rage, while humanistic lore and popular proverb pour forth in a continuous stream of vivid pictures. He was himself quite aware of the violent character of his attacks on his enemies. At times he meets criticism of these with resentful denial: those who charge him with too great sharpness have no other way of polluting his name, and the worst of these attacks come from those who have not read his works.[117] At other times he confesses his fault readily enough. "It is right that you exhort me to restraint," he writes his admirer Pellicanus, the Franciscan prior of Basel. "I myself have this feeling, but I am not master of myself. I am swept on by some spirit, when I am not conscious of wishing ill to anyone. Indeed these people also press upon me very furiously, so that I do not notice the Evil One. So, pray for me that I may know, speak, and write what is becoming to the Word and to me, not what they deserve." [118]

The chill, dark months of the North German winter must have passed swiftly, for Martin's life in university and cloister was a fury of activity. His responsibilities in the faculty and with his students were heavy; and he intervenes again and again with Spalatin in matters of university appointment and parish livings.[119] His pen is steadily active. In the middle of January the *Cause and Reason* and his Postil are still in press; [120] the pamphlet on Emser follows and he is at work on his *Instruction for Penitents*.[121] In February he keeps three presses busy.[122] "Many regard it as impossible," he says, "that I can live under such circumstances. I have now so much to do that three of me could not finish in six years. However, through God's grace I am active, well, happy, and of good courage and," he adds ironically, "have leisure." [123] His abundant energy, joined to increased facility in expressing himself, lead to an ever-expanding length in his

---

[117] Letter from Luther to Spalatin, Feb. 27, 1521, *WAB*, II, 270.

[118] Letter of end of February, *WAB*, II, 274.

[119] See his effort to have Carlstadt appointed as provost of the university on January 22 (letter to Spalatin, *WAB*, II, 252), and his withdrawal of this recommendation a week later (letter of January 29, *WAB*, II, 256).

[120] *Grund und Ursach aller Artikel . . . so durch römische Bulle . . . verdammt sind* and *Enarrationes epistolarum . . . quas postillas vocant.* See letter to Spalatin, Jan. 16, *WAB*, II, 249, ll. 26 f.

[121] *WA*, VII, 284.

[122] Letter to Staupitz, Feb. 9, *WAB*, II, 264, and n. 20, *ibid.*, p. 265. See also Luther's letter to Spalatin, Feb. 3, *WAB*, II, 260.

[123] *Auf des Bocks zu Leipzig Antwort. WA*, VII, 275, ll. 17 ff.

polemical writings as the winter goes by.[124] As always, he starts to print while his manuscript is still in preparation, and the results show themselves in defective arrangement, frequent repetitions, and great prolixity.

Early in January, 1521 Elector Frederick arrived in Worms.[125] One of his preoccupations must have been an early interview with the emperor regarding the invitation to Luther. Whether this interview took place does not appear in the sources.[126] It is not clear when Luther learned of the emperor's invitation of November 28, 1520, and the elector's refusal to bring him to Worms under the conditions imposed. It was obviously not until the middle of January that he knew of Charles's revocation of the invitation on December 17, for he mentions it with regret on January 14 to Staupitz and Link.[127] Whatever may have taken place at Worms in the early days of the month, Frederick and his advisers apparently felt that the situation should be met by reiterating Luther's formal "Offer" which, as we have said, had probably been brought to the attention of the emperor's councilors in Cologne. Now it was to go to Charles in person. In response to a request, submitted through Spalatin, Martin writes to the elector on January 25, enclosing the printed copy of the "Offer" of the preceding August.[128] In his letter to the elector, Martin thanks him for his intervention and especially that he has taken, not himself merely, but the whole German nation under his protection. He begs that Frederick intercede with the emperor for a safe-conduct so that he may appear before a jury of "pious, scholarly, sensible, and Christian men, clerical and lay, well founded in the Bible and having expert knowledge in divine and human laws." In the meantime, he begs

[124] An extreme example is his reply to the Italian Catharinus's *Apologia*, written in March. Luther promised four sheets (about sixteen pages), but when the work came from the press in June it was more than four times that long. See *WA*, VII, 699 ff.

[125] Spalatin, "Chronicon sive Annales," in Mencke, *Scriptores Rerum Germanicarum*, II, 605.

[126] *DRA*, II, 476, n. 2, assumes that it did take place and that Charles had given consent to Luther's coming.

[127] *WAB*, II, 246, l. 24; p. 247, l. 9. The sources are obscure. On December 29 Martin seems to have returned copies of Charles's letter of invitation of November 28 and Frederick's reply, and at the same time expressed his willingness to go to Worms. Letter from Luther to Spalatin, *WAB*, II, 243 f. and n. 10. Apparently he as yet knew nothing of the emperor's withdrawal of the invitation on December 17, possibly because the Saxon court was at that time en route to Worms. Nevertheless the news traveled fast to other parts of Germany. Lazarus Spengler had heard it in Nuremberg on December 21. *DRA*, II, 476, n. 1.

[128] *WAB*, II, 253 ff. Again the sources are defective and the situation somewhat obscure. Apparently before the end of the year Spalatin had prepared the way by sending Martin suggestions for a letter to the elector which was to be written when the proper time should come. Letter from Luther to Spalatin, Dec. 29, 1520, *WAB*, II, 243, l. 45 and n. 11. On January 14 Luther notified Spalatin that the letter to the elector was being sent. *WAB*, II, 249, ll. 15 f. and n. 13. The reference may be to that of January 25. If so, the reason for the delay in sending it does not appear.

that all attacks on him be withheld, with a tactful reference to the burning of his books and his own reprisal at Wittenberg. In conclusion he offers to appear before the Diet in order to show that what he has written and taught was "for the salvation of Christianity as a whole, for the benefit of the entire German nation, for the extermination of dangerous abuses and superstitions, and for the unburdening of all Christianity from so many unceasing, innumerable, un-Christian and damnable restrictions, hardships, and blasphemies." [129]

After speeding this letter on its way, Luther continued to live as usual, and so far as our sources give the picture, without anxiety or impatience. How much he learned of what was going on in Worms cannot be said. Of Aleander's activities he can have known little, although he repeats a widely circulated remark ascribed to the nuncio, that even if the Germans shook off the yoke of the Romans, the latter would take care that they should be worn out by attacks on each other and thus perish in their own blood, to which Luther adds that he has always maintained that this was the monstrous intention of the Romans.[130] He hears of Aleander's statement regarding the bull of the Florentine Council, containing the alleged acceptance by the Greek Church of Rome's dogmas, and declares he will publish a document on the subject.[131] After the Diet had been in session for six days Martin records with satisfaction that thus far the "nuntius apostatus" has accomplished nothing.[132]

[129] *WAB*, II, 253 ff.
[130] Letter from Luther to Link, Feb. 3, *WAB*, II, 258.
[131] Letter from Luther to Spalatin, Feb. 3, *WAB*, II, 260. The promised rebuttal seems not to have been written. In any case it could hardly have been available for use by the Saxon councilors when they prepared the note on this question for the elector on February 14. See *DRA*, II, 501, n. 1.
[132] Letter to Lang, March 6, *WAB*, II, 277; letter to Link, March 7, *WAB*, II, 282.

32

THE DIET IN SESSION

EVEN before Christmas representatives of the estates were to be seen on the roads leading toward Worms from all parts of the empire. Princes, like William, duke of Bavaria, with five hundred horse, and Philip, the landgrave of Baden, with six hundred; great bishops, like those of Würzburg and Bamberg, with attendant princes and knights and troops of retainers; the lesser nobility; representatives of the cities; councilors versed in the law, canon and civil; ambassadors from England, France, Venice, Poland, and Hungary, and even the Turkish island of Djerba—all found their way along the highways of the left bank of the Rhine or crowded the ferries that crossed the wintry stream from the east. In spite of the efforts of Emperor Maximilian through the two decades preceding, robber barons still plied their trade, and the representatives of cities and the lower nobility, especially those who were concerned in feuds, chose their roads with care and came under military protection, for there were dangers in the Frankish lands to the north from those who did not respect a safe-conduct even when issued by an electoral archbishop. On the way the French ambassador was robbed when crossing the land of Jülich on the lower Rhine;[1] and later, during the session of the Diet, its members were disturbed by the news that a merchant convoy had been held up and pillaged at Kronberg, presumably by a dependent of Franz von Sickingen, and an Italian merchant murdered in sight of the walls of Worms.[2] The strife for food and lodgings grew acute, and there were wild scenes in the taverns, where knives were drawn. Rank and power asserted themselves everywhere: the soldiers of the princes confiscated wood for fuel, and in spite of attempts at regulation by the imperial officials, the prices of food and drink were raised to fantastic figures by the citizens and the monks in the cloisters, which did duty as hostels.[3]

[1] Sanuto, *I Diarii*, XXIX, 580 f.
[2] Lazarus Spengler's report, April, 1521, *DRA*, II, 889.
[3] See letters of Frankfort and Strasbourg delegates, Dec. 23, 1520, and Jan. 7, 1521, *DRA*, II, 770 ff.

Even the elector Frederick had difficulty in finding quarters for his brother the co-regent of Saxony.[4]

After the session opened, the streets and squares offered a picture of all that was colorful in Germany, where half a century earlier wealth and ease of life had made a deep impression on the Italian humanist Eneo Silvio Piccolomini. Merchants from Spain, the Netherlands, and Italy as well as those from Germany displayed their wares,[5] and the titanic indulgence in food and drink characteristic of the sixteenth century startled more than one serious-minded visitor. Philip of Hesse, then scarcely seventeen years of age, later a strong protagonist of the Reformation, carried off the prize for the splendor of his court and his cleverness in jousting.[6] The German tendency to combine conviviality with business drew the attention of observers. Spengler, a councilor of Nuremberg, reports that seventy-two nobles drank twelve hundred measures of Frankish wine in one evening. The same observer, who had a keen eye for clerical weaknesses and had been included by Eck among the followers of Luther in the bull *Exsurge,* notes that the leading prelates especially spent most of their time, even in Lent, in banqueting and gambling, and that at a single sitting one of them lost sixty thousand guilders.[7] A humanistic visitor, Dietrich Butzbach, remarked that scarcely a night passed without three or four murders, in spite of the fact that the imperial provost had more than one hundred persons executed. "It goes on here quite as in Rome, with murdering, stealing; all the streets are full of whores; there is no Lent here, but jousting, whoring, eating of meat, mutton, pigeons, eggs, milk, and cheese, and there are such doings as in the mountain of Dame Venus." [8]

Many of those who found their way to Worms had little interest in the great problems that were to make this the most important Diet for nearly two hundred years. Private feuds and state embroglios, like the quarrel over the Hildesheim canonicate between the dukes of Brunswick and Lüneburg, which had dragged on for several years and now came before the Diet for settlement; complaints of South German cities against the Swabian League, a political-military association for the insurance of peace and the protection of the interests of the Swabian states; questions of precedence between territorial princes and among the cities—all called for interminable audiences before the emperor or before commissions and umpires appointed by him. Innumerable disputes of a lesser nature, especially between ecclesiastical establishments and the greedy nobility, were to be adjusted. Far more im-

---

[4] *DRA,* II, 774.   [5] *DRA,* II, 815.   [6] *Ibid.,* p. 816.
[7] Spengler's report, *DRA,* II, 889.   [8] *DRA,* II, 817.

portant than these were the complaints which had come before every Diet for many years of attacks on merchant caravans by the lawless knights in defiance of the "eternal peace" proclaimed a quarter of a century earlier by Emperor Maximilian. These questions and the pleas of Hungary for aid against the heathen Turk testified to the inner and outer weakness of the empire, whose loose organization made it difficult to maintain order within and paralyzed military effort abroad.

The great problem that confronted the Diet at this turning point in German history was, therefore, how to deal with the lack of national cohesion, a problem made especially pressing through the accession of a foreign-born emperor. To this end it was necessary to set up a representative agency to administer the empire and to reorganize the judicial system and the forces for the protection of life and property. The question of administration was of the highest importance to the greater territorial princes since it involved political and financial sanctions. Throughout the constitutional struggles since Maximilian's accession to the throne in 1493, the princes had sought to prevent any stiffening of the imperial power that might limit their own rights. For the emperor, whose vast dominion had still to be consolidated through a war with France and possibly also with the Pope and Venice, these questions were less important than that of the support which the estates were to give for his march on Rome with a sufficient force to protect himself from the French in Milan and to secure the imperial crown from the Pope.

Placed in this way amid conditions that would have been difficult for any ruler, whatever his ability, Charles began his reign under the additional handicaps of youth and inexperience. He spoke no word of German, and knew as yet little of German conditions. He had no military strength at hand with which he could enforce his will.[9] The revolt still raging in Castile deprived him of revenue from that quarter. He was therefore dependent on the Germans for troops with which to undertake the march to Rome and for money to finance that expedition and to prepare for the conflict with France. His great support lay in the loyalty of the Germans to the imperial crown. In spite of all the disintegrating and centrifugal forces, in spite of the weakness of the wearers of imperial dignity during one hundred and

---

[9] In April, 1521, just before Luther's arrival at Worms, Aleander heard that a henchman of Sickingen's had threatened to lead a troop to Worms and hew the prelates and the priests of the Diet to pieces. He adds that it would be easy, as the emperor did not have "four cripples" with whom to defend himself. Letter from Aleander to Medici, April 15(?), Brieger, "Aleander und Luther, 1521," *Quellen und Forschungen zur Geschichte der Reformation*, I, 132, and Kalkoff, *Depeschen*, p. 156.

fifty years preceding, the prestige of the duly elected emperor and the house of Habsburg was still great. From the wars of Maximilian in Italy the national enthusiasm had received new impulses which were reflected in the powerful appeals to the greatness of Germany's past by humanists like Jakob Wimpfeling and Ulrich von Hutten. In Charles, therefore, men of all classes hoped to find a national leader.

The installation of the new emperor brought a repetition of the solemn devotions and age-old feudal formulas whereby the estates of the empire were instituted in their dominions. In addition to these ceremonies, the emperor had many gifts of real value to bestow. Custom provided that a new sovereign should have the privilege of filling the first vacancies occurring in the churches, cathedral chapters, and cloisters of the empire after his coronation. These *preces primariae* [10] were, like the political offices bestowed by a new president of a republic, a powerful means of rewarding favorites. They secured for the emperor the loyal service of councilors and clerks and won support from the greedy lower nobility, always in search of sinecures for themselves or members of their families.

Charles was very young and political affairs were in the hands of his intimate advisers, largely a Burgundian and Netherlands group. They were playing an intricate game carried on with all the two-facedness and deceit that marked most sixteenth-century diplomacy. In January, 1521, the zero hour for the beginning of the emperor's duel with Francis I was rapidly approaching; but neither antagonist was as yet ready to break with the other. Both were engaged in negotiations with the Swiss cantons, a source of sturdy mercenary soldiers: Francis in order to enlist troops and Charles in order to prevent his doing so. A third contestant in the game was the Pope, who looked with covetous eyes toward Ferrara as an addition to the papal states. Since Charles's election, Pope Leo had been negotiating with both adversaries, and through astute diplomacy he had succeeded by October, 1520, in engaging six thousand Swiss soldiers, who reached the papal states in April of the following year. During the session of the Diet his diplomats were bound by a written agreement with the emperor to make no treaty against the interests of Charles. Nevertheless, at the very time the session opened they engaged secretly with King Francis to strip the emperor of the kingdom of Naples.[11] In dealing with Rome the inner council of the emperor, too, constantly had a political objective in view, a situation which was suspected by Aleander in December, as his letters indicate, and which

[10] See Kalkoff, *Der Wormser Reichstag,* pp. 9 f.
[11] See *DRA,* II, 61, n. 5.

became clearer to him as the days went by, although he had no opportunity
to see behind the curtain of papal diplomacy.

Into this international game there intruded two powerful movements
among the German people: the national resentment over the abuses in the
Church, and the heresy of Luther. If these movements could have been
united under the leadership of the sovereign, the future political and religious
history of Germany would have been very different. That they were not
united at Worms lay partly in the character of Luther himself, whose program was essentially spiritual, despite his appeal to the nobility, and partly
in the character of Charles.

Youthful as he was, the emperor impressed the Germans in attendance
on the Diet by his balance and fairness of judgment, his geniality of manner,
and his earnest piety.[12] Through all the storms of the Diet Aleander never
hints in his letters to Rome a doubt of Charles's loyalty to the Catholic faith
and to the pope as head of the Church, although he rails again and again
at the unreliability and trickiness of the imperial advisers. Trained in an
atmosphere of Franco-Burgundian orthodoxy, Charles began his career with
a strong feeling of responsibility for the preservation of the unity of the
Church. The characteristics of certain later leaders of the Counter Reformation are already evident in the young Habsburg: loyalty to the traditions and
dogmas of the Church, coupled with indifference towards its institutions and
a hostility toward its representatives that turned easily into contempt. To
such a personality an attack on the unity of the Church was in truth "a
rending of the seamless coat of Christ."

Of all the questions that confronted the Diet, those which had been raised
by Luther in his *Address to the Christian Nobility* undoubtedly had the
foremost place in the popular mind. Aleander ascribes this popularity to
Luther's abusive language and to Hutten's satires rather than to an understanding of Luther's doctrines.[13] To some extent his limited view is cor-
roborated by the pamphlet literature, which began to pour forth from the
German press toward the end of 1520. Here humanistic authors support
Luther as a champion of Church reform and a defender of the law of Christ
in all its purity in the *Address to the Christian Nobility,* and they dwell
especially on the pope as Antichrist. Yet they show little understanding of
the principle of evangelical faith as the kernel of Luther's doctrine.[14] In

---

[12] *DRA,* II, 816; *ibid.,* p. 888.

[13] Letter from Aleander to Medici, Dec. 1520, Brieger, "Aleander," p. 30, and Kalkoff,
Depeschen, p. 48.

[14] See Gottfried Blochwitz, "Die antirömischen deutschen Flugschriften der frühen Reformationszeit," *ARG,* XXVII (1930), 245 and *passim.*

regard to indulgences, however, it now seemed as if everyone was "Martinish." [15] Evidence of the powerful sympathy for Luther struck the attention of observers as soon as the crowds began to filter into Worms. The representatives of the imperial city of Frankfort, who were among the first to arrive, heard that the invitation to Luther had been recalled because the papal embassy thought themselves too weak to contend against him; [16] and on the eve of the assembly of the Diet, the English ambassador Spinelly reported to his master Wolsey that there was a strong feeling in Luther's favor.[17] The Venetian minister Andrea Rosso heard talk of twenty thousand followers of Luther in Germany and of a popular resistance ready to meet any attempt against him.[18] Hostility to Rome was outspoken: at the funeral of the young Cardinal of Croy, celebrated with great pomp on January 22, 1521, the prior of the Dominicans at Augsburg, Johann Faber, delivered a sermon which condemned Luther, to be sure, but astonished its hearers by summoning the emperor to the conquest of Italy.[19]

This was the situation which Aleander faced when the Diet finally came together. He urges the Pope's chancellor to see that a restraining hand is laid upon the papal lawyers and benefice hunters so as not to inflame German feeling any further.[20] He fears that Rome does not understand the situation in Germany, where nine tenths of the people are shouting "Luther!" and the other tenth "Death to the Roman Court!" and all are crying out for a council to be held in Germany. He finds that the Germans have lost all respect for the ban of excommunication and even laugh at it; the monks will not or dare not preach against Luther, whose works rain down upon Aleander, the presses for printing them having been set up under his very nose.[21] He is obliged to tremble for his own safety. On the street people pass him with a German curse, laying their hands on their swords.[22] His greatest hindrance is the burning discontent of the princes with Rome. In February this had taken form in a list of complaints against clerical greed and the cruel operation of the canon law, drawn up by one of the most faithful sons of the Church, George, duke of Saxony, for presentation to the

[15] DRA, II, 817.
[16] Letters of Frankfort and Strasbourg delegates, Dec. 23, DRA, II, 771.
[17] Letter of Jan. 24, DRA, II, 779 f.
[18] Sanuto, I Diarii, XXIX, 572 f. See also DRA, II, 781.
[19] Balan, Monumenta, pp. 41 f. See also Aleander's letter to the papal vice-chancellor, April 15(?), Brieger, "Aleander," p. 139, and Kalkoff, Depeschen, p. 164. The sermon led to a formal protest by Aleander. See Sanuto, I Diarii, XXIX, 617 ff.; see also DRA, II, 781 and notes.
[20] Letter to Medici, Feb. 6, Brieger, "Aleander," pp. 43 ff., and Kalkoff, Depeschen, pp. 63 f. The letters from the middle of December up to the present one are lacking.
[21] Letter to Medici, Feb. 8, Brieger, "Aleander," pp. 48 f., and Kalkoff, Depeschen, pp. 69 ff.
[22] Brieger, "Aleander," p. 56, and Kalkoff, Depeschen, p. 81.

Diet. Aleander secured the list by stealth and forwarded it to Rome.[23] He is especially aghast when he sees a picture circulating in Worms that represents Luther with dove, cross, and halo. He even hears people declare openly that the monk is without sin and place him above St. Augustine.[24] Two enemies cause him especial anxiety, Erasmus and Hutten. The former he sees as the source of all evil. Aleander suspects him of undermining him with his Roman patrons. Face to face with Erasmus, he is obliged to dissimulate his real feelings for fear of stirring up too many old enemies at once, although many people regard the Dutch humanist as the author of some of the books ascribed to Luther and as the one who has aroused the whole tumult throughout Germany.[25] Hutten, less than a day's ride away at the Ebernburg, is lashing public opinion into a fury by his writings. He appears pictured in public prints, sword in hand, as a defender of Luther.[26]

At last Rome sent real assistance to Aleander. On January 28 Medici sent the nuncio an encouraging letter,[27] and what was more to the point, letters from the Pope for delivery to the emperor and to other persons in attendance on the Diet and a draft for four hundred guilders.[28] The letter to Charles was a strong one, urging him to carry out the condemnation prescribed in the bull *Exsurge* and to use this opportunity to show himself a worthy successor of his ancestors and support the unity and peace of the Church.[29] Another document enclosed was the papal bull of January 3, *Decet Romanum*,[30] which repeated and emphasized the condemnations of the bull *Exsurge*. The accompanying letter named three other heretics along with Luther: Hutten, Pirckheimer, and Spengler, and appointed the archbishop of Mainz as chief inquisitor.[31] The new papal bull could be of little use, however, for thus far its predecessor had failed of general execution. Indeed Aleander did not publish the new bull, probably from fear of violent reprisals by Hutten. Early in April he asked Vice-Chancellor Medici for another papal condemnation of Luther, omitting the name of the militant knight.[32] The bull

[23] Letter to Medici, Feb. 18, Brieger, "Aleander," p. 64, and Kalkoff, *Depeschen*, p. 89.

[24] Letters to Medici, Dec., 1520, and Feb., 1521, Brieger, "Aleander," pp. 40, 55, and Kalkoff, *Depeschen*, pp. 58, 79 f.

[25] Letters to Medici, Feb. 8 and Feb. 12, Brieger, "Aleander," pp. 51 f., 56, 59, and Kalkoff, *Depeschen*, pp. 74 f., 80, 84.

[26] Brieger, "Aleander," p. 56, and Kalkoff, *Depeschen*, p. 80.

[27] See Balan, *Monumenta*, pp. 43 f.

[28] Brieger, "Aleander," p. 58, and Kalkoff, *Depeschen*, p. 82.

[29] Dated January 18. Balan, *Monumenta*, pp. 34 ff.; see also *DRA*, II, 495 f., n. 1.

[30] See Lünig, *Spicilegium ecclesiasticum des Teutschen Reichs-Archivs*, XV, 376 ff.

[31] Accompanying the bull was a letter to the archbishop of Mainz, the two nuncios at Worms, and Eck, in which the Pope reserved for himself the absolution of heretical Germans. Text in Balan, *Monumenta*, pp. 17 ff.

[32] Brieger, "Aleander," p. 129, and Kalkoff, *Depeschen*, p. 155. See also his letter of April

Decet Romanum was not made public until the following October.[33] The Pope's letter to the emperor, however, had an immediate influence on the progress of affairs.

After many delays the Diet assembled. It had been called for January 6, but the usual struggles for precedence among the princes intervened and continued so long that it was rumored that the meeting would be adjourned to Augsburg. On January 27, however, the assembly was opened with a Mass in the cathedral. The only important absentee was Joachim, elector of Brandenburg, and he was on the way to Worms. He had finally made peace with the emperor without at the same time breaking off his negotiations with Francis for financial reward and a family alliance, and with these he continued actively throughout the session. Elector Frederick of Saxony, who had traveled in a leisurely way and stopped off for a visit with the Landgrave of Hesse at Marburg, was the first of the great princes to reach Worms. He came with the dignity becoming the head of one of the most powerful states and accompanied by a full retinue of councilors. The ailing old man, impatient of the heavy expenditures, wished earnestly that he might be at home.[34] An important undertaking which lay before him was to carry through the projected marriage of his nephew and heir with the emperor's young sister, Catherine. The affair of Luther must also have weighed heavily upon him. It was indeed one of the major problems that confronted the empire and estates. As we have seen, a conference was probably held between Frederick and Charles at an early date. Whatever its result, the elector seems to have felt that the prospects of a public hearing for Martin would be strengthened through the presentation directly to the emperor of the "Offer," a copy of which was, as we noted previously, forwarded by Luther on January 25 at Spalatin's request. Any hopes that the Saxons may have entertained for a favorable result were soon shattered. When the paper was handed to the emperor, apparently on February 6, he tore it up.[35] Aleander gathered up the fragments and hastened to send them to Rome.[36]

29, Brieger, "Aleander," p. 168, and Kalkoff, *Depeschen*, p. 200; also Kalkoff, "Zu Luthers römischem Prozess," *ZKG*, XXV, 138. The papal breve of January 3, naming the archbishop of Mainz as chief inquisitor, was also withheld from publication, owing, as Aleander says, to the fear of the archbishop. Indeed, Aleander had not yet ventured to present to Elector Frederick the strong letter of the Pope written the preceding July, for the original is still among the nuncio's papers. See Kalkoff, "Zu Luthers römischem Prozess," p. 141. For the text of the papal letter to Frederick, see Balan, *Monumenta*, pp. 1 ff.

[33] Paquier, *L'Humanisme et la Réforme*, p. 220, n. 1.

[34] Letter from Frederick to Duke John, Jan. 12, *DRA*, II, 773 ff.

[35] For an anonymous letter of February 7, 1521, describing the scene, see Balan, *Monumenta*, pp. 52 f.

[36] According to Aleander, the document was handed to the emperor by a certain "Mons. di

This temperamental outburst was no doubt due in some measure to the
efforts of Aleander. The tireless nuncio had devoted himself since the end
of November to bringing to pass the issuance of an imperial edict in fulfillment of the bull. Without such a declaration he felt himself powerless; [37]
but, in spite of the support of Charles, he informs Medici that the issue of
the edict was prevented by the wire-pulling of the elector Frederick and by
repeated attacks on Rome on the part of the German princes, although he
had drawn up a Latin draft for the edict and attended ten meetings of the
full council. This draft was probably prepared at the instance of the commission appointed at the end of December, which, according to an Italian
observer in Worms,[38] was headed by a reliable supporter of the Pope,
Cardinal Schinner, bishop of Sitten. When the matter came before the German council, its president, Cardinal Matthäus Lang of Salzburg, demanded
that two German councilors be added to the commission. This was done,
but in spite of repeated trials nothing was accomplished, out of deference, as
Cardinal Schinner thought, to the elector of Saxony. Finally on February 3,
the imperial council debated the matter for four hours and, as a result of the
good conduct of affairs by Charles, a decision seems to have been reached on
the form of the edict, which now needed only the final approval of the
council before being translated into German.

At last, on February 12, Aleander was suddenly called upon by the emperor to address the estates on the following day, Ash Wednesday. This he
did for three hours, traversing the entire situation in its religious and national aspects, and noting with much pleasure the reflection of his effort in
the furious and threatening countenances of the Lutheran princes in his
audience.[39] On the next day he reported his speech to Rome with great self-
satisfaction. At the opening of this session the Pope's letter to the emperor
of January 18 was read, and it proved an effective prelude to Aleander's
address. As at the meeting of the council in December, he showed a good
understanding of the prejudices of his hearers when he emphasized Luther's

---

Cistein." See his letter of Feb. 8, Brieger, "Aleander," p. 55; Kalkoff, *Depeschen*, p. 78. See
also *DRA*, II, 476, n. 3.

[37] Letter of February 8, Brieger, "Aleander," pp. 49 f., and Kalkoff, *Depeschen*, p. 72.

[38] The following account of the affair rests on an anonymous Italian letter from Worms,
dated February 7, 1521, in the Vatican archives. Balan, *Monumenta*, pp. 50 ff. This is supplemented by a somewhat confused recital of Aleander's in his letter of Feb. 8, Brieger, "Aleander,"
pp. 49 f., and Kalkoff, *Depeschen*, pp. 72 f. See also *DRA*, II, 507, n. 2.

[39] See his letter to Medici, Feb. 14, Brieger, "Aleander," p. 62: ". . . feci per Deum im-
perterritus, come io fosse stato a lezzer una lezzione a XX fanciulli." The Saxon elector was
absent on the plea of illness, and Aleander's speech was taken down by Chancellor Brück,
whose manuscript is preserved in the Weimar archives. *DRA*, II, 495 ff.

condemnation of the Council of Constance;[40] and he again took the opportunity to set forth his discovery of the acknowledgment of papal supremacy by Paleologus, not forgetting to refer to his own career as scholar and to deny hotly the reports of his Jewish descent.[41] According to Aleander [42] the emperor expressed his will at this meeting that the edict be issued with the consent of the princes, and this was repeated on the next day to the council of princes by one of the imperial advisers. The debate among the princes became so violent that Aleander reports Saxony and Brandenburg almost came to blows.[43] According to another source, the report by the chancellor of the bishop of Strasbourg, the emperor laid the matter of the edict before several electors and princes who were in consultation with him, and these, after conferring among themselves, asked that it be referred to the estates on February 15, when, on account of Frederick's illness, the matter was laid over for four days.[44] Whatever the deviations in the reports on these events, it is clear that there was stiff opposition among the German princes to the issuance of the edict in the form presented.[45]

In this draft [46] the edict condemns Luther's attack on the papal see, the Church councils, and the unity of the Church in vigorous terms. It forbids on pain of the ban and super-ban the reading, printing, or distribution of his books which were condemned by the bull, and it commands that they be burned. It imposes silence on Luther, and directs that he be arrested and turned over to the emperor, or held subject to further action. His adherents are also to be treated as guilty of offenses against the state.

The debate on the draft and the manner of its issuance lasted for some days. The uneasy nuncio found little comfort in the assurance of the imperial chancellor that the emperor was not tying his hands but would proceed with the knowledge of the princes though without their counsel.[47] Even Count Palatine Louis, whom the papal emissaries had counted on as one of the

---

[40] See Brück's report, DRA, II, 503.

[41] Ibid., pp. 501 and 506 f. For these charges, see Acta academiae Lovaniensis, EA, XXXV, 309. See further Hutten, Opera, III, 460, 468, 469.

[42] Letter from Aleander to Medici, February 27, Brieger, "Aleander," pp. 68 f., and Kalkoff, Depeschen, pp. 92 f.

[43] Brieger, "Aleander," p. 70, and Kalkoff, Depeschen, p. 93.

[44] DRA, II, 164. See also DRA, II, 508, n. 1 for a review of the sources.

[45] According to a letter from Aleander to Eck, February 16, all of the electoral princes agreed with the emperor except the Saxon who was absent "on pretense of illness," but the other princes asked for six days' grace and received them. Balan, Monumenta, p. 59. For an attempt to interpret the conflicting reports on the discussion of the draft of the edict, see DRA, II, 514, n. 1.

[46] It exists in several contemporary German versions, with variant readings. DRA, II, 509 ff.

[47] Letter to Medici, Feb. 27, Brieger, "Aleander," p. 69, and Kalkoff, Depeschen, p. 92. The latter translates the passage incorrectly. See DRA, II, 508, n. 1.

faithful, "roared like a bull" in favor of Luther and against the Pope.[48] In spite of the fact that the majority in the council of electors sided with the emperor, the dispute seems to have ended with both parties dissatisfied.[49] When on February 19 the answer of the estates was laid before Charles, it was in effect a refusal to sacrifice Luther without a hearing.[50] The plain man in Germany, it said, had been greatly aroused by Luther's teaching and writing, and disorder threatened in case the monk should be condemned unheard. The estates were therefore of the opinion that he ought to be examined by scholarly experts, though without debate, as to whether he would stand by what he had written against Christian faith. In case he did, the estates agreed to approve and execute the edict. They closed with the prayer that the emperor might consider the complaints and abuses among the Germans due to Roman misrule and they asked for an investigation of these.[51] Aleander trembled at the very prospect of a disputation where Luther would appear before German judges,[52] and he hastily sent a letter to Gattinara, urging that the emperor resist such a diminution of his authority.[53] In reply to the estates, the emperor refused, according to Aleander, to permit complaints against the Church to be confused with Luther's case, and declared that Martin should be permitted only to say whether he had written the books and whether he wished to defend what he had said against the Church.[54]

Thus the negotiations went on. The emperor summoned the German council and discussed the matter until ten at night but without result. Finally a commission was set up consisting of bishops and doctors. Opinion in favor of summoning Luther seemed general.[55] Aleander was in a state

[48] Brieger, "Aleander," pp. 72 f., and Kalkoff, *Depeschen*, p. 97.

[49] Aleander ascribes this to the "tricks" of the Saxon, Brieger, "Aleander," p. 70, and Kalkoff, *Depeschen*, p. 93.

[50] It exists in several versions, published with the variants in *DRA*, II, 514 ff.

[51] At the end of January Gattinara had told the English ambassador Tunstall that 100,000 Germans were ready to sacrifice their lives before they would permit that Luther be suppressed without a hearing. See Tunstall's letter to Wolsey, Jan. 29, *DRA*, II, 783.

[52] Letter to Medici, Brieger, "Aleander," p. 71, and Kalkoff, *Depeschen*, pp. 94 f. In *DRA*, II, 517, nn. 1 and 2, it is pointed out that when Aleander wrote this letter on February 27 he apparently had not seen the draft of the reply of the estates and so exaggerates its demands. Another Italian observer at Worms, presumably Saxetta, according to *DRA*, II, 804 and n. 2, was of the opinion that the princes behaved as if the emperor could determine nothing without their counsel. See his letter of Feb. 25, *ibid.*, p. 805.

[53] February, 18(?), Brieger, "Aleander," pp. 65 f., and Kalkoff, *Depeschen*, p. 94, n. 2.

[54] Letter to Medici, Feb. 27, Brieger, "Aleander," p. 72, and Kalkoff, *Depeschen*, p. 96.

[55] Aleander says that the bishop of Salzburg told him that all the princes and estates were calling for it, Brieger, "Aleander," p. 74, and Kalkoff, *Depeschen*, p. 99. This is confirmed by Gattinara's statement to Tunstall referred to in note 51 above.

of despair.[56] As discussion in the commission went on, he hovered near Chievres, who did not regard the matter as serious, and Gattinara, who thought that a council of the Church should be summoned. He heard reports of violent scenes in the commission. When he visited the emperor on February 28, he found that His Majesty also seemed to have grown uncertain. In the meantime news continues to come in of the spread of heresy in Flanders, Holland, and North Germany, and of the distribution of Luther's books in Spain; yes, word even comes to him that Cranach's "Passion of Christ and Antichrist," which Aleander describes to Medici in exaggerated terms, is hanging in the residence of the Saxon elector.[57] The nervousness of the nuncio finds an outlet in vehement complaints about Erasmus and his own enemies in Rome, who, he is sure, are circulating lies against him.

It is highly probable that the compromise character of the resolution by the estates was due to the efforts of Frederick. His relations with Charles were being strengthened by new ties of self-interest. Soon after the Diet convened, on February 3, the marriage of his nephew and heir with the Infanta Catherine was celebrated *per verba de presenti* [58] in the presence of the elector, Chièvres, Gattinara and others; and there was, at least in the minds of the Saxons, every prospect that the emperor's sister would soon appear in Germany for the final celebration of the union. Frederick was therefore undoubtedly willing to tread the path of compromise, if one could be found acceptable to his conscience. Some time early in February, probably the week before Aleander brought on a crisis at the session of February 13, a conference was held between the Saxon chancellor Brück and the emperor's Franciscan confessor, Jean Glapion. This "most proud and most Minorite monk," as Luther called him a year later,[59] was regarded by

[56] "Se Martino vene, gran pericolo è di mal et pegio." Brieger, "Aleander," p. 75, and Kalkoff, *Depeschen*, p. 99.

[57] Letter of February 28, Brieger, "Aleander," p. 82, and Kalkoff, *Depeschen*, p. 107.

[58] *DRA*, II, 833 f., n. 3, See also Johann G. Droysen, "Über das Verlöbnis der Infantin Katharina mit Herzog Johann Friedrich von Sachsen 1519," *Berichte über die Verhandlungen der königlich sächsischen Gesellschaft der Wissenschaften zu Leipzig, phil.-hist. Klasse*, V (1853), 151 f., for an account of the whole affair. See also Ranke, *Deutsche Geschichte im Zeitalter der Reformation*, I, 257 f. The match had probably been offered to Frederick as bait to secure his support of Charles in the imperial election. Actually negotiations had begun on August 22, 1518, and were not broken off until 1524, Droysen, "Über das Verlöbnis," p. 165; see also Spalatin, *Friedrichs des Weisen Leben*, ed. by Neudecker and Preller, pp. 58 ff. Early in May, 1521, Charles had promised to send his sister within six months after his return to Spain, but it is very doubtful whether Charles's councilors ever had any serious intention of uniting the Spanish dynasty with a German provincial line. They merely played a trick especially common in the diplomacy of the Renaissance, and in the end the Saxons garnered nothing but humiliation.

[59] Letter to Johann Lang, June 26, 1522, *WAB*, II, 565.

Aleander as having great influence on the young emperor. Glapion was not without diplomatic experience, and may perhaps have been utilized by the councilors of Charles to seek an agreement with the Saxon prince.[60] He enjoyed the full confidence of Aleander, at whose prompting the Pope had sent the confessor an especial letter of favor.

Some time before the meeting of the princes in mid-February, then, the Franciscan conferred repeatedly with chancellor Brück.[61] Glapion began his efforts at compromise, which he desired should be held secret, with a tactful approach, complimenting Luther's early reformatory writings and taking pains, as the conference went on, to express his approval of the monk's position with respect to indulgences and the misuse of the Mass, and disclaiming for himself any responsibility in the burning of Luther's books. On the other hand he would make no concessions on questions of the sacraments, and arraigned severely Luther's attack on these in the *Babylonian Captivity*. With true diplomatic adroitness he suggested that this might not have been written by Luther, and that it would be easy for Martin to disclaim it and to make a declaration of loyalty to the Church; or he might explain that he had written in anger and give consent that his works be interpreted in an orthodox sense. The confessor further pointed out the danger of civil war in Germany if Luther's declaration of individual independence in religious matters should extend to the political field, the same argument which Aleander had thought most effective with the secular princes.

Glapion submitted a list of heretical declarations, drawn mostly from the *Babylonian Captivity*,[62] which Luther was to recant, and these were duly noted down by Chancellor Brück. Somewhat later another list was submitted which Spalatin then forwarded to Luther for his consideration.[63] It seems likely that Aleander had made a contribution to this, for in addition to the sentences from the *Babylonian Captivity* there were added others from Luther's defense, *Assertion of All the Articles*, which had just come from the press and had not escaped the watchful eye of the nuncio.[64] Finally

---

[60] Letter from Aleander to Medici, Feb. 18, Brieger, "Aleander," p. 64, and Kalkoff, *Depeschen*, p. 88. See *Depeschen*, p. 38, n. 1, for sources regarding Glapion. Authorities differ as to the sincerity of his efforts. Some even go so far as to think that the emperor's confessor was inspired by reformatory ideas. Kalkoff regards him as nothing more than a plotter.

[61] Brück drew up a long report of this conference, *DRA*, II, 477 ff. An important variant, *ibid.*, p. 491, ll. 26 ff., may have been a first draft, as suggested by the vividness of its style. See Kalkoff, *Der Wormser Reichstag*, p. 218, n. 3.

[62] See *DRA*, II, 478, n. 1. These were afterwards translated by Spalatin; they are published with Brück's Latin copy in Förstemann, *Neues Urkundenbuch*, pp. 37 f. and 40 f.

[63] Förstemann, *Neues Urkundenbuch*, pp. 44 f.; Spalatin's German translation, *ibid.*, pp. 46 f.

[64] See *EA*, XXXVII, 24. Knaake, *WA*, VII, 606, thinks that these articles were submitted by Aleander to the imperial commission that was examining the affair of Luther from February

Glapion suggested that the question between Luther and the Pope should be laid before a neutral commission and that in the meantime Luther should stop writing and his books be sequestrated by a neutral authority. At the same time the Pope and his agents would also cease from book-burnings and keep silent.[65] The notes of this proposed agreement are preserved among Aleander's papers and read somewhat differently from the minutes dictated to the Saxon chancellor by the Franciscan confessor.[66] In the Aleander version a recantation by Luther is the prime objective. Good and learned men are to be sent to Luther to inquire if the works circulated under his name are his. If he does not recant or explain them in an orthodox sense, the emperor is to proceed against him.

As was to be expected, this effort to induce Luther to recant shared the fate of previous ones. We find in Martin's papers the *Articles to Be Revoked*,[67] with his notes attached. His responses are very brief; are, indeed, scarcely more than reiterations of the heresies listed, such as "it is true," "it is not true." In the meantime Charles was giving evidence of his earnestness in the suppression of heresy.[68] On the afternoon of March 1 he summoned the estates to discuss the edict,[69] laying various questions before them: where and when Luther was to be heard; whether the heretical books should not be destroyed, no matter who was their author; and whether in case Luther did not present himself or recant, the estates should not support the emperor in treating him as an open heretic.[70] On the following day the emperor gave a written answer to the declaration of the estates of February 19.[71] In a conciliatory tone he agrees to give Luther a safe-conduct to come for a hearing; and tactfully separating the Lutheran question from the complaints against Rome, promises to confer with the estates regarding action on the religious grievances when these shall have been formulated. At the same time he laid before them the text of the edict which he wished them to approve. This second draft of the edict [72] corresponds closely in its first part to the earlier form, but then proceeds to a more careful formula-

---

19 to March 1. On March 19 Luther had the heretical list in his hands. See his letter to Spalatin on that day, *WAB*, II, 289. See also Kalkoff, *Der Wormser Reichstag*, p. 258, n. 3.

[65] Brück's reports, *DRA*, II, 488.

[66] Balan, *Monumenta*, pp. 116 f.; see *DRA*, II, 488, n. 1.

[67] *Articuli revocandi*. *WA*, VII, 606.

[68] His personal zeal in defense of the faith had been shown by his intervention with the Vienna University on behalf of the bull. See his urgent letter to the university, March, 1521 in Balan, *Monumenta*, pp. 16 f.; also Aleander's letter to Medici, Feb. 28, Brieger, "Aleander," p. 83, and Kalkoff, *Depeschen*, p. 109. See also *DRA*, II, 524, n. 1.

[69] Report of the Frankfort delegate, Fürstenberg, March 2, *DRA*, II, 812.

[70] See the memorandum in *DRA*, II, 518, No. 70, which agrees with Fürstenberg's report.

[71] *DRA*, II, 519 f.   [72] *DRA*, II, 520 ff.

tion, in line with the reading of the bull of condemnation. Again the deft hand of Aleander is to be seen in the emphasis on Martin's defense of Huss, his attack on the Council of Constance, and his leading astray the common people. It is to be seen also in the concluding declaration, on behalf of the empire and the estates, that they will cling loyally to the faith of their fathers and support the pope.

In spite of the steadiness of the emperor, Aleander was dancing on hot iron. He pours forth bitter complaints to Medici on March 4 about the fickleness of the imperial council, whose members are continually reversing themselves and allowing the matter to drag.[73] His great fear is that the Diet may adjourn without action, and he warns against sending a legate from Rome, lest the Germans make use of the opportunity to extract a new concordat.[74] The program of Charles seemed indeed to be a compromise with the friends of Luther. On March 6 he drew up a personal letter to "dear, honored, and pious Dr. Martin Luther of the Augustinian Order," enclosing a safe-conduct and inviting him in the name of himself and the estates to come to Worms within twenty-one days, "in order to receive information from him regarding the doctrine and the books which have from time to time come from him." [75] When this letter was ready, however, the emperor and his advisers hesitated to forward it. Aleander saw the safe-conduct on or about March 8, and resigned himself to the expectation that the arch-heretic would appear in Worms on the second day of Easter.[76] But the court seems to have feared that a direct invitation would show too much honor to one of Luther's reputation, and an attempt was made to get Frederick to assume responsibility for the summons, a suggestion which the elector declined with all promptness.[77] The nuncio learns that the safe-conduct, which was granted "in spite of us and in spite of repeated promises," [78] is to be sent through no mere courier, but by the imperial herald himself,[79] and he passes this on to Medici in a subsequent letter. In the same letter he expresses especial resentment that a heretic should be addressed, as

[73] Brieger, "Aleander," p. 86, and Kalkoff, *Depeschen*, pp. 111 f.

[74] The displacement of Aleander by one or more diplomats of high rank was under consideration in Rome at this time. Brieger, "Aleander," p. 86, n. 1.

[75] See the somewhat conflicting evidence regarding dates in *DRA*, II, 527, n. 1. For texts of originals of citation and safe-conduct see *WAB*, II, 280 f.

[76] Letter to Medici, March 8, Brieger, "Aleander," p. 94.

[77] See the memorandum to the Saxon councilors for Frederick, Cyprian, "Nützliche Urkunden," I, 11, 211 f. On March 11 the elector drew up a safe-conduct for his own territories, with a letter to Martin in which he was careful to place the responsibility for his coming on the emperor. *WAB*, II, 286 f. See also *DRA*, II, 533 and n. 1.

[78] "Invitis nobis et contra le promesse fatteci più volte da questoro." Letter to Medici, March 8, Brieger, "Aleander," p. 94, and Kalkoff, *Depeschen*, p. 118.

[79] To Medici, March 15, 16, Brieger, "Aleander," p. 101, and Kalkoff, *Depeschen*, p. 120. According to Aleander this change was decided upon on March 11.

he was in the emperor's letter of citation, as "honored" and "devout and beloved," additional evidence to his mind that the emperor's advisers are anxious to have Luther come.

Meanwhile the discussions concerning the form of the imperial edict had continued, and on March 6 the estates delivered their answer to the emperor. It has been lost, but the notes of the episcopal councilor of Strasbourg indicate that the Germans stood by their action of February 19, asking that Luther be heard and rejecting the second draft of the edict.[80] Charles was, however, in earnest. The draft was revised promptly, taking a form, as we shall see later, which Aleander, who was working secretly through the secretary of the German chancellery, hoped would put an end to this "ribald heresy." [81] But the printing dragged on and the publication of the official draft did not take place until nearly three weeks later, on March 26.[82]

The reasons for this lay again in the political situation. Charles was pulling all the levers to get help from the estates for the march to Rome which was to bring final recognition of his title as over-lord of the Holy Roman Empire and confirm his sovereignty in southern Italy. It was quite clear to all that the struggle with Francis would have to be fought out in great part in Italy, where the Pope, strengthened now by the enlistment of six thousand Swiss mercenaries, sought to fish in troubled waters in order to extend his dominions. Charles's treatment of the Diet, and particularly of the electoral princes, therefore, had to be as conciliatory as was consistent with his military program. It was apparent even to an outsider like Cuthbert Tunstall, the English ambassador, that in spite of the general desire, particularly on the part of the poorer German nobility, for the march on Rome,[83] each of the estates was utilizing the crisis to further its own interests.[84] The effort to win the Swiss cantons to an alliance against France needed the support of the estates, for the Swiss were, traditionally at least, still a part of the empire. Negotiations regarding intervention with the Swiss cities went on between the emperor and the German princes through the month of March until Charles grew weary of the endless hesitations and delays and proceeded to deal with the Cantons alone. The result, however, was that a month later all except Zurich concluded an alliance with France.[85]

---

[80] DRA, II, 166, and n. 2.
[81] Letter to Medici, March 8, Brieger, "Aleander," p. 91, and Kalkoff, Depeschen, p. 114.
[82] Regarding the dates, see DRA, II, 529, n. 1.
[83] Letter from Tunstall to Wolsey, Feb. 9, DRA, II, 793 f.
[84] Letter from Tunstall to Wolsey, March 6, DRA, II, 814.
[85] For the sources, see DRA, II, 361 f.

Difficulties, indeed, clustered thickly about the imperial advisers. Francis was busily at work seeking direct contact with the German electors,[86] one of whom, Joachim of Brandenburg, was in French pay. Just as the edict was reaching its final form about the middle of March, the rugged *condottiere,* Robert de la Mark, the brother of Aleander's patron, the ambitious archbishop of Liége, invaded Luxemburg with French troops. The startling news of this move against the hereditary lands of the emperor may well have aroused a suspicion that the French king was acting with papal connivance. Aleander, who was in a good position to look into the cards, suspected at once a connection between this sudden invasion by the mercenary chief and the delay in publishing the edict.[87] In these crucial days the nuncio received a hint from Chièvres that the case of Luther was being played up against the papal court. "See to it that the Pope does his duty," said the imperial councilor, "and goes along directly with us, and we will do all His Holiness desires," [88] adding that if the Pope crossed the emperor's plans, he would get into difficulties from which it would be hard to escape. The nuncio, on tenterhooks of anxiety, warns the Roman vice-chancellor to observe the greatest caution not to clash with the emperor and the entire German people.[89]

In general, however, the results of Aleander's efforts were such as to give him grounds for encouragement in spite of the coming of Luther to Worms The papal court had given ear to his earnest entreaties of February [90] regarding the disposition of cases before the Roman tribunal involving abuses which had evoked bitter complaints in Germany. Now, in the middle of March, the nuncio was delighted to receive from the Pope another personal letter for the emperor,[91] and an urgent appeal to clerical persons and to the princes.[92] Aleander notes with pleasure the beneficial effect of the papal favors which he had solicited for influential members of the court. The emperor's chamberlain is delighted at a decision in an old suit regarding his brother.[93] The opponents, to be sure, seem to have been in

---

[86] See his appeal to the electors, December 27, 1520, *DRA*, II, 381.

[87] "Sed dicet quispiam: quid hoc ad Martini negocium?" Letter to Medici, February 15, 16, Brieger, "Aleander," p. 101, and Kalkoff, *Depeschen*, p. 122. See also Brieger, "Aleander," p. 281.

[88] Letter to Medici, March 8, Brieger, "Aleander," p. 92, and Kalkoff, *Depeschen*, p. 115.

[89] March 8. See also letter of March 15 and 16, Brieger, "Aleander," p. 102, and Kalkoff, *Depeschen*, p. 117.

[90] Brieger, "Aleander," pp. 43 f., and Kalkoff, *Depeschen*, pp. 63 f.

[91] Dated February 25, 1521. Balan, *Monumenta*, pp. 65 f.

[92] *Ibid.*, pp. 66 f.

[93] Letter to Medici, March 15–16, Brieger, "Aleander," pp. 106 f., and Kalkoff, *Depeschen*, pp. 128 f. See also Kalkoff, *Der Wormser Reichstag*, pp. 135 f.

the right, but Armerstorff, the chamberlain, is, according to Aleander,[94] a bosom friend and relative of Hutten, who threatens with fire and sword, while in Germany nowadays there is no longer fear of excommunication or other papal weapons.[95] Complaints pour in on Aleander from every side and he feels it "necessary to use every honest and possible means in order not to fail in our duty toward the enemies of the Church and to the peace of Christianity." [96] He sends for Roman consideration a list of papal favors which would be well invested: a dispensation for the minor son of the emperor's doorkeeper, so that he may accept a benefice; permission to accept a third benefice for a zealous brother whose life is endangered because he preached against the Lutherans; one hundred Rhenish crowns for Dr. Jakob Spiegel, the scholarly imperial secretary, in return for confidential information; [97] a provostship to cool the Lutheran ardor of Wolfgang Capito, chief preacher at the Mainz cathedral and a leader among hostile humanists; the naming of Father Glapion in every letter from Rome, so as to hold in line the one responsible for strengthening the emperor's conscience.[98] Above all, the nuncio urges that the German "courtesans" in Rome, who are responsible for "all these derogations, surrogations, ingressions, regressions, reservations, cessions, accessions, . . . fifty livings in one hand, and similar novelties, concerning which all Germany is making an outcry, . . . should restrain themselves a little . . . until this tempest passes." [99]

The acute ear of the Italian told him that his appeals to the fears of the Germans had not been in vain. The enthusiasm for Luther was not what it had been three months before. In spite of the great excitement, in comparison with which the revolt of Henry IV against Gregory VII was like "violets and roses"; in spite of those "mad dogs," the humanists, armed with letters and weapons, and boasting that they are no longer senseless beasts like their ancestors, and that "the Tiber has flowed into the Rhine," [100] the nuncio felt that sympathy of the princes for Luther had fallen off sharply since his Ash Wednesday speech made clear to them Martin's attitude toward the sacraments and his approval of Huss. Now one hears nothing of him, when in earlier days people talked constantly of him in public and private.[101]

[94] Brieger, "Aleander," p. 107, and Kalkoff, *Depeschen,* p. 129.
[95] Brieger, "Aleander," p. 107, and Kalkoff, *Depeschen,* p. 130.
[96] Brieger, "Aleander," p. 110, and Kalkoff, *Depeschen,* p. 133.
[97] Brieger, "Aleander," pp. 110 f., and Kalkoff, *Depeschen,* pp. 134 f.
[98] Letter to Medici, March 19(?), Brieger, "Aleander," p. 113, and Kalkoff, *Depeschen,* pp. 136 f.
[99] Brieger, "Aleander," p. 109, and Kalkoff, *Depeschen,* p. 132.
[100] Brieger, "Aleander," p. 108, and Kalkoff, *Depeschen,* pp. 130 f.
[101] Brieger, "Aleander," p. 105, and Kalkoff, *Depeschen,* p. 126.

Finally on March 17 or 18 the first imperial edict against Luther came from the press,[102] and on the 26th, as we have seen, the long-expected document was posted in Worms, where it was solemnly proclaimed on the following day. It was issued by the emperor without participation of the estates of the empire. Affairs had now developed so that Charles felt free to assert himself and go alone as his conscience bade. On March 24 he put an end to the long conferences with the Diet concerning negotiations with the Swiss. On the same day the estates postponed discussion of the Roman campaign until after the regulation of internal reforms.[103] The end of the period of tension left the emperor free, for the moment at least, to proceed with regard to Luther without considering the wishes of Germany's estates.[104] The document that had been brought into being with so much difficulty came forth clothed in the heavy style of the German chancelleries as had the previous drafts, but it was sharper and more to the point.[105] All princes and officials of the empire are informed that Luther has by his writings opposed and harmed holy faith and Christian doctrine and that the Pope has condemned his books. Emperor and estates, it continues, have resolved to admit no innovation and confusion in faith and have summoned Luther to a recantation. Now, as is his duty, the emperor commands that all books and writings of Luther condemned in the bull, even though good may be mingled in them with "evil substance and error," shall be turned over to the authorities and passed on to the emperor, and that nothing contained in them is to be copied, printed, bought, or sold under pain of the ban of the empire. Two days later Aleander forwarded a copy of this document to Rome.[106] He notes with regret that it does not command the burning of Luther's books like the "fine one," that is, a former version of the edict, drawn "according to our intention," but he takes comfort from the Diet's declaration of loyalty to the old faith. He is especially delighted that the wagonloads of books that had been shipped from the Frankfort fair to Worms must now be returned at once.

Among the representatives of the estates the publication of the edict aroused a feeling of discontent. There seems to have been an understanding at the meeting with the emperor that there was to be a truce until Luther

[102] See the postscript to Aleander's letter of March 19, *DRA*, II, 827, and Kalkoff, *Depeschen*, p. 139. The postscript is lacking in Brieger's "Aleander."

[103] *DRA*, II, 394 ff.

[104] According to Aleander, the German council had previously advised the emperor that he alone was charged with the execution of the bull. Letter to Medici, March 4, Brieger, "Aleander," pp. 87 f., and Kalkoff, *Depeschen*, p. 112.

[105] Text in *DRA*, II, 531 ff.

[106] On March 29. Brieger, "Aleander," p. 116, and Kalkoff, *Depeschen*, pp. 141 f.

could be heard.[107] The Saxons particularly regarded the issuance of the edict as a breach of faith.[108] Many believed that now Luther would not come.[109] The councilors of Frederick began to raise the question whether, in view of this declaration that Luther was a heretic, the emperor and Diet would be bound to keep faith with him and observe the safe-conduct.[110] The betrayal of Huss was not forgotten.

When the edict, whatever its defects, was published one great objective of the Roman party at Worms was attained. Nevertheless the coming of Luther hung on the horizon like a cloud heavy with danger. In the electoral college there was something like a stalemate, for in addition to the electors of Saxony and the Palatinate, the archbishop of Cologne seems to have been inclined to sympathize with a reformatory program.[111] The nuncios felt therefore little confidence in the council of the princes. The bishops seemed disinclined to exert their power, a hesitation which Aleander ascribes to their fear of the knights under Sickingen and Hutten. This last unruly spirit had stood in the background as a continual threat of violence ever since Aleander crossed into Germany. Hutten seems to have been excited to the point of explosion by Aleander's Ash Wednesday speech, and in March he published a letter of bitter abuse addressed to the nuncios,[112] followed by another filled with violent invectives against the cardinals, bishops, and priests assembled at Worms.[113] Finally he turned directly to the emperor with an address full of railing against the Roman emissaries.[114] The influence upon the public mind of the attacks on Rome by the German humanists in recent months was immense, and Aleander did not underrate it. He urges the Pope to mobilize some Italian poets and rhetoricians in order that they may study the Bible and wield their pens like the Germans, only they are to do it for the defense of the faith, instead of turning out "four verses

---

[107] Kalkoff, *Die Entstehung des Wormser Edikts*, pp. 147, 151, 174 ff., assumes an "agreement" and a stipulation to this effect on the part of the estates. This is an exaggeration, but it is certain that, contrary to certain implications in the edict, the estates had not approved its issuance. See also Kalkoff, *Der Wormser Reichstag*, p. 314.

[108] Letter from Frederick to John, April 8, in Förstemann, *Neues Urkundenbuch*, p. 14. See also letter from Aleander to Medici, March 29, Brieger, "Aleander," p. 116, and Kalkoff, *Depeschen*, p. 143. See further Kalkoff, *Der Wormser Reichstag*, p. 314 and n. 2.

[109] Report of the delegate from Nördlingen, March 18. *Ibid.*, p. 310.

[110] In April Chancellor Brück analyzed the question in a memorandum for Spalatin and decided that the electors and the temporal princes would see to it that the safe-conduct was observed. *DRA*, II, 534 ff.

[111] Kalkoff has assembled some evidence for this. See *Der Wormser Reichstag*, p. 312.

[112] Hutten, *Opera*, I, Index, pp. 72 ff.

[113] *Ibid.*, II, 21 ff. See letter of Aleander to Medici, April 5: "con tanto veleno che sarebbe per intoxicar el mondo." Brieger, "Aleander," p. 123, and Kalkoff, *Depeschen*, p. 147.

[114] Hutten, *Opera*, II, 38 ff. Aleander calls it, "Una lettera bestiale," letter of April 5. Brieger, "Aleander," p. 122, and Kalkoff, *Depeschen*, p. 146.

a month and abusing each other about a word."[115] Regarding Hutten's threats of violence, Aleander feared that he could not rely on the protection of the emperor, since Charles, as the nuncio writes, does not feel himself safe from murder by Hutten and his accomplices even in the heart of Worms. It was therefore resolved to send a messenger of peace to the Ebernburg.[116]

The emissary who was selected for this purpose was the emperor's chamberlain, Paul von Armerstorff, according to Aleander a relative and great friend of Hutten, who had recently visited Sickingen's castle.[117] The purpose of his mission, which was reported for the public ear as undertaken on the responsibility of the chamberlain alone, was not solely to quiet Hutten, for Armerstorff took with him the astute imperial confessor Glapion, who carried a plan for another attempt at mediation. Its first objective, however, was to prevent Luther's coming to Worms. At the Ebernburg, where the two emissaries conferred at some time between April 5 and 9,[118] the results were most promising.[119] Hutten promptly wrote a letter of apology to the emperor,[120] agreeing to abstain from further attacks and engaging for service under Charles.[121] Glapion evidently acquitted himself well by winning the circle at the Ebernburg to cooperate toward some form of compromise. He disputed "an entire day" with Martin Bucer and demonstrated to his own satisfaction the heretical character of Luther's doctrine.[122] On Sickingen

[115] Letter of April 5, Brieger, "Aleander," p. 126, and Kalkoff, *Depeschen*, p. 151.

[116] Brieger, "Aleander," pp. 123 f., and Kalkoff, *Depeschen*, pp. 148 f. There seems no reason to brush aside Aleander's statement as an exaggeration, as is done by the editors of *DRA*, II, 537 f., n. 3. The nuncio reports the situation after a personal interview with the emperor. Charles was certainly no coward, and a month later he ridiculed the elector of Mainz for his fear of the Ebernburg group. Sickingen, "the terror of Germany," as Aleander calls him in his letter of April 5 (Brieger, "Aleander," p. 125, and Kalkoff, *Depeschen*, p. 150), was surrounded by a band of entirely lawless knights, and although he had been to this point loyal to the emperor, he was quite capable of a sudden desperate undertaking, as his record shows. Certainly there was no force in Worms at that time prepared to resist a sudden raid by the eager troop that would have followed the knight in an attack on the hated bishops.

[117] Aleander to Medici, April 5, Brieger, "Aleander," p. 124, see also p. 289, n. 4; Kalkoff, *Depeschen*, p. 149.

[118] Brieger, "Aleander," p. 124, and Kalkoff, *Depeschen*, p. 149. See also letter of April 13 or 15 in Brieger, "Aleander," p. 133 and Kalkoff, *Depeschen*, p. 157. Glapion was back in Worms on April 9. See also Otto Waltz, "Epistolae Reformatorum," *ZKG*, II, 127.

[119] According to Aleander, the mission arrived just in time, as Sickingen's troops would have been ready in ten days to take Worms and cut all the priests and prelates into pieces. Letter to Medici, April 13 or 15, Brieger, "Aleander," p. 132, and Kalkoff, *Depeschen*, p. 156.

[120] April 8. Hutten, *Opera*, II, 47 ff.

[121] He was to receive 400 gold florins annually. See, however, Aleander's letter of April 5. Brieger, "Aleander," p. 124, and Kalkoff, *Depeschen*, p. 149.

[122] According to Aleander's report to Medici on April 13 or 15. Brieger, "Aleander," p. 133, and Kalkoff, *Depeschen*, p. 157. Bucer expressed himself somewhat more modestly. See his letter to an unknown recipient, in which he says only "Disputavimus diem totum." Waltz, "Epistolae Reformatorum," p. 125. As the recipient of the letter Waltz suggests Spalatin.

also the Franciscan claimed to have made an impression, although the sturdy mercenary, who knew Luther's German writings by heart, declared finally that the Church must reform itself and that he would risk his property (*robba*) and the life of himself and his children in Luther's cause.[123] Hutten separated his affair from Luther, but demanded that the priests be chastised and deprived of their great riches, a statement which caused Aleander to dip well down into his store of abusive epithets when reporting it.[124] The nuncio was assured by the emperor's councilors that the ideas of the Ebernburg were backed by the whole knighthood of Germany.

The plan of the Franciscan confessor to divert Martin from appearing in Worms found support among the Sickingen group. Hutten a day or two later laid the suggestion tentatively before Spalatin,[125] and Bucer about the same time also addressed a letter supposedly to the elector's chaplain, urging a more cautious attitude on Luther's part.[126] Whether Father Glapion was sincerely hopeful of an arrangement that would satisfy both Luther and the Pope or whether he merely tried to hold Martin away from Worms at any cost cannot be said with certainty, although it was clearly his first objective to attain the latter goal in an indirect way so as not to offend the estates. There seems to have been some idea among the Saxons that the confessor honestly wished for a reform in the Church, although Spalatin was suspicious of trickiness on his part,[127] and a few days after the Ebernburg meeting claimed to have evidence of his duplicity.[128] Hutten and Sickingen trusted him fully and made plans for inviting Luther to turn aside from his journey to Worms and join them at the Ebernburg in an effort to reach an agreement.[129] In furtherance of this plan Bucer met Luther at Oppenheim just before he entered the city of the Diet, but the effort was in vain.[130] Martin proceeded on his way.

In the meantime the subject of these debates continued to preach and teach and write with resignation if not always with serenity. To him "life is a cross"; [131] but even when he had received and was pondering on the articles

[123] Brieger, "Aleander," p. 133, and Kalkoff, *Depeschen*, p. 158.

[124] "Sciagurato, homicida, miserabile, vitioso, scalzo et ignudo." Brieger, "Aleander," p. 134, and Kalkoff, *Depeschen*, p. 158.

[125] See letter from Spalatin to Frederick, *ca.* April 10, *DRA*, II, 538 f.

[126] Waltz, "Epistolae Reformatorum," p. 125.

[127] "Ich besorg, der beichtvater sei ein socius." *DRA*, II, 540. See also the report of Brück, *DRA*, II, 477 ff.

[128] *DRA*, II, 540, n. 1.

[129] Hutten laments this later. Hutten, *Opera*, II, 210 f.

[130] The sole evidence for this is Luther's statement a dozen years later in *TR*, V, No. 5342b, and IV, No. 5107, but there is no reason to doubt it. See also *TR*, V, No. 5342a.

[131] Letter from Luther to Pellicanus at the end of February, *WAB*, II, 273.

to be revoked at Worms, he found sufficient detachment to transmit to Spalatin suggestions for such matters as university appointments and private commissions of friends.[132] Solemnly he advises a pastor friend not to accept a call to Zwickau unless he is willing to lead the sheep away from the pope and to drive him away like a wolf. "Daily I experience more how proudly and completely Satan rules, so that horror seizes me when I look upon the Church." [133] One must make an enemy either of the pope or of Christ. It is not for himself that he asks prayers, but for God's word,

for I am not at all anxious about myself, in whose blood, still warm (remarkably enough) many thousand murderers incur guilt throughout the whole world, and the most sacred adversary of Christ, the commander in chief, with a mass of murderers presses forward with all his force to destroy me . . . Christ will give me the courage to despise these ministers of Satan while I live and to conquer him in death. . . . Formerly I called him the vicar of Christ; now I revoke that and say that he is the enemy of Christ and the apostle of the devil.[134]

Attacks were now increasing upon Luther from many directions. Early in March word comes that the Louvain theologian Jakob Latomus is preparing to bring out a work against him.[135] Two Italians are reported to have written attacking his position. One of these polemics, that of the Dominican jurist, Ambrosius Catharinus,[136] the receipt of which had rejoiced the heart of Aleander in the middle of February,[137] came into Martin's hands on March 7. He at once brands the work as the farrago of a narrow and stolid Thomist and promises a brief answer that will stir the "bile of the Italian beast into motion!" [138] Murner has written three books against him: never has so furious a clamor been raised against any man as by the Franciscans and Dominicans in attacking him, but "it is remarkable how I rejoice." [139] Indeed, the line between friends and foes was being drawn more and more sharply. Three humanist friends had already sounded a retreat: first the Augsburg canon Adelmann, who made his peace with Eck and received absolution in the November preceding; [140] and as a result of his action,

---

[132] Letter to Spalatin, March 19, *WAB*, II, 289.

[133] Letter to Nikolaus Hausmann, March 22, *WAB*, II, 290.

[134] Letter to an unknown, March 24, *WAB*, II, 292 f.

[135] Letter from Luther to Spalatin, March 6, *WAB*, II, 275. The work appeared in May at Antwerp. See *ibid.*, p. 276, n. 7.

[136] *Apologia pro veritate catholicae et apostolicae fidei ac doctrinae adversus impia ac valde pestifera Martini Lutheri dogmata* (Florence, Dec. 20, 1520). See *WAB*, II, 276, n. 8.

[137] Letter to Medici, in Brieger, "Aleander," p. 63, and Kalkoff, *Depeschen*, pp. 87 f.

[138] Letter to Spalatin, March 7, *WAB*, II, 283. His answer was ready on April 1, but was not published until June. See *WA*, VII, 700.

[139] Letter to Spalatin, March 6, *WAB*, II, 275.

[140] November 9. See F. X. Thurnhofer, "Bernhard Adelmann von Adelmannsfelden," *Erläuterungen und Ergänzungen zu Janssens Geschichte des deutschen Volkes*, II, 1, 89 ff.

the Nuremberg councilors Pirckheimer and Spengler, on the advice of the city fathers, made their submission and were received by Eck into the "community of the Mother Church" two months later.[141]

In place of the South German humanists, powerful support is promised from the North. One of his correspondents is Heinrich, duke of Freiberg;[142] and he hears that King Christian of Denmark has intervened with the University at Copenhagen to prevent the condemnation of his work.[143]

Martin sees clearly now that his relation to the hierarchy is at an end. A decade later he declared that at the time of the Augsburg hearing in 1518 Staupitz had released him from his monastic vows.[144] Now he writes to his old associate Lang with rejoicing that he is freed "from the order and laws of the pope and excommunicated by authority of the bull,"[145] although he does not intend to abandon the monastic garb nor his cell in Wittenberg, and continues to sign himself "Augustinian" and to speak of "our prior." This sense of freedom strengthens his resolve in the face of imminent danger. When the *Articles to Be Revoked* reached him through Spalatin, he wrote in response on the same day that he would reply to the emperor with a refusal to come to Worms if the invitation was solely that he might recant. If he were summoned there to be killed, he would go: "I will not run away, Christ helping me, or abandon the Word in the battle." He is sure that these men of blood will not be at peace until they have killed him.[146]

In the meantime his German reply to the bull, *The Reason and Cause of All the Articles,* came at last from the press. It had been ground out in the midst of many duties, and installments had gone to Spalatin as they came from the printer's hand.[147] The author rated this work higher than the Latin *Assertion.*[148] It is addressed to the simple man, who is not a master of Latin, for Martin had now become fully conscious of the power which the mother tongue gave him for a direct and forceful appeal to the individual heart. In this reply to his enemies he is not intent on theological refinements; the freedom of the will, for example, receives much less attention than in the Latin version. Instead, he insures himself of room to swing his weapon with telling blows, reinforced by homely picture and earthy proverb.

[141] Drews, *Willibald Pirckheimers Stellung zur Reformation,* pp. 63 f. The two Nurembergers made efforts toward an appeal to the Pope, but were finally compelled to make their peace directly with Eck. *Ibid.,* pp. 72 f.

[142] Letter from Luther to Spalatin, March 7, *WAB,* II, 283.

[143] *Ibid.* See also p. 284, n. 6.

[144] *TR,* I, Nos. 225, 409, 884; II, No. 2250.

[145] March 6. *WAB,* II, 277.

[146] Letter to Spalatin, March 19, *WAB,* II, 289.

[147] See *WA,* VII, 299.

[148] Letter to Spalatin, Jan. 21, 1521, *WAB,* II, 251.

The German work [149] is much longer than its Latin predecessor. It opens with a contrast between scholars and believers in a tone to strike the imagination of the lay mind. The bull which has been launched against him is "disgraceful, contemptible, abusive." [150] He has not wanted to teach everyone: what he really wanted was "to creep into his corner," but they "have drawn him on so as to win praise and honor for themselves by means of him." [151] All through history, from Moses to St. Augustine, God has selected one prophet at a time and never from among the highest priests, but lowly persons, like Amos, the shepherd, or those in an unimportant position like St. Augustine. "If I am not a prophet, nevertheless I am sure that God's word is with me, and not with them." [152] All heresy has come from bishops and scholars. There were many asses in the world in Balaam's time, but God spoke through Balaam's ass alone. Christ and the Apostles were also charged with bringing in new things; as for him, he is preaching nothing new. The cause of Christ has perished at the hands of bishops and scholars. He will put faith in no one who cannot prove his doctrine by Scripture. He is not terrified by the hatred and persecution of the "big fellows," [153] but feels cheered and strengthened.

In the same tone, one far more vigorous and personal than in the Latin version, Martin proceeds to defend the condemned articles. Here, as always when he appeals to the individual, he puts the reality of sin in the foreground and turns for support to Paul. His language is unrestrained in denunciation of those who juggle words in attempting to classify gradations of sin. To regard a sin as a "defect" or an "infirmity" would bring us in the end to call a tree a stone, or a horse a cow.[154]

To try to bring about repentance by merely contemplating sin and its baleful effects is "a hypocrisy made up out of nothing but dirty lies and seductions." [155] Penitence must precede the contemplation of sin as love precedes works. There must be a great earnestness and a deep anguish if the old nature is to be put aside. When the lightning strikes a tree or a man it does two things: first, it tears apart the tree and quickly destroys the man; second, it turns the face of the dead man and the split or break in the tree toward itself, toward heaven. So the grace of God frightens, pursues, drives, and at the same time turns man toward itself. "My dear Pope" knows less about true deeds of penitence and grace than some great block lying on

---

[149] *Grund und Ursach aller Artikel D. Martin Luthers, so durch römische Bulle unrechtlich verdammt sind. WA,* VII, 308 ff. Both Luther's MS and the first (Wittenberg) edition are printed in *WA,* VII, 308 ff.

[150] *Ibid.,* p. 309, l. 25. [151] *Ibid.,* p. 311, ll. 17 f. [152] *Ibid.,* p. 313, ll. 21 f.
[153] *Ibid.,* p. 317, l. 10. [154] *Ibid.,* p. 341, ll. 14 ff. [155] *Ibid.,* p. 361.

the ground; nevertheless he wants to judge and decide about them.[156] Furthermore, the Pope claims the power to transform into a true penitence the so-called "attrition," a kind of "gallows penitence," as Luther calls it, of a person who neither believes nor repents.[157]

Even though the Pope and his followers actually agree with certain of his ideas, Martin continues, they regard them as heretical: "I believe that if I were to say that there is one God and to confess all the articles of faith, it would all have to be heresy only because I say it. So pious and sincere are the Pope and his followers toward me." [158] With growing sarcasm he denounces the Pope for making Christ a liar and heretic: "I would sooner have believed that the heavens were falling than that such things would emanate from the Pope . . . the Pope worse than all devils . . . sits in God's place and condemns faith, which no devil has ever done. Oh, it is coming to an end with you, you child of destruction and Antichrist." [159] "Now condemn and burn books, Pope. So shall God cast you down and throw you into insanity, because you always strive against divine truth." [160]

In discussing absolution through faith rather than penitence, Martin contrasts the attitude of those who are proud of their penitence with that of the humble centurion in Acts. In contrast with him, the Pope in his triple tiara decked with gold rides on a stallion before God and defies Him, ready to drive Him out of heaven in case God will not forgive his sins. "Where are you heading, you diabolical arrogance?" [161] The Pope does more harm than a simple priest can do, for "You cheat countries and people out of money, property, body and soul, and lead them with you into the abyss of hell." [162]

Martin then proceeds to discuss the Bohemian heresy at great length. He defies the Pope to find in Scripture any argument against the double form of the sacrament. The Pope is a heretic, a renegade, himself banned and accursed: "He still raises his shameless, abusive voice to the skies and charges falsely the Greek Christians with being schismatics and renegades, while he is the first and only chief cause and originator of all apostasy." [163] "The Pope is not the lord but the servant of the sacrament." [164] As for the belated papal declaration on indulgences, "The old dragon from the pit of hell speaks in this bull." [165]

There follows a long attack, with much repetition of arguments, on the

[156] *Ibid.*, p. 365.   [157] *Ibid.*, p. 365, ll. 32 ff.   [158] *Ibid.*, p. 367, ll. 33 ff.
[159] *Ibid.*, p. 373, ll. 15 ff.   [160] *Ibid.*, p. 375, ll. 14 ff.   [161] *Ibid.*, p. 377, ll. 23 ff.
[162] *Ibid.*, p. 381, ll. 27 ff.   [163] *Ibid.*, p. 395, ll. 33 ff.   [164] *Ibid.*, p. 397, ll. 23 f.
[165] *Ibid.*, p. 405, ll. 19 f.

papal claim to succession from St. Peter, punctuated by frequent exclamations such as, "Pope, it is too much!" "Stop, Pope, that's enough of the game!" Ironically Martin states that the Church, by means of the Pope's new articles of faith, is leading Christ to school.[166] John Huss, on the other hand, has now become for Martin "Saint John." [167] When he comes to the article condemning as heretical the statement that a pious man sins in his good works, he questions the Pope's authorities: "Who? You, Gregory [the Great]? You are in the Pope's ban, and a heretic much worse than Luther." [168] As regards the burning of heretics, he compares the Pope to the Jews who turned Christ over to Pilate. "I call the Pope the greatest murderer that the earth has ever borne, for he murders body and soul. God be praised that I am a heretic in his eyes and those of his papists." [169] Why does he not go to Rome, as Christ went to Jerusalem, they ask? It is enough if he does not flee, but waits till they fetch him, like Christ, and lead him whither they will; then he will run after them and urge them to kill him. There follows a diatribe against the war with the Turks undertaken through sale of the Pope's indulgences. A restatement of his views on pride, free will, and purgatory constitute the remainder of the work.

Amid these vigorous polemics Martin continued his work as preacher and confessor within and without the cloister. He felt especially responsible for those who came troubled by fears that reading of his books might imperil their souls, and he heard of others being cross-questioned by confessing priests who were hostile to his ideas. His concern was shared by colleagues like Spalatin, who were anxious that something be done to pacify disturbed souls; and it was probably due to a suggestion of the elector's chaplain that Luther set himself to prepare a pamphlet instructing and comforting persons seeking guidance in this matter.[170] The *Instruction concerning Forbidden Books for Those Confessing* [171] was dashed off during the busy days of mid-winter [172] and a copy went to Spalatin at Worms about the middle of February.[173] The little pamphlet became popular at once. It was reprinted thirteen times in the same year in Wittenberg, Basel, Augsburg, and Halberstadt.[174]

Confessors, as Martin hears, are inquiring of their penitents whether they have copies of his books or are reading them. He advises them to answer

[166] *Ibid.*, p. 423, ll. 32 f.   [167] *Ibid.*, p. 431, l. 31.   [168] *Ibid.*, p. 437, ll. 10 ff.
[169] *Ibid.*, p. 441, ll. 21 ff.
[170] Letter from Melanchthon to Spalatin, March 2, 1521, *CR*, I, 360 f.
[171] *Ein Unterricht der Beichtkinder über die verbotenen Bücher. WA*, VII, 290 ff.
[172] On February 3 Luther reports to Spalatin that it is ready for printing. *WAB*, II, 260.
[173] Letter to Spalatin, Feb. 17, *WAB*, II, 266.
[174] *WA*, VII, 285 f.

that the matter is now in the hands of scholars and is still a subject of debate. If they are pressed further, they should say with humility that the priest is a confessor, not a chastiser; that the penitent need confess only what his conscience requires of him; and that it is his right to demand absolution. The responsibility for holding back something, therefore, lies with the one confessing, and the priest has no right to turn the holy sacrament into a disputation. If the priest is urgent and mentions the bull, the penitent is to answer that this instrument is not accepted by many pious persons. If absolution is not given, the confessant is to withdraw: "Where man does not absolve, God absolves," for one may be sure of absolution if one has confessed and asked for it. The confessor who refuses absolution is a robber who takes away what is ours. Those bold spirits who have the forbidden books and insist on keeping them should ask the confessor to absolve them at their own risk, and in case he refuses, tell him in the words of St. Peter: "We must obey God rather than man" (Acts 5.29). Just as all the world persecuted Christ and yet He was not in the wrong, so Luther's doctrine has not been disproved, but only attacked by force. The penitent who is refused absolution can go freely to the sacrament, since he is certainly absolved before God. They may take away the sacrament, but not its power and grace, for these depend on our faith. In case the sacrament is refused because no absolution has been given, the unshriven penitent can "let sacrament, altar, priests, and church go," and need think nothing of it if he must pass the whole year without the sacrament: "It is not your fault." [175] There has always been persecution for the sake of God's word: we ought to be grateful that we are found worthy of it.

Martin warns his readers not to confuse his works with libelous books and broadsides which are justly forbidden and which he also detests. His books are not anonymous, but always bear his name. Finally he urges priests and officials not to torment the consciences of their parishioners, otherwise confession, the most wholesome of all things, will be swept away in the confusion.

While Martin was keeping three presses busy, he found time to complete a work of devotion that had been long under his hand, *A Commentary on the Epistles and Gospels, the So-Called Postils*.[176] Here he turns to Latin and puts into the hands of the clergy a handbook for use in the Advent season. Many months before, in October, 1519, the elector had tried to divert Luther from the bitter mood of the Eck controversy by suggesting an interpreta-

[175] *Ibid.*, p. 295, ll. 2 ff.
[176] *Enarrationes epistolarum et evangeliorum, quas postillas vocant. WA*, VII, 463 ff.

tion of the Epistles and Gospels prescribed for Sundays and feast days.[177] After some hesitation Martin fell in with the idea. He evidently wanted to do something to simplify the customary interpretations and replace the traditions of medieval preaching on time-honored texts. Two months later he wrote Spalatin that he was at work.[178] The elector's chaplain was especially anxious that he should undertake the interpretation of the Lenten Scripture selections, and this Martin was eager to do, but by the following February he had brought the commentary only down to the third Sunday of Advent.[179] Early in June [180] he writes Spalatin that the work is being got ready for the press; but by mid-January, 1521, not more than three folios had been printed.[181] At last, on March 6, he is able to send the court chaplain the whole Advent postil.[182] It is to be a "taste" in order to see how the work is judged before he proceeds further with it.[183] It was evidently highly popular with the clergy, for it was printed in Wittenberg, Strasbourg, and Basel six times during the year.[184]

In the dedication to Elector Frederick, Luther excuses his delay by the necessity for a contest with "innumerable reptiles and great animals." [185] Like Nehemiah and Ezra, he has had to fight off the Arabs with one hand and build up the "old wall" with the other. It is not his ambition to write eloquent Latin, but "in the purest and simplest sense of the Gospel" to oppose ignorant and ill-informed glossaries and to set the words of God alone against fables and visions.[186]

His method is to interpret in simple Latin the familiar scriptural passages read at the Advent services. The dominating thought of his exegesis is the contrast between the law of justice and the work of faith. In spite of Martin's wish to make the interpretation simple and direct, many passages show traces of the older form of pulpit exposition. Conflicts between the evangelists as to whether Christ rode into Jerusalem on an ass or the foal of an ass still play a part. Certain of his mystical interpretations are as saturated with the medieval spirit as those of Father Otfried. The ass is the will of man oppressed by the many demands of the law; the foal of the ass is the spirit or will subdued by Christ. The vestments strewn in the path of Christ are the works and fruits of the martyrs and patriarchs who pre-

---

[177] To Spalatin, Oct. 16(?), 1519, *WAB*, I, 538.

[178] December 18. *WAB*, I, 594.

[179] Letter to Spalatin, Feb. 8, 1520, *WAB*, II, 36, l. 26.   [180] *WAB*, II, 120.

[181] Letter to Spalatin, January 16, *WAB*, II, 249.   [182] *WAB*, II, 275.

[183] "Pro gustu aliquo." Letter to Spalatin, Feb. 27, *WAB*, II, 270, l. 22.

[184] *WA*, VII, 459 ff. A German translation was published at Basel.

[185] *Ibid.*, p. 464, ll. 8 f.   [186] *Ibid.*, p. 465, ll. 10 ff.

ceded Him. The branches of trees and leaves are passages from sacred Scriptures. These and similar analogies are developed by Martin with obvious satisfaction at the success with which the hidden truth is thereby extracted from the Gospel narrative.

In the main, however, he seeks to penetrate the scriptural readings with a spiritual understanding. Eloquently he sets forth the release of mankind from law in a vivid contrast between the gift of the Tables on Sinai and the entry of Christ into Jerusalem, and here once more he draws on his cloister experiences to interpret the just God as the God who justifies. Once more we see how fully he has absorbed the ideology of Paul. Over against the magic world of faith stands the realm of works, with its terror: the impossibility of loving the law as we love sin. The law teaches man the extent of his hostility to God; confronting it is the "counter-concupiscence" of the Gospel,[187] which heals the corruption of the years and teaches the love of the law and the hatred of sin.

The devotional tone of the work is rarely interrupted by a discordant note from the conflict in which Martin was engaged. From time to time, however, we feel that the fighting spirit within him is straining at its leash. He pauses to raise a warning hand at the Church's division of things into sacred and profane or to slur at the vain hope of many people that they can win peace of conscience through pilgrimages and indulgences; or he scores the lack of moderation on the part of the Church authorities that was responsible for the schism of the Greeks and Bohemians. Here and there we hear a note of antagonism to the hierarchy, like that in the *Babylonian Captivity* and the attacks on the papal bull. He condemns those who think that absolution by pope or bishop is more important than by the simple priest. He contrasts the humility of John the Baptist, a voice crying in the wilderness, with the spirit of the bishops and clergy, who surpass all men in pomp, luxury, delights, and wealth. He closes with a long plea that people be instructed in the service of the heart. The aim of his commentary has been to ascertain whether men and the times are ripe for his message: "Let this be a sufficient preface, so that I may find out what is the fruit of my labor. I send out these four Sundays for the time, in order to see with what countenance Christians receive the Gospel of Christ after the hard and long Babylonian Captivity." [188]

A similar mingling of the spirit of devotion with traces of that of combat appears in another work, a translation and interpretation of the Magnificat, the exultant song of the Virgin that has played an important rôle in the

---

[187] *Ibid.*, p. 504, l. 10.   [188] *Ibid.*, p. 537, ll. 11 ff.

liturgy of the Church at all times and in Luther's day was sung especially at the Vesper service.[189] This work seems to have sprung not from a desire to meet the need of parishioners or clergy, but from an impulse of personal gratitude on Luther's part. In the fall of 1520 young John Frederick, as we have seen, had sent to the Wittenberg professor a letter of admiration and loyalty, filled with the enthusiasm of youth for a fighter in a cause which the Saxon prince himself was destined to serve in the following decade. Martin was evidently touched by these words of cheer, and in recognition resolved to dedicate to the future ruler of his state an interpretation of the great song of Mary. Apparently the work was begun early in December.[190] At the end of February Martin is busy with it,[191] and on March 19 it went to press.[192] Most of it seems to have been done in March and three folios were sent to John Frederick at the end of that month.[193] The fourth was in press but its completion was postponed until after the visit to Worms, and it was finally brought to an end during the early days of his stay at the Wartburg.[194] It appeared in print toward the end of August or early in September.[195]

In his dedication to John Frederick, Luther points out that great princes, who above all men need to fear and honor God, should learn and keep in mind the song of the Virgin. Then follows a prayer to the Blessed Mother to give him the spirit to interpret her song helpfully and thoroughly. The work itself begins with a translation of the simple yet sublime verses into homely and poetic German. In his introduction he points out God's attitude toward the lowly, so different from that of men, who have respect only for the rich and powerful and turn away from poverty, shame, distress, and anxiety. In contrast to the honored daughters of the priests and councilors in Jerusalem stands the poor daughter of a common citizen of Nazareth, the tender Virgin and simple maid who looked after the cattle and the house. She, however, attained to an honor of which the daughters of Sir Annas and Sir Caiphas were unworthy.

In scholastic manner Luther then goes on to analyze the words of the song.

---

[189] Das Magnificat verdeutscht und ausgelegt. Ibid., pp. 544 ff.

[190] See the letter from Spalatin to the elector, Dec. 3, 1520, in Waltz, Epistolae Reformatorum, p. 121.

[191] Letter to Spalatin, Feb. 27, 1521, WAB, II, 270. The dedication is dated March 10. See WA, VII, 545.

[192] Letter to Spalatin, March 19, WAB, II, 289.

[193] Letter from Luther to John Frederick, March 31, WAB, II, 295.

[194] Letter to Spalatin, May 14, WAB, II, 337. On June 10 the manuscript was sent from the Wartburg to Spalatin, who seems to have been impatient for its printing. WAB, II, 354.

[195] See WA, VII, 539. In the next five years there were eight reprints in Wittenberg, one of which was later translated into Latin. Ibid., pp. 540 f.

Like the tabernacle of Moses, man consists of a holy of holies, a holy place, and a court: spirit, soul, and body. When the spirit is holy, the whole man is sanctified, a thought which leads to an excursus on the familiar topic of the difference between works and faith. True praise is not that which is given in return for benefits and advantages alone. Mary allows God to work with her according to His will and receives whatever He gives in joy and confidence, while others love and praise God only for His kindness to them, in this way defiling all of God's gifts. In a little parable he tells a vision of a humble Cinderella at the Mass, who, alone of the sisters, receives with meekness the blows and rough treatment inflicted on her by a mysterious spirit of the altar, since she seeks nothing for herself and holds Christ dearer than his gifts. With Mary's pure spirit he contrasts the attitude of those who give praise only for benefits received. "God is not their saviour but His blessings are their saviour, and with these God must be their servant. These are the wretched children of Israel who in the desert were not satisfied with the bread from heaven, but wanted to eat meat, soup, and garlic." [196] With such persons all churches and cloisters are filled.

This brings him to distinguish between humility of the heart and that humility which seeks merely to win a reward. Humility, as used by Paul, means turning to slight and despised things, not to something that brings great returns. "Real humility never knows that it is humble." [197] If the greeting of the angel had come to a daughter of Caiphas, she would have accepted it as an honor and thought that it was fine and well done. "Oh, there is great pride under humble clothes, words, and gestures, and the world is now full of those who despise themselves, yet do not want to be despised by anyone else. . . . The Virgin, on the other hand, displays nothing but her nothingness, in which she was quite willing to dwell and remain. She never thought of honor or position, indeed, she did not realize that she was humble. Humility is so tender and so charming that it cannot bear to look upon itself." [198] On the other side, there are those who bring their good works as gifts and often put on the garb of a monk in the hour of death, seeking to profit by the works and the clothes of others. The painters do wrong who present the sublimity of the Virgin, so that we feel the contrast between her and ourselves rather than a contrast between the Virgin and God. The Virgin and the saints stand before us as an example of the inexhaustible goodness of God, even in the depths of their poverty.

Shall we pray to the Virgin for help? In answer to this question Martin

[196] *Ibid.*, p. 559, ll. 9 ff.   [197] *Ibid.*, p. 562, ll. 19 f.   [198] *Ibid.*, p. 563, ll. 24 ff.

remarks that he fears there is more idolatry in the world now than ever before. The honor paid to the Virgin means only that she was chosen to be the mother of God, an instrument like the wood of which the cross was made. We should be careful not to misuse the name of the Queen of Heaven. She can give no help. That must come from God alone, as the Virgin points out when she calls God a mighty and active power. "See how purely she ascribes all things to God, taking to herself no merit, honor, nor fame." [199]

Martin then turns to the Virgin's glorification of God's mercy. He draws a picture of the proud and obstinate man, full of insolent certainty that he has God's favor. "He is more sure and certain of abundant gratitude and merit with God than the very angels in heaven." [200] People like that proceed on their way even if the world must go to pieces. Such a person at present is the Pope with his crowd of followers. This leads to a lengthy discussion of the proper attitude of the Christian in defense of his "rights," [201] where Martin sets forth a truly medieval, ascetic philosophy with respect to the goods of this world. The Israelites fought and killed to accomplish God's will, not for material gain. Justice is a gift of God, but He may also take it away in order to see whether we are able to suffer injustice. Gain and advantage depend on God: if He wants us to have them, He will give them to us or permit us to win them ourselves in ways we have never thought of. This brings up an important question for the future ruler of Saxony, that of the right to protect his land and people by force. Such action, Luther argues, is justifiable, because it is not done for his own advantage but for the welfare of his neighbors. On the other hand it is a poor sort of protection to lay a whole district under tribute because a knight has perhaps carried off the property of a citizen. Christ did not root out the tares from the land for fear that the wheat might also be destroyed. In spiritual matters one must be ready to suffer shame, persecution, to be called a seducer, heretic, and criminal for the sake of the faith and the Gospel.

Unseen of man, unlimited by time, God humbles the mighty and exalts the lowly. When good men have been cast down and their strength seems exhausted, then God's strength comes to their assistance. Christ was powerless on the cross, but it was there He showed the greatest power by overcoming sin, death, the world, and the devil. God allows the proud to swell up with success because He has withdrawn from them; then He punctures the bubble just at the moment when they have become convinced that they are the best and wisest of all men. Obviously Martin has to restrain himself in order not to name the spiritual rulers whom he has in mind: "These are

---

[199] *Ibid.*, p. 575, ll. 13 ff. [200] *Ibid.*, p. 579, ll. 8 f. [201] *Ibid.*, pp. 580 ff.

the most poisonous, most harmful people on earth; theirs is a great abyss of devilish pride for which there is no help since they do not listen. They pay no attention to what is said but let it apply to poor sinners; "Whoever may need such instruction, it is not for them." John calls them a generation of vipers and Christ likewise. "Such are the true sinners, who do not fear God and only serve the purpose of being destroyed by God in their arrogance, because none persecute justice and truth more than they, though, as they say, for the sake of God and justice. Therefore in this respect they must be rated first among the three enemies of God. The rich are the least, the powerful are much worse, but scholars like these are the worst of all, for they push on the others. . . ." [202] Justice and truth have to find the wise, the powerful, and the rich against them; that is the way of the world. "The evil spirit has a dainty mouth, he likes to eat the best, the nicest, and the most choice, as the bear likes honey. Therefore the scholars, the holy deceivers, the great lords, the rich are the devil's dainties, while the poor, lowly, humble, unimportant, despised are God's choice ones." [203]

The interpretation is lengthy and grows in bitterness of tone toward the end, but returns at last to a gentler note of spiritual counsel. It closes with a solemn warning to the young prince against the danger of pride mentioned in the Virgin's prayer. This is the greatest, mightiest, and most harmful enemy of mankind. He suggests a brief prayer for princes expressive of consecration and humility and adds to it a translation of Solomon's prayer at Gibeon.

The work is a striking expression of the ideology of the transitional age, still medieval in its spiritual forms, but struggling to free itself from the bonds of convention. A tone of mystical devotion to the words and symbols of the Bible rises and falls within its scholastic framework; the adoration of the believing soul, the monastic attitude toward society, the intensity of the struggle against theological and hierarchical enemies, and the yearning for a return to the simple patterns of early Christian faith mingle in a stirring appeal to the young prince, deeply devout in his character and soon to become the ruler of a people.

The same earnest tone pervades a sermon *On the Proper Reception of the Sacred Body of Christ,* which was probably preached on the Thursday before Easter, March 28.[204] Here Martin makes an eloquent plea for a spiritual attitude toward the Mass. Again and again he strikes at the formality of the

---

[202] *Ibid.,* pp. 588, l. 33 ff. [203] *Ibid.,* p. 590, ll. 33 ff.

[204] *Sermon von der würdigen Empfahung des heiligen wahren Leichnams Christi, getan am Gründonnerstag* (March 28, 1521). *WA,* VII, 692 ff. See *WA,* IX, 640 ff., where the sermon appears in Poliander's text in a more extended form.

papal command for attendance on the Mass, even by those who live in open sin. On the contrary, only those should go to it who really hunger and thirst for the sacrament, and such believers will not wait for a command but will be driven by an inner urge. No one should abstain because he discovers evil in his heart, for the recognition of sin and the longing for purity is the beginning of hunger. He wishes that the priest might speak the mystical words of the service: "Take, eat this my body," loudly in German, and not secretly, for these are the "sweet words" of invitation and promise upon which the broken and humbled soul must build. He waves aside the benefits that are held out as rewards for attendance on the Mass, such as the assertion that the worshipper grows no older during the service. The promise of Christ is not temporal but spiritual help. Once more he points to faith as that which cleanses of sin and brings healing. Those are far off the road who frighten us with the fearful and solemn character of the Mass, for the Mass brings purity and help. The Lord does not drive men to the sacrament, but entices those heavily burdened with sin to come to Him for refreshment. He closes with an anathema against those who obey the command of the Church through fear: "Woe to all teachers who not only keep silent about the use and power of the holy sacrament but stand in the way of it with their crazy doings and writings." [205]

Neither these writings nor the tension of waiting for the summons to Worms hindered Martin in his office of sympathetic ministration to tormented souls. We have already seen how he responded to the call of the elector for consolation in the embattled days of the preceding summer. A similar call seems to have come to Martin in the early spring for a "sister" who was in trouble, and his answer, which has been preserved in two forms, was probably delivered as a sermon.[206] *"Consolation for a Person in Great Temptation"*: here again Luther points the suffering soul to God's promises. Her fate is that of all and she must submit to God's will. Praising Him as David did is the strongest medicine for depression. Out of his own life's experience Martin declares that the evil spirit of melancholy cannot be driven away with sadness and laments and anguish, but is exorcized only by praising God.[207]

---

[205] *WA*, VII, 697, ll. 27 ff.

[206] The two sources are Kaspar Creutziger's collection of Luther's consolatory works, published in 1545 (*WA*, VII, 779 f.), and the Poliander MS, where it bears the date 1521 (*WA*, IX, 314 ff.).

[207] *WA*, VII, 784.

33

MARTIN BEFORE THE DIET

THE effect of the edict seems to have been slight. A month after its issuance Lazarus Spengler, the Nuremberg delegate at Worms, reports that the placards were torn down and that books were not being turned in, but continued to be offered for sale.[1] To the diplomatic heads in the Rhenish city this was now of far less importance than the cloud arising beyond the Thuringian Mountains. The citation of Luther had been drawn up, as we have seen, at the end of the first week in March, and, after some hedging on the part of the imperial councilors, it was finally dispatched on March 15 or 16.[2] The bearer of the summons was no ordinary messenger but an imperial official of high dignity, Kaspar Sturm, the herald of the empire. It had been conceded by the emperor that Luther should have protection on the way,[3] but the pomp and dignity with which the summons was carried out implied an imperial recognition of the importance of the offender that aroused bitter protest on the part of the papal envoys.[4] Sturm was a sturdy representative of the Rhenish gentry, and had already given evidence that he shared the hostility of this class toward Rome. His anti-clerical attitude was well known to Aleander, who decorates him with a few choice Italian terms of abuse.[5] He regarded him as just the man to set in motion miraculous legends about Luther.

In about ten days Sturm rode into Wittenberg and delivered the document, formidable with its imperial seals, at the Augustinian Cloister.[6] The

[1] *DRA*, II, 891.

[2] See Kalkoff, *Depeschen*, p. 121, n. 1; Brieger, "Aleander und Luther, 1521," *Quellen und Forschungen zur Geschichte der Reformation*, I, 279, n. 1; *DRA*, II, 825, n. 2.

[3] The safe-conduct read, ". . . mit freiem, sicherm glait hin und wider." *DRA*, II, 520.

[4] See letter from Aleander to Medici, April 13 or 15, Brieger, "Aleander," pp. 134 f., and Kalkoff, *Depeschen*, p. 159.

[5] For example, "un matto protervo . . . sbajaffone." Brieger, "Aleander," p. 139, and Kalkoff, *Depeschen*, p. 164.

[6] The dates in the sources are given as March 23, 26, or 29. All three appear in the *Table Talk*. See *TR*, IV, No. 5123 and notes. The latest date seems the most probable. See *Luthers Tischreden in der Mathesischen Sammlung*, ed. by Ernst Kroker, p. 168, n. 5.

message arrived on the eve of the Easter holidays, and Martin delayed his departure until the festival was over. He was so little hurried in spirit at this time that he found leisure to write to Duke John Frederick a moderate and practical letter in answer to a series of questions of outmoded scholastic sort, and also to dedicate to Link his *Answer to Ambrosius Catharinus*.[7]

In the meantime the electoral authorities had seen to it that he was equipped with funds, and the city of Wittenberg provided a wagon with three horses. Three companions from the university and the cloister went with him: Nikolaus Amsdorf, the theologian; Johann Petzensteiner, a brother Augustinian; and young Peter Suaven, a Pomeranian of noble birth and humanistic training who had seen Luther in action at the Leipzig disputation. For this party the university gave twenty guilders toward the traveling expenses.[8]

On Tuesday, April 2, the little cavalcade crossed the Elbe and headed southward. Its route lay through Leipzig and the lands of hostile Duke George, who had furnished a safe-conduct for the journey.[9] In spite of official enmity, the city council of Leipzig honored Martin with a draft of wine when he reached that city,[10] where he spent the night of April 4. At Naumburg, picturesquely clustered about its great cathedral in the valley of the Saale, the route turned westward over the hills to Weimar, a road well known to Martin from his early Wittenberg days, and last traveled three years before when, flushed with ardor for the attack on indulgences, he had gone this way to the Heidelberg convention of his order. Faring along amid the first touches of spring, the little party whiled away the hours, not in casual conversation, but as cloistered discipline and university usage prescribed, with a discussion of a typical scholastic theme, the Book of Joshua as a pre-image of the Gospel.[11] Somewhere early in the journey they met an acquaintance from the Wittenberg library coming from the Rhineland, who gave them the first news of the publication of the imperial edict at Worms; and even before he reached Erfurt, if Luther's memory in later years may be trusted,[12] the document itself stared him in the face from the gates of the towns through which they passed. Perhaps he first saw it in Weimar

---

[7] March 31 and April 1, respectively. *WAB*, II, 294 f.

[8] For sources regarding the journey see "Neun Briefe von Hel. Eobanus, Joach. Camerarius . . . an Justus Jonas . . . ," ed. by Karl Förstemann, in *Neue Mitteilungen aus dem Gebiet historisch-antiquarischer Forschungen des thüringisch-sächsischen Vereins*, III, 1 (1837), 110 ff. See also *WAB*, II, 297, n. 9, and Gustav Bauch, "Zu Luthers Briefwechsel," *ZKG*, XVIII (1898), 408.

[9] March 8. Enders, *Briefwechsel*, III, 108 f.

[10] Letter from Veit Warbeck to John of Saxony(?), April 16, *DRA*, II, 851.

[11] Letter from Luther to Melanchthon, Eckartsberga, April 7, *WAB*, II, 296.

[12] *TR*, III, No. 3357a, p. 282.

where, as he gratefully recalled, Duke John, the co-ruler of the Ernestine Saxon lands, gave him further funds for the journey.[13]

Before he left Wittenberg, Martin seems to have been somewhat uncertain as to whether danger might not attend his passing through Erfurt, and he had appointed a rendezvous for his friend Lang at Eisenach, in case he should have to avoid the university town.[14] Whatever uncertainty he may have felt as to his reception was dispelled when he approached the city of his alma mater. Long before the little party reached the gates it was met by a crowd of students and other supporters of Luther, who led him into the city and through the narrow streets to the well-remembered gate of the Augustinian cloister. This was April 6, and the following day, a Sunday, he preached in the Augustinian chapel, whither crowds streamed to hear him. One of their number, a student from Dresden, recalled many years later that the portico of the church ("Porkirche") cracked from the multitude and a panic was averted only by the comforting words of Luther, who reminded his hearers that this was a trick of the devil.[15] Martin's friends at the university evidently rejoiced in his triumph. His enemies, like old Professor Arnold von Usingen, nursed their resentment in silence. The most gifted poet of the faculty, perhaps Germany's most gifted Latin poet in the whole humanistic age, Helius Eobanus Hessus, produced four elegies in his honor.[16] One of these celebrated in true humanistic fashion Martin's enthusiastic welcome, for which the river-god Herias (Gera) delivers a greeting. Germany's poet laureate who, like many other humanists, later washed his hands of the Lutheran cause, in these early days of the movement gave Martin his blessing for the coming great adventure: "Magna piis pro te Germania stabit in armis."

In his sermon Martin spoke on the Gospel of the day,[17] and according to the transcript of one hearer, at least, made no mention of his journey or its purpose. His sermon is a forceful declaration of hostility to the whole philosophy of "works," as implied in prescriptions of the Church for fasting and prayer, and once more sets forth Martin's old thesis of justification by faith. Here was plainly an opportunity to attack scholastic theology in a citadel closely associated in his memory with the subtleties of Occam and his

---

[13] *TR*, V, No. 5342b.

[14] Letter from Luther to Lang, March 29, *WAB*, II, 293.

[15] Daniel Greser, later superintendent in Dresden, in his *Curriculum vitae*, quoted in *WA*, VII, 803.

[16] See Lossius, *Anfang und Fortgang der Reformation*. The quotation appears in a poem reprinted by Lossius, "Ad Martinum Erphurdia abeuntem, Elegia Quarta," pp. 271 f. See also Krause, *Helius Eobanus Hessus*, II, 325, and IV, 274.

[17] *Ein Sermon auf dem Hinwege gen Worms zu Erfurt getan. WA*, VII, 808 ff. The sermon was issued in seven prints in 1521.

school, and Martin seized the occasion with both hands. The preachers who mingle with the Gospel heathen teachings like those of Aristotle, Plato, and Socrates, or who relate stories of Dietrich of Bern and other fables; the cruelty of the clergy who feed Christ's sheep "like butchers on Easter eve"; the simplicity of the priest or monk who thinks that saying rosaries and kneeling before the altar or singing Psalms will save him, and who is therefore trying to ride to heaven with the devil—these familiar themes are treated with vigor in an earthy tone that certifies to the faithful transcription of Luther's style by the hearer who has preserved the sermon for us. All the philosophy one needs, he declares, is a knowledge of Greek, Latin, and German. He is well aware that he is causing vexation to many people, thinking no doubt of his old teacher Usingen among others, but "I will and must speak the truth if it costs me my head twenty times over." [18] It is the recognition of God in our hearts that enables us to disregard human laws and papal bans. "Let the pope put forth as many laws as he will, I will keep them only so far as I please." [19]

The enthusiasm of the crowd and the honor shown him in this city of many associations must have cheered Martin to the point of elation. This appears in his letter to Melanchthon, written from Gotha, which the party seems to have reached on the evening of the eventful Sunday at Erfurt. Here he makes reference to this "Palm Sunday" of his, but leaves a description of it to another correspondent.[20] This is just one of a number of instances which show that quite naïvely in his own mind he parallels his Worms adventure to Christ's entry into Jerusalem and His trial and crucifixion.[21] Now in deadly seriousness he wonders whether his pompous entry into the university city was a temptation of the devil or a sign that his own death is approaching: "What will happen at Worms?"

The enthusiasm at Erfurt had its echo all along the route through Saxon lands. He preached in Gotha, whence his journey led over the hills to Eisenach where he preached again; [22] then the party proceeded down through pleasant Hessian country to Frankfort on the Main. To the academic and cloistered mind money seemed to vanish very rapidly on such a journey. To the academic and cloistered body, the hardships of the route, the evenings "surrounded by men, drinks, and conversation" [23] brought on an illness

---

[18] *Ibid.*, p. 812, ll. 18 f.   [19] *Ibid.*, p. 813, ll. 18 f.   [20] *WAB*, II, 296 and n. 10.

[21] Clemen, *Beiträge zur Reformationsgeschichte*, III, 9 f. See also Fritz Behrend, "Die Leidensgeschichte des Herrn als Form im politisch-literarischen Kampf besonders im Reformationszeitalter," *ARG*, XIV (1917), 49 ff.

[22] Letter from Veit Warbeck to Duke John(?), April 16, *DRA*, II, 851. Georg Buchwald, in "Luther-Kalendarium," *SVRG*, XLVII, II (1929), 19, states that he also preached in Weimar.

[23] Letter from Luther to Melanchthon, April 7, *WAB*, II, 296, ll. 20 f.

which hung to him throughout the week from Erfurt to Frankfort.[24] Martin believes he sees in this illness an attempt by the devil to keep him from Worms; so too the edict clearly seems a device to terrorize him. Nevertheless his spirit is unshaken. "We will enter Worms," he writes Spalatin from Frankfort, "in spite of all the gates of hell and the powers of the air . . . so make ready the lodgings." [25] Another day had brought the party across the Rhine and up its broad valley to Oppenheim, just a few miles from Worms and almost in view of the towers of the cathedral. Here, while they are waiting for morning to complete their journey, a visitor comes to the inn and confers with Luther. This was the young ex-monk Martin Bucer, who brought the invitation from Sickingen and Hutten to come to the Ebernburg. Our only source for this interview is a series of statements which Luther made years later in his *Table Talk*.[26] These differ widely, but all tend to show that he turned a deaf ear to the invitation. He and his friends could not forget the breach of imperial faith with Huss a century before, and the potential dangers attending the journey to Worms must have appeared in more and more vivid colors as they drew nearer to the city. Though they had traveled safely thus far, Martin could not free himself of the feeling that some trap might still have been set for him. This, at least, was his recollection years later.[27]

On April 16, at ten in the morning, the party, which had been increased at Erfurt by the rector of the university, Justus Jonas, an old friend of Luther's, and two companions from the university, rode through the gates of Worms. It was in truth a tumultuous entry.[28] A crowd on horse and on foot had gone out several miles to meet them, among them members of Frederick's court. Escorted by the clattering troop, the group passed up the street, through lines of spectators flattened against the walls, the imperial herald riding ahead. Behind, in his wagon with three others, sat the monk-professor, the focus of all eyes, as the procession rumbled over the narrow streets to the house of the Knights of St. John, about which some two thou-

---

[24] Letter from Luther to Spalatin, April 14, *WAB*, II, 298.

[25] *Ibid*. See also the letter to Melanchthon, *WAB*, II, 296. This may have been the origin of the often quoted, "Although there were as many devils there as tiles on the roof," which was possibly due to a slip of memory by Spalatin, who transmits it in his *Annales Reformationis* (II, 38 in Cyprian's edition). See *TR*, V, Nos. 5342a and 5342b, and *EA*, LXIV, 368.

[26] *TR*, III, No. 3357a, p. 282; IV, No. 5107; V, No. 5342b.

[27] *TR*, IV, No. 5107; V, Nos. 5342b and 5375b.

[28] Contemporary accounts by eye-witnesses are those of Veit Warbeck, the Saxon councilor, in a letter apparently to Duke John, Worms, April 16, *DRA*, II, 850 f.; Dr. Konrad Peutinger to the Augsburg council, April 19, *DRA*, II, 859 and n. 1; Georg Vogler, secretary of the Nuremberg commission at the Diet, to Johann Tettelbach, April 19, *DRA*, II, 853, n. 1.

sand people now surged, in spite of the fact that this was the hour of the morning lunch, as a spectator reports.[29]

We can well understand the consternation with which the papal envoys heard of these doings. Aleander now saw his worst fears realized. He had received news of the honors at Erfurt, and he rages especially against the herald, Sturm, who has permitted Luther's journey to become a triumphal progress.[30] He exerts himself now to do all he can to diminish the effect of Martin's appearance and check-mate the "tricks" of the Saxon prince. In the emperor himself he has full confidence, but none whatever in his advisers, whose "unreliability would make the stones go crazy." [31] They have refused to recognize the imminent peril to the general welfare and the safety of Christianity, and the despairing envoy fears that the "world is rushing into chaos" and expects the overturning (*commutatione*) of all Germany. Against the lukewarmness of the court, Aleander is obliged, as he confesses with bitterness, to use sweet words, to promise "Mary and the mountains" and the "head and hair of the Pope." [32] He looks into the future with deep pessimism and writes with truly prophetic earnestness of the results which are to follow in Germany: "In such a manner does the Saxon dragon raise his head; in such a manner do the Lutheran serpents multiply and hiss far and wide." [33]

It is, indeed, more than doubtful whether the emperor's advisers had believed that Luther would come to Worms after all.[34] Aleander now had the satisfaction of seeing them on tenterhooks. When the unruly monk, fresh from his enthusiastic reception along the road, stood before the gates the councilors turned in dismay to the papal representatives for advice. They were urged to have Martin come in as secretly as possible; and to lodge him in the bishop's palace, in which the emperor was staying, where he could be held incommunicado from all suspected persons and questioned without commotion.[35] Aleander had no faith, however, that the matter would be properly safeguarded. In the morning he heard the uproar of Luther's entry and soon news was brought him of the crowds that gathered around the heretic. He was appalled to learn that a priest had been seen to touch the

[29] Report of Fürstenberg to the Frankfort council, April 19, *DRA,* II, 863.

[30] Letter from Aleander to Medici, April 13 or 15, Brieger, "Aleander," pp. 134 f., and Kalkoff, *Depeschen,* p. 159.

[31] Brieger, "Aleander," p. 136, and Kalkoff, *Depeschen,* p. 161.

[32] Brieger, "Aleander," p. 137, and Kalkoff, *Depeschen,* p. 162.

[33] Brieger, "Aleander," p. 138, and Kalkoff, *Depeschen,* p. 163.

[34] Note Spalatin's report to Frederick of Father Glapion's fright when he hears Luther is on the way, *DRA,* II, 540, n. 1; also the fear of the Argonese secretary, according to Brück's report to Spalatin, *DRA,* II, 537. Aleander claimed that he never doubted Martin's coming.

[35] "Simpliciter." Brieger, "Aleander," p. 141, and Kalkoff, *Depeschen,* p. 166.

monk's garment three times like that of a saint. Ominous too was the fact that the crowd which had assembled about Luther's lodgings contained not only simple folk but members of the lower nobility of all grades, both lay and clerical.[36] Aleander hastens to report all this to Medici, not forgetting to add other dramatic details, such as the "demonic eyes" of the heretic, and the "deus erit pro me," spoken as he descended from the wagon; also that Luther had sat down to dinner with a large company and that the "whole world"[37] was now coming to see him. "The Duke of Saxony is already ruling and commanding . . . against God and against reason."

"Modern France dates from May 5, 1789; modern Germany dates from the appearance of Luther before the Diet of Worms."[38] This statement by a scholarly French Catholic reflects the extraordinary attention that this episode has received among all who study the history of Germany from whatever standpoint. The actors and observers at Worms were fully cognizant of its wide interest throughout Europe and foresaw something of its importance for posterity. Here, as in few great historical crises, the interest lay with one figure alone; whatever the religious affiliations of the reporter, his attention was concentrated on the behavior of Martin, on his words and gestures. The other *dramatis personae* figure in the accounts only in order to bring out more clearly the rôle played by the monk.

Unfortunately there were among the array of princes, prelates, nobility, gentry, burghers, and doctors of the law who made up the audience which squeezed into the small hall of the bishop's palace on the first day of Martin's hearing no sworn and certified clerks. Consequently in the crowd and confusion of that day and the following some statements were lost and some misunderstood. Particularly the final words of Luther have led to unending debate. Nevertheless the importance of the occasion was so well recognized that many noted on paper or committed to memory at the time the words and acts of the participants. It is therefore possible to construct out of a number of versions a picture of the proceedings that can hardly be inaccurate in any essential detail.

Two accounts were published within a few weeks after Luther's departure from Worms and professed to cover the entire proceedings. Both were by friends of Luther; both are diary-like and undoubtedly go back ultimately to day-by-day notes. The longer of these, *The Acts and Deeds of Luther at the Worms Diet*,[39] is in Latin, and comes, in all probability, from the pen

---

[36] *Acta et res gestae. DRA,* II, 546.
[37] Letter of April 16, Brieger, "Aleander," p. 143, and Kalkoff, *Depeschen,* p. 167.
[38] Paquier, *L'Humanisme et la Réforme,* p. 193.
[39] *Acta et res gestae D.M. Lutheri in comitiis principum Vuormaciae* (1521). *DRA,* II,

of one of the Saxon group, possibly Spalatin.[40] The briefer account is in German, *The Whole Negotiations Carried on with Luther*.[41] This seems also to have been prepared at Worms by one of the friends of Martin,[42] and treats the affair in summary form. Both accounts seek to be complete, though on a very different scale. Their sympathies are strongly with Luther. The author of the Latin report is well aware that he is writing history and that he is responsible for an objective and detailed account of events. Now and then the seams are visible where he has put together the day-by-day notes that formed his source; [43] but he aims evidently at the style of a Latin historian. The speeches of the participants are given first in direct quotation, then fall into the indirect. A further account, although for only a part of Luther's stay at Worms, is in German, *Certain Especially Important Transactions in Dr. Martin Luther's Affair . . . from Thursday after Misericordia to Friday after Jubilate*.[44] This takes up the narrative after the conclusion of Luther's hearings before the Diet and carries it on until his departure from Worms (April 19–26). Occasionally it supplements the story in the Latin *Acts and Deeds*. Evidently both accounts were based on the same notes. *Certain Especially Important Transactions,* however, races along in informal popular style and is more eager to put in an oar for Luther than the Latin account.[45] All three reports found wide distribution. Their popularity, however, did not compare with a report containing only the speeches delivered on the second day of the hearing, April 18, entitled *Luther's Answer at Worms*. This seems to have come out almost immediately and was published in Latin and in both High and Low German.[46]

---

541 ff., reproduces a Strasbourg print, with not very important variants from two other contemporary prints. The version *Acta reverendi patris* in *EA*, XXXVII, 5 ff., is a revision of the *Acta et res gestae* and without historical value. See *DRA*, II, 542 f., and n. 3.

[40] A natural supposition, but certain inner evidence makes Spalatin's authorship doubtful. See *ibid.*, p. 541, n. 1; also *WA*, VII, 820. Kalkoff (*Der Wormser Reichstag*, pp. 329 ff.), concludes that Jonas was the author.

[41] *Die ganze Handlung so mit dem hochgelehrten D.M.L. . . . ergangen ist. DRA*, II, 569 ff., gives a text with use of five contemporary prints. See also *WA*, VII, 861 f.

[42] Kalkoff, *Der Wormser Reichstag*, p. 328, ascribes it to Spalatin, but this theory is not convincing. See *DRA*, II, 569, n. 2.

[43] For example, an "adhuc" ("thus far") has slipped in, *DRA*, II, 558, l. 23 and n. 6; see also the present form "quaerunt": "occasio . . . quam non impigre quaerunt Romani legati," *ibid.*, p. 560, l. 2.

[44] *Etliche sunderliche fleissige Handlungen in D.M.L. Sachen durch geistliche und weltliche Fürsten des Reichs . . .* (1521). *DRA*, II, 600 ff. See *WA*, VII, 841 ff., where it appears with the corresponding part of *Acta et res gestae*.

[45] See *DRA*, II, 599 f., n. 1. Julius Köstlin and other authorities ascribe the authorship to the author of the Latin report, who, as mentioned above, may have been Spalatin. See Kalkoff, *Der Wormser Reichstag*, pp. 328 ff. The style, however, lacks the stiffness which seems generally to mark Spalatin's German.

[46] See *DRA*, II, 572, n. 1; *WA*, VII, 816 f.; 857 ff.

The High German version, by Spalatin, enjoyed especially wide popularity.[47]

Aleander, aware how important it was that the reporting of the events should not be left in the hands of Luther and his sympathizers, and stung by the publication of *Luther's Answer at Worms,* prepared to issue in due legal form a chronological report with notarial certification.[48] This was put together in Latin with the envoy's assistance by Johann von Eck, the legal official of the archbishop of Trier, and was sent to the Vatican, where it remained unpublished.[49] Here the official of the archbishop gives Luther's speeches at length and evidently after careful editing. The narrative lacks the dramatic tension of the chronicle accounts and is somewhat stiff and pompous in style, but is an important supplement to the versions with Lutheran bias. It furnishes evidence that the papal official who questioned Luther took full advantage of his position to impress the hierarchical view on the representatives of the estates.[50]

In addition to these chronicles and summaries, certain personal accounts also appeared. Among these were two by participants in colloquies with Luther: Hieronymus Vehus, the chancellor of the margrave of Baden,[51] and Johann Cochlaeus, a Frankfort cleric, who was enlisted for service by Aleander.[52] Aleander himself in day-by-day letters to Rome gave a diary of happenings.[53] Finally a Spanish report, sent from Worms to the Council at Castile, gives a somewhat detailed account.[54]

Naturally the stirring days at Worms played an important rôle in Luther's thinking throughout his later life. His recollection of events as reflected in his *Table Talk* was inexact, although not without historical value for certain incidents.[55] Most important are two letters, one written from Friedberg in

---

[47] *WA,* VII, 859 ff.

[48] Letter from Aleander to Medici, May 8, Brieger, "Aleander," p. 193, and Kalkoff, *Depeschen,* p. 216.

[49] First printed in Balan, *Monumenta,* pp. 175 ff., as *Acta comparitionis Lutheri in Diaeta Wormatiensi.* See also reprint in *DRA,* II, 588 ff. It is also reprinted in part in *WA,* VII, 825 ff., parallel with *Acta et res gestae.*

[50] Although the speeches of the official were no doubt edited for papal consumption, there is no reason to doubt their essential authenticity. Lazarus Spengler, writing within a fortnight after the hearing, reports the speeches more fully than the *Acta et res gestae.* See *DRA,* II, 886 f., n. 2. Konrad Peutinger notes that the Trier official urged Luther's recantation "mit vill Worten." *DRA,* II, 860, l. 13.

[51] Letter from Vehus to the margrave of Baden, June 3, *DRA,* II, 612 ff.

[52] Letter from Cochlaeus to a friend, June 12, *DRA,* II, 624 ff.

[53] Letters of April 17, 19, and a long summary letter of April 27, Brieger, "Aleander," pp. 144 ff. The last two were signed by Caracciolo, but as Luther would say, "stylus et saliva" are Aleander's.

[54] *DRA,* II, 632 ff., dated May 16. Translated by Kalkoff in "Briefe, Depeschen und Berichte vom Wormser Reichstag 1521," *SVRG,* LIX (1898), 49 ff. The authorship is uncertain. For a later MS, see Kalkoff, *Der Wormser Reichstag,* p. 336, n. 3.

[55] See *DRA,* II, 540, n. 2. The account said to have been given at Eisleben in the later

Hesse two days after he left Worms, addressed to the emperor,[56] and the other six days later to Count Albert of Mansfeld.[57] Both are apologies and were intended to clarify his position. They are somewhat formal statements, especially the letter to the emperor, which Martin in all likelihood prepared at the suggestion of the Saxon councilors before leaving Worms.[58]

The day following Luther's arrival at Worms, Wednesday, April 17, the indefatigable Aleander had gone early in the morning with the emperor's confessor, Glapion, to set the stage for the hearing and restrict it within the narrowest limits that the situation permitted. Intent as he was that the heretical professor should not be given too large an audience nor an opportunity to do more than answer the formal questions, he drew up a confidential written program for the emperor.[59] In accord with this, the hereditary marshal, Ulrich von Pappenheim, appeared at four in the afternoon at Luther's lodgings in the house of the Knights of St. John and summoned him to come before the emperor and estates assembled in the bishop's palace, where Charles had taken residence.[60] Martin followed him thither accompanied by the imperial herald and several Saxon councilors and friends. A crowd blocked the streets and looked down from the roofs, so that the party was obliged to go by a round-about way (*quasi furtim*).[61] Luther was led at once before the emperor and Diet, packed into the small hall to the point of suffocation. In accordance with the plan of Aleander,[62] Luther was warned that he was not to speak except in answer to questions. Having done all they could to render impossible anything resembling a disputation, the papal envoys both remained away from the session, probably to avoid exciting the resentment of Luther's sympathizers among the estates.

When Martin stood in the midst of the crowd, facing the emperor, observed of all observers, his little group of followers and advisers drew closely about him. Among them were, no doubt, his companions from Wittenberg, Jonas from Erfurt, and one or more of the Saxon elector's councilors. The author of the Spanish report noted that these men forced

---

years of his life is in the main confirmed by other sources. "Historie, wie es Doct. Martin Luther auf dem Reichstage zu Worms . . . ergangen sei," *EA*, LXIV, 366 ff.

[56] *WAB*, II, 307 ff. [57] *WAB*, II, 321 ff.

[58] See Kalkoff, *Der Wormser Reichstag*, p. 325.

[59] Letter to Medici, April 17, Brieger, "Aleander," p. 145, and Kalkoff, *Depeschen*, pp. 168 f.

[60] The old palace was destroyed by French invaders at the end of the seventeenth century. It lay not far from the cathedral.

[61] *Acta et res gestae, DRA*, II, 547, l. 7.

[62] Letter to Medici, April 17, Brieger, "Aleander," p. 145, and Kalkoff, *Depeschen*, p. 169.

their way about him so as to separate him from the crowd.[63] Standing there he appeared in the eyes of this observer "a man . . . of forty years of age, more or less, vigorous in expression and physique, eyes without distinction, mobile of countenance and frivolously changing his expression. He wore the habit of the Order of St. Augustine, with leathern girdle, his tonsure large and recently shaven, his hair close clipped." This picture of the monk corresponds strikingly with the well-known portrait from the school of the Wittenberg artist Lucas Cranach, painted in the preceding year. Martin stands here at Worms, however, not for a portrait, but with all the muscles of his stocky body tense, his head, white from the razor except for its fringe of hair, leaning forward, the haggard face flushed with excitement and strained in expectation of the great moments to come. Facing him was young Charles, who, like the other Italian and Spanish observers, doubtless found Martin's person unattractive and undistinguished. As the emperor looked upon the thick-set figure with the gaunt face rising from the monkish cowl, he is said to have exclaimed: "This man will never make me a heretic!" [64] Before him on a bench lay a pile of books, as Luther recalled many years afterward.[65] There were a score or more works, both in Latin and German, including in all probability the two recent attacks on Emser. They had been assembled by Aleander for the hearing, and as listed in his papers, comprised the chief and crucial works of Martin.[66] Their author gazed upon them, wondering, as he later recalled, how they could have brought them all together.[67]

The tense silence was broken by the jurist Johann von Eck, a man of imposing height and sonorous voice. Addressing Martin first in Latin and then in German, he said: "Martin Luther, His Imperial Majesty has summoned you for two reasons: to know whether you acknowledge as by you the books before you, which have been attributed to you; and then, if you do acknowledge them, whether you stand by them or wish to revoke any of them." [68] The imperial secretary then read the list of books.

[63] *DRA*, II, 632 f.

[64] "Questiu mai me farebbe heretico." Letter from Aleander to Medici, April 29, Brieger, "Aleander," p. 170, and Kalkoff, *Depeschen*, p. 196. There is no reason to doubt that the remark was correctly reported to Aleander.

[65] *EA*, LXIV, 369.

[66] For the list, see Balan, *Monumenta*, pp. 183 f., and *DRA*, II, 548, n. 1. See also letter from Aleander to Medici, April 17, Brieger, "Aleander," p. 146, and Kalkoff, *Depeschen*, p. 170.

[67] "Historie, wie es Doct. Martin Luther . . . ergangen sei," *EA*, LXIV, 369.

[68] *Acta et res gestae*, *DRA*, II, 547. The prelude to the question in Von Eck's report is long and rhetorical. *Ibid.*, p. 588.

With a bow to the emperor,[69] Martin answered first in German and then in Latin.[70] He spoke briefly and to the point. He could and would not deny that the books named were his. As to whether he would maintain or revoke them, however, that was a question of faith and the salvation of souls, and concerned the Divine Word. It would therefore be rash and dangerous to proceed without due consideration. The Spanish report as well as the Lutheran chroniclers noted that he added here the words of Christ, "Whoever denies me before men, him will I deny before my Father in heaven." He finished by requesting time for deliberation so that he might answer the question without damage to God's word or danger to his own soul.

This, or in effect this, Martin spoke with a low voice so that his reply was unintelligible to some.[71] Critical observers in the small audience hall read in his face an expression of fear.[72] To hostile eyes his manner was nervous and his gestures and expression disagreeable.[73] Plainly the monk, accustomed to face only uncritical audiences in lecture room and church, and used to the limitations prescribed by the forms of the academic disputation, was shaken by the stern ordeal. When he saw himself in the presence of the mightiest of the land, surrounded by some friendly faces, to be sure, but also by many that were hostile and contemptuous, nervousness and loss of confidence seized hold of him. This did not, however, mean any weakening of his resolution; and his request for time to reflect is not to be interpreted as meaning that even at this moment of greatest intensity he considered the possibility of revocation. Most probably the Saxon councilors had advised him in advance to give this answer. These men were not only devoted to his cause [74] but also represented the rights of a territorial state and its subjects under the terms of the imperial agreement of the preceding year. Luther's books had already been sequestrated. It seems that the tactics of the papal party were now to get an answer from him that could be used to exact from the estates approval of the edict of outlawry, and then to get the heretic away from Worms as quickly as possible.[75] The obvious counter

[69] "Hizo suo acathamiento á el emperador." Spanish report, DRA, II, 633, ll. 26 f.

[70] For evidence as to the sequence of the languages used, see DRA, II, 550, n. 1.

[71] Report of Fürstenberg to the Frankfort council, April 19, DRA, II, 863; report of the Strasbourg delegation, April 18, DRA, II, 851, ll. 24 f.

[72] "Als ob er erschrocken und ensatz wer," Fürstenberg's report, DRA, II, 863; "con mucha ansia," Spanish report, DRA, II, 634.

[73] Ibid. See also Aleander's remark on Martin's continual turning about of his head. Letter of April 17, Brieger, "Aleander," p. 147, and Kalkoff, Depeschen, p. 171.

[74] For an interesting survey of the councilors of Elector Frederick, see Kalkoff, Der Wormser Reichstag, pp. 212 f., n. 3.

[75] This was Luther's opinion expressed on May 3 to Albert of Mansfeld. WAB, II, 321 ff.

move was request for time to be used by Luther and his advisers in giving careful consideration to the answer.

As was its custom in considering questions of procedure, the Diet then broke up into its separate estates for consultation.[76] The fear that Martin would use the requested time to prepare a long disputatory address filled with propaganda is clearly reflected in the answer by Johann von Eck: the monk is censured for not having known from the imperial summons what he would be asked, and for not being ready with his answer; nevertheless a respite of twenty-four hours is granted on condition that the answer be made verbally and not in writing.[77] The official of Trier, in rendering this decision, made a long address which had probably been prepared beforehand as a general indictment of Luther. It is omitted from the Lutheran accounts, but its general tenor is well attested in other sources.[78] In highly oratorical language, with a free use of legalistic expressions, he warns Martin against seeking to divide the Church and trouble the peace of the Christian state, pointing to the revolutionary effects of his personal and distorted interpretations of the Scriptures, so that many have been seduced and condemned to the infernal regions for his errors. He urges the errant monk to reconsider, with a promise of grace from the emperor and from the Pope through the emperor. The orator, coached in advance by Aleander, makes clear the position of Charles, who has pledged himself to stand by the Christian Church and the Apostolic See and now threatens justice against the heretic. The speech closed with a lengthy rebuttal of Martin's right to claim further time for deliberation, and, as we have said, a final granting of his plea by the emperor.[79]

It is probable that this long speech interested Luther less than the encouraging remarks that came to him while the jurist was making his oration. If we may believe the authors of the *Acts and Deeds*,[80] many used the opportunity to wish him good courage and called out cheering words, to which the scribe gives a scriptural form. This encouragement was continued after

---

[76] As a foreigner, Aleander notes this form of procedure. Letter of April 17, Brieger, "Aleander," p. 146, and Kalkoff, *Depeschen*, p. 170.

[77] *Acta et res gestae*, DRA, II, 549.

[78] Undoubtedly Von Eck edited his remarks somewhat before sending them to Rome; but the speech was probably delivered essentially as recorded in the Vatican MS, printed in *DRA*, II, 588 ff., since Aleander in his letter to Rome the same day, April 17, gives the gist of it. See Brieger, "Aleander," p. 147, and Kalkoff, *Depeschen*, pp. 170 ff., where, however, the official's points are in a different sequence. The Spanish reporter summarized it correctly. *DRA*, II, 634.

[79] Von Eck's report, DRA, II, 590, ll. 16 ff.

[80] *DRA*, II, 549, ll. 11 ff.

he returned to his lodgings, where, as he recalled many years later,[81] noblemen, probably members of the Franconian knighthood, came in numbers to assure him that all of his opponents would be destroyed before he should be burned. On the other hand Aleander, at least, felt that the monk had lost heavily through the impression made by his personal appearance, especially on the emperor. According to the nuncio, Charles declared his disgust with the fantastic opinions of the "ribald" monk (*ribaldo*), and his impatience with the behavior of the duke of Saxony.[82] The nuncio closed his day's report to Rome with a prayer that the coming of this Antichrist might yet work out for the best.

The following day the hearing was transferred to a larger hall in the bishop's palace.[83] The hour had been set at five in the afternoon, but on account of other business of the princes, Luther was not admitted until six, waiting the while in a great crowd.[84] Evidently he looked forward to the ordeal with cheerfulness, for Dr. Peutinger of Augsburg went over to him in the courtyard and was jovially greeted with an inquiry about the welfare of his family.[85] In the hall the press was so great that the emperor could scarcely get to his place, as the Spanish observer noted.[86] At the request of Charles, the Trier inquisitor had been coached early in the morning by the papal envoys.[87] After a prologue of considerable length,[88] reproving the monk for his lack of readiness with a definite answer, Dr. von Eck now demanded a reply to the second question of yesterday. Again the jurist spoke, first in Latin, and, as the Lutheran chroniclers noted, with the vehemence of a prosecuting attorney,[89] and then in German. Luther answered first in German and then turned his answer into Latin.

The notes of the Lutheran reporter show that Martin now felt himself master of the situation. The speech which he delivered, "with becoming modesty and yet with Christian vehemence and forcefulness," according to his supporters, was a formal and carefully prepared statement of his position.

---

[81] "Historie, wie es Doct. Martin Luther . . . ergangen sei." *EA*, LXIV, 369.

[82] Letter of April 17, Brieger, "Aleander," p. 148, and Kalkoff, *Depeschen*, p. 172.

[83] According to the Spanish report, *DRA*, II, 634, l. 20. Note the reading "una sala baxa grande" in a Paris copy of this report. A. Morel Fatio, "Le premier témoignage Espagnol sur les Interrogatoires de Luther à la Diète de Worms en Avril 1521," *Bulletin Hispanique*, XVI (1914), 35 ff. See Kalkoff, *Der Wormser Reichstag*, p. 336, n. 3, supported by Konrad Peutinger's letter to Augsburg, April 19, *DRA*, II, 860.

[84] *DRA*, II, 549, ll. 21 ff.; p. 574, l. 15.

[85] *DRA*, II, 862, ll. 11 ff.   [86] *DRA*, II, 634, ll. 25 f.

[87] Letter from Aleander to Medici, April 17, Brieger, "Aleander," p. 145, and Kalkoff, *Depeschen*, p. 168.

[88] Here again the account in the Von Eck report is longer than that in the *Acta et res gestae*. See *DRA*, II, 591, ll. 4 ff.

[89] In *Acta et res gestae* it is noted that he spoke "virulentius" in Latin. *DRA*, II, 550, l. 12.

Only a fragment of the German draft remains, in Luther's own hand,[90] containing merely the introduction. It is difficult to say when the statement was prepared. In view of Martin's habit of drafting under pressure and his custom of writing his sermons out only after delivery, it is not impossible that it was drawn up after the preceding day's session. The citation he had received in Wittenberg had, after all, not indicated the exact nature of the questions he would be asked since it stated merely that the emperor wished to receive information concerning Luther's teaching and books. On the other hand, Martin knew of the posting of the imperial edict well before he entered Worms, and must certainly have been aware that according to this he would be asked if he admitted authorship of his writings and was willing to recant. It seems likely, therefore, that he had already planned an answer in tentative form but, in accord with the strategy of the Saxon advisers as postulated above, had asked for time so that he might formulate his response carefully. What he wished to say was of course quite clear in his mind, for it had been repeated many times in sermons and polemical writings. Now it was necessary to bring it into a form so dignified and tactful as to disarm resentment and yet leave no doubt as to his position. The restraining hand of Frederick's councilors is evident; in no way, however, does this impair the force or sincerity of Luther's style as we have it in the Latin version.[91] In view of the fact that there exists only a fragment of the German address, it is probable there was no time to complete this before the hearing. Martin's bilingual ability was sufficient and his memory powerful, however, so that his delivery of the German speech impressed his advisers by its vigor. According to his own account in later years, a Latin form was called for after he had finished. What with the heat ("I was sweating heavily") and embarrassment at the proximity of the great ones of the earth, he had difficulty in rendering it at first, but then controlled himself and repeated the speech in Latin.[92]

"Truly with the help of Christ I will not revoke even a dot in all eternity." This resolution Martin recorded in a brief letter to a distinguished humanist of the older generation in Vienna, a letter written immediately after his re-

---

[90] *WA*, VII, 815.

[91] The address, from Luther's MS, was printed almost immediately at Wittenberg, Hagenau, Strasbourg, and Augsburg, together with Von Eck's speech following Luther's address and Luther's final answer "without horns and teeth." *WA*, VII, 816 f.; German translation, *ibid.*, pp. 858 ff.; see also *DRA*, II, 572, n. 1. The response of Luther was widely circulated; it was incorporated into the Lutheran chronicle, *Acta et res gestae*, and in a somewhat altered form into the Aleander–Von Eck report. An examination of these two chronicles shows that Luther's speech and the answer of the official are awkwardly inserted in both. See *DRA*, II, 550 ff. and 591 ff.; also p. 551, n. 1.

[92] *EA*, LXIV, 370.

turn from the first hearing.[93] With this determination he proceeded now to take advantage of the opportunity to formulate for the emperor and estates his position, as he had done the year before in the "Offer." This was not the disputation before neutral judges that he had long hoped for, but it was at least an arena in which to explain and justify his stand.

The address shows, as we have seen, marks of careful preparation. It begins with a *captatio benevolentiae* directed to the emperor and the assembled lords and gentry for any improper use of titles and formalities of which he might be guilty. Concerning the first question asked him the day before, he reasserts his answer: The books are all his, unless some interfering hand has changed them. As regards the second question, like an experienced debater he puts the burden of proof on the other side. The books are not all of one kind. Some deal with faith and morals and these have been accepted as useful even by his enemies. To condemn these would be to condemn the truth as universally recognized by friend and foe. A second group attacks the papacy and its acts. No one can deny, he asserts boldly, that through the laws of the pope and doctrines of man the conscience of the Christian world is held prisoner and the substance of the German people destroyed with incredible tyranny. In proof he cites statutes from the canon law which he regards as opposed to the Gospel and the opinion of the Fathers. To revoke attacks upon these misuses would be to give strength to tyranny and open, not merely windows, but doors to a "worse raging" than ever before. Licentiousness and weakness would rule with impunity over the poor German people. "Then, good God! I would be an instrument for evil and tyranny." [94]

As the bitter wave of Martin's resentment threatened to gather force, the emperor imposed silence with regard to this question and bade him go ahead on another line.[95] The third group of books, he then declares, was written against the defenders of Roman tyranny. Here Luther concedes that he may have gone further in the violence of his attacks than befitted his profession: "For I do not set myself up to be a saint, nor do I argue about my life, but about the doctrines of Christ." [96] These works also he cannot revoke, for again this would lead to a greater raging of tyranny.

He cannot revoke; but like Christ before the high priest, he is ready to hear charges against any evil in his doctrines. If the Lord himself did not

[93] To Johann Cuspinianus, April 17, *WAB*, II, 300.

[94] *DRA*, II, 553, l. 19.

[95] Reported only by Aleander, to Medici on April 19, but highly probable. Brieger, "Aleander," p. 152, and Kalkoff, *Depeschen*, p. 175.

[96] *DRA*, II, 553, ll. 24 f.

refuse to listen to testimony against his teaching, how much more must poor scum of the earth (*faex*) like himself expect it? "Therefore I beg, in the name of God's mercy, that Your Majesty and you, illustrious rulers, whoever may be able, whether of high or low estate, testify and point out my errors, overcome me with the writings of the prophets and evangelists, for if I shall be thus instructed I will be most ready to recant any error and will, indeed, be the first to hurl my little books into the flames."[97] From this his opponents may see that he has weighed all dangers and dissensions that his doctrines have caused; indeed, he is delighted that zeal and disputing arise, for that is the course and the result of God's word. What he fears is that "this best young Prince Charles," in whom so many hopes rest, may begin his reign in misfortune. He points to many rulers in Scripture who tried to pacify and establish their kingdom by the wisest schemes, but without God, who "taketh the wise in their own craftiness" and "removeth the mountains and they know it not." With a humility that could scarcely have been altogether sincere, he adds: "I do not say this because so many persons of the highest rank need my doctrine or my warning, but because my native Germany ought not to be deprived of my due service. Herewith I commend myself to Your Majesty and to your governors with the humble prayer that you do not suffer me to be delivered over without cause as an abominable person to the fanaticism of my adversaries. I have spoken."[98]

This speech as we have it in Luther's original Latin is a vigorous presentation of his position, bolstered by numerous scriptural quotations and references. The response of the inquisitor, which appears at length in the Aleander–Von Eck report to Rome, is a formal indictment of Martin as a heretic.[99] The orator first reproves him for vehemence and bitterness unbecoming the monastic cloth. He then points out that Martin's claim that much truth is contained in his books is merely a repetition of a defense made for Arian and other heretics whose books were burned. Now also he seeks refuge in the same excuse advanced by all heretics, that he is willing to be instructed. All his false doctrines, Von Eck continues, are but heresies previously set forth by the Picards, the Waldensians, the Poor of London, Wyclif, Huss, and others. It is not proper to attempt to revise anything that the Catholic Church has determined. The speaker points a rhetorical finger at the rejoicing of Jews and infidels over these dissensions, and solemnly chides Martin for supposing that he can interpret the meaning of Scripture which the "most sacred doctors have sought for, sweating day and night."[100]

[97] *Ibid.*, p. 554, ll. 12 ff.
[98] *Ibid.*, p. 555, ll. 5 ff.
[99] *DRA*, II, 591 ff.
[100] *Ibid.*, p. 593, ll. 21 ff.

In an eloquent, if somewhat florid, peroration he arraigns him for thus setting up his own opinion against the sacred orthodox faith established by
Christ, revealed by the Apostles, illustrated by miracles, confirmed by martyrs,
cleared from obscurities by the sacred doctrines, confirmed by the councils,
discussed by the learned, defined by the Church, transmitted by the Fathers
at death, and put beyond all range of discussion by pope and emperor, in
order to make an end of argument and altercation among those rash persons who will not submit to the decision of Holy Church. At the conclusion
of this flight of eloquence, the orator warns Martin that he can expect no
disputation regarding matters of faith and demands a "sincere, candid, unambiguous answer, without horns," as to whether he is willing to revoke
his books and errors.[101]

The long-expected moment had come, and Martin was ready: "If then,
Your Majesty and rulers ask for a simple answer, I will give it without
horns and without teeth,[102] as follows: Unless I am shown by the testimony
of Scripture and by evident reasoning (for I do not put faith in pope or
councils alone, because it is established that they have often erred and
contradicted themselves), unless I am overcome by means of the scriptural
passages that I have cited, and unless my conscience is taken captive by the
words of God, I am neither able nor willing to revoke anything, since to
act against one's conscience is neither safe nor honest." He then added in
German, "God help me, amen!"[103]

This conclusion of Luther's brought to an end the second day's hearing.
In the simplicity of the ancient and popular German formula with which
Martin terminated his statement the resolution of the fateful hour stands

---

[101] "Quamobrem eadem sepius inculcanda et repetenda puto, ut sincere et candide, non
ambigue, non cornute respondeas, an libros tuos et errores inibi contentos, abs te disseminatos,
revocare et retractare velis, necne. . . ." *Ibid.*, ll. 40 ff. *Acta et res gestae*, which omits the
official's long speech, except for a brief exposition of the unimpeachable character of the condemnations and definitions of a council of the Church, also puts the question more briefly,
dropping, as so often, into the first person: "Orator imperii . . . dixit . . . a me peti sim-
plex, non cornutum responsum, an velim revocare vel non?" *DRA*, II, 555, ll. 10 ff.

[102] ". . . neque cornutum neque dentatum." *Ibid.*, ll. 15 f. Considerable ink has flowed
concerning the meaning of these words. "Cornutum" points probably to the "syllogismus
cornutus," or sophistical syllogism of the manuals of logic; an answer "without horns" would
then be a straightforward answer. "Dentatum" is more obscure. The most obvious explanation
seems that "without teeth" naturally suggested itself as a parallel to "without horns." See
R. Meissner, " 'Ohne Hörner und Zähne,' " *ARG*, III, iv (1906), 321 ff. See also Kalkoff,
Der Wormser Reichstag, pp. 348 f.

[103] *DRA*, II, 555, ll. 14 ff. The final "Gott helf mir, amen!" and its variants have given
rise to endless discussion. According to note 1, *ibid.*, an investigation of the manuscript relationship shows that the traditional additions to the conclusion of Luther's answer, "Ich kann
nicht anders. . . . Hier stehe ich," were a Wittenberg expansion and without justification
in the sources.

in a form far more dramatic than the later and more often quoted "Here I stand; God help me, I cannot do otherwise." This latter form rests on a tradition evidently dating from the early baroque age, which could not appreciate the simple "God help me!"

The chronicles of the proceedings from the Lutheran side do not bring them to an end with this reply. It marked, however, the crucial moment. Darkness was approaching and the air was fetid from the crowd, which now surged out, leaving half-understood the protests of Von Eck at Luther's assertion that the council could err in matters of faith, and Martin's offer to prove it had erred.[104] Once more, therefore, the question of the council comes to the fore. It was the point which the papal representatives could count upon most readily to prejudice the German princes against Martin. The Hussite wars, with their heavy toll on life and property, were still in the memory of everyone; and it was the Council of Constance that had condemned Huss and joined hands with the emperor to violate his safe-conduct. To reject the findings of the Council of Constance was therefore, in the eyes of many, not only heresy, but something like treason. Aleander, fully aware of this, notes in a report of the hearing which he put together hastily on the following day for the Medici, that Von Eck had previously demanded that Martin should revoke what he had written "against the sacred Council of Constance," and also the familiar response of Martin that he took his stand on the words of the Bible.[105]

As Martin and his friends pushed their way down the narrow street, a good part of the audience followed with a great hubbub. The enthusiasm for Luther's cause and the touchiness of the lower nobility in his defense broke out in an uproar, as Martin recalled years afterwards,[106] when the approach of two attendants sent to guard him started a rumor that he was to be taken away to prison. This would have been impossible at the moment for anything short of an army. The fervor of the Frankish knights and the Saxon group had been heated white by the monk's bold and uncompromising defense. Even the cool-headed jurists who represented the cities caught something of the contagion.[107] Martin, too, was in a buoyant mood. Observers, who crowded the room so that even the electoral princes could scarcely find seats, noted the change in Luther from the day before. His

[104] *Acta et res gestae, DRA,* II, 558, ll. 1 ff.; see also Von Eck's report, *DRA,* II, 594, ll. 4 ff.
[105] Aleander and Caracciolo to Medici, April 19, Brieger, "Aleander," p. 153, and Kalkoff, *Depeschen,* p. 175.
[106] *EA,* LXIV, 370 f.
[107] See the report of Fürstenberg on the following day to the Frankfort council. *DRA,* II, 864 ff.

voice was now bold and showed no signs of fear.[108] It was not surprising,
now that the great moment had passed, that Martin's soul rebounded with
elation. His decision had been declared to emperor and estates and to all
the world. As he went out through the crowd surrounded by his German
friends, the observer who drew the Spanish report of the hearing noted the
monk's mood and marked that he and his comrades "raised their arms,
moving the hands and fingers, as the Germans do for a signal of victory at
the tournament."[109] When he came into his lodgings he threw up his
hand with the same triumphant gesture, shouting joyfully to his friends:
"I've come through, I've come through!"[110] A sinister incident occurred
as Luther and his party came out into the court of the palace. The women and
esquires who were waiting at the entrance for the Spaniards to come out,
raised the cry, "To the flames!"[111] Lutheran observers did not hear this
grisly reminder of the pains of heresy, but only the cat-calls and satirical
shouts that continued to resound after the departing Martin.[112]

Luther had now given his answer. With a speed that caused consternation
among some of the representatives of the estates, Emperor Charles resolved
upon a counter action. Evidently his conscience had been stung by the debate and the arguments of the jurist Von Eck, which must have mobilized
again the lessons of loyalty to Church and dynasty taught him by his
Spanish-Burgundian tutors. At eight o'clock the next morning, April 19,
he summoned the estates[113] and laid before them a declaration which he
had written down in French, his native language. This statement by Charles
is brief, but categorical.[114] It begins by calling attention to the tradition of
loyalty of his four imperial, royal, and ducal lines of ancestors to the Church
of Rome, to its decrees, ceremonies, and customs. As successor to this great
heritage he is resolved to support its religious traditions, including the
ordinances of the Council of Constance. From his nontheological viewpoint
Charles remarks that obviously the opinion of a single brother must be

---

[108] *Ibid.*, l. 7; see also the report of Dr. Jakob Krel, April 20, *DRA*, II, 885 f.

[109] *DRA*, II, 636, ll. 20 ff. Aleander also reports this to Medici. Brieger, "Aleander," p. 153.

[110] "Ich bin hindurch, ich bin hindurch." Letter from Sixtus Ölhafen to Hector Pömer of
Nuremberg, April 18, *DRA*, II, 853, ll. 18 ff.

[111] *DRA*, II, 636, ll. 24 ff.   [112] *DRA*, II, 558, ll. 6 f.

[113] See *Acta et res gestae*, *DRA*, II, 558, ll. 8 ff.: "principes, electores, duces, cuiuscumque status
ordines, qui consultationibus adesse solent." The Roman envoys, Aleander and Caracciolo,
April 19, speak only of electors and princes. Brieger, "Aleander," p. 153, and Kalkoff,
Depeschen, p. 177. This is confirmed by Ludwig of Bavaria in his letter to Wilhelm, duke
of Bavaria, April 20, *DRA*, II, 869.

[114] Text in *DRA*, II, 594 ff. The original MS is among papers of Henry VIII in the London
Record Office; a Latin translation from Vatican archives is reprinted in Balan, *Monumenta*,
pp. 213 f.

wrong when weighed against that of one thousand years of Christianity, and he declares that he will support the Church with power, friends, body, blood, life, and soul, to prevent the dishonor that would fall upon him and the noble German nation through the rise of any suspicion of heresy or of damage to Christianity. In view of Luther's response, he now regrets there was delay in proceeding against him, and he proposes, without further hearings, to send him back under the safe-conduct and then proceed against him as a notorious heretic. The estates are invited to carry out their promise of February 19, like good Christians.

Evidently the promptness and finality of this declaration took the estates by surprise. Instead of the long debates and repeated postponements which were the usual procedure of the Diet when important questions were on the agenda, they had now a peremptory demand for action on a definite program. The papal envoys rubbed their hands with satisfaction over the pious spirit of the young emperor and his resolute way with the hesitating princes, and were equally gratified to learn that some of the latter had turned pale when they heard the paper read. It was better after all that things had taken the course they had, and Aleander utters a contented "et haec olim meminisse juvabit" in retrospect at the trials and dangers of the past months.[115]

---

[115] Aleander and Caracciolo to Medici, April 19, Brieger, "Aleander," p. 155, and Kalkoff, · *Depeschen*, p. 178.

34

REFUSAL TO COMPROMISE

WHILE the debate in the Diet went on through the afternoon of Friday and the following day, Martin sat quietly in his lodgings awaiting a decision. Many, of all ranks, came to see him: some, friends and devoted followers, others drawn by curiosity. Among the latter was a brilliant figure among the German princes, Philip, the young Landgrave of Hesse, who had just attained his majority and appeared at his first Diet attended by a splendid retinue. This prince, now eighteen years old, was later to show himself a weird mixture of religious enthusiasm, arbitrary violence, and ill-disciplined passions. He talked with Martin, and as the latter recalled many years after, left him with a somewhat ambiguous declaration: "If you are right, Doctor, may God help you." [1] That the friendship of high and low showed itself also in concrete efforts for the comfort and safety of the monk, seems likely; but concerning such acts we learn only of the presentation of a jug of Einbeck beer, and that comes from a somewhat doubtful source.[2]

The tense excitement in Worms had not abated. It was now increased on the night of April 19–20 by the posting of broadsides for and against Luther.[3] It was even said that a hostile note had been insinuated into the emperor's chamber, stating: "Woe to the land whose ruler is a boy!" [4] One broadside, which was posted at the town hall, claimed to have the support of four hundred of the lesser nobility and eight thousand men-at-arms. It glowed with rage against the princes, especially the archbishop of Mainz, and in the name of divine justice threatened all the clergy who supported these rulers.[5] The impression made by this poster was intensified by the signature,

[1] "Historie, wie es Doct. Martin Luther . . . ergangen sei," *EA*, LXIV, 373; *TR*, II, 2783c and III, 3357b.

[2] Nikolaus Selneccer, *Vitam Divi Lutheri*, p. 108. Cf. *DRA*, II, 559, n. 1.

[3] *Acta et res gestae, DRA*, II, 559; *Etliche sunderliche Handlungen, DRA*, II, 601, ll. 9 ff.

[4] Report of the Frankfort delegates, April 24, *DRA*, II, 872, ll. 35 f. Cochlaeus, *Commentaria de actis et scriptis Martini Lutheri*, p. 36, gives a somewhat different account.

[5] This placard was thought worth noting by several chroniclers and correspondents. See *DRA*, II, 559, n. 2; also the Spanish report, *DRA*, II, 637. Kalkoff thinks the author was

a threefold "Bundschuh," the slogan and symbol of the bands of outraged and vengeful peasants who had been troubling the Southwest of Germany intermittently for a generation and whose threat now hung like a cloud on the horizon. On the same night, their battle-cry resounded through the streets of Worms, to the vast alarm of the inhabitants.[6] Nothing came of these threats, but Aleander ascribed to them a direct influence on the turn of events that put an end to the immediate liquidation of Luther's case and threw everything once more into the crucible. According to the information of the papal representative, the electoral council under pressure of the emperor's firmness, had voted on Friday, four to two, to carry out the edict against Luther. A confirmation of this appears in a Latin memorandum now in the Vatican archives,[7] which was drawn by Elector Joachim and specifies the steps that Charles expected from the estates in carrying out the imperial edict banning Luther's books and teaching. That this plan did not go through Aleander now ascribes, in part, at least, to a sudden panic that befell Albert, elector of Mainz, because of the threatening broadside,[8] so that the latter hastened to the emperor with a scheme for a new hearing of Luther by scholars in the presence of certain of the electors. Thus the bogey of Aleander, a disputation before umpires regarding a cause already decided by the Pope, again threatened to become a reality. The emperor, however, ridiculed the fears of Albert and quashed the new scheme by refusing to budge one iota from his resolve to condemn Luther's works.[9]

It is interesting that none of the threats of violence which had terrified Albert came from the most unruly spirit among the humanists, Ulrich von Hutten, who, though close by at Sickingen's castle, held in suspense for the moment pen and sword against the partisans of Rome. Apparently, as we have seen, he had yielded to the diplomacy of the imperial confessor, Glapion, and accepted service with Charles on terms that silenced, in the days of Luther's Worms adventure, his attacks on the hierarchy and their fol-

---

the humanist Hermann von dem Busche, one of his favorites! See, e.g., his *Ulrich von Hutten und die Reformation, passim.*

[6] Letter from Aleander and Caracciolo to Medici, April 27, Brieger, "Aleander," pp. 157 f., and Kalkoff, *Depeschen,* p. 182.

[7] Text in Balan, *Monumenta,* pp. 184 f.; also *DRA,* II, 596 f. See also *ibid.,* p. 596, n. 3.

[8] The Roman envoys do not name the archbishop in their letter to Rome on April 27, but designate him as "uno di questi Principi, a chi più pertiene deffender questa causa." Brieger, "Aleander," p. 158, and Kalkoff, *Depeschen,* p. 182. The reference is unescapably to Albert, who in addition to being *ex officio* chancellor of the empire was primate of the Catholic hierarchy in Germany.

[9] *Ibid.* The envoy's account of this episode lacks confirmation, but seems plausible. The air was full of rumors, of which doubtless many more came to the ears of Albert than to the emperor's.

lowers.[10] In January Martin had written to the Ebernburg warning the
knight that the cause of the Gospel could not be furthered by violence.[11] On
the day of Luther's arrival in Worms Hutten sent a letter of encouragement,
utterly dissimilar in tone to any that had gone before.[12] It was replete with
quotations from the Psalms, adjurations to Luther to be strong in the Lord,
and assurances of his continued support. Evidently Martin found time to
write the knight of negotiations that were in progress after the formal
hearings, for within a week another letter came from the Ebernburg.[13] Here
we have no stiff, conventionalized theological phrase-making, but a whiff of
the real Hutten. He breathes fury against his opponents and hails Luther
for standing up unterrified against them. Had not the prudence of his friends
restrained him, he states, he would have carried an attack up to the walls of
Worms itself. With a dozen rhetorical caprioles he congratulates Luther on
his firmness and bids him stand fast to the end, promising that when the
proper hour arrives he will himself again rush forth with God-stirred spirit.

Whether it was the fright of Albert or the authority and trickery of the
elector of Saxony, as Aleander thinks,[14] the united estates showed, on
April 20, that they were not ready to turn thumbs down on the Saxon
monk. Their action is preserved in the Vatican archives in the form of a
French address to the emperor,[15] emphasizing the importance of the affair
and presenting their suggestions. In order that Luther, who had announced
himself ready to accept scriptural proof of his error, might not be able
to say that none had been offered him, and in order that the common
people should not say that he had been condemned unheard, and because
they regard such action toward him as a work of Christian charity to bring
him back to the way of truth and the sacred fold, they recommend that a
commission off three or four persons, "serious and instructed in sacred
Scriptures," point out to Martin which of his articles are contrary to faith
and the councils and their ordinances (*constitutiones*), and explain to him
the reasons underlying these ordinances. If he should be brought to recant,

[10] Kalkoff, *Ulrich von Hutten und die Reformation*, pp. 362 f., assumes that Hutten accepted
the offer brought him by Armerstorff and Glapion. It seems probable in view of the cessation
of his attacks.

[11] Luther's letter is lost; it may never have reached Hutten. See Martin's reference to it in
his letter to Spalatin, January 16, 1521, *WAB*, II, 249.

[12] April 17. *WAB*, II, 301 f.

[13] April 20 (25?), 1521. *WAB*, II, 303 f. The letter exists in three forms and raises a technical problem. See *ibid.*, p. 303, n. 1.

[14] Letter from Aleander and Caracciolo to Medici, April 27, Brieger, "Aleander," p. 159, and
Kalkoff, *Depeschen*, p. 184.

[15] Balan, *Monumenta*, pp. 188 ff.; *DRA*, II, 598 f.

evils would be prevented; if not, he might return to his home, and the road would then be clear to proceed against him.

This petition revived the fears of the papal envoys that wires might be pulled to bring the heretic to recant certain things while permitting him to uphold his complaints against the pope, thereby regaining for him the popularity he had lost through his opposition to the Council of Constance.[16] The emperor, however, opposed no objection to efforts to get Luther to recant and promised in case he did so to intercede for him with the Pope. In no event, however, would he or his council take part in another hearing. He stipulated also that Luther was not to remain in Worms more than three days longer.[17]

The way was now open for direct intervention by the estates. On Monday, the 22nd, after receipt of the emperor's note of assent, the estates delegated for the conference with Luther a commission representing the electors, princes, lower nobility, and cities, including two doctors of law.[18] This group met at six o'clock the next morning, April 23, to lay its plans,[19] and on the same day two priests came to summon Luther on behalf of the head of the commission, the archbishop of Trier, to a conference early the next morning.[20] At six o'clock on the 24th Martin betook himself to the archbishop's quarters escorted by the imperial herald, who by the terms of the safe-conduct was responsible for his welfare. Three advisers accompanied him: Hieronymus Schurf, a Saxon councilor in law; Nikolaus von Amsdorf, the theologian; and Justus Jonas, who had studied in both fields of learning

[16] Aleander had expressed fear of this in his letter to Medici on April 13 or 15 and was taking preventive steps. Brieger, "Aleander," p. 141, and Kalkoff, *Depeschen*, p. 166. In his coaching of Von Eck he must have guarded especially against any loophole through which Luther might escape a complete revocation or an absolute refusal. The idea that the question directed at Martin about his books on April 18 was different from that of the preceding day, giving him an opening to revoke those of his works that dealt with questions of faith and insist on those directed against Roman abuses, was developed by Adolf Hausrath in *Aleander und Luther auf dem Reichstage zu Worms*, pp. 262 ff. It has now been thoroughly exploded. See Kalkoff, *Der Wormser Reichstag*, pp. 338 f. The questions were intended to be the same on both days. Any partial revocation by Luther would have put the hierarchical party at Worms in the greatest embarrassment, as the papal bull had been careful to avoid differentiation between the orthodox and heretical in Luther's writing.

[17] *Etliche sunderliche Handlungen*, DRA, II, 601, ll. 14 ff. The Frankfort delegates confirm on April 24 the emperor's offer to serve as middleman between the Pope and Luther. *DRA*, II, 872, ll. 18 f.

[18] *Etliche sunderliche Handlungen*, DRA, II, 602, states that the commission consisted of one representative of the four estates. It is obvious, however, that there were two from each. Kalkoff, *Der Wormser Reichstag*, p. 23, makes it seem likely that this was a selection from the standing committee of the Diet.

[19] See the report of Hieronymus Vehus, *DRA*, II, 613, ll. 21 ff.

[20] *Etliche sunderliche Handlungen*, DRA, II, 602, ll. 7 ff., shows slight variations here from the *Acta et res gestae*, DRA, II, 560, ll. 4 ff.

and was a humanist as well.[21] When Martin stood before the members of the commission he saw some familiar faces: his old enemy, Duke George of Saxony; the wily Elector Joachim; the bishop of the Brandenburg diocese, Martin's immediate ecclesiastical superior, who had shown himself willing to carry water on both shoulders; and the Augsburg humanist, Peutinger, known to him from the days of his meeting with Cajetan. At the head of the table sat Richard Greiffenklau, Archbishop of Trier, whose friendship with Elector Frederick had suggested his selection as umpire in Luther's affair two years earlier.[22] The commission seems to have made a diligent effort to find ground for a compromise. The interrogator who came forward to represent it was Doctor Hieronymus Vehus, chancellor of the margrave of Baden. The lawyer from southwestern Germany demonstrated in his introductory speech that his selection as spokesman in this friendly effort was a wise one. He took up one after another the positions where Martin had established himself with especial obstinacy, and by apparent concessions and appeals to Luther's rational sense and to his loyalty to the Church, he sought to remove the obstacles to compromise. The practical work of the councils for enabling the Church to meet the changing conditions of humanity, the disorders that would ensue from Luther's books if they were permitted to continue to circulate, the danger especially that the work *On the Freedom of a Christian* would lead to abuses because many would shake off all yokes of obedience, the necessity of laws for promoting unity of faith, the snares which the devil was laying to have all Martin's works condemned when many of them contained much truth —all these ideas were set forth in a florid rhetorical style, interlarded with many scriptural quotations and exhortations, with much about "utility, salubrity, . . . dangers, conscience and public and private safety," and much about the great clemency of the princes.[23] He dwelt with especial emphasis on the function and authority of the councils, an indication that the commission was preparing to do what Aleander had feared from the beginning: secure a compromise with Luther by opening a vista to reform through a council to be held in Germany. This would have aided Luther

---

[21] Spalatin, *Annales Reformationis*, in Cyprian edition, II, 42. See also report of Vehus, *DRA*, 613, ll. 30 ff.

[22] The personnel of the commission is the same in all the sources, including Luther's letter to Albert of Mansfeld, May 3, 1521, *WAB*, II, 322. In addition to those named in my text, it included Christoph von Stadion, bishop of Augsburg; two representatives of the lower nobility, Georg von Wertheim and the head of the Teutonic Order, Dietrich von Klein; and the sturdy representative of the Free City of Strasbourg, Hans Bock.

[23] *Acta et res gestae*, *DRA*, II, 561 f. *Etliche sunderliche Handlungen*, *DRA*, II, 602 f., emphasizes especially Vehus's exposition of the function of the council of the Church. For Vehus's own report, drafted some six weeks later, see *DRA*, II, 611 ff.

to make a conditional revocation of his attacks on the sacraments in his *Babylonian Captivity* and would have ignored the attacks on papal authority. The tone of the appeal was conciliatory in character and addressed itself to reason and sentiment alike. On the whole, it made a favorable impression on the Roman envoys [24] and won Luther's admiration for its cleverness and good arrangement.[25]

In replying, Luther took his stand on familiar ground. He did not censure *all* councils, but only that of Constance, because it had rejected the word of God in condemning Huss's contention that the Church is the whole body of the elect, which is an article of Christian faith found in the Apostles' Creed.[26] He is troubled not because the councils have differed in their decisions, but because they have made contrary rulings: "It were better that no clerical ordinances were made than that they should be useless ones." He is fully aware that the Scriptures forbid obstinacy, but the articles of faith are not his, they are God's. To him, as he points out, there are two classes of offenses, those against Christian living and those against faith and doctrine. The former may be avoided as the devil's work; but in matters of faith offenses last from the beginning to the end of the world, for the word of God is a stone of offense to learned men. He admits the duty of obedience to magistrates and powers; he admits that one must yield his individual opinion, and offers to do so, so long as he is not forced to deny God's word: "I can never make the Lord Christ other than God himself made Him; if we insist on fending off offense and hardship, we then bring them on ourselves in earnest, for the sacred word of God has always looked as if it were going to cause the earth to collapse and the heavens to fall." [27] In conclusion he offers again to allow himself to be instructed, provided he is shown his error by means of Scripture.

The commission seems to have devoted itself with great earnestness to the task of discovering a formula, and it appears to have sought one on a path that led away from Rome and might therefore be tried by the heretic monk with greater confidence. Talk of a reforming council, to be

---

[24] Letter from Aleander and Caracciolo to Medici, April 27, Brieger, "Aleander," pp. 160 f., and Kalkoff, *Depeschen*, pp. 185 ff.

[25] Letter to Albert, May 3, *WAB*, II, 322, l. 52.

[26] "Tantum una est sacra universalis ecclesia, quae est numerus praedestinatorum." *Ibid.*, p. 324, ll. 109 f.

[27] *Etliche sunderliche Handlungen, DRA*, II, 605, ll. 3 ff. This source gives Luther's response, partly in direct, partly in indirect form, at considerable length and with something of his own vivid style. The text is in some respects defective. The *Acta et res gestae* is briefer and colder. Cf. *DRA*, II, 562, ll. 8 ff.

held in Germany, had been going about in the empire for two years and had found much support at Worms during the winter, as Aleander reports frequently to Rome. One of the chief protagonists of such a movement was Duke George of Saxony himself.[28] Such a council would obviously be under the influence of the lay authorities. It was probably this solution that the committee of the Diet had planned and this that Doctor Vehus had in mind when he repeated the request that Martin submit his writings to the judgment of the emperor and empire. Luther replied that he was very willing to submit his writings to representatives of the empire, indeed he was willing to submit them to the most humble person for attack, discussion, and interpretation, but those who judged them must do so by means of divine Scripture. The word of God is so clear, he asserted, and he could not yield unless he was shown his error by God's word. He asks for no favors except that he should not be forced to go against the evident word of God.[29] At the conclusion of his remarks Elector Joachim asked whether he would yield if convicted by evidence from Holy Scriptures. Luther answered, "Yes, . . . or by clear and evident arguments." [30]

Vehus had closed his address with an apology for mixing in theological matters. All instructions had been against a disputation; but the belief of the age that truth could be discovered by this means was strong. After the others had gone, the archbishop called Luther, Schurf, and Amsdorf into a smaller room (*triclinium*) and confronted them here with his own jurist, Von Eck, the orator of the week before, and Johann Cochlaeus. The latter was a cleric of energetic Franconian stock, a former defender of Luther. He had now turned against Martin, and had by his own account come to Worms the preceding week and made contact with Aleander through the humanist Wolfgang Capito.[31] At four o'clock on the morning of the conference between the commission and Luther, Cochlaeus declares, Aleander sent for him and instructed him to go to the house of the archbishop of Trier and remain there until called into colloquy with Luther, where he was to take part in no disputation but to act as an observer for the Roman envoys.

Von Eck opened the argument with the statement, repeated from the week before, that all heresies have their rise from Holy Scripture. He then attacked especially Luther's position that the Holy Catholic Church

---

[28] A "general council" for a "general reformation" was the final plea in the list of complaints submitted by Duke George to the Diet commission in February. *DRA*, II, 666, ll. 3 ff.

[29] Again there are considerable deviations between the two Lutheran reports, pointing perhaps to parallel chronicles as sources at this point.

[30] *DRA*, II, 563, ll. 18 f.   [31] *Ibid.*, n. 2.

was the totality of the saved. Schurf and Cochlaeus took part in the debate, which apparently led nowhere. According to the German chronicler, Von Eck and Cochlaeus both talked at once, and Luther could not get in a word.[32] The excitement of the meeting may be reproduced in imagination from an account by Cochlaeus, written soon afterwards to a friend,[33] and from observations on the colloquy which the papal envoys incorporated in a letter to Medici on April 27.[34] It was, as Luther wrote the following week to the duke of Mansfeld, "a pointless disputation." The official of the archbishop of Trier made another rhetorical address of exhortation; Cochlaeus begged Luther to think of the noble genius Melanchthon and other young scholars whom he was destroying. An argument developed over the authority of the council and Luther repeated his attack on that of Constance, interspersing his arguments, as usual, with scriptural texts, which Cochlaeus found were poorly remembered and without much application to the question.[35] When the eager and aggressive Cochlaeus, who found himself rudely treated by Luther's companion, Schurf, began to introduce the jargon of the disputation, Luther waved aside all syllogisms in favor of Scripture. The report of this leads Aleander to a bitter attack on Luther's habit of interpreting everything according to his own head and thrusting aside all opposing views as inadmissible. Aleander's information was that many who had talked with Martin observed that he was "not a grammarian nor a dialectician nor anything of a logician, but merely an insane man," and he repeats the prevalent belief that Luther did not write most of the books ascribed to him. Martin told someone in confidence, he declares, that those books about which the greatest noise was made were composed by his comrades.[36] The outstanding feature of this "pointless" disputation was Luther's iteration of his thesis that the Council of Constance was wrong in condemning the article of Huss which held that the Church is the whole number of the elect. When the arrival of the dinner hour had broken up the discussion Cochlaeus made, as he reports, a final attack on Luther for his abuse of the Pope. Martin defended himself with the excuse that Leo was a public person. "As if," Cochlaeus remarks, "atrocious insults *per se* were not more atrocious when made against a public than against a private person!" [37]

[32] *DRA*, II, 607, ll. 6 ff.; *DRA*, II, 564, and n. 1.

[33] *Colloquium Cochlaei cum Luthero*, cited in *DRA*, II, 624 ff.

[34] Letter from Aleander and Caracciolo, Brieger, "Aleander," p. 161, and Kalkoff, *Depeschen*, pp. 186 f.

[35] *DRA*, II, 627, ll. 3 ff.

[36] Brieger, "Aleander," p. 163, and Kalkoff, *Depeschen*, p. 188.

[37] *DRA*, II, 627, ll. 24 ff. Cochlaeus reports that Martin went off "glorying like a victor."

Apparently both sides went away with a feeling of victory. After dinner, the zealous Cochlaeus visited Luther's quarters and had a lively discussion with Martin and several of his group. The scene in Luther's room, as pictured by Cochlaeus in his *Colloquium with Luther* and confirmed, at least in certain points, by contemporary letters and other writings of Cochlaeus,[38] affords a vivid glimpse of Luther's exciting days at Worms: on the one side, Cochlaeus, surrounded by a group of Martin's friends, clerical and noble, and fencing warily so as to avoid being drawn into a disputation against so many, but when opportunity permits, pouring forth earnest appeals to Luther; on the other side, Luther, jovial, poking fun at a cloister brother for his pride in learning and refusing to take serious questions seriously, until the ardent Cochlaeus offers to meet him in disputation at equal risk, if Luther would give up his safe-conduct. At this the suspicious friends of Martin immediately scented a trap.[39] According to this account, obviously one-sided yet bearing many marks of truth, the young supporters crowding about Luther included noblemen, all violent with loyalty to him and with a passionate spirit of national opposition to Rome.

Nevertheless, among the older heads the desire for some form of compromise persisted. This led to an intimate conference between Luther and Cochlaeus in the former's bedroom, where Cochlaeus found the monk modest, full of admiration for young Melanchthon, grateful for Cochlaeus's well-meant intervention, and moved to sorrowful tears on more than one occasion.[40] Cochlaeus's account is of importance, not merely because of its intimate picture of Luther at a time of the highest crisis, in which the warm-hearted sentimentality of Martin stands forth in refreshing contrast to the superhuman Titanism of Luther at Worms as pictured in the orthodox tradition. It also shows how closely he was surrounded in this crisis by a group of ardent personal followers, especially younger humanists

---

Aleander, on the other hand, learned from the archbishop of Trier that the arguments of Von Eck so drove Martin into a corner that the archbishop hoped he was going to surrender on the spot. Brieger, "Aleander," p. 162, and Kalkoff, *Depeschen,* p. 187.

[38] The Lutheran chronicles at Worms were of course very hostile toward Cochlaeus, whose aggressiveness and self-confidence aroused the resentment of all Martin's followers: "Argutiis odiosissimis," *Acta et res gestae, DRA,* II, 564, ll. 12 f. However, the objective student will recognize the factual importance of his narrative and will not withhold recognition of the courage with which he strove to win Luther back amid the taunts and threats of the irritated and violent Saxons.

[39] *DRA,* II, 629, ll. 19 ff. See *EA,* LXIV, 373, where Luther says that one of his followers among the knights, Vollrat von Watzdorf, would have given Cochlaeus a "bloody conduct" if others had not stopped him.

[40] In a later work Cochlaeus repeated the story of the tears, calling forth a vigorous denial from Luther. "Adversus armatum virum Cocleum Martinus Lutherus," *EA,* XXXVIII, 48.

who were convinced that they were championing the cause of enlightenment against barbarism.[41]

How far did the written and personal exhortations of men like Hutten strengthen Martin's resistance to compromise? What importance is to be ascribed to the presence at Worms of young and enthusiastic scholars like Jonas, who had sworn loyalty to his flag? What to the adulation with which he had been greeted on the way to Worms and which surrounded his lodgings in that city?

We have already pointed out that Martin felt behind him at this time the ardent backing of two classes, the theologians of humanistic sympathies and the Franconian knights. It was the former who were to flood Germany with pamphlet literature in advocacy of the Reformation in the next two years. The tide of this was just beginning to sweep in. As has been stated, there is in that literature very little understanding of Luther's theological ideas. What appealed to the eager and at times almost incoherent authors of these polemics was the social import of such works as the *Address to the Christian Nobility* and *The Freedom of a Christian*. They showed only a languid interest in Luther's ideas on the enslaved will and redemption from sin. These ideas were even further from the knowledge of men of Hutten's social class, the economically depressed knights of the empire. Their goal was the destruction of the money- and position-grabbing hierarchy, where their demands did not go further and call for complete freedom from Rome.

We may conclude on the basis of Martin's relationship to Hutten that he would not have sacrificed his convictions for the support of these men. On the other hand, there were many whose acclaim or backing did not require compromise, at least at this time, and their attitude could not help buoy him up in the difficult situation in which he found himself at Worms. Nevertheless, two factors were at least equally important in sustaining him in his ordeal: the depth of his own convictions and the unwillingness or inability of his prosecutors at Worms to make any real compromise.

Martin's convictions, like those of every truly dedicated reformer, were deep to the point of irrationality. Indeed, it was not only his followers who did not completely grasp his ideas; we may doubt whether Martin himself had penetrated below the surface of some of them, whether, for instance, he was clear as to what he meant by the "universal Church." Nevertheless,

---

[41] Cochlaeus relates that the next day he met Jonas, and that the young Erfurt humanist, who had under Luther's influence deserted the law for theology, taunted him with being the only champion of the barbarian ignoramuses against more than a thousand scholars, *Colloquium Cochlaei, DRA*, II, 631, ll. 23 ff.

his thinking and theories had all developed organically out of one theological root. His position respecting the error of the Council of Constance; the falsity of papal pretensions to temporal power, including its emphasis on pious deeds and works; the injustice of the canon law; the spirituality of the processes of grace—all of these as set forth in the polemics of the three preceding years go back to his basic idea—one might even say, experience—of man's utter worthlessness and the reality of individual faith. It was this conception of faith that brought as its corollary a supreme trust in the Scriptures as the sole law book of Christian men. After 1517, as Martin's confidence in Church tradition sank, this idea gained in clarity until it became crystallized with the Leipzig disputation. Following that, lines radiated from it to include so many aspects of the relation of the Church to the individual and society that compromise on any point was impossible as soon as its implications were faced in Luther's mind. Thus, the question of the authority of the council, on which so much stress was laid by theological and legal minds at Worms, was interlocked with the whole framework of Luther's ideology. He could never have made this clear to his interlocutors; it is doubtful, as we have said, whether the causal relationship was entirely clear to him, so completely was his whole system emotionalized. To those, therefore, who sought to persuade or defeat him by rational argument, his steadfastness must have seemed pure obstinacy.

With ideas so organically developed and so deeply interwoven with his emotions Martin came before the Diet. The atmosphere in Worms was hardly favorable to compromise. Martin had reiterated his willingness to be heard before competent scholars who were to refute him on the basis of Scripture. It must remain a question whether he actually believed that such a hearing could lead him to change his views, convinced as he was that he had based his thinking on the authority of Scripture. The rift in German Christianity, which was to become of such incalculable influence on the history of Europe in the next four hundred years, had revealed itself to Martin and to others at the Leipzig disputation, and after that no bridge could span it. Whatever his feelings in this respect, however, it is clear that the leaders at Worms did not and indeed could not provide such a hearing. Nor were they themselves in a position to shake Martin's convictions or abandon their own. The apologist for Luther is prone to create the impression that everything hinged at the Diet upon the stubborn unwillingness of his opponents to see the manifest truth as he had revealed it. The error in this is too obvious to require denial. Most of the representatives of empire and Church were ready to engage in political maneuvering and to make certain limited concessions to Martin's supporters, but neither the emperor nor the Pope could yield on the basic questions which Martin had brought up. At worst these men and their advisers and followers were concerned with preserving and increasing their own powers and those of the institutions or dynasties they represented; at best they were sincere adherents of the established order in Church and state. Even the men who made further attempts after the formal hearing to find a basis for peaceful settlement with Luther were not concerned with a free debate on fundamental theological issues. Their function was to quiet the disturber of the peace in such a way as to satisfy his backers as well as emperor and Pope.

Considering this attitude on the part of the leaders at Worms, there can be no question that Martin was aware of the danger to his freedom of expression or even to his life. Even the observer of the present day can do no more than conjecture that the political situation made extreme measures against the heretic unlikely; an observer at the Diet, however politically astute, could hardly have been more reassuring. Martin himself, as we have seen, was haunted by grim premonitions on his way from Wittenberg.[42] We know also that he did not find the ordeal at Worms easy to face. Despite the strong likelihood that his request on the first day of the hearing for further time to consider was a planned move on the part of the Saxon party, as we have said, one cannot rule out entirely the suggestion that it was due to his own loss of assurance. Even on the second day, with the statement well prepared, he did not maintain his composure without effort. In the course of the subsequent hearings, too, there is at least the possibility that Martin may have thought for a passing moment of compromise, though this, as we shall see below, may have been merely an erroneous impression on the part of the lawyers. On a more certain foundation rests Martin's own dissatisfaction with his replies at Worms. He writes to Spalatin from the Wartburg[43] that his conscience troubles him because he restrained himself at Worms on the advice of his friends, instead of exhibiting something of the prophet Elijah.

In the light of the situation at Worms and its effect on Martin, then, there can be no doubt that he was strengthened and encouraged by friendship and loyalty, by the acclaim of the people, the offers of refuge, and especially the support, however cautious, of Elector Frederick. It is no derogation to Martin's outstanding courage to admit this. But it would

[42] Letter from Luther to Spalatin, April 14, 1521, *WAB*, II, 298. See also his letter to Melanchthon, April 7, *WAB*, II, 296.

[43] Sept. 9, 1521. *WAB*, II, 388, ll. 21 ff.

require a complete misjudgment of his character and personality to suggest that but for this support he would have abandoned the truth as he had come to see it after so long a development. Indeed, if one may go by the letter to Spalatin referred to above, his friends could be a hindrance as well as a help. It must be recalled, too, that if the support of others bolstered his faith in the justice of his cause, it was also his supreme self-confidence that enlisted support.

However little Martin may have believed in the possibility of compromise, the Saxon court evidently still thought that a formula might be found to satisfy both parties. The attitude of Frederick toward Martin had all along undoubtedly been determined in part by political and dynastic considerations. At the same time it seems also to have been motivated by a feeling of loyalty on the part of the elector toward one whom he believed sincere and whose independence and courage he had learned to admire.[44] This motive grew stronger as the appearance of Luther in Worms drew nearer. "Would to God," Frederick writes to his brother John two weeks before Martin's arrival, "that I could with propriety do something to help Martin. I certainly would not fail him." [45] In the course of the Worms hearing, when, according to Aleander, Frederick had just succeeded in getting the estates to appoint the commission for further efforts with Luther, the elector implies uncertainty in another letter to his brother as to how far Martin is in the right, but is resentful at the determination of his opponents to brand everyone a heretic who takes the part of the professor.[46] By this time Frederick had plainly become fearful over the situation.[47] Aleander's devices and the emperor's attitude had driven Luther's defenders into their last trenches. In view of this state of affairs the Saxon councilors could leave no stone unturned. They must, if possible, find a way to delay, if they could not finally prevent the issuance of the imperial edict outlawing Luther which had been threatening since December.

[44] It may be repeated that I do not share the opinion, first developed by Theodor Kolde and supported radically by Paul Kalkoff, that Frederick had an understanding of Luther's ideas, still less that he matured careful plans with Erasmus and others for a policy of religious reform. Frederick's character was greatly dependent on religious support, and deeply conservative. He was also a conscientious ruler and a resourceful politician, concentrated on an effort to preserve and enhance the importance of the Saxon state within the empire, and to this end obliged constantly to apply temporary expedients to temporary emergencies. His attitude toward Martin was determined in large part by his political program, as has been stated above, and also by a growing loyalty toward his subject, but not by any change in his religious convictions.

[45] April 8, 1521. *DRA*, II, 844.

[46] Letter from Frederick to Duke John, April 23, *DRA*, II, 871.

[47] See Spalatin, *Annales Reformationis*, in Cyprian ed., II, 50.

A move in this direction followed immediately on the failure of the conference between the commission of the Diet and the Saxon group. As Vehus was crossing the market place, he met Peutinger, who related a conversation he had just had with the Saxon councilor Schurf. The latter had proposed in haste that Luther submit his writings to the emperor and estates with the reservation "that nothing should be done against evangelical doctrine and God's word." [48] This opened the way for further negotiations, which were this time to be of a man-to-man nature. As a result, Martin that evening received a message from the archbishop telling him that his safe-conduct had been extended for two days more.[49] Early the next morning (April 25) the two lawyers, Vehus and Peutinger, came to see Luther [50] and explored with him, alone for the most part,[51] the possibilities of Schurf's suggestion. Chancellor Vehus reported that Martin showed himself friendly and grateful throughout. He noted three obstacles as Luther formulated his position. First, he would not submit his writings without a definite preface stating that the word of God must be free and independent and not subject to human judgment. Second, he hesitated to submit his writings to those who had already condemned and burned them and who had issued an edict against him before a hearing. Third, he wondered whether there was not so much prejudice against his writings as to prevent an agreement regarding them on the part of the estates.[52] The two doctors of law met these arguments systematically, offering, among other things, to see that Luther's books were put in the hands only of unprejudiced persons. With adroitness they praised the evangelical character of Martin's preaching, its spirituality, and his warfare against indulgences, but expressed

[48] Hieronymus Vehus's report, *DRA*, II, 618. On the same afternoon, April 24, Vehus reported to the estates on the conference of the commission with Luther. *Ibid.*, p. 619.

[49] *Acta et res gestae*, *DRA*, II, 565, ll. 5 f.; *Etliche sunderliche Handlungen*, *DRA*, II, 607, ll. 28 ff. According to Aleander, after adjournment of the commission's conference with Luther, the archbishop of Trier came to the session of the princes where he met members of the emperor's privy council, and it was agreed that the time had come to send the "dog" away. Brieger, "Aleander," p. 163, and Kalkoff, *Depeschen*, p. 189. However, it was decided to ask the emperor's permission for Trier to see Martin alone, since he had hopes that he could change him. This was given and the nervous Roman envoys urged the archbishop to hurry, for fear that Luther might make a partial recantation. The archbishop was in no case to deviate from the prescribed form. See Aleander's letter to the archbishop of Trier, April 24(?), expressing his earnest hope that whatever is done, the principle of papal authority be put first: "nisi pontificiae autoritatis ratio in primis habeatur." Balan, *Monumenta*, p. 192.

[50] Vehus sets the hour at six. *DRA*, II, 619, ll. 10 ff. (There is a tendency in these records to begin the day's business at six!) The German chronicler says between seven and eight. *Etliche sunderliche Handlungen*, *DRA*, II, 608, ll. 3 ff.

[51] The Saxon councilor, Schurf, and a colleague of his were present a part of the time, according to Vehus's report. *DRA*, II, 619, ll. 15 f. Luther recalled in later years that Elector Frederick had suggested that he take along witnesses. *EA*, LXIV, 371 f.

[52] Vehus's German is not altogether clear here. *DRA*, II, 620, ll. 6 ff.

the fear that now through his obstinacy in unnecessary things the reprinting and circulation of all his works might be forbidden. They suggested, therefore, that he omit the things which were good for the sake of those which were better.[53] He was to submit his writings to the emperor and the estates for consideration and abide by their opinion, declaring at the same time that he had sought nothing in his works and doctrines except God's evangelical truth and the welfare of mankind. The lawyers also pointed out that this would be a more effective way of making a reservation than the proposed preface. They came away under the impression that Luther was not altogether displeased with their proposal[54] and that he would take it into consideration. Luther, when recording the interview twice during the following week, declared that he had agreed to submit his writings on condition that he was to be shown his errors by Scripture or clear and evident reasoning.[55]

When they came together in the afternoon for a continuation of the discussion, the two lawyers found conditions less favorable. A number of knights and scholars came in and the jurists were hard pressed in regard to Scripture. Luther restated his reservation clearly and categorically, though, according to Vehus, "with becoming modesty."[56] The talk turned to the unjust condemnation of Huss's articles by the council, and Peutinger suggested that the only way to a settlement would be for Luther to lay his writings before a future council. The lawyers understood Luther's answer to be "Yes," provided a council was not too long delayed and that he himself should know what articles were supposed to contain error and would be submitted to the council,[57] while the Lutheran chroniclers add that a decision on the articles should be dependent on the word of God.[58]

It is evident that the two lawyers did not catch the force of Luther's reservation, that *he* was to decide which articles should be submitted to the council and obviously also that he was to judge whether a decision

---

[53] Vehus's report, *ibid.*, p. 621, ll. 21 f. The German chronicler states, "So wer je unter zwaien ubeln eins zu erwelen." *Etliche sunderliche Handlungen, DRA*, II, 608, ll. 9 f.

[54] "Nit ganz missfellig." *DRA*, II, 621, l. 36.

[55] In his letter to Emperor Charles, April 28, *WAB*, II, 308, l. 39; to the estates of the Empire, April 28, *WAB*, II, 315, ll. 39 f. See also his letter to Albert, May 3: "Das sy nicht wider Gott beschlussen." *WAB*, II, 326, l. 192. In the *Table Talk* Luther's recollection of the interviews with the two lawyers is confused. He combines the two into one.

[56] Vehus's report, *DRA*, II, 622, ll. 9 f.   [57] *Ibid.*, ll. 25 ff.

[58] *Etliche sunderliche Handlungen, DRA*, II, 609, ll. 15 ff.: "man solt aus seinen büchern mit seinem wissen artikel zihen, die er auf erkantnus des kunftigen concilii sol stellen, doch also das ein kunftigs concilium aus und mit kraft des götlichen worts daruber spreche." The wording is practically the same in *Acta et res gestae, DRA*, II, 565, ll. 20 ff. It is similarly formulated in Luther's résumé to Emperor Charles, *WAB*, II, 308, ll. 40 f.

reached by the council accorded with the word of God. They also understood Luther to agree to a cessation of lectures, writing, and preaching
respecting articles which were regarded as erroneous, although he claimed
the right otherwise to lecture and write on God's word as well as preach
it. This was the report which Vehus and Peutinger took to the archbishop,
apparently under the impression that the difficult matter was approaching
a solution. The Lutheran chroniclers deny categorically and vigorously that
Martin promised to submit certain articles to the council and in the meantime keep silence respecting them: "Something which Martin never even
thought of, as up to now he had always refused to deny or to postpone
anything that belonged to the word of God." [59]

The archbishop of Trier now decided to confer with Luther privately.
This conference was Martin's final contact with the Roman hierarchy. At
its conclusion the last bridge that might have led to compromise was broken
down. It was, we should recall, this prince of the Church whom Martin had
sought as an umpire two years before. Now an interview between them had
come when umpires could no longer serve. Regarding the conference we
have indirect reports from both parties.[60] According to the Lutherans and to
Martin's brief reference in his letter to the count of Mansfeld,[61] the archbishop treated him with kindness and Martin talked to him with perfect
frankness. At one point in the proceedings Spalatin appeared, apparently
in response to a summons, for consultation.[62] The optimistic report of the
two doctors of the law at once turned out to be an illusion. The archbishop
put three possibilities before Luther: reference to the emperor and the
estates; reference to the emperor and a group of German prelates nominated
by the Pope; the submission of certain articles, selected with Martin's approval, to a future council for decision.[63] He then asked which articles might

[59] *DRA*, II, 565, ll. 25 ff. Vehus resented bitterly the implied charge of deceit. This was
indeed the reason he prepared the report of his activity in the matter. See *DRA*, II, 623, ll. 14 ff.
In reviewing the matter later on Martin characterized the proposal to refer the question to the
council as a trap laid for him by the archbishop. *EA*, LXIV, 372.

[60] *Acta et res gestae*, *DRA*, II, 566 f.; *Etliche sunderliche Handlungen*, *DRA*, II, 609, ll.
23 ff.; Spalatin, briefly, in his *Annales Reformationis* in Cyprian, II, 44 f.; the papal envoys
in their letter of April 27 to Medici, based on information from the archbishop of Trier;
Brieger, "Aleander," p. 164 and Kalkoff, *Depeschen*, pp. 190 f.; Christoph von Schwarzenberg,
in a letter written on the same day to Ludwig, duke of Bavaria, based on conversations with
Luther and the archbishop, *DRA*, II, 874 f. There are no essential differences in the reports
as to the facts of the colloquy, though the sequence of events is not the same in all.

[61] May 3, 1521. *WAB*, II, 326, ll. 193 ff.

[62] He is not named by the chroniclers. The Latin reporter in *DRA*, II, 566, l. 12, says merely
"a friend," but his presence is confirmed by Spalatin himself in his *Annales Reformationis*,
Cyprian ed., II, 44.

[63] Here Schwarzenberg's report seems the most factual. Aleander gives four alternatives:

go before a future council. Martin immediately made an exception of those which the Council of Constance had condemned. The archbishop interjected that he feared these would be the very ones to be selected. A further disillusionment was Martin's statement that he could not and would not keep silence regarding articles of that kind. "I would rather lose life and head than desert so clearly the word of God." [64] On the other hand, concerning articles which were not found in the Bible, he would be willing to accept the decision of a council so far as it was not against the word of God. In reply to what may have been a final question of the archbishop, what then could be done about the matter, Luther answered that there was nothing better than the reply of Gamaliel (Acts 5.38), namely, that the emperor and the estates should report to Rome that unless his affair was of God, it would perish of itself in three years, yes, in two years. In conclusion, Martin asked that the archbishop secure dismissal for him from the emperor. Thus they parted in friendliness.

The offers of the archbishop of Trier have usually been regarded by Lutheran authorities as insincere. The Italian envoys who found the proposals entirely unacceptable from the papal standpoint, seemed also to regard them as not having been made in good faith, though they accepted the archbishop's excuse for exceeding his authority, viz., that the alternatives proffered to Luther were not intended to have any validity until they should receive papal approval. The wiliness of Archbishop Greiffenklau is well attested in the biography of this hard-boiled prince at a period when Church diplomacy was as deficient in good faith as state diplomacy. It is not, however, unlikely that he was as ready to deceive the Italians as to deceive Luther. To the papal envoys he declared that the bait which was offered Martin was to entice him to revoke even a small part of his errors (*pur una particola*), which would then turn the people against him.[65] An examination of the sources makes it seem more likely that a partial revocation, weak enough to be palatable to a sensitive conscience, and the reference of other matters to a council, was a compromise seriously planned by the Diet commission. The Venetian envoys report this to their government the same week, adding that the purpose was "to keep control of the Pope

Pope and emperor, the emperor alone, the emperor and estates, a future council. In his report to Aleander the archbishop claims to have included in the last alternative the condition that Martin should revoke at once the worst of his errors, but in none of the other accounts does the word "revocation" occur. See Brieger, "Aleander," p. 164, and Kalkoff, *Depeschen*, p. 191.

[64] *DRA*, II, 567, ll. 8 ff.

[65] Letter of April 27, Brieger, "Aleander," p. 165, and Kalkoff, *Depeschen*, pp. 191 f.

and make him submissive to the wishes of the emperor." [66] They add that this plan had, to some extent, the approval of Charles. It is certain that although Father Glapion and Martin did not meet in conference at Worms, the emperor's confessor did bring to Martin's attention his project for a partial revocation, which had been discussed with the Saxon court so actively two months before; [67] and it is by no means certain that the Franciscan guardian of the royal conscience was, despite Roman flattery, free from participation in political, anti-Roman schemes which Aleander so often suspected in the inner council of the emperor. [68] Luther himself, as the papal envoys remark, spared the pretended friends of the Pope the necessity for adjusting their political moves to their duty to Rome. His refusal to compromise rescued papal diplomacy from a difficult situation.

It is due to Aleander, who bases his statement on the authority of the archbishop of Trier, that we have the only evidence of a direct attempt to bribe Luther. The archbishop claims to have told Martin that in case he was deterred from revoking for fear of his comrades, who were said to frighten him with threats of death, he would make him a rich prior in the neighborhood of one of his castles, keep him at his table and in his council and assure him of the emperor's protection and the Pope's favor. "Luther refused everything." [69] That the conversation was of an especially intimate and cordial nature is evident in the softened tone with which the archbishop is treated by the Lutheran chroniclers, and also by the prelate's statement, as reported by Christoph von Schwarzenberg, that Martin had told him something in confidence which he could not repeat. [70] This was confirmed later by Aleander, whose curiosity was intensely aroused as to Martin's mysterious statement, which the archbishop held secret under the seal of the confessional. The envoy believed that he had ferreted out its subject—the names of the real authors of the books attributed to Luther. [71]

[66] Letter from Francesco Corner and Gasparo Contarini to the Doge, April 28, DRA, II, 880, ll. 12 f.

[67] See the letter from the papal envoys to Medici, April 27, Brieger, "Aleander," p. 165, and Kalkoff, Depeschen, p. 192. See also Etliche sunderliche Handlungen, DRA, II, 602, ll. 13 f.

[68] Kalkoff as we have seen, is firmly convinced of the confessor's thorough trickiness. See his Der Wormser Reichstag., pp. 243 f. Aleander was, in the main, assured of his loyalty to the papal cause. The student of the available sources will have his doubts on this point.

[69] "A tutto negó." Brieger, "Aleander," p. 164; and Kalkoff, Depeschen, p. 191. Cochlaeus also gives Luther assurances of protection in a secure place by the emperor or the archbishop of Trier. Colloquium Cochlaei, DRA, II, 630, ll. 26 ff.

[70] Letter to Ludwig of Bavaria, DRA, II, 874, ll. 29 ff.

[71] Letter to Medici, May 15, Brieger, "Aleander," pp. 212 f., and Kalkoff, Depeschen, pp. 239 f. Aleander was laying a scheme to induce the archbishop, "for the honor of God and the peace of the Church," as he states in his letter, to violate this promise made to a destroyer of the confessional and a notorious heretic. It seems possible that the archbishop was mystifying

After the conference, the archbishop departed at once and laid the matter before the emperor, praising God, according to Aleander,[72] for having relieved him of such a scandal. Luther went on an errand of mercy to the house of a knight sick unto death, Hans von Minkwitz, to bring him Christian consolation. "I am leaving tomorrow," he declared.[73] Both sides, indeed, had exhausted all efforts to find a solution. The Roman envoys, who hastened on the heels of the archbishop to the emperor, felt that a stone had been rolled from their hearts when the emperor took steps immediately to give Martin formal orders for departure. A little later [74] three imperial representatives, Von Eck, a secretary of the emperor, and a chancellor of Lower Austria, summoned Luther on behalf of the privy council and gave him a formal document of dismissal. This pointed out that although he had been urged often by emperor and estates, he had been unwilling to return to the bosom and unity of the Church. The emperor must therefore take the only course open to an advocate of the Catholic faith. Martin had twenty-one days within which to return to his home under safe-conduct, and he was warned not to stir up people by preaching or writing on the way. To this formal dismissal Luther responded briefly: "As it has pleased God, so it has been done. Blessed be the name of the Lord." He expressed his thanks to the emperor and the estates for a gracious hearing and for promising and intending to observe his safe-conduct. "I have never desired in these things anything except a reformation by means of sacred Scripture, and for this I have earnestly striven. For the rest, I would suffer for his imperial majesty and the empire all things, life and death, fame and infamy, reserving absolutely nothing for myself except liberty of confessing and testifying freely to the word of God." [75]

"So we parted." [76] Henceforth the German people were to be divided into two camps, with two series of traditions, two galaxies of religious

---

Aleander and that Luther's confidential communication was of a political nature, possibly information that had come to him of the impending attack on the territory of Trier, which was launched a few months later by Franz von Sickingen. See Kalkoff, *Depeschen*, p. 239, n. 1.

[72] Brieger, "Aleander," p. 165, and Kalkoff, *Depeschen*, p. 192.

[73] Spalatin, *Annales Reformationis*, Cyprian ed., II, 46.

[74] *Acta et res gestae, DRA*, II, 567, l. 18. According to Spalatin, about three hours after the end of the conference. *Annales Reformationis*, Cyprian ed., II, 47. According to *Etliche sunderliche Handlungen, DR*, II, 610, l. 20, between five and six hours.

[75] *DRA*, II, 568, ll. 8 ff. Somewhat more briefly in Luther's letter to Albert, *WAB*, II, 327. The answer, according to the German chronicle, was in Latin. See *DRA*, II, 610, ll. 32 ff. It was probably prepared in writing beforehand. According to Spalatin, the little address was made by Luther to his friends after he received his dismissal and returned to his lodgings. *Annales Reformationis*, Cyprian ed., II, 47 f.

[76] Letter to Mansfeld, *WAB*, II, 326.

heroes, and to a considerable degree, two fundamentally different views of life. The reports of friend and foe testify that the last night in Worms was not spent in solemn thoughts, but rather in a festive celebration. A crowd of distinguished people came to visit Luther,[77] and Aleander adds a note that Martin drank many glasses of Malmsey wine, "of which he is very fond." [78] On the next morning, the 26th, about ten o'clock, two carts rumbled away from Luther's lodging, bearing the little party. Aleander was informed that twenty horsemen who met them outside the gate were sent by Sickingen for Luther's protection. This is possibly a misunderstanding of the troop with which Kaspar Sturm, the imperial herald, was waiting for the party at Oppenheim.[79] The elector had provided Martin with forty guilders to cover the journey back to Wittenberg, although according to Spalatin [80] Luther had been informed the night before he departed of a plan, known to a few of the inside circle of the Saxon court, which was to take him, not to Wittenberg, but into hiding. The departure, indeed, relieved the tension on both sides: the papal envoys had been constantly in fear of an outbreak of disorder on the part of the resentful humanists and the lesser nobility; the Saxon party, and Luther's friends in general, were nervous regarding the safe-conduct, for it was noised about in Worms that this pledge need not be kept with the new heretic any more than with Huss.[81] Luther, Spalatin, and Hutten all believed that Aleander and Caracciolo were laying traps to have him arrested at Worms, apparently a groundless suspicion, for it lacks confirmation either in Aleander's writings or other sources.[82]

"Are these your books?" "Yes." "Will you revoke them or not?" "No." "Then get out!" Thus Martin sums up the Worms experience to his friend, Lucas Cranach in Wittenberg, in a letter written the second day after he left Worms,[83] which is marked by genial humor in spite of its serious undertone. As he fared northward through the Rhine country and passed in review the preceding ten days, a mood of bitterness seized him. "O, we blind Germans, how childishly we behave, allowing ourselves to be duped

---

[77] *DRA*, II, 611, ll. 12 ff.

[78] Brieger, "Aleander," p. 166, and Kalkoff, *Depeschen*, p. 193.

[79] *DRA*, II, 568, ll. 24 ff.

[80] Spalatin, *Annales Reformationis*, Cyprian ed., II, 50. See the intimation of some plan on April 23 in Frederick's letter to John, *DRA*, II, 871. See also *ibid.*, n. 1.

[81] Letter of Lazarus Spengler to an anonymous correspondent, end of April(?), *DRA*, II, 891, ll. 33 ff.

[82] See Jules Paquier's spirited defense of Aleander in this matter. In an examination of all the private papers of the envoy, extending through two later missions to Germany, in which he comes back often to the Worms experience, Paquier found not the slightest hint of regret that Charles honored the safe-conduct of Luther. *L'Humanisme et la Réforme*, pp. 242 f.

[83] April 28. *WAB*, II, 305.

and made fools of so wretchedly by the Romans." [84] This mood is reflected in the letter to Cranach and again several days later in a long letter from Eisenach to Albert of Mansfeld, in which Martin summarizes his treatment at Worms.[85] This very personal review of his experience was published late in the summer.[86] Vividly it all passes once more in Martin's mind: the surprise of the papal group that he had come at all; the sequestration of his books, like a slap in the face, on the eve of his appearance; the hearings and the conferences with his adversaries; the clever and the stodgy councilors in law and the chattering Cochlaeus; the crowds of friendly and hostile faces. The slogan which in retrospect rings constantly throughout is, "Nothing against God's word." Around this had centered all questions about revocations, the whole dispute about submission to emperor, estates, or council. Because of this they had parted.

Probably on advice of the Saxon councilors, Martin reviews the whole situation also in a formal letter to the emperor. This document is dated at the small city of Friedberg, just outside of Frankfort, two days after he left Worms.[87] It is in Latin. A rather awkward German translation, probably by Spalatin, was laid before the estates two days later,[88] then printed and widely circulated.[89] In his letter to Charles, Martin reviews his offers to revoke as well as the discussion regarding the reference to a council, with the reservation that nothing be submitted by him or decided by others that was against the Gospel of God. "Here was the chief point of the controversy." [90] This position he fortifies from Scripture. In material things we owe obedience to temporal authority, but in what concerns God's word and eternal welfare, man may not submit to man. He has left Worms because there was no hope of an examination of his books on the basis of God's word. With thanks to the emperor for preserving his safe-conduct, he offers once more to go before neutral and learned judges; to be shown his errors by emperor, estates, or whomever it may be; to submit his books and accept judgment on them, save only as concerns "God's clear, evident, and free word." [91] He closes with a prayer for the

---

[84] *Ibid.*

[85] May 3. *WAB*, II, 321 ff. Luther says that the letter was written at the request of Rudolf von Watzdorf, a retainer of the Mansfeld house.

[86] Two prints appeared, in Augsburg and in Leipzig; also a Latin translation, perhaps earlier. *WAB*, II, p. 320.

[87] *WAB*, II, 307 ff. The original MS is the property of the Lutherhalle in Wittenberg, thanks to the generosity of the late J. P. Morgan.

[88] *WAB*, II, 310 f.

[89] Ten prints from 1521 are listed by Otto Clemen, *WAB*, II, 312 ff.

[90] "Hic fuit controversiae totius cardo." *WAB*, II, 308, ll. 47 f.

[91] *Ibid.*, p. 309, l. 106.

emperor, the empire, and the most noble German nation. "If Christ himself prayed for his enemies on the cross, how much more should I pray for Your Majesty, the empire, my very dear rulers, and the whole German fatherland."

Thus Martin closes the chapter and turns his face northward. Once before, at the end of 1518, when the Dominicans launched their first attack on him, he had planned flight from Wittenberg, possibly then also with the connivance of the court. Now the Saxon plan that he should disappear had been well matured; [92] and when Martin rode out of Worms he knew that his destination was not to be Wittenberg. Despite the imperial prohibition of preaching on the journey, he did preach at Hersfeld and Eisenach; and while the papal group in Worms were raging at this new infamy, his wagon climbed up the Thuringian ridge to the village of Möhra, where he dined in a garden near the priest's house and preached again, this time to peasant and miner folk, nearly all of whom were his relatives.[93] The next day, as he drove on through the Thuringian forest, a group of armed men halted the wagon and carried him off to the Wartburg castle, ancient seat of the Thuringian rulers, perched on the northwestern declivity of the great transverse ridge.

"The Jews must sing their song of triumph around the cross," he had written to Cranach from Frankfort, but "Easter Day will come for us, too, when we can sing hallelujah! . . . 'A little while and ye shall not see me, and again a little while and ye shall see me,' said Christ. I hope that will be the way of it now again. But may God's will be done, as the best in heaven or on earth." [94]

[92] The plan may go back as far as February 15, when it seems to be forecast in a memorandum drawn up by the Saxon councilors. See Kalkoff, *Der Wormser Reichstag*, p. 227, n. 1. The night before Martin left Worms, Frederick had discussed the matter with his councilors. See Freiherr von Thüna, "Friedrich von Thun," *Zeitschrift des Vereins für thüringische Geschichte und Altertumskunde*, N.F. VI (1889), 349. See also *TR*, V, No. 5353.

[93] C. A. H. Burkhardt, "Luther in Möhra 1521," *Neues Archiv für sächsische Geschichte*, X (1889), 330 ff. See also Julius Köstlin, *Martin Luther*, ed. by Gustav Kawerau, p. 432 and n. 1, p. 773.

[94] April 28, 1521. *WAB*, II, 305, ll. 17 f.

CONCLUSION

LUTHER had come victorious from his ordeal at Worms—victorious through his own resolute adherence to his convictions, through the aid also of circumstances and the loyalty of friends and supporters. A long road still lay ahead. His weaknesses were manifest: intransigency in theological views, proneness to vehemence, narrowness of social concepts. These were to lead to intolerance of sectarian movements, pitiless harshness toward the peasants, incredibly poor judgment in the matter of Philip of Hesse. But Luther also had qualities to offset these: sincere desire for the truth, courage, determination, power of organization, an outstanding gift for identifying himself with the language and thought of the simple man. These were the qualities that permitted him to carry through what he had begun. And whatever the judgment of friend or foe, such was the power of his personality that despite the many factors which aided him in making reform possible at this time, Protestantism must forever bear the impress of his hand as the molding force which brought the existing potentialities into being and gave them their characteristic form.

LIST OF ABBREVIATIONS

"Acten"   "Acten der Erfurter Universität," in *Geschichtsquellen der Provinz Sachsen*

ARG   *Archiv für Reformationsgeschichte*

Const.   *Constitutiones Fratrum heremitarum Sancti Augustini ad apostolicorum privilegiorum formana pro reformatione Alemanie*

Corp. Cath. *Corpus Catholicorum*

CR   *Corpus Reformatorum*

DRA   *Deutsche Reichstagsakten*

EA   Luther, *Sämmtliche Werke* (Erlangen)

Ref.-Act.   *Vollständige Reformations-Acta und Documenta*

RgST   *Reformationsgeschichtliche Studien und Texte*

SVRG   *Schriften des Vereins für Reformationsgeschichte*

ThStKr   *Theologische Studien und Kritiken*

TR   *Tischreden, 1531–1546.* In *WA*

WA   *D. Martin Luthers Werke* (Weimar)

WAB   *Briefwechsel.* In *WA*

ZKG   *Zeitschrift für Kirchengeschichte*

SELECTED BIBLIOGRAPHY

Abbagnano, Nicola. 1931. Guglielmo di Ockham. Lanciano.

Acta Academiae Lovaniensis. 1520. In *EA,* Vol. XXXV.

"Acten der Erfurter Universität." 1881, 1884. Ed. by J. C. H. Weissenborn, in *Geschichtsquellen der Provinz Sachsen,* Vol. VIII, Teile ı, ıı.

Alexander de Villa-Dei. 1893. "Das Doctrinale des Alexander de Villa-Dei," ed. by D. Reichling, in *Monumenta Germaniae pedagogica,* Vol. XII.

Alfeld [Alveld], Augustin von. 1520. Super apostolica Sede an videlicet divino sit jure nec ne. . . . Declaratio. Leipzig.

—— 1926. "Wyder den wittenbergischen Abgot Martin Luther" (1524), ed. by K. Büschgens, in *Corp. Cath.,* Vol. XI.

—— 1926. "Erklärung des Salve Regina" (1527), ed. by Leonhard Lemmens, in *Corp. Cath.,* Vol. XI.

Allen, Percy S., ed. 1906–. Opus epistolarum Des. Erasmi Roterdami. Oxford.

Allgemeine Deutsche Biographie. 1875–. Leipzig.

Analecta Augustiniana. 1912, 1917, 1919. Rome. Vols. IV, VII, VIII.

Appel, Helmut. 1938. "Anfechtung und Trost im Spätmittelalter und bei Luther," *SVRG,* Vol. LVI, Heft ı.

Archiv für Reformationsgeschichte. 1903–. Leipzig, Berlin.

Arnold von Usingen, Bartholomäus. 1499. Parvulus philosophie naturalis figuralis interpretatio. Leipzig.

—— 1501. Compendium naturalis philosophie et studio singulari M. Bartholomei de Usingen. In Gymnasio Erphurdiensi publice litterarie perfectum.

—— 1514. Summa in totam physicem: hoc est philosophiam naturalem conformiter siquidem vere sophie: que est theologia . . . elucubrata et edita.

Augustine (Saint). 1489. Opuscula plurima.

—— 1489. De trinitate. Basel.

—— 1489. De civitate Dei. Basel.

Balan, Petrus. 1884. Monumenta Reformationis Lutheranae ex Tabulariis secretioribus S. Sedis 1521–1525. Regensburg.

Bale, John. 1902. Index Brittaniae Scriptorum. Oxford.

Barge. Hermann. 1905. Andreas Bodenstein von Karlstadt. Leipzig.

Barnikol, Ernst. 1917. Luther in Magdeburg und die dortige Brüderschule. Reprinted from *Theologische Arbeiten aus dem rheinischen wissenschaftlichen Predigerverein,* Neue Folge XVII. Tübingen.

Baronio, C., and O. Rinaldi. 1755. Annales ecclesiastici (Tomus Duodecimus). Vol. XXXI. Lucae.

Bauch, Gustav. 1894. "Zur Cranachforschung," *Repertorium für Kunstwissenschaft,* Vol. XVII.

—— 1897. "Wittenberg und die Scholastik," *Neues Archiv für sächsische Geschichte und Altertumskunde,* Vol. XVIII.

—— 1898. "Andreas Karlstadt als Scholastiker," *ZKG,* Vol. XVIII.

—— 1898. "Zu Luthers Briefwechsel," *ZKG,* Vol. XVIII.

—— 1901. "Christoph Scheurl in Wittenberg," *Neue Mitteilungen aus dem Gebiet historisch-antiquarischer Forschungen,* Vol. XXI, Heft 1.

—— 1904. Die Universität Erfurt im Zeitalter des Frühhumanismus. Breslau.

Bauer, Karl. 1901. "Die Heidelberger Disputation Luthers," *ZKG,* Vol. XXI.

—— 1928. Die Wittenberger Universitätstheologie und die Anfänge der Deutschen Reformation. Tübingen.

Bavarus, Valentin. 1549. Rhapsodiae et dicta quedam ex ore Doctoris Martini Lutheri. . . .

Beatus Rhenanus. 1886. Briefwechsel des Beatus Rhenanus, ed. by A. Horawitz and K. Hartfelder. Leipzig.

Becker, Hans. 1928. "Herzog Georg von Sachsen als kirchlicher und theologischer Schriftsteller," *ARG,* Vol. XXV.

Behrend, Fritz. 1917. "Die Leidensgeschichte des Herrn als Form im politisch-literarischen Kampf besonders im Reformationszeitalter," *ARG,* Vol. XIV.

Below, Georg von. 1917. "Die Ursachen der Reformation," in *Historische Bibliothek,* Vol. XXXVIII.

Benary, Friedrich. 1919. Zur Geschichte der Stadt und der Universität Erfurt am Ausgang des Mittelalters. Ed. by Alfred Overmann. Gotha.

Berbig, Georg. 1906. Spalatin und sein Verhältnis zu Martin Luther . . . bis zum Jahre 1525. Halle a. S.

Bertram, M. P. 1908. "Der Erfurter Dorfpfarrer im ausgehenden Mittelalter," *Zeitschrift des Vereins für Kirchengeschichte der Provinz Sachsen,* Vol. V.

Besler, N. 1732. "Vita Nicolai Besleri Augustiniani ab ipso conscripta," in *Fortgesetzte Sammlung von alten und neuen theologischen Sachen.* Leipzig.

Biblia Latina (Froben). 1509. Basel.

Biel, Gabriel. 1488. Lectura super canone Missae. Reutlingen.

—— 1499. Epithomata et collectorium pariter collectorium circa quattuor Sententiarium libros. Tübingen.

—— 1499. Epithoma expositionis canonis Missae. Tübingen.

Biereye, Johannes. 1917. Die Erfurter Lutherstätten nach ihrer geschichtlichen Beglaubigung. Erfurt.

Biereye, Johannes. 1929. "Über die Wohnung Luthers und einiger zeitgenössischer Humanisten in Erfurt," in *Beiträge zur thüringischen und sächsischen Geschichte. Festschrift für Otto Dobenecker.* Jena.

Blochwitz, Gottfried. 1930. "Die antirömischen deutschen Flugschriften der frühen Reformationszeit," *ARG,* Vol. XXVII.

Böhmer, Heinrich. 1914. Luthers Romfahrt. Leipzig.

―― 1918. Luther im Lichte der neueren Forschung. Leipzig. 5th ed.

―― 1920–21. "Luther und der 10. December 1520," in *Jahrbuch der Luthergesellschaft,* Vols. II–III.

―― 1923. "Luthers erste Vorlesung," *Berichte über die Verhandlungen der sächsischen Akademie der Wissenschaften zu Leipzig, phil.-hist. Klasse,* Vol. LXXV, Heft 1.

―― 1925. Der junge Luther. Gotha.

Bömer, Aloys, ed. 1924. Epistolae obscurorum virorum. Heidelberg.

Braun, Wilhelm. 1908. Die Bedeutung der Concupiszens in Luthers Leben und Lehre. Berlin.

Brieger, Theodor. 1884. "Aleander und Luther, 1521," *Quellen und Forschungen zur Geschichte der Reformation,* Vol. I.

―― 1890. "Kritische Erörterungen zur neuen Luther-Ausgabe," *ZKG,* Vol. XI.

―― 1896. "Über die handschriftlichen Protokolle der Leipziger Disputation," in *Beiträge zur Reformationsgeschichte. Festgabe für Julius Köstlin.* Gotha.

―― 1897. Das Wesen des Ablasses am Ausgange des Mittelalters. Leipzig.

―― 1909. "Einiges über die Leipziger Disputation von 1519," in *Die Universität Leipzig 1409–1909. Gedenkblätter zum 30. Juli 1909.* Leipzig.

―― 1910. "Die Gliederung der 95 Thesen Luthers," in *Studien und Versuche zur neueren Geschichte, Max Lenz gewidmet.* Berlin.

Büchi, Albert. 1928. "Das Ende der Betrügerin Anna Laminit in Freiburg i. Uechtland," *ZKG,* Vol. XLVII, Neue Folge X.

Buchwald, Georg. 1896. "Archivalische Mitteilungen über Bücherbezüge der kurfürstlichen Bibliothek und Georg Spalatins in Wittenberg," *Archiv für Geschichte des deutschen Buchhandels,* Vol. XVIII.

―― 1918. "Wann hat Luther die Priesterweihe empfangen?" *ZKG,* Vol. XXXVII.

―― 1925. Die Predigten D. Martin Luthers. Gütersloh.

―― 1927, "Ist Luther am 9. Oktober 1512 in Leipzig gewesen?" *Beiträge zur sächsischen Kirchengeschichte,* Vol. XXXVI.

―― 1929. "Luther-Kalendarium," *SVRG,* Vol. XLVII, Heft 11.

―― 1929. "Zu Spalatins Reisen, insbesondere nach Wittenberg in Angelegenheit der Kurfürstlichen Bibliothek," *Archiv für Bibliographie,* Vol. II.

Buchwald, Georg, and E. Wolf. 1927. Tübinger Predigten des Joh. von Staupitz. Leipzig.

Burgdorf, Martin. 1911. Johann Lange, der Reformator Erfurts. Kassel.

Burgdorf, Martin. [1928]. Der Einfluss der Erfurter Humanisten auf Luthers Entwicklung bis 1510. Leipzig.

Burkhardt, C. A. H. 1874. "Das tolle Jahr zu Erfurt," *Archiv für sächsische Geschichte,* Vol. XII.

———— 1889. "Luther in Möhra 1521," *Neues Archiv für sächsische Geschichte,* Vol. X.

Cajetan. See Vio, Thomas de.

Cammermeister, Hartung. 1896. "Die Chronik Hartung Cammermeisters," ed. by R. Reiche, in *Geschichtsquellen der Provinz Sachsen,* Vol. XXXV.

Catharinus, Ambrosius. 1520. Apologia pro veritate catholicae et apostolicae fidei ac doctrinae adversus impia ac valde pestifera Martini Lutheri dogmata. Florence.

Catholic Encyclopedia. 1907–12. Ed. by Charles G. Herbermann and others. New York.

Cleary, P. 1914. The Church and Usury. Dublin.

Clemen, Otto. 1897. "Litterarische Nachspiele zur Leipziger Disputation," *Beiträge zur sächsischen Kirchengeschichte,* Vol. XII.

———— 1900–. Beiträge zur Reformationsgeschichte aus Büchern und Handschriften der Zwickauer Ratsschulbibliothek. Berlin.

———— 1902. "Kleine Beiträge zur sächsischen Gelehrtengeschichte in der Reformationszeit," *Neues Archiv für sächsische Geschichte,* Vol. XXIII.

———— 1908. "Über die Verbrennung der Bannbulle durch Luther," *ThStKr,* Vol. LXXXI.

———— 1912. "Beiträge zur Lutherforschung," in *Aus Deutschlands kirchlicher Vergangenheit. Festschrift zum 70. Geburtstag von Th. Brieger.* Leipzig.

———— 1929. "Das lateinische Original von Luthers 'Vater-Unser vorwärts und rückwärts' vom Jahre 1516," *ZKG,* Vol. XLVIII, Neue Folge XI.

Cochlaeus, Johann. 1524. Ad semper victricem Germaniam paraklesis.

———— 1533. Auf Luthers Trostbrieff an etliche zu Leipzig. Dresden.

———— 1549. Commentaria de actis et scriptis Martini Lutheri. Mainz.

Constitutiones Fratrum heremitarum Sancti Augustini. 1504.

Corpus Catholicorum. 1919–. Münster.

Corpus Reformatorum. 1834–. Ed. by Karl Gottlieb Bretschneider and Heinrich Ernst Bindseil. Halle. Vols. 1–28: Philip Melanchthon, *Opera quae supersunt omnia.*

Cossio, A. 1902. Il cardinale Gaetano e la Riforma. Cividale.

Creutzberg, H. A. 1907. Die Jugend des päpstlichen Nuntius Karl von Miltitz und sein Aufenthalt in Rom. Freiburg i. B.

Cruel, R. 1879. Geschichte der deutschen Predigt. Detmold.

Cyprian, Ernst S. 1717, 1718. "Nützliche Urkunden zur Erläuterung der ersten Reformationsgeschichte," in *Tentzels Historischer Bericht vom Anfang und ersten Fortgang der Reformation Lutheri.* Leipzig. Vols. I, II.

Dannenbauer, Heinrich. 1930. "Luther als religiöser Volksschriftsteller 1517–20," in *Sammlung gemeinverständlicher Vorträge und Schriften aus dem Gebiet der Theologie und Religionsgeschichte.* Tübingen, No. 145.

Degering, Hermann. 1916. "Aus Luthers Frühzeit," *Zentralblatt für Bibliothekswesen,* Vol. XXXII.

———— 1933. Luthers Randbemerkungen zu Gabriel Biels Collectorium in quattuor libros sententiarium und zu dessen Sacri canonis missae expositio, Lyon 1514. Weimar.

De Jongh, H. 1911. L'Ancienne Faculté de Théologie de Louvain. Louvain.

Denifle, Heinrich. 1885. Die Universitäten des Mittelalters. Berlin. Vol. I.

———— 1904, 1906. Luther und Luthertum. Mainz.

Denifle, Heinrich, ed. 1889–. Chartularium universitatis Parisiensis. Paris.

De Ram, P. F. X. 1843. "Disquisitio Historica de iis quae contra Lutherum Lovanienses Theologi Egerunt," *Nouveaux Mémoires de l'Académie Royale . . . de Bruxelles,* Vol. XVI.

Deutsche Reichstagsakten unter Kaiser Karl V. 1893, 1896. Jüngere Reihe I, ed. by August Kluckhohn; II, ed. by Adolf Wrede. Gotha.

De Wette, Wilhelm M. L. 1828. Dr. Martin Luthers Briefe, Sendschreiben und Bedenken. Berlin.

Doebner, R., ed. 1903. "Annalen und Akten der Brüder des gemeinsamen Lebens im Lüchtenhofe zu Hildesheim," *Quellen und Darstellungen zur Geschichte Niedersachsens,* Vol. IX.

Drescher, Karl, ed. 1917. Lutherstudien zur 4. Jahrhundertfeier der Reformation. Weimar.

Dresser, Matthias. 1593. De Festis Diebus Christianorum. Leipzig.

———— 1598. Martini Lutheri Historia. Leipzig.

Drews, Paul. 1887. Willibald Prickheimers Stellung zur Reformation. Leipzig.

Droysen, Johann G. 1853. "Über das Verlöbnis der Infantin Katharina mit Herzog Johann Friedrich von Sachsen 1519," *Berichte über die Verhandlungen der königlich sächsischen Gesellschaft der Wissenschaften zu Leipzig, phil.-hist. Klasse,* Vol. V.

Du Cange, C. 1938. Glossarium mediae et infimae Latinitatis. Paris. Vol. IV.

Eccius Dedolatus Autore Joanne francisco Cotta Lembergio, Poeta Laureato. 1891. Ed. by Max Herrmann and Siegfried Szamatolski, in *Lateinische Literaturdenkmäler des XV. und XVI. Jahrhunderts.* Berlin. Vol. II.

Eck, Johannes. 1854. Letter to Christoph Tengler, in *Notizenblatt. Beilage zum Archiv für Kunde österreichischer Geschichtsquellen,* Vol. IV.

———— 1917. "Zwei unbekannte Briefe Johann Ecks an Johann Cuspinian," ed. by Hans von Ankwicz, in *Mitteilungen des Instituts für österreichische Geschichtsforschung.* Innsbruck. Vol. XXXVII.

———— 1919. "Defensio contra Amarulentas D. Andreae Bodenstein Carolstatini Invectiones" (1518), ed. by Joseph Greving, in *Corp. Cath.,* Vol. I.

Eck, Johannes. 1923. "Disputatio Viennae Pannoniae habita" (1517), ed. by Therese Virnich, in *Corp. Cath.,* Vol. VI.

—— 1929. "Gegen Martin Luthers Anklage wider das Konzil von Konstanz in Sachen des Johannes Hus und des Hieronymus von Prag," one of "Vier deutsche Schriften gegen Martin Luther . . . ," ed. by K. Meisen and F. Zoepfl, in *Corp. Cath.,* Vol. XIV.

Ellinger, Georg. 1929. Geschichte der neulateinischen Literatur Deutschlands im 16. Jahrhundert. Berlin. Vol. I.

Ellwein, Eduard, trans. 1927. Martin Luther, Vorlesung über den Römerbrief 1515–1516. Munich.

Emser, Hieronymus. 1921. "De disputatione Lipsicensi, quantum ad Boemos obiter deflexa est" (1519), ed. by F. X. Thurnhofer, in *Corp. Cath.,* Vol. IV.

—— 1921. "A venatione Luteriana aegocerotis assertio" (1519), ed. by F. X. Thurnhofer, in *Corp. Cath.,* Vol. IV.

Enders, Ernst Ludwig, ed. 1884–. Luthers Briefwechsel. Frankfurt a. M. and elsewhere.

—— 1890, 1892. "Luther und Emser. Ihre Streitschriften aus dem Jahre 1521," *Neudrucke deutscher Literaturwerke des XVI. und XVII. Jahrhunderts,* Vols. I, Nos. 83–84; II, Nos. 96–98.

Eobanus Hessus. 1506. De recessu studentum.

Erasmus, Desiderius. 1516. Novum instrumentum cum annotationibus. Basel.

—— 1703. Erasmi Opera omnia. Ed. by Joannes Clericus. Lugduni. Vol. III.

—— 1906–. Opus epistolarum Des. Erasmi Roterdami. Ed. by Percy S. Allen. Oxford.

—— 1933. Erasmi opuscula. Ed. by W. K. Ferguson. The Hague.

Ericeus, N. 1566. Sylvula Sententiarum. Frankfurt.

Eschenhagen, Edith. 1927. "Beiträge zur sozial- und Wirtschaftsgeschichte der Stadt Wittenberg in der Reformationszeit," *Jahrbuch der Luthergesellschaft,* Vol. IX.

Eulenburg, F. 1904. "Die Frequenz der deutschen Universitäten von ihrer Gründung bis zur Gegenwart," *Abhandlung der sächsischen Gesellschaft der Wissenschaften,* Vol. XXIV, Heft II.

Ficker, Johannes. 1908, 1929. Anfänge reformatorischer Bibelauslegung. Leipzig. Vol. I: Luthers Vorlesung über den Römerbrief 1515–1516; Vol. II: Luthers Vorlesung über den Hebräerbrief.

—— 1918. "Luther, 1517," *SVRG,* Vol. XXXVI.

—— 1927–28. "Luthers erste Vorlesung—welche?" *ThStKr,* Vol. C.

—— 1928. "Luther als Professor," *Hallische Universitätsreden,* Vol. XXXIV.

Flavio, Giovanni B. 1639. Oratio de vita sanctissimi viri maximeque Reverendi D. Thomae de Vio Caietani, cardinalis S. Xysti, in *Thomae de Vio, D. Caietani Opera omnia, quotquot in Sacrae Scripturae expositionem reperiuntur.* Lugduni. Vol. I.

Fontana, V. M. 1666. Theatrum Dominicarum. Rome.

Förstemann, Karl E., ed. 1837. "Neun Briefe . . . an Justus Jonas . . . ," *Neue Mitteilungen aus dem Gebiet historisch-antiquarischer Forschungen des thüringisch-sächsischen Vereins,* Vol. III, Heft 1.

———— 1841. Album Academiae Vitebergensis 1502–1602. Leipzig.

———— 1842. Neues Urkundenbuch zur Geschichte der evangelischen Kirchen-Reformation. Hamburg.

———— 1838. Liber decanorum Facultatis Theologicae Academiae Vitebergensis. Leipzig.

Freytag, Gustav. 1911. "Bilder aus der deutschen Vergangenheit," Part II, in *Gesammelte Werke.* Leipzig, Vol. XIX.

Friedensburg, Walter. 1898. Quellen und Forschungen aus italienischen Archiven und Bibliotheken. Rome. Vol. I.

———— 1917. Geschichte der Universität Wittenberg. Halle.

———— 1926. "Urkundenbuch der Universität Wittenberg," *Geschichtsquellen der Provinz Sachsen,* Neue Reihe III, Vol. I (1502–1611).

Geiger, Ludwig. 1871. Johann Reuchlin. Leipzig.

Gelbke, Karl. 1890. "Die Volkszahl der Stadt Eisleben von der Mitte des 15. Jahrhunderts bis zur Gegenwart," *Mansfelder Blätter. Mitteilungen des Vereins für Geschichte und Altertümer der Grafschaft Mansfeld zu Eisleben,* Vol. IV.

Germann, Oskar. 1899. "Sebastian Fröschel, sein Leben und seine Schriften," *Beiträge zur sächsischen Kirchengeschichte,* Vol. XIV.

Gesellschaft für deutsche Erziehungs- und Schulgeschichte. 1891, 1892. Mitteilungen. Berlin. Vols. I, II.

Gess, Felician. 1888. "Luthers Thesen und der Herzog von Sachsen," *ZKG,* Vol. IX.

———— 1895. "Leipzig und Wittenberg. Ein Beitrag zur sächsischen Reformationsgeschichte," *Neues Archiv für sächsische Geschichte,* Vol. XVI.

———— 1905. Briefe und Akten zur Kirchenpolitik Herzog Georgs von Sachsen. Leipzig.

Graf, Wilhelm. 1930. "Dr. Christoph Scheurl von Nürnberg," *Beiträge zur Kulturgeschichte des Mittelalters und der Renaissance,* Vol. XLIII.

Greving, Joseph. 1906. "Johann Eck als junger Gelehrter. Eine literar- und dogmengeschichtliche Untersuchung über seinen Chrysopassus praedestinationis aus dem Jahre 1514," *RgST,* Vol. I.

———— 1908. "Joh. Ecks Pfarrbuch für U. L. Frau in Ingolstadt. Ein Beitrag zur Kenntnis der pfarrkirchlichen Verhältnisse im 16. Jahrhundert," *RgST,* Vol. IV–V.

———— 1912. "Briefmappe. Erstes Stück," *RgST,* Vol. XXI–XXII.

Grisar, Hartmann. 1918–19, 1922. "Lutheranalekten," *Historisches Jahrbuch,* Vols. XXXIX, XLII.

———— 1911. Luther. Freiburg i. B. 3 vols.

———— 1927. Martin Luthers Leben und sein Werk. Freiburg i. B.

Grohmann, J. C. A. 1801. Annalen der Universität Wittenberg. Meissen.

Hain, L. T. 1826. Repertorium Bibliographicum. Stuttgart and Tübingen.

Hartlieb, J. 1599. De fide meretricum in suos amatores. . . . Frankfurt.

Hausrath, Adolf. 1894. Martin Luthers Romfahrt nach einem gleichzeitigen Pilgerbuch. Berlin.

——— 1897. Aleander und Luther auf dem Reichstage zu Worms. Berlin.

Haussleiter, Johannes. 1903. Die Universität Wittenberg vor dem Eintritt Luthers nach der Schilderung des Magisters Andreas Meinhardi vom Jahre 1507. Leipzig.

Helbig, G. 1930. Martin Luthers Vorlesung über den Hebräerbrief 1517–18. Leipzig.

Held, F. 1929. Augustins Enarrationes in Psalmos als exegetische Vorlage für Luthers erste Psalmenvorlesung. Kiel.

Helmbold, H. 1915. "Geschichte der Stadt Eisenach," *Bau- und Kunstdenkmäler Thüringens,* Vol. III, Heft 1.

Hennes, J. H. 1858. Albrecht von Brandenburg. Mainz.

Hermelink, Heinrich. 1912. "Text und Gedankengang der Theologia Deutsch," in *Aus Deutschlands kirchlicher Vergangenheit. Festschrift zum 70. Geburtstag von Th. Brieger.* Leipzig.

——— 1935. "Die neuere Lutherforschung," *Theologische Rundschau,* Vol. VII.

Herrmann, F. 1902. "Miscellen zur Reformationsgeschichte," *ZKG,* Vol. XXIII.

Herrmann, Karl. 1875. "Selbstbiographie," *Mitteilungen des Vereins zur Geschichte des alten Erfurt,* Vol. VII.

Hildebrandt, Ernst. 1925. "Die kurfürstliche Schloss- und Universitätsbibliothek zu Wittenberg, 1512–1547," *Zeitschrift für Buchkunde,* Vol. II.

Hirsch, Emanuel. 1918. "Randglossen zu Lutbertexten," *ThStKr,* Vol. XCI.

——— 1919. "Luthers Eintritt ins Kloster," *ThStKr,* Vol. XCII.

——— 1920. "Initium theologiae Lutheri," in *Festgabe für J. Kaftan.* Tübingen.

——— 1929. "Luther über die oratio mentalis," *Zeitschrift für systematische Theologie,* Vol. VI.

Hirsch, Emanuel, and Hanns Rückert. 1929. Luthers Vorlesung über den Hebräerbrief. Berlin and Leipzig.

Hochstetter, Erich. 1927. Studien zur Metaphysik und Erkenntnislehre Wilhelms von Ockham. Berlin and Leipzig.

Hoffmann, F. W. 1845–50. Geschichte der Stadt Magdeburg. Magdeburg.

Holl, Karl. 1923. "Luther," in *Gesammelte Aufsätze zur Kirchengeschichte.* Tübingen, Vol. I, Heft III.

Horawitz, Adalbert, and Karl Hartfelder. 1886. Briefwechsel des Beatus Rhenanus. Leipzig.

Huizinga, Johan. 1924. Erasmus. Trans. by F. Hopman. New York.

Hunzinger, A. W. 1908. "Luther und die deutsche Mystik," *Neue kirchliche Zeitschrift (Luthertum),* Vol. XIX.

Huss, John. 1520. De causa Boemica.

Hutten, Ulrich von. 1859–. Ulrichi Hutteni opera. Ed. by Eduard Böcking. Leipzig.

Hyma, Albert. 1925. The Christian Renaissance: a History of the Devotio Moderna. New York.

Iwand, H. J. 1930. Rechtfertigungslehre und Christusglaube. Leipzig.

Janssen, Johannes. 1897, 1904. Geschichte des deutschen Volkes seit dem Ausgang des Mittelalters. Ed. by Ludwig von Pastor. Freiburg i. B. Vols I, VII.

Joachimsen, Paul. 1927. Review of Paul Kalkoff's *Huttens Vagantenzeit und Untergang,* in *Historische Zeitschrift,* Vol. CXXXVI.

Jovy, Ernest. 1913. François Tissard et Jérome Aléandre. Contribution à l'histoire des études grecques en France. Vitry-le-François. Vol. III.

Jürgens, Karl. 1846. Luthers Leben. Leipzig. Vol. I.

Kaegi, Werner. 1924–25. "Hutten und Erasmus," *Historische Vierteljahrschrift,* Vol. XXII.

Kalkoff, Paul. 1897. Die Depeschen des Nuntius Aleander vom Wormser Reichstage 1521. Halle a. S.

—— 1898. "Briefe, Depeschen und Berichte über Luther vom Wormser Reichstage 1521, aus dem Englischen, Italienischen und Spanischen übersetzt," *SVRG,* Vol. LIX.

—— 1903. "Die Anfänge der Gegenreformation in den Niederlanden," *SVRG,* Vol. XXI, Nos. 79, 81.

—— 1903–4. "Die Vermittlungspolitik des Erasmus und sein Anteil an den Flugschriften der ersten Reformationszeit," *ARG,* Vol. I.

—— 1904. "Zu Luthers römischem Prozess," *ZKG,* Vol. XXV.

—— 1905. Forschungen zu Luthers römischem Prozess. Rome.

—— 1907. Ablass und Reliquienverehrung an der Schlosskirche zu Wittenberg unter Friedrich dem Weisen. Gotha.

—— 1908. Aleander gegen Luther. Studien zu ungedruckten Aktenstücken aus Aleanders Nachlass. Leipzig.

—— 1910. "Zu Luthers römischem Prozess," *ZKG,* Vol. XXXI.

—— 1911. Die Miltitziade. Leipzig.

—— 1911. "Zu Luthers römischem Prozess (Fortsetzung)," *ZKG,* Vol. XXXII.

—— 1911–12. "Die von Cajetan verfasste Ablassdekretale und seine Verhandlungen mit dem Kurfürsten von Sachsen in Weimar, den 28. und 29. Mai 1519," *ARG,* Vol. IX.

—— 1912. "Zu Luthers römischem Prozess (Schluss)," *ZKG,* Vol. XXXIII, Heft I.

—— 1912. "G. B. Flavio als Biograph Kajetans und sein Bericht über Luthers Verhör in Augsburg," *ZKG,* Vol. XXXIII, Heft II.

—— 1913. Die Entstehung des Wormser Edikts. Leipzig.

—— 1914. "Die Bulle Exsurge," *ZKG,* Vol. XXXV.

—— 1914. "Luthers Antwort auf Kajetans Ablassdekretale (30. Mai 1519)," *ARG,* Vol. XI.

—— 1918. "Die Bulle Exsurge," *ZKG,* Vol. XXXVII.

—— 1919. "Erasmus, Luther und Friedrich der Weise. Eine reformationsgeschichtliche Studie," *SVRG*, Vol. CXXXII.

Kalkoff, Paul. 1920. Ulrich von Hutten und die Reformation. Leipzig.

―――― 1921. "Die Vollziehung der Bulle Exsurge," *ZKG*, Vol. XXXIX, Neue Folge II.

―――― 1921. "Ein neuaufgefundenes Original der Bulle 'Exsurge Domine'," *ZKG*, Vol. XXXIX, Neue Folge II.

―――― 1922. Der Wormser Reichstag von 1521. Munich.

―――― 1924. "Die Kaiserwahl Friedrichs des Weisen," *ARG*, Vol. XXI.

―――― 1925. Huttens Vagantenzeit und Untergang. Weimar.

―――― 1925. "Kleine Nachträge zu 'Luthers römischem Prozess'," *ZKG*, Vol. XLIV, Neue Folge VII.

―――― 1926. "Die Crotus-Legende und die deutschen Triaden," *ARG*, Vol. XXIII, Nos. 89, 90.

―――― 1926. Die Reformation in der Reichsstadt Nürnberg nach den Flugschriften ihres Ratsschreibers Lazarus Spengler. Halle.

―――― 1926. Humanismus und Reformation in Erfurt. Halle.

―――― 1927. "Die Erfurter theologische Fakultät gegenüber der Bulle 'Exsurge'," *Historisches Jahrbuch*, Vol. XLVII.

―――― 1927. "Die Übersetzung der Bulle 'Exsurge'," *ZKG*, Vol. XLV, Neue Folge VIII.

―――― 1928. "Die Stellung der deutschen Humanisten zur Reformation," *ZKG*, Vol. XLVI, Neue Folge IX.

Kaufmann, Georg. 1896. Die Geschichte der deutschen Universitäten. Stuttgart. Vol. II.

Kawerau, Gustav. 1881. "Welche Schule in Magdeburg hat Luther besucht?" *Geschichtsblätter für Stadt und Land Magdeburg*, Vol. XVI.

―――― 1898. "Hieronymus Emser," *SVRG*, Vol. LXI.

―――― 1911. "Aus den Actis generalatus Aegidii Viterbiensis," *ZKG*, Vol. XXXII.

―――― 1917. "Luthers Randglossen zum Marienpsalter 1515," *ThStKr*, Vol. XC.

Kiessling, Elmer C. 1935. The Early Sermons of Luther and Their Relation to the Pre-Reformation Sermon. Grand Rapids, Mich.

Kirchhoff, Alfred. 1870. Die ältesten Weistümer der Stadt Erfurt. Halle.

Kirn, Paul. 1926. "Friedrich der Weise und die Kirche," *Beiträge zur Kulturgeschichte des Mittelalters und der Renaissance*, Vol. XXX.

Klingner, Erich. 1912. Luther und der deutsche Volksaberglaube. Berlin.

Knaake, J. F. K. 1900. "Bemerkungen zum Briefwechsel der Reformatoren," *ThStKr*, Vol. LXXIII.

Knepper, Joseph. 1902. "Jakob Wimpfeling," in *Erläuterungen und Ergänzungen zu Janssens Geschichte des deutschen Volkes*. Vol. III, Hefte II–IV. Freiburg i. B.

Knoll, A. M. 1933. Der Zins in der Scholastik. Innsbruck.

Köhler, Walter. 1895. Die Quellen zu Luthers Schrift "An den christlichen Adel deutscher Nation." Halle.

―――― 1900. Luther und die Kirchengeschichte. Erlangen.

―――― 1902. "Dokumente zum Ablassstreit von 1517," in *Sammlung ausge-*

wählter kirchen- und dogmengeschichtlicher Quellenschriften, Reihe II, Heft III. Tübingen and Leipzig.

—— 1913. "Die Mystik in Luthers 'Freiheit eines Christenmenschen'," *Zeitschrift für Theologie und Kirche*, Vol. XXIII.

Kohlmeyer, Ernst. 1922. Die Entstehung der Schrift Luthers An den christlichen Adel deutscher Nation. Gütersloh.

Kolde, Theodor. 1876. Luthers Stellung zu Concil und Kirche. Gütersloh.

—— 1878. "Innere Bewegungen unter den deutschen Augustinern und Luthers Romreise," *ZKG*, Vol. II.

—— 1879. Die deutsche Augustiner-Kongregation und Johann von Staupitz. Gotha.

—— 1883. Analecta Lutherana. Gotha.

—— 1890. "Wittenberger Disputationsthesen aus den Jahren 1516 bis 1522," *ZKG*, Vol. XI.

—— 1898. "Das religiöse Leben in Erfurt beim Ausgang des Mittelalters," *SVRG*, Vol. LXIII.

Köstlin, Julius. 1871. "Geschichtliche Untersuchungen über Luthers Leben vor dem Ablassstreite," *ThStKr*, Vol. XLIV.

—— 1884. "Rezensionen," *ThStKr*, Vol. LVII, Heft II.

—— 1903. Martin Luther. Ed. by G. Kawerau. Berlin. 5th ed.

Krause, Karl. 1879. Helius Eobanus Hessus. Gotha.

Krüger, G. 1917. "Luthers Tractatus de Indulgentiis," *ThStKr*, Vol. XC.

Krumhaar, K. 1855. Die Grafschaft Mansfeld im Reformationszeitalter. Eisleben.

—— 1869. Versuch einer Geschichte von Stadt und Schloss Mansfeld.

Lauchert, Friedrich. 1912. "Die italienischen literarischen Gegner Luthers," in *Erläuterungen und Ergänzungen zu Janssens Geschichte des deutschen Volkes*. Freiburg i. B. Vol. VIII.

Laurence, Richard, ed. 1839. "Unterricht der Visitatoren," in *The Visitation of the Saxon Reformed Church in the Years 1527 and 1528*. Dublin.

Lefèvre [Jacques Lefèvre d'Étaples, Faber Stapulensis]. 1509. Psalterium Quintuplex, gallicanum, romanum, hebraicum, vetus, conciliatum. Paris.

Lemmens, Leonhard. 1899. "Pater Augustin von Alfeld," in *Erläuterungen und Ergänzungen zu Janssens Geschichte des deutschen Volkes*. Freiburg i. B. Vol. I, Heft IV.

—— 1911. "Aus ungedruckten Franziskanerbriefen des XVI. Jahrhunderts," *RgST*, Vol. XX.

—— 1918. "Zur Biographie des P. Augustin von Alfeld," *Franziskanische Studien*, Vol. V. Münster.

Leopold, F. H. 1803. Wittenberg und die umliegende Gegend. Meissen.

Lezius, Friedrich. 1895. Zur Charakteristik des religiösen Standpunktes des Erasmus. Gütersloh.

Lindener, Michael. 1883. "Katzipori," *Bibliothek des Litterarischen Vereins in Stuttgart*. Tübingen. Vol. CLXIII.

Lombard, Peter. 1489. Textus Sententiarum cum conclusionibus ac titulis questionum sancti Thome. Basel.

Löscher, Valentin E. 1720–. Vollständige Reformations-Acta und Documenta. Leipzig.

Lossius, K. F. 1817. Anfang und Fortgang der Reformation; oder Helius Eobanus Hesse und seine Zeitgenossen. Gotha.

Lünig, Johann C. 1716. Spicilegium ecclesiasticum des Teutschen Reichs-Archivs. Leipzig. Vol. XV.

Luther, Johann. 1933. Vorbereitung und Verbreitung von Martin Luthers 95 Thesen. Berlin and Leipzig.

Luther, Johann, and M. Perlbach. 1907. "Ein neuer Bericht über Luthers Verbrennung der Bannbulle," *Abhandlungen der preussischen Akademie der Wissenschaften.*

Luther, Martin. 1551–69. Der erste Teil der Bücher . . . D. Mart. Luth., Wittenberg, Gedruckt durch Peter Seitz. (Vol. I, 1567).

——— 1826–57. Sämmtliche Werke. Erlangen (later Frankfurt a. M.). Vols. I–XL: *D. Martini Lutheri Exegetica Opera Latina.*

——— 1883–. D. Martin Luthers Werke. Kritische Gesamtausgabe. Ed. by J. K. F. Knaake, Gustav Kawerau, Ernst Thiele, Georg Buchwald, and others. Weimar.

——— 1884–. Doktor Martin Luthers Briefwechsel. Ed. by Ernst L. Enders. Frankfurt a. M. and elsewhere.

——— 1903. Luthers Tischreden in der Mathesischen Sammlung. Ed. by Ernst Kroker. Leipzig.

——— 1905. Luthers Werke. Ergänzungsband II, ed. by Otto Scheel. Berlin.

——— 1912–21. D. Martin Luthers Tischreden 1531–1546. Ed. by Karl Drescher, Ernst Kroker, and others. Weimar.

——— 1914–. Ausgewählte Werke. Unter Mitwirkung von H. Barge, G. Buchwald, P. Kalkoff. . . . Ed. by H. Borcherdt. Munich.

——— 1924. Luthers Werke für das christliche Haus. Ed. by Georg Buchwald, Gustav Kawerau, Julius Köstlin, and others. Leipzig. 4th ed.

——— 1925. Luthers Werke in Auswahl. Vol. I, ed. by Otto Clemen. Bonn.

——— 1930–48. D. Martin Luthers Briefwechsel. Ed. by Otto Clemen and others. Weimar.

Mathesius, Johann. 1846. Das Leben Dr. Martin Luthers. Ed. by G. H. von Schubert. Stuttgart.

——— 1898, 1906. "Luthers Leben in Predigten," in *Ausgewählte Werke,* Vol. III. Ed. by G. Loesche. Prague.

Meinhard, Andreas. 1508. Dialogus illustrate ac Augustissime urbis Albiorene vulgo Vittenberg dicte Situm Amenitatem ac Illustrationem docens Tirocinia nobilium artium iacientibus Editus. Leipzig.

——— 1509. Dye zaigung des hochlobwirdigen hailigthums der Stifft kirchen aller hailigen zu wittenburg. Wittenberg.

Meissinger, Karl A. 1910. Luthers Exegese in der Frühzeit. Leipzig.

Meissner, R. 1906. " 'Ohne Hörner und Zähne'," *ARG*, Vol. III, Heft IV.

Melanchthon, Philip. 1926. "Melanchthons Briefwechsel," Part I, in *Supplementa Melanchthoniana*, Vol. VI, ed. by Otto Clemen. Leipzig.

Mencke, Johann B. 1728. Scriptores rerum Germanicarum. Leipzig. Vol. II.

Merker, Paul. 1923. Der Verfasser des Eccius Dedolatus und anderer Reformations-dialoge. Halle.

Mestwerdt, Paul. 1917. Die Anfänge des Erasmus. Leipzig.

Meyner, A. M. 1856. Geschichte der Stadt Wittenberg. Wittenberg.

Migne, J.-P. 1854-. Patrologiae cursus completus. Paris.

Mirbt, Carl. 1924. Quellen zur Geschichte des Papsttums und des römischen Katholizismus. Tübingen. 4th ed.

Möllenberg, W. 1906. "Hans Luther, Dr. Martin Luthers Vater," *Zeitschrift des Harzvereins für Geschichte und Altertumskunde*, Vol. XXXIX.

Morel-Fatio, A. 1914. "Le Premier Témoignage Espagnol sur les Interrogatoires de Luther à la Diète de Worms en Avril 1521," *Annales de la Faculté des Lettres de Bordeaux*, Vol. XXXVI, and *Bulletin Hispanique*, Vol. XVI.

Mosen, Paul. 1890. Emser, der Vorkämpfer Roms gegen die Reformation. Halle.

Muffel, Nikolaus. 1876. "Nikolaus Muffels Beschreibung der Stadt Rom," ed. by W. Vogt, in *Bibliothek des Litterarischen Vereins in Stuttgart*. Tübingen. Vol. CXXVIII.

Müller, Anton V. 1912. Luthers theologische Quellen. Giessen.

——— 1917. "Beweggründe und Umstände bei Luthers Eintritt ins Kloster," *ThStKr*, Vol. XC.

——— 1918. Luther und Tauler. Bern.

——— 1920. Luthers Werdegang bis zum Turmerlebnis. Gotha.

——— 1921. "Der Augustiner Observantismus und die Kritik und Psychologie Luthers," *ARG*, Vol. XVIII.

——— 1921. "Nochmals Luthers Eintritt ins Kloster," *ThStKr*, Vol. XCIII.

Müller, Karl G. 1903. "Luthers römischer Prozess," *ZKG*, Vol. XXIV.

Müller, Nikolaus. 1911. Die Wittenberger Bewegung 1521 und 1522. Leipzig.

Mustard, Wilfred P. 1911. The Eclogues of Baptista Mantuanus. Baltimore, Md.

Muther, Theodor. 1866. Aus dem Universitäts- und Gelehrtenleben im Zeitalter der Reformation. Erlangen.

Mutianus (Konrad Mudt). 1890. "Der Briefwechsel des Conradius Mutianus," ed. by Karl Gillert, in *Geschichtsquellen der Provinz Sachsen*, Vol. XVIII, Teile I, II.

Myconius, Friedrich. 1718. Historia Reformationis 1517-1542. In E. S. Cyprian, "Nützliche Urkunden zur Erläuterung der ersten Reformationsgeschichte," in *Tentzels Historischer Bericht vom Anfang und ersten Fortgang der Reforma-tion Lutheri*, Vol. II, Heft III.

Neubauer, Theodor T. 1913. "Die sozialen und wirtschaftlichen Verhältnisse der

Stadt Erfurt vor Beginn der Reformation," *Mitteilungen des Vereins für die Geschichte und Altertumskunde von Erfurt,* Vol. XXXIV.

Neubauer, Theodor T. 1914. "Zur Geschichte der mittelalterlichen Stadt Erfurt," *Mitteilungen des Vereins für die Geschichte und Altertumskunde von Erfurt,* Vol. XXXV.

────── 1917. Luthers Frühzeit. Erfurt.

Neumann, Max. 1865. Geschichte des Wuchers in Deutschland. Halle.

Nitzsch, Friedrich. 1833. Luther und Aristoteles. Kiel.

O'Connor, Sister Mary Catharine. 1942. The Art of Dying Well. New York.

Oecolampadius (Johann Huszgen). 1927. Briefe und Akten zum Leben Oecolampads, Vol. I, ed. by E. Staehelin. Leipzig.

Oergel, Georg. 1894. "Urkunden zur Geschichte des Collegium majus zu Erfurt," *Mitteilungen des Vereins für Geschichte und Altertumskunde von Erfurt,* Vol. XVI.

────── 1899. Vom jungen Luther. Erfurt.

Oldecop, Johan. 1891. "Die Chronik des Johan Oldecop," *Bibliothek des Litterarischen Vereins in Stuttgart.* Tübingen. Vol. CXC.

Oppermann, Otto. 1897. "Das sächsische Amt Wittenberg im Anfang des 16. Jahrhunderts," *Leipziger Studien aus dem Gebiet der Geschichte,* Vol. IV, Heft II.

Panzer, G. 1798. Annales typographici. Nuremberg. Vol. VI.

Paquier, Jules. 1900. L'Humanisme et la Réforme. Jérôme Aléandre (1480–1529). Paris.

Pastor, Ludwig von. 1886–1933. Geschichte der Päpste seit dem Ausgang des Mittelalters. Freiburg i. B. Vol. III, 1. und 2. Auflage; Vols. IV–VIII, 1. bis 4. Auflage.

────── 1905. "Die Reise des Kardinals Luigi d'Aragona durch Deutschland, die Niederlande, Frankreich und Oberitalien, 1517 bis 1518, beschreiben von Antonio de Beatis," in *Erläuterungen und Ergänzungen zu Janssens Geschichte des deutschen Volkes.* Freiburg i. B. Vol. IV, Heft IV.

────── 1925. Die Stadt Rom zu Ende der Renaissance. Freiburg i. B.

Paullini, Chr. Franz. 1698. Rerum et Antiquitatum Germanicarum Syntagma. Frankfurt.

Paulsen, Friedrich. 1881. "Organisation und Lebensordnung der deutschen Universitäten im Mittelalter," *Historische Zeitschrift,* Vol. XLV, Neue Folge IX.

────── 1919. Geschichte des gelehrten Unterrichts, Leipzig. Vol. I.

Paulus, Nikolaus. 1893. "Der Augustiner Barth. Arnoldi von Usingen, Luthers Lehrer und Gegner," *Strassburger theologische Studien,* Vol. I, Heft III.

────── 1899. Johann Tetzel, der Ablassprediger. Mainz.

────── 1903. "Die deutschen Dominikaner im Kampfe gegen Luther 1518–1563," in *Erläuterungen und Ergänzungen zu Janssens Geschichte des deutschen Volkes.* Freiburg i. B. Vol. IV, Hefte I, II.

—— 1906. "Zu Luthers Schrift über das Mönchsgelübde," *Historisches Jahrbuch,* Vol. XXVII.

Pellicanus (Konrad Kürsner). 1877. Das Chronikon des Konrad Pellicanus. Ed. by B. Riggenbach. Basel.

—— 1892. Die Hauschronik Konrad Pellikans von Rufach. Trans. by Th. Vulpinus (Th. Renaud). Strasbourg.

—— 1950. "The Chronicle of Conrad Pellican, 1478–1556," trans. by F. C. Ahrens. Ph.D. dissertation, Columbia University.

Pineau, J. B. 1923. Érasme et la Papauté. Paris.

Pirckheimer, Willibald. 1610. Bilibaldi Pirckheimeri . . . Opera. Ed. by M. Goldast. Frankfurt.

Plitt, Gustav. 1876. Jodocus Trutfetter von Eisenach, der Lehrer Luthers. Erlangen.

Prantl, Karl von. 1855–70. Geschichte der Logik im Abendlande. Leipzig.

Preuss, Hans. 1931. Martin Luther der Künstler. Gütersloh.

Rade, D. M. 1913. "Luthers 'De libertate Christiana' mystisch?" *Zeitschrift für Theologie und Kirche,* Vol. XXIII.

Ranke, Leopold von. 1909. Deutsche Geschichte im Zeitalter der Reformation. Leipzig. Vol. I, 8th ed.

Rashdall, Hastings. 1936. The Universities of Europe in the Middle Ages. Oxford.

Ratzeberger, Matthäus. 1850. Die handschriftliche Geschichte Ratzebergers über Luther und seine Zeit. Ed. by C. Neudecker. Jena.

Realenzyklopädie für protestantische Theologie und Kirche. 1896–. Leipzig.

Reformationsgeschichtliche Studien und Texte. 1906–. Münster.

Rein, W. 1863. "Kurze Geschichte und mittelalterliche Physiognomie der Stadt Eisenach," *Zeitschrift des Vereins für thüringische Geschichte und Altertumskunde,* Vol. V.

Reu, Johann M. 1917. Thirty-five Years of Luther Research. Chicago.

—— 1929. Dr. Martin Luther's Small Catechism. Chicago.

—— 1934. Luther's German Bible. Columbus, Ohio.

Reuchlin, Johannes. 1875. "Johann Reuchlins Briefwechsel," ed. by L. Geiger, in *Bibliothek des Litterarischen Vereins in Stuttgart.* Tübingen. Vol. CXXVI.

Reusch, F. H. 1883. Index der verbotenen Bücher. Bonn. Vol. I.

Richter, Max. 1900. Die Stellung des Erasmus zu Luther und zur Reformation. Leipzig.

Riederer, J. B. 1762. Beytrag zu den Reformationsurkunden. Altdorf.

—— 1764. Nachrichten zur Kirchen- Gelehrten- und Bücher-Geschichte. Altdorf. Vol. I.

Ritter, Gerhard. 1921, 1922. "Studien zur Spätscholastik," Parts I and II, *Sitzungsberichte der Heidelberger Akademie der Wissenschaften,* Vols. XII, XIII.

—— 1923. "Die geschichtliche Bedeutung des deutschen Humanismus," *Historische Zeitschrift,* Vol. CXXVII.

—— 1936. Die Heidelberger Universität. Heidelberg. Vol. I.

Rommel, Herbert. 1930. Über Luthers Randbemerkungen von 1509–10. Kiel.

Roth, Friedrich. 1881. Augsburgs Reformationsgeschichte 1517–1527. Munich.

—— 1924. "Die geistliche Betrügerin Anna Laminit von Augsburg," *ZKG*, Vol. XLIII, Neue Folge VI.

Rothe, Johann. 1859. "Düringische Chronik," in *Thüringische Geschichtsquellen*. Jena. Vol. III.

Sanuto, Marino. 1889, 1890. I Diarii di Marino Sanuto. Venice. Vols. XXV, XXVI; XXVIII, XXIX.

Schauerte, Heinrich. 1919. "Die Busslehre des Joh. Eck," *RgST*, Vols. XXXVIII, XXXIX.

Schaumkell, E. 1893. Der Kultus der heiligen Anna am Ausgange des Mittelalters. Freiburg i. B. and Leipzig.

Scheel, Otto. Martin Luther. Tübingen. Vol. I, 1st ed., 1916; 2d ed., 1921. Vol. II, 1st and 2d eds., 1917; 3d and 4th eds., 1930.

—— 1929. Dokumente zu Luthers Entwicklung. Tübingen.

—— 1929. Review of M. Burgdorf's *Der Einfluss der Erfurter Humanisten auf Luthers Entwicklung bis 1510*, in *Theologische Literaturzeitung*, Vol. LIV, Heft III.

Scheurl, Christoph. 1867–72. Briefbuch. Ed. by F. von Soden and J. K. F. Knaake. Potsdam.

—— 1872. "Christoph Scheurls Geschichtbuch der Christenheit von 1511 bis 1521," ed. by J. K. F. Knaake, *Jahrbücher des deutschen Reichs und der deutschen Kirche*, Vol. I, Heft I.

Schlecht, Joseph. 1922. "Briefmappe II," *RgST*, Vol. XL.

Schlüsselberg, Conrad. 1610. Oratio de vita et morte . . . Lutheri. Rostock.

Schnürer, Gustav. 1935. "Warum wurde Erasmus nicht ein Führer der kirchlichen Erneuerung?" *Historisches Jahrbuch*, Vol. LV.

Schott, A. 1928. Das Messbuch der heiligen Kirche. Freiburg i. B. 33d ed.

Schottenloher, Karl. 1915. "Magister Andreas Lutz in Ingolstadt, der Drucker der Bulle 'Exsurge Domine' (1519–1524)," *Zentralblatt für Bibliothekswesen*, Vol. XXXII.

Schriften des Vereins für Reformationsgeschichte. 1883–. Halle a. S.

Schubert, Hans von. 1912. "Die Vorgeschichte der Berufung Luthers auf den Reichstag zu Worms 1521," *Sitzungsberichte der Heidelberger Akademie der Wissenschaften, phil.-hist. Klasse*, Abhandlung VI.

—— 1918. "Luthers Vorlesung über den Galaterbrief," *Abhandlungen der Heidelberger Akademie der Wissenschaften, phil.-hist. Klasse*, Vol. V.

Schubert, Hans von, and K. Meissinger. 1920. "Zu Luthers Vorlesungstätigkeit," *Sitzungsberichte der Heidelberger Akademie der Wissenschaften, phil.-hist. Klasse*, Abhandlung IX.

Schulte, Aloys. 1904. Die Fugger in Rom. Leipzig.

—— 1904. "Die römischen Verhandlungen über Luther 1520," *Quellen und Forschungen aus italienischen Archiven und Bibliotheken*. Rome. Vol. VI.

Schulze, Gerhard. 1926. "Die Vorlesung Luthers über den Galaterbrief von 1531 und der gedruckte Kommentar von 1535," *ThStKr,* Vol. XCVIII–XCIX.

Schum, Wilhelm. 1887. Beschreibendes Verzeichnis der amplonianischen Handschriftensammlung zu Erfurt. Berlin.

Seckendorf, Veit. 1688. Commentarius historicus et apologeticus . . . de Lutheranismo; sive, De reformatione religionis ductu Martini Lutheri. Frankfurt and Leipzig. Vol. I.

Seidemann, J. K. 1843. Die Leipziger Disputation im Jahre 1519. Dresden and Leipzig.

—— 1844. Karl von Miltitz, eine chronologische Untersuchung zum besseren Verständnisse der Quellen. Dresden.

Seifert, Friedrich. 1883. Die Reformation in Leipzig. Leipzig.

Seitz, Otto, ed. 1903. Der authentische Text der Leipziger Disputation. Berlin.

Selneccer, Nicolaus. 1575. Historica Narratio et oratio de D. Martino Luthero. . . . Leipzig.

—— 1587. Vitam Divi Lutheri. Wittenberg.

Siebeck, H. 1897. "Occams Erkenntnislehre in ihrer historischen Stellung," *Archiv für Geschichte der Philosophie,* Vol. X, Neue Folge III.

Smith, Preserved. 1913. "Luther's Early Development in the Light of Psycho-Analysis," *American Journal of Psychology,* Vol. XXIV.

—— 1923. Erasmus, a Study of His Life, Ideals, and Place in History. New York.

Smith, Preserved, and Charles M. Jacobs, eds. and trans. 1913. Luther's Correspondence and Other Contemporary Letters. Philadelphia. Vol. I.

Spalatin, Georg. 1718. Annales Reformationis. In E. S. Cyprian, "Nützliche Urkunden zur Erläuterung der ersten Reformationsgeschichte," in *Tentzels Historischer Bericht vom Anfang und ersten Fortgang der Reformation Lutheri.* Leipzig. Vol. II.

—— 1728. "Chronicon sive Annales Georgii Spalatini," ed. by J. B. Mencke, in *Scriptores rerum Germanicarum.* Leipzig. Vol. II.

—— 1854. Friedrichs des Weisen Leben und Zeitgeschichte. Ed. by C. Neudecker and L. Preller. Jena.

Stange, Carl. 1904. "Die ältesten ethischen Disputationen Luthers," *Quellenschriften zur Geschichte des Protestantismus.* Leipzig. Vol. I.

—— 1937. Erasmus und Julius II. Berlin.

Stauber, Anton. 1900. Das Haus Fugger. Augsburg.

Steinlein, P. 1912. "Luthers Doktorat," *Neue kirchliche Zeitschrift (Luthertum),* Vol. XXIII, Heft 11.

Stolle, Konrad. 1854. "Konrad Stolles Thüringische-Erfurtische Chronik," in *Bibliothek des Litterarischen Vereins in Stuttgart.* Stuttgart, Vol. XXXII.

—— 1900. "Memoriale thüringsch-erfurtische Chronik," ed. by R. Thiele, in *Geschichtsquellen der Provinz Sachsen,* Vol. XXXIX.

Störmann, Anton. 1916. "Die städtischen Gravamina gegen den Klerus," *RgST,* Vol. XXIV–XXVI.

Stracke, Ernst. 1926. "Luthers grosses Selbstzeugnis 1545 über seine Entwicklung zum Reformator," *SVRG,* Vol. XLIV, Heft 1.

Strauss, D. F. 1874. Ulrich von Hutten. Leipzig. 2d ed.

Strobel, G. Th. 1792. Neue Beyträge zur Litteratur besonders des 16. Jahrhunderts. Nuremberg and Altdorf. Vol. III, Heft II.

Strohl, Henri. 1922. L'Évolution religieuse de Luther. Strasbourg.

———— 1924. L'Épanouissement de la pensée religieuse de Luther. Strasbourg.

Tentzels Historischer Bericht vom Anfang und ersten Fortgang der Reformation Lutheri. 1717, 1718. Leipzig. Vols. I, II.

Tettau, W. J. A., Freiherr von. 1885. "Beiträge zu einer vergleichenden Topographie und Statistik von Erfurt," *Mitteilungen des Vereins für die Geschichte und Altertumskunde von Erfurt,* Vol. XII.

Thiele, Ernst. 1917. "Die Originalhandschriften Luthers," in *Luther-Studien zur 4. Jahrhundertfeier der Reformation.* Weimar.

Thiele, Richard, ed. 1906. "Erphurdianus Antiquitatum Variloquus incerti auctoris," *Geschichtsquellen der Provinz Sachsen,* Vol. XLII.

Theologische Studien und Kritiken. 1828–. Hamburg.

Thomas Aquinas, Saint. 1882–1948. S. Thomae Aquinatis opera omnia iussu impensaque Leonis XIII P.M. edita. Ed. by Thomas de Vio (Cajetan). Rome.

Thomas, Hedwig. 1920. Zur Würdigung der Psalmenvorlesung Luthers. Weimar.

Thüna, Freiherr von. 1889. "Friedrich von Thun," *Zeitschrift des Vereins für thüringische Geschichte und Altertumskunde,* Neue Folge VI.

Thurnhofer, Franz X. 1900. "Bernhard Adelmann von Adelmannsfelden, Humanist und Luthers Freund (1457–1523)," in *Erläuterungen und Ergänzungen zu Janssens Geschichte des deutschen Volkes.* Freiburg i. B. Vol. II, Heft 1.

———— 1917. "Willibald Pirkheimer und Hieronymus Emser," in *Beiträge zur Geschichte der Renaissance und Reformation. Festschrift für J. Schlecht.* Munich.

Tschackert, P. 1897. "Justus Jonas' Bericht aus dem Jahre 1538 über Martin Luthers Eintritt in das Kloster (1505)," *ThStKr,* Vol. LXX.

Ulmann, Heinrich. 1891. Kaiser Maximilian I. Stuttgart.

"Urkundenbuch der Stadt Magdeburg." 1896. Ed. by G. Hertel, in *Geschichtsquellen der Provinz Sachsen,* Vol. XXVIII.

Usingen, Arnold von. See Arnold von Usingen, Bartholomäus.

Vacant, A., and E. Mangenot. 1909. Dictionnaire de Théologie Catholique. Paris. Vol. I.

Vio, Thomas de (Cajetan). 1639. Thomae de Vio, D. Caietani Opera omnia, quotquot in Sacrae Scripturae expositionem reperiuntur. Lugduni.

———— 1925. De divina institutione pontificatus Romani pontificis. Ed. by F. Lauchert, in *Corp. Cath.,* Vol. X.

Vogelsang, Erich. 1929. Die Anfänge von Luthers Christologie nach der ersten Psalmenvorlesung. Berlin and Leipzig.

—— 1930. "Luthers Hebräerbrief-Vorlesung," *Arbeiten zur Kirchengeschichte*. Berlin. Vol. XVII.

—— 1931. "Zur Datierung der frühsten Lutherpredigten," *ZKG*, Vol. L, 3. Folge I.

Voigt, H. 1928. "Die entscheidendste Stunde in Luthers religiöser Entwicklung," *Zeitschrift des Vereins für die Kirchengeschichte in der Provinz Sachsen*, Vol. XXIII–XXIV.

Wackernagel, Philip. 1864. Das deutsche Kirchenlied. Leipzig. Vol. I.

Walch, J. G. 1740–. D. Martin Luthers Sämtliche Schriften. Halle.

Walser, Fritz. 1928. "Die politische Entwickelung Ulrichs von Hutten während der Entscheidungsjahre der Reformation," *Historische Zeitschrift*, Beiheft 14.

Waltz, Otto. 1878. "Epistolae Reformatorum," *ZKG*, Vol. II.

Weicker, Bernhard. 1901. "Die Stellung der Kurfürsten zur Wahl Karls V im Jahre 1519," *Historische Studien*, Vol. XXII.

Weissenborn, J. C. H. 1877. "Die Urkunden für die Geschichte des Dr. Amplonius Ratingk de Fago auch genannt Amplonius de Berka," *Mitteilungen des Vereins für die Geschichte und Altertumskunde von Erfurt*, Vol. VIII.

—— 1880. "Die Urkunden zur Geschichte des M. Amplonius de Fago aus Rheinbergen," *Mitteilungen des Vereins für die Geschichte und Altertumskunde von Erfurt*. Vol. IX.

Weller, E. 1864. Repertorium typographicum. Nördlingen. Vol. III.

Wendorf, Hermann. 1930. Martin Luther, der Aufbau seiner Persönlichkeit. Leipzig.

—— 1932–33. "Der Durchbruch der neuen Erkenntnis Luthers im Lichte der handschriftlichen Überlieferung," Parts I and II, *Historische Vierteljahrschrift*, Vol. XXVII.

Werdermann, Hermann. 1929. Luthers Wittenberger Gemeinde wiederhergestellt aus seinen Predigten. Gütersloh.

Werlich, Johann. See Thiele, Richard, ed.

Wetzer and Welte. 1882–1901. Kirchenlexikon. Freiburg i. B. 2d ed.

Wiedemann, Theodor. 1865. Dr. Johann Eck, Professor der Theologie an der Universität Ingolstadt. Regensburg.

Wimpfeling, Jakob. 1505. De integritate libellus. Strasbourg.

Wolf, Ernst. 1927. "Staupitz und Luther," in *Quellen und Forschungen zur Reformationsgeschichte*. Leipzig, Vol. IX.

Wolff, Johann. 1907. "Drei Beichtbüchlein nach den zehn Geboten," ed. by F. Falk, *RgST*, Vol. II.

Wustmann, Gustav. 1885. Aus Leipzigs Vergangenheit. Leipzig.

Zarncke, Friedrich. 1857. Die deutschen Universitäten im Mittelalter. Leipzig.

Zeitschrift für Kirchengeschichte. 1876–. Gotha, Tübingen.

INDEX